FUEL INJECTION DIAGNOSIS AND REPAIR

CHILTON'S

Covers all domestic and import vehicles

ABCDE
FGHIJ
KLMNO

GAYLORD MG

Chilton is a registered trademark of W.G. Nichols, Inc., and has been licensed to Haynes North America, Inc.

Contents

Contents

6 IMPORT DIAGNOSTIC TROUBLE CODE RETRIEVAL

7 TRUCK DIAGNOSTIC TROUBLE CODE RETRIEVAL

8 FUEL INJECTION SYSTEM COMPONENT SERVICE

9 GLOSSARY

MASTER INDEX

SAFETY NOTICE

Proper service and repair procedures are vital to the safe, reliable operation of all motor vehicles, as well as the personal safety of those performing repairs. This manual outlines procedures for servicing and repairing vehicles using safe, effective methods. The procedures contain many NOTES, CAUTIONS and WARNINGS which should be followed, along with standard procedures to eliminate the possibility of personal injury or improper service which could damage the vehicle or compromise its safety.

It is important to note that repair procedures and techniques, tools and parts for servicing motor vehicles, as well as the skill and experience of the individual performing the work vary widely. It is not possible to anticipate all of the conceivable ways or conditions under which vehicles may be serviced, or to provide cautions as to all possible hazards that may result. Standard and accepted safety precautions and equipment should be used when handling toxic or flammable fluids, and safety goggles or other protection should be used during cutting, grinding, chiseling, prying, or any other process that can cause material removal or projectiles.

Some procedures require the use of tools specially designed for a specific purpose. Before substituting another tool or procedure, you must be completely satisfied that neither your personal safety, nor the performance of the vehicle will be endangered.

Although information in this manual is based on industry sources and is complete as possible at the time of publication, the possibility exists that some car manufacturers made later changes which could not be included here. While striving for total accuracy, the authors or publishers cannot assume responsibility for any errors, changes or omissions that may occur in the compilation of this data.

PART NUMBERS

Part numbers listed in this reference are not recommendations by Haynes North America, Inc. for any product brand name. They are references that can be used with interchange manuals and aftermarket supplier catalogs to locate each brand supplier's discrete part number.

SPECIAL TOOLS

Special tools are recommended by the vehicle manufacturer to perform their specific job. Use has been kept to a minimum, but where absolutely necessary, they are referred to in the text by the part number of the tool manufacturer. These tools can be purchased, under the appropriate part number, from your local dealer or regional distributor, or an equivalent tool can be purchased locally from a tool supplier or parts outlet. Before substituting any tool for the one recommended, read the SAFETY NOTICE at the top of this page.

ACKNOWLEDGMENTS

The publisher expresses appreciation to the following companies for their generous assistance:

AutoXray® Automotive Diagnostic Systems - Tempe, AZ
B&B Electronics Manufacturing Company® - Ottowa, IL

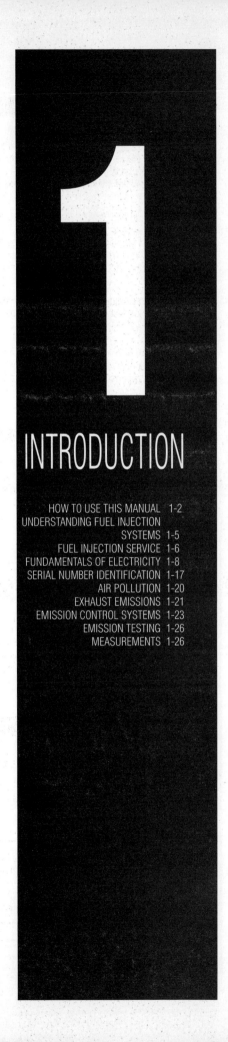

1
INTRODUCTION

HOW TO USE THIS MANUAL

Introduction

▶ See Figure 1

Servicing vehicles that are equipped with fuel injection may seem intimidating to the do-it-yourselfer, but this shouldn't be the case. As long as you keep a basic understanding of how fuel injection works in your mind as you troubleshoot your vehicle, you should be able to diagnose and repair your fuel injection system with relative ease.

Vehicles have evolved greatly since the days of carburetors. Purely mechanical carburetors gradually evolved to feedback, or electronically controlled carburetors to help improve their efficiency. Electronic fuel injection systems gradually replaced carburetors because of their ability to precisely regulate the fuel/air ratio mixture supplied to the engine. This not only lowered vehicle emissions, but also increased fuel economy. Since the days of early fuel injection, many more electronic control devices have been added to vehicles for the main purpose of fuel management and lowering emissions.

Modern electronic fuel injection systems use many electronic components. These components can basically be grouped into three categories—computers, sensors, and actuators. The sensors receive data which is processed by the computer. In turn, the computer signals actuators to perform functions to provide more engine power, help reduce exhaust emissions and improve fuel economy.

Additionally, modern day fuel injection systems feature self-diagnostic capabilities built into their control units. The self-diagnostics aid you in your repair work by providing Diagnostic Trouble Codes (DTCs). The Diagnostic Trouble Codes help to identify faulty component(s) or system(s).

Fuel injected vehicles CAN be serviced by the do-it-yourselfer. This manual will show you how easily it can be done by following logical step by step procedures.

In addition, useful information on tools, safety procedures, and preventive maintenance is also included in this manual. The information on basic electricity and testing will help you understand and test circuits and electrical components on your vehicle.

The following descriptions of each section will help familiarize you with the contents of this book. The remaining sections will give you the background required to accomplish fuel injection service and repair.

These sections include:

- Understanding Fuel Injection Systems
- Fuel Injection Service
- Fundamentals of Electricity
- Serial Number Identification
- Air Pollution
- Exhaust Emission
- Emission Controls
- Emission Testing
- Measurements

Tools, Equipment and Safety

▶ See Figure 2

Section 2 focuses on automotive tools and equipment. From basic hand tools to special diagnostic tools, the importance of tool quality is discussed, along with guidelines for planning your tool purchases. This section also covers; recommendations for your work area, necessary supplies an equipment, and specific safety tips. Many useful illustrations are pro-

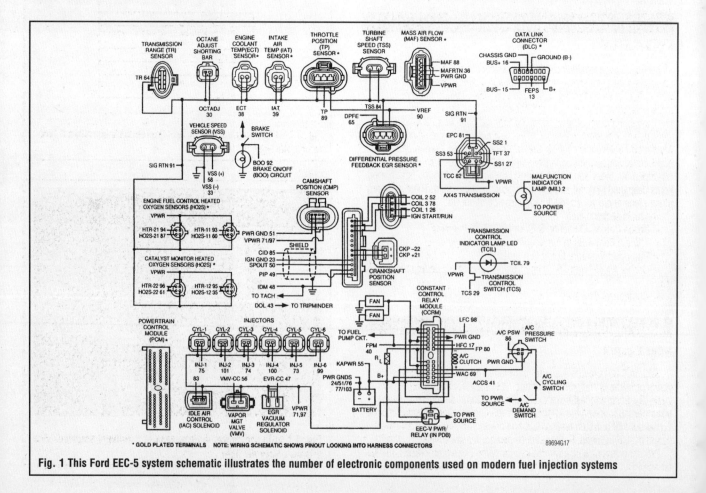

* GOLD PLATED TERMINALS   NOTE: WIRING SCHEMATIC SHOWS PINOUT LOOKING INTO HARNESS CONNECTORS

89694G17

Fig. 1 This Ford EEC-5 system schematic illustrates the number of electronic components used on modern fuel injection systems

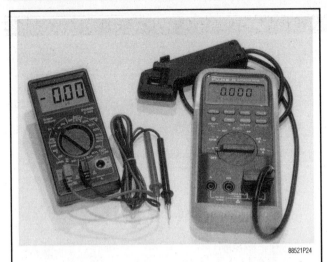

Fig. 2 The combination multimeter is the most important diagnostic tool when diagnosing fuel injection problems

vided, as well as information pertaining to the function of many tools and the proper use of each.

The specific topics are:
- What Tools Do I Need?
- Basic Automotive Tools
- Special Diagnostic Tools
- The Work Area
- Supplies and Equipment
- Safe Vehicle Servicing Tips

System and Component Operation

▶ See Figure 3

Section 3 will provide you with an overview of how mechanical and computer-controlled fuel injection systems and their individual components operate. This information will also help you understand how the different systems interact with each other. A basic understanding of system function and interaction is very useful for performing effective troubleshooting.

Constant Injection System (CIS), Throttle Body Fuel Injection (TBI), Multi-port Fuel Injection (MFI), Central Multi-port Fuel Injection (CMFI) and Central Sequential Fuel Injection (CSFI) system operations are described. An overview of each system is given, then the individual components described in detail and a typical location is provided. There are many illustrations to aid you in identifying these components.

The main sections are:
- Bosch Constant Injection System (CIS) Fuel Injection
- Throttle Body Fuel Injection (TBI) System
- Multi-port Fuel Injection (MFI) System
- Central Multi-port (CMFI) and Central Sequential Fuel Injection (CSFI)
- Component Operation

Basic Maintenance and Troubleshooting

▶ See Figure 4

Section 4 will provide you with information on general vehicle maintenance procedures and troubleshooting. There is also information about basic diagnosis and testing. It explains how you can perform may of the tasks needed to keep your vehicle in top running condition. Useful information about fuel pressure testing, fuel line connectors and using a vacuum gauge is also included. Proper service procedures are covered in detail.

Preventive maintenance procedures for items like the air cleaner, fuel filter and PCV valve are covered . Performing preventative maintenance on

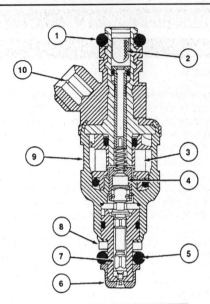

Item	Description
1	Fuel Injection Supply Manifold O-Ring Seal
2	Integral Filter Screen
3	Coil
4	Armature
5	Intake Manifold O-Ring Seal
6	End Cap
7	Stainless Steel Needle and Valve Body
8	Washer
9	Body
10	Coil Terminal Blade

Fig. 3 This cutaway view of an MFI fuel injector provides a hint at how the injector operates

Fig. 4 A little preventive maintenance will prevent surprises like this very dirty air filter

your vehicle will contribute to the proper operation of the fuel injection and emissions systems.

The following subjects are covered in great detail:
- Preventitive Maintenance
- Troubleshooting—Where Do I Start?
- Jump Starting
- Releiving Fuel System Pressure
- Fuel Line Connectors
- Fuel System Pressure Testing
- Fuel System Adjustments
- Engine Will Not Start
- Troubleshooting With a Vacuum Gauge

Diagnostic Trouble Codes

▶ See Figure 5

Sections 5, 6 and 7 contain Diagnostic Trouble Codes (DTCs) for domestic and imported vehicles. Modern electronic fuel injection systems use many electronic components. Each of these components is monitored by the vehicle's control unit. If a fault should occur, a self-diagnostic feature of the control unit will record a diagnostic trouble code and in most cases warn the driver of the failure.

As fuel injection systems have become more complex, so has the self-diagnostic capabilities of the systems. In this section we will discuss the differences between pre-OBD trouble codes, OBD-I trouble codes and the later model OBD-II codes.

The procedures to access and clear codes are outlined. If a special tool is needed to access or clear codes, it will be stated in the text. At the end of each manufacturer's section, the Diagnostic Trouble Codes (DTC)s are listed.

The domestic manufacturers covered are:
- Chrysler Corporation
- Ford Motor Company
- General Motors Corporation

The import manufacturers covered are:
- Acura
- Audi
- Honda
- Hyundai
- Infiniti
- Isuzu
- Kia
- Lexus
- Mazda
- Mitsubishi
- Nissan
- Porsche
- Saab
- Subaru
- Suzuki
- Toyota
- Volkswagen
- Volvo

Fuel Injection System Component Service

Section 8 contains information concerning the testing, replacement, and adjustment of the fuel injection components. Most components used on modern day injections systems are listed the index alphabetically for easy reference. Once you have diagnosed the cause of your vehicle's problem, this section will enable you to perform the needed tests. Appropriate notes, warnings, and cautions are provided in the text. Ignition, fuel, and emission components are included.

Clearly written procedures will guide you through removal and installation, and adjustment instructions are given, if they are applicable.

A full list of the covered components may be found in the Section 8 Table of Contents. The following list includes some of the major components covered in the section:
- Camshaft Position (CMP) Sensor
- Coolant Temperature Sensor (CTS)
- Crankshaft Position (CKP) Sensor
- EGR Solenoid Valve
- EGR Valve
- Intake Air Temperature (IAT) Sensor
- Knock Sensor
- Manifold Absolute Pressure (MAP) Sensor
- Mass Airflow (MAF) Sensor
- Oxygen Sensor (O_2)
- Positive Crankcase Ventilation (PCV) Valve
- Throttle Position (TPS) Sensor
- Vacuum Switching Valve (VSV)

Glossary

Section 9 is a glossary of automotive words, terminology, and abbreviations. In keeping with the subject material of this manual, many of the definitions pertain to emission, fuel, and ignition systems. A large portion of the definitions are universal, but we have also included many manufacturer-specific terms which will be useful to the do-it-yourselfer. Some basic electrical definitions are included.

Generally, you will find any definitions you need within the text when a word, term, or abbreviation is first used. If you need to refresh your memory later, simply look in the glossary to save time. Using the glossary on its own, as a learning tool, can help you enhance your automotive knowledge without even opening the hood of your vehicle.

Section 9's heading is:
- Abbreviations and Definitions

89694P31

Fig. 5 The diagnostic link connector provides a single source to tap into the fuel injection self-diagnostic system

UNDERSTANDING FUEL INJECTION SYSTEMS

Basic Fuel Injection Overview

▶ See Figures 6, 7 and 8

In general, fuel injection systems can be categorized into two groups—Port injection and Throttle Body injection.

Port injection systems are characterized by fuel injectors mounted in or near the cylinder head. The injectors spray the fuel charge directly behind the intake valve. The air and fuel are mixed in the valve bowl and then consumed by the engine. Electronic versions of Port type injection are called Multi-port Fuel Injection (MFI) and Sequential Multi-port Fuel Injection (SFI). A mechanical version used mainly on imported vehicles is called a Constant Injection Systems (CIS) or Constant Injection System Electronic (CIS-E).

Throttle Body Injection (TBI) uses one or two injectors mounted atop a conventional intake manifold (much like a carburetor) that spray the fuel charge down through a butterfly valve. The fuel charge is drawn into the intake manifold, mixed with the incoming air and distributed to the cylinders in the conventional manner.

Central Multi-Port (CMFI) and the Central Sequential (CSFI) fuel injection systems are two variations of Port fuel injection. At first glance, they appear similar to the TBI system, however they have a centrally mounted unit in the intake manifold with one (CMFI) or multiple (CSFI), injectors in the unit. These injector(s) are connected to lines running to poppet valves at each intake port.

With the exception of the mechanical CIS fuel injection, all systems discussed in this manual are combined with electronics and various engine sensors to provide a precise fuel management system. These systems meet all the demands for improved fuel economy, increased performance and lower emissions more precisely and reliably than is possible with a conventional carburetor.

Fuel-injected engines average ten percent more power and fuel economy with lower emissions than a carbureted engine. Even "feedback" carburetors with computer controls couldn't achieve the accurate fuel metering necessary to meet the lower emission levels required by Federal standards. Because of its precise control, fuel injection allows the engine

Fig. 7 This TBI unit sits on top of a conventional intake manifold, much like a carburetor and contains two injectors

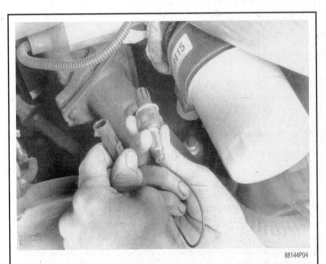

Fig. 8 Most electronic fuel injection systems use at least one oxygen sensor to sniff the exhaust gases

to operate with a Stoichiometric or optimum fuel ratio of 14.7 parts air to one part fuel throughout the entire engine rpm range, under all operating conditions. Stoichiometric (14.7:1) fuel mixtures assure that all the carbon and hydrogen is burned in the combustion chamber during the power stroke. This produces the lowest combination of emissions from unburned hydrocarbons, carbon monoxide and oxides of nitrogen in the exhaust gases.

Most electronic fuel injection systems use an oxygen sensor to measure the oxygen content of the exhaust gases. This information is used by the control unit to constantly adjust and "fine tune" the fuel mixture in response to changing temperature, load and altitude conditions. In addition, this degree of fuel control allows the catalytic converter to function at peak efficiency for optimum emission control.

Fig. 6 This is a fuel rail assembly from a typical MFI or SFI system. Note that each port has its own injector

FUEL INJECTION SERVICE

Can You Do It?

▶ See Figure 9

Probably the first real question you're asking yourself is, "Can I really do this?" The answer is, sure, why not?

You don't have to be an experienced mechanic to perform preventative maintenance on the fuel system on your vehicle. Really! If you have a basic set of hand tools, and a few, readily available and inexpensive specialty tools, and are at all familiar with their use, you should have few, if any, real problems.

In addition to preventative maintenance, most fuel system components may be replaced without extreme difficulty. Identifying whether those components are operating properly can be a little more difficult. With the exception of CIS mechanical injection system, almost all of the other fuel systems components are electronically controlled. This will require an understanding of the "Fundamentals of Electricity" later in this section, and at minimum a high quality digital multi-meter.

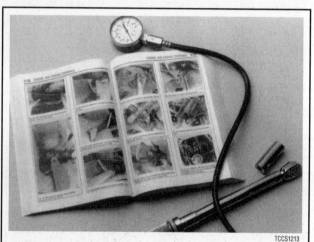

TCCS1213

Fig. 9 With the proper tools and a good information source, like this Chilton Total Car Care manual, you should be able to perform most maintenance procedures yourself

Where to Begin

Always start with a complete visual inspection of the fuel system and its related components. Read the information in this book and refer to the Chilton Total Car Care (TCC) Manual for your specific vehicle for information on your fuel system. The more you know about the operation of your specific system and its components the better the odds of you finding the problem the first time.

Before removing or replacing any components, read through the entire procedure. This will give you the overall view of what tools and supplies will be required. There is nothing more frustrating than having to walk to the bus stop on Monday morning because you were short one bolt on Sunday afternoon. So read ahead and plan ahead. Each operation should be approached logically and all procedures thoroughly understood before attempting any work.

This book contains maintenance, testing, and removal and installation procedures. While repair is not considered practical for most fuel system components, we tell you how to remove the part and then how to install the new or rebuilt replacement. Due to the complexity of most components used on modern fuel injected vehicles, backyard repair of fuel injection components is just not practical.

Avoiding Trouble

Many procedures in this book require you to "label and disconnect . . ." a group of lines, hoses or wires. Don't be lulled into thinking you can remember where everything goes — you won't. If you reconnect or install a part incorrectly, the vehicle's brakes will operate poorly, if at all. If you hook up electrical wiring incorrectly, you may instantly learn a very expensive lesson.

A piece of masking tape, for example, on a hose and a piece on its fitting will allow you to assign your own label such as the letter A or a short name. As long as you remember your own code, the lines can be reconnected by matching similar letters or names. Do remember that tape will dissolve in gasoline or other fluids. If a component is to be washed or cleaned, use another method of identification. A permanent felt-tipped marker can be very handy for marking metal parts. Remove any tape or paper labels after assembly.

SAFETY is the most important thing to remember when working on a vehicle, especially on the fuel system (since you are working with a combustible substance). Be sure to read the information on shop safety in Section 2 of this book.

Keep a log of everything you have checked and replaced. This will be a time and money saver if you should have to seek professional help.

Maintenance or Repair?

Proper maintenance is the key to long and trouble-free vehicle life, and the work can yield its own rewards. A properly maintained vehicle performs better than one that is neglected. As a conscientious owner and driver, set aside a Saturday morning, say once a month, to check or replace items which could cause major problems later. Keep your own personal log to jot down which services you performed, how much the parts cost you, the date, and the exact odometer reading at the time. Keep all receipts for parts purchased, so that they may be referred to in case of related problems or to determine operating expenses. As a do-it-yourselfer, these receipts are the only proof you have that the required maintenance was performed. In the event of a warranty problem, these receipts will be invaluable.

The literature provided with your vehicle when it was originally delivered includes the factory recommended maintenance schedule. If you no longer have this literature, replacement copies are usually available from the dealer, or, you can purchase a Chilton Total Car Care (TCC) Manual that is written just for your vehicle.

It's necessary to mention the difference between maintenance and repair. Maintenance includes routine inspections, adjustments, and replacement of parts that show signs of normal wear. Maintenance compensates for wear or deterioration. Repair implies that something has broken or is not working. A need for repair is often caused by lack of maintenance. Example: replacement of the air and fuel filter is maintenance recommended by the manufacturer at specific mileage intervals. Failure to do this can impair the operation of the fuel system, requiring very expensive repairs. While no maintenance program can prevent items from breaking or wearing out, a general rule can be stated: MAINTENANCE IS CHEAPER THAN REPAIR.

Two basic mechanic's rules should be mentioned here. First, whenever the left side of the vehicle is referred to, it is meant to specify the driver's side. Conversely, the right side of the vehicle means the passenger's side. Second, most screws and bolts are removed by turning counterclockwise, and tightened by turning clockwise. An easy way to remember: righty, tighty; lefty loosey. Corny, but effective.

Safety is always the most important rule. Constantly be aware of the dangers involved in working on a vehicle and take the proper precautions. See the information in this section regarding SERVICING YOUR VEHICLE SAFELY and the SAFETY NOTICE on the acknowledgment page.

Professional Help

▶ **See Figures 10 and 11**

No, we're not suggesting a psychiatrist. If you are not the type who is prone to taking a wrench to something NEVER FEAR. The procedures in this book cover topics at a level virtually anyone will be able to handle. And just the fact that you purchased this book shows your interest in better understanding your vehicle.

So where are we going with this? Simple, not only do we believe that you are capable of diagnosing and maintaining your own vehicle, but that maintaining it yourself is preferable in most cases. At the very least, you should fully understand how the systems in your vehicle work and what proper maintenance entails. You may decide that you would prefer most service be performed by a mechanic (and that's your call). Understanding what that mechanic has done to your vehicle will allow you to keep an eye on its condition.

Don't believe for a second that we are taking anything away from the professionals who dedicate their lives to being first rate mechanics. In some cases it is better for the do-it-yourselfer to bring their vehicle to a well equipped professional shop. The point we are try to make is that the more personal involvement you have in the maintenance of your vehicle, the better your odds are of coming out a winner.

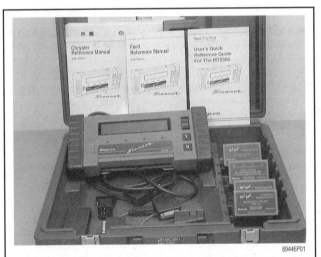

Fig. 10 A professional diagnostic scan tool is priced out of reach for the average do-it-yourselfer . . .

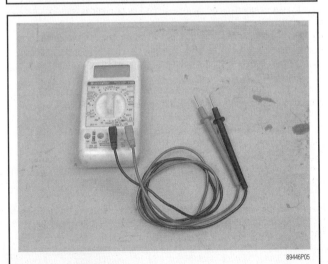

Fig. 11 . . . however, most basic diagnostics can be handled with a high quality multimeter

Avoiding the Most Common Mistakes

▶ **See Figure 12**

Before tackling any fuel system problems you should ask yourself a few questions.
1. Do I fully understand what is wrong?
2. Have I checked the basics:
    a. Is there fuel in the tank?
    b. Is the battery in good condition?
    c. Have I performed a visual inspection of belts, hoses, wires, and vacuum lines?
3. When was preventative maintenance last performed?
4. Do I understand the system and its operation used on this vehicle?
5. Do I understand how the components operate in this system?
6. Have I checked for diagnostic codes?

Only after you have answered yes to the above questions should you proceed. Even some professionals have been known to skip the basics looking for a quick fix to the problem only to find hours later that the vehicle has a bad battery.

Two tests should easily confirm the mechanical integrity of the fuel supply and return systems. These are the pressure and volume tests. You will find information in Section 4, Basic Maintenance and Troubleshooting.

Establish a test plan and follow it. Keep notes on everything you have done. Should it be necessary to get professional assistance, this will save the mechanic time, and you money.

Pay attention to the instructions provided. Thoroughly read and understand the test procedures before performing them.

Always take your time and be patient; once you have some experience, working on your vehicle may well become an enjoyable hobby.

Fig. 12 Fuel pressure can be checked using an inexpensive fuel pressure gauge

FUNDAMENTALS OF ELECTRICITY

▶ **See Figures 13 and 14**

A good understanding of basic electrical theory and how circuits work is necessary to successfully perform the service and testing outlined in this manual. Therefore, this section should be read before attempting any diagnosis and repair.

All matter is made up of tiny particles called molecules. Each molecule is made up of two or more atoms. Atoms may be divided into even smaller particles called protons, neutrons and electrons. These particles are the same in all matter and differences in materials (hard or soft, conductive or non-conductive) occur only because of the number and arrangement of these particles. In other words, the protons, neutrons and electrons in a drop of water are the same as those in an ounce of lead, there are just more of them (arranged differently) in a lead molecule than in a water molecule. Protons and neutrons packed together form the nucleus of the atom, while electrons orbit around the nucleus much the same way as the planets of the solar system orbit around the sun.

The proton is a small positive natural charge of electricity, while the neutron has no electrical charge. The electron carries a negative charge equal to the positive charge of the proton. Every electrically neutral atom contains the same number of protons and electrons, the exact number of which determines the element. The only difference between a conductor and an insulator is that a conductor possesses free electrons in large quantities, while an insulator has only a few. An element must have Very few free electrons to be a good insulator and vice-versa. When we speak of electricity, we're talking about these free electrons.

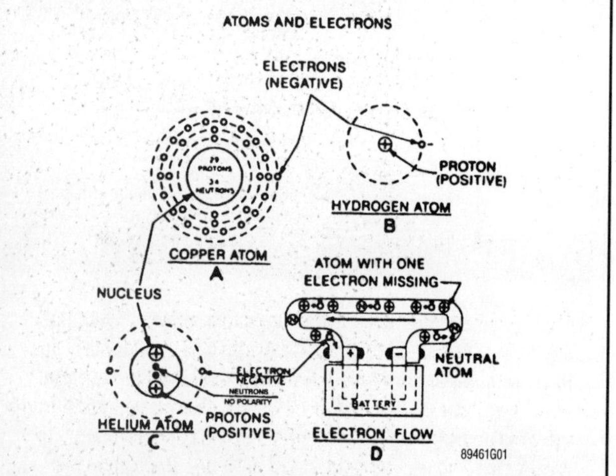

In a conductor, the movement of the free electrons is hindered by collisions with the adjoining atoms of the element (matter). This hindrance to movement is called RESISTANCE and it varies with different materials and temperatures. As temperature varies, the movement of the free electrons increases and decreases, causing collision rates to fluctuate and therefore varying resistance to the movement of the electrons. The number of collisions (resistance) also varies with the number of electrons flowing (current). Current is defined as the movement of electrons through a conductor such as a wire. In a conductor (such as copper) electrons can be caused to leave their atoms and move to other atoms. This flow is continuous in that every time an atom gives up an electron, it collects another one to take its place. This movement of electrons is called electric current and is measured in amperes. When 6.28 billion-billion (yes that's right, billion-billion) electrons pass a certain point in the circuit in one second, the amount of current flow is called 1 ampere.

The force or pressure which causes electrons to flow in any conductor (such as a wire) is called VOLTAGE. It is measured in volts and is similar to the pressure that causes water to flow in a pipe. Voltage is the difference in electrical pressure measured between 2 different points in a circuit. In a 12 volt system, for example, the force measured between the two battery posts is 12 volts. Two important concepts are voltage potential and polarity. Voltage potential is the amount of voltage or electrical pressure at a certain point in the circuit with respect to another point. For example, if the voltage potential at one post of the 12 volt battery is 0, the voltage potential at the other post is 12 volts with respect to the first post. One post of the battery is said to be positive (+); the other post is negative (-) and the conventional direction of current flow is from positive to negative in an electrical circuit. It should be noted that the electron flow in the wire is opposite the current flow. In other words, when the circuit is energized, the current flows from positive to negative, but the electrons actually move from negative to positive. The voltage or pressure needed to produce a current flow in a circuit must be greater than the resistance present in the circuit. In other words, if the voltage drop across the resistance is greater than or equal to the voltage input, the voltage potential will be zero—no voltage will flow through the circuit. Resistance to the flow of electrons is measured in ohms. One volt will cause 1 ampere to flow through a resistance of 1 ohm.

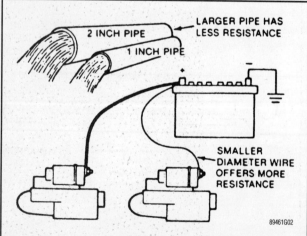

Fig. 13 Typical atoms of Copper (A), Hydrogen (B) and Helium (C). Electron flow in a battery circuit (D).

Units Of Electrical Measurement

▶ **See Figure 15**

There are 3 fundamental characteristics of a direct-current electrical circuit: volts, amperes and ohms.

VOLTAGE in a circuit controls the intensity with which the loads in the circuit operate. The brightness of a lamp, the heat of an electrical defroster, the speed of a motor are all directly proportional to the voltage, if the resistance in the circuit and/or mechanical load on electric motors remains constant. Voltage available from the battery is constant (normally 12 volts), but as it operates the various loads in the circuit, voltage decreases (drops).

AMPERE is the unit of measurement of current in an electrical circuit. One ampere is the quantity of current that will flow through a resistance of 1 ohm at a pressure of 1 volt. The amount of current that flows in a circuit is controlled by the voltage and the resistance in the circuit. Current flow is directly proportional to resistance. Thus, as voltage is increased or decreased, current is increased or decreased accordingly. Current is decreased as resistance is increased. However, current is also increased as resistance is decreased. With little or no resistance in a circuit, current is high.

Fig. 14 Electrical resistance can be compared to water flow through a pipe. The smaller the wire (pipe), the more resistance the flow of electrons (water).

OHM is the unit of measurement of resistance, represented by the Greek letter Omega (Ω). One ohm is the resistance of a conductor through which a current of one ampere will flow at a pressure of one volt. Electrical resistance can be measured on an instrument called an ohmmeter. The loads (electrical devices) are the primary resistances in a circuit. Loads such as lamps, solenoids and electric heaters have a resistance that is essentially fixed; at a normal fixed voltage, they will draw a fixed current. Motors, on the other hand, do not have a fixed resistance. Increasing the mechanical load on a motor, (such as might be caused by a misadjusted track in a power window system) will decrease the motor speed. The drop in motor rpm has the effect of reducing the internal resistance of the motor because the current draw of the motor varies directly with the mechanical load on the motor, although its actual resistance is unchanged. Thus, as the motor load increases, the current draw of the motor increases, and may increase up to the point where the motor stalls (cannot move the mechanical load).

Circuits are designed with the total resistance of the circuit taken into account. Troubles can arise when unwanted resistances enter into a circuit. If corrosion, dirt, grease, or any other contaminant occurs in places like switches, connectors and grounds, or if loose connections occur, resistances will develop in these areas. These resistances act like additional loads in the circuit and cause problems.

OHM'S LAW

Ohm's law is a statement of the relationship between the 3 fundamental characteristics of an electrical circuit. These rules apply to direct current (DC) only.

Ohm's law provides a means to make an accurate circuit analysis without actually seeing the circuit. If, for example, one wanted to check the condition of the rotor winding in a alternator whose specifications indicate that the field (rotor) current draw is normally 2.5 amperes at 12 volts, simply connect the rotor to a 12 volt battery and measure the current with an ammeter. If it measures about 2.5 amperes, the rotor winding can be assumed good.

An ohmmeter can be used to test components that have been removed from the vehicle in much the same manner as an ammeter. Since the voltage and the current of the rotor windings used as an earlier example are known, the resistance can be calculated using Ohms law. The formula would be ohms equals volts divided by amperes.

If the rotor resistance measures about 4.8 ohms when checked with an ohmmeter, the winding can be assumed good. By plugging in different specifications, additional circuit information can be determined such as current draw, etc.

Electrical Circuits

▶ See Figures 16 thru 26

An electrical circuit must start from a source of electrical supply and return to that source through a continuous path. Circuits are designed to handle a certain maximum current flow. The maximum allowable current flow is designed higher than the normal current requirements of all the loads in the circuit. Wire size, connections, insulation, etc., are designed to prevent undesirable voltage drop, overheating of conductors, arcing of contacts and other adverse effects. If the safe maximum current flow level is exceeded, damage to the circuit components will result; it is this condition that circuit protection devices are designed to prevent.

Protection devices are fuses, fusible links or circuit breakers designed to open or break the circuit quickly whenever an overload, such as a short circuit, occurs. By opening the circuit quickly, the circuit protection device prevents damage to the wiring, battery and other circuit components. Fuses and fusible links are designed to carry a preset maximum amount of current and to melt when that maximum is exceeded, while circuit breakers merely break the connection and may be manually reset. The maximum amperage rating of each fuse is marked on the fuse body and all contain a see-through portion that shows the break in the fuse element when blown.

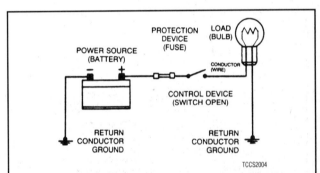

Fig. 16 This example illustrates a simple circuit. When the switch is closed, power from the positive (+) battery terminal flows through the fuse and the switch, and then to the light bulb. The light illuminates and the circuit is completed through the ground wire back to the negative (-) battery terminal. In reality, the two ground points shown in the illustration are attached to the metal frame of the vehicle, which completes the circuit back to the battery

$$I = \frac{E}{R} \quad \text{or} \quad AMPERES = \frac{VOLTS}{OHMS}$$

$$R = \frac{E}{I} \quad \text{or} \quad OHMS = \frac{VOLTS}{AMPERES}$$

$$E = I \times R \quad \text{or} \quad VOLTS = AMPERES \times OHMS$$

Fig. 15 Ohms law is the basis for all electrical measurement. By simply plugging in two values, the third can be calculated using this formula.

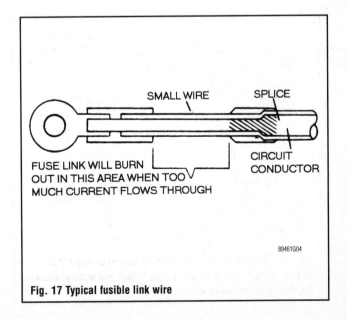

Fig. 17 Typical fusible link wire

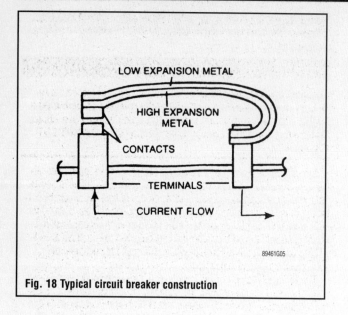

Fig. 18 Typical circuit breaker construction

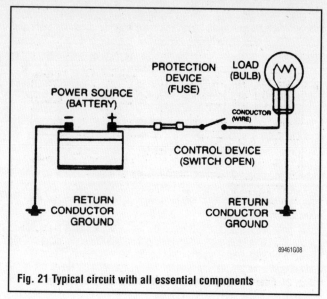

Fig. 21 Typical circuit with all essential components

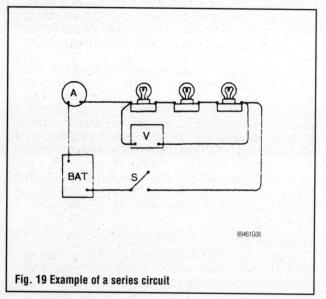

Fig. 19 Example of a series circuit

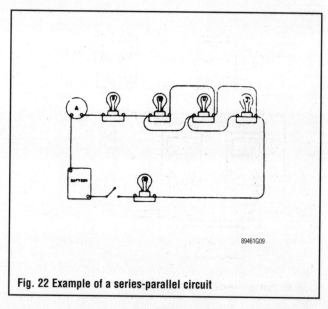

Fig. 22 Example of a series-parallel circuit

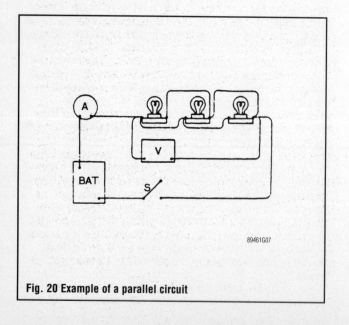

Fig. 20 Example of a parallel circuit

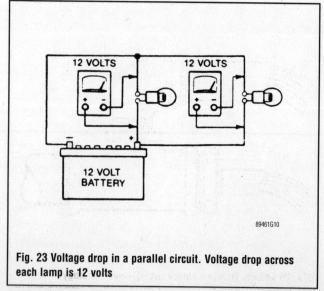

Fig. 23 Voltage drop in a parallel circuit. Voltage drop across each lamp is 12 volts

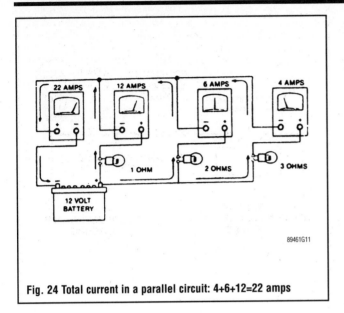

Fig. 24 Total current in a parallel circuit: 4+6+12=22 amps

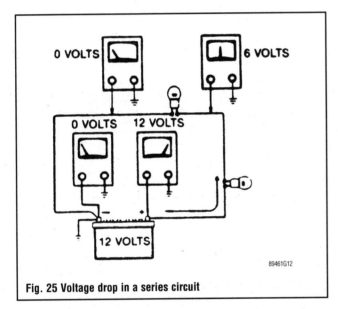

Fig. 25 Voltage drop in a series circuit

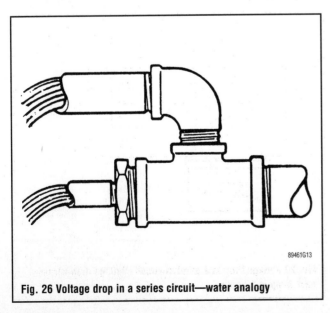

Fig. 26 Voltage drop in a series circuit—water analogy

Fusible link maximum amperage rating is indicated by gauge or thickness of the wire. Never replace a blown fuse or fusible link with one of a higher amperage rating.

✱✱ CAUTION

Resistance wires, like fusible links, are also spliced into conductors in some areas. Do not make the mistake of replacing a fusible link with a resistance wire. Resistance wires are longer than fusible links and are stamped 'RESISTOR—DO NOT CUT OR SPLICE.'

Circuit breakers consist of 2 strips of metal which have different coefficients of expansion. As an overload or current flows through the bimetallic strip, the high-expansion metal will elongate due to heat and break the contact. With the circuit open, the bimetal strip cools and shrinks, drawing the strip down until contact is re-established and current flows once again. In actual operation, the contact is broken very quickly if the overload is continuous and the circuit will be repeatedly broken and remade until the source of the overload is corrected.

The self-resetting type of circuit breaker is the one most generally used in automotive electrical systems. On manually reset circuit breakers, a button will pop up on the circuit breaker case. This button must be pushed in to reset the circuit breaker and restore power to the circuit. Always repair the source of the overload before resetting a circuit breaker or replacing a fuse or fusible link. When searching for overloads, keep in mind that the circuit protection devices protect only against overloads between the protection device and ground.

There are 2 basic types of circuit; Series and Parallel. In a series circuit, all of the elements are connected in chain fashion with the same amount of current passing through each element or load. No matter where an ammeter is connected in a series circuit, it will always read the same. The most important fact to remember about a series circuit is that the sum of the voltages across each element equals the source voltage. The total resistance of a series circuit is equal to the sum of the individual resistances within each element of the circuit. Using ohms law, one can determine the voltage drop across each element in the circuit. If the total resistance and source voltage is known, the amount of current can be calculated. Once the amount of current (amperes) is known, values can be substituted in the Ohms law formula to calculate the voltage drop across each individual element in the series circuit. The individual voltage drops must add up to the same value as the source voltage.

A parallel circuit, unlike a series circuit, contains 2 or more branches, each branch a separate path independent of the others. The total current draw from the voltage source is the sum of all the currents drawn by each branch. Each branch of a parallel circuit can be analyzed separately. The individual branches can be either simple circuits, series circuits or combinations of series-parallel circuits. Ohms law applies to parallel circuits just as it applies to series circuits, by considering each branch independently of the others. The most important thing to remember is that the voltage across each branch is the same as the source voltage. The current in any branch is that voltage divided by the resistance of the branch. A practical method of determining the resistance of a parallel circuit is to divide the product of the 2 resistances by the sum of 2 resistances at a time. Amperes through a parallel circuit is the sum of the amperes through the separate branches. Voltage across a parallel circuit is the same as the voltage across each branch.

By measuring the voltage drops the resistance of each element within the circuit is being measured. The greater the voltage drop, the greater the resistance. Voltage drop measurements are a common way of checking circuit resistances in automotive electrical systems. When part of a circuit develops excessive resistance (due to a bad connection) the element will show a higher than normal voltage drop. Normally, automotive wiring is selected to limit voltage drops to a few tenths of a volt. In parallel circuits, the total resistance is less than the sum of the individual resistances; because the current has 2 paths to take, the total resistance is lower.

Magnetism and Electromagnets

▶ See Figures 27, 28 and 29

Electricity and magnetism are very closely associated because when electric current passes through a wire, a magnetic field is created around the wire. When a wire carrying electric current is wound into a coil, a magnetic field with North and South poles is created just like in a bar magnet. If an iron core is placed within the coil, the magnetic field becomes stronger because iron conducts magnetic lines much easier than air. This arrangement is called an electromagnet and is the basic principle behind the operation of such components as relays, buzzers and solenoids.

A relay is basically just a remote-controlled switch that uses a small amount of current to control the flow of a large amount of current. The simplest relay contains an electromagnetic coil in series with a voltage source (battery) and a switch. A movable armature made of some magnetic material pivots at one end and is held a small distance away from the electromagnet by a spring or the spring steel of the armature itself. A contact point, made of a good conductor, is attached to the free end of the armature with another contact point a small distance away. When the relay is switched on (energized), the magnetic field created by the current flow attracts the armature, bending it until the contact points meet, closing a cir-

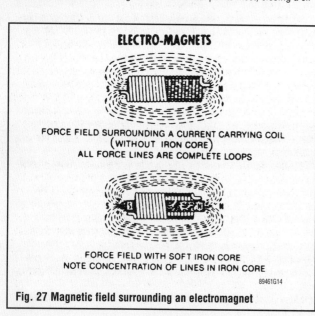

FORCE FIELD SURROUNDING A CURRENT CARRYING COIL (WITHOUT IRON CORE) ALL FORCE LINES ARE COMPLETE LOOPS

FORCE FIELD WITH SOFT IRON CORE NOTE CONCENTRATION OF LINES IN IRON CORE

89461G14

Fig. 27 Magnetic field surrounding an electromagnet

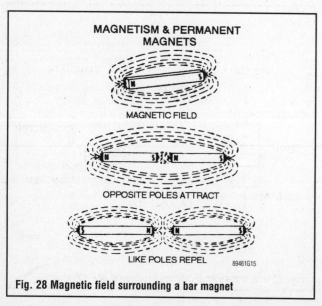

MAGNETIC FIELD

OPPOSITE POLES ATTRACT

LIKE POLES REPEL

89461G15

Fig. 28 Magnetic field surrounding a bar magnet

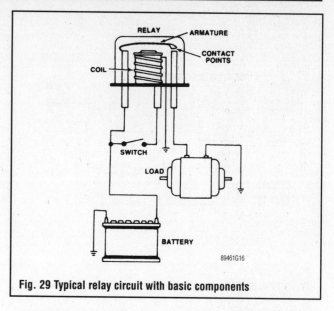

89461G16

Fig. 29 Typical relay circuit with basic components

cuit and allowing current to flow in the second circuit through the relay to the load the circuit operates. When the relay is switched off (de-energized), the armature springs back and opens the contact points, cutting off the current flow in the secondary, or controlled, circuit. Relays can be designed to be either open or closed when energized, depending on the type of circuit control a manufacturer requires.

A buzzer is similar to a relay, but its internal connections are different. When the switch is closed, the current flows through the normally closed contacts and energizes the coil. When the coil core becomes magnetized, it bends the armature down and breaks the circuit. As soon as the circuit is broken, the spring-loaded armature remakes the circuit and again energizes the coil. This cycle repeats rapidly to cause the buzzing sound.

A solenoid is constructed like a relay, except that its core is allowed to move, providing mechanical motion that can be used to actuate mechanical linkage to operate a door or trunk lock or control any other mechanical function. When the switch is closed, the coil is energized and the movable core is drawn into the coil. When the switch is opened, the coil is de-energized and spring pressure returns the core to its original position.

Basic Solid State

The term 'solid state' refers to devices utilizing transistors, diodes and other components which are made from materials known as semiconductors. A semiconductor is a material that is neither a good insulator nor a good conductor; principally silicon and germanium. The semiconductor material is specially treated to give it certain qualities that enhance its function therefore becoming either P-type (positive) or N-type (negative) material. Most semiconductors are constructed of silicon and can be designed to function either as an insulator or conductor.

DIODES

▶ See Figures 30 and 31

The simplest semiconductor function is that of the diode or rectifier (the 2 terms mean the same thing). A diode will pass current in one direction only, like a one-way valve, because it has low resistance in one direction and high resistance on the other. Whether the diode conducts or not depends on the polarity of the voltage applied to it. A diode has 2 electrodes, an anode and a cathode. When the anode receives positive (+) voltage and the cathode receives negative (-) voltage, current can flow easily through the diode. When the voltage is reversed, the diode becomes nonconducting and only allows a very slight amount of current to flow in the circuit. Because the semiconductor is not a perfect insulator, a small amount of reverse current leakage will occur, but the amount is usually too

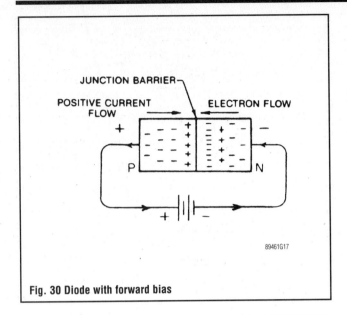

Fig. 30 Diode with forward bias

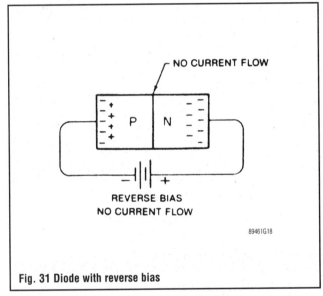

Fig. 31 Diode with reverse bias

small to consider. The application of voltage to maintain the current flow described is called 'forward bias.'

A light-emitting diode (LED) is made of a particular type of crystal that glows when current is passed through it. LED's are used in display faces of many digital or electronic instrument clusters. LED's are usually arranged to display numbers (digital readout), but can be used to illuminate a variety of electronic graphic displays.

Like any other electrical device, diodes have certain ratings that must be observed and should not be exceeded. The forward current rating (or bias) indicates how much current can safely pass through the diode without causing damage or destroying it. Forward current rating is usually given in either amperes or milliamperes. The voltage drop across a diode remains constant regardless of the current flowing through it. Small diodes designed to carry low amounts of current need no special provision for dissipating the heat generated in any electrical device, but large current carrying diodes are usually mounted on heat sinks to keep the internal temperature from rising to the point where the silicon will melt and destroy the diode. When diodes are operated in a high ambient temperature environment, they must be de-rated to prevent failure.

Another diode specification is its peak inverse voltage rating. This value is the maximum amount of voltage the diode can safely handle when operating in the blocking mode. This value can be anywhere from 50–1000

volts, depending on the diode. If voltage amount is exceeded, it will damage the diode just as too much forward current will. Most semiconductor failures are caused by excessive voltage or internal heat.

One can test a diode with a small battery and a lamp with the same voltage rating. With this arrangement one can find a bad diode and determine the polarity of a good one. A diode can fail and cause either a short or open circuit, but in either case it fails to function as a diode. Testing is simply a matter of connecting the test bulb first in one direction and then the other and making sure that current flows in one direction only. If the diode is shorted, the test bulb will remain on no matter how the light is connected.

TRANSISTORS

♦ See Figures 32 thru 38

The transistor is an electrical device used to control voltage within a circuit. A transistor can be considered a 'controllable diode' in that, in addition to passing or blocking current, the transistor can control the amount of current passing through it. Simple transistors are composed of 3 pieces of semiconductor material, P and N type, joined together and enclosed in a container. If 2 sections of P material and 1 section of N material are used, it is known as a PNP transistor; if the reverse is true, then it is known as an NPN transistor. The 2 types cannot be interchanged.

Most modern transistors are made from silicon (earlier transistors were made from germanium) and contain 3 elements; the emitter, the collector and the base. In addition to passing or blocking current, the transistor can control the amount of current passing through it and because of this can function as an amplifier or a switch. The collector and emitter form the main current carrying circuit of the transistor. The amount of current that flows through the collector-emitter junction is controlled by the amount of current in the base circuit. Only a small amount of base-emitter current is necessary to control a large amount of collector-emitter current (the amplifier effect). In automotive applications, however, the transistor is used primarily as a switch.

When no current flows in the base-emitter junction, the collector-emitter circuit has a high resistance, like to open contacts of a relay. Almost no current flows through the circuit and transistor is considered OFF. By bypassing a small amount of current into the base circuit, the resistance is low, allowing current to flow through the circuit and turning the transistor ON. This condition is known as 'saturation' and is reached when the base current reaches the maximum value designed into the transistor that allows current to flow. Depending on various factors, the transistor can turn on and off (go from cutoff to saturation) in less than one millionth of a second.

Much of what was said about ratings for diodes applies to transistors,

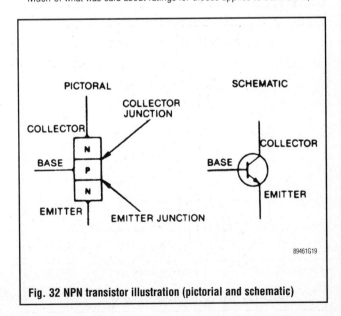

Fig. 32 NPN transistor illustration (pictorial and schematic)

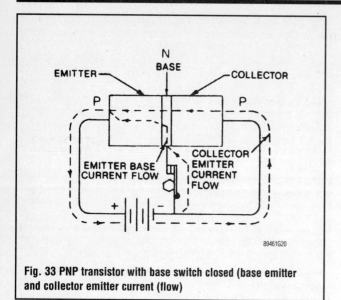

Fig. 33 PNP transistor with base switch closed (base emitter and collector emitter current (flow)

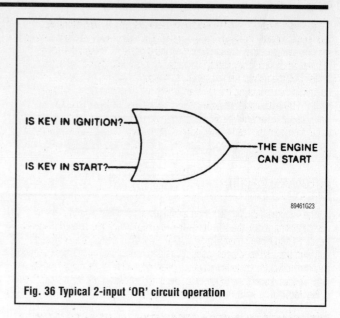

Fig. 36 Typical 2-input 'OR' circuit operation

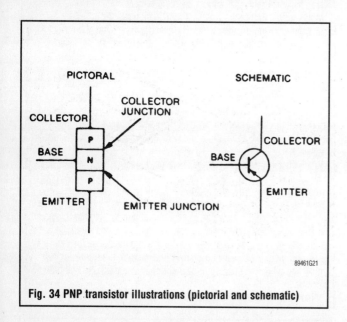

Fig. 34 PNP transistor illustrations (pictorial and schematic)

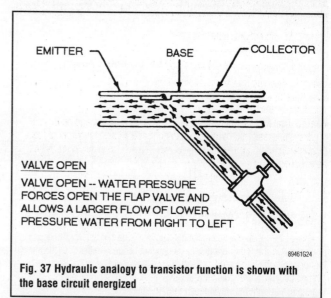

Fig. 37 Hydraulic analogy to transistor function is shown with the base circuit energized

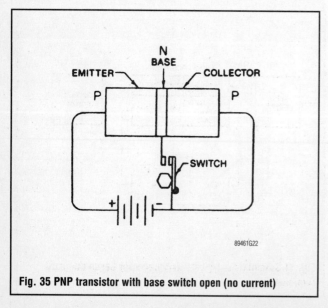

Fig. 35 PNP transistor with base switch open (no current)

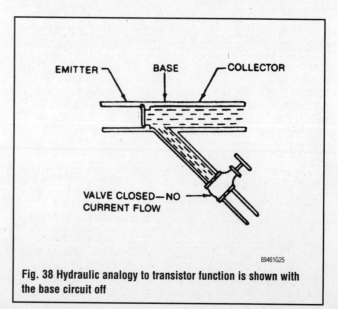

Fig. 38 Hydraulic analogy to transistor function is shown with the base circuit off

since they are constructed of the same materials. When transistors are required to handle relatively high currents, such as in voltage regulators or ignition systems, they are generally mounted on heat sinks in the same manner as diodes. They can be damaged or destroyed in the same manner if their voltage ratings are exceeded. A transistor can be checked for proper operation by measuring the resistance with an ohmmeter between the base-emitter terminals and then between the base-collector terminals. The forward resistance should be small, while the reverse resistance should be large. Compare the readings with those from a known good transistor. As a final check, measure the forward and reverse resistance between the collector and emitter terminals.

INTEGRATED CIRCUITS

The integrated circuit (IC) is an extremely sophisticated solid state device that consists of a silicone wafer (or chip) which has been doped, insulated and etched many times so that it contains an entire electrical circuit with transistors, diodes, conductors and capacitors miniaturized within each tiny chip. Integrated circuits are often referred to as 'computers on a chip' and are largely responsible for the current boom in electronic control technology.

Microprocessors, Computers and Logic Systems

GENERAL INFORMATION

Mechanical or electromechanical control devices lack the precision necessary to meet the requirements of modern control standards. They do not have the ability to respond to a variety of input conditions common to fuel injection, antilock brakes, climate control and electronic suspension operation. To meet these requirements, manufacturers have gone to solid state logic systems and microprocessors to control the basic functions of fuel, suspension, brake and temperature control, as well as other systems and accessories.

LOGIC

▶ See Figures 39, 40 and 41

One of the more vital roles of microprocessor-based systems is their ability to perform logic functions and make decisions. Logic designers use a shorthand notation to indicate whether a voltage is present in a circuit (the number 1) or not present (the number 0). Their systems are designed to respond in different ways depending on the output signal (or the lack of it) from various control devices.

There are 3 basic logic functions or 'gates' used to construct a microprocessor control system: the AND gate, the OR gate or the NOT gate. Stated simply, the AND gate works when voltage is present in 2 or more circuits which then energize a third (A and B energize C). The OR gate works when voltage is present at either circuit A or circuit B which then energizes circuit C. The NOT function is performed by a solid state device called an 'inverter' which reverses the input from a circuit so that, if voltage is going in, no voltage comes out and vice versa. With these three basic building blocks, a logic designer can create complex systems easily. In actual use, a logic or decision making system may employ many logic gates and receive inputs from a number of sources (sensors), but for the most part, all utilize the basic logic gates discussed above.

Stripped to its bare essentials, a computerized decision-making system is made up of 3 subsystems:

- Input devices (sensors or switches)
- Logic circuits (computer control unit)
- Output devices (actuators or controls)

The input devices are usually nothing more than switches or sensors that provide a voltage signal to the control unit logic circuits that is read as a 1 or 0 (on or off) by the logic circuits. The output devices are anything from a warning light to solenoid-operated valves, motors, linkage, etc. In most cases, the logic circuits themselves lack sufficient output power to

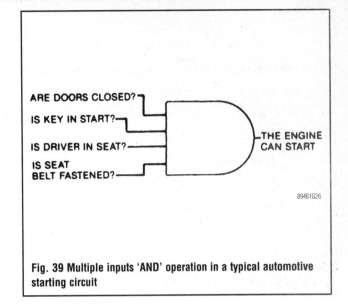

Fig. 39 Multiple inputs 'AND' operation in a typical automotive starting circuit

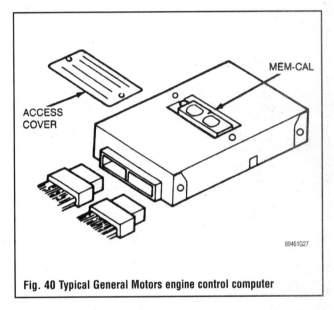

Fig. 40 Typical General Motors engine control computer

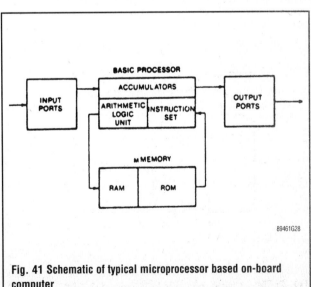

Fig. 41 Schematic of typical microprocessor based on-board computer

operate these devices directly. Instead, they operate some intermediate device such as a relay or power transistor which in turn operates the appropriate device or control. Many problems diagnosed as computer failures are really the result of a malfunctioning intermediate device like a relay. This must be kept in mind whenever troubleshooting any microprocessor-based control system.

As computer capacity is improved by the manufacturers, so does sensor technology. A few years ago, the on-board computer would receive a message from an engine sensor in a 'go or no-go' form; for example the coolant temperature would either be above or below 150°F (66°C). Today's systems allow the same sensor to pass progressively more voltage as the engine warms up. The engine computer now knows exactly what temperature the coolant is at all times. With this information the computer can react to the changing voltage signal from the sensor instantly and control other engine functions based on engine warm-up or over heating conditions.

MICROPROCESSORS

The logic systems discussed above are called `hardware' systems, because they consist only of the physical electronic components (gates, resistors, transistors, etc.). Hardware systems do not contain a program and are designed to perform specific or `dedicated' functions, which cannot readily be changed. For many simple automotive control requirements, such dedicated logic systems are perfectly adequate. When more complex logic functions are required, or where it may be desirable to alter these functions (e.g. from one model vehicle to another) a true computer system is used. A computer can be programmed through its software to perform many different functions and, if that program is stored on a separate integrated circuit chip called a ROM (Read Only Memory), it can be easily changed simply by plugging in a different ROM with the desired program. Most on-board automotive computers are designed with this capability. The on-board computer method of engine control offers the manufacturer a flexible method of responding to data from a variety of input devices and of controlling an equally large variety of output controls. The computer response can be changed quickly and easily by simply modifying its software program.

The microprocessor is the heart of the microcomputer. It is the thinking part of the computer system through which all the data from the various sensors passes. Within the microprocessor, data is acted upon, compared, manipulated or stored for future use. A microprocessor is not necessarily a microcomputer, but the differences between the 2 are becoming very minor. Originally, a microprocessor was a major part of a microcomputer, but nowadays microprocessors are being called 'single-chip microcomputers'. They contain all the essential elements to make them behave as a computer, including the most important ingredient—the program.

All computers require a program. In a general-purpose computer, the program can be easily changed to allow different tasks to be performed. In a 'dedicated' computer, such as most on-board automotive computers, the program isn't quite so easily altered. These automotive computers are designed to perform one or several specific tasks, such as maintaining the passenger compartment temperature at a specific, predetermined level. A program is what makes a computer smart; without a program a computer can do absolutely nothing. The term 'software' refers to the computer's program that makes the hardware perform the function needed.

The software program is simply a listing in sequential order of the steps or commands necessary to make a computer perform the desired task. Before the computer can do anything at all, the program must be fed into it by one of several possible methods. A computer can never be 'smarter' than the person programming it, but it is a lot faster. Although it cannot perform any calculation or operation that the programmer himself cannot perform, its processing time is measured in millionths of a second.

MEMORY

▶ See Figures 42 and 43

Because a computer is limited to performing only those operations (instructions) programmed into its memory, the program must be broken down into a large number of very simple steps. Two different programmers

can come up with 2 different programs, since there is usually more than one way to perform any task or solve a problem. In any computer, however, there is only so much memory space available, so an overly long or inefficient program may not fit into the memory. In addition to performing arithmetic functions (such as with a trip computer), a computer can also store data, look up data in a table and perform the logic functions previously discussed. A Random Access Memory (RAM) allows the computer to store bits of data temporarily while waiting to be acted upon by the program. It may also be used to store output data that is to be sent to an output device. Whatever data is stored in a RAM is lost when power is removed from the system by turning OFF the ignition key, for example.

Computers have another type of memory called a Read Only Memory (ROM) which is permanent. This memory is not lost when the power is removed from the system. Most programs for automotive computers are stored on a ROM memory chip. Data is usually in the form of a look-up table that saves computing time and program steps. For example, a computer designed to control the amount of distributor advance can have this information stored in a table. The information that determines distributor advance (engine rpm, manifold vacuum and temperature) is coded to produce the correct amount of distributor advance over a wide range of engine operating conditions. Instead of the computer computing the required advance, it simply looks it up in a pre-programmed table. However, not all electronic control functions can be handled in this manner; some must be computed. On an antilock brake system, for example, the computer must measure the rotation of each separate wheel and then calculate how much brake pressure to apply in order to prevent one wheel from locking up and causing a loss of control.

There are several ways of programming a ROM, but once programmed the ROM cannot be changed. If the ROM is made on the same chip that contains the microprocessor, the whole computer must be altered if a program change is needed. For this reason, a ROM is usually placed on a separate chip. Another type of memory is the Programmable Read Only Memory (PROM) that has the program 'burned in' with the appropriate programming machine. Like the ROM, once a PROM has been programmed, it cannot be changed. The advantage of the PROM is that it can be produced in small quantities economically, since it is manufactured with a blank memory. Program changes for various vehicles can be made readily. There is still another type of memory called an EPROM (Erasable PROM) which can be erased and programmed many times.

Engines coupled to electronically controlled transmissions employ a control module to oversee both engine and transmission operation. This unit may be referred to as the Electronic Control Module (ECM), the Powertrain Control Module (PCM) or the Vehicle Control Module (VCM). The integrated functions of engine and transmission control allow accurate gear selection and improved fuel economy.

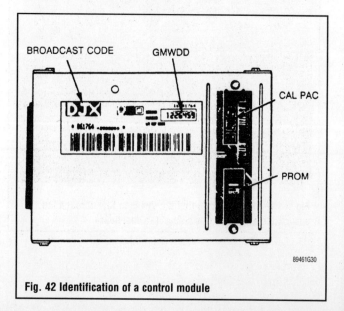

Fig. 42 Identification of a control module

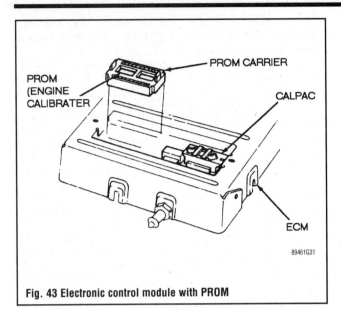

PROM (ENGINE CALIBRATER)

PROM CARRIER

CALPAC

ECM

89461G31

Fig. 43 Electronic control module with PROM

For engine diagnostics, the ECM and VCM may be considered identical to an PCM system, although the combined unit will display additional codes relating to transmission function and components.

➡**When the term control module is used in this manual it will refer to the engine control computer regardless that the manufacturer may call it a Powertrain Control Module (PCM), Electronic Control Module (ECM) or Vehicle Control Module (VCM).**

SERIAL NUMBER IDENTIFICATION

Vehicle Identification Number

▶ **See Figures 44, 45, 46 and 47**

The Vehicle Identification Number (VIN), usually located at the left side of the dashboard and viewable through the windshield, is the number that will tell you just about every thing you need to know concerning your vehicle. Since 1981 the VIN is a standardized 17 digit number. Each digit of this number has a specific meaning or designation. For example: the 8th digit usually designates the engine code, the 10th digit designates the model year of the vehicle etc.

The VIN number may be interpreted as follows:

- The first three digits are the World Manufacturer Identification number.
- The next five digits are the Vehicle Description Section.
- The remaining nine digits are the production numbers.

➡**If the vehicle has been altered in some way or the engine or transmission has been changed the VIN may not coincide with the change that has been made. In a case like this, look for the serial number on the component to be sure the correct parts are ordered.**

For a complete explanation of the Vehicle Identification Number for your specific vehicle, consult a 'Chilton Total Car Care (TCC) Manual'.

86801500

Fig. 44 The best place to find the VIN is to look through the windshield at the driver's side of the dashboard

89691P04

Fig. 45 On some vehicles, the manufacturer's label is located in the door pillar area

Fig. 46 Some manufacturers also place identification numbers on the firewall in the engine compartment

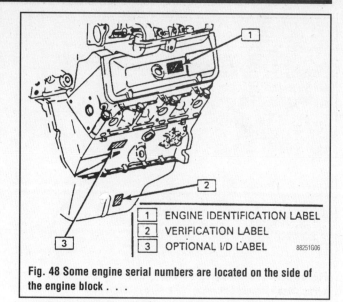

1	ENGINE IDENTIFICATION LABEL
2	VERIFICATION LABEL
3	OPTIONAL I/D LABEL

Fig. 48 Some engine serial numbers are located on the side of the engine block . . .

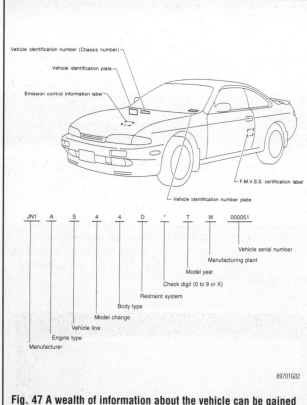

Fig. 47 A wealth of information about the vehicle can be gained by translating the code of the VIN

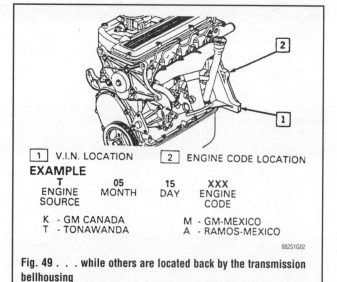

1	V.I.N. LOCATION	2 ENGINE CODE LOCATION

EXAMPLE

T	05	15	XXX
ENGINE SOURCE	MONTH	DAY	ENGINE CODE

K - GM CANADA   M - GM-MEXICO
T - TONAWANDA   A - RAMOS-MEXICO

Fig. 49 . . . while others are located back by the transmission bellhousing

Engine Serial Number

▶ **See Figures 48, 49, 50 and 51**

Most engine serial numbers consists of an engine series identification number followed by a production number which corresponds to the production number of the VIN. The number may be found in various places, depending upon the particular engine.

For complete information on engine serial numbers for your specific vehicle, consult a 'Chilton Total Car Care (TCC) Manual'.

Fig. 50 Ford is famous for placing engine serial numbers on their valve covers

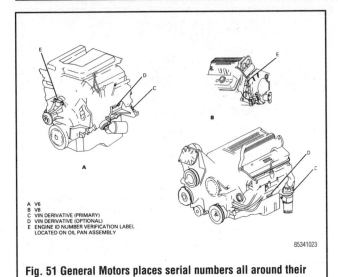

A V6
B V8
C VIN DERIVATIVE (PRIMARY)
D VIN DERIVATIVE (OPTIONAL)
E ENGINE ID NUMBER VERIFICATION LABEL
 LOCATED ON OIL PAN ASSEMBLY

85341023

Fig. 51 General Motors places serial numbers all around their V8 engines

Transmission Serial Number

▶ See Figure 52

It is slightly easier to find transmission serial numbers since there are less places for the factory to hide them. Most serial numbers are located on the side of the transmission case. However, some manufacturers have placed them on the fluid pan, or on the bellhousing.

For complete information on transmission serial numbers for your specific vehicle, consult a 'Chilton Total Car Care (TCC) Manual'.

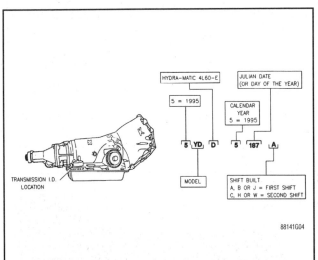

88141G04

Fig. 52 Typical transmission serial number location. Serial numbers can be translated using manufacturer's codes

Transfer Case Serial Number

▶ See Figure 53

Much like transmissions, transfer case serial numbers are usually stamped on the side of the transfer case. However, serial numbers can be located anywhere on the case.

For complete information on transfer case serial numbers for your specific vehicle, consult a 'Chilton Total Car Care (TCC) Manual'.

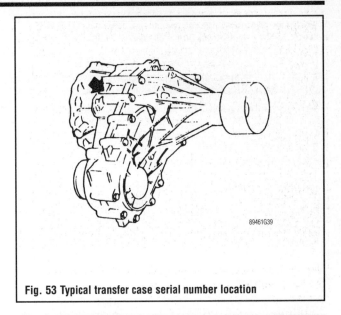

89461G39

Fig. 53 Typical transfer case serial number location

Vehicle Emissions Control Information (VECI) label

▶ See Figure 54

The Vehicle Emissions Control Information (VECI) label provides a wealth of information pertaining to the engine's emission control system. Most labels identifies the engine's Cubic Inch Displacement (CID) and size in Liter(s). They can also provide information for tune-up, such as spark plug gap, ignition timing, idle speed and valve lash specifications.

In some cases, the VECI label will provide a specific adjustment procedure. This is usually the case if a connector must be unplugged to set the base ignition timing. Some labels will also incorporate the vacuum routing of your engine's emission control system.

The VECI label should be considered the best source for information concerning your vehicle. It reflects the latest information available from the manufacturer and often times provides changes made during the production run that may not have made it into the service manuals.

➡ **Always keep in mind that the vehicle you are working on may have had an engine change. If this is the case, you will have to identify the engine (year and code) you now the have in the vehicle. If the vehicle is missing the VECI label, a new one can be ordered from your local dealer.**

86712037

Fig. 54 Vehicle Emission Control Information (VECI) label located in the engine compartment

The VECI label is usually located in or around the engine compartment. On some vehicles, the decal will be found directly under the hood. Others may have it on the strut tower or radiator support.

For complete information on VECI labels for your specific vehicle, consult a 'Chilton Total Car Care (TCC) Manual'.

AIR POLLUTION

The earth's atmosphere, at or near sea level, consists approximately of 78 percent nitrogen, 21 percent oxygen and 1 percent other gases. If it were possible to remain in this state, 100 percent clean air would result. However, many varied causes allow other gases and particulates to mix with the clean air, causing the air to become unclean or polluted.

Certain of these pollutants are visible while others are invisible, with each having the capability of causing distress to the eyes, ears, throat, skin and respiratory system. Should these pollutants become concentrated in a specific area and under certain conditions, death could result due to the displacement or chemical change of the oxygen content in the air. These pollutants can also cause great damage to the environment and to the many man made objects that are exposed to the elements.

To better understand the causes of air pollution, the pollutants can be categorized into 3 separate types, natural, industrial and automotive.

Natural Pollutants

Natural pollution has been present on earth since before man appeared and continues to be a factor when discussing air pollution, although it causes only a small percentage of the overall pollution problem existing in our country today. It is the direct result of decaying organic matter, wind born smoke and particulates from such natural events as plain and forest fires (ignited by heat or lightning), volcanic ash, sand and dust which can spread over a large area of the countryside.

Such a phenomenon of natural pollution has been recently seen in the form of volcanic eruptions, with the resulting plume of smoke, steam and volcanic ash blotting out the sun's rays as it spreads and rises higher into the atmosphere. As it travels into the atmosphere the upper air currents catch and carry the smoke and ash, while condensing the steam back into water vapor. As the water vapor, smoke and ash traveled on their journey, the smoke dissipates into the atmosphere while the ash and moisture settle back to earth in a trail hundreds of miles long. In some cases, lives are lost and millions of dollars of property damage result. Ironically, man can only stand by and watch it happen.

Industrial Pollution

Industrial pollution is caused primarily by industrial processes, the burning of coal, oil and natural gas, which in turn produce smoke and fumes. Because the burning fuels contain large amounts of sulfur, the principal ingredients of smoke and fumes are sulfur dioxide and particulate matter. This type of pollutant occurs most severely during still, damp and cool weather, such as at night. Even in its less severe form, this pollutant is not confined to just cities. Because of air movements, the pollutants move for miles over the surrounding countryside, leaving in its path a barren and unhealthy environment for all living things.

Working with Federal, State and Local mandated regulations and by carefully monitoring the emissions, big business has greatly reduced the amount of pollutant emitted from its industrial sources, striving to obtain an acceptable level. Because of the mandated industrial emission clean up, many land areas and streams in and around the cities that were formerly barren of vegetation and life, have now begun to move back in the direction of nature's intended balance.

Automotive Pollutants

The third major source of air pollution is automotive emissions. The emissions from the internal combustion engine were not an appreciable problem years ago because of the small number of registered vehicles and the nation's small highway system. However, during the early 1950's, the trend of the American people was to move from the cities to the surround-ing suburbs. This caused an immediate problem in transportation because the majority of suburbs were not afforded mass transit conveniences. This lack of transportation created an attractive market for the automobile manufacturers, which resulted in a dramatic increase in the number of vehicles produced and sold, along with a marked increase in highway construction between cities and the suburbs. Multi-vehicle families emerged with a growing emphasis placed on an individual vehicle per family member. As the increase in vehicle ownership and usage occurred, so did pollutant levels in and around the cities, as suburbanites drove daily to their businesses and employment, returning at the end of the day to their homes in the suburbs.

It was noted that a fog and smoke type haze was being formed and at times, remained in suspension over the cities, taking time to dissipate. At first this smog, derived from the words 'smoke and fog', was thought to result from industrial pollution but it was determined that automobile emissions shared the blame. It was discovered that when normal automobile emissions were exposed to sunlight for a period of time, complex chemical reactions would take place.

It is now known that smog is a photo chemical layer which develops when certain oxides of nitrogen (NOx) and unburned hydrocarbons (HO) from automobile emissions are exposed to sunlight. Pollution was more severe when smog would become stagnant over an area in which a warm layer of air settled over the top of the cooler air mass, trapping and holding the cooler mass at ground level. The trapped cooler air would keep the emissions from being dispersed and diluted through normal air flows. This type of air stagnation was given the name 'Temperature Inversion'.

Temperature Inversion

In normal weather situations, the surface air is warmed by heat radiating from the earth's surface and the sun's rays and will rise upward, into the atmosphere. Upon rising it will cool through a convection type heat exchange with the cooler upper air. As warm air rises, the surface pollutants are carried upward and dissipated into the atmosphere.

When a temperature inversion occurs, we find the higher air is no longer cooler but warmer than the surface air, causing the cooler surface air to become trapped. This warm air blanket can extend from above ground level to a few hundred or even a few thousand feet into the air. As the surface air is trapped, so are the pollutants, causing a severe smog condition. Should this stagnant air mass extend to a few thousand feet high, enough air movement with the inversion takes place to allow the smog layer to rise above ground level but the pollutants still cannot dissipate. This inversion can remain for days over an area, with the smog level only rising or lowering from ground level to a few hundred feet high. Meanwhile, the pollutant levels increase, causing eye irritation, respiratory problems, reduced visibility, plant damage and in some cases, disease.

This inversion phenomenon was first noted in the Los Angeles, California area. The city lies in terrain resembling a basin and with certain weather conditions, a cold air mass is held in the basin while a warmer air mass covers it like a lid.

Because this type of condition was first documented as prevalent in the Los Angeles area, this type of trapped pollution was named 'Los Angeles Smog', although it occurs in other areas where a large concentration of automobiles are used and the air remains stagnant for any length of time.

Gasoline Engine Pollutants

Consider the internal combustion engine as a machine in which raw materials must be placed so a finished product comes out. As in any machine operation, a certain amount of wasted material is formed. When we relate this to the internal combustion engine, we find that through the input of air and fuel, we obtain power during the combustion process to drive the vehicle. The by-product or waste of this power is, in part, heat and exhaust gases with which we must dispose.

Heat Transfer

The heat from the combustion process can rise to over 4,000°F (2,204°C). The dissipation of this heat is controlled by a ram air effect, the use of cooling fans to cause air flow and having a liquid coolant solution surrounding the combustion area to transfer the heat of combustion through the cylinder walls and into the coolant. The coolant is then directed to a thin-finned, multi-tubed radiator, from which the excess heat is transferred to the atmosphere by 1 of the 3 heat transfer methods, conduction, convection or radiation.

The cooling of the combustion area is an important part in the control of

exhaust emissions. To understand the behavior of the combustion and transfer of its heat, consider the air/fuel charge. It is ignited and the flame front burns progressively across the combustion chamber until the burning charge reaches the cylinder walls. Some of the fuel in contact with the walls is not hot enough to burn, thereby snuffing out or quenching the combustion process. This leaves unburned fuel in the combustion chamber. This unburned fuel is then forced out of the cylinder and into the exhaust system, along with the exhaust gases.

Many attempts have been made to minimize the amount of unburned fuel in the combustion chambers due to the snuffing out or quenching, by increasing the coolant temperature and lessening the contact area of the coolant around the combustion area. Design limitations within the combustion chambers prevent the complete burning of the air/fuel charge, so a certain amount of the unburned fuel is still expelled into the exhaust system, regardless of modifications to the engine.

EXHAUST EMISSIONS

Composition Of The Exhaust Gases

The exhaust gases emitted into the atmosphere are a combination of burned and unburned fuel. To understand the exhaust emission and its composition, we must review some basic chemistry.

When the air/fuel mixture is introduced into the engine, we are mixing air, composed of nitrogen (78 percent), oxygen (21 percent) and other gases (1 percent) with the fuel, which is 100 percent hydrocarbons (HC), in a semi-controlled ratio. As the combustion process is accomplished, power is produced to move the vehicle while the heat of combustion is transferred to the cooling system. The exhaust gases are then composed of nitrogen, a diatomic gas (N_2), the same as was introduced in the engine, carbon dioxide (CO_2), the same gas that is used in beverage carbonation and water vapor (H_2O). The nitrogen (N_2), for the most part passes through the engine unchanged, while the oxygen (O_2) reacts (burns) with the hydrocarbons (HC) and produces the carbon dioxide (CO_2) and the water vapors (H_2O). If this chemical process would be the only process to take place, the exhaust emissions would be harmless. However, during the combustion process, other compounds are formed which are considered dangerous. These pollutants are carbon monoxide (CO), hydrocarbons (HC), oxides of nitrogen (NOx) oxides of sulfur (SOx) and engine particulates.

HYDROCARBONS

Hydrocarbons (HC) are essentially fuel which was not burned during the combustion process or which has escaped into the atmosphere through fuel evaporation. The main sources of incomplete combustion are rich air/fuel mixtures, low engine temperatures and improper spark timing. The main sources of hydrocarbon emission through fuel evaporation on most vehicles used to be the vehicle's fuel tank and carburetor bowl.

To reduce combustion hydrocarbon emission, engine modifications were made to minimize dead space and surface area in the combustion chamber. In addition, the air/fuel mixture was made leaner through the improved control which fuel injection offers and by the addition of external controls to aid in further combustion of the hydrocarbons outside the engine. Two such methods were the addition of an air injection system, to inject fresh air into the exhaust manifolds and the installation of a catalytic converter, a unit that is able to burn traces of hydrocarbons without affecting the internal combustion process or fuel economy. The vehicles covered in this manual may utilize either, both or none of these methods, depending on the year and model.

To control hydrocarbon emissions through fuel evaporation, modifications were made to the fuel tank to allow storage of the fuel vapors during periods of engine shut-down. Modifications were also made to the air intake system so that at specific times during engine operation, these vapors may be purged and burned by blending them with the air/fuel mixture.

CARBON MONOXIDE

Carbon monoxide is formed when not enough oxygen is present during the combustion process to convert carbon (C) to carbon dioxide (CO_2). An increase in the carbon monoxide (CO) emission is normally accompanied by an increase in the hydrocarbon (HC) emission because of the lack of oxygen to completely burn all of the fuel mixture.

Carbon monoxide (CO) also increases the rate at which the photo chemical smog is formed by speeding up the conversion of nitric oxide (NO) to nitrogen dioxide (NO_2). To accomplish this, carbon monoxide (CO) combines with oxygen (O_2) and nitric oxide (NO) to produce carbon dioxide (CO_2) and nitrogen dioxide (NO_2). ($CO + O_2 + NO = CO_2 + NO_2$).

The dangers of carbon monoxide, which is an odorless and colorless toxic gas are many. When carbon monoxide is inhaled into the lungs and passed into the blood stream, oxygen is replaced by the carbon monoxide in the red blood cells, causing a reduction in the amount of oxygen being supplied to the many parts of the body. This lack of oxygen causes headaches, lack of coordination, reduced mental alertness and should the carbon monoxide concentration be high enough, death could result.

NITROGEN

Normally, nitrogen is an inert gas. When heated to approximately 2,500°F (1,371°C) through the combustion process, this gas becomes active and causes an increase in the nitric oxide (NOx) emission.

Oxides of nitrogen (NOx) are composed of approximately 97–98 percent nitric oxide (NO). Nitric oxide is a colorless gas but when it is passed into the atmosphere, it combines with oxygen and forms nitrogen dioxide (NO_2). The nitrogen dioxide then combines with chemically active hydrocarbons (HC) and when in the presence of sunlight, causes the formation of photo chemical smog.

OZONE

To further complicate matters, some of the nitrogen dioxide (NO_2) is broken apart by the sunlight to form nitric oxide and oxygen. (NO_2 + sunlight = NO + O). This single atom of oxygen then combines with diatomic (meaning 2 atoms) oxygen (O_2) to form ozone (O_3). Ozone is one of the smells associated with smog. It has a pungent and offensive odor irritates the eyes and lung tissues, affects the growth of plant life and causes rapid deterioration of rubber products. Ozone can be formed by sunlight as well as electrical discharge into the air.

The most common discharge area on the automobile engine is the secondary ignition electrical system, especially when inferior quality spark plug cables are used. As the surge of high voltage is routed through the secondary cable, the circuit builds up an electrical field around the wire, acting upon the oxygen in the surrounding air to form the ozone. The faint glow along the cable with the engine running that may be visible on a dark night, is called the 'corona discharge'. It is the result of the electrical field passing from a high along the cable, to a low in the surrounding air, which forms the ozone gas. The combination of corona and ozone has been a major cause of cable deterioration. Recently, different and better quality insulating materials have lengthened the life of the electrical cables.

Although ozone at ground level can be harmful, ozone is beneficial to the earth's inhabitants. By having a concentrated ozone layer called the 'ozonosphere', between 10 and 20 miles (16–32km) up in the atmosphere, much of the ultra violet radiation from the sun's rays are absorbed and screened. If this ozone layer were not present, much of the earth's surface would be burned, dried and unfit for human life.

There is much discussion concerning the ozone layer and its density. A feeling exists that this protective layer of ozone is slowly diminishing and corrective action must be directed to this problem. Much experimentation is presently being conducted to determine if a problem exists and if so, the short and long term effects of the problem and how it can be remedied.

OXIDES OF SULFUR

Oxides of sulfur (SOx) were initially ignored in the exhaust system emissions, since the sulfur content of gasoline as a fuel is less than $\frac{1}{10}$ of 1 percent. Because of this small amount, it was felt that it contributed very little to the overall pollution problem. However, because of the difficulty in solving the sulfur emissions in industrial pollution and the introduction of catalytic converter to the automobile exhaust systems, a change was mandated. The automobile exhaust system, when equipped with a catalytic converter, changes the sulfur dioxide (SO_2) into the sulfur trioxide (SO_3).

When this combines with water vapors (H_2O), a sulfuric acid mist (H_2SO_4) is formed and is a very difficult pollutant to handle since it is extremely corrosive. This sulfuric acid mist that is formed, is the same mist that rises from the vents of an automobile battery when an active chemical reaction takes place within the battery cells.

When a large concentration of vehicles equipped with catalytic converters are operating in an area, this acid mist will rise and be distributed over a large ground area causing land, plant, crop, paints and building damage.

PARTICULATE MATTER

A certain amount of particulate matter is present in the burning of any fuel, with carbon constituting the largest percentage of the particulates. In gasoline, the remaining particulates are the burned remains of the various other compounds used in its manufacture. When a gasoline engine is in good internal condition, the particulate emissions are low but as the engine wears internally, the particulate emissions increase. By visually inspecting the tail pipe emissions, a determination can be made as to where an engine defect may exist. An engine with light gray or blue smoke emitting from the tail pipe normally indicates an increase in the oil consumption through burning due to internal engine wear. Black smoke would indicate a defective fuel delivery system, causing the engine to operate in a rich mode. Regardless of the color of the smoke, the internal part of the engine or the fuel delivery system should be repaired to prevent excess particulate emissions.

Diesel and turbine engines emit a darkened plume of smoke from the exhaust system because of the type of fuel used. Emission control regulations are mandated for this type of emission and more stringent measures are being used to prevent excess emission of the particulate matter. Electronic components are being introduced to control the injection of the fuel at precisely the proper time of piston travel, to achieve the optimum in fuel ignition and fuel usage. Other particulate after-burning components are being tested to achieve a cleaner emission.

Good grades of engine lubricating oils should be used, which meet the manufacturers specification. Cut-rate oils can contribute to the particulate emission problem because of their low flash or ignition temperature point. Such oils burn prematurely during the combustion process causing emissions of particulate matter.

The cooling system is an important factor in the reduction of particulate matter. With the cooling system operating at a temperature specified by the manufacturer, the optimum of combustion will occur. The cooling system must be maintained in the same manner as the engine oiling system, as each system is required to perform properly in order for the engine to operate efficiently for a long time.

Other Automobile Emission Sources

Before emission controls were mandated on the internal combustion engines, other sources of engine pollutants were discovered, along with the exhaust emission. It was determined the engine combustion exhaust produced 60 percent of the total emission pollutants, fuel evaporation from the fuel tank and carburetor vents produced 20 percent, with the another 20 percent being produced through the crankcase as a by-product of the combustion process.

CRANKCASE EMISSIONS

Crankcase emissions are made up of water, acids, unburned fuel, oil fumes and particulates. The emissions are classified as hydrocarbons (HC) and are formed by the small amount of unburned, compressed air/fuel mixture entering the crankcase from the combustion area during the compression and power strokes, between the cylinder walls and piston rings. The head of the compression and combustion help to form the remaining crankcase emissions.

Since the first engines, crankcase emissions were allowed to vent into the atmosphere through a road draft tube, mounted on the lower side of the engine block. Fresh air came in through an open oil filler cap or breather. The air passed through the crankcase mixing with blow-by gases. The motion of the vehicle and the air blowing past the open end of the road draft tube caused a low pressure area at the end of the tube. Crankcase emissions were simply drawn out of the road draft tube into the air.

To control the crankcase emission, the road draft tube was deleted. A hose and/or tubing was routed from the crankcase to the intake manifold so the blow-by emission could be burned with the air/fuel mixture. However, it was found that intake manifold vacuum, used to draw the crankcase emissions into the manifold, would vary in strength at the wrong time and not allow the proper emission flow. A regulating type valve was needed to control the flow of air through the crankcase.

Testing, showed the removal of the blow-by gases from the crankcase as quickly as possible, was most important to the longevity of the engine. Should large accumulations of blow-by gases remain and condense, dilution of the engine oil would occur to form water, soot, resins, acids and lead salts, resulting in the formation of sludge and varnishes. This condensation of the blow-by gases occur more frequently on vehicles used in numerous starting and stopping conditions, excessive idling and when the engine is not allowed to attain normal operating temperature through short runs.

FUEL EVAPORATIVE EMISSIONS

Gasoline fuel is a major source of pollution, before and after it is burned in the automobile engine. From the time the fuel is refined, stored, pumped and transported, again stored until it is pumped into the fuel tank of the vehicle, the gasoline gives off unburned hydrocarbons (HC) into the atmosphere. Through redesigning of the storage areas and venting systems, the pollution factor was diminished, but not eliminated, from the refinery standpoint. However, the automobile remained the primary source of vaporized, unburned hydrocarbon (HC) emissions.

Fuel pumped from an underground storage tank is cool but when exposed to a warmer ambient temperature, will expand. Before controls were mandated, an owner would fill the fuel tank with fuel from an underground storage tank and park the vehicle for some time in warm area, such as a parking lot. As the fuel would warm, it would expand and should no provisions or area be provided for the expansion, the fuel would spill out the filler neck and onto the ground, causing hydrocarbon (HC) pollution and creating a severe fire hazard. To correct this condition, the vehicle manufacturers added overflow plumbing and/or gasoline tanks with built in expansion areas or domes.

However, this did not control the fuel vapor emission from the fuel tank. It was determined that most of the fuel evaporation occurred when the vehicle was stationary and the engine not operating. Most vehicles carry 5–25 gallons (19–95 liters) of gasoline. Should a large concentration of vehicles be parked in one area, such as a large parking lot, excessive fuel vapor emissions would take place, increasing as the temperature increases.

To prevent the vapor emission from escaping into the atmosphere, the fuel system is designed to trap the fuel vapors while the vehicle is stationary, by sealing the fuel system from the atmosphere. A storage system is used to collect and hold the fuel vapors from the fuel injection system and the fuel tank when the engine is not operating. When the engine is started, the storage system is then purged of the fuel vapors, which are drawn into the engine and burned with the air/fuel mixture.

EMISSION CONTROL SYSTEMS

When viewed as a whole, emission control systems can be extremely confusing. However, it is possible to ease some of the confusion by dividing the overall emissions system into several easily understood smaller systems.

There are five popular systems used to reduce emissions: the crankcase ventilation system, the evaporative emission control system, the Exhaust Gas Recirculation (EGR) system, the air injection system and the catalytic converter system. In addition to these emission systems, some vehicles incorporate an electronically controlled fuel system (feedback system) which further reduces emissions.

➡ **Not all vehicles are equipped with these emission systems.**

CRANKCASE VENTILATION SYSTEMS

♦ **See Figures 55 and 56**

Since the early sixties, all cars have been equipped with crankcase ventilation systems.

When the engine is running, a small portion of the gases which are formed in the combustion chamber leak past the piston rings and enter the crankcase. Since these gases are under pressure, they tend to escape from the crankcase and enter the atmosphere. If these gases are allowed to remain in the crankcase for any length of time, they contaminate the engine oil and cause sludge to build up in the crankcase. If the gases are allowed to escape to the atmosphere, they pollute the air with unburned hydrocarbons. The job of the crankcase ventilation system is to recycle these gases back into the engine combustion chamber where they are re-burned.

The crankcase (blow-by) gases are recycled as the engine is running by drawing clean filtered air through the air filter and into the crankcase. As the air passes through the crankcase, it picks up the combustion gases and carries them out of the crankcase, through the oil separator, through the PCV valve or orifice, and into the induction system. As they enter the intake manifold, they are drawn into the combustion chamber where they are re-burned.

The most critical component in the system is the PCV valve that controls

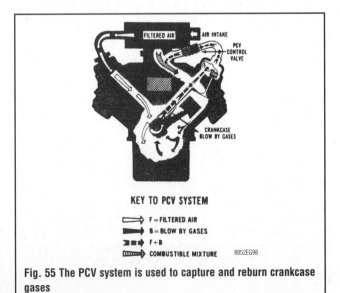

KEY TO PCV SYSTEM

⇨ F = FILTERED AIR
▬▶ B = BLOW BY GASES
▤▶ F + B
▦▶ COMBUSTIBLE MIXTURE   8852EG98

Fig. 55 The PCV system is used to capture and reburn crankcase gases

the amount of gases that are recycled. At low engine speeds, the valve is partially closed, limiting the flow of gases. As engine speed increases, the valve opens to admit greater quantities of air to the intake manifold. Some systems do not use a PCV valve. They simply use a restrictor or orifice in the ventilation hose to meter the crankcase gases.

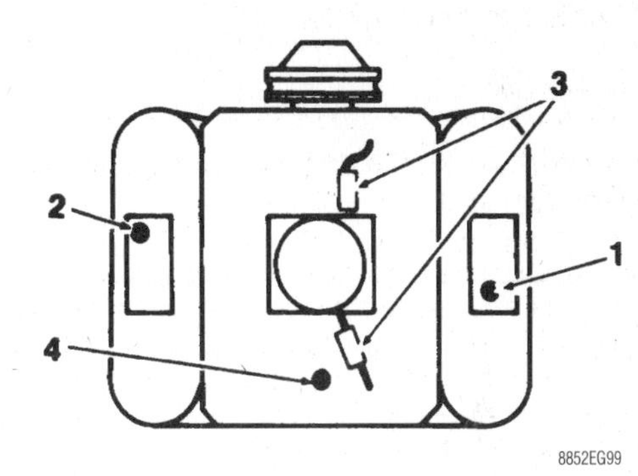

If the PCV valve/orifice becomes blocked or plugged, the gases cannot be vented from the crankcase. Since they are under pressure, they will find their own way out of the crankcase. This alternate route is usually a weak oil seal or gasket in the engine. As the gas escapes by the gasket, it usually creates an oil leak. Besides causing oil leaks, a clogged PCV valve also allows these gases to remain in the crankcase for an extended period, promoting the formation of sludge in the engine.

EVAPORATIVE EMISSION CONTROL SYSTEM

♦ **See Figures 57 and 58**

The evaporative emission control system is designed to prevent fuel tank and carburetor bowl (if equipped) vapors from being emitted into the atmosphere. Fuel vapors are absorbed and stored by a fuel vapor charcoal canister. The canister stores them until certain engine conditions are met and the vapors can be purged and burned by the engine.

The charcoal canister purge cycle is controlled different ways: either by a thermostatic vacuum switch, a solenoid or by a timed vacuum source. The thermostatic switch is installed in the coolant passage and prevents canister purge when the engine is below a certain temperature. The solenoid is usually controlled by a computer and is used on feedback controlled fuel systems. The computer determines when canister purge is appropriate. Depending on the system, this can be engine operating temperature, engine speed, evaporative system pressure or any combination of these. The timed vacuum source uses a manifold vacuum controlled diaphragm to control canister purge. When the engine is running, full manifold vacuum is applied to the top tube of the purge valve which lifts the valve diaphragm and opens the valve.

[Figure 56 — top right]

8852EG99

Fig. 56 Likely PCV valve locations—(1–2) in the valve cover, (3) at the carburetor/throttle body or (4) in the intake manifold.

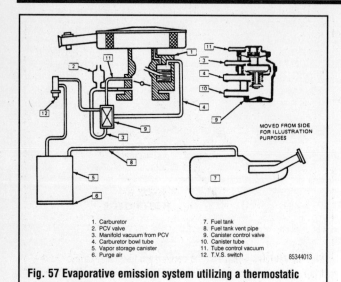

1. Carburetor
2. PCV valve
3. Manifold vacuum from PCV
4. Carburetor bowl tube
5. Vapor storage canister
6. Purge air
7. Fuel tank
8. Fuel tank vent pipe
9. Canister control valve
10. Canister tube
11. Tube control vacuum
12. T.V.S. switch

MOVED FROM SIDE FOR ILLUSTRATION PURPOSES

85344013

Fig. 57 Evaporative emission system utilizing a thermostatic vacuum switch

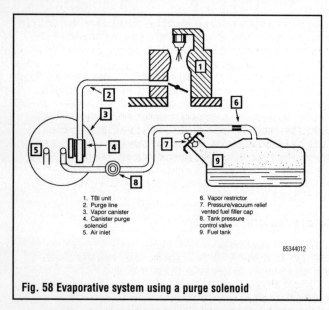

1. TBI unit
2. Purge line
3. Vapor canister
4. Canister purge solenoid
5. Air inlet
6. Vapor restrictor
7. Pressure/vacuum relief vented fuel filler cap
8. Tank pressure control valve
9. Fuel tank

85344012

Fig. 58 Evaporative system using a purge solenoid

A vent located in the fuel tank, allows fuel vapors to flow to the charcoal canister. A tank pressure control valve, used on some high altitude applications, prevents canister purge when the engine is not running. The fuel tank cap does not normally vent to the atmosphere, but is designed to provide both vacuum and pressure relief.

AIR INJECTION SYSTEMS

▶ See Figure 59

Introducing a controlled amount of air into the exhaust stream promotes further oxidation of the gases. This in turn reduces the amount of carbon monoxide and hydrocarbons. The carbon monoxide and hydrocarbons are converted to carbon dioxide and water, the harmless by-products of combustion. Some systems use an air pump, while other use negative exhaust pulses to draw air (pulse air).

The air pump, usually driven by a belt, simply pumps air under a pressure of only a few pounds into each exhaust port. Between the nozzles and the pump is a check valve to keep the hot exhaust gases from flowing back into the pump and hoses thereby destroying them. Most pumps also utilize a gulp valve or a diverter valve. Early systems used a gulp valve, while later systems use diverter valves. They both operate on the same principle. During deceleration, as the throttle is closed, the fuel mixture tends to get too

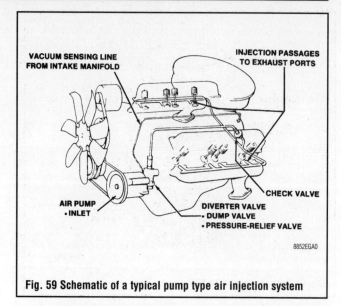

VACUUM SENSING LINE FROM INTAKE MANIFOLD

INJECTION PASSAGES TO EXHAUST PORTS

AIR PUMP •INLET

CHECK VALVE

DIVERTER VALVE • DUMP VALVE • PRESSURE-RELIEF VALVE

8852EGA0

Fig. 59 Schematic of a typical pump type air injection system

rich. If the air continued to be pumped during deceleration, an explosion in the exhaust system could occur that could blow the muffler apart. During deceleration, the air is either diverted into the atmosphere or into the intake system.

On pulse air systems, clean air (from the air cleaner) is drawn through a silencer, the check valve(s) and then into the exhaust ports. The negative exhaust pulses opens the reed valve in the check valve assembly, allowing air to flow into the exhaust port.

Some feedback controlled vehicles utilize an oxidizing catalytic converter. Under certain operating conditions, the air is diverted into the catalytic converter to help oxidize the exhaust gases.

EXHAUST GAS RECIRCULATION (EGR) SYSTEMS

▶ See Figures 60, 61 and 62

The EGR system's purpose is to control oxides of nitrogen (NOx) which are formed during the combustion process. NOx emissions at low combustion temperatures are not severe, but when the combustion temperatures go over 2500° F, the production of NOx in the combustion chambers shoots way up. The end products of combustion are relatively inert gases derived from the exhaust gases. These are redirected (under certain conditions) through the EGR valve and back into the combustion chamber. These inert

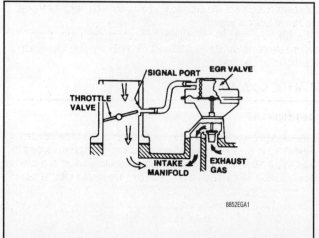

SIGNAL PORT   EGR VALVE

THROTTLE VALVE

INTAKE MANIFOLD   EXHAUST GAS

8852EGA1

Fig. 60 The EGR system redirects exhaust gas into the combustion chamber to lower combustion temperatures—vacuum operated EGR valve

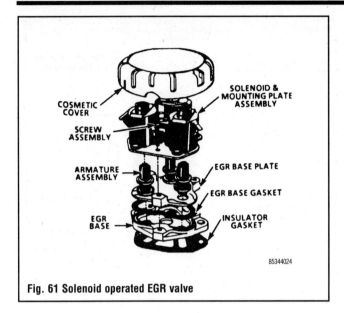

Fig. 61 Solenoid operated EGR valve

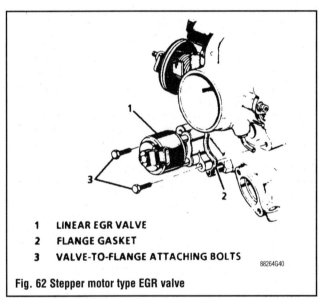

1   **LINEAR EGR VALVE**
2   **FLANGE GASKET**
3   **VALVE-TO-FLANGE ATTACHING BOLTS**

Fig. 62 Stepper motor type EGR valve

gases displace a certain amount of oxygen in the chamber. Since not as much oxygen is present, the explosion is not as hot. This helps lower peak combustion temperatures.

The EGR valve can either be actuated by a vacuum diaphragm, a solenoid or a stepper motor. On feedback controlled vehicles, the EGR system is controlled by the computer.

CATALYTIC CONVERTER

▶ **See Figure 63**

The catalytic converter is a muffler-like container built into the exhaust system to aid in the reduction of exhaust emissions. The catalyst element is coated with a noble metal such as platinum, palladium, rhodium or a combination of them. When the exhaust gases come into contact with the cata-

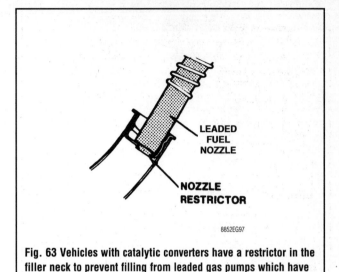

Fig. 63 Vehicles with catalytic converters have a restrictor in the filler neck to prevent filling from leaded gas pumps which have a larger pump nozzle

lyst, a chemical reaction occurs which reduces the pollutants into harmless substances such as water and carbon dioxide. Oxidizing catalysts require the addition of oxygen to spur the catalyst into reducing the engine's HC and CO emissions into H_2O and CO_2.

While catalytic converters are built in a variety of shapes and sizes, they all fall into two general types, the pellet, or bead type and the monolithic type. Construction may differ slightly, but the object is the same—to present the largest possible surface area to passing exhaust gases. Older vehicles use bead/pellet type converters. The exhaust gas must pass through a bed of these pellets. This type of converter is rather restrictive. The cross-section of a monolithic type converter resembles a honeycomb. The exhaust gases are exposed to a greater amount of surface area in these converters, as a result they are more efficient. They also tend to be less restrictive.

Catalytic Converter Precautions

1. Use only unleaded fuel.
2. Avoid prolonged idling; the engine should run no longer than 20 min. at curb idle and no longer than 10 min. at fast idle.
3. Don't disconnect any of the spark plug leads while the engine is running. If any engine testing procedure requires disconnecting or bypassing a control component, perform the procedure as quickly as possible. A misfiring engine can overheat the catalyst and damage the oxygen sensor.
4. Make engine compression checks as quickly as possible.
5. Whenever under the vehicle or around the catalytic converter, remember that it has a very high outside or skin temperature. During operation, the catalyst must reach very high temperatures to work efficiently. Be very wary of burns, even after the engine has been shut off for a while. Additionally, because of the heat, never park the vehicle on or over flammable materials, particularly dry grass or leaves. Inspect the heat shields frequently and correct any bends or damage.
6. In the unlikely event that the catalyst must be replaced, DO NOT dispose of the old one where anything containing grease, gas or oil can come in contact with it. The catalytic reaction may occur with these substances, which can start a fire.

EMISSION TESTING

In addition to mandating that vehicles must be equipped with emission controls, the law may also require that vehicles in certain areas be tested to ensure that they remain within specified limits for emissions.

This type of testing began long after emission controls were being installed, but it was discovered that some areas still had growing pollution problems. Part of the reason for this was that some vehicles had been poorly maintained, or had emission control devices altered or removed.

Early forms of testing generally involved running the vehicle at idle, or some other steady speed, and inserting the probe of the emissions analyzer into the tailpipe in order to obtain the readings. Exhaust gases such as hydrocarbons (HC) and carbon monoxide (CO) were typically measured, either as parts per million (PPM) or as a percentage of exhaust gas content. Certain information, such as the Vehicle Identification Number (VIN), vehicle type, vehicle or engine year, number of cylinders, mechanic number and inspection station number would have to be entered into the machine, in order to promote accurate and honest testing.

After the testing was completed, there was generally a printout of the results, including a Pass/Fail message. Even though this type of testing criteria goes back to the California Bureau of Automotive Repair (BAR) standard of 1979, (known as BAR 80), it is still used in some areas, with whatever variations are required by individual states or localities.

One of the newest programs is referred to as IM240. The abbreviation stands for Inspection/Maintenance 240 Seconds.

Some states require this type of emissions testing. It was mandated to begin on January 1, 1995. There have been delays and modifications to the program in some cases, and earlier program starting dates in some locations.

There are two types of IM240 tests, Basic and Enhanced. Factors such as population and pollution levels in a given area are used to determine which test will be utilized. Major metropolitan areas would be more apt to require the Enhanced test, while lightly populated rural areas may not use any type of IM240 testing at all.

The Basic test is similar to some current IM programs. The Enhanced test, which takes 240 seconds to perform, is designed to provide a more accurate picture of a vehicle's emissions during an actual operating cycle, not just at idle. This is done by testing the vehicle on a chassis dynamometer. Emissions are constantly monitored as the vehicle idles, accelerates, cruises at two different road speeds, and decelerates.

In areas using IM240, testing will be performed on 1968 and later model passenger cars and light trucks.

The following exhaust by-products are measured:
- Hydrocarbons (HC)
- Carbon Monoxide (CO)
- Carbon Dioxide (CO_2)
- Nitrogen Oxides (NOx)

The exhaust gas is more thoroughly checked for pollutants than it was with pre-IM240 testing methods. The measurements are made in grams per mile for these tests.

The following tests may be performed, depending on the model year of the vehicle:
- Evaporative Performance Test
- Evaporative System Integrity Test

The Evaporative Performance Test checks that the fuel vapors stored in the purge canister are being delivered to the engine for combustion at an acceptable rate.

The Evaporative System Integrity Test is a pressure test of all items in the fuel system, including the fuel cap, which control fuel vapors. Any loss of pressure greater than the standards permit will cause the vehicle to fail the test. Furthermore, if the pressure does not release when the fuel cap is removed, the vehicle will fail the test.

If you reside in an area where you will need to have the Enhanced Test performed on your vehicle, there are a few things you can check before you go to the test station which will expedite the testing procedure. All tires must be in good condition, with no cords or steel belts showing through the tread. The tire pressure should be at the correct level, or it will have to be adjusted before the test can be done. No space saver spare tires may be mounted on the vehicle.

Additionally, no vehicle with an exhaust leak will be permitted to test, and any vehicle which is in an overheated condition must be back at normal operating temperature before the test can be performed. Switch accessories OFF, when possible, before turning the vehicle over to the mechanic.

Should the vehicle require repair(s) to pass the test, keep in mind that basic items such as a clogged air filter or Positive Crankcase Ventilation (PCV) valve may cause an emission test failure. Therefore, it is good practice to perform preventive maintenance before taking the vehicle for the test. Preventive maintenance is discussed in Section 4 of this book. In addition to servicing items that may need attention, be sure to perform a visual inspection for anything that might cause poor running or increased emissions, such as loose connections or vacuum hoses.

MEASUREMENTS

Most of the world uses the metric system. So, if you have an imported vehicle, you can be pretty certain that it was built with metric fasteners and put together using metric measured clearances and adjustments.

In the United States, most people still use the English system, which nowadays should be called the U.S. system. However, if your U.S. made vehicle was built after 1980, most, if not all, of the fasteners and measurements are metric. So, we have included the following conversion charts for your convenience.

ENGLISH TO METRIC CONVERSION: MASS (WEIGHT)

Current **mass** measurement is expressed in pounds and ounces (lbs. & ozs.). The metric unit of **mass** (or weight) is the kilogram (kg). Even although this table does not show conversion of masses (weights) larger than 15 lbs, it is **easy to** calculate larger units by following the data immediately below.

To convert ounces (oz.) to grams (g): multiply th number of ozs. by 28
To convert grams (g) to ounces (oz.): multiply the number of grams by .035

To convert pounds (lbs.) to kilograms (kg): multiply the number of lbs. by .45
To convert kilograms (kg) to pounds (lbs.): multiply the number of kilograms by 2.2

lbs	kg	lbs	kg	oz	kg	oz	kg
0.1	0.04	0.9	0.41	0.1	0.003	0.9	0.024
0.2	0.09	1	0.4	0.2	0.005	1	0.03
0.3	0.14	2	0.9	0.3	0.008	2	0.06
0.4	0.18	3	1.4	0.4	0.011	3	0.08
0.5	0.23	4	1.8	0.5	0.014	4	0.11
0.6	0.27	5	2.3	0.6	0.017	5	0.14
0.7	0.32	10	4.5	0.7	0.020	10	0.28
0.8	0.36	15	6.8	0.8	0.023	15	0.42

ENGLISH TO METRIC CONVERSION: TEMPERATURE

To convert Fahrenheit (°F) to Celsius (°C): take number of °F and subtract 32; multiply result by 5; divide result by 9

To convert Celsius (°C) to Fahrenheit (°F): take number of °C and multiply by 9; divide result by 5; add 32 to total

Fahrenheit (F)		Celsius (C)		Fahrenheit (F)		Celsius (C)		Fahrenheit (F)		Celsius (C)	
°F	°C	°C	°F	°F	°C	°C	°F	°F	°C	°C	°F
−40	−40	−38	−36.4	80	26.7	18	64.4	215	101.7	80	176
−35	−37.2	−36	−32.8	85	29.4	20	68	220	104.4	85	185
−30	−34.4	−34	−29.2	90	32.2	22	71.6	225	107.2	90	194
−25	−31.7	−32	−25.6	95	35.0	24	75.2	230	110.0	95	202
−20	−28.9	−30	−22	100	37.8	26	78.8	235	112.8	100	212
−15	−26.1	−28	−18.4	105	40.6	28	82.4	240	115.6	105	221
−10	−23.3	−26	−14.8	110	43.3	30	86	245	118.3	110	230
−5	−20.6	−24	−11.2	115	46.1	32	89.6	250	121.1	115	239
0	−17.8	−22	−7.6	120	48.9	34	93.2	255	123.9	120	248
1	−17.2	−20	−4	125	51.7	36	96.8	260	126.6	125	257
2	−16.7	−18	−0.4	130	54.4	38	100.4	265	129.4	130	266
3	−16.1	−16	3.2	135	57.2	40	104	270	132.2	135	275
4	−15.6	−14	6.8	140	60.0	42	107.6	275	135.0	140	284
5	−15.0	−12	10.4	145	62.8	44	112.2	280	137.8	145	293
10	−12.2	−10	14	150	65.6	46	114.8	285	140.6	150	302
15	−9.4	−8	17.6	155	68.3	48	118.4	290	143.3	155	311
20	−6.7	−6	21.2	160	71.1	50	122	295	146.1	160	320
25	−3.9	−4	24.8	165	73.9	52	125.6	300	148.9	165	329
30	−1.1	−2	28.4	170	76.7	54	129.2	305	151.7	170	338
35	1.7	0	32	175	79.4	56	132.8	310	154.4	175	347
40	4.4	2	35.6	180	82.2	58	136.4	315	157.2	180	356
45	7.2	4	39.2	185	85.0	60	140	320	160.0	185	365
50	10.0	6	42.8	190	87.8	62	143.6	325	162.8	190	374
55	12.8	8	46.4	195	90.6	64	147.2	330	165.6	195	383
60	15.6	10	50	200	93.3	66	150.8	335	168.3	200	392
65	18.3	12	53.6	205	96.1	68	154.4	340	171.1	205	401
70	21.1	14	57.2	210	98.9	70	158	345	173.9	210	410
75	23.9	16	60.8	212	100.0	75	167	350	176.7	215	414

TCCS1C01

ENGLISH TO METRIC CONVERSION: LENGTH

To convert inches (ins.) to millimeters (mm): multiply number of inches by 25.4

To convert millimeters (mm) to inches (ins.): multiply number of millimeters by .04

Inches	Decimals	Milli-meters	Inches to millimeters inches	mm	Inches	Decimals	Milli-meters	Inches to millimeters inches	mm
1/64	0.051625	0.3969	0.0001	0.00254	33/64	0.515625	13.0969	0.6	15.24
1/32	0.03125	0.7937	0.0002	0.00508	17/32	0.53125	13.4937	0.7	17.78
3/64	0.046875	1.1906	0.0003	0.00762	35/64	0.546875	13.8906	0.8	20.32
1/16	0.0625	1.5875	0.0004	0.01016	9/16	0.5625	14.2875	0.9	22.86
5/64	0.078125	1.9844	0.0005	0.01270	37/64	0.578125	14.6844	1	25.4
3/32	0.09375	2.3812	0.0006	0.01524	19/32	0.59375	15.0812	2	50.8
7/64	0.109375	2.7781	0.0007	0.01778	39/64	0.609375	15.4781	3	76.2
1/8	0.125	3.1750	0.0008	0.02032	5/8	0.625	15.8750	4	101.6
9/64	0.140625	3.5719	0.0009	0.02286	41/64	0.640625	16.2719	5	127.0
5/32	0.15625	3.9687	0.001	0.0254	21/32	0.65625	16.6687	6	152.4
11/64	0.171875	4.3656	0.002	0.0508	43/64	0.671875	17.0656	7	177.8
3/16	0.1875	4.7625	0.003	0.0762	11/16	0.6875	17.4625	8	203.2
13/64	0.203125	5.1594	0.004	0.1016	45/64	0.703125	17.8594	9	228.6
7/32	0.21875	5.5562	0.005	0.1270	23/32	0.71875	18.2562	10	254.0
15/64	0.234375	5.9531	0.006	0.1524	47/64	0.734375	18.6531	11	279.4
1/4	0.25	6.3500	0.007	0.1778	3/4	0.75	19.0500	12	304.8
17/64	0.265625	6.7469	0.008	0.2032	49/64	0.765625	19.4469	13	330.2
9/32	0.28125	7.1437	0.009	0.2286	25/32	0.78125	19.8437	14	355.6
19/64	0.296875	7.5406	0.01	0.254	51/64	0.796875	20.2406	15	381.0
5/16	0.3125	7.9375	0.02	0.508	13/16	0.8125	20.6375	16	406.4
21/64	0.328125	8.3344	0.03	0.762	53/64	0.828125	21.0344	17	431.8
11/32	0.34375	8.7312	0.04	1.016	27/32	0.84375	21.4312	18	457.2
23/64	0.359375	9.1281	0.05	1.270	55/64	0.859375	21.8281	19	482.6
3/8	0.375	9.5250	0.06	1.524	7/8	0.875	22.2250	20	508.0
25/64	0.390625	9.9219	0.07	1.778	57/64	0.890625	22.6219	21	533.4
13/32	0.40625	10.3187	0.08	2.032	29/32	0.90625	23.0187	22	558.8
27/64	0.421875	10.7156	0.09	2.286	59/64	0.921875	23.4156	23	584.2
7/16	0.4375	11.1125	0.1	2.54	15/16	0.9375	23.8125	24	609.6
29/64	0.453125	11.5094	0.2	5.08	61/64	0.953125	24.2094	25	635.0
15/32	0.46875	11.9062	0.3	7.62	31/32	0.96875	24.6062	26	660.4
31/64	0.484375	12.3031	0.4	10.16	63/64	0.984375	25.0031	27	690.6
1/2	0.5	12.7000	0.5	12.70					

ENGLISH TO METRIC CONVERSION: TORQUE

To convert foot-pounds (ft. lbs.) to Newton-meters: multiply the number of ft. lbs. by 1.3

To convert inch-pounds (in. lbs.) to Newton-meters: multiply the number of in. lbs. by .11

in lbs	N-m	in lbs	N-m	in lbs	N-m	in lbs	N-m	in lbs	N-m
0.1	0.01	1	0.11	10	1.13	19	2.15	28	3.16
0.2	0.02	2	0.23	11	1.24	20	2.26	29	3.28
0.3	0.03	3	0.34	12	1.36	21	2.37	30	3.39
0.4	0.04	4	0.45	13	1.47	22	2.49	31	3.50
0.5	0.06	5	0.56	14	1.58	23	2.60	32	3.62
0.6	0.07	6	0.68	15	1.70	24	2.71	33	3.73
0.7	0.08	7	0.78	16	1.81	25	2.82	34	3.84
0.8	0.09	8	0.90	17	1.92	26	2.94	35	3.95
0.9	0.10	9	1.02	18	2.03	27	3.05	36	4.0

ENGLISH TO METRIC CONVERSION: TORQUE

Torque is now expressed as either foot-pounds (ft./lbs.) or inch-pounds (in./lbs.). The metric measurement unit for torque is the Newton-meter (Nm). This unit—the Nm—will be used for all SI metric torque references, both the present ft./lbs. and in./lbs.

ft lbs	N-m	ft lbs	N-m	ft lbs	N-m	ft lbs	N-m
0.1	0.1	33	44.7	74	100.3	115	155.9
0.2	0.3	34	46.1	75	101.7	116	157.3
0.3	0.4	35	47.4	76	103.0	117	158.6
0.4	0.5	36	48.8	77	104.4	118	160.0
0.5	0.7	37	50.7	78	105.8	119	161.3
0.6	0.8	38	51.5	79	107.1	120	162.7
0.7	1.0	39	52.9	80	108.5	121	164.0
0.8	1.1	40	54.2	81	109.8	122	165.4
0.9	1.2	41	55.6	82	111.2	123	166.8
1	1.3	42	56.9	83	112.5	124	168.1
2	2.7	43	58.3	84	113.9	125	169.5
3	4.1	44	59.7	85	115.2	126	170.8
4	5.4	45	61.0	86	116.6	127	172.2
5	6.8	46	62.4	87	118.0	128	173.5
6	8.1	47	63.7	88	119.3	129	174.9
7	9.5	48	65.1	89	120.7	130	176.2
8	10.8	49	66.4	90	122.0	131	177.6
9	12.2	50	67.8	91	123.4	132	179.0
10	13.6	51	69.2	92	124.7	133	180.3
11	14.9	52	70.5	93	126.1	134	181.7
12	16.3	53	71.9	94	127.4	135	183.0
13	17.6	54	73.2	95	128.8	136	184.4
14	18.9	55	74.6	96	130.2	137	185.7
15	20.3	56	75.9	97	131.5	138	187.1
16	21.7	57	77.3	98	132.9	139	188.5
17	23.0	58	78.6	99	134.2	140	189.8
18	24.4	59	80.0	100	135.6	141	191.2
19	25.8	60	81.4	101	136.9	142	192.5
20	27.1	61	82.7	102	138.3	143	193.9
21	28.5	62	84.1	103	139.6	144	195.2
22	29.8	63	85.4	104	141.0	145	196.6
23	31.2	64	86.8	105	142.4	146	198.0
24	32.5	65	88.1	106	143.7	147	199.3
25	33.9	66	89.5	107	145.1	148	200.7
26	35.2	67	90.8	108	146.4	149	202.0
27	36.6	68	92.2	109	147.8	150	203.4
28	38.0	69	93.6	110	149.1	151	204.7
29	39.3	70	94.9	111	150.5	152	206.1
30	40.7	71	96.3	112	151.8	153	207.4
31	42.0	72	97.6	113	153.2	154	208.8
32	43.4	73	99.0	114	154.6	155	210.2

TCCS1C03

ENGLISH TO METRIC CONVERSION: FORCE

Force is presently measured in pounds (lbs.). This type of measurement is used to measure spring pressure, specifically how many pounds it takes to compress a spring. Our present force unit (the pound) will be replaced in SI metric measurements by the Newton (N). This term will eventually see use in specifications for electric motor brush spring pressures, valve spring pressures, etc.

To convert pounds (lbs.) to Newton (N): multiply the number of lbs. by 4.45

lbs	N	lbs	N	lbs	N	oz	N
0.01	0.04	21	93.4	59	262.4	1	0.3
0.02	0.09	22	97.9	60	266.9	2	0.6
0.03	0.13	23	102.3	61	271.3	3	0.8
0.04	0.18	24	106.8	62	275.8	4	1.1
0.05	0.22	25	111.2	63	280.2	5	1.4
0.06	0.27	26	115.6	64	284.6	6	1.7
0.07	0.31	27	120.1	65	289.1	7	2.0
0.08	0.36	28	124.6	66	293.6	8	2.2
0.09	0.40	29	129.0	67	298.0	9	2.5
0.1	0.4	30	133.4	68	302.5	10	2.8
0.2	0.9	31	137.9	69	306.9	11	3.1
0.3	1.3	32	142.3	70	311.4	12	3.3
0.4	1.8	33	146.8	71	315.8	13	3.6
0.5	2.2	34	151.2	72	320.3	14	3.9
0.6	2.7	35	155.7	73	324.7	15	4.2
0.7	3.1	36	160.1	74	329.2	16	4.4
0.8	3.6	37	164.6	75	333.6	17	4.7
0.9	4.0	38	169.0	76	338.1	18	5.0
1	4.4	39	173.5	77	342.5	19	5.3
2	8.9	40	177.9	78	347.0	20	5.6
3	13.4	41	182.4	79	351.4	21	5.8
4	17.8	42	186.8	80	355.9	22	6.1
5	22.2	43	191.3	81	360.3	23	6.4
6	26.7	44	195.7	82	364.8	24	6.7
7	31.1	45	200.2	83	369.2	25	7.0
8	35.6	46	204.6	84	373.6	26	7.2
9	40.0	47	209.1	85	378.1	27	7.5
10	44.5	48	213.5	86	382.6	28	7.8
11	48.9	49	218.0	87	387.0	29	8.1
12	53.4	50	224.4	88	391.4	30	8.3
13	57.8	51	226.9	89	395.9	31	8.6
14	62.3	52	231.3	90	400.3	32	8.9
15	66.7	53	235.8	91	404.8	33	9.2
16	71.2	54	240.2	92	409.2	34	9.4
17	75.6	55	244.6	93	413.7	35	9.7
18	80.1	56	249.1	94	418.1	36	10.0
19	84.5	57	253.6	95	422.6	37	10.3
20	89.0	58	258.0	96	427.0	38	10.6

TCCS1C04

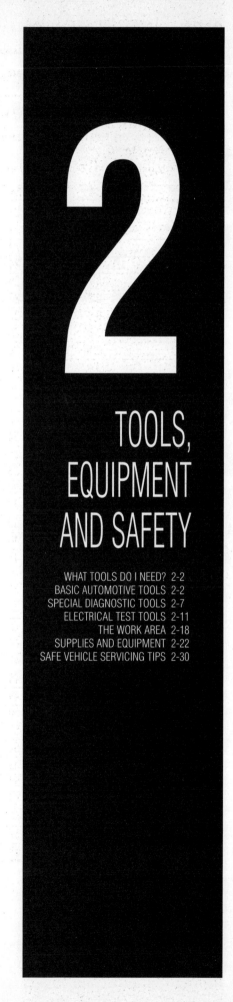

2

TOOLS, EQUIPMENT AND SAFETY

WHAT TOOLS DO I NEED?

Analyze Your Needs

Nearly everybody needs some tools, whether they are fixing a kitchen sink, or overhauling the engine in the family car. As far as car repairs go, pliers and a can of oil won't to get you very far down the path of do-it-your-self service. Nevertheless, you don't have to equip your garage like the local service station either. Somewhere between these two extremes is a level that suits the average do-it-yourselfer. Just where that point is depends on your ability and your interest. The strategy is to match your tools and equipment to the tasks you would like to tackle.

First, sort things out in an orderly manner. Think about your repair work in three levels: Basic, average and advanced. Before you purchase any tools, sit down and determine your level of expertise with the job you need to accomplish and how much it will cost. Knowing what repairs you can or want to do is the most important step. Obviously, if all your intend to do is change the oil and spark plugs you don't need many tools. If you plan some extensive repair work, you are going to end up with a complete collection of tools. Many expensive tools can be rented from automotive parts jobbers or tool rental centers. This allows many of us to do special repairs on an occasional basis.

BASIC AUTOMOTIVE TOOLS

Common Tools

▶ **See Figures 1 thru 15**

Naturally, without the proper tools it is impossible to properly service your vehicle. It would be impossible to catalog each tool that you would

need to perform every operation in this book. It would also be unwise for the amateur to rush out and buy an expensive set of tools on the theory that one or more may be needed at sometime.

The best approach is to proceed slowly, gathering together a good quality set of those tools that are used most frequently. Don't be misled by the low cost of bargain tools. It is far better to spend a little more for better

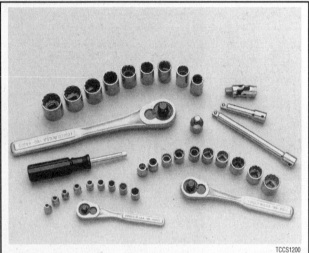

TCCS1200

Fig. 1 All but the most basic procedure will require an assortment of ratchets and sockets

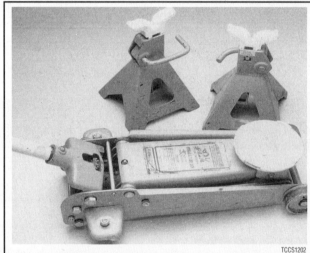

TCCS1202

Fig. 3 A hydraulic floor jack and a set of jackstands are essential for lifting and supporting the vehicle

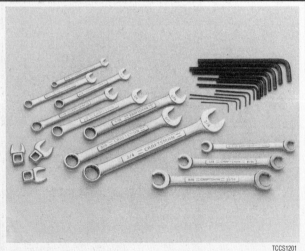

TCCS1201

Fig. 2 In addition to ratchets, a good set of wrenches and hex keys will be necessary

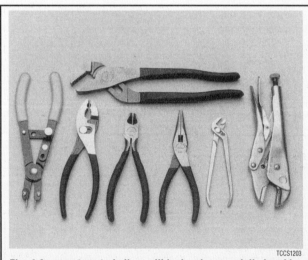

TCCS1203

Fig. 4 An assortment of pliers will be handy, especially for old rusted parts and stripped bolt heads

quality. Forged wrenches, 6-point sockets and fine tooth ratchets are by far preferable to their less expensive counterparts. As any good mechanic can tell you, there are few worse experiences than trying to work on a vehicle with bad tools. Your monetary savings will be far outweighed by frustration and mangled knuckles.

Certain tools, plus a basic ability to handle them, are required to get started. A basic tool set and a torque wrench, are good for a start. Begin accumulating those tools that are used most frequently (tools associated with routine maintenance/tune-up and engine repair). In addition to the normal assortment of screwdrivers and pliers, you should have the following tools for routine maintenance:

• Metric wrenches, sockets and combination open end/box end wrenches in sizes from 3–19mm, and a spark plug socket (⅝ inch or 16mm). If possible, buy various length socket drive extensions. One break in this department is that the metric sockets available in the U.S. will fit SAE ratchet handles and extensions you may already have (¼ in., ⅜ in., and ½ in. drive).

• Jackstands for support.
• Oil filter wrench.
• Oil filler spout or funnel.
• Grease gun for chassis lubrication.
• Hydrometer or battery tester for checking the battery.

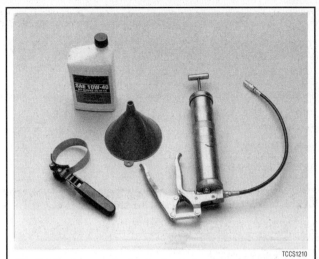

TCCS1210

Fig. 7 A few inexpensive lubrication tools will make regular service easier

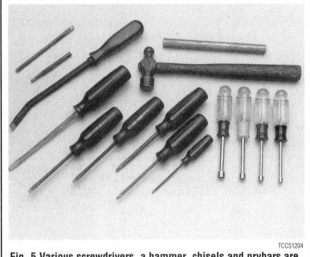

TCCS1204

Fig. 5 Various screwdrivers, a hammer, chisels and prybars are necessary to have in your toolbox

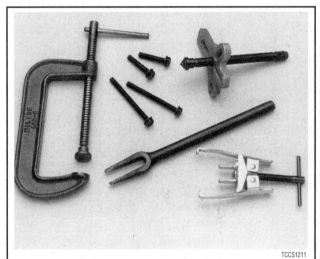

TCCS1211

Fig. 8 Various pullers, clamps and separator tools are needed for the repair of many components

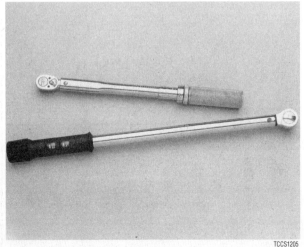

TCCS1205

Fig. 6 Many repairs will require the use of a torque wrench to assure the components are properly fastened

TCCS1212

Fig. 9 A variety of tools and gauges are needed for spark plug service

- A low flat pan for draining oil.
- Lots of rags for wiping up the inevitable mess.

In addition to the above items, there are several others that are not absolutely necessary, but handy to have around. These include oil-dry, a transmission fluid funnel and the usual supply of lubricants and fluids, although these can be purchased as needed. This is a basic list for routine maintenance, but only your personal needs and desires can accurately determine your list of tools.

The second list of tools is for tune-ups. While these tools are slightly more sophisticated, they need not be outrageously expensive. There are several inexpensive tach/dwell meters on the market that are every bit as good for the average mechanic as a costly professional model. Just be sure that it goes to at least 1200–1500 rpm on the tach scale and that it works on 4, 6 and 8-cylinder engines. A basic list of tune-up equipment could include:

- Tach/dwell meter.
- Spark plug wrench.
- Timing light (a DC light that works from the vehicle's battery is best).
- Wire spark plug gauge/adjusting tools.

Here again, be guided by your own needs. In addition to these basic tools, there are several other tools and gauges you may find useful. These include:

- A compression gauge. The screw-in type is slower to use, but eliminates the possibility of a faulty reading due to escaping pressure.
- A manifold vacuum gauge.
- A test light.
- A Digital Volt-Ohmmeter (DVOM) . This meter allows direct testing of electrical components and grounds.

As a final note, you will probably find a torque wrench necessary for most work. The beam type models are perfectly adequate, although the newer click (breakaway) type are more precise, and you don't have to crane your neck to see a torque reading in awkward situations. The breakaway torque wrenches are more expensive and should be recalibrated periodically.

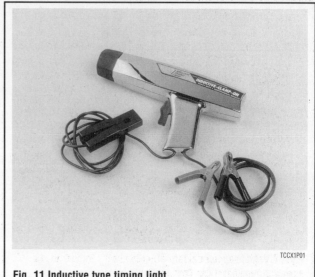
Fig. 11 Inductive type timing light

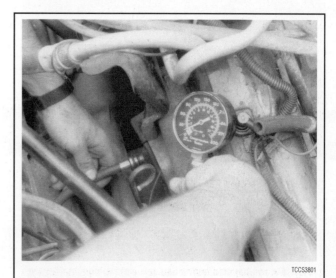
Fig. 12 Compression gauge

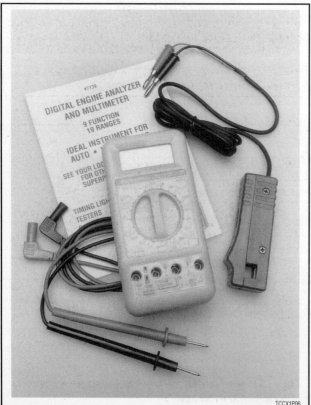
Fig. 10 Most modern automotive multimeters incorporate many helpful functions. This one also functions as an engine analyzer

Fig. 13 Vacuum/fuel pressure test gauge

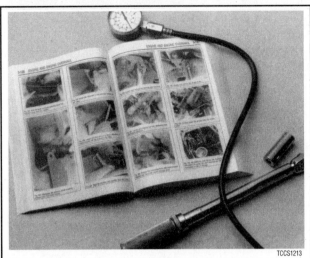

Fig. 14 Vehicle specific information is always important, so have a Chilton Total Car Care manual handy

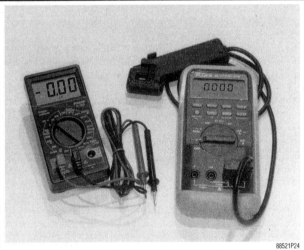

Fig. 15 A combination multimeter is the most important tool you own when trying to diagnose fuel injection problems

Correct tightening of bolts is an extremely important item on today's automobiles. The torque specification for each fastener will be given in the procedure whenever a specific torque value is required.

➡**Always Refer to a Chilton Total Car Care (TCC) repair manual for exact removal, installation and tightening instructions when replacing components.**

Special Tools

Normally, special factory tools are avoided for repair procedures, since these many not be readily available for the do-it-yourself mechanic. Diagnosis of fuel systems requires quiet a few special tools. However, these are mentioned later in this section. When it is possible to perform the job with more commonly available tools, it will be pointed out, but occasionally, a special tool was designed to perform a specific function and should be used. Before substituting another tool, you should be convinced that neither your safety nor the performance of the vehicle will be compromised.

Special tools can usually be purchased from an automotive parts store or from your dealer. In some cases, special tools may be rented.

Electric Power Tools

▶ **See Figures 16 and 17**

Power tools are most often associated with woodworking. However, there are a few which are very helpful in automotive work.

The most common and most useful power tool is the bench grinder. You'll need a grinder with a grinding stone on one side and a wire brush wheel on the other. The brush wheel is indispensable for cleaning parts and the stone can be used to remove rough surfaces and for reshaping, where necessary.

Almost as useful as the bench grinder is the drill. Drills can come in very handy when a stripped or broken fastener is encountered.

Power ratchets and impact wrenches can come in very handy. Power ratchets can save a lot of time and muscle when removing and installing long bolts or nuts on long studs, especially where there is little room to swing a manual ratchet. Electric impact wrenches can be invaluable in a lot of automotive work, especially wheel lugs and axle shaft nuts. They don't have much use on fuel system repair, though.

Fig. 16 Three types of common power tools. Left to right: a hand-held grinder, drill and impact wrench

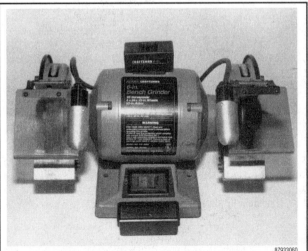

Fig. 17 The bench grinder can be used to clean just about every part removed from the vehicle

Air Tools and Compressors

♦ **See Figures 18 and 19**

Air-powered tools are not necessary for fuel system work. They are, however, useful for speeding up many jobs and for the rapid removal of parts. If you don't have air tools, and you want them, be prepared for an initial outlay of a lot of money.

The first thing you need is a compressor. Compressors are available in electrically driven and gas engine driven models. As long as you have electricity, you don't need a gas engine driven type.

The common shop-type air compressor is a pump mounted on a tank. The pump compresses air and forces it into the tank where it is stored until you need it. The compressor automatically turns the pump on when the air pressure in the tank falls below a certain preset level.

There are all kinds of air powered tools, including ratchets, impact wrenches, saws, drills, sprayers, nailers, scrapers, riveters, grinders and sanders. In general, air powered tools are much cheaper than their electric counterparts.

When deciding what size compressor unit you need, you'll be driven by two factors: the Pounds per Square Inch (PSI) capacity of the unit and the deliver rate in Cubic Feet per Minute (CFM). For example, most air powered ratchets require 90 psi at 4–5 cfm to operate at peak efficiency.

Grinders and saws may require up to 7 cfm at 90 psi. So, before buying the compressor unit, decide what types of tools you'll want so that you don't short-change yourself on the compressor purchase.

If you decide that a compressor and air tools aren't for you, you can have the benefit of air pressure rather cheaply. Purchase an air storage tank, available in sizes up to 20 gallons at most retail stores that sell auto products. These storage tanks can safely store air pressure up to 125 psi and come with a high pressure nozzle for cleaning things and an air chuck for filling tires. The tank can be filled using the common tire-type air compressor.

Jacks and Jackstands

♦ **See Figures 20 and 21**

Jacks and safety stands (jackstands) will be needed for just about anything that you'll do on the lower end of a vehicle.

Your vehicle was supplied with a jack for emergency road repairs. This jack is fine for changing a flat tire or other short-term procedures not requiring you to go beneath the vehicle. For any real work, you MUST use a floor jack.

Never place the jack under the radiator, engine or transmission components. Severe and expensive damage will result when the jack is raised. Additionally, never jack under the floorpan or bodywork; the metal will deform.

Fig. 18 This compressor operates off ordinary house current and provides all the air pressure you'll need

Fig. 20 Floor jacks come in all sizes and capacities. Top is a large 2¼ ton models; underneath is a compact 2 ton model

Fig. 19 An air storage tank

Fig. 21 Jackstands are necessary for holding your vehicle up off the ground. Top are 6 ton models; bottom are 4 ton models

Check your owner's manual or a Chilton Total Car Care for proper jacking and support locations on your vehicle. Many vehicles have crossmembers at the front and rear of the sub-frames that are suitable for jacking, but be careful not to mistake a thin metal skid plate or plastic trim piece as a crossmember.

There are usually reinforced pinch welds along the sides of the vehicle (just in front of the rear wheel and just behind the front wheel) that are used with the vehicle's emergency jack and can be used to raise the vehicle or that can be used with a pair of jackstands. In this case, a block of wood with a cut down the middle in order to cradle the pinch weld will help prevent stress or damage to the metal.

If you have a truck or an older framed vehicle, jackstands can be used almost anywhere along the frame for support. Always use a pair of stands directly across from each other (no closer to the front or rear of the vehicle than the other stand) to help keep the vehicle properly balanced.

✳✳ WARNING

Always position a block of wood or small rubber pad on top of the jack or jackstand to protect the lifting point's finish when lifting or supporting the vehicle.

Whenever you plan to work under the vehicle, you must support it on jackstands or ramps. Never use cinder blocks or stacks of wood to support the vehicle, even if you're only going to be under it for a few minutes. Never crawl under the vehicle when it is supported only by the tire-changing jack or other floor jack.

✳✳ CAUTION

Refer to the jacking precautions and the safety information later in this section before attempting to raise or support the vehicle. Failure to follow proper jacking procedures could result in severe injury or death.

Small hydraulic, screw, or scissors jacks are satisfactory for raising the vehicle. Drive-on trestles or ramps are also a handy and safe way to both raise and support the vehicle. Be careful though, some ramps may be too steep to drive your vehicle onto without scraping the front bottom panels. Never support the vehicle on any suspension member (unless specifically instructed to do so by a repair manual) or by an underbody panel.

SPECIAL DIAGNOSTIC TOOLS

Frequent references to specific test equipment will be found in the text. This usually refers to scan tools used to communicate with electronic control units or special electronic testers. Among other features, scan tools combine many standard testers into a single device for quick and accurate circuit diagnosis. For many tests, a multimeter, test light, or other general test equipment can be substituted but the technician must be aware of the risk involved. The general test equipment may not be capable of safely testing the system or may generate incomplete or inaccurate test results. Some tests require activating system components and often this can only be done with scan tools or other special equipment.

Most test equipment is available through aftermarket tool manufacturers, but some can only be obtained through the vehicle manufacturer. Care should be taken that all test equipment being used is designed to diagnose that particular system accurately without damaging control modules or other components.

➡**When using special test equipment, the manufacturer's instructions provided with the tester should be read and clearly understood before attempting any test procedures.**

Specialty Testers

FREQUENCY PROCESSOR

Some older DVOM's are not equipped to read frequency. There is at least one unit on the market that converts frequency signals to a millivolt signal that any DVOM can read. It is a simple box with input and output jacks and a `wake-up' circuit that automatically turns the unit on when needed. Its range of 10–5000 Hz makes it useful for checking rpm sensors, mass air flow sensors, Hall effect sensors and more. Instructions provided with the processor show how to interpret the readings

BREAK-OUT BOX

The electronic Break-Out Box (BOB) is used to tap into the wiring of a control unit. The main connector to the electronic control unit is connected to the break-out box and another wire harness is connected from the box to the control unit. The break-out box then allows the technician to access each circuit while it is operating without piercing the wire or causing damage to the connectors. All testing with the DVOM can be done safely at these terminals, eliminating the risk of damage due to backprobing at the control unit. Many times a break-out box is the only way to test a control unit function.

An Intelligent Break-Out Box (IBOB) connects to the vehicle diagnostic connector and has connector ports for a scan tool and/or a computer. On earlier electronic control units that do not generate a data stream, an IBOB will collect input/output data while the engine is running and present it to a scan tool or PC. Additionally, some manufacturers provide plastic overlays for the break-out box. This allows the box to be used on a variety of models; different overlays identify the changes in wire use or labeling. With the proper cable adapters, an IBOB can be used with any engine, body or ABS control unit on any vehicle.

OSCILLOSCOPE

▸ **See Figures 22 and 23**

An oscilloscope is a voltmeter that presents a graphic picture of the voltage reading over time. Unlike a DVOM, it can show a voltage that exists for only a fraction of a second or occurs only at a specific time. Ignition oscilloscopes have been around for many years, but the latest generation of service bay oscilloscopes are more like those found in electronics labs. They can read voltages as small as one millivolt and can show a spike that occurs for as little as 10 nanoseconds (1 ns = one billionth of a second). Both the voltage and time scales are adjustable, so the same tool can be used to measure the fast, high voltage signal of the secondary ignition system and slow stable signals such as a temperature sensor. Another major feature of all oscilloscopes is an extremely high input impedance, meaning the oscilloscope imposes negligible current draw on the circuit being measured that might influence that measurement. Many times an oscilloscope is the only tool that can be used to measure low voltage, frequency, or duty cycle signals.

Like a timing light, an oscilloscope must be triggered. The trigger can be internal (automatic) or can come from an external source. On a multi-channel oscilloscope, displaying the external trigger signal can show the timing of two events. For example, by taking the trigger from a suspected faulty fuel injector, it is possible to see the oxygen sensor signal only at the time of that injection event. The voltage level required to trigger the oscilloscope can also be adjusted, providing a simple method to look for low level or intermittent faults that may not set a code.

A digital oscilloscope converts the analog input signal to a digital form. A digital signal can be stored and played back by itself or along with another trace. Some units can also display the signal as numbers, min/max values, change value and average value. If the oscilloscope is equipped with a computer port, the digitized traces and other data can also be downloaded to save and/or print out. There is computer software available to aid organization and analysis of waveforms.

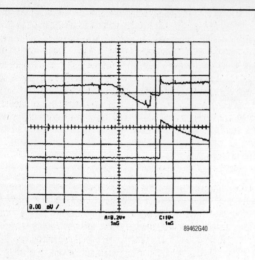

Fig. 22 The oxygen sensor trace (top) shows a delayed cross-over coinciding with an injector pulse (bottom trace)

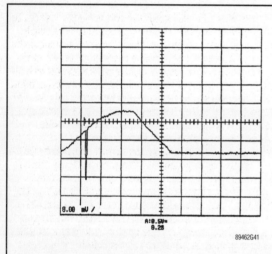

Fig. 23 An intermittent fault in the throttle position sensor shows clearly on the scope trace

With its extremely fast sampling rate and graphic display, an oscilloscope can easily show a malfunction that occurs too fast for a voltmeter to show. For example, by adjusting the time sweep of the oscilloscope to show the full up-and-down stroke of a throttle position sensor, an intermittent fault in the signal can be clearly shown. A voltmeter may also detect the fault but cannot change the display fast enough to show the resistance spike. A storage oscilloscope with min/max value capability can locate intermittent faults that even other oscilloscopes cannot.

Any oscilloscope used for automotive testing must be designed for use with automobiles. Standard lab oscilloscopes are usually not able to cope with the relatively harsh automotive electronic environment. Automotive oscilloscopes are available in a variety of types with a variety of features. Some are portable hand held models that operate on batteries or vehicle power. Even though they are small, the newest portable units include multi-trace and storage capabilities and are rugged enough to be used under the hood or on road tests. Larger models mounted in a console are often part of a top-of-the-line engine analyzer package. Most of the major diagnostic tool manufacturers produce at least one oscilloscope model.

As vehicles become more sophisticated and electronic controls become more powerful, an oscilloscope is fast becoming a necessary diagnostic tool. When the technician becomes proficient with an oscilloscope, many other diagnostic tools become unnecessary.

SCAN TOOL

▶ See Figures 24 and 25

This is the generic name for portable diagnostic equipment that communicates directly with an electronic control unit. The major vehicle manufacturers each have their own scan tool that is used by dealership technicians, such as GM's Tech 1, Ford's Star Tester, Nissan's Consult and Honda's PGM Tester. Some of these are available through the dealer parts network or are sold outside the network under another name. Others such as Volkswagen's VAG 1551 are available only to authorized dealerships.

Scan tools are used to read and erase trouble codes stored in the control unit memory and to provide a direct data transfer link with the control unit's On Board Diagnostic (OBD) system. Reading the control unit memory through the scan tool is more complete than reading codes with the flashing light on the instrument panel. Some information is only available through the scan tool, such as the number of engine starts since the fault first appeared. Data transfer provides a real time display of control unit input/output signals. Data such as the oxygen sensor reading or idle control motor duty cycle can be displayed while the engine is running. The scan tool can also be used as a volt/ohmmeter to check selected circuits without disconnecting them.

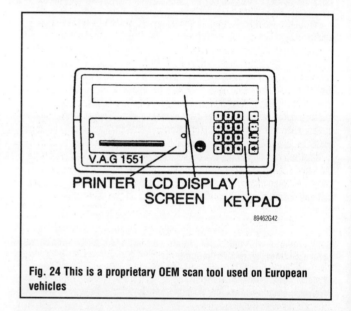

Fig. 24 This is a proprietary OEM scan tool used on European vehicles

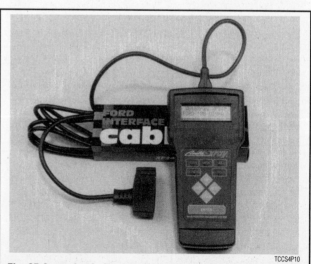

Fig. 25 A popular do-it-yourselfer scan tool shown with a Ford interface cable

Some scan tools are designed to simulate sensor inputs to test the sensor circuit, the control unit and the output device. On many vehicles, the scan tool can communicate with every control unit on the vehicle through a single diagnostic connector. Some of the more advanced scan tools are equipped with a data memory to store test data during a road test.

Aftermarket scan tools require adapters to match the different vehicle diagnostic connectors. A cartridge that plugs into the scan tool contains software needed for communicating with the different control units. The software is the tool's real power and is continuously evolving to enhance its capabilities. As the tool manufacturer's data base has grown, software now in includes VIN-specific information that addresses some of the most common trouble codes and driveability problems that don't always generate codes. Tests are menu-driven and many of the specifications are included right there in the program. Depending on the vehicle and the amount of computer control used, systems which may be viewed or investigated with a scan tool include:

1. Control Modules
2. Fuel/ignition systems
3. Electronic transmission control
4. Charging system
5. Suspension control functions
6. Anti-Lock brake system.
7. Passive restraint system
8. Anti-theft system
9. Climate Control Systems
10. Body electrical systems including power systems, sunroofs, and defoggers.

Aftermarket scan tools work well with most vehicles, but no scan tool can be used on all models and all are limited in their ability to communicate with European models. The Federal On-Board Diagnostic (OBD) specification requires all vehicles to have the same diagnostic connector and diagnostic trouble codes and to use the same data transfer language. This makes it possible to use a single scan tool to communicate with all engine control units from all manufacturers. Some manufacturers began production of OBD vehicles for the 1994 model year and all new vehicles must comply by the 1998 model year but the results have been mixed. As vehicle control units and scan tools become more powerful, data acquisition and test capabilities will also improve dramatically with each new generation of control unit and scan tool software.

EXHAUST GAS ANALYZER

Exhaust gas analysis has long been an extremely valuable and versatile diagnostic tool. It can be used to troubleshoot fuel and ignition systems, locate vacuum leaks or EGR malfunctions, even diagnose mechanical problems such as worn valve guides. On most vehicles, it is the only way to accurately check air/fuel mixture.

The federal government regulates three exhaust gas components: hydrocarbons (HC), carbon monoxide (CO), and oxides of nitrogen (NOx). HC and CO are relatively easy to measure and have long been tested in states that require emissions inspections. Measuring carbon dioxide (CO_2) and oxygen (O_2) are also valuable diagnostic aids but NOx cannot be accurately measured at idle or no-load conditions. However as states enact tighter Inspection and Maintenance programs, service bay NOx analyzers and test procedures are being developed. For complete diagnostic and certification testing, a five-gas analyzer is required.

Most gas analyzers include a single tailpipe sample probe, sample pump along with a filtration system and a detector cell for each of the gasses being measured. Most stand-alone four-gas analyzers used for emissions inspections are equipped with a small microprocessor that includes testing and calibration programs, a self diagnostic program and a built-in printer. Other units are designed as part of a complete diagnostic station and are connected to a PC based computer, printer and monitor screen. There is at least one portable four-gas analyzer that is used along with the same manufacturer's scan tool. The scan tool's software guides the user through test procedures based on the gas and sensor readings.

There is also a series of small, hand-held oxygen and CO monitors available that do not require a sample pump and filter system. The measur-

ing cell is built into the tailpipe probe and the monitor is battery operated. Since there is only a wire between the probe and the monitor, these units can easily be used on a road test. They are also equipped with a memory that can record three minutes of test data. The CO monitor can be particularly useful for routine air/fuel adjustments. Each unit is available with its own display, with voltage outputs to use a DVOM display, or with computer ports and PC based software that includes test procedures.

All gas analyzers must be calibrated at least once per day. Industry standard calibration gasses are usually available through parts stores or tool outlets.

ENGINE ANALYZER

A large, fully-equipped engine analyzer usually includes an oscilloscope, exhaust gas analyzer, vacuum and pressure sensors, a timing light and probe, electrical measuring equipment, and a computer. With a variety of electrical connections and a tail pipe probe, this analyzer can check the primary and secondary ignition systems, fuel injection controls and injectors, EGR systems, engine vacuum and compression, as well as starting and charging systems. The computer can be used to read the engine control unit's data stream through the vehicle diagnostic connector. Even on earlier vehicles with no sensors or data stream, an engine analyzer is still a powerful diagnostic tool.

The computer is the real power behind an engine analyzer. The computer's ability to determine the ignition pulse at cylinder number one can be used to index all other engine events to particular cylinders. For example, the analyzer can measure the starter current needed to move each piston to Top Dead Center (TDC), indicating the relative compression of each cylinder. The analyzer can also display spark plug firing voltage and duration on the oscilloscope. A spark plug that requires more voltage with less duration could indicate a faulty injector. The analyzer can detect and clearly show all the differences between cylinders. The computer can help the technician diagnose the data, determine the necessary repairs and even provide a print-out to present a clear explanation to the vehicle owner.

These analyzers are a major investment and are well supported by the manufacturer. They are frequently updated with a computer floppy disc that includes new vehicle information and test procedures. Some machines include CD-ROM equipment to read service manuals that are available on disc. They may also include a modem to communicate with the manufacturer or other computers via telephone. As vehicles and other shop equipment become more sophisticated, it should be possible to keep a computer based engine analyzer up to date and useful almost indefinitely.

Specific Test Equipment

There are many special diagnostic tools for testing individual components or systems, such as a Hall effect sensor, idle air control motor, fuel injectors, secondary ignition systems, and others. Most are designed for use on as many vehicles as possible. Some are designed to test parts or systems on specific vehicles. Generally, these devices allow the technician to quickly test components or sub-systems without going through a long diagnostic procedure. However, there is a risk of incorrect diagnosis. These tools can only be dependable if the technician is familiar with their use and understands what the test results really mean. A simple vacuum leak or loose connection may produce the same test result as a faulty component.

LEAK DETECTORS

A battery powered, hand-held vacuum leak detector uses a microphone and amplifier that detects noise in the ultrasonic range. Air moving through a vacuum leak will generate sound waves in the 40 kHz range, well above the range of human hearing. The detector will sound a beeper when a leak is found. Because of the high frequency sensed by the detector, it is not generally affected by normal engine or shop noises.

Leak detectors for air conditioning systems have a vacuum pump and probe to draw an air sample into the detecting cell. The cell detects halogen gas that is common to all air conditioning refrigerants. Most are capable of indicating the type of Freon in the system, as well as the rate of leakage. There are battery powered hand-held models and larger AC powered units suitable for mounting on an air conditioning service cart. The newest models are capable of detecting R134a and the sensitivity can be adjusted for possible background interference.

A combustible gas leak detector reacts to hydrocarbons present in fuels, exhaust gases, coolants, and lubricants. Models with adjustable sensitivity are typically used to look for fuel vapor leaks, head gasket leaks, and to measure the amount of exhaust leaking into the interior of a vehicle. With some imagination, this can be an extremely useful tool.

PYROMETER

A pyrometer measures a wide range of temperatures with a probe that only needs to touch the item being measured. As a general diagnostic tool, a hand held pyrometer can quickly locate hot or cold spots in a cooling system, a seized brake caliper, a dry bearing, test heater and A/C performance or even find a weak cylinder by measuring exhaust manifold runner temperatures. Most pyrometers are available with special probes for penetration and for measuring tire temperatures. There are even optical infrared non-contact pyrometers that measure temperature by the heat emission of a surface. This is useful as the surface to be measured does not have to actually touched with a probe. They can be calibrated quickly, have a very wide temperature range and can usually be switched to display Fahrenheit or Celsius degrees. With a little imagination, this can be an extremely useful tool.

IDLE AIR CONTROL TESTER

This is a kit used to isolate and test idle air control solenoids, motors, and signals. Some are made for use with a specific system, others include adapters for use with many different vehicles. The device can activate solenoid valves and control motors to test the full range of motion with the engine not running. It can also be used to control idle speed for timing adjustment or other engine tests. Some can also check the control unit output signal to the idle air control motor. These functions can also be accomplished with scan tools but this tester can be faster and easier to use for some tests.

FUEL INJECTOR TESTER

▶ **See Figure 26**

This device can quickly check the coil resistance and current draw of an electric fuel injector while it is under load. Each injector is tested individually and the results are reported on a DVOM or oscilloscope. This information makes it possible to electronically check injector balance and detect intermittent faults. When used with equipment that measures fuel pressure and injection quantity, every function of the fuel system can be tested.

OXYGEN SENSOR TESTER

This kit usually includes a propane enrichment control valve, special connectors and test instructions, as well as the hose and fittings needed for connecting the valve to an intake manifold. The kit allows the technician to control air/fuel mixture and check the oxygen sensor response time. When the oxygen sensor is disconnected, forcing the control unit into open loop, sensor output voltage or resistance can be read with a DVOM. The instructions also include procedures for testing the control unit's response to the oxygen sensor signal.

SENSOR SIMULATOR

This device is used to take a sensor `out of the loop' and simulate its input signals to the control unit. It can simulate every type of voltage, resistance, and frequency signal one at a time to test the control unit's response to the input. The simulator can also measure any sensor output signal by back-probing the sensor connector. In addition to displaying the reading

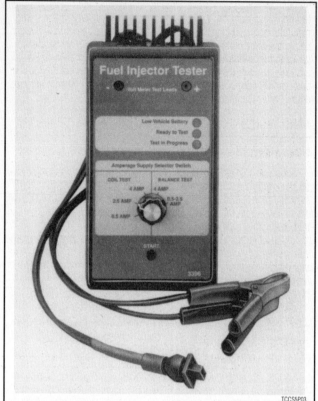

Fig. 26 A fuel injector tester measures voltage drop while the injector is being activated

TCCS5P03

directly, some units can also output the reading to an oscilloscope, scan tool, or other diagnostic equipment.

Mechanical Test Equipment

VACUUM GAUGE

▶ **See Figure 27**

Most gauges are graduated in inches of Mercury (in. Hg), although a device called a manometer reads vacuum in inches of water (in. H2O). The

TCCS4P04

Fig. 27 Hand-held manifold vacuum gauge

vacuum reading usually varies between 18 and 22 in. Hg at sea level. To test engine vacuum, the vacuum gauge must be connected to a source of manifold vacuum. Many engines have a plug in the intake manifold that can be removed and replaced with an adapter fitting. Connect the vacuum gauge to the fitting with a suitable rubber hose or, if no manifold plug is available, connect the vacuum gauge to any device using manifold vacuum, such as EGR valves, etc. The vacuum gauge can be used to determine the amount of vacuum reaching a component.

HAND VACUUM PUMP

♦ **See Figure 28**

Intake manifold vacuum is used to operate various systems and devices on all cars. To correctly diagnose and solve problems in vacuum control systems, a vacuum source is necessary for testing. In some cases, vacuum can be taken from the intake manifold when the engine is running, but vacuum is normally provided by a hand vacuum pump.

Small, hand-held vacuum pumps come in a variety of designs and provide a source of vacuum for testing components without the engine operating. Most have a built-in vacuum gauge and allow a component to be tested without removing it from the vehicle. Operate the pump lever or plunger, applying the correct amount of vacuum required for the test. The level of vacuum in inches of Mercury (in. Hg) is indicated on the pump gauge. For some testing, an additional vacuum gauge may be necessary.

COMPRESSION GAUGE

A compression gauge measures the amount of pressure in pounds per square inch (psi) that a cylinder is producing. Some gauges have a hose that screws into the spark plug hole while others have a tapered rubber tip which is held by hand in the spark plug hole. Engine compression depends on the sealing ability of the rings, valves, head gasket and spark plug gaskets. If any of these parts are not sealing properly, compression will be lost and the power output of the engine will be reduced. The compression in each cylinder should be measured and the variation between cylinders

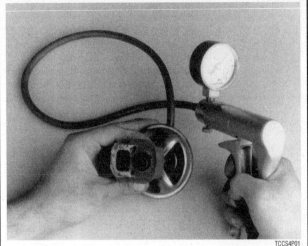

TCCS4P01

Fig. 28 Hand-held vacuum pump is handy for checking vacuum controlled devices

should be noted. The engine should be cranked through 5 or 6 compression strokes while warm, with all plugs removed, ignition disabled and throttle valves wide open.

FUEL PRESSURE GAUGE

A fuel pressure gauge is required to test the operation of the fuel delivery and injection systems. Some systems also need a 3-way valve to check the fuel pressure in various modes of operation. Gauges may require special adapters for making fuel connections. Always observe the cautions outlined in the fuel system service section of your repair manual when working around any pressurized fuel system.

ELECTRICAL TEST TOOLS

Organized Troubleshooting

When diagnosing a specific problem, there are certain troubleshooting techniques that are standard:

1. Establish when the problem occurs. Does the problem appear only under certain conditions? Were there any noises, odors, or other unusual symptoms? Make notes on any symptoms found, including warning lights and trouble codes, if applicable.

2. Isolate the problem area. To do this, make some simple tests and observations; then eliminate the systems that are working properly. Check for obvious problems such as broken wires, split or disconnected vacuum hoses. Always check the obvious before assuming something complicated is the cause. Be suspicious of fuses, switches and connectors; as the wiring itself rarely fails.

3. Test for problems systematically to determine the cause once the problem area is isolated. Are all the components functioning properly? Is there power going to electrical switches and motors? Is there vacuum at vacuum switches and/or actuators? Doing careful, systematic checks will often turn up most causes on the first inspection without wasting time checking components that have little or no relationship to the problem.

4. Test all repairs after the work is done to make sure that the problem is fixed. Some causes can be traced to more than one component, so a careful verification of repair work is important to pick up additional malfunctions that may cause a problem to reappear or a different problem to arise. A blown fuse, for example, is a simple problem that may require more than another fuse to repair.

Experience has shown that most problems tend to be the result of a fairly simple and obvious cause, such as loose or corroded connectors; making careful inspection of components during testing is essential to quick and accurate troubleshooting. Frequent references to special test equipment will be found in the text. These devices or a compatible equivalent are necessary to perform some of the more complicated test procedures listed. Testers are available from a variety of aftermarket sources as well as from the vehicle manufacturer. Care should be taken that any test equipment being used is designed to diagnose that particular system accurately without damaging the computer control modules or components being tested.

➡ **Pinpointing the exact cause of trouble in an electrical system can sometimes be accomplished only by the use of special test equipment. In addition to the information covered in this section, the manufacturer's instructions booklet provided with the tester should be read and clearly understood before attempting any test procedures.**

Test Equipment

♦ **See Figure 29**

Pinpointing the exact cause of trouble in an electrical circuit is most times accomplished by the use of special test equipment. The following describes different types of commonly used test equipment and briefly explains how to use them in diagnosis. In addition to the information covered below, the tool manufacturer's instructions booklet (provided with the tester) should be read and clearly understood before attempting any test procedures.

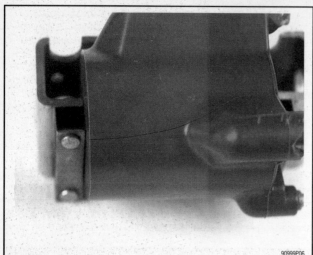

Fig. 29 All the electronic test equipment in the shop won't help you find a mechanical problem like this cracked coil

JUMPER WIRES

✲✲ CAUTION

Never use jumper wires made from a thinner gauge wire than the circuit being tested. If the jumper wire is of too small a gauge, it may overheat and possibly melt. Never use jumpers to bypass high resistance loads in a circuit. Bypassing resistance, in effect, creates a short circuit. This may, in turn, cause damage and fire. Jumper wires should only be used to bypass lengths of wire or to simulate switches.

Jumper wires are simple, yet extremely valuable, pieces of test equipment. They are basically test wires which are used to bypass sections of a circuit. Although jumper wires can be purchased, they are usually fabricated from lengths of standard automotive wire and whatever type of connector (alligator clip, spade connector or pin connector) that is required for the particular application being tested. In cramped, hard-to-reach areas, it is advisable to have insulated boots over the jumper wire terminals in order to prevent accidental grounding. It is also advisable to include a standard automotive fuse in any jumper wire. This is commonly referred to as a "fused jumper." By inserting an in-line fuse holder between a set of test leads, a fused jumper wire can be used for bypassing open circuits while still protecting the circuit. Use a 5 amp fuse to provide protection against voltage spikes.

Jumper wires are used primarily to locate open electrical circuits, on either the ground (-) side of the circuit or on the power (+) side. If an electrical component fails to operate, connect the jumper wire between the component and a good ground. If the component operates only with the jumper installed, the ground circuit is open. If the ground circuit is good, but the component does not operate, the circuit between the power feed and component may be open. By moving the jumper wire successively back from the component toward the power source, you can isolate the area of the circuit where the open is located. When the component stops functioning, or the power is cut off, the open is in the segment of wire between the jumper and the point previously tested.

You can sometimes connect the jumper wire directly from the battery to the "hot" terminal of the component, but first make sure the component uses 12 volts in operation. Some electrical components, such as fuel injectors or sensors, may be designed to operate on about 4 to 5 volts, and running 12 volts directly to these components will cause damage.

TEST LIGHTS

▶ See Figure 30

The test light is used to check circuits and components while electrical current is flowing through them. It is used for voltage and ground tests. To use a 12 volt test light, connect the ground clip to a good ground and probe wherever necessary with the pick. The test light will illuminate when voltage is detected. This does not necessarily mean that 12 volts (or any particular amount of voltage) is present; it only means that some voltage is present. It is advisable before using the test light to touch its ground clip and probe across the battery posts or terminals to make sure the light is operating properly.

✲✲ WARNING

Do not use a test light to probe electronic ignition, spark plug or coil wires. Never use a pick-type test light to probe wiring on computer controlled systems unless specifically instructed to do so. Any wire insulation that is pierced by the test light probe should be taped and sealed with silicone after testing.

Like the jumper wire, the 12 volt test light is used to isolate opens in circuits. But, whereas the jumper wire is used to bypass the open to operate the load, the 12 volt test light is used to locate the presence of voltage in a circuit. If the test light illuminates, there is power up to that point in the circuit; if the test light does not illuminate, there is an open circuit (no power). Move the test light in successive steps back toward the power source until the light in the handle illuminates. The open is between the probe and a point which was previously probed.

The self-powered test light is similar in design to the 12 volt test light, but contains a 1.5 volt penlight battery in the handle. It is most often used in place of a multimeter to check for open or short circuits when power is isolated from the circuit (continuity test).

The battery in a self-powered test light does not provide much current. A weak battery may not provide enough power to illuminate the test light even when a complete circuit is made (especially if there is high resistance in the circuit). Always make sure that the test battery is strong. To check the battery, briefly touch the ground clip to the probe; if the light glows brightly, the battery is strong enough for testing.

➡A self-powered test light should not be used on any computer controlled system or component. The small amount of electricity transmitted by the test light is enough to damage many electronic automotive components.

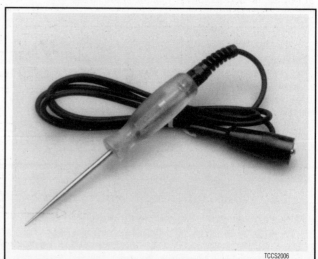

Fig. 30 A 12 volt test light is used to detect the presence of voltage in a circuit

MULTIMETERS

Multimeters are an extremely useful tool for troubleshooting electrical problems. They can be purchased in either analog or digital form and have a price range to suit any budget. A multimeter is a voltmeter, ammeter and ohmmeter (along with other features) combined into one instrument. It is often used when testing solid state circuits because of its high input impedance (usually 10 megaohms or more). A brief description of the multimeter main test functions follows:

• Voltmeter—the voltmeter is used to measure voltage at any point in a circuit, or to measure the voltage drop across any part of a circuit. Voltmeters usually have various scales and a selector switch to allow the reading of different voltage ranges. The voltmeter has a positive and a negative lead. To avoid damage to the meter, always connect the negative lead to the negative (-) side of the circuit (to ground or nearest the ground side of the circuit) and connect the positive lead to the positive (+) side of the circuit (to the power source or the nearest power source). Note that the negative voltmeter lead will always be black and that the positive voltmeter will always be some color other than black (usually red).

• Ohmmeter—the ohmmeter is designed to read resistance (measured in ohms) in a circuit or component. Most ohmmeters will have a selector switch which permits the measurement of different ranges of resistance (usually the selector switch allows the multiplication of the meter reading by 10, 100, 1,000 and 10,000). Some ohmmeters are "auto-ranging" which means the meter itself will determine which scale to use. Since the meters are powered by an internal battery, the ohmmeter can be used like a self-powered test light. When the ohmmeter is connected, current from the ohmmeter flows through the circuit or component being tested. Since the ohmmeter's internal resistance and voltage are known values, the amount of current flow through the meter depends on the resistance of the circuit or component being tested. The ohmmeter can also be used to perform a continuity test for suspected open circuits. In using the meter for making continuity checks, do not be concerned with the actual resistance readings. Zero resistance, or any ohm reading, indicates continuity in the circuit. Infinite resistance indicates an opening in the circuit. A high resistance reading where there should be none indicates a problem in the circuit. Checks for short circuits are made in the same manner as checks for open circuits, except that the circuit must be isolated from both power and normal ground. Infinite resistance indicates no continuity, while zero resistance indicates a dead short.

✳✳ WARNING

Never use an ohmmeter to check the resistance of a component or wire while there is voltage applied to the circuit.

• Ammeter—an ammeter measures the amount of current flowing through a circuit in units called amperes or amps. At normal operating voltage, most circuits have a characteristic amount of amperes, called "current draw" which can be measured using an ammeter. By referring to a specified current draw rating, then measuring the amperes and comparing the two values, one can determine what is happening within the circuit to aid in diagnosis. An open circuit, for example, will not allow any current to flow, so the ammeter reading will be zero. A damaged component or circuit will have an increased current draw, so the reading will be high. The ammeter is always connected in series with the circuit being tested. All of the current that normally flows through the circuit must also flow through the ammeter; if there is any other path for the current to follow, the ammeter reading will not be accurate. The ammeter itself has very little resistance to current flow and, therefore, will not affect the circuit, but it will measure current draw only when the circuit is closed and electricity is flowing. Excessive current draw can blow fuses and drain the battery, while a reduced current draw can cause motors to run slowly, lights to dim and other components to not operate properly.

Troubleshooting Electrical Systems

▶ See Figure 31

When diagnosing a specific problem, organized troubleshooting is a must. The complexity of a modern vehicle demands that you approach any problem in a logical, organized manner. There are certain troubleshooting techniques which are standard:

• Establish when the problem occurs. Does the problem appear only under certain conditions? Were there any noises, odors or other unusual symptoms?

• Isolate the problem area. To do this, make some simple tests and observations, then eliminate the systems that are working properly. Check for obvious problems, such as broken wires and loose or dirty connections. Always check the obvious before assuming something complicated is the cause.

• Test for problems systematically to determine the cause once the problem area is isolated. Are all the components functioning properly? Is there power going to electrical switches and motors. Performing careful, systematic checks will often turn up most causes on the first inspection, without wasting time checking components that have little or no relationship to the problem.

• Test all repairs after the work is done to make sure that the problem is fixed. Some causes can be traced to more than one component, so a careful verification of repair work is important in order to pick up additional malfunctions that may cause a problem to reappear or a different problem to arise. A blown fuse, for example, is a simple problem that may require more than another fuse to repair. If you don't look for a problem that caused a fuse to blow, a shorted wire (for example) may go undetected.

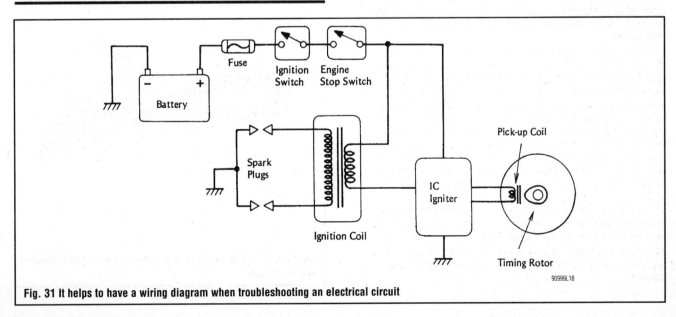

Fig. 31 It helps to have a wiring diagram when troubleshooting an electrical circuit

90999L18

Experience has shown that most problems tend to be the result of a fairly simple and obvious cause, such as loose or corroded connectors, bad grounds or damaged wire insulation which causes a short. This makes careful visual inspection of components during testing essential to quick and accurate troubleshooting.

Open Circuits

TESTING

▶ See Figure 32

This test already assumes the existence of an open in the circuit and it is used to help locate the open portion.

1. Isolate the circuit from power and ground.
2. Connect the self-powered test light or ohmmeter ground clip to the ground side of the circuit and probe sections of the circuit sequentially.
3. If the light is out or there is infinite resistance, the open is between the probe and the circuit ground.
4. If the light is on or the meter shows continuity, the open is between the probe and the end of the circuit toward the power source.

TCCA6P10

Fig. 32 The infinite reading on this multimeter (1 .) indicates that the circuit is open

Short Circuits

TESTING

✳✳ WARNING

Never use a self-powered test light to perform checks for opens or shorts when power is applied to the circuit under test. The test light can be damaged by outside power.

1. Isolate the circuit from power and ground.
2. Connect the self-powered test light or ohmmeter ground clip to a good ground and probe any easy-to-reach point in the circuit.
3. If the light comes on or there is continuity, there is a short somewhere in the circuit.
4. To isolate the short, probe a test point at either end of the isolated circuit (the light should be on or the meter should indicate continuity).
5. Leave the test light probe engaged and sequentially open connectors or switches, remove parts, etc. until the light goes out or continuity is broken.
6. When the light goes out, the short is between the last two circuit components which were opened.

Available Voltage

TESTING

This test determines voltage available from the battery and should be the first step in any electrical troubleshooting procedure after visual inspection. Many electrical problems, especially on computer controlled systems, can be caused by a low state of charge in the battery. Excessive corrosion at the battery cable terminals can cause poor contact that will prevent proper charging and full battery current flow.

1. Set the voltmeter selector switch to the 20V position.
2. Connect the multimeter negative lead to the battery's negative (-) post or terminal and the positive lead to the battery's positive (+) post or terminal.
3. Turn the ignition switch **ON** to provide a load.
4. A well charged battery should register over 12 volts. If the meter reads below 11.5 volts, the battery power may be insufficient to operate the electrical system properly.

Voltage Drop

TESTING

When current flows through a load, the voltage beyond the load drops. This voltage drop is due to the resistance created by the load and also by small resistance's created by corrosion at the connectors and damaged insulation on the wires. The maximum allowable voltage drop under load is critical, especially if there is more than one load in the circuit, since all voltage drops are cumulative.

1. Set the voltmeter selector switch to the 20 volt position.
2. Connect the multimeter negative lead to a good ground.
3. Operate the circuit and check the voltage prior to the first component (load).
4. There should be little or no voltage drop in the circuit prior to the first component. If a voltage drop exists, the wire or connectors in the circuit are suspect.
5. While operating the first component in the circuit, probe the ground side of the component with the positive meter lead and observe the voltage readings. A small voltage drop should be noticed. This voltage drop is caused by the resistance of the component.
6. Repeat the test for each component (load) down the circuit.
7. If a large voltage drop is noticed, the preceding component, wire or connector is suspect.

Resistance

TESTING

▶ See Figure 33

✳✳ WARNING

Never use an ohmmeter with power applied to the circuit. The ohmmeter is designed to operate on its own power supply. The normal 12 volt electrical system voltage could damage the meter!

1. Isolate the circuit from the vehicle's power source.
2. Ensure that the ignition key is **OFF** when disconnecting any components or the battery.
3. Where necessary, also isolate at least one side of the circuit to be checked, in order to avoid reading parallel resistances. Parallel circuit resistances will always give a lower reading than the actual resistance of either of the branches.
4. Connect the meter leads to both sides of the circuit (wire or component) and read the actual measured ohms on the meter scale. Make sure the selector switch is set to the proper ohm scale for the circuit being tested, to avoid misreading the ohmmeter test value.

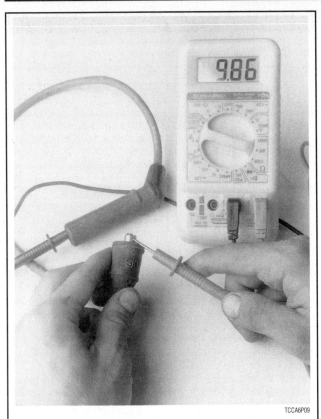

Fig. 33 Spark plug wires can be checked for excessive resistance using an ohmmeter

Wire and Connector Repair

Almost anyone can replace damaged wires, as long as the proper tools and parts are available. Wire and terminals are available to fit almost any need. Even the specialized weatherproof, molded and hard shell connectors are now available from aftermarket suppliers.

Be sure the ends of all the wires are fitted with the proper terminal hardware and connectors. Wrapping a wire around a stud is never a permanent solution and will only cause trouble later. Replace wires one at a time to avoid confusion. Always route wires exactly the same as the factory.

➡ If connector repair is necessary, only attempt it if you have the proper tools. Weatherproof and hard shell connectors require special tools to release the pins inside the connector. Attempting to repair these connectors with conventional hand tools will damage them.

Reading Wiring Diagrams

▶ See Figures 34 thru 39

For many people, reading wiring diagrams, or schematics, is a black art. It isn't as bad as it seems, since wiring diagrams are really nothing more than connect-the-dots with wires!

If you look at the sample diagrams, you will see that they contain information such as wire colors, terminal connections and components. The boxes may contain information such as internal configurations as would be handy to figure out what is going on inside a relay or switch.

There is a standard set of symbols used in wiring diagrams to denote various components. If the wiring diagram doesn't provide a reference for the symbols, you should be able to pick out their meanings from other information given.

The wiring diagram will use abbreviations for wire colors. There will be a chart somewhere in the wiring diagram or in the manual you are using to decode them.

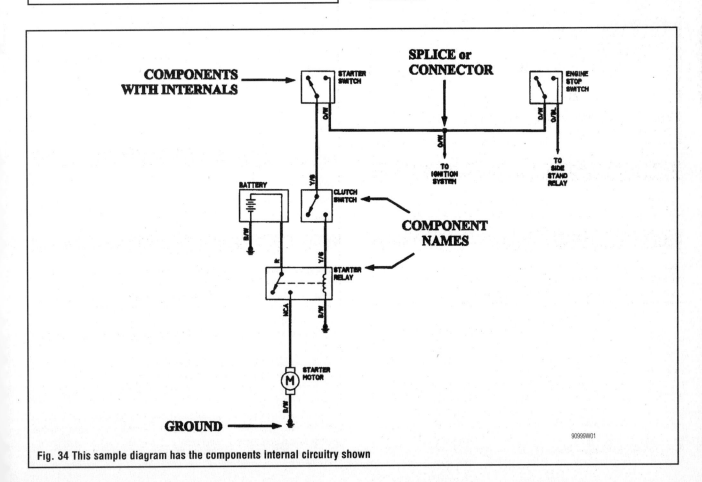

Fig. 34 This sample diagram has the components internal circuitry shown

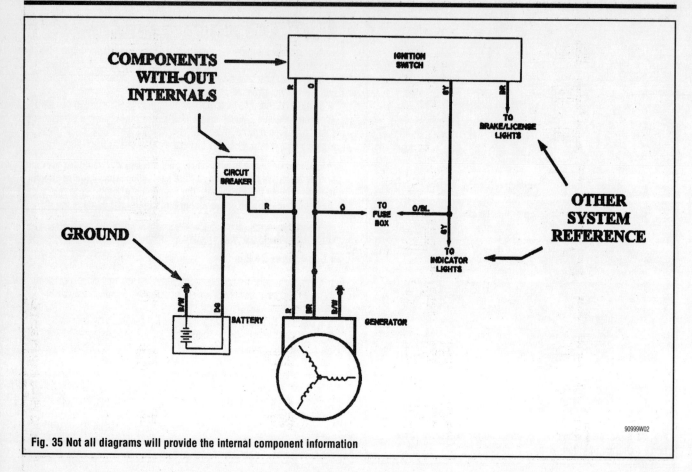

Fig. 35 Not all diagrams will provide the internal component information

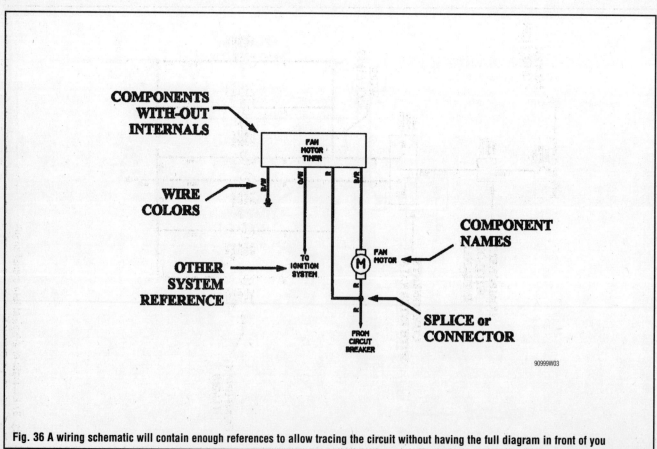

Fig. 36 A wiring schematic will contain enough references to allow tracing the circuit without having the full diagram in front of you

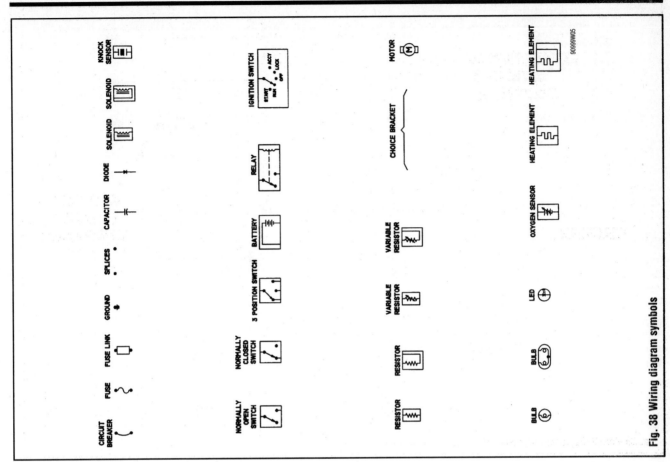

Fig. 38 Wiring diagram symbols

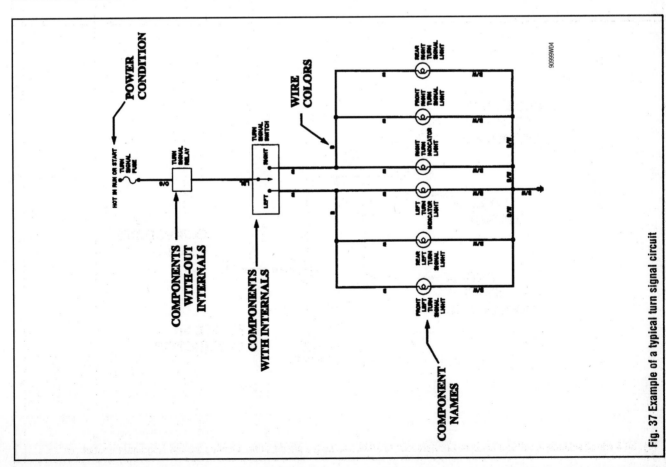

Fig. 37 Example of a typical turn signal circuit

BLACK	B	PINK	PK
BROWN	BR	PURPLE	P
RED	R	GREEN	G
ORANGE	O	WHITE	W
YELLOW	Y	LIGHT BLUE	LBL
GRAY	GY	LIGHT GREEN	LG
BLUE	BL	DARK GREEN	DG
VIOLET	V	DARK BLUE	DBL
TAN	T	NO COLOR AVAILABLE	NCA

90999W06

Fig. 39 Examples of some wire color abbreviations

THE WORK AREA

Floor Space and Working Height

▶ See Figure 40

The average one car garage will give you more than enough workspace. A floor plan of 16 ft. X 12 ft. is more than sufficient for shelving, workbenches, tool shelves or boxes and parts storage areas. 12 X 16 works out to 192 square feet. You may think that this sounds like a lot of room, but when you start building shelves, and constructing work benches almost most half of that can be eaten up!

In addition, you may wonder why a lot of floor space is needed. There are several reasons, not the least of which is the safety factor. You'll be working around a large, heavy, metal object — your vehicle. You don't want to be tripping, falling, crashing into things or hurting yourself, all because your vehicle takes up most of your workspace. Accidents can happen! You can easily trip over a jack handle or work stand leg or drop a heavy part or tool. You'll need room to take evasive action!

Most garages have concrete floors. Your creeper rolls best on a smooth surface. If your garage floor has cracks with raised sections or blocks with deep grooves, you may have a problem. The wheels can hang up on these cracks or grooves causing you to get stuck under the vehicle.

As for working height, overhead clearance is a problem, only if you have a tall vehicle, such as an RV or sport utility vehicle, or, if you're doing more than fuel system work. If doing engine work, for example, you might need an engine crane. To lift an engine from or install an engine in a vehicle, the crane cane needs as much as 10 ft. overhead.

Storage Areas

SHELVES

▶ See Figures 41, 42 and 43

You can't have enough shelf space. Adequate shelf space means that you don't have to stack anything on the floor, where it would be in the way.

Shelves aren't tough. You can make your own or buy modular or prefab units. The best modular units are those made of interlocking shelves and

TCCA1P18

Fig. 40 Example of an engine stand

87932001

Fig. 41 Typical homemade wood shelves, crammed with stuff. These shelves are made from spare pressure treated decking

uprights of ABS plastic. They're lightweight and easy to assemble, and their load-bearing capacity is more than sufficient. Also, they are not subject rust or rot as are wood and metal shelves.

Probably the cheapest and best shelves are ones that you make yourself from one inch shelving with 2 X 4 uprights. You can make them as long, wide and high as you want. For at least the uprights, use pressure treated wood. Its resistance to rot is more than worth the additional cost.

TOOL CHESTS

▶ See Figures 44 and 45

There are many types and sizes of tool chests. Their greatest advantage is that they can hold a lot of tools, securely, in a relatively small area. If you decide that you need one, make sure that you buy one that's big enough and mobile enough for the work area. Remember, you get what you pay for, so purchase a good brand name, and it should last a lifetime.

There are several things to look for in a tool chest, depending on how much you plan on using it, and just how many tools you plan to stuff in it. Check the overall construction. In general, bolted-together chests are stronger than riveted or tabbed, because they are sturdier. Drawers that ride on ball bearings are better than compound slide drawers, because they can hold more and are easier to open/close. Heavy-duty, ball bearing casters are better than bushing type wheels, because they will roll better and last longer. Steel wheels are better than plastic, as they are less prone to damage. Compare different boxes, you'll have to make up your own mind exactly what style is best for you.

Fig. 42 Modular plastic shelves, such as these are inexpensive, weatherproof and easy to assemble

Fig. 43 These shelves were made from the frame of old kitchen cabinets

87932031

Fig. 44 Different types of mobile, steel tool chests

87932033

Fig. 45 A good tool chest has several drawers, each designed to hold a different type tool

WORK BENCHES

▶ **See Figure 46**

As with the shelving, work benches can be either store-bought or home-made. The store-bought workbenches can be steel or precut wood kits. Either are fine and are available at most building supply stores or through tool catalogs.

Homemade benches, as with the shelves have the advantage of being made-to-fit your workshop. A freestanding workbench is best, as opposed to one attached to an outside wall. The freestanding bench can take more abuse since it doesn't transfer the shock or vibration to wall supports.

A good free-standing workbench should be constructed using 4 X 4 pressure treated wood as legs, 2 X 6 planking as header boards and ¾ inch plywood sheathing as a deck. Diagonal supports can be 2 X 4 studs and it's always helpful to construct a full size ¾ inch plywood shelf under the bench. Not only can you use the shelf for storage but also it gives great rigidity to the whole bench structure. Assembling the bench with screws rather than nails takes longer but adds strength and gives you the ability to take the whole thing apart if you ever want to move it.

LIGHTING

▶ **See Figures 47 and 48**

The importance of adequate lighting can't be over emphasized. Good lighting is not only a convenience but also a safety feature. If you can see what you're working on you're less likely to make mistakes, have a wrench slip or trip over an obstacle. On most vehicles, everything is about the same color and usually dirty. During disassembly, a lot of frustration can be avoided if you can see all the bolts, some of which may be hidden or obscured.

For overhead lighting, at least two twin tube 36 inch fluorescent shop lights should be in place. Most garages are wired with standard light bulbs attached to the wall studs at intervals. Four or five of these lights, at about a 6 foot height combined with the overhead lighting should suffice. However, no matter where the lights are, your body is going to block some of it so a droplight or clip-on type work light is a great idea. These lights can be mounted on the engine stand, or even the engine itself.

VENTILATION

At one time or another, you'll be working with chemicals that may require adequate ventilation. Now, just about all garages have a big car-sized door and all sheds or workshops have a door. In bad weather the door will have to be closed so at least one window that opens is a necessity. An exhaust fan or regular ventilation fan is a great help, especially in hot weather.

HEATERS

If you live in an area where the winters are cold, as do many of us, it's nice to have some sort of heat where we work. If your workshop or garage is attached to the house, you'll probably be okay. If your garage or shop is detached, then a space heater of some sort — electric, propane or kerosene — will be necessary. NEVER run a space heater in the presence of flammable vapors! When running a non-electric space heater, always allow for some means of venting the carbon monoxide!

ELECTRICAL REQUIREMENTS

Obviously, your workshop should be wired according to all local codes. As to what type of service you need, that depends on your electrical load. If you have a lot of power equipment and maybe a refrigerator, TV, stereo or whatever, not only do you have a great shop, but your amperage requirements may exceed your wiring's capacity. If you are at all in doubt, consult your local electrical contractor.

Fig. 46 Homemade workbenches

Fig. 47 At least two of this type of twin tube fluorescent light is essential

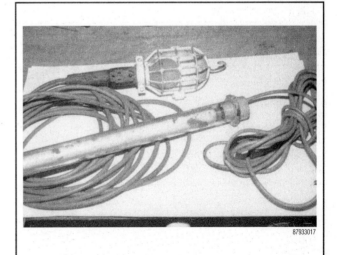

Fig. 48 Two types of droplights. Incandescent and fluorescent

SUPPLIES AND EQUIPMENT

Fluid Disposal

Used fluids such as engine oil, transmission fluid, antifreeze and brake fluid are hazardous wastes and must be disposed of properly. Before draining any fluids, consult with your local authorities; in many areas waste oil, etc. is being accepted as a part of recycling programs. A number of service stations and auto parts stores are also accepting waste fluids for recycling.

Be sure of the recycling center's policies before draining any fluids, as many will not accept different fluids that have been mixed together.

Chemicals and Supplies

There is a whole range of chemicals that you'll need. The most common types are, lubricants, penetrants and sealers. Keep these handy, on some convenient shelf.

When a particular chemical is not being used, keep it capped, upright and in a safe place. These substances may be flammable or irritants or caustic and should always be stored properly, used properly and handled with care. Always read and follow all label directions and be sure to always wear hand and eye protection!

LUBRICANTS & PENETRANTS

▶ **See Figure 49**

In this category, a well-prepared automotive shop should have:
- Clean engine oil. Whatever you use regularly in your engine will be fine.
- Lithium grease.
- Chassis lube
- Assembly lube
- Silicone grease
- Silicone spray
- Penetrating oil

Clean engine oil is used to coat certain bolts, screws and nuts prior to installation. This is always a good practice since the less friction there is on a fastener, the less chance there will be of breakage and crossthreading. Also, an oiled bolt will give a truer torque value and be less likely to rust or seize. An obvious exception would be wheel lugs. These are not oiled.

Lithium grease, chassis lube, silicone grease or a synthetic brake caliper grease can all be used pretty much interchangeably. All can be used for coating rust-prone fasteners and for facilitating the assembly of parts that are a tight fit. The main advantages of silicone grease are that it's slipperier than most similar lubricants and it has a higher melting point.

Fig. 49 A variety of penetrants and lubricants is a staple of any DIYer's garage

87933516

➡Silicone dielectric grease is a non-conductor that is often used to coat the terminals of wiring connectors before fastening them. It may sound odd to coat metal portions of a terminal with something that won't conduct electricity, but here is it how it works. When the connector is fastened the metal-to-metal contact between the terminals will displace the grease (allowing the circuit to be completed). The grease that is displaced will then coat the non-contacted surface and the cavity around the terminals, SEALING them from atmospheric moisture that could cause corrosion.

Silicone spray is a good lubricant for hard-to-reach places and parts that shouldn't be gooped up with grease.

Penetrating oil may turn out to be one of your best friends during disassembly. The most familiar penetrating oils are Liquid Wrench® and WD-40®. These products have hundreds of uses. For your purposes, they are vital!

Before disassembling any part, check the fasteners. If any appear rusted, soak them thoroughly with the penetrant and let them stand while you do something else. This simple act can save you hours of tedious work trying to extract a broken bolt or stud.

Engine assembly lube. There are several types of this product available. Essentially it is a heavy-bodied lubricant used for coating moving parts prior to assembly. For engine work, the idea is that is stays in place until the engine starts for the first time and dissolves in the engine oil as oil pressure is achieved. This way, expensive parts receive needed protection until everything is working. For non-engine work, it comes in handy for assembling tight-fitting parts.

SEALANTS

▶ **See Figure 50**

Sealants are an indispensable part of almost all automotive work. The purpose of sealants is to establish a leak-proof bond between or around assembled parts. Most sealers are used in conjunction with gaskets, but some are used instead of conventional gasket material in newer engines.

The most common sealers are the non-hardening types such as Permatex® No.2 or its equivalents. These sealers are applied to the mating surfaces of each part to be joined, then a gasket is put in place and the parts are assembled.

One very helpful type of non-hardening sealer is the "high tack" type. This type is a very sticky material that holds the gasket in place while the parts are being assembled. This stuff is really a good idea when you don't have enough hands or fingers to keep everything where it should be.

The stand-alone sealers are the Room Temperature Vulcanizing (RTV) silicone gasket makers. On many newer vehicles, this material is used instead of a gasket. In those instances, a gasket may not be available or, because of the shape of the mating surfaces, a gasket shouldn't be used. This stuff, when used in conjunction with a conventional gasket, produces the surest bonds.

It does have its limitations though. When using this material, you will have a time limit. It starts to set-up within 15 minutes or so, so you have to assemble the parts without delay. In addition, when squeezing the material out of the tube, don't drop any glops into the engine. The stuff will form and set and travel around the oil gallery, possibly plugging up a passage. Also, most types are not fuel-proof. Check the tube for all cautions.

CLEANERS

▶ **See Figures 51, 52 and 53**

You'll have two types of cleaners to deal with: parts cleaners and hand cleaners. The parts cleaners are for the vehicle; the hand cleaners are for you.

There are many good, non-flammable, biodegradable parts cleaners on the market. These cleaning agents are safe for you, the parts and the envi-

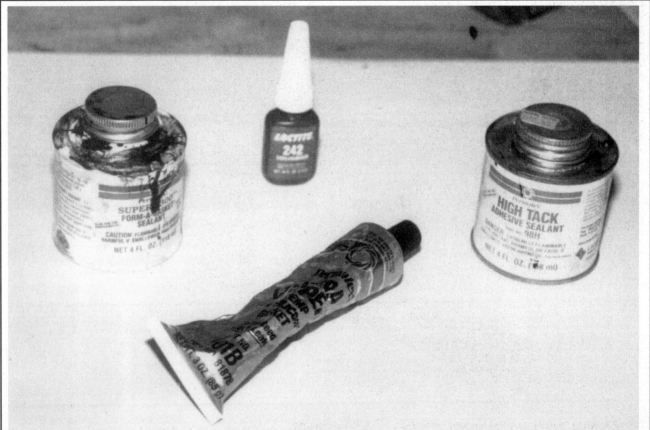

Fig. 50 Sealants are essential. These four types are all that you'll need

Fig. 51 Three types of cleaners. Some are caustic; some are not. Always read and follow label instructions

Fig. 52 This is one type of hand cleaner that not only works well but smells pretty good too

Fig. 53 The best thing to clean up all types of spills is "kitty litter"

ronment. Therefore, there is no reason to use flammable, caustic or toxic substances to clean your parts or tools.

As far as hand cleaners go, the waterless types are the best. They have always been efficient at cleaning, but left behind a pretty smelly odor. Recently though, just about all of them have eliminated the odor and added stuff that actually smells good. Make sure that you pick one that contains lanolin or some other moisture-replenishing additive. Cleaners not only remove grease and engine oil but also skin oil.

One other note: most women know this already but most men don't. Use a hand lotion when you're all cleaned up. It's okay. Real men DO use hand lotion!

SHOP TOWELS

▶ See Figure 54

One of the most important elements in doing shop work is a good supply of shop towels. Regular paper towels just don't cut it! Most auto parts stores sell packs of shop towels, usually 50–100 in a pack. They are relatively cheap and can be washed over and over. Always keep them handy.

One of the best shop towels known to science, is the old-fashioned cloth diaper. They're highly absorbent and rugged, but, in these days of disposable diapers, are hard to find.

Fig. 54 A pack of shop towels

Fasteners

▶ See Figures 55 and 56

Although there are a great variety of fasteners found in the modern vehicle, the most commonly used retainer is the threaded fastener (nuts, bolts, screws, studs, etc). Most threaded retainers may be reused, provided that they are not damaged in use or during the repair. Some retainers (such as stretch bolts or torque prevailing nuts) are designed to deform when tightened or in use and should not be reinstalled.

Whenever possible, we will note any special retainers which should be replaced during a procedure. But you should always inspect the condition of a retainer when it is removed and replace any that show signs of damage. Check all threads for rust or corrosion that can increase the torque necessary to achieve the desired clamp load for which that fastener was originally selected. Additionally, be sure that the driver surface of the fastener has not been compromised by rounding or other damage. In some cases a driver surface may become only partially rounded, allowing the driver to catch in only one direction. In many of these occurrences, a fastener may be installed and tightened, but the driver would not be able to

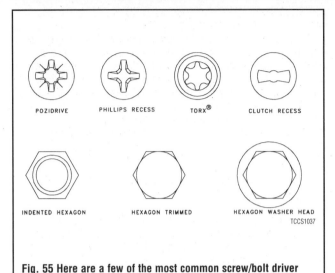

Fig. 55 Here are a few of the most common screw/bolt driver styles

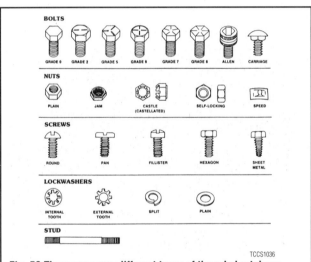

Fig. 56 There are many different types of threaded retainers found on vehicles

grip and loosen the fastener again. (This could lead to frustration down the line should that component ever need to be disassembled again).

If you must replace a fastener, whether due to design or damage, you must ALWAYS be sure to use the proper replacement. In all cases, a retainer of the same design, material and strength should be used. Markings on the heads of most bolts will help determine the proper strength of the fastener. The same material, thread and pitch must be selected to assure proper installation and safe operation of the vehicle afterwards.

Thread gauges are available to help measure a bolt or stud's thread. Most automotive and hardware stores keep gauges available to help you select the proper size. In a pinch, you can use another nut or bolt for a thread gauge. If the bolt you are replacing is not too badly damaged, you can select a match by finding another bolt that will thread in its place. If you find a nut that threads properly onto the damaged bolt, then use that nut to help select the replacement bolt. If however, the bolt you are replacing is so badly damaged (broken or drilled out) that its threads cannot be used as a gauge, you might start by looking for another bolt (from the same assembly or a similar location on your vehicle) which will thread into the damaged bolt's mounting. If so, the other bolt can be used to select a nut; the nut can then be used to select the replacement bolt.

In all cases, be absolutely sure you have selected the proper replacement. Don't be shy, you can always ask the store clerk for help.

Be aware that when you find a bolt with damaged threads, you may also find the nut or drilled hole it was threaded into has also been damaged. If this is the case, you may have to drill and tap the hole, replace the nut or otherwise repair the threads. NEVER try to force a replacement bolt to fit into the damaged threads.

BOLTS & SCREWS

▶ **See Figure 57**

Technically speaking, bolts are hexagon head or cap screws. For the purposes of this book, however, cap screws will be called bolts because that is the common terminology for them. Both bolts and screws are turned into drilled or threaded holes to fasten two parts together. Frequently, bolts require a nut on the other end, but this is not always the case. Screws seldom, if ever, require a nut on the other end.

Screws are supplied with slotted or Phillips heads. For obvious reasons, screws are not generally used where a great deal of torque is required. Most of the screws you will encounter will be used to retain components where strength is not a factor.

Threaded retainers (such as bolts and screws) come in various sizes, designated as 8–32, 10–32, or ¼–32. The first number indicates the minor diameter, and the second number indicates the number of threads per inch (or distance between threads in mm).

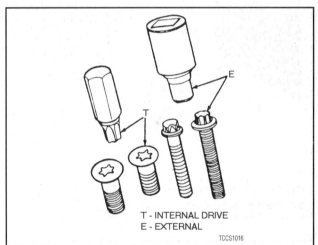

T - INTERNAL DRIVE
E - EXTERNAL

Fig. 57 Special fasteners such as these Torx® head bolts are used by manufacturers to discourage people from working on vehicles without the proper tools

NUTS

Nuts have only one use: they simply hold the other end of the bolt or stud and, thereby, hold the two parts together. There are a variety of nuts used on vehicles, but a standard hexagon head (six-sided) nut is the most common.

Castellated and slotted nuts are designed for use with a cotter pin and are usually used when it is extremely important that the nuts do not work loose (in wheel bearings, for example). Other nuts are self-locking nuts that have a slot cut in the side.

When the nut is tightened, the separated sections pull together and lock the nut onto the bolt. Interference nuts have a collar of soft metal or fiber. The bolt cuts threads in the soft material that then jams in the threads and prevents the nut and bolt from working loose.

A jam nut is a second hexagon nut that is used to hold the first nut in place. They are usually found where some type of adjustment is needed; parking brake cables, for instance.

Pawlnuts are single thread nuts that provide some locking action when they have been turned down on the nut.

Speed nuts are simply rectangular bits of sheet metal that are pushed down over a bolt, screw, or stud to provide locking action.

STUDS

Studs are simply pieces of threaded rod. They are similar to bolts and screws in their thread configuration, but they have no heads. One end is turned into a threaded hole and the other end is generally secured by same type of nut. Unless the nut is self-locking, a lockwasher or jam nut is generally used underneath it.

LOCKWASHERS

Lockwashers are a form of washer. They may be either split or toothed, and they are always installed between a nut or screw head and the actual part being held. The split washer is crushed flat and locks the nut in place by spring tension. The toothed washer provides many edges to improve the locking effect and is usually used on smaller bolts and screws.

BOLT & SCREW TERMINOLOGY

Bolts and screws are identified by type, major diameter, minor diameter, pitch or threads per inch, class, length, thread length, and the size of the wrench required.

Major Diameter

▶ See Figure 58

This is the widest diameter of the bolt as measured from the top of the threads on one side to the top of the threads on the other side.

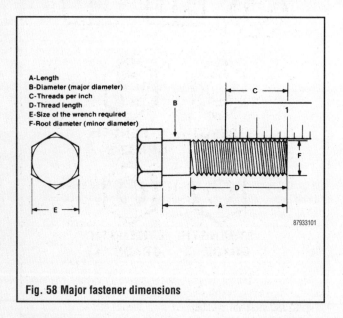

A-Length
B-Diameter (major diameter)
C-Threads per inch
D-Thread length
E-Size of the wrench required
F-Root diameter (minor diameter)

87933101

Fig. 58 Major fastener dimensions

Minor Diameter

This is the diameter obtained by measuring from the bottom of the threads on one side of the bolt to the bottom of the threads on the other side. In other words, it is the diameter of the bolt if it does not have any threads.

Pitch Or Threads Per Inch

▶ See Figure 59

Thread pitch is the distance between the top of one thread to the top of the next. It is simply the distance between one thread and the next. There

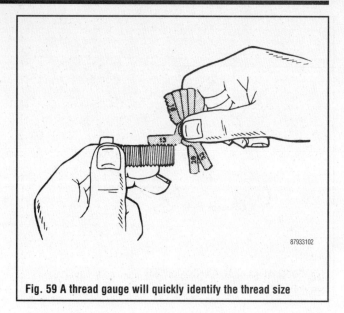

87933102

Fig. 59 A thread gauge will quickly identify the thread size

are two types of threads in general use today. Unified National Coarse thread, and Unified National Fine. These are usually known simply as either fine or coarse thread.

Anyone who has been working on vehicles for any length of time can tell the difference between the two simply by looking at the screw, bolt, or nut. The only truly accurate way to determine thread pitch is to use a thread pitch gauge. There are some general rules to remember, however.

Coarse thread screws and bolts are used frequently when they are being threaded into aluminum or cast iron because the finer threads tend to strip more easily in these materials. Also, as a bolt or screw's diameter increases, thread pitch becomes greater.

Thread Class

Thread class is a measure of the operating clearance between the internal nut threads and the external threads of the bolt. There are three classes of fit, 1, 2, or 3. In addition, there are letter designations to designate either internal (class A) or external (class B) threads.

Class 1 threads are a relatively loose fit and are used when ease of assembly and disassembly are of paramount importance.

Class 2 bolts are most commonly encountered in automotive applications and give an accurate, but not an overly tight, fit.

Class 3 threads are used when utmost accuracy is needed. You might find a class 3 bolt and nut combination on an airplane, but you won't encounter them very often on a vehicle.

Length and Thread Length

Screw length is the length of the bolt or screw from the bottom of the head to the bottom of the bolt or screw. Thread length is exactly that, the length of the threads.

Types Or Grades Of Bolts & Screws

▶ See Figure 60

The tensile strength of bolts and screws varies widely. Standards for these fasteners have been established by the Society of Automotive Engineers (SAE). Distinctive markings on the head of the bolt will identify its tensile strength.

These outward radiating lines are normally called points. A bolt with no points on the head is a grade 1 or a grade 2 bolt. This type of bolt is suitable for applications in which only a low-strength bolt is necessary.

On the other hand, a grade 5 bolt is found in a number of automotive applications and has double the tensile strength of a grade 2 bolt. A grade 5 bolt will have three embossed lines or points on the head.

going to do much good. It is also possible to run a metric nut down on an U.S. measure bolt and find that it is too loose to provide sufficient strength.

Metric bolts are marked in a manner different from that of U.S. measure bolts. Most metric bolts have a number stamped on the head. This metric grade marking won't be an even number, but something like 4.6 or 10.9. The number indicates the relative strength of the bolt. The higher the number, the greater the strength of the bolt. Some metric bolts are also marked with a single-digit number to indicate the bolt strength. Metric bolt sizes are also identified in a manner different from that of U.S. measure fasteners.

If, for example, a metric bolt were designated 14 x 2, that would mean that the major diameter is 14 mm (.56 in.), and that the thread pitch is 2 mm (.08 in.). More important, metric bolts are not classified by number of threads per inch, but by the distance between the threads, and the distance between threads does not quite correspond to number of threads per inch. For example, 2 mm between threads is about 12.7 threads per inch.

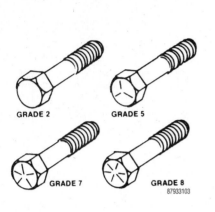

Fig. 60 Markings on U.S. measure bolts indicate the relative strength of the bolt

Grade 8 bolts are the best and are frequently called aircraft grade bolts. Grade 8 bolts have six points on the head.

Metric Bolts

▶ **See Figures 61, 62, 63 and 64**

While metric bolts may seem to be the same as their U.S. measure counterparts, they definitely are not. The pitch on a metric bolt is different from that of an U.S. measure bolt. It is entirely possible to start a metric bolt into a hole with U.S. measure threads and run it down a few turns. Then it is going to bind. Recognizing the problem at this point is not

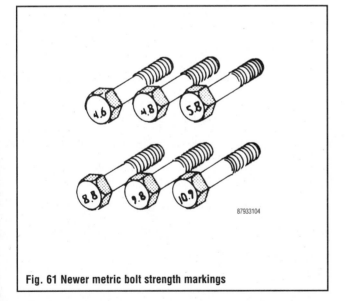

Fig. 61 Newer metric bolt strength markings

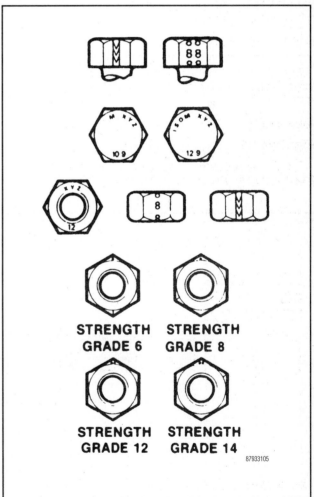

Fig. 62 ISO strength markings

	Mark	Class		Mark	Class
Hexagon head bolt	4— (Bolt head No. 4)	4T	Stud bolt	No mark	4T
	5—	5T			
	6—	6T			
	7—	7T			
	8—	8T			
	9—	9T			
	10—	10T			
	11—	11T			
	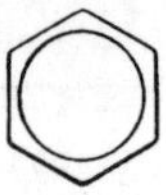 No mark	4T		Grooved	6T
Hexagon flange bolt w/ washer hexagon bolt	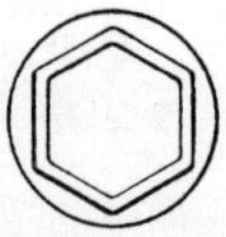 No mark	4T			
Hexagon head bolt	 Two protruding lines	5T			
Hexagon flange bolt w/ washer hexagon bolt	 Two protruding lines	6T	Welded bolt		4T
Hexagon head bolt	 Three protruding lines	7T			
Hexagon head bolt	 Four protruding lines	8T			

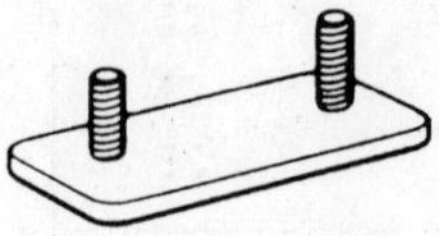

TCCS1240

Fig. 63 Metric bolt strength indicator marks

Class	Diameter mm	Pitch mm	Specified torque					
			Hexagon head bolt			Hexagon flange bolt		
			N·m	kgf·cm	ft·lbf	N·m	kgf·cm	ft·lbf
4T	6	1	5	55	48 in.·lbf	6	60	52 in.·lbf
	8	1.25	12.5	130	9	14	145	10
	10	1.25	26	260	19	29	290	21
	12	1.25	47	480	35	53	540	39
	14	1.5	74	760	55	84	850	61
	16	1.5	115	1,150	83	—	—	—
5T	6	1	6.5	65	56 in.·lbf	7.5	75	65 in.·lbf
	8	1.25	15.5	160	12	17.5	175	13
	10	1.25	32	330	24	36	360	26
	12	1.25	59	600	43	65	670	48
	14	1.5	91	930	67	100	1,050	76
	16	1.5	140	1,400	101	—	—	—
6T	6	1	8	80	69 in.·lbf	9	90	78 in.·lbf
	8	1.25	19	195	14	21	210	15
	10	1.25	39	400	29	44	440	32
	12	1.25	71	730	53	80	810	59
	14	1.5	110	1,100	80	125	1,250	90
	16	1.5	170	1,750	127	—	—	—
7T	6	1	10.5	110	8	12	120	9
	8	1.25	25	260	19	28	290	21
	10	1.25	52	530	38	58	590	43
	12	1.25	95	970	70	105	1,050	76
	14	1.5	145	1,500	108	165	1,700	123
	16	1.5	230	2,300	166	—	—	—
8T	8	1.25	29	300	22	33	330	24
	10	1.25	61	620	45	68	690	50
	12	1.25	110	1,100	80	120	1,250	90
9T	8	1.25	34	340	25	37	380	27
	10	1.25	70	710	51	78	790	57
	12	1.25	125	1,300	94	140	1,450	105
10T	8	1.25	38	390	28	42	430	31
	10	1.25	78	800	58	88	890	64
	12	1.25	140	1,450	105	155	1,600	116
11T	8	1.25	42	430	31	47	480	35
	10	1.25	87	890	64	97	990	72
	12	1.25	155	1,600	116	175	1,800	130

TCCS1241

Fig. 64 Determining the strength of metric fasteners

SAFE VEHICLE SERVICING TIPS

▶ **See Figures 65, 66, 67 and 68**

It is virtually impossible to anticipate all of the hazards involved with automotive maintenance and service but care and common sense will prevent most accidents.

The rules of safety for mechanics range from "don't smoke around gasoline" to "use the proper tool for the job." The trick to avoiding injuries is to develop safe work habits and take every possible precaution.

Do's

• Do keep a fire extinguisher and first aid kit handy.
• Do wear safety glasses or goggles when cutting, drilling, grinding or prying, even if you have 20–20 vision. If you wear glasses for the sake of vision, wear safety goggles over your regular glasses.
• Do shield your eyes whenever you work around the battery. Batteries contain sulfuric acid. In case of contact with the eyes or skin, flush the area with water or a mixture of water and baking soda, then seek immediate medical attention.

• Do use safety stands (jackstands) for any under vehicle service. Jacks are for raising vehicles; jackstands are for making sure the vehicle stays raised until you want it to come down. Whenever the vehicle is raised, block the wheels remaining on the ground and set the parking brake.
• Do use adequate ventilation when working with any chemicals or hazardous materials. Like carbon monoxide, the asbestos dust resulting from some brake lining wear can be hazardous in sufficient quantities.
• Do disconnect the negative battery cable when working on the electrical system. The secondary ignition system contains EXTREMELY HIGH VOLTAGE. In some cases it can even exceed 50,000 volts.
• Do follow manufacturer's directions whenever working with potentially hazardous materials. Most chemicals and fluids are poisonous if taken internally.
• Do properly maintain your tools. Loose hammerheads, mushroomed punches and chisels, frayed or poorly grounded electrical cords, excessively worn screwdrivers, spread wrenches (open end), cracked sockets, slipping ratchets, or faulty droplight sockets can cause accidents.
• Likewise, keep your tools clean; a greasy wrench can slip off a bolt head, ruining the bolt and often harming your knuckles in the process.

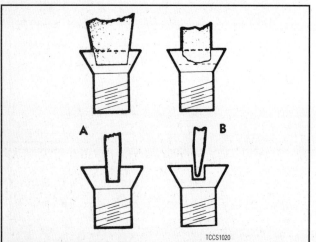

Fig. 65 Screwdrivers should be kept in good condition to prevent injury or damage that could result if the blade slips from the screw

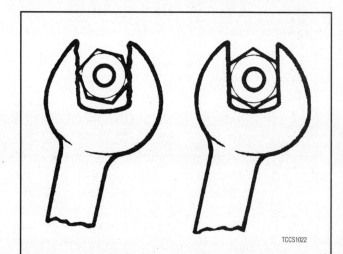

Fig. 67 Using the correct size wrench will help prevent the possibility of rounding-off a nut

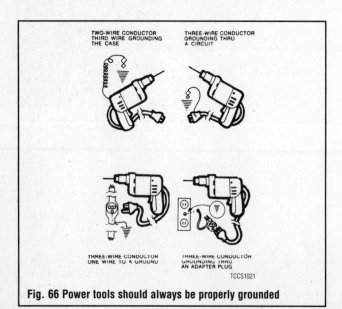

Fig. 66 Power tools should always be properly grounded

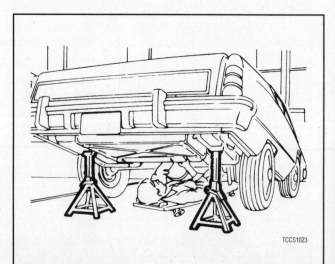

Fig. 68 NEVER work under a vehicle unless it is supported using safety stands (jackstands)

• Do use the proper size and type of tool for the job at hand. Do select a wrench or socket that fits the nut or bolt. The wrench or socket should sit straight, not cocked.

• Do, when possible, pull on a wrench handle rather than push on it, and adjust your stance to prevent a fall.

• Do be sure that adjustable wrenches are tightly closed on the nut or bolt and pulled so that the force is on the side of the fixed jaw.

• Do strike squarely with a hammer; avoid glancing blows.

• Do set the parking brake and block the drive wheels if the work requires a running engine.

Don't's

• Don't run the engine in a garage or anywhere else without proper ventilation—EVER! Carbon monoxide is poisonous; it takes a long time to leave the human body and you can build up a deadly supply of it in your system by simply breathing in a little every day. You may not realize you are slowly poisoning yourself. Always use power vents, windows, fans and/or open the garage door.

• Don't work around moving parts while wearing loose clothing. Short sleeves are much safer than long, loose sleeves. Hard-toed shoes with neoprene soles protect your toes and give a better grip on slippery surfaces. Jewelry such as watches, fancy belt buckles, beads or body adornment of any kind is not safe working around a vehicle. Long hair should be tied back under a hat or cap.

• Don't use pockets for toolboxes. A fall or bump can drive a screwdriver deep into your body. Even a rag hanging from your back pocket can wrap around a spinning shaft or fan.

• Don't smoke when working around gasoline, cleaning solvent or other flammable material.

• Don't smoke when working around the battery. When the battery is being charged, it gives off explosive hydrogen gas.

• Don't use gasoline to wash your hands; there are excellent soaps available. Gasoline contains dangerous additives that can enter the body through a cut or through your pores. Gasoline also removes all the natural oils from the skin so that bone dry hands will suck up oil and grease.

• Don't service the air conditioning system unless you are equipped with the necessary tools and training. When liquid or compressed gas refrigerant is released to atmospheric pressure it will absorb heat from whatever it contacts. This will chill or freeze anything it touches. Although refrigerant is normally non-toxic, R-12 becomes a deadly poisonous gas in the presence of an open flame. One good whiff of the vapors from burning refrigerant can be fatal.

• Don't use screwdrivers for anything other than driving screws! A screwdriver used as a prying tool can snap when you least expect it, causing injuries. At the very least, you'll ruin a good screwdriver.

• Don't use a bumper or emergency jack (that little ratchet, scissors, or pantograph jack supplied with the vehicle) for anything other than changing a flat! These jacks are only intended for emergency use out on the road; they are NOT designed as a maintenance tool. If you are serious about maintaining your vehicle yourself, invest in a hydraulic floor jack of at least a 1½ ton capacity, and at least two sturdy jackstands.

SAFETY EQUIPMENT

▶ See Figure 69

Fire Extinguishers

▶ See Figure 70

There are many types of safety equipment. The most important of these is the fire extinguisher. You'll be well off with two 5 lbs. extinguishers rated for oil, chemical and wood.

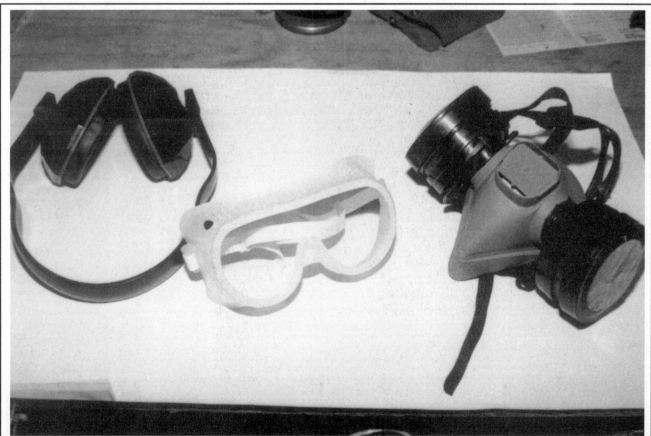

Fig. 69 Three essential pieces of safety equipment. Left to right: ear protectors, safety goggles and respirator

87932514

Fig. 70 A good, all-purpose fire extinguisher

First Aid

Next you'll need a good first aid kit. Any good kit that can be purchased from the local drug store will be fine. It's a good idea, in addition, to have something easily accessible in the event of a minor injury, such a hydrogen peroxide or other antiseptic that can be poured onto or applied to a wound immediately. Remember, your hands will be dirty. Just as you wouldn't want dirt entering the fuel system that has been opened, you certainly don't want bacteria entering a blood stream that has just been opened!

Work Gloves

▶ **See Figure 71**

Unless you think scars on your hands are cool, enjoy pain and like wearing bandages, get a good pair of work gloves. Canvass or leather are the best. And yes, we realize that there are some jobs involving small parts that can't be done while wearing work gloves. These jobs are not the ones usually associated with hand injuries.

A good pair of rubber gloves such as those usually associated with dish washing is also a great idea. There are some liquids such as solvents and penetrants that don't belong on your skin. Avoid burns and rashes. Wear these gloves.

And lastly, an option. If you're tired of being greasy and dirty all the time, go to the drug store and buy a box of disposable latex gloves like medical professionals wear. You can handle greasy parts, perform small tasks, wash parts, etc. all without getting dirty! These gloves take a surprising amount of abuse without tearing and aren't expensive. Note however, that it has been reported that some people are allergic to the latex or the powder used inside the gloves.

Work Boots

It's up to you, but I think that a good, comfortable pair of steel-toed work boots is a sensible idea. Primarily because heavy parts always get dropped sooner or later.

Good work boots also provide better support, — you're going to be on your feet a lot — are oil-resistant, and they keep your feet warm and dry.

To keep the boots protected, get a spray can of silicone-based water repellent and spray the boots when new, and periodically thereafter.

Eye Protection

Don't begin this, or for that matter, any job without a good pair of work goggles or impact resistant glasses! When doing any kind of work, it's all

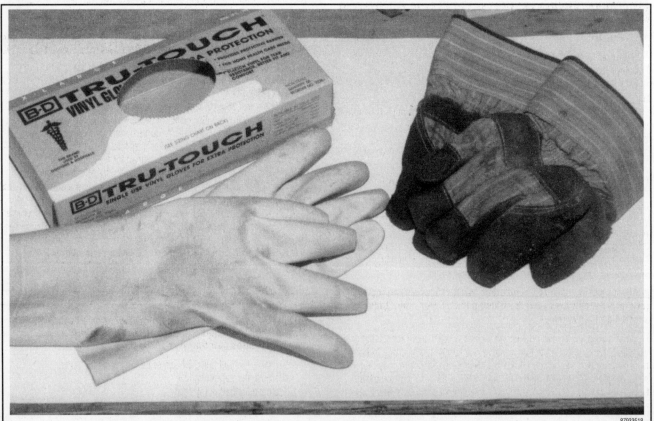
Fig. 71 Three different types of work gloves. The box contains latex gloves

too easy to avoid eye injury through this simple precaution. And don't just buy eye protection and leave it on the shelf. Wear it all the time! Things have a habit of breaking, chipping, splashing, spraying, splintering and flying around. And, for some reason, your eye is always in the way!

If you wear vision correcting glasses as a matter of routine, get a pair made with polycarbonate lenses. These lenses are impact resistant and are available at any optometrist.

Ear Protection

Often overlooked is hearing protection. Power equipment is noisy! Loud noises damage your ears. It's as simple as that!

The simplest and cheapest form of ear protection is a pair of noise-reducing ear plugs. Cheap insurance for your ears. And, they even come with their own, cute little carrying case.

More substantial, more protection and more money is a good pair of noise reducing earmuffs. They protect from all but the loudest sounds. Hopefully those are sounds that you'll never encounter since they're usually associated with disasters or rock concerts.

Work Clothes

Everyone has "work clothes". Usually this consists of old jeans and a shirt that has seen better days. That's fine. In addition, a denim work apron is a nice accessory. It's rugged, can hold some tools, and you don't feel bad wiping your hands or tools on it. That's what it's for.

If you're so inclined, overalls are a superb work garment. They're rugged and are equipped with numerous pockets, loops and places to put stuff. When bending or reaching, you won't have to worry about your shirt pulling out. Also, they cover your shirt like a work apron.

When working in cold weather, a one-piece, thermal work outfit is invaluable. Most are rated to below zero (Fahrenheit) temperatures and are ruggedly constructed.

Jacking

▶ See Figure 72

Your vehicle was supplied with a jack for emergency road repairs. This jack is fine for changing a flat tire or other short-term procedures not requiring you to go beneath the vehicle. If it is used in an emergency situation, carefully follow the instructions provided either with the jack or in your owner's manual. Do not attempt to use the jack on any portions of the vehicle other than specified by the vehicle manufacturer. Always block the diagonally opposite wheel when using a jack.

A more convenient way of jacking is the use of a garage or floor jack. Never place the jack under the radiator, engine or transmission components. Severe and expensive damage will result when the jack is raised. Additionally, never jack under the floor-pan or bodywork; the metal will deform.

Whenever you plan to work under the vehicle, you must support it on jackstands or ramps. Never use cinder blocks or stacks of wood to support the vehicle, even if you're only going to be under it for a few minutes. Never crawl under the vehicle when it is supported only by the tire-changing jack or other floor jack.

➡**Always position a block of wood or small rubber pad on top of the jack or jackstand to protect the lifting point's finish when lifting or supporting the vehicle.**

Small hydraulic, screw, or scissors jacks are satisfactory for raising the vehicle. Drive-on trestles or ramps are also a handy and safe way to both raise and support the vehicle. Be careful though, some ramps may be too steep to drive your vehicle onto without scraping the front bottom panels. Never support the vehicle on any suspension member (unless specifically instructed to do so by a repair manual) or by an underbody panel.

TCCS1202

Fig. 72 Do yourself a favor, if you plan to work on your vehicle, buy a good quality floor jack and set of jackstands

JACKING PRECAUTIONS

The following safety points cannot be overemphasized:
• Always block the opposite wheel or wheels to keep the vehicle from rolling off the jack.
• When raising the front of the vehicle, firmly apply the parking brake.
• When the drive wheels are to remain on the ground, leave the vehicle in gear to help prevent it from rolling.
• Always use jackstands to support the vehicle when you are working underneath. Place the stands beneath the vehicle's jacking brackets. Before climbing underneath, rock the vehicle a bit to make sure it is firmly supported.

Fuel System Precautions

The following warning should be obvious, however it bears repeating them just to remind you that working around your vehicle's fuel system can be very dangerous.

• Observe all applicable safety precautions when working around fuel. Whenever servicing the fuel system, always work in a well ventilated area. Do not allow fuel spray or vapors to come in contact with a spark or open flame. Keep a dry chemical fire extinguisher near the work area. Always keep fuel in a container specifically designed for fuel storage; also, always properly seal fuel containers to avoid the possibility of fire or explosion.
• Don't smoke when working around gasoline, cleaning solvent or other flammable material!
• Be advised that the fuel system on most modern fuel injected vehicles is under constant pressure. Yes, even when the ignition is **OFF**. Before servicing any components on a fuel injection system, the pressure must be relieved. Failure to relieve fuel system pressure may result in personal injury or damage to your vehicle.

RELIEVING FUEL SYSTEM PRESSURE

➡**This is a generic procedure for most fuel injected vehicles. Always Refer to a Chilton Total Car Care (TCC) repair manual for exact procedures covering your vehicle.**

1. Disable the fuel pump by one of the following methods:
• Remove the fuel pump fuse.
• Remove the fuel pump relay.
• Locate and disconnect the fuel pump wiring.

➡ **When removing the fuel pump fuse or relay to disable the fuel pump, it is important to make certain that the fuel injectors are not part of this circuit. If the injectors do not operate, the residual fuel system pressure will not be relieved.**

2. Crank the engine and allow it to operate until it stalls. Once the engine has stalled, crank the starter for an additional 5 seconds.

3. Place a rag over the connection in which you intend to disconnect and carefully separate the connections. Use the rag to absorb any remaining fuel.

GUIDE TO TOOLS FOR DO-IT-YOURSELF REPAIRS

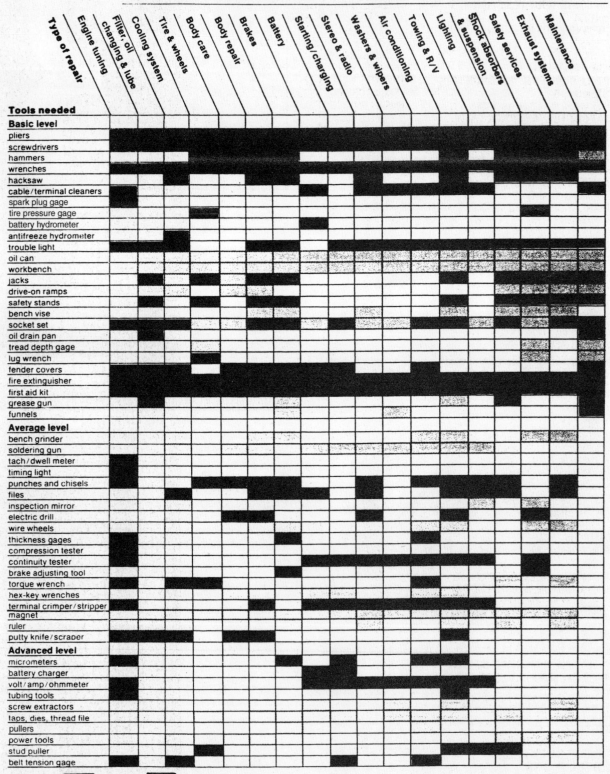

Need to have ■ Nice to have ☐

88521C01

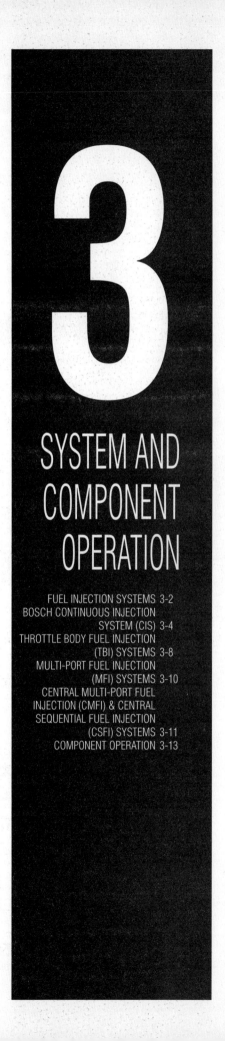

3

SYSTEM AND COMPONENT OPERATION

FUEL INJECTION SYSTEMS

General Information

Fuel injection systems have been used on vehicles for many years. The earliest ones were purely mechanical. As technology advanced, electronic fuel injection systems became more popular. Early mechanical and electronic fuel injection systems did not use feedback controls. As emissions became more of a concern, feedback controls were adapted to both types of fuel injection systems.

Both mechanical and electronic fuel injection systems can be found on gasoline engines. Diesel engines are most commonly found with mechanical type systems, although the newest generations of these engines have been using electronic fuel injection. Following is a description of the most common fuel injection systems.

The Fuel Delivery System

The fuel delivery system consists of all the components which supply the engine with fuel. This includes the tank itself, all the lines, one or more fuel filters, a fuel pump (mechanical or electric), and the fuel metering components (carburetor or fuel injection system).

FUEL TANK

Fuel tanks are normally located at the rear of the vehicle, although on rear or mid engine vehicles they are usually located at the front. The tank contains a fuel gauge sending unit, a filler tube and on most fuel injected vehicles, a fuel pump. In most tanks, there is also a fine mesh screen "sock" attached to the pickup tube. This is used to filter out large particles which could easily clog the fuel lines, fuel pump and fuel filter.

Since the advent of emission controls, tanks are equipped with a control system to prevent fuel vapor from being discharged into the atmosphere. A vent line in the tank is connected to an activated carbon or charcoal filled canister in the engine compartment. Vapors from the tank are stored in this canister, until they can be purged later for combustion in the engine. On many carbureted engines, the float bowl is also vented to this canister.

FUEL PUMP

Mechanical Pumps

▶ See Figures 1 and 2

Mechanical pumps are usually found on carbureted engines or on engines that utilize a mechanical fuel injection system.

Mechanical fuel pumps on carbureted engines are usually mounted on the side of the engine block or cylinder head and operated by an eccentric on the engine's camshaft. The rocker arm of the pump rests against the camshaft eccentric, and as the camshaft rotates, it actuates the rocker arm. Some engines use a pushrod between the rocker arm and camshaft eccentric. Inside the fuel pump, the rocker arm is connected to a flexible diaphragm. A spring, mounted underneath, maintains pressure on the diaphragm. As the rocker arm is actuated, it pulls the diaphragm down and then releases it. Once the diaphragm is released, the spring pushes it back up. This continual diaphragm motion causes a partial vacuum and pressure in the space above the diaphragm. The vacuum draws the fuel from the tank and the pressure pushes it toward the carburetor or injection pump. A check valve is used in the pump to prevent fuel from being pumped back into the tank.

Certain mechanical fuel injection systems also utilize a mechanical fuel pump, typically some diesel engines and early gasoline fuel injection systems. Many of them use a fuel pump essentially identical to the carbureted fuel system's.

Some, however, use a vane type fuel pump mounted directly to the injection pump/fuel distributor assembly. The injection pump/fuel distributor assembly is driven by the timing belt, chain or gears which in turn drives the fuel pump. The vanes draw the fuel in through the inlet port then

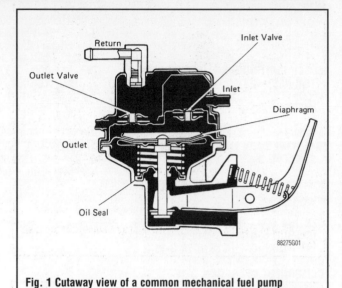

Fig. 1 Cutaway view of a common mechanical fuel pump

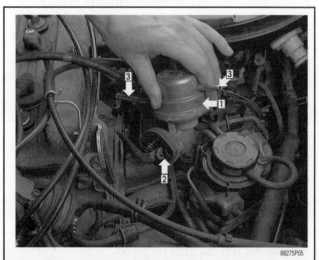

Fig. 2 Mechanical fuel pump parts include a diaphragm (1), lever arm (2) and fuel line connections (3)

squeeze the fuel into a tight passage. The fuel then exits pressurized through the outlet port.

Electric Pumps

▶ See Figures 3 and 4

There are two general types of electric fuel pumps: the impeller type and the bellows type. Electric pumps can be found on all types of fuel systems.

The impeller type pump uses a vane or impeller that is driven by an electric motor. These pumps are often mounted in the fuel tank, though they are sometimes found below or beside the tank. The vanes or impeller draw the fuel in through the inlet port then squeeze the fuel into a tight passage. This pressurizes the fuel. The pressurized fuel then exits through the outlet port.

The bellows type pump is rare. This pump is ordinarily mounted in the engine compartment and contains a flexible metal bellows operated by an electromagnet. As the electromagnet is energized, it pulls the metal bellows up—this draws the fuel from the tank into the pump. When the electromagnet is de-energized, the bellows returns to its original position. A check valve closes to prevent the fuel from returning to the tank. The only place for the fuel to go now is through the outlet port.

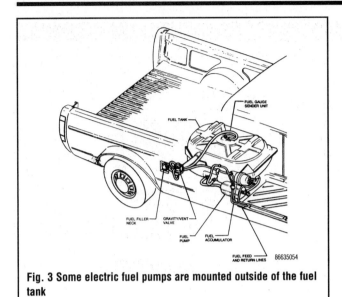

Fig. 3 Some electric fuel pumps are mounted outside of the fuel tank

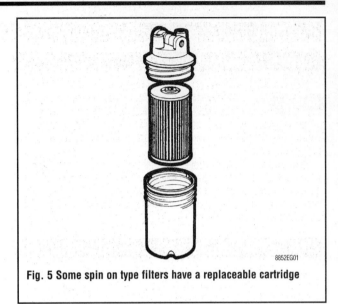

Fig. 5 Some spin on type filters have a replaceable cartridge

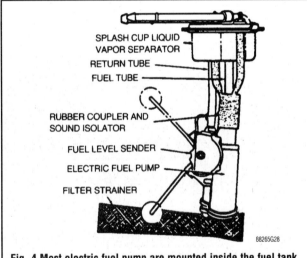

Fig. 4 Most electric fuel pump are mounted inside the fuel tank and are part of the fuel level sending unit

Fig. 6 This type of disposable in-line filter is secured by clamps

FUEL FILTERS

In addition to the mesh screen attached to the pickup tube, all fuel systems have at least one other filter located somewhere between the fuel tank and the fuel metering components. On some models, the filter is part of the fuel pump itself, on others, it is located in the fuel line, and still others locate the filter at the carburetor or throttle body inlet.

Inline and Spin On Filters

▶ See Figures 5, 6, 7 and 8

Inline and spin on filters are located between the fuel pump and fuel metering components. They are connected to fuel lines either by clamps, banjo bolts, flare fittings or quick-disconnect fittings. Most are "throwaway" units with a paper element encased in a housing. Some have a clear plastic housing that allows you to view the amount of dirt trapped in the filter. Some filters consist of a replaceable pleated paper cartridge installed in a permanent filter housing. Their use is limited mostly to diesel and heavy-duty gasoline engines.

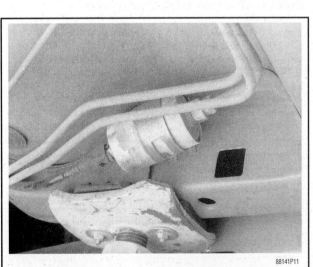

Fig. 7 Many in-line filters are mounted along the frame rail under the vehicle . . .

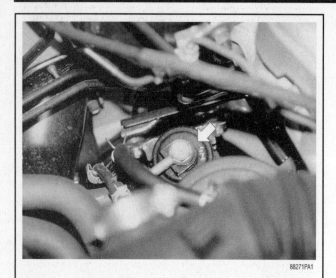

Fig. 8 . . . others can be found in the engine compartment

Throttle Body Inlet Filters

▶ **See Figures 9, 10 and 11**

Fuel filters can also be located in the carburetor or throttle body inlet.
For carburetors, they consist of a small paper or bronze filter that is
installed in the inlet housing. They are extremely simple in design and are
about as efficient as an in-line type. The bronze filter is the least common
and must be installed with the small cone section facing out. One type is

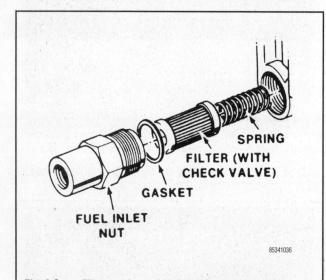

Fig. 9 Some filters are located in the carburetor inlet fitting . . .

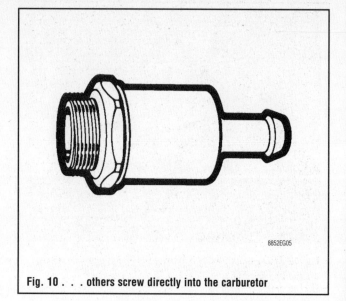

Fig. 10 . . . others screw directly into the carburetor

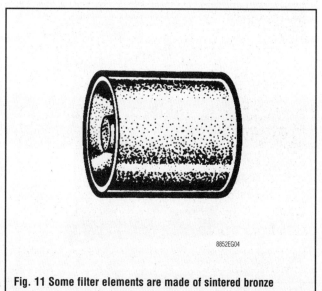

Fig. 11 Some filter elements are made of sintered bronze

held in place by a threaded metal cap that attaches to the fuel line and
screws into the carburetor fuel inlet. On another type, the fuel filter threads
directly into the carburetor.

On throttle body units, these filters are used as a supplement to the primary in-line filter. They usually consist of a conical screen, similar in
appearance to an air conditioning orifice tube. They can be accessed after
removing the fuel line from the throttle body unit.

BOSCH CONTINUOUS INJECTION SYSTEM (CIS)

Bosch Continuous Injection Systems

CIS SYSTEM

▶ **See Figures 12 thru 21**

The Continuous Injection System (CIS) is an independent mechanical
system. The basic operating principle is to continuously inject fuel into the
intake side of the engine by means of an electric pump. The amount of fuel
delivered is metered by an air flow measuring device. Some CIS systems
are feedback controlled.

The primary fuel circuit consists of an electric pump, which pulls fuel
from the tank. Fuel then passes through an accumulator. The accumulator is
basically a container in the fuel line. It houses a spring-loaded diaphragm
that provides fuel damping and delays pressure build-up when the engine
is first started. When the engine is shut down, the expanded chamber in the
accumulator keeps the system under enough pressure for good hot restarts

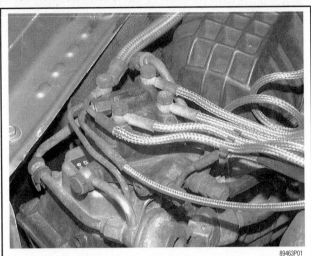

Fig. 12 The fuel distributor is unique to CIS systems and delivers the appropriate amount of fuel to each injectors

Fig. 15 Electronic cold start injectors meter extra fuel into the engine to richen the fuel mixture for starting

Fig. 13 The air cleaner on CIS systems is usually located below the fuel distributor

Fig. 16 The throttle body meters the air coming into the CIS system

Fig. 14 On some vehicles, a frequency valve responds to signals from the oxygen sensor (Lambda) to control fuel pressure

Fig. 17 A control pressure regulator is used to vary the fuel pressure to the distributor. This in turn varies the fuel mixture

Fig. 18 Fuel injectors are located in the intake runners near the cylinder head

Fig. 19 The injectors provide a constant spray of fuel and are held in by O-rings

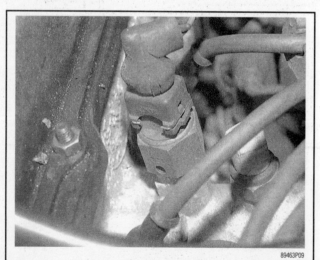

Fig. 20 A thermo-time switch is used to control the cold start injector

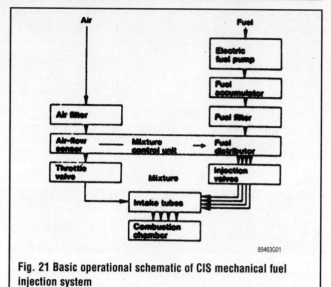

Fig. 21 Basic operational schematic of CIS mechanical fuel injection system

with no vapor locking. Fuel flows through a large, paper element filter to the mixture control assembly.

The mixture control assembly is the heart of the CIS system. It houses the airflow sensor and the fuel distributor. The air sensor is a round plate attached to a counterbalanced lever. The plate and lever are free to move up-and-down on a fulcrum. Accelerator pedal linkage connects to a throttle butterfly, which is upstream (closer to the manifold and intake valves) of the air sensor. Stepping on the accelerator pedal opens the throttle valve. Increased air, demanded by the engine, is sucked through the air cleaner and around the air sensor plate.

In the air funnel, where the air sensor plate is located, the quantity of intake air lifts the plate until an equilibrium is reached between air flow and hydraulic counter-pressure acting on the lever through a plunger. This is the control plunger. In this balanced position, the plunger stays at a level in the fuel distributor to open small metering slits, one for each cylinder in the engine. Fuel under controlled pressure from the pump goes through the slits to the injectors' supply opening. The slit meters the right amount of fuel.

In order to maintain a precise fuel pressure, a pressure regulator, or pressure relief valve, is located in the primary fuel circuit of the fuel distributor. Excess fuel is diverted back to the tank through a return line. To make sure the amount of fuel going through the control plunger slits depends only on their area, an exact pressure differential must always be maintained at the openings. This pressure is controlled by a differential-pressure valve. There's one valve for each cylinder. The valve consists of a spring loaded steel diaphragm and an outlet to the injectors. The diaphragm separates the upper and lower chambers.

The valve keeps an exact pressure differential of 1.42 psi between upper chamber pressure and lower chamber pressure. Both pressures act on the spring loaded steel diaphragm which opens the outlet to the injectors. The size of the outlet opening is always just enough to maintain that 1.42 psi pressure differential at the metering slit. The diaphragm opens more if a larger amount of fuel flows. If less fuel enters the upper chamber, the diaphragm opens less and less fuel goes to the injectors. An exact pressure differential between upper and lower chamber is kept constant. Diaphragm movement is actually only a thousandths of an inch (few hundreths of a millimeter). On feedback controlled CIS systems, a frequency valve regulates the pressure differential at the metering slits and as a result is able to control mixture ratio. The frequency valve uses a signal from a control unit which is generated by an oxygen sensor.

The control pressure regulator can alter the pressure on the control plunger according to engine and outside air temperature. For warm-up running, it lowers the pressure so that the air sensor plate can go higher for the same air flow. This exposes more metering slit area, and more fuel flows for a richer mixture. For cold starts, a separate injector is used to squirt fuel into the intake manifold. This injector is electronically controlled. A thermo-time switch, screwed into the engine, limits the amount of time the valve is open and at higher temperatures, cuts it off.

CIS-E SYSTEMS

▶ See Figures 22 and 23

CIS-E is an electronically controlled continuous fuel injection system. This system utilizes the basic CIS mechanical system for injection, with electrically controlled correction functions. The electronic portion of the system consists of an airflow sensor position indicator, coolant temperature sensor, throttle valve switches, idle air stabilizer and the differential pressure regulator.

When the ignition switch is turned **ON**, the electric fuel pump is activated causing pressurized fuel to move from the tank to the accumulator. Fuel pulsations exerted by the fuel pump are then damped or smoothed out by the accumulator. The pressurized fuel is directed through the fuel filter and to the fuel distributor. A differential pressure regulator located on the side of fuel distributor is used to control the air/fuel mixture. The control pressure regulator is not used in the CIS-E fuel injection system. The system pressure regulator valve has been removed from the fuel distributor and replaced by an external, diaphragm type, pressure regulator. This regulator contains an additional port which is used to return fuel from the differential pressure regulator.

The differential pressure regulator is an electro-magnetic operated pressure regulator. It receives an electronic signal in milliamps from the control unit. The higher the milliamp signal the higher the differential between the upper and lower chamber pressures, resulting in a richer mixture. The lower the milliamp signal the lower the differential pressure resulting in a leaner mixture.

In the CIS-E fuel injection system, system pressure is always present in the upper chamber of the fuel distributor. The metering slit in the control plunger regulates the amount of fuel delivered to the upper chamber depending on the airflow sensor position and control plunger position. The amount of fuel delivered to the injectors and consequently fuel mixture, is adjusted by the differential pressure regulator.

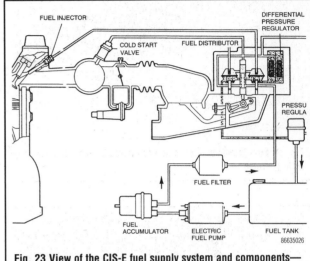

Fig. 23 View of the CIS-E fuel supply system and components—CIS similar

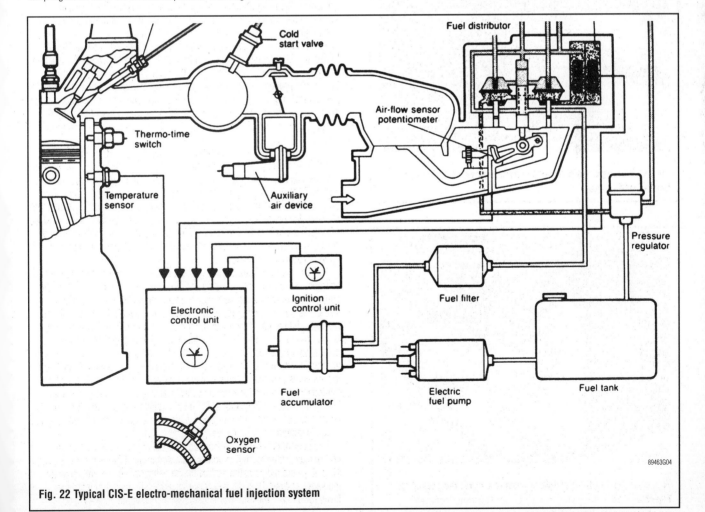

Fig. 22 Typical CIS-E electro-mechanical fuel injection system

THROTTLE BODY FUEL INJECTION (TBI) SYSTEMS

TBI Operation

▶ See Figures 24, 25, 26 and 27

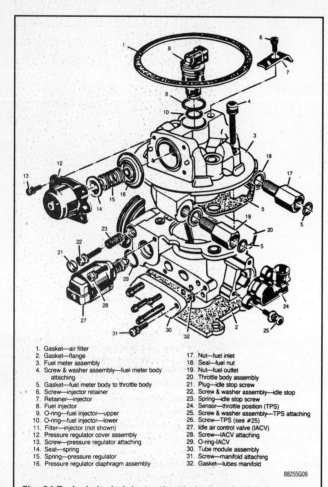

1. Gasket—air filter
2. Gasket—flange
3. Fuel meter assembly
4. Screw & washer assembly—fuel meter body attaching
5. Gasket—fuel meter body to throttle body
6. Screw—injector retainer
7. Retainer—injector
8. Fuel injector
9. O-ring—fuel injector—upper
10. O-ring—fuel injector—lower
11. Filter—injector (not shown)
12. Pressure regulator cover assembly
13. Screw—pressure regulator attaching
14. Seat—spring
15. Spring—pressure regulator
16. Pressure regulator diaphragm assembly
17. Nut—fuel inlet
18. Seal—fuel nut
19. Nut—fuel outlet
20. Throttle body assembly
21. Plug—idle stop screw
22. Screw & washer assembly—idle stop
23. Spring—idle stop screw
24. Sensor—throttle position (TPS)
25. Screw & washer assembly—TPS attaching
26. Screw—TPS (see #25)
27. Idle air control valve (IACV)
28. Screw—IACV attaching
29. O-ring-IACV
30. Tube module assembly
31. Screw—manifold attaching
32. Gasket—tubes manifold

88255G09

Fig. 24 Typical single injector throttle body and related components

The appearance of throttle body injection systems is similar to the carbureted fuel system. Although not as efficient as multi-port systems, TBI does offer better driveability and lower emissions than carbureted systems.

The TBI assembly is centrally located on the intake manifold where air and fuel are distributed through a up to four bores in the throttle body, similar to a carbureted engine. Air for combustion is controlled by up to four throttle valves that are connected to the accelerator pedal linkage by a throttle shafts and lever assembly.

All fuel injection and on most vehicles ignition functions are controlled by a control module. The control module accepts inputs from various sensors and switches, calculates the optimum air/fuel mixture and operates the various output devices to provide peak performance within specific emissions limits. The control module will attempt to maintain the air/fuel mixture of 14.7:1 in order to optimize catalytic converter operation. If a system failure occurs that is not serious enough to stop the engine, the control module will illuminate a malfunction indicator lamp, set and store a fault code and on some vehicles, operate the engine in a limp home mode. In the limp home mode the control module delivers fuel according to predetermined parameters. Driveability will be definitely effected but the vehicle should still be driveable.

Fuel is supplied to the engine from a high pressure electric fuel pump. Fuel pumps are usually mounted in the fuel tank in the same assembly that includes the fuel tank sending unit. However, some manufacturers may mount the pump on the chassis. Electricity to the pump is usually provided through a relay.

Depending on the manufacturer, fuel pressure prior to startup is maintained by two different methods. The first method is via a check ball or valve in the fuel pump to prevent fuel drainback. The second method is to run the electric fuel pump for a few seconds to pressurize the system prior to startup. It is important to know which system you have, as the system which maintains pressure must have that pressure released prior to servicing.

One or more fuel injectors are used to meter fuel to the engine. Fuel injectors are essentially solenoid valves that the control module pulses on and off many times per second. Each time the injector is turned on, a spray of fuel is supplied to the engine. The control unit pulse width, or injector on time, determines how much fuel is supplied to the engine during various conditions.

The Fuel Pressure (FP) regulator is usually part of the throttle body assembly. The regulator diaphragm is operated by intake manifold vacuum, making system pressure partly dependent on engine load.

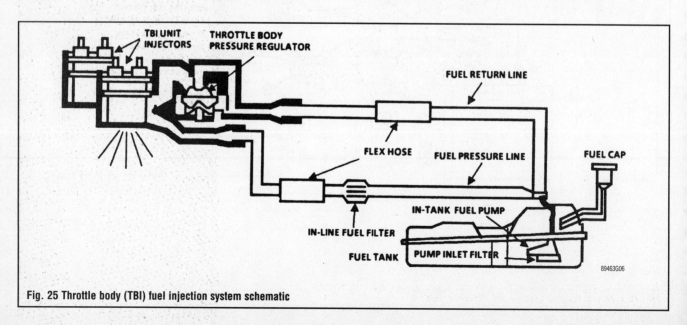

Fig. 25 Throttle body (TBI) fuel injection system schematic

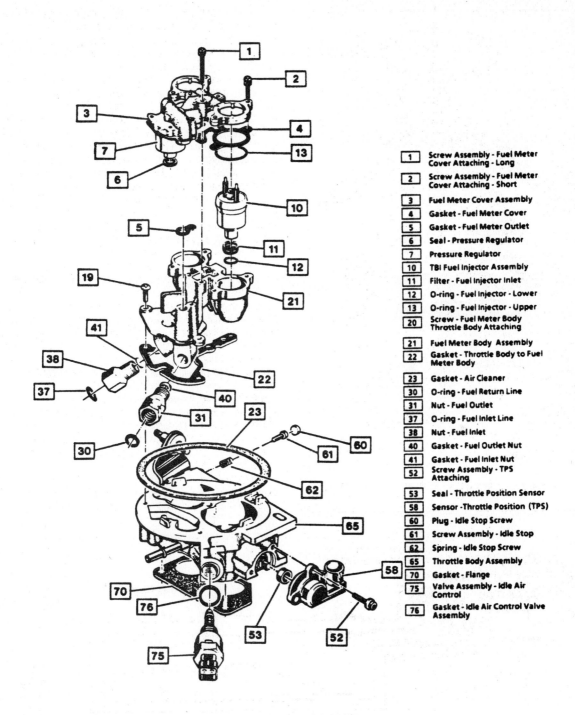

1	Screw Assembly - Fuel Meter Cover Attaching - Long
2	Screw Assembly - Fuel Meter Cover Attaching - Short
3	Fuel Meter Cover Assembly
4	Gasket - Fuel Meter Cover
5	Gasket - Fuel Meter Outlet
6	Seal - Pressure Regulator
7	Pressure Regulator
10	TBI Fuel Injector Assembly
11	Filter - Fuel Injector Inlet
12	O-ring - Fuel Injector - Lower
13	O-ring - Fuel Injector - Upper
20	Screw - Fuel Meter Body Throttle Body Attaching
21	Fuel Meter Body Assembly
22	Gasket - Throttle Body to Fuel Meter Body
23	Gasket - Air Cleaner
30	O-ring - Fuel Return Line
31	Nut - Fuel Outlet
37	O-ring - Fuel Inlet Line
38	Nut - Fuel Inlet
40	Gasket - Fuel Outlet Nut
41	Gasket - Fuel Inlet Nut
52	Screw Assembly - TPS Attaching
53	Seal - Throttle Position Sensor
58	Sensor - Throttle Position (TPS)
60	Plug - Idle Stop Screw
61	Screw Assembly - Idle Stop
62	Spring - Idle Stop Screw
65	Throttle Body Assembly
70	Gasket - Flange
75	Valve Assembly - Idle Air Control
76	Gasket - Idle Air Control Valve Assembly

89463G07

Fig. 26 Exploded view of a typical throttle body assembly

1. IAC valve
2. TP sensor
3. Fuel Injector
4. Throttle body
5. Fuel pressure regulator
6. Fuel heater

89463P21

Fig. 27 Typical multiple injector throttle body and related components

The Idle Air Control (IAC) valve controls the amount of air allowed to bypass the throttle plate. The control module can closely control idle speed using this valve, even when the engine is cold or when there is a high engine load at idle.

Other system components include a Throttle Position Sensor (TPS), Manifold Absolute Pressure Sensor (MAP), Intake Air Temperature Sensor (IAT), Coolant Temperature Sensor (CTS), Power Steering Pressure (PSP) switch, Crankshaft Position Sensor (CKP), Camshaft Position Sensor (CMP) and an Oxygen Sensor (O2).

MULTI-PORT FUEL INJECTION (MFI) SYSTEMS

MFI Operation

▶ See Figures 28 and 29

Multi-port fuel injection is the most common type of fuel injection system found today. Regardless of the manufacturer, they all function in the same basic way. On these systems an equal amount of fuel is delivered to each cylinder.

These systems all use sensors which transmit operating conditions to the computer. Information from these sensors is processed by the computer which then determines the proper air/fuel mixture. This signal is sent the to fuel injectors which open and inject fuel into their ports. The longer the injector is held open, the richer the fuel mixture. Most fuel injection systems need the following information to operate properly:

1. Temperature sensors—This includes both air and coolant temperature. The computer uses this information to determine how rich or lean the mixture should be. The colder the temperature, the richer the mixture.

2. Throttle position sensors or switches—The computer uses this information to determine the position of the throttle valve(s). Some vehicles use sensors which relay the exact position of the throttle valve(s) at all times. Others use switches which only relay closed and wide-open throttle positions (some may also use a mid-throttle switch). These switches and sensors help determine engine load.

3. Airflow sensors—These sensors also help the computer determine engine load by indicating the amount of air entering the engine. There are several different types of airflow sensors, but in the end, they all do the same job.

4. Manifold pressure sensors—If a vehicle is not equipped with an airflow sensor, it uses a manifold pressure sensor to determine engine load (Note that some vehicles with an airflow sensor may also have a manifold pressure sensor. This is used as a fail-safe if the airflow sensor fails). As engine load increases, so does intake manifold air pressure.

5. Engine speed and position sensors—Engine speed/position sensors can be referenced from the crankshaft, camshaft or both. In addition to helping determine engine load, these sensors also tell the computer when the injectors should be fired.

These systems operate at a relatively high pressure (usually at least 30 psi). To control the fuel pressure, a fuel pressure regulator is used. As engine load increases, more fuel pressure is needed. This is due to the richer mixture (more fuel needed) and to overcome the increased air pressure in the ports. Any unused fuel is diverted back to the fuel tank using a return line.

The fuel injectors can be fired as a batch, a bank or sequentially. On batch fire systems, all of the injectors are fired simultaneously, usually at top dead center of the compression stroke for cylinder number one. Bank fire systems are divided into two separate injector banks. The first bank fires when cylinder number one is at top dead center of the compression stroke. The second bank is usually fired when the number one cylinder is at top dead center of the exhaust stroke. On sequential systems, each injector is fired as its cylinder is at top dead center of its compression stroke. This tends to be the most fuel efficient system.

Feedback fuel injection systems use an oxygen sensor to precisely monitor the air/fuel mixture. Using the signal generated by the oxygen sensor, the computer varies the pulse-width of the fuel injectors. The longer the injector on time (longer pulse width) the richer the fuel mixture.

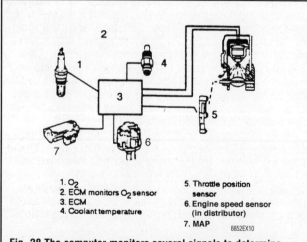

1. O_2
2. ECM monitors O_2 sensor
3. ECM
4. Coolant temperature
5. Throttle position sensor
6. Engine speed sensor (in distributor)
7. MAP

8852EX10

Fig. 28 The computer monitors several signals to determine injector pulse width. Non-feedback systems do not use an oxygen sensor

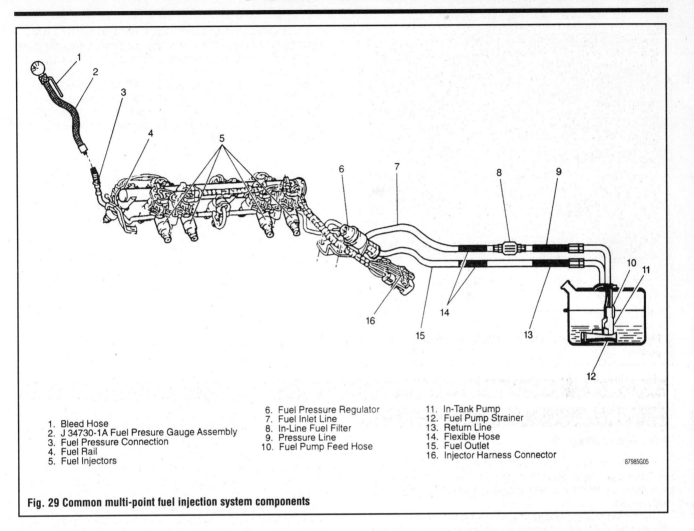

1. Bleed Hose
2. J 34730-1A Fuel Presure Gauge Assembly
3. Fuel Pressure Connection
4. Fuel Rail
5. Fuel Injectors
6. Fuel Pressure Regulator
7. Fuel Inlet Line
8. In-Line Fuel Filter
9. Pressure Line
10. Fuel Pump Feed Hose
11. In-Tank Pump
12. Fuel Pump Strainer
13. Return Line
14. Flexible Hose
15. Fuel Outlet
16. Injector Harness Connector

87985G05

Fig. 29 Common multi-point fuel injection system components

CENTRAL MULTI-PORT FUEL INJECTION (CMFI) & CENTRAL SEQUENTIAL FUEL INJECTION (CSFI) SYSTEMS

CMFI & CSFI Operation

♦ See Figures 30, 31, 32 and 33

The Central Multi-port Fuel Injection (CMFI) and Central Sequential Fuel Injection (CSFI) systems are typically found on General Motors V-6 and V-8 engines. The systems appear similar to a TBI system in that an throttle body assembly (CMFI/CSFI unit) is centrally mounted on the intake manifold. The major differences come in the incorporation of a split (upper and lower) intake manifold assembly with a variable tuned plenum (using an intake manifold tuning valve) and the CMFI unit's single fuel injector which feeds 6 or 8 poppet valves (1 for each individual cylinder). On the Central Sequential Fuel Injection (CSFI) there are 6 or 8 injectors, one for each poppet valve. Individual injectors allows sequential fuel injection to occur in the same order as the cylinders are fired.

The non-serviceable CMFI/CSFI injection unit consists of a fuel meter body, gasket seal, fuel pressure regulator, fuel injector(s) and 6 or 8 poppet nozzles with fuel tubes. The assembly is housed in the lower intake manifold.

As with most other electronic fuel injection systems, all injection and ignition functions are controlled by a control module. The module accepts inputs from various sensors and switches, calculates the optimum air/fuel

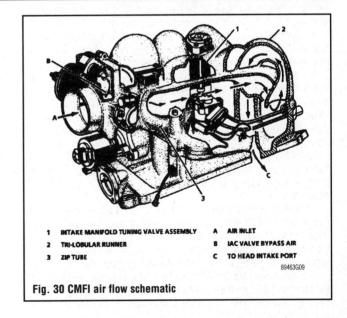

1	INTAKE MANIFOLD TUNING VALVE ASSEMBLY	A	AIR INLET
2	TRI-LOBULAR RUNNER	B	IAC VALVE BYPASS AIR
3	ZIP TUBE	C	TO HEAD INTAKE PORT

89463G09

Fig. 30 CMFI air flow schematic

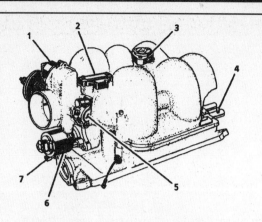

1   VALVE ASSEMBLY - IDLE AIR CONTROL (IAC)

2   SENSOR - MANIFOLD ABSOLUTE PRESSURE (MAP)

3   VALVE ASSEMBLY - INTAKE MANIFOLD TUNING

4   CONNECTION - FUEL PRESSURE

5   SENSOR - THROTTLE POSITION (TP)

6   VALVE ASSEMBLY - EXHAUST GAS RECIRCULATION (EGR)

7   SENSOR - ENGINE COOLANT TEMPERATURE

89463G10

Fig. 31 Various CMFI engine components are mounted to the intake manifolds (the CMFI unit is located under the upper intake)

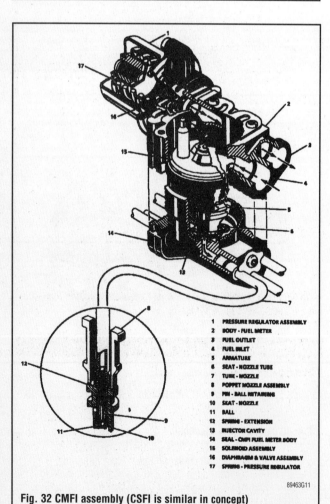

1   PRESSURE REGULATOR ASSEMBLY
2   BODY - FUEL METER
3   FUEL OUTLET
4   FUEL INLET
5   ARMATURE
6   SEAT - NOZZLE TUBE
7   TUBE - NOZZLE
8   POPPET NOZZLE ASSEMBLY
9   PIN - BALL RETAINING
10   SEAT - NOZZLE
11   BALL
12   SPRING - EXTENSION
13   INJECTOR CAVITY
14   SEAL - CMFI FUEL METER BODY
15   SOLENOID ASSEMBLY
16   DIAPHRAGM & VALVE ASSEMBLY
17   SPRING - PRESSURE REGULATOR

89463G11

Fig. 32 CMFI assembly (CSFI is similar in concept)

89463P17

Fig. 33 The upper intake manifold shrouds the fuel injectors and lines on this CSFI unit. The manifold is made of plastic

mixture and operates the various output devices to provide peak performance within specific emissions limits. The module will attempt to maintain the ideal air/fuel mixture of 14.7:1 in order to optimize catalytic converter operation. If a system failure occurs that is not serious enough to stop the engine, the module will illuminate a malfunction indicator lamp and will continue to operate the engine, although it may need to operate in fail-safe mode.

Fuel is supplied to the injector through an electric fuel pump assembly which is mounted in the vehicle's fuel tank. The module provides a signal to operate the fuel pump though the fuel pump relay and oil pressure switch. The CMFI/CSFI unit internal pressure regulator maintains a system pressure of approximately 55–61 psi (380–420 kPa). When the injector is energized by the control module, an armature lifts allowing pressurized fuel to travel down the fuel tubes to the poppet valves. In the poppet valves, fuel pressure (working against the extension spring force) will cause the nozzle ball to open from its seat and fuel will flow from the nozzle. It takes approximately 51 psi (350 kPa) to force fuel from the poppet nozzle. Once the module de-energizes the injector, the armature will close, allowing fuel pressure in the tubes to drop and the spring force will close off fuel flow.

Other components which may be used include a Throttle Position Sensor (TPS), Manifold Absolute Pressure Sensor (MAP), Mass Airflow Sensor (MAF), Intake Air Temperature Sensor (IAT), Coolant Temperature Sensor (CTS), Power Steering Pressure (PSP) switch, Crankshaft Position Sensor (CKP), Camshaft Position Sensor (CMP) and an Oxygen Sensor (O2).

The idle air control valve is a stepper motor that controls the amount of air allowed to bypass the throttle plate. With this valve the computer control module can closely control idle speed even when the engine is cold or when there is a high engine load at idle.

The computer module used on CMFI/CSFI vehicles has a learning capability which is used to provide corrections for a particular engine's condition. If the battery is disconnected to clear diagnostic codes, or for safety during a repair, the learning process must start all over again. A change may be noted in vehicle performance. In order to "teach" the vehicle, make sure the vehicle is at normal operating temperature, then drive at part throttle, under moderate acceleration and idle conditions, until normal performance returns.

COMPONENT OPERATION

The following section is an alphabetical listing of fuel injection components followed by a brief description and operation. As fuel injection systems evolve, more and more components are being used to both enhance driveability and improve fuel efficiency. To further complicate matters, manufacturers often change the names of components even though the component operation stays the same. By better understanding the function of individual components as pieces of a larger system, your understanding of how your entire fuel injection system functions will be enhanced.

It must be understood that although the list of fuel injection components in this section is long, not every component is used on every system. For further information on the appropriate components for your particular vehicle, consult a Chilton's Total Car Care (TCC) manual.

Air Flow Sensor

▶ See Figures 34, 35 and 36

This component is used on CIS mechanical injection systems. This device measures the amount of air drawn in by the engine. It operates according to the suspended body principle, using a counterbalanced sensor plate that is connected to the fuel distributor control plunger by a lever system. A small leaf spring assures that the sensor plate assumes the correct zero position when the engine is stationary.

The air flow sensor consists of an air venturi tube in which an air flow sensor plate moves. The air flowing into the venturi from the air cleaner lifts the air flow sensor plate, allowing the air to flow through. The greater the amount of air, the higher the sensor plate will be raised.

The air flow sensor plate is fitted to a lever which is compensated by a counterweight. The lever acts on the control plunger in the fuel distributor that is pressed down by the control pressure, thus counteracting the lifting force of the air flow sensor plate.

The height to which the air flow sensor plate is raised is governed by the magnitude of the air flow.

The air/fuel mixture varies with the engine load. The inclination of the venturi walls therefore varies in stages in order to provide a correct air/fuel mixture at all loads. Thus, the mixture is enriched at full load and leaned at idle.

The lever acts on the control plunger in the fuel distributor by means of an adjustable link with a needle bearing at the contact point. The basic fuel setting, and thus the CO setting, is adjusted by means of the adjustment screw on the link. This adjustment is made with a special tool and access to the screw can be gained through a hole in the air flow sensor between the air venturi and the fuel distributor. The CO adjustment is sealed on later models.

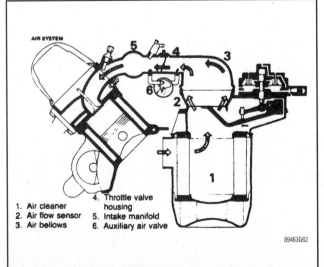

1. Air cleaner
2. Air flow sensor
3. Air bellows
4. Throttle valve housing
5. Intake manifold
6. Auxiliary air valve

89463G62

Fig. 34 Air flow through typical K-Jetronic induction system

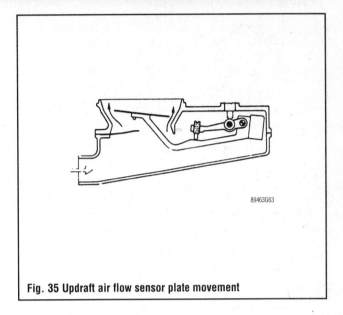

89463G63

Fig. 35 Updraft air flow sensor plate movement

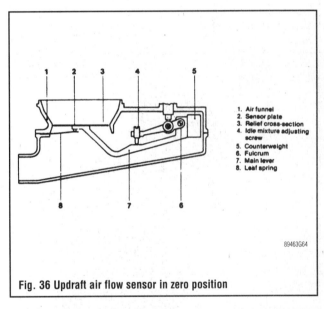

1. Air funnel
2. Sensor plate
3. Relief cross-section
4. Idle mixture adjusting screw
5. Counterweight
6. Fulcrum
7. Main lever
8. Leaf spring

89463G64

Fig. 36 Updraft air flow sensor in zero position

A rubber bellows connects the air flow sensor to the throttle valve housing.

➡On KE systems, the sensor plate rest position is angled upward, not horizontal as is the K system.

Auxiliary Air Regulator

▶ See Figures 37 and 38

This component is used on CIS mechanical injection systems. The auxiliary air regulator allows more air/fuel mixture when the engine is cold in order to improve driveability and provide idle stabilization. The increased air volume is measured by the air flow sensor and fuel is metered accordingly. The auxiliary air regulator contains a specially shaped plate attached to a bi-metal spring. The plate changes position according to engine temperature, allowing the moist air to pass when the engine is cold. As the temperature rises, the bi-metal spring slowly closes the air passage. The bi-metal spring is also heated electrically, allowing the opening time to be

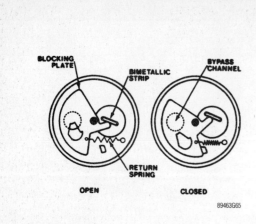

Fig. 37 Internal components of the auxiliary air regulator showing cold (open) and warm (closed) positions

Fig. 39 Barometric pressure sensor on a TBI equipped engine

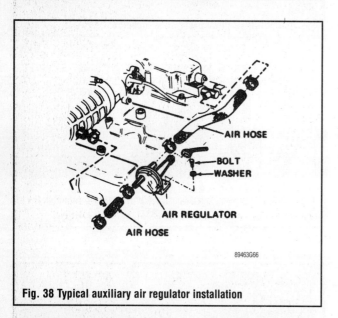

Fig. 38 Typical auxiliary air regulator installation

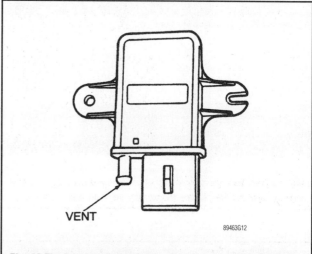

Fig. 40 The Barometric pressure sensor doesn't use the vacuum connection. MAP and BARO sensors look alike on most vehicles

limited according to engine type. The auxiliary air regulator does not function when the engine is warm.

Barometric Pressure (BAP) Sensor

▶ See Figures 39 and 40

The barometric pressure sensor is used to compensate for altitude variations. From this signal, the control module modifies the air/fuel ratio, spark timing, idle speed, and EGR flow. The barometric sensor is a design that produces a frequency based on atmospheric pressure (altitude).

Camshaft Position Sensor

▶ See Figures 41, 42 and 43

The control module uses the camshaft position sensor to determine the position of the No. 1 piston during its power stroke. This signal is used to calculate the ignition and fuel injection timing. On most vehicles, if the camshaft position sensor signal is lost while the engine is running, the fuel injection system will shift to a calculated fuel injection mode and the engine will continue to run. However, once an attempt is made to restart the engine, the engine will not fire.

Canister Purge Valve

▶ See Figures 44 and 45

The canister purge valve is sometimes called a purge control or cutoff solenoid valve. This solenoid valve controls vacuum to the purge valve in the charcoal canister. Prior to certain conditions being met, the solenoid valve is energized and blocks vacuum to the purge valve. After those conditions are met, the solenoid valve is de-energized and vacuum can be applied to the purge valve. This releases the collected vapors from the evaporative canister into the intake manifold. On systems not using an electronically controlled solenoid, a Thermo Vacuum Valve (TVV) is used to control purge.

Cold Start (Valve) Injector

▶ See Figure 46

The cold start injector is used in the CIS-E and CIS Motronic systems. The injector delivers extra fuel into the intake manifold during cold starts. It is controlled by the control module. Operation of the injector is determined by the coolant temperature, to prevent excess fuel from being injected.

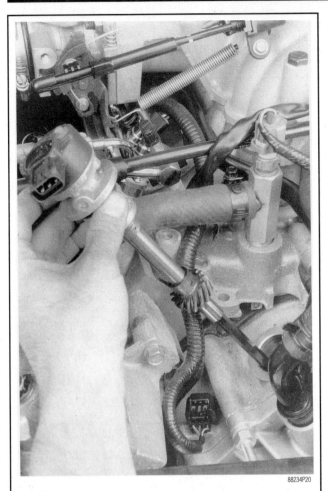

Fig. 41 Camshaft position sensors for some engines are a direct replacement for the distributor, as seen in this Ford engine

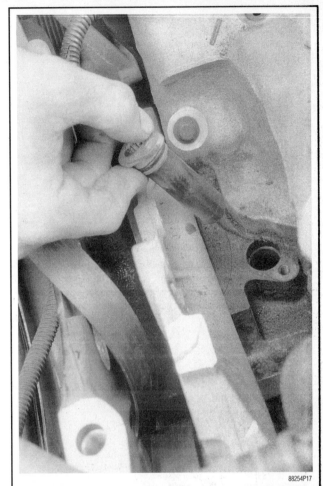

Fig. 43 Most camshaft position sensors are located either in the engine block or cylinder head, adjacent to the camshaft(s)

Fig. 42 Other camshaft position sensors are located inside the distributor, as seen by the location of this connector on a GM engine

Fig. 44 Vacuum control solenoid valves, like this one for the canister purge, are used to turn vacuum component on and off

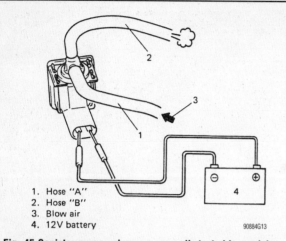

1. Hose "A"
2. Hose "B"
3. Blow air
4. 12V battery

90884G13

Fig. 45 Canister purge valves are normally tested by applying and removing voltage while using a hand vacuum pump to test for leakage

89463P20

Fig. 47 The control unit on this vehicle is mounted inside the engine compartment. Note the aluminum fins to cool the unit

89463P04

Fig. 46 Electronic cold start injectors meter extra fuel into the engine to richen the fuel mixture for starting

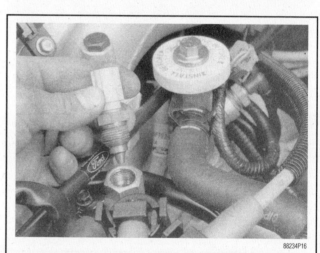

88234P16

Fig. 48 Coolant temperture sensors are usually found on the intake manifold or cylinder head and are mounted so they protrude into the coolant passage

Control Unit

▶ See Figure 47

The control unit, sometimes referred to as the Electronic Control Unit (ECM), Powertrain Control Unit (control module), Vehicle Control Unit (VCM) or other variants, is a digital computer that controls engine, transmission and other component functions on the vehicle. The main purpose of the control unit is to receive data from various sensors around the vehicle, perform computations and comparisons with its internal programs and output signals to various actuators. The control unit can be mounted anywhere in the vehicle, but usually is located under the dash or center console, in the kick panels or under the hood in the engine compartment.

Coolant Temperature Sensor

▶ See Figures 48 and 49

The coolant temperature sensor, also known as a temperature switch, is a thermistor (a resistor which changes value based on temperature) mounted in the engine coolant stream. The sensor provides the control module with engine temperature information.

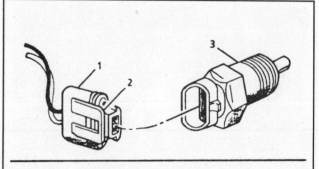

1	HARNESS CONNECTOR
2	LOCKING TAB
3	SENSOR

85344062

Fig. 49 Typical coolant temperature sensor

Two types of sensors are common: the negative temperature coefficient and the positive temperature coefficient. Negative temperature coefficient sensors will show low resistance with high temperature. Positive temperature coefficient sensors will show high resistance with high temperature.

Crankshaft Position Sensor

▶ See Figures 50, 51 and 52

The crankshaft sensor is sometimes called an engine position sensor, TDC sensor or cylinder sensor. These sensors can be located on the engine (usually near the crankshaft), near the flywheel or inside the distributor.

Most systems use either a magnetic reluctance type sensor or a Hall effect sensor. These sensors can be differentiated by the number of wires leading to them and the wire function. Normally, magnectic reluctance sensors use two wires. Hall effect sensors use three wires. The first provides power to the sensor. The second is ground. The last wire is the signal back to the control module.

Magnetic reluctance sensors are combined with a reluctors (toothed wheels). As the reluctor turns the high and low parts of the teeth on the reluctor cause the gap between the sensor and reluctor to change. This change in gap causes the magnetic field near the sensor to change. The

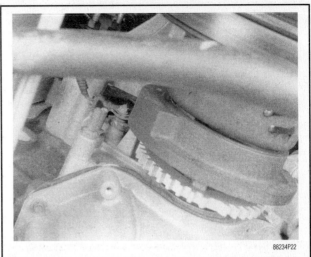

Fig. 52 The sensor rings teeth cause changes in the magnetic field of the sensor which are read by the control module

control module reads this change in voltage to determine engine speed and crankshaft position. It is interesting to note that a magnetic reluctance sensor generates its own voltage during operation.

A Hall effect sensor has a metal pulse ring and a pick-up assembly. They can be located either on the engine or inside the distributor. The signal is a digital on/off type signal. When the pulse ring travels through the pickup, a permanent magnet inside the pick-up creates a magnetism which induces voltage. The pulse ring has slots, or one large slot, in the ring which as they pass, the pick-up loses the magnetism and voltage is lost, thus the on/off signal.

Differential Pressure Regulator

▶ See Figure 53

This regulator is used in the CIS-E and CIS Motronic systems only. The differential pressure regulator controls the fuel flow in the lower chamber of the fuel distributor. This helps to determine the fuel mixture. The regulator designates 0 milliamps (mA) as a reference point. When the vehicle is at normal operating temperature and all engine controls are operating properly, the regulator operates with current from the control module between +10 mA (rich) to -10 mA (lean) ranges.

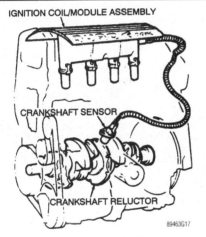

Fig. 50 Crankshaft sensors on some 4-cylinder engines are mounted to the side of the engine block and mate with a reluctor that is part of the crankshaft

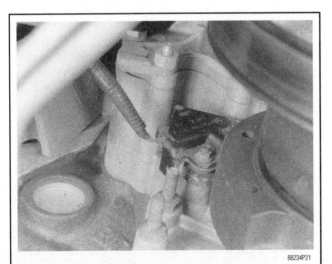

Fig. 51 Crankshaft position sensors on other engines are mounted near the harmonic balancer

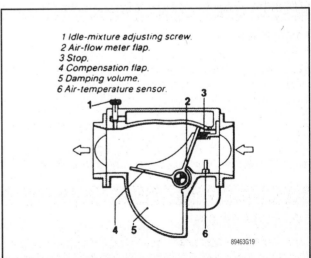

1 Idle-mixture adjusting screw.
2 Air-flow meter flap.
3 Stop.
4 Compensation flap.
5 Damping volume.
6 Air-temperature sensor.

Fig. 53 CIS injection air flow sensor is used to control fuel mixture and pressure regulation

When the starter is operated, current to the differential pressure regulator is increased to enrich the fuel mixture. This will occur whenever the engine is started, and the amount of increase will be regulated by the coolant temperature. When the temperature is extremely cold, the current can be as high as 140 mA.

During cold acceleration, current can raise to approximately 6 mA to enrich the fuel mixture. Enrichment is determined by the engine speed and signals from the temperature sensor.

During full load operation, the full throttle switch closes, sending a signal to the control module. The control module sends a signal approximately 3 mA greater than the signal that is currently present. This signal will vary, depending on the engine speed and altitude.

When the vehicle is decelerated, fuel to the injectors is shutoff by reversing the current to -50 mA to -60 mA. The engine speed, at which this reversing will occur, is regulated by the coolant temperature. Current will also be reversed when engine speed reaches 6600 rpm. The differential pressure regulator is attached to the fuel distributor.

Dual Crank Sensor / Combination Sensor

▶ See Figure 54

The dual crank sensor is unique to GM vehicles. The sensor is usually mounted on a pedestal at the front of the engine near the harmonic balancer. The sensor consists of 2 Hall Effect switches, which depend on 2 metal interrupter rings mounted on the balancer to activate them. Windows in the interrupters activate the hall effect switches as they provide a patch for the magnetic field between the switches transducers and magnets. When one of the hall effect switches is activated, it grounds the signal line to the control module, pulling that signal line's (Sync Pulse or Crank) applied voltage low, which is interpreted as a signal.

Because of the way the signal is created by the dual crank sensor, the signal circuit is always either at a high or low voltage (square wave signal). Three crank signal pulses and one SYNC PULSE are created during each crankshaft revolution. The crank signal is used by the control module to create a reference signal that is also a square wave signal similar to the crank signal. The reference signal is used to calculate the engine rpm and crankshaft position by the control module. The SYNC PULSE is used by the control module to begin the ignition coil firing sequence. Both the crank sensor and the SYNC PULSE signals must be received by the ignition module for the engine to start. A misadjusted sensor or bent interrupter ring could cause rubbing of the sensor resulting in potential driveability problems, such as rough idle, poor performance, or a nor start condition.

✳✳ WARNING

Failure to have the correct clearance will damage the crankshaft sensor.

The dual crank sensor is not adjustable for ignition timing but positioning of the interrupter ring is very important. A dual crank sensor that is damaged, due to mispositioning or a bent interrupter ring, can result in a hesitation, sag stumble or dieseling condition.

To determine if the dual crank sensor could be at fault, a special scanning tool will be necessary along with the testing charts in your vehicle service manual. If the engine rpm, using a special scan tool while driving the vehicle, shows an erratic display this indicates that a proper reference pulse has not been received by the control module, which may be the result of a malfunctioning dual crank sensor.

EGR Solenoid Valve

▶ See Figures 55, 56, 57 and 58

EGR solenoid valves control the flow of vacuum to the EGR valve. The valves are operated by the control module based on engine operating con-

1. EGR valve
2. EGR backpressure transducer
3. EGR solenoid valve

89704P21

Fig. 55 As seen on this engine, the EGR solenoid is usually located near the EGR valve

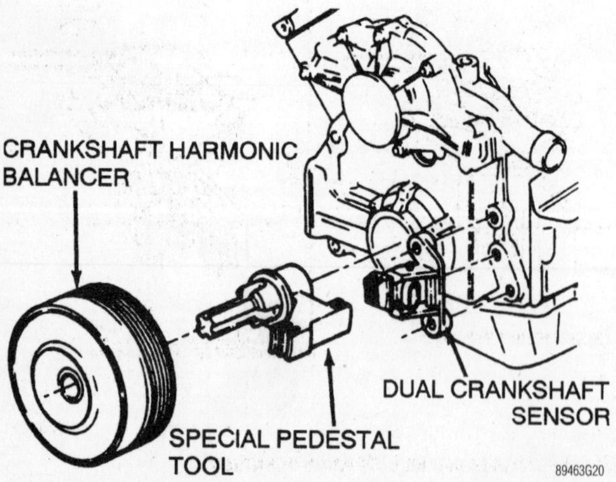

CRANKSHAFT HARMONIC BALANCER

DUAL CRANKSHAFT SENSOR

SPECIAL PEDESTAL TOOL

89463G20

Fig. 54 Some GM engines use a Dual Crank sensor, in place of camshaft and crankshaft sensors

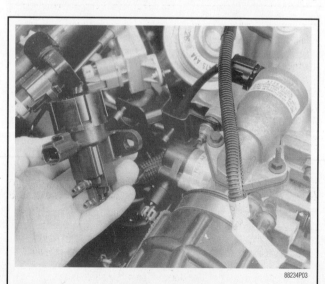

88234P03

Fig. 56 This is a typical EGR solenoid valve

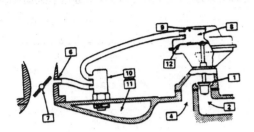

1. EGR valve
2. Exhaust gas
4. Intake flow
6. Vacuum port
7. Throttle valve
8. Vacuum chamber
9. Valve return spring
10. Thermal vacuum switch
11. Coolant
12. Diaphragm

89463G21

Fig. 57 Example of a Thermostatic Vacuum Switch (TVS) controlled EGR system

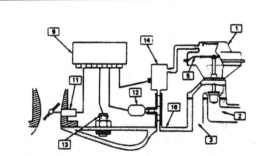

1. EGR valve
2. Exhaust gas
3. Intake air
5. Diaphragm
9. Electronic control module
10. Manifold vacuum
12. Manifold pressure sensor
13. Coolant temperature sensor
14. EGR control solenoid

89463G22

Fig. 58 Example of a solenoid controlled EGR system

ditions. When conditions are proper, ground is provided through the control module to open the solenoid. Vacuum is allowed to pass to the EGR valve. When conditions are not proper, the control module ungrounds the solenoid, thus closing off the flow of vacuum to the EGR valve.

A second type of solenoid valve is commonly used on early model fuel injection systems. This valve is not electronically controlled, but rather controlled by engine coolant temperature. A thermostatic sensor in the bottom of the valve is attached to a spool valve. The sensor is inserted into the coolant passage on the intake manifold or in the cylinder head. As the sensor warms with the coolant temperature, the spool valve moves, allowing vacuum to bypass to the EGR valve.

Exhaust Gas Recirculation Valve

Almost all vehicles built since the 1970's are equipped with an EGR system. These systems usually consist of an EGR valve, vacuum lines to the intake manifold, cast-in exhaust passages in the intake manifold and electronic solenoid valves or thermostatic vacuum valves to control the flow of vacuum to the EGR valve.

However, on most modern systems, a fully electronic EGR valve is used. These valves are completely computer controlled and use stepper motors to regulate the ports which control exhaust gas flow.

No matter what the system type, the function of the system is the same. The system is designed to reintroduce exhaust gas into the combustion chamber, thus lowering combustion temperatures and reducing the formation of Oxides of Nitrogen (NOx). The amount of exhaust that is reintroduced into the combustion cycle is determined by factors such as engine speed, engine vacuum, exhaust system backpressure, coolant temperature and throttle position.

There are actually four types of EGR systems: Ported, Positive Backpressure, Negative Backpressure and Digital. The principle of all the systems is the same; the only difference is in the method used to control how the EGR valve opens.

Too much EGR flow at idle, cruise or during cold operation may result in the engine stalling after cold start, the engine stalling at idle after deceleration, vehicle surge during cruise and rough idle. If the EGR valve is always open, the vehicle may not idle. Too little or no EGR flow allows combustion temperatures to rise, which could result in spark knock (detonation), engine overheating and/or emission test failure.

Some manufacturers use an identification system to help with what type of EGR valve is used.

• Positive backpressure EGR valves will have a "P" stamped on the top side of the valve below the date built.

• Negative backpressure EGR valves will have a "N" stamped on the top side of the valve below the date built.

• Port EGR valves have no identification stamped below the date built.

PORTED VALVE

♦ **See Figures 59 and 60**

In the ported system, the amount of exhaust gas admitted into the intake manifold depends on a ported vacuum signal. A ported vacuum signal is one taken from above the throttle plates; thus, the vacuum signal (amount of vacuum) is dependent on how far the throttle plates are opened. When the throttle is closed (idle or deceleration) there is no vacuum signal. Thus, the EGR valve is closed, and no exhaust gas enters the intake manifold. As the throttle is opened, a vacuum is produced, which opens the EGR valve, admitting exhaust gas into the intake manifold.

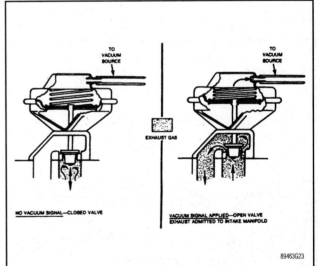

89463G23

Fig. 59 Ported vacuum EGR valve operation

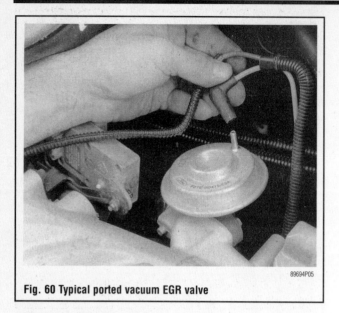

Fig. 60 Typical ported vacuum EGR valve

POSITIVE BACKPRESSURE VALVE

♦ See Figure 61

This valve operates the same as the ported, except, it has an internal air bleed that acts as a vacuum regulator. The bleed valve controls the amount of vacuum inside the vacuum chamber during operation. When the valve receives sufficient exhaust backpressure through the hollow shaft, it closes the bleed; at this point the EGR valve opens.

ÊThis valve will not open, with vacuum applied to it, while the engine is idling or stopped.

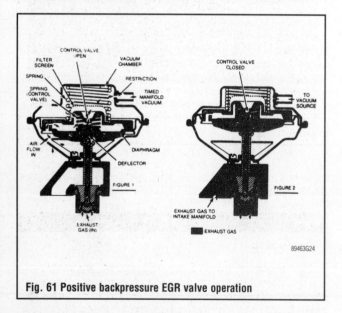

Fig. 61 Positive backpressure EGR valve operation

NEGATIVE BACKPRESSURE VALVE

♦ See Figure 62

This valve is similar to the positive backpressure type, except, the bleed valve spring is moved from above the diaphragm to below it. The bleed valve is normally closed.

At certain manifold pressures, the EGR valve will open. When the manifold vacuum combines with the negative exhaust backpressure, the bleed hole opens and the EGR valve closes.

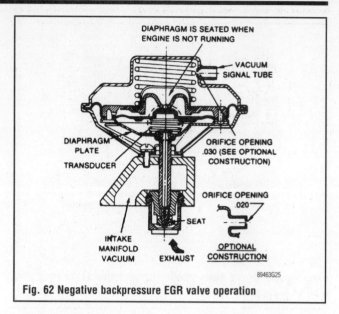

Fig. 62 Negative backpressure EGR valve operation

➡This valve will open when vacuum is applied and the engine is not running.

DIGITAL EGR VALVE

♦ See Figure 63

The digital EGR valve is designed to control the flow of EGR independent of intake manifold vacuum. The valve controls EGR flow through 3 solenoid-opened orifices, which increase in size, to produce 7 possible combinations. When a solenoid is energized, the armature with attached shaft and swivel pintle, is lifted, opening the orifice.

The digital EGR valve is opened by the control module as it grounds each solenoid circuit individually. The flow of exhaust gas is regulated by the control module which uses information about engine temperature and load to determine an appropriate rate of flow.

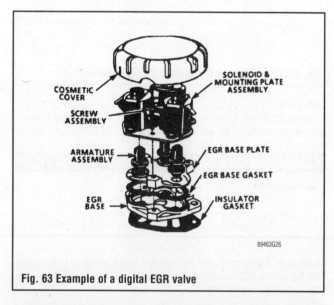

Fig. 63 Example of a digital EGR valve

EGR Valve Position Sensor

♦ See Figures 64 and 65

When equipped, an EGR valve position sensor, sometimes known as an EGR valve lift sensor, is mounted on EGR valve. It signals the control unit of

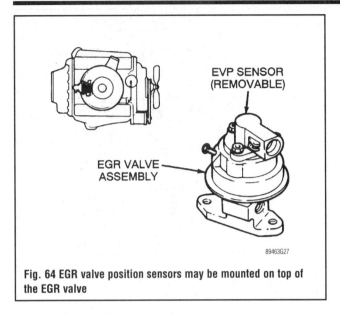

Fig. 64 EGR valve position sensors may be mounted on top of the EGR valve

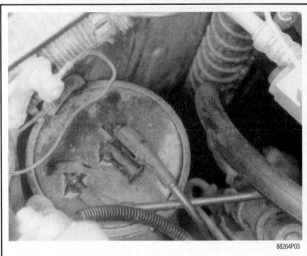

Fig. 66 Typical evaporative canisters are round and use vacuum lines at the top of the canister to transfer vapors

Fig. 65 This EGR valve contains an integral position sensor

Fig. 67 EGR temperature sensors are usually located on or near the EGR valve. This one is located in the intake manifold adjacent to the valve

EGR opening so that it may subtract EGR flow from total air flow into the manifold. In this way, EGR flow is excluded from air flow information used to determine mixture requirements.

Evaporative Canister

▶ See Figure 66

The evaporative canister contains activated carbon, which absorbs fuel vapor. The canister is usually located in the engine compartment near the front of the vehicle.

Fuel vapors from the fuel tank and lines are stored in the evaporative canister until the engine is operated. At this time the vapors will be purged from the canister into the engine for combustion. Vacuum to the canister may be controlled by an purge control solenoid valve.

Exhaust Gas Temperature Sensor

▶ See Figure 67

Exhaust gas temperature sensors are most often found on vehicle equipped with California emissions. The sensors monitor exhaust gas tem-

perature and transmit signals to the control module. Exhaust gas temperature is used to determine proper air/fuel ratio and also can be used to check the efficiency of the EGR system.

Fuel Accumulator

▶ See Figure 68

This component is used on CIS mechanical injection systems. This device maintains the fuel system pressure at a constant level under all operating conditions. The pressure regulator, incorporated into the fuel distributor housing, keeps delivery pressure at approximately 73 psi (5.0 bar). Because the fuel pump delivers more fuel than the engine can use, a plunger shifts in the regulator to open a port which returns excess fuel to the tank. When the engine is **OFF** and the primary pressure drops, the pressure regulator closes the return port and prevents further pressure reduction in the system.

The fuel accumulator has a check valve which keeps residual fuel pressure from dropping below a pre-determined pressure when the engine or fuel pump are **OFF**.

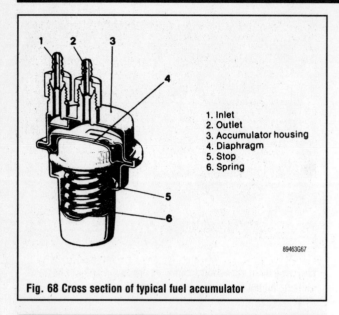

1. Inlet
2. Outlet
3. Accumulator housing
4. Diaphragm
5. Stop
6. Spring

89463G67

Fig. 68 Cross section of typical fuel accumulator

Fuel Distributor

▶ **See Figure 69**

This component is used on CIS mechanical injection systems.

K-JETRONIC

The fuel distributor meters the correct amount of fuel to the individual cylinders according to the position of the air flow sensor plate. A control plunger opens or closes metering slits in the barrel, allowing more or less fuel to pass into the system. Control pressure assures that the plunger follows the movement of the sensor plate immediately. Control pressure is tapped from primary fuel pressure through a restriction bore. It acts through a damping restriction on the control plunger, eliminating any oscillations of the sensor plate due to a pulsating air flow. 1978 and later models incorporate a "push valve" in the fuel distributor to maintain pressure when the engine is switched off. The push valve is a one-way device mounted in the primary pressure regulator which is held open in normal operation by the pressure regulator plunger. Differential pressure valves in the fuel distributor hold the drop in pressure at the metering slits at a constant value.

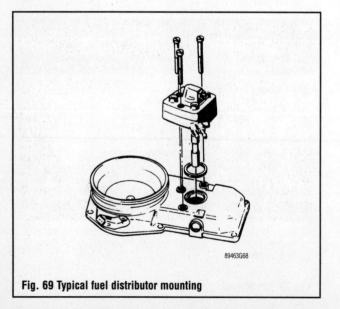

89463G68

Fig. 69 Typical fuel distributor mounting

KE-JETRONIC

The internal components and operation of the KE type fuel distributor is slightly different than the K model. With the engine running, a constant system pressure of approximately 79 psi (5.4 bar) is present at the fuel inlet. The plate valve is adjusted depending on current intensity and in this manner determines the flow rate, in combination with a fixed orifice (0.3mm in diameter) at the fuel distributor outlet. The pressure change in the lower chamber causes movement of the diaphragm and regulates the fuel volume flowing to the injectors.

During cold start and warm-up, current at the Electro Hydraulic Actuator (EHA) is approximately 8–120 milliamps. The plate valve is positioned in the direction of the intake port and the differential pressure drop in the lower chamber is approximately 6–22 psi (0.4–1.5 bar). With increasing coolant temperature, the current at the actuator drops to approximately 8 milliamps and the differential pressure drops at the same rate, down to approximately 6 psi (0.4 bar). For acceleration enrichment, the current to the actuator is determined by the coolant temperature and the amount of sensor plate deflection. The plate valve is moved closer to the intake port and the differential pressure decreases by approximately 22 psi (1.5 bar).

➡**Acceleration enrichment is canceled at approximately 176°F (80°C).**

The airflow sensor position indicator operates with approximately 8 volts supplied constantly. During acceleration, a voltage signal is transmitted to the control unit, depending on the position of the airflow sensor plate. The control unit provides acceleration enrichment as an impulse which increases the instantaneous current value. During acceleration enrichment, Lambda (oxygen sensor) control is influenced by the control unit.

➡**With the accelerator pedal at idle, the micro switch on the side of the airflow sensor is closed and no enrichment is possible.**

The throttle valve switch receives a constant 8 volt signal from the control unit. With the throttle valve fully open (switch closed), approximately 8 mA of current flows to the electro hydraulic actuator, independent of engine speed. At full load enrichment, the plate valve moves in the direction of the intake port and the differential pressure in the lower chamber of the fuel distributor is approximately 6 psi (0.4 bar) below system pressure. Under deceleration, the circuit to the control unit is closed by the micro switch. The speed at which deceleration shutoff occurs depends on coolant temperature. The lower the temperature, the higher the speed at which restart of fuel injection begins. With the micro switch closed, the current at the actuator is approximately 45 mA and the plate valve moves away from the intake port. The pressure difference between the upper and lower chamber is cancelled and system pressure is present in the lower chamber. Operational signals from the control unit will change the direction of the current flow at the actuator plate valve; the plate valve then opens. When the lower chamber pressure changes, pressure and spring force push the diaphragm against the ports to the injectors and cut off the fuel supply.

Fuel Injector(s)

MECHANICAL FUEL INJECTORS

▶ **See Figures 70 and 71**

Mechanical injectors are most commonly used on CIS mechanical injection systems. The fuel injection valves are mounted in the intake manifold at the cylinder head, and continuously inject atomized fuel upstream of the intake valves.

A spring loaded valve is contained in each injector, calibrated to open at a predetermined fuel start pressure. The valves may also contain a small fuel filter.

The fuel injector (one per cylinder) delivers the fuel allocated by the fuel distributor into the intake tubes directly in front of the intake valves. The injectors are secured in a special holder in order to insulate them from

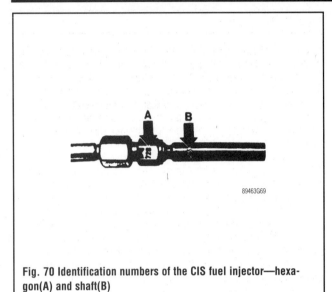

Fig. 70 Identification numbers of the CIS fuel injector—hexagon(A) and shaft(B)

Fig. 72 Individual throttle body injectors are serviceable by removing the electrical connector and unscrewing the injector from the mounting bracket

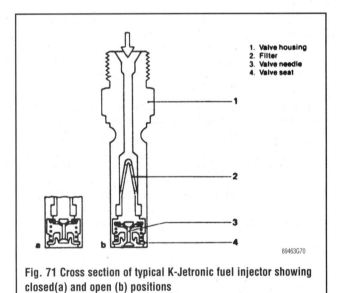

1. Valve housing
2. Filter
3. Valve needle
4. Valve seat

Fig. 71 Cross section of typical K-Jetronic fuel injector showing closed(a) and open (b) positions

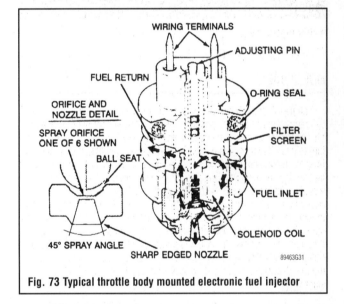

WIRING TERMINALS

ADJUSTING PIN

FUEL RETURN

O-RING SEAL

ORIFICE AND
NOZZLE DETAIL

SPRAY ORIFICE
ONE OF 6 SHOWN

FILTER
SCREEN

BALL SEAT

FUEL INLET

45° SPRAY ANGLE

SHARP EDGED NOZZLE

SOLENOID COIL

Fig. 73 Typical throttle body mounted electronic fuel injector

engine heat. The insulation is necessary to prevent vapor bubbles from forming in the fuel injection lines which would lead to poor starting when the engine is hot. The fuel injectors have no metering function: they open when the appropriate pressure is reached and are fitted with a valve needle that "chatters" at high frequency to atomize the fuel. When the engine is **OFF**, the injection valve closes tightly, forming a seal that prevents fuel from dripping into the intake tubes.

ELECTRONIC FUEL INJECTORS

▶ **See Figures 72, 73, 74, 75 and 76**

An electronic fuel injector is an electric solenoid driven by the control module. The control module, based on sensor inputs, determines when and how long the fuel injector should operate. When an electric current is supplied to the injector, a spring loaded ball is lifted from its seat. This allows fuel to flow through spray orifices and deflect off the sharp edge of the injector nozzle. This action causes the fuel to form an angled, cone shaped spray pattern before entering the air stream in the intake manifold.

Fuel is supplied to the injector via a fuel rail on MFI engines or a fuel supply line on most other electronically fuel injected engines. Fuel that is not used by the injectors is returned to the fuel tank.

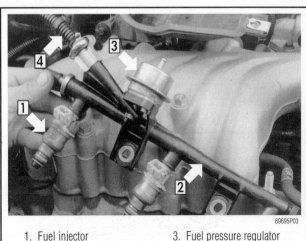

1. Fuel injector
2. Fuel rail
3. Fuel pressure regulator
4. Fuel feed hose

Fig. 74 Typical multi-point fuel injection system components

Fig. 75 The fuel injectors are located above the throttle plates on this TBI unit . . .

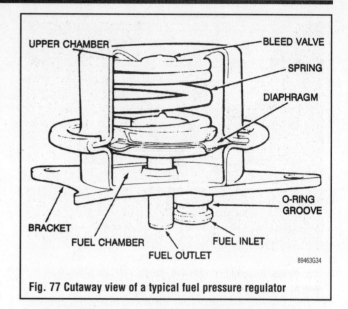

Fig. 77 Cutaway view of a typical fuel pressure regulator

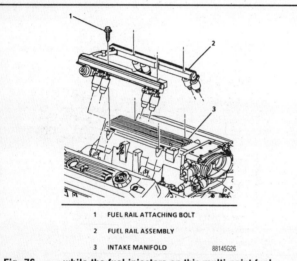

1　FUEL RAIL ATTACHING BOLT

2　FUEL RAIL ASSEMBLY

3　INTAKE MANIFOLD

Fig. 76 . . . while the fuel injectors on this multi-point fuel injection unit are located in the intake manifold

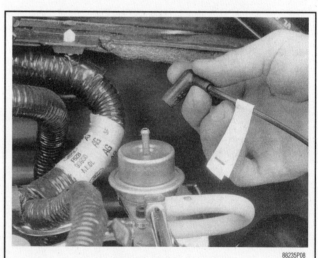

Fig. 78 Most fuel pressure regulators work vacuum. A vacuum leak in this line can cause a driveability problem

Fuel Pressure Regulator

▶ **See Figures 77, 78, 79, 80 and 81**

The pressure regulator is a vacuum operated device located downstream of the fuel injector. Its function is to maintain a constant pressure across the fuel injector tip. The regulator uses a spring loaded rubber diaphragm to uncover a fuel return port. When the fuel pump becomes operational, fuel flows past the injector into the regulator, and is restricted from flowing any further by the blocked return port. When fuel pressure reaches the predetermined setting, it pushes on the diaphragm, compressing the spring, and uncovers the fuel return port. The diaphragm and spring will constantly move from an open to closed position to keep the fuel pressure constant.

Idle Air Control (IAC) Solenoid

▶ **See Figures 82, 83 and 84**

The purpose of the idle air control solenoid system is to control engine idle speed while preventing stalls due to changes in engine load. Most electronically fuel injected engines use the IAC assembly, usually mounted on the throttle body, to control bypass air around the throttle plate. By

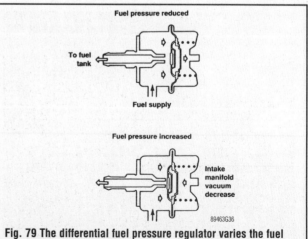

Fig. 79 The differential fuel pressure regulator varies the fuel flow back to the fuel tank in response to manifold vacuum. The lower the vacuum, the less fuel flows back to the fuel tank, increasing the injection pressure.

Fig. 80 On TBI equipped vehicles, the fuel pressure regulator is mounted to the throttle body behind the injectors

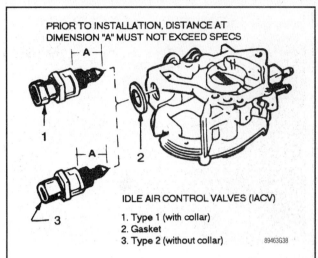

PRIOR TO INSTALLATION, DISTANCE AT DIMENSION "A" MUST NOT EXCEED SPECS

IDLE AIR CONTROL VALVES (IACV)

1. Type 1 (with collar)
2. Gasket
3. Type 2 (without collar)

Fig. 83 Some IAC solenoids are threaded into the throttle body—typical TBI fuel injection

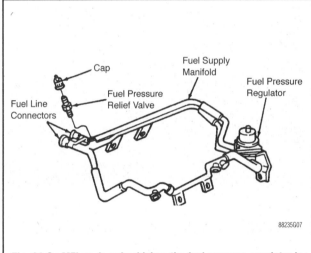

Fig. 81 On MFI equipped vehicles, the fuel pressure regulator is mounted at the end of the fuel rail

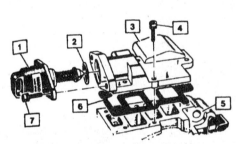

1. Idle air control (IAC) valve assembly
2. Idle air control valve O-ring
3. Idle air/vacuum signal housing assembly
4. Idle air/vacuum signal assembly screw
5. Throttle body assembly
6. Idle air/vacuum signal assembly gasket
7. Idle air control valve screw

Fig. 84 Some IAC solenoids are bolted onto bosses that connect to the throttle body—typical MFI fuel injection

extending or retracting a conical valve, a controlled amount of air can move around the throttle plate. If rpm is too low, more air is diverted around the throttle plate to increase rpm. During idle, the proper position of the IAC is calculated by the control module based on current engine conditions.

Idle Speed Control (ISC) Solenoid

The idle speed control or stepper motor does just what its name implies; it controls the idle speed. The ISC is used to maintain low engine speeds while at the same time preventing stalling due to engine load changes. The system consists of a motor assembly mounted on the throttle body which moves the throttle lever so as to open or close the throttle blades.

Intake Air Temperature (IAT) Sensor

♦ See Figure 85

This device, also known as a Manifold Air Temperature Sensor (MAT) is a thermistor normally placed in the intake air stream. It acts much like the water temperature sensor but with a reduced thermal capacity for quicker response. The injector duration determined by the control module is altered for different operating conditions by the signals sent from this sensor.

Fig. 82 This CSFI idle air control solenoid adjusts air bypassing the throttle body to control idle speed

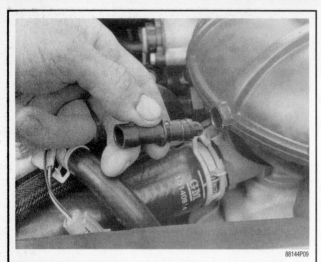

Fig. 85 Most IAT sensors are mounted in the intake air hose near the throttle body

Knock (Detonation) Sensor

♦ See Figure 86

The knock sensor is a piezoelectric device that is usually located on the cylinder block or head. It generates an electrical impulse which is directly proportional to the frequency of the knock which is detected. A buffer then sorts these signals and eliminates all noise except for those frequency ranges which signal detonation. This information is used by the control module to alter ignition timing advance for best performance.

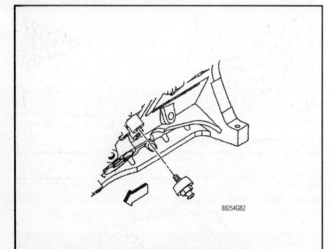

Fig. 86 Knock sensors attach directly to the cylinder block or head and detect vibrations associated with detonation

Line Pressure Regulator

♦ See Figure 87

This component is used on CIS mechanical injection systems. The line pressure regulator ensures that the pressure in the circuit remains constant when the fuel pump is in operation and also controls the recirculation of fuel to the tank. When the fuel pump is switched off, the regulator will cause a rapid pressure drop to the rest pressure, which is maintained by means of the O-ring seal and the quantity of fuel contained in the fuel accumulator. The purpose of the rest pressure is to prevent the fuel from vapor-

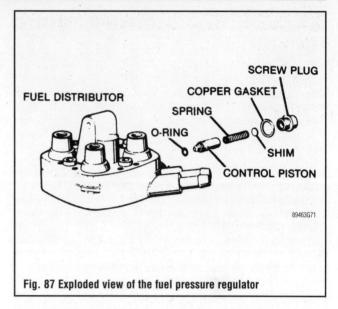

Fig. 87 Exploded view of the fuel pressure regulator

izing in the circuit when the engine is warm, which would otherwise make restarting difficult.

The line pressure regulator forms an integral unit with a shut-off valve to which the return fuel line from the control pressure regulator is connected. When the fuel pump is operating, the shut-off valve is actuated mechanically by the control pressure regulator, whereupon the return fuel from the control pressure regulator bypasses the shut-off valve to the return line.

When the fuel pump stops running and the line pressure regulator valve is pressed into its seating, the shut-off valve is also pressed into its seating, preventing the fuel system from emptying through the control pressure return.

Main Relay

♦ See Figure 88

The main relay is energized when the control module receives information that the ignition switch is **ON** and a either a cranking or engine rpm signal is present. Part of the function of the main relay is to close the relay circuit for the fuel pump system.

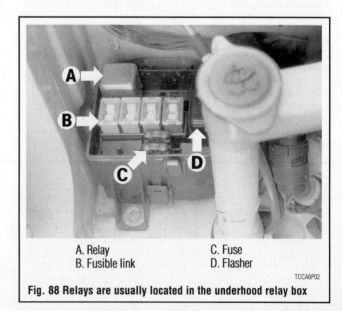

A. Relay   C. Fuse
B. Fusible link   D. Flasher

Fig. 88 Relays are usually located in the underhood relay box

Malfunction Indicator Lamp

▶ See Figure 89

Most modern fuel injected vehicles use some kind of malfunction indicator lamp to warn the driver when a system fault has occurred. Over the years the name of this light has changed significantly. Some of the common names are derivatives of the terms: Service, Check Engine or Malfunction. Some manufacturers will not even use a word but opt to just put a picture of an engine.

Regardless of the term or picture used, these red or yellow lamps should only illuminate briefly for a bulb check when the key is turned ON. If the lamp illuminates while driving, there is a fault in the fuel injector or emissions system and the vehicle should not be driven.

Once the malfunction lamp is illuminated, the control module will store a fault code associated with the problem. Once lit, most lamps will not go out until the problem is repaired.

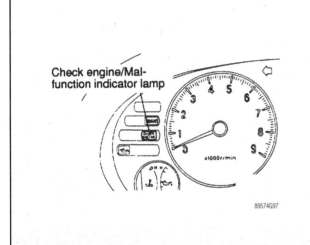

Fig. 89 Malfunction indicator lamp is usually found on the instrument panel

Manifold Absolute Pressure Sensor

▶ See Figures 90, 91 and 92

The Manifold Absolute Pressure (MAP) sensor or atmospheric pressure sensor, measures the changes in the intake manifold pressure which result from engine load and speed changes. The pressure measured by the MAP sensor is the difference between barometric pressure (outside air) and manifold pressure (vacuum). A closed throttle engine coastdown would produce a relatively low MAP value, while wide-open throttle would produce a high value. This high value is produced when the pressure inside the manifold is the same as outside the manifold, and 100% of outside air is being measured. MAP output is the opposite of what you would measure on a vacuum gauge. The use of this sensor also allows the control module to adjust automatically for different altitude.

There are 2 basic types of MAP sensors. The Piezoresitive (PRT) design (used on most vehicles except Ford) provides a DC voltage proportional to pressure. The Silicon Capacitive Absolute Pressure (SCAP) design provides a variable frequency. The control module sends a 5 volt reference signal to the MAP sensor. As the MAP changes, the electrical resistance or frequency of the sensor also changes. By monitoring the sensor output signal the control module can determine the manifold pressure. On a typical PRT design, the higher pressure, lower vacuum (high voltage) requires more fuel, while a lower pressure, higher vacuum (low voltage) requires less fuel. The control module uses the MAP sensor to control fuel delivery and ignition timing.

Fig. 90 The manifold absolute pressure sensor provides the control unit with engine load information

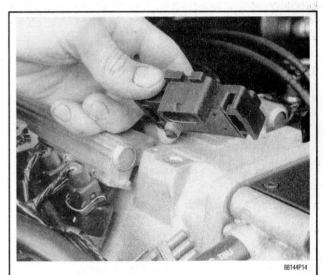

Fig. 91 Sensors can be located on the engine . . .

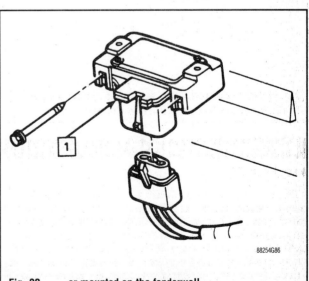

Fig. 92 . . . or mounted on the fenderwell

Mass Air Flow Sensor

♦ See Figures 93 and 94

The Mass Air Flow (MAF) sensor or airflow meter, measures the volume of air which passes through it. The control module uses this information to calculate proper fuel delivery. A large quantity of air indicates acceleration, while a small quantity indicates deceleration or idle.

Many domestic and european manufacturers use sensors that function on a hot wire principle. A wire is heated to a certain temperature. The amount of voltage necessary to keep the wire at that temperature with air flowing over it is used to calculate airflow.

Some import manufacturers use a mechanical door system where by a door is pushed by the incoming air. The wider the door is open, the larger the amount of air flow.

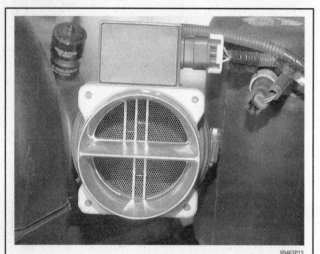

Fig. 93 The sensor measures the volume of air which passes through this screen

Fig. 94 The MAF sensor is usually located between the air cleaner element and the throttle body

Oil Pressure Switch

♦ See Figure 95

The oil pressure switch can be mounted anywhere on the engine. Some vehicles use the oil pressure switch as a parallel power supply with the fuel

Fig. 95 A common location for the oil pressure switch is near the oil filter

pump relay and will provide voltage to the fuel pump, after a certain oil pressure is reached. This switch will also help prevent engine seizure by shutting off the power to the fuel pump and causing the engine to stop when the oil pressure drops dangerously low.

Oxygen Sensor

♦ See Figures 96 and 97

Oxygen sensors supply signals to the control module which indicate a rich or lean condition during engine operation. This input data assists the module in determining the proper air/fuel ratio.

A low voltage signal from the sensor indicates too much oxygen in the exhaust (lean condition) and a high voltage signal indicates too little oxygen in the exhaust (rich condition).

Oxygen sensors are located in the exhaust system, usually in the exhaust manifold or near the catalytic converter. Modern vehicles may use 4 or more oxygen sensors. In this case, sensors are mounted near the exhaust manifolds and after the catalytic converters.

Two types of oxygen sensors exist—heated and non-heated. A small electric heating unit is used to pre-warm the sensor to operating temperature quickly. This reduces the time the engine is in an uncontrolled (Open Loop) operation.

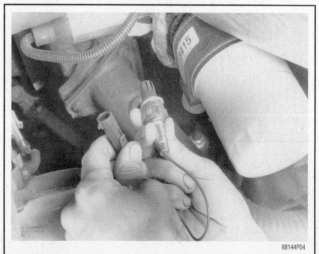

Fig. 96 Oxygen sensors can be found mounted in the exhaust manifold . . .

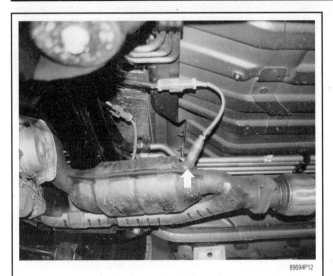

Fig. 97 . . . and near the catalytic converter

Sensors also come in a number of wire configurations. Most heated sensors are 4-wire. Unheated sensors can come in one, two or three wire configurations.

Park/Neutral Switch

▶ See Figure 98

The park/neutral switch, also known as the neutral safety switch, indicates to the control module when the transmission is in **P** or **N**. This information is used by the control module for torque converter clutch, EGR, and the idle air control valve operation.

On late model vehicles the switch may be known as a transmission range sensor. The difference between this and a traditional park/neutral switch is that the range sensor can determine not only Park and Neutral positions but also all other gear ranges.

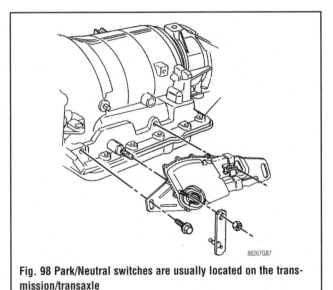

Fig. 98 Park/Neutral switches are usually located on the transmission/transaxle

Positive Crankcase Ventilation Valve

▶ See Figures 99 and 100

A closed Positive Crankcase Ventilation (PCV) system is used on most fuel injected vehicles. This system cycles incompletely burned fuel which works its way past the piston rings back into the intake manifold for reburning with the fuel/air mixture. The oil filler cap is sealed and the air is drawn from the top of the crankcase into the intake manifold through either a valve with a variable orifice or a hose with a fixed orifice.

Variable orifice valves (commonly known as the PCV valves) regulate the flow of air into the manifold according to the amount of manifold vacuum. When the throttle plates are open fairly wide, the valve is fully open. However, at idle speed, when the manifold vacuum is at maximum, the PCV valve reduces the flow.

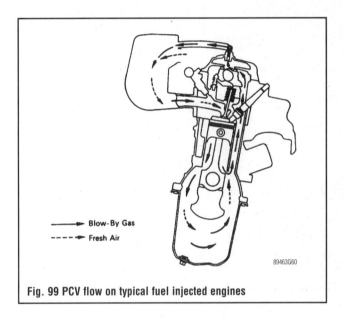

Fig. 99 PCV flow on typical fuel injected engines

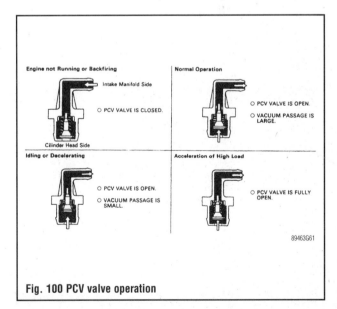

Fig. 100 PCV valve operation

A plugged valve or hose may cause a rough idle, stalling or low idle speed, oil leaks in the engine and/or sludging and oil deposits within the engine and air cleaner. A leaking valve or hose could cause an erratic idle or stalling.

PROM (EEPROM)

▶ See Figure 101

The control module consists of 3 parts; a controller (the control module without a PROM), a calibrator called a PROM (Programmable Read Only Memory) and/or a Cal-Pak. Some PROM chips are replaceable, while others require that the entire control unit be replaced.

A third more recent type of control unit allows the memory unit to be reprogrammed in the vehicle. These control units are said to have EEPROM (Electrically Erasable Programmable Read Only Memory). Calibration information, which is particular to the vehicle application, must be programmed into these modules prior to installing them in the vehicle

On some vehicles a calibrator (CAL-PAK) is used to allow one control module to be used for many different vehicles. The CAL-PAK is located inside the control module and has information on the vehicle's weight, engine, transmission, axle ratio and other components.

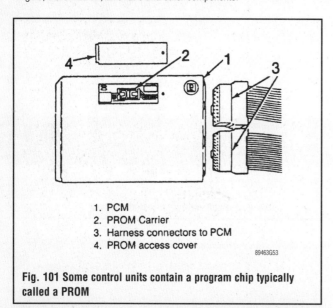

1. PCM
2. PROM Carrier
3. Harness connectors to PCM
4. PROM access cover

89463G53

Fig. 101 Some control units contain a program chip typically called a PROM

Secondary Throttle Sensor

The secondary throttle sensor is used on some vehicles with traction control. It responds to the movement of the throttle motor, which is controlled by the Traction Control Module (TCM). This sensor is a type of potentiometer that transforms the secondary valve position into output voltage, and emits the voltage signal to the TCM. In addition, the sensor detects the opening and closing speed along with the position of the secondary throttle valve and feeds the voltage signal to the TCM.

When the secondary throttle valve opening becomes smaller than the ordinary throttle valve opening due to traction control operation, then, and only then, the signal from the secondary throttle valve is used for engine control in place of the signal from the ordinary throttle sensor. The signal of the secondary throttle valve is sent to the control module.

Starter Signal

On some fuel injection systems, the START position on the ignition switch causes a signal to be sent to the control module. During cranking, the control module will increase the amount of fuel injected into the engine

according to the engine temperature. The amount of fuel that is injected is gradually reduced when the starter switch is released.

Thermo-Time Switch

▶ See Figure 102

Thermo-Time switches are used on CIS mechanical injection systems. The switch actuates the cold start valve. It has a bi-metal spring which senses coolant temperature and an electric coil which limits the cold start valve spray to 12 seconds. A thermo-time switch also measures water temperature and opens the cold start valve, located on the intake header, a varying amount of each time the engine is started, depending on the conditions. With a hot engine (coolant temperature over 95°F /35°C), the injector should not operate. If it does, the thermo-time switch is defective. In addition, on a cold engine, the cold start valve should not inject fuel for more than 12 seconds (during starter cranking). If it does, the thermo-time switch is defective.

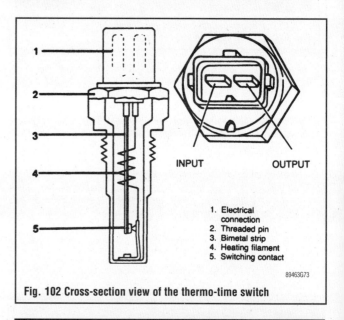

INPUT   OUTPUT

1. Electrical connection
2. Threaded pin
3. Bimetal strip
4. Heating filament
5. Switching contact

89463G73

Fig. 102 Cross-section view of the thermo-time switch

Throttle Body

THROTTLE BODY INJECTION SYSTEMS

▶ See Figure 103

The TBI throttle body assembly replaces a conventional carburetor and is mounted on top of the intake manifold. The throttle body houses the fuel injector(s), pressure regulator, throttle position sensor, idle air control solenoid (idle speed control solenoid).

Air flow through the throttle body is controlled throttle blades located in the base of the unit. The throttle body itself provides the chamber for metering atomizing and distributing fuel throughout the air entering the engine.

MULTI-PORT FUEL INJECTION SYSTEMS

▶ See Figures 104 and 105

The MFI throttle body assembly replaces is mounted on the intake manifold (plenum) in-line with the air intake hose. The throttle bodyhouses the throttle position sensor, idle air control solenoid (idle speed control solenoid) and on some vehicles the intake air temperature sensor.

On most vehicles, it connects to the accelerator pedal via a solid or cable type accelerator linkage.

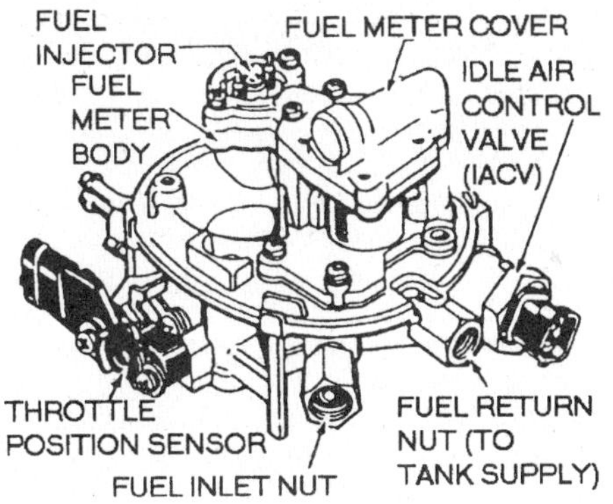

FUEL
INJECTOR
FUEL
METER
BODY
FUEL METER COVER
IDLE AIR
CONTROL
VALVE
(IACV)
THROTTLE
POSITION SENSOR
FUEL INLET NUT
FUEL RETURN
NUT (TO
TANK SUPPLY)

89463G54

Fig. 103 Throttle body mounted components—typical TBI fuel system shown

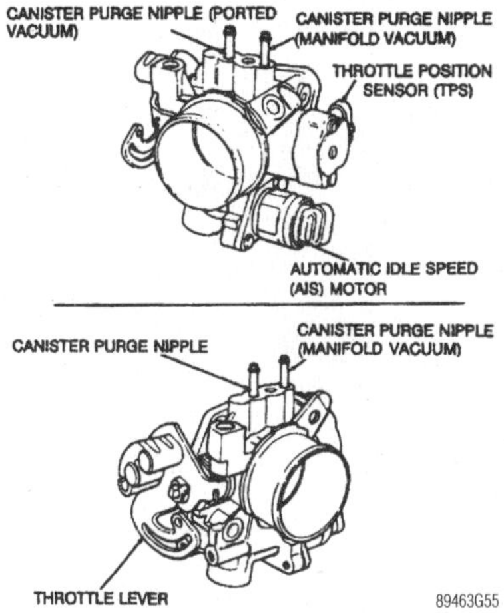

CANISTER PURGE NIPPLE (PORTED VACUUM)   CANISTER PURGE NIPPLE (MANIFOLD VACUUM)
THROTTLE POSITION SENSOR (TPS)
AUTOMATIC IDLE SPEED (AIS) MOTOR
CANISTER PURGE NIPPLE   CANISTER PURGE NIPPLE (MANIFOLD VACUUM)
THROTTLE LEVER

89463G55

Fig. 104 Throttle body mounted components—typical MFI fuel system shown

ATTENTION
DO NOT CLEAN INSIDE THROTTLE BODY OR
ADJUST HARD STOP SCREW. HAS COATING ON THROTTLE PLATE AND BORE

89695P01

Fig. 105 Some throttle bodies are coated with a protective anti-sludge compound. Do not attempt to clean these with solvent

Throttle Position Sensor

▶ **See Figures 106, 107 and 108**

The Throttle Position Sensor (TPS) may also be called a throttle angle valve, throttle potentiometer or a throttle valve switch. It is connected to the throttle shaft and is controlled by the throttle mechanism. A 5-volt reference signal is sent to the TPS from the control module. As the throttle valve angle is changed (accelerator pedal moved), the resistance of the TPS also changes. At a closed throttle position, the resistance of the TPS is high, so the output voltage to the control module will be low (approximately 0.5 volt). As the throttle plate opens, the resistance decreases so that, at wide-open throttle, the output voltage should be approximately 5 volts. At closed throttle position, the voltage at the TPS should be less than 1.25 volts. By monitoring the output voltage from the TPS, the control module can determine fuel delivery based on throttle valve angle (driver demand).

Problems may occur causing the TPS to become misadjusted, shorted, open or loose. Misadjustment might result in poor idle or poor wide-open throttle performance. An open TPS signals the control module that the throttle is always closed, resulting in poor performance. This usually sets a code. A shorted TPS gives the control module a constant wide-open throttle signal will store a code. A loose TPS indicates to the control module that

89463P22

Fig. 106 On TBI equipped vehicles, the throttle position sensor (front) and idle air control valve (rear) are both mounted on the throttle body

8166

89463P11

Fig. 107 Throttle positions sensors are usually mounted on the side of the throttle body, in-line with the throttle shaft

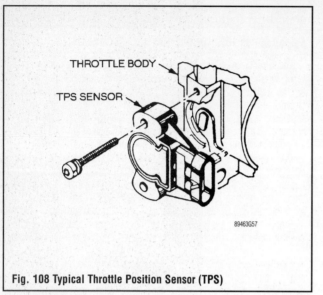

Fig. 108 Typical Throttle Position Sensor (TPS)

the throttle is moving. This causes intermittent bursts of fuel from the injector and an unstable idle. Once the fault code is set, the control module will use an artificial default value and some vehicle performance will return.

Throttle Valve

This component is used on CIS mechanical injection systems. The throttle valve housing is connected to the intake manifold and, in addition to the throttle valve, it contains the idling air passage and the idling adjustment screw, connections for the hoses to the auxiliary air valve, and the cold start valve and the vacuum outlet for ignition timing.

Vehicle Speed Sensor

▶ **See Figure 109**

The vehicle speed sensor is mounted behind the speedometer in the instrument cluster or the transmission/transaxle. It provides electrical pulses to the control module which indicate road speed. The control module uses this information in may of its calculations.

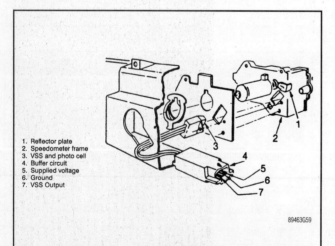

1. Reflector plate
2. Speedometer frame
3. VSS and photo cell
4. Buffer circuit
5. Supplied voltage
6. Ground
7. VSS Output

Fig. 109 Typical instrument panel mounted Vehicle Speed Sensor (VSS). Many newer models use a sensor in the transmission/transaxle.

Warm-Up Regulator

▶ **See Figures 110 and 111**

This component is used on CIS mechanical injection systems. When the engine is cold, the warm-up regulator reduces control pressure, causing the metering slits in the fuel distributor to open further. This enrichment process prevents combustion miss during the warm-up phase of engine operation and is continually reduced as temperature rises. The warm-up regulator is a spring controlled flat seat diaphragm-type valve with an electrically heated bi-metal spring. When cold, the bi-metal spring overcomes the valve spring pressure, moving the diaphragm and allowing more fuel to be diverted Out of the control pressure circuit thereby lowering the control pressure. When the bi-metal spring is heated electrically or by engine temperature the valve spring pushes the diaphragm up, allowing less fuel to be diverted thereby raising the control pressure. When the bi-metal spring lifts fully off the `valve spring the warm-up enrichment is completed and control pressure is maintained at normal level by the valve spring. The warm-up regulator should be checked when testing fuel pressure.

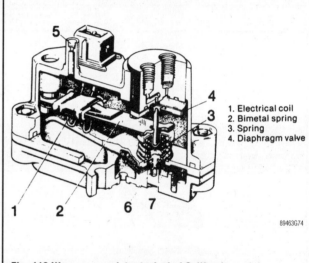

1. Electrical coil
2. Bimetal spring
3. Spring
4. Diaphragm valve

Fig. 110 Warm-up regulator typical of California models

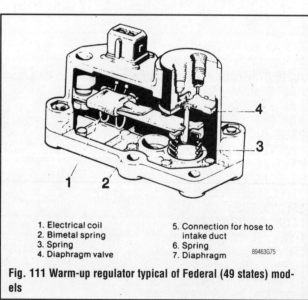

1. Electrical coil
2. Bimetal spring
3. Spring
4. Diaphragm valve
5. Connection for hose to intake duct
6. Spring
7. Diaphragm

Fig. 111 Warm-up regulator typical of Federal (49 states) models

4

BASIC MAINTENANCE AND TROUBLE-SHOOTING

PREVENTIVE MAINTENANCE

Fuel System

Late model fuel injection systems allow only minute quantities of air and fuel to reach the combustion chamber in order to produce minimal emissions. Nevertheless, these diminutive amounts of air and fuel are easily obstructed by intake and fuel injector deposits. These deposits cause many driveability problems that range from hesitation and rough idle to detonation problems. But this problem is not inevitable; it can be prevented through fuel system maintenance.

Fuel system maintenance is required to reduce the amount of deposits in the fuel and intake system. These deposits are caused by dirt in the fuel, poorly maintained engines, and engine compartment heat. To begin with, the intake and fuel system deposits can be reduced substantially by replacing the fuel filter at the manufacturer's recommended intervals or as part of a tune-up.

The remainder of these deposits can be removed by cleaning the system. However, there are several levels of cleaning. The system is cleaned by the vehicle's owner if they use a high detergent gasoline or gas tank additives. The high detergent gasoline differs according to each distributor according to how well their holding tanks are maintained.

On the other hand, the gas tank additives can go a long way to reducing the overall amount of deposits. For example, one additive may concentrate on breaking up carbon deposits in the combustion chamber while another focuses on reducing intake valve deposits. Therefore, consult the additive manufacturer for the recommended usage interval. Likewise, verify that a particular additive is catalytic converter and oxygen sensor safe before stocking it or recommending it to your customers. Additionally, these companies also have an all-in-one cleaner that cleanses the whole system.

➡ **Some vehicle manufacturers do not recommend the use of fuel system additives. Always check your owner's manual or warranty booklet prior to using these additives in your vehicle. This is especially important if your vehicle is still under warranty.**

The other method of removing deposits is clean the system using high pressure cleaning equipment. This method is usually performed by professional technicians, however, aftermarket suppliers have recently been marketing kits for the do-it-yourselfer. The intervals at which a fuel system requires professional cleaning varies according to the way the vehicle is operated and whether or not it is properly maintained.

The majority of the vehicles on the road today will benefit from a high pressure cleaning at 24–30,000 mile (38,600–48,200 km) intervals.

Combining the high pressure fuel system cleaning and regular use of fuel system additives is an excellent way to prevent intake and fuel in which can cause irregular idles and poor fuel mileage.

Air Cleaner

The air cleaner element should be replaced at the recommended maintenance intervals. If your vehicle is operated under severely dusty conditions or severe operating conditions, more frequent changes will certainly be necessary. Inspect the element at least twice a year. Early spring and early fall are good times for an inspection. Remove the element and check for any perforations or tears in the filter. Check the cleaner housing for signs of dirt or dust that may have leaked through the filter element or in through the snorkel tube. Position a droplight on one side of the element and look through the filter at the light. If no glow of light can be seen through the element material, replace the filter. If holes in the filter element are apparent, or signs of dirt seepage through the filter are evident, replace the filter.

REMOVAL & INSTALLATION

▶ See Figures 1 and 2

Air cleaners come a wide selection of shapes and sizes. Most common are either round or rectangular. In any event, air filter element replacement is usually pretty simple.

Fig. 1 The air filter element may be cleaned with low pressure compressed air

Fig. 2 An extremely neglected filter element. Allowing the filter to get this dirty drastically reduces economy and power

If your vehicle is equipped with a round type air cleaner, it probably has one or two wing nuts and/or some clips holding the air cleaner lid in place. Just remove the wing nuts and unclip the retaining clips. Lift the lid off and remove the element.

If your vehicle is equipped with a rectangular type air cleaner, unclip the retaining clips and lift off the air cleaner lid. remove the element from the assembly. Some these units may not be as easily accessible and may require removing a hose or two, but all in all it's pretty simple to do.

Air Cleaner Assembly (Housing)

▶ See Figures 3, 4 and 5

1. Disconnect all hoses, ducts and vacuum tubes from the air cleaner assembly, after tagging them for easy identification.
2. Remove the top cover wing nuts and grommet (if so equipped). Some models also utilize four to five side clips to further secure the top of the assembly. Simply pull the overcenter tab and release the clip. On most later vehicles, air cleaners are secured solely by means of clips (air box-to-cleaner housing). Remove the cover and lift out the filter element.
3. Remove any side mount brackets and/or retaining bolts, then lift off the air cleaner assembly.

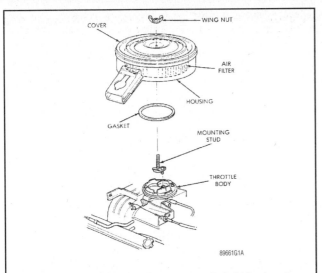

Fig. 3 Round air cleaner housings are usually held in place by wing nuts and/or clips

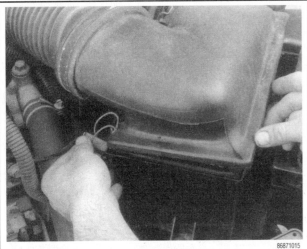

Fig. 4 Rectangular air cleaner housings are used on newer vehicles and mainly held in place by clips

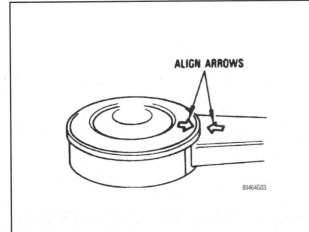

Fig. 5 Many air cleaner assemblies have arrows on the housing and lid—always make sure they align

4. Clean or replace the filter element as detailed previously. Wipe clean all surfaces of the air cleaner housing and cover. Check the condition of the mounting gasket and replace if it appears worn or broken.

5. Reposition the air cleaner assembly, then install the mounting bracket and/or bolts.

6. Reposition the filter element in the case and install the cover being careful not to overtighten the wingnut(s). On round-style cleaners, be certain that the arrows on the cover lid and the snorkel match up properly.

➡ Filter elements on many engines have a TOP and BOTTOM side; be sure they are inserted correctly.

7. Reconnect all hoses, ductwork and vacuum lines.

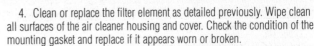

❈❈ **WARNING**

Never operate the engine without the air filter element in place.

Air Cleaner Element

▸ See Figures 6, 7, 8, 9 and 10

The air cleaner element can be replaced by removing the air cleaner housing lid and lifting the air cleaner filter element from it's housing.

Fig. 6 Loosen the air intake hose clamp before removing the filter element

Fig. 7 Disconnect the air intake hose, being careful not to lose the retaining clamp

Fig. 8 Unfasten the side retaining clamps so that the air filter housing can be opened

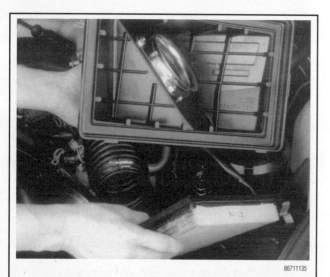

Fig. 9 Remove the air filter element from the air filter housing

Fig. 10 View of the air filter element. Make sure that the element is installed in the housing properly before fastening the side clamps

Crankcase Ventilation Filter

◗ See Figures 11 and 12

Certain models may utilize an air cleaner-mounted crankcase ventilation filter. If so, it should also be cleaned or replaced at the same time as the regular air filter element. To replace the filter, remove the air cleaner top cover and pull the filter from its housing on the side of the air cleaner assembly. Push a new filter into the housing and reinstall the cover. If the filter and plastic holder need replacement, remove the clip mounting the feeder tube to the air cleaner housing, then remove the assembly from the air cleaner.

Fig. 11 The crankcase ventilation filter is an integral part of the PCV system. A dirty filter will decrease system performance

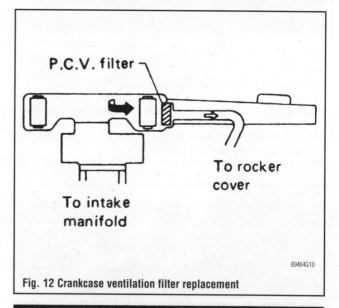

Fig. 12 Crankcase ventilation filter replacement

Fuel Filter

REMOVAL & INSTALLATION

◗ See Figures 13, 14, 15, 16 and 17

✳✳ CAUTION

Never smoke when working around or near gasoline! Provide plenty of ventilation and make sure that there is no active ignition source near your work area!

Never attempt to remove the fuel filter without first relieving the fuel system pressure!

The procedure below is a general procedure, consult a "Chilton Total Car Care (TCC) Manual" for specific procedure concerning your vehicle.

1. Relieve the fuel pressure from the fuel line as follows:
    a. Remove the fuel pump fuse or relay at the fuse box.
    b. Start the engine.
    c. After the engine stalls, crank the engine two or three times to make sure that the fuel pressure is released.
    d. Turn the ignition switch **OFF**.
2. Raise and support the vehicle as necessary.
3. Three types of connections are normally made at the fuel filter.
    a. If the filter is connected by rubber hoses, loosen the hose clamps and separate the filter from the rubber hoses.
    b. If the filter is connected by clips, disengage the clips and pull the fuel lines from the filter.
    c. If the filter is connected with fittings using banjo bolts, unscrew the bolts and disconnect the filter from the fuel lines.

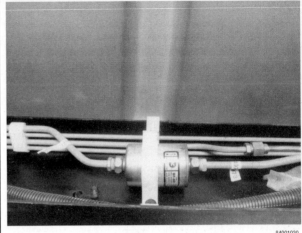

Fig. 15 This is a flare nut and hard line installation. Always use a backup wrench to prevent twisting the hard line

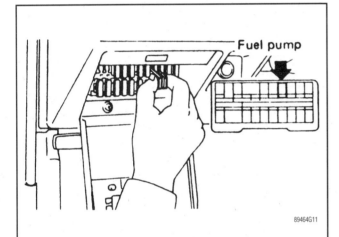

Fig. 13 Remove the fuel pump fuse or relay when releasing the fuel pressure—the fuse or relay location may vary

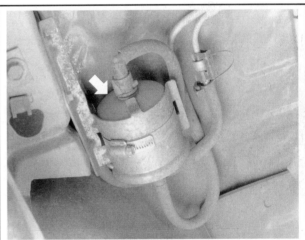

Fig. 16 Fuel filters attached using clips can be easily removed by unfastening the clips and pulling back the fuel lines

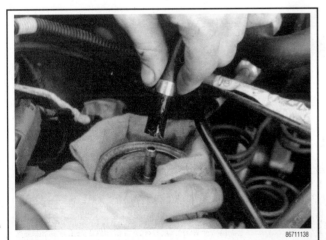

Fig. 14 A typical rubber hose and nipple connection. Always replace the rubber hoses and hose clamps when replacing the fuel filter

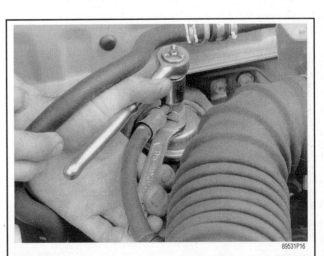

Fig. 17 Disconnecting a fuel filter connected with a banjo bolt. Note the use of a backup wrench to prevent damage to the fuel line

d. If the filter is connected by flare nut and hard fuel line, use a flare nut wrench to loosen the fittings and disconnect the hard lines from the filter.

➡**When loosening flare nuts, always use a flare nut wrench and a backup wrench to prevent twisting the hard fuel line.**

4. Wrap a shop towel or absorbent rag around the filter to prevent fuel spillage.

5. Remove the fuel filter.

To install:

6. Install the new fuel filter, being careful to observe the correct direction of flow.

7. Once the filter is properly positioned in the vehicle, connect the fuel lines as follows:

a. If the filter is connected by rubber hoses, install new hoses and tighten clamps securely.

b. If the filter is connected by clips, install new O-rings and push fuel lines into filter. Install new retaining clips.

c. If the filter is connected with fittings using banjo bolts, carefully screw the bolts into the filter and tighten securely.

d. If the filter is connected by flare nuts and hard fuel line, carefully screw the flare nuts into the filter and tighten using a flare nut wrench and a backup wrench.

8. Lower the vehicle if raised

9. Reinstall the fuel pump fuse or relay. Start the engine and check for fuel leaks.

✳✳ WARNING

Always use a high pressure-type fuel filter specifically designed to work with your fuel system.

PCV Valve

◆ **See Figures 18, 19 and 20**

The PCV valve regulates crankcase ventilation during various engine operating conditions. At high vacuum (idle speed and partial load range) the valve will open slightly, and at low vacuum (full throttle) it will open fully. This causes vapor to be removed from the crankcase by the engine vacuum and then be sucked into the combustion chamber where it is burned.

➡**The PCV system will not function properly unless the oil filler cap is tightly sealed. Check the gasket on the cap and be certain it is not leaking. Replace the cap and/or gasket, if necessary, to ensure proper sealing.**

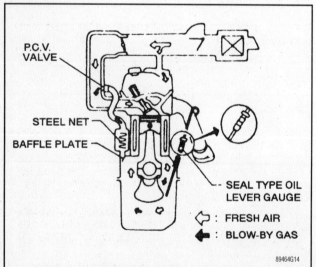

P.C.V.
VALVE

STEEL NET

BAFFLE PLATE

SEAL TYPE OIL
LEVER GAUGE

⇨ : FRESH AIR

➡ : BLOW-BY GAS

89464G14

Fig. 18 Typical PCV system operation

88194P01

Fig. 19 Most PCV valves are installed by simply pushing them into a grommet on the valve cover

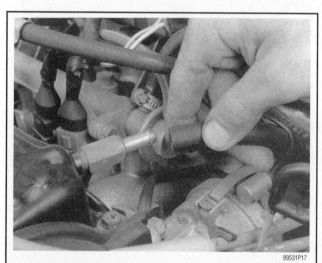

89531P17

Fig. 20 Some PCV valves are screwed into the valve cover and must be removed using a wrench

TESTING

◆ **See Figure 21**

1. Inspect the ventilation hoses and lines for leaks or clogging. Clean or replace as necessary.

2. With the engine running at idle, locate the PCV and disconnect the ventilation hose.

3. Place a finger over the hose and check for the presence of vacuum. If no vacuum is present, trace the hose back to its source at the throttle body or intake manifold and inspect for clogs.

4. Next perform the same test with the PCV valve connected to the hose. If vacuum is not present with the PCV valve connected, the valve is faulty.

5. A final check of the PCV valve can be made by simply shaking the valve. If a rattling noise is heard (the sound of the check ball in the valve), the valve is functioning properly.

6. If the PCV valve failed either of the preceding two checks (and the ventilation hose is not clogged or broken), the valve will require replacement.

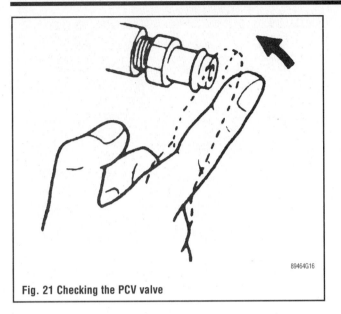

Fig. 21 Checking the PCV valve

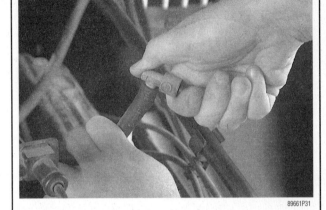

Fig. 23 With a twisting motion, disconnect the valve from the vacuum hose

REMOVAL & INSTALLATION

▶ **See Figures 22, 23 and 24**

    1. If not already done, disconnect the ventilation hose from the PCV valve.

    2. Remove the PCV valve. If its base is threaded, unscrew the valve; otherwise, simply pull the valve from its retaining grommet.

    To install:

    3. Depending on the type of valve, either screw in the replacement PCV valve or push it into its retaining grommet.

    4. Slide the ventilation hose onto the end of the PCV valve.

➡**For more detailed information on the PCV system for your vehicle, consult a "Chilton Total Car Care (TCC) Manual".**

Battery

➡**On a maintenance-free sealed battery, a built-in hydrometer or "eye" is used for checking the fluid level and specific gravity readings. If your battery is equipped with an eye, use it for checking the condition of the battery by observing the color of the eye. A green colored eye indicates good condition and a dark colored eye indicates the need for service. Replacement batteries could be either the sealed (maintenance-free) or non-sealed type.**

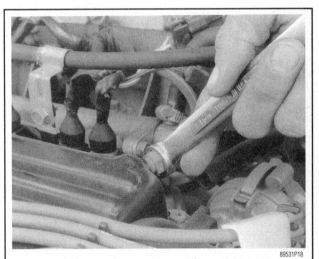

Fig. 24 PCV valves which screw into the valve cover must be removed using a suitable wrench

Almost all current replacement batteries are of the sealed maintenance free type.

FLUID LEVEL (EXCEPT MAINTENANCE-FREE SEALED BATTERIES)

▶ **See Figure 25**

    Check the battery electrolyte level at least once a month, or more often in hot weather or during periods of extended operation. The level can be checked through the case on translucent polypropylene batteries; the cell caps must be removed on other models. The electrolyte level in each cell should be kept filled to the bottom of the split ring inside, or to the line marked on the outside of the case.

    If the level is low, add only distilled water, or colorless, odorless drinking water, through the opening until the level is correct. Each cell is completely separate from the others, so each must be checked and filled individually.

    If water is added in freezing weather, the vehicle should be driven several miles to allow the water to mix with the electrolyte. Otherwise, the battery could freeze.

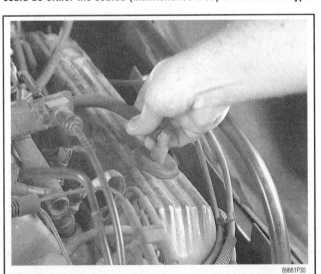

Fig. 22 Remove the PCV valve from the valve cover grommet

Fig. 25 Fill each battery cell to the bottom of the split ring with distilled water

Fig. 27 On non-maintenance free batteries with translucent cases, the electrolyte level can be viewed through the case; on other type, as shown, the cell caps must be removed

SPECIFIC GRAVITY (EXCEPT MAINTENANCE-FREE BATTERIES)

▶ **See Figures 26, 27 and 28**

➡**On a maintenance-free sealed battery, a built-in eye is used for checking the specific gravity readings. Refer to the battery case for further instructions.**

At least once a year, check the specific gravity of the battery. It should be 1.26–1.28 at room temperature.

The specific gravity can be checked with the use of a hydrometer, an inexpensive instrument available from many sources, including auto parts stores. The hydrometer has a squeeze bulb at one end and a nozzle at the other. Battery electrolyte is sucked into the hydrometer until the float is lifted from its seat. The specific gravity is then read by noting the position of the float. Generally, if after charging, the specific gravity of any two cells varies more than 50 points (0.50), the battery is bad and should be replaced.

It is not possible to check the specific gravity in this manner on sealed (maintenance-free) batteries. Instead, the indicator built into the top of the case must be relied on to display any signs of battery deterioration. On most batteries if the indicator is a light color, the battery can be assumed to be OK. If the indicator is a dark color, the specific gravity

BATTERY STATE OF CHARGE AT ROOM TEMPERATURE	
Specific Gravity Reading	Charged Condition
1.260–1.280	Fully Charged
1.230–1.250	3/4 Charged
1.200–1.220	1/2 Charged
1.170–1.190	1/4 Charged
1.140–1.160	Almost no Charge
1.110–1.130	No Charge

89464G19

Fig. 28 Battery state of charge at room temperature—Generalized Specifications

is low, and the battery should be charged or replaced. There should be specific notations on the battery you are working with as to what color the indicator will be depending on the batteries state of charge.

CABLES AND CLAMPS

▶ **See Figures 29 thru 36**

Once a year, the battery terminals and the cable clamps should be checked and cleaned, if necessary. Make sure that the ignition switch is turned to the **OFF** position. Loosen the clamps and remove the cables, negative cable first. On batteries with posts on top, the use of a puller specially made for this purpose is recommended. These are inexpensive, and available in most auto parts stores. Side terminal battery cables are secured with a bolt.

Clean the cable clamps and the battery terminal with a wire brush, until all corrosion, grease, etc., is removed and the metal is shiny. It is especially important to clean the inside of the clamp thoroughly, since a small deposit of foreign material or oxidation there will prevent a sound electrical connection and inhibit either starting or charging. Special tools are available for cleaning these parts, one type for top post batteries and another type for side terminal batteries.

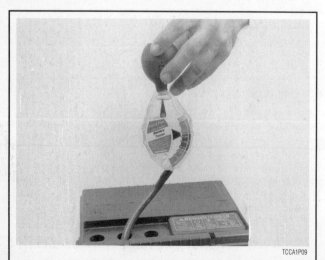

Fig. 26 The specific gravity of the battery acid can be checked with a simple float-type hydrometer

Before installing the cables, loosen the battery hold-down clamp or strap, remove the battery and check the battery tray. Clear it of any debris, and check it for soundness. Rust should be wire brushed away, and the metal given a coat of anti-rust paint. Install the battery and tighten the hold-down clamp or strap securely, but be careful not to overtighten, as doing so may crack the battery case.

After the clamps and terminals are clean, reinstall the cables, negative cable last; do not hammer on the clamps to install. Tighten the clamps securely, but do not distort them. Give the clamps and terminals a thin external coat of grease after installation, to retard corrosion.

Check the cables at the same time that the terminals are cleaned. If the cable insulation is cracked or broken, or if the ends are frayed, the cable should be replaced with a new cable of the same length and gauge.

☀☀ CAUTION

Keep flame or sparks away from the battery; it gives off explosive hydrogen gas! Battery electrolyte contains sulfuric acid! If you should splash any on your skin or in your eyes, flush the affected area with plenty of clear water. If it lands in your eyes, get medical help immediately!

Fig. 31 Clean the inside of the clamps with a wire brush or the special tool

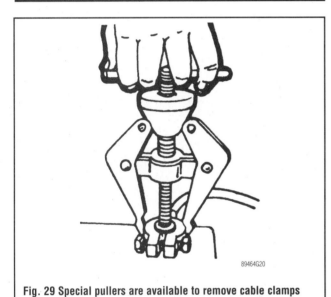
Fig. 29 Special pullers are available to remove cable clamps

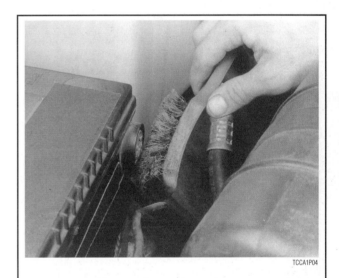
Fig. 32 Cleaning the posts . . .

Fig. 30 Clean the battery posts with a wire brush or the special tool shown

Fig. 33 . . . and cable ends of a side terminal battery using a wire brush

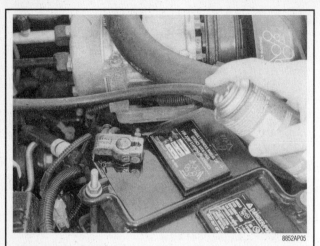

Fig. 34 Once the terminals are clean, apply a liberal amount of petroleum jelly or battery terminal protectant to prevent corrosion

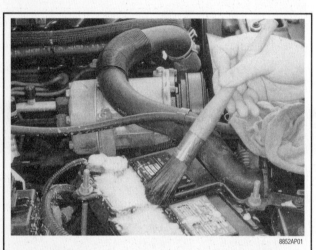

Fig. 35 Battery case maintenance can be performed using a mixture of baking soda and water to neutralize and any acid deposits

Fig. 36 A light coating of dielectric grease promotes a sound connection between the battery cable and the terminal. It also prevents corrosion from forming

REPLACEMENT

When it becomes necessary to replace the battery, be sure to select a new battery with a cold cranking power rating equal to or greater than the battery originally installed. Deterioration, embrittlement and just plain aging of the battery cables, starter motor and associated wires makes the battery's job all the more difficult in successive years. The slow increase in electrical resistance over time makes it prudent to install a new battery with a greater capacity than the old.

REMOVAL

▶ **See Figures 37, 38, 39, 40 and 41**

1. Make sure the ignition switch is turned **OFF**.
2. Disconnect the negative battery cable from the terminal, then disconnect the positive cable. Special pullers are available to remove the clamps.

➡**To avoid sparks, always disconnect the negative cable first and reconnect it last.**

3. Unscrew and remove the battery hold-down clamp.

Fig. 37 On top post batteries, loosen the terminal retaining nut, then remove the terminal from the post

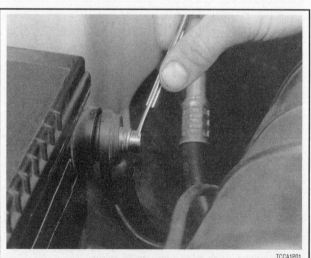

Fig. 38 On side post batteries, loosen the terminal retaining bolt and disconnect the terminal from the battery

TCCA1P10

Fig. 39 Unscrew the battery hold down . . .

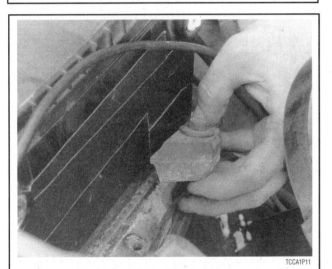

TCCA1P11

Fig. 40 . . . and remove it from the battery tray

TCCA1P12

Fig. 41 Lift the battery from the vehicle using the strap handle, if so equipped, or by using a battery lifting tool

4. Remove the battery, being careful not to spill any of the acid.

➡Spilled acid can be neutralized with a baking soda and water solution. If you somehow get acid into your eyes, flush it out with lots of clean water and get to a doctor as quickly as possible.

To install:

5. Clean the battery posts thoroughly.

6. Clean the cable clamps using the special tools or a wire brush, both inside and out.

7. Install the battery, then fasten the hold-down clamp.

8. Connect the positive and then the negative cable. Do not hammer them into place. Coat the terminals with grease to prevent corrosion.

※※ WARNING

Make sure that the battery is connected properly before you turn on the ignition switch. Reversed polarity can burn out the alternator and regulator in a matter of seconds.

Drive Belts

MODERN DRIVE BELTS DON'T SHOW THEIR AGE

On today's vehicles, it's very difficult to tell the difference between an automotive drive belt with 50,000 miles (80,450 km) of wear, and another belt with 10,000 miles (16,090 km) of wear. A basic change in drive belt construction—one that produced a longer-lasting belt—also makes it difficult to spot indications of belt wear.

Virtually all automotive drive belts produced in the U.S. and Europe are made without a cover. These "bandless" belts don't show wear like their predecessors. Although bandless belts are designed to outlast banded belts on similar drives, they provide no early warning of failure.

There are two main causes of drive belt failure. The most common is fatigue of the load-bearing, tensile cords leading to belt failure from the inside out. Tensile cord failure is due to a gradual weakening of the tensile cords that results from a combination of side stress, bending stress, and centrifugal force imposed on the belt as it travels around the pulleys.

Because this type of failure takes place inside the belt, there is no easy way to determine when the belt is about to break. Statistics show the chance of drive belt failure on an average vehicle goes up sharply after four years.

For this reason, many drive belt manufacturers recommend that all engine drive belts be replaced on a four-year basis.

In this way, the replacement can be done at the vehicle owner's convenience, rather than on an emergency basis.

The other major cause of drive belt failure is improper tension. This causes the belt to slip as it travels around the pulleys, generating heat build-up. Excessive heat eventually causes the rubber compounds in the belt to break down, and crack, leading to belt failure.

Indicators of belt tension problems include:

• Belt squeal, especially on the fan or power steering drives.

• Battery discharge sometimes caused by a slipping alternator belt.

• Excessive sidewall wear that allows the belt to ride lower than normal in the pulley grooves.

• Absences of overcord (the belt's top protective covering).

• Cracking of the bottom and sides of the belt.

In addition, small engine compartments on today's vehicles make belts more susceptible to heat and contamination from petroleum products. High temperatures can cause belts to dry, harden and crack. If a belt becomes oil soaked, it cannot grip the pulley. Petroleum products also break down the rubber compounds in the belt.

The best way to check belt tension is with a tension gauge. Because of smaller engine compartments and shorter belt spans between pulleys, the old finger deflection method of checking tension are not as accurate.

BELT INSPECTION

▶ **See Figures 42, 43, 44, 45 and 46**

V-Belts

Many vehicles utilize one or more V-belts to drive engine accessories (such as the alternator, water pump, power steering pump or A/C compressor off the crankshaft.

V-belts should be checked every 3,000 miles (4,800 km) or 3 months for evidence of wear such as cracking, fraying and incorrect tension. Determine the belt tension at a point halfway between the pulleys by pressing on the belt with moderate thumb pressure. The belt should deflect about ¼ inch (6mm) over a 7–10 inch (178–254mm) span, or ½ inch (13mm) over a 13–16 inch (330–406mm) span. If the deflection is found too much or too little, perform the tension adjustments.

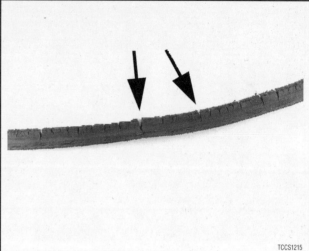

Fig. 44 Deep cracks in this belt will cause flex, building up heat that will eventually lead to belt failure

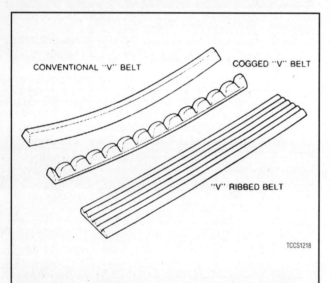

Fig. 42 There are typically three types of accessory drive belts found on vehicles today

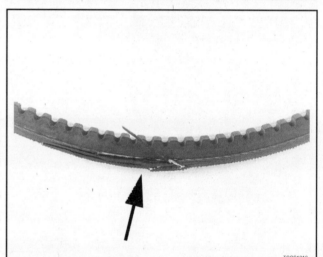

Fig. 45 The cover of this belt is worn, exposing the critical reinforcing cords to excessive wear

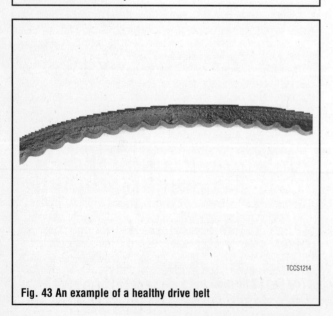

Fig. 43 An example of a healthy drive belt

Fig. 46 Installing too wide a belt can result in serious belt wear and/or breakage

Serpentine Belts

▶ See Figures 47 and 48

Many late model vehicles utilize single, ribbed, serpentine belts to drive engine accessories, such as the alternator, water pump, power steering pump or A/C compressor off the crankshaft.

The serpentine belt and pulleys should be inspected every 3,000 miles (4,800 km) or 3 months for evidence of wear such as cracking, fraying, incorrect alignment and incorrect tension. Proper maintenance of the belt and pulleys can extend normal belt life.

✳✳ WARNING

DO NOT use belt dressings in an attempt to extend belt life. Belt dressing will soften the serpentine belt, causing deterioration. Oil or grease contamination on the belt or pulleys will have the same effect. Keep the drive belt system clear of oil, grease, coolant or other contaminants.

Fig. 47 Serpentine drive belts require little attention other than periodic inspection or replacement

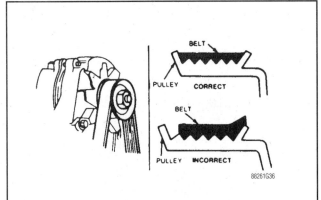

Fig. 48 When checking the serpentine belt, be sure it is properly seated in each of the pulleys

Serpentine Belt Pulley Inspection

▶ See Figure 49

Pulley inspection is most easily accomplished with the drive belt removed so you can freely turn the pulleys and to provide an unobstructed view of each pulley.

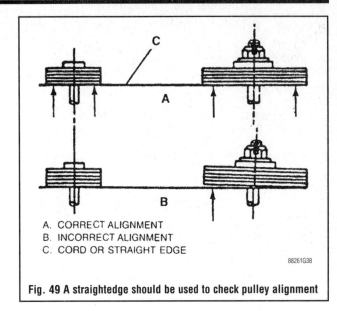

A. CORRECT ALIGNMENT
B. INCORRECT ALIGNMENT
C. CORD OR STRAIGHT EDGE

Fig. 49 A straightedge should be used to check pulley alignment

1. Visually inspect each of the pulleys for chips, nicks, cracks, tool marks, bent sidewalls, severe corrosion or other damage. Replace any pulley showing these signs as they will eventually lead to belt failure.
2. Place a straightedge or position a length of string across any 2 pulleys making sure it touches all points. When using string, be sure it is straight and not bent at one spot in order to contact all points on the pulley.

➡**An assistant is helpful to hold the straightedge or string during the next steps.**

3. Turn each pulley 1/2 revolution and recheck with the straightedge or string.
4. Full contact must be made at all points checked. If contact is not made at all of the points, the pulley may be warped or the shaft may be bent. Replace any damaged parts to assure proper belt life.

Serpentine Belt Inspection

1. Visually check the belt for signs of damage. Routine inspection may reveal cracks in the belt ribs. These cracks will not impair belt performance and are NOT a basis for belt replacement. HOWEVER, if your inspection reveals that sections of the belt are missing, the belt must be replaced to avoid a possible failure.
2. Visually check the belt for proper routing (when compared with the engine compartment label). Make sure the belt is fully seated on all pulleys.
3. Check the automatic drive belt tensioner. The belt is considered serviceable if no wear or damage was found in the previous visual inspections and if the arrow on the tensioner assembly is pointing within the acceptable used belt length range on the tensioner spindle.

ADJUSTING TENSION

V-Belts

▶ See Figure 50

➡**The following procedures require the use of a Belt Tension Gauge.**

If a belt tension gauge is not available, you can adjust tension using the deflection measurements, but this is not as exact. Keep in mind that too tight or too loose an adjustment can damage the components that the belt drives. Too tight will increase preload on the bearings, leading to early failure, while too loose could cause slippage or jerky movements. Of the two possibilities, you would prefer the belt to be a little loose, rather than a little tight. The belt should deflect about ¼ inch (6mm) over a 7–10 inch (178–254mm) span, or ½ inch (13mm) over a 13–16 inch (330–406mm) span.

If a belt tension gauge is available:

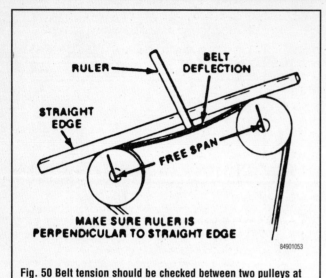

Fig. 50 Belt tension should be checked between two pulleys at the longest unsupported span of belt

1. If the belt is cold, operate the engine (at idle speed) for 15 minutes; the belt will seat itself in the pulleys allowing the belt fibers to relax or stretch. If the belt is hot, allow it to cool, until it is warm to the touch.

➡A used belt is one that has been rotated at least one complete revolution on the pulleys. This begins the belt seating process and it must never be tensioned to the new belt specifications.

2. Disconnect the negative battery cable for safety.
3. Loosen the component-to-mounting bracket bolts.
4. Place a Belt Tension Gauge, place the tension gauge at the center of the belt between the longest span.
5. Applying belt tension pressure, adjust the drive belt tension to the correct specifications.
6. While holding the correct tension on the component, tighten the component-to-mounting bracket bolt.
7. When the belt tension is correct, remove the tension gauge and connect the negative battery cable.

Serpentine Belts

▶ **See Figure 51**

Most late model vehicles are equipped with a single serpentine belt and spring loaded tensioner. The proper belt adjustment is automatically maintained by the tensioner, therefore, no periodic adjustment is needed until the pointer is past the scale on the tensioner. For more information, please refer to the information on serpentine belt and pulley inspection found earlier in this section.

DRIVE BELT ROUTING

▶ **See Figure 52**

A label is normally provided in the engine compartment which details the proper belt routing for the original engine installed in that vehicle. Check the routing label (or vehicle emission control information label) for an illustration which resembles your motor first. If no label is present or if the label does not match your engine (perhaps an engine swap was performed on older vehicles before you were the owner).

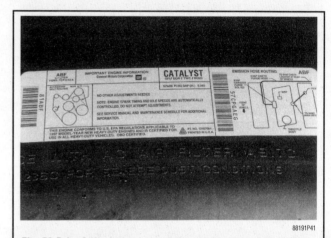

Fig. 52 Drive belt routing is normally provided on a label in the engine compartment

DRIVE BELT REPLACEMENT

V-Belts

▶ **See Figures 53, 54, 55 and 56**

1. Disconnect the negative battery cable for safety.
2. Loosen the component-to-mounting bracket bolts.
3. Rotate the component to relieve the tension on the drive belt.
4. Slip the drive belt from the pulleys and remove it from the engine.

Fig. 51 Typical automatic belt tensioner showing wear indicator marks

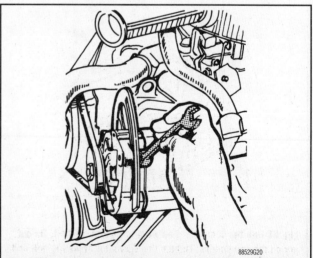

Fig. 53 Loosen the adjusting bolt. If necessary, loosen the bolt that the component pivots on.

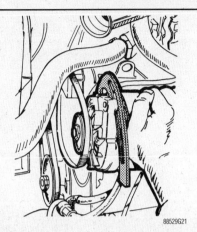

Fig. 54 Push the component in until there is enough slack in the belt to remove it. Remove the belt from the component pulley and the crankshaft pulley. If the component belt is behind another belt, the interfering belt will also have to be removed.

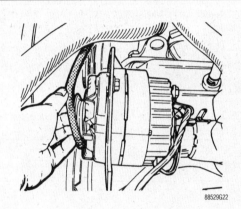

Fig. 55 Install the new belt over the crankshaft and component pulleys. Be sure you have the correct belt. It should fit even with the top of the pulley groove and should not require too much movement of the alternator to properly tension it.

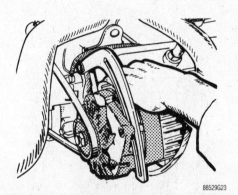

Fig. 56 Pull the component outward to tighten the belt. Do not pry on the component. Tighten the alternator adjusting bolt and pivot bolts (if loosened). Check the belt tension, and recheck it in about 200 miles; new belts will stretch with use.

➡**If the engine uses more than one belt, it may be necessary to remove other belts that are in front of the one being removed.**

5. To install, reverse the removal procedures. Adjust the component drive belt tension to specifications.

Serpentine Belts

◆ **See Figure 57**

For serpentine belts replacement is a relatively simple matter of rotating the tensioner off the belt (to relieve tension) and holding the tensioner in this position as the belt is slipped from its pulley. Depending on the model, engine and year of production, there are various methods of rotating the tensioner, but all require a breaker bar, large ratchet or wrench.

1. Before you begin, visually confirm the belt routing to the engine compartment label (if present). If you cannot make a match (perhaps it is not the original motor), scribble your own diagram before proceeding.
2. Disconnect the negative battery cable for safety.
3. Install the appropriate sized breaker bar, wrench, or socket to the tensioner arm or pulley, as applicable.
4. Rotate the tensioner and slip the belt from the tensioner pulley.

Fig. 57 Rotate the tensioner using a wrench or specially designed tensioner tool and hold in this position while removing the belt from the pulleys

5. Once the belt is free from the tensioner, CAREFULLY rotate the tensioner back into position. DO NOT allow the tensioner to suddenly snap into place or damage could occur to the assembly.
6. Slip the belt from the remaining pulleys (this can get difficult if there is little room to work between components). Work slowly and be patient.
7. Once the belt is free, remove it from the engine compartment.

To install:

8. Route the belt over all the pulleys except one, and the tensioner. Refer to engine compartment label before beginning.
9. Rotate the tensioner pulley and hold it while you finish slipping the belt into position. Slowly allow the tensioner into contact with the belt. DO NOT allow the tensioner to suddenly snap into place or damage could occur to the assembly.
10. Check to see if the correct V-groove tracking is around each pulley.

✶✶ WARNING

Improper V-groove tracking will cause the belt to fail in a short period.

11. Connect the negative battery cable.

Evaporative Canister

SERVICING

▶ See Figures 58, 59, 60, 61 and 62

Check the evaporation control system, if so equipped, every 15,000 miles (24,000 km) or every 12 months. Check the fuel and vapor lines/hoses for proper connections, correct routing, and condition. Replace damaged or deteriorated parts as necessary.

To check the operation of the carbon canister purge control valve, disconnect the rubber hose between the canister control valve and the T-fitting at the T-fitting. Apply vacuum to the hose leading to the control valve. The vacuum condition should be maintained indefinitely. If the control valve leaks, remove the top cover of the valve and check for a dislocated or cracked diaphragm. If the diaphragm is damaged, a repair kit containing a new diaphragm, retainer, and spring is available and should be installed.

Some carbon canisters have a replaceable air filter in the bottom of the canister. The filter element should be checked once a year or every 15,000 miles (24,000 km); more frequently if the vehicle is operated in dusty areas. Replace the filter by pulling it out of the bottom of the canister and installing a new one.

Fig. 60 Remove the lines to the evaporative canister assembly before removing the canister

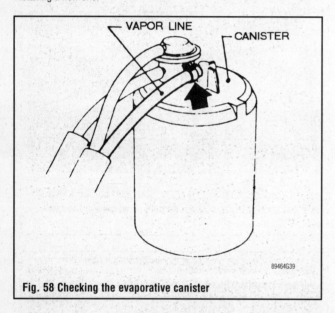

Fig. 58 Checking the evaporative canister

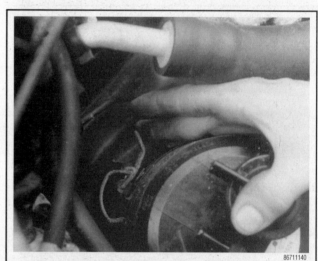

Fig. 61 Some canisters are retained by a simple clamp, while others are bolted into the vehicle

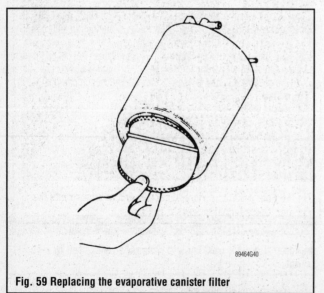

Fig. 59 Replacing the evaporative canister filter

Fig. 62 Lift the canister from the vehicle carefully and store in an upright position

Hoses

INSPECTION

▶ See Figures 63 and 64

Inspect the condition of the radiator hoses, heater hoses and clamps periodically. Early spring and late fall are often good times to perform this, as well as other routine maintenance.

Make sure the engine and cooling system are cold. Visually inspect for cracked, rotted or collapsed hoses, and replace as necessary. Run your hand along the length of the hose. If a weak or swollen spot is noted when squeezing the hose wall, replace the hose.

Fig. 63 Check for over tightened clamps which will cause the hose to bulge

Fig. 64 A bulging hose like this may be ready to blow

REPLACEMENT

▶ See Figures 65, 66 and 67

1. Drain the coolant into a suitable container (if the coolant is to be reused). If the coolant is to be replaced, place it in a suitable container and take it to a recycling point.

✳✳ WARNING

When draining the coolant, keep in mind that cats and dogs are attracted by ethylene glycol antifreeze, and are quite likely to drink any that is left in an uncovered container or in puddles on the ground. This will prove fatal in sufficient quantity. Always drain the coolant into a sealable container.

2. Loosen the hose clamps at each end of the hose that requires replacement.

Fig. 65 Loosen the drain plug at the lower portion of the radiator to allow coolant to drain. If drainage is slow, ensure the radiator cap is removed

Fig. 66 Pour a 50/50 mixture of coolant and antifreeze into the radiator. Use a funnel to prevent spillage

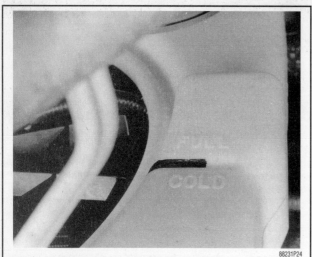

Fig. 67 Ensure the coolant level is at the proper level on the overflow bottle

3. Twist, pull and slide the hose off the radiator, water pump, thermostat housing or heater connection.

4. Clean the hose mounting connections. Inspect the hose clamps and replace any that are rusted or worn.

5. Position the hose clamps on the new hose.

6. Coat the connection surfaces with a water resistant sealer or equivalent and slide the hose into position. Make sure the hose clamps are located beyond the raised bead of the connector (if equipped) and centered in the clamping area of the connection.

7. Tighten the clamps evenly. Do not overtighten.

8. Refill the cooling system.

9. Start the engine and allow it to reach normal operating temperature. Check for coolant leaks, then top off the coolant level as necessary.

ADDITIONAL PREVENTIVE MAINTENANCE CHECKS

Antifreeze

▶ **See Figure 68**

At least every other year on Glycol based coolants, the engine cooling system should be inspected, flushed, and refilled with fresh coolant. If the

coolant is left in the system too long, it loses its ability to prevent rust and corrosion. If the coolant has too much water, it won't protect against freezing.

Silicate free coolants such as DEX-COOL® can go for 100,000 miles (160,000 km) or 5 years, whichever comes first. However, if you add a silicate coolant to the system (even in small amounts) premature engine, heater core or radiator corrosion may result. In addition, the coolant will have to be changed sooner (12,000 miles (19,300 km) or every year, just like other vehicles not using DEX-COOL® or other Silicate-free coolant).

Radiator Cap

▶ **See Figures 69 and 70**

For efficient operation of the vehicle's cooling system, the radiator cap should have a holding pressure which meets manufacturer's specifications. A cap which fails to hold the specified pressure should be replaced.

Fig. 69 Inspect the radiator cap gasket and seal. Replace the cap if either is damaged

Fig. 68 Use a coolant hydrometer to check the condition of the coolant in your engine

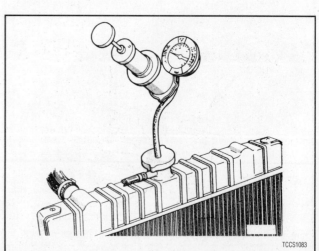

Fig. 70 The cooling system should be pressure checked to ensure it is leak free. The same tester will also check the radiator cap

TROUBLESHOOTING, WHERE DO I START?

Logical Diagnostic Procedures

Diagnosis of a driveability problem requires attention to detail and following the diagnostic procedures in the correct order. Resist the temptation to begin extensive testing before completing the preliminary diagnostic steps. The preliminary or visual inspection must be completed in detail before diagnosis begins. In many cases this will shorten diagnostic time and often cure the problem without the need for involved electronic testing.

There are two basic ways to check your vehicle fuel system for problems. These are by symptom diagnosis and by the on-board computer self-diagnostic system. The first place to start is always the preliminary inspection. Intermittent problems are the most difficult to locate. If the problem is not present at the time you are testing you may not be able to locate the fault.

PRELIMINARY INSPECTION

▶ See Figures 71, 72, 73 and 74

The visual inspection of all components is possibly the most critical step of diagnosis. A detailed examination of connectors, wiring and vacuum hoses can often lead to a repair without further diagnosis. Also, take into consideration if the vehicle has been serviced recently. Sometimes things

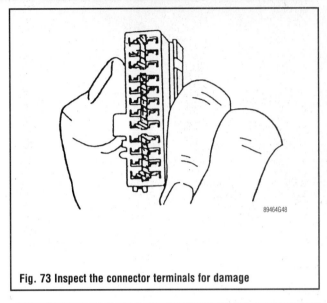

Fig. 73 Inspect the connector terminals for damage

Fig. 71 Perform underhood inspection of all wiring and hoses

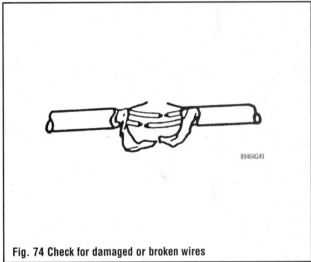

Fig. 74 Check for damaged or broken wires

get reconnected in the wrong place, or not at all. A careful inspector will check the undersides of hoses as well as the integrity of hard-to-reach hoses blocked by the air cleaner or other components. Correct routing for vacuum hoses can be obtained from your specific vehicle service manual, "Chilton Total Car Care Manual", or Vehicle Emission Control Information (VECI) label in the engine compartment of the vehicle. Wiring should be checked carefully for any sign of strain, burning, crimping or terminals pulled out from a connector.

Checking connectors at components or in harnesses is required; usually, pushing them together will reveal a loose fit. Also, check electrical connectors for corroded, bent, damaged, improperly seated pins, and bad wire crimps to terminals. Pay particular attention to ground circuits, making sure they are not loose or corroded. Remember to inspect connectors and hose fittings at components not mounted on the engine, such as the evaporative canister or relays mounted on the fender aprons. Any component or wiring in the vicinity of a fluid leak or spillage should be given extra attention during inspection.

Additionally, inspect maintenance items such as belt condition and tension, battery charge and condition and the radiator cap carefully. Any of these very simple items may affect the system enough to set a fault code.

DIAGNOSIS BY SYMPTOM

Before the advent of the self-diagnostic system, diagnosis by symptom was the only method for investigation of an automotive problem. An attempt

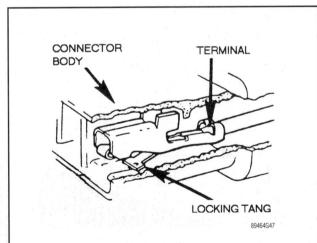

Fig. 72 Check the individual terminals and wiring connectors for damage

	Throttle Position Sensor	Coolant Temperature Sensor	MAP or MAF sensor	Air Temperature Sensor	Ignition Coil	Distributor	Spark Plug Wires	Fuel Filter	Air Filter	Vacuum Leak	Engine Mechanical	Knock Sensor / Spark Control	EGR System	Idle Control System	Camshaft sensor/Dist. pick-up	Oxygen Sensor	Ignition Module / Engine Computer	Torque Converter Clutch	PCV System
No Start	u	u	u		•	•		•		u	•			u	•		•		
Hard Start	•	•	•		•	•	•			•									u
Hesitation	•		•		•	•	•	•	•	•	•			•					
Stalling	•				•	•	•	•	•	•	•			•				•	u
Poor Idle	•				•	•	•			•				•	•				•
Dieseling								•				•		•					
Engine Lamp ON	•	•	•	•								•	•	•	•	•			
Knocks or Pings							•					•		•		•	•	•	•
High Hydrocarbons	u	u	u		•	•	•	u	•	u	•			u		•			
Black Smoke	u	•	•	•						•						•			
Blue Smoke											•								
Poor Fuel Mileage	•	•	•	•	•	•	•		•	•	•			•		•		•	u
Lack of Power	•	•	•	•	•	•	•	•	•	•	•							•	u
Back fires		•			•	•	•		•	•	•						•		u
Runs Poor Cold	•				•	•	•		•	•	•	u	•			•		u	u
Runs Poor Hot	•	•	•	•	•	•	•	•	•	•	•	•	u	•	•	•	•	u	u
High speed surging			•	•				•										•	u

u: Although possible it is unlikely this component is at fault. A totally open or shorted circuit, or severe component fault may cause this condition.

was made to solve problems by reviewing the symptoms and performing tests on suspected components until a defective component was located. The problem was then corrected and the vehicle checked for any other problems. This method is still used frequently today when a driveability complaint is made, but no code is set in the electronic control unit's memory.

When diagnosing by symptom the first step is to find out if the problem really exists. This may sound like a waste of time but you must be able to recreate the problem before you begin testing. This is called an "operational check". Each operational check will give either a positive or negative answer (symptom). A positive answer is found when the check gives a positive result (the horn blows when you press the horn button). A negative answer is found when the check gives a negative result (the radio does not play when you turn the knob on). After performing several operational checks, a pattern may develop. This pattern is used in the next step of diagnosis to determine related symptoms.

In order to determine related symptoms, perform operational checks on circuits related to the problem circuit (the radio does not work and the dash lights do not go on). These checks can be made without the use of any test equipment. Simply follow the wires in the wiring harness or, if available, obtain a copy of your vehicle's specific wiring diagram. If you see that the radio and the dash lights are on the same circuit, first check the radio to see if it works. Then check the dash lights. If the neither the radio or dash lights work, this tells you that there is a problem in that circuit. Perform additional operational checks on that circuit and compile a list of symptoms.

When analyzing your answers, a defect will always lie between a check which gave a positive answer and one which gave a negative answer. Look at your list of symptoms and try to determine probable areas to test. If you get negative answers on related circuits, then maybe the problem is at the common junction. After you have determined what the symptoms are and where you are going to look for defects, develop a plan for isolating the trouble. Ask a knowledgeable automotive person which components frequently fail on your vehicle. Also notice which parts or components are easiest to reach and how can you accomplish the most by doing the least amount of checks.

A common way of diagnosis is to use the split-in-half technique. Each test that is made essentially splits the trouble area in half. By performing this technique several times the area where a problem is located becomes smaller and smaller until the problem can be isolated in a single wire or component. This area is most commonly between the two closest checkpoints that produced a negative answer and a positive answer.

After the problem is located, perform the repair procedure. This may involve replacing a component, repairing a component or damaged wire, or making an adjustment.

➡**Never assume a component is defective until you have thoroughly tested it.**

The final step is to make sure the complaint is corrected. Remember that the symptoms that you uncover may lead to several problems that require separate repairs. Repeat the diagnosis and test procedures repeatedly until all negative symptoms are corrected.

DIAGNOSIS BY STORED TROUBLE CODE

▶ **See Figures 75, 76, 77 and 78**

When a fault code is detected, it appears as a flash of the Malfunction Indicator Lamp (MIL) on the instrument panel. This indicates that an abnormal signal in the system has been recognized by the control module.

When diagnosing by code, the first step is to read any fault codes from the control module using a scan tool. On some vehicles, fault codes can be read as flashes of the MIL after grounding terminals on the DLC. The fault codes will identify the area to perform more in-depth testing. After the fault codes have been read, proceed to test each of the components and component circuits indicated. Continue performing individual component tests until the failed component is located, Remember, fault codes do indicate the presence of a failure, but they do not identify the failed component directly.

Fig. 75 Stored fault code information is normally accessed through the Data Link Connector (DLC)

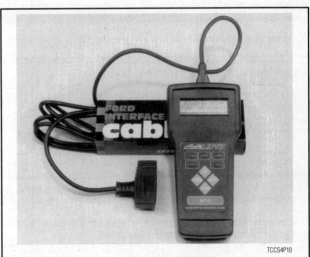

Fig. 76 Inexpensive scan tools, such as this Auto Xray®, are available to interface with almost any vehicle

Fig. 77 The data display function of the Auto Xray® can also provide live sensor voltage information

Fig. 78 The AutoTap®, from B&B Electronics, connects to a personal computer and retrieves stored codes and live data

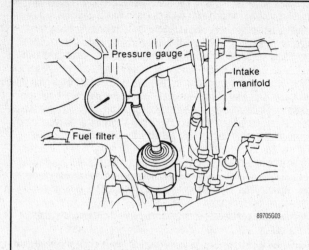

Fig. 80 On some systems, the pressure gauge is simply connected in-line

Two Important Tests

FUEL SYSTEM BASICS

◆ **See Figures 79, 80 and 81**

Two simple tests-pressure and volume-can easily verify the mechanical integrity of the vehicle's fuel supply and return systems. Problems within the fuel supply or return system can cause many driveability problems because the control system can't compensate for a mechanical problem. Nor can the system adjust the air/fuel mixture when the system is in open loop or back-up mode. Moreover, a control system's parameters are programmed based on a set flow rate and system pressure. Therefore, even if the computer were adjusting the air/fuel mixture, the computer's calculations would be wrong whenever the system pressure or volume was incorrect.

➡**When testing fuel system pressure, always use a pressure gauge that is capable of handling the system pressure. Old style vacuum/pressure gauges will not work with most fuel injection systems**

The fuel system's pressure can be thoroughly verified by performing both static and dynamic tests. Dynamic tests are used to determine the system's

overall operating condition while the engine is running. For example, if the pressure is low, the problem is most likely to be in the supply or high side of the system. Likewise, if the fuel pressure is high, the problem is going to be on the return or low side of the fuel system. All pressure tests should be taken on the high or supply side of the fuel system.

If a dynamic test reveals that the pressure is below manufacturer specifications, the problem is caused by one or more of the following items: weak pumps, clogged or restricted fuel filter or lines, external leaks bad check valves, or a faulty fuel pressure regulator. But if a test reveals pressures above the desired specification, then the problem is caused by one or more of these items: restricted or clogged return lines, faulty EVAP systems, vacuum leak at the pressure regulator, or a defective fuel pressure regulator.

However, if the pressure is high on a return less fuel system, the cause, most likely, is a defective pressure regulator or clogged/faulty injectors. The causes are slightly different on return less systems because the regulator is located in or near the fuel tank and there is no fuel return line used on these systems. However, the systems which use a remotely mounted fuel pressure regulator require a short return line. Thus, there is no excess fuel beyond the injectors and the measured pressure is already the regulated pressure.

Many manufacturers are switching to return less fuel systems because of the advantages they provide. One advantage is lower evaporative emissions which allows less frequent purge cycles and the use of smaller canisters. The evaporative emissions are lower on a return-less fuel system because

Fig. 79 Never attempt to test a high pressure fuel injection system with a standard vacuum/pressure tester

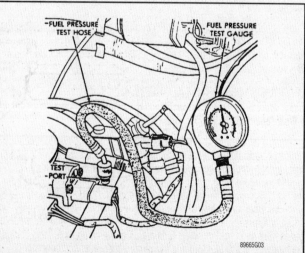

Fig. 81 Most modern systems use a Schrader valve on the fuel rail as a test port. These require a special fitting for your gauge

the fuel doesn't absorb any heat from the engine compartment. This prevents it from turning into a vapor as it returns to the fuel tank.

Another example of how return-less fuel systems are different from conventional fuel injection systems is that they may not use a frame/engine compartment mounted fuel filter. Most return-less systems use a combination fuel filter/pressure regulator which is mounted on top of the fuel pump module. The fuel pump module is located in the tank. Other return-less systems use an in-line filter on the frame that incorporates an integral fuel pressure regulator. These systems also utilize a short return line from the fuel filter to the fuel pump module in the tank. Yet, others use a regular frame/engine mounted filter in conjunction with a fuel pressure regulator and filter assembly in the tank.

Previously we mentioned that a static pressure test should also be performed. This test can be performed before or after a dynamic test with the engine off. These tests are useful for determining the sealing capacity of the system. If the fuel system leaks down after the engine is shut off, the vehicle will experience extended crank times while the system builds up enough fuel pressure to start. If the system is prone to losing residual pressure too quickly, it also usually suffers from low fuel pressure during the dynamic test. In addition to verifying that the system is holding residual pressure, a static test can also verify that the system is receiving the initial priming pulse at startup.

However, don't assume that the correct amount of fuel is being delivered just because the system pressure is within specifications. The only way to measure fuel volume is to open the fuel system into a graduated container and measure the fuel output while cranking the engine. Some manufacturers specify that a certain amount of fuel be dispersed over a short period of time, but generally the pump should be able to supply at least one pint over a period of 20 seconds. If the fuel output is below the recommended specification, there is a restriction in the fuel supply or the fuel pump is weak.

In summary, pressure and volume tests provide information about the overall condition of the fuel system. The information obtained from these tests will set the direction and path of your diagnosis.

JUMP STARTING

Jump Starting a Dead Battery

▶ See Figure 82

Whenever a vehicle must be jump started, precautions must be followed in order to prevent the possibility of personal injury. Remember that batteries contain a small amount of explosive hydrogen gas which is a by-product of battery charging. Sparks should always be avoided when working around batteries, especially when attaching jumper cables. To minimize the possibility of accidental sparks, follow the procedure carefully.

✳✳ WARNING

NEVER hook the batteries up in a series circuit or the entire electrical system will go up in smoke, especially the starter!

Vehicles equipped with a diesel engine utilize two 12 volt batteries, one on either side of the engine compartment. The batteries are connected in a parallel circuit (positive terminal to positive terminal, negative terminal to negative terminal). Hooking the batteries up in parallel circuit increases battery cranking power without increasing total battery voltage output. Output remains at 12 volts. On the other hand, hooking two 12 volt batteries up in a series circuit (positive terminal to negative terminal, positive terminal to negative terminal) increases total battery output to 24 volts (12 volts plus 12 volts).

Jump Starting Precautions

1. Be sure that both batteries are of the same voltage. Most vehicles on the road today utilize a 12 volt charging system.
2. Be sure that both batteries are of the same polarity (have the same grounded terminal; in most cases NEGATIVE).
3. Be sure that the vehicles are not touching or a short circuit could occur.
4. On serviceable batteries, be sure the vent cap holes are not obstructed.

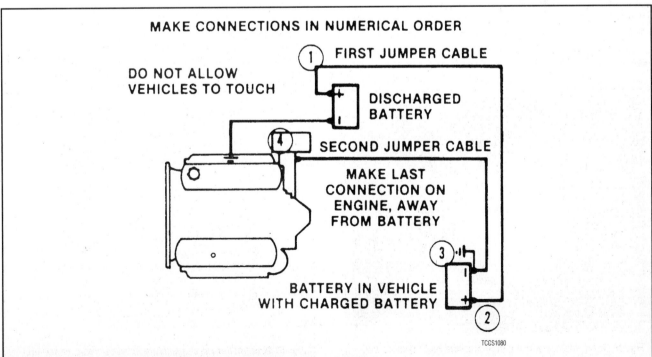

Fig. 82 Connect the jumper cables to the batteries and engine in the order shown

5. Do not smoke or allow sparks anywhere near the batteries.

6. In cold weather, make sure the battery electrolyte is not frozen. This can occur more readily in a battery that has been in a state of discharge.

7. Do not allow electrolyte to contact your skin or clothing.

Jump Starting Procedure

1. Make sure that the voltages of the 2 batteries are the same. Most batteries and charging systems are of the 12 volt variety.

2. Pull the jumping vehicle (with the good battery) into a position so the jumper cables can reach the dead battery and that vehicle's engine. Make sure that the vehicles do NOT touch.

3. Place the transmissions of both vehicles in NEUTRAL or PARK, as applicable, then firmly set their parking brakes.

➡**If necessary for safety reasons, both vehicle's hazard lights may be operated throughout the entire procedure without significantly increasing the difficulty of jump starting the dead battery.**

4. Turn all lights and accessories **OFF** on both vehicles. Make sure the ignition switches on both vehicles are turned to the **OFF** position.

5. Cover the battery cell caps with a rag, but do not cover the terminals.

6. Make sure the terminals on both batteries are clean and free of corrosion or proper electrical connection will be impeded. If necessary, clean the battery terminals before proceeding.

7. Identify the positive (+) and negative (-) terminals on both batteries.

8. Connect the first jumper cable to the positive (+) terminal of the dead battery, then connect the other end of that cable to the positive (+) terminal of the booster (good) battery.

9. Connect one end of the other jumper cable to the negative (-) terminal of the booster battery and the other cable clamp to an engine bolt head, alternator bracket or other solid, metallic point on the dead battery's engine.

Try to pick a ground on the engine that is positioned away from the battery, in order to minimize the possibility of the 2 clamps touching should one loosen during the procedure. DO NOT connect this clamp to the negative (-) terminal of the bad battery.

✳✳ CAUTION

Be very careful to keep the jumper cables away from moving parts (cooling fan, belts, etc.) on both engines.

10. Check to make sure that the cables are routed away from any moving parts, then start the donor vehicle's engine. Run the engine at moderate speed for several minutes to allow the dead battery a chance to receive some initial charge.

11. With the donor vehicle's engine still running slightly above idle, try to start the vehicle with the dead battery. Crank the engine for no more than 10 seconds at a time and let the starter cool for at least 20 seconds between tries. If the vehicle does not start within 3 tries, it is likely that something else is also wrong.

12. Once the vehicle is started, allow it to run at idle for a few seconds to make sure that it is properly operating.

13. Turn on the headlights, heater blower and, if equipped, the rear defroster of both vehicles in order to reduce the severity of voltage spikes and subsequent risk of damage to the vehicles' electrical systems when the cables are disconnected.

14. Carefully disconnect the cables in the reverse order of connection. Start with the negative cable that is attached to the engine ground, then the negative cable on the donor battery. Disconnect the positive cable from the donor battery, then disconnect the positive cable from the formerly dead battery. Be careful when disconnecting the cables from the positive terminals not to allow the alligator clips to touch any metal on either vehicle or a short circuit and sparks will occur.

RELIEVING FUEL SYSTEM PRESSURE

Pressure relief

Since fuel injection systems are pressurized, it is necessary to relieve the pressure prior to opening the system for repairs or testing. Multi-Port fuel injection systems are commonly equipped with a Schrader valve which, when used in conjunction with a fuel pressure gauge the system pressure may be relieved. Relieving the fuel system pressure is also necessary on TBI, Bosch CIS, and other fuel injection systems that are not equipped with a Schrader valve type pressure test port. Without a Schrader valve, the system has to be opened and have a pressure gauge connected in-line with the system's supply in order to measure pressure.

The pressure can be relieved using one of two methods. The first and easiest method is to disable the vehicle's fuel pump and crank the engine over. If the system is already primed, the engine will start and then stall. After the engine stalls, crank the engine over for an additional 20 seconds while the fuel pump(s) is disabled. This will ensure that all the fuel pressure has been released. However, even with the pressure released, there may still be some fuel remaining in the lines. So have a shop rag or container ready to catch it when the lines are opened. The other method is to use a fuel pressure gauge's release valve on the systems equipped with a Schrader valve type of pressure test port.

Furthermore, many TBI systems have a constant bleed passage which reduces the system's residual pressure to zero after the engine is shut off. However, it is still good practice to relieve the system pressure before opening it as a precaution to prevent an injury.

Disabling the fuel pump

Removing the fuel pump fuse or relay from the fuse block is the most commonly used method. But this won't work for all vehicles because some fuses or relays protect the ignition and/or the fuel injector circuits as well. For exam-

ple, on vehicles manufactured by Ford (all except Explorer), the fuel pump is disabled by disconnecting the inertia switch. In addition, on pre-1990 BMW models, the fuel pump can be disabled by disconnecting its ground.

However, there is a universal method that will work on all fuel injected systems. This method entails disconnecting the fuel pump electrical connector. Nevertheless, make sure to disconnect all the connectors because some systems use multiple fuel pumps. Alternatively, you can always follow the manufacturer's recommended fuel pressure relief procedure. For specific procedures on your vehicle, consult your "Chilton Total Car Care Manual".

FUEL PRESSURE RELIEF

◗ **See Figures 83, 84 and 85**

This is a generic procedure for most electronically fuel injected vehicles. For specific procedures on your vehicle, consult your "Chilton Total Car Care (TCC) Manual".

1. Disable the fuel pump by one of the following methods:
- Remove the fuel pump fuse.
- Remove the fuel pump relay.
- Locate and disconnect the fuel pump wiring.

➡**When removing the fuel pump fuse or relay to disable the fuel pump, it is important to make certain that the fuel injectors are not part of this circuit. If the injectors do not operate the residual fuel system pressure will not be relieved.**

2. Start the engine and operate it until it stalls. Once the engine has stalled, crank the starter for an additional 10 seconds.

3. Place a rag over the connection in which you intend to disconnect and carefully separate the connections. Use the rag to absorb any remaining fuel.

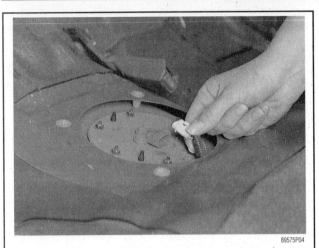

Fig. 83 On some vehicles, the fuel pump wiring can be accessed through a removable plate under the rear seat or in the trunk

Fig. 84 Other vehicles have the fuel pump connector located along the frame rail at the rear of the vehicle

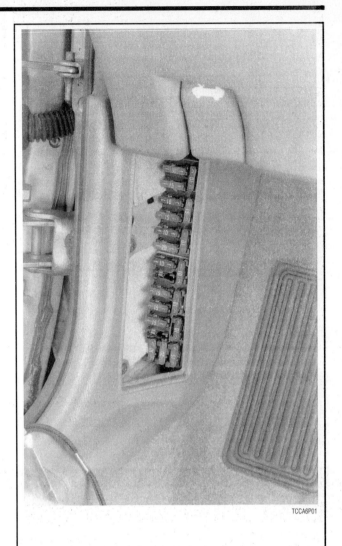

Fig. 85 A safe way to relieve fuel system pressure on most systems is to remove the fuel pump fuse or relay and crank the engine

SPECIAL FUEL LINE CONNECTORS

Thread Connectors

▶ See Figure 86

Probably the most common type of fuel system connector is the threaded connection. On these connections tightening the flare nut or threaded connection seals the fuel line. There are other types of threaded connectors that may use an O-ring type seal. Always check the condition of the O-rings on this type of connection.

➡ **Always use two wrenches when tightening threaded connectors and be careful not to twist or kink the fuel line while tightening.**

Chrysler Connectors

Chrysler vehicles use different types of quick-connect fittings. These are used to attach various fuel system components. These are: a single-tab type, a two-tab type, a plastic retainer ring type or a latch clip type.

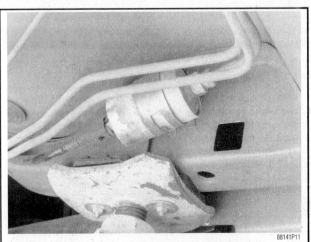

Fig. 86 This fuel filter illustrates the difference between a threaded connector (right) and a tab style connector (left)

SINGLE-TAB TYPE

▶ **See Figure 87**

This type of fitting is equipped with a single pull tab. The tab is removable. After the tab is removed, the quick-connect fitting can be separated from the fuel system component.

➡ **The interior components (O-rings, spacers) of this type of quick-connect fitting are not serviced separately, but new pull tabs are available. Do not attempt to repair damaged fittings or fuel lines/ tubes. If repair is necessary, replace the complete fuel tube assembly.**

❋❋ CAUTION

The fuel system is under a constant pressure (even with the engine off). Before servicing any fuel system hoses, fittings or lines, the fuel system pressure must be released

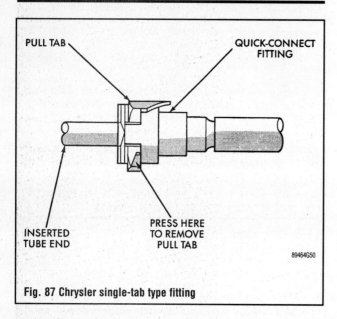

Fig. 87 Chrysler single-tab type fitting

Removal & Installation

▶ **See Figures 88 and 89**

1. Perform the fuel pressure release procedure.
2. Disconnect negative battery cable from battery.
3. Clean the fitting of any foreign material before disassembly.
4. Press the release tab on the side of fitting to release pull tab.

❋❋ WARNING

If this release tab is not pressed prior to releasing the pull tab, the pull tab will be damaged.

5. While pressing the release tab on the side of the fitting, use a screwdriver to pry up the pull tab.
6. Raise the pull tab until it separates from the quick-connect fitting. Discard the old pull tab.
7. Disconnect the quick-connect fitting from the fuel system component being serviced.
8. Inspect the quick-connect fitting body and fuel system component for damage. Replace as necessary.
9. Prior to connecting the quick-connect fitting to component being serviced, check condition of fitting and component. Clean the parts with a lint-free cloth. Lubricate them with clean engine oil.

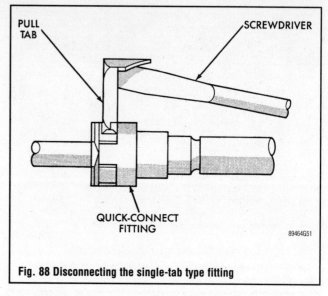

Fig. 88 Disconnecting the single-tab type fitting

10. Insert the quick-connect fitting into the fuel tube or fuel system component until the built-on stop on the fuel tube or component rests against back of fitting.
11. Obtain a new pull tab. Push the new tab down until it locks into place in the quick-connect fitting.
12. Verify a locked condition by firmly pulling on fuel tube and fitting .
13. Connect negative cable to battery
14. Start engine and check for leaks.

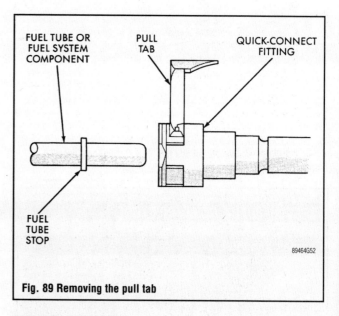

Fig. 89 Removing the pull tab

TWO-TAB TYPE FITTING

▶ **See Figure 90**

This type of fitting is equipped with tabs located on both sides of the fitting . These tabs are supplied for disconnecting the quick-connect fitting from component being serviced.

➡ **The interior components (O-rings, spacers) of this type of quick-connect fitting are not serviced separately, but new pull tabs are available. Do not attempt to repair damaged fittings or fuel lines/ tubes. If repair is necessary, replace the complete fuel tube assembly.**

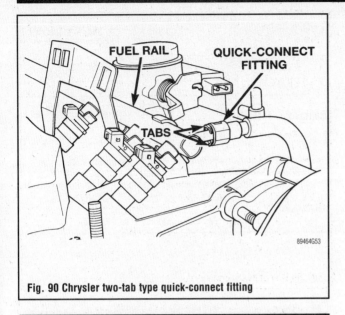

Fig. 90 Chrysler two-tab type quick-connect fitting

✳✳ CAUTION

The fuel system is under a constant pressure (even with the engine off). Before servicing any fuel system hoses, fittings or lines, the fuel system pressure must be released

Removal & Installation

▶ See Figure 91

1. Perform the fuel pressure release procedure.
2. Disconnect negative battery cable from the battery.
3. Clean the fitting of any foreign material before disassembly.
4. To disconnect the quick-connect fitting, squeeze the plastic retainer tabs against the sides of the quick-connect fitting with your fingers. Tool use is not required for removal and may damage plastic retainer. Pull the fitting from the fuel system component being serviced. The plastic retainer will remain on the component being serviced after fitting is disconnected. The O-rings and spacer will remain in the quick- connect fitting connector body.
5. Inspect the quick-connect fitting body and component for damage. Replace as necessary.

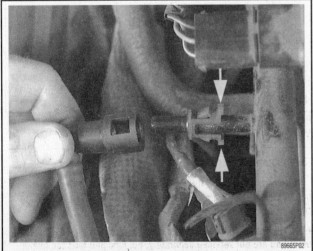

Fig. 91 To release the two-tab fitting, squeeze the tabs together and pull the fuel line away from the fitting

✳✳ WARNING

When the quick-connect fitting was disconnected, the plastic retainer will remain on the component being serviced. If this retainer must be removed, very carefully release the retainer from the component with two small screwdrivers. After removal, inspect the retainer for cracks or any damage.

6. Prior to connecting the quick-connect fitting to component being serviced, check condition of fitting and component. Clean the parts with a lint-free cloth. Lubricate them with clean engine oil.
7. Insert the quick-connect fitting to the component being serviced and into the plastic retainer. When a connection is made, a click will be heard.
8. Verify a locked condition by firmly pulling on fuel tube and fitting.
9. Connect the negative cable to battery.
10. Start the engine and check for leaks.

PLASTIC RETAINER RING TYPE FITTING

▶ See Figure 92

This type of fitting can be identified by the use of a full-round plastic retainer ring usually black in color.

➡The interior components (O-rings, spacers) of this type of quick-connect fitting are not serviced separately, but new pull tabs are available. Do not attempt to repair damaged fittings or fuel lines/ tubes. If repair is necessary, replace the complete fuel tube assembly.

✳✳ CAUTION

The fuel system is under a constant pressure (even with the engine off). Before servicing any fuel system hoses, fittings or lines, the fuel system pressure must be released.

Removal & Installation

1. Perform the fuel pressure release procedure.
2. Disconnect negative battery cable from the battery.
3. Clean the fitting of any foreign material before disassembly.
4. To release the fuel system component from the quick-connect fitting, firmly push the fitting towards the component being serviced while firmly pushing the plastic retainer ring into the fitting. With the plastic ring depressed, pull the fitting from the component. The plastic retainer

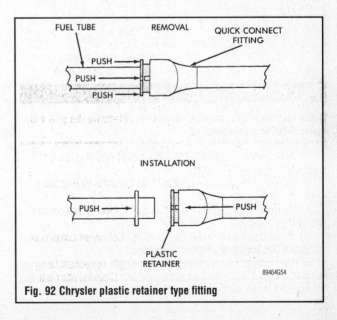

Fig. 92 Chrysler plastic retainer type fitting

ring must be pressed squarely into the fitting body. If this retainer is cocked during removal, it may be difficult to disconnect fitting. Use an open-end wrench on the shoulder of the plastic retainer ring to aid in disconnection.

5. After disconnection, the plastic retainer ring will remain with the quick-connect fitting connector body.

6. Inspect fitting connector body, plastic retainer ring and fuel system component for damage. Replace as necessary.

7. Prior to connecting the quick-connect fitting to component being serviced, check condition of fitting and component. Clean the parts with a lint-free cloth. Lubricate them with clean engine oil.

8. Insert the quick-connect fitting into the component being serviced until a click is felt.

9. Verify a locked condition by firmly pulling on fuel tube and fitting .

10. Connect the negative battery cable to the battery.

11. Start the engine and check for leaks.

Ford Connectors

➥Quick-connect (push type) fuel line fittings must be disconnected using proper procedure or the fitting may be damaged. There are two types of retainers used on the push connect fittings. Line sizes of ⅜ and ⁵⁄₁₆ in. diameter use a hairpin clip retainer. The ¼ in. diameter line connectors use a duck-bill clip retainer. In addition, some engines use spring-lock connections, secured by a garter spring, which require Ford Tool T81P-19623-G (or equivalent) for removal.

HAIRPIN CLIP FITTING

REMOVAL & INSTALLATION

▶ See Figure 93

1. Clean all dirt and grease from the fitting. Spread the two clip legs about ⅛ in. (3mm) each to disengage from the fitting and pull the clip outward from the fitting. Use finger pressure only; do not use any tools.

2. Grasp the fitting and hose assembly and pull away from the steel line. Twist the fitting and hose assembly slightly while pulling, if the assembly sticks.

3. Inspect the hairpin clip for damage, replacing the clip if necessary. Reinstall the clip in position on the fitting.

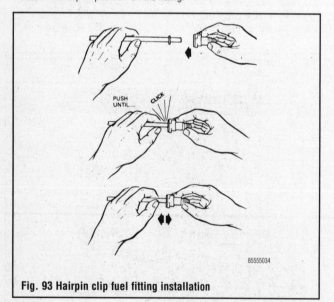

Fig. 93 Hairpin clip fuel fitting installation

4. Inspect the fitting and inside of the connector to ensure freedom from dirt or obstruction. Install the fitting into the connector and push together. A click will be heard when the hairpin snaps into the proper connection. Pull on the line to insure full engagement.

DUCKBILL CLIP FITTING

Removal & Installation

▶ See Figure 94

1. A special tool is available from Ford and other manufacturers for removing the retaining clips. Use Ford Tool T82L-9500-AH or equivalent. If the tool is not on hand, go onto step 2. Align the slot on the push connector disconnect tool with either tab on the retaining clip. Pull the line from the connector.

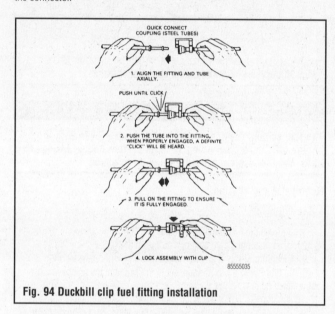

Fig. 94 Duckbill clip fuel fitting installation

2. If the special clip tool is not available, use a pair of narrow 6-inch slip-jaw pliers with a jaw width of 0.2 in (5mm) or less. Align the jaws of the pliers with the openings of the fitting case and compress the part of the retaining clip that engages the case. Compressing the retaining clip will release the fitting, which may be pulled from the connector. Both sides of the clip must be compressed at the same time to disengage.

3. Inspect the retaining clip, fitting end and connector. Replace the clip if any damage is apparent.

4. Push the line into the steel connector until a click is heard, indicating the clip is in place. Pull on the line to check engagement.

SPRING LOCK COUPLING

Removal & Installation

▶ See Figures 95 thru 100

The spring lock coupling is held together by a garter spring inside a circular cage. When the coupling is connected together, the flared end of the female fitting slips behind the garter spring inside the cage of the male fitting. The garter spring and cage then prevent the flared end of the female fitting from pulling out of the cage. As an additional locking feature, most vehicles have a horseshoe-shaped retaining clip that improves the retaining reliability of the spring lock coupling.

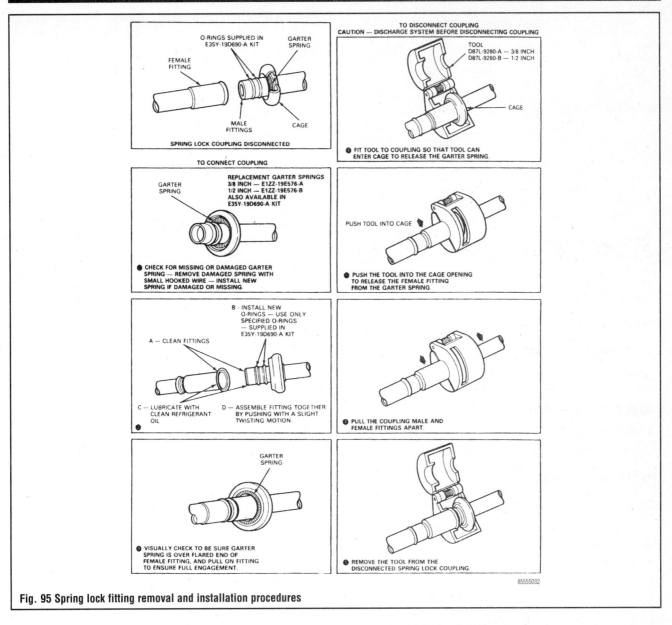

Fig. 95 Spring lock fitting removal and installation procedures

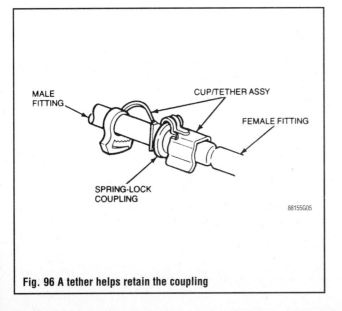

Fig. 96 A tether helps retain the coupling

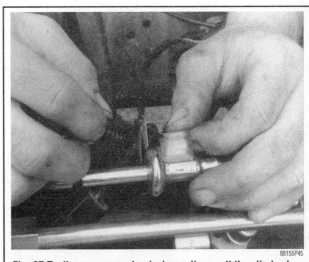

Fig. 97 To disengage a spring lock coupling, pull the clip back off the coupling after cleaning the area . . .

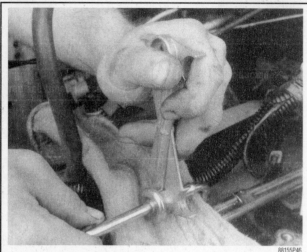

Fig. 98 . . . then insert a removal tool into the coupling to release the spring

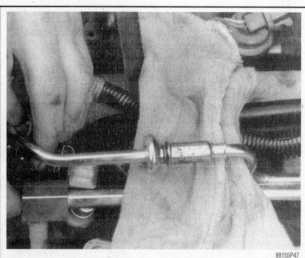

Fig. 99 Use a rag to catch any spilled fuel while pulling the coupling apart . . .

Fig. 100 . . . and be sure to check the O-rings for damage; replace them if necessary

General Motors Connectors

QUICK-CONNECT FITTINGS

Removal & Installation

◗ See Figures 101, 102, 103, 104 and 105

➥This procedure requires tool .137088 or an equivalent aftermarket fuel line quick-connect separator.

1. Grasp both sides of the fitting. Twist the female connector ¼ turn in each direction to loosen any dirt within the fittings. Using compressed air, blow out the dirt from the quick-connect fittings at the end of the fittings.

✳✳ CAUTION

Safety glasses MUST be worn when using compressed air to avoid eye injury due to flying dirt particles!

2. For plastic (hand releasable) fittings, squeeze the plastic retainer release tabs, then pull the connection apart.
3. For metal fittings, choose the correct size tool for the fitting to be disconnected. Insert the proper tool into the female connector, then push inward to release the locking tabs. Pull the connection apart.
4. If it is necessary to remove rust or burrs from the male tube end of a quick-connect fitting, use emery cloth in a radial motion with the tube end to prevent damage to the O-ring sealing surfaces. Using a clean shop towel, wipe off the male tube ends. Inspect all connectors for dirt and burrs. Clean and/or replace it required.
   To install:
5. Apply a few drops of clean engine oil to the male tube end of the fitting.
6. Push the connectors together to cause the retaining tabs/fingers to snap into place.
7. Once installed, pull on both ends of each connection to make sure they are secure.

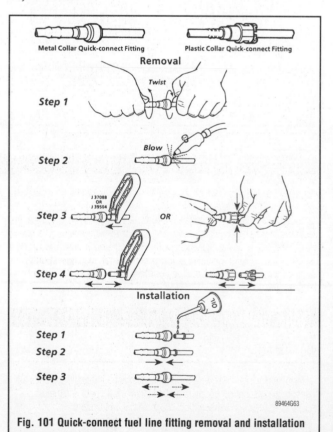

Fig. 101 Quick-connect fuel line fitting removal and installation

Fig. 102 Before disconnecting any fuel lines, make sure to clean all the dirt from around the fittings (see arrows)

Fig. 104 . . . then push inward to release the locking tabs and pull the connector apart

Fig. 103 For metal fittings, insert the tool into the female connector . . .

Fig. 105 View of the female connectors (A) and O-ring (B), once the line is disconnected

FUEL SYSTEM PRESSURE TESTING

In both Electronic and Mechanical fuel injection, one of the most critical tests to be performed is the fuel pressure test. This test will require a special fuel injection pressure gauge kit, usually consisting of a mechanical or electronic pressure gauge along with special adapters to connect this gauge to the fuel system. Many gauge sets will contain their own installation and test procedures. The information below is generic, for specific test pressures and procedures please refer to your test equipment or Chilton Total Car Care manual.

Gauge Installation

ADAPTER KITS

Designed for use with your specific gauge, each kit usually includes all hoses, quick disconnect couplers and adapters, both male & female, needed to access the fuel supply of the fuel injection system.

PRELIMINARY INSPECTION

Inspect all fuel hoses, connections and pipes from the fuel tank to the engine for signs of leakage or deterioration, and repair or replace as needed. Inspect the quality and quantity of fuel in the fuel tank. Inspect the condition of the fuel filter, battery cranking system, ignition system, related electrical wiring and connections, and engine grounds

✳✳ CAUTION

Before connecting the fuel pressure gauge, residual fuel pressure in the system should be released. See "Relieving Fuel System Pressure" in this section for instructions. On certain CMFI and CSFI vehicles there will still be pressure in the system, so be careful when making connections to these systems. Hold a shop towel around the fittings when making the gauge connection or disconnecting lines, to absorb any spilled fuel.

INSTALLING THE FUEL INJECTION PRESSURE TEST GAUGE

All fuel injection systems need to have the gauge installed without interrupting the normal fuel flow to the injector(s). Some vehicles have fittings (Schrader valves) for connecting the gauge, some won't. On vehicles without Schrader valves, the gauge must be tee'd into the pressure line of the system.

On some vehicles a manifold and valve assembly will be used with only one leg of the manifold attached to the vehicle. In these cases be certain that the valve is positioned so the unattached hose is blocked.

INSTALLING A MANIFOLD

When testing a fuel system you want to tie into the fuel flow. On some vehicles this can be done very easily by using an adapter hose that ties into the Schrader valve. In these cases the vehicle manufacturer had you in mind when designing the fuel injection system. Simply use an adapter and connect to the fuel rail directly.

Attaching the Adapters With Manifold Assembly

If there is no Schrader valve you will need to use a special adapter that should be supplied in your kit. Once the adapter is identified, relieve the fuel pressure (refer to the' Fuel Pressure Release Procedure'). Once the fuel pressure is relieved, disconnect the fuel line adapter and attach the male and female adapter in place. Doing this allows the use of a manifold hose assemblies to tie into the fuel flow.

INITIAL TESTS

When beginning a fuel pressure test on a vehicle which is a "no start", be certain there is sufficient fuel in the tank. One way this can be accomplished is by attaching the appropriate adapter to the vehicle and using a 1 liter volume sample bottle. If the vehicle can fill the bottle half way in about 15 seconds, there should be sufficient fuel available to proceed with the diagnostic tests. This is also an excellent way to visually inspect the fuel for contamination.

MANUALLY ACTIVATING THE FUEL PUMP

On most fuel injected vehicles the fuel pump will be activated for a few seconds by turning the ignition key to the **ON** position.

REMOVING THE MANIFOLD

When removing the manifold be sure there is no residual pressure in the fuel line. Remove the fittings from the base of the hose assemblies and any adapters being used. Once the manifold and adapters are removed, inspect the fitting connections and clean and replace any O-rings or washers that may be worn before reattaching the fuel line. Check for leaks after reconnecting the vehicle fuel rail system.

Troubleshooting Common Fuel System Problems

ALL SYSTEMS

Fuel Pressure is Low

Check and replace the fuel filter if necessary. Check the electrical supply and ground to fuel pump, and repair if needed. Block the return line, and if fuel pressure rises the problem is most likely in the fuel pressure regulator.

✷✷ WARNING

Do not pinch plastic or braided steel lines.

If fuel pressure is still low, check for: leaking injectors, leaking fuel pressure regulator diaphragm, faulty fuel pump, restricted fuel pump sock, leaking fuel pump pressure hose connection in fuel tank, no fuel in the fuel tank or restricted fuel pressure line.

Fuel Pressure is High

Remove return line at throttle body or rail and attach a hose to the engine return fitting. Insert the other end of the hose into a suitable container and retest the pressure. If it is now normal, check and repair restriction in the fuel return line. If the pressure is still high, replace or repair the fuel pressure regulator as needed.

Fuel Pressure Leak Down Tests

TBI systems may, or may not, hold pressure after the fuel pump turns off. GM TBI vehicles, 1981-83 Chrysler Imperial 318 EFI, Isuzu TBI, Renault Alliance and Encore TBI don't hold pressure. Most others will hold pressure after the pump shuts off (key **ON**, engine **OFF**. If this type of system bleeds down after the pump shuts off, block off the return line and cycle the key again.

✷✷ WARNING

Do not pinch plastic or braided steel lines.

Observe the following:
- If pressure now holds, the problem is the fuel pressure regulator.
- If the pressure still drops, block off the feed line the instant the fuel pressure reaches maximum. If it now holds pressure after the pump shuts off, the problem is in the fuel pump or the coupling in the tank.
- If the pressure still drops, the problem is either a leaking injector or a fuel pressure regulator diaphragm leaking into the vacuum hose.

CIS SYSTEMS

Bosch K-JETRONIC

When checking fuel pressure on Bosch K-Jetronic systems, abnormal pressure readings should be handled in the following manner:

SYSTEM PRESSURE IS LOW

- Verify the voltage and the ground are available at fuel pump.
- Verify the fuel filter condition.
- Verify there is no fuel leakage.
- Carefully restrict the fuel return line while monitoring the system pressure. If system pressure can be brought to within specifications while restricting return line, the problem is in the fuel pressure regulator (either internal fuel distributor slide valve type regulator or external diaphragm type regulator).
- Verify there are no restrictions in fuel lines.

SYSTEM PRESSURE HIGH.

Verify there is no restriction in return side fuel circuit. Remove the return side line and run it into a suitable container. If the system pressure returns to specifications, the restriction in the return circuit If the system pressure does not return to specifications, the problem is with the fuel pressure regulator (either internal fuel distributor slide valve type regulator or external diaphragm type regulator).

FALLING REST PRESSURE

All K-Jetronic fuel pumps are equipped with a non-return valve. In some cases this check valve is replaceable, separate from the pump.

If the rest pressure falls, energize the fuel pump long enough to pressurize system. Restrict the fuel return line and monitor the system pressure. If the system pressure still falls, the problem is with the non-return valve on the fuel pump or with the fuel accumulator. If the pressure does not fall, the problem is with the pressure regulator (either internal fuel distributor slide valve type regulator or external diaphragm type regulator).

To test the non-return valve on the fuel pump, energize the fuel pump long enough to pressurize the system. Restrict fuel line between pump and fuel tank and monitor system pressure. If pressure no longer falls, the problem is with the non-return valve. If the pressure continues to fall, the problem is a faulty accumulator.

Bosch K & KE Test Procedures

Due to the high pressures involved, the proper test procedures are essential when servicing Bosch K & KE Series injection systems.

Use the following steps:

1. When checking the fuel pressure on a K or K Lambda system, the gauge should be hooked up in the following manner:

a. Remove the fuel line from the center top port of the fuel distributor (this is the line that goes to the control pressure regulator).

b. Place the gauge and shut off valve assembly so that the shut-off valve is on the control pressure regulator side.

c. Connect the shut-off valve side of the gauge to the control pressure regulator fuel line, then connect the gauge side to the center top port of the fuel distributor. Start the engine or manually energize the fuel pump (consult you Chilton Total Car Care manual for fuel pump relay location and bypass procedure).

d. With the gauge in this position and the shut-off valve closed, system pressure is measured.

2. When checking fuel pressure on a KE system, the gauge should be hooked up in the following manner:

a. Remove the fuel line to the cold start injector.

b. Place the gauge and shut-off valve assembly so that the shut-off valve is on the fuel distributor side.

c. Connect the shut-off valve side of the gauge and shut-off valve assembly to the fuel distributor test port.

d. Connec t the gauge side to the cold start injector fuel line. Start the engine, or manually energize the fuel pump (consult a Chilton Total Car Care manual for fuel pump relay location and bypass procedure). With the gauge in this position and the shut-off valve open, differential pressure is measured; with the shut-off valve closed, system pressure is measured. (Note: An alternative method of measuring differential pressure is to dead head the gauge to the fuel distributor test port. Only differential pressure is measured in this case.)

3. To check system rest pressure, the gauge should be hooked up in the same manner as for testing system pressure. The system should hold a specific rest pressure for a specific amount of time.

4. After testing, be sure to replace banjo washers with new ones and be sure to test system for leaks.

FUEL SYSTEM ADJUSTMENTS

Idle Mixture Adjustments

Most vehicles today use a rather complex electronic fuel injection system which is regulated by a series of temperature, altitude and air flow sensors which feed information into a control module. The control module then relays an electronic signal to the injector nozzle(s), which allow(s) a predetermined amount of fuel into the combustion chamber. In this way all mixture control adjustments are regulated by the control module, therefore on these vehicles no manual adjustments are necessary or possible.

➡**For specific information on your vehicle's systems, consult a "Chilton Total Car Care (TCC) Manual" for your vehicle.**

Idle Speed Adjustments

No periodic service adjustments are necessary on most computer controlled fuel systems. However, if the vehicle you are working with requires adjustment or an idle check, a general procedure is shown below. Consult a "Chilton Total Car Care (TCC) Manual" for your specific vehicle for more detailed information. Also, always refer to the instructions or specifications found on the Vehicle Emission Control Information (VECI) label found underhood for additional or updated information which is applicable to your particular vehicle.

✳ CAUTION

For manual transmission models, set parking brake and check idle speed in N position. For automatic transmission equipped models, shifted into D for idle speed checks. When in Drive, the parking brake must be fully applied with both front and rear wheels chocked.

1. Turn **OFF** the: headlights, heater blower, air conditioning, and rear window defogger. If the vehicle has power steering, make sure the wheels are in the straight ahead position. The ignition timing must be correct to get an effective idle speed adjustment. Connect a tachometer (a special adapter harness may be needed) according to the instrument manufacturer's directions.

Start the engine and warm the engine so it reaches normal operating temperature. The water temperature indicator should be in the middle of the gauge.

✳ CAUTION

NEVER run the engine in a closed garage. Always make sure there is proper ventilation to prevent carbon monoxide poisoning.

2. Run engine at 2000 rpm for about 2 minutes under no load.

3. Race the engine to 2000–3000 rpm a few times under no load and then allow it to return to idle speed.

4. Apply the parking brake securely. If equipped with an automatic, put the transmission into **D**.

5. Adjust the idle speed by turning the idle speed adjusting screw.

6. Turn the engine **OFF** and remove the tachometer. Road test for proper operation.

ENGINE WILL NOT START

➡**The procedure below is a general procedure, consult a "Chilton Total Car Care (TCC) Manual" for specific information concerning your vehicle.**

No Start Testing

▶ **See Figures 106 and 107**

1. Connect a voltmeter across the battery terminals. If battery voltage is not at least 12 volts, charge and test the battery before proceeding.

2. Turn the key to the **START** position and observe the voltmeter. If the engine turned over and battery voltage remained above 9.6 volts, go to next step. If the engine failed to crank and/or voltage was below 9.6 volts, proceed as follows:

a. If the instrument panel lights dim, load test the battery, check the battery terminals and cables, test the starter motor and verify the engine turns.

b. If the instrument panel lights do not dim, check the battery terminal connections, the ignition switch/wiring and the starter.

3. Using a spark tester, check for spark at two or more spark plugs. If okay go to next step, if not okay, perform No Spark Testing.

4. Cycle the ignition switch on and off, several times, while listening for fuel pump operation. If fuel pump operates, proceed to next step. If fuel pump does not operate, begin testing of the fuel pump circuit.

5. Verify adequate fuel in the tank, then connect a fuel pressure gauge and check fuel pressure. If fuel pressure is within specifications, proceed to next step, if not okay continue on checking the fuel pump and supply system.

6. Disconnect the fuel injector connector and connect a Noid® light to the wiring harness. Crank the engine, while watching the light. Perform this test on at least two injectors before proceeding. If the light does not flash, go to the next step. If the light flashes, check the engine valve timing and overall mechanical condition of the engine. If okay, items such as; poor fuel quality, faulty injectors and computer controlled devices should be checked. Although these items are less likely, a shorted TPS or faulty coolant temperature sensor, are possibilities.

7. Check and verify the Malfunction Indicator Lamp (MIL) is operating properly. If the light does not operate, check the control module and related wiring. If the MIL lamp is operational, check the injector wiring and circuitry.

No Spark Testing

▶ See Figure 108

1. Check for spark at two or more spark plugs. If spark does not exist go to next step, if spark is okay, check spark plugs, fuel system and engine mechanical condition.

2. Check for spark from the ignition coil wire. If spark does not exist go to next step, if spark is okay, check distributor cap, rotor and ignition wires.

3. Check the ignition coil wire with an ohmmeter. Resistance should not exceed 1000 ohms per inch of cable. If wire resistance exceeds specification, replace the wire and retest. If wire is okay, proceed to the next step.

4. Connect a test light to the negative side of the ignition coil. Turn the key to the **ON** position and observe the test light. If the light remains brightly lit, proceed to the next step. If the light did not light, or glowed dim, check the ignition switch and power supply circuit.

5. Observe the light while cranking the engine. If the light was flashing during cranking, check the ignition coil. If the light did not flash, verify the distributor rotates smoothly, then test the ignition module, pick-up coil or hall effect switch.

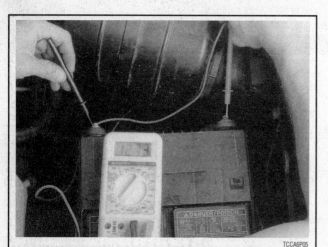

TCCA6P05

Fig. 106 Battery voltage should remain over 9.6 volts while the engine is cranking and should stay above 12 volts with the engine at rest

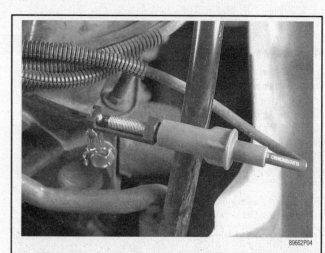

89662P04

Fig. 108 An adjustable spark tester can be used with most ignition systems. When in doubt, use a spark plug removed from the engine to test for spark

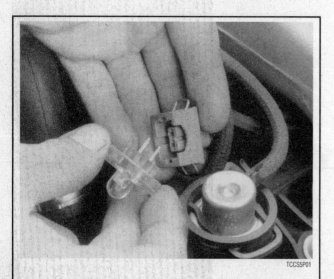

TCCS5P01

Fig. 107 A noid light is used to test voltage to the fuel injector

5

DOMESTIC DIAGNOSTIC TROUBLE CODE RETRIEVAL

DOMESTIC VEHICLE DIAGNOSTIC TROUBLE CODE RETRIEVAL

Introduction

Most cars today are equipped with an On-Board Diagnostic (OBD) system. During the late '70s manufacturers started using electronics to control engine functions and diagnose engine faults. This was primarily to meet stringent new EPA emission standards. Through the years OBD have become more sophisticated. OBD-II, a new standard introduced in the mid-'90s, provides almost complete engine control and also monitors parts of the chassis, body and accessory devices, as well as the diagnostic control network of the vehicle.

OBD was brought about to combat a persistent smog problem in the LA basin. The State of California started requiring emission control systems on 1966 model cars. The federal government extended these controls nationwide in 1968.

Congress passed the Clean Air Act in 1970 and established the Environmental Protection Agency (EPA). From the EPA, series of emission standards for maintenance of vehicles has been brought forth. To meet these standards, manufacturers were forced to electronically control their fuel feed and ignition systems. Sensors measure engine performance and adjustments are made automatically to the systems to provide optimum performance with minimum emissions. These sensors also provided vehicle owners with their earliest diagnostic assistance.

In the beginning there were few standards and each manufacturer had their own systems and signals. In 1988, the Society of Automotive Engineers (SAE) set a standard connector plug and set of diagnostic test codes. The EPA adapted most of the SAE standards and gradually mandated compliance from the manufacturers.

The EPA has been charged with reducing "mobile emissions" from cars and trucks and given the power to require manufacturers to build cars which meet increasingly stiff emissions standards. The manufacturers must further maintain the emission standards of the cars for the useful life of the vehicle.

OBD-II is a natural progression of the initial standards developed by the SAE and implemented by the EPA and California Air Resources Board (CARB). The standards were implemented January 1, 1996.

OBD-II provides a universal inspection and diagnosis method to be sure the car is performing to OEM standards. While there is argument as to the exact standards and methodology employed, the fact is there is a need to reduce vehicle emitted pollution levels in our cities, and we have to live with these requirements.

What System Do I Have?

So how do I know if my car has OBD-I or OBD-II. All cars built since January 1, 1996 have OBD-II systems. Manufacturers started incorporating OBD-II in various models as early as 1994. Some early OBD-II cars were not 100% compliant.

It is safe to say that if you own a pre-1994 model year vehicle, you have some variant of an OBD-I system. Remember, OBD-I was very manufacturer specific and great differences may exist between models of the same manufacturer and year.

It is also safe to say that if you own a 1996 or later model year vehicle, you have OBD-II. Here it gets a little easier. Since there are a standard set of generic codes for OBD-II, which are published here, each make and model will display the same code for the same fault.

There are also manufacturer specific codes, which like OBD-I are specific to each manufacturer. However, the manufacturers have pretty much used the same codes across their model lines.

The real problem with comes with vehicles built between 1994 and 1995. These were transition years and many manufacturers installed systems that were better than traditional OBD-I systems, yet still did not comply with OBD-II regulations.

The surest way to tell which version of OBD you have is to look for some indication on the Vehicle Emissions Control Information (VECI) sticker in the engine compartment. A second, less accurate, way to check is to look at the Data Link Connector (DLC) in the engine compartment or under the dash. If the connector has 16 pins and is trapezoidal in shape, you can be pretty sure you have an OBD-II system.

➡ Some manufacturers started using the 16 pin OBD-II connector prior to full implementation of the system on their vehicles.

How Do I Read The Codes?

OBD-I vehicles have connectors in various positions around the vehicle. Some likely spots are under the dashboard, under the hood, in the center console, in the trunk or hatch area or under the seats. Some vehicles do not use a connector but have several buttons and lights directly on the control module.

Each manufacturer has a specific sequence that must be performed exactly to enable the code to be read. These sequences range from the simple (ground two terminals on a connector) to the ridiculous (cycle the ignition key 15 times). However, most manufacturers codes could be read without the use of any special equipment.

All OBD-II cars have a connector located in the passenger compartment easily accessible from the driver's seat. Check under the dash or near the ashtray. A cable is plugged into the OBD-II connector and a scan tool is used to read the fault codes. This can range from a simple hand-held meter that provides a coded read-out of the various diagnostic functions, up to a large console computer-based unit costing used by some high tech professional mechanics.

Most scan tools use replaceable cartridges, making them compatible with all cars. Each tool contains software that analyzes the signals received from the car and displays a text or diagrammed readout of any malfunctions found. Some of the higher end models even suggest possible solutions to the problems.

Several manufacturers have started to market smaller scan tools. Units for the advanced do-it-yourselfer or small shop technician can provide a variety of levels of data, some approaching the sophistication of the big shop consoles.

A detailed description of how to access codes is included with each manufacturer section.

A Word About Scan Tools

▶ See Figures 1 and 2

The check engine light on your dashboard has been winking at you randomly for months. Perhaps this partly explains why your car just doesn't

89465P01

Fig. 1 AutoTap®from B&B electronics is an OBD-II compatible scan tool you can hook up to your personal computer

Fig. 2 The AutoXray® is more like a traditional scan tool which comes complete with various adapters to fit many makes and models

feel quite right and your gasoline credit card bill is enormous. Maybe this time, instead of taking it to the mechanic its time to start looking into things yourself.

First, you'll need a scan tool. In the past, scan tools were the private domain of mechanics and dealerships due to their high cost. Now the do-it-yourselfer can choose from many entry-level scan testers designed for the small shop and home mechanic. The ones we tested have control panels and screens you can understand. So if you've learned to use a PC, a scan tool is much easier. Even the (Picture) harness adapter fits only one way in the diagnostic plug. So if it doesn't fit right, you've got the wrong one.

Plugging in the scan tool is quite easy, as long as you have the correct adapters. Most kits come with adapters to enable one scan tool to fit a number of vehicles. Once you plug it the scan tool can begin the job with a list of trouble codes, including those that aren't accompanied by malfunction indicator lamp. If only the entire procedure were this easy. The trouble code is a good start, but many problems will not set a code at all, so you'll need to do some good old-fashioned diagnosis.

What Do Codes Tell Me?

OBD signals are most often sought in response to a "Malfunction Indicator Lamp (MIL)" appearing on the dashboard or driveability problems experienced with the vehicle. The data provided by OBD can often pinpoint the specific component that has malfunctioned, saving substantial time and cost compared to guess-and-replace repairs.

The MIL shows three different types of signals. Occasional flashes show momentary malfunctions. It stays **ON** if the problem is of a more serious nature, affecting the emissions output or safety of the vehicle. A constantly flashing MIL is a sign of a major problem which can cause serious damage if the engine is not stopped immediately. In all cases an electronic picture called a "freeze frame" is taken to show all sensor readings at the time of the fault. This picture is recorded in the vehicle's control module and can be accessed to provide additional clues during diagnosis.

OBD-I TROUBLE CODES

Introduction

It should be remembered that OBD-I codes, for the most part, are manufacturer, model and sometimes year specific. Reading the codes is also specific to the individual manufacturer. Special tools may be necessary to gain access to the control modules. If reading codes does require special tools, the procedures given here will reference those tools.

➡ The term control module is a generic term used for the engine control computer. These computers are known by various names including Electronic Control Module (ECM), Powertrain Control Module (PCM), Vehicle Control Module (VCM), Single Board Engine Controller (SBEC), Engine Control Assembly (ECA) and Engine Control Unit (ECU).

➡ The term Malfunction Indicator Lamp (MIL) is a generic term used to indicate the instrument panel mounted, engine computer controlled lamp which warns the driver there has been a fault in the system. Some common names for this lamp are the Check Engine Light and the Service Engine Soon Light. Sometimes just the word Engine will appear.

Reading and Clearing Codes

▶ See Figures 3, 4, 5, 6 and 7

It should be noted that with very few exceptions, reading and clearing of OBD-I trouble codes, can be performed without using a scan tool. However, by using a scan tool, the codes can be obtained much quicker and other functions of the system can readily be accessed. This should not be tremendous cause for concern as, as several manufacturers have developed scan tools that are well within the price range of the average do-it-yourselfer. Also, many mechanics will hook up a scan tool to your vehicle for a minimal charge.

Fig. 3 Hooking up the scan tool is as easy as plugging into the diagnostic link connector

Fig. 4 Inexpensive scan tools, such as this one from AutoXray®, are available to interface with the OBD-I electronics in your vehicle

Fig. 5 Among other features, a scan tool combines many standard testers into a single device for quick and accurate diagnosis

Fig. 6 Although some times no DTC's are found, that does not rule out a problem

Fig. 7 Once the scan tool finds a trouble code it will display the appropriate code number and description

Chrysler Corporation

SELF DIAGNOSTICS

The control module is designed to test it's own input and output circuits, If a fault is found in a major system, this information is stored in the control module for eventual display to the technician. Information on this fault can be displayed to the technician by means of the instrument panel check engine light or by connecting a diagnostic read-out tester and reading a numbered display code, which directly relates to a general fault. Some inputs and outputs are checked continuously and others are checked under certain conditions. If the problem is repaired or no longer exists, the control module cancels the fault code after approximately 50 key ON/OFF cycles.

When a fault code is detected, it appears as either a flash of the check engine light on the instrument panel or by watching the Diagnostic Readout Box version II (DRB-II). This indicates that an abnormal signal in the system has been recognized by the control module. Fault codes do indicate the presence of a failure but they don't identify the failed component directly.

Visual Inspections

This is possibly the most critical step of diagnosis. A detailed examination of all connectors, wiring and vacuum hoses can often lead to a repair without further diagnosis. Performance of this step relies on the skill of the technician performing it; a careful inspector will check the undersides of hoses as well as the integrity of hard-to-reach hoses blocked by the air cleaner or other components. Wiring should be checked carefully for any sign of strain , burning, crimping or terminal pull-out from a connector.

Checking connectors at components or in harnesses is required; usually, pushing them together will reveal a loose fit. Pay particular attention to ground circuits, making sure they are not loose or corroded. Remember to inspect connectors and hose fittings at components not mounted on the engine, such as the evaporative canister or relays mounted on the fender aprons. Any component or wiring in the vicinity of a fluid leak or spillage should be given extra attention during inspection.

Additionally, inspect maintenance items such as belt condition and tension, battery charge and condition and the radiator cap carefully. Any of these very simple items may affect the system enough to set a fault.

Fault Codes

Fault codes are numbers that tell the technician which circuit is bad. Fault codes do indicate the presence of a failure but they don't identify the failed component directly. Therefore, a fault code a result and not always the reason for the problem.

Indicator Codes

Indicator codes are numbers that tell the technician if particular sequences or conditions have occurred. Such a condition where the indicator code will be displayed is at the beginning or the end of a diagnostic test. Indicator codes will not generate a check engine light or engine running test code.

Actuator Test Mode (ATM) Codes

Starting in 1985, ATM test codes are numbers that identify the various circuits used by the technician during the diagnosis procedure. In 1989, the control module and test equipment changed design. The actuator test functions where expanded, but access to these functions may have changed, dependent on vehicle or test equipment being used.

Engine Running Test Codes

Engine running test codes where introduced on fuel injected vehicles. These codes are used to access sensor readouts while the engine is running and place the engine in particular operating conditions for diagnosis. Feedback carburetor system does not offer engine running sensor test mode.

Check Engine (MIL) Light

This is possibly the most critical step of diagnosis. A detailed examination of connectors, wiring and vacuum hoses can often lead to a repair without further diagnosis. A careful inspector will check the undersides of hoses as well as the integrity of hard-to-reach hoses blocked by the air cleaner or other component. Wiring should be checked carefully for any sign of strain, burning, crimping, or terminals pulled-out from a connector. Checking connectors at components or in harnesses is required; usually, pushing them together will reveal a loose fit.

The check engine or Maintenance Indicator Lamp (MIL) light has 2 modes of operation: diagnostic mode and switch test mode.

If a DRB-II diagnostic tester is not available, the control module can show the technician fault codes by flashing the check engine light on the instrument panel in the diagnostic mode. In the switch test mode, after all codes are displayed, switch function can be confirmed. The light will turn on and off when a switch is turned **ON** and **OFF**.

Although the light can be used as a diagnostic tool, it cannot do the following:

Once the light starts to display fault codes, it cannot be stopped. If the technician loses count, he must start the test procedure again.

The light cannot display all of the codes or any blank displays.

The light cannot tell the technician if the oxygen feed-back system is lean or rich and if the idle motor and detonation systems are operational.

The light cannot perform the actuation test mode; sensor test mode or engine running test mode.

➡ Be advised that the check engine light can only perform a limited amount of functions and is not to be used as a substitute for a diagnostic tester. All diagnostic procedure described herein are intended for use with a Diagnostic Readout Box II (DRB-II) or equivalent tool.

Limp-In Mode

The limp-in mode is the attempt by the control module to compensate for the failure of certain components by substituting information from other sources. If the control module senses incorrect data or no data at all from the MAP sensor, throttle position sensor or coolant temperature sensor, the system is placed into limp-in mode and the check engine light on the instrument panel is activated. This mode will keep the vehicle drive able until the customer can get it to a service facility.

Test Modes

There are 5 modes of testing required for the proper diagnosis of the system. They are as follows:

Diagnostic Test Mode—This mode is used to access the fault codes from the control module's memory.

Circuit Actuation Test Mode (ATM Test)—This mode is used to turn a certain circuit on and off in order to test it. ATM test codes are used in this mode.

Switch Test Mode—This mode is used to determine if specific switch inputs are being received by the control module .

Sensor Test Mode—This mode looks at the output signals of certain sensors as they are received by the control module when the engine is not running. Sensor access codes are read in this mode. In addition, this mode is used to clear the control module memory of stored codes.

Engine Running Test Mode—This mode looks at sensor output signals as seen by the control module when the engine is running. In addition, this mode is used to determine some specific running conditions necessary for diagnosis.

READING TROUBLE CODES

Obtaining Codes

▶ See Figures 8, 9 and 10

Entering the Jeep or Eagle self-diagnostic system requires the use of a special adapter that connects with the Diagnostic Readout Box II (DRB-II). These systems require the adapter because all of the system diagnosis is done Off-Board instead of On-Board like most vehicles. The adapter, which is a computer module itself, measures signals at the diagnostic connector and converts the signals into a form that the DRBII can use to perform tests. On vehicles other than Jeep and Eagle the following procedures will obtain stored Diagnostic Trouble Codes (DTC).

USING THE DASH MIL LAMP

Codes display on vehicles built before 1989 are displayed in numerical order, after 1989 codes are displayed in order of occurrence.

1. Connect the readout box to the diagnostic connector located in the engine compartment near control module.
2. Start the engine, if possible, cycle the transmission selector and the A/C switch if applicable. Shut off the engine.
3. Turn the ignition switch **ON—OFF, ON—OFF, ON—OFF, ON** within 5 seconds.
4. Observe the check engine light on the instrument panel.
5. Just after the last **ON** cycle, the dash warning (MIL) lamp will begin flashing the stored codes.
6. The codes are transmitted as two digit flashes.
7. Example would be Code 21 will be displayed as a FLASH FLASH pause FLASH.

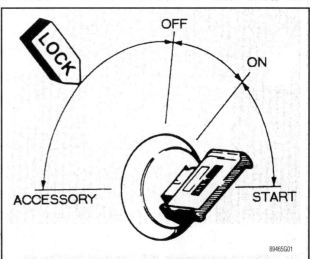

89465G01

Fig. 8 Turn the ignition switch ON and OFF three times to enter self-diagnostics

8. Be ready to write down the codes as they appear; the only way to repeat the codes is to start over at the beginning.

SCAN TOOL

The scan tool is the preferred choice for fault recovery and system diagnosis. Some hints on using the DRB-II include:

• To use the HELP screen, press and hold F3 at any time.

• To restart the DRB-II at any time, hold the MODE button and press ATM at the same time.

• Pressing the up or down arrows will move forward or backward one item within a menu.

• To select an item, either press the number of the item or move the cursor arrow to the selection, then press ENTER.

• To return to the previous display (screen), press ATM.

• Some test screens display multiple items. To view only one, move the cursor arrow to the desired item, then press ENTER.

To read stored faults with the DRB-II:

1. With the ignition switch **OFF**, connect the tool to the diagnostic connector near the engine controller under the hood. On some 1988 and earlier models cycling, the ignition key **ON—OFF** three times may be necessary to enter diagnostics. On 1989 and newer models, simply turn the ignition switch **ON** to access the read fault code data.

2. Start the engine if possible. Cycle the transmission from **P** to a forward gear, then back to **P**. Cycle the air conditioning **ON** and **OFF**. Turn the ignition switch **OFF**.

3. Turn the ignition switch **ON** but do not start the engine. The DRB-II will begin its power-up sequence; do not touch any keys on the scan tool during this sequence.

4. Reading faults must be selected from the FUEL/IGN MENU. To reach this menu on the DRB-II:

a. When the initial menu is displayed after the power-up sequence, use the down arrow to display choice 4) SELECT SYSTEM and select this choice.

b. Once on the — SELECT SYSTEM — screen, choose 1) ENGINE. This will enter the engine diagnostics section of the program.

c. The screen will momentarily display the engine family and SBEC identification numbers. After a few seconds the screen displays the choices 1) With A/C and 2) Without A/C. Select and enter the correct choice for the vehicle.

d. When the — ENGINE SYSTEM — screen appears, select 1) FUEL/IGNITION from the menu.

e. On the next screen, select 2) READ FAULTS

5. If any faults are stored, the display will show how many are stored (1 of 4 faults, etc.) and issue a text description of the problem, such as

COOLANT SENSOR VOLTAGE TOO LOW. The last line of the display shows the number of engine starts since the code was set. If the number displayed is 0 starts, this indicates a hard or current fault. Faults are displayed in reverse order of occurrence; the first fault shown is the most current and the last fault shown is the oldest.

6. Press the down arrow to read each fault after the first. Record the screen data carefully for easy reference.

7. If no faults are stored in the controller, the display will state NO FAULTS DETECTED and show the number of starts since the system memory was last erased.

8. After all faults have been read and recorded, press ATM.

9. Refer to the appropriate diagnostic path. Remember that the fault message identifies a circuit problem, not a component. Use of the charts is required to sequentially test a circuit and identify the fault.

```
----- FUEL/IGN FAULTS -----
NO FAULTS DETECTED

X STARTS SINCE ERS
```

```
1 OF X FAULTS
[message
appears here]
X STARTS SINCE SET
```
89465G03

Fig. 10 Example of the DRB-II display screen while reading trouble codes

Switch Test

The control module only recognizes 2 switch input states — HI and LOW. For this reason the control module cannot tell the difference between a selected switch position and an open circuit, short circuit or an open switch. However, if one of the switches is toggled, the controller does have the ability to respond to the change of state in the switch. If the change is displayed, it can be assumed that entire switch circuit to the control module is operational.

1988 AND EARLIER

After all codes have been shown and has indicated Code 55 end of message, actuate the following component switches. The digital display must change its numbers between 00 and 88 and the check engine light will blink when the following switches are activated and released:

Brake pedal
Gear shift selector
A/C switch
Electric defogger switch (1984)

1989 AND LATER

To enter the switch test mode, activate read input states or equivalent function on the readout box for the following switch tests:

Z1 Voltage Sense
Speed Control Set
Speed Control **ON/OFF**
Speed Control Resume
A/C Switch Sense
Brake Switch
Park/neutral Switch

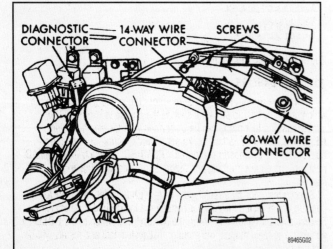
89465G02

Fig. 9 Typical view of the Powertrain Control Module diagnostic link connector

SCAN TOOL FUNCTIONS

✳✳ CAUTION

Always apply the parking brake and block the wheels before performing any diagnostic procedures with the engine running. Failure to do so may result in personal injury and/or property damage.@TX:After stored faults have been read and recorded, the scan tool may be used to investigate states and functions of various components. This ability compliments but does not replace the use of diagnostic charts. The DRB-II functions are useful in identifying circuits that are or are not operating correctly as well as checking component function or signal.

When diagnosing an emissions-related problem, keep in mind that the SBEC system only enters closed loop mode under certain conditions. The single most important criteria for entry into closed loop operation is that the engine be at normal operating temperature; i.e., fully warmed up. The engine is considered to be at normal operating temperature if any of the following are true: the electric cooling fan cycles on at least once or the upper radiator hose is hot to the touch or the heater is able to deliver hot air.

In open loop operation, the signal from the oxygen sensor is ignored by the engine controller and the fuel injection is controlled by pre-programmed values within the computer. Once closed loop operation is begun, the signal from the oxygen sensor is used by the engine controller to constantly adjust the fuel injection to maintain the proper air/fuel ratio. The system will switch in and out of closed loop operation depending on sensor signals and driver input. In most cases, the system will be in closed loop operation during normal driving, acceleration or deceleration and idle. Wide open throttle will cause the system to momentarily switch to open loop operation. Additionally, some engine control systems will momentarily switch to open loop under hard acceleration or deceleration until the MAP sensor signal stabilizes.

The DRB-II may be operated in the following diagnostic modes from the FUEL/IGN MENU screen.

State Display

The State Display programs allow the operator to view the present conditions in the SBEC system. These choices are displayed on the FUEL/IGN STATE screen and offer the choices of MODULE INFO, SENSORS, INPUTS/OUTPUTS, or MONITORS. Viewing system data through these windows can be helpful in observing the effects of repairs or to compare the problem vehicle to a known-good vehicle.

MODULE INFO

This choice identifies the engine and transmission family and provides the SBEC identification number. It is always wise to check this screen first to insure that the correct controller is installed in the vehicle. The SBEC identification number must be used if the unit is to be replaced.

SENSORS

This function displays current data being transmitted from the fuel and ignition sensors to the engine controller. Examples of sensor data available include MAP voltage, throttle position sensor voltage and percentage, RPM, coolant temperature, voltage sensor, total spark advance, and vehicle speed.

Many other sensors may be monitored depending on engine/transmission combinations. Data for each sensor is displayed in the appropriate units, such as volts, mph, in. Hg, degrees F, etc.

1988 AND EARLIER

1. Put the system into the diagnostic test mode and wait for Code 55 to appear on the display screen.
2. Press the ATM button on the diagnostic tool to activate the display. If a specific sensor read test is desired, hold the ATM button down until the desired test code appears.

3. Slide the READ/HOLD switch to the **HOLD** position to display the corresponding sensor output.

Sensor Read Test Display codes:Code 01 Battery temperature sensor; display voltage divided by 10 equals sensor temperature

Code 02 Oxygen sensor voltage; display number divided by 10 equals sensor voltage

Code 03 Charge temperature sensor voltage; display number divided by 10 equals sensor voltage

Code 04 Engine coolant temperature sensor; display number multiplied by 10 equals degrees of engine coolant sensor

Code 05 Throttle position sensor voltage; display number divided by 10 equals sensor voltage or temperature

Code 06 Peak knock sensor voltage; display number is sensor voltage

Code 07 Battery voltage; display number is battery voltage

Code 08 Map sensor voltage; display number divided by 10 equals sensor voltage

Code 09 Speed control switches:

Display is blank—Cruise **OFF**

Display shows 00—Cruise **ON**

Display shows 10—Cruise **SET**

Display shows 01—Cruise **RESUME**

Code 10—Fault code erase routine; display will flash 0's for 4 seconds

1989 AND LATER

To enter the sensor test mode, activate read sensor voltage or read sensor values or equivalent functions on the readout box for the following sensor displays:

Read Sensor Voltage
Battery temperature sensor
Oxygen sensor input
Throttle body temperature sensor
Coolant temperature sensor
Throttle position
Minimum throttle
Battery voltage
MAP sensor voltage

Read Sensor Values
Throttle body temperature
Coolant temperature
MAP gauge reading
AIS motor position
Added adaptive fuel
Adaptive fuel factor
Barometric pressure
Engine speed
Module spark advance
Vehicle speed
Oxygen sensor state

Engine Running Test Mode

1988 AND EARLIER

The Engine Running Test Mode monitors the sensors on the vehicle which check operating conditions while the engine is running. The engine running test mode can be performed with the engine idling in **NEUTRAL** and with parking brake set or under actual driving conditions. With the diagnostic readout box READ/HOLD switch in the **READ** position, the engine running test mode is initiated after the engine is started.

Select a test code by switching the READ/HOLD switch to the **READ** position and pressing the actuator button until the desired code appears. Release actuator button and switch the READ/HOLD switch to the **HOLD** position. The logic module will monitor that system test and results will be displayed.

Only fuel injected engine offer this function. The Feedback carburetor system does not offer engine running sensor test mode.

ENGINE RUNNING TEST DISPLAY CODES

Code 61 Battery temperature sensor; display number divided by 10 equals voltage**Code 62** Oxygen sensor; display number divided by 10 equals voltage

Code 63 Fuel injector temperature sensor; display number divided by 10 equals voltage

Code 64 Engine coolant temperature sensor; display number multiplied by 10 equals degrees F

Code 65 Throttle position sensor; display number divided by 10 equals voltage

Code 67 Battery voltage sensor; display is voltage

Code 68 Manifold vacuum sensor; display is in. Hg

Code 69 Minimum throttle position sensor; display number divided by 10 equals voltage

Code 70 Minimum airflow idle speed sensor; display number multiplied by 10 equals rpm (see minimum air flow check procedure)

Code 71 Vehicle speed sensor; display is mph

Code 72 Engine speed sensor; display number multiplied by 10 equals rpm

FUEL/IGNITION INPUT/OUTPUT

The engine controller recognizes only two states of electrical signals, voltage high or low. In some cases this corresponds to a switch or circuit being on or off; in other circuits a voltage signal may change from low voltage to higher voltage as a sensor opens. The controller cannot recognize the difference between a selected switch position and an open or shorted circuit.

In this test mode, the change in the circuit may be viewed as the switch is operated. For example, if the BRAKE SWITCH state is selected, the display should change from Low to High as the brake pedal is pressed. If a change in a circuit is displayed as the switch is used, it may be reasonably assumed that the entire switch circuit into the engine controller is operating correctly.

Depending on the engine/transmission in the vehicle, some of the switch states which may be checked include the air conditioning switch, brake switch, park/neutral switch, fuel flow signal, air conditioning clutch relay, radiator fan relay, check engine lamp, overdrive solenoid(s), lock-up solenoid and the speed control vent or vacuum solenoids. The scan tool will recognize the correct choices for each vehicle and only offer the appropriate systems on the screen.

MONITORS

On vehicles built before 1991, this display is called ENGINE PARAMETERS. 1991 and newer vehicles name the screen MONITORS. This display allows close observation of groups of related signals. For example, if RPM is chosen, the screen will display data for many of the factors affecting the rpm such as throttle position sensor, advance, air conditioning status, park/neutral status, AIS status and coolant temperature.

One of the screens within this test is NO START. When this display is selected, the screen shows the initial data sent to the engine controller during cranking. Using this screen to identify missing or unusual signals can shorten diagnostic time.

Actuator Tests

The purpose of the circuit actuation mode test is to check for proper operation of the output circuits that the control module cannot internally recognize. The control module can attempt to activate these outputs and allow the technician to affirm proper operation. Most of the tests performed in this mode issue an audible click or visual indication of component operation (click of relay contacts, injector spray, etc.). Except for intermittent conditions, if a component functions properly when it is tested, it can be assumed that the component, attendant wiring and driving circuit are functioning properly.

1988 AND EARLIER

The Actuator Test Mode 10 Code number was introduced in 1985. In 1983–84 ATM function only provided 3 ignition sparks, 2 AIS motor cycles and 1 injector pulse.

1. Put the system into the diagnostic test mode and wait for 55 to appear on the display screen.

2. Press ATM button on the tool to activate the display. If a specific ATM test is desired, hold the ATM button down until the desired test code appears.

3. The computer will continue to turn the selected circuit on and off for as long as 5 minutes or until the ATM button is pressed again or the ignition switch is turned to the **OFF** position.

4. If the ATM button is not pressed again, the computer will continue to cycle the selected circuit for 5 minutes and then shut the system off. Turning the ignition to the **OFF** position will also turn the test mode off.

Actuator Test Display Codes:

Code 01 Spark activation—once every 2 seconds

Code 02 Injector activation—once every 2 seconds

Code 03 AIS activation—one step open, one step closed every 4 seconds

Code 04 Radiator fan relay—once every 2 seconds

Code 05 A/C WOT cutout relay—once every 2 seconds

Code 06 ASD relay activation—once every 2 seconds

Code 07 Purge solenoid activation—one toggle every 2 seconds (The A/C fan will run continuously and the A/C switch must be in the **ON** position to allow for actuation)

Code 08 Speed control activation—speed control vent and vacuum every 2 seconds (Speed control switch must be in the **ON** position to allow for activation)

Code 09 Alternator control field activation—one toggle every 2 seconds

Code 10 Shift indicator activation—one toggle every 2 seconds

Code 11 EGR diagnosis solenoid activation—one toggle every 2 seconds

1989 AND LATER

This family of tests is chosen from the FUEL/IGN MENU screen. The actuator tests allow the operation of the output circuits not recognized by the engine controller to be checked by energizing them on command. Testing in this fashion is necessary because the controller does not recognize the function of all the external components. If an output to a relay is triggered, and the relay is heard to click, it may be reasonably assumed that both the output circuit and the relay are operating properly. In this mode, most of the tests cause a response that may be seen or heard, although close attention may be necessary to notice the change.

Once selected, the ACTUATOR TEST screen offers a choice of items to be activated. Depending on engine and fuel system, some of the choices include:

- Stop all tests
- Engine rpm
- Ignition coil
- Fuel injector
- Fuel system
- Solenoid/relay
- AIS motor

The engine speed may be set to a desired level through the ENGINE RPM screen. Once a system is chosen, related screens will appear allowing detailed selection of which relay, injector or component is to be operated.

Exiting Diagnostic Test

By turning the ignition switch to the **OFF** position, the test mode system is exited. With a Diagnostic Readout Box attached to the system and the ATM control button not pressed, the computer will continue to cycle the selected circuits for 5 minutes and then automatically shut the system down.

Clearing Codes

Stored faults should only be cleared by use of the DRB-II or similar scan tool. Disconnecting the battery will clear codes but is not recommended as doing so will also clear all other memories on the vehicle and may affect driveability. Disconnecting the control module connector will also clear codes, but on newer models it may store a power loss code and will affect driveability until the vehicle is driven and the control module can relearn it's driveability memory.

The —ERASE—screen will appear when ATM is pressed at the end of the stored faults. Select the desired action from ERASE or DON'T ERASE. If ERASE is chosen, the display asks ARE YOU SURE? Pressing ENTER erases stored faults and displays the message FAULTS ERASED. After the faults are erased, press ATM to return the FUEL/IGN MENU.

DIAGNOSTIC TROUBLE CODES

Chrysler Domestic Built Fuel Injection System

Code 88 Display used for start of test.**Code 11** Camshaft signal or Ignition signal—no reference signal detected during engine cranking.**Code 12** Memory to controller has been cleared within 50–100 engine starts.

Code 13 MAP sensor pneumatic signal—no variation in MAP sensor signal is detected or no difference is recognized between the engine MAP reading and the stored barometric pressure reading..

Code 14 MAP voltage too high or too low.

Code 15 Vehicle speed sensor signal—no distance sensor signal detected during road load conditions.

Code 16 Knock sensor circuit—Open or short has been detected in the knock sensor circuit.

Code 16 Battery input sensor—battery voltage sensor input below 4 volts with engine running.

Code 17 Low engine temperature—engine coolant temperature remains below normal operating temperature during vehicle travel; possible thermostat problem.

Code 21 Oxygen sensor signal—neither rich or lean condition is detected from the oxygen sensor input.

Code 22 Coolant voltage low—coolant temperature sensor input below the minimum acceptable voltage/Coolant voltage high—coolant temperature sensor input above the maximum acceptable voltage.

Code 23 Air Charge or Throttle Body temperature voltage HIGH/LOW—charge air temperature sensor input is above or below the acceptable voltage limits.

Code 24 Throttle Position sensor voltage high or low.

Code 25 Automatic Idle Speed (AIS) motor driver circuit—short or open detected in 1 or more of the AIS control circuits.

Code 26 Injectors No. 1, 2, or 3 peak current not reached, high resistance in circuit.

Code 27 Injector control circuit—bank output driver stage does not respond properly to the control signal.

Code 27 Injectors No. 1, 2, or 3 control circuit and peak current not reached.

Code 31 Purge solenoid circuit—open or short detected in the purge solenoid circuit.

Code 32 Exhaust Gas Recirculation (EGR) solenoid circuit—open or short detected in the EGR solenoid circuit/EGR system failure—required change in fuel/air ratio not detected during diagnostic test.

Code 32 Surge valve solenoid—open or short in turbocharger surge valve circuit—some 1993 vehicles.

Code 33 Air conditioner clutch relay circuit—open or short detected in the air conditioner clutch relay circuit. If vehicle doesn't have air conditioning ignore this code.

Code 34 Speed control servo solenoids or MAX speed control circuit HIGH/LOW— open or short detected in the vacuum or vent solenoid circuits or speed control switch input above or below allowable voltage.

Code 35 Radiator fan control relay circuit—open or short detected in the radiator fan relay circuit.

Code 35 Idle switch shorted—switch input shorted to ground—some 1993 vehicles.

Code 36 Wastegate solenoid—open or short detected in the turbocharger wastegate control solenoid circuit.

Code 37 Part Throttle Unlock (PTU) circuit for torque converter

clutch—open or short detected in the torque converter part throttle unlock solenoid circuit.

Code 37 Baro Reed Solenoid—solenoid does not turn off when it should.

Code 37 Shift indicator circuit (manual transaxle).

Code 37 Transaxle temperature out of range—some 1993 models.**Code 41** Charging system circuit—output driver stage for generator field does not respond properly to the voltage regulator control signal.

Code 42 Fuel pump or no Auto shut-down (ASDZ) relay voltage sense at controller.

Code 43 Ignition control circuit—peak primary circuit current not respond properly with maximum dwell time.

Code 43 Ignition coil #1, 2, or 3 primary circuits—peak primary was not achieved within the maximum allowable dwell time.

Code 44 Battery temperature voltage— problem exists in the control module battery temperature circuit or there is an open or short in the engine coolant temperature circuit.

Code 44 Fused J2 circuit in not present in the logic board; used on the single engine module controller system.

Code 45 Turbo boost limit exceeded—MAP sensor detects overboost.

Code 44 Overdrive solenoid circuit—open or short in overdrive solenoid circuit.

Code 46 Battery voltage too high—battery voltage sense input above target charging voltage during engine operation.

Code 47 Battery voltage too low—battery voltage sense input below target charging voltage.

Code 51 Air/fuel at limit—oxygen sensor signal input indicates LEAN air/fuel ratio condition during engine operation.

Code 52 Air/fuel at limit—oxygen sensor signal input indicates RICH air/fuel ratio condition during engine operation.

Code 52 Logic module fault—1984 vehicles.

Code 53 Internal controller failure— internal engine controller fault condition detected during self test.

Code 54 Camshaft or (distributor sync.) reference circuit—No camshaft position sensor signal detected during engine rotation.

Code 55 End of message.

Code 61 Baro read solenoid—open or short detected in the baro read solenoid circuit.

Code 62 EMR mileage not stored— unsuccessful attempt to update EMR mileage in the controller EEPROM.

Code 63 EEPROM write denied— unsuccessful attempt to write to an EEPROM location by the controller.

Code 64 Flex fuel sensor—Flex fuel sensor signal out of range—(new in 1993)—CNG Temperature voltage out of range—CN gas pressure out of range.

Code 65 Manifold tuning valve—an open or short has been detected in the manifold tuning valve solenoid circuit (3.3L and 3.5L LH-Platform).

Code 66 No CCD messages or no BODY CCD messages or no EATX CCD messages—messages from the CCD bus or the BOOY CCD or the EATX CCO were not received by the control module.

Code 76 Ballast bypass relay—open or short in fuel pump relay circuit.

Code 77 Speed control relay—an open or short has been detected in the speed control relay.

Code 88 Display used for start of test.

Code Error Fault code error—Unrecognized fault 10 received by DRBII.

➡**If more than one definition is listed for a code or the code is not listed here, consult your "Chilton Total Car Care (TCC) Manual" to obtain the specific meaning for your vehicle. This list is for reference and does not mean that a component is defective. The code identifies the circuit and component that require further testing.**

Chrysler Import Built Fuel Systems

1984–1988 COLT, VISTA, SUMMIT AND D50

Code 1 Oxygen sensor.
Code 2 Crank angle sensor.

Code 2 Ignition signal.
Code 3 Air flow sensor.
Code 4 Barometric pressure sensor.
Code 5 Throttle Position Sensor (TPS).
Code 6 Motor Position Sensor (MPS).
Code 6 Idle Speed Control (ISC) position sensor.
Code 7 Engine Coolant Temperature Sensor.
Code 8 No. 1 cylinder TDC Sensor.
Code 8 Vehicle speed sensor.

➡ Some 1988 Multi-Point injected vehicles use 1989 2-digit codes.

➡ If more than one definition is listed for a code or the code is not listed here, consult your "Chilton Total Car Care (TCC) Manual" to obtain the specific meaning for your vehicle. This list is for reference and does not mean that a component is defective. The code identifies the circuit and component that require further testing.

1988–1993 COLT, SUMMIT, VISTA, LASER, TALON, STEALTH AND D50

Code 11 Oxygen sensor.
Code 12 Air flow sensor.
Code 13 Intake Air Temperature Sensor.
Code 14 Throttle Position Sensor (TPS).
Code 15 SC Motor Position Sensor (MPS).
Code 21 Engine Coolant Temperature Sensor.
Code 22 Crank angle sensor.
Code 23 No. 1 cylinder TDC (Camshaft position) Sensor.
Code 24 Vehicle speed sensor.
Code 25 Barometric pressure sensor.
Code 31 Knock (KS) sensor.
Code 32 Manifold pressure sensor.
Code 36 Ignition timing adjustment signal.
Code 39 Oxygen sensor (rear—turbocharged).
Code 41 Injector.
Code 42 Fuel pump.
Code 43 EGR—California.
Code 44 Ignition Coil—power transistor unit (No. 1 and No. 4 cylinders) on 3.0L Stealth.
Code 52 Ignition Coil—power transistor unit (No. 2 and No. 5 cylinders) on 3.0L Stealth.
Code 53 Ignition coil, power transistor unit (No. 3 and No. 6 cylinders).
Code 55 IAC valve position sensor.
Code 59 Heated oxygen sensor.
Code 61 Transaxle control unit cable (automatic transmission).
Code 62 Warm up control valve position sensor (non-turbo).

Jeep and Eagle Built Fuel Systems

1988–90 2.5L, 3.0L AND 4.0L ENGINE

Code 1000 Ignition line low.
Code 1001 Ignition line high.
Code 1002 Oxygen heater line.
Code 1004 Battery voltage low.
Code 1005 Sensor ground line out of limits.
Code 1010 Diagnostic enable line low.
Code 1011 Diagnostic enable line high.
Code 1012 MAP line low.
Code 1013 MAP line high.
Code 1014 Fuel pump line low.
Code 1015 Fuel pump line high.
Code 1016 Charge air temperature sensor low.
Code 1017 Charge air temperature sensor high.
Code 1018 No serial data from the ECU.
Code 1021 Engine failed to start due to mechanical, fuel, or ignition problem.
Code 1022 Start line low.
Code 1024 ECU does not see start signal.

Code 1025 Wide open throttle circuit low.
Code 1027 ECU sees wide open throttle.
Code 1028 ECU does not see wide open throttle.
Code 1031 ECU sees closed throttle.
Code 1032 ECU does not see closed throttle.
Code 1033 Idle speed increase line low.
Code 1034 Idle speed increase line high.
Code 1035 Idle speed decrease line low.
Code 1036 Idle speed decrease line high.
Code 1037 Throttle position sensor reads low.
Code 1038 Park/Neutral line high.
Code 1040 Latched B+ line low.
Code 1041 Latched B+ line high.
Code 1042 No Latched B+ ½ volt drop.
Code 1047 Wrong ECU.
Code 1048 Manual vehicle equipped with automatic ECU.
Code 1949 Automatic vehicle equipped with manual ECU.
Code 1050 Idle RPM's less than 500.
Code 1051 Idle RPM's greater than 2000.
Code 1052 MAP sensor out of limits.
Code 1053 Change in MAP reading out of limits.
Code 1054 Coolant temperature sensor line low.
Code 1055 Coolant temperature sensor line high.
Code 1056 Inactive coolant temperature sensor.
Code 1057 Knock circuit shorted.
Code 1058 Knock value out of limits.
Code 1059 A/C request line low.
Code 1060 A/C request line high.
Code 1061 A/C select line low.
Code 1062 A/C select line high.
Code 1063 A/C clutch line low.
Code 1064 A/C clutch line high.
Code 1065 Oxygen reads rich.
Code 1066 Oxygen reads lean.
Code 1067 Latch relay line low.
Code 1068 Latch relay line high.
Code 1070 A/C cutout line low.
Code 1071 A/C cutout line high.
Code 1073 ECU does not see speed sensor signal.
Code 1200 ECU defective.
Code 1202 Injector shorted to ground.
Code 1209 Injector open.
Code 1218 No voltage at ECU from power latch relay.
Code 1220 No voltage at ECU from EGR solenoid.
Code 1221 No injector voltage.
Code 1222 MAP not grounded.
Code 1223 No ECU tests run.

➡ Prior to 1988 vehicles used an Off-Board Diagnostic system which required special diagnostic equipment to read codes. 1991–95 Jeep and Eagle vehicles used the Chrysler Domestic Built Engine Control system. The code list for Chrysler Built Domestic Fuel injection System also covers 1991–95 Jeep and Eagle vehicles.

Ford Motor Company

EEC-IV AND EEC-V SYSTEMS

This system includes all Ford Motor Company vehicles with the exception of imported vehicles like the Capri, Festiva, Probe 2.0L, 2.2L and 2.5L engine and the Escort and Tracer equipped with the 1.8L engine.

Most 1984–94 Ford domestic built vehicles employ the 4th generation Electronic Engine Control system, commonly designated EEC-IV, to manage fuel, ignition and emissions on vehicle engines. In 1994 the EEC-V system was introduced on some models. The diagnostic system on EEC-V provides 3 digit codes in place of 2 digit codes and monitors more components.

Engine Control System

The control module is given responsibility for the operation of the emission control devices, cooling fans, ignition and advance and in some cases, automatic transmission functions. Because the EEC-IV oversees both the ignition timing and the fuel injector operation, a precise air/fuel ratio will be maintained under all operating conditions. The ECA is a microprocessor or small computer which receives electrical inputs from several sensors, switches and relays on and around the engine.

Based on combinations of these inputs, the ECA controls outputs to various devices concerned with engine operation and emissions. The engine control assembly relies on the signals to form a correct picture of current vehicle operation. If any of the input signals is incorrect, the ECA reacts to what ever picture is painted for it. For example, if the coolant temperature sensor is inaccurate and reads too low, the ECA may see a picture of the engine never warming up. Consequently, the engine settings will be maintained as if the engine were cold. Because so many inputs can affect one output, correct diagnostic procedures are essential on these systems.

One part of the ECA is devoted to monitoring both input and output functions within the system. This ability forms the core of the self-diagnostic system. If a problem is detected within a circuit, the controller will recognize the fault, assign it an identification code, and store the code in a memory section. Depending on the year and model, the fault code(s) may be represented by two or three digit numbers. The stored code(s) may be retrieved during diagnosis.

While the EEC-IV system is capable of recognizing many internal faults, certain faults will not be recognized. Because the computer system sees only electrical signals, it cannot sense or react to mechanical or vacuum faults affecting engine operation. Some of these faults may affect another component which will set a code. For example, the ECA monitors the output signal to the fuel injectors, but cannot detect a partially clogged injector. As long as the output driver responds correctly, the computer will read the system as functioning correctly. However, the improper flow of fuel may result in a lean mixture. This would, in turn, be detected by the oxygen sensor and noticed as a constantly lean signal by the ECA. Once the signal falls outside the pre-programmed limits, the engine control assembly would notice the fault and set an identification code.

Additionally, the EEC-IV system employs adaptive fuel logic. This process is used to compensate for normal wear and variability within the fuel system. Once the engine enters steady-state operation, the engine control assembly watches the oxygen sensor signal for a bias or tendency to run slightly rich or lean. If such a bias is detected, the adaptive logic corrects the fuel delivery to bring the air/fuel mixture towards a centered or 14.7:1 ratio. This compensating shift is stored in a non-volatile memory which is retained by battery power even with the ignition switched off. The correction factor is then available the next time the vehicle is operated.

➡ If the battery cable(s) are disconnected for longer than 5 minutes, the adaptive fuse factor will be lost. After repair, it will be necessary to drive the car at least 10 miles to allow the processor to relearn the correct factors. The driving period should include steady-throttle open road driving if possible. During the drive, the vehicle may exhibit driveability symptoms not noticed before. These symptoms should clear as the ECA computes the correction factor. The ECA will also store Code 19 indicating loss of power to the controller.

FAILURE MODE EFFECTS MANAGEMENT (FMEM)

The engine controller assembly contains back-up programs which allow the engine to operate if a sensor signal is lost. If a sensor input is seen to be out of range—either high or low—the FMEM program is used. The processor substitutes a fixed value for the missing sensor signal. The engine will continue to operate, although performance and driveability may be noticeably reduced. This function of the controller is sometimes referred to as the limp-in or fail-safe mode. If the missing sensor signal is restored, the FMEM system immediately returns the system to normal operation. The dashboard warning lamp will be lit when FMEM is in effect.

HARDWARE LIMITED OPERATION STRATEGY (HLOS)

This mode is only used if the fault is too extreme for the FMEM circuit to handle. In this mode, the processor has ceased all computation and control; the entire system is run on fixed values. The vehicle may be operated but performance and driveability will be greatly reduced. The fixed or default settings provide minimal calibration, allowing the vehicle to be carefully driven in for service. The dashboard warning lamp will be lit when HLOS is engaged. Codes cannot be read while the system is operating in this mode.

Dashboard Warning Lamp

The check engine dashboard warning lamp is referred to as the Malfunction Indicator Lamp (MIL). The lamp is connected to the engine control assembly and will alert the driver to certain malfunctions within the EEC-IV system. When the lamp is lit, the ECA has detected a fault and stored an identity code in memory. The engine control system will usually enter either FMEM or HLOS mode and driveability will be impaired.

The light will stay on as long as the fault causing it is present. Should the fault self-correct, the MIL will extinguish but the stored code will remain in memory.

Under normal operating conditions, the MIL should light briefly when the ignition key is turned **ON**. As soon as the ECA receives a signal that the engine is cranking, the lamp will be extinguished. The dash warning lamp should remain out during the entire operating cycle.

➡ On the Continental, the check engine message is displayed on the message center. When a fault is detected, the message is accompanied by a 1 second tone every 5 seconds. The tone stops after 1 minute. When the Continental system enters HLOS, the additional message CHECK DCL is displayed. DCL refers to the Data Communications Link running between the engine controller and the message center.

SELF DIAGNOSTICS

Diagnosis of a driveability problem requires attention to detail and following the diagnostic procedures in the correct order. Resist the temptation to begin extensive testing before completing the preliminary diagnostic steps. The preliminary or visual inspection must be completed in detail before diagnosis begins. In many cases this will shorten diagnostic time and often cure the problem without electronic testing.

Visual Inspection

This is possibly the most critical step of diagnosis. A detailed examination of all connectors, wiring and vacuum hoses can often lead to a repair without further diagnosis. Performance of this step relies on the skill of the technician performing it; a careful inspector will check the undersides of hoses as well as the integrity of hard-to-reach hoses blocked by the air cleaner or other components. Wiring should be checked carefully for any sign of strain, burning, crimping or terminal pull-out from a connector.

Checking connectors at components or in harnesses is required; usually, pushing them together will reveal a loose fit. Pay particular attention to ground circuits, making sure they are not loose or corroded. Remember to inspect connectors and hose fittings at components not mounted on the engine, such as the evaporative canister or relays mounted on the fender aprons. Any component or wiring in the vicinity of a fluid leak or spillage should be given extra attention during inspection.

Additionally, inspect maintenance items such as belt condition and tension, battery charge and condition and the radiator cap carefully. Any of these very simple items may affect the system enough to set a fault.

Diagnostic Connector Location

▶ See Figure 11

The Diagnostic Link Connectors (DLC) are located a 6 basic locations:
- Near the bulkhead (right or left side of vehicle)
- Near the wheel well (right or left side of vehicle)

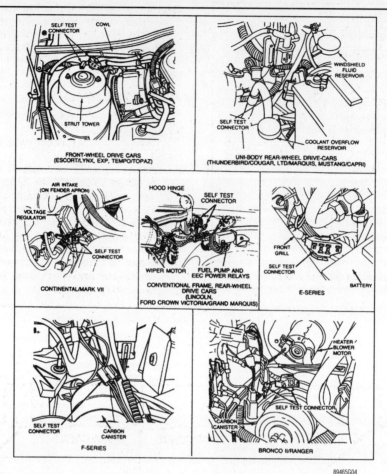

Fig. 11 Typical diagnostic link connector locations. Locations may vary on different years and models

• Near the front corner of the engine compartment (right or left side of vehicle)

READING TROUBLE CODES

The EEC-IV system may be interrogated for stored codes using the Quick Test procedures. These tests will reveal faults immediately present during the test as well as any intermittent codes set within the previous 80 warm up cycles. If a code was set before a problem self-corrected (such as a momentarily loose connector), the code will be erased if the problem does not reoccur within 80 warm-up cycles.

The Quick Test procedure is divided into 2 sections, Key **ON** Engine **OFF** (KOEO) and Key **ON** Engine Running (KOER). These 2 procedures must be performed correctly if the system is to run the internal self-checks and provide accurate fault codes. Codes will be output and displayed as numbers on the hand scan tool, i.e. 23. Code 23 would be displayed as 2 needle sweeps and pause and 3 more needle sweeps. For codes being read on an analog voltmeter, the needle sweeps indicate the code digits in the same manner as the lamp flashes on other systems.

In all cases, the codes 11 or 111 are used to indicate PASS during testing. Note that the PASS code may appear, followed by other stored codes. These are codes from the continuous memory and may indicate intermittent faults, even though the system does not presently contain the fault. The PASS designation only indicates the system passes all internal tests at the moment.

Once the Quick Test has been performed and all fault codes recorded, refer to the code charts. The charts direct the use of specific pinpoint tests for the appropriate circuit and will allow complete circuit testing.

✳✳ CAUTION

To prevent injury and/or property damage, always block the drive wheels, firmly apply the parking brake, place the transmission in Park or Neutral and turn all electrical loads off before performing the Quick Test procedures.

Reading Codes With Analog Voltmeter

▶ **See Figures 12, 13 and 14**

➡**There are inexpensive tools available at auto parts stores that make reading and clear Ford engine codes very easy. Reading the voltmeter needle sweeps is sometimes difficult. Always check the code more than once to make certain it was read correctly.**

In the absence of a scan tool, an analog voltmeter may be used to retrieve stored fault codes. Set the meter range to read DC 0–15 volts. Connect the (+) lead of the meter to the battery positive terminal and connect the (-) lead of the meter to the self-test output pin of the diagnostic connector.

Follow the directions given for performing the KOEO and KOER tests. To activate the tests, use a jumper wire to connect the signal return pin on the

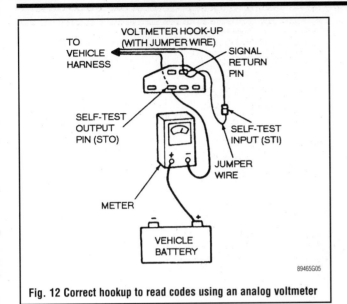

Fig. 12 Correct hookup to read codes using an analog voltmeter

diagnostic connector to the self-test input connector. The self-test input line is the separate wire and connector with or near the diagnostic connector.

The codes will be transmitted as groups of needle sweeps. This method may be used to read either 2 or 3 digit codes. The Continuous Memory codes are separated from the KOEO codes by 6 seconds, a single sweep and another 6 second delay.

KEY ON ENGINE OFF TEST

1. Connect the scan tool to the self-test connectors. Make certain the test button is unlatched or up.
2. Start the engine and run it until normal operating temperature is reached.
3. Turn the engine **OFF** for 10 seconds.
4. Activate the test button on the STAR tester.
5. Turn the ignition switch **ON** but do not start the engine. For vehicles with 4.9L engines, depress the clutch during the entire test. For vehicles with the 7.3L diesel engine, hold the accelerator to the floor during the test.
6. The KOEO codes will be transmitted. Six to nine seconds after the last KOEO code, a single separator pulse will be transmitted. Six to nine seconds after this pulse, the codes from the Continuous Memory will be transmitted.
7. Record all service codes displayed. Do not depress the throttle on gasoline engines during the test.

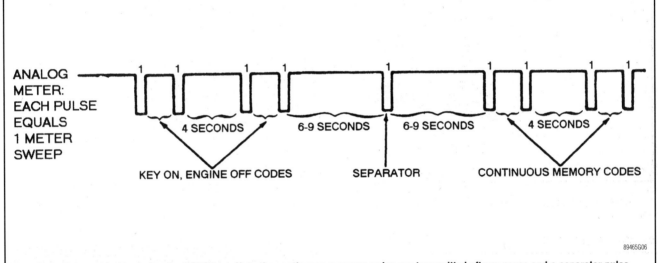

Fig. 13 Code transmission during the KOEO test. Note the continuous memory codes are transmitted after a pause and a separator pulse

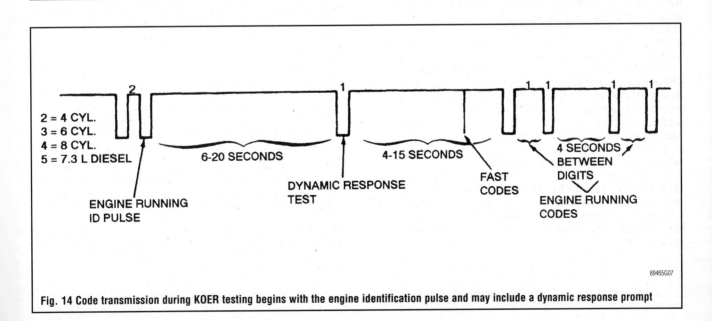

Fig. 14 Code transmission during KOER testing begins with the engine identification pulse and may include a dynamic response prompt

KEY ON ENGINE RUNNING TEST

♦ **See Figures 15, 16, 17 and 18**

1. Make certain the self-test button is released or de-activated on the STAR tester.

2. Start the engine and run it at 2000 rpm for two minutes. This action warms up the oxygen sensor.

3. Turn the ignition switch **OFF** for 10 seconds.

4. Activate or latch the self-test button on the scan tool.

5. Start the engine. The engine identification code will be transmitted. This is a single digit number representing ½ the number of cylinders in a gasoline engine. On the STAR tester, this number may appear with a zero, i.e., 20 = 2. For 7.3L diesel engines, the 10 code is 5. The code is used to confirm that the correct processor is installed and that the self-test has begun.

6. If the vehicle is equipped with a Brake On/Off (BOO) switch, the brake pedal must be depressed and released after the ID code is transmitted.

7. If the vehicle is equipped with a Power Steering Pressure Switch (PSPS), the steering wheel must be turned at least ½ turn and released within 2 seconds after the engine ID code is transmitted.

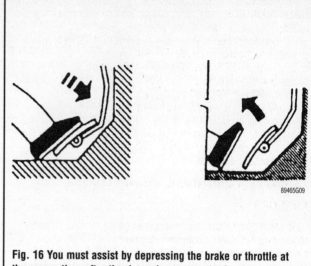

Fig. 16 You must assist by depressing the brake or throttle at the proper time after the dynamic response code

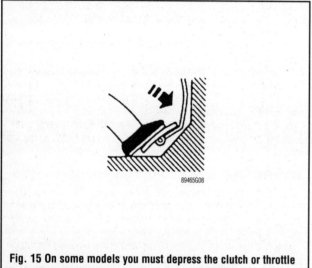

Fig. 15 On some models you must depress the clutch or throttle to the floor for the dynamic portion of the KOER test

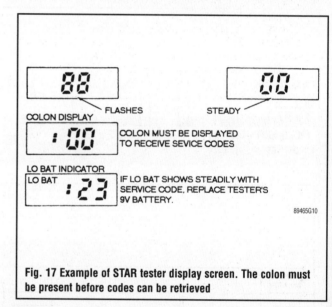

Fig. 17 Example of STAR tester display screen. The colon must be present before codes can be retrieved

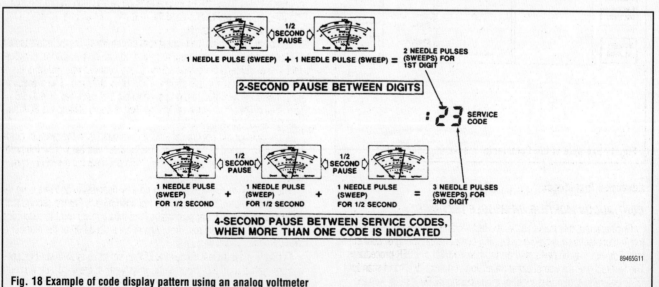

Fig. 18 Example of code display pattern using an analog voltmeter

8. If the vehicle is equipped with the E4OD transmission, the Overdrive Cancel Switch (OCS) must be cycled after the engine ID code is transmitted.

9. Certain Ford vehicles will display a Dynamic Response code 6–20 seconds after the engine ID code. This will appear as one pulse on a meter or as a 10 on the STAR tester. When this code appears, briefly take the engine to wide open throttle. This allows the system to test the throttle position, MAF and MAP sensors.

10. All relevant codes will be displayed and should be recorded. Remember that the codes refer only to faults present during this test cycle. Codes stored in Continuous Memory are not displayed in this test mode.

11. Do not depress the throttle during testing unless a dynamic response code is displayed

TESTING WITH CONTINENTAL MESSAGE CENTER

▶ See Figure 19

The stored fault codes may be displayed on the electronic message screen in Continentals so equipped. To perform the KOEO test, press all 3 buttons on the electronic instrument cluster (GAUGE SELECT, ENGLISH/METRIC, SPEED ALARM or SELECT, RESET and SYSTEM CHECK) simultaneously. Turn the ignition switch **ON** and release the buttons; stored codes will be displayed on the screen.

To perform the KOER test:

1. Hold in all 3 buttons, start the engine and release the buttons.

2. Press the SELECT or GAUGE SELECT button 3 times. The message **dEALEr 4** should appear at the bottom of the message panel.

3. Initiate the test by using a jumper wire to connect the signal return pin on the diagnostic connector to the self-test input connector. The self-test input line is the separate wire and connector with or near the diagnostic connector.

4. The stored codes will be output to the vehicle display.

5. To exit the test, turn the ignition switch **OFF** and disconnect the jumper wire.

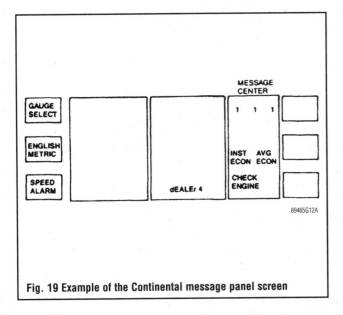

Fig. 19 Example of the Continental message panel screen

Advanced Test Modes

CONTINUOUS MONITOR OR WIGGLE TEST MODE

Once entered, this mode allows the technician to attempt to recreate intermittent faults by wiggling or tapping components, wiring or connectors. The test may be performed during either KOEO or KOER procedures. The test requires the use of either an analog voltmeter or a hand scan tool.

To enter the continuous monitor mode during KOEO testing, turn the ignition switch **ON**. Activate the test, wait 10 seconds, then deactivate and reactivate the test; the system will enter the continuous monitor mode. Tap, move or wiggle the harness, component or connector suspected of causing the problem; if a fault is detected, the code will store in the memory. When the fault occurs, the dash warning lamp will illuminate, the STAR tester will light a red indicator (and possibly beep) and the analog meter needle will sweep once.

To enter this mode in the KOER test:

1. Start the engine and run it at 2000 rpm for two minutes. This action warms up the oxygen sensor.

2. Turn the ignition switch **OFF** for 10 seconds.

3. Start the engine.

4. Activate the test, wait 10 seconds, then deactivate and reactivate the test; the system will enter the continuous monitor mode.

5. Tap, move or wiggle the harness, component or connector suspected of causing the problem; if a fault is detected, the code will store in the memory.

6. When the fault occurs, the dash warning lamp will illuminate, the STAR tester will light a red indicator (and possibly beep) and the analog meter needle will sweep once.

OUTPUT STATE CHECK

This testing mode allows the operator to energize and de-energize most of the outputs controlled by the EEC-IV system. Many of the outputs may be checked at the component by listening for a click or feeling the item move or engage by a hand placed on the case. To enter this check:

1. Enter the KOEO test mode.

2. When all codes have been transmitted, depress the accelerator all the way to the floor and release it.

3. The output actuators are now all **ON**. Depressing the throttle pedal to the floor again switches the all the actuator outputs **OFF**.

4. This test may be performed as often as necessary, switching between **ON** and **OFF** by depressing the throttle.

5. Exit the test by turning the ignition switch **OFF**, disconnecting the jumper at the diagnostic connector or releasing the test button on the scan tool.

CYLINDER BALANCE TEST

This test is only for SEFI engines. On SEFI engine the EEC-IV system allows a cylinder balance test to be performed on engines equipped with the Sequential Electronic Fuel Injection system. Cylinder balance testing identifies a weak or non-contributing cylinder.

Enter the cylinder balance test by depressing and releasing the throttle pedal within 2 minutes of the last code output in the KOER test. The idle speed will become fixed and engine mm is recorded for later reference. The engine control assembly will shut off the fuel to the highest numbered cylinder (4, 6 or 8), allow the engine to stabilize and then record the rpm. The injector is turned back on and the next one shut off and the process continues through cylinder No. 1.

The controller selects the highest rpm drop from all the cylinders tested, multiplies it by a percentage and arrives at an rpm drop value for all cylinders. For example, if the greatest drop for any cylinder was 150 rpm, the processor applies a multiple of 65% and arrives at 98 mm. The processor then checks the recorded rpm drops, checking that each was at least 98 rpm. If all cylinders meet the criteria, the test is complete and the ECA outputs Code 90 indicating PASS.

If one cylinder did not drop at least this amount, then the cylinder number is output instead of the 90 code. The cylinder number will be followed by a zero, so 30 indicates cylinder No. 3 did not meet the minimum rpm drop.

The test may be repeated a second time by depressing and releasing the throttle pedal within 2 minutes of the last code output. For the second test, the controller uses a lower percentage (and thus a lower rpm) to determine the minimum acceptable rpm drop. Again, either Code 90 or the number of the weak cylinder will be output.

Performing a third test causes the ECA to select an even lower percentage and rpm drop. If a cylinder is shown as weak in the third test, it should be considered non-contributing. The tests may be repeated as often as needed if the throttle is depressed within two minutes of the last code output. Subsequent tests will use the percentage from the third test instead of selecting even lower values.

Continuous Memory Codes

These codes are retained in memory for 80 warm-up cycles. To clear the codes for the purposes of testing or confirming repair, perform the KOEO test. When the fault codes begin to be displayed, de-activate the test by either disconnecting the jumper wire (meter, MIL or message center) or releasing the test button on the hand scanner. Stopping the test during code transmission will erase the Continuous Memory. Do not disconnect the negative battery cable to clear these codes; the Keep Alive memory will be cleared and a new code, 19, will be stored for loss of ECA power.

KEEP ALIVE MEMORY

The Keep Alive Memory (KAM) contains the adaptive factors used by the processor to compensate for component tolerances and wear. It should not be routinely cleared during diagnosis. If an emissions related part is replaced during repair, the KAM must be cleared. Failure to clear the KAM may cause severe driveability problems since the correction factor for the old component will be applied to the new component.

To clear the Keep Alive Memory, disconnect the negative battery cable for at least 5 minutes. After the memory is cleared and the battery reconnected, the vehicle must be driven at least 10 miles so that the processor may relearn the needed correction factors. The distance to be driven depends on the engine and vehicle, but all drives should include steady-throttle cruise on open roads. Certain driveability problems may be noted during the drive because the adaptive factors are not yet functioning.

To prevent the replacement of good components, remember that the EEC-IV system has no control over the following items:
- Fuel quantity and quality
- Damaged or faulty ignition components
- Internal engine condition — rings, valves,
- Starter and battery circuit
- Dual Hall sensor
- TFI or DIS module
- Distributor condition or function
- Camshaft sensor
- Crankshaft sensor
- Ignition or DIS coil
- Engine governor module

Any of these systems can cause erratic engine behavior easily mistaken for an EEC-IV problem.

SCAN TOOL FUNCTIONS

Although stored codes may be read by using an analog voltmeter by counting the needle sweeps, the use of hand-held scan tools such as Ford's second generation SUPER STAR II tester or equivalent is recommended. There are many manufacturers of these tools; the purchaser must be certain that the tool is proper for the intended use.

➡**The engine and 4EAT fault codes on NON-NAAO vehicles may only be read with the SUPER STAR II or its equivalent. The regular STAR tester or voltmeter may be capable not retrieve the stored codes.**

The SUPER STAR II tester is designed to communicate directly with the EEC system and interpret the electrical signals. The scan tool allows any stored faults to be read from the engine controller memory. Use of the scan tool provides additional data during troubleshooting but does not eliminate the use of the charts. The scan tool makes collecting information easier; the data must be correctly interpreted by an operator familiar with the system.

An adapter cable will be required to connect the scan tool to the vehicle; the adapter(s) may differ depending on the vehicle being tested.

DIAGNOSTIC TROUBLE CODES

Ford EEC-IV Diagnostic Engine Codes

The code definitions listed general 2-digit codes for Ford Vehicles using the Ford EEC-IV engine control system. In 1991 Ford started introducing vehicles that use 3-digit codes. The code definitions for both the 2 and 3-digit codes are found in this section. For a specific code definition or component test procedure consult a "Chilton Total Car Care (TCC) Manual" for your vehicle. A diagnostic code does not mean the component is defective. For example a Code 29 is a vehicle speed sensor code. This does not mean the sensor is defective, but to check the sensor and related components. A defective speedometer cable or transmission problem will also set this code.

Ford EEC Non-NAAO Vehicles

The Capri, Festiva, Probe, Escort and Tracer are referred to as NON-NAAO (Not North American Automotive Operations) produced vehicles. The fuel system used on these vehicles is called Electronic Engine Control (EEC). This EEC system components and operation are basically the same as the EEC-IV system. The self-diagnostic function on the EEC system differs from the EEC-VI system and is covered under NON-NAAO vehicle.

The Non-NAAO EEC system self-diagnostics and code retrieval many be different than domestic built Ford engines. The code descriptions are mostly the same for all of the NON-NAAO vehicles. Take note that not all vehicles use all codes. The transaxle codes were introduced in 1992 some Capri, Escort, Probe and Tracer models. Late model Probe and Escort may be equipped with EEC-IV fuel control system, the diagnostic link connector (DLC) will be of the EEC-IV design.

Ford EEC-IV System 2-Digit Diagnostic Trouble Codes

1981-94 PASSENGER CAR
1984-94 LIGHT TRUCK

Code 11 System Pass.
Code 12 (R) Idle control fault—RPM Unable To Reach Upper Limit Self-Test.
Code 13 (C) DC Motor Did Follow Dashpot.
Code 13 (O) DC Motor Did Not Move.
Code 13 (R) Idle control fault—Cannot control RPM during Self-Test low RPM check.
Code 14 (C) Engine RPM signal fault—Profile Ignition Pickup (PIP) circuit failure or RPM sensor.
Code 15 (C) EEC Processor, power to Keep Alive Memory (KAM) interrupted or test failed.
Code 15 (O) Power Interrupted To Processor or EEC Processor ROM Test failure.
Code 16 (O,R) RPM too low to perform Exhaust Gas Oxygen (EGO) sensor test or fuel control error.
Code 17 (O) CFI Fuel Control System fault—Rich/Lean condition indicated; 3.8L V-6 / 5.0L V-8 (1984).
Code 17 (R) RPM Below Self-Test Limit, Set Too Low.
Code 18 (C) Ignition diagnostic monitor (IDM) circuit failure, loss of RPM signal or SPOUT circuit grounded.
Code 18 (O) Ignition Diagnostic Monitor (IDM) circuit.
Code 18 (R) SPOUT or SAW circuit open.
Code 19 (C) Cylinder Identification (CID) Sensor Input failure.
Code 19 (O) Failure in EEC Processor internal voltage.
Code 19 (R) Erratic RPM During EGR Test or RPM Too Low During ISC Off Test.
Code 21 Engine Coolant Temperature (ECT) out of Self-Test range.
Code 22 (O,R) Manifold Absolute Pressure (MAP)/Barometric Pressure (BP/BARO) Sensor circuit out of Self-Test range.

Code 23 Throttle Position (TP) Sensor out of Self-Test range.

Code 24 (O,R) Air Charge (ACT) or Intake Air (IAT) Temperature out of Self-Test range.

Code 25 (R) Knock not sensed during dynamic response test.

Code 26 (O,R) Transmission Fluid Temp (TFT) out of Self-Test range.

Code 26 (O,R) Vane Air (VAF) or Mass Air (MAF) sensor out of self-test range.

Code 28 (C) Loss Of Primary Tach, Right Side.

Code 29 (C) Insufficient input from Vehicle Speed Sensor (VSS) or Programmable Speedometer/Odometer Module (PSOM).

Code 31 EGR valve position sensor circuit below minimum voltage.

Code 32 EGR Valve Position (EVP) sensor circuit voltage below closed limit.

Code 33 (C) Throttle Position (TP) sensor noisy/harsh on line.

Code 33 (R,C) EGR valve position sensor circuit, EGR valve opening not detected.

Code 34 EGR valve circuit out of self-test range or valve not closing.

Code 35 EGR valve circuit above maximum voltage—except 2.3L HSC with Feedback Carburetor System.

Code 38 (C) Idle Track Switch Circuit Open.

Code 39 (C) AXOD Torque Converter or Bypass Clutch Not Applying Properly.

Code 41 (R,C) Oxygen Sensor circuit indicates system always lean.

Code 42 (R,C) Oxygen Sensor circuit indicates system always rich, right side if 2 sensors used.

Code 43 (C) Oxygen Sensor Out Of Test Range—on 1992 and earlier vehicles.

—**or**—Throttle Position Sensor failure—on 1993 and newer vehicles.

Code 43 (R) Exhaust Gas Oxygen (EGO) sensor cool down has occurred during testing—2.3L HSC and 2.8L FBC truck.

Code 44 (R) Air injection control system failure (right side cylinders, if a split system).

Code 45 (C) Coil 1 primary circuit failure.

Code 45 (R) Air injection control system air flow misdirected.

Code 46 (C) Coil Primary Circuit failure.

Code 46 (R) Thermactor air not bypassed during Self-Test.

Code 47 (C) 4x4 switch is closed—on Truck.

Code 47 (R) Airflow low at idle—on fuel injected engines.

—**or**—4 x 4 switch is closed—on Truck.

—**or**—Fuel control system/Exhaust Gas Oxygen (EGO) Sensor fault—on 2.3L HSC and 2.8L FBC truck.

Code 48 (C) Coil Primary Circuit failure; Except 2.3L Truck

—**or**—Loss Of Secondary Tach, Left Side—with 2.3L Truck engine.

Code 48 (R) Airflow high at base idle.

Code 49 (C) Electronic Transmission Shift Error—on Truck and 1992 and later cars.

—**or**—SPOUT Signal Defaulted To 10 Degrees BTDC or SPOUT Open—Up to 1991 passenger cars.

Code 51 (O,C) Engine Coolant Temperature (ECT) circuit open or out of range during self-test.

Code 52 (O) Power Steering Pressure Switch (PSPS) circuit open.

Code 52 (R) Power Steering Pressure Switch (PSPS) circuit did not change states.

Code 53 (O,C) Throttle Position (TP) circuit above maximum voltage.

Code 54 (O,C) Air Charge (ACT) or Intake Air (IAT) Temperature circuit open.

Code 55 (R) Key Power Input To Processor—open circuit.

Code 56 (O,C) Mass Air (MAF) or Vane Air (VAF) Flow circuit above maximum voltage—Port fuel injected engines.

—**or**—Transmission oil temperature (TOT) circuit open—on vehicles with automatic transaxle.

Code 57 (C) AXOD Circuit failure—on vehicles with automatic overdrive transaxle.

—**or**—Octane Adjust Circuit failure—on some 1992 and newer cars.

Code 58 (R) Idle Tracking Switch circuit fault.

Code 59 (C) Automatic Transmission Shift Error—on 1991 and newer.

—**or**—AXOD 4/3 or Neutral Pressure Switch Failed Open—on 3.0L EFI and 3.8L AXOD—vehicles with automatic overdrive transaxle.

Code 59 (O) AXOD 4/3 Pressure Switch Failed Closed—on 3.8L engine AXOD—vehicles with automatic transaxle.

—**or**—Idle Adjust Service Pin In Use—on 2.9L EFI engine.

—**or**—Low Speed Fuel Pump Circuit failure—on 3.0L SHO engine.

Code 61 (O,C) Engine Coolant Temperature (ECT) circuit grounded.

Code 62 (C) Converter clutch error.

Code 62 (O) Electronic Transmission Shift Error.

Code 63 (O,C) Throttle Position (TP) circuit below minimum voltage.

Code 64 (O,C) Air Charge (ACT) or Intake Air (IAT) Temperature circuit grounded.

Code 65 (C) Fuel System Failed To Enter Closed Loop Mode or key power.

Code 65 (O) Key Power Check—Possible Charging System over voltage condition.

Code 65 (R) Overdrive Cancel Switch (OCS) circuit did not switch.

Code 66 (C) Mass Air (MAF) or Vane Air (VAF) Flow circuit below minimum voltage—engine with Port fuel injection.

—**or**—Transmission Oil Temperature (TOT) circuit grounded—vehicles with automatic transaxle.

Code 67 (O,C) Manual Lever Position (MLP) sensor out of range and A/C ON.

Code 67 (O,C) Neutral/Drive Switch (NDS) circuit open/A/C on during Self-Test.

Code 67 (O,R) Neutral Drive Circuit Failed or A/C Input High

—**or**—Clutch Switch Circuit failed—on vehicles with manual transaxle

—**or**—Manual Lever Position Sensor out of range—on vehicles with automatic transaxle.

Code 68 (C) Transmission Fluid Temp (TFT) transmission over temp (over heated).

Code 68 (O) Idle Tracking Switch circuit—on 2.8L FBC truck only.

—**or**—Air temperature sensor—except FBC truck.

Code 68 (R,C) Air Temperature Sensor Circuit failure on 1.9L EFI engine.

—**or**—Idle Tracking Switch Circuit failure—on CFI engine.

—**or**—Transmission Temperature Circuit.

Code 69 (O,C) Transmission Shift Error.

Code 70 (C) Data Communications Link Circuit failure.

Code 71(C) Software Re-Initialization Detected—on 1.9L EFI and 2.3L Turbo.

—**or**—Idle Tracking Switch failure—on CFI engine.

—**or**—Message Center Control Circuit failure—on vehicles with Message Center Control Center.

—**or**—Power Interrupt Detected—except vehicles with 3.8L AXOD (automatic overdrive transaxle).

Code 72 (R) Insufficient Manifold Absolute Pressure (MAP) change during Dynamic Response Test.

Code 73 (R) Insufficient Throttle Position (TP) change during Dynamic Response Test.

Code 74 (R,C) Brake On/Off (BOO) circuit open/not actuated during Self-Test.

Code 75 (R) Brake On/Off (BOO) circuit closed/EEC processor input open.

Code 76 (R) Insufficient Airflow Output Change During Test.

Code 77 (R) Brief Wide Open Throttle (WOT) not sensed during Self-Test/operator error (Dynamic Response/Cylinder Balance Tests).

Code 78 (C) Power Interrupt Detected.

Code 79 (O) A/C on/Defrost on during Self-Test.

Code 81(C) MAP Sensor Has Not Changing Normally.

Code 81(O) Air Management Circuit failure.

Code 82 (O) Supercharger Bypass Circuit failure, 3.8L SC engine.

—**or**—Air Management Circuit failure, Except 3.8L SC engine.

—**or**—EGR Solenoid Circuit failure, 2.3L OHC engine.

Code 83 OIC—Low speed fuel pump relay circuit failure.

Code 83 (O) High Speed Electro Drive Fan Circuit failure, Except 2.3L OHC and 3.0L SHO engine.

—**or**—Low Speed Fuel Pump Relay Circuit failure, 3.0L SHO engine.

Code 84 (O) EGR Vacuum Regulator (EVR) circuit failure.

Code 84 (R) EGR Solenoid Circuit failure.
Code 85 (C) Adaptive Lean Limit Reached.
Code 85 (O) Canister Purge (CANP) circuit failure.
Code 86 (C) Adaptive Rich Limit Reached.
Code 86 (O) Shift Solenoid (SS) circuit failure.
—**or**—Wide Open Throttle (WOT) A/C Cutoff Solenoid circuit—on Carbureted engine
Code 87 Fuel Pump circuit fault.
Code 88 (C) Loss Of Dual Plug Input control.
Code 88 (O) Electro Drive Fan Circuit failure.—fuel injected engine
—**or**—Throttle Kicker, feedback carburetor system
Code 89 (O)—Transmission solenoid circuit failure.
Code 89 (O) Clutch Converter Override (CCO) circuit failure.
—**or**—Exhaust Heat Control (EHC) Solenoid circuit—3.8L CFI engine
Code 91(C) No Heated Exhaust Gas Oxygen (HEGO) sensor switching detected—left HEGO.
Code 91(O) Shift Solenoid 1 (SS1) circuit failure.
Code 91(R) Heated Exhaust Gas Oxygen (HEGO) sensor circuit indicates system lean—left HEGO.
Code 92 (O) Shift Solenoid Circuit failure.
Code 92 (R) Oxygen Sensor Circuit failure.
Code 93 (O) Throttle Position Sensor (TPS) input low at maximum DC motor extension—OR—Shift solenoid circuit failure.
Code 93 (O) Coast Clutch Solenoid (CCS) circuit failure.
Code 94 (O) Torque Converter Clutch (TCC) solenoid circuit failure.
Code 94 (O) Converter Clutch Control (CCC) Solenoid circuit failure.
Code 94 (R) Thermactor Air System inoperative, left side.
Code 95 (O,C) Fuel Pump secondary circuit failure/Fuel Pump circuit open—EEC processor to motor ground.
Code 96 (O,C) Fuel Pump secondary circuit failure/Fuel Pump circuit open—battery to EEC processor.
Code 97 (O) Overdrive Cancel Indicator Light (OCIL) circuit failure.
Code 98 (R) Electronic control assembly failure.
Code 98 (O) Electronic Pressure Control (EPC) Driver open in EEC processor.
Code 98 (R) Hard fault is present—FMEM mode.
Code 99 (O,C) Electronic Pressure Control (EPC) circuit failure.
Code 92 (O) Shift Solenoid 2 (SS2) circuit failure.
Code 92 (R) Heated Exhaust Gas Oxygen (HEGO) sensor circuit indicates system rich—left HEGO.
Code 93 (O) Throttle Position Sensor Input Low At Max DC Motor Extension, CFI engine.
—**or**—Shift Solenoid Circuit failure—Except CFI engine.
Code 94 (O) Converter Clutch Solenoid Circuit failure.
Code 94 (R) Thermactor Air System Inoperative.
Code 95 (O,C) Fuel Pump Circuit failure, ECA To ground.
Code 96 (O,C) Fuel Pump Circuit failure.
Code 97 (O) Transmission Indicator Circuit failure.
Code 98 (O) Electronic Pressure Control Circuit failure.
Code 98 (R) Electronic Control Assembly failure.
Code 99 (O,C) Electronic Pressure Control Circuit or Transmission Shift failure.
Code 99 (R) EEC System Has Not Learned To Control Idle: Ignore Codes 12 & 13.

➡️**If more than one definition is listed for a code or the code is not listed here, consult your "Chilton Total Car Care (TCC) Manual" to get the specific meaning for your vehicle. This list is to be used as a reference for testing and does not mean a specific component is defective.**

(O) Key On, Engine Off
(R) Engine running
(C) Continuous Memory
No Code—Unable to Run Self Test or Output Codes, or list does not apply to vehicle tested, refer to service manual

Ford EEC-IV System 3-Digit Diagnostic Trouble Codes

1991-95 PASSENGER CAR AND LIGHT TRUCK

Code 111 System pass.
Code 112 Intake Air Temperature (IAT) Sensor circuit below minimum voltage.
Code 113 Intake Air Temperature (IAT) Sensor circuit above maximum voltage.
Code 114 Intake Air Temperature (IAT) higher or lower than expected.
Code 116 Engine Coolant Temperature (ECT) higher or lower than expected.
Code 117 Engine Coolant Temperature (ECT) Sensor circuit below minimum voltage.
Code 118 Engine Coolant Temperature (ECT) Sensor circuit above maximum voltage.
Code 121 Closed throttle voltage higher or lower than expected.
Code 121 Indicates Throttle Position voltage inconsistent with Mass Air Flow (MAF) Sensor.
Code 122 Throttle Position (TP) Sensor circuit below minimum voltage.
Code 123 Throttle Position (TP) Sensor circuit above maximum voltage.
Code 124 Throttle Position (TP) Sensor circuit voltage higher than expected.
Code 125 Throttle Position (TP) Sensor circuit voltage lower than expected.
Code 126 Manifold Absolute Pressure/Barometric Pressure (MAP/BARO) Sensor higher or lower than expected.
Code 128 Manifold Absolute Pressure (MAP) Sensor vacuum hose damaged/disconnected.
Code 129 Insufficient Manifold Absolute Pressure (MAP)/Mass Air Flow (MAF) change during Dynamic Response Test—KOER.
Code 136 Lack of Heated Oxygen Sensor (HO2S-2) switches during KOER, indicates lean—Bank # 2.
Code 137 Lack of Heated Oxygen Sensor (HO2S-2) switches during KOER, indicates rich—Bank # 2.
Code 138 Cold Start Injector (CSI) flow insufficient—KOER.
Code 139 No Heated Oxygen Sensor (HO2S-2) switches detected—Bank # 2.
Code 141 Fuel system indicates lean.
Code 144 No Heated Oxygen Sensor (HO2S-1) switches detected—Bank # 1.
Code 157 Mass Air Flow (MAF) Sensor circuit below minimum voltage.
Code 158 Mass Air Flow (MAF) Sensor circuit above maximum voltage.
Code 159 Mass Air Flow (MAF) higher or lower than expected.
Code 167 Insufficient Throttle Position (TP) change during Dynamic Response Test—KOER.
Code 171 Fuel system at adaptive limits, Heated Oxygen Sensor (HO2S-I) unable to switch—Bank # 1.
Code 172 Lack of Heated Oxygen Sensor (HO2S-1) switches, indicates lean—Bank # 1.
Code 173 Lack of Heated Oxygen Sensor (HO2S-1) switches, indicates rich—Bank # 1.
Code 174 Heated Oxygen Sensor (HO2S) switching time is slow—Right side—1992 vehicles only.
Code 175 Fuel system at adaptive limits, Heated Oxygen Sensor (HO2S-2) unable to switch—Bank # 2.
Code 176 Lack of Heated Oxygen Sensor (HO2S-2) switches, indicates lean—Bank # 2.
Code 177 Lack of Heated Oxygen Sensor (HO2S-2) switches, indicates rich—Bank # 2.
Code 178 Heated Oxygen Sensor (HO2S) switching time is slow—Left side—1992 vehicles only.
Code 179 Fuel system at lean adaptive limit at part throttle, system rich—Bank # 1.

Code 181 Fuel system at rich adaptive limit at part throttle, system lean—Bank # 1.

Code 182 Fuel system at lean adaptive limit at idle, system rich—Right side—1992 vehicles only.

Code 183 Fuel system at rich adaptive limit at idle, system lean—Right side—1992 vehicles only.

Code 184 Mass Air Flow (MAF) higher than expected.

Code 185 Mass Air Flow (MAF) lower than expected.

Code 186 Injector pulse width higher or Mass Air Flow (MAF) lower than expected (without BARO Sensor).

Code 187 Injector pulse width lower than expected (with BARO Sensor.

Code 187 Injector pulse width lower or Mass Air Flow (MAF) higher than expected (without BARO Sensor).

Code 188 Fuel system at lean adaptive limit at part throttle, system rich—Bank # 2.

Code 189 Fuel system at rich adaptive limit at part throttle, system lean—Bank # 2.

Code 191 Adaptive fuel lean limit is reached at idle—Left side—1992 vehicles only.

Code 192 Adaptive fuel rich limit is reached at idle—Left side—1992 vehicles only.

Code 193 Flexible Fuel (FF) Sensor circuit failure.

Code 211 Profile Ignition Pickup (PIP) circuit failure.

Code 212 Loss of Ignition Diagnostic monitor (IDM) input to Powertrain Control Module (control module)/SPOUT circuit grounded.

Code 213 SPOUT circuit open.

Code 214 Cylinder Identification (CID) circuit failure.

Code 215 Powertrain Control Module (PCM) detected Coil 1 Primary circuit failure (EI).

Code 216 Powertrain Control Module (PCM) detected Coil 2 Primary circuit failure (EI).

Code 217 Powertrain Control Module (PCM) detected Coil 3 Primary circuit failure (EI).

Code 218 Loss of Ignition Diagnostic Monitor (IDM) signal—left side (dual plug EI).

Code 219 Spark Timing defaulted to 10 degrees—SPOUT circuit open (EI).

Code 221 Spark Timing error (EI).

Code 222 Loss of Ignition Diagnostic Monitor (IDM) signal—right side (dual plug EI).

Code 223 Loss of Dual Plug Inhibit (DPI) control (Dual Plug EI).

Code 224 Powertrain Control Module (PCM) detected Coil 1,2,3,or 4 Primary circuit failure (Dual Plug EI).

Code 225 Knock not sensed during Dynamic Response Test—KOER.

Code 226 Ignition Diagnostic Monitor (IDM) signal not received (EI).

Code 232 Powertrain Control Module (PCM) detected Coil 1,2,3,or 4 Primary circuit failure (EI).

Code 238 Powertrain Control Module (PCM) detected Coil 4 Primary circuit failure (EI).

Code 241 Ignition Control Module (1CM) to Powertrain Control Module (PCM) Ignition Diagnostic Monitor (IDM) Pulse Width Transmission error (EI).

Code 244 Cylinder Identification (CID) circuit fault present when Cylinder Balance Test requested.

Code 311 Secondary Air Injection (AIR) system inoperative during KOER—Bank # 1 with dual HO2S.

Code 312 Secondary Air Injection (AIR) misdirected during KOER.

Code 313 Secondary Air Injection (AIR) not bypassed during KOER.

Code 314 Secondary Air Injection (AIR) system inoperative during KOER—Bank # 2 with dual HO2S.

Code 326 EGR (PFE/DPFE) circuit voltage lower than expected.

Code 327 EGR (EVP/PFE/DPFE) circuit below minimum voltage.

Code 328 EGR (EVP) closed valve voltage lower than expected.

Code 332 Insufficient EGR flow detected/EGR Valve opening not detected (EVP/PFE/DPFE).

Code 334 EGR (EVP) closed valve voltage higher than expected.

Code 335 EGR (PFE/DPFE) Sensor voltage higher or lower than expected during KOEO

Code 336 Exhaust pressure high/EGR (PFE/DPFE) circuit voltage higher than expected.

Code 337 EGR (EVP/PFE/DPFE) circuit above maximum voltage.

Code 338 Engine Coolant Temperature (ECT) lower than expected (thermostat test).

Code 339 Engine Coolant Temperature (ECT) higher than expected (thermostat test).

Code 341 Octane Adjust service pin open.

Code 411 Cannot control RPM during KOER low rpm check.

Code 412 Cannot control RPM during KOER high rpm check.

Code 415 Idle Air Control (IAC) system at maximum adaptive lower limit.

Code 416 Idle Air Control (IAC) system at upper adaptive learning limit.

Code 452 Insufficient input from Vehicle Speed Sensor (VSS) to PCM.

Code 453 Servo leaking down (KOER IVSC test).

Code 454 Servo leaking up (KOER IVSC test).

Code 455 Insufficient RPM increase (KOER IVSC test).

Code 456 Insufficient RPM decrease (KOER IVSC test).

Code 457 Speed Control Command Switch(s) circuit not functioning (KOEO IVSC test).

Code 458 Speed Control Command Switch(s) stuck/circuit grounded (KOEO IVSC test).

Code 459 Speed Control ground circuit open (KOEO IVSC test).

Code 511 Powertrain Control Module (PCM) Read Only Memory (ROM) test failure (KOEO).

Code 512 Powertrain Control Module (PCM) Keep Alive Memory (KAM) test failure.

Code 513 Powertrain Control Module (PCM) internal voltage failure—KOEO.

Code 519 Power Steering Pressure (PSP) Switch circuit open—KOEO.

Code 521 Power Steering Pressure (PSP) Switch circuit did not change states—KOER.

Code 522 Vehicle not in park or neutral during KOEO/Park/Neutral Position (PNP) Switch circuit open.

Code 524 Low speed Fuel Pump circuit open—battery to PCM.

Code 525 Indicates vehicle in gear/A/C on.

Code 526 Neutral Pressure Switch (NPS) circuit closed, A/C on—1992 vehicles only.

Code 527 Park/Neutral Position (PNP) Switch open—A/C on, KOEO.

Code 528 Clutch Pedal Position (CPP) switch circuit failure.

Code 529 Data Communications Link (DCL) or PCM circuit failure.

Code 532 Cluster Control Assembly (CCA) circuit failure.

Code 533 Data Communications Link (DCL) or Electronic Instrument Cluster (EIC) circuit failure.

Code 536 Brake On/Off (BOO) circuit failure/not actuated during KOER.

Code 538 Insufficient RPM change during KOER Dynamic Response Test.

Code 538 Invalid Cylinder Balance Test due to throttle movement during test—SF1 only.

Code 538 Invalid Cylinder Balance test due to Cylinder Identification (CID) circuit failure.

Code 539 A/C on/Defrost on during Self-Test.

Code 542 Fuel Pump secondary circuit failure.

Code 543 Fuel Pump secondary circuit failure.

Code 551 Idle Air Control (IAC) circuit failure—KOEO.

Code 552 Secondary Air Injection Bypass (AIRB) circuit failure—KOEO.

Code 553 Secondary Air Injection Diverter (AIRD) circuit failure—KOEO.

Code 554 Fuel Pressure Regulator Control (FPRC) circuit failure.

Code 556 Fuel Pump Relay primary circuit failure.

Code 557 Low speed Fuel Pump primary circuit failure.

Code 558 EGR Vacuum Regulator (EVR) circuit failure -KOEO.

Code 559 Air Conditioning On (ACON) Relay circuit failure-KOEO.

Code 563 High Fan Control (HFC) circuit failure—KOEO.

Code 564 Fan Control (FC) circuit failure—KOEO.

Code 565 Canister Purge (CANP) circuit failure—KOEO.

Code 566 3–4 Shift Solenoid circuit failure, A4LD transmission—KOEO.

Code 567 Speed Control Vent (SCVNT) circuit failure—KOEO IVSC test.

Code 568 Speed Control Vacuum (SCVAC) circuit failure—KOEO IVSC test.

Code 569 Auxiliary Canister Purge (CANP2) circuit failure—KOEO.

Code 571 EGRA solenoid circuit failure KOEO.

Code 572 EGRV solenoid circuit failure KOEO.

Code 578 A/C Pressure Sensor circuit shorted (VCRM) mode.

Code 579 Insufficient A/C pressure change (VCRM) mode.

Code 581 Power to fan circuit over current (VCRM) mode.

Code 582 Fan circuit open (VCRM) mode.

Code 583 Power to Fuel Pump over current (VCRM) mode.

Code 584 Power ground circuit open (Pin 1) (VCRM) mode.

Code 585 Power to A/C Clutch over current (VCRM) mode.

Code 586 A/C Clutch circuit open (VCRM) mode.

Code 587 Variable Control Relay Module (VCRM) communication failure.

Code 593 Heated Oxygen Sensor Heater (HO2S HTR).

Code 617 1–2 Shift error.

Code 618 2–3 Shift error.

Code 619 3–4 Shift error.

Code 621 Shift Solenoid 1 (SS1) circuit failure—KOEO.

Code 622 Shift Solenoid 2 (SS2) circuit failure—KOEO.

Code 623 Transmission Control Indicator Lamp (TCIL) circuit failure.

Code 624 Electronic Pressure Control (EPC) circuit failure.

Code 625 Electronic Pressure Control (EPC) driver open in PCM.

Code 626 Coast Clutch Solenoid (CCS) circuit failure—KOEO.

Code 627 Torque Converter Clutch (TCC) solenoid circuit failure.

Code 628 Excessive Converter Clutch slippage.

Code 629 Torque Converter Clutch (TCC) solenoid circuit failure.

Code 631 Transmission Control Indicator Lamp (TCIL) circuit failure—KOEO.

Code 632 Transmission Control Switch (TCS) circuit did not change states during KOER.

Code 633 4 x 4L Switch closed during KOEO.

Code 634 Manual Lever Position (MLP) voltage higher or lower than expected/ error in Transmission Select Switch (TSS) circuit(s).

Code 636 Transmission Oil Temperature (TOT) higher or lower than expected.

Code 637 Transmission Oil Temperature (TOT) Sensor circuit above maximum voltage/circuit open.

Code 638 Transmission Oil Temperature (TOT) Sensor circuit below minimum voltage/circuit shorted.

Code 639 Insufficient input from Transmission Speed Sensor (TSS)

Code 641 Shift Solenoid 3 (SS3) circuit failure.

Code 643 Torque Converter Clutch (TCC) circuit failure.

Code 645 Incorrect gear ratio obtained for first gear.

Code 646 Incorrect gear ratio obtained for second gear.

Code 647 Incorrect gear ratio obtained for third gear.

Code 648 Incorrect gear ratio obtained for fourth gear.

Code 649 Electronic Pressure Control (EPC) higher or lower than expected.

Code 651 Electronic Pressure Control (EPC) circuit failure.

Code 652 Torque Converter Clutch (TCC) Solenoid circuit failure.

Code 654 Manual Lever Position (MLP) Sensor not indicating park during KOEO.

Code 655 Manual Lever Position (MLP) Sensor indicating not in neutral during Self-Test.

Code 656 Torque Converter Clutch (TCC) continuous slip error.

Code 657 Transmission Over Temperature condition occurred.

Code 659 High vehicle speed in park indicated.

Code 667 Transmission Range sensor circuit voltage below minimum voltage.

Code 668 Transmission Range sensor circuit voltage above maximum voltage.

Code 675 Transmission Range sensor circuit voltage out of range.

Code 691 4x4 Low switch open or short circuit.

Code 692 Transmission state does not match calculated ratio.

Code 998 Hard fault present—FMEM Mode.

➥If specific cylinder banks or sides are referred to in any of the above codes, but the vehicle code is being obtained from has a 4 cylinder engine, or only one Oxygen Sensor, disregard the bank/side reference, but the code definition and components it pertains to is always the same.

General Motors Corporation

SELF DIAGNOSTICS

The control module is used on today's vehicles has a built in self testing system. This self-test ability is called self-diagnosis. The self-diagnosis system will test many or all of the sensors and controlled devices for proper function. When a malfunction is detected, this system will store a code in memory that's related to that specific circuit. The computer can later be accessed to obtain fault codes recorded in memory using the procedures for Reading Codes. This helps narrow down what area to begin testing.

Fault code meanings can vary from year to year even on the same model. It is extremely important after retrieving a fault code to verify its meaning with a proper manual. Servicing a code incorrectly will not only lead to the wrong conclusion but could also cause damage if tested or serviced incorrectly.

Since the control module is programmed to recognize the presence and value of electrical inputs, it will also note the lack of a signal or a radical change in values. It will, for example, react to the loss of signal from the vehicle speed sensor or note that engine coolant temperature has risen beyond acceptable (programmed) limits. Once a fault is recognized, a numeric code is assigned and held in memory. The dashboard warning lamp—check engine —will illuminate to advise the operator that the system has detected a fault.

More than one code may be stored. Although not every engine uses every code and the same code may carry different meanings relative to each engine or engine family. For example, on the 3.3L (VIN N), Code 46 indicates a fault found in the power steering pressure switch circuit. The same code on the 5.7L (VIN F) engine indicates a fault in the VATS anti-theft system.

In the event of an control module failure, the system will default to a pre-programmed set of values. These are compromise values that allow the engine to operate, although possibly at reduced efficiency. This is also known as the default, limp-in or back-up mode. Driveability is almost always affected when the control module enters this mode.

Service Precautions

• Protect the on-board solid-state components from rough handling or extremes of temperature.

• Always turn the ignition **OFF** when connecting or disconnecting battery cables, jumper cables, or a battery charger. Failure to do this can result in control module or other electronic component damage.

• Remove the control module before any arc welding is performed to the vehicle.

• Electronic components are very susceptible to damage caused by electrostatic discharge (static electricity). To prevent electronic component damage, do not touch the control module connector pins or soldered components on the control module circuit board.

Visual Inspection

This is possibly the most critical step of diagnosis. A detailed examination of all connectors, wiring and vacuum hoses can often lead to a repair without further diagnosis. Also, take into consideration if the vehicle has been serviced recently? Sometimes things get reconnected in the wrong place, or not at all. A careful inspector will check the undersides of hoses as well as the integrity of hard-to-reach hoses blocked by the air cleaner or other components. Correct routing for vacuum hoses can be obtained from your specific vehicle service manual or Vehicle Emission Control Information (VECI) label in the engine compartment of the vehicle. Wiring should be checked carefully for any sign of strain, burning, crimping or terminals pulled-out from a connector.

Checking connectors at components or in harnesses is required; usually, pushing them together will reveal a loose fit. In addition, check electrical connectors for corroded, bent, damaged, improperly seated pins, and bad wire crimps to terminals. Pay particular attention to ground circuits, making sure they are not loose or corroded. Remember to inspect connectors and hose fittings at components not mounted on the engine, such as the evaporative canister or relays mounted on the fender aprons. Any component or wiring in the vicinity of a fluid leak or spillage should be given extra attention during inspection.

➡**There are many problems with connectors on electronic engine control systems. Due to the low voltage signals that these systems use any dirt, corrosion or damage will affect their operation. Note that some connectors use a special grease on the contacts to prevent corrosion. Do not wipe this grease off, it is a special type for this purpose. You can obtain this grease from your vehicle dealer or parts distributor.**

Additionally, inspect maintenance items such as belt condition and tension, battery charge and condition and the radiator cap carefully. Any of these very simple items may affect the system enough to set a fault.

Dashboard Warning Lamp

▶ **See Figure 20**

The primary function of the dash warning lamp is to advise the operator that a fault has been detected, and, in most cases, a code stored. Under normal conditions, the dash warning lamp will illuminate when the ignition is turned **ON**. Once the engine is started and running, the control module will perform a system check and extinguish the warning lamp if no fault is found.

Additionally, the dash warning lamp can be used to retrieve stored codes after the system is placed in the Diagnostic Mode. Codes are transmitted as a series of flashes with short or long pauses. When the system is placed in the Field Service Mode (available on fuel injected model), the dash lamp will indicate open loop or closed loop function.

Intermittent Problems

If a fault occurs intermittently, such as a loose connector pin breaking contact as the vehicle hits a bump, the control module will note the fault as it occurs and energize the dash warning lamp. If the problem self-corrects, as with the terminal pin again making contact, the dash lamp will extinguish after 10 seconds but a code will remain stored in the POM memory. When an unexpected code appears during an intermittent failure that self-corrected; the codes are still useful in diagnosis and should not be discounted.

Diagnostic Connector Location

▶ **See Figures 21 and 22**

The Assembly Line Communication Link (ALCL) or Assembly Line Diagnostic Link (ALDL) is a Diagnostic Link Connector (DLC) located in the passenger compartment. It has terminals which are used in the assembly plant to check that the engine is operating properly before it leaves the plant.

This DLC is where you connect you jumper the terminals to place the engine control computer into self-diagnostic mode. The standard term DLC is sometimes referred to as the ALCL or the ALDL in different manuals. Either way it is referred to, they all still perform the same function.

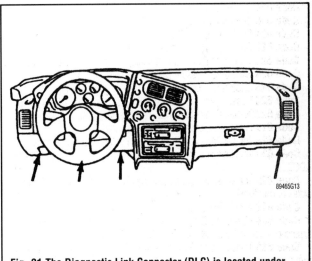

89465G13

Fig. 21 The Diagnostic Link Connector (DLC) is located under the instrument panel near the steering column on most vehicles

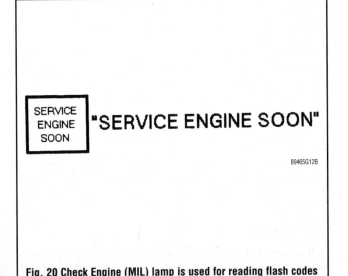

89465G12B

Fig. 20 Check Engine (MIL) lamp is used for reading flash codes

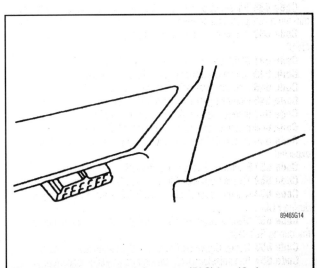

89465G14

Fig. 22 The Diagnostic Link Connector (DLC) is a 12 pin connector with a notch keyway

READING TROUBLE CODES

Reading Codes (Except Cadillac)

Since the inception of electronic engine management systems on General Motors vehicles, there has been a variety of connectors provided to the technician for retrieving Diagnostic Trouble Codes (DTC)s. Additionally, there have been a number of different names given to these connectors over the years; Assembly Line Communication Link (ALCL), Assembly Line Diagnostic Link (ALDL), Data Link Connector (DLC). Actually when the system was initially introduced to the 49 states in 1979, early 1980, there was no connector used at all. On these early vehicles there was a green spade terminal taped to the ECM harness and connected to the diagnostic enable line at the computer. When this terminal was grounded with the key **ON**, the system would flash any stored diagnostic trouble codes. The introduction of the ALCL was found to be a much more convenient way of retrieving fault codes. This connector was located underneath the instrument panel on most GM vehicles, however on some models it will not be found there. On early Corvettes the ALCL is located underneath the ashtray, it can be found in the glove compartment of some early FWD Oldsmobiles, and between the seats in the Pontiac Fiero. The connector was first introduced as a square connector with four terminals, then progressed to a flat five terminal connector, and finally to what is still used in 1993, a 12 terminal double row connector. To access stored Diagnostic Trouble Codes (DTC) from the square connector, turn the ignition **ON** and identify the diagnostic enable terminal (usually a white wire with a black tracer) and ground it. The flat five terminal connector is identified from left to right as A, B, C, D, and E. There is a space between terminal D and E which permits a spade to be inserted for the purposes of diagnostics when the ignition key is **ON**. On this connector terminal D is the diagnostic enable line, and E is a ground. The 12 terminal double row connector has been continually expanded through the years as vehicles acquired more on-board electronic systems such as Anti-lock Brakes. Despite this, the terminals used for engine code retrieval have remained the same. The 12 terminal connector is identified from right-to-left on the top row A-F, and on the bottom row from left-to-right, G-L. To access engine codes turn the ignition **ON** and insert a jumper between terminals A and B. Terminal A is a ground, and terminal B is the diagnostic request line. Stored trouble codes can be read through the flashing of the **Check Engine Light** or on later vehicles the **Service Engine Soon** lamp. Trouble codes are identified by the timed flash of the indicator light. When diagnostics are first entered the light will flash once, pause; then two quick flashes.

This reads as Code 12 which indicates that the diagnostic system is working. This code will flash indefinitely if there are no stored trouble codes. If codes are stored in memory, Code 12 will flash three times before the next code appears. Codes are displayed in the next highest numerical sequence. For example, Code 13 would be displayed next if it was stored in memory and would read as follow: flash, pause, flash, flash, flash, long pause, repeat twice. This sequence will continue until all codes have been displayed, and then start all over again with Code 12.

Clearing Codes (Except Cadillac)

EXCEPT RIVIERA, TORONADO AND TROFEO

To clear any Diagnostic Trouble Codes (DTCs) from the control module memory, either to determine if the malfunction will occur again or because repair has been completed, power feed must be disconnected for at least 30 seconds. Depending on how the vehicle is equipped, the system power feed can be disconnected at the positive battery terminal pigtail, the inline fuse holder that originates at the positive connection at the battery, or the control module fuse in the fuse block. The negative battery terminal may be disconnected but other on-board memory data such as preset radio tuning will also be lost. To prevent system damage, the ignition switch must be in the **OFF** position when disconnecting or reconnecting power.

When using a Diagnostic Computer such as Tech 1, or equivalent scan tool to read the diagnostic trouble codes, clearing the codes is done in the same manner. On some systems, DTCs may be cleared through the Tech 1, or equivalent scan tool.

On Riviera, Toronado and Trofeo, clearing codes is part of the dashboard display menu or diagnostic routine. Because of the amount of electronic equipment on these vehicles, clearing codes by disconnecting the battery is not recommended.

RIVIERA, TORONADO AND TROFEO (NON-CRT/DID VEHICLES)

Using the On-Board Diagnostic Display System

First turn the ignition to the **ON** position. On Riviera depress the **OFF** and TEMP buttons on the ECCP at the same time and hold until all display segments light. This is known as the Segment Check. On Toronado and Trofeo follow the same procedure, however, depress the **OFF** and WARMER buttons on the ECOP instead. After diagnostics is entered, any DTCs stored in computer memory will be displayed. Codes may be stored for the control module. Following the display of DTCs, the first available system for testing will be displayed. For example, "EC?" would be displayed on Riviera for ECM testing, while on Toronado and Trofeo the message "ECM?" will appear. The message is more clear on these vehicles due to increased character space in the IPC display area.

1. Depress the "FAN UP" button on the ECCP until the message "DATA EC?" appears on the display for Riviera, or "ECM DATA?" is displayed on Toronado and Trofeo.
2. Depress the "FAN DOWN" button on the ECCP until the message "CLR E CODE" appears on the display for Riviera, or "ECM CLEAR CODES?" is displayed on Toronado and Trofeo.
3. Depressing the "FAN UP" button on the ECCP will result in the message "E CODE CLR" or "E NOT CLR" on Riviera, "ECM CODES CLEAR" or "ECM CODES NOT CLEAR" on Toronado and Trofeo. This message will appear for 3 seconds. After 3 seconds, the display will automatically return to the next available test type for the selected system. It is a good idea to either cycle the ignition once or test drive the vehicle to ensure the code(s) do not reset.

TORONADO AND TROFEO (CRT/DID EQUIPPED)

Using the On-Board Diagnostic Display System

First turn the ignition switch to the **ON** position. Depress the "OFF" hardkey and "WARM" softkey on the CRT/DID at the same time and hold until all display segments light. This is the "Segment Check." During diagnostic operation, all information will be displayed on the Driver Information Center (DIC) located in the Instrument Panel Cluster (IPC). Because of the limited space available single letter identifiers are often used for each of the major computer systems. These are: E for ECM, B for BCM, I for IPC and R for SIR. After diagnostics is entered, any DTCs stored in computer memory will be displayed. Codes may be stored for the control module. Following the display of DTCs, the first available system for testing will be displayed. This will be displayed as "ECM?".

1. Depress the "YES" softkey until the display reads "ECM DATA?".
2. Depress the "NO" softkey until the display reads "ECM CLEAR CODES?".
3. Depressing the "YES" softkey will result in either the message "ECM CODES CLEAR" or "ECM CODES NOT CLEAR" being displayed, indicating whether or not the codes were successfully cleared. This message will appear for 3 seconds. After 3 seconds the display will automatically return to the next available test type for the selected system. It is a good idea to either cycle the ignition once or test drive the vehicle to ensure the code(s) do not reset.

Reading And Clearing Cadillac Engine Codes

The Cadillac Cimmaron used the 12 terminal DLC and codes can be accessed in the conventional manner as all other General Motors vehicles. The rear wheel drive Cadillac equipped with either the 4.1L V6, 5.0L V8, or the 5.7L V8 all can also be accessed in the conventional manner using the DLC.

1980–1983 DIGITAL FUEL INJECTION

1. Turn the ignition switch **ON**.
2. Depress the "OFF" and "WARMER" buttons on the Electronic Climate Control (ECC) panel simultaneously and hold until .. is displayed.

3. The numerals 88 should then appear indicating that all display segments are functional. Diagnosis should not be attempted unless the entire 88 is displayed or misdiagnosis will result.

4. If trouble codes are present they will appear on the digital ECC panel as follows:

   a. The lowest numbered code will be displayed for approximately two seconds.

   b. Progressively higher numbered codes, if present, will be displayed consecutively for two second intervals until the highest code has been displayed.

   c. 88 is again displayed.

   d. Parts A, B, and C will be repeated a second time.

   e. After the trouble codes have been displayed Code 70 will then appear. 70 indicates that the ECM is prepared for the switch test procedure.

5. If no trouble codes are stored in memory, 88 will appear for a longer time, and then the ECM will display Code 70.

Clearing Codes

While still in the diagnostic mode, press the "OFF" and "HIGH" buttons simultaneously until 00 appears. Trouble codes are now removed from the system memory.

➡ **The fuel data panel will go blank when the system is displaying in the diagnostic mode.**

1984 DIGITAL FUEL INJECTION

1. Turn the ignition switch **ON**.

2. Depress the "OFF" and "WARMER" buttons on the Electronic Climate Control (ECC) panel simultaneously and hold until .. is displayed.

3. "-1.8.8" should then appear indicating that all display segments are functional. Diagnosis should not be attempted unless the entire "-1.8.8" is displayed or misdiagnosis will result.

4. If trouble codes are present they will appear on the digital ECC panel as follows:

   a. The lowest numbered code will be displayed for approximately two seconds.

   b. Progressively higher numbered codes, if present, will be displayed consecutively for two second intervals until the highest code has been displayed.

   c. 88 is again displayed.

   d. Parts A, B, and C will be repeated a second time.

   e. After the trouble codes have been displayed Code 70 will then appear. 70 indicates that the ECM is prepared for the switch test procedure.

5. If no trouble codes are stored in memory, "-1.8.8" will appear for a longer time, and then the ECM will display Code 70.

Clearing Codes

While still in the diagnostic mode, press the "OFF" and "HIGH" buttons simultaneously until ".0.0" appears. Trouble codes are now removed from the system memory.

➡ **The fuel data panel will go blank when the system is displaying in the diagnostic mode.**

1985–1986 DIGITAL FUEL INJECTION

1. Turn the ignition switch **ON**.

2. Depress the "OFF" and "WARMER" buttons on the Climate Control Panel (CCP) simultaneously and hold until "-188" is displayed.

3. "-188" should then appear indicating that all display segments are functional. Diagnosis should not be attempted unless the entire "-188" is displayed or misdiagnosis will result.

4. If trouble codes are present they will appear on the Fuel Data Center (FDC) panel as follows:

   a. Display of trouble codes will begin with an "8.8.8" on the FDC panel for approximately one second. ". . . E" will then be displayed which indicates beginning of the ECM stored trouble codes. The initial pass of ECM codes includes all the detected malfunctions whether or not

they are currently present. If no ECM codes are stored the ". . . E" display will be bypassed.

   b. Following the display of ". . . E" the lowest numbered ECM code will be displayed for approximately two seconds. All ECM codes will be prefixed with an E (i.e. E12, E13, etc.).

   c. Progressively higher numbered codes, if present, will be displayed consecutively for two second intervals until the highest code has been displayed.

   d. ".E.E" is again displayed which indicates the start of the second pass of ECM trouble codes. On the second pass only current faults (hard codes) will be displayed. Codes displayed on the first pass are history failures or (soft codes). If all displayed codes were history codes the ".E.E" will be bypassed.

   e. When all ECM codes have been displayed, BCM codes will appear with the prefix F in the same manner as the ECM did.

5. After the display of all codes, or if no codes were stored, Code .7.0 will appear indicating the start of the switch tests.

Clearing Codes

While still in the diagnostic mode, press the "OFF" and "HIGH" buttons simultaneously until "E.0.0" appears. Trouble codes are now removed from the ECM memory.

1987–1993 DEVILLE AND FLEETWOOD

1. Turn the ignition switch **ON**.

2. Depress the "OFF" and "WARMER" buttons on the Climate Control Panel (CCP) simultaneously and hold until "-188" is displayed.

3. "-188" should then appear indicating that all display segments are functional. Diagnosis should not be attempted unless the entire "-188" is displayed or misdiagnosis will result.

4. If trouble codes are present they will appear on the Fuel Data Center (FDC) panel as follows:

   a. Display of trouble codes will begin with an "8.8.8" on the FDC panel for approximately one second. ". . . E" will then be displayed which indicates beginning of the ECM stored trouble codes. The initial pass of ECM codes includes all the detected malfunctions whether or not they are currently present. If no ECM codes are stored the ". . . E" display will be bypassed.

   b. Following the display of ". . . E" the lowest numbered ECM code will be displayed for approximately two seconds. All ECM codes will be prefixed with an E (i.e. E12, E13, etc.).

   c. Progressively higher numbered codes, if present, will be displayed consecutively for two second intervals until the highest code has been displayed.

   d. ".E.E" is again displayed which indicates the start of the second pass of ECM trouble codes. On the second pass only current faults (hard codes) will be displayed. Codes displayed on the first pass are history failures or (soft codes). If all displayed codes were history codes the ".E.E" will be bypassed.

   e. When all ECM codes have been displayed, BCM codes will appear with the prefix F in the same manner as the ECM did.

5. After the display of all codes, or if no codes were stored, Code .7.0 will appear indicating the start of the switch tests.

Clearing Codes

While still in the diagnostic mode, press the "OFF" and "HIGH" buttons simultaneously until "E.0.0" appears. Trouble codes are now removed from the ECM memory.

1987–1993 ALLANTE, ELDORADO AND SEVILLE

1. Turn the ignition switch **ON**.

2. Depress the "OFF" and "WARMER" buttons on the Climate Control Panel (CCP) simultaneously and hold until the segment check appears on the Instrument Panel Cluster (IPC) and the Climate Control Driver Information Center (CCDIC).

3. Diagnosis should not be attempted unless all of the segments of the vacuum fluorescent display are working as this could lead to misdiagnosis. On the IPC however the turn signal indicators do not light during this check.

4. After the service mode is entered, any trouble codes stored in the computer memory will be displayed, starting with ECM codes prefixed with an E.

5. If no trouble codes are present, the message NO ECM CODES will be displayed. Some later systems will display NO X CODES present, with X representing the system selected such as ECM, BCM, SIR, etc.

Clearing Codes

6. While still in the service mode, and the ECM diagnostic code display has been completed press the HI button on the CCP.

7. This action should cause the display to read "ECM DATA?".

8. Press the LO button on the CCP until the display reads "ECM CLEAR CODES?".

9. Press the HI button on the CCP and the display should read "ECM CODES CLEAR".

10. After approximately 3 seconds, all stored ECM codes will be erased.

➡ **The Cadillac Cimmaron used the 12 terminal DLC and codes can be accessed in the conventional manner. The rear wheel drive Cadillac equipped with either the 4.1 L V6, 5.0L V8, or the 5.7L V8 all can be accessed in the conventional manner using the DLC.**

DIAGNOSTIC TROUBLE CODES

Except Front Wheel Drive Cadillac

Code 12 No engine RPM reference pulses—System Normal.
Code 13 Oxygen Sensor (O2S) circuit open—left side on 2 sensor system.
Code 14 Engine Coolant Temperature (ECT) sensor—possible circuit high or shorted sensor.
Code 15 Engine Coolant Temperature (ECT) sensor—circuit low or open circuit.
Code 16 Direct ignition system (DIS), fault line circuit.
— **or** — Distributor ignition system (low resolution pulse).
— **or** — Missing 2x reference circuit
— **or** — OPTI-Spark ignition timing system (low resolution pulse).
— **or** — System voltage out of range.
Code 17 Camshaft Position Sensor (CPS) or spark reference circuit error.
Code 18 Crank/Cam error.
Code 19 Crankshaft Position Sensor (CPS) circuit.
Code 21 Throttle Position (TP) sensor circuit—signal voltage out of range, probably high.
Code 22 Throttle Position (TP) sensor circuit—signal voltage low.
Code 23 Intake Air Temperature (IAT or MAT) sensor circuit—temperature out of range, low.
— **or** — Open or grounded M/C solenoid—Feedback Carburetor system.
Code 24 Vehicle Speed Sensor (VSS) circuit.
Code 25 Intake Air Temperature (IAT or MAT) sensor circuit—temperature out of range, high.
Code 26 Quad-Driver Module #1 circuit.
— **or** — Transaxle gear switch circuit.
Code 27 Quad-Driver Module circuit.
— **or** — Transaxle gear switch, probably 2nd gear switch circuit.
Code 28 Quad-Driver Module (QDM) #2 circuit.
— **or** — Transaxle gear switch, probably 3rd gear switch circuit.
Code 29 Transaxle gear switch, probably 4th gear switch circuit.
Code 31 Camshaft sensor circuit fault.
— **or** — Park/Neutral Position (PNP) switch circuit.
— **or** — Wastegate circuit signal.
Code 32 Exhaust Gas Recirculation (EGR) circuit fault.
— **or** — Barometric Pressure Sensor circuit low—Feedback Carburetor system.
Code 33 Manifold Absolute Pressure (MAP) sensor—signal voltage out of range, high.
— **or** — Mass Air Flow (MAE) sensor—signal voltage out of range, probably high.

Code 34 Manifold Absolute Pressure (MAP) sensor—circuit out of range voltage, low.
— **or** — Mass Air Flow (MAF) sensor circuit (gm/sec low).
Code 35 Idle Air Control (IAC) or idle speed error.
— **or** — Idle Speed Control (ISC) circuit—throttle switch shorted—Feedback Carburetor system.
Code 36 Ignition system circuit error.
— **or** — Transaxle shift problem—4T60E Transaxle.
Code 38 Brake input circuit fault—Torque converter clutch signal.
Code 39 Clutch input circuit fault—Torque converter clutch signal.
Code 41 Cam sensor or cylinder select circuit fault—ignition control (IC) reference pulse system fault.
— **or** — Electronic Spark Timing (EST) circuit open or shorted.
Code 42 Electronic Spark Timing (EST) circuit grounded.
— **or** — Ignition Control (IC) circuit grounded or faulty bypass line.
Code 43 Knock Sensor (KS) or Electronic Spark Control (ESC) circuit fault.
Code 44 Oxygen Sensor (O2S), left side on 2 sensor system—lean exhaust indicated.
Code 45 Oxygen Sensor (O2S), left side on 2 sensor system—rich exhaust indicated.
Code 46 Personal Automotive Security System (PASS-Key II) circuit.
— **or** — Power Steering Pressure Switch (PSPS) circuit.
Code 47 PCM-BCM data circuit.
Code 48 Misfire diagnosis.
Code 51 Calibration error, faulty MEM-CAL, ECM or EEPROM failure.
Code 52 Engine oil temperature sensor circuit, low temperature indicated.
— **or** — Fuel Calpac missing.
— **or** — Over voltage condition.
— **or** — EGR Circuit fault.
Code 53 Battery voltage error.
— **or** — EGR problem.
— **or** — Personal Automotive Security System (PASS-Key) circuit.
Code 54 EGR #2 problem.
— **or** — Fuel pump circuit (low voltage).
— **or** — Shorted mixture control solenoid circuit—Feedback Carburetor system.
Code 55 A/D Converter error.
— **or** — PCM error or not grounded.
— **or** — EGR #3 problem.
— **or** — Fuel lean monitor.
— **or** — Grounded voltage reference, faulty oxygen sensor, fuel lean—Feedback Carburetor system.
Code 56 Quad-Driver Module (QDM) #2 circuit.
— **or** — Secondary air inlet valve actuator vacuum sensor circuit signal high—5.7L (VIN J).
Code 57 Boost control problem.
Code 58 Vehicle Anti-theft System fuel enable circuit.
Code 61 A/C system performance.
— **or** — Cruise vent solenoid circuit fault.
— **or** — Oxygen Sensor (O2S)—degraded signal.
— **or** — Secondary port throttle valve system fault—5.7L (VIN J).
— **or** — Transaxle gear switch signal.
Code 62 Cruise vacuum solenoid circuit fault.
— **or** — Engine oil temperature sensor, high temperature indicated.
— **or** — Transaxle gear switch signal circuit fault.
Code 63 Oxygen Sensor (O2S), right side—circuit open.
— **or** — Cruise system problem (speed error).
— **or** — Manifold Absolute Pressure (MAP) sensor—circuit out of range.
Code 64 Oxygen Sensor (O2S), right side—lean exhaust indicated.
Code 65 Oxygen Sensor (O2S), right side—rich exhaust indicated.
— **or** — Cruise servo position circuit.
— **or** — Fuel injector circuit low current.
Code 66 A/C pressure sensor circuit fault, probably low pressure.
— **or** — Engine power switch, voltage high or low or PCM fault—5.7L (VIN J).

Code 67 A/C pressure sensor circuit, sensor or A/C clutch circuit failure.
— **or** — Cruise switch circuit fault.
Code 68 A/C compressor relay (shorted circuit).
— **or** — Cruise system fault.
Code 69 A/C clutch circuit or head pressure high.
Code 70 A/C refrigerant pressure sensor circuit (high pressure).
Code 71 A/C evaporator temperature sensor circuit (low temperature).
Code 72 Gear selector switch circuit.
Code 73 A/C evaporator temperature sensor circuit (high temperature).
Code 75 Digital EGR #1 solenoid error.
Code 76 Digital EGR #2 solenoid error.
Code 77 Digital EGR #3 solenoid error.
Code 79 Vehicle Speed Sensor (VSS) circuit signal high.
Code 80 Vehicle Speed Sensor (VSS) circuit signal low.
Code 81 Brake input circuit fault—Torque converter clutch signal.
Code 82 Ignition Control (IC) 3X signal error.
Code 85 PROM error.
Code 86 Analog/Digital ECM error.
Code 87 EEPROM error.
Code 99 Power management.

➡ **If more than one definition is listed for a code or the code is not listed here, consult your "Chilton Total Car Care (TCC) Manual" to get the specific meaning for your vehicle. This list is for reference and does not mean a specific component is defective.**

Front Wheel Drive Cadillac

Cadillac Codes may start with an "E", "EO", "P" or "P0" dependent on model or type of code display. This prefix has been left off the following code description list.
Code 12 No spark reference from ignition control module or distributor.
Code 13 Oxygen sensor No.1 not ready.
Code 14 Engine Coolant Temperature (ECT) sensor circuit shorted.
Code 15 Engine Coolant Temperature (ECT) sensor circuit open.
Code 16 System voltage out of range.
Code 17 Oxygen sensor No.2 not ready.
Code 19 Fuel pump circuit shorted.
Code 20 Fuel pump circuit open.
Code 21 Throttle Position Sensor (TPS) circuit shorted.
Code 22 Throttle Position Sensor (TPS) circuit open.
Code 23 Electronic Spark Timing (EST) circuit fault or Ignition Control (IC) circuit problem.
Code 24 Vehicle Speed Sensor (VSS) circuit problem.
Code 26 Throttle Position (TP) switch circuit shorted.
Code 27 Throttle Position (TP) switch circuit open.
Code 28 Transaxle pressure switch problem.
Code 29 Transaxle shift "B" solenoid problem.
Code 30 Idle Speed Control (ISO) RPM out of range.
Code 31 Manifold Absolute Pressure (MAP) sensor circuit shorted.
Code 32 Manifold Absolute Pressure (MAP) sensor circuit open.
Code 33 Extended travel brake switch input circuit problem.
Code 34 Manifold Absolute Pressure (MAP) sensor signal too high.
Code 35 Ignition ground voltage out of range.
Code 36 EGR valve pintle position out of range.
Code 37 Intake Air Temperature (IAT) Manifold Air Temperature (MAT) circuit shorted.
Code 38 Intake Air Temperature (IAT) sensor, Manifold Air Temperature (MAT) circuit open.
Code 39 Torque Converter Clutch (TCC) engagement problem.
Code 40 Power Steering Pressure Switch (PSPS) open.
Code 41 Cam sensor circuit fault.
Code 42 Oxygen sensor No.1 LEAN exhaust signal.
Code 43 Oxygen sensor No.1 RICH exhaust signal.
Code 44 Oxygen sensor No.2 LEAN exhaust signal.
Code 45 Oxygen sensor No.2 RICH exhaust signal.

Code 46 Bank-to-bank fueling difference.
Code 47 ECM—Body Control Module (BCM) or IPC/PCM data fault.
Code 48 EGR control system fault.
Code 50 2nd gear pressure circuit fault.
Code 51 MEM-CAL error or PROM checksum mismatch.
Code 52 ECM memory reset indicator or PCM keep alive memory reset.
Code 53 Spark reference signal interrupt from Ignition Control (IC) module.
Code 55 Closed throttle angle out of range or Throttle Position Sensor (TPS) misadjusted.
Code 56 Transaxle input speed sensor circuit problem.
Code 57 Shorted transaxle temperature sensor circuit.
Code 58 Personal Automotive Security System (PASS) control fault.
Code 59 Open transaxle temperature sensor circuit.
Code 60 Cruise—transaxle not in drive.
Code 61 Cruise—vent solenoid circuit fault.
Code 62 Cruise—vacuum solenoid circuit fault.
Code 63 Cruise—vehicle speed and set speed difference.
Code 64 Cruise—vehicle acceleration too high.
Code 65 Cruise—servo position sensor failure.
Code 66 Cruise—engine RPM too high.
Code 67 Cruise—set/coast or resume/accel input shorted.
Code 68 Cruise Control Command (CCC) fault or servo position out of range.
Code 69 Traction control active in cruise.
Code 70 Intermittent Throttle Position (TP) sensor signal.
Code 71 Intermittent Manifold Absolute Pressure (MAP) sensor signal.
Code 73 Intermittent Engine Coolant Temperature (ECT) sensor signal.
Code 74 Intermittent Intake Air Temperature (IAT) sensor signal.
Code 75 Vehicle Speed Sensor (VSS) signal intermittent.
Code 76 Transaxle pressure control solenoid circuit malfunction.
Code 80 Fuel system rich or TP Sensor/idle learn not complete.
Code 81 Cam to 4X reference correlation problem.
Code 83 24X Reference signal high.
Code 85 Idle throttle angle too high, Throttle body service required.
Code 86 Undefined gear ratio.
Code 88 Torque Converter Clutch (TOO) not disengaging.
Code 89 Long shift and maximum adapt.
Code 90 Viscous Converter Clutch (VOC) brake switch input fault.
Code 91 Park/neutral switch fault.
Code 92 Heated windshield fault.
Code 93 Traction control system PWM link failure.
Code 94 Transaxle shift `A' solenoid problem.
Code 95 Engine stall detected.
Code 96 Torque converter overstress.
Code 97 Park/neutral to drive/reverse at high throttle angle.
Code 98 High RPM P/N to D/R shift under Idle Speed Control (ISO).
Code 99 Cruise control servo not applied in cruise.
Code P102 Shorted Brake Booster Vacuum (BBV) sensor.
Code P103 Open Brake Booster Vacuum (BBV) sensor.
Code P105 Brake Booster Vacuum (BBV) too low.
Code P106 Stop lamp switch input circuit problem.
Code P107 PCM/BCM data link problem.
Code P108 PROM checksum mismatch.
Code P109 POM keep alive memory reset.
Code P110 Generator L-terminal circuit problem.
Code P112 Total EEPROM failure.
Code P117 Shift `A/Shift `B' circuit output open or shorted.
Code P131 Active Knock Sensor (KS) failure.
Code P132 Knock Sensor (KS) circuit failure.
Code P137 Loss of ABS/TCS data.

➡ **If more than one definition is listed for a code or the code is not listed here, consult your "Chilton Total Car Care (TCC) Manual" to get the specific meaning for your vehicle. This list is for reference and does not mean a specific component is defective.**

OBD-II TROUBLE CODES

➡The term control module is a generic term used for the engine control computer. These computers are known by various names including Electronic Control Module (ECM), Powertrain Control Module (PCM), Vehicle Control Module (VCM), Single Board Engine Controller (SBEC), Engine Control Assembly (ECA) and Engine Control Unit (ECU).

➡The term Malfunction Indicator Lamp (MIL) is a generic term used to indicate the instrument panel mounted, engine computer controlled lamp which warns the driver there has been a fault in the system. Some common names for this lamp are the Check Engine Light and the Service Engine Soon Light. Sometimes just the word Engine will appear.

Introduction

The Federal Clean Air Act of 1990 mandated that all vehicles sold in the United States by the 1996 model year must adhere to the California Air Resources Board (CARB) requirements. These requirements took the form of a monitoring system that we now call OBD-II. The objective was to put into effect a method of monitoring the Electronic Engine Management and Emission Control Systems that would not only aid in their diagnosis, as was the case with OBD-I, but to also alert the driver of an OBD-II equipped vehicle of the early stages of an Emission Control component or system failure.

Reading and Clearing Codes

▶ See Figures 23, 24, 25, 26 and 27

It should be noted that with very few exceptions, reading and clearing of OBD-II trouble codes, must be performed using an OBD-II compliant scan tool. This should not be tremendous cause for concern as, as several manufacturers have developed scan tools that are well within the price range of the average do-it-yourselfer. Also, many mechanics will hook up a scan tool to your vehicle for a minimal charge.

Diagnostic Test Modes

Common diagnostic test modes have been created in a way that makes them common to all manufacturers. What this means is that no matter what vehicle you're testing or which piece of scanning equipment you have, all

TCCS4P10

Fig. 24 Inexpensive scan tools, such as this one from AutoXray®, are available to interface with the OBD-II electronics in your vehicle

TCCS4P06

Fig. 25 Among other features, a scan tool combines many standard testers into a single device for quick and accurate diagnosis

89694P31

Fig. 23 Hooking up the scan tool is as easy as plugging into the diagnostic link connector

89664P05

Fig. 26 Although some times no DTC's are found, that does not rule out a problem

89664P06

Fig. 27 Once the scan tool finds a trouble code it will display the appropriate code number and description

the tests that you need to perform will be the same for all manufacturers using the same terms and trouble codes. There 6 Test Modes as follows:
• Mode 1—Parameter Identification (PID)—accessing of live data, digital and analog values for inputs and outputs etc. Mode 1 is very similar to OBD I Data Scanning.
• Mode 2—Freeze Frame Data Access—This feature is a built-in freeze frame device right inside the control module. Data will be captured for all emissions related values at the time of a recognized fault, that will be available for the individual to retrieve at a suitable and convenient time.
• Mode 3—This enables all scan tools to retrieve stored DTCs. The DTC can be displayed alone or with descriptive text.
• Mode 4—This is ability of the scan tool to clear all control module emission-related diagnostic information. When the control module is reset like this, an Inspection/Maintenance Readiness code will be stored. (P1000) This only illustrates that the control module is awaiting further vehicle operating modes to complete further on-board monitoring and testing.
• Mode 5—This is the monitoring of the oxygen sensors to determine catalytic converter efficiency.
• Mode 6—Output State Mode (OTM)—allows the individual to energize and de-energize many of the controlled output devices. Through the use of the scanner, the devices can be manually controlled to determine real time functionality.

System Monitoring

To comply with EPA regulations, the OBD-II control module is equipped with software designed to allow it to extensively monitor vehicle emission control systems and components. Once the ignition is turned **ON** or the engine is started, and certain test conditions are met, the control module runs a series of monitors to test the emission control systems and components. Test conditions include different inputs such as time since startup, run-time, engine speed and temperature, transaxle gear position, and the engine open or closed loop status. Once the monitor is started, the control module attempts to run it to completion. If a particular monitor fails a test, a code is set and operating conditions at that time are recorded in memory. If the same component or system fails twice in succession, the Malfunction Indicator Lamp (MIL) is activated.

Monitors are divided into two types: Main Monitors and the Comprehensive Component Monitors.
• Catalyst Monitor
• EGR Monitor
• EVAP Monitor
• Fuel System Monitor
• Misfire Monitor

• Oxygen Sensor Monitor
• Oxygen Sensor Heater Monitor

Certain monitors, in particular the fuel system and misfire monitors, have limitations that are different from the others. The first time either of these monitors fail, the MIL is activated, and engine conditions at the time of the fault are recorded. In order for the control module to turn **OFF** an MIL related to these two monitors, it must determine that no faults are present with engine operating conditions similar to when it detected the fault. To qualify, the engine must be operated within a specified speed range, engine load range and temperature range. This is known as a drive cycle.

System monitoring has been improved over OBD-I by checking and double checking all input and output systems. The interesting thing about OBD-II is that this system has made it more difficult to illuminate the MIL by tightening up the parameters that causes the MIL to come on. Many of the conditions that cause the light to come on are now set out in what are referred to as the following:
• Warm-up Cycle—is operation of the vehicle to the point of warming the coolant by at least 40 degrees Fahrenheit over the last engine off and reaching at least 160 degrees Fahrenheit.
• Drive Cycles—take the warm-up cycle one step further by operating the vehicle to the point whereby it will go into closed loop and include the operating conditions that are necessary to initiate or even complete a specific OBD-II monitor or it will verify a symptom or its repair. A "monitor" is a new term that describes an operating strategy that can run internal tests of a specific system, component or function. This is very similar to on-board computer self tests.
• OBD-II Trip—is often referred to as a trip, and again takes the above mentioned steps further in progression. Beginning with an engine off period, after the engine is started, the vehicle must travel a specified distance to allow the following five OBD-II monitors to complete all of their tests:
1. Misfires
2. Fuel System
3. Comprehensive components
4. EGR
5. HO2S

OBD-II Drive Cycle This is a very specific combination of driving conditions that have been set out by the Federal Clean Air Act. Completion of all the conditions of this cycle ensures that all monitors have completed their required tests. This cycle is the most comprehensive of all the cycles and is illustrated in repair and diagnostic manuals through the use of a chart. In order for all monitors to take place the following must happen:
1. Cold Start. In order to be classified as a cold start the engine coolant temperature must be below 50C (122F) and within 6C (11F) of the ambient air temperature at startup. Do not leave the key on prior to the cold start or the heated oxygen sensor diagnostic may not run.
2. Idle. The engine must be run for two and a half minutes with the air conditioner on and rear defroster on. The more electrical load you can apply the better. This will test the O2 heater, Passive Air, Purge "No Flow", Misfire and if closed loop is achieved, Fuel Trim.
3. Accelerate. Turn off the air conditioner and all the other loads and apply half throttle until 88km/hr (55mph) is reached. During this time the Misfire, Fuel Trim, and Purge Flow diagnostics will be performed.
4. Hold Steady Speed. Hold a steady speed of 88km/hr (55mph) for 3 minutes. During this time the O2 response, air Intrusive, EGR, Purge, Misfire, and Fuel Trim diagnostics will be performed.
5. Decelerate. Let off the accelerator pedal. Do not shift, touch the brake or clutch. It is important to let the vehicle coast along gradually slowing down to 32km/hr (20 mph). During this time the EGR, Purge and Fuel Trim diagnostics will be performed.
6. Accelerate. Accelerate at 3/4 throttle until 88-96 km/hr (55-60mph). This will perform the same diagnostics as in step 3.
7. Hold Steady Speed. Hold a steady speed of 88km/hr (55mph) for five minutes. During this time, in addition to the diagnostics performed in step 4, the catalyst monitor diagnostics will be performed. If the catalyst is marginal or the battery has been disconnected, it may take 5 complete driving cycles to determine the state of the catalyst.
8. Decelerate. This will perform the same diagnostics as in step 5. Again, don't press the clutch or brakes or shift gears.

Trouble Code Description

▶ **See Figure 28**

In the past, trouble code descriptions varied between manufacturers, years, makes and models. OBD-II requires that all vehicle manufacturers use a common Diagnostic Trouble Code (DTC) numbering system. Since the generic listing was not specific enough, most manufacturers came up with their own DTC listings which are called manufacturer specific codes. Both generic and manufacturer specific codes are 5 digits. The numbers can be decoded as follows:

The first digit is a letter which identifies the function of the device or circuit which has the fault. This digit can be either:

- P—Powertrain
- B—Body
- C—Chassis
- U—Network or data link code

The second digit is either a 0 or 1 and indicates whether the code is generic or manufacturer specific.

- 0—Generic
- 1—Manufacturer Specific

The third digit represents the specific vehicle circuit or system that has the fault. Listed below are the number identifiers for the powertrain system.

- 1—Fuel and Air Metering
- 2—Fuel and Air Metering (Injector Circuit Malfunctions Only)
- 3—Ignition System or Misfire
- 4—Auxiliary Emission Control
- 5—Vehicle Speed Control and Idle Control System
- 6—Computer and Auxiliary Outputs
- 7—Transmission
- 8—Transmission

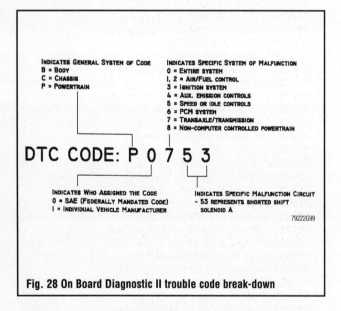

Fig. 28 On Board Diagnostic II trouble code break-down

The last two digits indicate the specific trouble code.

On OBD-II vehicles there are two different types of DTCs: Stored and Pending. For a DTC to become Stored, certain malfunction conditions must occur. The condition(s) required to Store codes are different for every DTC and vary by vehicle manufacturer.

In order for some DTCs to become Stored, a malfunction condition has to happen more than once. If the malfunction conditions are required to occur more than once, the potential malfunction is called a Pending DTC. The DTC remains pending until the malfunction condition occurs the required number of times to make the code stored. If the malfunction condition does not occur again after a set time the pending DTC will be cleared.

SAE Generic OBD-II Trouble Codes

On board diagnostic requirements have been defined by the OBD-II legislation in California and the Federal Clean Air Act. These requirements include the need for standardization of various parts of the system, including some of the Diagnostic Trouble Codes.

Prior to OBD-II, there was no uniformity in these numeric Diagnostic Trouble Codes (DTC) between manufacturers, and in some cases, even within the same manufacturer across different product lines. The Society of Automotive Engineers (SAE) codes from document J2012 provide some recommended uniformity for these codes.

In this section you will find the SAE recommended Industry Common Trouble codes for the powertrain control system. The fact that a code is recommended as a Industry Common Code does not imply that it is a Required Code (Legislated), an Emission Related Code, or that it indicates a fault that will cause the Malfunction Indicator Light to be illuminated.

In the following sections you will find the manufacturer specific codes. These are fault codes that will not generally be used by a majority of the manufacturers due to basic system differences, implementation differences, or diagnostic strategy differences. Each vehicle manufacturer or supplier who designs and specifies diagnostic algorithms, software, and diagnostic trouble codes have been strongly encouraged to remain consistent across their product line when assigning codes in the manufacturer controlled area.

P0100 Mass or Volume Air Flow Circuit Malfunction

P0101 Mass or Volume Air Flow Circuit Range/Performance Problem

P0102 Mass or Volume Air Flow Circuit Low Input

P0103 Mass or Volume Air Flow Circuit High Input

P0104 Mass or Volume Air Flow Circuit Intermittent

P0105 Manifold Absolute Pressure/Barometric Pressure Circuit Malfunction

P0106 Manifold Absolute Pressure/Barometric Pressure Circuit Range/Performance Problem

P0107 Manifold Absolute Pressure/Barometric Pressure Circuit Low Input

P0108 Manifold Absolute Pressure/Barometric Pressure Circuit High Input

P0109 Manifold Absolute Pressure/Barometric Pressure Circuit Intermittent

P0110 Intake Air Temperature Circuit Malfunction

P0111 Intake Air Temperature Circuit Range/Performance Problem

P0112 Intake Air Temperature Circuit Low Input

P0113 Intake Air Temperature Circuit High Input

P0114 Intake Air Temperature Circuit Intermittent

P0115 Engine Coolant Temperature Circuit Malfunction

P0116 Engine Coolant Temperature Circuit Range/Performance Problem

P0117 Engine Coolant Temperature Circuit Low Input

P0118 Engine Coolant Temperature Circuit High Input

P0119 Engine Coolant Temperature Circuit Intermittent

P0120 Throttle/Pedal Position Sensor/Switch "A" Circuit Malfunction

P0121 Throttle/Pedal Position Sensor/Switch "A" Circuit Range/Performance Problem

P0122 Throttle/Pedal Position Sensor/Switch "A" Circuit Low Input

P0123 Throttle/Pedal Position Sensor/Switch "A" Circuit High Input

P0124 Throttle/Pedal Position Sensor/Switch "A" Circuit Intermittent

P0125 Insufficient Coolant Temperature For Closed Loop Fuel Control

P0126 Insufficient Coolant Temperature For Stable Operation

P0130 O2 Circuit Malfunction (Bank no. 1 Sensor no. 1)

P0131 O2 Sensor Circuit Low Voltage (Bank no. 1 Sensor no. 1)

P0132 O2 Sensor Circuit High Voltage (Bank no. 1 Sensor no. 1)

P0133 O2 Sensor Circuit Slow Response (Bank no. 1 Sensor no. 1)

P0134 O2 Sensor Circuit No Activity Detected (Bank no. 1 Sensor no. 1)

P0135 O2 Sensor Heater Circuit Malfunction (Bank no. 1 Sensor no. 1)

P0136 O2 Sensor Circuit Malfunction (Bank no. 1 Sensor no. 2)

P0137 O2 Sensor Circuit Low Voltage (Bank no. 1 Sensor no. 2)

P0138 O2 Sensor Circuit High Voltage (Bank no. 1 Sensor no. 2)
P0139 O2 Sensor Circuit Slow Response (Bank no. 1 Sensor no. 2)
P0140 O2 Sensor Circuit No Activity Detected (Bank no. 1 Sensor no. 2)
P0141 O2 Sensor Heater Circuit Malfunction (Bank no. 1 Sensor no. 2)
P0142 O2 Sensor Circuit Malfunction (Bank no. 1 Sensor no. 3)
P0143 O2 Sensor Circuit Low Voltage (Bank no. 1 Sensor no. 3)
P0144 O2 Sensor Circuit High Voltage (Bank no. 1 Sensor no. 3)
P0145 O2 Sensor Circuit Slow Response (Bank no. 1 Sensor no. 3)
P0146 O2 Sensor Circuit No Activity Detected (Bank no. 1 Sensor no. 3)
P0147 O2 Sensor Heater Circuit Malfunction (Bank no. 1 Sensor no. 3)
P0150 O2 Sensor Circuit Malfunction (Bank no. 2 Sensor no. 1)
P0151 O2 Sensor Circuit Low Voltage (Bank no. 2 Sensor no. 1)
P0152 O2 Sensor Circuit High Voltage (Bank no. 2 Sensor no. 1)
P0153 O2 Sensor Circuit Slow Response (Bank no. 2 Sensor no. 1)
P0154 O2 Sensor Circuit No Activity Detected (Bank no. 2 Sensor no. 1)
P0155 O2 Sensor Heater Circuit Malfunction (Bank no. 2 Sensor no. 1)
P0156 O2 Sensor Circuit Malfunction (Bank no. 2 Sensor no. 2)
P0157 O2 Sensor Circuit Low Voltage (Bank no. 2 Sensor no. 2)
P0158 O2 Sensor Circuit High Voltage (Bank no. 2 Sensor no. 2)
P0159 O2 Sensor Circuit Slow Response (Bank no. 2 Sensor no. 2)
P0160 O2 Sensor Circuit No Activity Detected (Bank no. 2 Sensor no. 2)
P0161 O2 Sensor Heater Circuit Malfunction (Bank no. 2 Sensor no. 2)
P0162 O2 Sensor Circuit Malfunction (Bank no. 2 Sensor no. 3)
P0163 O2 Sensor Circuit Low Voltage (Bank no. 2 Sensor no. 3)
P0164 O2 Sensor Circuit High Voltage (Bank no. 2 Sensor no. 3)
P0165 O2 Sensor Circuit Slow Response (Bank no. 2 Sensor no. 3)
P0166 O2 Sensor Circuit No Activity Detected (Bank no. 2 Sensor no. 3)
P0167 O2 Sensor Heater Circuit Malfunction (Bank no. 2 Sensor no. 3)
P0170 Fuel Trim Malfunction (Bank no. 1)
P0171 System Too Lean (Bank no. 1)
P0172 System Too Rich (Bank no. 1)
P0173 Fuel Trim Malfunction (Bank no. 2)
P0174 System Too Lean (Bank no. 2)
P0175 System Too Rich (Bank no. 2)
P0176 Fuel Composition Sensor Circuit Malfunction
P0177 Fuel Composition Sensor Circuit Range/Performance
P0178 Fuel Composition Sensor Circuit Low Input
P0179 Fuel Composition Sensor Circuit High Input
P0180 Fuel Temperature Sensor "A" Circuit Malfunction
P0181 Fuel Temperature Sensor "A" Circuit Range/Performance
P0182 Fuel Temperature Sensor "A" Circuit Low Input
P0183 Fuel Temperature Sensor "A" Circuit High Input
P0184 Fuel Temperature Sensor "A" Circuit Intermittent
P0185 Fuel Temperature Sensor "B" Circuit Malfunction
P0186 Fuel Temperature Sensor "B" Circuit Range/Performance
P0187 Fuel Temperature Sensor "B" Circuit Low Input
P0188 Fuel Temperature Sensor "B" Circuit High Input
P0189 Fuel Temperature Sensor "B" Circuit Intermittent
P0190 Fuel Rail Pressure Sensor Circuit Malfunction
P0191 Fuel Rail Pressure Sensor Circuit Range/Performance
P0192 Fuel Rail Pressure Sensor Circuit Low Input
P0193 Fuel Rail Pressure Sensor Circuit High Input
P0194 Fuel Rail Pressure Sensor Circuit Intermittent
P0195 Engine Oil Temperature Sensor Malfunction
P0196 Engine Oil Temperature Sensor Range/Performance
P0197 Engine Oil Temperature Sensor Low
P0198 Engine Oil Temperature Sensor High
P0199 Engine Oil Temperature Sensor Intermittent
P0200 Injector Circuit Malfunction
P0201 Injector Circuit Malfunction—Cylinder no. 1
P0202 Injector Circuit Malfunction—Cylinder no. 2
P0203 Injector Circuit Malfunction—Cylinder no. 3
P0204 Injector Circuit Malfunction—Cylinder no. 4
P0205 Injector Circuit Malfunction—Cylinder no. 5
P0206 Injector Circuit Malfunction—Cylinder no. 6
P0207 Injector Circuit Malfunction—Cylinder no. 7
P0208 Injector Circuit Malfunction—Cylinder no. 8

P0209 Injector Circuit Malfunction—Cylinder no. 9
P0210 Injector Circuit Malfunction—Cylinder no. 10
P0211 Injector Circuit Malfunction—Cylinder no. 11
P0212 Injector Circuit Malfunction—Cylinder no. 12
P0213 Cold Start Injector no. 1 Malfunction
P0214 Cold Start Injector no. 2 Malfunction
P0215 Engine Shutoff Solenoid Malfunction
P0216 Injection Timing Control Circuit Malfunction
P0217 Engine Over Temperature Condition
P0218 Transmission Over Temperature Condition
P0219 Engine Over Speed Condition
P0220 Throttle/Pedal Position Sensor/Switch "B" Circuit Malfunction
P0221 Throttle/Pedal Position Sensor/Switch "B" Circuit Range/Performance Problem
P0222 Throttle/Pedal Position Sensor/Switch "B" Circuit Low Input
P0223 Throttle/Pedal Position Sensor/Switch "B" Circuit High Input
P0224 Throttle/Pedal Position Sensor/Switch "B" Circuit Intermittent
P0225 Throttle/Pedal Position Sensor/Switch "C" Circuit Malfunction
P0226 Throttle/Pedal Position Sensor/Switch "C" Circuit Range/Performance Problem
P0227 Throttle/Pedal Position Sensor/Switch "C" Circuit Low Input
P0228 Throttle/Pedal Position Sensor/Switch "C" Circuit High Input
P0229 Throttle/Pedal Position Sensor/Switch "C" Circuit Intermittent
P0230 Fuel Pump Primary Circuit Malfunction
P0231 Fuel Pump Secondary Circuit Low
P0232 Fuel Pump Secondary Circuit High
P0233 Fuel Pump Secondary Circuit Intermittent
P0234 Engine Over Boost Condition
P0261 Cylinder no. 1 Injector Circuit Low
P0262 Cylinder no. 1 Injector Circuit High
P0263 Cylinder no. 1 Contribution/Balance Fault
P0264 Cylinder no. 2 Injector Circuit Low
P0265 Cylinder no. 2 Injector Circuit High
P0266 Cylinder no. 2 Contribution/Balance Fault
P0267 Cylinder no. 3 Injector Circuit Low
P0268 Cylinder no. 3 Injector Circuit High
P0269 Cylinder no. 3 Contribution/Balance Fault
P0270 Cylinder no. 4 Injector Circuit Low
P0271 Cylinder no. 4 Injector Circuit High
P0272 Cylinder no. 4 Contribution/Balance Fault
P0273 Cylinder no. 5 Injector Circuit Low
P0274 Cylinder no. 5 Injector Circuit High
P0275 Cylinder no. 5 Contribution/Balance Fault
P0276 Cylinder no. 6 Injector Circuit Low
P0277 Cylinder no. 6 Injector Circuit High
P0278 Cylinder no. 6 Contribution/Balance Fault
P0279 Cylinder no. 7 Injector Circuit Low
P0280 Cylinder no. 7 Injector Circuit High
P0281 Cylinder no. 7 Contribution/Balance Fault
P0282 Cylinder no. 8 Injector Circuit Low
P0283 Cylinder no. 8 Injector Circuit High
P0284 Cylinder no. 8 Contribution/Balance Fault
P0285 Cylinder no. 9 Injector Circuit Low
P0286 Cylinder no. 9 Injector Circuit High
P0287 Cylinder no. 9 Contribution/Balance Fault
P0288 Cylinder no. 10 Injector Circuit Low
P0289 Cylinder no. 10 Injector Circuit High
P0290 Cylinder no. 10 Contribution/Balance Fault
P0291 Cylinder no. 11 Injector Circuit Low
P0292 Cylinder no. 11 Injector Circuit High
P0293 Cylinder no. 11 Contribution/Balance Fault
P0294 Cylinder no. 12 Injector Circuit Low
P0295 Cylinder no. 12 Injector Circuit High
P0296 Cylinder no. 12 Contribution/Balance Fault
P0300 Random/Multiple Cylinder Misfire Detected
P0301 Cylinder no. 1—Misfire Detected
P0302 Cylinder no. 2—Misfire Detected

P0303 Cylinder no. 3—Misfire Detected
P0304 Cylinder no. 4—Misfire Detected
P0305 Cylinder no. 5—Misfire Detected
P0306 Cylinder no. 6—Misfire Detected
P0307 Cylinder no. 7—Misfire Detected
P0308 Cylinder no. 8—Misfire Detected
P0309 Cylinder no. 9—Misfire Detected
P0310 Cylinder no. 10—Misfire Detected
P0311 Cylinder no. 11—Misfire Detected
P0312 Cylinder no. 12—Misfire Detected
P0320 Ignition/Distributor Engine Speed Input Circuit Malfunction
P0321 Ignition/Distributor Engine Speed Input Circuit Range/Performance
P0322 Ignition/Distributor Engine Speed Input Circuit No Signal
P0323 Ignition/Distributor Engine Speed Input Circuit Intermittent
P0325 Knock Sensor no. 1—Circuit Malfunction (Bank no. 1 or Single Sensor)
P0326 Knock Sensor no. 1—Circuit Range/Performance (Bank no. 1 or Single Sensor)
P0327 Knock Sensor no. 1—Circuit Low Input (Bank no. 1 or Single Sensor)
P0328 Knock Sensor no. 1—Circuit High Input (Bank no. 1 or Single Sensor)
P0329 Knock Sensor no. 1—Circuit Input Intermittent (Bank no. 1 or Single Sensor)
P0330 Knock Sensor no. 2—Circuit Malfunction (Bank no. 2)
P0331 Knock Sensor no. 2—Circuit Range/Performance (Bank no. 2)
P0332 Knock Sensor no. 2—Circuit Low Input (Bank no. 2)
P0333 Knock Sensor no. 2—Circuit High Input (Bank no. 2)
P0334 Knock Sensor no. 2—Circuit Input Intermittent (Bank no. 2)
P0335 Crankshaft Position Sensor "A" Circuit Malfunction
P0336 Crankshaft Position Sensor "A" Circuit Range/Performance
P0337 Crankshaft Position Sensor "A" Circuit Low Input
P0338 Crankshaft Position Sensor "A" Circuit High Input
P0339 Crankshaft Position Sensor "A" Circuit Intermittent
P0340 Camshaft Position Sensor Circuit Malfunction
P0341 Camshaft Position Sensor Circuit Range/Performance
P0342 Camshaft Position Sensor Circuit Low Input
P0343 Camshaft Position Sensor Circuit High Input
P0344 Camshaft Position Sensor Circuit Intermittent
P0350 Ignition Coil Primary/Secondary Circuit Malfunction
P0351 Ignition Coil "A" Primary/Secondary Circuit Malfunction
P0352 Ignition Coil "B" Primary/Secondary Circuit Malfunction
P0353 Ignition Coil "C" Primary/Secondary Circuit Malfunction
P0354 Ignition Coil "D" Primary/Secondary Circuit Malfunction
P0355 Ignition Coil "E" Primary/Secondary Circuit Malfunction
P0356 Ignition Coil "F" Primary/Secondary Circuit Malfunction
P0357 Ignition Coil "G" Primary/Secondary Circuit Malfunction
P0358 Ignition Coil "H" Primary/Secondary Circuit Malfunction
P0359 Ignition Coil "I" Primary/Secondary Circuit Malfunction
P0360 Ignition Coil "J" Primary/Secondary Circuit Malfunction
P0361 Ignition Coil "K" Primary/Secondary Circuit Malfunction
P0362 Ignition Coil "L" Primary/Secondary Circuit Malfunction
P0370 Timing Reference High Resolution Signal "A" Malfunction
P0371 Timing Reference High Resolution Signal "A" Too Many Pulses
P0372 Timing Reference High Resolution Signal "A" Too Few Pulses
P0373 Timing Reference High Resolution Signal "A" Intermittent/Erratic Pulses
P0374 Timing Reference High Resolution Signal "A" No Pulses
P0375 Timing Reference High Resolution Signal "B" Malfunction
P0376 Timing Reference High Resolution Signal "B" Too Many Pulses
P0377 Timing Reference High Resolution Signal "B" Too Few Pulses
P0378 Timing Reference High Resolution Signal "B" Intermittent/Erratic Pulses
P0379 Timing Reference High Resolution Signal "B" No Pulses

P0380 Glow Plug/Heater Circuit "A" Malfunction
P0381 Glow Plug/Heater Indicator Circuit Malfunction
P0382 Glow Plug/Heater Circuit "B" Malfunction
P0385 Crankshaft Position Sensor "B" Circuit Malfunction
P0386 Crankshaft Position Sensor "B" Circuit Range/Performance
P0387 Crankshaft Position Sensor "B" Circuit Low Input
P0388 Crankshaft Position Sensor "B" Circuit High Input
P0389 Crankshaft Position Sensor "B" Circuit Intermittent
P0400 Exhaust Gas Recirculation Flow Malfunction
P0401 Exhaust Gas Recirculation Flow Insufficient Detected
P0402 Exhaust Gas Recirculation Flow Excessive Detected
P0403 Exhaust Gas Recirculation Circuit Malfunction
P0404 Exhaust Gas Recirculation Circuit Range/Performance
P0405 Exhaust Gas Recirculation Sensor "A" Circuit Low
P0406 Exhaust Gas Recirculation Sensor "A" Circuit High
P0407 Exhaust Gas Recirculation Sensor "B" Circuit Low
P0408 Exhaust Gas Recirculation Sensor "B" Circuit High
P0410 Secondary Air Injection System Malfunction
P0411 Secondary Air Injection System Incorrect Flow Detected
P0412 Secondary Air Injection System Switching Valve "A" Circuit Malfunction
P0413 Secondary Air Injection System Switching Valve "A" Circuit Open
P0414 Secondary Air Injection System Switching Valve "A" Circuit Shorted
P0415 Secondary Air Injection System Switching Valve "B" Circuit Malfunction
P0416 Secondary Air Injection System Switching Valve "B" Circuit Open
P0417 Secondary Air Injection System Switching Valve "B" Circuit Shorted
P0418 Secondary Air Injection System Relay "A" Circuit Malfunction
P0419 Secondary Air Injection System Relay "B" Circuit Malfunction
P0420 Catalyst System Efficiency Below Threshold (Bank no. 1)
P0421 Warm Up Catalyst Efficiency Below Threshold (Bank no. 1)
P0422 Main Catalyst Efficiency Below Threshold (Bank no. 1)
P0423 Heated Catalyst Efficiency Below Threshold (Bank no. 1)
P0424 Heated Catalyst Temperature Below Threshold (Bank no. 1)
P0430 Catalyst System Efficiency Below Threshold (Bank no. 2)
P0431 Warm Up Catalyst Efficiency Below Threshold (Bank no. 2)
P0432 Main Catalyst Efficiency Below Threshold (Bank no. 2)
P0433 Heated Catalyst Efficiency Below Threshold (Bank no. 2)
P0434 Heated Catalyst Temperature Below Threshold (Bank no. 2)
P0440 Evaporative Emission Control System Malfunction
P0441 Evaporative Emission Control System Incorrect Purge Flow
P0442 Evaporative Emission Control System Leak Detected (Small Leak)
P0443 Evaporative Emission Control System Purge Control Valve Circuit Malfunction
P0444 Evaporative Emission Control System Purge Control Valve Circuit Open
P0445 Evaporative Emission Control System Purge Control Valve Circuit Shorted
P0446 Evaporative Emission Control System Vent Control Circuit Malfunction
P0447 Evaporative Emission Control System Vent Control Circuit Open
P0448 Evaporative Emission Control System Vent Control Circuit Shorted
P0449 Evaporative Emission Control System Vent Valve/Solenoid Circuit Malfunction
P0450 Evaporative Emission Control System Pressure Sensor Malfunction
P0451 Evaporative Emission Control System Pressure Sensor Range/Performance
P0452 Evaporative Emission Control System Pressure Sensor Low Input

P0453 Evaporative Emission Control System Pressure Sensor High Input

P0454 Evaporative Emission Control System Pressure Sensor Intermittent

P0455 Evaporative Emission Control System Leak Detected (Gross Leak)

P0460 Fuel Level Sensor Circuit Malfunction

P0461 Fuel Level Sensor Circuit Range/Performance

P0462 Fuel Level Sensor Circuit Low Input

P0463 Fuel Level Sensor Circuit High Input

P0464 Fuel Level Sensor Circuit Intermittent

P0465 Purge Flow Sensor Circuit Malfunction

P0466 Purge Flow Sensor Circuit Range/Performance

P0467 Purge Flow Sensor Circuit Low Input

P0468 Purge Flow Sensor Circuit High Input

P0469 Purge Flow Sensor Circuit Intermittent

P0470 Exhaust Pressure Sensor Malfunction

P0471 Exhaust Pressure Sensor Range/Performance

P0472 Exhaust Pressure Sensor Low

P0473 Exhaust Pressure Sensor High

P0474 Exhaust Pressure Sensor Intermittent

P0475 Exhaust Pressure Control Valve Malfunction

P0476 Exhaust Pressure Control Valve Range/Performance

P0477 Exhaust Pressure Control Valve Low

P0478 Exhaust Pressure Control Valve High

P0479 Exhaust Pressure Control Valve Intermittent

P0480 Cooling Fan no. 1 Control Circuit Malfunction

P0481 Cooling Fan no. 2 Control Circuit Malfunction

P0482 Cooling Fan no. 3 Control Circuit Malfunction

P0483 Cooling Fan Rationality Check Malfunction

P0484 Cooling Fan Circuit Over Current

P0485 Cooling Fan Power/Ground Circuit Malfunction

P0500 Vehicle Speed Sensor Malfunction

P0501 Vehicle Speed Sensor Range/Performance

P0502 Vehicle Speed Sensor Circuit Low Input

P0503 Vehicle Speed Sensor Intermittent/Erratic/High

P0505 Idle Control System Malfunction

P0506 Idle Control System RPM Lower Than Expected

P0507 Idle Control System RPM Higher Than Expected

P0510 Closed Throttle Position Switch Malfunction

P0520 Engine Oil Pressure Sensor/Switch Circuit Malfunction

P0521 Engine Oil Pressure Sensor/Switch Range/Performance

P0522 Engine Oil Pressure Sensor/Switch Low Voltage

P0523 Engine Oil Pressure Sensor/Switch High Voltage

P0530 A/C Refrigerant Pressure Sensor Circuit Malfunction

P0531 A/C Refrigerant Pressure Sensor Circuit Range/Performance

P0532 A/C Refrigerant Pressure Sensor Circuit Low Input

P0533 A/C Refrigerant Pressure Sensor Circuit High Input

P0534 A/C Refrigerant Charge Loss

P0550 Power Steering Pressure Sensor Circuit Malfunction

P0551 Power Steering Pressure Sensor Circuit Range/Performance

P0552 Power Steering Pressure Sensor Circuit Low Input

P0553 Power Steering Pressure Sensor Circuit High Input

P0554 Power Steering Pressure Sensor Circuit Intermittent

P0560 System Voltage Malfunction

P0561 System Voltage Unstable

P0562 System Voltage Low

P0563 System Voltage High

P0565 Cruise Control On Signal Malfunction

P0566 Cruise Control Off Signal Malfunction

P0567 Cruise Control Resume Signal Malfunction

P0568 Cruise Control Set Signal Malfunction

P0569 Cruise Control Coast Signal Malfunction

P0570 Cruise Control Accel Signal Malfunction

P0571 Cruise Control/Brake Switch "A" Circuit Malfunction

P0572 Cruise Control/Brake Switch "A" Circuit Low

P0573 Cruise Control/Brake Switch "A" Circuit High

P0574 Through P0580 Reserved for Cruise Codes

P0600 Serial Communication Link Malfunction

P0601 Internal Control Module Memory Check Sum Error

P0602 Control Module Programming Error

P0603 Internal Control Module Keep Alive Memory (KAM) Error

P0604 Internal Control Module Random Access Memory (RAM) Error

P0605 Internal Control Module Read Only Memory (ROM) Error

P0606 PCM Processor Fault

P0608 Control Module VSS Output "A" Malfunction

P0609 Control Module VSS Output "B" Malfunction

P0620 Generator Control Circuit Malfunction

P0621 Generator Lamp "L" Control Circuit Malfunction

P0622 Generator Field "F" Control Circuit Malfunction

P0650 Malfunction Indicator Lamp (MIL) Control Circuit Malfunction

P0654 Engine RPM Output Circuit Malfunction

P0655 Engine Hot Lamp Output Control Circuit Malfunction

P0656 Fuel Level Output Circuit Malfunction

P0700 Transmission Control System Malfunction

P0701 Transmission Control System Range/Performance

P0702 Transmission Control System Electrical

P0703 Torque Converter/Brake Switch "B" Circuit Malfunction

P0704 Clutch Switch Input Circuit Malfunction

P0705 Transmission Range Sensor Circuit Malfunction (PRNDL Input)

P0706 Transmission Range Sensor Circuit Range/Performance

P0707 Transmission Range Sensor Circuit Low Input

P0708 Transmission Range Sensor Circuit High Input

P0709 Transmission Range Sensor Circuit Intermittent

P0710 Transmission Fluid Temperature Sensor Circuit Malfunction

P0711 Transmission Fluid Temperature Sensor Circuit Range/Performance

P0712 Transmission Fluid Temperature Sensor Circuit Low Input

P0713 Transmission Fluid Temperature Sensor Circuit High Input

P0714 Transmission Fluid Temperature Sensor Circuit Intermittent

P0715 Input/Turbine Speed Sensor Circuit Malfunction

P0716 Input/Turbine Speed Sensor Circuit Range/Performance

P0717 Input/Turbine Speed Sensor Circuit No Signal

P0718 Input/Turbine Speed Sensor Circuit Intermittent

P0719 Torque Converter/Brake Switch "B" Circuit Low

P0720 Output Speed Sensor Circuit Malfunction

P0721 Output Speed Sensor Circuit Range/Performance

P0722 Output Speed Sensor Circuit No Signal

P0723 Output Speed Sensor Circuit Intermittent

P0724 Torque Converter/Brake Switch "B" Circuit High

P0725 Engine Speed Input Circuit Malfunction

P0726 Engine Speed Input Circuit Range/Performance

P0727 Engine Speed Input Circuit No Signal

P0728 Engine Speed Input Circuit Intermittent

P0730 Incorrect Gear Ratio

P0731 Gear no. 1 Incorrect Ratio

P0732 Gear no. 2 Incorrect Ratio

P0733 Gear no. 3 Incorrect Ratio

P0734 Gear no. 4 Incorrect Ratio

P0735 Gear no. 5 Incorrect Ratio

P0736 Reverse Incorrect Ratio

P0740 Torque Converter Clutch Circuit Malfunction

P0741 Torque Converter Clutch Circuit Performance or Stuck Off

P0742 Torque Converter Clutch Circuit Stuck On

P0743 Torque Converter Clutch Circuit Electrical

P0744 Torque Converter Clutch Circuit Intermittent

P0745 Pressure Control Solenoid Malfunction

P0746 Pressure Control Solenoid Performance or Stuck Off

P0747 Pressure Control Solenoid Stuck On

P0748 Pressure Control Solenoid Electrical

P0749 Pressure Control Solenoid Intermittent

P0750 Shift Solenoid "A" Malfunction

P0751 Shift Solenoid "A" Performance or Stuck Off

P0752 Shift Solenoid "A" Stuck On

P0753 Shift Solenoid "A" Electrical
P0754 Shift Solenoid "A" Intermittent
P0755 Shift Solenoid "B" Malfunction
P0756 Shift Solenoid "B" Performance or Stuck Oft
P0757 Shift Solenoid "B" Stuck On
P0758 Shift Solenoid "B" Electrical
P0759 Shift Solenoid "B" Intermittent
P0760 Shift Solenoid "C" Malfunction
P0761 Shift Solenoid "C" Performance Or Stuck Oft
P0762 Shift Solenoid "C" Stuck On
P0763 Shift Solenoid "C" Electrical
P0764 Shift Solenoid "C" Intermittent
P0765 Shift Solenoid "D" Malfunction
P0766 Shift Solenoid "D" Performance Or Stuck Oft
P0767 Shift Solenoid "D" Stuck On
P0768 Shift Solenoid "D" Electrical
P0769 Shift Solenoid "D" Intermittent
P0770 Shift Solenoid "E" Malfunction
P0771 Shift Solenoid "E" Performance Or Stuck Oft
P0772 Shift Solenoid "E" Stuck On
P0773 Shift Solenoid "E" Electrical
P0774 Shift Solenoid "E" Intermittent
P0780 Shift Malfunction
P0781 1–2 Shift Malfunction
P0782 2–3 Shift Malfunction
P0783 3–4 Shift Malfunction
P0784 4–5 Shift Malfunction
P0785 Shift/Timing Solenoid Malfunction
P0786 Shift/Timing Solenoid Range/Performance
P0787 Shift/Timing Solenoid Low
P0788 Shift/Timing Solenoid High
P0789 Shift/Timing Solenoid Intermittent
P0790 Normal/Performance Switch Circuit Malfunction
P0801 Reverse Inhibit Control Circuit Malfunction
P0803 1–4 Upshift (Skip Shift) Solenoid Control Circuit Malfunction
P0804 1–4 Upshift (Skip Shift) Lamp Control Circuit Malfunction

Chrysler Corporation

READING CODES

With Scan Tool

Reading the control module memory is on of the first steps in OBD-II system diagnostics. This step should be initially performed to determine the general nature of the fault. Subsequent readings will determine if the fault has been cleared.

Reading codes can be performed by any of the methods below:
• Read the control module memory with the Generic Scan Tool (GST)
• Read the control module memory with the vehicle manufacturer's specific tester

To read the fault codes, connect the scan tool or tester according to the manufacturer's instructions. Follow the manufacturer's specified procedure for reading the codes.

Without Scan Tool

On all 1995–97 vehicles, as well as the 1998 Sebring coupe and Avenger models with a 2.0L engine, DTC's can be accessed by observing the 2-digit number (referred to as an OBD-II Equivalent code) displayed by the Malfunction Indicator Lamp (MIL). The MIL is shown on the instrument panel as the Check Engine lamp. This method should be used as a "quick test" only. You should always use a scan tool to get the most detailed information.

➡**Be advised that the MIL can only perform a limited number of functions, and it is a good idea to have the system checked with a scan tool to double check the circuit function.**

Within a period of 5 seconds, cycle the ignition key **ON – OFF – ON – OFF – ON**.

1. Count the number of times the MIL (check engine lamp) on the instrument panel flashes on and off. The number of flashes represents the trouble code. There is a short pause between the flashes representing the 1st and 2nd digits of the code. Longer pauses are used to separate individual 2-digit trouble codes.

An example of a flashed DTC is as follows:
• Lamp flashes 4 times, pauses, then flashes 6 more times. This denotes a DTC number 46.
• Lamp flashes 5 times, pauses, then flashes 5 more times. This indicates a DTC number 55.

DTC 55 will always be the last code to be displayed.

CLEARING CODES

With Scan Tool

Control module reset procedures are a very important part of OBD-II System diagnostics. This step should be done at the end of any fault code repair and at the end of any driveability repair.

Clearing codes can be performed by any of the methods below:
• Clear the control module memory with the Generic Scan Tool (GST)
• Clear the control module memory with the vehicle manufacturer's specific tester
• Turn the ignition off and remove the negative battery cable for at least 1 minute.

Removing the negative battery cable may cause other systems in the vehicle to loose their memory. Prior to removing the cable, ensure you have the proper reset codes for radios and alarms.

➡**The MIL will may also be de-activated for some codes if the vehicle completes three consecutive trips without a fault detected with vehicle conditions similar to those present during the fault.**

Without Scan Tool

Control module reset procedures are a very important part of OBD-II System diagnostics. This step should be done at the end of any fault code repair and at the end of any driveability repair.

Clearing codes can be performed by turning the ignition off and removing the negative battery cable for at least 1 minute. Removing the negative battery cable may cause other systems in the vehicle to loose their memory. Prior to removing the cable, ensure you have the proper reset codes for radios and alarms.

➡**The MIL will may also be de-activated for some codes if the vehicle completes three consecutive trips without a fault detected with vehicle conditions similar to those present during the fault.**

CHRYSLER SPECIFIC OBD-II TROUBLE CODES

P1290 CNG Fuel System Pressure Too High—3.3L CNG vehicles only
P1291 No Temp Rise Seen From Intake Air Heaters
P1292 CNG Pressure Sensor Voltage Too High—3.3L CNG vehicles only
P1293 CNG Pressure Sensor Voltage Too Low—3.3L CNG vehicles only
P1294 Target Idle Not Reached
P1296 No 5-Volts To MAP Sensor
P1297 No Change In MAP From Start To Run
P1391 Intermittent Loss Of CMP Or CKP
P1398 Misfire Adaptive Numerator At Limit
P1486 EVAP Leak Monitor Pinched Hose Or Obstruction Found
P1491 Radiator Fan Control Relay Circuit
P1492 Battery Temp Sensor Voltage Too High
P1493 Battery Temp Sensor Voltage Too Low
P1494 Leak Detection Pump Pressure Switch Or Mechanical Fault
P1495 Leak Detection Pump Solenoid Circuit

P1498 Auxiliary 5-Volt Supply Output Too Low
P1697 PCM Failure SRI Mile Not Stored
P1698 PCM Failure EEPROM Write Denied
P1756 Governor Pressure Not Equal To Target @ 15–20 PSI
P1757 Governor Pressure Above 3 PSI In Gear With 0 MPH
P1762 Governor Pressure Sensor Offset Volts Too Low Or High
P1763 Governor Pressure Sensor Volts Too High
P1764 Governor Pressure Sensor Volts Too Low
P1765 Trans 12-Volt Supply Relay Control Circuit
P1899 P/N Switch Stuck In Park Or In Gear

CHRYSLER OBD-II TROUBLE CODE EQUIVALENTS

If a scan tool is not available for code retrieval, the following codes may be retrieved without one.

11 No crank reference signal at PCM
11 Timing belt skipped t tooth or more
11 Intermittent loss of CMP or CKP
11 Misfire adaptive numerator at limit
12 Battery disconnect
13 Slow change in idle MAP sensor signal (VIN N engine)
13 No change in MAP from start to run
14 MAP sensor voltage too low
14 MAP sensor voltage too high
14 No 5 volts to MAP sensor
15 5 volt supply output too low
16 No vehicle speed sensor signal
16 Knock sensor signal
17 Engine cold too long
17 Closed loop temperature not reached
21 Front 02S shorted to voltage
21 Front 02S stays at center
21 Rear 02S shorted to voltage
21 Rear 02S stays at center
21 Upstream 02S shorted to ground
21 Upstream 02S shorted to voltage
21 Upstream 02S response
21 Upstream 02S stays at center
21 Upstream 02S heater failure
21 Downstream 02S shorted to ground
21 Downstream 02S shorted to voltage
21 Downstream 025 response
21 Downstream 02S signal inactive
21 Downstream 02S heater failure
21 Front bank upstream 02S shorted to ground (6 cylinder)
21 Front bank upstream 02S shorted to voltage (6 cylinder)
21 Front bank upstream 02S slow response 6 cylinder)
21 Front bank upstream 02S stays at center (6 cylinder)
21 Front bank upstream 025 heater failure (6 cylinder)
21 Front bank downstream 025 shorted to ground (6 cylinder)
21 Front bank downstream 02S shorted to voltage (6 cylinder)
21 Front bank downstream 02S stays at center (6 cylinder)
21 Front bank downstream 02S heater failure (6 cylinder)
22 ECT sensor voltage too low
22 ECT sensor voltage too high
23 Intake air temperature voltage low
23 Intake air temperature voltage high
24 TPS voltage does not agree with MAP
24 Throttle position sensor voltage low
24 Throttle position sensor voltage high
24 No 5 volts to TPS
25 Idle air control motor circuits
25 Target idle not reached
25 Vacuum leak found (IAC fully seated)
27 Injector #I control circuit
27 Injector #2 control circuit
27 Injector#3control circuit
27 Injector #4 control circuit

27 Injector #5 control circuit (6 cylinder)
27 Injector #6 control circuit (6 cylinder)
31 EVAP purge flow monitor failure
31 EVAP system small leak
31 EVAP solenoid circuit
31 EVAP system large leak
31 EVAP leak monitor pinched hose
31 Leak detection pump pressure switch
31 EVAP emission vent solenoid switch or mechanical failure
31 Leak detection pump solenoid circuit
31 EVAP emission vent solenoid circuit
31 High speed radiator fan ground control relay circuit
32 EGR system failure
32 EGR solenoid circuit
33 A/C pressure sensor volts too high
33 A/C pressure sensor volts too low
33 A/C clutch relay circuit
34 Speed control switch always low
34 Speed control switch always high
31 Speed control solenoid circuit
35 High speed condenser fan control relay circuit
35 High fan and high fan ground control relay circuit
35 High speed radiator fan control relay circuit
35 High speed fan control relay circuit
35 Low speed fan control relay circuit
37 Park/Neutral switch failure
41 Alternator field not switching properly
42 Auto shutdown relay circuit
42 No ASD relay output voltage at PCM
42 Fuel level sending unit volts too low
42 Fuel level sending unit volts too high
42 Fuel level unit no change over miles
42 Fuel pump relay control circuit
43 Multiple cylinder misfire
43 Cylinder #I misfire
43 Cylinder #2 misfire
43 Cylinder #3mislire
43 Cylinder #4 misfire
43 Cylinder #5 misfire
43 Cylinder #6 misfire
43 Ignition coil #1 primary circuit
43 Ignition coil #2 primary circuit
44 Ambient temperature sensor
44 Battery temperature sensor volts out of limit
44 Battery temperature sensor voltage too high
44 Battery temperature sensor voltage too low
45 Transaxle fault present
46 Charging system voltage too high
47 Charging system voltage too low
51 Fuel system lean (4 cylinder)
51 Rear bank fuel system lean (6 cylinder)
51 Front bank fuel system lean (6 cylinder)
52 Fuel system rich (4 cylinder)
52 Rear bank fuel system rich (6 cylinder)
52 Front bank fuel system rich (6 cylinder)
53 Internal controller failure
53 PCM failure SPI communications
53 Internal controller failure
53 PCM failure SPI communications
54 No cam signal at PCM
55 Completion or fault code display on Check Engine Lamp
62 PCM failure SRI mile not stared
63 PCM failure EEPROM write denied
64 Catalytic converter efficiency failure
64 Rear bank catalytic converter efficiency failure
65 Power steering switch failure
65 Brake switch performance circuit
66 No CCD message from body controller

66 No CCD message from TCM
71 5 volt output low speed control power circuit
72 Catalytic Converter efficiency failure
72 Front bank catalytic converter efficiency failure
77 Malfunction detected with power feed to speed control servo

Ford Motor Company

READING CODES

Reading the control module memory is on of the first steps in OBD-II system diagnostics. This step should be initially performed to determine the general nature of the fault. Subsequent readings will determine if the fault has been cleared.

Reading codes can be performed by any of the methods below:
- Read the control module memory with the Generic Scan Tool (GST)
- Read the control module memory with the vehicle manufacturer's specific tester

To read the fault codes, connect the scan tool or tester according to the manufacturer's instructions. Follow the manufacturer's specified procedure for reading the codes.

CLEARING CODES

Control module reset procedures are a very important part of OBD-II System diagnostics. This step should be done at the end of any fault code repair and at the end of any driveability repair.

Clearing codes can be performed by any of the methods below:
- Clear the control module memory with the Generic Scan Tool (GST)
- Clear the control module memory with the vehicle manufacturer's specific tester
- Turn the ignition off and remove the negative battery cable for at least 1 minute.

Removing the negative battery cable may cause other systems in the vehicle to loose their memory. Prior to removing the cable, ensure you have the proper reset codes for radios and alarms.

➡ **The MIL will may also be de-activated for some codes if the vehicle completes three consecutive trips without a fault detected with vehicle conditions similar to those present during the fault.**

FORD SPECIFIC OBD-II TROUBLE CODES

1994–95 Models

P1000 OBD-II Monitor Testing not complete
P1100 Mass Air Flow (MAF) sensor intermittent
P1101 Mass Air Flow (MAF) sensor out of Self-Test range
P1112 Intake Air Temperature (IAT) sensor intermittent
P1116 Engine Coolant Temperature (ECT) sensor out of Self-Test range
P1117 Engine Coolant Temperature (ECT) sensor intermittent
P1120 Throttle Position (TP) sensor out of range low
P1121 Throttle Position (TP) sensor inconsistent with MAF sensor
P1124 Throttle Position (TP) sensor out of Self-Test range
P1125 Throttle Position (TP) sensor circuit intermittent
P1130 Lack of HO2S 11 switch, adaptive fuel at limit
P1131 Lack of HO2S 11 switch, sensor indicates lean (Bank #1)
P1132 Lack of HO2S 11 switch, sensor indicates rich (Bank #1)
U1135 Ignition switch signal missing or incorrect
P1137 Lack of HO2S 12 switch, sensor indicates lean (Bank #1)
P1138 Lack of HO2S 12 switch, sensor indicates rich (Bank #1)
P1150 Lack of HO2S 21 switch, adaptive fuel at limit
P1151 Lack of HO2S 21 switch, sensor indicates lean (Bank #2)
P1152 Lack of HO2S 21 switch, sensor indicates rich (Bank #2)
P1157 Lack of HO2S 22 switch, sensor indicates lean (Bank #2)
P1158 Lack of HO2S 22 switch, sensor indicates rich (Bank #2)
P1220 Series Throttle Control malfunction

P1224 Throttle Position Sensor (TP-B) out of Self-test range
P1233 Fuel Pump driver Module off-line
P1234 Fuel Pump driver Module off-line
P1235 Fuel Pump control out of range
P1236 Fuel Pump control out of range
P1237 Fuel Pump secondary circuit malfunction
P1238 Fuel Pump secondary circuit malfunction
P1260 THEFT detected—engine disabled
P1270 Engine RPM or vehicle speed limiter reached
P1351 Ignition Diagnostic Monitor (IDM) circuit input malfunction
P1352 Ignition coil A primary circuit malfunction
P1353 Ignition coil B primary circuit malfunction
P1354 Ignition coil C primary circuit malfunction
P1355 Ignition coil D primary circuit malfunction
P1358 Ignition Diagnostic Monitor (IDM) signal out of Self-Test range
P1359 Spark output circuit malfunction
P1364 Ignition coil primary circuit malfunction
P1390 Octane Adjust (OCT ADJ) out of Self-Test range
P1400 Differential Pressure Feedback Electronic (DPFE) sensor circuit low voltage detected
P1401 Differential Pressure Feedback Electronic (DPFE) sensor circuit high voltage detected
P1403 Differential Pressure Feedback Electronic (DPFE) sensor hoses reversed
P1405 Differential Pressure Feedback Electronic (DPFE) sensor upstream hose off or plugged
P1406 Differential Pressure Feedback Electronic (DPFE) sensor downstream hose off or plugged
P1407 Exhaust Gas Recirculation (EGR) no flow detected (valve stuck closed or inoperative)
P1408 Exhaust Gas Recirculation (EGR) flow out of Self-Test range
P1409 Electronic Vacuum Regulator (EVR) control circuit malfunction
P1414 Secondary Air Injection system monitor circuit high voltage
P1443 Evaporative emission control system—vacuum system purge control solenoid or purge control valve malfunction
P1444 Purge Flow Sensor (PFS) circuit low input
P1445 Purge Flow Sensor (PFS) circuit high input
U1451 Lack of response from Passive Anti-Theft system (PATS) module—engine disabled
P1460 Wide Open Throttle Air Conditioning Cut-off (WAC) circuit malfunction
P1461 Air Conditioning Pressure (ACP) sensor circuit low input
P1462 Air Conditioning Pressure (ACP) sensor circuit high input
P1463 Air Conditioning Pressure (ACP) sensor insufficient pressure change
P1469 Low air conditioning cycling period
P1473 Fan Secondary High with fan(s) off
P1474 Low Fan Control primary circuit malfunction
P1479 High Fan Control primary circuit malfunction
P1480 Fan Secondary low with low fan on
P1481 Fan Secondary low with high fan on
P1500 Vehicle Speed Sensor (VSS) circuit intermittent
P1505 Idle Air Control (IAC) system at adaptive clip
P1506 Idle Air control (IAC) overspeed error
P1518 Intake Manifold Runner Control (IMRC) malfunction (stuck open)
P1519 Intake Manifold Runner Control (IMRC) malfunction (stuck closed)
P1520 Intake Manifold Runner Control (IMRC) circuit malfunction
P1507 Idle Air control (IAC) under speed error
P1605 Powertrain Control Module (POM)—Keep Alive Memory (KAM) test error
P1650 Power steering Pressure (PSP) switch out of Self-Test range
P1651 Power steering Pressure (PSP) switch input malfunction
P1701 Reverse engagement error
P1703 Brake On/Off (BOO) switch out of Self-Test range
P1705 Manual Lever Position (MLP) sensor out of Self-Test range
P1709 Park or Neutral Position (PNP) switch out of Self-test range
P1729 4X4 Low switch error

P1711 Transmission Fluid Temperature (TFT) sensor out of Self-Test range
P1741 Torque Converter Clutch (TCC) control error
P1742 Torque Converter Clutch (TCC) solenoid mechanically failed (turns MIL on)
P1743 Torque Converter Clutch (TCC) solenoid mechanically failed (turns TOIL on)
P1744 Torque Converter Clutch (TCC) system mechanically stuck in off position
P1748 Electronic Pressure Control (EPC) solenoid circuit low input (open circuit)
P1747 Electronic Pressure Control (EPC) solenoid circuit high input (short circuit)
P1749 Electric Pressure Control (EPC) solenoid failed low
P1751 Shift Solenoid #1(SS1) performance
P1756 Shift Solenoid #2 (SS2) performance
P1780 Transmission Control Switch (TCS) circuit out of Self-Test range

1996–99 Models

P1000 OBD-II Monitor Testing Not Complete More Driving Required
P1001 Key On Engine Running (KOER) Self-Test Not Able To Complete, KOER Aborted
P1100 Mass Air Flow (MAF) Sensor Intermittent
P1101 Mass Air Flow (MAF) Sensor Out Of Self-Test Range
P1111 System Pass 49 State Except Econoline
P1112 Intake Air Temperature (IAT) Sensor Intermittent
P1116 Engine Coolant Temperature (ECT) Sensor Out Of Self-Test Range
P1117 Engine Coolant Temperature (ECT) Sensor Intermittent
P1120 Throttle Position (TP) Sensor Out Of Range (Low)
P1121 Throttle Position (TP) Sensor Inconsistent With MAF Sensor
P1124 Throttle Position (TP) Sensor Out Of Self-Test Range
P1125 Throttle Position (TP) Sensor Circuit Intermittent
P1127 Exhaust Not Warm Enough, Downstream Heated Oxygen Sensors (HO2S) Not Tested
P1128 Upstream Heated Oxygen Sensors (HO2S) Swapped From Bank To Bank
P1129 Downstream Heated Oxygen Sensors (HO2S) Swapped From Bank To Bank
P1130 Lack Of Upstream Heated Oxygen Sensor (HO2S 11) Switch, Adaptive Fuel At Limit (Bank #1)
P1131 Lack Of Upstream Heated Oxygen Sensor (HO2S 11) Switch, Sensor Indicates Lean (Bank #1)
P1132 Lack Of Upstream Heated Oxygen Sensor (HO2S 11) Switch, Sensor Indicates Rich (Bank#1)
P1137 Lack Of Downstream Heated Oxygen Sensor (HO2S 12) Switch, Sensor Indicates Lean (Bank#1)
P1138 Lack Of Downstream Heated Oxygen Sensor (HO2S 12) Switch, Sensor Indicates Rich (Bank#1)
P1150 Lack Of Upstream Heated Oxygen Sensor (HO2S 21) Switch, Adaptive Fuel At Limit (Bank #2)
P1151 Lack Of Upstream Heated Oxygen Sensor (HO2S 21) Switch, Sensor Indicates Lean (Bank#2)
P1152 Lack Of Upstream Heated Oxygen Sensor (HO2S 21) Switch, Sensor Indicates Rich (Bank #2)
P1157 Lack Of Downstream Heated Oxygen Sensor (HO2S 22) Switch, Sensor Indicates Lean (Bank #2)
P1158 Lack Of Downstream Heated Oxygen Sensor (HO2S 22) Switch, Sensor Indicates Rich (Bank#2)
P1169 (HO2S 12) Signal Remained Unchanged For More Than 20 Seconds After Closed Loop
P1170 (HO2S 11) Signal Remained Unchanged For More Than 20 Seconds After Closed Loop
P1173 Feedback A/F Mixture Control (HO2S 21) Signal Remained Unchanged For More Than 20 Seconds After Closed Loop
P1184 Engine Oil Temp Sensor Circuit Performance
P1195 Barometric (BARO) Pressure Sensor Circuit Malfunction (Signal Is From EGR Boost Sensor)

P1196 Starter Switch Circuit Malfunction
P1209 Injection Control Pressure (ICP) Peak Fault
P1210 Injection Control Pressure (ICP) Above Expected Level
P1211 Injection Control Pressure (ICP) Not Controllable—Pressure Above/Below Desired
P1212 Injection Control Pressure (ICP) Voltage Not At Expected Level
P1218 Cylinder Identification (CID) Stuck High
P1219 Cylinder Identification (CID) Stuck Low
P1220 Series Throttle Control Malfunction (Traction Control System)
P1224 Throttle Position Sensor "B" (TP-B) Out Of Self-Test Range (Traction Control System)
P1230 Fuel Pump Low Speed Malfunction
P1231 Fuel Pump Secondary Circuit Low With High Speed Pump On
P1232 Low Speed Fuel Pump Primary Circuit Malfunction
P1233 Fuel Pump Driver Module Off-line (MIL DTC)
P1234 Fuel Pump Driver Module Disabled Or Off-line (No MIL)
P1235 Fuel Pump Control Out Of Range (MIL DTC)
P1236 Fuel Pump Control Out Of Range (No MIL)
P1237 Fuel Pump Secondary Circuit Malfunction (MIL DTC)
P1238 Fuel Pump Secondary Circuit Malfunction (No DMIL)
P1250 Fuel Pressure Regulator Control (FPRC) Solenoid Malfunction
P1260 THEFT Detected—Engine Disabled
P1261 High To Low Side Short—Cylinder #1 (Indicates Low side Circuit Is Shorted To B+ Or To The High Side Between The IDM And The Injector)
P1262 High To Low Side Short—Cylinder #2 (Indicates Low side Circuit Is Shorted To B+ Or To The High Side Between The IDM And The Injector)
P1263 High To Low Side Short—Cylinder #3 (Indicates Low side Circuit Is Shorted To B+ Or To The High Side Between The IDM And The Injector)
P1264 High To Low Side Short—Cylinder #4 (Indicates Low side Circuit Is Shorted To B+ Or To The High Side Between The IDM And The Injector)
P1265 High To Low Side Short—Cylinder #5 (Indicates Low side Circuit Is Shorted To B+ Or To The High Side Between The IDM And The Injector)
P1266 High To Low Side Short—Cylinder #6 (Indicates Low side Circuit Is Shorted To B+ Or To The High Side Between The IDM And The Injector)
P1267 High To Low Side Short—Cylinder #7 (Indicates Low side Circuit Is Shorted To B+ Or To The High Side Between The IDM And The Injector)
P1268 High To Low Side Short—Cylinder #8 (Indicates Low side Circuit Is Shorted To B+ Or To The High Side Between The IDM And The Injector)
P1270 Engine RPM Or Vehicle Speed Limiter Reached
P1271 High To Low Side Open—Cylinder #1 (Indicates A High To Low Side Open Between The Injector And The IDM)
P1272 High To Low Side Open—Cylinder #2 (Indicates A High To Low Side Open Between The Injector And The IDM)
P1273 High To Low Side Open—Cylinder #3 (Indicates A High To Low Side Open Between The Injector And The IDM)
P1274 High To Low Side Open—Cylinder #4 (Indicates A High To Low Side Open Between The Injector And The IDM)
P1275 High To Low Side Open—Cylinder #5 (Indicates A High To Low Side Open Between The Injector And The IDM)
P1276 High To Low Side Open—Cylinder #6 (Indicates A High To Low Side Open Between The Injector And The IDM)
P1277 High To Low Side Open—Cylinder #7 (Indicates A High To Low Side Open Between The Injector And The IDM)
P1278 High To Low Side Open—Cylinder #8 (Indicates A High To Low Side Open Between The Injector And The IDM)
P1280 Injection Control Pressure (ICP) Circuit Out Of Range Low
P1281 Injection Control Pressure (ICP) Circuit Out Of Range High
P1282 Injection Control Pressure (ICP) Excessive
P1283 Injection Pressure Regulator (IPR) Circuit Failure
P1284 Injection Control Pressure (ICP) Failure—Aborts KOER Or CCT Test

P1285 Cylinder Head Temperature (CHT) Over Temperature Sensed
P1288 Cylinder Head Temperature (CHT) Sensor Out Of Self-Test Range
P1289 Cylinder Head Temperature (CHT) Sensor Circuit Low Input
P1290 Cylinder Head Temperature (CHT) Sensor Circuit High Input
P1291 IDM To Injector High Side Circuit #1 (Right Bank) Short To GND Or B+
P1292 IDM To Injector High Side Circuit #2 (Right Bank) Short To GND Or B+
P1293 IDM To Injector High Side Circuit Open Bank #1 (Right Bank)
P1294 IDM To Injector High Side Circuit Open Bank #2 (Left Bank)
P1295 Multiple IDM/Injector Circuit Faults On Bank #1 (Right)
P1296 Multiple IDM/Injector Circuit Faults On Bank#2 (Left)
P1297 High Sides Shorted Together
P1298 IDM Failure
P1299 Engine Over Temperature Condition
P1309 Misfire Detection Monitor Is Not Enabled
P1316 Injector Circuit/IDM Codes Detected
P1320 Distributor Signal Interrupt
P1336 Crankshaft Position Sensor (Gear)
P1345 No Camshaft Position Sensor Signal
P1351 Ignition Diagnostic Monitor (IDM) Circuit Input Malfunction
P1351 Indicates Ignition System Malfunction
P1352 Indicates Ignition System Malfunction
P1353 Indicates Ignition System Malfunction
P1354 Indicates Ignition System Malfunction
P1355 Indicates Ignition System Malfunction
P1356 PIPs Occurred While IDM Pulse width Indicates Engine Not Turning
P1357 Ignition Diagnostic Monitor (IDM) Pulse width Not Defined
P1358 Ignition Diagnostic Monitor (IDM) Signal Out Of Self-Test Range
P1359 Spark Output Circuit Malfunction
P1364 Spark Output Circuit Malfunction
P1390 Octane Adjust (OCT ADJ) Out Of Self-Test Range
P1391 Glow Plug Circuit Low Input Bank #1 (Right)
P1392 Glow Plug Circuit High Input Bank #1 (Right)
P1393 Glow Plug Circuit Low Input Bank #2 (Left)
P1394 Glow Plug Circuit High Input Bank #2 (Left)
P1395 Glow Plug Monitor Fault Bank #1
P1396 Glow Plug Monitor Fault Bank #2
P1397 System Voltage Out Of Self Test Range
P1400 Differential Pressure Feedback EGR (DPFE) Sensor Circuit Low Voltage Detected
P1401 Differential Pressure Feedback EGR (DPFE) Sensor Circuit High Voltage Detected/EGR Temperature Sensor
P1402 EGR Valve Position Sensor Open Or Short
P1403 Differential Pressure Feedback EGR (DPFE) Sensor Hoses Reversed
P1405 Differential Pressure Feedback EGR (DPFE) Sensor Upstream Hose Off Or Plugged
P1406 Differential Pressure Feedback EGR (DPFE) Sensor Downstream Hose Off Or Plugged
P1407 Exhaust Gas Recirculation (EGR) No Flow Detected (Valve Stuck Closed Or Inoperative)
P1408 Exhaust Gas Recirculation (EGR) Flow Out Of Self-Test Range
P1409 Electronic Vacuum Regulator (EVR) Control Circuit Malfunction
P1410 Check That Fuel Pressure Regulator Control Solenoid And The EGR Check Solenoid Connectors Are Not Swapped
P1411 Secondary Air Injection System Incorrect Downstream Flow Detected
P1413 Secondary Air Injection System Monitor Circuit Low Voltage
P1414 Secondary Air Injection System Monitor Circuit High Voltage
P1442 Evaporative Emission Control System Small Leak Detected
P1443 Evaporative Emission Control System—Vacuum System, Purge Control Solenoid Or Purge Control Valve Malfunction
P1444 Purge Flow Sensor (PFS) Circuit Low Input
P1445 Purge Flow Sensor (PFS) Circuit High Input
P1449 Evaporative Emission Control System Unable To Hold Vacuum

P1450 Unable To Bleed Up Fuel Tank Vacuum
P1455 Evaporative Emission Control System Control Leak Detected (Gross Leak)
P1460 Wide Open Throttle Air Conditioning Cut-Off Circuit Malfunction
P1461 Air Conditioning Pressure (ACP) Sensor Circuit Low Input
P1462 Air Conditioning Pressure (ACP) Sensor Circuit High Input
P1463 Air Conditioning Pressure (ACP) Sensor Insufficient Pressure Change
P1464 Air Conditioning (A/C) Demand Out Of Self-Test Range/A/C On During KOER Or CCT Test
P1469 Low Air Conditioning Cycling Period
P1473 Fan Secondary High, With Fan(s) Off
P1474 Low Fan Control Primary Circuit Malfunction
P1479 High Fan Control Primary Circuit Malfunction
P1480 Fan Secondary Low, With Low Fan On
P1481 Fan Secondary Low, With High Fan On
P1483 Power To Fan Circuit Over current
P1484 Open Power/Ground To Variable Load Control Module (VLCM)
P1485 EGR Control Solenoid Open Or Short
P1486 EGR Vent Solenoid Open Or Short
P1487 EGR Boost Check Solenoid Open Or Short
P1500 Vehicle Speed Sensor (VSS) Circuit Intermittent
P1501 Vehicle Speed Sensor (VSS) Out Of Self-Test Range/Vehicle Moved During Test
P1502 Invalid Self Test—Auxiliary Powertrain Control Module (APCM) Functioning
P1504 Idle Air Control (IAC) Circuit Malfunction
P1505 Idle Air Control (IAC) System At Adaptive Clip
P1506 Idle Air Control (IAC) Overspeed Error
P1507 Idle Air Control (IAC) Underspeed Error
P1512 Intake Manifold Runner Control (IMRC) Malfunction (Bank#1 Stuck Closed)
P1513 Intake Manifold Runner Control (IMRC) Malfunction (Bank#2 Stuck Closed)
P1516 Intake Manifold Runner Control (IMRC) Input Error (Bank #1)
P1517 Intake Manifold Runner Control (IMRC) Input Error (Bank #2)
P1518 Intake Manifold Runner Control (IMRC) Malfunction (Stuck Open)
P1519 Intake Manifold Runner Control (IMRC) Malfunction (Stuck Closed)
P1520 Intake Manifold Runner Control (IMRC) Circuit Malfunction
P1521 Variable Resonance Induction System (VRIS) Solenoid #1 Open Or Short
P1522 Variable Resonance Induction System (VRIS) Solenoid#2 Open Or Short
P1523 High Speed Inlet Air (HSIA) Solenoid Open Or Short
P1530 Air Condition (A/C) Clutch Circuit Malfunction
P1531 Invalid Test—Accelerator Pedal Movement
P1536 Parking Brake Applied Failure
P1537 Intake Manifold Runner Control (IMRC) Malfunction (Bank#1 Stuck Open)
P1538 Intake Manifold Runner Control (IMRC) Malfunction (Bank#2 Stuck Open)
P1539 Power To Air Condition (A/C) Clutch Circuit Overcurrent
P1549 Problem In Intake Manifold Tuning (IMT) Valve System
P1550 Power Steering Pressure (PSP) Sensor Out Of Self-Test Range
P1601 Serial Communication Error
P1605 Powertrain Control Module (PCM)—Keep Alive Memory (KAM) Test Error
P1608 PCM Internal Circuit Malfunction
P1609 PCM Internal Circuit Malfunction (2.5L Only)
P1625 B+ Supply To Variable Load Control Module (VLCM) Fan Circuit Malfunction
P1626 B+ Supply To Variable Load Control Module (VLCM) Air Conditioning (A/C) Circuit
P1650 Power Steering Pressure (PSP) Switch Out Of Self-Test Range
P1651 Power Steering Pressure (PSP) Switch Input Malfunction

P1660 Output Circuit Check Signal High
P1661 Output Circuit Check Signal Low
P1662 Injection Driver Module Enable (IDM EN) Circuit Failure
P1663 Fuel Delivery Command Signal (FDCS) Circuit Failure
P1667 Cylinder Identification (CID) Circuit Failure
P1668 PCM—IDM Diagnostic Communication Error
P1670 EF Feedback Signal Not Detected
P1701 Reverse Engagement Error
P1701 Fuel Trim Malfunction (Villager)
P1703 Brake On/Off (BOO) Switch Out Of Self-Test Range
P1704 Digital Transmission Range (TR) Sensor Failed To Transition State
P1705 Transmission Range (TR) Sensor Out Of Self-Test Range
P1705 TP Sensor (AT) Villager
P1705 Clutch Pedal Position (CPP) Or Park Neutral Position (PNP) Problem
P1706 High Vehicle Speed In Park
P1709 Park Or Neutral Position (PNP) Or Clutch Pedal Position (CPP) Switch Out Of Self-Test Range
P1709 Throttle Position (TP) Sensor Malfunction (Aspire 1.3L, Escort/Tracer 1.8L, Probe 2.5L)
P1711 Transmission Fluid Temperature (TFT) Sensor Out Of Self-Test Range
P1714 Shift Solenoid "A" Inductive Signature Malfunction
P1715 Shift Solenoid "B" Inductive Signature Malfunction
P1716 Transmission Malfunction
P1717 Transmission Malfunction
P1719 Transmission Malfunction
P1720 Vehicle Speed Sensor (VSS) Circuit Malfunction
P1727 Coast Clutch Solenoid Inductive Signature Malfunction
P1728 Transmission Slip Error—Converter Clutch Failed
P1729 4x4 Low Switch Error
P1731 Improper 1–2 Shift
P1732 Improper 2–3 Shift
P1733 Improper 3–4 Shift
P1734 Improper 4–5 Shift
P1740 Torque Converter Clutch (TCC) Inductive Signature Malfunction
P1741 Torque Converter Clutch (TCC) Control Error
P1742 Torque Converter Clutch (TCC) Solenoid Failed On (Turns On MIL)
P1743 Torque Converter Clutch (TCC) Solenoid Failed On (Turns On TCIL)
P1744 Torque Converter Clutch (TCC) System Mechanically Stuck In Off Position
P1744 Torque Converter Clutch (TCC) Solenoid Malfunction (2.5L Only)
P1746 Electronic Pressure Control (EPC) Solenoid Open Circuit (Low Input)
P1747 Electronic Pressure Control (EPC) Solenoid Short Circuit (High Input)
P1748 Electronic Pressure Control (EPC) Malfunction
P1749 Electronic Pressure Control (EPC) Solenoid Failed Low
P1751 Shift Solenoid#1 (SS1) Performance
P1754 Coast Clutch Solenoid (CCS) Circuit Malfunction
P1756 Shift Solenoid#2 (SS2) Performance
P1760 Overrun Clutch SN
P1761 Shift Solenoid #(SS2) Performance
P1762 Transmission Malfunction
P1765 3–2 Timing Solenoid Malfunction (2.5L Only)
P1779 TCIL Circuit Malfunction
P1780 Transmission Control Switch (TCS) Circuit Out Of Self-Test Range
P1781 4x4 Low Switch, Out Of Self-Test Range
P1783 Transmission Over Temperature Condition
P1784 Transmission Malfunction
P1785 Transmission Malfunction
P1786 Transmission Malfunction

P1787 Transmission Malfunction
P1788 3–2 Timing/Coast Clutch Solenoid (3–2/CCS) Circuit Open
P1789 3–2 Timing/Coast Clutch Solenoid (3–2/CCS) Circuit Shorted
P1792 Idle (IDL) Switch (Closed Throttle Position Switch) Malfunction
P1794 Loss Of Battery Voltage Input
P1795 EGR Boost Sensor Malfunction
P1797 Clutch Pedal Position (CPP) Switch Or Neutral Switch Circuit Malfunction
P1900 Cooling Fan
U1021 SCP Indicating The Lack Of Air Conditioning (A/C) Clutch Status Response
U1039 OBD-II Monitor not complete
U1039 Vehicle Speed Signal (VSS) Missing Or Incorrect
U1051 Brake Switch Signal Missing Or Incorrect
U1073 SCP Indicating The Lack Of Engine Coolant Fan Status Response
U1131 SCP Indicating The Lack Of Fuel Pump Status Response
U1135 SCP Indicating The Ignition Switch Signal Missing Or Incorrect
U1256 SCP Indicating A Communications Error
U1451 Lack Of Response From Passive Anti-Theft System (PATS) Module—Engine Disabled

General Motors Corporation

READING CODES

Reading the control module memory is on of the first steps in OBD-II system diagnostics. This step should be initially performed to determine the general nature of the fault. Subsequent readings will determine if the fault has been cleared.

Reading codes can be performed by any of the methods below:
• Read the control module memory with the Generic Scan Tool (GST)
• Read the control module memory with the vehicle manufacturer's specific tester

To read the fault codes, connect the scan tool or tester according to the manufacturer's instructions. Follow the manufacturer's specified procedure for reading the codes.

CLEARING CODES

Control module reset procedures are a very important part of OBD-II System diagnostics. This step should be done at the end of any fault code repair and at the end of any driveability repair.

Clearing codes can be performed by any of the methods below:
• Clear the control module memory with the Generic Scan Tool (GST)
• Clear the control module memory with the vehicle manufacturer's specific tester
• Turn the ignition off and remove the negative battery cable for at least 1 minute.

Removing the negative battery cable may cause other systems in the vehicle to loose their memory. Prior to removing the cable, ensure you have the proper reset codes for radios and alarms.

➥**The MIL will may also be de-activated for some codes if the vehicle completes three consecutive trips without a fault detected with vehicle conditions similar to those present during the fault.**

GM SPECIFIC OBD-II TROUBLE CODES

P1106 MAP Sensor Voltage Intermittently High
P1107 MAP Sensor Voltage Intermittently Low
P1111 IAT Sensor Circuit Intermittent High Voltage
P1112 IAT Sensor Circuit Intermittent Low Voltage
P1114 ECT Sensor Circuit Intermittent Low Voltage
P1115 ECT Sensor Circuit Intermittent High Voltage
P1121 TP Sensor Voltage Intermittently High

P1122 TP Sensor Voltage Intermittently Low
P1133 HO2S Insufficient Switching Sensor
P1133 HO2S Insufficient Switching Bank #1, Sensor #1
P1134 HO2S #1 Transition Time Ratio
P1134 HO2S Transition Time Ratio Bank #1, Sensor #1
P1153 HO2S Insufficient Switching Sensor Bank #2, Sensor #1
P1154 HO2S Transition Time Ratio Bank #2, Sensor #1
P1345 Crankshaft/Camshaft (CKP/CMP) Correlation
P1350 Ignition Control (IC) Circuit Malfunction
P1351 Ignition Control (IC) Circuit High Voltage
P1361 Ignition Control (IC) Circuit Not Toggling
P1361 Ignition Control (IC) Circuit Low Voltage
P1380 Electronic Brake Control Module (EBCM) DTC Detected Rough Road Data Unusable
P1 381 Misfire Detected, No EBCM/PCM/VCM Serial Data
P1406 EGR Pintle Position Circuit Fault
P1415 AIR System Bank #1
P1416 AIR System Bank #2
P1441 EVAP Control System Flow During Non-Purge

P1442 EVAP Vacuum Switch Circuit
P1450 Barometric Pressure Sensor Circuit Fault
P1451 Barometric Pressure Sensor Performance
P1460 Cooling Fan Control System Fault
P1500 Starter Signal Circuit Fault
P1510 Back-up Power Supply Fault
P1508 IAC System Low RPM
P1509 IAC System High RPM
P1520 PNP Circuit
P1530 Ignition Timing Adjustment Switch Circuit
P1600 PCM Battery Circuit Fault
P1635 5-Volt Reference "A" Circuit
P1639 5-Volt Reference "B" Circuit
P1641 MIL Control Circuit
P1651 Fan #1 Relay Control Circuit
P1652 Fan #2 Relay Control Circuit
P1654 A/C Relay Control
P1655 EVAP Purge Solenoid Control Circuit
P1672 Low Engine Oil Level Light Control Circuit

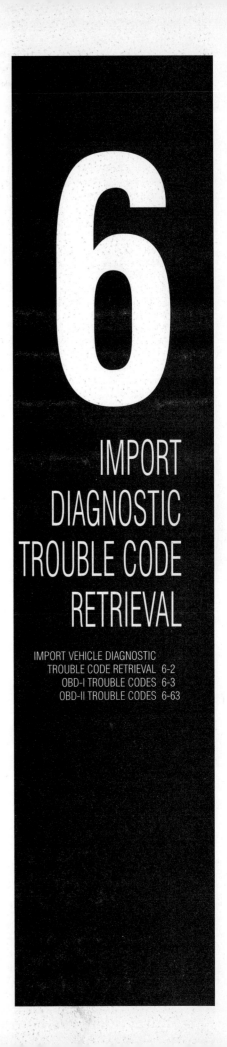

6

IMPORT DIAGNOSTIC TROUBLE CODE RETRIEVAL

IMPORT VEHICLE DIAGNOSTIC TROUBLE CODE RETRIEVAL

Introduction

Most cars today are equipped with an On-Board Diagnostic (OBD) system. During the late '70s manufacturers started using electronics to control engine functions and diagnose engine faults. This was primarily to meet stringent new EPA emission standards. Through the years OBD have become more sophisticated. OBD-II, a new standard introduced in the mid-'90s, provides almost complete engine control and also monitors parts of the chassis, body and accessory devices, as well as the diagnostic control network of the vehicle.

OBD was brought about to combat a persistent smog problem in the LA basin. The State of California started requiring emission control systems on 1966 model cars. The federal government extended these controls nationwide in 1968.

Congress passed the Clean Air Act in 1970 and established the Environmental Protection Agency (EPA). From the EPA, series of emission standards for maintenance of vehicles has been brought forth. To meet these standards, manufacturers were forced to electronically control their fuel feed and ignition systems. Sensors measure engine performance and adjustments are made automatically to the systems to provide optimum performance with minimum emissions. These sensors also provided vehicle owners with their earliest diagnostic assistance.

In the beginning there were few standards and each manufacturer had their own systems and signals. In 1988, the Society of Automotive Engineers (SAE) set a standard connector plug and set of diagnostic test codes. The EPA adapted most of the SAE standards and gradually mandated compliance from the manufacturers.

The EPA has been charged with reducing "mobile emissions" from cars and trucks and given the power to require manufacturers to build cars which meet increasingly stiff emissions standards. The manufacturers must further maintain the emission standards of the cars for the useful life of the vehicle.

OBD-II is a natural progression of the initial standards developed by the SAE and implemented by the EPA and California Air Resources Board (CARB). The standards were implemented January 1, 1996.

OBD-II provides a universal inspection and diagnosis method to be sure the car is performing to OEM standards. While there is argument as to the exact standards and methodology employed, the fact is there is a need to reduce vehicle emitted pollution levels in our cities, and we have to live with these requirements.

What System Do I Have?

So how do I know if my car has OBD-I or OBD-II. All cars built since January 1, 1996 have OBD-II systems. Manufacturers started incorporating OBD-II in various models as early as 1994. Some early OBD-II cars were not 100% compliant.

It is safe to say that if you own a pre-1994 model year vehicle, you have some variant of an OBD-I system. Remember, OBD-I was very manufacturer specific and great differences may exist between models of the same manufacturer and year.

It is also safe to say that if you own a 1996 or later model year vehicle, you have OBD-II. Here it gets a little easier. Since there are a standard set of generic codes for OBD-II, which are published here, each make and model will display the same code for the same fault.

There are also manufacturer specific codes, which like OBD-I are specific to each manufacturer. However, the manufacturers have pretty much used the same codes across their model lines.

The real problem with comes with vehicles built between 1994 and 1995. These were transition years and many manufacturers installed systems that were better than traditional OBD-I systems, yet still did not comply with OBD-II regulations.

The surest way to tell which version of OBD you have is to look for some indication on the Vehicle Emissions Control Information (VECI) sticker in the engine compartment. A second, less accurate, way to check is to look at the Data Link Connector (DLC) in the engine compartment or under the dash. If the connector has 16 pins and is trapezoidal in shape, you can be pretty sure you have an OBD-II system.

➡**Some manufacturers started using the 16 pin OBD-II connector prior to full implementation of the system on their vehicles.**

How Do I Read The Codes?

OBD-I vehicles have connectors in various positions around the vehicle. Some likely spots are under the dashboard, under the hood, in the center console, in the trunk or hatch area or under the seats. Some vehicles do not use a connector but have several buttons and lights directly on the control module.

Each manufacturer has a specific sequence that must be performed exactly to enable the code to be read. These sequences range from the simple (ground two terminals on a connector) to the ridiculous (cycle the ignition key 15 times). However, most manufacturers codes could be read without the use of any special equipment.

All OBD-II cars have a connector located in the passenger compartment easily accessible from the driver's seat. Check under the dash or near the ashtray. A cable is plugged into the OBD-II connector and a scan tool is used to read the fault codes. This can range from a simple hand-held meter that provides a coded read-out of the various diagnostic functions, up to a large console computer-based unit costing used by some high tech professional mechanics.

Most scan tools use replaceable cartridges, making them compatible with all cars. Each tool contains software that analyzes the signals received from the car and displays a text or diagrammed readout of any malfunctions found. Some of the higher end models even suggest possible solutions to the problems.

Several manufacturers have started to market smaller scan tools. Units for the advanced do-it-yourselfer or small shop technician can provide a variety of levels of data, some approaching the sophistication of the big shop consoles.

A detailed description of how to access codes is included with each manufacturer section.

A Word About Scan Tools

▶ **See Figures 1 and 2**

The malfunction indicator light on your dashboard has been winking at you randomly for months. Perhaps this partly explains why your car just

89465P01

Fig. 1 AutoTap® from B&B electronics is an OBD-II compatible scan tool you can hook up to your personal computer

Fig. 2 The AutoXray® is more like a traditional scan tool which comes complete with various adapters to fit many makes and models

TCCS4P10

doesn't feel quite right and your gasoline credit card bill is enormous. Maybe this time, instead of taking it to the mechanic its time to start looking into things yourself.

First, you'll need a scan tool. In the past, scan tools were the private domain of mechanics and dealerships due to their high cost. Now the do-it-yourselfer can choose from many entry-level scan testers designed for the small shop and home mechanic. The ones we tested have control panels and screens you can understand. So if you've learned to use a PC, a scan tool is much easier. Even the harness adapter fits only one way in the diagnostic plug. So if it doesn't fit right, you've got the wrong one.

Plugging in the scan tool is quite easy, as long as you have the correct adapters. Most kits come with adapters to enable one scan tool to fit a number of vehicles. Once you plug it the scan tool can begin the job with a list of trouble codes, including those that aren't accompanied by malfunction indicator lamp. If only the entire procedure were this easy. The trouble code is a good start, but many problems will not set a code at all, so you'll need to do some good old-fashioned diagnosis.

What Do Codes Tell Me?

OBD signals are most often sought in response to a "Malfunction Indicator Lamp (MIL)" appearing on the dashboard or driveability problems experienced with the vehicle. The data provided by OBD can often pinpoint the specific component that has malfunctioned, saving substantial time and cost compared to guess-and-replace repairs.

The MIL shows three different types of signals. Occasional flashes show momentary malfunctions. It stays **ON** if the problem is of a more serious nature, affecting the emissions output or safety of the vehicle. A constantly flashing MIL is a sign of a major problem which can cause serious damage if the engine is not stopped immediately. In all cases an electronic picture called a "freeze frame" is taken to show all sensor readings at the time of the fault. This picture is recorded in the vehicle's control module and can be accessed to provide additional clues during diagnosis.

OBD-I TROUBLE CODES

Introduction

It should be remembered that OBD-I codes, for the most part, are manufacturer, model and sometimes year specific. Reading the codes is also specific to the individual manufacturer. Special tools may be necessary to gain access to the control modules. If reading codes does require special tools, the procedures given here will reference those tools.

➡The term **control module** is a generic term used for the engine control computer. These computers are known by various names including Electronic Control Module (ECM), Powertrain Control Module (PCM), Vehicle Control Module (VCM), Single Board Engine Controller (SBEC), Engine Control Assembly (ECA) and Engine Control Unit (ECU).

➡The term **Malfunction Indicator Lamp (MIL)** is a generic term used to indicate the instrument panel mounted, engine computer controlled lamp which warns the driver there has been a fault in the system. Some common names for this lamp are the malfunction indicator light and the Service Engine Soon Light. Sometimes just the word Engine will appear.

Reading and Clearing Codes

▶ **See Figures 3, 4, 5, 6 and 7**

It should be noted that with very few exceptions, reading and clearing of OBD-I trouble codes, can be performed without using a scan tool. However, by using a scan tool, the codes can be obtained much quicker and other functions of the system can readily be accessed. This should not be tremendous cause for concern as, as several manufacturers have developed scan tools that are well within the price range of the average do-it-yourselfer. Also, many mechanics will hook up a scan tool to your vehicle for a minimal charge.

89694P31

Fig. 3 Hooking up the scan tool is as easy as plugging into the diagnostic link connector

Acura

GENERAL INFORMATION

Programmed Fuel Injection (PGM-FI) System is a fully electronic microprocessor based engine management system. The Electronic Control Unit (ECU) is given responsibility for control of injector timing and duration, intake air control, ignition timing, cold start enrichment, fuel pump control, fuel cut-off, A/C compressor operation, alternator control as well as EGR function and canister purge cycles.

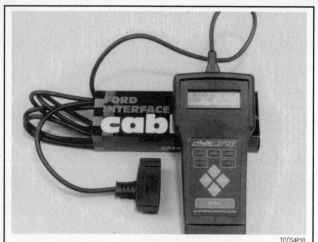

Fig. 4 Inexpensive scan tools, such as this one from AutoXray®, are available to interface with the OBD-I electronics in your vehicle

Fig. 5 Among other features, a scan tool combines many standard testers into a single device for quick and accurate diagnosis

Fig. 6 Although some times no DTC's are found, that does not rule out a problem

Fig. 7 Once the scan tool finds a trouble code it will display the appropriate code number and description

The ECU receives electric signals from many sensors and sources on and around the engine. The signals are processed against pre-programmed values; correct output signals from the ECU are determined by these calculations. The ECU contains additional memories, back-up and fail-safe functions as well as self diagnostic capabilities.

SELF DIAGNOSTICS

Service Precautions

- Do not operate the fuel pump when the fuel lines are empty.
- Do not operate the fuel pump when removed from the fuel tank.
- Do not reuse fuel hose clamps.
- The washer(s) below any fuel system bolt (banjo fittings, service bolt, fuel filter, etc.) must be replaced whenever the bolt is loosened. Do not reuse the washers; a high-pressure fuel leak may result.
- Make sure all ECU harness connectors are fastened securely. A poor connection can cause an extremely high voltage surge and result in damage to integrated circuits.
- Keep all ECU parts and harnesses dry during service. Protect the ECU and all solid-state components from rough handling or extremes of temperature.
- Use extreme care when working around the ECU or other components; the airbag or SRS wiring may be in the vicinity. On these vehicles, the SRS wiring and connectors are yellow; do not cut or test these circuits.
- Before attempting to remove any parts, turn the ignition switch **OFF** and disconnect the battery ground cable.
- Always use a 12 volt battery as a power source for the engine, never a booster or high-voltage charging unit.
- Do not disconnect the battery cables with the engine running.
- Do not disconnect any wiring connector with the engine running or the ignition **ON** unless specifically instructed to do so.
- Do not apply battery power directly to injectors.
- Whenever possible, use a flashlight instead of a drop light.
- Keep all open flame and smoking material out of the area.
- Use a shop cloth or similar to catch fuel when opening a fuel system. Consider the fuel-soaked rag to be a flammable solid and dispose of it in the proper manner.
- Relieve fuel system pressure before servicing any fuel system component.
- Always use eye or full-face protection when working around fuel lines, fittings or components.
- Always keep a dry chemical (class B-C) fire extinguisher near the area.

READING TROUBLE CODES

▶ See Figures 8, 9 and 10

1986–90 LEGEND
1986–91 INTEGRA

When a fault is noted, the ECU stores an identifying code and illuminates the malfunction indicator light. The code will remain in memory until cleared; the dashboard warning lamp may not illuminate during the next ignition cycle if the fault is no longer present. Not all faults noted by the ECU will trigger the dashboard warning lamp although the fault code will be set in memory. For this reason, troubleshooting should be based on the presence of stored codes, not the illumination of the warning lamp while the car is operating.

Stored codes are displayed by a flashing LED on the ECU. When the CHECK ENGINE warning lamp has been on or reported on, lift or remove the carpet from the right front passenger footwell. The ECU is below a protective cover; the LED may be viewed through a small window without removing the ECU cover. Turn the ignition switch **ON**; the LED will display any stored codes by rhythmic flashing. Note that 1986–90 Legends have two LEDs on the controller; one is red and one is amber. The red one will

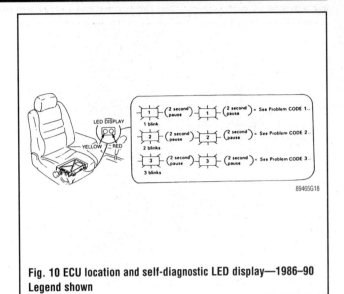

Fig. 10 ECU location and self-diagnostic LED display—1986–90 Legend shown

flash the fault codes; the amber one is used during idle adjustment and is not related to this procedure. 1986–91 Integra use a single LED which is used to display codes only.

Codes 1–9 are indicated by a series of short flashes; two-digit codes use a number of long flashes for the first digit followed by the appropriate number of short flashes. For example, Code 43 would be indicated by 4 long flashes followed by 3 short flashes. Codes are separated by a longer pause between transmissions. The position of the codes during output can be helpful in diagnostic work. Multiple codes transmitted in isolated order indicate unique occurrences; a display of showing 1–1–1–pause–9–9–9 indicates two problems or problems occurring at different times. An alternating display, such as 1–9–1–9–1, indicates simultaneous occurrences of the faults.

When counting flashes to determine codes, a code not valid for the vehicle may be found. In this case, first recount the flashes to confirm an accurate count. If necessary, turn the ignition switch **OFF**, then recycle the system and begin the count again. If the Code is not valid for the vehicle, the ECU must be replaced.

1992–95 INTEGRA
1991–95 LEGEND, NSX AND VIGOR
1995 2.5TL

When a fault is noted, the ECU stores an identifying code and illuminates the malfunction indicator light. The code will remain in memory until cleared; the dashboard warning lamp may not illuminate during the next ignition cycle if the fault is no longer present. Not all faults noted by the ECU will trigger the dashboard warning lamp although the fault code will be set in memory. For this reason, troubleshooting should be based on the presence of stored codes, not the illumination of the warning lamp while the car is operating.

Beginning in 1991 on the Legend and in 1992 on Integra, codes are read thorough the use of the malfunction indicator light or more commonly know today as the Malfunction Indicator Lamp (MIL). NSX and Vigor are read in the same manner. The 1995 Legend equipped with the 2.7L V6 engine and the 2.5TL utilize OBD-II trouble codes.

Additionally, all models are equipped with a service connector in side the cabin of the vehicle. If the service connector is jumped, the CHECK ENGINE lamp will display the stored codes in the same fashion. The 2-pin service connector is located under the extreme right dashboard on Integra, Legend, 2.5TL and NSX; on Vigor models, it is found behind the right side of the center console well under the dashboard.

Codes 1–9 are indicated by a series of short flashes; two-digit codes use a number of long flashes for the first digit followed by the appropriate number of short flashes. For example, Code 43 would be indicated by 4 long

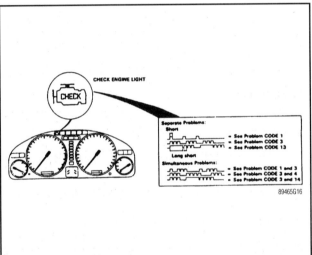

Fig. 8 Fault code display pattern and malfunction indicator light location—1986–95 Acura

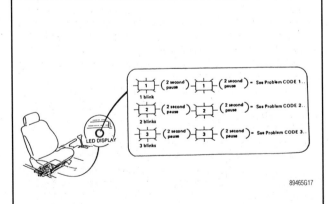

Fig. 9 ECU location and self-diagnostic LED display—1986–91 Integra shown

flashes followed by 3 short flashes. Codes are separated by a longer pause between transmissions. The position of the codes during output can be helpful in diagnostic work. Multiple codes transmitted in isolated order indicate unique occurrences; a display of showing 1–1–1–pause–9–9–9 indicates two problems or problems occurring at different times. An alternating display, such as 1–9–1–9–1, indicates simultaneous occurrences of the faults.

When counting flashes to determine codes, a code not valid for the vehicle may be found. In this case, first recount the flashes to confirm an accurate count. If necessary, turn the ignition switch **OFF**, then recycle the system and begin the count again. If the Code is not valid for the vehicle, the ECU must be replaced.

➡**On vehicles with automatic transaxles, the S, D or D4 lamp may flash with the CHECK ENGINE lamp if certain codes are stored. For Legend and NSX, this may occur with Codes 6, 7 or 17. On Vigor and Integra it may occur with codes 6, 7 or 13. In addition, the TCS lamp on NSX may flash with codes 3, 5, 6,13,15,16,17, 35 or 36. In all cases, proceed with the diagnosis based on the engine code shown. After repairs, recheck the lamp. If the additional warning lamp is still lit, proceed with diagnosis for that system.**

CLEARING CODES

1986–95 Vehicles

Stored codes are removed from memory by removing power to the ECU. Disconnecting the power may also clear the memories used for other solid-state equipment such as the clock and radio. For this reason, always make note of the radio presets before clearing the system. Additionally, some radios contain anti-theft programming; obtain the owner's code number before clearing the codes.

While disconnecting the battery will clear the memory, this is not the recommended procedure. The memory should be cleared after the ignition is switched **OFF** by removing the appropriate fuse for at least 10 seconds. The correct fuses and their locations are:
- 1990 and earlier Legend—ALTERNATOR SENSE, in the underhood fuse and relay panel.
- 1991 and later Legend—ACG, in the dashboard fuse panel. Removing this fuse also cancels the memory for the power seats.
- Integra, U.S. vehicles—BACK UP, in the underhood fuse and relay panel.
- Integra, Canadian vehicles—HAZARD/BACK UP in the underhood fuse and relay panel.
- Vigor—BACK UP, located in the underhood fuse and relay panel. Removing this fuse will cancel memories for the clock and radio.
- 1991–94 NSX—CLOCK, located in the main fuse and relay panel in the front luggage compartment, right side. Removing this fuse will cancel memories for the clock and radio.
- 1995 NSX—CLOCK, located in the main fuse and relay panel in the front luggage compartment, right side. Removing this fuse will cancel memories for the clock and radio.
- 1995 2.5TL—BACK UP, located in the underhood fuse and relay panel. Removing this fuse will cancel memories for the clock and radio.

DIAGNOSTIC TROUBLE CODES

1986–93 Integra 1.6l (1590cc)

Code 0 Electronic Control Unit
Code 1 Oxygen Content
Code 2 Replace Engine Control Unit with known-good unit
Code 3 Manifold Absolute Pressure
Code 4 Replace Engine Control Unit with known-good unit
Code 5 Manifold Absolute Pressure
Code 6 Coolant Temperature
Code 7 Throttle Angle
Code 8 Crank Angle (TDC)
Code 9 Crank Angle (Cyl)

Code 10 Intake Air Temperature
Code 12 EGR system (if equipped)
Code 13 Atmospheric Pressure
Code 14 Electronic Air Control
Code 15 Ignition output signal
Code 16 Fuel injector
Code 17 Vehicle speed sensor
Code 19 Lock up solenoid valve
Code 20 Electric load (to 1989)
Code 43 Fuel supply system

1986–87 Legend 2.5L (2494cc) C25A1

Code 0 Electronic Control Unit
Code 1 Oxygen Content
Code 2 Replace Engine Control Unit with known-good unit
Code 3 Manifold Absolute Pressure
Code 4 Replace Engine Control Unit with known-good unit
Code 5 Manifold Absolute Pressure
Code 6 Coolant Temperature
Code 7 Throttle Angle
Code 8 Crank Angle (TDC)
Code 9 Crank Angle (Cyl)
Code 10 Intake Air Temperature
Code 12 EGR system (if equipped)
Code 13 Atmospheric Pressure
Code 14 Electronic Air Control
Code 15 Ignition output signal
Code 16 Fuel injector
Code 17 Vehicle speed sensor
Code 20 Electric load (to 1989)
Code 43 Fuel supply system

1987–90 Legend 2.7L (2675cc) C27A1

Code 0 Electronic Control Unit (ECU)
Code 1 Front Oxygen Content
Code 2 Rear Oxygen Content
Code 3 Manifold Absolute Pressure (MAP)
Code 4 Crank angle
Code 5 Manifold Absolute Pressure (MAP)
Code 6 Coolant Temperature
Code 7 Throttle angle
Code 8 Crank Angle—Top Dead Center
Code 9 Crank Angle—Number 1 Cylinder
Code 10 Intake Air temperature
Code 12 Exhaust Gas Recirculation system
Code 13 Atmospheric pressure
Code 14 Electronic Idle Control
Code 15 Ignition output signal
Code 17 Vehicle speed pulsar
Code 18 Ignition timing adjustment
Code 30 A/T FI Signal A (if equipped)
Code 31 A/T FI Signal B (if equipped)

1991–93 Integra 1.8L (1834cc) B18A1

1992–93 Integra 1.7L (1678cc) B17A1

1994–95 Integra 1.8L (1834cc) B18B1

1994–95 Integra 1.8L (1797cc) B18C1

Code 0 Electronic Control Unit
Code 1 Oxygen Content
Code 3 Manifold Absolute Pressure
Code 4 Crank Angle sensor
Code 5 Manifold Absolute Pressure
Code 6 Coolant Temperature

Code 7 Throttle Angle
Code 8 TDC Position
Code 9 No.1 Cylinder Position
Code 10 Intake Air Temperature
Code 12 EGR system
Code 13 Atmospheric Pressure
Code 14 Electronic Air Control
Code 15 Ignition output signal
Code 16 Fuel injector
Code 17 Vehicle speed sensor
Code 20 Electric Load Detector
Code 21 VTEC Solenoid Valve (1.8L GS-R)
Code 22 VTEC Oil Pressure Switch (1.8L GS-R)
Code 30 TCM Signal "A"
Code 31 TCM Signal "B"
Code 41 HO2S Heater
Code 43 Fuel supply system

1991–95 Legend 3.2L (3206cc) C32A1

Code 0 Electronic Control Unit (ECU)
Code 1 Left Oxygen Sensor
Code 2 Right Oxygen Sensor
Code 3 Manifold Absolute Pressure (MAP)
Code 4 Crank angle 1
Code 5 Manifold Absolute Pressure (MAP)
Code 6 Coolant Temperature
Code 7 Throttle angle
Code 9 Crank Angle-Number 1 Cylinder
Code 10 Intake Air temperature
Code 12 Exhaust Gas Recirculation (EGR) system
Code 13 Atmospheric pressure
Code 14 Electronic Air Control (EACV)
Code 15 Ignition output signal
Code 17 Vehicle speed pulsar
Code 18 Ignition timing adjustment
Code 23 Left Knock Sensor
Code 30 A/T FI Signal A
Code 35 Traction Control System Circuit
Code 36 Traction Control System Circuit
Code 41 Left Oxygen Sensor Heater
Code 42 Right Oxygen Sensor Heater
Code 43 Left Fuel Supply System
Code 44 Right Fuel Supply System
Code 45 Left Fuel Supply Metering
Code 46 Right Fuel Supply Metering
Code 53 Right Knock Sensor
Code 54 Crank angle 2
Code 59 No.1 Cylinder Position 2 (Cylinder Sensor)

1991–95 NSX 3.0L (2977cc) C30A1

Code 0 ECU
Code 1 Front Oxygen Sensor
Code 2 Rear Oxygen Sensor
Code 3 Manifold Absolute Pressure (MAP)
Code 4 Crank angle A
Code 5 Manifold Absolute Pressure (MAP)
Code 6 Coolant Temperature
Code 7 Throttle angle
Code 9 Crank Angle-Number 1 Cylinder/Position A
Code 10 Intake Air temperature
Code 12 Exhaust Gas Recirculation (EGR) system
Code 13 Atmospheric pressure
Code 14 Electronic Air Control (EACV)
Code 15 Ignition output signal
Code 16 Fuel Injector
Code 17 Vehicle speed pulsar

Code 18 Ignition timing adjustment
Code 22 VTEC System; front, bank 2
Code 23 Front Knock Sensor
Code 30 A/T FI Signal A
Code 31 A/T FI Signal B
Code 35 TC STB signal
Code 36 TCFC signal
Code 37 Accelerator Position; Sensors 1, 2 or 1 and 2 circuits
Code 40 Throttle Position or Throttle Valve Control Motor Circuits 1 or 2
Code 41 Front Oxygen Sensor Heater; (circuit malfunction; bank 2 sensor 1)
Code 42 Rear Primary Heated Oxygen Sensor Heater (circuit malfunction)
Code 43 Front Fuel Supply System
Code 44 Rear Fuel Supply System
Code 45 Front Fuel Supply Metering; front bank 2
Code 46 Rear Fuel Supply Metering; rear bank 1
Code 47 Fuel Pump
Code 51 Rear Spool Solenoid Valve
Code 52 VTEC System; rear, bank 1
Code 53 Rear Knock Sensor
Code 54 Crank Angle B
Code 59 No. 1 Cylinder Position B (Cylinder Sensor)
Code 61 Front Heated Oxygen Sensor (slow response; bank 2 sensor 1)
Code 62 Rear Primary Heated Oxygen Sensor (slow response; bank 1 sensor 1)
Code 63 Front Secondary Oxygen Sensor (slow response or circuit voltage high or low)
Code 65 Front Secondary Heated Oxygen Sensor (circuit malfunction; bank 2 sensor 2)
Code 64 Rear Secondary Oxygen Sensor (slow response or circuit voltage high or low)
Code 66 Rear Secondary Heated Oxygen Sensor (circuit malfunction; bank 1 sensor 2)
Code 67 Front Catalytic Converter System
Code 68 Rear Catalytic Converter System
Code 80 Exhaust Gas Recirculation (EGR) system
Code 86 Coolant temperature
Code 70 Automatic Transaxle; the D indicator light and MIL may come on simultaneously.
Code 71 Misfire detected; cylinder No. 1 or random misfire
Code 72 Misfire detected; cylinder No. 2 or random misfire
Code 73 Misfire detected; cylinder No. 3 or random misfire
Code 74 Misfire detected; cylinder No. 4 or random misfire
Code 75 Misfire detected; cylinder No. 5 or random misfire
Code 76 Misfire detected; cylinder No. 6 or random misfire
Code 79 Spark Plug Voltage Detection; circuit malfunction; (Front Bank (Bank 2) or (Rear Bank (Bank 1)
Code 79 Spark Plug Voltage Detection; circuit malfunction; (Front Bank (Bank 2) or (Rear Bank (Bank 1)
Code 79 Spark Plug Voltage Detection Module; reset circuit malfunction; (Front Bank (Bank 2)) or (Rear Bank (Bank 1)
Code 92 Evaporative Emission Control System

1992–94 Vigor 2.5L (G25A1)

Code 0 Electronic Control Unit
Code 1 HO2S circuit
Code 3 Manifold Absolute Pressure
Code 4 Crank Angle Sensor
Code 5 Manifold Absolute Pressure
Code 6 Coolant Temperature
Code 7 Throttle Angle
Code 8 TDC and or Crankshaft Position sensors
Code 9 No. 1 Cylinder Position
Code 10 Intake Air Temperature
Code 12 EGR system
Code 13 Atmospheric Pressure

Code 14 Electronic Air Control
Code 15 Ignition output signal
Code 16 Fuel injector
Code 17 Vehicle speed sensor
Code 18 Ignition Timing Adjuster
Code 20 Electric Load Detector
Code 30 A/T FI Signal
Code 31 A/T FI Signal
Code 41 HO2S Heater
Code 43 Fuel supply system
Code 45 Fuel Supply Metering
Code 50 Mass Air Flow (MAF) circuit—2.5TL
Code 53 Rear Knock Sensor
Code 54 Crankshaft Speed Fluctuation sensor—2.5TL
Code 61 HO2S sensor heater—2.5TL
Code 65 Secondary HO2S sensor—2.5TL
Code 67 Catalytic Converter System—2.5TL
Code 70 Automatic transaxle or A/T FI Data line—2.5TL
Code 71 Misfire detected; cylinder No. 1 or random misfire
Code 72 Misfire detected; cylinder No. 2 or random misfire
Code 73 Misfire detected; cylinder No. 3 or random misfire
Code 74 Misfire detected; cylinder No. 4 or random misfire
Code 75 Misfire detected; cylinder No. 5 or random misfire
Code 76 Random misfire detected—2.5TL
Code 80 EGR system—2.5TL
Code 86 Coolant Temperature circuit—2.5TL
Code 92 Evaporative Emission Control System—2.5TL

Audi

GENERAL INFORMATION

Motronic And Multi Point Injection (MPI) Systems

The Motronic and MPI fuel injection systems are similar and share most components and modes of operation. Audi uses Motronic to describe the fuel injection system on the V8 Quattro, S4, 200 Quattro and the 200 Quattro Wagon. Audi uses MPI to describe the systems used on the 90 Quattro, Coupe Quattro and the 2.8L V6 equipped 100 series vehicles.

The Motronic and MPI fuel injection systems are self-learning adaptive systems. They continuously learn using a sophisticated feedback system that readjusts various control settings. These new values are then stored in the ECU memory. The adaptive capability allows the systems to compensate for changes in the engine's operating conditions, such as intake leaks, altitude changes or any other system malfunction. If the battery or ECU is disconnected, the vehicle must be driven so ECU can "re-learn" its operating conditions.

Operation of the fuel injection system is based on the information received by the various sensors. This keeps the system constantly updated on engine speed, coolant temperature, throttle position and the intake air volume.

On the V8, the power supply to ECU is at terminal 18, through a 5 amp fuse (S27) in the main fuse/relay panel. Power from fuse S27 energizes the power supply relay in the ECU when engine speed reaches 25 rpm. The main fuse/relay panel is located behind the side kick panel cover on the passenger's side.

A Hall effect signal from the right distributor helps the ECU establish a reference point to start the fuel injection process. After the engine is running, the reference sender and speed sensor provide the necessary information to the ECU for ignition and fuel injection.

The ECU has a self-diagnostic feature. Any faults detected by the sensors are sent to the ECU and are recorded in the ECU memory. Fault codes can be displayed using LED tester US 1115 and a jumper wire.

Continuous Injection System (CIS-E)

▶ **See Figure 11**

The CIS-E system incorporates 2 control units. An Ignition Control Unit (ICU) or Knock Sensor Control Unit (KSCU, on 5000S only) and a Fuel Injection Control Unit (FICU).

The CIS-E system also has self-diagnosis and troubleshooting capabilities. Input and output signals from various sensors, switches and signaling devices are constantly monitored for faults. These faults are stored in the control unit memory. Faults can be displayed by a flashing 4 digit code sequence from an LED light located on the instrument panel.

CIS-Motronic Fuel Injection System

The CIS Motronic system used on Audi 80 and 90 models use a single Electronic Control Unit (ECU), located behind the A/C evaporator assembly. The ECU controls the fuel delivery, ignition system and operation of the emission control components. The CIS Motronic system also incorporates self-diagnostic capabilities. The CIS-Motronic system consists of the following components:

• Ignition coil with power stage
• Differential pressure regulator
• Cold start valve
• Idle stabilizer valve
• Ignition distributor with Hall sender
• Knock sensor
• Coolant temperature sensor
• Idle/Full throttle switches
• Air sensor potentiometer
• Oxygen sensor
• Carbon canister frequency valve
• Carbon canister ON/OFF valve
• CIS Motronic control unit

The ECU receives signals from various sensors, switches and signaling components which are constantly monitored for faults. These faults are stored in the ECU memory. Faults can be displayed by using a suitable test light connected between the battery positive terminal and the test lead, located next to the fuel distributor in the engine compartment. Characteristics of the CIS-Motronic system are as follows:

• Fuel injection control
• Oxygen sensor regulation with adaptive learning capability
• MAP type ignition control with individual cylinder knock regulation
• Idle speed control
• Fuel tank ventilation control
• Permanent fault memory for self-diagnosis

SELF DIAGNOSTICS

Service Precautions

• Do not disconnect the battery or power to the control module before reading the fault codes. On the Motronic SMPI and Audi SMPI systems, fault code memory is erased when power is interrupted.

• Make sure the ignition switch is **OFF** before disconnecting any wiring.

• Before removing or installing a control module, disconnect the negative battery cable. The unit receives power through the main connector at all times and will be permanently damaged if improperly powered up or down.

• Keep all parts and harnesses dry during service. Protect the control module and all solid-state components from rough handling or extremes of temperature.

• Do not apply voltage to engine control module to simulate output signals.

• When coil wire, terminal 4, is disconnected from distributor, always ground using a jumper wire.

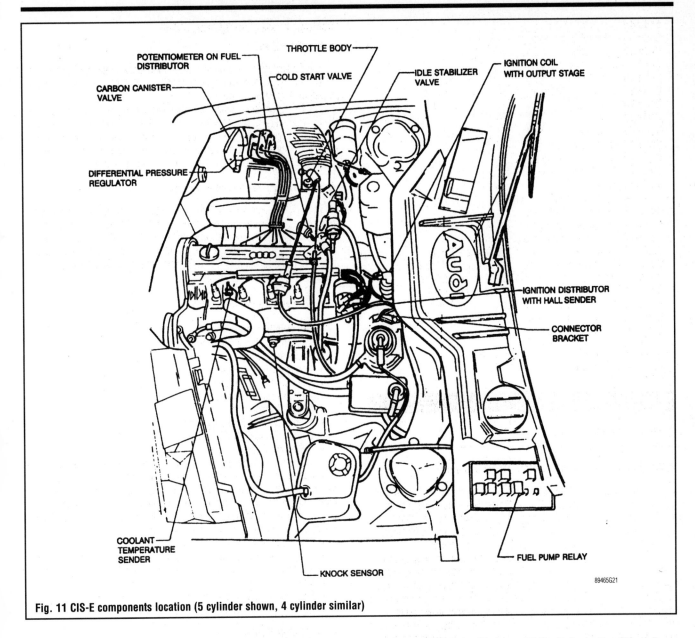

Fig. 11 CIS-E components location (5 cylinder shown, 4 cylinder similar)

- Do not try to start the engine with the fuel injectors removed.
- In emergency starting situations, use a fast charge for cranking up to 15 seconds only and not more than 16.5 volts; allow at least 1 minute between attempts.

Generating Codes

Before attempting to read trouble codes, the vehicle must be driven for at least 5 minutes to set codes in the computer's memory. This procedure is referred to as "generating codes".

CIS SYSTEMS

1. The engine must be running to generate fault codes. Read all the Steps in this procedure before starting.
2. On 1985–88 models, turn the ignition switch **ON** without starting the engine to make sure the engine warning light works, if equipped. If it does not light with the ignition **ON**, engine not running, but does light when attempting to retrieve fault codes, either the wiring between the control units is faulty or the ignition control unit is faulty.
3. On 1989–92 California models only, turn the ignition switch **ON** without starting the engine to make sure the engine warning light On Board

Diagnostics (OBD) works. If it does not light with the ignition **ON**, engine not running, then turn ignition **OFF** and bridge terminals of diagnostic connectors using adapter (cable 357 971 51 4E) or an equivalent tool. Now turn ignition **ON**, but do not start the engine. The engine warning light OBD will light up, if it does not light the wiring between the control modules is faulty or the ignition control module is faulty. Consult a wiring diagram and complete the necessary repairs before continuing.

4. Fuel pump relay and fuses 13, 19, 24 and 28 on 1985–88 models or 13, 19, 21, 24, 27 and 28 on 1989–92 models, must be good and all ground connections in the engine compartment must be good. Also, make sure the air conditioning is **OFF**.

5. To generate fault codes, the vehicle must be driven with air conditioner **OFF**, for at least 5 minutes at normal operating temperature. The engine must be kept above 3000 RPM for the majority of the test drive with at least one full throttle application. On turbocharged engines, full boost should be reached during the full throttle acceleration. After the test drive, allow the engine to idle for at least 2 minutes before retrieving codes.

6. Do not turn the ignition switch **OFF** or the temporary memory will be erased. If the engine stalls, do not restart it. The codes will still be in memory.

7. If the engine will not run, operate the starter for at least 6 seconds and leave the ignition switch **ON**.

READING TROUBLE CODES

▶ **See Figures 12, 13, 14 and 15**

➡Vehicles that do not have a malfunction indicator light or Malfunction Indicator Lamp (MIL) codes can only be accessed by the use of special equipment. US 1115 LED tester, VAG 1551 diagnostic tester or equivalent special testers can only be used to retrieve diagnostic codes from these vehicles. When using special diagnostic equipment, always observe the tool manufacturer's instructions.

With Flash Tester

1985-94 VEHICLES

1. On California models equipped with a engine warning light, an LED tester is not required. On models not equipped with a engine warning light, connect the US 1115 LED tester or equivalent to the test connectors under the left-hand side of dash and above the pedals.

2. On 1985-88 models with a engine warning light, locate the fuel pump relay on the main fuse/relay panel. Insert a spare fuse into the terminals on top of the relay for at least 4 seconds, then remove the fuse to activate the diagnostic program. The engine warning light on the instrument panel or the LED tester will begin to flash the first code. It will continue to flash this code until the fuse is installed.

3. On all models, codes should be retrieved with the engine running at idle. If engine will not start, operate the starter for approximately 6 seconds and leave the ignition switch **ON**. On CIS systems the engine should be left running after the generating codes procedure.

4. On 1989-94 models, so equipped, locate the test connectors above the pedals and connect the tester. To connect the LED tester, connect the positive terminal of the LED tester to the positive terminal in connector A. Connect the negative terminal of the LED tester to the only terminal in connector B. Connect one end of a jumper wire to the negative terminal in connector A, touch the other end of the jumper wire to the terminal in connector B for at least 4 seconds.

5. Fault codes will now be displayed as flashing by the tester or by the engine warning light on California models. Touch the jumper wire to the terminal in connector B for another 4 seconds to advance to the next code. Do not leave jumper wire connected for ten seconds or memory will be erased. Engine idle speed may increase slightly when reading injection control module codes.

6. All flash codes are 4 digits, with about 2.5 seconds between digits. Codes are displayed in order of importance, usually beginning with ignition system codes. Count the flashes and write down the code, then proceed onto the next code. Read all codes, before starting any repairs. If the first code is 4444 or 0000 there are no faults present. 0000 is represented by

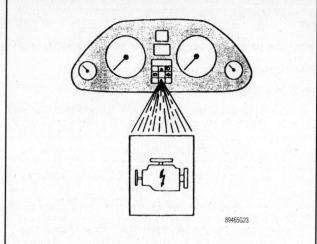

Fig. 13 Location of the fault indicator light in the instrument panel—Vehicles equipped with an ENGINE WARNING light

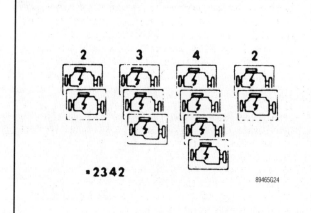

Fig. 14 Example of the indicator light sequence for Code 2342—vehicles equipped with an ENGINE WARNING LIGHT

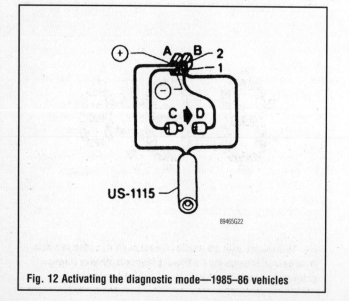

Fig. 12 Activating the diagnostic mode—1985-86 vehicles

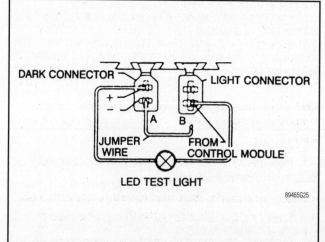

Fig. 15 On 1989—94, connect the LED tester and momentarily connect jumper terminals A and B to read fault codes

the light **ON** for 2.5 seconds with 2.5 second intervals between. When all fault codes have been reported (0000 or 4444 displayed), turn the ignition **OFF**.

➡ On CIS systems codes are erased when the ignition is turned OFF.

With Diagnostic Tester

1987–89 VEHICLES

1. On all 1987–88 models, the VAG 1551 or equivalent diagnostic tester can be connected to the terminals on top of the fuel pump relay. For power to the tester, a separate power supply wire must be connected to the positive battery terminal. On 1989 models, the tester can be connected to the diagnostic terminals above the pedals. The terminals are shaped so they cannot be connected incorrectly. Power for the tester is supplied through fuse 21.

2. With the tester connected, turn the ignition switch **ON**, but do not start the engine or the codes will be erased.

3. Select menu option 2, Blink Code Output. Press and release, then press and hold the run (arrow) key until the program starts, then release the key. An asterisk (*) will appear and flash the codes, which the tester will count and report on the screen as numbers. If Code 4444 is displayed, no faults are found in memory.

4. Press the run key to advance to the next code. Read all the fault codes before starting repairs.

5. All engine system fault codes will be displayed first. If there are other control units on the vehicle, press the run key again to access those codes.

6. When the End of the Report Code 0000 is displayed and there are no other control units on the vehicle, pressing the run key again may return to the main menu or it may erase the codes. To stop the program without erasing the codes, turn the ignition switch **OFF** and press the clear button once.

1990–91 VEHICLES

1. Connect the VAG 1551 or equivalent diagnostic tester to the diagnostic terminals above the pedals or in the passenger side foot well. The terminals are shaped so they cannot be connected incorrectly. Power for the tester is supplied through fuse 21 or 27.

2. On all models, codes should be retrieved with the engine running at idle. If the engine will not start, operate the starter for at least 5 seconds and leave the ignition switch **ON**. On CIS systems, the engine should be left running after the procedure for generating codes.

3. Operate the tester to select menu option 2, Blink Code Output or Fault Memory Recall. An asterisk (*) will appear and flash the codes, which the tester will count and report on the screen as numbers. If Code 4444 is displayed, no faults are found in memory.

4. If the engine is not running, some codes will be displayed. These codes can be ignored if the engine has been intentionally stalled but should be investigated if the engine will not start.

5. Press the run key to advance to the next code. Read all the fault codes before starting repairs.

6. When the End of the Report Code 0000 is displayed and there are no other control units on the vehicle, pressing the run key again may return to the main menu or it may erase the codes. To stop the program without erasing the codes, turn the ignition switch **OFF** and press the clear button once.

1992–94 VEHICLES WITH 2.2L AND 2.8L ENGINES

Diagnostic trouble codes (DTCs) may be accessed using the VAG 1551 scan tool.

1. Turn the ignition switch to the **OFF** position.

2. Connect the VAG1551/1 diagnostic lead to the data link connectors (DLCs) in the underhood relay box.

➡ Observe the connector shape when connecting diagnostic leads.

3. Connect the black lead of the VAG1551/1 diagnostic lead to the DLC 1, and the white lead to the DLC 4.

4. Connect the VAG15S1/1 diagnostic lead to the VAG 1551 scan tool. The scan tool should read—VAG self diagnosis—1 Rapid Data Transmission or 2 Flash Code Output.

5. Additional operating instructions may be accessed by pressing the help key on the VAG 1551 scan tool. Press the arrow key to continue fault tracing.

1992–94 VEHICLES WITH 4.2L ENGINE

Diagnostic trouble codes (DTCs) may be accessed using the VAG 1551 scan tool.

1. Turn the ignition switch to the **OFF** position.

2. Connect the VAG1551/1 diagnostic lead to the data link connectors (DLC) under the passenger side foot well carpet.

➡ Observe the connector shape when connecting diagnostic leads.

3. Connect the black lead of the VAG1551/1 diagnostic lead to the DLC 1, and the white lead to the DLC 2 and the blue lead to the DLC 4.

4. Connect the VAG1551/1 diagnostic lead to the VAG 1551 scan tool. The scan tool should read—VAG self diagnosis—Rapid Data Transmission or 2 Flash Code Output.

5. Additional operating instructions may be accessed by pressing the help key on the VAG 1551 scan tool. Press the arrow key to continue fault tracing.

With On Board Diagnostic (OBD) Display

1992–94 VEHICLES

▶ **See Figure 16**

The air conditioning system On-Board Diagnostic (OBD) can be accessed without the need of a scan tool. The air conditioning control head contains a 61 channel OBD display.

1. To start the display, turn the ignition **ON** or start the engine.

2. Press and hold down RECIRCULATION button 1 and press and hold down upper AIR DISTRIBUTION button 2.

3. Release both buttons and "O1c" will be displayed, "O1c" indicates channel 1, "O2c" indicates channel 2, etc.

4. To change to a different channel, press the temperature + button to go to the next higher channel or the temperature -button to go to the next lower channel.

5. To call up information about a particular channel, select the desired channel and press RECIRCULATION button 1.

➡ Diagnostic channel 1 "O1c" contains the DTC's. There are also graphics channels 1 and 2 in diagnostic channel 52, to aid in diagnosis.

6. When using channel 52, graphics channels 1 and 2, a segment of an 88.8 display will appear. This appears when there is a compressor off situa-

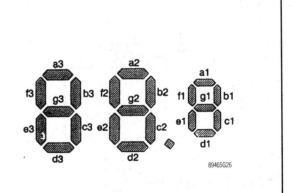

Fig. 16 Vehicles with automatic climate control, codes can also be accessed through the On Board Diagnostic display through graphics channels 1 and 2 display—1992–94 vehicles

tion. Each segment has an alpha numeric denomination, which can be used to diagnose a particular air conditioning compressor off problem.

7. To leave the memory display, press AUTO button or switch the ignition **OFF**.

8. The VAG 1551 is needed to erase codes from memory. See clearing codes using diagnostic tester section.

GENERATING OUTPUT SIGNALS

Without Diagnostic Tester

1985–86 VEHICLES

1. Insert the fuse in the opening on top of the fuel pump relay for 4 seconds.

2. Remove the fuse from the fuel pump relay.

3. The fault code will be displayed by observing the indicator light in the instrument cluster and counting the flashes.

4. To display the next code repeat Steps 1 and 2.

5. Each code will repeat until the fuse is inserted into the fuel pump relay.

6. The diagnosis procedure will be cancelled if the engine speed is raised above 2000 rpm or the ignition switch is turned **OFF**.

1987–89 VEHICLES

1. With the ignition switch **OFF**, insert the spare fuse in the top of the fuel pump relay or connect the jumper wire to the test connectors.

2. Turn the ignition switch **ON**. The first code will be displayed. If the first code is for the fuel pump relay, or the pump begins to run, remove the fuse or jumper wire quickly to prevent flooding the engine.

3. To go to the next output signal, momentarily remove the fuse from the fuel pump relay or disconnect the jumper wire. The next item on the output code list will be activated when the full throttle switch is closed. Be sure to use the correct output code list, the sequence is not the same on all engines.

4. When the full throttle switch is closed, each solenoid or frequency valve can be checked by listening or touching the valve to detect operation. Cold start valves are operated for only 10 seconds.

5. When the last output test has been completed, Code 0000 will be displayed. At this time, the fault code memory can be erased or the test can be repeated by turning the ignition switch **OFF** and **ON** again.

6. If the starter is operated at any point in the output test, the control unit will switch to reporting input signal codes.

1990–94 VEHICLES

1. With the ignition switch **OFF**, connect the LED test light and the jumper wire to the test connectors.

2. Turn the ignition switch **ON**. The first code will be displayed. If the first code is for the fuel pump relay, or the pump begins to run, remove the jumper wire quickly to prevent flooding the engine.

3. To go to the next output signal, momentarily disconnect the jumper wire. The next item on the output code list will be activated when the full throttle switch is closed. Be sure to use the correct output code list, the sequence is not the same on all engines.

4. When the full throttle switch is closed, each solenoid or frequency valve can be checked by listening or touching the valve to detect operation. Cold start valves on CIS systems are operated for only 10 seconds.

5. When the last output test has been completed, Code 0000 will be displayed. At this time, the fault code memory can be erased.

6. If the starter is operated at any point in the output test, the control module will switch to reporting input signal codes.

With Diagnostic Tester

1987–91 VEHICLES

1. Follow the procedure for retrieving fault codes. After all codes have been reported, turn the ignition switch OFF and press the clear button.

2. Select the Blink Code Output program on the tester. Press and hold the run key until the Continuous Short Circuit message appears on the screen, then turn the ignition switch **ON** without starting the engine.

3. Press and release the run key. The first output code should appear on the display. If the first output signal is for the fuel pump relay, remove the fuse for the fuel pump quickly after that test to avoid flooding the engine.

4. The code for each item in the output signal test will appear in the order listed. Press the run key to change to the next item on the list.

5. Except for the cold start valve, the output signal will be activated, as long as the code appears on the screen. As each item is activated, touch each valve to physically check that it is vibrating or humming.

6. When the test is completed, turn the ignition switch **OFF** to stop the test. The test can be repeated by turning the ignition switch **ON**.

1992–94 VEHICLES

1. Go to Step 3, if not using Rapid Data Transfer. Turn the ignition **ON**, but do not start the car.

➡**The engine must not be running when output checks are being performed. The output check mode will not work if the car is running.**

2. After selecting mode 1, Rapid Data Transfer, and the Select Function display appears, enter 01 for engine electronics. Now the control module coding and engine identification numbers will appear. After the coding is deciphered and the information matches your engine, press the Run key to continue. If the Fault In Communication display appears, one of the four displays indicating an open/short wire will appear or possibly the control module may be defective. Pushing the Help button will give you a list of possible causes for this problem. This problem must be corrected before continuing.

3. When the Select Function message appears, select 03 for Output Check Diagnosis. Each output check being tested will be displayed on the VAG 1551. Press the Run key to advance the next output check. The output check displayed on the screen will be performed until the next output check is selected.

➡**When testing the fuel pump, do not run the test too long or the engine could become flooded. When the output checks are finished the Select Function Menu will appear. The output tests can be run again by selecting function 03. Turn the ignition OFF for approximately 20 seconds, before selecting Output Check Diagnosis again.**

4. Follow the procedure for retrieving fault codes. After all codes have been reported, turn the ignition switch **OFF** and press the clear C button.

5. Select the Blink Code Output program on the tester, then turn the ignition **ON**, but do not start the engine. Output checks can only be performed with the engine NOT RUNNING. The tests will be stopped if the engine is started or a speed impulse is recognized.

6. Press and release the Run key. The first output code should appear on the display. If the first output signal is for the fuel pump relay, remove the fuse for the fuel pump quickly after that test to avoid flooding the engine.

➡**During output checks diagnosis, the carbon canister solenoid valve, idle stabilizer valve and cold start valve are checked audibly or by touch. Avoid background noise while audibly checking these components.**

7. The code for each item in the output signal test will appear in the order listed for your particular engine. Press the Run key to change to the next item on the list.

8. Except for the cold start valve, the output signal will be activated, as long as the code appears on the screen. As each item is activated, touch each valve to physically check that it is vibrating or humming.

9. When the test is completed, turn the ignition switch **OFF** to stop the test. The test can be repeated by turning the ignition switch **ON**.

CLEARING CODES

Without Diagnostic Tester

1985–88 VEHICLES

1. On California vehicles, the output signals must be tested before codes can be erased. Leave the ignition switch **ON**.

2. After the last output signal code is displayed, install the fuse for at least 4 seconds and remove it again. The engine warning light should come **ON** for 2.5 seconds, then go **OFF** for 2.5 seconds, displaying Code 0000.

3. Install the fuse again for at least 10 seconds, then remove it. If the engine warning light stays **ON**, all codes have been erased.

4. On Federal vehicles, after activating the fault code memory, the codes will automatically be erased when the ignition switch is turned **OFF** or when the engine is started.

1989–94 VEHICLES

1. The output signals must be tested before codes can be erased. Leave the ignition switch **ON**.

2. After the last output signal code is displayed, connect the test connector jumper wire for at least 4 seconds and remove it again. The engine warning light or flash tester light should come **ON** for 2.5 seconds, then go **OFF** for 2.5 seconds, displaying Code 0000.

3. Connect the jumper wire again for at least 10 seconds, then remove it. If the engine warning light or tester light stays **ON**, all codes have been erased.

With Diagnostic Tester

1985–88 VEHICLES

When all control unit memory codes have been retrieved and Code 0000 is displayed, press and hold the run key with the ignition switch **ON** to clear all codes.

1989–91 VEHICLES—EXCEPT CIS-E III

When all control module memory codes have been retrieved and code 0000 or End of output is displayed, press the run key, now press 05 and the codes will be erased using mode 1 (Rapid Data Transfer). Mode 1 will display a message saying:

Fault memory is erased! after erasing the codes. In mode 2 (Blink Code Output), press and hold the run key with the ignition **ON** and all codes will be cleared.

➡️**This procedure erases all control module codes, make sure you have checked all control modules for DTC's before performing the erasing codes procedure.**

1992–94 VEHICLES—EXCEPT CIS-E III

Diagnostic trouble codes (DTCs) may be erased after they are retrieved using the VAG 1551 scan tool.
1. Turn the ignition switch to the **OFF** position.
2. Connect the VAG1551 scan tool as outlined in Generating Output Signals.
3. Press 01 on the VAG scan tool to select VAG address "Engine Electronics".
4. Press the arrow button until the display reads "Select Function XX".
5. Press the Q on the VAG scan tool and view all DTCs.
6. Press the 05 on the VAG scan tool to select 02—Cancel Fault Code Memory. Press Q to erase all DTCs.
7. Road test the vehicle and reactivate DTC memory to ensure all faults have been eliminated.

1989–92 VEHICLES—CIS-E III

After activating the fault code memory, the codes will automatically be erased when the ignition switch is turned **OFF** or when the engine is started.

➡️**CIS-E III California models have permanent memory and will retain the fault codes after the ignition is turned off. This memory can be erased by following the erasure method using the VAG 1551 diagnostic tester. Control module part numbers can be used to identify the control modules and determine whether the CIS-E III system has permanent or temporary memory.**

DIAGNOSTIC TROUBLE CODES

1985–89 VEHICLES

2.1L (MC), 2.2L (MC), 2.0L (3A) AND 2.3L (NG, NF) ENGINES

Code 1111 Ignition control unit or fuel injection control unit
Code 1231 Transmission speed sensor
Code 2111 Engine speed sensor
Code 2112 Ignition reference sensor
Code 2113 Hall sensor
Code 2121 Idle switch
Code 2122 Engine speed/Hall sensor
Code 2123 Full throttle switch
Code 2132 No data being transmitted from fuel injection control unit to ignition control unit
Code 2141 Knock control 1, knock sensor 1 for cylinder 2; knock control 2, knock sensor 2 for cylinder 4
Code 2142 Knock sensor 1 on cylinder 2; knock sensor 2 on cylinder 4
Code 2143 Knock control 1, knock sensor 1 for cylinder 2; knock control 2, knock sensor 2 for cylinder 4
Code 2144 Knock sensor 1 on cylinder 2; knock sensor 2 on cylinder 4
Code 2212 Throttle valve potentiometer (position sensor)
Code 2221 Vacuum hose to pressure sensor in control unit
Code 2222 Pressure sensor in control unit
Code 2223 Altitude sensor
Code 2232 Air sensor potentiometer (position sensor)
Code 2233 Reference (supply) voltage
Code 2234 MPI control unit supply voltage
Code 2242 CO potentiometer
Code 2312 Engine coolant temperature (ECT) sensor
Code 2322 Intake air temperature (IAT) sensor
Code 2341 Oxygen sensor control unit is at its limit
Code 2342 Oxygen sensor (does not control)
Code 4431 Idle stabilizer valve
Code 4444 No faults stored in memory
Code 0000 End of diagnosis

1990–94 Vehicles

2.0L (3A), 2.3L (NG, NF, 7A), 2.2L (MC, 3B, AAN), 2.8L (AAH), 3.6L (PT) AND 4.2L (ABH) ENGINES

Code 00000 or 0000 No faults in memory (1992–93 all engines except 2.8L and 1992 2.3L)
Code 00000 or 0000 End of diagnosis (1990–91 all engines; 1992–94 2.8L and 1992 2.3L)
Code 00000 or 4444 No faults in memory (1990–91 all engines; 1992–94 2.8L and 1992 2.3L)
Code 00281 or 1231 Vehicle speed sender signal is missing
Code 00513 or 2111 Engine speed (RPM) sensor has no change in signal
Code 00513 or 2231 Air mass sensor has open/short in circuit
Code 00514 or 2112 Crankshaft position (CKP) sensor has no change in signal
Code 00515 or 2113 Hall sender has fault in basic setting or open/short in circuit
Code 2114 Hall sender is not on reference point or out of adjustment
Code 00516 or 2121 Idle switch (closed throttle position switch 4.2L ABH) has open/short in circuit
Code 00517 or 2123 Full throttle switch
Code 00518 or 2212 Throttle position (TP) sensor has open/short in circuit
Code 00519 or 2222 Manifold vacuum sensor signal is out of range
Code 00520 or 2232 Air mass sensor signal is missing/signal out of limit
Code 00521 or 2242 CO potentiometer position sensor (2.3L 7A 1990–91)

Code 00522 or 2312 Engine coolant temperature (ECT) sensor signal is out of range

Code 00523 or 2322 Intake air temperature (IAT) sensor has open/short in circuit

Code 00524 or 2142 Knock sensor (KS) 1 has no change in signal, possible open/short between KS and ECM

Code 00525 or 2342 Oxygen sensor signal is out of range

Code 00528 or 2223 Pressure sensor (altitude sensor 1990-91) has open/short in circuit

Code 00529 or 2122 Engine RPM signal missing (2.3L NG,NF)

Code 00531 or 2233 Air mass sensor reference voltage signal missing; voltage high (2.3L 7A 1990-91)

Code 00532 or 2234 Supply voltage signal is too high or low

Code 00533 or 2231 Idle speed regulation, the idle speed is too low or too high

Code 00535 or 2141 Knock sensor regulation has exceeded its maximum control limit (1992 2.3L NG)

Code 00536 or 2141 First & second knock regulation, the maximum control limits have been exceeded (4.2L ABH engine)

Code 00536 or 2143 Second knock control has exceeded its control limits (1992-93 2.8L AAH)

Code 00537 or 2341 Oxygen sensor signal is out of range

Code 2343 Air/fuel mixture rich (2.0L engine)

Code 2344 Air/fuel mixture lean (2.0L engine)

Code 00538 or 2241 Second knock control (1991 2.2L 3B)

Code 00540 or 2144 Knock sensor 2 has no change in signal, possible open/short between KS and ECM

Code 00543 or 2214 Engine speed signal is too high, the RPM exceeds maximum limit

Code 00544 or 2224 Wastegate frequency valve has exceeded maximum boost pressure (Manifold dump valve 1990-91 2.2L MC)

Code 00545 or 2314 Engine/Transmission electrical connection has ground between ECM and TCM

Code 00546 or 2132 Fuel injection/ignition control data link (2.3L NG, NF)

Code 00553 or 2324 Mass air flow (MAF) sensor signal

Code 00554 or 2331 Oxygen control for cylinders (4-6) exceeded control limits (1992-93 2.8L AAH)

Code 00555 or 2332 Oxygen sensor 2 (G108) signal is missing (1992-93 2.8L AAH)

Code 00560 or 2411 EGR system not working properly

Code 00560 or 2441 EGR system has false readings (1992-93 2.8L AAH, California)

Code 00561 or 2413 Fuel mixture too rich

Code 00575 or 2221 Manifold pressure signal missing (1990-91 2.2L MC)

Code 00577 or 2141 Knock regulation cylinder 1 has exceeded control limit

Code 00578 or 2141 Knock regulation cylinder 2 has exceeded control limit

Code 00579 or 2141 Knock regulation cylinder 3 has exceeded control limit

Code 00580 or 2143 Knock regulation cylinder 4 has exceeded control limit

Code 00581 or 2143 Knock regulation cylinder 5 has exceeded control limit

Code 00824 or 3424 Engine warning light is defective

Code 4312 EGR frequency valve (2.3L 7A 1990-91)

Code 4331 Carbon canister solenoid valve 2

Code 01242 or 4332 Ignition final control circuit problem (1992-93 2.8L AAH)

Code 01247 or 4343 Carbon canister solenoid has short/open in circuit

Code 01249 or 4411 Fuel Injector cylinder 1 (& 5 on 3.6/4.2L) open/short injector circuit, fuse 23 open (fuse 13 on 2.8L)

Code 01250 or 4412 Fuel Injector cylinder 2 (& 7 on 3.6/4.2L) open/short injector circuit, fuse 23 open (fuse 13 on 2.8L)

Code 01251 or 4413 Fuel Injector cylinder 3 (& 6 on 3.6/4.2L) open/short injector circuit, fuse 23 open (fuse 13 on 2.8L)

Code 01252 or 4414 Fuel Injector cylinder 4 (& 8 on 3.6/4.2L) open/short injector circuit, fuse 23 open (fuse 13 on 2.8L)

Code 01253 or 4415 Fuel Injector cylinder 5 (code applies to 2.8L) has open/short in injector circuit, fuse 13 is open, ECM

Code 01253 or 4416 Fuel Injector cylinder 6 (code applies to 2.8L) has open/short in injector circuit, fuse 13 is open, ECM

Code 01253 or 4421 Fuel Injector cylinder 5 (code does not apply to 6 & 8 cylinder engines) has open/short in injector circuit, fuse 23 is open

Code 01254 or 4422 Fuel Injector cylinder 6 has open/short in circuit (1992-93 2.8L AAH)

Code 01257 or 4431 Idle air control (IAC) has open/short in circuit, fuse 2 is open

Code 01262 or 4442 Boost pressure limiting valve has open/short in circuit, thermo-fuse S75 for EVAP frequency valve is blown

Code 01265 or 4312 EGR valve has open/short in circuit (1992-93 2.8L AAH)

Code 65535 or 1111 Control module is defective

Code 65535 or 2324 Engine control module (ECM) is defective (1992-93 4.2L ABH) Ignore this code if displayed as an intermittent

Honda

GENERAL INFORMATION

Honda utilizes one type of fuel injection system. This is Programmed Fuel Injection (PGM-FI) system. This system began in 1985 and was available in the Accord and Civic. As of 1992, all Hondas are fuel injected.

SELF DIAGNOSTICS

Service Precautions

• Make sure all ECM harness connectors are fastened securely. A poor connection can cause an extremely high voltage surge and result in damage to integrated circuits.
• Keep all ECM parts and harnesses dry during service. Protect the ECM and all solid-state components from rough handling or extremes of temperature.
• Use extreme care when working around the ECM or other components. The airbag or SRS wiring may be in the vicinity. On these vehicles, the SRS wiring and connectors are yellow. Do not cut or test these circuits.
• Before attempting to remove any parts, turn the ignition switch **OFF** and disconnect the battery ground cable.
• Always use a 12 volt battery as a power source for the engine, never a booster or high-voltage charging unit.
• Do not disconnect the battery cables with the engine running.
• Do not disconnect any wiring connector with the engine running or the ignition **ON** unless specifically instructed.
• Do not apply battery power directly to injectors.
• Whenever possible, use a flashlight instead of a droplight.
• Relieve fuel system pressure before servicing any fuel system component.
• Always use eye or full-face protection when working around fuel lines, fittings or components.

READING TROUBLE CODES

♦ **See Figures 17, 18, 19 and 20**

1985-89 VEHICLES

When a fault is noted, the ECU stores an identifying code and illuminates the malfunction indicator light. The code will remain in memory until cleared; the dashboard warning lamp may not illuminate during the next ignition cycle if the fault is no longer present. Not all faults noted by the

ECU will trigger the dashboard warning lamp although the fault code will be set in memory. For this reason, troubleshooting should be based on the presence of stored codes, not the illumination of the warning lamp while the car is operating.

Stored codes are displayed by either a single flashing LED (Light Emitting Diode) light, or an illuminated light pattern of 4 LED lights on the ECU. When the CHECK ENGINE warning lamp has been on or reported on, check the ECU LED for presence of codes.

The location of the malfunction is determined by observing the LED display. Earlier Hondas used 2 types of LED displays: a single LED and a 4 LED display. After 1987 all models use the single LED display.

Systems with a single LED indicate the malfunction with a series of flashes. The number of flashes indicates a code which identifies the location of the component or system malfunction. The code will flash, followed by a 2 second pause, repeat, followed by another 2 second pause, then move to the next code.

On systems with 4 LED's a display pattern identifies the malfunction. The LED's are numbered 1, 2, 4 and 8 as counted from right-to-left. The code is determined by observing which LED's are lit on the display. Each code is displayed once, followed by a 2 second pause, then the next code is displayed.

The LED's are part of the Electronic Control Module (ECM). Depending on the vehicles, the ECU is located in the following places:

- 1985–89 Accord—Under the driver side front seat
- 1985–87 Civic and CRX— Under the passenger side seat
- 1988–89 Civic and CRX— Under the passenger side foot-well, below the dashboard
- 1987 Prelude—Behind driver side rear seat trim panel
- 1988–89 Prelude—Under the passenger side foot well, below the dash. (The LED may be viewed through a small window without removing the ECU cover).

Turn the ignition switch **ON**; the LED will display any stored codes.

On the 1985 Accord and 1985–87 Civic/CRX having the 4 LED display, codes are indicated by a specific pattern of LED lights illuminated on the ECU.

On 1986–89 Accord, 1988–89 Civic, and Prelude having the single LED display, codes 1–9 are indicated by a series of short flashes; two-digit codes use a number of long flashes for the first digit followed by the appropriate number of short flashes. For example, Code 43 would be indicated by 4 long flashes followed by 3 short flashes. Codes are separated by a longer pause between transmissions. The position of the codes during output can be helpful in diagnostic work. Multiple codes transmitted in isolated order indicate unique occurrences; a display of showing 1–1–1 pause 9–9–9 indicates two problems or problems occurring at different times. An alternating display, such as 1–9–1–9–1, indicates simultaneous occurrences of the faults.

When counting flashes to determine codes, a code not valid for the vehicle may be found. In this case, first recount the flashes to confirm an accurate count. If necessary, turn the ignition switch **OFF**, then recycle the system and begin the count again. If the Code is not valid for the vehicle, the ECU must be replaced.

➡On vehicles with electronically controlled automatic transaxles, the 5, D or D4 lamp may flash with the CHECK ENGINE lamp if certain codes are stored. If this does occur, proceed with the diagnosis based on the engine code shown. After repairs, recheck the lamp. If the additional warning lamp is still lit, proceed with diagnosis for that system.

1990–95 VEHICLES

When a fault is noted, the ECM stores an identifying code and illuminates the malfunction indicator light. The code will remain in memory until cleared. The dashboard warning lamp may not illuminate during the next ignition cycle if the fault is no longer present. Not all faults noted by the ECM will trigger the dashboard warning lamp although the fault code will be set in memory. For this reason, troubleshooting should be based on the presence of stored codes, not the illumination of the warning lamp while the car is operating.

In 1990, the Accord and Prelude were equipped with a 2-pin service connector in addition to the LED. if the service connector is jumpered, with

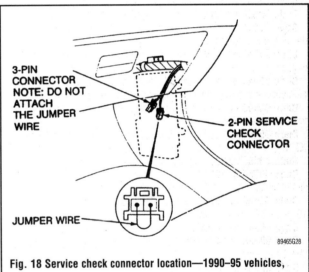

Fig. 18 Service check connector location—1990–95 vehicles, except Prelude

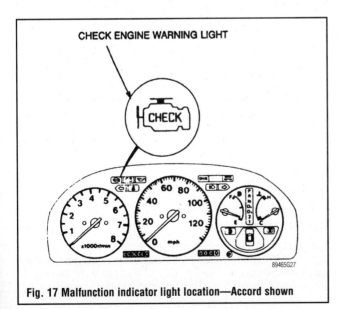

Fig. 17 Malfunction indicator light location—Accord shown

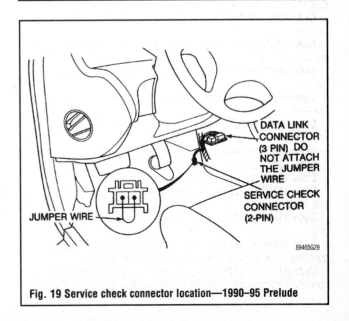

Fig. 19 Service check connector location—1990–95 Prelude

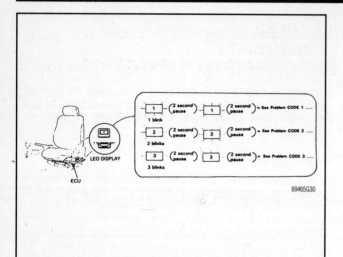

Fig. 20 Electronic Control Module location and Code flash indications— Accord shown

the ignition key in the **ON** position, the CHECK ENGINE lamp will display the stored codes in a series of flashes. The 2-pin service connector is located under the passenger side of dash on the Accord and behind the center console on the Prelude.

As of 1992, the LED on the ECU was eliminated and all vehicles obtain codes by jumping the 2-pin connector when the ignition switch is **ON**. The malfunction indicator light will then flash codes present in the ECU memory.

Diagnostic Codes 1–9 are indicated by a series of short flashes; two-digit codes use a number of long flashes for the first digit followed by the appropriate number of short flashes. For example, Code 43 would be indicated by 4 long flashes followed by 3 short flashes. Codes are separated by a longer pause between transmissions. The position of the codes during output can be helpful in diagnostic work. Multiple codes transmitted in isolated order indicate unique occurrences; a display showing 1–1–1 pause 9–9–9 indicates two problems or problems occurring at different times. An alternating display, such as 1–9–1–9–1, indicates simultaneous occurrences of the faults.

When counting flashes to determine codes, a code not valid for the vehicle may be found. In this case, first recount the flashes to confirm an accurate count. If necessary, turn the ignition switch **OFF**, then recycle the system and begin the count again. If the code is not valid for the vehicle, the ECM must be replaced.

➡On vehicles with electronically controlled automatic transaxles, the D4 lamp may flash with the CHECK ENGINE lamp if certain codes are stored. If this does occur, proceed with the diagnosis based on the engine code shown. After repairs, recheck the lamp. If the additional warning lamp is still lit, proceed with diagnosis for that system.

CLEARING CODES

1985–87 VEHICLES

The memory for the PGM-FI CHECK ENGINE lamp on the dashboard will be erased when the ignition switch is turned **OFF**; however, the memory for the LED display will not be canceled. Thus, the CHECK ENGINE lamp will not come on when the ignition switch is again turned **ON** unless the trouble is once more detected. Troubleshooting should be done according to the LED display even if the CHECK ENGINE lamp is off.

After making repairs, disconnect the battery negative cable from the battery negative terminal for at least 10 seconds and reset the ECU memory. After reconnecting the cable, check that the LED display is turned off.

Turn the ignition switch **ON**. The PGM-FI CHECK ENGINE lamp should come on for about 2 seconds. If the CHECK ENGINE lamp won't come on, check for:—Blown CHECK ENGINE lamp bulb—Blown fuse (causing faulty back up light, seat belt alarm, clock, memory function of the car radio)—Open circuit in Yellow wire—Open circuit in wiring and control unit.

After the PGM-FI CHECK ENGINE lamp and self-diagnosis indicators have been turned on, turn the ignition switch **OFF**. If the LED display fails to come on when the ignition switch is turned **ON** again, check for:—Blown fuses, especially No. 10 fuse—Open circuit in wire between ECU fuse.

Replace the ECU only after making sure that all couplers and connectors are connected securely.

1988–90 VEHICLES

The memory for the PGM-FI CHECK ENGINE lamp on the dashboard will be erased when the ignition switch is turned **OFF**; however, the memory for the LED display will not be canceled. Thus, the CHECK ENGINE lamp will not come on when the ignition switch is again turned **ON** unless the trouble is once more detected. Troubleshooting should be done according to the LED display even if the CHECK ENGINE lamp is off.

To clear the ECU trouble code memory, remove the ECU memory power fuse for at least 10 seconds. The correct fuse to remove is:
  1988–89 Accord—CLOCK fuse from the underhood relay box
  1988–90 Accord—BACK UP fuse from the underhood relay box
  Civic—HAZARD fuse at the main fuse box
  Prelude with PGM-FI—CLOCK fuse from the underhood relay box

➡**Removing these fuses will also erase the clock, radio station presets, and the radio anti-theft codes. Make sure you have the anti-theft code and station presets before removing fuse so they may be reset when repairs are complete.**

1990–95 VEHICLES

Stored codes are removed from memory by removing power to the ECU. Disconnecting the power may also clear the memories used for other solid-state equipment such as the clock and radio. For this reason, always make note of the radio presets before clearing the system. Additionally, some radios contain anti-theft programming; obtain the owner's code number before clearing the codes.

While disconnecting the battery will clear the memory, this is not the recommended procedure. The memory should be cleared after the ignition is switched **OFF** by removing the appropriate fuse for at least 10 seconds. The correct fuses and their locations are:
  Accord—BACK UP fuse from the underhood relay box
  Civic—HAZARD fuse at the main fuse box
  Civic del Sol—BACK UP fuse from the underhood relay box
  Odyssey—BACK UP fuse from the underhood relay box
  Prelude with PGM-FI—CLOCK fuse from the underhood relay box

➡**Removing these fuses will also erase the clock, radio station presets, and the radio anti-theft codes. Make sure you have the anti-theft code and station presets before removing fuse so they may be reset when repairs are complete.**

DIAGNOSTIC TROUBLE CODES

1985–87 4-LED System

ACCORD

▶ **See Figure 21**

This list includes vehicles with fuel injection engines: 1.5L (EW3), 1.5L (DI5A3), 1.8L (ES3) Engine.

Code definition as shown in illustration for the 4-LED type ECM.

ECM TROUBLE CODES

Code	Explanation
○ ○ ○ ○ (Dash Warning Light ON only)	Loose or poorly connected power line to Electronic Control Unit (ECU). Short circuit in combination meter or warning light wire. Faulty ECU
○ ○ ○ ● (1)	Disconnected oxygen sensor coupler. Spark plug misfire. Short or open circuit in oxygen sensor circuit. Faulty oxygen sensor
○ ○ ● ○ (2)	Faulty Electronic Control Unit (ECU)
○ ○ ● ● (2 1)	Disconnected Manifold Absolute Pressure (MAP) sensor coupler. Short or open circuit in MAP sensor wire. Faulty MAP sensor
○ ● ○ ○ (4)	Faulty Electronic Control Unit (ECU)
○ ● ○ ● (4 1)	Disconnected Manifold Absolute Pressure (MAP) sensor piping
○ ● ● ○ (4 2)	Disconnected coolant temperature sensor coupler. Open circuit in coolant temperature sensor wire. Faulty coolant temperature sensor (thermostat housing)
○ ● ● ● (4 2 1)	Disconnected throttle angle sensor coupler. Open or short circuit in throttle angle sensor wire. Faulty throttle angle sensor
● ○ ○ ○ (8)	Short or open circuit in crank angle sensor wire. Crank angle sensor wire interfering with high tension wire. Crank angle sensor at fault
● ○ ○ ● (8)	Short or open circuit in crank angle sensor wire. Crank angle sensor wire interfering with high tension wire. Crank angle sensor at fault
● ○ ● ○ (8 2)	Disconnected intake air temperature sensor. Open circuit in intake air temperature sensor wire. Faulty intake air temperature sensor
● ○ ● ● (8 2 1)	Disconnected idle mixture adjuster sensor coupler. Shorted or disconnected idle mixture adjuster sensor wire. Faulty idle mixture adjuster sensor
● ● ○ ○ (8 4)	Disconnected Exhaust Gas Recirculation (EGR) control system coupler. Shorted or disconnected EGR control wire. Faulty EGR control system
● ● ○ ● (8 4 1)	Disconnected atmospheric pressure sensor coupler. Shorted or disconnected atmospheric pressure sensor wire. Faulty atmospheric pressure sensor
● ● ● ○ (8 4 2)	Faulty Electronic Control Unit (ECU)
● ● ● ● (8 4 2 1)	Faulty Electronic Control Unit (ECU)

89465G31

Fig. 21 4-LED Code definition—1985 Accord 1.8L (ES3), 1985–86 Civic Si 1.5L (EW3), 1987 Civic/CRX Si 1.5L (D15A3) fuel injected engines

1985–95 Vehicles

ACCORD, CIVIC, DEL SOL, ODYSSEY AND PRELUDE

This list includes all of the following fuel injected engines:
1.5L (D15B1, D15B2, D15B6, D15B7, D15B8, D15Z1), 1.6L (B16A3, D16A6, D16Z6), 2.0L (A20A3, BS, BT, B20A5) 2.1L (B21A) 2.2L (F22A1, F22A4, F22A6, F22B1, F22B2, H22A1), 2.3L (H23A1) and 2.7L (C27A4) Engines

Code 0 Electronic Control Module (ECM)

Code 1 Heated oxygen sensor (or Oxygen content) **or** Oxygen content A (A20A3, B20A5)

Code 2 Oxygen content B (A20A3, B20A5) **or** Electronic Control Module (ECM) (BS, BT—1986 only) and (A20A3— 1987 only)

Code 3 Manifold Absolute Pressure (MAP)

Code 4 Crankshaft position sensor

Code 5 Manifold Absolute Pressure (MAP)

Code 6 Engine coolant temperature (ECT)

Code 7 Throttle position sensor (TP sensor)

Code 8 Top dead center sensor (TDC sensor)

Code 9 No. 1 cylinder position sensor

Code 10 Intake air temperature sensor (IAT sensor)

Code 11 Electronic Control Module (ECM) (BS, BT -1986 only) and (A20A3 **1987 only**)

Code 12 Exhaust Gas Recirculation (EGR) System (except Del Sol and Civic & CRX 1 .6L DI 6A6)

Code 13 Barometric pressure sensor (BARO sensor)

Code 14 Idle air control (IAC valve) except 1987——A20A3 engine.**or** 1986 BS, BT and 1987 A20A3 Engines, Code 14 or high is possible faulty Electronic Control Module (ECM)

Code 15 Ignition output signal

Code 16 Fuel Injector

Code 17 Vehicle Speed sensor (VSS)

Code 19 A/T lock-up control solenoid valve A/B (D15B1, D15B2, D15B6, D15B7, D15B8, D15Z1, D16A6, D16Z6)

Code 20 Electric load detector (ELD)

Code 21 V-TEC control solenoid (D15Z1, D16Z6, H22A1)

Code 22 V-TEC pressure switch (D15Z1, D16Z6, H22A1)

Code 23 Knock sensor (H22A1-DOHC—VTEC)

Code 30 A/T FI Signal A (F22A1, F22A4, F22A6)

Code 31 A/T FI Signal B (F22A1, F22A4, F22A6)

Code 41 Heated Oxygen Sensor Heater (F22A1, F22A4)

Code 43 Fuel supply system (except D15B1, D15B2, D15B6, B20A5, B21A, D16A6)

Code 45 Fuel supply metering

Code 48 Heated oxygen sensor (D15Z1 engine only, except Calif. emission)

Code 61 Front Heated Oxygen Sensor

Code 63 Rear Heated Oxygen Sensor

Code 65 Rear Heated Oxygen Sensor Heater

Code 67 Catalytic Converter System

Code 70 Automatic Transaxle or A/F FI Data line

Code 71 Misfire detected; cylinder No. 1 or random misfire

Code 72 Misfire detected; cylinder No. 2 or random misfire

Code 73 Misfire detected; cylinder No. 3 or random misfire

Code 74 Misfire detected; cylinder No. 4 or random misfire

Code 75 Misfire detected; cylinder No. 5 or random misfire

Code 76 Misfire detected; cylinder No. 6 or random misfire

Code 80 Exhaust Gas Recirculation (EGR) system

Code 86 Coolant temperature

Code 92 Evaporative Emission Control System

Hyundai

GENERAL INFORMATION

Hyundai utilizes a Multi-point Fuel Injection (MFI) system that was introduced in 1989 on the Sonata. In 1990, the Excel was available with fuel injection also. Scoupe, Elantra and Accent came only with MFI.

SELF DIAGNOSTICS

Service Precautions

• Keep the ECU parts and harnesses dry during service. Protect the ECU and all solid-state components from rough handling or temperature extremes.

• Use extreme care when working around the ECU or other components.

• Disconnect the negative battery cable before attempting to disconnect or remove any electronic parts.

• Disconnect the negative battery cable and ECU connector before performing arc welding on the vehicle.

• Disconnect and remove the ECU from the vehicle before subjecting the vehicle to the temperatures experienced in a heated paint booth.

READING TROUBLE CODES

⬧ **See Figures 22, 23, 24 and 25**

➡Self-diagnosis pertains to fuel injected vehicles only. 1993–94 Scoupe and 1995 Accent have the ability to read diagnostic codes through the Malfunction Indicator Lamp (MIL) and therefore special equipment is not required to retrieve codes. All other vehicles however, do not process this ability, therefore either a Multi-Use Tester or and Analog voltmeter must be used to retrieve codes. When using special diagnostic equipment, always observe the tool manufacturer's instructions.

1989–95 Vehicles

USING MULTI-USE TESTER

1. Turn the ignition switch to the **OFF** position.
2. Connect the multi-use tester to the diagnosis connector in the fuse box.
3. Connect the power-source terminal of the multi-use tester to the cigar lighter.
4. Turn the ignition switch to the **ON** position.
5. Follow the manufacturer's instructions to retrieve the trouble codes. The codes will be displayed in numerical order.

USING ANALOG VOLTMETER

1. Connect the voltmeter to the self-diagnosis connector.
2. Turn the ignition switch to the **ON** position.
3. Observe the voltmeter to read the trouble codes. The code is determined by noting the duration of the voltmeter sweeps. A sweep of long duration indicates the multiple of ten digit, while a sweep of short duration indicates the single digit. For example, the code number 12 is indicated by

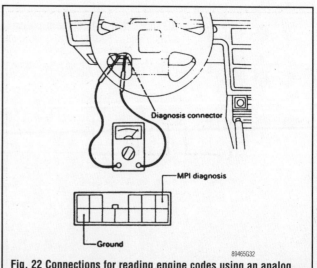

Fig. 22 Connections for reading engine codes using an analog voltmeter—1989–91 Hyundai

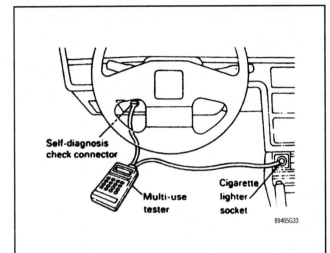

Fig. 23 Connections for reading engine codes using a multi-use tester—1989–91 Hyundai

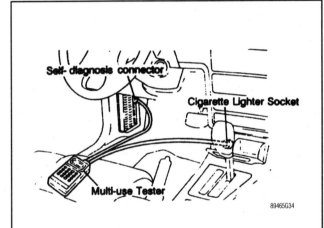

Fig. 24 Connections for reading engine codes using a multi-use tester—1992–95 Hyundai

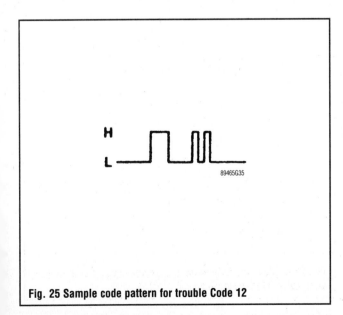

Fig. 25 Sample code pattern for trouble Code 12

1 sweep of long duration followed by 2 sweeps of short duration and so on. The trouble codes will be displayed in numerical order.

USING ENGINE (MIL) LAMP

The 1993-94 Scoupe and 1995 Accent has the ability to read codes by using the Maintenance Indicator Lamp (MIL).
1. Turn the ignition switch **ON** but do not start the vehicle.
2. Ground the L-wire (PIN 10) in the diagnostic terminal for 2 ½ seconds.
3. The first code to flash should be (4444) which will flash until the L-wire is disconnected.
4. Ground the L-wire again for 2 ½ seconds and record flash codes until the end of output code (3333) is flashed.

CLEARING CODES

1989–95 Vehicles

1. Turn the ignition switch to the **OFF** position.
2. Disconnect the negative battery cable for at least 15 seconds.
3. Disconnect the multi-use tester or analog voltmeter.
4. Reconnect the negative battery cable.

DIAGNOSTIC TROUBLE CODES

1989–94 Excel

1992–95 Elantra

1991–92 Scoupe

1989–95 Sonata

Code 11 Oxygen sensor—check harness and connector, fuel pressure, fuel injectors, oxygen sensor, check for intake air leaks
Code 12 Air flow sensor—check harness, connector and air flow sensor
Code 13 Air temperature sensor—check harness, connector and air temperature sensor
Code 14 Throttle position sensor—check harness and connector, throttle position sensor, idle position switch
Code 15 Motor position sensor—check harness and connector, motor position sensor
Code 21 Engine coolant temperature sensor—check harness and connector, engine coolant temperature sensor
Code 22 Crank angle sensor—check harness, connector and distributor assembly
Code 23 No. 1 cylinder top dead center sensor—check harness, connector and distributor assembly
Code 24 Vehicle speed sensor. (reed switch)—check harness and connector, and vehicle speed sensor
Code 25 Barometric pressure sensor—check harness, connector and barometric pressure sensor
Code 41 Injector—check harness and connector, injector coil resistance
Code 42 Fuel pump—check harness and connector, control relay
Code 43 EGR—check harness and connector, EGR temperature sensor, EGR valve, EGR control solenoid valve, EGR valve control vacuum (California)
Code 44 Ignition coil fault, faulty power transistor
Code 59 Oxygen (HO2S) sensor fault

1993–95 Scoupe

1995 Accent

Code 1122 Electronic Control Unit failure—RAM/ROM
Code 1169 Electronic Control Unit failure
Code 1233 Electronic Control Unit failure—ROM
Code 1234 Electronic Control Unit failure—RAM
Code 2121 Boost sensor control valve
Code 3112 Injector No.1

Code 3114 AC opening failure
Code 3116 Injector No. 3
Code 3117 Airflow sensor
Code 3121 Boost pressure sensor failure
Code 3122 AC closing failure
Code 3128 HO2S sensor
Code 3135 Evaporative purge control solenoid valve
Code 3137 Alternator output/low battery
Code 3145 Coolant temperature sensor
Code 3149 A/C compressor
Code 3152 Turbo boost to high
Code 3153 Throttle position sensor
Code 3159 Vehicle speed sensor
Code 3211 Knock sensor
Code 3222 Phase sensor
Code 3224 ECM—knock evolution sensor
Code 3232 Crankshaft position sensor
Code 3233 ECM—knock evolution sensor
Code 3234 Injector No. 2
Code 3235 Injector No. 4
Code 3241 ECM-injector or purge control valve
Code 3242 ECM-IAC motor or A/C relay
Code 3243 Electronic Control Unit failure
Code 4133 Electronic Control Unit failure
Code 4151 Air/fuel control
Code 4152 Air/fuel adaptive failure
Code 4153 Air/fuel adaptive (multiple) failure
Code 4154 Air/fuel adaptive (additive) failure
Code 4155 ECM—A/C relay, IAC motor, injector or PCV
Code 4156 Boost sensor control deviation failure

Infiniti

GENERAL INFORMATION

The Infiniti Electronic Concentrated Control System (ECCS) is an air flow controlled, sequential port fuel injection and engine control system. It is used on all models equipped with 2.0L, 3.0L and 4.5L engines. The ECCS electronic control unit consists of a microcomputer, an inspection lamp, a diagnostic mode selector and connectors for signal input and output, powers and grounds.

The safety relay prevents electrical damage to the electronic control unit, or ECU, and the injectors in case the battery terminals are accidentally connected in reverse. The safety relay is built into the fuel pump control circuit.

Ignition timing is controlled in response to engine operating conditions. The optimum ignition timing in each driving condition is pre-programmed in the computer. The signal from the control unit is transmitted to the power transistor and this signal controls when the transistor turns the ignition coil primary circuit on and off (hence, the ignition timing). The idle speed is also controlled according to engine operating conditions, temperature and gear position. On manual transmission models, if battery voltage is less than 12 volts for a few seconds, a higher idle speed will be maintained by the control unit to improve charging function.

There is a fail-safe system built into the ECCS control unit. This system makes engine starting possible if a portion of the ECU's central processing unit circuit fails. Also, if a major component such as the crank angle sensor or the air flow meter were to malfunction, the ECU substitutes or borrows data to compensate for the fault. For example, if the output voltage of the air flow meter is extremely low, the ECU will substitute a pre-programmed value for the air flow meter signal and allows the vehicle to be driven as long as the engine speed is kept below 2000 rpm. Or, if the cylinder head temperature sensor circuit is open, the control unit clamps the warm up enrichment at a certain amount. This amount is almost the same as that when the cylinder head temperature is between 68–176°F (20–80°C).

If the fuel pump circuit malfunctions, the fuel pump relay comes on until the engine stops. This allows the fuel pump to receive power from the relay.

The electronic control unit controls the following functions:
- Injector pulse width
- Ignition timing
- Intake valve timing control (Q45)
- Air regulator control (G20)
- Exhaust gas recirculation (EGR) solenoid valve operation
- Exhaust gas sensor heater operation
- Idle speed
- FICD solenoid valve operation (G20 and M30)
- Fuel pump relay operation
- Fuel pump voltage (M30 and Q45)
- Fuel pressure regulator control (M30)
- AIV control (G20)
- Carbon canister control solenoid valve operation
- Air conditioner relay operation (During early wide-open throttle)
- Radiator fan operation (G20)
- Traction control system (TCS) operation (Q45, if equipped)
- Self-diagnosis
- Fail-safe mode operation

SELF DIAGNOSTICS

Service Precautions

- Do not disconnect the injector harness connectors with the engine running.
- Do not apply battery power directly to the injectors.
- Do not disconnect the ECU harness connectors before the battery ground cable has been disconnected.
- Make sure all ECU connectors are fastened securely. A poor connection can cause an extremely high surge voltage in the coil and condenser and result in damage to integrated circuits.
- When testing the ECU with a DVOM make sure that the probes of the tester never touch each other as this will result in damage to a transistor in the ECU.
- Keep the ECCS harness at least 4 in. away from adjacent harnesses to prevent an ECCS system malfunction due to external electronic noise.
- Keep all parts and harnesses dry during service.
- Before attempting to remove any parts, turn **OFF** the ignition switch and disconnect the battery ground cable.
- Always use a 12 volt battery as a power source.
- Do not attempt to disconnect the battery cables with the engine running or the ignition key **ON**.
- Do not clean the air flow meter with any type of detergent.
- Do not attempt to disassemble the ECCS control unit under any circumstances.
- Avoid static electricity build-up by properly grounding yourself prior to handling any ECU or related parts.

READING TROUBLE CODES

♦ See Figures 26 and 27

➡**Diagnostic codes may be retrieved by observing code flashes through the LED lights located on the Electronic Control Module (ECM). A special Nissan Consult monitor tool can be used, but is not required. When using special diagnostic equipment, always observe the tool manufacturer's instructions.**

1990–95 Vehicles

2-MODE DIAGNOSTIC SYSTEM

Infiniti vehicles use a 2-mode diagnostic system incorporated in the ECU that uses inputs from various sensors to determine the correct air/fuel ratio. If any of the sensors malfunction, the ECU will store the code in memory.

An Infiniti/Nissan Consult monitor may be used to retrieve these codes by simply connecting the monitor to the diagnosis connector located on the driver's side near the hood release.

Turn the ignition switch **ON** and press START, ENGINE and then SELE-DIAG RESULTS, the results will then be output to the monitor.

The conventional CHECK ENGINE or red LED ECU light may be used for self-diagnostics. The conventional 2-mode diagnostic system is broken into 2 separate modes each capable of 2 tests, an ignition switch **ON** or engine running test as outlined below:

MODE 1—BULB CHECK

In this mode the RED indicator light on the ECU and the malfunction indicator light should be **ON**. To enter this mode simply turn the ignition switch **ON** and observe the light.

MODE 1—MALFUNCTION WARNING

In this mode the ECU is acknowledging if there is a malfunction by illuminating the RED indicator light on the ECU and the malfunction indicator light. If the light turns **OFF**—, the system is normal. To enter this mode, simply start the engine and observe the light

MODE 2—SELF-DIAGNOSTIC CODES

In this mode the ECU will output all malfunctions via the malfunction indicator light or the red LED on the ECU. The code may be retrieved by counting the number of flashes. The longer flashes indicate the first digit and the shorter flashes indicate the second digit. To enter this mode proceed as follows:
1. Turn the ignition switch **ON**, but do not start the vehicle.
2. Turn the ECU diagnostic mode selector fully clockwise for 2 seconds, then turn it back fully counterclockwise.
3. Observe the red LED on the ECU or malfunction indicator light for stored codes.

MODE 2—EXHAUST GAS SENSOR MONITOR

In this mode the red LED on the ECU or malfunction indicator light will display the condition of the fuel mixture and whether the system is in closed loop or open loop. When the light flashes **ON**, the exhaust gas sensor is indicating a lean mixture. When the light stays **OFF**, the sensor is indicating a rich mixture. If the light remains **ON** or **OFF**, it is indicating an open loop system. If the system is equipped with 2 exhaust gas sensors, the left side will operate first. If already in Mode 2, proceed to Step 3 for exhaust gas sensor monitor.
1. Turn the ignition switch **ON**.
2. Turn the diagnostic switch **ON**, by turning the switch fully clockwise for 2 seconds and then fully counterclockwise.
3. Start the engine and run until thoroughly warm. Raise the idle to 2,000 rpm and hold for approximately 2 minutes. Ensure the red LED or malfunction indicator light flash **ON** and **OFF** more than 5 times every 10 seconds with the engine speed at 2,000 rpm.

➡**If equipped with 2 exhaust gas sensors, switch to the right sensor by turning the ECU mode selector fully clockwise for 2 seconds and then fully counterclockwise with the engine running.**

CLEARING CODES

1990–95 VEHICLES

All control unit diagnostic codes may be cleared by disconnecting the negative battery for a period of 15 seconds. The codes will be cleared when mode 1 is re-entered from mode 2. The Nissan Consult Monitor or equivalent can also be used to clear codes.

DIAGNOSTIC TROUBLE CODES

1990–95 Vehicles

Code 16 TCS Signal
Code 21 Ignition signal missing in primary coil
Code 31 ECM (engine ECCS control unit)
Code 32 EGR circuit
Code 33 Heated oxygen sensor circuit
Code 34 Knock Sensor (KS) circuit
Code 35 EGR temperature sensor circuit
Code 42 Fuel temperature sensor circuit
Code 43 Throttle sensor circuit
Code 45 Injector leak
Code 46 Secondary throttle sensor circuit
Code 51 Injector circuit
Code 53 Heated oxygen sensor circuit (right bank)
Code 54 A/T controller circuit
Code 55 No malfunctioning in the above circuit
Code 11 Crankshaft position sensor
Code 12 Mass Air flow sensor
Code 13 Engine coolant temperature sensor circuit
Code 14 Vehicle speed sensor

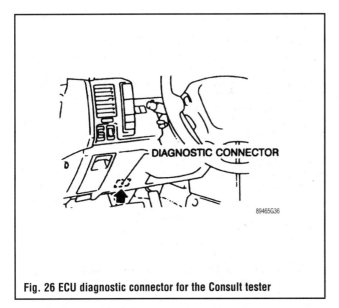

Fig. 26 ECU diagnostic connector for the Consult tester

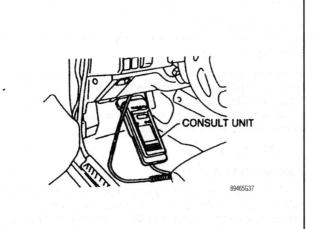

Fig. 27 Reading diagnostic codes using the Consult tester

Isuzu

GENERAL INFORMATION

Isuzu vehicles use Throttle Body Fuel Injection (TBI) systems or Multi-port Fuel Injection System (MFI).

The Throttle Body (TBI) fuel injection system was put into production in 1989. It is used on 2.8L and 3.1L engines. The system functions much the same as a multi-port fuel injection system but with one exception—fuel is injected into the intake manifold rather than into each individual cylinder. This system may also control the ignition system.

The I-TEC Multi-port Fuel Injection (MFI) system was first used in 1985 and continues to be used today. The system constantly monitors and controls engine operation through the use of data sensors, an Electronic Control Module (ECM) and other components. Individual fuel injectors are mounted at each cylinder and provide a metered amount of fuel as required by current operating conditions. This system may also control the ignition system and, as equipped, the turbocharger system.

SELF DIAGNOSTICS

All vehicles covered in this section have self-diagnostic capabilities. The ECM diagnostics are in the form of trouble codes stored in the system's memory. When a trouble code is detected by the control module, it will turn the malfunction indicator lamp **ON** until the code is cleared. An intermittent problem will set a code. The lamp will turn **OFF** if the problem goes away, but the trouble code will stay in memory until ECM power is interrupted.

Service Precautions

• Keep all ECM parts and harnesses dry during service. Protect the ECM and all solid-state components from rough handling or extremes of temperature.

• Use extreme care when working around the ECM or other solid-state components. Do not allow any open circuit to short or ground in the ECM circuit. Voltage spikes may cause damage to solid-state components.

• Before attempting to remove any parts, turn the ignition switch **OFF** or disconnect the negative battery cable.

• Remove the ECM before any arc welding is performed to the vehicle.

• Electronic components are very susceptible to damage caused by electrostatic discharge (static electricity). To prevent electronic component damage, do not touch the control module connector pins or soldered components on the control module circuit board.

READING TROUBLE CODES

♦ **See Figures 28, 29 and 30**

➡**Diagnostic codes may be retrieve through the use of the malfunction indicator light or Malfunction Indicator Lamp (MIL). A special Scan tool can be used, but is not required. When using special diagnostic equipment, always observe the tool manufacturer's instructions.**

1982–86 Vehicles

The trouble code system is actuated by connecting a diagnostic lead to ground. The location of the diagnostic lead differs from model-to-model and, in some cases from year-to-year within the same model.

I-Mark RWD models for 1982–86; the trouble code test leads are usually taped to the wiring harness under the instrument panel, at the right side of the steering column and just above the accelerator pedal.

I-Mark FWD models for 1985–86; a 3 terminal connector, also known as the Assembly Line Diagnostic Link (ALDL) or Assembly Line Communications Link (ALCL) is located near the ECM connector. Connect a jumper wire between A and C.

Impulse for 1983–86; connect diagnostic lead terminals together (1 male and 1 female). Terminals are located under dash near the top of the driver's side kick panel.

Trooper II for 1985; connect the diagnostic lead terminals together (1 male and 1 female). The terminals are located under dash, on the passenger's side, behind the radio. The terminal leads for 1986 models are located near the ALDL connector, under dash, on the driver's side behind the cigarette lighter.

Pick-up truck for 1982; connect the diagnostic lead terminals together (1

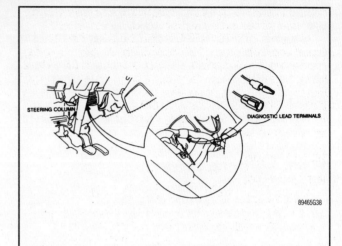

Fig. 28 Diagnostic lead location—1982–85 I-Mark (RWD) shown without Scan Tool

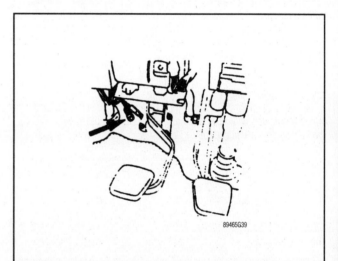

Fig. 29 Diagnostic connector—1987–89 vehicles, except Trooper

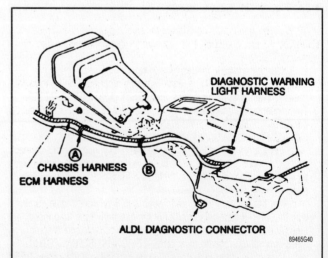

Fig. 30 Assembly Line Diagnostic link (ALDL) connector—1988–91 Trooper with 2.6L engine

male and 1 female). The terminals are branched from the harness near the ECM, under the dash on the driver's side behind the hood release.

The trouble code is determined by counting the flashes of the "Check Engine" lamp. Trouble Code 12 will flash first, indicating that the self-diagnostic system is working. Code 12 consists of 1 flash, short pause, then 2 flashes. There will be a longer pause and Code 12 will repeat 2 more times. Each code flashes 3 times. The cycle will then repeat itself until the engine is started or the ignition switch is turned **OFF**. In most cases, the codes will be checked with the engine running since no codes other than 12 or 51 will be present on initial key **ON**.

1987–94 Vehicles

WITH SCAN TOOL

1. Turn the ignition key to the **OFF** position.
2. Connect the scan tool to the Assembly Line Diagnostic Link (ALDL).
3. Turn **ON** the ignition for scan tool to access engine computer.

With Scan Tool

1987–89 VEHICLES

1. With the ignition turned **ON**, and the engine stopped, the CHECK ENGINE lamp should be **ON**. This is a bulb check to indicate the light is working properly.
2. For the I-Mark, connect a jumper wire between the A and C terminals of the Assembly Line Diagnostic Link (ALDL). The connector is located next to the ECM near the heater blower motor.
3. For the Impulse, Trooper and Pickup; connect the trouble code TEST lead (white cable) to the ground lead (black cable). It is located 8 in. from the ECM connector next to the clutch pedal or center console.
4. The malfunction indicator light will begin to flash a trouble Code 12. Code 12 consists of 1 flash, short pause and then 2 more flashes. There will be a longer pause and then a Code 12 will repeat 2 more times. The check indicates that the self-diagnostic system is working. This cycle will repeat itself until the engine is started or the ignition switch is turned **OFF**. If more than a single fault code is stored in the memory, the lowest number code will flash 3 times followed by the next highest code number until all the codes have been flashed. The faults will then repeat in the same order. In most cases, codes will be checked with the engine running since no codes other than Codes 12 and 51 will be present on the initial key **ON**. Remove the jumper wire from the test terminal before starting the engine.

➡ **The fault indicated by trouble Code 15 takes 5 minutes of engine operation before it will display.**

1990–94 VEHICLES

▶ **See Figures 31, 32, 33 and 34**

1. With the ignition turned **ON** and the engine stopped, the CHECK ENGINE lamp should be **ON**. This is a bulb check to indicate the light is working properly.
2. Enter the diagnostic modes as follows:
    a. For the Impulse, Stylus, and Trooper; jumper the 1 and 3 terminals (outer terminals) of the white Assembly Line Diagnostic Link (ALDL). The connector for Impulse and Stylus is located behind the kick panel on the passenger side of the vehicle. On Trooper, the ALDL connector is located behind the left side of the center console.
    b. For the Amigo, Pickup, and Rodeo with 4 cylinder engine; connect the trouble code TEST lead (white cable) and a ground lead (black cable) together. It is located 8 in. from the ECM connector (next to the clutch pedal or brake pedal).
    c. For the Amigo, Pickup, and Rodeo with 6 cylinder engine; jumper wire the A and B terminals together of the Assembly Line Diagnostic Link (ALDL). The ALDL is located in the center console and is sometimes covered by a plastic cover labeled DIAGNOSTIC CONNECTOR. Read the trouble codes with the ignition switch **ON** and the engine **OFF**.
3. The malfunction indicator light will begin to flash a trouble Code 12. Code 12 consists of 1 flash, a short pause and then 2 more flashes. There

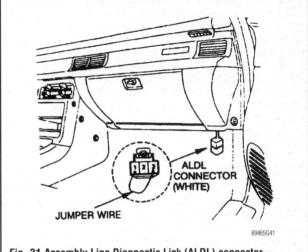

Fig. 31 Assembly Line Diagnostic Link (ALDL) connector—1990–93 Impulse and Stylus

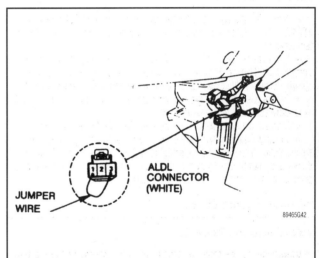

Fig. 32 Assembly Line Diagnostic Link (ALDL) connector—1992–94 Trooper

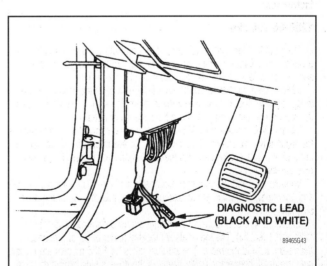

Fig. 33 Assembly Line Diagnostic Link (ALDL) connector—1990–94 Amigo, Pickup and Rodeo (4 cylinder engines)

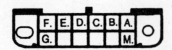

A. Ground
B. Diagnostic terminal
C. A.I.R system (if used)
D. Check engine light

E. Serial data
F. Torque Converter
   Clutch (TCC)
G. Fuel pump
M. Serial data

89465G44

Fig. 34 Assembly Line Diagnostic Link (ALDL) connector—1990–94 Amigo, Pickup and Rodeo (6 cylinder engines)

will be a longer pause and a Code 12 will repeat 2 more times. Code 12 indicates that the self-diagnostic system is working. If any other faults are present, the faults will be displayed 3 times each in the same fashion. Fault codes are flashed from lowest to highest after the Code 12. Remember to remove the jumper wire from the ALDL connector before starting the engine. After all codes have been displayed, the cycle will repeat itself until the engine is started or the ignition switch is turned **OFF**.

➡ **The fault indicated by trouble Code 15 takes 5 minutes of engine operation before it will display (4 cylinder engine only).**

CLEARING CODES

1982–86 VEHICLES

The trouble code memory is fed a continuous 12 volts even with the ignition switch in the **OFF** position. After a fault has been corrected, it will be necessary to remove the voltage for 10 seconds to clear any stored codes. Voltage can be removed by disconnecting the 14 pin ECM connector or by removing the fuse marked `ECM' or fuse No. 4 on some models. Since all memory will be lost when removing the fuse, it will be necessary to reset the clock and other electrical equipment.

1987–94 VEHICLES

The trouble code memory is fed a continuous 12 volts even with the ignition switch in the **OFF** position. After a fault has been corrected, it will be necessary to remove the voltage for 30 seconds to clear any stored codes. The quickest way to remove the voltage is to remove the ECM fuse from the fuse block or the MAIN 60A fuse for 10 seconds. The voltage can also be removed by disconnecting the negative battery cable. This will mean electronic instrumentation, such as a clock and radio, would have to be reset.

1987–89 I-Mark; to clear the trouble codes; turn the ignition switch **OFF** and remove the ECM (30 amp) slow blow fuse located in the engine compartment fuse block for 30 seconds.

1987–89 Impulse; turn the ignition switch **OFF** and disconnect the ECM 13-pin connector or remove the No. 4 fuse from the fuse block for 30 seconds. The electronic functions with memory have to be reset after removing the No. 4 fuse.

1987–89 Pickup and Trooper; turn the ignition switch **OFF** and disconnect the ECM 13-pin connector or remove the No. 4 fuse from the fuse block for 30 seconds.

The 60 amp slow blow fuse may be removed from the fuse block in the engine compartment. However, the electronic functions with memory have to be reset after removing the No. 4 fuse for 30 seconds.

1990–93 I-Mark, Impulse and Stylus; to clear the trouble codes, turn the ignition switch **OFF** and remove the ECM (30 amp) fusible link (FL 3) located in the engine compartment relay and fuse block for 30 seconds.

1992–94 Amigo, Pickup, Rodeo and Trooper; To clear the trouble codes; turn the ignition switch **OFF** and remove the ECM fuse from the under-dash fuse block for 30 seconds. Removing the number 3 fuse from the under dash fuse panel will result in having to reset all the electronic functions with memory in the vehicle. This applies to trucks with 4-cylinder engines.

Removing the 60 amp slow blow fuse from the fuse block in the engine compartment will also erase codes.

DIAGNOSTIC TROUBLE CODES

1983–94 Vehicles

1985–87 2.0L TURBO EFI (VIN F) ENGINE

1983–89 2.0L EFI (VIN A) ENGINE

1988–89 2.3L EFI (VIN L) ENGINE

1988–94 2.6L EFI (VIN E) ENGINE

Code 12 Normal
Code 13 Oxygen sensor circuit
Code 14 Engine Coolant Temperature (ECT) sensor—grounded
Code 15 Engine Coolant Temperature (ECT) sensor—incorrect signal (open circuit on 1988–94 2.6L)
Code 16 Engine Coolant Temperature (ECT) sensor—open circuit
Code 21 Throttle Valve Switch (TVS) system—idle contact and full contact made simultaneously
Code 22 Starter—no signal input
Code 23 Ignition power transistor—output terminal grounded
Code 25 Vacuum Switching Valve (VSV)—output terminal grounded or open
Code 26 Canister purge/Vacuum Switching Valve (VSV)—open or grounded
Code 27 Canister purge/Vacuum Switching Valve (VSV)—faulty transistor or bad ground circuit
Code 32 EGR temperature sensor—faulty sensor or harness
Code 33 Fuel injector system—output terminal grounded or open
Code 34 EGR/Vacuum switching valve—output terminal grounded or open
Code 35 Ignition power transistor—open circuit
Code 41 Crank Angle sensor (CAS)—no signal or faulty signal
Code 43 Throttle Valve Switch—idle contact closed continuously
Code 44 Fuel metering system—lean signal (Oxygen sensor—low voltage)
Code 45 Fuel metering system—rich signal (Oxygen sensor-high voltage)
Code 51 Faulty ECM
Code 52 Faulty ECM
Code 53 Vacuum Switching Valve (VSV)—grounded or faulty power transistor
Code 54 Ignition power transistor—grounded or faulty power transistor
Code 55 Faulty ECM
Code 61 Air Flow Sensor (AFS)—grounded, shorted, open or broken HOT wire
Code 62 Air Flow Sensor (AFS)—broken COLD wire
Code 63 Vehicle Speed Sensor (VSS)—no signal input
Code 64 Fuel injector system—grounded or faulty transistor
Code 65 Throttle Valve Switch (TVS)—full contact closed continuously
Code 66 Knock sensor—grounded or open circuit
Code 71 Throttle Position Sensor (TPS)—turbo control system—abnormal signal
Code 72 EGR/Vacuum switching valve—output terminal grounded or open
Code 73 EGR/Vacuum switching valve—faulty transistor or grounded system

1987–89 1.5L TURBO EFI (VIN 9) ENGINE

1989 1.6L EFI (VIN 5) ENGINE

1991–92 1.6L TURBO EFI (VIN 4) ENGINE

1989–91 2.8L TBI (VIN R) ENGINE

1991–94 3.1L TBI (VIN Z) ENGINE

Code 12 Normal
Code 13 Oxygen sensor circuit
Code 14 Engine Coolant Temperature (ECT) sensor—high temperature indicated
Code 15 Engine Coolant Temperature (ECT) sensor—low temperature indicated
Code 21 Throttle Position Sensor (TPS)—voltage high
Code 22 Throttle Position Sensor (TPS)—voltage low
Code 23 Intake Air Temperature (IAT)—low temperature indicated
Code 24 Vehicle Speed Sensor (VSS)—no input signal
Code 25 Intake Air Temperature (IAT)—high temperature indicated
Code 31 Turbocharger wastegate control
Code 32 EGR system fault
Code 33 Manifold Absolute Pressure (MAP) sensor—voltage high
Code 34 Manifold Absolute Pressure (MAP) sensor—voltage low
Code 42 Electronic Spark Timing (EST) circuit fault
Code 43 Electronic Spark Control (ESC)—knock failure circuit
Code 44 Oxygen sensor circuit—lean exhaust
Code 45 Oxygen sensor circuit—rich exhaust
Code 51 PROM error—faulty or incorrect PROM
Code 52 CALPAK error—faulty or incorrect CALPAK
Code 54 Fuel Pump Circuit—low voltage
Code 55 ECM error

1990–91 1.6L EFI (VIN 5) ENGINE

1992–94 1.8L EFI (VIN 8) ENGINE

1991–94 2.3L EFI (VIN 5(6)) ENGINE

1992–94 3.2L EFI (VIN V/W) ENGINE

Code 13 Oxygen sensor circuit
Code 14 Engine Coolant Temperature (ECT) sensor—out of range
Code 21 Throttle Position Sensor (TPS)—out of range
Code 23 Intake Air Temperature (IAT)—out of range
Code 24 Vehicle Speed Sensor (VSS)—no input signal
Code 32 EGR system fault
Code 33 Manifold Absolute Pressure (MAP) sensor—out of range
Code 44 Oxygen sensor circuit—lean exhaust
Code 45 Oxygen sensor circuit—rich exhaust
Code 51 ECM failure

Lexus

GENERAL INFORMATION

This system is broken down into 3 major systems: the Fuel System, Air Induction System and the Electronic Control System. The air induction system provides sufficient clean air for the engine operation. This system includes the throttle body, air intake ducting and cleaner and idle control components. Lexus equips the ES300, SC300 and SC400 with a system of induction tuning that changes the induction path length. The Intake Air Control Valve (IACV) changes the length of the induction path to broaden the power curve by matching the resonance characteristics of the intake charge with the engine speed. When the IACV opens, the effective length of the intake tract is shortened, boosting top end power. With the IACV closed, the intake tract is long, boosting the low end torque.

Lexus engines are equipped with a computer which centrally controls the electronic fuel injection, electronic spark advance and the exhaust gas recirculation valve. The systems can be diagnosed by means of an Electronic Control Unit (ECU).

The ECU receives signals from the various sensors indicating changing engine operations conditions such as:
- Intake air flow
- Intake air temperature
- Coolant temperature sensor
- Engine rpm
- Acceleration/deceleration
- Exhaust oxygen content

These signals are utilized by the ECU to determine the injection duration necessary for an optimum air/fuel ratio.

SELF DIAGNOSTICS

Service Precautions

- Keep all ECU parts and harnesses dry during service. Protect the ECU and all solid-state components from rough handling or extremes of temperature.
- Before attempting to remove any parts, turn the ignition switch **OFF** and disconnect the battery ground cable.
- Make sure all harness connectors are fastened securely. A poor connection can cause an extremely high voltage surge, resulting in damage to integrated circuits.
- Always use a 12 volt battery as a power source.
- Do not attempt to disconnect the battery cables with the engine running.
- Do not attempt to disassemble the ECU unit under any circumstances.
- If installing a 2-way or CB radio, mobile phone or other radio equipment, keep the antenna as far as possible away from the electronic control unit. Keep the antenna feeder line at least 8 in. away from the EFI harness and do not run the lines parallel for a long distance. Be sure to ground the radio to the vehicle body.
- When performing ECU input/output signal diagnosis, remove the water proofing rubber plug, if equipped, from the connectors to make it easier to insert tester probes into the connector. Always reinstall it after testing.
- Always insert test probes into a connector from the wiring side when checking continuity, amperage or voltage.
- When connecting or disconnecting pin connectors from the ECU, take care not to bend or break any pin terminals. Check that there are no bends or breaks on ECU pin terminals before attempting any connections.
- When measuring supply voltage of ECU-controlled components, keep the tester probes separated from each other and from accidental grounding. If the tester probes accidentally make contact with each other during measurement, a short circuit will damage the ECU.
- Use great care when working on or around air bag systems. Wait at least 20 seconds after turning the ignition switch to **LOCK** and disconnecting the negative battery cable before performing any other work. The air bag system is equipped with a back-up power system which will keep the system functional for 20 seconds without battery power.
- All air bag connectors are a standard yellow color. The related wiring is encased in standard yellow sheathing. Testing and diagnostic procedures must be followed exactly when performing diagnosis on this system. Improper procedures may cause accidental deployment or disable the system when needed.
- Never attempt to measure the resistance of the air bag squib. Detonation may occur.

READING TROUBLE CODES

▶ **See Figure 35**

1990–95

All models contain a self-diagnostic system. Stored fault codes are transmitted through the blinking of the CHECK ENGINE warning lamp. This occurs when the system is placed in normal diagnostic mode or in test mode. Normal diagnostic mode is used to read stored codes while the vehicle is stopped. The test mode is used after the vehicle is driven under certain conditions. In test mode, while the ECU monitors, the technician will simulate conditions of the suspected fault in an attempt to cause the malfunction. When a malfunction is found, the CHECK ENGINE lamp will illuminate to alert the technician that the fault is presently occurring.

When troubleshooting 1995 ES300 and LS400 models, an OBD-II scan tool or equivalent generic scan tool must be used.

To read the fault codes, the following initial conditions must be met:
1. Battery voltage at or above 11 volts.
2. Throttle fully closed.
3. Transmission in **N**.
4. All electrical systems and accessories **OFF**.

Normal Diagnostic Mode

1. Turn the ignition **ON** but do not start the engine.
2. Use a jumper wire to connect terminals TE1 and E1 of the check connector in the engine compartment or of the TDCL connector below the left side of the dash, if so equipped.
3. Fault codes will be transmitted through the controlled flashing of the CHECK ENGINE warning lamp.
4. If no malfunction was found or no code was stored, the lamp will flash 2 times per second with no other pauses or patterns. This confirms that the diagnostic system is working but has nothing to report. This light pattern may be referred to as the system normal signal. It should be present when no other codes are stored.
5. If faults are present, the CHECK lamp will blink the number of the code(s). All codes are 2 digits; the pulsing of the light represents the digits, not the count. For example, Code 25 is displayed as 2 flashes, a pause and 5 flashes.
6. If more than 1 code is stored, the next will be transmitted after a 2 ½ second pause.

➡**If multiple codes are stored, they will be transmitted in numerical order from lowest to highest. This does not indicate the order of fault occurrence.**

7. When all codes have been transmitted, the entire pattern will repeat after a 4 ½ second pause. The cycle will continue as long as the diagnostic terminals are connected.
8. After recording the codes, disconnect the jumper at the diagnostic connector and turn the ignition **OFF**.

Test Mode

1. Turn the ignition switch **OFF**.
2. Use a jumper wire to connect the TE2 and E1 terminals of the check connector or TDCL. The test mode cannot be initiated if the connection between TE2 and E1 is made with the key in the **ON** position.

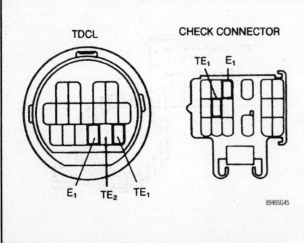

Fig. 35 Jump terminals TE1 and EI to enter normal diagnostic mode, Jump terminals TE2 and E1 to enter test mode—Lexus

3. Turn the ignition switch **ON**, but do not start the engine. The malfunction indicator light should flash. If the light does not flash, check the TE1 terminal circuit.
4. Start the engine and simulate the conditions of the problem or malfunction.
5. When the road test is complete, connect the TE1 and E1 terminals of the TDCL or check connector and read trouble codes.
6. After the codes are read and noted, disconnect the jumpers from the connector. When the engine is not cranked a code for starter signal and cam position sensors will be set, but this is not abnormal. If any of the sensed switches are used, the transmission shift lever, throttle or air conditioner, the switch condition code will be set, but this is not abnormal either.

CLEARING CODES

▶ **See Figure 36**

1990–95 VEHICLES

Although the CHECK ENGINE lamp will reset itself after a repair is made, the original fault code will still be stored in memory. It is therefore necessary to clear the code after repairs are completed.
1. Turn the ignition **OFF**.
2. Remove the 20 amp EFI fuse from junction fuse box No. 2
3. Wait at least 10 seconds before reinstalling the EFI fuse.
4. Road test vehicle and check to see that no fault codes are present.

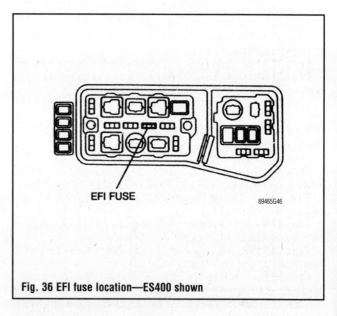

Fig. 36 EFI fuse location—ES400 shown

DIAGNOSTIC TROUBLE CODES

1990–95 Vehicles

Constant blinking of malfunction indicator light: Normal system operation
Code 12 Rpm NE, G1 or G2 signal to ECU—missing for 2 seconds or more after STA turns **ON**
Code 13 Rpm NE signal to ECU—missing for 50 msec. or more with engine speed above 1000 rpm, between 2 pulses of the G signal, NE signal of other than 12 pulses to ECU, or deviance of G1, G2 and NE signal continues for 1 second with engine warm and idling.
Code 14 Igniter IGF1 signal to ECU—missing for 8 successive ignitions
Code 15 Igniter IGF2 signal to ECU—missing for 8 successive ignitions
Code 16 ECT control signal—normal signal missing from ECT CPU (1990–94)
Code 16 A/T control system—normal signal missing from between the engine CPU and A/T CPU in the ECM (1995)
Code 17 No. 1 cam position sensor—G1 signal to ECU missing

Code 18 No. 2 cam position sensor—G2 signal to ECU missing

Code 21* Left bank main oxygen sensor signal—signal voltage is remains between 0.35–0.70 V for 60 seconds or more at driving speed between 40–50 mph, AC **ON** and ECT in 4th gear or open/short sensor heater circuit

Code 22 Engine Coolant Temperature sensor circuit—open/short for 0.5 seconds or more

Code 24 Intake air temperature sensor circuit—open/short for 0.5 seconds or more

Code 25* Air/fuel ratio LEAN malfunction—voltage output from oxygen sensor is less than 0.45 V for 90 seconds with engine racing at 2000 rpm, feedback frequency 5 Hz or more with main oxygen sensor signal centered at 0.45 V and idle switch **ON**, or feedback value of right and left banks differs by more than a certain percentage.

Code 26* Air/fuel ratio RICH malfunction—feedback frequency 5 Hz or more with main oxygen sensor signal centered at 0.45 V and idle switch **ON**, or feedback value of right and left banks differs by more than a certain percentage.

Code 27* Left bank sub-oxygen sensor signal—output of main oxygen sensor is 0.45 V or more and output of sub-oxygen sensor is 0.45 V or less with engine at wide open throttle for 4 seconds or more and sensors warmed.

Code 28* Right bank main oxygen sensor signal—signal voltage is remains between 0.35–0.70 V for 60 seconds or more at driving speed between 40–50 mph, AC **ON** and ECT in 4th gear or open/short sensor heater circuit

Code 29* Right bank sub-oxygen sensor signal—output of main oxygen sensor is 0.45 V or more and output of sub-oxygen sensor is 0.45 V or less with engine at wide open throttle for 4 seconds or more and sensors warmed.

Code 31 Air flow meter circuit signal to ECU—missing for 2 seconds when engine speed is above 300 rpm

Code 32 Air flow meter circuit—E2 circuit open or VC and VS shorted

Code 35 HAC sensor circuit—open/short for 0.5 seconds or more/Baro sensor

Code 41 Throttle Position Sensor signal—open or short in the throttle position sensor circuit.

Code 42 Vehicle speed sensor circuit—engine RPM over 2350, and VSS shows zero miles per hour.

Code 43 Starter signal to ECU missing

Code 47 Sub-throttle position sensor signal (VTA2)—open/short for at least 0.5 seconds or signal outputs exceed 1.45 V with idle contacts **ON**.

Code 51 AC signal **ON**, IDL contacts off, or shift in R, D, 2 or 1 range—during check mode

Code 52 No. 1 knock sensor signal—missing from ECU for 3 revolutions when engine speed is between 1600–5200 rpm

Code 53 Knock control signal—ECU knock control malfunction detected with engine speed between 650–5200 rpm

Code 55 No. 2 knock sensor signal—missing from ECU for 3 revolutions when engine speed is between 1600–5200 rpm

Code 71* EGR gas temperature below 149°F (65°C) for 90 seconds or more during EGR control

Code 78* Fuel pump control signal—open or short in the fuel pump control circuit

➡ ***2 trip detection logic code: A single occurrence of this fault will be temporarily stored in memory. The malfunction indicator light will NOT illuminate until fault is detected a second time (during a separate ignition cycle).**

Mazda

GENERAL INFORMATION

Mazda utilizes Electronic Gas Injection (EGI). This was first available in the 1984 RX-7. The 626 picked it up in 1986, and the 323 in 1987. In 1988, all models except B2200 and B2600 pickup trucks came equipped with fuel injection. Mazda uses various variations of EGI. Navajo uses the Ford EEC-IV system. However, the EEC-IV system will not be covered in this section.

SELF DIAGNOSTICS

Service Precautions

• Before connecting or disconnecting the ECU harness connectors, make sure the ignition switch is **OFF** and the negative battery cable is disconnected to avoid the possibility of damage to the control unit.

• When performing ECU input/output signal diagnosis, remove the pin terminal retainer from the connectors to make it easier to insert tester probes into the connector.

• When connecting or disconnecting pin connectors from the ECU, take care not to bend or break any pin terminals. Check that there are no bends or breaks on ECU pin terminals before attempting any connections.

• Before replacing any ECU, perform the ECU input/output signal diagnosis to make sure the ECU is functioning properly or not.

• After checking through EGI troubleshooting, perform the EFI self-diagnosis and driving test.

• When measuring supply voltage of ECU controlled components with a circuit tester, separate 1 tester probe from another. If the 2 tester probes accidentally make contact with each other during measurement, a short circuit will result and may damage the ECU.

READING TROUBLE CODES

➡**Diagnostic codes may be retrieve through the use of the malfunction indicator light or Malfunction Indicator Lamp (MIL). Special System Checker No. 83, Digital Code Checker and a Self-diagnosis Checker are all special diagnostic equipment used to retrieve codes, however these tools are not required. When using special diagnostic equipment, always observe the tool manufacturer's instructions.**

1984–86 Vehicles With System Checker Tool 83

▶ **See Figures 37 and 38**

On 1984–85 GLC, 626 and RX-7, 1986 323 and 1986 B2000 Pick-up, the System Checker No. 83 (tool No. 49-G030-920), is used to detect and indicate any problems of each sensor, damaged wiring, poor contact or a short circuit between each of the sensor control units. Trouble is indicated by a red lamp and a buzzer. If there are more than 2 problems at a time, the indicator lamp turns **ON** in the numerical order of the code number. Even if the problem is corrected during indication, 1 cycle will be indicated, If after a malfunction has occurred and the ignition key is switched **OFF**, the malfunction indicator for the feedback system will not be displayed on the checker.

Read engine trouble codes using the following procedures:

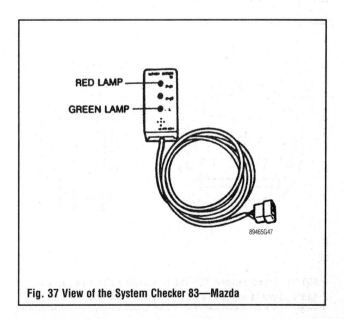

Fig. 37 View of the System Checker 83—Mazda

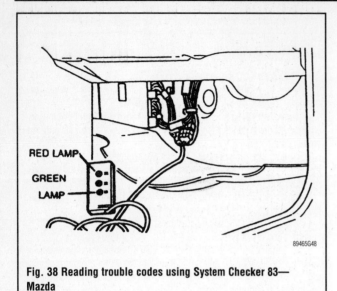

Fig. 38 Reading trouble codes using System Checker 83—Mazda

1984–85 GLC

1. Operate the engine until normal operating temperatures are reached. Allow the engine to run at idle.

2. Connect System Checker tool No. 83 (49-G030-920) to the check connector, located near the ECU.

3. Check whether the trouble indication light turns **ON**.

➡**Trouble is indicated by a red light and a buzzer.**

4. If the light turns **ON**, check for cause of problems.

➡**If the trouble code is code number 3 (feedback system), proceed as follows:**

5. Start the engine, letting it run until it reaches normal operating temperature. Connect a tachometer to the engine.

6. Connect a dwell meter (90 degrees, 4 cylinder) to the yellow wire in the service (check) connector of the air/fuel solenoid valve.

7. Run the engine at idle and note the reading on the dwell meter.

8. If the dwell meter reading is 0° degrees, the probable causes are as follows:

    a. The wiring harness from the IG to the check connector BrY terminal is open.

    b. The wiring harness from the check connector Y terminal to the control unit (F) terminal is grounded.

    c. The transistor in the control unit for the air/fuel solenoid is short circuit.

9. If the dwell meter reading is 27°, check whether the green lamp (feedback signal) illuminates or does not illuminate.

10. If the oxygen sensor signal lamp does not illuminate, proceed as follows:

    a. If the green lamp does not illuminate, the air is sucked from the intake system or the air is sucked from the exhaust manifold.

    b. Carburetor jets are clogged.

    c. The valve of the air/fuel solenoid is stuck to the lower position, giving a lean air/fuel mixture condition.

11. If the oxygen sensor signal lamp illuminates, proceed as follows:

    a. If green lamp turns **ON**, the mixture is richer than stoichiometric air/fuel ratio.

    b. If the green lamp turns **ON** and **OFF**, the 02 sensor signal is fed to the control unit.

    c. If the green lamp turns **OFF**, the mixture is leaner than stoichiometric.

1984–85 626 AND B2200

1. Operate the engine until normal operating temperatures are reached. Allow the engine to run at idle.

2. Connect System Checker tool No. 83 (49-G030-920) to the check connector, located near the ECU.

3. Check whether the trouble indication light turns **ON**.

➡**If there is more than 2 problems at the same time, the indicator lamp lights on in the numerical order of the code number. Even if the problem is corrected during indication, 1 cycle will be Indicated. If after a malfunction has occurred the Ignition key is switched off, the malfunction indicator for the feedback system will not be displayed on the checker. The control unit has a built In fall-safe mechanism. If a malfunction occurs during driving, the control unit will on its own initiative, send out a command and driving performance will be affected. The commands are as follows:**

    a. Water Thermo-Sensor—the control unit outputs a constant 176°F (80°C) command.

    b. Feed-Back Sensor—the control unit holds air/fuel solenoid to dwell meter reading 18° (duty 0%) for 626 or 27° (duty 30%) for B2200.

    c. Vacuum Sensor—the control unit prevents operation of the EGR valve, and holds the air/fuel solenoid to a duty of 0%.

    d. EGR Position Sensor—the control unit prevents operation of the EGR valve.

➡**If the trouble code is code number 3 (feedback system), proceed as follows:**

4. Start the engine, letting it run until it reaches normal operating temperature. Connect a tachometer to the engine.

5. Connect a dwell meter (90 degrees, 4 cylinder) to the yellow wire in the service (check) connector of the air/fuel solenoid valve.

6. Run the engine at idle and note the reading on the dwell meter.

7. If the dwell meter reading is 0° degrees, the probable causes are as follows:

    a. The wiring harness from the IG to the check connector BrY terminal is open.

    b. The wiring harness from the check connector Y terminal to the control unit (F) terminal is grounded.

    c. The transistor in the control unit for the air/fuel solenoid is open.

8. If the dwell meter reading is 90°, the probable causes are as follows:

    a. The wiring harness from the IG to the check connector BrY terminal is open.

    b. The wiring harness from the check connector BrY terminal to the control unit (F) terminal is grounded.

    c. The transistor in the control unit for the air/fuel solenoid is short circuited.

9. If the dwell meter reading is 18°, check whether the green lamp (feedback signal) illuminates or does not illuminate.

10. If the oxygen sensor signal lamp does not illuminate, proceed as follows:

    a. If the green lamp does not illuminate, the air is sucked from the intake system or the air is sucked from the exhaust manifold.

    b. Carburetor jets are clogged.

    c. The valve of the air/fuel solenoid is stuck to the lower position, giving a lean air/fuel mixture condition.

11. If the oxygen sensor signal lamp illuminates, proceed as follows:

    a. If green lamp turns **ON**, the mixture is richer than stoichiometric air/fuel ratio.

    b. If the green lamp turns **ON** and **OFF**, the 02 sensor signal is fed to the control unit.

    c. If the green lamp turns **OFF**, the mixture is leaner than stoichiometric.

1984–85 RX-7 AND 1986 323

1. Operate the engine until normal temperatures are reached.

2. Allow the engine to run at idle.

3. Check whether the trouble indication light turns **ON**.

➡**Trouble is indicated by a red light and a buzzer.**

4. If the light turns **ON**, check the ECM code problems indicated.

With Digital Code Checker and Self-diagnosis Checker

▶ **See Figures 39 and 40**

The Digital Code Checker tool No. 49-G01829A0 for 1986 or Self-Diagnosis Checker tool No. 49-H018-9A1 are used to retrieve code numbers of malfunctions which have happened and were memorized or are continuing. The malfunction is indicated by the code number and buzzer.

If there is more 1 malfunction, the code numbers will display on the self diagnosis checker 1 by 1 in numerical order. In the case of malfunctions, 09, 13 and 01, the code numbers are displayed in order of 01, 09 and then 13.

The ECU has a built in fail-safe mechanism for the main input sensors. If a malfunction occurs, the emission control unit will substitute values; this will slightly effect the driving performance but the vehicle may still be driven.

The ECU continuously checks for malfunctions of the input devices within 2 seconds after turning the ignition switch to the **ON** position and the test connector is grounded.

The malfunction indicator light indicates a pattern the same as the buzzer of the self-diagnosis checker when the self-diagnosis check connector is grounded. When the self-diagnosis check connector is not grounded, the lamp illuminates steady while the malfunction recovers. However, the malfunction code is memorized in the emission control unit.

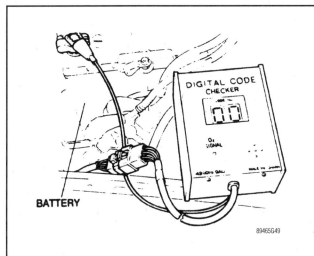

Fig. 39 Reading trouble codes using the Digital Code Checker— Mazda

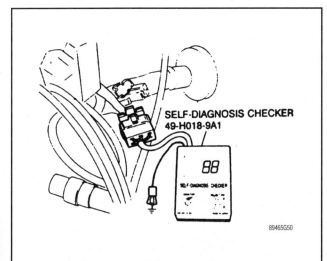

Fig. 40 Reading trouble codes using the Self-Diagnosis Checker—1986 Mazda

Read engine trouble codes using the following procedures:

1988 VEHICLES EXCEPT RX-7

1. Warm the engine to normal operating temperatures, by keeping the engine speed below 400 rpm.
2. Connect the Digital Code Checker No.
3. Wait for 3 minutes for the code(s) to register.
4. If the code number flashes, a buzzer will automatically sound, indicating the code number.
5. Note the code number and check the causes, repair as necessary.

1986 RX-7

1. Start the engine and allow it to reach operating temperature.
2. Connect the Digital Code Checker for trouble codes.
3. Check the Digital Code Checker for trouble codes.

➡ **After turning the Ignition switch to the ON position, the buzzer will sound for 3 seconds.**

AFTER REPAIR PROCEDURE

➡ **This procedure is used on all vehicles 1986 and later.**

1. Clear all trouble codes from the ECU memory.
2. After clearing codes, connect the Digital Code Checker or the Self-Diagnosis Checker to the test connector.
3. If necessary to use a jumper wire, connect it between the test connector (green: pin 1) and a ground.
4. Turn the ignition switch **ON**, but do not start the engine for 6 seconds.
5. Operate the engine until normal operating temperatures are reached, then, run it at 2000 rpm for 2 minutes.
6. Verify that no code numbers are displayed.

1987–94 Vehicles With Self-Diagnosis Checker

▶ **See Figure 41**

The self-diagnosis checker (49-H0I8-9A1) and System Selector (49-B0I9-9A0), are used to retrieve code numbers of malfunctions which have happened and were memorized or are continuing. The malfunction is indicated by a code number.

If there is more than 1 malfunction, the code numbers will display on the self-diagnosis checker in numerical order. The ECU has a built in fail-safe mechanism for the main input sensors. If a malfunction occurs, the emission control unit will substitute values. This will affect driving performance, but the vehicle may still be driven.

The ECU continuously checks for malfunctions of the input devices. But the ECU checks for malfunctions of the output devices within 3 seconds after the green (1 pin) test connector or TEN terminal of the diagnosis connector is grounded and the ignition switch is turned to the **ON** position.

Read engine trouble codes using the following procedures:

1987–91 323, MIATA AND PROTEGE

1. Connect the tester to the check connector at the rear of the left side wheel housing and to the negative battery cable.
2. Set the tester select switch to the A setting.
3. With a jumper wire, ground the 1-pin test connector.
4. Turn the ignition switch **ON**.
5. Make sure that 88 flashes on the monitor and that the audible buzzer sounds for 3 seconds after turning the ignition switch **ON**.
6. If 88 does not flash, check the main relay, power supply circuit and the check connector wiring.
7. If 88 flashes and the buzzer sounds for more than 20 seconds, replace the engine control unit and repeat Steps 3 and 4.
8. Note any other code numbers that are present and refer to the code chart. Repair if necessary.

1992 626, MX-6, MPV, B2200 AND B2600i

The check connector is located at the rear of the left side wheel house on 626/MX-6, front of the left side wheel house on MPV, above the right side wheel house on B2200 and near the fuel filter on B2600i.

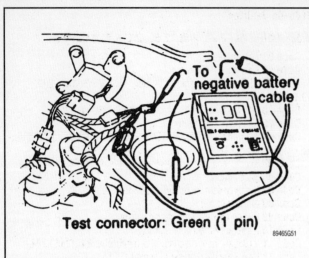

Test connector: Green (1 pin)

89465G51

Fig. 41 Reading trouble codes using the Self-Diagnosis Checker—1987–94 Mazda

1. Connect the tester to the check connector and to ground.
2. Set the tester select switch to the A setting.
3. With a jumper wire, ground the 1 pin test connector.
4. Turn the ignition switch **ON**.
5. Make sure that 88 flashes on the monitor and that the audible buzzer sounds for 3 seconds after turning the ignition switch **ON**.
6. If 88 does not flash, check the main relay, power supply circuit and the check connector wiring.
7. If 88 flashes and the buzzer sounds for more than 20 seconds, replace the engine control unit and perform steps number 1 through 6 again.

➡**Before replacing the ECU on the MPV or B2600i, check for a short circuit between ECU terminal IB for JE engine and 1F for G6 engine and the 6 pin check connector.**

8. Note and record any other code numbers that are present.

1992–94 323, PROTEGE, 929, MIATA (MX-5), MX-3 AND 1993–94 RX-7

1. Connect the system selector to the diagnosis connector at the rear of the left side wheel housing.
2. Set the SYSTEM SELECT switch to the 1 setting.
3. Set the TEST switch to the **SELF—TEST** position.
4. Connect the self-diagnosis checker, the system selector and ground.
5. Set the self-diagnosis checker SELECT switch to the A position.
6. Turn the ignition switch **ON**.
7. Make sure that 88 flashes on the monitor and that the audible buzzer sounds for 3 seconds after turning the ignition switch **ON**.
8. If 88 does not flash, check the main relay, power supply circuit and the diagnosis connector wiring.
9. If 88 flashes and the buzzer sounds for more than 20 seconds, check for a short between ECU terminal 1F and the FEN terminal of the diagnosis connector. Replace the engine control unit if necessary and perform Steps 1 through 7 again.
10. Note and record any other code numbers that are present.

1993–94 626 AND MX-6

1. Connect the system selector to the diagnosis connector at the rear of the left side wheel housing.
2. Set the SYSTEM SELECT switch to the 1 setting.
3. Set the TEST switch to the **SELF—TEST** position.
4. Connect the self-diagnosis checker the system selector and ground.
5. Set the self-diagnosis checker SELECT switch to the A position.
6. Turn the ignition switch **ON**.

7. Make sure that 88 flashes on the monitor and that the audible buzzer sounds for 3 seconds after turning the ignition switch **ON.**
8. If 88 does not flash, check the main relay, power supply circuit and the diagnosis connector wiring.
9. If 88 flashes and the buzzer sounds for more than 20 seconds, check for a short between PCM terminal 1F (manual trans.), (1G auto trans.) and the FEN terminal of the diagnosis connector. Replace the engine control unit if necessary and perform Steps 1 through 7 again.
10. Note and record any other code numbers that are present.

1984–94 Vehicles Without Self-Diagnosis Checker

The malfunction indicator light indicates a pattern the same as the buzzer of the self-diagnosis checker when the green (1 pin) test connector or FEN terminal of the diagnosis connector is grounded. When the green (1 pin) test connector or FEN terminal of the diagnosis connector is not grounded, the lamp illuminates steady while malfunction of the main input sensor occurs and goes out if the malfunction recovers. However, the malfunction code is memorized in the control unit.

CLEARING CODES

1984–86 Vehicles

ALL VEHICLES

1. Turn the ignition switch **OFF**.
2. Disconnect the negative battery cable.
3. Depress the brake pedal for at least 5 seconds.
4. Reconnect the negative battery cable.

1987–91 Vehicles

ALL VEHICLES

1. Cancel the memory of the malfunction by disconnecting the negative battery cable and depressing the brake pedal for at least 20 seconds, then reconnect the negative battery cable.
2. Except Miata, MX-3, 323 and Protege, connect the Self-Diagnosis Checker 49-H018-9A1 to the check connector. Ground the test connector (green: 1 pin) using a jumper wire.
3. On Miata, MX-3, 323 and Protege, connect Self-Diagnosis Checker (49-B0I9-9A0) to the diagnosis connector.
4. Turn the ignition switch **ON**, but do not start the engine for approximately 6 seconds.
5. Start the engine and allow it to reach normal operating temperature. Then run the engine at 2000 rpm for 2 minutes. Check that no code numbers are displayed.

1992–94 Vehicles

323, MX-3 (B6 ENGINE), MX-5/MIATA

1. Disconnect the negative battery cable.
2. Press the brake pedal for at least 20 seconds.
3. Connect the negative battery cable.
4. Connect the self-diagnosis tester to the diagnosis connector.
5. Turn the ignition switch **ON**.
6. Start and warm-up the engine.
7. Run engine at 2,000 rpm for 3 minutes.
8. Verify that no more codes are stored.

1992 626, MX-6, B2200 (EGI) AND B2600I

1. Disconnect the negative battery cable.
2. Press the brake pedal for at least 5 seconds.
3. Connect the negative battery cable.
4. Connect the self-diagnosis tester and ground the test connector.
5. Turn the ignition switch to the **ON** position for 6 seconds.
6. Start and warm-up the engine.
7. Run engine at 2,000 rpm for 2 minutes (3 minutes on truck).

8. Verify that no more codes are stored.

1993–94 626 AND MX-6 (FS ENGINE)

1. Disconnect the negative battery cable.
2. Press the brake pedal for at least 20 seconds.
3. Connect the negative battery cable.
4. Connect the self-diagnosis tester to the diagnosis connector.
5. Turn the ignition switch **ON**.
6. Start and warm-up the engine.
7. Run engine at 2,000 rpm for 2 minutes.
8. Verify that no more codes are stored.

1993–94 626 AND MX-6 (KL ENGINE), MX-3 (K8 ENGINE) AND 1993–94 RX-7

1. Disconnect the negative battery cable.
2. Press the brake pedal for at least 20 seconds.
3. Connect the negative battery cable.
4. Connect the self-diagnosis tester to the diagnosis connector.
5. Turn the ignition switch **ON**.
6. Verify that no more codes are stored.

929

1. Turn the ignition switch **OFF**.
2. Disconnect the negative battery cable for 20 seconds.

MPV (JE ENGINE)

1. Disconnect the negative battery cable for at least 20 seconds.
2. Connect the negative battery cable.
3. Connect a jumper wire between the 1 pin test connector and ground.
4. Turn the ignition **ON** and verify that no codes are present.
5. Start the engine and again verify that no codes are present.

MPV (G6 ENGINE)

1. Disconnect the negative battery cable for at least 20 seconds.
2. Connect the negative battery cable.
3. Connect the self-diagnosis tester and ground the test connector.
4. Turn the ignition switch to the **ON** position for 6 seconds.
5. Start and warm-up the engine.
6. Run engine at 2,000 rpm for 3 minutes.
7. Verify that no more codes are stored.

DIAGNOSTIC TROUBLE CODES

1984–94 Except RX-7

1984–85 Vehicles

2.0L ENGINE (CODE FE)

Code 01 Engine speed
Code 02 Water thermo-sensor
Code 03 Oxygen sensor
Code 04 Vacuum sensor
Code 05 EGR position sensor

1986–87 Vehicles

1.6L, 2.0L AND 2.2L ENGINES

Code 01 Ignition pulse
Code 02 Air flow meter
Code 03 Water thermo-sensor
Code 04 Intake air thermo or Temperature sensor
Code 05 Feedback system
Code 06 Atmospheric pressure sensor (1986 1.6L)
Code 08 EGR position sensor
Code 09 Atmospheric pressure sensor
Code 22 No. 1 Cylinder sensor (2.2L turbocharged)

1988–94 Vehicles

1.6L, 1.8L, 2.0L, 2.2L, 2.5L, 2.6L AND 3.0L ENGINES

Code 01 Ignition pulse
Code 02 Ne signal—distributor
Code 02 NE 2 signal—crankshaft (1992–93 1.8L V6, 1994 2.0L, 1992–94 3.0L)
Code 03 G1 signal—distributor (2.2L turbo, 1988–91 3.0L)
Code 03 G signal—distributor
Code 04 G2 signal—distributor (2.2L turbo, 1988–91 3.0L); NE 1 signal—distributor (1992–94 1.8L V6, 1994 2.0L, 1992–93 3.0L)
Code 05 Knock sensor and control unit (Left side on 1992–94 3.0L)
Code 06 Speed signal
Code 07 Knock sensor; right side (1992–94 3.0L)
Code 08 Air flow meter
Code 09 Engine coolant temperature sensor
Code 10 Intake air temperature sensor
Code 11 Intake air thermo-sensor—dynamic chamber (3.0L, 2.6L)
Code 13 Intake manifold pressure sensor (1.3L)
Code 14 Atmospheric pressure sensor (in ECU on 2.6L and 1994 2.5L)
Code 15 Oxygen sensor
Code 15 Oxygen sensor; left side on 1992–94 1.8L V6, 1994 2.5L, 1990–94 3.0L
Code 16 EGR position sensor
Code 17 Closed loop system
Code 17 Closed loop system; left side on 1992–94 1.8L V6, 1993-94 2.5L 1990–94 3.0L
Code 23 Heated oxygen sensor; right side on 1992–94 1.8L V6, 1994 2.5L 1990–91 3.0L
Code 24 Closed loop system; right side on 1992–94 1.8L V6, 1993 2.5L 1990–91 3.0L
Code 25 Solenoid valve—pressure regulator
Code 26 Solenoid valve—purge control
Code 26 Solenoid valve—purge control No. 2 (1988–89 3.0L)
Code 27 Solenoid valve—purge control No. 1 (1988–89 3.0L)
Code 27 Solenoid valve—No. 2 purge control (1989 1.6L)
Code 28 Solenoid valve—EGR vacuum
Code 29 Solenoid valve—EGR vent
Code 30 Relay (cold start injector 3.0L)
Code 34 ISC valve
Code 34 Idle air control valve (1993–94 2.0L and 2.5L, 1.6L, 1.8L, 2.6L, 3.1L)
Code 36 Oxygen sensor heater relay (1990 3.0L)
Code 36 Right side oxygen sensor heater (1992–94 3.0L)
Code 37 Left side oxygen sensor heater (1992–94 3.0L)
Code 37 Coolant fan relay
Code 40 Oxygen sensor heater relay (1991 3.0L)
Code 40 Solenoid (triple induction system) and oxygen sensor relay (1988–89 3.0L)
Code 41 Solenoid valve—VRIS (1989–94 MPV 3.0L)
Code 41 Solenoid valve—VRIS 1 (1992–94 1.8L V6, 1993 2.5L)
Code 41 Solenoid valve—VICS (3.0L)
Code 42 Solenoid valve—Waste gate (turbocharged)
Code 46 Solenoid valve—VRIS 2 (1992–94 1.8L V6, 1993 2.5L)
Code 65 A/C signal—PCMT (1992–94 3.0L)
Code 67 Coolant fan relay No. 1 (1993 2.5L)
Code 67 Coolant fan relay No. 2 (1992–94 1.8L V6)
Code 68 Coolant fan relay No. 2, No.3 with ATX (1993 2.5L)
Code 69 Engine coolant temperature sensor—fan (1992–94 1.8L V6, 1993 2.0L and 2.5L)

1984–94 RX-7

1.3L ROTARY ENGINE

Code 01 Crank angle sensor (1984–87)
Code 01 Ignition coil—trailing (1988–91)
Code 02 Air flow meter (1984–87)

Code 02 Ne signal—crank angle sensor (1988–91)
Code 03 Water thermo-sensor (1984–87)
Code 03 G signal—crank angle sensor (1988–91)
Code 04 Intake air temperature sensor—in the air flow meter (1984–87)
Code 05 Oxygen sensor (1984–87)
Code 05 Knock sensor (1993)
Code 06 Throttle sensor (1984–87)
Code 06 Speedometer sensor (1993)
Code 07 Boost sensor / Pressure sensor (1984–87 turbo)
Code 08 Air flow meter (1988–91)
Code 09 Atmospheric pressure sensor (1984–87)
Code 09 Water thermo-sensor (1988–94)
Code 10 Intake air thermo-sensor—in air flow meter (1988–91)
Code 11 Intake air thermo-sensor (1988–93)
Code 12 Coil with igniter—trailing (1984–87)
Code 12 Throttle sensor—wide open throttle (1988–94)
Code 13 Intake manifold pressure sensor (1988–94)
Code 14 Atmospheric pressure sensor (1988–94, in ECU on 1993)
Code 15 Intake air temperature sensor—in dynamic chamber (1984–87)
Code 15 Oxygen sensor (1988–94)
Code 16 EGR switch (1993 California)
Code 17 Closed loop system (1988–93)
Code 18 Throttle sensor—closed or narrow throttle (1988–94)
Code 20 Metering oil pump position sensor (1988–94)
Code 23 Fuel thermo-sensor (1993)
Code 25 Solenoid valve—pressure regulator control (1993)
Code 26 Metering oil pump stepping motor (1993)
Code 27 Step motor—metering oil pump (1988–91)
Code 27 Metering oil pump (1993)
Code 28 Solenoid valve—EGR (1993)
Code 30 Solenoid valve—split air bypass (1988–94)
Code 31 Solenoid valve—relief No. 1 (1988–94)
Code 32 Solenoid valve—switching (1988–94)
Code 33 Solenoid valve—port air bypass (1988–94)
Code 34 Solenoid valve—bypass air control (1988–91)
Code 34 Solenoid valve—idle speed control (1993)
Code 37 Metering oil pump (1988–93)
Code 38 Solenoid valve—accelerated warm-up system (1988–94)
Code 39 Solenoid valve—relief No. 2 (1993)
Code 40 Auxiliary port valve (1988–91)
Code 40 Solenoid valve—purge control (1993)
Code 41 Solenoid valve—variable dynamic effect Intake control (1988–91)
Code 42 Solenoid valve—turbo boost pressure regulator (1988–91)
Code 42 Solenoid valve—turbo pre-control (1993)
Code 43 Solenoid valve—wastegate control (1993)
Code 44 Solenoid valve—turbo control (1993)
Code 45 Solenoid valve—charge control (1993)
Code 46 Solenoid valve—charge relief (1993)
Code 50 Solenoid valve—double throttle control (1993)
Code 51 Fuel pump relay (1988–94)
Code 54 Air pump relay (1993)
Code 71 Injector—front secondary (1988–94)
Code 73 Injector—rear secondary (1988–94)
Code 76 Slip lockup off signal—EC-AT CU (1993)
Code 77 Torque reduced—EC-AT CU (1993)

Mitsubishi

GENERAL INFORMATION

The Electronic Fuel Injection (EFI) system, used on Mitsubishi vehicles, is classified as a Multi-Point Injection (MPI) system. The MPI system controls the fuel flow, idle speed, and ignition timing. The basic function of the MPI system is to control the air/fuel ratio in accordance with all engine operating conditions. An Electronic Control Unit (ECU) is the heart of the MPI system. Based on data from various sensors, the ECU computes the desired air/fuel ratio.

SELF DIAGNOSTICS

Service Precautions

• Before connecting or disconnecting the ECU harness connectors, make sure the ignition switch is **OFF** and the negative battery cable is disconnected to avoid the possibility of damage to the control unit.
• When performing ECU input/output signal diagnosis, remove the pin terminal retainer from the connectors to make it easier to insert tester probes into the connector.
• When connecting or disconnecting pin connectors from the ECU, take care not to bend or break any pin terminals. Check that there are no bends or breaks on ECU pin terminals before attempting any connections.
• Before replacing any ECU, perform the ECU input/output signal diagnosis to make sure the ECU is functioning properly.
• When measuring supply voltage of ECU-controlled components with a circuit tester, separate 1 tester probe from another. If the 2 tester probes accidentally make contact with each other during measurement, a short circuit will result and damage the ECU.

READING TROUBLE CODES

▶ See Figures 42, 43, 44 and 45

➡All though the malfunction indicator light or Malfunction Indicator Lamp (MIL) will illuminate when there is trouble detected, diagnostic codes can only be retrieved with the use of either a analog voltmeter or a Multi-use Tester. When using diagnostic equipment, always observe the tool manufacturer's instructions.

1984–86 Vehicles

WITH ECI/MPI TESTER

Refer to manufacturer's tester manual regarding diagnosis with this tester.

1985–94 Vehicles

WITH ANALOG VOLTMETER

The voltmeter can be used to retrieve code numbers of malfunctions that have happened and were memorized or are continuing to happen. On the voltmeter, the malfunction is indicated by a sweep of the needle. The voltmeter

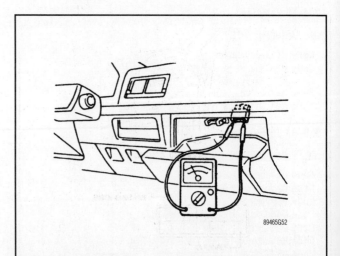

89465G52

Fig. 42 Diagnosis terminal connector location—Galant, Montero, Sigma, Starion and Van/Wagon

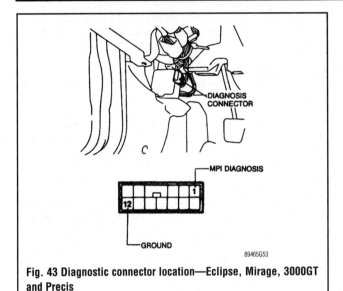

Fig. 43 Diagnostic connector location—Eclipse, Mirage, 3000GT and Precis

should be connected to the data link connector located under the driver side dashboard. Connect the voltmeter between the Multi-Point Injection (MPI) terminal and the ground terminal. Turn the ignition switch **ON** if the normal condition exists, the voltmeter pointer will indicate a normal pattern. A normal pattern is indicated by constant needle sweeps. If a problem exists in the system, the voltmeter pointer will indicate it in a series of pointer sweeps. For example, a Code 3 would be 3 consecutive short sweeps of the voltmeter needle.

If there is more than 1 malfunction, the low code numbers will first be indicated and after a 2 second pause (no code indication) the higher code will be indicated.

WITH MULTI-USE TESTER

To read the trouble codes using the Multi-Use Tester (MB991341 or equivalent) follow the steps below:
1. Turn the ignition switch **OFF**.
2. Insert the power supply terminal to the cigarette lighter socket.
3. Connect the tester connector to the diagnosis connector in the glove compartment, under the hood or under the driver side dashboard.
4. Turn the ignition switch **ON** and push the DIAG key.
5. Observe the trouble code and make the necessary repairs.

On most models the CHECK ENGINE malfunction indicator light will light up and remain illuminated to indicate that there is a problem in the system. After this light has been reported to be **ON**, the system should be checked for malfunction codes.

CLEARING CODES

Without Multi-Use Tester

1984–86 vehicles; engine codes can be cleared by disconnecting the negative battery terminal or by disconnecting ECU connector for 15 seconds or longer.

1987–94 vehicles; engine codes can be cleared by disconnecting the negative battery terminal for 10 seconds or longer.

With Multi-Use Tester

Engine codes may also be cleared by setting the ignition switch to the **ON** position and using the malfunction code ERASE signal.

DIAGNOSTIC TROUBLE CODES

1984–88 Vehicles

CORDIA, GALANT, MIRAGE, STARION, TREDIA, AND VAN/WAGON

Code 1 Oxygen sensor
Code 2 Crank angle sensor
Code 2 Ignition signal
Code 3 Air flow sensor
Code 4 Barometric pressure sensor
Code 5 Throttle Position Sensor (TPS)
Code 6 Motor Position Sensor (MPS)
Code 6 Idle Speed Control (ISC) position sensor
Code 7 Engine Coolant Temperature Sensor
Code 8 No. 1 cylinder TDC Sensor
Code 8 Vehicle speed sensor

➡**Some 1988 Multi-Port injected vehicles use 1989 2-digit codes**

1989–94 Vehicles

DIAMANTE, ECLIPSE, 3000GT, GALANT, MIRAGE, MONTERO, PRECIS, SIGMA, STARION, EXPO, MONTERO, TRUCK AND VAN/WAGON

Code 11 Oxygen sensor
Code 12 Air flow sensor
Code 13 Intake Air Temperature Sensor

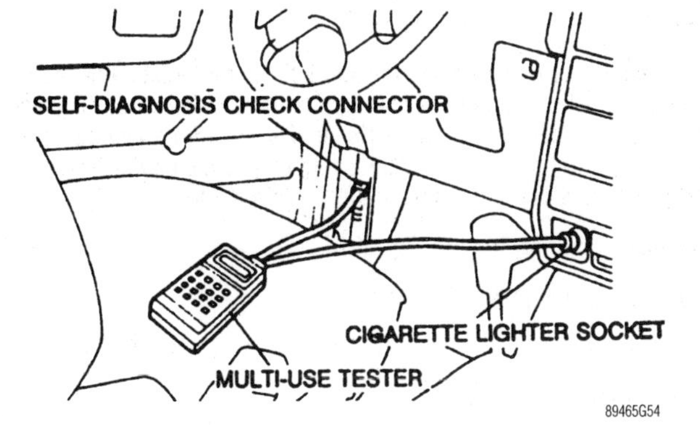

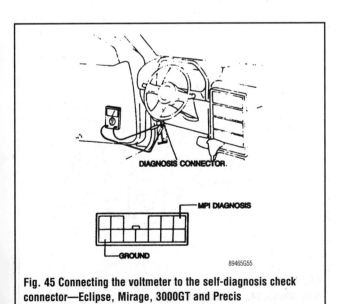

Fig. 44 Connecting the multi-use tester to the self-diagnosis check connector—Eclipse, Mirage, 3000GT and Precis

Fig. 45 Connecting the voltmeter to the self-diagnosis check connector—Eclipse, Mirage, 3000GT and Precis

Code 14 Throttle Position Sensor (TPS)
Code 15 SC Motor Position Sensor (MPS)
Code 21 Engine Coolant Temperature Sensor
Code 22 Crank angle sensor
Code 23 No. 1 cylinder TDC (Camshaft position) Sensor
Code 24 Vehicle speed sensor
Code 25 Barometric pressure sensor
Code 31 Knock (KS) sensor
Code 32 Manifold pressure sensor
Code 36 Ignition timing adjustment signal
Code 39 Oxygen sensor (rear-turbocharged)
Code 41 Injector
Code 42 Fuel pump
Code 43 EGR-California
Code 44 Ignition Coil; power transistor unit (No. 1 and No. 4 cylinders) on 3.0L
Code 52 Ignition Coil; power transistor unit (No. 2 and No. 5 cylinders) on 3.0L
Code 53 Ignition Coil; power transistor unit (No. 3 and No. 6 cylinders)
Code 55 AC valve position sensor
Code 59 Heated oxygen sensor
Code 61 Transaxle control unit cable (automatic transmission)
Code 62 Warm-up control valve position sensor (non-turbo)

Nissan

GENERAL INFORMATION

Nissan uses the ECCS is a fuel injection system that may be either throttle body injection or Multi-port injection. The ECCS system was available as of 1984.

SELF DIAGNOSTICS

Service Precautions

• Do not disconnect the injector harness connectors with the engine running.
• Do not apply battery power directly to the injectors.
• Do not disconnect the ECU harness connectors before the battery ground cable has been disconnected.
• Make sure all ECU connectors are fastened securely. A poor connection can cause an extremely high surge voltage in the coil and condenser and result in damage to integrated circuits.
• When testing the ECU with a DVOM make sure that the probes of the tester never touch each other as this will result in damage to a transistor in the ECU.
• Keep the ECCS harness at least 4 in. away from adjacent harnesses to prevent an ECCS system malfunction due to external electronic noise.
• Keep all parts and harnesses dry during service.
• Before attempting to remove any parts, turn **OFF** the ignition switch and disconnect the battery ground cable.
• Always use a 12 volt battery as a power source.
• Do not attempt to disconnect the battery cables with the engine running or the ignition key **ON**.
• Do not clean the air flow meter with any type of detergent.
• Do not attempt to disassemble the ECCS control unit under any circumstances.
• Avoid static electricity build-up by properly grounding yourself prior to handling any ECU or related parts.

READING TROUBLE CODES

▶ **See Figures 46, 47 and 48**

➡Diagnostic codes may be retrieved by observing the code flashes through the LED lights located on the Electronic Control Module

(ECM). A special Nissan Consult monitor tool can be used, but is not required. When using special diagnostic equipment, always observe the tool manufacturer's instructions.

Electronic Fuel Injection

1984–94 VEHICLES

Two types of diagnostic systems are used in Nissan vehicles: the 2-mode diagnostic system and the 5-mode diagnostic system. The 2 mode system is used in some vehicles starting in 1990, ultimately, all vehicles used the 2-mode system after 1991 with the exception of 1991–94 Maxima (VG30E engine), Pathfinder and Truck. These vehicles continued to use the 5-mode system. The 5-mode system began in 1984.

5-Mode Diagnostic System

The 5-mode diagnostic system is incorporated in the ECU which uses inputs from various sensors to determine the correct air/fuel ratio. If any of the sensors malfunction, the ECU will store the code in memory. The 5-mode diagnostic system is capable of various tests as outlined below. When using these modes, the ECM may have to be removed from its mounting bracket to better access the mode selector switch.

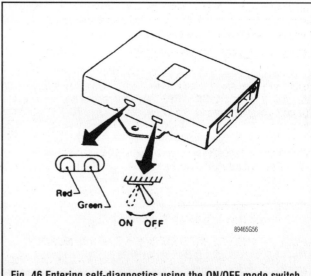

Fig. 46 Entering self-diagnostics using the ON/OFF mode switch

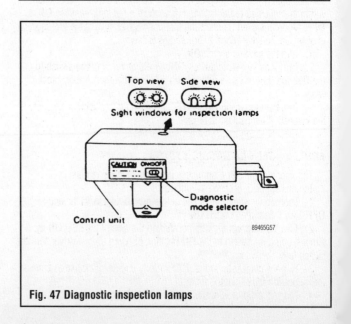

Fig. 47 Diagnostic inspection lamps

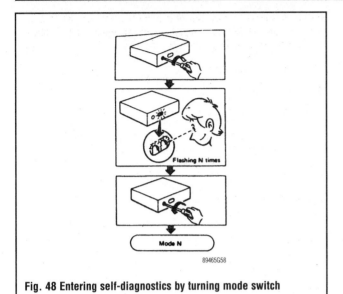

Fig. 48 Entering self-diagnostics by turning mode switch

➡Vehicles are equipped with a malfunction indicator light on the instrument panel. If any systems are malfunctioning, the light will illuminate the same time as the red lamp while the engine is running and the system is in Mode 1.

MODE 1—HEATED OXYGEN SENSOR

During closed loop operation the green lamp turns **ON** when a lean condition is detected and turns **OFF** under a rich condition. During open loop the green lamp remains **ON** or **OFF**. This mode is used to check Heated Oxygen sensor functions for correct operation. To enter Mode 1, proceed as follows:
1. Turn the ignition switch **ON**.
2. Turn the diagnostic switch located on the side of the ECU **ON** by either flipping the switch to the **ON** position or turning the screw switch fully clockwise.
3. Turn the diagnostic switch **OFF** or fully counterclockwise as soon as the inspection lamps flash 1 time.
4. The self-diagnostic system is now in Mode 1.

MODE 2—MIXTURE RATIO FEEDBACK CONTROL MONITOR

The green inspection lamp is operating in the same manner as in Mode 1. During closed loop operation the red inspection lamp turns **ON** and **OFF** simultaneously with the green lamp when the mixture ratio is controlled within the specified value. During open loop the red lamp remains **ON** or **OFF**. Mode 2 is used for checking that optimum control of the fuel mixture is obtained. To enter Mode 2, proceed as follows:
1. Turn the ignition switch **ON**.
2. Turn the diagnostic switch **ON**, by either flipping the switch to the **ON** position or use a screwdriver and turn the switch fully clockwise.
3. Turn the diagnostic switch **OFF** or fully counterclockwise as soon as the inspection lamps flash 2 times.
4. The self-diagnostic system is now in Mode 2.

MODE 3—SELF-DIAGNOSIS SYSTEM

This mode of the self-diagnostics is for stored code retrieval.
To enter Mode 3, proceed as follows:
1. Thoroughly warm the engine before proceeding. With the engine **OFF**, turn the ignition switch **ON**.
2. Turn the diagnostic switch located on the side of the ECU **ON** by either flipping the switch to the **ON** position or using a screwdriver, turn the switch fully clockwise.
3. Turn the diagnostic switch **OFF** or fully counterclockwise as soon as the inspection lamps flash 3 times.
4. The self-diagnostic system is now in Mode 3.

➡When the battery is disconnected or self-diagnostic Mode 4 is selected after using Mode 3, all stored codes will be cleared. However, if the ignition key is turned OFF and then the procedure is followed to enter Mode 4 directly, the stored codes will not be cleared.

5. The codes will now be displayed by the red and green inspection lamps flashing. The red lamp will flash first and the green lamp will follow. The red lamp is the tens and the green lamp is the units, that is, the red lamp flashes 1 time and the green lamp flashes 2 times, this would indicate a Code 12.

MODE 4—ON/OFF SWITCHES

This mode checks the operation of the Vehicle Speed Sensor (VSS), Closed Throttle Position (CTP) and starter switches. Entering this mode will also clear all stored codes in the ECU. To enter Mode 4, proceed as follows:
1. Turn the ignition switch **ON**.
2. Turn the diagnostic switch located on the side of the ECU **ON** by either flipping the switch to the **ON** position or turning the mode switch fully clockwise.
3. Turn the diagnostic switch **OFF** or fully counterclockwise as soon as the inspection lamps flash 4 times.
4. The self-diagnostic system is now in Mode 4.
5. Turn the ignition switch to the **START** position and verify the red inspection lamp illuminates. This verifies that the starter switch is working.
6. Depress the accelerator and verify the red inspection lamp goes **OFF**. This verifies that the CTP switch is working.
7. Raise and properly support the vehicle and verify the lamp goes **ON** when the vehicle speed is above 12 mph (20 km/h). This verifies that the VSS is working
8. Turn the ignition switch **OFF**.

MODE 5—REAL TIME DIAGNOSTICS

◆ See Figures 49 and 50

In this mode the ECU is capable of detecting and alerting the technician the instant a malfunction in the crank angle sensor, air flow meter, ignition signal or the fuel pump occurs while operating/driving the vehicle. Items which are noted to be malfunctioning are not stored in the ECU's memory. To enter Mode 5, proceed as follows:
1. Turn the ignition switch **ON**.
2. Turn the diagnostic switch located on the side of the ECU **ON** by either flipping the switch to the **ON** position or by turning the switch fully clockwise.
3. Turn the diagnostic switch **OFF** or fully counterclockwise as soon as the inspection lamps flash 5 times.

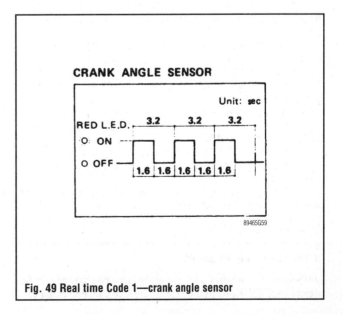

Fig. 49 Real time Code 1—crank angle sensor

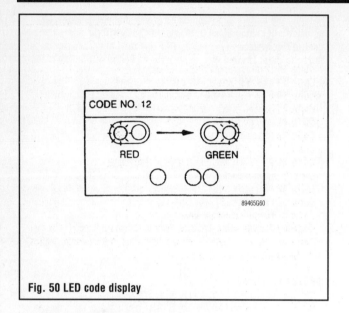

Fig. 50 LED code display

4. The self-diagnostic system is now in Mode 5.
5. Ensure the inspection lamps are not flashing. If they are, count the number of flashes within a 3.2 second period:
- 1 Flash = Crank angle sensor
- 2 Flashes = Air flow meter
- 3 Flashes = Fuel pump
- 4 Flashes = Ignition signal

2-Mode Diagnostic System

▶ See Figures 51, 52 and 53

The 1992—94 300ZX, Stanza, 240SX, Sentra/NX Coupe, Maxima (VE30DE engine), and the 1993–94 Altima and Quest use a 2-mode diagnostic system incorporated in the ECU which uses inputs from various sensors to determine the correct air/fuel ratio. If any of the sensors malfunction the ECU will store the code in memory.

A Nissan Consult monitor, or equivalent may be used to retrieve these codes by simply connecting the monitor to the diagnostic connector located on the driver's side near the hood release. Turn the ignition switch to **ON** and press START, ENGINE and then SELF-DIAG RESULTS, the results will then be output to the monitor.

The conventional CHECK ENGINE or red LED ECU light may also be used for self-diagnostics. The conventional 2-Mode diagnostic system is

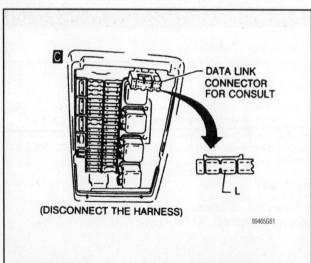

Fig. 51 Data Link connector location—1993–94 Altima and Stanza shown

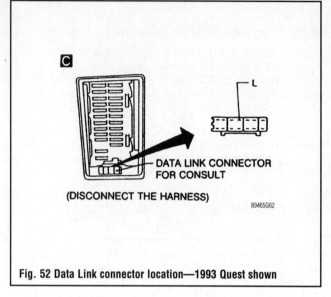

Fig. 52 Data Link connector location—1993 Quest shown

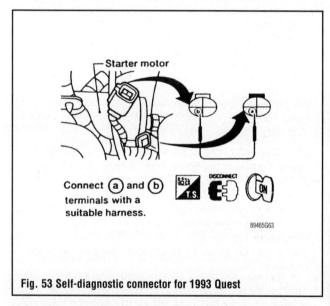

Fig. 53 Self-diagnostic connector for 1993 Quest

broken into 2 separate modes each capable of 2 tests, an ignition switch **ON** or engine running test as outlined below:

MODE 1—BULB CHECK

In this mode the RED indicator light on the ECU and the malfunction indicator light should be **ON**. To enter this mode simply turn the ignition switch **ON** and observe the light.

MODE 1—MALFUNCTION WARNING

In this mode the ECU is acknowledging if there is a malfunction by illuminating the RED indicator light on the ECU and the malfunction indicator light. If the light turns **OFF**, the system is normal. To enter this mode, simply start the engine and observe the light.

MODE 2—SELF-DIAGNOSTIC CODES—EXCEPT QUEST

In this mode the ECU will output all malfunctions via the malfunction indicator light or the red LED on the ECU. The code may be retrieved by counting the number of flashes. The longer flashes indicate the first digit and the shorter flashes indicate the second digit. To enter this mode proceed as follows:
1. Turn the ignition Switch **ON**, but do not start the vehicle.
2. Turn the ECU diagnostic mode selector fully clockwise for 2 seconds, then turn it back fully counterclockwise.

3. Observe the red LED on the ECU or malfunction indicator light for stored codes.

MODE 2—SELF-DIAGNOSTIC CODES—QUEST

In this mode the ECU will output all malfunctions via the malfunction indicator light or the red LED on the ECU. The code may be retrieved by counting the number of flashes. The longer flashes indicate the first digit and the shorter flashes indicate the second digit. To enter this mode proceed as follows:

1. Turn the ignition switch **ON**, but do not start the vehicle.
2. Disconnect harness connectors and connect terminals A and B with a jumper wire.
3. Wait 2 seconds, remove the jumper wire and reconnect the harness connector.
4. Observe the malfunction indicator light for stored codes.

MODE 2—EXHAUST GAS SENSOR MONITOR

In this mode the red LED on the ECU or malfunction indicator light will display the condition of the fuel mixture and whether the system is in closed loop or open loop. When the light flashes **ON**, the exhaust gas sensor is indicating a lean mixture. When the light stays **OFF**, the sensor is indicating a rich mixture. If the light remains **ON** or **OFF**, it is indicating an open loop system. If the system is equipped with 2 exhaust gas sensors, the left side will operate first. If already in Mode 2, proceed to Step C to enter the exhaust gas sensor monitor.

1. On all models except Quest, perform the following steps:
   a. Turn the ignition switch **ON**.
   b. Turn the diagnostic switch **ON**, by turning the switch fully clockwise for 2 seconds and then fully counterclockwise.
   c. Start the engine and run until thoroughly warm. Raise the idle to 2,000 rpm and hold for approximately 2 minutes. Ensure the red LED or malfunction indicator light flashes **ON** and **OFF** more than 5 times every 10 seconds with the engine speed at 2,000 rpm.

➡If equipped with 2 exhaust gas sensors, switch to the right sensor by turning the ECU mode selector fully clockwise for 2 seconds and then fully counterclockwise with the engine running.

2. On Quest models, perform the following steps:
   a. Turn the ignition switch **ON**.
   b. Disconnect harness connectors and connect terminals A and B with a jumper wire.
   c. Wait 2 seconds, remove the jumper wire and reconnect the harness connectors.
   d. Start the engine and run until thoroughly warm. Raise the idle to 2,000 rpm and hold for approximately 2 minutes. Ensure the red LED or malfunction indicator light flashes **ON** and **OFF** more than 5 times every 10 seconds with the engine speed at 2,000 rpm.

CLEARING CODES

Except Mode 5, 3 and 2 Systems

All control unit diagnostic codes may be cleared by disconnecting the negative battery cable for a period of 15 seconds. Entering Mode 4 of the Electronic Fuel Injection system diagnostics will also clear stored ECM engine codes.

Mode 5, 3 and 2 Systems

On 5-mode systems, enter mode 4 immediately after using mode 3 and the codes will be cleared. On 2-mode systems, the codes will be cleared when mode 1 is re-entered from mode 2. The Nissan Consult Monitor or equivalent can also be used to clear codes on 2-mode systems.

DIAGNOSTIC TROUBLE CODES

1984–87 Vehicles

Code 11 Crankshaft position sensor circuit
Code 12 Mass Air flow sensor circuit
Code 13 Engine coolant temperature sensor circuit
Code 21 Ignition signal circuit
Code 22 Fuel pump circuit
Code 23 Idle switch circuit
Code 24 Transmission switch
Code 31 AC switch, fast idle control of load signal
Code 32 Starter signal
Code 33 EGR gas sensor
Code 34 Detonation (Knock) sensor
Code 41 Air or Fuel temperature sensor
Code 42 Throttle sensor (or BP sensor in Canada)
Code 43 Mixture feedback control slips out (or low battery in Canada)
Code 44 No Malfunctioning circuits

1988–94 Vehicles

Code 11 Crankshaft position sensor circuit
Code 12 Mass Air flow sensor circuit
Code 13 Engine coolant temperature sensor circuit
Code 14 Vehicle speed sensor circuit
Code 15 Mixture ratio feedback control slips out (1988)
Code 21 Ignition signal circuit
Code 22 Fuel pump circuit (to 1991)
Code 23 Idle switch circuit (to 1991)
Code 24 Fuel Switch circuit or O.D. switch circuit (to 1990)
Code 25 AAC valve circuit (to 1991)
Code 31 Electronic Control Module (ECM) or A/C circuit
Code 32 Exhaust Gas Recirculation (EGR) function
Code 33 Oxygen sensor circuit (left side, if two)
Code 34 Knock sensor circuit
Code 35 Exhaust gas temperature sensor circuit
Code 41 Air temperature sensor circuit
Code 42 Fuel temperature sensor circuit
Code 43 Throttle position sensor circuit
Code 44 No malfunctioning circuits
Code 45 Injector leak
Code 51 Injector circuit
Code 53 Heated oxygen sensor circuit (right side)
Code 54 Signal circuit from A/T control unit to ECM
Code 55 No malfunctioning in the above circuits

Porsche

GENERAL INFORMATION

Except 911 Turbo

Porsche vehicles use 2 forms of electronic fuel injection. The 928 uses LH-Jetronic fuel injection. The 911, 944 and the 968 use Digital Motor Electronics (DME) fuel injection. Both systems are advanced versions of their fuel injection systems and provide excellent control of emissions, fuel economy and performance.

911 Turbo

The Porsche 911 Turbo has always been a specialized vehicle. The latest version is a hybrid of the 911 Carrera 2 body and the proven 3.3L turbocharged engine. While the 3.6L engine of the Carrera 2 uses Digital Motor Electronics as the fuel injection system, the 911 Turbo has used since its introduction the traditional Continuous Injection System (CIS).

SELF DIAGNOSTICS

Service Precautions

- Do not disconnect the battery or power to the control unit before reading the fault codes. Fault code memory is erased when power is interrupted.
- Make sure the ignition switch is **OFF** before disconnecting any wiring.
- Before removing or installing a control unit, disconnect the negative battery cable. The unit receives power through the main connector at all times and will be permanently damaged if improperly powered up or down.
- Keep all parts and harnesses dry during service. Protect the control unit and all solid-state components from rough handling or extremes of temperature.
- All air bag system wiring is in a yellow harness. Use extreme care when working around this wiring. Do not test these circuits without first disconnecting the air bag units.

READING TROUBLE CODES

➡Vehicles prior to 1991 with self diagnostic capability require the use of special tool 9288 Tester or 9268 flash tester to retrieve diagnostics codes. On 1991 and later models, the flash codes can be read on the malfunction indicator light on the instrument panel. When using special diagnostic equipment, always observe the tool manufacturer's instructions.

➡1987 vehicles with LH and EZK systems did not have OBD capability.

1987–93 Vehicles

WITH 9288 DIAGNOSTIC TESTER

When the tester is attached to the diagnostic connector, the control units will present country and application codes to the tester for display on the screen. The tester will then provide a menu with instructions for retrieving fault codes from the control unit memory. If the tester display shows fault not present, this indicates the fault is intermittent or the conditions under which the fault occurs do not exist at this time. The necessary conditions will be displayed on the screen. If the display shows signal not plausible, the input or output signal does exist but is out of the correct operating range.

WITHOUT 9288 DIAGNOSTIC TESTER

The control unit is equipped with a self diagnostic program that will detect emissions related malfunctions and turn the malfunction indicator light **ON** while the engine is running. Emissions related fault codes stored in the control unit can be read with the 9268 flash tester. On 1991 and later models, the flash codes can be read on the malfunction indicator light on the instrument panel. Only faults that may effect exhaust emissions are reported as flash codes. All other codes are only accessible with the 9288 Diagnostic Tester.

1. If required, connect the flash tester to the diagnostic connector using the adapter connector.
2. Turn the ignition switch **ON** without starting the engine.
3. Fully press the accelerator pedal to close the full load switch. After about 3 seconds the malfunction indicator light or tester will flash.
4. When the pedal is released, flash codes will be reported. All codes are 4 digits. Each digit will be flashed with about 2.5 seconds between digits. When the whole code has been displayed, the light will stay **ON** or **OFF**. Count the flashes and write the numbers down. If Code 1500 or 2500 is displayed, no codes are stored in memory.
5. Repeat Steps 3 and 4 until Code 1000 appears, indicating all codes have been reported. On 928 models, the EZK unit will display Code 2000 when all codes have been reported.

➡On all 928 models, if the first digit is 2, the fault is in the EZK ignition system control unit.

If the second digit is 1, the detected fault is current. If the second digit is 2, the detected fault has not occurred during the last running of the vehicle but did occur within the last 50 engine starts. The remaining 2 digits indicate which component or circuit is at fault.

CLEARING CODES

1987–93 VEHICLES

The fault code memory should be cleared before returning the vehicle to service. All Codes in memory and the idle control adaptation are lost when the control unit or the battery is disconnected. To avoid the loss of the learned idle program, use the instructions on the 9288 tester to clear the memory. If this tester is not available, disconnect the battery or control unit to clear the memory. It will be necessary to drive the vehicle for at least 6 minutes and run the engine at idle for about 10 minutes so the control unit can learn idle speed, timing and mixture parameters. Make sure the engine is at operating temperature and that all accessories are **OFF**. The throttle-at-idle position switch must be closed and functioning or system adaptation will not take place.

DIAGNOSTIC TROUBLE CODES

Code 1223 Coolant temperature sensor
Code 1224 Air temperature sensor
Code 1231 Battery voltage
Code 1232 Throttle idle switch
Code 1233 Throttle full load switch
Code 1251 Fuel injector group 1, even numbers
Code 1252 Fuel injector group 2, odd numbers
Code 1261 Fuel pump relay
Code 1262 Idle speed control actuator
Code 1263 Carbon canister purge valve
Code 1264 Oxygen sensor heater relay
Code 1221 Control unit self test
Code 1215 Airflow sensor
Code 1221 Oxygen sensor
Code 1222 Oxygen regulation

SAAB

GENERAL INFORMATION

▶ **See Figures 54, 55, 56 and 57**

The LH-Jetronic fuel injection system was introduced in the Saab 900 in 1985. The 9000 picked it up in 1986. The 1990 models and in some markets 1991–94 models are equipped with an LH 2.4 fuel system Electronic Control Unit (ECU). Most 1991–94 models, are equipped with an LH 2.4.2 fuel system ECU, except the 1991 9000 with the B234 engine, which has an LH 2.4.1 fuel system ECU. Turbocharged 900 models are also equipped with an Automatic Performance Control (APC) ECU and 9000 models are equipped with an integrated Direct Ignition-Automatic Performance Control (DI/APC) control unit, which control ignition functions and turbocharger-related functions.

The LH-system ECU has the particular fuel system identification marked on it for identification. Visually, the LH 2.4 fuel system can be differentiated from the LH 2.4.2 fuel system by the pins on the Automatic Idle Control (AIC) valve. The LH 2.4 fuel system AIC valve has 2 pins and the LH 2.4.2 fuel system AIC valve has 3 pins.

The LH 2.4.1 fuel system differs from the LH 2.4 fuel system in that the cold start injector has been discontinued. The direct ignition system has taken over this function. Also, the vehicle speed sensor is used in the control of the AIC function to tell the fuel system ECU whether the car is moving or at a standstill.

The LH 2.4 (some markets) and LH 2.4.2 fuel systems with the Electronic Throttle System (ETS), used on the 1992–94 9000 with traction control, differ from the systems without ETS in the following ways: The electronically controlled throttle eliminates the need for automatic idling and load control throughout the load range, the throttle angle transmitter is located in the actuator motor, which is integrated with the throttle housing and the electronically controlled throttle system carries out compensation for the air conditioning. Vehicles with ETS also have an Automatic Slip Reduction (ASR) control unit that carries out other traction control system functions.

Visually, the throttle housing on engines with ETS is larger, is vacuum operated and has an emergency cable, but in other respects this system operates in the same way as the LH 2.4 and 2.4.2 systems without ETS.

The central component of the LH-Jetronic fuel injection system is the air mass meter that measures the mass of air flow instead of the volume. The microprocessor measures how much electrical energy is used when air flow passes an electrically heated platinum wire in the air mass meter. The higher the rate of air flow, the higher the energy necessary to keep the temperature of the wire constant. At the same time, the microprocessor monitors the engine speed and temperature, calculating the exact amount of fuel needed for optimum performance. The microprocessor also incorporates an rpm limiter that ensures that no opening signals will be transmitted to the injectors at engine speeds above 6000 rpm.

The LH-Jetronic fuel injection system provides the air mass meter with a self-cleaning function. During burn-off the platinum wire in the air mass meter is quickly heated to about 1800°F (1000°C) for a 1 second duration, 4 seconds after the ignition is switched **OFF**. This burns away any deposits on the wire that would be detrimental to efficient operation.

The APC system on turbocharged vehicles enables the engine to achieve optimum performance and good fuel economy, regardless of the grade of fuel being used. A knock sensor, in conjunction with the pressure transducer and ignition system information, detects knocking in the engine and sends an electrical signal to the microprocessor inside the ECU. The ECU processes these signals and sends electrical pulses to a solenoid valve that controls the charging pressure in the intake manifold. The turbocharger is designed to come into operation at fairly low engine speeds, thereby providing a high torque within the speed range of normal driving. It is water cooled and the coolant for the bearing housing is supplied by a pipe connected to the cooling system.

Charging pressure is regulated by a pressure regulator valve (known as a wastegate). The charging pressure regulator is fitted to the exhaust side of the engine and regulates the flow of exhaust gas to the compressor. The valve remains closed when the engine load is low. As the demand on the engine is increased, the wastegate opens.

The DI/APC system was updated in 1991 to include an air temperature sensor, located upstream of the throttle housing. The boost pressure is governed by the position of the throttle valve, but it is subject to temperature compensation based on information supplied by the new air temperature sensor. The separate pressure-switch function is discontinued, with the pressure-sensing function now being regulated by the DI/APC system ECU. The load signal provided by the air mass meter is sent to the LH-system ECU, which will keep the DI/APC system ECU informed of boost status.

Starting in 1991 there is also a spark plug burn-off function that occurs when the engine is stopped. The burn-off function, which operates in all

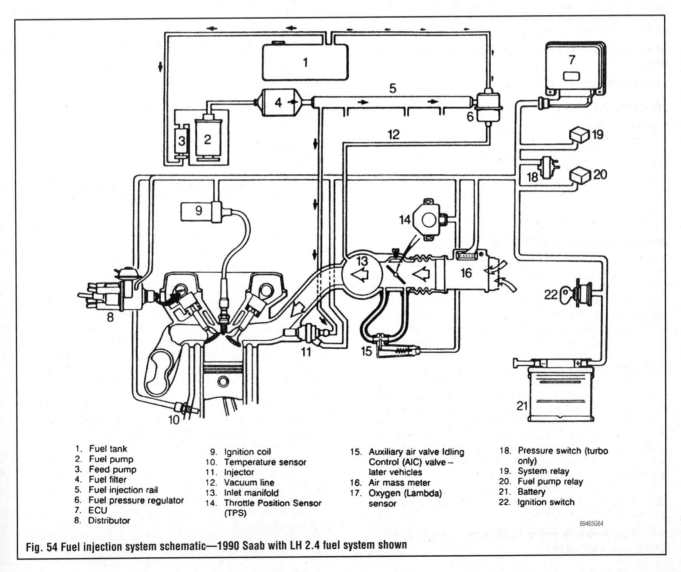

1. Fuel tank
2. Fuel pump
3. Feed pump
4. Fuel filter
5. Fuel injection rail
6. Fuel pressure regulator
7. ECU
8. Distributor
9. Ignition coil
10. Temperature sensor
11. Injector
12. Vacuum line
13. Inlet manifold
14. Throttle Position Sensor (TPS)
15. Auxiliary air valve Idling Control (AIC) valve – later vehicles
16. Air mass meter
17. Oxygen (Lambda) sensor
18. Pressure switch (turbo only)
19. System relay
20. Fuel pump relay
21. Battery
22. Ignition switch

Fig. 54 Fuel injection system schematic—1990 Saab with LH 2.4 fuel system shown

cylinders simultaneously, lasts for 5 seconds at a frequency corresponding to 6000 rpm.

Turbocharged California vehicles, except the 1991–94 9000 Turbo with the B234 engine, are equipped with an electronically controlled EGR system. A modulating valve functions as a 3-way valve as it controls the vacuum to the EGR valve. A vacuum regulator is incorporated in the modulating valve to maintain a constant vacuum to the EGR valve. A vacuum storage tank is connected via a vacuum check valve to the intake manifold. The check valve prevents the loss of vacuum in the tank during

acceleration. An EGR temperature sensor provides information to the LH-system ECU. If the temperature deviates from a normal range, a problem is indicated due to improper exhaust gas flow in the EGR pipe and a fault code will be set.

The LH-Jetronic system also incorporates an emergency system known as a limp home function. If a malfunction is detected, the limp home feature of the ECU is actuated, enabling the vehicle to continue its journey, but with somewhat diminished performance. If the vehicle is operated in this mode, the malfunction indicator light (CEL) on the display panel will be illumi-

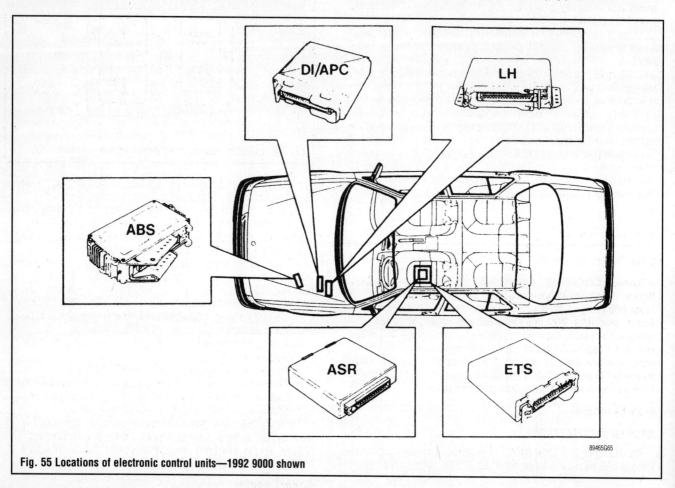

Fig. 55 Locations of electronic control units—1992 9000 shown

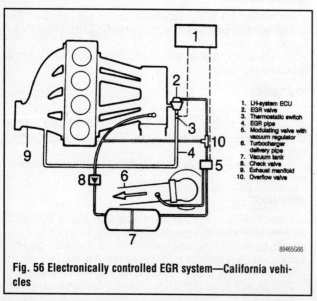

Fig. 56 Electronically controlled EGR system—California vehicles

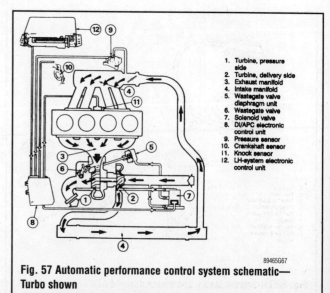

Fig. 57 Automatic performance control system schematic—Turbo shown

nated. An integrated fault-storing capability enables diagnosis to be carried out efficiently.

SELF DIAGNOSTICS

Service Precautions

• Before connecting or disconnecting ECU harness connectors, make sure the ignition switch is **OFF** and the negative battery cable is disconnected to avoid the possibility of damage to the control unit.

• When connecting or disconnecting pin connectors from the ECU, take care not to bend or break any pin terminals. Check that there are no bends or breaks on ECU pin terminals before attempting any connections.

• Before replacing any ECU, perform ECU input/output signal diagnosis to determine if the ECU is functioning properly.

• When measuring supply voltage of ECU controlled components with a circuit tester, separate 1 tester probe from another. If the 2 tester probes accidentally make contact with each other during measurement, a short circuit may result and damage the ECU.

• Always disarm the airbag (SRS) system when working on the airbag or ABS system.

• Always verify the ignition is switched **OFF** before connecting or disconnecting any electrical connections, especially connections to a control unit.

READING TROUBLE CODES

▶ **See Figures 58 and 59**

➡**Diagnostic codes may be retrieved by observing the code flashes through the malfunction indicator light or Malfunction Indicator Lamp (MIL) only on vehicles listed under "Without Diagnostic Tester" procedure. With this procedure a basic jumper switch (momentary type) is required to activate the computer. Other vehicles would require the use of special diagnostic tools: LH System tester or a ISAT Tester to retrieve codes. Read all procedures before attempting to perform checks. When using special diagnostic tools always observe the tool manufacturer's instructions.**

1985–94 Vehicles

WITH LH SYSTEM TESTER

The Saab LH system tester 8394223 has been developed to simplify service and fault diagnosis work on the LH fuel injection system. The tester

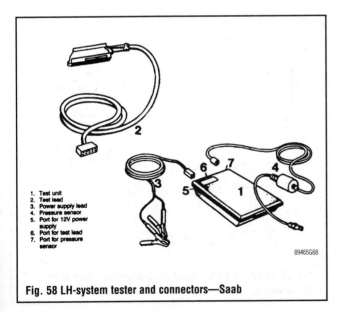

1. Test unit
2. Test lead
3. Power supply lead
4. Pressure sensor
5. Port for 12V power supply
6. Port for test lead
7. Port for pressure sensor

89465G68

Fig. 58 LH-system tester and connectors—Saab

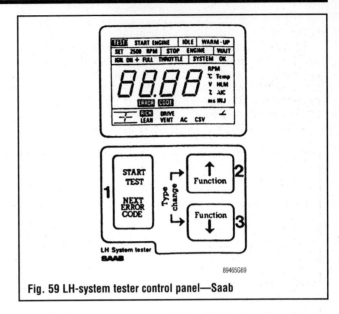

Fig. 59 LH-system tester control panel—Saab

consists of a test unit, power supply lead, test lead incorporating a 2-way 35-pin connector and a pressure sensor with magnetic base.

The tester is equipped with an automatic program for diagnosing faults, both permanent and intermittent, while the vehicle is operating. Faults detected are then stored in memo for recall after the vehicle is road-tested. Connect the diagnostic tester, or equivalent, as follows:

1. Insert the power supply lead between the door and body where there is a break in the seal, then run it under the back of the hood on the left hand side.

2. Clean the battery terminals to ensure proper contact with lead clips.

3. Connect the power supply lead to the tester first, then connect the lead clips to the battery.

4. Remove the cover on the left side over the space behind the false bulkhead panel.

5. Remove the ABS system ECU and bracket, if equipped.

6. Remove the LH system ECU connector. Connect the test lead between the LH-system ECU and the vehicle's wiring loom. Fit a couple of ties around the connector and ECU to hold them tightly together.

The tester, designed to perform 3 basic functions, monitor mode, test mode and fuel mode, is now in start mode. If at any time the operation in progress must be interrupted, simultaneously press all 3 control buttons and the tester will revert to the starting point.

MONITOR MODE

The monitor mode can be selected either by switching the ignition **ON**, or if the ignition is **OFF**, by pressing the START TEST button when MON appears on the tester display.

When in monitor mode, the tester is used to manually control parameter and functional checks.

TEST MODE

Test mode can only be selected from the monitor mode. Once the LH system version has been selected, the test mode can be activated. Press the START TEST button to select the test mode. TEST will now appear on the display.

In the test mode, the program instructs by way of prompts in the upper part of the display.

FUEL MODE

To select the fuel mode, the ignition must be **OFF**. Initially, MON will be displayed on the tester for approximately 5 seconds. During this time, if required, the monitor mode can be selected. If none of the tester buttons are activated, FUEL will appear on the display for approximately 2 seconds. To activate the fuel mode, press the START button when FUEL is displayed.

When the tester is in fuel mode the following checks can be performed:

- Fuel pump delivery flow
- Fuel pressure and fuel-pressure regulator
- Residual pressure
- Fuel pump delivery pressure Delivery flow from injectors

WITHOUT DIAGNOSTIC TESTER

▶ See Figures 60, 61 and 62

This method can be used to retrieve fault codes from 1988–94 Saab models equipped with LH 2.4, LH 2.4.1 and LH 2.4.2 fuel injection systems. These systems are capable of an internal self-diagnostic checks and have the ability to store up to 3 intermittent faults at a time. Serious malfunctions are always given priority and must be rectified before the memory can store information on minor faults. The built in diagnosis function also has the capability to manually test the components and signals of the LH system.

The Saab switched jumper lead 8393886, or equivalent, is necessary to conduct these tests.

Connect the switched jumper lead for as follows:

For the Saab 900, Use the switched jumper lead to connect the No. 3 pin in the 3-pin test socket, on the right-hand side in the engine compartment, to the battery ground (negative terminal).

For the Saab 9000, use the switched jumper lead to connect the 3-pin socket, in the test box on the left-hand side of the engine compartment, to the battery ground (negative terminal).

1. Switch the ignition ON. The malfunction indicator light should now illuminate.

2. Set the jumper switch to ON (grounding ECU pin 16). The malfunction indicator light should now be extinguished.

3. Watch the malfunction indicator light carefully. After about 2.5 seconds, it will flash briefly, signifying that the first error code is about to display.

4. As soon as the light has flashed, turn the jumper switch OFF.

5. The first of a possible 3 error codes will now be displayed by a series of short flashes. The number 1 is represented by a single flash followed by a long pause. The number 2 is represented by 2 flashes separated from each other by a short pause, but separated from the next number by a long pause. The number 3 would consist of 3 flashes separated by short pauses and followed by a long pause, and so on. For example Code 12112 would consist of: flash-long pause, flash-short pause, flash-long pause, flash-long pause, flash-long pause, flash-short pause, flash-long pause. The code will be displayed repeatedly until the next test step is taken.

6. To check for any additional error codes, turn the jumper switch ON.

7. Watch the malfunction indicator light carefully. After a short flash, turn the jumper switch OFF.

8. If present, the next error code will now display in the same fashion as the first.

9. If there are no more faults stored or all faults have been remedied, an uninterrupted series of flashes will be displayed.

10. Follow the same procedure until all faults have been identified and corrected.

11. To restart the test procedure (return to the first fault), set the jumper switch to ON.

12. After 2 short flashes, turn the jumper switch OFF. The fault code for the first fault should now be displayed.

13. Proceed with the test from Step 5.

TESTING COMPONENTS AND SIGNALS

1. Connect the jumper lead in the same manner as for reading fault codes.
2. Set the jumper switch to ON.
3. Turn the ignition switch ON and wait for a short flash of the malfunction indicator light.
4. Immediately following the flash, turn the jumper switch OFF.
5. The moment the malfunction indicator light begins flashing, the fuel pump should begin running for about 1 second (if it is not faulty). There will be no identification codes sent during this test.
6. To move on to the next test, set the jumper switch to ON.
7. After a short flash, set the jumper switch to OFF. A test code (NOT FAULT CODE) will be displayed and the corresponding component will activate.

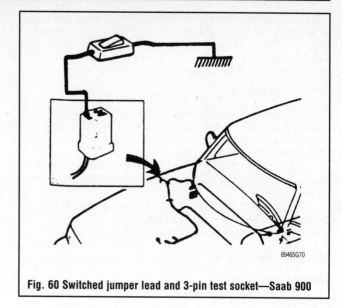

Fig. 60 Switched jumper lead and 3-pin test socket—Saab 900

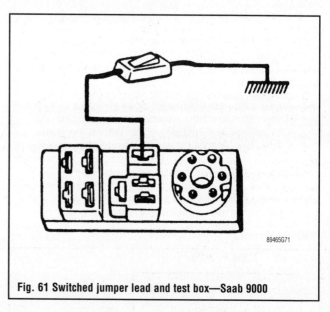

Fig. 61 Switched jumper lead and test box—Saab 9000

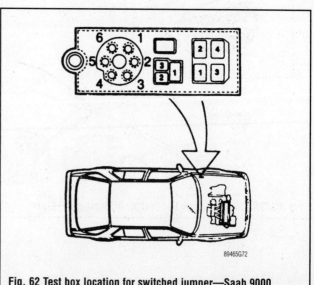

Fig. 62 Test box location for switched jumper—Saab 9000

8. Continue through the remaining items in the test sequence in the same method—set switch to **ON**, wait for a short flash, set the switch to **OFF**.

Components and signals are checked in the following order:
- Fuel pump (no code displayed).
- Injection valves (1.5 ms-10 Hz).
- AIC valve (switches between open and closed positions).
- EVAP Canister Purge valve (switches between closed and open)—CHECK ENGINE flashing stops. EGR valve operates—CHECK ENGINE flashing stops. Drive signal (changes when shifting from D to N)—CHECK ENGINE flashing stops.
- Air conditioning operates—CHECK ENGINE flashing stops. Throttle position switch position (changes as accelerator is depressed)—CHECK ENGINE flashing stops.
- Throttle position switch WOT position (changes as accelerator is pressed down to the floor)—CHECK ENGINE flashing stops.
- Fuel pump operates—CHECK ENGINE flashing stops.

1990–94 Vehicles

WITH SAAB ISAT TESTER

♦ See Figures 63 and 64

The Saab SAT tester is also available to extract fault codes, both constant and intermittent, or to issue command codes.

Read codes with the ISAT tester, or equivalent, as follows:
1. Never unplug connector from the ECU or disconnect a battery lead before the fault data stored in the ECU has been transferred to the tester.
2. Connect the diagnostic tester to the diagnostic socket. The diagnosis socket is a black 10-pin connector located under the RH front seat.
3. Turn the ignition to the **ON** position.
4. Press the No. 1 on the ISAT to identify that you are checking the LH system.

The Trionic system engine fault codes can be read in the same manner, but the Saab adapter # 8611188 must be used with SAT and current EPROM update.

Fig. 64 ISAT tester—Saab

EZK IGNITION CODES

♦ See Figure 65

The EZK ignition system is capable of self diagnostics only with the aid of the system tester 8394058, or equivalent. The test should be performed only in the event that a malfunction is suspected or when adjusting ignition timing. Read fault codes as follows:
1. With the ignition switch **OFF**, connect the tester to the test box on the left-hand side of the engine compartment on the Saab 9000 or to the test socket located forward of the electrical distribution box on the Saab 900.
2. Turn the ignition switch **ON** and start engine. The fault indication LED (green) on the tester should illuminate for about 2 seconds while the starter motor is running.
3. Warm the engine to normal operating temperature, making sure that the engine is briefly run above 2300 rpm at some point during warm-up.
4. Run engine at idling speed and check tester LEDs for flashing. (mal-

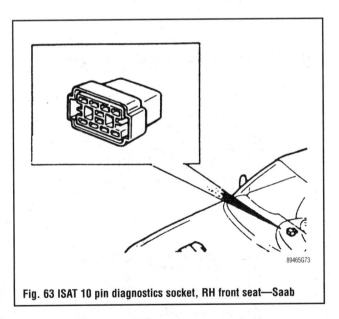

Fig. 63 ISAT 10 pin diagnostics socket, RH front seat—Saab

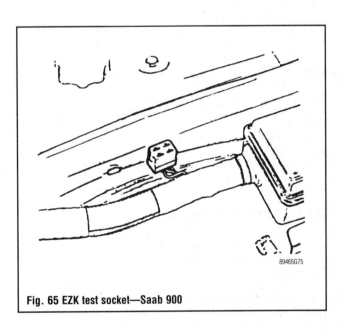

Fig. 65 EZK test socket—Saab 900

function indicator light will flash at a corresponding rate to any green LED fault indication.) The red LED light indicates spark knocking.

5. The fault code is determined by counting the number of LED flashes.

➡**The EZK ignition fault codes can also be read with the Saab ISAT tester. To pull the ignition codes, follow the procedure for reading LH fuel system codes with ISAT. The EZK codes will be displayed with the fuel system fault codes. The malfunction indicator light will illuminate steady if the EZK or fuel system has a fault in memory.**

DI/APC IGNITION CODES

The Saab combined Direct Ignition and Automatic Performance Control (DI/APC) system is controlled by the LH fuel injection ECU. The DI/APC system is an adaptive system which compensates for engine wear and other conditions which would adversely affect engine performance. With the aid of the Saab ISAT tester, or equivalent, it is possible to extract fault codes, both constant and intermittent or to issue command codes.

READ CODES WITH THE SAT TESTER AS FOLLOWS:

1. Never unplug connector from the ECU or disconnect a battery lead before the fault data stored in the ECU has been transferred to the ISAT.
2. The diagnosis socket is a black 10-pin connector located under the RH front seat.
3. Turn the ignition switch to the **ON** position.
4. Press No. 2 on the SAT tester to identify the DI/APC system and follow the instructions in the ISAT manual that accompany the tester to

ELECTRONIC THROTTLE CONTROL (ETS) CODES

A Saab ISAT tester must be used to access the fault codes. Make sure to use the correct code chart when diagnosing fault codes, the codes differ for automatic and manual transmissions. Read codes with SAT tester as follows:

1. Never unplug connector from the ECU or disconnect a battery lead before the fault data stored in the ECU has been transferred to the tester.
2. Connect the diagnostic tester to the diagnostic socket. The diagnosis socket is a black 10-pin diagnostic connector located under the RH front seat.
3. Turn the ignition to the **ON** position.
4. Press the No. 3 on the ISAT to identify that you are checking the ETS system.

CLEARING CODES

1985–94 Vehicles

WITH LH SYSTEM TESTER

After completing repairs, reset the tester to the start mode by pressing all 3 control buttons at the same time. If fault codes are still found, disconnect the battery for at least 10 minutes or road test vehicle for 10 minutes or until malfunction indicator light extinguishes. The fault code should erase itself after extended operation with the repaired component.

WITH SAAB ISAT TESTER

After repairs are completed, the ISAT command code 900 is used to clear diagnostic memory.

WITHOUT SYSTEM TESTER

1. Set the jumper switch to **ON**.
2. After 3 short flashes, turn the jumper switch **OFF**.
3. The malfunction indicator light will now either flash in a continuous series of long flashes (this represents Code 00000) or display the Code 12444, indicating that the contents of the memory have been erased.

EZK Ignition Codes

The EZK ignition does not store intermittent fault codes. All codes should clear when repair procedures are carried out.

DI/APC Ignition Codes

After repairs are completed, the ISAT command Code 900 is used to clear diagnostic memory.

Electronic Throttle Control (ETS) System Codes

After repairs are completed, the SAT command Code 900 is used to clear diagnostic memory. A confirmation code "11111" will be displayed after the codes have been successfully erased. If this display is not received, repeat the code erasure procedure.

DIAGNOSTIC TROUBLE CODES

1988–94 Flash Codes

Fault codes on 1988–94 vehicles using LH 2.4, 2.4.1 and LH 2.4.2 fuel injected systems may be read without the use of a diagnostic tester.

Code 00000 No more faults or faults not detected
Code 12111 Oxygen sensor adaptation fault; air/fuel mixture during idling
Code 12112 Oxygen sensor adaptation fault; air/fuel mixture with engine running
Code 12113 Idling control (IAC) adaptation fault; pulse ratio too low
Code 12114 Idling control (IAC) adaptation fault; pulse ratio too high
Code 12211 Incorrect battery voltage with engine running (below 10V or over 16V)
Code 12212 Throttle Position Sensor; faulty idling contacts (grounding when throttle open)
Code 12213 Throttle Position Sensor; faulty full-throttle contacts (grounding when engine idling)
Code 12214 Engine Coolant Temperature sensor signal; faulty (signal below -90 degrees or above 160 degrees Centigrade)
Code 12221 Mass Air Flow (MAF) sensor signal; missing (engine in limp-home mode)
Code 12222 Idling adjustment (IAC); faulty
Code 12223 Air/Fuel mixture; lean
Code 12224 Air/Fuel mixture; rich
Code 12225 Heated Oxygen sensor; faulty or preheating defective (engine temperature must be 80 degrees Centigrade
Code 12231 No ignition signal; (always occurs with the engine switched off)
Code 12232 Memory voltage greater than 1V
Code 12233 Change made in EPROM (ROM fault 1992 and newer)
Code 12241 Fuel injector malfunction (1992 and newer)
Code 12242 Mass Air Flow (MAF) sensor; No filament burn-off (1992 and newer)
Code 12243 Vehicle Speed Sensor (VSS) signal; missing
Code 12244 No drive signal to pin 30 in ECM (automatic transmission, 1992 and newer)
Code 12245 EGR function faulty
Code 12251 Throttle Position (TP) sensor is faulty (1992 and newer)
Code 12252 EVAP canister purge valve not working (1992 and newer)
Code 12253 PRE-Ignition signal lasts more than 20 seconds (1992 and newer)
Code 12254 Engine RPM signal is missing (1992 and newer)

1985–94 LH-Tester

Fault codes on 1985–94 vehicles using LH 2.2 and LH 2.4 fuel injection systems may be read by using an LH system tester.

Code E001 No ignition pulse
Code E002 No signal from Coolant Temperature Sensor (CTS) (LH 2.2) or Throttle Position Sensor (TPS); idling contacts not closing on idling (LH 2.4)
Code E003 Throttle Position Sensor (TPS); idling contacts not closing on idling (LH 2.2) or Throttle Position Sensor (TPS); full load contacts constantly open (LH 2.4)
Code E004 Battery voltage to Electronic Control Unit (ECU) memory; missing

Code E005 Electronic Control Unit (ECU) pin 5 not grounding
Code E006 Air Mass Meter (AMM) not grounding
Code E007 No signal from Air Mass Meter (AMM)
Code E008 Air Mass Meter (AMM); no filament burn-off function
Code E009 No power to system relay
Code E010 No signal from Electronic Control Unit (ECU) pin 10 to Automatic Idle Control (AIC) valve
Code E011 Electronic Control Unit (ECU) pin 11 not grounding
Code E012 Throttle Position sensor (TPS)—full throttle contacts constantly open
Code E013 No injection pulse (LH 2.2) or No signal from temperature sensor (LH 2.4)
Code E014 Air Mass Meter (AMM)—break in CO—adjusting circuit
Code E017 Fuel pump relay—control circuit faulty (LH 2.2) or break in ground circuit continuity (LH 2.4)
Code E018 No power at + 15 supply terminal
Code E020 Faulty signal from Oxygen sensor (LH 2.2) or Fuel pump relay; faulty control circuit (LH 2.4)
Code E021 System relay; faulty control circuit
Code E023 No signal from Automatic Idle Control (AIC) valve
Code E024 No load signal (LH 2.2) or Lambda sensor; faulty signal (LH 2.4)
Code E025 Electronic Control Unit (ECU) pin 25 not grounding
Code E033 Signal to Automatic Idle Control (AIC) valve from Electronic Control Unit (ECU); missing
Code E035 No power at +15 supply terminal
Code E101 Starter motor revolutions too low
Code E102 Short in Coolant Temperature Sensor (CTS) circuit (LH 2.2) or Throttle Position Sensor (TPS); idling contacts not opening on increase from idling to 2500 rpm (LH 2.4)
Code E103 Throttle Position Sensor (TPS); idling contacts not opening on increase from idling to 2500 rpm (LH 2.2) or Throttle Position Sensor (TPS); full load contacts constantly closed (LH 2.4)
Code E107 Low signal from Air Mass Meter (AMM)
Code E108 Air Mass Meter (AMM); filament burn-off function constantly actuated
Code E109 Low voltage from system relay
Code E112 Throttle Position Sensor (TPS)—full load contacts constantly closed

Code E113 Erratic or No Injection Pulse
Code E120 Lambda sensor—signal too low
Code E207 High signal from Air Mass Meter (AMM)
Code E213 Continuous pulses to injectors
Code E218 Continuous pulses from injectors
Code E220 Lambda sensor—signal too high
Code E320 DI/APC system Electronic Control Unit (ECU)—pre-ignition signal constantly actuated
Code E328 Pre-ignition signal constantly grounded
Code AICO Automatic Idle Control (AIC) valve pulse ratio—faulty
Code GLOU (Glow) Air Mass Meter (AMM) filament burn-off function operating
Code CI Turbo
Code C2 Turbo with AIC
Code C3 Turbo with AIC and catalytic converter
Code C4 Turbo with AIC and Saab DI
Code C5 Non-Turbo with AIC
Code FPU Fuel pump relay and system relay operating
Code FUEL Fuel mode
Code OFF Starting point for injection valve test
Code FIn Injection valve open
Code MON Monitor mode

Subaru

GENERAL INFORMATION

Single Point Fuel Injection

▶ **See Figure 66**

The SPFI is used on the Loyale 1.8L engine only. The system electronically controls the amount of injection from the fuel injector, and supplies the optimum air/fuel mixture under all operating conditions of the engine. Features of the SPFI system are as follows:
1. Precise control of the air/fuel mixture is accomplished by an increased number of input signals transmitting engine operating conditions to the control unit.

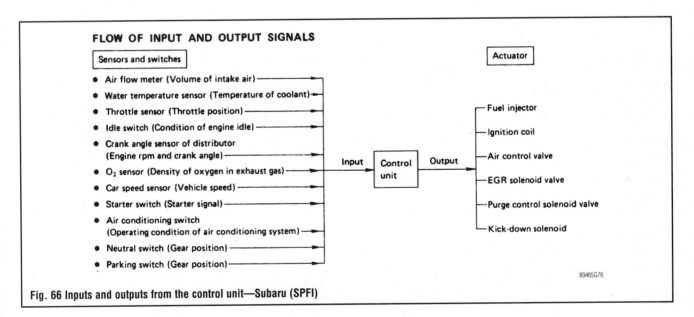

Fig. 66 Inputs and outputs from the control unit—Subaru (SPFI)

2. The use of hot wire type air flow meter not only eliminates the need for high altitude compensation, but improves driving performance at high altitudes.

3. The air control valve automatically regulates the idle speed to the set value under all engine operating conditions.

4. Ignition timing is electrically controlled, thereby allowing the use of complicated spark advances characteristics.

5. Wear of the air flow meter and fuel injector is automatically corrected so that they maintain their original performance.

6. Troubleshooting can easily be accomplished by the built-in self-diagnosis function.

Multi-Point Fuel Injection

▶ See Figure 67

The MPFI system supplies the optimum air/fuel mixture to the engine under all various operating conditions. System fuel, which is pressurized at a constant pressure, is injected into the intake air passage of the cylinder head. The amount of fuel injected is controlled by the intermittent injection system where the electro-magnetic injection valve (fuel injector) opens only for a short period of time, depending on the amount of fuel required for 1 cycle of operation. During system operation, the amount of injection is determined by the duration of an electric pulse sent to the fuel injector, which permits precise metering of the fuel.

Each of the operating conditions of the engine are converted into electric signals, resulting in additional features of the system, such as improved

adaptability and easier addition of compensating element. The MPFI system also incorporates the following features:

- Reduced emission of exhaust gases
- Reduction in fuel consumption
- Increased engine output
- Superior acceleration and deceleration
- Superior starting and warm-up performance in cold weather since compensation is made for coolant and intake air temperature
- Good performance with turbocharger, if equipped

SELF DIAGNOSTICS

Service Precautions

- Before connecting or disconnecting ECU harness connectors, make sure the ignition switch is **OFF** and the negative battery cable is disconnected to avoid the possibility of damage to the control unit.
- When connecting or disconnecting pin connectors from the ECU, take care not to bend or break any pin terminals. Check that there are no bends or breaks on ECU pin terminals before attempting any connections.
- Before replacing any ECU, perform ECU input/output signal diagnosis to determine if the ECU is functioning properly.
- When measuring supply voltage of ECU-controlled components with a circuit tester, separate 1 tester probe from another. If the 2 tester probes accidentally make contact with each other during measurement, a short circuit may result and damage the EC U.

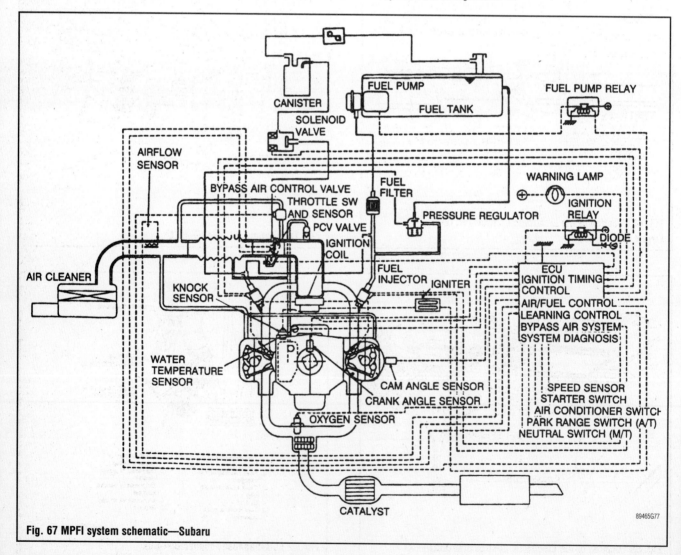

Fig. 67 MPFI system schematic—Subaru

READING TROUBLE CODES

1987–92 Fuel Injected Vehicles

▶ **See Figures 68, 69, 70, 71 and 72**

The self-diagnosis system has 4 modes: U-check mode, read memory mode, D-check mode and clear memory mode. Two connectors, Read memory and Test mode, are used. In addition, the malfunction indicator light is utilized. Connectors are used in various combinations to select the proper test mode and the lamps are used to read codes. No scan tool is necessary to extract codes.

➡**The engine should be running when in the D-check or clear memory modes.**

U-CHECK MODE

The U-check is a user-oriented mode in which only the components necessary for start-up and drive are diagnosed. On occurrence of a fault, the malfunction indicator light is turned **ON** to indicate that system inspection is necessary. The diagnosis of less significant components which do not adversely effect start-up and driving are excluded from this mode.

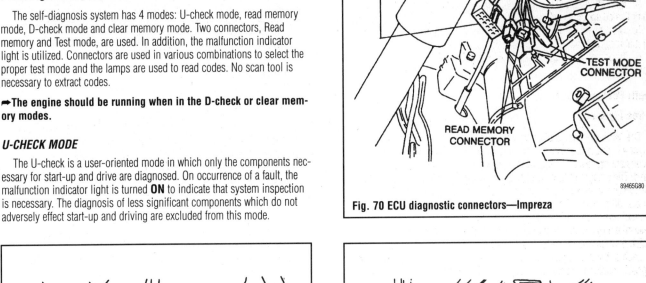

Fig. 70 ECU diagnostic connectors—Impreza

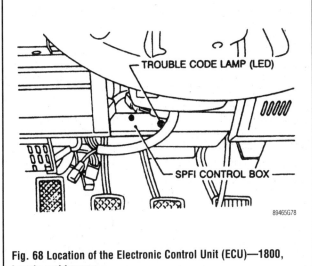

Fig. 68 Location of the Electronic Control Unit (ECU)—1800, Loyale and Legacy

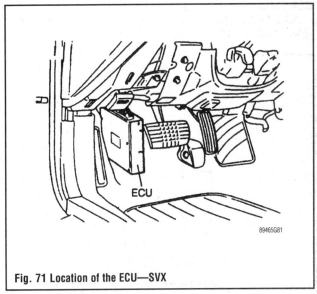

Fig. 71 Location of the ECU—SVX

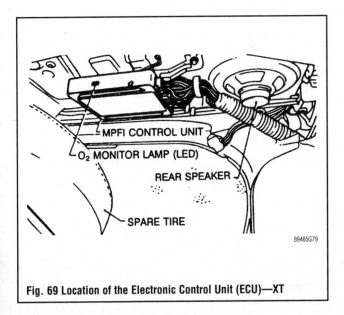

Fig. 69 Location of the Electronic Control Unit (ECU)—XT

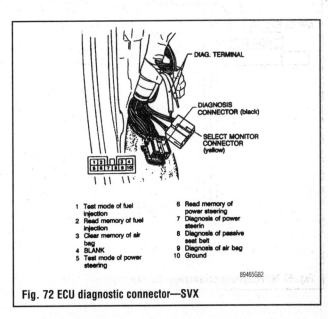

1 Test mode of fuel injection
2 Read memory of fuel injection
3 Clear memory of air bag
4 BLANK
5 Test mode of power steering
6 Read memory of power steering
7 Diagnosis of power steerin
8 Diagnosis of passive seat belt
9 Diagnosis of air bag
10 Ground

Fig. 72 ECU diagnostic connector—SVX

READ MEMORY MODE

The Read memory mode is used to detect faults which recently occurred but are not currently present.

1. Turn the ignition switch **OFF**.
2. Connect the Read memory connector.
3. Turn the ignition switch **ON** with the engine **OFF**.
4. If the malfunction indicator light turns **ON**, trouble code(s) are present.
5. If the oxygen monitor lamp turns **ON**, trouble code(s) are being produced; confirm the trouble code(s).
6. Disconnect the read memory connector.
7. Perform the D-check mode.

D-CHECK MODE

The D-check mode is used to check the current status of the entire system.

1. Start the engine and warm it to normal operating temperatures.
2. Turn the ignition switch **OFF**.
3. Connect the test mode connector.
4. Turn the ignition switch **ON** with the engine **OFF**.
5. Make sure the malfunction indicator light turns **ON**; there should also be noise from the operation of the fuel pump.
6. Depress the accelerator pedal completely. Return it to ½ throttle position and hold it there for 2 seconds, then release the pedal completely.
7. Start the engine: If the malfunction indicator light indicates a trouble code, confirm code. If the malfunction indicator light turns **OFF**, continue test.
8. Race the engine briefly with the throttle fully opened.
9. Drive the vehicle above 5 mph, at engine speeds above 1500 rpm, for at least 1 minute.
10. If the malfunction indicator light blinks, there are no trouble codes. If the malfunction indicator light stays **ON**, trouble codes are present and must be read.

CLEARING CODES

1984–94 Fuel Injected Vehicles

1. Start the engine and warm it to normal operating temperatures.
2. Turn the ignition switch **OFF**.
3. Connect the test mode connector and the read memory connector.
4. Turn the ignition switch **ON** with the engine **OFF**.
5. Make sure the malfunction indicator light turns **ON**.
6. Depress the accelerator pedal completely. Return it to ½ throttle position and hold it there for 2 seconds then release the pedal completely.
7. Start the engine; the malfunction indicator light should turn OFF.
8. Race the engine with the throttle fully opened for a second or two.
9. Drive the vehicle above 5 mph, at engine speeds above 1500 rpm, for at least 1 minute.
10. The malfunction indicator light should blink showing that there are no trouble codes. If the malfunction indicator light stays **ON**, read the trouble codes and re-perform the D-check mode.

DIAGNOSTIC TROUBLE CODES

1984–94 Fuel Injected

1984–86 VEHICLES

1.6L (VIN 2 SPFI),

1.8L (VIN 4 & 5 SPFI),

1.8L (VIN 4, 5 & 7 MPFI)

2.7L (VIN 8 & 9 MPFI)

Code 11 No ignition pulse**Code 12** Starter switch; continuously in **OFF** position
Code 13 Starter switch; continuously in **ON** position
Code 14 Air flow meter

Code 15 Atmospheric pressure switch (1.8L VIN 4 & 5 SPFI 1986 only)
Code 16 Crank angle sensor (1.8L VIN 4 & 5 SPFI 1986 only)
Code 17 Starter switch (1.8L VIN 4 & 5 SPFI 1986 only)
Code 21 Air flow meter flap seized
Code 22 Pressure (Vacuum) switch
Code 23 Throttle sensor
Code 24 Wide Open Throttle (WOT) sensor
Code 25 Throttle sensor (1.8L VIN 4 & 5 SPEI 1986 only)
Code 31 Vehicle Speed Sensor (VSS)
Code 32 Oxygen sensor
Code 33 Coolant Temperature Sensor (CTS)
Code 34 Intake Air Thermo sensor (IAT)
Code 35 EGR solenoid
or Air flow meter (1.8L VIN 4 & 5 SPFI 1986 only)
Code 41 Open or ground in sensor
Code 42 Fuel injector
Code 43 Kick-down Low Hold (KDLH) relay
Code 46 Neutral safety switch (1.8L VIN 4 & 5 SPFI 1986 only)
Code 53 Fuel pump (1.8L VIN 4 & 5 SPFI 1986 only)
Code 55 Kick-down Low Hold (KDLH) relay (1.8L VIN 4 & 5 SPFI 1986 only)
Code 57 Canister purge control (1.8L VIN 4 & 5 SPFI 1986 only)
Code 58 Air control valve (1.8L VIN 4 & 5 SPFI 1986 only)
Code 62 EGR control system (1.8L VIN 4 & 5 SPFI 1986 only)
Code 88 Faulty ECU (1.8L VIN 4 & 5 SPFI 1986 only)

1987–94 VEHICLES

1.2L (VIN 7 & 8 MPFI),

1.8L (VIN 4 & 5 SPFI),

1.8L (VIN 2, 4, 5 & 7 MPFI),

2.2L (VIN 6 MPFI),

2.7L (VIN 8 & 9 MPFI) AND

3.3L (VIN 3)

Code 11 Crank angle sensor
Code 12 Starter switch
Code 13 Crank angle (Cam or Cylinder distinction) sensor
Code 14 Fuel injector (1.8L VIN 4 & 5 SPFI)
or Fuel injector No. 1 (1.2L VIN 7 & 8 MPFI), (1.8L VIN 2 MPFI), (2.2L VIN 6 MPFI) and (3.3L VIN 3 MPFI)**or** Fuel injectors No. 1 and No. 2 (1.8L VIN 4 & 5 MPFI)
or Fuel injectors No. 5 and No. 6 (2.7L VIN 8 & 9 MPFI)
Code 15 Fuel injector No. 2 (1.2L VIN 7 & 8 MPFI), (1.8L VIN 2 MPFI), (2.2L VIN 6 MPFI) and (3.3L VIN 3 MPFI)
or Fuel injectors No. 3 and No. 4 (1.8L VIN 4 & 5 MPFI)
or Fuel injectors No. 1 and No. 2 (2.7L VIN 8 & 9 MPFI)
Code 16 Fuel injector No. 3
Code 17 Fuel injector No. 4
Code 18 Fuel injector No. 5
Code 19 Fuel injector No. 6
Code 21 Coolant Temperature Sensor (CTS)
Code 22 Knock sensor (1.8L VIN 2 MPFI), (2.2L VIN 6 MPFI), (2.7L VIN 8 & 9 MPFI)
Code 22 Knock sensor 1; right (3.3L VIN 3 MPFI)
Code 23 Air flow meter
Code 24 Air control valve
Code 25 Fuel injectors No. 3 and No. 4; abnormal injector output (2.7L VIN 8 & 9 MPFI)
Code 26 Air temperature sensor; abnormal signal (1 .2L VIN 7 & 8 MPFI)
Code 28 Knock sensor 2; left (3.3L VIN 3 MPFI)
Code 29 Crank angle sensor 2 (3.3L VIN 3 MPFI)
Code 31 Throttle sensor
Code 32 Oxygen sensor 1; right (3.3L VIN 3 MPFI)
Code 33 Vehicle speed sensor 2 (1.8L VIN 2 MPFI), (3.3L VIN 3 MPFI)

Code 34 EGR solenoid valve or (California) clogged EGR line

Code 35 Purge control solenoid valve

Code 36 Air suction valve; faulty valve function **or** Igniter; abnormal signal

Code 37 Oxygen sensor 2; left (3.3L VIN 3 MPFI)

Code 38 Engine torque control (3.3L VIN 3 MPFI)

Code 41 AF (Air/Fuel) learning control **or** System too lean (1.8 VIN 4 & 5 MPFI), (2.7L VIN 8 & 9 MPFI)

Code 42 Idle switch

Code 43 Power switch

Code 44 Duty solenoid valve (wastegate control); valve inoperative

Code 45 Kick-down control relay (1.8L VIN 4 & 5 SPFI)

Code 45 A: Atmospheric pressure sensor; faulty sensor (2.2L VIN 6 MPFI 1991 only)

Code 45 B: Pressure exchange solenoid valve; valve inoperative (2.2L VIN 6 MPFI 1991 only)

Code 45 Atmospheric pressure sensor (1.2L VIN 7 & 8 MPFI), (2.2L VIN 6 MPFI 1992 1993), (3.3L VIN 3 MPFI)

Code 49 Air flow sensor

Code 51 Neutral switch

Code 52 Clutch switch; signal remains **ON** or **OFF** (Front Wheel Drive/Manual Transaxle only) (1.2L VIN 7 & 8 MPFI)

Code 52 Parking switch (2.2L VIN 6 MPFI), (3.3L VIN 3 MPFI)

Code 55 EGR gas temperature sensor

Code 56 EGR System; faulty EGR function (1.8L VIN 2 MPFI)

Code 56 EGR system (California) (3.3L VIN 3 MPFI)

Code 61 Parking switch; continuously in **ON** position

Code 62 Electric load signal; headlight HI/LO signal or rear defogger signal remains **ON** or **OFF**

Code 63 Blower fan switch; signal remains **ON** or **OFF**

Code 65 Vacuum pressure sensor; abnormal signal

➡**If more than one definition is listed for a code or the code is not listed here, consult your "Chilton Total Car Care" manual to obtain the specific meaning for your vehicle. This list is for reference and does not mean that a component is defective. The code identifies the circuit and component that require further testing.**

Suzuki

GENERAL INFORMATION

The Suzuki Electronic Fuel Injection (EFI) system supplies the vehicle's combustion chambers with air/fuel mixture of optimized ratio under varying driving conditions. Fuel delivery through the injector is controlled electrically by the Electronic Control Module (ECM).

SELF DIAGNOSTICS

Service Precautions

• Keep the ECM parts and harnesses dry during service. Protect the ECM and all solid-state components from rough handling or temperature extremes.

• Use extreme care when working around the ECM or other components.

• Disconnect the negative battery cable before attempting to disconnect or remove any parts.

• Disconnect the negative battery cable and ECM connector before performing arc welding on the vehicle.

• Disconnect and remove the ECM from the vehicle before subjecting the vehicle to the temperatures experienced in a heated paint booth.

READING TROUBLE CODES

1989–95 Vehicles

▶ **See Figures 73, 74, 75 and 76**

On Swift and Samurai, the ECM memory is activated by connecting the spare fuse to the diagnosis switch terminal and turning the ignition switch **ON**. The fuse panel is located under the instrument panel, near the driver's

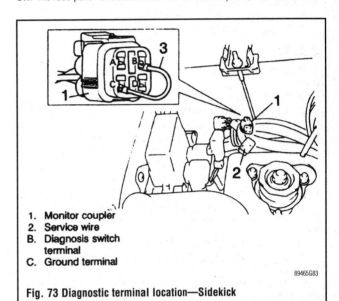

1. Monitor coupler
2. Service wire
B. Diagnosis switch terminal
C. Ground terminal

Fig. 73 Diagnostic terminal location—Sidekick

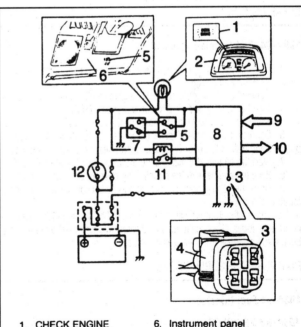

1. CHECK ENGINE light
2. Cluster
3. Diagnosis switch terminal
4. Monitor coupler
5. Cancel switch
6. Instrument panel
7. Mileage sensor
8. ECM
9. Sensed information
10. Output
11. Main relay
12. Ignition Switch

Fig. 74 "Check Engine" light circuit (Federal)—Sidekick

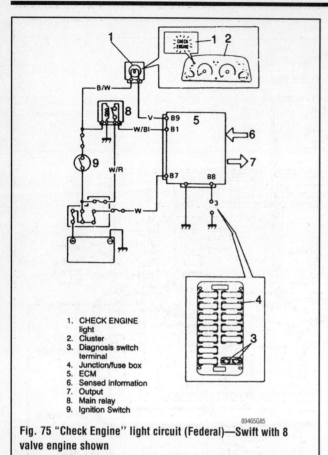

1. CHECK ENGINE
   light
2. Cluster
3. Diagnosis switch
   terminal
4. Junction/fuse box
5. ECM
6. Sensed information
7. Output
8. Main relay
9. Ignition Switch

89465G85

Fig. 75 "Check Engine" light circuit (Federal)—Swift with 8 valve engine shown

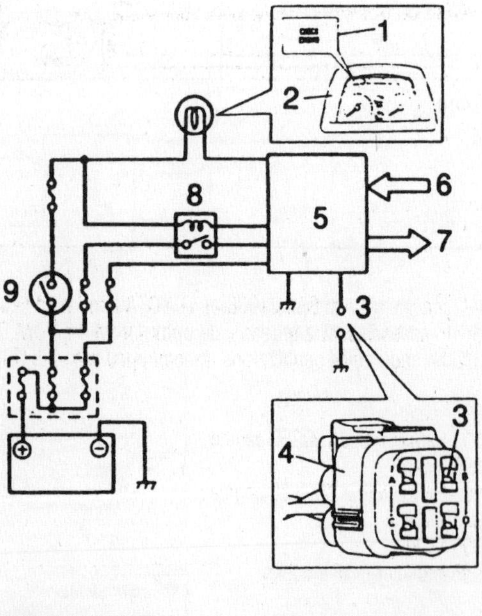

1. CHECK ENGINE
   light
2. Cluster
3. Diagnosis switch
   terminal
4. Fuse box
5. ECM
6. Sensed information
7. Output
8. Main relay
9. Ignition switch

89465G86

Fig. 76 "Check Engine" light circuit (California and Canada)—Sidekick

side kick panel. On Sidekick models, the diagnostic terminals B and C must be grounded. The diagnostic terminal is located under the hood, on the right rear side.

The diagnostic codes are flashed by the malfunction indicator light or Malfunction Indicator Lamp (MIL) on the dash. The memory displays the codes in numerical order from lowest to highest. The order in which the codes are displayed does not necessarily indicate the order in which the malfunction occurred. The ECM displays each code 3 times, then moves on the next code in numerical order. The entire sequence is repeated as long as the diagnosis switch terminal is grounded and the ignition switch is in the **ON** position.

CLEARING CODES

1989–95 VEHICLES

When repairs have been completed, erase the ECM back-up memory by disconnecting the negative battery cable or the ECM harness connector for 30 seconds or longer.

DIAGNOSTIC TROUBLE CODES

1986–95 Vehicles

Code 12 Normal
Code 13 Oxygen sensor circuit
Code 14 Engine Coolant Temperature (ECT) Sensor circuit—low temperature indicated, signal voltage high
Code 15 Engine Coolant Temperature (ECT) Sensor circuit—high temperature indicated, signal voltage low
Code 21 Throttle Position Sensor (TPS) circuit—signal voltage high
Code 22 Throttle Position Sensor (TPS) circuit—signal voltage low
Code 23 Air Temperature Sensor (ATS) circuit—low temperature indicated, signal voltage high
Code 24 Vehicle Speed Sensor (VSS) circuit
Code 25 Air Temperature Sensor (ATS) circuit—high temperature indicated, signal voltage low
Code 31 Pressure Sensor (PS) circuit—high pressure indicated, signal voltage high
Code 32 Pressure Sensor (PS) circuit—low pressure indicated, signal voltage low
Code 33 Mass Air Flow Sensor (MAS) circuit—signal voltage high
Code 34 Mass Air Flow Sensor (MAS) circuit—signal voltage low
Code 41 Ignition signal
Code 42 Crank Angle Sensor (CAS) circuit (except 1989–90 Sidekick) or Fifth switch circuit, Lock-up signal circuit (1989–90 Sidekick)
Code 44 Idle switch of Throttle Position Sensor (TPS)—open circuit
Code 45 Idle switch of Throttle Position Sensor (TPS)—shorted circuit
Code 51 Exhaust Gas Recirculation (EGR) system and/or Recirculated Exhaust Gas Temperature Sensor (REGTS) system—California vehicle
Code 52 Fuel Injector—California vehicle
Code 53 Ground circuit—California vehicle
Code 54 Fifth gear switch circuit
Code 71 Test switch circuit

Toyota

GENERAL INFORMATION

◆ See Figure 77

Toyota fuel injected vehicles use the Multi-port Fuel Injection (MFI) system. The Multi-port Fuel Injection system was first used in 1980 and continues in use today.

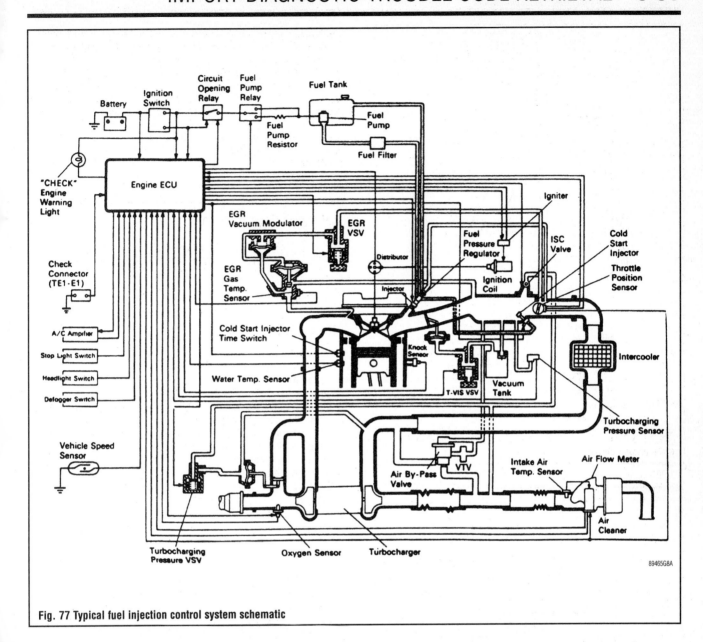

Fig. 77 Typical fuel injection control system schematic

SELF DIAGNOSTICS

As the engine control computers became capable of more functions, self-diagnostic and memory circuits were added. These systems allow the ECU to note a fault, assign an identity code and store the code in memory for later retrieval.

All fuel injected control engine units possess the ability to provide fault codes during diagnosis. The number, type and meaning of engine codes vary by year and model.

While most fault codes are held in an electronic memory and are retained even after the ignition is switched **OFF**, certain codes are only held or displayed as long as the ignition is **ON**. If the fault is present at the next restart, the code will reset.

When a controller or ECU notes a fault, the dash warning lamp for the appropriate system will be lit to advise the operator. If the dash lamp is normally lit during system operation, as in the case of cruise control, the lamp will flash when a fault is found. The illumination or flashing of the dash lamp indicates that the controller has detected a fault and placed itself into the back-up or default mode.

Beginning in 1995 some models were equipped with an on board diagnostic system known as OBD-II. To diagnose this system an OBD-II scan tool, complying with SAE J1978 or TOYOTA hand held tester is necessary to access codes and read data output from the ECM. The following model and engine applications are equipped with the OBD-II system:

- 1995 Tercel
- 1995 Camry with a 1MZ-FE engine
- 1995 Avalon
- 1995 Previa with a 2TZ-FZE engine
- 1995 Tacoma
- 1995 T100
- 1996 and later—All models

Service Precautions

- Keep all ECU parts and harnesses dry during service. Protect the ECU and all solid-state components from rough handling or extremes of temperature.
- Before attempting to remove any parts, turn the ignition switch **OFF** and disconnect the battery ground cable.
- Make sure all harness connectors are fastened securely. A poor connection can cause an extremely high voltage surge, resulting in damage to integrated circuits.

- Always use a 12 volt battery as a power source.
- Do not attempt to disconnect the battery cables with the engine running.
- Do not attempt to disassemble the ECU unit under any circumstances.
- If installing a 2-way or CB radio, mobile phone or other radio equipment, keep the antenna as far as possible away from the electronic control unit. Keep the antenna feeder line at least 8 in. away from the EFI harness and do not run the lines parallel for a long distance. Be sure to ground the radio to the vehicle body.
- When performing ECU input/output signal diagnosis, remove the water-proofing rubber plug, if equipped, from the connectors to make it easier to insert tester probes into the connector. Always reinstall it after testing.
- When connecting or disconnecting pin connectors from the ECU, take care not to bend or break any pin terminals. Check that there are no bends or breaks on ECU pin terminals before attempting any connections.
- When measuring supply voltage of ECU-controlled components, keep the tester probes separated from each other and from accidental grounding. If the tester probes accidentally make contact with each other during measurement, a short circuit will damage the ECU.
- Use great care when working on or around air bag systems. Wait at least 20 seconds after turning the ignition switch to LOCK and disconnecting the negative battery cable before performing any other work. The air bag system is equipped with a back-up power system which will keep the system functional for 20 seconds without battery power.
- All air bag connectors are a standard yellow color; the related wiring is encased in standard yellow sheathing. Testing and diagnostic procedures must be followed exactly when performing diagnosis on this system. Improper procedures may cause accidental deployment or disable the system when needed.
- Never attempt to measure the resistance of the air bag squib; detonation may occur.

READING TROUBLE CODES

The following procedures are for all vehicles except those equipped with the OBD-II system. Accessing OBD-II system codes can only be accomplished with the use of a OBD-II scan tool, complying with SAE J1978 or TOYOTA hand held tester. The following models are equipped with the OBD-II system:
- 1995 Tercel
- 1995 Camry with a 1MZ-FE engine
- 1995 Avalon
- 1995 Previa with a 2TZ-FZE engine
- 1995 Tacoma
- 1995 T100
- 1996 and later—All models

1983–86 Vehicles

▶ See Figures 78, 79, 80, 81 and 82

The diagnostic codes can be read by the number of blinks of the "Check Engine" warning light when the proper terminals of the check connector are short-circuited. If the vehicle is equipped with a super monitor display, the diagnostic code is indicated on the display screen. The initial conditions for entering the self-diagnostics are as follows:
1. The battery voltage of the vehicle should be above 11 volts. The throttle valve must be in a fully closed position (throttle position sensor IDL points closed).
2. If equipped with an automatic transmission, place it in **P** or **N**.
3. Turn the air conditioning switch **OFF**.
4. Start the engine and allow it reach normal operating temperature.

EXCEPT SUPER MONITOR DISPLAY—NORMAL MODE

1. Turn the ignition switch to the **ON** position. Do not start the engine. Remove the protective rubber cap and, with a jumper wire connect the terminals of the check connector.
2. Read the diagnostic code as indicated by the number of flashes of the "Check Engine" warning light.

➡On some early models, install an analog voltmeter to the EFI service connector. Read diagnostic codes by voltmeter needle deflection between 0V–2.5V–5V. The voltmeter needle will fluctuate between 5V and 2.5V every 0.6 seconds.

3. If the system is operating normally (no malfunction), the light will blink once every ¼ second. On single digit code number systems, the light will blink once every 3 or 4.5 seconds.

4. In the event of a malfunction, the light will blink once every ½ second (on some models it may be 1, 2 or 3 seconds). The 1st number of blinks will equal the 1st digit of a 2-digit diagnostic code. After a 1.5 second pause, the 2nd number of blinks will equal the 2nd number of a 2-digit diagnostic code. If there are 2 or more codes, there will be a 2.5 second pause between each. On single digit code number systems the light will blink a number of times equal to the malfunction code indication every 2 or 4.5 seconds.

5. After all the codes have been output, there will be a 4.5 second pause and they will be repeated as long as the terminals of the check connector are shorted.

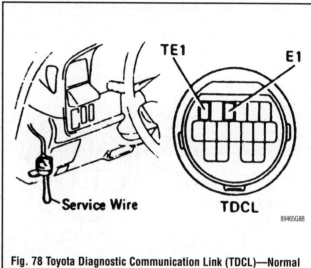

Fig. 78 Toyota Diagnostic Communication Link (TDCL)—Normal Mode

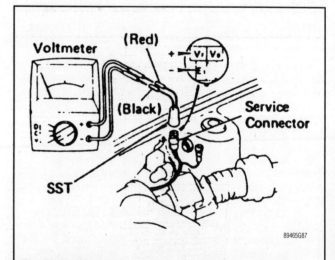

Fig. 79 Installing analog voltmeter to EFI service connector—1983–84 Celica Supra

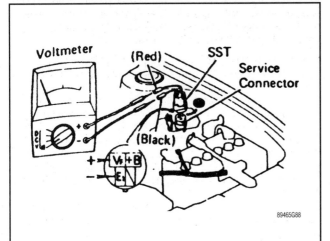

Fig. 80 Installing analog voltmeter to EFI service connector—1983–84 Cressida

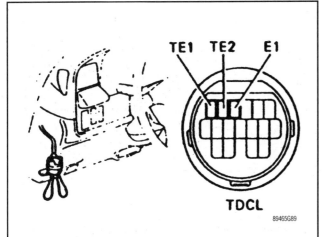

Fig. 81 Toyota Diagnostic Communication Link (TDCL)—Test Mode

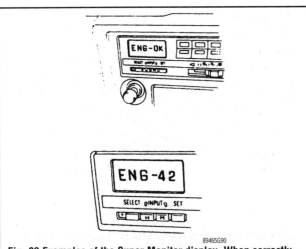

Fig. 82 Examples of the Super Monitor display. When correctly engaged, the screen will provide system identifiers such as ENG, ABS or ECT and the fault code(s)

➡In event of multiple trouble codes, indication will begin from the smaller value and continue to the larger in order.

6. After the diagnosis check, remove the jumper wire from the check connector and install the protective rubber cap.

TEST MODE

The Cressida provides a diagnostic test mode for vehicle servicing.

1. Using a jumper wire, connect the TE2 and E1 terminals of the Toyota Diagnostic Communication Link (TDCL), then turn the ignition switch **ON** to begin the diagnostic test mode.

2. Start the engine and drive the vehicle at a speed of 10 mph or more. Simulate the conditions where the malfunction has been reported to happen.

3. Using a jumper wire, connect the TE2 and E1 terminals of the TDCL connector.

4. Read the diagnosis code as indicated by the number of "Check Engine" light flashes.

5. After diagnosis check remove the jumper wires.

SUPER MONITOR DISPLAY

The super monitor display system was offered as an option on some late model Toyota vehicles.

1. Turn the ignition switch **ON** but do not start the engine.

2. Simultaneously push and hold in the SELECT and INPUT M keys for at least 3 seconds. The letters DIAG will appear on the screen.

3. After a short pause, hold the SET key in for at least 3 seconds. If the system is normal (no malfunctions), ENG-OK will appear on the screen.

4. If there is a malfunction, the code number for it will appear on the screen. In event of 2 or more numbers, there will be a 3 second pause between each (example:EN-42).

1987–89 Vehicles

◆ See Figures 83, 84, 85 and 86

Stored fault codes are transmitted through the blinking of the CHECK engine warning lamp. This occurs only when the system is placed into the diagnostic mode; it does not occur while the vehicle is being driven.To read the fault codes:

1. The following initial conditions must be met:
   a. Battery voltage at or above 11 volts.
   b. Throttle fully closed.
   c. Transmission in **N** or **P**.
   d. All electrical systems and accessories **OFF**.

2. Turn the ignition **ON** but do not start the engine.

3. Use a jumper wire to connect terminals T and E1 at the diagnostic connector. On 1988 California Supra and all 1989 vehicles except Corolla, MR2 and Tercel, connect terminals TE1 and E1. For 1988 Corolla EX, FX/16 and 1988–89 Vans, jumper the 2 pins of the service connector. On 1989 Corolla, MR2 and Tercel, connect terminals T and E1.

4. The fault codes will be transmitted through the controlled flashing of the CHECK engine warning lamp.

5. If no malfunction was found or no code was stored, the lamp will flash 2 times per second with no other pauses or patterns. This confirms that the diagnostic system is working but has nothing to report. This light pattern may be referred to as the System Normal signal; it should be present when no other codes are stored.

6. The CHECK lamp will blink the number of the code(s). All codes are 2 digits; the pulsing of the light represents the digits, not the count. For example, Code 25 is displayed as 2 flashes a pause and 5 flashes.

7. If more than 2 codes are stored, the next will be transmitted after a 2½ second pause.

➡If multiple codes are stored, they will be transmitted in numerical order from lowest to highest. This does not indicate the order of fault occurrence.

8. When all codes have been transmitted, the entire pattern will repeat after a 4½ second pause. The repeats continue as long as the diagnostic terminals are connected.

9. After recording the codes, disconnect the jumper at the diagnostic connector and turn the ignition **OFF**.

SUPER MONITOR SYSTEM

This procedure is used on Cressida and Supra equipped with Super Monitor.
1. The following initial conditions must be met:
    a. Battery voltage at or above 11 volts.
    b. Throttle fully closed.
    c. Transmission in **N** or **P**.
    d. All electrical systems and accessories **OFF**.
2. Turn the ignition **ON** but do not start the engine.
3. Simultaneously press and hold the SELECT and INPUT M keys for at least 2 seconds. The letters DIAG will appear on the screen, showing that the system is in the diagnostic mode.
4. After a short pause, hold in the SET key for at least 2 seconds.
5. If the system is normal, with no faults stored, the message ENG OK will appear on the screen. If faults are stored, the code number will appear on the screen with a system designator; for example, ENG-42. If 2 or more codes are stored, each will appear after a 3 second pause.

1990-95 Vehicles

Stored fault codes are transmitted through the blinking of the CHECK engine warning lamp. This occurs only when the system is placed into the diagnostic mode; it does not occur while the vehicle is being driven.
To read the fault codes:
1. The following initial conditions must be met:
    a. Battery voltage at or above 11 volts.
    b. Throttle fully closed.
    c. Transmission in **N** or **P**.
    d. All electrical systems and accessories **OFF**.
2. Turn the ignition **ON** but do not start the engine.
3. Except for 1990–94 Tercel and 1990 MR2, use a jumper wire to connect terminals TE1 and E1 at the diagnostic connector in the engine compartment or at the TDCL connector below the left dashboard if so equipped. On Tercel and MR2 as noted, connect terminals T and E1 at the diagnostic connector.
4. The fault codes will be transmitted through the controlled flashing of the CHECK ENGINE warning lamp.
5. If no malfunction was found or no code was stored, the lamp will flash 2 times per second with no other pauses or patterns. This confirms that the diagnostic system is working but has nothing to report. This light pattern may be referred to as the System Normal signal; it should be present when no other codes are stored.

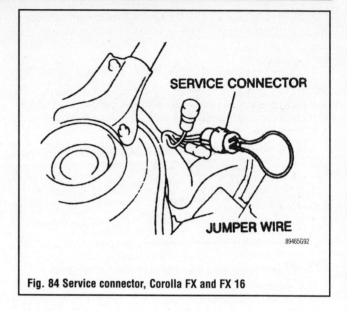

Fig. 84 Service connector, Corolla FX and FX 16

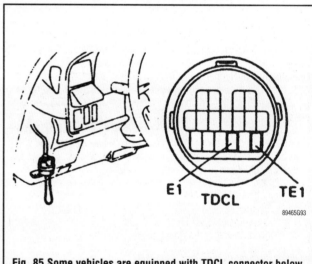

Fig. 85 Some vehicles are equipped with TDCL connector below the dash

Fig. 83 To read the engine codes, the computer must be put into the diagnostic mode by connecting the proper terminals

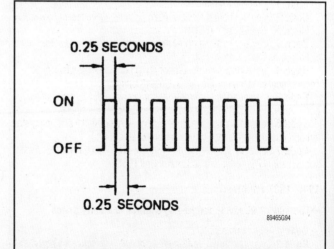

Fig. 86 The System Normal signal is transmitted by a steady flashing of the lamp

6. The CHECK lamp will blink the number of the code(s). All codes are 2-digit; the pulsing of the light represents the digits, not the count. For example, Code 25 is displayed as 2 flashes, a pause and 5 flashes.

7. If more than 1 code is stored, the next will be transmitted after a 2 ½ second pause.

➡**If multiple codes are stored, they will be transmitted in numerical order from lowest to highest. This does not indicate the order of fault occurrence.**

8. When all codes have been transmitted, the entire pattern will repeat after a 4 ½ second pause. The repeats continue as long as the diagnostic terminals are connected.

9. After recording the codes, disconnect the jumper at the diagnostic connector and turn the ignition **OFF**.

CLEARING CODES

1986–95

Stored codes will remain in memory until cleared. The correct method of clearing codes is to turn the ignition switch **OFF**, then remove the proper fuse. On all vehicles except as noted below, remove the EFI fuse. Each fuse must be removed for at least 10 seconds. The time required may be longer in cold weather.

Disconnecting the negative battery cable will also clear the memory but is not recommended due to other on-board memories being cleared as well. Once the system power is restored, re-check for stored codes. Only the System Normal indication should be present. If any other code is stored, the clearing procedure must be repeated or additional repairs performed; the old code will remain stored along with any new ones.

After repairs, it is recommended to clear the memory before test driving the vehicle. Upon returning from the drive, interrogate the memory; if the original code is again present, the repair was unsuccessful.

Except, EFI Fuse
- Corolla—15A Stop fuse
- 1990–94 MR2—7.5 AMP fuse
- Starlet—yellow fusible link
- 1990–94 Tercel—Stop fuse
- 1990–94 Corolla—15A Stop fuse

DIAGNOSTIC TROUBLE CODES

1983–1984 Engines

Code 1 Normal operation
Code 2 Open or shorted air flow meter circuit—defective air flow meter or Electronic Control Unit (ECU)
Code 3 Open or shorted air flow meter circuit—defective air flow meter or Electronic Control Unit (ECU)
Code 4 Open Water Thermo-sensor (THW) circuit—defective Water Thermo-sensor (THW) or Electronic Control Unit (ECU)
Code 5 Open or shorted oxygen sensor circuit—lean or rich indication—defective oxygen sensor or Electronic Control Unit (ECU)
Code 6 No ignition signal—defective ignition system circuit, Integrated Ignition Assembly (IIA) or Electronic Control Unit (ECU)
Code 7 Defective Throttle Position Sensor (TPS) circuit, Throttle Position Sensor (TPS) or Electronic Control Unit (ECU)

1985–1987 Engines

➡**The 1985 2.0L (2S-E and 3Y-EC) engines use 1984 Codes**

Code 1 Normal operation
Code 2 Open or shorted air flow meter circuit—defective air flow meter or Electronic Control Unit (ECU)

Code 3 No signal from igniter 4 times in succession—defective igniter or main relay circuit, igniter or Electronic Control Unit (ECU)
Code 4 Open Water Thermo-sensor (THW) circuit—defective Water Thermo-sensor (THW) or Electronic Control Unit (ECU)
Code 5 Open or shorted oxygen sensor circuit—lean or rich indication—defective oxygen sensor or Electronic Control Unit (ECU)
Code 6 No engine revolution sensor (Ne) signal to Electronic Control Unit (ECU) or Ne value being over 1000 rpm in spite of no Ne signal to ECU—defective igniter circuit, igniter, distributor or Electronic Control Unit (ECU)
Code 7 Open or shorted Throttle Position Sensor (TPS) circuit, Throttle Position Sensor (TPS) or Electronic Control Unit (ECU)
Code 8 Open or shorted intake air thermo-sensor circuit—defective intake air thermo-sensor circuit or Electronic Control Unit (ECU)
Code 10 No starter switch signal to Electronic Control Unit (ECU) with vehicle speed at 0 and engine speed over 800 rpm—defective speed sensor circuit, main relay circuit, igniter switch to starter circuit, igniter switch or Electronic Control Unit (ECU)
Code 11 Short circuit in check connector terminal T with the air conditioning switch **ON** or throttle switch (IDL) contact point **OFF**—defective air conditioner switch, Throttle Position Sensor (TPS) circuit, Throttle Position Sensor (TPS) or Electronic Control Unit (ECU)
Code 12 Knock control sensor signal has not reached judgement level in succession—defective knock control sensor circuit, knock control sensor or Electronic Control Unit (ECU)
Code 13 Knock CPU faulty

1988–95 Engines

—-Constant blinking of indicator light: No faults detected
Code 11 Momentary interruption in power supply to ECU; up to 1991
Code 12 Engine revolution (NE or G) signal to ECU; missing within several seconds after engine is cranked
Code 13 Rpm NE signal to ECU; missing when engine speed is above 1000 rpm
Code 14 Igniter (IGF) signal to ECU; missing 4–11 times in succession
Code 16 ECT control signal—normal signal missing from ECT CPU (1990-94)
Code 16 A/T control system—normal signal missing from between the engine CPU and A/T CPU in the ECM (1995)
Code 21 Main oxygen sensor signal; voltage output does not exceed a set value on the lean and rich sides continuously for a certain period of time or open/short sensor heater circuit
Code 22 Water temperature sensor circuit (THW); open/short for 500 msec. or more
Code 23 Intake air temperature signal (THA)
Code 24 Intake air temperature sensor circuit (THA); open/short for 500 msec. or more
Code 25 Air/fuel ratio LEAN malfunction; Oxygen sensor output is less than 0.45 V for at least 90 seconds when oxygen sensor is warmed up (engine racing at 2000 rpm). California only: air/fuel ratio feedback compensation/adaptive control: feedback value continues at upper (LEAN) limit, or is not renewed, for a certain period of time.
Code 26 Air/fuel ratio RICH malfunction; California only: Air/fuel ratio feedback compensation/adaptive control: feedback value continues at lower (RICH) limit, or is not renewed, for a certain period of time.
Code 27 Sub-oxygen sensor signal; detection of sensor/signal deterioration or open/short sensor heater circuit (California only)
Code 28 No. 2 oxygen sensor signal/heater signal
Code 31 Air flow meter circuit; open or shorted when idle contacts are closed**Code 31** Vacuum (Manifold absolute pressure) sensor signal; open/short circuit
Code 32 Air flow meter circuit; circuit open or shorted when idling
Code 34 Turbocharging pressure signal; excessive pressure
Code 35 Altitude compensation (HAC) sensor signal; open/short
Code 35 Turbocharging pressure sensor signal; open/short

Code 36 Turbocharging pressure sensor signal; open or short detected for 0.5 sec or more in the turbocharging pressure sensor signal circuit; 1992–94

Code 41 Throttle position sensor circuit (VTA); open/short

Code 42 Vehicle speed sensor circuit

Code 43 No starter switch (STA) signal to ECU until engine speed reaches 800 rpm when cranking

Code 51 A/C signal **ON**, DL contact **OFF**, or shift position in R, D, 2 or 1 range; with check terminals T and EI connected

Code 52 Knock sensor signal (KNK); open/short

Code 53 Knock control signal in ECU; ECU knock control faulty

Code 55 Knock sensor (rear side) signal in ECU; ECU knock control faulty

Code 71 EGR system malfunction; EGR gas temperature signal (THG) is below water temperature sensor signal or below intake air temperature sensor signal plus 86°F (30°C), after driving for 240 seconds in EGR operation range (California only)

Code 72 Fuel cut solenoid signal circuit (FCS) open; up to 1991

Code 78 Fuel pump control signal input circuit to pump (FPC) open

Code 81 TCM communication; open detected in ECT1 circuit for 2 or more seconds

Code 83 TCM communication; open detected in ESA1 circuit 0.5 sec after idle

Code 84 TCM communication; open in ESA2 circuit for 0.5 seconds after idle

Code 85 TCM communication; open in ESA3 circuit for more than 0.5 seconds after idle

Volkswagen

GENERAL INFORMATION

CIS-E Fuel Injection

▶ **See Figures 87, 88 and 89**

The CIS-E Motronic system is the latest development of the electronically controlled mechanical Continuous Injection System (CIS). This system uses injectors, fuel pump and air flow sensor that are similar to those on earlier systems. The fuel distributor is equipped with an electronically controlled differential pressure regulator. This is operated by the ECU to control the fuel pressure in the lower chamber of the fuel distributor, which controls air/fuel mixture.

The ECU is now equipped with an adaptive learning program which allows it to learn and remember the normal operating range of the mixture control output signal. This gives the system the capability to compensate for changes in altitude, slight vacuum leaks or other changes due to things such as engine wear. Cold engine driveability and emissions are improved. The new ECU also is capable of cold start enrichment without the use of a thermo-time switch. The Fox still uses the thermo-time switch on CIS equipped vehicles.

The fuel injector pressure has been increased for better fuel atomization and residual pressure. The threads on the new injectors are different so they

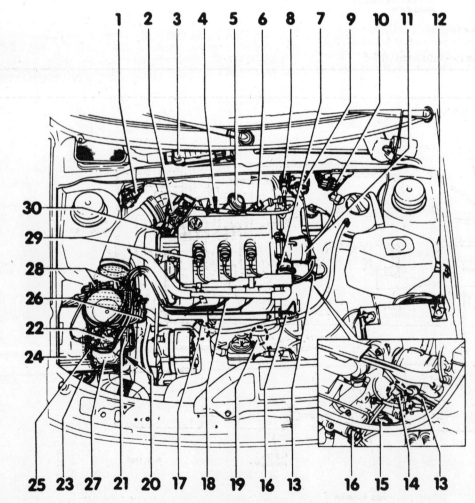

1. Oxygen sensor harness connector on right engine mount
2. Throttle body
3. Control module
4. Intake air temperature sensor—California only
5. EGR valve—California only
6. Exhaust tap
7. Idle stabilizer valve
8. Ignition coil power output stage
9. Ignition coil
10. 6-pin wiring harness connector
11. Distributor
12. EGR vacuum amplifier—California only
13. Ignition timing sensor or plug wire 4
14. EGR vacuum valve—California only
15. Coolant temperature sensor
16. Cold start valve
17. Knock sensor I
18. Fuel injector
19. Knock sensor II
20. Heated air intake control door
21. Differential pressure regulator
22. Fuel distributor
23. Charcoal canister below air cleaner
24. Air filter
25. Potentiometer
26. Fuel pressure regulator
27. Air flow sensor
28. Charcoal canister solenoid valves
29. Spark plug
30. Throttle switch harness connectors

89465G95

Fig. 87 Engine compartment layout—Volkswagen GTI 16V and Passat shown

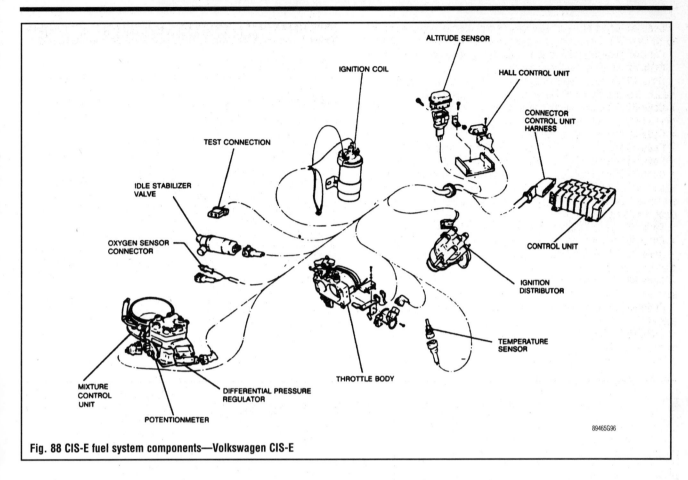

Fig. 88 CIS-E fuel system components—Volkswagen CIS-E

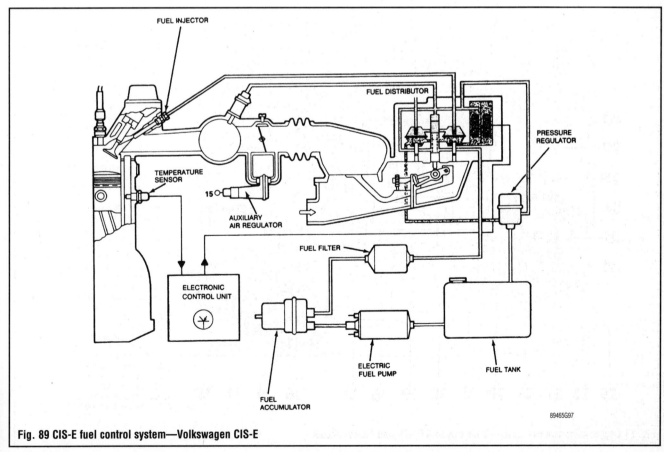

Fig. 89 CIS-E fuel control system—Volkswagen CIS-E

cannot be interchanged with older units. Some of the other components used on the CIS-E system are similar to those used on the fully electronic engine management systems. Some of the testing procedures are the same but the parts are not necessarily interchangeable.

Motronic and Motronic 2.9 Multiport Fuel Injection (MFI) Systems

Motronic and Motronic 2.9 systems are developments of the electronically controlled Multiport Fuel Injection (MFI) system. The two systems are almost identical. The engine control module (ECM) monitors engine intake air quantity using the Mass Air Flow (MAF) sensor. This is a true mass air measurement system. Using input from the MAF and other sensors, the ECM can calculate the length of time the injectors should be opened, and also controls the ignition system timing.

The ECM is equipped with an adaptive learning program which allows it to learn and remember the normal operating range of the mixture control output signal. This allows the system to compensate for changes in altitude, slight vacuum leaks or other changes due to other things such as engine wear. Cold engine driveability and emissions are improved.

The ECM is also equipped with a fault memory. If the sensor signal or output solenoid feedback signal is outside preprogrammed parameters, the ECM will store a fault code representing the fault and sensor involved. The ECM will also illuminate the Malfunction Indicator Lamp (MIL) to inform the vehicle operator that the vehicle requires service.

Mono-Motronic Throttle Body Fuel Injection (TBI) System

The Mono-Motronic system is development of the electronically controlled Throttle Body Fuel Injection (TBI) system. Based on outputs from the Throttle Position (TP), Engine Coolant Temperature (ECT) and Intake Air Temperature/Fuel Injector Temperature (IAT/FIT) sensors, the Engine Control Module (ECM) can infer intake air flow by air temperature and throttle position. This is a speed-density type control system. The ECM calculates the length of time the injector(s) should be opened, and with input from other sensors, also controls ignition timing.

The ECM is equipped with an adaptive learning program which allows it to learn and remember the normal operating range of the mixture control output signal. This allows the system to compensate for changes in altitude, slight vacuum leaks or other changes due to other things such as engine wear. Cold engine driveability and emissions are improved. The ECM is also equipped with a fault memory. If the sensor signal or output solenoid feedback signal is outside preprogrammed parameters, the ECM will store a fault code representing the fault and sensor involved. The ECM will also illuminate the Malfunction Indicator Lamp (MIL) to inform the vehicle operator that the vehicle requires service.

Digifant Multiport Fuel Injection (MFI) System

The Digifant Motronic system is development of the electronically controlled Multiport Fuel Injection (MFI) system. This system is quite similar on all models, but there is one significant difference among the three engines, intake air flow is measured using one of two systems. The 1.8L NA engine is equipped with a Vane Air Flow (VAF) sensor. This is a true mass air measurement system. The 1.8L SC and 2.5L NA engines use a Manifold Absolute Pressure (MAP) sensor. Along with output from the Intake Air Temperature (IAT) sensor, the ECM can infer intake air flow by air temperature and pressure. This is a speed-density type control system. Using either measurement system, the ECM calculates the length of time the injectors should be opened, and with input from other sensors, also controls ignition timing.

The ECM is equipped with an adaptive learning program which allows it to learn and remember the normal operating range of the mixture control output signal. This allows the system to compensate for changes in altitude, slight vacuum leaks or other changes due to other things such as engine wear. Cold engine driveability and emissions are improved.

The ECM is also equipped with a fault memory. If the sensor signal or output solenoid feedback signal is outside preprogrammed parameters, the ECM will store a fault code representing the fault and sensor involved. The

ECM will also illuminate the Malfunction Indicator Lamp (MIL) to inform the vehicle operator that the vehicle requires service. Some vehicles equipped with both the Digifant Motronic system and California specification emissions equipment also have the capability of flashing diagnostic codes.

SELF DIAGNOSTICS

Service Precautions

• Do not disconnect the battery or the control unit before reading the fault codes. On the Motronic system, fault code memory is erased when power is interrupted.
• Make sure the ignition switch is **OFF** before disconnecting any wiring.
• Before removing or installing a control unit, disconnect the negative battery cable. The unit receives power through the main connector at all times and will be permanently damaged if improperly powered up or down.
• Keep all parts and harnesses dry during service. Protect the control unit and all solid-state components from rough handling or extremes of temperature.

READING TROUBLE CODES

Only California vehicles with the Digifant II and Digifant I systems were equipped with the capability of flashing diagnostic codes.

On the Digifant II system codes were viewed through a combination rocker switch/indicator light. The following California vehicles were equipped with the Digifant II system:
   1988–90 Golf, Jetta and GTI with 2.0L 16 valve engine
   1990 Cabriolet with engine code 2H
On the Digifant I system a jumper cable would have to be connected and then the codes would flash from the malfunction indicator light on the dash. The following California vehicles were equipped with the Digifant I system:
   1990–93 Fox—Digifant I
   1991–93 Cabriolet—Digifant I
   1991–92 Corado—Digifant I
On all other systems, codes can only be retrieved with the use of a special diagnostic tester, the VAG 1551. This tester is available at car dealerships. The VAG 1551 tester can be used on all vehicles that have code capability.

➡**Some diagnostic codes may be retrieved by connecting special jumper cable 357 971 514E or an equivalent to the check connectors. Others for the most part are going to require the use of a special VAG 1551 tester and adapter to retrieve any remaining codes.**

Digifant II System

ROCKER SWITCH METHOD

California models are the only vehicles equipped with the On-Board Diagnostic (OBD) lamp. On these models, codes may be accessed by 2 methods. The first is the use of a combination rocker switch/lamp located on the instrument panel. The second is used by the dealers, they use a special tool called the VAG 1551.

An indicator light labeled CHECK is located in a rocker switch on the instrument panel. Each time the engine is started, the indicator light will flash once to inform the operator the bulb is working.

The light will come on and stay on if a fault develops in the engine management system. It will also display diagnostic codes to assist in trouble diagnosis.

A diagnostic code consists of 4 groups of flashes. There is a 2.5 second pause (light **OFF**), between each group of flashes.

The indicator light will come on for two and half seconds prior to displaying a fault code when the diagnostic procedure has been activated. The fault code will continue repeating while the ignition is **ON**.

If the fault is not repaired the indicator light will come on and stay on when the ignition is turned **ON** to signify the fault still exists.

The following California vehicles were equipped with the Digifant II system:
1988–90 Golf, Jetta and GTI with 2.0L 16 valve engine
1990 Cabriolet with engine code 2H
Prior to checking for codes, drive the vehicle for 10 minutes or more.

1. Turn the ignition to the **ON** position, do not start the engine.

2. Press and hold down the rocker switch for 4–6 seconds then release the switch. The CHECK indicator lamp will begin flashing a diagnostic code.

3. Press and hold down the rocker switch again for 4–6 seconds then release it. The indicator lamp will flash the next diagnostic code and will continue until all codes have been displayed.

When all diagnostic codes have been displayed, the indicator lamp will flash a series of 2.5 second flashes **ON** and 2.5 seconds **OFF**. This is an "End Of Fault Sequence" code.

If there are no faults stored in the control unit memory, the indicator lamp will flash Code 4444.

➡**Occasionally the control unit will sense various deviations or changes in the air/fuel mixture. Because of the sensitivity of this system a fault code may set without any apparent problem showing up. This is a normal function with systems of this type.**

Digifant I System

JUMPER CABLE METHOD

California models are the only vehicles equipped with the On-Board Diagnostic (OBD) lamp. On these models codes may be access by 2 methods. The first is the use of a special jumper cable connected to the diagnostic connector. The second is used by the dealers, they use a special tool called the VAG 1551.

The following California vehicles were equipped with the Digifant I system:
1990–93 Fox—Digifant I
1991–93 Cabriolet—Digifant I
1991–92 Corado—Digifant I

1. Verify that all the fuses and grounds in the engine compartment are good.

2. Turn the ignition key **ON**.

3. Connect jumper cable 357 971 514E or equivalent to the connectors located in the center console. The black end of jumper wire connects to the black diagnostic connector in the console. The white end of the jumper wire connects to white diagnostic connector in the console.

4. Connect the jumper wire for about 5 seconds. When the OBD light begins flashing, remove the jumper wire.

5. Count the flashes of the light to get codes, each separate flash, in one code, will be have a short interval in between. Each interval between codes will be about 2.5 seconds. Count flashes until either Code 4444 or 0000 appears. To end this procedure turn the ignition switch **OFF**.

6. Output checks can not be performed without a diagnostic tester.

WITH DIAGNOSTIC TESTER

This method is used by the Dealers and requires the use of the special tester VAG 1551. The following vehicles can only be accessed using this tester:
1991–92 Golf, Jetta—Digifant I system
1993–94 Corado—with VR6 Engine—Motronic system
All CIS-E Motronic and Motronic systems

1. Make sure ignition switch is **OFF** and that all fuses are good. Make sure all grounds in engine compartment are good, especially those for the battery and control module.

2. Make sure the air conditioning system is **OFF**.

3. Connect the VAG 1551 diagnostic tester using VAG 1551/1 Adapter cable or equivalent. The diagnostic connectors are located in the center console, under the shifter. The shifter knob and console cover must be removed to access diagnostic connectors. Connect diagnostic connector 1 (black) to the black connector on the scan tool. Connect diagnostic connector 2 (white) to the white connector on the scan tool. The blue connector is not required.

4. Turn the ignition switch **ON**; now start the vehicle and let it idle. If vehicle will not start, crank engine for 6 seconds and leave ignition **ON**.

5. Turn the tester **ON** and make sure it is receiving power. The screen will display 2 menu options; Rapid Data Transfer and Blink Code Output:

6. If you choose to use mode 02, Blink Code Output, skip to Step 10.

7. Select mode 01, Rapid Data Transfer, and address word 01. Now press the Q button to enter your selection. The tester will display a control unit part number, the system it controls and an application (country) code.

a. If the information is displayed and is correct, press the (run) key to continue. The display "Select function XX" will appear.

b. If "Control unit does not answer" is displayed, use the Help key to display a list of possible causes. When the problem is repaired, return to step 1 and start over again.

8. When function 02 is selected, the control module will report fault codes to the diagnostic tester.

9. When all codes have been reported, proceed to the Output Check diagnosis or select function 06 to exit the fault code memory without erasing the codes. Repair and erase the faults, then check and see if all faults have been corrected.

10. The following steps will retrieve engine codes by using Blink Code Output.

11. To operate the VAG 1551 tester in Blink Code Output, select menu option # 2. An asterisk will appear and flash the codes, which the tester will count and report on the screen as numbers. If Code 4444 or 0000 is displayed, no faults are found in memory.

➡**On vehicles that use 4444 for no codes present, the 0000 will stand for output ended.**

12. If the engine is not running, some codes may be displayed. These can be ignored if the engine was intentionally stalled, but should be investigated if the engine will not start.

13. Press the (run) key to advance to the next code. Read through entire code list before starting repairs.

14. When the 0000 (output ended) code is displayed, pressing the (run) key again will proceed to another control module. If no other control modules are to be tested, the following display will appear: Blink Code Output is ended. To stop the program without erasing the codes, turn the ignition key **OFF** and press the clear C button once.

15. Repair and erase the faults, then check to see if all faults have been corrected.

OUTPUT CHECK DIAGNOSIS

Only the Motronic system is equipped with this program. It allows testing most of the engine output devices without running the engine. The program cannot be run without the VAG 1551 Diagnostic Tester or equivalent. During the test, four output devices are activated in the following order:
Differential pressure regulator
Carbon canister frequency valve
Idle stabilizer valve
Cold start valve

Testing the differential pressure regulator requires a multi-meter that will read milliamps. The other items can be checked with a voltmeter, test light or by listening and feeling for valve activation. The cold start valve is activated for a limited time to avoid flooding the engine.

1. Connect the diagnostic tester, turn the ignition switch **ON** and confirm that the tester will communicate with the control unit. See the procedure for retrieving fault codes.

2. Select Rapid Data Transfer and Function 03. When the test is started by pressing the Q button (enter), the first output signal is generated.

3. Each time the Run button is pressed, the tester will send an output signal to the next device on the list.

4. When the last item has been tested, select Function 06 to exit the program. To repeat the test, turn the ignition switch **OFF** and **ON** again.

➡**Leave the ignition OFF for approximately 20 seconds, before selecting Output Check diagnosis again.**

CLEARING CODES

1988–95 Vehicles

WITHOUT DIAGNOSTIC TESTER

1. To erase codes, wait until Code 4444 or 0000 is displayed.
2. Turn ignition switch **OFF** and connect jumper wire to diagnostic connectors again.
3. Turn the ignition switch **ON** and leave connectors jumpered for about 5 seconds, When Code 4444 or 0000 appears the codes will be erased.
4. Turn the ignition switch **OFF** and remove jumper wire.

WITH DIAGNOSTIC TESTER

For both engine and automatic transaxle, after all fault codes have been retrieved, select Function 05 and press the Q button to enter the selection. The memory will be erased only if all fault codes have been retrieved. Test drive the vehicle for at least 10 minutes, including at least 1 full throttle application above 3000 rpm. Check the fault code memory again to make sure all faults have been repaired.

DIAGNOSTIC TROUBLE CODES

1988–95 Vehicles

➡ **The 5 digit code groups are used with a diagnostic tester. The 4 digit code groups are the flashing codes.**

00000 or 4444 No faults in memory
00281 or 1231 Vehicle Speed Sensor (VSS) signal is missing
00282 or 1232 Throttle actuator solenoid or wiring harness
00513 or 2111 Engine RPM sensor signal is missing
00514 or 2112 Ignition reference sensor signal is missing
00515 or 2113 Hall sender signal is missing
00516 or 2121 Idle switch has open short in circuit
00517 or 2123 Full throttle switch
00518 or 2212 Throttle position sensor
00519 or 2222 Manifold absolute pressure (MAP) sensor
00520 or 2232 Air flow sensor signal is missing
00521 or 2242 CO potentiometer
00522 or 2312 Engine coolant temperature (ECT) sensor
00523 or 2322 Intake air temperature (IAT) sensor
00524 or 2142 Knock sensor 1 signal is missing
00525 or 2342 Oxygen sensor signal missing
00527 or 2412 Intake air temperature (IAT) sensor has open/short in circuit
00532 or 2234 Supply voltage is too high
00533 or 2231 Idle speed regulation out of limit
00535 or Both 2141/2142 Knock sensor or control program
00537 or 2341 Oxygen sensor signal out of limit
00540 or 2144 Knock sensor 2 signal is missing
00543 or 2214 RPM exceeds maximum limit
00545 or 2314 Engine/Transmission electrical connection
00549 or 2314 Fuel consumption signal
00552 or 2323 Air flow sensor signal missing
00553 or 2324 Mass Air Flow (MAF) sensor signal is out of range
00558 or NA Adaptive mixture control lean (Fuel injector leak, EVAP purge system)
00559 or NA Adaptive mixture control rich (vacuum leak)
00560 or 2411 EGR temperature sensor circuit
00561 or 2413 Mixture adaptation limits are out of range
00585 or 2411 EGR temperature sensor circuit (2.8L AAA engine only)
00586 EGR controlling system, EGR valve is sticking or false signals
00587 Adjustment limit mixture regulator is lean
00609 Ignition output 1 circuit
00624 A/C compressor engagement circuit has mechanical or electrical malfunction
00640 or 3434 Heated Oxygen sensor relay has open/short circuit
01025 Malfunction indicator lamp (MIL) circuit

01242 or 4332 Output stages in engine control module (ECM)
01247 or 4343 EVAP frequency valve 1 has open/short in circuit
01249 or 4411 Fuel injector #1 circuit has open/short
01250 or 4412 Fuel injector #2 circuit has open/short
01251 or 4413 Fuel injector #3 circuit has open/short
01252 or 4414 Fuel injector #4 circuit has open/short
01253 or 4421 Fuel injector #5 circuit has open/short
01254 or 4422 Fuel injector #6 circuit has open/short
01257 or 4431 Idle Air Control (IAC) valve has open/short in circuit or a mechanical malfunction
01259 or 4433 Fuel pump relay is faulty or short circuited
01265 or 4312 EGR frequency valve has open/short in circuit
65535 or 1111 Engine Control Module (ECM) is defective
0000 End of output
NA Not Available

Volvo

GENERAL INFORMATION

▶ **See Figure 90**

The LH-Jetronic 2.2 was used on models through 1990, The LH-Jetronic 2.4 and 3.1 fuel injection systems are used on 1990 and newer 240, 700 and 900 series vehicles. The LH Jetronic 3.2 fuel injection system is used on the 1993 and later 850. The Motronic 1.8 was used on the 1992 and later 960. The Motronic 4.3 is used on 1994 and later 850 Turbo. On all fuel systems except the LH 2.2 system are monitored by a self-diagnostic system that lights up a warning lamp on the instrument panel. The LH-Jetronic 2.2 does not have self-diagnostic ability. Many different fault codes can be set, however only three can be stored at any one time. Fault tracing can be carried out by utilizing the diagnostic unit.

SELF DIAGNOSTICS

Service Precautions

- Do not operate the fuel pump when the fuel lines are empty.
- Do not operate the fuel pump when removed from the fuel tank.
- Do not reuse fuel hose clamps.
- The washer(s) below any fuel system bolt (banjo fittings, service bolt, fuel filter, etc.) must be replaced whenever the bolt is loosened. Do not reuse the washers; a high-pressure fuel leak may result.
- Make sure all ECU harness connectors are fastened securely. A poor connection can cause an extremely high voltage surge and result in damage to integrated circuits.
- Keep all ECU parts and harnesses dry during service. Protect the ECU and all solid-state components from rough handling or extremes of temperature.
- Use extreme care when working around the ECU or other components; the airbag or SRS wiring may be in the vicinity. On these vehicles, the SRS wiring and connectors are yellow; do not cut or test these circuits.
- Before attempting to remove any parts, turn the ignition switch **OFF** and disconnect the battery ground cable.
- Always use a 12 volt battery as a power source for the engine, never a booster or high-voltage charging unit.
- Do not disconnect the battery cables with the engine running.
- Do not disconnect any wiring connector with the engine running or the ignition **ON** unless specifically instructed to do so.
- Do not apply battery power directly to injectors.
- Whenever possible, use a flashlight instead of a drop light.
- Keep all open flame and smoking material out of the area. a Use a shop cloth or similar to catch fuel when opening a fuel system. Consider the fuel-soaked rag to be a flammable solid and dispose of it in the proper manner.
- Relieve fuel system pressure before servicing any fuel system component.

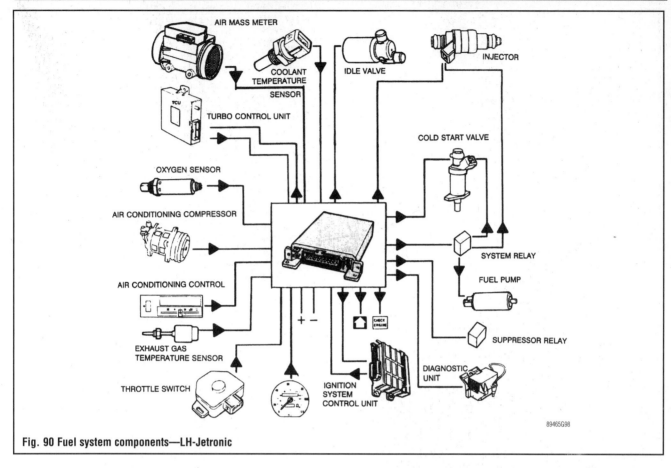

Fig. 90 Fuel system components—LH-Jetronic

• Always use eye or full-face protection when working around fuel lines, fittings or components.

• Always keep a dry chemical (class B-C) fire extinguisher near the area.

READING TROUBLE CODES

On-board engine diagnostics were not available on vehicles prior to 1988.

1988–94 Vehicles

▶ See Figures 91 and 92

1. Open diagnostic socket cover and install selector cable into socket No. 2 for fuel injection codes or socket No. 6 (except Motronic systems) for ignition codes.
2. Turn ignition to the **ON** position.
3. Enter control system 1 by pressing the button once. Hold the button for at least 1 second, but not more than 3.
4. Watch the diode light and count the number of flashes in the 3 flash series indicating a fault code. The flash series are separated by 3 second intervals. Note fault codes.

→**If there are no fault codes in the diagnostic unit, the diode will flash 1-1-1 and the fuel system is operating correctly.**

5. If diode light does not flash when button is pressed, or no code is flashed there is a problem with the soft-diagnostic system, proceed as follows:
    a. Check ground connections on the intake manifold, and the ground connection for the Lambda-sond at the right front mudguard.
    b. Check the fuses for the pump relay and the primary pump. On 240 models, fuses are located inside the engine compartment on the left side wheel well housing. On 760/780 models, fuses are located in the center console, just below the radio. On 740/940 models, fuses are located

behind the ashtray. Access can be gained by removing the ashtray, and pressing upward on the tab marked "electrical fuses press". On 850 models, the fuses are located on the left side of the engine compartment behind the strut mount plate. The fuses on 960 models are located on the far left side of the dashboard. The driver's door must be open to gain access to the fuses.
    c. Remove glove compartment, and check control unit ground connections.
    d. Turn ignition switch to the **OFF** position. Remove control unit connector and connector protective sleeve.
    e. Check diagnostic socket, (Steps 5e-5j), by connecting a voltmeter

Fig. 91 Diagnostic test connector location—850 shown (right front of engine compartment)

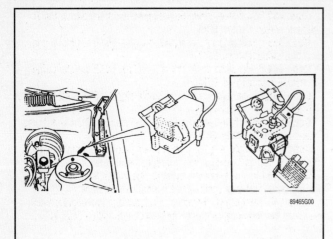

89465G00

Fig. 92 Diagnostic socket box location—240, 740, 940 and 960 shown

between ground and No. 4 connection on the control unit connector. Reading should be 12 volts. If no voltage is present, check lead between control unit connector and fuse No. 1 in the fuse/relay box.

f. Turn the ignition to the **ON** position, and install selector cable into the No. 2 socket on the diagnostic socket. Connect a voltmeter between ground and No. 12 connection on the control unit connector. Reading should be 12 volts. Press the button on diagnostic socket and note reading. Reading on the voltmeter should be 0 volts. If no voltage at the control unit is present, take reading at the diagnostic socket connector. If reading remains at 12 volts when button is pressed, check diagnostic socket.

g. Connect a voltmeter between ground and the red/black lead on the diagnostic socket connector. Reading should be 12 volts.

h. Connect a suitable ohmmeter between ground and the brown/black lead in the diagnostic socket connector. Reading should be 0 ohms.

i. Turn ignition to the **OFF** position. Connect ohmmeter between diagnostic socket selector cable and the pin under selector button. Ohmmeter should read infinity. Press button, and note reading. Reading should be 0 ohms.

j. Connect a suitable diode/multimeter tester, or equivalent, between the diagnostic socket diode light and the selector cable. Connect red test pin from the tester to pin under diode light and black test pin from tester to selector cable. A reading on the tester indicates correct diode light function. With no reading on tester, replace diagnostic socket.

k. Check the system relay/primary relay by connecting a voltmeter between ground and the No. 9 connection on the control unit connector, then connect a jumper wire between ground and No. 21 connection on the control unit connector. The relay should activate and the reading should be 12 volts.

6. Press the diagnostic socket button. Note any additional fault codes.

➡**The diagnostic system memory is full when it contains 3 fault codes. Until those codes are corrected and the memory erased, the system cannot give information on any other problems.**

7. Press the diagnostic socket button for the third time to see if a third fault code is stored in the memory. If the diode light flashes the same Code 1–1–1, there are no other codes in the memory.

CLEARING CODES

1989–94 Vehicles

1. Turn the ignition switch to the **ON** position.
2. Read fault codes.
3. Press diagnostic socket button 1 time and hold for approximately 5

seconds. Release button. After 3 seconds the diode light should light up. While the light is still lit, press the button again and hold for approximately 5 seconds. After releasing the button, the diode light should go off.

4. To ensure that the memory is erased, press the button 1 time, for 1 second but not more than 3 seconds. The diode light should flash Code 1–1–1.

5. Start and run engine. If engine will not start, correct the problem before proceeding and start over with step 1.

6. Check to see if new fault codes have been stored in the memory by pressing the diagnostic socket button 1 time, for 1 second but not more than 3 seconds.

7. If fault Code 1–1–1 flashes, it indicates that there are no additional fault codes stored in its memory.

DIAGNOSTIC TROUBLE CODES

1989–94 Vehicles

Code 111 No fault
Code 112 Fault in control module
Code 113 Heated oxygen sensor at maximum enrichment limit; injector clogged, break in lead, etc.
Code 115 Fuel injector 1; wiring harness, ECM
Code 121 Air Mass Meter (MAF) or air pressure sensor signal; missing/faulty
Code 122 Air temperature sensor signal; missing/faulty
Code 123 Engine temperature sensor signal faulty or missing
Code 125 Fuel injector 2; wiring harness, ECM
Code 131 Engine Speed Signal
Code 132 Battery voltage; too low or too high
Code 133 Throttle (Shutter) switch; idle setting faulty
Code 135 Fuel injector 3; wiring harness, ECM
Code 142 Fault in control module
Code 143 Front knock sensor signal missing/faulty
Code 144 Load signal missing from fuel system control module
Code 145 Fuel injector 4; wiring harness, ECM
Code 153 Rear HO2S signal; wiring harness, ECM
Code 154 EGR system leakage; EGR valve, EGR transfer pipes
Code 155 Fuel injector 5; wiring harness, ECM
Code 212 Oxygen sensor (Lambda-sond) signal; missing/faulty
Code 213 Throttle switch; full load setting faulty
Code 214 Timing pick-up signal; missing intermittently
Code 214 Vehicle speed sensor signal intermittent
Code 221 Adaptive Heated Oxygen sensor running rich at part load
Code 222 System relay; signal is missing/faulty
Code 223 Idling valve signal; missing/faulty
Code 224 Missing/faulty temperature sensor circuit; signal missing/faulty
Code 225 A/T pressure sensor signal; sensor/wiring harness faulty
Code 231 Adaptive Heated Oxygen sensor running lean at part load
Code 232 Adaptive Oxygen sensor (Lambda-sond) control; lean or rich, idle
Code 233 Adaptive idling control out of limits
Code 234 Faulty throttle control; engine runs with safety retarded timing (about 10 degrees); up to 1991
Code 241 Exhaust gas recirculation system; sensor senses flow of exhaust back to engine is too small
Code 242 Turbo control valve; not operating
Code 243 Throttle switch signal; missing/faulty
Code 245 AC solenoid closing signal; wiring harness/faulty
Code 311 Speedometer signal missing
Code 312 Signal for knock-controlled enrichment missing
Code 314 Camshaft position sensor signal; missing/faulty
Code 321 Cold start valve signal is missing or shorted to ground
Code 322 Air mass meter burn-off signal missing
Code 324 Camshaft position sensor signal intermittent
Code 325 Memory failure; ECM wiring harness

Code 335 Request to illuminate MIL from TCM; TCM, wiring harness
Code 342 A/T blocking relay; current too high
Code 411 Throttle switch signal; missing/faulty
Code 416 Boost pressure reduction request from TCM; TCM wiring harness/faulty
Code 413 EGR temperature sensor signal; missing or incorrect
Code 421 Boost pressure sensor in control module
Code 423 Throttle position sensor signal; missing/faulty
Code 424 Load signal from fuel system; RPM too low for boost
Code 431 Coolant temperature sensor signal; missing
Code 432 High temperature warning in control box (temp. above 85°C)
Code 433 Rear knock sensor signal; missing/faulty
Code 435 Front HO2S slow response; front HO2S
Code 436 Rear HO2S compensation; rear HO2S
Code 443 TWC efficiency; TWC converter
Code 444 Acceleration sensor signal; acceleration sensor wiring harness
Code 451 Misfire, cylinder 1; Spark plug, spark plug wire, distributor, ignition coil, wiring harness
Code 452 Misfire, cylinder 2; Spark plug, spark plug wire, distributor, ignition coil, wiring harness
Code 453 Misfire, cylinder 3; Spark plug, spark plug wire, distributor, ignition coil, wiring harness
Code 454 Misfire, cylinder 4; Spark plug, spark plug wire, distributor, ignition coil, wiring harness
Code 455 Misfire, cylinder 5; Spark plug, spark plug wire, distributor, ignition coil, wiring harness
Code 512 Heated oxygen sensor at maximum lean running limit
Code 513 High temperature warning in control box (temp. above 95°C)
Code 514 Engine cooling fan, Low speed signal; engine cooling fan relay wiring harness
Code 521 Front HO2S preheating; Front HO2S, wiring harness
Code 522 Rear HO2S preheating; Rear HO2S, wiring harness
Code 531 Power stage group A; fuel injectors, EVAP canister purge solenoid, wiring harness, ECM

Code 532 Power stage group B; fuel injectors, EVAP canister purge solenoid, wiring harness, ECM
Code 533 Power stage group C; fuel injectors, EVAP canister purge solenoid, wiring harness, ECM
Code 534 Power stage group D; fuel injectors, EVAP canister purge solenoid, wiring harness, ECM
Code 535 TC Wastegate Control Solenoid signal; TC Wastegate Control Solenoid, wiring harness, ECM
Code 541 EVAP Canister purge Solenoid signal; EVAP Canister Purge Solenoid, wiring harness, ECM
Code 542 Multiple cylinder misfire; Spark plug, spark plug wire, distributor cap and rotor, ignition coil, wiring harness, ECM
Code 543 Misfire at least one cylinder; Spark plug, spark plug wire, distributor cap and rotor, ignition coil, wiring harness, ECM
Code 544 Multiple cylinder misfire TWC damage; Spark plug, spark plug wire, distributor cap and rotor, ignition coil, wiring harness, ECM, TWC converter
Code 545 Misfire at least one cylinder, TWC damage; Spark plug, spark plug wire, distributor cap and rotor, ignition coil, wiring harness, TWC converter
Code 551 Misfire in cylinder 1, TWC damage; Cylinder 1 spark plug, spark plug wire, distributor cap, ignition coil, wiring harness, TWC converter
Code 552 Misfire in cylinder 2, TWC damage; Cylinder 1 spark plug, spark plug wire, distributor cap, ignition coil, wiring harness, TWC converter
Code 553 Misfire in cylinder 3, TWC damage; Cylinder 1 spark plug, spark plug wire, distributor cap, ignition coil, wiring harness, TWC converter

➡**Code combination explanations are as follows:**

Code 113, 221 & 232 In the part load range; Air/Fuel mixture is lean and on idle
Code 113 & 221 Air/Fuel mixture is lean in the part load range
Code 113 & 231 Air/Fuel mixture is probably rich in the part load range

OBD-II TROUBLE CODES

➡The term control module is a generic term used for the engine control computer. These computers are known by various names including Electronic Control Module (ECM), Powertrain Control Module (PCM), Vehicle Control Module (VCM), Single Board Engine Controller (SBEC), Engine Control Assembly (ECA) and Engine Control Unit (ECU).

➡The term Malfunction Indicator Lamp (MIL) is a generic term used to indicate the instrument panel mounted, engine computer controlled lamp which warns the driver there has been a fault in the system. Some common names for this lamp are the malfunction indicator light and the Service Engine Soon Light. Sometimes just the word Engine will appear.

Introduction

The Federal Clean Air Act of 1990 mandated that all vehicles sold in the United States by the 1996 model year must adhere to the California Air Resources Board (CARB) requirements. These requirements took the form of a monitoring system that we now call OBD-II. The objective was to put into effect a method of monitoring the Electronic Engine Management and Emission Control Systems that would not only aid in their diagnosis, as was the case with OBD-I, but to also alert the driver of an OBD-II equipped vehicle of the early stages of an Emission Control component or system failure.

Reading and Clearing Codes

▶ **See Figures 93, 94, 95, 96 and 97**

It should be noted that with very few exceptions, reading and clearing of OBD-II trouble codes, must be performed using an OBD-II compliant scan

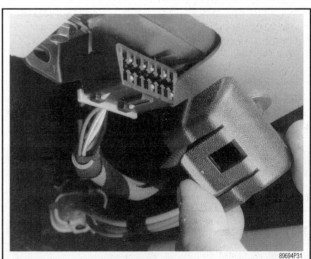

Fig. 93 Hooking up the scan tool is as easy as plugging into the diagnostic link connector

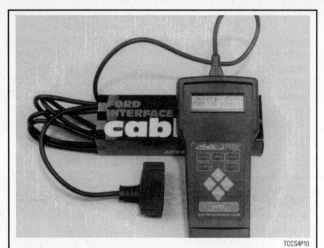

Fig. 94 Inexpensive scan tools, such as this one from AutoXray®, are available to interface with the OBD-II electronics in your vehicle

TCCS4P10

Fig. 95 Among other features, a scan tool combines many standard testers into a single device for quick and accurate diagnosis

TCCS4P06

Fig. 96 Although some times no DTC's are found, that does not rule out a problem

89664P05

Fig. 97 Once the scan tool finds a trouble code it will display the appropriate code number and description

89664P06

tool. This should not be tremendous cause for concern as, as several manufacturers have developed scan tools that are well within the price range of the average do-it-yourselfer. Also, many mechanics will hook up a scan tool to your vehicle for a minimal charge.

Diagnostic Test Modes

Common diagnostic test modes have been created in a way that makes them common to all manufacturers. What this means is that no matter what vehicle you're testing or which piece of scanning equipment you have, all the tests that you need to perform will be the same for all manufacturers using the same terms and trouble codes. There 6 Test Modes as follows:

• Mode 1—Parameter Identification (PID)—accessing of live data, digital and analog values for inputs and outputs etc. Mode 1 is very similar to OBD-I Data Scanning.

• Mode 2—Freeze Frame Data Access—This feature is a built-in freeze frame device right inside the control module. Data will be captured for all emissions related values at the time of a recognized fault, that will be available for the individual to retrieve at a suitable and convenient time.

• Mode 3—This enables all scan tools to retrieve stored DTCs. The DTC can be displayed alone or with descriptive text.

• Mode 4—This is ability of the scan tool to clear all control module emission-related diagnostic information. When the control module is reset like this, an Inspection/Maintenance Readiness code will be stored. (P1000) This only illustrates that the control module is awaiting further vehicle operating modes to complete further on-board monitoring and testing.

• Mode 5—This is the monitoring of the oxygen sensors to determine catalytic converter efficiency.

• Mode 6—Output State Mode (OTM)—allows the individual to energize and de-energize many of the controlled output devices. Through the use of the scanner, the devices can be manually controlled to determine real time functionality.

System Monitoring

To comply with EPA regulations, the OBD-II control module is equipped with software designed to allow it to extensively monitor vehicle emission control systems and components. Once the ignition is turned **ON** or the engine is started, and certain test conditions are met, the control module runs a series of monitors to test the emission control systems and components. Test conditions include different inputs such as time since startup, run-time, engine speed and temperature, transaxle gear position, and the engine open or closed loop status. Once the monitor is started, the control module attempts to run it to completion. If a particular monitor fails a test, a code is set and operating conditions at that time are recorded in memory. If the same component or system fails twice in succession, the Malfunction Indicator Lamp (MIL) is activated.

Monitors are divided into two types: Main Monitors and the Comprehensive Component Monitors.

- Catalyst Monitor
- EGR Monitor
- EVAP Monitor
- Fuel System Monitor
- Misfire Monitor
- Oxygen Sensor Monitor
- Oxygen Sensor Heater Monitor

Certain monitors, in particular the fuel system and misfire monitors, have limitations that are different from the others. The first time either of these monitors fail, the MIL is activated, and engine conditions at the time of the fault are recorded. In order for the control module to turn **OFF** an MIL related to these two monitors, it must determine that no faults are present with engine operating conditions similar to when it detected the fault. To qualify, the engine must be operated within a specified speed range, engine load range and temperature range. This is known as a drive cycle.

System monitoring has been improved over OBD-I by checking and double checking all input and output systems. The interesting thing about OBD-II is that this system has made it more difficult to illuminate the MIL by tightening up the parameters that causes the MIL to come on. Many of the conditions that cause the light to come on are now set out in what are referred to as the following:

- Warm-up Cycle—is operation of the vehicle to the point of warming the coolant by at least 40 degrees Fahrenheit over the last engine off and reaching at least 160 degrees Fahrenheit.

- Drive Cycles—take the warm-up cycle one step further by operating the vehicle to the point whereby it will go into closed loop and include the operating conditions that are necessary to initiate or even complete a specific OBD-II monitor or it will verify a symptom or its repair. A "monitor" is a new term that describes an operating strategy that can run internal tests of a specific system, component or function. This is very similar to on-board computer self tests.

- OBD-II Trip—is often referred to as a trip, and again takes the above mentioned steps further in progression. Beginning with an engine off period, after the engine is started, the vehicle must travel a specified distance to allow the following five OBD-II monitors to complete all of their tests:

1. Misfires
2. Fuel System
3. Comprehensive components
4. EGR
5. HO2S

OBD-II Drive Cycle This is a very specific combination of driving conditions that have been set out by the Federal Clean Air Act. Completion of all the conditions of this cycle ensures that all monitors have completed their required tests. This cycle is the most comprehensive of all the cycles and is illustrated in repair and diagnostic manuals through the use of a chart. In order for all monitors to take place the following must happen:

1. Cold Start. In order to be classified as a cold start the engine coolant temperature must be below 50°C (122°F) and within 6°C (11°F) of the ambient air temperature at startup. Do not leave the key on prior to the cold start or the heated oxygen sensor diagnostic may not run.

2. Idle. The engine must be run for two and a half minutes with the air conditioner on and rear defroster on. The more electrical load you can apply the better. This will test the O2 heater, Passive Air, Purge "No Flow", Misfire and if closed loop is achieved, Fuel Trim.

3. Accelerate. Turn off the air conditioner and all the other loads and apply half throttle until 88km/hr (55mph) is reached. During this time the Misfire, Fuel Trim, and Purge Flow diagnostics will be performed.

4. Hold Steady Speed. Hold a steady speed of 88km/hr (55mph) for 3 minutes. During this time the O2 response, air Intrusive, EGR, Purge, Misfire, and Fuel Trim diagnostics will be performed.

5. Decelerate. Let off the accelerator pedal. Do not shift, touch the brake or clutch. It is important to let the vehicle coast along gradually slowing down to 32km/hr (20 mph). During this time the EGR, Purge and Fuel Trim diagnostics will be performed.

6. Accelerate. Accelerate at 3/4 throttle until 88-96 km/hr (55-60mph). This will perform the same diagnostics as in step 3.

7. Hold Steady Speed. Hold a steady speed of 88km/hr (55mph) for five minutes. During this time, in addition to the diagnostics performed in step 4, the catalyst monitor diagnostics will be performed. If the catalyst is marginal or the battery has been disconnected, it may take 5 complete driving cycles to determine the state of the catalyst.

8. Decelerate. This will perform the same diagnostics as in step 5. Again, don't press the clutch or brakes or shift gears.

Trouble Code Description

♦ See Figure 98

In the past, trouble code descriptions varied between manufacturers, years, makes and models. OBD-II requires that all vehicle manufacturers use a common Diagnostic Trouble Code (DTC) numbering system. Since the generic listing was not specific enough, most manufacturers came up with their own DTC listings which are called manufacturer specific codes. Both generic and manufacturer specific codes are 5 digits. The numbers can be decoded as follows:

The first digit is a letter which identifies the function of the device or circuit which has the fault. This digit can be either:

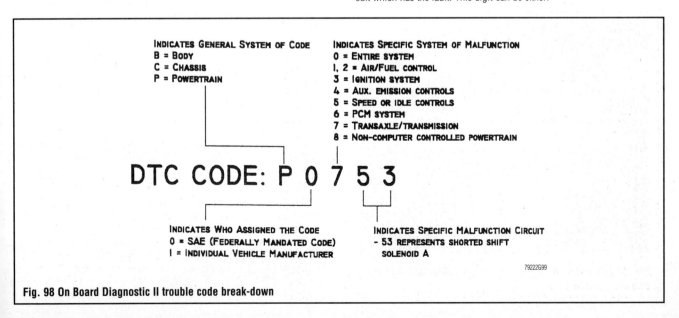

INDICATES GENERAL SYSTEM OF CODE
B = BODY
C = CHASSIS
P = POWERTRAIN

INDICATES SPECIFIC SYSTEM OF MALFUNCTION
0 = ENTIRE SYSTEM
1, 2 = AIR/FUEL CONTROL
3 = IGNITION SYSTEM
4 = AUX. EMISSION CONTROLS
5 = SPEED OR IDLE CONTROLS
6 = PCM SYSTEM
7 = TRANSAXLE/TRANSMISSION
8 = NON-COMPUTER CONTROLLED POWERTRAIN

DTC CODE: P 0 7 5 3

INDICATES WHO ASSIGNED THE CODE
0 = SAE (FEDERALLY MANDATED CODE)
I = INDIVIDUAL VEHICLE MANUFACTURER

INDICATES SPECIFIC MALFUNCTION CIRCUIT
- 53 REPRESENTS SHORTED SHIFT SOLENOID A

79222G99

Fig. 98 On Board Diagnostic II trouble code break-down

- P—Powertrain
- B—Body
- C—Chassis
- U—Network or data link code

The second digit is either a 0 or 1 and indicates whether the code is generic or manufacturer specific.

- 0—Generic
- 1—Manufacturer Specific

The third digit represents the specific vehicle circuit or system that has the fault. Listed below are the number identifiers for the powertrain system.

- 1—Fuel and Air Metering
- 2—Fuel and Air Metering (Injector Circuit Malfunctions Only)
- 3—Ignition System or Misfire
- 4—Auxiliary Emission Control
- 5—Vehicle Speed Control and Idle Control System
- 6—Computer and Auxiliary Outputs
- 7—Transmission
- 8—Transmission

The last two digits indicate the specific trouble code.

On OBD-II vehicles there are two different types of DTCs: Stored and Pending. For a DTC to become Stored, certain malfunction conditions must occur. The condition(s) required to Store codes are different for every DTC and vary by vehicle manufacturer.

In order for some DTCs to become Stored, a malfunction condition has to happen more than once. If the malfunction conditions are required to occur more than once, the potential malfunction is called a Pending DTC. The DTC remains pending until the malfunction condition occurs the required number of times to make the code stored. If the malfunction condition does not occur again after a set time the pending DTC will be cleared.

SAE Generic OBD-II Trouble Codes

On board diagnostic requirements have been defined by the OBD-II legislation in California and the Federal Clean Air Act. These requirements include the need for standardization of various parts of the system, including some of the Diagnostic Trouble Codes.

Prior to OBD-II, there was no uniformity in these numeric Diagnostic Trouble Codes (DTC) between manufacturers, and in some cases, even within the same manufacturer across different product lines. The Society of Automotive Engineers (SAE) codes from document J2012 provide some recommended uniformity for these codes.

In this section you will find the SAE recommended Industry Common Trouble codes for the powertrain control system. The fact that a code is recommended as a Industry Common Code does not imply that it is a Required Code (Legislated), an Emission Related Code, or that it indicates a fault that will cause the Malfunction Indicator Light to be illuminated.

In the following sections you will find the manufacturer specific codes. These are fault codes that will not generally be used by a majority of the manufacturers due to basic system differences, implementation differences, or diagnostic strategy differences. Each vehicle manufacturer or supplier who designs and specifies diagnostic algorithms, software, and diagnostic trouble codes have been strongly encouraged to remain consistent across their product line when assigning codes in the manufacturer controlled area.

P0100 Mass or Volume Air Flow Circuit Malfunction

P0101 Mass or Volume Air Flow Circuit Range/Performance Problem

P0102 Mass or Volume Air Flow Circuit Low Input

P0103 Mass or Volume Air Flow Circuit High Input

P0104 Mass or Volume Air Flow Circuit Intermittent

P0105 Manifold Absolute Pressure/Barometric Pressure Circuit Malfunction

P0106 Manifold Absolute Pressure/Barometric Pressure Circuit Range/Performance Problem

P0107 Manifold Absolute Pressure/Barometric Pressure Circuit Low Input

P0108 Manifold Absolute Pressure/Barometric Pressure Circuit High Input

P0109 Manifold Absolute Pressure/Barometric Pressure Circuit Intermittent

P0110 Intake Air Temperature Circuit Malfunction

P0111 Intake Air Temperature Circuit Range/Performance Problem

P0112 Intake Air Temperature Circuit Low Input

P0113 Intake Air Temperature Circuit High Input

P0114 Intake Air Temperature Circuit Intermittent

P0115 Engine Coolant Temperature Circuit Malfunction

P0116 Engine Coolant Temperature Circuit Range/Performance Problem

P0117 Engine Coolant Temperature Circuit Low Input

P0118 Engine Coolant Temperature Circuit High Input

P0119 Engine Coolant Temperature Circuit Intermittent

P0120 Throttle/Pedal Position Sensor/Switch "A" Circuit Malfunction

P0121 Throttle/Pedal Position Sensor/Switch "A" Circuit Range/Performance Problem

P0122 Throttle/Pedal Position Sensor/Switch "A" Circuit Low Input

P0123 Throttle/Pedal Position Sensor/Switch "A" Circuit High Input

P0124 Throttle/Pedal Position Sensor/Switch "A" Circuit Intermittent

P0125 Insufficient Coolant Temperature For Closed Loop Fuel Control

P0126 Insufficient Coolant Temperature For Stable Operation

P0130 O2 Circuit Malfunction (Bank no. 1 Sensor no. 1)

P0131 O2 Sensor Circuit Low Voltage (Bank no. 1 Sensor no. 1)

P0132 O2 Sensor Circuit High Voltage (Bank no. 1 Sensor no. 1)

P0133 O2 Sensor Circuit Slow Response (Bank no. 1 Sensor no. 1)

P0134 O2 Sensor Circuit No Activity Detected (Bank no. 1 Sensor no. 1)

P0135 O2 Sensor Heater Circuit Malfunction (Bank no. 1 Sensor no. 1)

P0136 O2 Sensor Circuit Malfunction (Bank no. 1 Sensor no. 2)

P0137 O2 Sensor Circuit Low Voltage (Bank no. 1 Sensor no. 2)

P0138 O2 Sensor Circuit High Voltage (Bank no. 1 Sensor no. 2)

P0139 O2 Sensor Circuit Slow Response (Bank no. 1 Sensor no. 2)

P0140 O2 Sensor Circuit No Activity Detected (Bank no. 1 Sensor no. 2)

P0141 O2 Sensor Heater Circuit Malfunction (Bank no. 1 Sensor no. 2)

P0142 O2 Sensor Circuit Malfunction (Bank no. 1 Sensor no. 3)

P0143 O2 Sensor Circuit Low Voltage (Bank no. 1 Sensor no. 3)

P0144 O2 Sensor Circuit High Voltage (Bank no. 1 Sensor no. 3)

P0145 O2 Sensor Circuit Slow Response (Bank no. 1 Sensor no. 3)

P0146 O2 Sensor Circuit No Activity Detected (Bank no. 1 Sensor no. 3)

P0147 O2 Sensor Heater Circuit Malfunction (Bank no. 1 Sensor no. 3)

P0150 O2 Sensor Circuit Malfunction (Bank no. 2 Sensor no. 1)

P0151 O2 Sensor Circuit Low Voltage (Bank no. 2 Sensor no. 1)

P0152 O2 Sensor Circuit High Voltage (Bank no. 2 Sensor no. 1)

P0153 O2 Sensor Circuit Slow Response (Bank no. 2 Sensor no. 1)

P0154 O2 Sensor Circuit No Activity Detected (Bank no. 2 Sensor no. 1)

P0155 O2 Sensor Heater Circuit Malfunction (Bank no. 2 Sensor no. 1)

P0156 O2 Sensor Circuit Malfunction (Bank no. 2 Sensor no. 2)

P0157 O2 Sensor Circuit Low Voltage (Bank no. 2 Sensor no. 2)

P0158 O2 Sensor Circuit High Voltage (Bank no. 2 Sensor no. 2)

P0159 O2 Sensor Circuit Slow Response (Bank no. 2 Sensor no. 2)

P0160 O2 Sensor Circuit No Activity Detected (Bank no. 2 Sensor no. 2)

P0161 O2 Sensor Heater Circuit Malfunction (Bank no. 2 Sensor no. 2)

P0162 O2 Sensor Circuit Malfunction (Bank no. 2 Sensor no. 3)

P0163 O2 Sensor Circuit Low Voltage (Bank no. 2 Sensor no. 3)

P0164 O2 Sensor Circuit High Voltage (Bank no. 2 Sensor no. 3)

P0165 O2 Sensor Circuit Slow Response (Bank no. 2 Sensor no. 3)

P0166 O2 Sensor Circuit No Activity Detected (Bank no. 2 Sensor no. 3)

P0167 O2 Sensor Heater Circuit Malfunction (Bank no. 2 Sensor no. 3)

P0170 Fuel Trim Malfunction (Bank no. 1)

P0171 System Too Lean (Bank no. 1)

P0172 System Too Rich (Bank no. 1)

P0173 Fuel Trim Malfunction (Bank no. 2)

P0174 System Too Lean (Bank no. 2)

P0175 System Too Rich (Bank no. 2)
P0176 Fuel Composition Sensor Circuit Malfunction
P0177 Fuel Composition Sensor Circuit Range/Performance
P0178 Fuel Composition Sensor Circuit Low Input
P0179 Fuel Composition Sensor Circuit High Input
P0180 Fuel Temperature Sensor "A" Circuit Malfunction
P0181 Fuel Temperature Sensor "A" Circuit Range/Performance
P0182 Fuel Temperature Sensor "A" Circuit Low Input
P0183 Fuel Temperature Sensor "A" Circuit High Input
P0184 Fuel Temperature Sensor "A" Circuit Intermittent
P0185 Fuel Temperature Sensor "B" Circuit Malfunction
P0186 Fuel Temperature Sensor "B" Circuit Range/Perfo-rmance
P0187 Fuel Temperature Sensor "B" Circuit Low Input
P0188 Fuel Temperature Sensor "B" Circuit High Input
P0189 Fuel Temperature Sensor "B" Circuit Intermittent
P0190 Fuel Rail Pressure Sensor Circuit Malfunction
P0191 Fuel Rail Pressure Sensor Circuit Range/Performance
P0192 Fuel Rail Pressure Sensor Circuit Low Input
P0193 Fuel Rail Pressure Sensor Circuit High Input
P0194 Fuel Rail Pressure Sensor Circuit Intermittent
P0195 Engine Oil Temperature Sensor Malfunction
P0196 Engine Oil Temperature Sensor Range/Performance
P0197 Engine Oil Temperature Sensor Low
P0198 Engine Oil Temperature Sensor High
P0199 Engine Oil Temperature Sensor Intermittent
P0200 Injector Circuit Malfunction
P0201 Injector Circuit Malfunction—Cylinder no. 1
P0202 Injector Circuit Malfunction—Cylinder no. 2
P0203 Injector Circuit Malfunction—Cylinder no. 3
P0204 Injector Circuit Malfunction—Cylinder no. 4
P0205 Injector Circuit Malfunction—Cylinder no. 5
P0206 Injector Circuit Malfunction—Cylinder no. 6
P0207 Injector Circuit Malfunction—Cylinder no. 7
P0208 Injector Circuit Malfunction—Cylinder no. 8
P0209 Injector Circuit Malfunction—Cylinder no. 9
P0210 Injector Circuit Malfunction—Cylinder no. 10
P0211 Injector Circuit Malfunction—Cylinder no. 11
P0212 Injector Circuit Malfunction—Cylinder no. 12
P0213 Cold Start Injector no. 1 Malfunction
P0214 Cold Start Injector no. 2 Malfunction
P0215 Engine Shutoff Solenoid Malfunction
P0216 Injection Timing Control Circuit Malfunction
P0217 Engine Over Temperature Condition
P0218 Transmission Over Temperature Condition
P0219 Engine Over Speed Condition
P0220 Throttle/Pedal Position Sensor/Switch "B" Circuit Malfunction
P0221 Throttle/Pedal Position Sensor/Switch "B" Circuit Range/Performance Problem
P0222 Throttle/Pedal Position Sensor/Switch "B" Circuit Low Input
P0223 Throttle/Pedal Position Sensor/Switch "B" Circuit High Input
P0224 Throttle/Pedal Position Sensor/Switch "B" Circuit Intermittent
P0225 Throttle/Pedal Position Sensor/Switch "C" Circuit Malfunction
P0226 Throttle/Pedal Position Sensor/Switch "C" Circuit Range/Performance Problem
P0227 Throttle/Pedal Position Sensor/Switch "C" Circuit Low Input
P0228 Throttle/Pedal Position Sensor/Switch "C" Circuit High Input
P0229 Throttle/Pedal Position Sensor/Switch "C" Circuit Intermittent
P0230 Fuel Pump Primary Circuit Malfunction
P0231 Fuel Pump Secondary Circuit Low
P0232 Fuel Pump Secondary Circuit High
P0233 Fuel Pump Secondary Circuit Intermittent

P0234 Engine Over Boost Condition
P0261 Cylinder no. 1 Injector Circuit Low
P0262 Cylinder no. 1 Injector Circuit High
P0263 Cylinder no. 1 Contribution/Balance Fault
P0264 Cylinder no. 2 Injector Circuit Low
P0265 Cylinder no. 2 Injector Circuit High
P0266 Cylinder no. 2 Contribution/Balance Fault
P0267 Cylinder no. 3 Injector Circuit Low
P0268 Cylinder no. 3 Injector Circuit High
P0269 Cylinder no. 3 Contribution/Balance Fault
P0270 Cylinder no. 4 Injector Circuit Low
P0271 Cylinder no. 4 Injector Circuit High
P0272 Cylinder no. 4 Contribution/Balance Fault
P0273 Cylinder no. 5 Injector Circuit Low
P0274 Cylinder no. 5 Injector Circuit High
P0275 Cylinder no. 5 Contribution/Balance Fault
P0276 Cylinder no. 6 Injector Circuit Low
P0277 Cylinder no. 6 Injector Circuit High
P0278 Cylinder no. 6 Contribution/Balance Fault
P0279 Cylinder no. 7 Injector Circuit Low
P0280 Cylinder no. 7 Injector Circuit High
P0281 Cylinder no. 7 Contribution/Balance Fault
P0282 Cylinder no. 8 Injector Circuit Low
P0283 Cylinder no. 8 Injector Circuit High
P0284 Cylinder no. 8 Contribution/Balance Fault
P0285 Cylinder no. 9 Injector Circuit Low
P0286 Cylinder no. 9 Injector Circuit High
P0287 Cylinder no. 9 Contribution/Balance Fault
P0288 Cylinder no. 10 Injector Circuit Low
P0289 Cylinder no. 10 Injector Circuit High
P0290 Cylinder no. 10 Contribution/Balance Fault
P0291 Cylinder no. 11 Injector Circuit Low
P0292 Cylinder no. 11 Injector Circuit High
P0293 Cylinder no. 11 Contribution/Balance Fault
P0294 Cylinder no. 12 Injector Circuit Low
P0295 Cylinder no. 12 Injector Circuit High
P0296 Cylinder no. 12 Contribution/Balance Fault
P0300 Random/Multiple Cylinder Misfire Detected
P0301 Cylinder no. 1—Misfire Detected
P0302 Cylinder no. 2—Misfire Detected
P0303 Cylinder no. 3—Misfire Detected
P0304 Cylinder no. 4—Misfire Detected
P0305 Cylinder no. 5—Misfire Detected
P0306 Cylinder no. 6—Misfire Detected
P0307 Cylinder no. 7—Misfire Detected
P0308 Cylinder no. 8—Misfire Detected
P0309 Cylinder no. 9—Misfire Detected
P0310 Cylinder no. 10—Misfire Detected
P0311 Cylinder no. 11—Misfire Detected
P0312 Cylinder no. 12—Misfire Detected
P0320 Ignition/Distributor Engine Speed Input Circuit Malfunction
P0321 Ignition/Distributor Engine Speed Input Circuit Range/Performance
P0322 Ignition/Distributor Engine Speed Input Circuit No Signal
P0323 Ignition/Distributor Engine Speed Input Circuit Intermittent
P0325 Knock Sensor no. 1—Circuit Malfunction (Bank no. 1 or Single Sensor)
P0326 Knock Sensor no. 1—Circuit Range/Performance (Bank no. 1 or Single Sensor)
P0327 Knock Sensor no. 1—Circuit Low Input (Bank no. 1 or Single Sensor)
P0328 Knock Sensor no. 1—Circuit High Input (Bank no. 1 or Single Sensor)

P0329 Knock Sensor no. 1—Circuit Input Intermittent (Bank no. 1 or Single Sensor)
P0330 Knock Sensor no. 2—Circuit Malfunction (Bank no. 2)
P0331 Knock Sensor no. 2—Circuit Range/Performance (Bank no. 2)
P0332 Knock Sensor no. 2—Circuit Low Input (Bank no. 2)
P0333 Knock Sensor no. 2—Circuit High Input (Bank no. 2)
P0334 Knock Sensor no. 2—Circuit Input Intermittent (Bank no. 2)
P0335 Crankshaft Position Sensor "A" Circuit Malfunction
P0336 Crankshaft Position Sensor "A" Circuit Range/Performance
P0337 Crankshaft Position Sensor "A" Circuit Low Input
P0338 Crankshaft Position Sensor "A" Circuit High Input
P0339 Crankshaft Position Sensor "A" Circuit Intermittent
P0340 Camshaft Position Sensor Circuit Malfunction
P0341 Camshaft Position Sensor Circuit Range/Performance
P0342 Camshaft Position Sensor Circuit Low Input
P0343 Camshaft Position Sensor Circuit High Input
P0344 Camshaft Position Sensor Circuit Intermittent
P0350 Ignition Coil Primary/Secondary Circuit Malfunction
P0351 Ignition Coil "A" Primary/Secondary Circuit Malfunction
P0352 Ignition Coil "B" Primary/Secondary Circuit Malfunction
P0353 Ignition Coil "C" Primary/Secondary Circuit Malfunction
P0354 Ignition Coil "D" Primary/Secondary Circuit Malfunction
P0355 Ignition Coil "E" Primary/Secondary Circuit Malfunction
P0356 Ignition Coil "F" Primary/Secondary Circuit Malfunction
P0357 Ignition Coil "G" Primary/Secondary Circuit Malfunction
P0358 Ignition Coil "H" Primary/Secondary Circuit Malfunction
P0359 Ignition Coil "I" Primary/Secondary Circuit Malfunction
P0360 Ignition Coil "J" Primary/Secondary Circuit Malfunction
P0361 Ignition Coil "K" Primary/Secondary Circuit Malfunction
P0362 Ignition Coil "L" Primary/Secondary Circuit Malfunction
P0370 Timing Reference High Resolution Signal "A" Malfunction
P0371 Timing Reference High Resolution Signal "A" Too Many Pulses
P0372 Timing Reference High Resolution Signal "A" Too Few Pulses
P0373 Timing Reference High Resolution Signal "A" Intermittent/Erratic Pulses
P0374 Timing Reference High Resolution Signal "A" No Pulses
P0375 Timing Reference High Resolution Signal "B" Malfunction
P0376 Timing Reference High Resolution Signal "B" Too Many Pulses
P0377 Timing Reference High Resolution Signal "B" Too Few Pulses
P0378 Timing Reference High Resolution Signal "B" Intermittent/Erratic Pulses
P0379 Timing Reference High Resolution Signal "B" No Pulses
P0380 Glow Plug/Heater Circuit "A" Malfunction
P0381 Glow Plug/Heater Indicator Circuit Malfunction
P0382 Glow Plug/Heater Circuit "B" Malfunction
P0385 Crankshaft Position Sensor "B" Circuit Malfunction
P0386 Crankshaft Position Sensor "B" Circuit Range/Performance
P0387 Crankshaft Position Sensor "B" Circuit Low Input
P0388 Crankshaft Position Sensor "B" Circuit High Input
P0389 Crankshaft Position Sensor "B" Circuit Intermittent
P0400 Exhaust Gas Recirculation Flow Malfunction
P0401 Exhaust Gas Recirculation Flow Insufficient Detected
P0402 Exhaust Gas Recirculation Flow Excessive Detected
P0403 Exhaust Gas Recirculation Circuit Malfunction
P0404 Exhaust Gas Recirculation Circuit Range/Performance
P0405 Exhaust Gas Recirculation Sensor "A" Circuit Low
P0406 Exhaust Gas Recirculation Sensor "A" Circuit High
P0407 Exhaust Gas Recirculation Sensor "B" Circuit Low
P0408 Exhaust Gas Recirculation Sensor "B" Circuit High
P0410 Secondary Air Injection System Malfunction
P0411 Secondary Air Injection System Incorrect Flow Detected
P0412 Secondary Air Injection System Switching Valve "A" Circuit Malfunction

P0413 Secondary Air Injection System Switching Valve "A" Circuit Open
P0414 Secondary Air Injection System Switching Valve "A" Circuit Shorted
P0415 Secondary Air Injection System Switching Valve "B" Circuit Malfunction
P0416 Secondary Air Injection System Switching Valve "B" Circuit Open
P0417 Secondary Air Injection System Switching Valve "B" Circuit Shorted
P0418 Secondary Air Injection System Relay "A" Circuit Malfunction
P0419 Secondary Air Injection System Relay "B" Circuit Malfunction
P0420 Catalyst System Efficiency Below Threshold (Bank no. 1)
P0421 Warm Up Catalyst Efficiency Below Threshold (Bank no. 1)
P0422 Main Catalyst Efficiency Below Threshold (Bank no. 1)
P0423 Heated Catalyst Efficiency Below Threshold (Bank no. 1)
P0424 Heated Catalyst Temperature Below Threshold (Bank no. 1)
P0430 Catalyst System Efficiency Below Threshold (Bank no. 2)
P0431 Warm Up Catalyst Efficiency Below Threshold (Bank no. 2)
P0432 Main Catalyst Efficiency Below Threshold (Bank no. 2)
P0433 Heated Catalyst Efficiency Below Threshold (Bank no. 2)
P0434 Heated Catalyst Temperature Below Threshold (Bank no. 2)
P0440 Evaporative Emission Control System Malfunction
P0441 Evaporative Emission Control System Incorrect Purge Flow
P0442 Evaporative Emission Control System Leak Detected (Small Leak)
P0443 Evaporative Emission Control System Purge Control Valve Circuit Malfunction
P0444 Evaporative Emission Control System Purge Control Valve Circuit Open
P0445 Evaporative Emission Control System Purge Control Valve Circuit Shorted
P0446 Evaporative Emission Control System Vent Control Circuit Malfunction
P0447 Evaporative Emission Control System Vent Control Circuit Open
P0448 Evaporative Emission Control System Vent Control Circuit Shorted
P0449 Evaporative Emission Control System Vent Valve/Solenoid Circuit Malfunction
P0450 Evaporative Emission Control System Pressure Sensor Malfunction
P0451 Evaporative Emission Control System Pressure Sensor Range/Performance
P0452 Evaporative Emission Control System Pressure Sensor Low Input
P0453 Evaporative Emission Control System Pressure Sensor High Input
P0454 Evaporative Emission Control System Pressure Sensor Intermittent
P0455 Evaporative Emission Control System Leak Detected (Gross Leak)
P0460 Fuel Level Sensor Circuit Malfunction
P0461 Fuel Level Sensor Circuit Range/Performance
P0462 Fuel Level Sensor Circuit Low Input
P0463 Fuel Level Sensor Circuit High Input
P0464 Fuel Level Sensor Circuit Intermittent
P0465 Purge Flow Sensor Circuit Malfunction
P0466 Purge Flow Sensor Circuit Range/Performance
P0467 Purge Flow Sensor Circuit Low Input
P0468 Purge Flow Sensor Circuit High Input
P0469 Purge Flow Sensor Circuit Intermittent
P0470 Exhaust Pressure Sensor Malfunction
P0471 Exhaust Pressure Sensor Range/Performance
P0472 Exhaust Pressure Sensor Low
P0473 Exhaust Pressure Sensor High
P0474 Exhaust Pressure Sensor Intermittent
P0475 Exhaust Pressure Control Valve Malfunction
P0476 Exhaust Pressure Control Valve Range/Performance

P0477 Exhaust Pressure Control Valve Low
P0478 Exhaust Pressure Control Valve High
P0479 Exhaust Pressure Control Valve Intermittent
P0480 Cooling Fan no. 1 Control Circuit Malfunction
P0481 Cooling Fan no. 2 Control Circuit Malfunction
P0482 Cooling Fan no. 3 Control Circuit Malfunction
P0483 Cooling Fan Rationality Check Malfunction
P0484 Cooling Fan Circuit Over Current
P0485 Cooling Fan Power/Ground Circuit Malfunction
P0500 Vehicle Speed Sensor Malfunction
P0501 Vehicle Speed Sensor Range/Performance
P0502 Vehicle Speed Sensor Circuit Low Input
P0503 Vehicle Speed Sensor Intermittent/Erratic/High
P0505 Idle Control System Malfunction
P0506 Idle Control System RPM Lower Than Expected
P0507 Idle Control System RPM Higher Than Expected
P0510 Closed Throttle Position Switch Malfunction
P0520 Engine Oil Pressure Sensor/Switch Circuit Malfunction
P0521 Engine Oil Pressure Sensor/Switch Range/Performance
P0522 Engine Oil Pressure Sensor/Switch Low Voltage
P0523 Engine Oil Pressure Sensor/Switch High Voltage
P0530 A/C Refrigerant Pressure Sensor Circuit Malfunction
P0531 A/C Refrigerant Pressure Sensor Circuit Range/Performance
P0532 A/C Refrigerant Pressure Sensor Circuit Low Input
P0533 A/C Refrigerant Pressure Sensor Circuit High Input
P0534 A/C Refrigerant Charge Loss
P0550 Power Steering Pressure Sensor Circuit Malfunction
P0551 Power Steering Pressure Sensor Circuit Range/Performance
P0552 Power Steering Pressure Sensor Circuit Low Input
P0553 Power Steering Pressure Sensor Circuit High Input
P0554 Power Steering Pressure Sensor Circuit Intermittent
P0560 System Voltage Malfunction
P0561 System Voltage Unstable
P0562 System Voltage Low
P0563 System Voltage High
P0565 Cruise Control On Signal Malfunction
P0566 Cruise Control Off Signal Malfunction
P0567 Cruise Control Resume Signal Malfunction
P0568 Cruise Control Set Signal Malfunction
P0569 Cruise Control Coast Signal Malfunction
P0570 Cruise Control Accel Signal Malfunction
P0571 Cruise Control/Brake Switch "A" Circuit Malfunction
P0572 Cruise Control/Brake Switch "A" Circuit Low
P0573 Cruise Control/Brake Switch "A" Circuit High
P0574–P0580 Reserved for Cruise Codes
P0600 Serial Communication Link Malfunction
P0601 Internal Control Module Memory Check Sum Error
P0602 Control Module Programming Error
P0603 Internal Control Module Keep Alive Memory (KAM) Error
P0604 Internal Control Module Random Access Memory (RAM) Error
P0605 Internal Control Module Read Only Memory (ROM) Error
P0606 PCM Processor Fault
P0608 Control Module VSS Output "A" Malfunction
P0609 Control Module VSS Output "B" Malfunction
P0620 Generator Control Circuit Malfunction
P0621 Generator Lamp "L" Control Circuit Malfunction
P0622 Generator Field "F" Control Circuit Malfunction
P0650 Malfunction Indicator Lamp (MIL) Control Circuit Malfunction
P0654 Engine RPM Output Circuit Malfunction
P0655 Engine Hot Lamp Output Control Circuit Malfunction
P0656 Fuel Level Output Circuit Malfunction
P0700 Transmission Control System Malfunction
P0701 Transmission Control System Range/Performance

P0702 Transmission Control System Electrical
P0703 Torque Converter/Brake Switch "B" Circuit Malfunction
P0704 Clutch Switch Input Circuit Malfunction
P0705 Transmission Range Sensor Circuit Malfunction (PRNDL Input)
P0706 Transmission Range Sensor Circuit Range/Performance
P0707 Transmission Range Sensor Circuit Low Input
P0708 Transmission Range Sensor Circuit High Input
P0709 Transmission Range Sensor Circuit Intermittent
P0710 Transmission Fluid Temperature Sensor Circuit Malfunction
P0711 Transmission Fluid Temperature Sensor Circuit Range/Performance
P0712 Transmission Fluid Temperature Sensor Circuit Low Input
P0713 Transmission Fluid Temperature Sensor Circuit High Input
P0714 Transmission Fluid Temperature Sensor Circuit Intermittent
P0715 Input/Turbine Speed Sensor Circuit Malfunction
P0716 Input/Turbine Speed Sensor Circuit Range/Performance
P0717 Input/Turbine Speed Sensor Circuit No Signal
P0718 Input/Turbine Speed Sensor Circuit Intermittent
P0719 Torque Converter/Brake Switch "B" Circuit Low
P0720 Output Speed Sensor Circuit Malfunction
P0721 Output Speed Sensor Circuit Range/Performance
P0722 Output Speed Sensor Circuit No Signal
P0723 Output Speed Sensor Circuit Intermittent
P0724 Torque Converter/Brake Switch "B" Circuit High
P0725 Engine Speed Input Circuit Malfunction
P0726 Engine Speed Input Circuit Range/Performance
P0727 Engine Speed Input Circuit No Signal
P0728 Engine Speed Input Circuit Intermittent
P0730 Incorrect Gear Ratio
P0731 Gear no. 1 Incorrect Ratio
P0732 Gear no. 2 Incorrect Ratio
P0733 Gear no. 3 Incorrect Ratio
P0734 Gear no. 4 Incorrect Ratio
P0735 Gear no. 5 Incorrect Ratio
P0736 Reverse Incorrect Ratio
P0740 Torque Converter Clutch Circuit Malfunction
P0741 Torque Converter Clutch Circuit Performance or Stuck Off
P0742 Torque Converter Clutch Circuit Stuck On
P0743 Torque Converter Clutch Circuit Electrical
P0744 Torque Converter Clutch Circuit Intermittent
P0745 Pressure Control Solenoid Malfunction
P0746 Pressure Control Solenoid Performance or Stuck Off
P0747 Pressure Control Solenoid Stuck On
P0748 Pressure Control Solenoid Electrical
P0749 Pressure Control Solenoid Intermittent
P0750 Shift Solenoid "A" Malfunction
P0751 Shift Solenoid "A" Performance or Stuck Off
P0752 Shift Solenoid "A" Stuck On
P0753 Shift Solenoid "A" Electrical
P0754 Shift Solenoid "A" Intermittent
P0755 Shift Solenoid "B" Malfunction
P0756 Shift Solenoid "B" Performance or Stuck Off
P0757 Shift Solenoid "B" Stuck On
P0758 Shift Solenoid "B" Electrical
P0759 Shift Solenoid "B" Intermittent
P0760 Shift Solenoid "C" Malfunction
P0761 Shift Solenoid "C" Performance Or Stuck Off
P0762 Shift Solenoid "C" Stuck On
P0763 Shift Solenoid "C" Electrical
P0764 Shift Solenoid "C" Intermittent
P0765 Shift Solenoid "D" Malfunction
P0766 Shift Solenoid "D" Performance Or Stuck Off
P0767 Shift Solenoid "D" Stuck On

P0768 Shift Solenoid "D" Electrical
P0769 Shift Solenoid "D" Intermittent
P0770 Shift Solenoid "E" Malfunction
P0771 Shift Solenoid "E" Performance Or Stuck Oft
P0772 Shift Solenoid "E" Stuck On
P0773 Shift Solenoid "E" Electrical
P0774 Shift Solenoid "E" Intermittent
P0780 Shift Malfunction
P0781 1–2 Shift Malfunction
P0782 2–3 Shift Malfunction
P0783 3–4 Shift Malfunction
P0784 4–5 Shift Malfunction
P0785 Shift/Timing Solenoid Malfunction
P0786 Shift/Timing Solenoid Range/Performance
P0787 Shift/Timing Solenoid Low
P0788 Shift/Timing Solenoid High
P0789 Shift/Timing Solenoid Intermittent
P0790 Normal/Performance Switch Circuit Malfunction
P0801 Reverse Inhibit Control Circuit Malfunction
P0803 1–4 Upshift (Skip Shift) Solenoid Control Circuit Malfunction
P0804 1–4 Upshift (Skip Shift) Lamp Control Circuit Malfunction

Acura

READING CODES

Reading the control module memory is on of the first steps in OBD-II system diagnostics. This step should be initially performed to determine the general nature of the fault. Subsequent readings will determine if the fault has been cleared.

Reading codes can be performed by any of the methods below:
- Read the control module memory with the Generic Scan Tool (GST)
- Read the control module memory with the vehicle manufacturer's specific tester

To read the fault codes, connect the scan tool or tester according to the manufacturer's instructions. Follow the manufacturer's specified procedure for reading the codes.

CLEARING CODES

Control module reset procedures are a very important part of OBD-II system diagnostics. This step should be done at the end of any fault code repair and at the end of any driveability repair.

Clearing codes can be performed by any of the methods below:
- Clear the control module memory with the Generic Scan Tool (GST)
- Clear the control module memory with the vehicle manufacturer's specific tester
- Turn the ignition off and remove the negative battery cable for at least 1 minute.

Removing the negative battery cable may cause other systems in the vehicle to loose their memory. Prior to removing the cable, ensure you have the proper reset codes for radios and alarms.

➡**The MIL may also be de-activated for some codes if the vehicle completes three consecutive trips without a fault detected with vehicle conditions similar to those present during the fault.**

ACURA SPECIFIC OBD-II TROUBLE CODES

P1106 Map Sensor Circuit Intermittent High Voltage
P1107 MAP Sensor Circuit Intermittent Low Voltage
P1111 IAT Sensor Circuit Intermittent High Voltage
P1112 IAT Sensor Circuit Intermittent Low Voltage
P1114 ECT Sensor Circuit Intermittent Low Voltage
P1115 ECT Sensor Circuit Intermittent High Voltage

P1121 TP Sensor Circuit Intermittent High Voltage
P1122 TP Sensor Circuit Intermittent Low Voltage
P1133 HO2S-11 Insufficient Switching (Bank 1 Sensor 1)
P1134 HO2S-11 Transition Time Ratio (Bank 1 Sensor 1)
P1153 HO2S-21 Insufficient Switching (Bank 2 Sensor I)
P1154 HO2S-21 Transition Time Ratio (Bank 2 Sensor 1)
P1171 Fuel System Lean During Acceleration
P1391 G-Acceleration Sensor Intermittent Low Voltage
P1390 G-Acceleration (Low G) Sensor Performance
P1392 Rough Road G-Sensor Circuit Low Voltage
P1393 Rough Road G-Sensor Circuit High Voltage
P1394 G-Acceleration Sensor Intermittent High Voltage
P1406 EGR Valve Pintle Position Sensor Circuit Fault
P1441 EVAP System Flow During Non-Purge
P1442 EVAP System Flow During Non-Purge
P1508 Idle Speed Control System-Low
P1509 Idle Speed Control System-High
P1618 Serial Peripheral Interface Communication Error
P1640 Output Driver Module `A' Fault
P1790 PCM ROM (Transmission Side) Check Sum Error
P1792 PCM EEPROM (Transmission Side) Check Sum Error
P1835 Kick Down Switch Always On
P1850 Brake Band Apply Solenoid Electrical Fault
P1860 TCC PWM Solenoid Electrical Fault
P1870 Transmission Component Slipping

1995 2.5TL And NSX

Code P1107 Barometric Pressure circuit; low input
Code P1108 Barometric Pressure circuit; high input
Code P1201 Misfire detected; cylinder 1
Code P1202 Misfire detected; cylinder 2
Code P1203 Misfire detected; cylinder 3
Code P1204 Misfire detected; cylinder 4
Code P1205 Misfire detected; cylinder 5
Code P1206 Misfire detected; cylinder 6
Code P1241 Throttle Valve Control Motor; circuit 1 malfunction
Code P1242 Throttle Valve Control Motor; circuit 2 malfunction
Code P1243 Throttle Position insufficient
Code P1244 Closed Throttle Position insufficient
Code P1246 Accelerator Position Sensor 1; circuit malfunction
Code P1247 Accelerator Position Sensor 2; circuit malfunction
Code P1248 Accelerator Position Sensor 1 and 2; incorrect correlation
Code P1259 VTEC System malfunction; (Rear Bank (Bank 1))
Code P1279 VTEC System malfunction; (Front Bank (Bank 2))
Code P1297 Electric load Detector circuit; low input
Code P1298 Electric load Detector circuit; high input
Code P1300 Random Misfire
Code P1301 Misfire detected; cylinder 1
Code P1302 Misfire detected; cylinder 2
Code P1303 Misfire detected; cylinder 3
Code P1304 Misfire detected; cylinder 4
Code P1305 Misfire detected; cylinder 5
Code P1306 Misfire detected; cylinder 6
Code P1316 Spark Plug Voltage Detection; circuit malfunction; (Front Bank (Bank 2))
Code P1317 Spark Plug Voltage Detection; circuit malfunction; (Rear Bank (Bank 1))
Code P1318 Spark Plug Voltage Detection Module; reset circuit malfunction; (Front Bank (Bank 2))
Code P1319 Spark Plug Voltage Detection Module; reset circuit malfunction; (Rear Bank (Bank 1))
Code P1336 Crankshaft Position Sensor; range and performance (on NSX, sensor B)
Code P1337 Crankshaft Position Sensor; low input (on NSX, circuit B)
Code P1359 Crankshaft Position Sensor and TDC Sensor—2.5TL
Code P1361 TDC Sensor; intermittent interruption—2.5TL
Code P1362 TDC Sensor; no signal—2.5TL

Code P1381 Cylinder Position Sensor; intermittent interruption (on NSX, Sensor A)**Code P1382** Cylinder Position Sensor; no signal (on NSX, Sensor A)

Code P1386 Cylinder Position Sensor B; intermittent interruption
Code P1387 Cylinder Position Sensor B; no signal
Code P1459 Evaporative Emission Purge Flow Switch malfunction
Code P1491 EGR Valve; insufficient lift detected
Code P1498 EGR Valve Lift Sensor; high voltage
Code P1508 Idle Air Control Valve; circuit failure—2.5TL
Code P1607 ECM internal circuit failure A
Code P1608 ECM internal circuit failure B
Code P1660 A/T FI Data Line; failure
Code P1671 A/T FI Data Line; no signal
Code P1672 A/T FI Data Line; failure
Code P1676 TCS FI Data Line; no signal
Code P1677 TCS FI Data Line; failure
Code P1681 A/T FI Signal A; low input—2.5TL
Code P1682 A/T FI Signal A; high input—2.5TL
Code P1686 A/T FI Signal B; low input—2.5TL
Code P1687 A/T FI Signal B; high input—2.5TL
Code P1705 Automatic Transaxle
Code P1706 Automatic Transaxle
Code P1753 Automatic Transaxle
Code P1758 Automatic Transaxle
Code P1768 Automatic Transaxle
Code P1788 Automatic Transaxle
Code P1790 Automatic Transaxle
Code P1791 Automatic Transaxle
Code P1792 Automatic Transaxle
Code P1793 Automatic Transaxle
Code P1795 Automatic Transaxle

Audi

READING CODES

Reading the control module memory is one of the first steps in OBD-II system diagnostics. This step should be initially performed to determine the general nature of the fault. Subsequent readings will determine if the fault has been cleared.

Reading codes can be performed by any of the methods below:
- Read the control module memory with the Generic Scan Tool (GST)
- Read the control module memory with the Vag 1550 tester

To read the fault codes, connect the scan tool or tester according to the manufacturer's instructions. Follow the manufacturer's specified procedure for reading the codes.

CLEARING CODES

Control module reset procedures are a very important part of OBD-II System diagnostics. This step should be done at the end of any fault code repair and at the end of any driveability repair.

Clearing codes can be performed by any of the methods below:
- Clear the control module memory with the Generic Scan Tool (GST)
- Clear the control module memory with the vehicle manufacturer's specific tester
- Turn the ignition off and remove the negative battery cable for at least 1 minute.

Removing the negative battery cable may cause other systems in the vehicle to loose their memory. Prior to removing the cable, ensure you have the proper reset codes for radios and alarms.

➡**The MIL will may also be de-activated for some codes if the vehicle completes three consecutive trips without a fault detected with vehicle conditions similar to those present during the fault.**

AUDI SPECIFIC OBD-II TROUBLE CODES

P1102 Oxygen Sensor Heating Circuit, Bank 1-Sensor 1 Short to B+
P1105 Oxygen Sensor Heating Circuit, Bank 1-Sensor 2 Short to B+
P1107 Oxygen Sensor Heating Circuit, Bank 2-Sensor I Short to B+
P1110 Oxygen Sensor Heating Circuit, Bank 2-Sensor 2 Short to B+
P1127 Long Term Fuel Trim Multiplicative, Bank 1 System Too Rich
P1128 Long Term Fuel Trim Multiplicative, Bank 1 System Too Lean
P1129 Long Term Fuel Trim Multiplicative, Bank2 System too Rich
P1130 Long Term Fuel Trim Multiplicative, Bank2 System too Lean
P1136 Long Term Fuel Trim Additive, Bank 1 System Too Lean
P1137 Long Term Fuel Trim Additive, Bank 1 System Too Rich
P1138 Long Term Fuel Trim Additive Fuel, Bank I System too Lean
P1139 Long Term Fuel Trim Additive Fuel, Bank 1 System too Rich
P1141 Load Calculation Cross Check Range/Performance
P1176 Oxygen Correction Behind Catalyst, B1 Limit Attained
P1177 Oxygen Correction Behind Catalyst. 82 Limit Attained
P1196 Oxygen Sensor Heater Circuit, Bank 1-Sensor 1 Electrical Malfunction
P1197 Oxygen Sensor Heater Circuit, Bank 2-Sensor I Electrical Malfunction
P1198 Oxygen Sensor Heater Circuit, BankI-Sensor2 Electrical Malfunction
P1198 Oxygen Sensor Heater Circuit, Bank 1-Sensor 2 Electrical Malfunction
P1199 Oxygen Sensor Heater Circuit, Bank 2-Sensor 2 Electrical Malfunction
P1201 Cylinder 1, Fuel Injection Circuit Electrical Malfunction
P1202 Cylinder 2, Fuel Injection Circuit Electrical Malfunction
P1203 Cylinder 3, Fuel Injection Circuit Electrical Malfunction
P1204 Cylinder 4, Fuel Injection Circuit Electrical Malfunction
P1205 Cylinder 5, Fuel Injection Circuit Electrical Malfunction
P1206 Cylinder 6, Fuel Injection Circuit Electrical Malfunction
P1207 Cylinder 7, Fuel Injection Circuit Electrical Malfunction
P1208 Cylinder 8, Fuel Injection Circuit Electrical Malfunction
P1213 Cylinder I-Fuel Injection Circuit Short to B+
P1214 Cylinder 2-Fuel Injection Circuit Short to B+
P1215 Cylinder 3 Fuel Injection Circuit Short to B+
P1216 Cylinder 4 Fuel Injection Circuit Short to B+
P1217 Cylinder 5 Fuel Injection Circuit Short to B+
P1218 Cylinder 6 Fuel Injection Circuit Short to B+
P1219 Cylinder 7, Fuel Injection Circuit Short to B+
P1219 Cylinder 8, Fuel Injection Circuit Short to B+
P1225 Cylinder I Fuel Injection Circuit Short to Ground
P1226 Cylinder 2 Fuel Injection Circuit Short to Ground
P1227 Cylinder 3 Fuel Injection Circuit Short to Ground
P1228 Cylinder 4 Fuel Injection Circuit Short to Ground
P1229 Cylinder 5 Fuel Injection Circuit Short to Ground
P1230 Cylinder 6 Fuel Injection Circuit Short to Ground
P1237 Cylinder I Fuel Injection Circuit Open Circuit
P1238 Cylinder 2 Fuel Injection Circuit Open Circuit
P1239 Cylinder 3 Fuel Injection Circuit Open Circuit
P1240 Cylinder 4 Fuel Injection Circuit Open Circuit
P1241 Cylinder 5 Fuel Injection Circuit Open Circuit
P1242 Cylinder 6 Fuel Injection Circuit Open Circuit
P1250 Fuel Level Too Low
P1280 Fuel Injection Air Control Valve Circuit Flow too Low
P1283 Fuel Injection Air Control Valve Circuit Electrical Malfunction
P1325 Cylinder I Knock Control Limit Attained
P1326 Cylinder 2 Knock Control Limit Attained
P1327 Cylinder 3 Knock Control Limit Attained
P1328 Cylinder 4 Knock Control Limit Attained

P1329 Cylinder 5 Knock Control Limit Attained
P1330 Cylinder 6 Knock Control Limit Attained
P1331 Cylinder 7, Knock Control Limit Attained
P1332 Cylinder 8, Knock Control Limit Attained
P1337 Camshaft Position Sensor, Bank 1 Short to Ground
P1338 Camshaft Position Sensor, Bank 1 Open Circuit/Short to B+
P1340 Boost Pressure Control Valve Short to B+
P1386 Internal Control Module Knock Control Circuit Error
P1391 Camshaft Position Sensor, Bank 2 Short to Ground
P1392 Camshaft Position Sensor, Bank 2 Open Circuit/Short to B+
P1410 Tank Ventilation Valve Circuit Short to B+
P1420 Secondary Air Injection Module Short To B+
P1421 Secondary Air Injection Module Short To Ground
P1421 Secondary Air Injection Valve Circuit Short to Ground
P1422 Secondary Air Injection System Control Valve Circuit Short To B+
P1422 Secondary Air Injection Valve Circuit Short to B+
P1425 Tank Vent Valve Short To Ground
P1425 Tank Vent Valve Short to Ground
P1426 Tank Vent Valve Open
P1426 Tank Vent Valve Open
P1432 Secondary Air Injection Valve Open
P1433 Secondary Air Injection System Pump Relay Circuit Open
P1434 Secondary Air Injection System Pump Relay Circuit Short to B+
P1435 Secondary Air Injection System Pump Relay Circuit Short to Ground
P1436 Secondary Air Injection System Pump Relay Circuit Electrical Malfunction
P1450 Secondary Air Injection System Circuit Short To B+
P1451 Secondary Air Injection System Circuit Short To Ground
P1452 Secondary Air Injection System Open Circuit
P1471 EVAP Emission Control LDP Circuit Short to B+
P1472 EVAP Emission Control LDP Circuit Short to Ground
P1473 EVAP Emission Control LDP Circuit Open Circuit
P1475 EVAP Emission Control LDP Circuit Malfunction/Signal Circuit Open
P1476 EVAP Emission Control LDP Circuit Malfunction/Insufficient Vacuum
P1477 EVAP Emission Control LDP Circuit Malfunction
P1500 Fuel Pump Relay Circuit Electrical Malfunction
P1501 Fuel Pump Relay Circuit Short to Ground
P1502 Fuel Pump Relay Circuit Short to B+
P1505 Closed Throttle Position Switch Does Not Close/Open Circuit
P1506 Closed Throttle Position Switch Does Not Open/Short to Ground
P1507 Idle System Learned Value Lower Limit Attained
P1508 Idle System Learned Value Upper Limit Attained
P1512 Intake Manifold Changeover Valve Circuit, Short to B+
P1515 Intake Manifold Changeover Valve Circuit, Short to Ground
P1516 Intake Manifold Changeover Valve Circuit, Open
P1519 Intake Camshaft Control, Bank I Malfunction
P1522 Intake Camshaft Control, Bank 2 Malfunction
P1543 Throttle Actuation Potentiometer Signal Too Low
P1544 Throttle Actuation Potentiometer Signal Too High
P1545 Throttle Position Control Malfunction
P1547 Boost Pressure Control Valve Short to Ground
P1548 Boost Pressure Control Valve Open
P1555 Charge Pressure Upper Limit Exceeded
P1556 Charge Pressure Negative Deviation
P1557 Charge Pressure Positive Deviation
P1558 Throttle Actuator Electrical Malfunction
P1559 Idle Speed Control Throttle Position Adaptation Malfunction
P1560 Maximum Engine Speed Exceeded
P1564 Idle Speed Control, Throttle Position Low Voltage During Adaptation

P1580 Throttle Actuator (B1) Malfunction
P1582 Idle Adaptation At Limit
P1602 Power Supply (B+) Terminal 30 Low Voltage
P1606 Rough Road Spec Engine Torque ABS-ECU Electrical Malfunction
P1611 MIL Call-up Circuit/Transmission Control Module Short to Ground
P1612 Electronic Control Module Incorrect Coding
P1613 MIL Call-up Circuit Open/Short to B+
P1624 MIL Request Signal Active
P1625 CAN-Bus Implausible Message from Transmission Control
P1626 CAN-Bus Missing Message from Transmission Control
P1640 Internal Control Module (EEPROM) Error
P1640 Internal Control Module (EEPROM) Error
P1681 Control Unit Programming not Finished
P1690 Malfunction Indicator Light Malfunction
P1693 Malfunction Indicator Light Short to B+
P1778 Solenoid EV7 Electrical Malfunction
P1780 Engine Intervention Readable

AUDI OBD-II TROUBLE CODE EQUIVALENTS

If a generic scan tool is not available for code retrieval, the following codes may be retrieved using the Vag 1551.
16486 Mass or Volume Air Flow Circuit Low Input
16487 Mass or Volume Air Flow Circuit High Input
16491 Manifold Absolute Pressure or Barometric Pressure Low Input
16492 Manifold Absolute Pressure or Barometric Pressure High Input
16496 Intake Air Temperature Circuit Low Input
16497 Intake Air Temperature Circuit High Input
16500 Engine Coolant Temperature Circuit Range/Performance
16501 Engine Coolant Temperature Circuit Low Input
16502 Oxygen Engine Coolant Temperature Circuit High Input
16504 Throttle Position Sensor A Circuit Malfunction
16505 Throttle/Pedal Position Sensor A Circuit Range/Performance
16506 Throttle/Pedal Position Sensor A Circuit Low Input
16507 Throttle/Pedal Position Sensor A Circuit High Input
16509 Insufficient Coolant Temperature For Closed Loop Fuel Control
16514 Oxygen Sensor Circuit, Bank 1-Sensor 1 Malfunction
16515 Oxygen Sensor Circuit, Bank 1-Sensor 1 Low Voltage
16516 Oxygen Sensor Circuit, Bank 1-Sensor 1 High Voltage
16517 Oxygen Sensor Circuit, Bank 1-Sensor 1 Slow Response
16518 Oxygen Sensor Circuit, Bank 1-Sensor 1 No Activity Detected
16519 Oxygen Sensor Heater Circuit, Bank 1-Sensor 1 Malfunction
16520 Oxygen Sensor Circuit, Bank 1-Sensor 2 Malfunction
16521 Oxygen Sensor Circuit, Bank 1-Sensor 2 Low Voltage
16522 Oxygen Sensor Circuit, Bank 1-Sensor 2 High Voltage
16524 Oxygen Sensor Circuit, Bank 1-Sensor 2 No Activity Detected
16525 Oxygen Sensor Heater Circuit, Bank 1-Sensor 2 Malfunction
16534 Oxygen Sensor Circuit, Bank 2-Sensor 1 Malfunction
16535 Oxygen Sensor Circuit, Bank 2-Sensor 1 Low Voltage
16536 Oxygen Sensor Circuit, Bank 2-Sensor 1 High Voltage
16537 Oxygen Sensor Circuit, Bank 2-Sensor 1 Slow Response
16538 Oxygen Sensor Circuit, Bank 2-Sensor 1 No Activity Detected
16540 Oxygen Sensor Circuit, Bank 2-Sensor 2 Malfunction
16541 Oxygen Sensor Circuit, Bank 2-Sensor 2 Low Voltage
16542 Oxygen Sensor Circuit, Bank 2-Sensor 2 High Voltage
16544 Oxygen Sensor Circuit, Bank 2-Sensor 2 No Activity Detected
16555 Oxygen System Too Lean, Bank 1
16556 Oxygen System Too Rich, Bank 1
16684 Random Multiple Misfire Detected
16685 Cylinder 1 Misfire Detected
16686 Cylinder 2 Misfire Detected
16687 Cylinder 3 Misfire Detected
16688 Cylinder 4 Misfire Detected

16689 Cylinder 5 Misfire Detected
16690 Cylinder 6 Misfire Detected
16705 Ignition Distributor Engine Speed Input Circuit Range/Performance
16706 Ignition /Distributor Engine Speed Input Circuit No Signal
16711 Knock sensor 1 Circuit Low Input
16712 Knock Sensor Circuit, High Input
16716 Knock sensor 2 Circuit Low Input
16716 Knock Sensor Circuit, Low Input
16717 Knock Sensor 2 Circuit, High Input
16725 Camshaft Position Sensor Circuit Range/Performance
16795 Secondary Air Injection System Incorrect Flow Detected
16806 Main Catalyst Efficiency Below Threshold (Bank 1)
16806 Main Catalyst, Bank I Efficiency Below Threshold
16824 Evaporative Emission Control System Malfunction
16825 EVAP Emission Contr. Sys. Incorrect Purge Flow
16826 EVAP Emission Contr. Sys. (Small Leak) Leak Detected
16839 EVAP Emission Contr. Sys. (Gross Leak) Leak Detected
16885 Vehicle Speed Sensor Range/Performance
16890 Idle Control System RPM Lower Than Expected
16891 Idle Control System RPM Higher Than Expected
16894 Closed Throttle Position Switch Malfunction
16944 System Voltage Malfunction
16946 System Voltage Low Voltage
16947 System Voltage High Voltage
16985 Internal Contr. Module Memory Check Sum Error
16988 Internal Contr. Module Random Access Memory (RAM) Error
16989 Internal Control Module Read Only Memory (ROM) Error
17091 Transmission Range Sensor Circuit Low Input
17092 Transmission Range Sensor Circuit High Input
17099 Input Turbine Speed Sensor Circuit Malfunction
17106 Output Speed Sensor Circuit No Signal
17109 Engine Speed Input Circuit Malfunction
17132 Pressure Control Solenoid Electrical
17137 Shift Solenoid A Electrical
17142 Shift Solenoid B Electrical
17147 Shift Solenoid C Electrical
17152 Shift Solenoid D Electrical
17157 Shift Solenoid E Electrical
16684 Random/Multiple Cylinder Misfire Detected
16685 Cylinder I Misfire Detected
16686 Cylinder 2 Misfire Detected
17510 Oxygen Sensor Heating Circuit, Bank 1-Sensor 1 Short to B+
17513 Oxygen Sensor Heating Circuit, Bank 1-Sensor 2 Short to B+
17515 Oxygen Sensor Heating Circuit, Bank 2-Sensor I Short to B+
17518 Oxygen Sensor Heating Circuit, Bank 2-Sensor 2 Short to B+
17535 Long Term Fuel Trim Multiplicative, Bank 1 System Too Rich
17536 Long Term Fuel Trim Multiplicative, Bank 1 System Too Lean
17537 Long Term Fuel Trim Multiplicative, Bank2 System too Rich
17538 Long Term Fuel Trim Multiplicative, Bank2 System too Lean
17544 Long Term Fuel Trim Additive, Bank 1 System Too Lean
17545 Long Term Fuel Trim Additive, Bank 1 System Too Rich
17546 Long Term Fuel Trim Additive Fuel, Bank I System too Lean
17547 Long Term Fuel Trim Additive Fuel, Bank 1 System too Rich
17549 Load Calculation Cross Check Range/Performance
17584 Oxygen Correction Behind Catalyst, B1 Limit Attained
17585 Oxygen Correction Behind Catalyst. 82 Limit Attained
17604 Oxygen Sensor Heater Circuit, Bank 1-Sensor 1 Electrical Malfunction
17605 Oxygen Sensor Heater Circuit, Bank 2-Sensor I Electrical Malfunction
17606 Oxygen Sensor Heater Circuit, Bank 1-Sensor 2 Electrical Malfunction

17606 Oxygen Sensor Heater Circuit, Bank 1-Sensor 2 Electrical Malfunction
17607 Oxygen Sensor Heater Circuit, Bank 2-Sensor 2 Electrical Malfunction
17609 Cylinder 1, Fuel Injection Circuit Electrical Malfunction
17610 Cylinder 2, Fuel Injection Circuit Electrical Malfunction
17611 Cylinder 3, Fuel Injection Circuit Electrical Malfunction
17612 Cylinder 4, Fuel Injection Circuit Electrical Malfunction
17613 Cylinder 5, Fuel Injection Circuit Electrical Malfunction
17614 Cylinder 6, Fuel Injection Circuit Electrical Malfunction
17615 Cylinder 7, Fuel Injection Circuit Electrical Malfunction
17616 Cylinder 8, Fuel Injection Circuit Electrical Malfunction
17621 Cylinder I-Fuel Injection Circuit Short to B+
17622 Cylinder 2-Fuel Injection Circuit Short to B+
17623 Cylinder 3 Fuel Injection Circuit Short to B+
17624 Cylinder 4 Fuel Injection Circuit Short to B+
17625 Cylinder 5 Fuel Injection Circuit Short to B+
17626 Cylinder 6 Fuel Injection Circuit Short to B+
17627 Cylinder 7, Fuel Injection Circuit Short to B+
17628 Cylinder 8, Fuel Injection Circuit Short to B+
17633 Cylinder I Fuel Injection Circuit Short to Ground
17634 Cylinder 2 Fuel Injection Circuit Short to Ground
17635 Cylinder 3 Fuel Injection Circuit Short to Ground
17636 Cylinder 4 Fuel Injection Circuit Short to Ground
17637 Cylinder 5 Fuel Injection Circuit Short to Ground
17638 Cylinder 6 Fuel Injection Circuit Short to Ground
17645 Cylinder I Fuel Injection Circuit Open Circuit
17646 Cylinder 2 Fuel Injection Circuit Open Circuit
17647 Cylinder 3 Fuel Injection Circuit Open Circuit
17648 Cylinder 4 Fuel Injection Circuit Open Circuit
17649 Cylinder 5 Fuel Injection Circuit Open Circuit
17650 Cylinder 6 Fuel Injection Circuit Open Circuit
17658 Fuel Level Too Low
17688 Fuel Injection Air Control Valve Circuit Flow too Low
17691 Fuel Injection Air Control Valve Circuit Electrical Malfunction
17733 Cylinder I Knock Control Limit Attained
17734 Cylinder 2 Knock Control Limit Attained
17735 Cylinder 3 Knock Control Limit Attained
17736 Cylinder 4 Knock Control Limit Attained
17737 Cylinder 5 Knock Control Limit Attained
17738 Cylinder 6 Knock Control Limit Attained
17739 Cylinder 7, Knock Control Limit Attained
17740 Cylinder 8, Knock Control Limit Attained
17745 Camshaft Position Sensor, Bank 1 Short to Ground
17746 Camshaft Position Sensor, Bank 1 Open Circuit/Short to B+
17954 Boost Pressure Control Valve Short to B+
17794 Internal Control Module Knock Control Circuit Error
17799 Camshaft Position Sensor, Bank 2 Short to Ground
17800 Camshaft Position Sensor, Bank 2 Open Circuit/Short to B+
17818 Tank Ventilation Valve Circuit Short to B+
17818 Tank Ventilation Valve Circuit Short to B+
17828 Secondary Air Injection Module Short To B+
17829 Secondary Air Injection Module Short To Ground
17829 Secondary Air Injection Valve Circuit Short to Ground
17830 Secondary Air Injection System Control Valve Circuit Short To B+
17830 Secondary Air Injection Valve Circuit Short to B+
17833 Tank Vent Valve Short To Ground
17833 Tank Vent Valve Short to Ground
17834 Tank Vent Valve Open
17834 Tank Vent Valve Open
17840 Secondary Air Injection Valve Open
17841 Secondary Air Injection System Pump Relay Circuit Open

17842 Secondary Air Injection System Pump Relay Circuit Short to B+

17843 Secondary Air Injection System Pump Relay Circuit Short to Ground

17844 Secondary Air Injection System Pump Relay Circuit Electrical Malfunction

17858 Secondary Air Injection System Circuit Short To B+

17859 Secondary Air Injection System Circuit Short To Ground

17860 Secondary Air Injection System Open Circuit

17879 EVAP Emission Control LDP Circuit Short to B+

17880 EVAP Emission Control LDP Circuit Short to Ground

17881 EVAP Emission Control LDP Circuit Open Circuit

17883 EVAP Emission Control LDP Circuit Malfunction/Signal Circuit Open

17884 EVAP Emission Control LDP Circuit Malfunction/Insufficient Vacuum

17885 EVAP Emission Control LDP Circuit Malfunction

17908 Fuel Pump Relay Circuit Electrical Malfunction

17909 Fuel Pump Relay Circuit Short to Ground

17910 Fuel Pump Relay Circuit Short to B+

17913 Closed Throttle Position Switch Does Not Close/Open Circuit

17914 Closed Throttle Position Switch Does Not Open/Short to Ground

17915 Idle System Learned Value Lower Limit Attained

17916 Idle System Learned Value Upper Limit Attained

17920 Intake Manifold Changeover Valve Circuit, Short to B+

17923 Intake Manifold Changeover Valve Circuit, Short to Ground

17924 Intake Manifold Changeover Valve Circuit, Open

17927 Intake Camshaft Control, Bank 2 Malfunction

17951 Throttle Actuation Potentiometer Signal Too Low

17952 Throttle Actuation Potentiometer Signal Too High

17953 Throttle Position Control Malfunction

17955 Boost Pressure Control Valve Short to Ground

17956 Boost Pressure Control Valve Open

17963 Charge Pressure Upper Limit Exceeded

17964 Charge Pressure Negative Deviation

17965 Charge Pressure Positive Deviation

17966 Throttle Actuator Electrical Malfunction

17967 Idle Speed Control Throttle Position Adaptation Malfunction

17968 Maximum Engine Speed Exceeded

17972 Idle Speed Control, Throttle Position Low Voltage During Adaptation

17988 Throttle Actuator (B1) Malfunction

17990 Idle Adaptation At Limit

18010 Power Supply (B+) Terminal 30 Low Voltage

18014 Rough Road Spec Engine Torque ABS-ECU Electrical Malfunction

18019 MIL Call-up Circuit/Transmission Control Module Short to Ground

18020 Electronic Control Module Incorrect Coding

18021 MIL Call-up Circuit Open/Short to B+

18032 MIL Request Signal Active

18033 CAN-Bus Implausible Message from Transmission Control

18034 CAN-Bus Missing Message from Transmission Control

18048 Internal Control Module (EEPROM) Error

18048 Internal Control Module (EEPROM) Error

18089 Control Unit Programming not Finished

18098 Malfunction Indicator Light Malfunction

18101 Malfunction Indicator Light Short to B+

18186 Solenoid EV7 Electrical Malfunction

18188 Engine Intervention Readable

Honda

READING CODES

With Scan Tool

Reading the control module memory is on of the first steps in OBD-II system diagnostics. This step should be initially performed to determine the general nature of the fault. Subsequent readings will determine if the fault has been cleared.

Reading codes can be performed by any of the methods below:
- Read the control module memory with the Generic Scan Tool (GST)
- Read the control module memory with the vehicle manufacturer's specific tester

To read the fault codes, connect the scan tool or tester according to the manufacturer's instructions. Follow the manufacturer's specified procedure for reading the codes.

Without Scan Tool

Honda also provides a way of reading OBD-II trouble code equivalents using a service connector and viewing the MIL. This method is similar to the flash codes from non-OBD-II vehicles.

To read codes, plug the service connector into the service check connector and turn the ignition on. The MIL will flash any stored trouble codes.

CLEARING CODES

Control module reset procedures are a very important part of OBD-II System diagnostics.

This step should be done at the end of any fault code repair and at the end of any driveability repair.

Clearing codes can be performed by any of the methods below:
- Clear the control module memory with the Generic Scan Tool (GST)
- Clear the control module memory with the vehicle manufacturer's specific tester
- Turn the ignition off and remove the negative battery cable for at least 1 minute.

Removing the negative battery cable may cause other systems in the vehicle to loose their memory. Prior to removing the cable, ensure you have the proper reset codes for radios and alarms.

➡**The MIL will may also be de-activated for some codes if the vehicle completes three consecutive trips without a fault detected with vehicle conditions similar to those present during the fault.**

HONDA SPECIFIC OBD-II TROUBLE CODES

P1106 Barometric Pressure Circuit Range/Performance Problem

P1107 Barometric Pressure Circuit Low Input

P1108 Barometric Pressure Circuit High Input

P1121 Throttle Position Lower Than Expected

P1122 Throttle Position Higher Than Expected

P1128 Manifold Absolute Pressure Lower Than Expected

P1129 Manifold Absolute Pressure Higher Than Expected

P1259 VTEC System Malfunction

P1297 Electrical Load Detector Circuit Low Input

P1298 Electrical Load Detector Circuit High Input

P1297 Electrical Load Detector Circuit Low Input

P1298 Electrical Load Detector Circuit High Input

P1336 Crankshaft Speed Fluctuation Sensor Intermittent Interruption

P1337 Crankshaft Speed Fluctuation Sensor No Signal

P1359 Crankshaft Position Top Dead Center Sensor/Cylinder Position Connector Disconnection

P1361 Top Dead Center Sensor Intermittent Interruption
P1362 Top Dead Center Sensor No Signal
P1381 Cylinder Position Sensor Intermittent Interruption
P1382 Cylinder Position Sensor No Signal
P1456 Evaporative Emission Control System Leak Detected (Fuel Tank System)
P1457 Evaporative Emission Control System Leak Detected (EVAP Control Canister Leak)
P1491 EGR Valve Lift Insufficient Detected
P1498 EGR Valve Lift Sensor High Voltage
P1519 Idle Air Control Valve Circuit Failure
P1508 Idle Air Control Valve Circuit Failure
P1607 Powertrain Control Module Internal Circuit Failure A
P1705 Automatic Transaxle
P1706 Automatic Transaxle
P1753 Automatic Transaxle
P1768 Automatic Transaxle
P1790 Automatic Transaxle
P1791 Automatic Transaxle

OBD-II Codes

1995 ACCORD

Code P1107 Barometric Pressure circuit; low input
Code P1108 Barometric Pressure circuit; high input
Code P1297 Electric load Detector circuit; low input
Code P1298 Electric load Detector circuit; high input
Code P1361 TDC Sensor; intermittent interruption
Code P1362 TDC Sensor; no signal
Code P1381 Cylinder Position Sensor; intermittent interruption
Code P1382 Cylinder Position Sensor; no signal
Code P1459 Evaporative Emission Purge Flow Switch malfunction
Code P1491 EGR Valve; insufficient lift detected
Code P1498 EGR Valve Lift Sensor; high voltage
Code P1508 Idle Air Control Valve; circuit failure
Code P1607 ECM internal circuit failure A
Code P1660 A/T FI Data Line; failure
Code P1681 A/T FI Signal A; low input
Code P1682 A/T FI Signal A; high input
Code P1686 A/T FI Signal B; low input
Code P1687 A/T FI Signal B; high input
Code P1705 Automatic Transaxle
Code P1706 Automatic Transaxle
Code P1753 Automatic Transaxle
Code P1758 Automatic Transaxle
Code P1768 Automatic Transaxle
Code P1786 Automatic Transaxle
Code P1790 Automatic Transaxle
Code P1791 Automatic Transaxle
Code P1792 Automatic Transaxle
Code P1794 Automatic Transaxle

HONDA OBD-II TROUBLE CODE EQUIVALENTS

If a scan tool is not available for code retrieval, the following codes may be retrieved without one.
1 O2 Sensor Circuit High Voltage (Bank no. 1 Sensor no. 1)
1 O2 Sensor Circuit Low Voltage (Bank no. 1 Sensor no. 1)
3 Manifold Absolute Pressure/Barometric Pressure Circuit Low Input
3 Manifold Absolute Pressure/Barometric Pressure Circuit High Input
4 Crankshaft Position Sensor "A" Circuit Malfunction
4 Crankshaft Position Sensor "A" Circuit Range/Performance
5 Manifold Absolute Pressure Higher Than Expected
5 Manifold Absolute Pressure Lower Than Expected
6 Engine Coolant Temperature Circuit High Input
6 Engine Coolant Temperature Circuit Low Input
7 Throttle Position Higher Than Expected
7 Throttle Position Lower Than Expected
7 Throttle/Pedal Position Sensor/Switch "A" Circuit High Input
7 Throttle/Pedal Position Sensor/Switch "A" Circuit Low Input
8 Crankshaft Position Top Dead Center Sensor/Cylinder Position Connector Disconnection
8 Top Dead Center Sensor Intermittent Interruption
8 Top Dead Center Sensor No Signal
9 Cylinder Position Sensor Intermittent Interruption
9 Cylinder Position Sensor No Signal
10 Intake Air Temperature Circuit High Input
10 Intake Air Temperature Circuit Low Input
12 EGR Valve Lift Insufficient Detected
12 EGR Valve Lift Sensor High Voltage
13 Barometric Pressure Circuit High Input
13 Barometric Pressure Circuit Low Input
13 Barometric Pressure Circuit Range/Performance Problem
14 Idle Air Control Valve Circuit Failure
14 Idle Air Control Valve Circuit Failure
14 Idle Control System Malfunction
20 Electrical Load Detector Circuit High Input
20 Electrical Load Detector Circuit High Input
20 Electrical Load Detector Circuit Low Input
20 Electrical Load Detector Circuit Low Input
22 VTEC System Malfunction
23 Knock Sensor no. 1—Circuit Malfunction (Bank no. 1 or Single Sensor)
80 Exhaust Gas Recirculation Flow Insufficient Detected
41 O2 Sensor Heater Circuit Malfunction (Bank no. 1 Sensor no. 1)
45 System Too Lean (Bank no. 1)
45 System Too Rich (Bank no. 1)
54 Crankshaft Speed Fluctuation Sensor Intermittent Interruption
54 Crankshaft Speed Fluctuation Sensor No Signal
61 O2 Sensor Circuit Slow Response (Bank no. 1 Sensor no. 1)
63 O2 Sensor Circuit High Voltage (Bank no. 1 Sensor no. 2)
63 O2 Sensor Circuit Low Voltage (Bank no. 1 Sensor no. 2)
63 O2 Sensor Circuit Slow Response (Bank no. 1 Sensor no. 2)
65 O2 Sensor Heater Circuit Malfunction (Bank no. 1 Sensor no. 2)
67 Catalyst System Efficiency Below Threshold (Bank no. 1)
70 Automatic Transaxle
70 Transmission Control System Malfunction
70 Input/Turbine Speed Sensor Circuit Malfunction
70 Output Speed Sensor Circuit Malfunction
70 Incorrect Gear Ratio
70 Torque Converter Clutch Circuit Malfunction
70 Shift Solenoid "A" Electrical
70 Shift Solenoid "B" Electrical
71 Cylinder no. 1—Misfire Detected
72 Cylinder no. 2—Misfire Detected
73 Cylinder no. 3—Misfire Detected
74 Cylinder no. 4—Misfire Detected
86 Engine Coolant Temperature Circuit Range/Performance Problem
90 Evaporative Emission Control System Leak Detected (EVAP Control Canister Leak)
90 Evaporative Emission Control System Leak Detected (Fuel Tank System)
91 Evaporative Emission Control System Pressure Sensor Low Input
91 Evaporative Emission Control System Pressure Sensor High Input

Hyundai

READING CODES

Reading the control module memory is on of the first steps in OBD-II system diagnostics. This step should be initially performed to determine the general nature of the fault. Subsequent readings will determine if the fault has been cleared.

Reading codes can be performed by any of the methods below:

- Read the control module memory with the Generic Scan Tool (GST)
- Read the control module memory with the vehicle manufacturer's specific tester

To read the fault codes, connect the scan tool or tester according to the manufacturer's instructions. Follow the manufacturer's specified procedure for reading the codes.

CLEARING CODES

Control module reset procedures are a very important part of OBD-II System diagnostics.

This step should be done at the end of any fault code repair and at the end of any driveability repair.

Clearing codes can be performed by any of the methods below:
- Clear the control module memory with the Generic Scan Tool (GST)
- Clear the control module memory with the vehicle manufacturer's specific tester

➡ **The MIL will may also be de-activated for some codes if the vehicle completes three consecutive trips without a fault detected with vehicle conditions similar to those present during the fault.**

HYUNDAI SPECIFIC OBD-II TROUBLE CODES

P1123 Long term fuel trim additive, air system too rich
P1124 Long term fuel trim additive, air system too lean
P1127 Long term fuel trim multiplicative, system too rich
P1128 Long term fuel trim multiplicative, system too lean
P1140 Load monitoring signal not plausible
P1400 EGR system monitor malfunction
P1510 Idle control valve opening coil circuit shorted
P1513 Idle control valve opening coil circuit open
P1552 Idle control valve closing coil circuit shorted
P1553 Idle control valve closing coil circuit open
P1586 Encoding signal circuit not rationale
P1605 Rough road sensor circuit malfunction
P1606 Rough road sensor not rationale
P1608 Rough road sensor not rational
P1611 MIL request signal circuit low input
P1613 MIL request signal circuit high input
P1614 MIL request signal circuit high input
P1615 Power stage group A, malfunction
P1624 Malfunctian of TCM component
P1665 Power stage group A malfunction
P1670 Power stage group B, malfunction
P1715 Open-circuited pulse generator
P1750 Open-circuited or shorted shift control solenoid, pressure control solenoid or damper clutch control solenoid valve

Infiniti

READING CODES

Reading the control module memory is on of the first steps in OBD-II system diagnostics. This step should be initially performed to determine the general nature of the fault. Subsequent readings will determine if the fault has been cleared.

Reading codes can be performed by any of the methods below:
- Read the control module memory with the Generic Scan Tool (GST)
- Read the control module memory with the vehicle manufacturer's specific tester

To read the fault codes, connect the scan tool or tester according to the manufacturer's instructions. Follow the manufacturer's specified procedure for reading the codes.

CLEARING CODES

Control module reset procedures are a very important part of OBD-II System diagnostics. This step should be done at the end of any fault code repair and at the end of any driveability repair.

Clearing codes can be performed by any of the methods below:
- Clear the control module memory with the Generic Scan Tool (GST)
- Clear the control module memory with the vehicle manufacturer's specific tester

➡ **The MIL will may also be de-activated for some codes if the vehicle completes three consecutive trips without a fault detected with vehicle conditions similar to those present during the fault.**

INFINITI SPECIFIC OBD-II TROUBLE CODES

P1120 Secondary Throttle Position Sensor Circuit Fault
P1125 Tandem Throttle Position Sensor Circuit Fault
P1210 Traction Control System Signal Fault
P1220 Fuel Pump Control Module Fault
P1320 Ignition Control Signal Fault
P1336 Crankshaft Position Sensor Circuit Fault
P1400 EGR/EVAP Control Solenoid Circuit Fault
P1401 EGR Temperature Sensor Circuit Fault
P1443 EVAP Canister Control Vacuum Switch Circuit Fault
P1445 EVAP Purge Volume Control Valve Circuit Fault
P1605 TCM A~T Diagnosis Communication Line Fault
P1705 Throttle Position Sensor (Switch) Circuit Fault
P1760 Overrun Clutch Solenoid Valve Circuit Fault
P1900 Cooling Fan Control Circuit Fault

Isuzu

READING CODES

Reading the control module memory is on of the first steps in OBD-II system diagnostics. This step should be initially performed to determine the general nature of the fault. Subsequent readings will determine if the fault has been cleared.

Reading codes can be performed by any of the methods below:
- Read the control module memory with the Generic Scan Tool (GST)
- Read the control module memory with the vehicle manufacturer's specific tester

To read the fault codes, connect the scan tool or tester according to the manufacturer's instructions. Follow the manufacturer's specified procedure for reading the codes.

CLEARING CODES

Control module reset procedures are a very important part of OBD-II System diagnostics. This step should be done at the end of any fault code repair and at the end of any driveability repair.

Clearing codes can be performed by any of the methods below:
- Clear the control module memory with the Generic Scan Tool (GST)
- Clear the control module memory with the vehicle manufacturer's specific tester
- Turn the ignition off and remove the negative battery cable for at least 1 minute.

Removing the negative battery cable may cause other systems in the vehicle to loose their memory. Prior to removing the cable, ensure you have the proper reset codes for radios and alarms.

➡ **The MIL will may also be de-activated for some codes if the vehicle completes three consecutive trips without a fault detected with vehicle conditions similar to those present during the fault.**

ISUZU SPECIFIC OBD-II TROUBLE CODES

P1106 Map Sensor Circuit Intermittent High Voltage
P1107 MAP Sensor Circuit Intermittent Low Voltage
P1111 IAT Sensor Circuit Intermittent High Voltage
P1112 IAT Sensor Circuit Intermittent Low Voltage
P1114 ECT Sensor Circuit Intermittent Low Voltage
P1115 ECT Sensor Circuit Intermittent High Voltage
P1121 TP Sensor Circuit Intermittent High Voltage
P1122 TP Sensor Circuit Intermittent Low Voltage
P1133 HO2S-11 Insufficient Switching (Bank 1 Sensor 1)
P1134 HO2S-11 Transition Time Ratio (Bank 1 Sensor 1)
P1153 HO2S-21 Insufficient Switching (Bank 2 Sensor I)
P1154 HO2S-21 Transition Time Ratio (Bank 2 Sensor 1)
P1171 Fuel System Lean During Acceleration
P1391 G-Acceleration Sensor Intermittent Low Voltage
P1390 G-Acceleration (Low G) Sensor Performance
P1392 Rough Road G-Sensor Circuit Low Voltage
P1393 Rough Road G-Sensor Circuit High Voltage
P1394 G-Acceleration Sensor Intermittent High Voltage
P1406 EGR Valve Pintle Position Sensor Circuit Fault
P1441 EVAP System Flow During Non-Purge
P1442 EVAP System Flow During Non-Purge **P1508** Idle Speed Control System-Low
P1509 Idle Speed Control System-High
P1618 Serial Peripheral Interface Communication Error
P1640 Output Driver Module `A' Fault
P1790 PCM ROM (Transmission Side) Check Sum Error
P1792 PCM EEPROM (Transmission Side) Check Sum Error
P1835 Kick Down Switch Always On
P1850 Brake Band Apply Solenoid Electrical Fault
P1860 TCC PWM Solenoid Electrical Fault
P1870 Transmission Component Slipping

Kia

READING CODES

Reading the control module memory is on of the first steps in OBD-II system diagnostics.

This step should be initially performed to determine the general nature of the fault. Subsequent readings will determine if the fault has been cleared.

Reading codes can be performed by any of the methods below:
- Read the control module memory with the Generic Scan Tool (GST)
- Read the control module memory with the vehicle manufacturer's specific tester

To read the fault codes, connect the scan tool or tester according to the manufacturer's instructions. Follow the manufacturer's specified procedure for reading the codes.

CLEARING CODES

Control module reset procedures are a very important part of OBD-II System diagnostics. This step should be done at the end of any fault code repair and at the end of any driveability repair.

Clearing codes can be performed by any of the methods below:
- Clear the control module memory with the Generic Scan Tool (GST)
- Clear the control module memory with the vehicle manufacturer's specific tester
- Turn the ignition off and remove the negative battery cable for at least 1 minute.

Removing the negative battery cable may cause other systems in the vehicle to loose their memory. Prior to removing the cable, ensure you have the proper reset codes for radios and alarms.

➡The MIL will may also be de-activated for some codes if the vehicle completes three consecutive trips without a fault detected with vehicle conditions similar to those present during the fault.

KIA SPECIFIC OBD-II TROUBLE CODES

P1102 HO2S-11 Heater Circuit High Voltage
P1105 HO2S-12 Heater Circuit High Voltage
P1115 HO2S-11 Heater Circuit Low Voltage
P1117 HO2S-12 Heater Circuit Low Voltage
P1123 Long Term Fuel Trim Adaptive Air System Low
P1124 Long Term Fuel Trim Adaptive Air System High
P1127 Long Term Fuel Trim Multiplicative Air System Low
P1128 Long Term Fuel Trim Multiplicative Air System High
P1140 Load Calculation Cross Check
P1170 HO2S-11 Circuit Voltage Stuck At Mid-Range
P1195 EGR Boost Or Pressure Sensor Circuit Fault
P1196 Ignition Switch Start Circuit Fault
P1213 Fuel Injector 1, 2, 3 Or 4 Circuit High Voltage
P1214 Fuel Injector 1, 2, 3 Or 4 Circuit High Voltage
P1215 Fuel Injector 1, 2, 3 Or 4 Circuit High Voltage
P1216 Fuel Injector 1, 2, 3 Or 4 Circuit High Voltage
P1225 Fuel Injector 1, 2, 5 Or 4 Circuit Low Voltage
P1226 Fuel Injector 1, 2, 5 Or 4 Circuit Low Voltage
P1227 Fuel Injector 1, 2, 5 Or 4 Circuit Low Voltage
P1228 Fuel Injector 1, 2, 5 Or 4 Circuit Low Voltage
P1250 Pressure Regulator Control Solenoid Circuit Fault
P1345 No SGC (CMP) Signal To PCM
P1386 Knock Sensor Control Zero Test
P1401 EGR Control Solenoid Circuit Signal Low
P1402 EGR Control Solenoid Circuit Signal High
P1402 EGR Valve Position Sensor Circuit Fault
P1410 EVAP Purge Control Solenoid Circuit High Voltage
P1412 EGR Differential Pressure Sensor Signal Low
P1413 EGR Differential Pressure Sensor Signal High
P1425 EVAP Purge Control Solenoid Circuit Low Voltage
P1449 Canister Drain Cut Valve Solenoid Circuit Fault
P1455 Fuel Tank Sending Unit Circuit Fault
P1458 Air Conditioning Compressor Clutch Signal Fault
P1485 EGR Vent Control Solenoid Circuit Fault
P1486 EGR Vacuum Control Solenoid Circuit Fault
P1487 EGR Boost Sensor Solenoid Circuit Fault
P1510 Idle Air Control Valve Closing Coil High Voltage
P1513 Idle Air Control Valve Closing Coil Low Voltage
P1515 A/T To M/T Codification
P1523 VICS Solenoid Valve Circuit Fault
P1552 Idle Air Control Valve Opening Coil Low Voltage
P1553 Idle Air Control Valve Opening Coil High Voltage
P1606 Chassis Accelerator Sensor Signal Circuit Fault
P1608 PCM Internal Fault
P1611 MIL Request Circuit Low Voltage
P1614 MIL Request Circuit High Voltage
P1616 Chassis Accelerator Sensor Signal Low Voltage
P1617 Chassis Accelerator Sensor Signal High Voltage
P1624 TCM to PCM MIL Request Circuit Fault
P1655 Unused Power Stage "B"
P1660 Unused Power Stage `A'
P1660 Unused Power Stage `B'
P1665 Power Stage Group `A'
P1743 Torque Converter Clutch Solenoid Circuit Fault
P1794 Battery Or Circuit Fault
P1797 Clutch Pedal Switch (MT) Or PIN Switch Circuit Fault

Lexus

READING CODES

Reading the control module memory is on of the first steps in OBD-II system diagnostics.

This step should be initially performed to determine the general nature of the fault. Subsequent readings will determine if the fault has been cleared.

Reading codes can be performed by any of the methods below:
- Read the control module memory with the Generic Scan Tool (GST)
- Read the control module memory with the vehicle manufacturer's specific tester

To read the fault codes, connect the scan tool or tester according to the manufacturer's instructions. Follow the manufacturer's specified procedure for reading the codes.

CLEARING CODES

Control module reset procedures are a very important part of OBD-II System diagnostics. This step should be done at the end of any fault code repair and at the end of any driveability repair.

Clearing codes can be performed by any of the methods below:
- Clear the control module memory with the Generic Scan Tool (GST)
- Clear the control module memory with the vehicle manufacturer's specific tester
- Turn the ignition off and remove the negative battery cable for at least 1 minute.

Removing the negative battery cable may cause other systems in the vehicle to loose their memory. Prior to removing the cable, ensure you have the proper reset codes for radios and alarms.

➡The MIL will may also be de-activated for some codes if the vehicle completes three consecutive trips without a fault detected with vehicle conditions similar to those present during the fault.

LEXUS SPECIFIC OBD-II TROUBLE CODES

P1100 Barometric Pressure Sensor Circuit Fault
P1200 Fuel Pump Relay Circuit Fault
P1300 Igniter Circuit Fault (Bank 1)
P1305 Igniter Circuit Fault (Bank 2)
P1335 Crankshaft Position Sensor Circuit Fault
P1400 Sub-Throttle Position Sensor Circuit Fault
P1401 Sub-Throttle Position Sensor Performance
P1500 Starter Signal Circuit Fault
P1510 Air Volume Too Low With Supercharger On
P1600 PCM Battery Back-up Circuit Fault
P1605 Knock Control CPU Fault
P1700 Vehicle Speed Sensor Circuit Fault
P1705 Direct Clutch Speed Sensor Circuit Fault
P1765 Linear Shift Solenoid Circuit Fault
P1780 Park Neutral Position Switch Fault

Mazda

READING CODES

Reading the control module memory is on of the first steps in OBD-II system diagnostics. This step should be initially performed to determine the general nature of the fault. Subsequent readings will determine if the fault has been cleared.

Reading codes can be performed by any of the methods below:
- Read the control module memory with the Generic Scan Tool (GST)
- Read the control module memory with the vehicle manufacturer's specific tester

To read the fault codes, connect the scan tool or tester according to the manufacturer's instructions. Follow the manufacturer's specified procedure for reading the codes.

CLEARING CODES

Control module reset procedures are a very important part of OBD-II System diagnostics. This step should be done at the end of any fault code repair and at the end of any driveability repair.

Clearing codes can be performed by any of the methods below:
- Clear the control module memory with the Generic Scan Tool (GST)
- Clear the control module memory with the vehicle manufacturer's specific tester
- Turn the ignition off and remove the negative battery cable for at least 1 minute.

Removing the negative battery cable may cause other systems in the vehicle to loose their memory. Prior to removing the cable, ensure you have the proper reset codes for radios and alarms.

➡The MIL will may also be de-activated for some codes if the vehicle completes three consecutive trips without a fault detected with vehicle conditions similar to those present during the fault.

MAZDA SPECIFIC OBD-II TROUBLE CODES

P1000 OBD-II Monitor Testing Not Complete More Driving Required
P1001 Key On Engine Running (KOER) Self-Test Not Able To Complete, KOER Aborted
P1100 Mass Air Flow (MAF) Sensor Intermittent
P1101 Mass Air Flow (MAF) Sensor Out Of Self-Test Range
P1110 Intake Air Temperature (IAT) Sensor Signal Circuit Fault
P1112 Intake Air Temperature (IAT) Sensor Intermittent
P1113 Intake Air Temperature (IAT) Sensor Intermittent
P1116 Engine Coolant Temperature (ECT) Sensor Out Of Self-Test Range
P1117 Engine Coolant Temperature (ECT) Sensor Intermittent
P1120 Throttle Position (TP) Sensor Out Of Range (Low)
P1121 Throttle Position (TP) Sensor Inconsistent With MAF Sensor
P1124 Throttle Position (TP) Sensor Out Of Self-Test Range
P1125 Throttle Position (TP) Sensor Circuit Intermittent
P1127 Exhaust Not Warm Enough, Downstream Heated Oxygen Sensors (HO2S) Not Tested
P1128 Upstream Heated Oxygen Sensors (HO2S) Swapped From Bank To Bank
P1129 Downstream Heated Oxygen Sensors (HO2S) Swapped From Bank To Bank
P1130 Lack Of Upstream Heated Oxygen Sensor (HO2S 11) Switch, Adaptive Fuel At Limit (Bank #1)
P1131 Lack Of Upstream Heated Oxygen Sensor (HO2S 11) Switch, Sensor Indicates Lean (Bank #1)
P1132 Lack Of Upstream Heated Oxygen Sensor (HO2S 11) Switch, Sensor Indicates Rich (Bank#1)
P1137 Lack Of Downstream Heated Oxygen Sensor (HO2S 12) Switch, Sensor Indicates Lean (Bank#1)
P1138 Lack Of Downstream Heated Oxygen Sensor (HO2S 12) Switch, Sensor Indicates Rich (Bank#1)
P1150 Lack Of Upstream Heated Oxygen Sensor (HO2S 21) Switch, Adaptive Fuel At Limit (Bank #2)
P1151 Lack Of Upstream Heated Oxygen Sensor (HO2S 21) Switch, Sensor Indicates Lean (Bank#2)
P1152 Lack Of Upstream Heated Oxygen Sensor (HO2S 21) Switch, Sensor Indicates Rich (Bank #2)
P1170 (HO2S 11) Signal Remained Unchanged For More Than 20 Seconds After Closed Loop
P1173 Feedback A/F Mixture Control (HO2S 21) Signal Remained Unchanged For More Than 20 Seconds After Closed Loop
P1195 Barometric (BARO) Pressure Sensor Circuit Malfunction (Signal Is From EGR Boost Sensor)

P1196 Starter Switch Circuit Malfunction
P1235 Fuel Pump Control Out Of Range (MIL DTC)
P1236 Fuel Pump Control Out Of Range (No MIL)
P1250 Fuel Pressure Regulator Control (FPRC) Solenoid Malfunction
P1252 Fuel Pressure Regulator Control (FPRC) Solenoid Malfunction
P1260 THEFT Detected—Engine Disabled
P1270 Engine RPM Or Vehicle Speed Limiter Reached
P1345 No Camshaft Position Sensor Signal
P1351 Ignition Diagnostic Monitor (IDM) Circuit Input Malfunction
P1351 Indicates Ignition System Malfunction
P1352 Indicates Ignition System Malfunction
P1353 Indicates Ignition System Malfunction
P1354 Indicates Ignition System Malfunction
P1358 Ignition Diagnostic Monitor (IDM) Signal Out Of Self-Test Range
P1359 Spark Output Circuit Malfunction
P1360 Ignition Coil "A" Secondary Circuit Fault
P1361 Ignition Coil "A" Secondary Circuit Fault
P1362 Ignition Coil "A" Secondary Circuit Fault
P1364 Spark Output Circuit Malfunction
P1365 Ignition Coil Secondary Circuit Fault
P1390 Octane Adjust (OCT ADJ) Out Of Self-Test Range
P1400 Differential Pressure Feedback EGR (DPFE) Sensor Circuit Low Voltage Detected
P1401 Differential Pressure Feedback EGR (DPFE) Sensor Circuit High Voltage Detected/EGR Temperature Sensor
P1402 EGR Valve Position Sensor Open Or Short
P1405 Differential Pressure Feedback EGR (DPFE) Sensor Upstream Hose Off Or Plugged
P1406 Differential Pressure Feedback EGR (DPFE) Sensor Downstream Hose Off Or Plugged
P1407 Exhaust Gas Recirculation (EGR) No Flow Detected (Valve Stuck Closed Or Inoperative)
P1408 Exhaust Gas Recirculation (EGR) Flow Out Of Self-Test Range
P1409 Electronic Vacuum Regulator (EVR) Control Circuit Malfunction
P1443 Evaporative Emission Control System—Vacuum System, Purge Control Solenoid Or Purge Control Valve Malfunction
P1444 Purge Flow Sensor (PFS) Circuit Low Input
P1445 Purge Flow Sensor (PFS) Circuit High Input
P1449 Evaporative Emission Control System Unable To Hold Vacuum
P1455 Evaporative Emission Control System Control Leak Detected (Gross Leak)
P1460 Wide Open Throttle Air Conditioning Cut-Off Circuit Malfunction
P1464 Air Conditioning (A/C) Demand Out Of Self-Test Range/A/C On During KOER Or CCT Test
P1474 Low Fan Control Primary Circuit Malfunction
P1485 EGR Control Solenoid Open Or Short
P1486 EGR Vent Solenoid Open Or Short
P1487 EGR Boost Check Solenoid Open Or Short
P1500 Vehicle Speed Sensor (VSS) Circuit Intermittent
P1501 Vehicle Speed Sensor (VSS) Out Of Self-Test Range/Vehicle Moved During Test
P1502 Invalid Self Test—Auxiliary Powertrain Control Module (APCM) Functioning
P1504 Idle Air Control (IAC) Circuit Malfunction
P1505 Idle Air Control (IAC) System At Adaptive Clip
P1506 Idle Air Control (IAC) Overspeed Error
P1507 Idle Air Control (IAC) Underspeed Error
P1508 Bypass Air Solenoid "1" Circuit Fault
P1509 Bypass Air Solenoid "2" Circuit Fault
P1521 Variable Resonance Induction System (VRIS) Solenoid #1 Open Or Short
P1522 Variable Resonance Induction System (VRIS) Solenoid #2 Open Or Short
P1523 High Speed Inlet Air (HSIA) Solenoid Open Or Short
P1524 Charge Air Cooler Bypass Solenoid Circuit Fault
P1525 ABV Vacuum Solenoid Circuit Fault
P1526 ABV Vent Solenoid Circuit Fault

P1529 Atmospheric balance Air Control Valve Fault
P1540 ABV System Fault
P1601 Serial Communication Error
P1602 Serial Communication Error
P1605 Powertrain Control Module (PCM)—Keep Alive Memory (KAM) Test Error
P1608 PCM Internal Circuit Malfunction
P1609 PCM Internal Circuit Malfunction
P1627 Serial Communication Error
P1628 Serial Communication Error
P1650 Power Steering Pressure (PSP) Switch Out Of Self-Test Range
P1651 Power Steering Pressure (PSP) Switch Input Malfunction
P1701 Reverse Engagement Error
P1703 Brake On/Off (BOO) Switch Out Of Self-Test Range
P1705 Transmission Range (TR) Sensor Out Of Self-Test Range
P1706 High Vehicle Speed In Park
P1709 Park Or Neutral Position (PNP) Or Clutch Pedal Position (CPP) Switch Out Of Self-Test Range
P1711 Transmission Fluid Temperature (TFT) Sensor Out Of Self-Test Range
P1720 Vehicle Speed Sensor (VSS) Circuit Malfunction
P1729 4x4 Low Switch Error
P1741 Torque Converter Clutch (TCC) Control Error
P1742 Torque Converter Clutch (TCC) Solenoid Failed On (Turns On MIL)
P1743 Torque Converter Clutch (TCC) Solenoid Failed On (Turns On TCIL)
P1746 Electronic Pressure Control (EPC) Solenoid Open Circuit (Low Input)
P1747 Electronic Pressure Control (EPC) Solenoid Short Circuit (High Input)
P1749 Electronic Pressure Control (EPC) Solenoid Failed Low
P1751 Shift Solenoid#1 (SS1) Performance
P1754 Coast Clutch Solenoid (CCS) Circuit Malfunction
P1756 Shift Solenoid#2 (SS2) Performance
P1761 Shift Solenoid #(SS2) Performance
P1780 Transmission Control Switch (TCS) Circuit Out Of Self-Test Range
P1781 4x4 Low Switch, Out Of Self-Test Range
P1783 Transmission Over Temperature Condition
P1794 PCM Battery Direct Power Circuit Fault
P1797 P/N Switch Open or Short Circuit Fault

Mitsubishi

READING CODES

Reading the control module memory is on of the first steps in OBD-II system diagnostics. This step should be initially performed to determine the general nature of the fault. Subsequent readings will determine if the fault has been cleared.

Reading codes can be performed by any of the methods below:
- Read the control module memory with the Generic Scan Tool (GST)
- Read the control module memory with the vehicle manufacturer's specific tester

To read the fault codes, connect the scan tool or tester according to the manufacturer's instructions. Follow the manufacturer's specified procedure for reading the codes.

CLEARING CODES

Control module reset procedures are a very important part of OBD-II System diagnostics. This step should be done at the end of any fault code repair and at the end of any driveability repair.

Clearing codes can be performed by any of the methods below:
- Clear the control module memory with the Generic Scan Tool (GST)
- Clear the control module memory with the vehicle manufacturer's specific tester

• Turn the ignition off and remove the negative battery cable for at least 1 minute.

Removing the negative battery cable may cause other systems in the vehicle to loose their memory. Prior to removing the cable, ensure you have the proper reset codes for radios and alarms.

➡The MIL will may also be de-activated for some codes if the vehicle completes three consecutive trips without a fault detected with vehicle conditions similar to those present during the fault.

MITSUBISHI SPECIFIC OBD-II TROUBLE CODES

P1100 Induction Control Motor Position Sensor Fault
P1101 Traction Control Vacuum Solenoid Circuit Fault
P1102 Traction Control Ventilation Solenoid Circuit Fault
P1103 Turbocharger Waste Gate Actuator Circuit Fault
P1104 Turbocharger Waste Gate Solenoid Circuit Fault
P1105 Fuel Pressure Solenoid Circuit Fault
P1294 Target Idle Speed Not Reached
P1295 No 5-Volt Supply To TP Sensor
P1296 No 5-Volt Supply To MAP Sensor
P1297 No Change In MAP From Start To Run
P1300 Ignition Timing Adjustment Circuit
P1390 Timing Belt Skipped One Tooth Or More
P1391 Intermittent Loss Of CMP Or CKP Sensor Signals
P1400 Manifold Differential Pressure Sensor Fault
P1443 EVAP Purge Control Solenoid "2" Circuit Fault
P1486 EVAP Leak Monitor Pinched Hose Detected
P1487 High Speed Radiator Fan Control Relay Circuit Fault
P1989 High Speed Condenser Fan Control Relay Fault
P1490 Low Speed Fan Control Relay Fault
P1492 Battery Temperature Sensor High Voltage
P1494 EVAP Ventilation Switch Or Mechanical Fault
P1495 EVAP Ventilation Solenoid Circuit Fault
P1496 5-Volt Supply Output Too Low
P1500 Generator FR Terminal Circuit Fault
P1600 PCM-TCM Serial Communication Link Circuit Fault
P1696 PCM Failure- EEPROM Write Denied
P1715 No CCD Messages From TCM
P1750 TCM Pulse Generator Circuit Fault
P1791 Pressure Control, Shift Control, TCC Solenoid Fault
P1899 PCM ECT Level Signal to TCM Circuit Fault

Nissan

➡This section also provides coverage for the Mercury Villager since it shares a platform with the Nissan Quest

READING CODES

With Scan Tool

Reading the control module memory is on of the first steps in OBD-II system diagnostics. This step should be initially performed to determine the general nature of the fault. Subsequent readings will determine if the fault has been cleared.

Reading codes can be performed by any of the methods below:
• Read the control module memory with the Generic Scan Tool (GST)
• Read the control module memory with the vehicle manufacturer's specific tester

To read the fault codes, connect the scan tool or tester according to the manufacturer's instructions. Follow the manufacturer's specified procedure for reading the codes.

Without Scan Tool

The ECM is capable of outputting data in four different modes, depending on the position of the mode switch and the ignition key. Modes are

switched by turning the mode screw on the side of the ECM, near the red LED. Additional modes are accessed by turning the ignition key on or off.

The ECM is located forward of the center console, behind an access panel on the Altima, and in the passenger's side kick panel on the 240SX.

With the ECM set in Mode 1 and the ignition in the **ON** position, a malfunction indicator lamp bulb check may be performed. When the engine is started, the ECM will illuminate the indicator lamps as a warning of a fault in the system.

Mode 2 is set by turning the mode selector screw fully clockwise, waiting 2 seconds, then turning the screw fully counterclockwise. With the ignition in the **ON** position, self-diagnostic results will be output as a series of lamp flashes. When the engine is started, the oxygen sensor monitor function is enabled and the red LED on the ECM is used to determine proper oxygen sensor function.

1. Remove the access cover and locate the mode adjusting screw and LED on the ECM.
2. Turn the ignition switch **ON**, but do not start the engine. Both the LED and the malfunction indicator lamp on the instrument panel should be illuminated. This is a bulb check.
3. Start the engine.

➡Switching modes is not possible while the engine is running.

4. If the LED or malfunction indicator lamp illuminates, there is a fault in the system.
5. Turn the mode selector screw fully clockwise. Wait 2 seconds, then turn the screw fully counterclockwise.
6. The diagnostic trouble codes will now be read from the ECM memory. They will appear as flashes of the malfunction indicator lamp, or the ECM's LED.
7. After all codes have been read, turn the mode selector screw fully clockwise to erase the codes.

➡Turn the mode adjusting screw to the fully counterclockwise position whenever the vehicle is in use.

8. Turn the ignition **OFF**.

➡When the ignition switch is turned OFF during diagnosis, power to the ECM will drop after approximately 5 seconds. The diagnosis will automatically return to Mode 1 at this time.

CLEARING CODES

With Scan Tool

Control module reset procedures are a very important part of OBD-II System diagnostics. This step should be done at the end of any fault code repair and at the end of any driveability repair.

Clearing codes can be performed by any of the methods below:
• Clear the control module memory with the Generic Scan Tool (GST)
• Clear the control module memory with the vehicle manufacturer's specific tester

➡The MIL will may also be de-activated for some codes if the vehicle completes three consecutive trips without a fault detected with vehicle conditions similar to those present during the fault.

Without Scan Tool

The easiest way to clear trouble codes without a scan tool is to turn the mode selector screw fully clockwise after all codes have been read.

➡Turn the mode adjusting screw to the fully counterclockwise position whenever the vehicle is in use.

Codes may also be erased by turning the ignition off and remove the negative battery cable for at least 1 minute. However, removing the negative battery cable may cause other systems in the vehicle to loose their memory. Prior to removing the cable, ensure you have the proper reset codes for radios and alarms.

NISSAN SPECIFIC OBD-II TROUBLE CODES

P1120 Secondary Throttle Position Sensor Circuit Fault
P1125 Tandem Throttle Position Sensor Circuit Fault
P1210 Traction Control System Signal Fault
P1220 Fuel Pump Control Module Fault
P1320 Ignition Control Signal Fault
P1336 Crankshaft Position Sensor Circuit Fault
P1400 EGR/EVAP Control Solenoid Circuit Fault
P1401 EGR Temperature Sensor Circuit Fault
P1443 EVAP Canister Control Vacuum Switch Circuit Fault
P1445 EVAP Purge Volume Control Valve Circuit Fault
P1605 TCM A~T Diagnosis Communication Line Fault
P1705 Throttle Position Sensor (Switch) Circuit Fault
P1760 Overrun Clutch Solenoid Valve Circuit Fault
P1900 Cooling Fan Control Circuit Fault

NISSAN OBD-II TROUBLE CODE EQUIVALENTS

If a scan tool is not available for code retrieval, the following codes may be retrieved without one.

0505 No Self Diagnostic Failure Indicated
0102 Mass or Volume Air Flow Circuit Malfunction
0401 Intake Air Temperature Circuit Malfunction
0103 Engine Coolant Temperature Circuit Malfunction
0403 Throttle/Pedal Position Sensor/Switch "A" Circuit Malfunction
0908 Insufficient Coolant Temperature For Closed Loop Fuel Control
0303 O2 Circuit Malfunction
0307 Closed Loop Control
0901 O2 Sensor Heater Circuit Malfunction (Bank no. 1 Sensor no. 1)
0707 O2 Sensor Circuit Malfunction (Bank no. 1 Sensor no. 2)
0902 O2 Sensor Heater Circuit Malfunction (Bank no. 1 Sensor no. 2)
0115 System Too Lean (Bank no. 1)
0114 System Too Rich (Bank no. 1)
0701 Random/Multiple Cylinder Misfire Detected
0608 Cylinder no. 1—Misfire Detected
0607 Cylinder no. 2—Misfire Detected
0606 Cylinder no. 3—Misfire Detected
0605 Cylinder no. 4—Misfire Detected
0304 Knock Sensor no. 1—Circuit Malfunction (Bank no. 1 or Single Sensor)
0802 Crankshaft Position Sensor "A" Circuit Malfunction
0101 Camshaft Position Sensor Circuit Malfunction
0302 Exhaust Gas Recirculation Flow Malfunction
0306 Exhaust Gas Recirculation Flow Excessive Detected
0702 Catalyst System Efficiency Below Threshold (Bank no. 1)
0104 Vehicle Speed Sensor Malfunction
0205 Idle Control System Malfunction
0301 Internal Control Module Read Only Memory (ROM) Error
1003 Transmission Range Sensor Circuit Malfunction (PRNDL Input)
1101 Inhibitor Switch Circuit
1208 Transmission Fluid Temperature Sensor Circuit Malfunction
1102 Output Speed Sensor Circuit Malfunction
1207 Engine Speed Input Circuit Malfunction
1103 Gear no. 1 Incorrect Ratio
1104 Gear no. 2 Incorrect Ratio
1105 Gear no. 3 Incorrect Ratio
1106 Gear no. 4 Incorrect Ratio
1204 Torque Converter Clutch Circuit Malfunction
1205 Pressure Control Solenoid Malfunction
1108 Shift Solenoid "A" Malfunction
1201 Shift Solenoid "B" Malfunction
0201 Ignition Control Signal Fault
0905 Crankshaft Position Sensor Circuit Fault
1005 EGR/EVAP Control Solenoid Circuit Fault
0305 EGR Temperature Sensor Circuit Fault
0804 TCM A~T Diagnosis Communication Line Fault

1206 Throttle Position Sensor (Switch) Circuit Fault
1203 Overrun Clutch Solenoid Valve Circuit Fault
1308 Cooling Fan Control Circuit Fault

Porsche

READING CODES

Reading the control module memory is on of the first steps in OBD-II system diagnostics. This step should be initially performed to determine the general nature of the fault. Subsequent readings will determine if the fault has been cleared.

Reading codes can be performed by any of the methods below:
- Read the control module memory with the Generic Scan Tool (GST)
- Read the control module memory with the vehicle manufacturer's specific tester

To read the fault codes, connect the scan tool or tester according to the manufacturer's instructions. Follow the manufacturer's specified procedure for reading the codes.

CLEARING CODES

Control module reset procedures are a very important part of OBD-II System diagnostics. This step should be done at the end of any fault code repair and at the end of any driveability repair.

Clearing codes can be performed by any of the methods below:
- Clear the control module memory with the Generic Scan Tool (GST)
- Clear the control module memory with the vehicle manufacturer's specific tester
- Turn the ignition off and remove the negative battery cable for at least 1 minute.

Removing the negative battery cable may cause other systems in the vehicle to loose their memory. Prior to removing the cable, ensure you have the proper reset codes for radios and alarms.

➡**The MIL will may also be de-activated for some codes if the vehicle completes three consecutive trips without a fault detected with vehicle conditions similar to those present during the fault.**

PORSCHE SPECIFIC OBD-II TROUBLE CODES

P1102 Oxygen Sensor Heating
P1105 Oxygen Sensor Heating
P1107 Oxygen Sensor Heating
P1110 Oxygen Sensor Heating
P1115 Oxygen Sensor Heating
P1117 Oxygen Sensor Heating
P1119 Oxygen Sensor Heating
P1121 Oxygen Sensor Heating
P1123 Oxygen Sensing Heating
P1124 Oxygen Sensing
P1125 Oxygen Sensing
P1126 Oxygen Sensing
P1127 Oxygen Sensing
P1128 Oxygen Sensing
P1129 Oxygen Sensing
P1130 Oxygen Sensing
P1136 Oxygen Sensing
P1137 Oxygen Sensing
P1138 Oxygen Sensing
P1139 Oxygen Sensing
P1140 Load Signal
P1157 Engine Compartment Temperature
P1158 Engine Compartment Temperature
P1213 Fuel Injector, Cylinder 1
P1214 Fuel Injector, Cylinder 2
P1215 Fuel Injector, Cylinder 3

P1216 Fuel Injector, Cylinder 4
P1217 Fuel Injector, Cylinder 5
P1218 Fuel Injector, Cylinder 6
P1225 Fuel Injector, Cylinder 1
P1226 Fuel Injector, Cylinder 2
P1227 Fuel Injector, Cylinder 3
P1228 Fuel Injector, Cylinder 4
P1229 Fuel Injector, Cylinder 5
P1230 Fuel Injector, Cylinder 6
P1237 Fuel Injector, Cylinder 1
P1238 Fuel Injector, Cylinder 2
P1239 Fuel Injector, Cylinder 3
P1240 Fuel injector, Cylinder 4
P1241 Fuel Injector, Cylinder 5
P1242 Fuel Injector, Cylinder 6
P1265 Airbag Signal
P1275 Oxygen Sensor Aging Ahead of Three Way Catalytic Converter
P1276 Oxygen Sensor Aging Ahead of Three Way Catalytic Converter
P1313 Misfire Cylinder 1, Emission Related
P1314 Misfire Cylinder 2, Emission Related
P1315 Misfire Cylinder 3, Emission Related
P1316 Misfire, Cylinder 4, Emission Related
P1317 Misfire, Cylinder 5, Emission Related
P1318 Misfire, Cylinder 6, Emission Related
P1319 Misfire Emission Related
P1324 Timing Chain out of Position, Bank 2
P1340 Timing Chain out of Position, Bank 1
P1384 Knock Sensor 1
P1385 Knock Sensor 2
P1386 Knock Sensor Test Pulse
P1386 Knock Control Test Pulse
P1397 Camshaft Position Sensor 2
P1411 Secondary Air Injection System
P1455 A/C Compressor Control
P1456 A/C Compressor Control
P1457 A/C Compressor Control
P1458 A/C Compressor Signal
P1501 Fuel Pump Relay End-Stage
P1502 Fuel Pump Relay End-Stage
P1510 Idle Air Control Valve
P1513 Idle Air Control Valve
P1514 Idle Control Valve
P1515 Intake Manifold Resonance Flap
P1516 Intake Manifold Resonance Flap
P1524 Camshaft Adjustment, Bank 2
P1530 Camshaft Adjustment, Bank 1
P1531 Camshaft Adjustment, Bank 1
P1539 Camshaft Adjustment, Bank 2
P1541 Fuel Pump Relay End-Stage
P1551 Idle Air Control Valve
P1552 Idle Air Control Valve
P1553 Idle Air Control Valve
P1555 Charge Pressure Characteristics
P1556 Charge Deviations
P1557 Charge Deviations
P1570 Immobilizer
P1571 Immobilizer
P1585 Misfire With Empty Fuel Tank
P1593 Intake Manifold Length Tuning 2
P1594 Intake Manifold Length Tuning 2
P1595 Intake Manifold Length Tuning 2
P1600 Voltage Supply
P1601 Voltage Supply
P1602 Voltage Supply
P1610 MIL Activated Externally
P1611 MIL Activated Externally
P1614 MIL Activated Externally
P1640 Engine Control Module

P1656 Coolant Shutoff Valve
P1671 Engine Compartment Purge Fan End-Stage
P1673 Fan End-Stage
P1689 Engine Control Module
P1691 Malfunction Indicator Lamp
P1692 Malfunction Indicator Lamp
P1693 Malfunction Indicator Lamp
P1704 Kickdown Switch
P1710 Speed Signal, Right Front
P1715 Speed Signal, Left Front
P1744 Manual Program Switch
P1746 Control Unit Defective (Relay)
P1748 Control unit defective (relay sticks)
P1749 Version coding
P1750 Voltage supply, solenoid valve pressure regulators 1
P1761 Shiftlock P/N
P1762 Shiftlock P/N
P1764 Instrument cluster triggering
P1765 Throttle-valve information error
P1770 Load signal from ECM
P1782 Engine Engagement
P1813 Pressure regulator 1
P1818 Pressure regulator 2
P1823 Pressure regulator 3
P1828 Pressure regulator 4

Saab

READING CODES

Reading the control module memory is on of the first steps in OBD-II system diagnostics. This step should be initially performed to determine the general nature of the fault. Subsequent readings will determine if the fault has been cleared.

Reading codes can be performed by any of the methods below:
- Read the control module memory with the Generic Scan Tool (GST)
- Read the control module memory with the vehicle manufacturer's specific tester

To read the fault codes, connect the scan tool or tester according to the manufacturer's instructions. Follow the manufacturer's specified procedure for reading the codes.

CLEARING CODES

Control module reset procedures are a very important part of OBD-II System diagnostics. This step should be done at the end of any fault code repair and at the end of any driveability repair.

Clearing codes can be performed by any of the methods below:
- Clear the control module memory with the Generic Scan Tool (GST)
- Clear the control module memory with the vehicle manufacturer's specific tester
- Turn the ignition off and remove the negative battery cable for at least 1 minute.

Removing the negative battery cable may cause other systems in the vehicle to loose their memory. Prior to removing the cable, ensure you have the proper reset codes for radios and alarms.

➡**The MIL will may also be de-activated for some codes if the vehicle completes three consecutive trips without a fault detected with vehicle conditions similar to those present during the fault.**

SAAB SPECIFIC OBD-II TROUBLE CODES

P1102 Front heated oxygen sensor, bank 1, control module input. Current in preheating circuit much too high.

P1105 Rear heated oxygen sensor, bank 1, control module input. Current in preheating circuit much too high.

P1115 Front heated oxygen sensor, bank 1, control module input. Current in preheating circuit much too low.

P1117 Rear heated oxygen sensor, bank 1, control module input. Current in preheating circuit much too low.

P1123 Additive adaptation, bank 1. Min value.

P1124 Additive adaptation, bank 1. Max value.

P1125 Additive adaptation, bank 2. Min value.

P1126 Additive adaptation, bank 2. Max value.

P1127 Multiplicative adaptation, bank 1. Min value.

P1128 Multiplicative adaptation, bank 1. Max value.

P1129 Multiplicative adaptation, bank 2. Min value.

P1130 Multiplicative adaptation, bank 2. Max value.

P1170 Closed loop. Malfunction.

P1171 Closed loop. Lean mixture.

P1172 Closed loop. Rich mixture.

P1213 Injector, cylinder 1, control module output. Shorting to battery positive (B+).

P1214 Injector, cylinder 2, control module output. Shorting to battery positive (B+).

P1215 Injector, cylinder 3, control module output. Shorting to battery positive (B+).

P1216 Injector, cylinder 4, control module output. Shorting to battery positive (B+).

P1217 Injector, cylinder 5, control module output. Shorting to battery positive (B+).

P1218 Injector, cylinder 6, control module output. Shorting to battery positive (B+).

P1225 Injector, cylinder 1, control module output. Open circuit or shorting to ground.

P1226 Injector, cylinder 2, control module output. Open circuit or shorting to ground.

P1227 Injector, cylinder 3, control module output. Open circuit or shorting to ground.

P1228 Injector, cylinder 4, control module output. Open circuit or shorting to ground.

P1229 Injector, cylinder 5, control module output. Open circuit or shorting to ground.

P1230 Injector, cylinder 6, control module output. Open circuit or shorting to ground.

P1386 Control module, electronic circuitry for processing knock sensor signals Internal fault.

P1396 Crankshaft position sensor, control module input. Malfunctioning, slotted ring has too many ribs.

P1410 EVAP canister purge valve, control module output. Shorting to battery positive (B+).

P1416 Tank level. Low level in conjunction with misfiring or fault in fuel system.

P1425 EVAP canister purge module output. Shorting to ground.

P1426 EVAP canister purge module output. Open circuit.

P1500 Battery voltage outside limits.

P1501 Fuel pump relay, control module output. Shorting to ground.

P1502 Fuel pump relay, control module output. Shorting to battery positive (B+)

P1510 Idle air control valve, open control module output. Shorting to battery positive (B+).

P1513 Idle air control valve, open control module output. Shorting to ground.

P1514 Idle air control valve, open function, control module output. Open circuit.

P1541 Fuel pump relay, control module out put.

P1549 Boost pressure control. Malfunction.

P1551 Idle air control valve, close function, control module output. Open circuit.

P1552 Idle air control valve, close function, control module output. Shorting to ground.

P1553 Idle air control valve, close function, control module output. Shorting to battery positive (B+).

P1576 Brake light switch. Shorting to battery positive (B+).

P1577 Brake light switch. Open circuit.

P1585 Fuel less than 10 liters.

P1611 CHECK ENGINE request, input signal to control module. Shorting to ground.

P1616 Rough road sensor. Control module input low, shorting to ground.

P1617 Rough road sensor. Control module input high; open circuit or shorting to battery positive (B+).

P1624 The automatic transmission has a stored emission-related fault.

P1664 Shift up, output signal from control module. Malfunction.

P1665 Intermittent fault which cannot identify any other specific diagnostic trouble code.

P1669 TCS active, input signal to control module.

P1670 Intermittent fault which cannot identify any other specific diagnostic trouble code.

P1675 Intermittent fault which cannot identify any other specific diagnostic trouble code.

P1680 Relay, secondary air injection. Control module output, open circuit or short circuit.

P1691 CHECK ENGINE, output signal from On control module. Open circuit.

P1692 CHECK ENGINE, output signal from On control module. Shorting to ground.

P1693 CHECK ENGINE, output signal from On control module. Open circuit or shorting to ground or battery positive (B+).

Subaru

READING CODES

Reading the control module memory is on of the first steps in OBD-II system diagnostics.

This step should be initially performed to determine the general nature of the fault. Subsequent readings will determine if the fault has been cleared.

Reading codes can be performed by any of the methods below:
- Read the control module memory with the Generic Scan Tool (GST)
- Read the control module memory with the vehicle manufacturer's specific tester

To read the fault codes, connect the scan tool or tester according to the manufacturer's instructions. Follow the manufacturer's specified procedure for reading the codes.

CLEARING CODES

Control module reset procedures are a very important part of OBD-II System diagnostics. This step should be done at the end of any fault code repair and at the end of any driveability repair.

Clearing codes can be performed by any of the methods below:
- Clear the control module memory with the Generic Scan Tool (GST)
- Clear the control module memory with the vehicle manufacturer's specific tester
- Turn the ignition **OFF** and disconnect the negative battery cable for at least 1 minute.

Removing the negative battery cable may cause other systems in the vehicle to loose their memory. Prior to removing the cable, ensure you have the proper reset codes for radios and alarms.

➡**The MIL will may also be de-activated for some codes if the vehicle completes three consecutive trips without a fault detected with vehicle conditions similar to those present during the fault.**

SUBARU SPECIFIC OBD-II TROUBLE CODES

P1100 Starter Switch Circuit Fault
P1101 Neutral Position Switch Circuit Fault (MT)

Suzuki

READING CODES

Reading the control module memory is on of the first steps in OBD-II system diagnostics. This step should be initially performed to determine the general nature of the fault. Subsequent readings will determine if the fault has been cleared.

Reading codes can be performed by any of the methods below:
- Read the control module memory with the Generic Scan Tool (GST)
- Read the control module memory with the vehicle manufacturer's specific tester

To read the fault codes, connect the scan tool or tester according to the manufacturer's instructions. Follow the manufacturer's specified procedure for reading the codes.

CLEARING CODES

Control module reset procedures are a very important part of OBD-II System diagnostics. This step should be done at the end of any fault code repair and at the end of any driveability repair.

Clearing codes can be performed by any of the methods below:
- Clear the control module memory with the Generic Scan Tool (GST)
- Clear the control module memory with the vehicle manufacturer's specific tester
- Turn the ignition off and remove the negative battery cable for at least 1 minute.

Removing the negative battery cable may cause other systems in the vehicle to loose their memory. Prior to removing the cable, ensure you have the proper reset codes for radios and alarms.

➡**The MIL will may also be de-activated for some codes if the vehicle completes three consecutive trips without a fault de-tected with vehicle conditions similar to those present during the fault.**

SUZUKI SPECIFIC OBD-II TROUBLE CODES

P1250 EFI Heater Circuit Fault
P1408 Manifold Differential Pressure Sensor Circuit Fault
P1410 Fuel Tank Pressure Control Solenoid Circuit Fault
P1450 Barometric Pressure Sensor Circuit Fault
P1451 Barometric Pressure Sensor Performance
P1460 Cooling Fan Control System Fault
P1500 Starter Signal Circuit Fault
P1510 Back-up Power Supply Fault
P1530 Ignition Timing Adjustment Switch Circuit
P1600 PCM Battery Circuit Fault
P1700 TCM Throttle Position Sensor Circuit Fault
P1705 TCM ECT Circuit Fault
P1715 PNP Switch Circuit Fault
P1717 AT Drive Range Signal Circuit Fault

Toyota

READING CODES

Reading the control module memory is on of the first steps in OBD-II system diagnostics. This step should be initially performed to determine the general nature of the fault. Subsequent readings will determine if the fault has been cleared.

Reading codes can be performed by any of the methods below:
- Read the control module memory with the Generic Scan Tool (GST)
- Read the control module memory with the vehicle manufacturer's specific tester

To read the fault codes, connect the scan tool or tester according to the manufacturer's instructions. Follow the manufacturer's specified procedure for reading the codes.

CLEARING CODES

Control module reset procedures are a very important part of OBD-II System diagnostics. This step should be done at the end of any fault code repair and at the end of any driveability repair.

Clearing codes can be performed by any of the methods below:
- Clear the control module memory with the Generic Scan Tool (GST)
- Clear the control module memory with the vehicle manufacturer's specific tester
- Turn the ignition off and remove the negative battery cable for at least 1 minute.

Removing the negative battery cable may cause other systems in the vehicle to loose their memory. Prior to removing the cable, ensure you have the proper reset codes for radios and alarms.

➡**The MIL will may also be de-activated for some codes if the vehicle completes three consecutive trips without a fault detected with vehicle conditions similar to those present during the fault.**

TOYOTA SPECIFIC OBD-II TROUBLE CODES

P1100 Barometric Pressure Sensor Circuit Fault
P1200 Fuel Pump Relay Circuit Fault
P1300 Igniter Circuit Fault (Bank 1)
P1305 Igniter Circuit Fault (Bank 2)
P1335 Crankshaft Position Sensor Circuit Fault
P1400 Sub-Throttle Position Sensor Circuit Fault
P1401 Sub-Throttle Position Sensor Performance
P1500 Starter Signal Circuit Fault
P1510 Air Volume Too Low With Supercharger On
P1600 PCM Battery Back-up Circuit Fault
P1605 Knock Control CPU Fault
P1700 Vehicle Speed Sensor Circuit Fault
P1705 Direct Clutch Speed Sensor Circuit Fault
P1765 Linear Shift Solenoid Circuit Fault
P1780 Park Neutral Position Switch Fault

Volkswagen

READING CODES

Reading the control module memory is one of the first steps in OBD-II system diagnostics. This step should be initially performed to determine the general nature of the fault. Subsequent readings will determine if the fault has been cleared.

Reading codes can be performed by any of the methods below:
- Read the control module memory with the Generic Scan Tool (GST)
- Read the control module memory with the Vag 1550 tester

To read the fault codes, connect the scan tool or tester according to the manufacturer's instructions. Follow the manufacturer's specified procedure for reading the codes.

CLEARING CODES

Control module reset procedures are a very important part of OBD-II System diagnostics. This step should be done at the end of any fault code repair and at the end of any driveability repair.

Clearing codes can be performed by any of the methods below:
- Clear the control module memory with the Generic Scan Tool (GST)
- Clear the control module memory with the vehicle manufacturer's specific tester
- Turn the ignition off and remove the negative battery cable for at least 1 minute.

Removing the negative battery cable may cause other systems in the vehicle to loose their memory. Prior to removing the cable, ensure you have the proper reset codes for radios and alarms.

➡ **The MIL will may also be de-activated for some codes if the vehicle completes three consecutive trips without a fault detected with vehicle conditions similar to those present during the fault.**

VOLKSWAGEN SPECIFIC OBD-II TROUBLE CODES

P1102 Oxygen Sensor Heating Circuit, Bank 1-Sensor 1 Short to B+
P1105 Oxygen Sensor Heating Circuit, Bank 1-Sensor 2 Short to B+
P1107 Oxygen Sensor Heating Circuit, Bank 2-Sensor I Short to B+
P1110 Oxygen Sensor Heating Circuit, Bank 2-Sensor 2 Short to B+
P1127 Long Term Fuel Trim Multiplicative, Bank 1 System Too Rich
P1128 Long Term Fuel Trim Multiplicative, Bank 1 System Too Lean
P1129 Long Term Fuel Trim Multiplicative, Bank2 System too Rich
P1130 Long Term Fuel Trim Multiplicative, Bank2 System too Lean
P1136 Long Term Fuel Trim Additive, Bank 1 System Too Lean
P1137 Long Term Fuel Trim Additive, Bank 1 System Too Rich
P1138 Long Term Fuel Trim Additive Fuel, Bank I System too Lean
P1139 Long Term Fuel Trim Additive Fuel, Bank 1 System too Rich
P1141 Load Calculation Cross Check Range/Performance
P1176 Oxygen Correction Behind Catalyst, B1 Limit Attained
P1177 Oxygen Correction Behind Catalyst. 82 Limit Attained
P1196 Oxygen Sensor Heater Circuit, Bank 1-Sensor 1 Electrical Malfunction
P1197 Oxygen Sensor Heater Circuit, Bank 2-Sensor I Electrical Malfunction
P1198 Oxygen Sensor Heater Circuit, Bank 1-Sensor 2 Electrical Malfunction
P1198 Oxygen Sensor Heater Circuit, Bank 1-Sensor 2 Electrical Malfunction
P1199 Oxygen Sensor Heater Circuit, Bank 2-Sensor 2 Electrical Malfunction
P1201 Cylinder 1, Fuel Injection Circuit Electrical Malfunction
P1202 Cylinder 2, Fuel Injection Circuit Electrical Malfunction
P1203 Cylinder 3, Fuel Injection Circuit Electrical Malfunction
P1204 Cylinder 4, Fuel Injection Circuit Electrical Malfunction
P1205 Cylinder 5, Fuel Injection Circuit Electrical Malfunction
P1206 Cylinder 6, Fuel Injection Circuit Electrical Malfunction
P1207 Cylinder 7, Fuel Injection Circuit Electrical Malfunction
P1208 Cylinder 8, Fuel Injection Circuit Electrical Malfunction
P1213 Cylinder I-Fuel Injection Circuit Short to B+
P1214 Cylinder 2-Fuel Injection Circuit Short to B+
P1215 Cylinder 3 Fuel Injection Circuit Short to B+
P1216 Cylinder 4 Fuel Injection Circuit Short to B+
P1217 Cylinder 5 Fuel Injection Circuit Short to B+
P1218 Cylinder 6 Fuel Injection Circuit Short to B+
P1219 Cylinder 7, Fuel Injection Circuit Short to B+
P1219 Cylinder 8, Fuel Injection Circuit Short to B+
P1225 Cylinder I Fuel Injection Circuit Short to Ground
P1226 Cylinder 2 Fuel Injection Circuit Short to Ground
P1227 Cylinder 3 Fuel Injection Circuit Short to Ground
P1228 Cylinder 4 Fuel Injection Circuit Short to Ground
P1229 Cylinder 5 Fuel Injection Circuit Short to Ground
P1230 Cylinder 6 Fuel Injection Circuit Short to Ground
P1237 Cylinder I Fuel Injection Circuit Open Circuit
P1238 Cylinder 2 Fuel Injection Circuit Open Circuit
P1239 Cylinder 3 Fuel Injection Circuit Open Circuit
P1240 Cylinder 4 Fuel Injection Circuit Open Circuit
P1241 Cylinder 5 Fuel Injection Circuit Open Circuit
P1242 Cylinder 6 Fuel Injection Circuit Open Circuit
P1250 Fuel Level Too Low
P1280 Fuel Injection Air Control Valve Circuit Flow too Low
P1283 Fuel Injection Air Control Valve Circuit Electrical Malfunction
P1325 Cylinder I Knock Control Limit Attained

P1326 Cylinder 2 Knock Control Limit Attained
P1327 Cylinder 3 Knock Control Limit Attained
P1328 Cylinder 4 Knock Control Limit Attained
P1329 Cylinder 5 Knock Control Limit Attained
P1330 Cylinder 6 Knock Control Limit Attained
P1331 Cylinder 7, Knock Control Limit Attained
P1332 Cylinder 8, Knock Control Limit Attained
P1337 Camshaft Position Sensor, Bank 1 Short to Ground
P1338 Camshaft Position Sensor, Bank 1 Open Circuit/Short to B+
P1340 Boost Pressure Control Valve Short to B+
P1386 Internal Control Module Knock Control Circuit Error
P1391 Camshaft Position Sensor, Bank 2 Short to Ground
P1392 Camshaft Position Sensor, Bank 2 Open Circuit/Short to B+
P1410 Tank Ventilation Valve Circuit Short to B+
P1420 Secondary Air Injection Module Short To B+
P1421 Secondary Air Injection Module Short To Ground
P1421 Secondary Air Injection Valve Circuit Short to Ground
P1422 Secondary Air Injection System Control Valve Circuit Short To B+
P1422 Secondary Air Injection Valve Circuit Short to B+
P1425 Tank Vent Valve Short To Ground
P1425 Tank Vent Valve Short to Ground
P1426 Tank Vent Valve Open
P1426 Tank Vent Valve Open
P1432 Secondary Air Injection Valve Open
P1433 Secondary Air Injection System Pump Relay Circuit Open
P1434 Secondary Air Injection System Pump Relay Circuit Short to B+
P1435 Secondary Air Injection System Pump Relay Circuit Short to Ground
P1436 Secondary Air Injection System Pump Relay Circuit Electrical Malfunction
P1450 Secondary Air Injection System Circuit Short To B+
P1451 Secondary Air Injection System Circuit Short To Ground
P1452 Secondary Air Injection System Open Circuit
P1471 EVAP Emission Control LDP Circuit Short to B+
P1472 EVAP Emission Control LDP Circuit Short to Ground
P1473 EVAP Emission Control LDP Circuit Open Circuit
P1475 EVAP Emission Control LDP Circuit Malfunction/Signal Circuit Open
P1476 EVAP Emission Control LDP Circuit Malfunction/Insufficient Vacuum
P1477 EVAP Emission Control LDP Circuit Malfunction
P1500 Fuel Pump Relay Circuit Electrical Malfunction
P1501 Fuel Pump Relay Circuit Short to Ground
P1502 Fuel Pump Relay Circuit Short to B+
P1505 Closed Throttle Position Switch Does Not Close/Open Circuit
P1506 Closed Throttle Position Switch Does Not Open/Short to Ground
P1507 Idle System Learned Value Lower Limit Attained
P1508 Idle System Learned Value Upper Limit Attained
P1512 Intake Manifold Changeover Valve Circuit, Short to B+
P1515 Intake Manifold Changeover Valve Circuit, Short to Ground
P1516 Intake Manifold Changeover Valve Circuit, Open
P1519 Intake Camshaft Control, Bank I Malfunction
P1522 Intake Camshaft Control, Bank 2 Malfunction
P1543 Throttle Actuation Potentiometer Signal Too Low
P1544 Throttle Actuation Potentiometer Signal Too High
P1545 Throttle Position Control Malfunction
P1547 Boost Pressure Control Valve Short to Ground
P1548 Boost Pressure Control Valve Open
P1555 Charge Pressure Upper Limit Exceeded
P1556 Charge Pressure Negative Deviation
P1557 Charge Pressure Positive Deviation
P1558 Throttle Actuator Electrical Malfunction
P1559 Idle Speed Control Throttle Position Adaptation Malfunction
P1560 Maximum Engine Speed Exceeded
P1564 Idle Speed Control, Throttle Position Low Voltage During Adaptation
P1580 Throttle Actuator (B1) Malfunction
P1582 Idle Adaptation At Limit

P1602 Power Supply (B+) Terminal 30 Low Voltage
P1606 Rough Road Spec Engine Torque ABS-ECU Electrical Malfunction
P1611 MIL Call-up Circuit/Transmission Control Module Short to Ground
P1612 Electronic Control Module Incorrect Coding
P1613 MIL Call-up Circuit Open/Short to B+
P1624 MIL Request Signal Active
P1625 CAN-Bus Implausible Message from Transmission Control
P1626 CAN-Bus Missing Message from Transmission Control
P1640 Internal Control Module (EEPROM) Error
P1640 Internal Control Module (EEPROM) Error
P1681 Control Unit Programming not Finished
P1690 Malfunction Indicator Light Malfunction
P1693 Malfunction Indicator Light Short to B+
P1778 Solenoid EV7 Electrical Malfunction
P1780 Engine Intervention Readable

VOLKSWAGEN OBD-II TROUBLE CODE EQUIVALENTS

If a generic scan tool is not available for code retrieval, the following codes may be retrieved using the Vag 1551.

16486 Mass or Volume Air Flow Circuit Low Input
16487 Mass or Volume Air Flow Circuit High Input
16491 Manifold Absolute Pressure or Barometric Pressure Low Input
16492 Manifold Absolute Pressure or Barometric Pressure High Input
16496 Intake Air Temperature Circuit Low Input
16497 Intake Air Temperature Circuit High Input
16500 Engine Coolant Temperature Circuit Range/Performance
16501 Engine Coolant Temperature Circuit Low Input
16502 Oxygen Engine Coolant Temperature Circuit High Input
16504 Throttle Position Sensor A Circuit Malfunction
16505 Throttle/Pedal Position Sensor A Circuit Range/Performance
16506 Throttle/Pedal Position Sensor A Circuit Low Input
16507 Throttle/Pedal Position Sensor A Circuit High Input
16509 Insufficient Coolant Temperature For Closed Loop Fuel Control
16514 Oxygen Sensor Circuit, Bank 1-Sensor 1 Malfunction
16515 Oxygen Sensor Circuit, Bank 1-Sensor 1 Low Voltage
16516 Oxygen Sensor Circuit, Bank 1-Sensor 1 High Voltage
16517 Oxygen Sensor Circuit, Bank 1-Sensor 1 Slow Response
16518 Oxygen Sensor Circuit, Bank 1-Sensor 1 No Activity Detected
16519 Oxygen Sensor Heater Circuit, Bank 1-Sensor 1 Malfunction
16520 Oxygen Sensor Circuit, Bank 1-Sensor 2 Malfunction
16521 Oxygen Sensor Circuit, Bank 1-Sensor 2 Low Voltage
16522 Oxygen Sensor Circuit, Bank 1-Sensor 2 High Voltage
16524 Oxygen Sensor Circuit, Bank 1-Sensor 2 No Activity Detected
16525 Oxygen Sensor Heater Circuit, Bank 1-Sensor 2 Malfunction
16534 Oxygen Sensor Circuit, Bank 2-Sensor 1 Malfunction
16535 Oxygen Sensor Circuit, Bank 2-Sensor 1 Low Voltage
16536 Oxygen Sensor Circuit, Bank 2-Sensor 1 High Voltage
16537 Oxygen Sensor Circuit, Bank 2-Sensor 1 Slow Response
16538 Oxygen Sensor Circuit, Bank 2-Sensor 1 No Activity Detected
16540 Oxygen Sensor Circuit, Bank 2-Sensor 2 Malfunction
16541 Oxygen Sensor Circuit, Bank 2-Sensor 2 Low Voltage
16542 Oxygen Sensor Circuit, Bank 2-Sensor 2 High Voltage
16544 Oxygen Sensor Circuit, Bank 2-Sensor 2 No Activity Detected
16555 Oxygen System Too Lean, Bank 1
16556 Oxygen System Too Rich, Bank 1
16684 Random Multiple Misfire Detected
16685 Cylinder 1 Misfire Detected
16686 Cylinder 2 Misfire Detected
16687 Cylinder 3 Misfire Detected
16688 Cylinder 4 Misfire Detected
16689 Cylinder 5 Misfire Detected
16690 Cylinder 6 Misfire Detected
16705 Ignition Distributor Engine Speed Input Circuit Range/Performance
16706 Ignition /Distributor Engine Speed Input Circuit No Signal
16711 Knock sensor 1 Circuit Low Input

16712 Knock Sensor Circuit, High Input
16716 Knock sensor 2 Circuit Low Input
16716 Knock Sensor Circuit, Low Input
16717 Knock Sensor 2 Circuit, High Input
16725 Camshaft Position Sensor Circuit Range/Performance
16795 Secondary Air Injection System Incorrect Flow Detected
16806 Main Catalyst Efficiency Below Threshold (Bank 1)
16806 Main Catalyst, Bank I Efficiency Below Threshold
16824 Evaporative Emission Control System Malfunction
16825 EVAP Emission Contr. Sys. Incorrect Purge Flow
16826 EVAP Emission Contr. Sys. (Small Leak) Leak Detected
16839 EVAP Emission Contr. Sys. (Gross Leak) Leak Detected
16885 Vehicle Speed Sensor Range/Performance
16890 Idle Control System RPM Lower Than Expected
16891 Idle Control System RPM Higher Than Expected
16894 Closed Throttle Position Switch Malfunction
16944 System Voltage Malfunction
16946 System Voltage Low Voltage
16947 System Voltage High Voltage
16985 Internal Contr. Module Memory Check Sum Error
16988 Internal Contr. Module Random Access Memory (RAM) Error
16989 Internal Control Module Read Only Memory (ROM) Error
17091 Transmission Range Sensor Circuit Low Input
17092 Transmission Range Sensor Circuit High Input
17099 Input Turbine Speed Sensor Circuit Malfunction
17106 Output Speed Sensor Circuit No Signal
17109 Engine Speed Input Circuit Malfunction
17132 Pressure Control Solenoid Electrical
17137 Shift Solenoid A Electrical
17142 Shift Solenoid B Electrical
17147 Shift Solenoid C Electrical
17152 Shift Solenoid D Electrical
17157 Shift Solenoid E Electrical
16684 Random/Multiple Cylinder Misfire Detected
16685 Cylinder I Misfire Detected
16686 Cylinder 2 Misfire Detected
17510 Oxygen Sensor Heating Circuit, Bank 1-Sensor 1 Short to B+
17513 Oxygen Sensor Heating Circuit, Bank 1-Sensor 2 Short to B+
17515 Oxygen Sensor Heating Circuit, Bank 2-Sensor I Short to B+
17518 Oxygen Sensor Heating Circuit, Bank 2-Sensor 2 Short to B+
17535 Long Term Fuel Trim Multiplicative, Bank 1 System Too Rich
17536 Long Term Fuel Trim Multiplicative, Bank 1 System Too Lean
17537 Long Term Fuel Trim Multiplicative, Bank2 System too Rich
17538 Long Term Fuel Trim Multiplicative, Bank2 System too Lean
17544 Long Term Fuel Trim Additive, Bank 1 System Too Lean
17545 Long Term Fuel Trim Additive, Bank 1 System Too Rich
17546 Long Term Fuel Trim Additive Fuel, Bank I System too Lean
17547 Long Term Fuel Trim Additive Fuel, Bank 1 System too Rich
17549 Load Calculation Cross Check Range/Performance
17584 Oxygen Correction Behind Catalyst, B1 Limit Attained
17585 Oxygen Correction Behind Catalyst. 82 Limit Attained
17604 Oxygen Sensor Heater Circuit, Bank 1-Sensor 1 Electrical Malfunction
17605 Oxygen Sensor Heater Circuit, Bank 2-Sensor I Electrical Malfunction
17606 Oxygen Sensor Heater Circuit, BankI-Sensor2 Electrical Malfunction
17606 Oxygen Sensor Heater Circuit, Bank 1-Sensor 2 Electrical Malfunction
17607 Oxygen Sensor Heater Circuit, Bank 2-Sensor 2 Electrical Malfunction
17609 Cylinder 1, Fuel Injection Circuit Electrical Malfunction
17610 Cylinder 2, Fuel Injection Circuit Electrical Malfunction
17611 Cylinder 3, Fuel Injection Circuit Electrical Malfunction
17612 Cylinder 4, Fuel Injection Circuit Electrical Malfunction
17613 Cylinder 5, Fuel Injection Circuit Electrical Malfunction
17614 Cylinder 6, Fuel Injection Circuit Electrical Malfunction
17615 Cylinder 7, Fuel Injection Circuit Electrical Malfunction

17616 Cylinder 8, Fuel Injection Circuit Electrical Malfunction
17621 Cylinder I-Fuel Injection Circuit Short to B+
17622 Cylinder 2-Fuel Injection Circuit Short to B+
17623 Cylinder 3 Fuel Injection Circuit Short to B+
17624 Cylinder 4 Fuel Injection Circuit Short to B+
17625 Cylinder 5 Fuel Injection Circuit Short to B+
17626 Cylinder 6 Fuel Injection Circuit Short to B+
17627 Cylinder 7, Fuel Injection Circuit Short to B+
17628 Cylinder 8, Fuel Injection Circuit Short to B+
17633 Cylinder I Fuel Injection Circuit Short to Ground
17634 Cylinder 2 Fuel Injection Circuit Short to Ground
17635 Cylinder 3 Fuel Injection Circuit Short to Ground
17636 Cylinder 4 Fuel Injection Circuit Short to Ground
17637 Cylinder 5 Fuel Injection Circuit Short to Ground
17638 Cylinder 6 Fuel Injection Circuit Short to Ground
17645 Cylinder I Fuel Injection Circuit Open Circuit
17646 Cylinder 2 Fuel Injection Circuit Open Circuit
17647 Cylinder 3 Fuel Injection Circuit Open Circuit
17648 Cylinder 4 Fuel Injection Circuit Open Circuit
17649 Cylinder 5 Fuel Injection Circuit Open Circuit
17650 Cylinder 6 Fuel Injection Circuit Open Circuit
17658 Fuel Level Too Low
17688 Fuel Injection Air Control Valve Circuit Flow too Low
17691 Fuel Injection Air Control Valve Circuit Electrical Malfunction
17733 Cylinder I Knock Control Limit Attained
17734 Cylinder 2 Knock Control Limit Attained
17735 Cylinder 3 Knock Control Limit Attained
17736 Cylinder 4 Knock Control Limit Attained
17737 Cylinder 5 Knock Control Limit Attained
17738 Cylinder 6 Knock Control Limit Attained
17739 Cylinder 7 Knock Control Limit Attained
17740 Cylinder 8 Knock Control Limit Attained
17745 Camshaft Position Sensor, Bank 1 Short to Ground
17746 Camshaft Position Sensor, Bank 1 Open Circuit/Short to B+
17954 Boost Pressure Control Valve Short to B+
17794 Internal Control Module Knock Control Circuit Error
17799 Camshaft Position Sensor, Bank 2 Short to Ground
17800 Camshaft Position Sensor, Bank 2 Open Circuit/Short to B+
17818 Tank Ventilation Valve Circuit Short to B+
17818 Tank Ventilation Valve Circuit Short to B+
17828 Secondary Air Injection Module Short To B+
17829 Secondary Air Injection Module Short To Ground
17829 Secondary Air Injection Valve Circuit Short to Ground
17830 Secondary Air Injection System Control Valve Circuit Short To B+
17830 Secondary Air Injection Valve Circuit Short to B+
17833 Tank Vent Valve Short To Ground
17833 Tank Vent Valve Short to Ground
17834 Tank Vent Valve Open
17834 Tank Vent Valve Open
17840 Secondary Air Injection Valve Open
17841 Secondary Air Injection System Pump Relay Circuit Open
17842 Secondary Air Injection System Pump Relay Circuit Short to B+
17843 Secondary Air Injection System Pump Relay Circuit Short to Ground
17844 Secondary Air Injection System Pump Relay Circuit Electrical Malfunction
17858 Secondary Air Injection System Circuit Short To B+
17859 Secondary Air Injection System Circuit Short To Ground
17860 Secondary Air Injection System Open Circuit
17879 EVAP Emission Control LDP Circuit Short to B+
17880 EVAP Emission Control LDP Circuit Short to Ground
17881 EVAP Emission Control LDP Circuit Open Circuit
17883 EVAP Emission Control LDP Circuit Malfunction/Signal Circuit Open
17884 EVAP Emission Control LDP Circuit Malfunction/Insufficient Vacuum
17885 EVAP Emission Control LDP Circuit Malfunction

17908 Fuel Pump Relay Circuit Electrical Malfunction
17909 Fuel Pump Relay Circuit Short to Ground
17910 Fuel Pump Relay Circuit Short to B+
17913 Closed Throttle Position Switch Does Not Close/Open Circuit
17914 Closed Throttle Position Switch Does Not Open/Short to Ground
17915 Idle System Learned Value Lower Limit Attained
17916 Idle System Learned Value Upper Limit Attained
17920 Intake Manifold Changeover Valve Circuit, Short to B+
17923 Intake Manifold Changeover Valve Circuit, Short to Ground
17924 Intake Manifold Changeover Valve Circuit, Open
17927 Intake Camshaft Control, Bank 2 Malfunction
17951 Throttle Actuation Potentiometer Signal Too Low
17952 Throttle Actuation Potentiometer Signal Too High
17953 Throttle Position Control Malfunction
17955 Boost Pressure Control Valve Short to Ground
17956 Boost Pressure Control Valve Open
17963 Charge Pressure Upper Limit Exceeded
717964 Charge Pressure Negative Deviation
17965 Charge Pressure Positive Deviation
17966 Throttle Actuator Electrical Malfunction
17967 Idle Speed Control Throttle Position Adaptation Malfunction
17968 Maximum Engine Speed Exceeded
17972 Idle Speed Control, Throttle Position Low Voltage During Adaptation
17988 Throttle Actuator (B1) Malfunction
17990 Idle Adaptation At Limit
18010 Power Supply (B+) Terminal 30 Low Voltage
18014 Rough Road Spec Engine Torque ABS-ECU Electrical Malfunction
18019 MIL Call-up Circuit/Transmission Control Module Short to Ground
18020 Electronic Control Module Incorrect Coding
18021 MIL Call-up Circuit Open/Short to B+
18032 MIL Request Signal Active
18033 CAN-Bus Implausible Message from Transmission Control
18034 CAN-Bus Missing Message from Transmission Control
18048 Internal Control Module (EEPROM) Error
18048 Internal Control Module (EEPROM) Error
18089 Control Unit Programming not Finished
18098 Malfunction Indicator Light Malfunction
18101 Malfunction Indicator Light Short to B+
18186 Solenoid EV7 Electrical Malfunction
18188 Engine Intervention Readable

Volvo

READING CODES

Reading the control module memory is on of the first steps in OBD-II system diagnostics. This step should be initially performed to determine the general nature of the fault. Subsequent readings will determine if the fault has been cleared.
Reading codes can be performed by any of the methods below:
- Read the control module memory with the Generic Scan Tool (GST)
- Read the control module memory with the vehicle manufacturer's specific tester

To read the fault codes, connect the scan tool or tester according to the manufacturer's instructions. Follow the manufacturer's specified procedure for reading the codes.

CLEARING CODES

Control module reset procedures are a very important part of OBD-II System diagnostics. This step should be done at the end of any fault code repair and at the end of any driveability repair.
Clearing codes can be performed by any of the methods below:
- Clear the control module memory with the Generic Scan Tool (GST)

• Clear the control module memory with the vehicle manufacturer's specific tester

• Turn the ignition off and remove the negative battery cable for at least 1 minute.

Removing the negative battery cable may cause other systems in the vehicle to loose their memory. Prior to removing the cable, ensure you have the proper reset codes for radios and alarms.

➡**The MIL will may also be de-activated for some codes if the vehicle completes three consecutive trips without a fault detected with vehicle conditions similar to those present during the fault.**

VOLVO SPECIFIC OBD-II TROUBLE CODES

P1307 Accelerometer signal
P1308 Accelerometer signal
P1326 Fault in engine control module (ECM) knock control circuit.
P1327 Fault in engine control module (ECM) knock control circuit.
P1328 Fault in engine control module (ECM) knock control circuit.
P1329 Fault in engine control module (ECM) knock control circuit.
P1401 Fault in engine control module (ECM) engine coolant temperature (ECT) sensor circuit NTC switching
P1403 Fault in engine control module (ECM) control module box temperature sensor
P1404 Fault in engine control module (ECM) control module box temperature sensor
P1405 Temperature warning greater than 230 degrees F
P1406 Temperature warning greater than 212 degrees F
P1505 Idle air control (IAC) valve opening signal
P1506 Idle air control (IAC) valve opening signal
P1507 Idle air control (IAC) valve closing signal
P1508 Idle air control (IAC) valve closing signal
P1604 Ignition discharge module (IDM) group D

89465P01

As time goes on, more manufacturers will release do-it-yourselfer friendly scan tools equipped to read OBD-II codes

P1605 Ignition discharge module (IDM) group E
P1617 Cable fault between AW 50–42 transmission control module (TCM) and Motronic 4.4 engine control module (ECM) (lamp lights)
PI618 Cable fault between AW 50-Q2 transmission control module (TCM) and Motronic 4.4 engine control module (ECM) (lamp lights)
P1619 Engine cooling fan (FC) low-speed, signal
P1620 Engine cooling fan (FC) low-speed, signal
P1621 Diagnostic trouble code (DTC) in automatic transmission control module(TCM)

7

TRUCK
DIAGNOSTIC
TROUBLE CODE
RETRIEVAL

TRUCK DIAGNOSTIC TROUBLE CODE RETRIEVAL

Introduction

Most cars today are equipped with an On-Board Diagnostic (OBD) system. During the late '70s manufacturers started using electronics to control engine functions and diagnose engine faults. This was primarily to meet stringent new EPA emission standards. Through the years OBD have become more sophisticated. OBD-II, a new standard introduced in the mid-'90s, provides almost complete engine control and also monitors parts of the chassis, body and accessory devices, as well as the diagnostic control network of the vehicle.

OBD was brought about to combat a persistent smog problem in the LA basin. The State of California started requiring emission control systems on 1966 model cars. The federal government extended these controls nationwide in 1968.

Congress passed the Clean Air Act in 1970 and established the Environmental Protection Agency (EPA). From the EPA, series of emission standards for maintenance of vehicles has been brought forth. To meet these standards, manufacturers were forced to electronically control their fuel feed and ignition systems. Sensors measure engine performance and adjustments are made automatically to the systems to provide optimum performance with minimum emissions. These sensors also provided vehicle owners with their earliest diagnostic assistance.

In the beginning there were few standards and each manufacturer had their own systems and signals. In 1988, the Society of Automotive Engineers (SAE) set a standard connector plug and set of diagnostic test codes. The EPA adapted most of the SAE standards and gradually mandated compliance from the manufacturers.

The EPA has been charged with reducing "mobile emissions" from cars and trucks and given the power to require manufacturers to build cars which meet increasingly stiff emissions standards. The manufacturers must further maintain the emission standards of the cars for the useful life of the vehicle.

OBD-II is a natural progression of the initial standards developed by the SAE and implemented by the EPA and California Air Resources Board (CARB). The standards were implemented January 1, 1996.

OBD-II provides a universal inspection and diagnosis method to be sure the car is performing to OEM standards. While there is argument as to the exact standards and methodology employed, the fact is there is a need to reduce vehicle emitted pollution levels in our cities, and we have to live with these requirements.

What System Do I Have?

So how do I know if my car has OBD-I or OBD-II. All cars built since January 1, 1996 have OBD-II systems. Manufacturers started incorporating OBD-II in various models as early as 1994. Some early OBD-II cars were not 100% compliant.

It is safe to say that if you own a pre-1994 model year vehicle, you have some variant of an OBD-I system. Remember, OBD-I was very manufacturer specific and great differences may exist between models of the same manufacturer and year.

It is also safe to say that if you own a 1996 or later model year vehicle, you have OBD-II. Here it gets a little easier. Since there are a standard set of generic codes for OBD-II, which are published here, each make and model will display the same code for the same fault.

There are also manufacturer specific codes, which like OBD-I are specific to each manufacturer. However, the manufacturers have pretty much used the same codes across their model lines.

The real problem with comes with vehicles built between 1994 and 1995. These were transition years and many manufacturers installed systems that were better than traditional OBD-I systems, yet still did not comply with OBD-II regulations.

The surest way to tell which version of OBD you have is to look for some indication on the Vehicle Emissions Control Information (VECI) sticker in the engine compartment. A second, less accurate, way to check is to look at the Data Link Connector (DLC) in the engine compartment or under the

dash. If the connector has 16 pins and is trapezoidal in shape, you can be pretty sure you have an OBD-II system.

→**Some manufacturers started using the 16 pin OBD-II connector prior to full implementation of the system on their vehicles.**

How Do I Read The Codes?

OBD-I vehicles have connectors in various positions around the vehicle. Some likely spots are under the dashboard, under the hood, in the center console, in the trunk or hatch area or under the seats. Some vehicles do not use a connector but have several buttons and lights directly on the control module.

Each manufacturer has a specific sequence that must be performed exactly to enable the code to be read. These sequences range from the simple (ground two terminals on a connector) to the ridiculous (cycle the ignition key 15 times). However, most manufacturers codes could be read without the use of any special equipment.

All OBD-II cars have a connector located in the passenger compartment easily accessible from the driver's seat. Check under the dash or near the ashtray. A cable is plugged into the OBD-II connector and a scan tool is used to read the fault codes. This can range from a simple hand-held meter that provides a coded read-out of the various diagnostic functions, up to a large console computer-based unit costing used by some high tech professional mechanics.

Most scan tools use replaceable cartridges, making them compatible with all cars. Each tool contains software that analyzes the signals received from the car and displays a text or diagrammed readout of any malfunctions found. Some of the higher end models even suggest possible solutions to the problems.

Several manufacturers have started to market smaller scan tools. Units for the advanced do-it-yourselfer or small shop technician can provide a variety of levels of data, some approaching the sophistication of the big shop consoles.

A detailed description of how to access codes is included with each manufacturer section.

A Word About Scan Tools

▶ **See Figures 1 and 2**

The check engine light on your dashboard has been winking at you randomly for months. Perhaps this partly explains why your car just doesn't feel quite right and your gasoline credit card bill is enormous. Maybe this

89465P01

Fig. 1 AutoTap® from B&B electronics is an OBD-II compatible scan tool you can hook up to your personal computer

Fig. 2 The AutoXray® is more like a traditional scan tool which comes complete with various adapters to fit many makes and models

time, instead of taking it to the mechanic its time to start looking into things yourself.

First, you'll need a scan tool. In the past, scan tools were the private domain of mechanics and dealerships due to their high cost. Now the do-it-yourselfer can choose from many entry-level scan testers designed for the small shop and home mechanic. The ones we tested have control panels and screens you can understand. So if you've learned to use a PC, a scan tool is much easier. Even the (Picture) harness adapter fits only one way in the diagnostic plug. So if it doesn't fit right, you've got the wrong one.

Plugging in the scan tool is quite easy, as long as you have the correct adapters. Most kits come with adapters to enable one scan tool to fit a number of vehicles. Once you plug it the scan tool can begin the job with a list of trouble codes, including those that aren't accompanied by malfunction indicator lamp. If only the entire procedure were this easy. The trouble code is a good start, but many problems will not set a code at all, so you'll need to do some good old-fashioned diagnosis.

What Do Codes Tell Me?

OBD signals are most often sought in response to a "Malfunction Indicator Lamp (MIL)" appearing on the dashboard or driveability problems experienced with the vehicle. The data provided by OBD can often pinpoint the specific component that has malfunctioned, saving substantial time and cost compared to guess-and-replace repairs.

The MIL shows three different types of signals. Occasional flashes show momentary malfunctions. It stays **ON** if the problem is of a more serious nature, affecting the emissions output or safety of the vehicle. A constantly flashing MIL is a sign of a major problem which can cause serious damage if the engine is not stopped immediately. In all cases an electronic picture called a "freeze frame" is taken to show all sensor readings at the time of the fault. This picture is recorded in the vehicle's control module and can be accessed to provide additional clues during diagnosis.

OBD-I DIAGNOSTIC TROUBLE CODES

Introduction

It should be remembered that OBD-I codes, for the most part, are manufacturer, model and sometimes year specific. Reading the codes is also specific to the individual manufacturer. Special tools may be necessary to gain access to the control modules. If reading codes does require special tools, the procedures given here will reference those tools.

→The term control module is a generic term used for the engine control computer. These computers are known by various names including Electronic Control Module (ECM), Powertrain Control Module (PCM), Vehicle Control Module (VCM), Single Board Engine Controller (SBEC), Engine Control Assembly (ECA) and Engine Control Unit (ECU).

→The term Malfunction Indicator Lamp (MIL) is a generic term used to indicate the instrument panel mounted, engine computer controlled lamp which warns the driver there has been a fault in the system. Some common names for this lamp are the Check Engine Light and the Service Engine Soon Light. Sometimes just the word Engine will appear.

Reading and Clearing Codes

▶ See Figures 3, 4, 5, 6 and 7

It should be noted that with very few exceptions, reading and clearing of OBD-I trouble codes, can be performed without using a scan tool. However, by using a scan tool, the codes can be obtained much quicker and other functions of the system can readily be accessed. This should not be tremendous cause for concern as, as several manufacturers have developed scan tools that are well within the price range of the average do-it-yourselfer. Also, many mechanics will hook up a scan tool to your vehicle for a minimal charge.

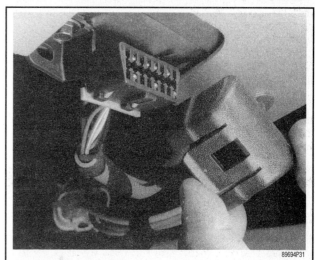

Fig. 3 Hooking up the scan tool is as easy as plugging into the diagnostic link connector

Chrysler Corporation Truck

SELF-DIAGNOSTICS

The Chrysler fuel injection systems combine electronic spark advance and fuel control. At the center of these systems is a digital, pre-programmed computer, known as an Powertrain Control Module (PCM). The PCM can also be referred to as the Single Module Engine Controller (SMEC) or as the Single Board Engine Controller (SBEC). The PCM regu-

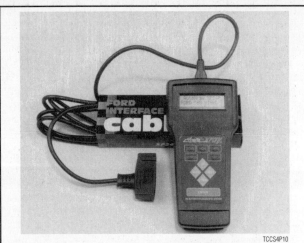

Fig. 4 Inexpensive scan tools, such as this one from AutoXray®, are available to interface with the OBD-I electronics in your vehicle

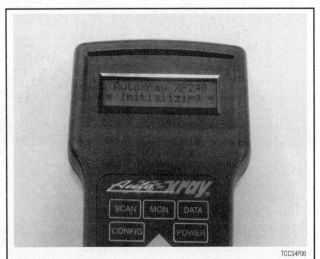

Fig. 5 Among other features, a scan tool combines many standard testers into a single device for quick and accurate diagnosis

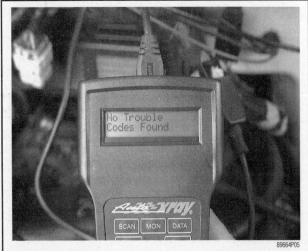

Fig. 6 Although some times no DTC's are found, that does not rule out a problem

Fig. 7 Once the scan tool finds a trouble code it will display the appropriate code number and description

lates ignition timing, air-fuel ratio, emission control devices, cooling fan, charging system idle speed and speed control. It has the ability to update and revise its commands to meet changing operating conditions.

Various sensors provide the input necessary for PCM to correctly regulate fuel flow at the injectors. These include the Manifold Absolute Pressure (MAP), Throttle Position Sensor (TPS), oxygen sensor, coolant temperature sensor, charge temperature sensor, and vehicle speed sensors.

In addition to the sensors, various switches are used to provide important information to the PCM. These include the neutral safety switch, air conditioning clutch switch, brake switch and speed control switch. These signals cause the PCM to change either the fuel flow at the injectors or the ignition timing or both.

The PCM is designed to test it's own input and output circuits, If a fault is found in a major system, this information is stored in the PCM for eventual display to the technician. Information on this fault can be displayed to the technician by means of the instrument panel malfunction indicator light or by connecting a diagnostic read-out tester and reading a numbered display code, which directly relates to a general fault. Some inputs and outputs are checked continuously and others are checked under certain conditions. If the problem is repaired or no longer exists, the PCM cancels the fault code after approximately 50 key **ON/OFF** cycles.

When a fault code is detected, it appears as either a flash of the check engine light on the instrument panel or by watching the Diagnostic Readout Box version II (DRB-II). This indicates that an abnormal signal in the system has been recognized by the PCM. Fault codes do indicate the presence of a failure but they don't identify the failed component directly.

Fault Codes

Fault codes are 2 digit numbers that tell the technician which circuit is bad. Fault codes do indicate the presence of a failure but they don't identify the failed component directly. Therefore a fault code a result and not always the reason for the problem.

Indicator Codes

Indicator codes are 2 digit numbers that tell the technician if particular sequences or conditions have occurred. Such a condition where the indicator code will be displayed is at the beginning or the end of a diagnostic test. Indicator codes will not generate a check engine light or engine running test code.

Actuator Test Mode (Atm) Codes

Starting in 1985, ATM test codes are 2 digit numbers that identify the various circuits used by the technician during the diagnosis procedure. In

1989 the PCM and test equipment changed design. The actuator test functions where expanded, but access to these functions may have changed, dependent on vehicle or test equipment being used.

Engine Running Test Codes

Engine running test codes where introduced on fuel injected vehicles. These are 2 digit numbers. The codes are used to access sensor readouts while the engine is running and place the engine in particular operating conditions for diagnosis. Feedback carburetor system does not offer engine running sensor test mode.

Check Engine Light

This is possibly the most critical step of diagnosis. A detailed examination of connectors, wiring and vacuum hoses can often lead to a repair without further diagnosis. A careful inspector will check the undersides of hoses as well as the integrity of hard-to-reach hoses blocked by the air cleaner or other component. Wiring should be checked carefully for any sign of strain, burning, crimping, or terminals pulled-out from a connector. Checking connectors at components or in harnesses is required; usually, pushing them together will reveal a loose fit.

The check engine or Maintenance Indicator Lamp (MIL) light has 2 modes of operation: diagnostic mode and switch test mode.

If a DRB-II diagnostic tester is not available, the PCM can show the technician fault codes by flashing the check engine light on the instrument panel in the diagnostic mode. In the switch test mode, after all codes are displayed, switch function can be confirmed. The light will turn on and off when a switch is turned ON and OFF.

Even though the light can be used as a diagnostic tool, it cannot do the following:

Once the light starts to display fault codes, it cannot be stopped. If the technician loses count, he must start the test procedure again. The light cannot display all of the codes or any blank displays.

The light cannot tell the technician if the oxygen feed-back system is lean or rich and if the idle motor and detonation systems are operational. The light cannot perform the actuation test mode, sensor test mode or engine running test mode.

➡Be advised that the check engine light can only perform a limited amount of functions and is not to be used as a substitute for a diagnostic tester. All diagnostic procedure described herein are intended for use with a Diagnostic Readout Box II (DRB-II) or equivalent tool.

Limp-In Mode

The limp-in mode is the attempt by the PCM to compensate for the failure of certain components by substituting information from other sources. If the PCM senses incorrect data or no data at all from the MAP sensor, throttle position sensor or coolant temperature sensor, the system is placed into limp-in mode and the check engine light on the instrument panel is activated. This mode will keep the vehicle drive able until the customer can get it to a service facility.

Test Modes

There are 5 modes of testing required for the proper diagnosis of the system. They are as follows:

Diagnostic Test Mode This mode is used to access the fault codes from the PCM's memory.

Circuit Actuation Test Mode (ATM Test) This mode is used to turn a certain circuit on and off in order to test it. ATM test codes are used in this mode.

Switch Test Mode This mode is used to determine if specific switch inputs are being received by the PCM.

Sensor Test Mode This mode looks at the output signals of certain sensors as they are received by the PCM when the engine is not running. Sensor access codes are read in this mode. Also this mode is used to clear the PCM memory of stored codes.

Engine Running Test Mode This mode looks at sensor output signals as seen by the PCM when the engine is running. Also this mode is used to determine some specific running conditions necessary for diagnosis.

READING CODES

Obtaining Trouble Codes

Entering the Jeep or Eagle self-diagnostic system requires the use of a special adapter that connects with the Diagnostic Readout Box II (DRB-II). These systems require the adapter because all of the system diagnosis is done Off-Board instead of On-Board like most vehicles. The adapter, which is a computer module itself, measures signals at the diagnostic connector and converts the signals into a form which the DRB can use to perform tests. On vehicles other than Jeep and Eagle the following procedures will obtain stored Diagnostic Trouble Codes (DTC).

USING THE CHECK ENGINE LAMP

Codes display on vehicles built before 1989 are displayed in numerical order, after 1989 codes are displayed in order of occurrence.

1. Connect the readout box to the diagnostic connector located in the engine compartment near PCM.
2. Start the engine, if possible, cycle the transmission selector and the A/C switch if applicable. Shut off the engine.
3. Turn the ignition switch ON—OFF, ON—OFF, ON -OFF, ON within 5 seconds.
4. Observe the CHECK ENGINE light on the instrument panel.
5. Just after the last ON cycle, the dash warning (MIL) lamp will begin flashing the stored codes.
6. The codes are transmitted as two digit flashes.
7. Example would be Code 21 will be displayed as a FLASH FLASH pause FLASH.
8. Be ready to write down the codes as they appear; the only way to repeat the codes is to start over at the beginning.

SCAN TOOL

◆ See Figures 8, 9 and 10

The scan tool is the preferred choice for fault recovery and system diagnosis. Some hints on using the DRB-II include:

• To use the HELP screen, press and hold F3 at any time.
• To restart the DRB-II at any time, hold the MODE button and press ATM at the same time.
• Pressing the up or down arrows will move forward or backward one item within a menu.
• To select an item, either press the number of the item or move the cursor arrow to the selection, then press ENTER.
• To return to the previous display (screen), press ATM.
• Some test screens display multiple items. To view only one, move the cursor arrow to the desired item, then press ENTER.

To read stored faults with the DRB-II:

1. With the ignition switch OFF, connect the tool to the diagnostic connector near the engine controller under the hood. On some 1988 and earlier models, cycling the ignition key ON-OFF three times may be necessary to enter the diagnostics. On 1989 and newer models, simply turn the ignition switch ON to access the read fault code data.
2. Start the engine if possible. Cycle the transmission from Park to a forward gear, then back to Park. Cycle the air conditioning ON and OFF. Turn the ignition switch OFF.
3. Turn the ignition switch ON but do not start the engine. The DRB-II will begin its power-up sequence; do not touch any keys on the scan tool during this sequence.
4. Reading faults must be selected from the FUEL/IGN MENU. To reach this menu on the DRB-II:

   a. When the initial menu is displayed after the power-up sequence, use the down arrow to display choice 4) SELECT SYSTEM and select this choice.

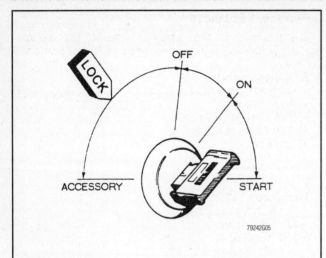

Fig. 8 Cycle the ignition switch ON-OFF three times to enter the diagnostic mode

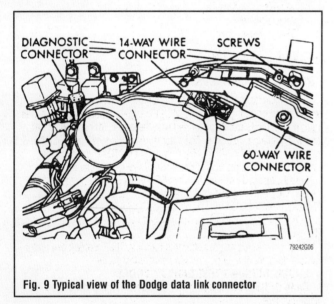

Fig. 9 Typical view of the Dodge data link connector

```
----- FUEL/IGN FAULTS -----
NO FAULTS DETECTED

X STARTS SINCE ERS
```

```
1 OF X FAULTS
[message
appears here]
X STARTS SINCE SET
```

Fig. 10 Example of the DRB-II display screen while reading the trouble codes

b. Once on the—SELECT SYSTEM—screen, choose 1) ENGINE. This will enter the engine diagnostics section of the program.

c. The screen will momentarily display the engine family and SBEC identification numbers. After a few seconds the screen displays the choices 1) With A/C and 2) Without A/C. Select and enter the correct choice for the vehicle.

d. When the—ENGINE SYSTEM—screen appears, select 1) FUEL/IGNITION from the menu.

e. On the next screen, select 2) READ FAULTS.

5. If any faults are stored, the display will show how many are stored (1 of 4 faults, etc.) and issue a text description of the problem, such as COOLANT SENSOR VOLTAGE TOO LOW. The last line of the display shows the number of engine starts since the code was set. If the number displayed is 0 starts, this indicates a hard or current fault. Faults are displayed in reverse order of occurrence; the first fault shown is the most current and the last fault shown is the oldest.

6. Press the down arrow to read each fault after the first. Record the screen data carefully for easy reference.

7. If no faults are stored in the controller, the display will state NO FAULTS DETECTED and show the number of starts since the system memory was last erased.

8. After all faults have been read and recorded, press ATM.

9. Refer to the appropriate diagnostic chart for a diagnostic path. Remember that the fault message identifies a circuit problem, not a component. Use of the charts is required to sequentially test a circuit and identify the fault.

SWITCH TEST

The PCM only recognizes 2 switch input states—HI and LOW. For this reason the PCM cannot tell the difference between a selected switch position and an open circuit, short circuit or an open switch. However, if one of the switches is toggled, the controller does have the ability to respond to the change of state in the switch. If the change is displayed, it can be assumed that entire switch circuit to the PCM is operational.

1988 AND EARLIER MODELS:

After all codes have been shown and has indicated Code 55 end of message, actuate the following component switches. The digital display must change its numbers between 00 and 88 and the CHECK ENGINE light will blink when the following switches are activated and released:

- Brake pedal
- Gear shift selector
- A/C switch
- Electric defogger switch (1984)

1989 AND NEWER MODELS:

To enter the switch test mode, activate read input states or equivalent function on the readout box for the following switch tests:

- Z1 Voltage Sense
- Speed Control Set
- Speed Control ON/OFF
- Speed Control Resume
- A/C Switch Sense
- Brake Switch
- Park/neutral Switch

SCAN TOOL FUNCTIONS

> **⁎⁎ CAUTION**
>
> **Always apply the parking brake and block the wheels before performing any diagnostic procedures with the engine running. Failure to do so may result in personal injury and/or property damage.**

After stored faults have been read and recorded, the scan tool may be used to investigate states and functions of various components. This ability compliments but does not replace the use of diagnostic charts. The DRB-II functions are useful in identifying circuits which are or are not operating correctly as well as checking component function or signal.

When diagnosing an emissions-related problem, keep in mind that the SBEC system only enters closed loop mode under certain conditions. The single most important criteria for entry into closed loop operation is that the engine be at normal operating temperature; i.e., fully warmed up. The engine is considered to be at normal operating temperature if any of the following are true: the electric cooling fan cycles on at least once or the upper radiator hose is hot to the touch or the heater is able to deliver hot air.

In open loop operation, the signal from the oxygen sensor is ignored by the engine controller and the fuel injection is controlled by pre-programmed values within the computer. Once closed loop operation is begun, the signal from the oxygen sensor is used by the engine controller to constantly adjust the fuel injection to maintain the proper air/fuel ratio. The system will switch in and out of closed loop operation depending on sensor signals and driver input. In most cases, the system will be in closed loop operation during normal driving, acceleration or deceleration and idle. Wide open throttle will cause the system to momentarily switch to open loop operation. Additionally, some engine control systems will momentarily switch to open loop under hard acceleration or deceleration until the MAP sensor signal stabilizes.

The DRB-II may be operated in the following diagnostic modes from the FUEL/IGN MENU screen.

Sensors

This function displays current data being transmitted from the fuel and ignition sensors to the engine controller. Examples of sensor data available include MAP voltage, throttle position sensor voltage and percentage, RPM, coolant temperature, voltage sensor, total spark advance, and vehicle speed. Many other sensors may be monitored depending on engine/transmission combinations.

Data for each sensor is displayed in the appropriate units, such as volts, mph, in. Hg, degrees F, etc.

1988 AND EARLIER MODELS

1. Put the system into the diagnostic test mode and wait for Code 55 to appear on the display screen.
2. Press the ATM button on the diagnostic tool to activate the display. If a specific sensor read test is desired, hold the ATM button down until the desired test code appears.
3. Slide the READ/HOLD switch to the HOLD position to display the corresponding sensor output.

Sensor Read Test Display codes:

Code 01 Battery temperature sensor; display voltage divided by 10 equals sensor temperature

Code 02 Oxygen sensor voltage; display number divided by 10 equals sensor voltage

Code 03 Charge temperature sensor voltage; display number divided by 10 equals sensor voltage

Code 04 Engine coolant temperature sensor; display number multiplied by 10 equals degrees of engine coolant sensor

Code 05 Throttle position sensor voltage; display number divided by 10 equals sensor voltage or temperature

Code 06 Peak knock sensor voltage; display number is sensor voltage

Code 07 Battery voltage; display number is battery voltage

Code 08 Map sensor voltage; display number divided by 10 equals sensor voltage

Code 09 Speed control switches:
- Display is blank—Cruise OFF
- Display shows 00—Cruise ON
- Display shows 10—Cruise SET
- Display shows 01—Cruise RESUME

Code 10 Fault code erase routine; display will flash 0's for 4 seconds

The State Display programs allow the operator to view the present conditions in the SBEC system. These choices are displayed on the FUEL IGN STATE screen and offer the choices of MODULE INFO, SENSORS, INPUTS/OUTPUTS or MONITORS. Viewing system data through these windows can be helpful in observing the effects of repairs or to compare the problem vehicle to a known-good vehicle.

1989 AND NEWER MODELS

To enter the sensor test mode, activate read sensor voltage or read sensor values or equivalent functions on the readout box for the following sensor displays:

Read Sensor Voltage
- Battery temperature sensor
- Oxygen sensor input
- Throttle body temperature sensor
- Coolant temperature sensor
- Throttle position
- Minimum throttle
- Battery voltage
- MAP sensor voltage

Read Sensor Values
- Throttle body temperature
- Coolant temperature
- MAP gauge reading
- AIS motor position
- Added adaptive fuel
- Adaptive fuel factor
- Barometric pressure
- Engine speed
- Module spark advance
- Vehicle speed
- Oxygen sensor state

Engine Running Test Mode

1988 AND EARLIER MODELS

The Engine Running Test Mode monitors the sensors on the vehicle which check operating conditions while the engine is running. The engine running test mode can be performed with the engine idling in NEUTRAL and with parking brake set or under actual driving conditions. With the diagnostic readout box READ/HOLD switch in the READ position, the engine running test mode is initiated after the engine is started.

Select a test code by switching the READ/HOLD switch to the READ position and pressing the actuator button until the desired code appears. Release actuator button and switch the READ/HOLD switch to the HOLD position. The logic module will monitor that system test and results will be displayed.

Only fuel injected engines offer this function. The Feedback carburetor system does not offer engine running sensor test mode.

ENGINE RUNNING TEST DISPLAY CODES:

Code 61 Battery temperature sensor; display number divided by 10 equals voltage

Code 62 Oxygen sensor; display number divided by 10 equals voltage

Code 63 Fuel injector temperature sensor; display number divided by 10 equals voltage

Code 64 Engine coolant temperature sensor; display number multiplied by 10 equals degrees F

Code 65 Throttle position sensor; display number divided by 10 equals voltage

Code 67 Battery voltage sensor; display is voltage

Code 68 Manifold vacuum sensor; display is in. Hg code 69—Minimum throttle position sensor; display number divided by 10 equals voltage

Code 70 Minimum airflow idle speed sensor; display number multiplied by 10 equals rpm (see minimum air flow check procedure)

Code 71 Vehicle speed sensor; display is mph Code 72—Engine speed sensor; display number multiplied by 10 equals rpm

Fuel/Ignition Input/Output:

The engine controller recognizes only two states of electrical signals, voltage high or low. In some cases this corresponds to a switch or circuit being on or off; in other circuits a voltage signal may change from low voltage to higher voltage as a sensor opens. The controller cannot recognize the difference between a selected switch position and an open or shorted circuit.

In this test mode, the change in the circuit may be viewed as the switch is operated. For example, if the BRAKE SWITCH state is selected, the display should change from Low to High as the brake pedal is pressed. If a change in a circuit is displayed as the switch is used, it may be reasonably assumed that the entire switch circuit into the engine controller is operating correctly.

Depending on the engine/transmission in the vehicle, some of the switch states which may be checked include the air conditioning switch, brake switch, park/neutral switch, fuel flow signal, air conditioning clutch relay, radiator fan relay, CHECK ENGINE lamp, overdrive solenoid(s), lock-up solenoid and the speed control vent or vacuum solenoids. The scan tool will recognize the correct choices for each vehicle and only offer the appropriate systems on the screen.

MONITORS

On vehicles built before 1991, this display is called ENGINE PARAMETERS. 1991 and newer vehicles name the screen MONITORS. This display allows close observation of groups of related signals. For example, if RPM is chosen, the screen will display data for many of the factors affecting the rpm such as throttle position sensor, advance, air conditioning status, park/neutral status, AIS status and coolant temperature.

One of the screens within this test is NO START. When this display is selected, the screen shows the initial data sent to the engine controller during cranking. Using this screen to identify missing or unusual signals can shorten diagnostic time.

Actuator Tests

The purpose of the circuit actuation mode test is to check for proper operation of the output circuits that the PCM cannot internally recognize. The PCM can attempt to activate these outputs and allow the technician to affirm proper operation. Most of the tests performed in this mode issue an audible click or visual indication of component operation (click of relay contacts, injector spray, etc.). Except for intermittent conditions, if a component functions properly when it is tested, it can be assumed that the component, attendant wiring and driving circuit are functioning properly.

1988 AND EARLIER MODELS

The Actuator Test Mode 10 Code number was introduced in 1985. In 1983–84 ATM function only provided 3 ignition sparks, 2 AIS motor cycles and 1 injector pulse.

1. Put the system into the diagnostic test mode and wait for Code 55 to appear on the display screen.
2. Press ATM button on the tool to activate the display. If a specific ATM test is desired, hold the ATM button down until the desired test code appears.
3. The computer will continue to turn the selected circuit on and off for as long as 5 minutes or until the ATM button is pressed again or the ignition switch is turned to the OFF position.
4. If the ATM button is not pressed again, the computer will continue to cycle the selected circuit for 5 minutes and then shut the system off. Turning the ignition to the OFF position will also turn the test mode off.

Actuator Test Display codes:
Code 01 Spark activation—once every 2 seconds
Code 02 Injector activation—once every 2 seconds
Code 03 AIS activation—one step open, one step closed every 4 seconds
Code 04 Radiator fan relay—once every 2 seconds code 05- A/C WOT cutout relay—once every 2 seconds
Code 06 ASD relay activation—once every 2 seconds code 07- Purge solenoid activation—one toggle every 2 seconds (The A/C fan will run continuously and the A/C switch must be in the ON position to allow for actuation)
Code 08 Speed control activation—speed control vent and vacuum every 2 seconds (Speed control switch must be in the ON position to allow for activation)
Code 09 Alternator control field activation—one toggle every 2 seconds
Code 10 Shift indicator activation—one toggle every 2 seconds
Code 11 EGR diagnosis solenoid activation—one toggle every 2 seconds

1989 AND NEWER MODELS

This family of tests is chosen from the FUEL/IGN MENU screen. The actuator tests allow the operation of the output circuits not recognized by the engine controller to be checked by energizing them on command. Testing in this fashion is necessary because the controller does not recognize the function of all the external components. If an output to a relay is triggered, and the relay is heard to click, it may be reasonably assumed that both the output circuit and the relay are operating properly. In this mode, most of the tests cause a response that may be seen or heard, although close attention may be necessary to notice the change.

Once selected, the ACTUATOR TEST screen offers a choice of items to be activated. Depending on engine and fuel system, some of the choices include:
- Stop all tests
- Engine rpm
- Ignition coil
- Fuel injector
- Fuel system
- Solenoid/relay
- AIS motor

The engine speed may be set to a desired level through the ENGINE RPM screen. Once a system is chosen, related screens will appear allowing detailed selection of which relay, injector or component is to be operated.

Exiting Diagnostic Test

By turning the ignition switch to the OFF position, the test mode system is exited. With a Diagnostic Readout Box attached to the system and the ATM control button not pressed, the computer will continue to cycle the selected circuits for 5 minutes and then automatically shut the system down.

CLEARING CODES

Stored faults should only be cleared by use of the DRB-II or similar scan tool. Disconnecting the battery will clear codes but is not recommended as doing so will also clear all other memories on the vehicle and may affect drive ability. Disconnecting the PCM connector will also clear codes, but on newer models it may store a power loss code and will affect driveability until the vehicle is driven and the PCM can relearn it's drive ability memory.

The—ERASE—screen will appear when ATM is pressed at the end of the stored faults. Select the desired action from ERASE or DON'T ERASE. If ERASE is chosen, the display asks ARE YOU SURE? Pressing ENTER erases stored faults and displays the message FAULTS ERASED. After the faults are erased, press ATM to return the FUEL/IGN MENU.

DIAGNOSTIC TROUBLE CODES

Dodge Built Fuel Injection System

Code 88 Display used for start of test
Code 11 Camshaft signal or Ignition signal—no reference signal detected during engine cranking
Code 12 Memory to controller has been cleared within 50-100 engine starts
Code 13 MAP sensor pneumatic signal—no variation in MAP sensor signal is detected or no difference is recognized between the engine MAP reading and the stored barometric pressure reading
Code 14 MAP voltage too high or too low
Code 15 Vehicle speed sensor signal—no distance sensor signal detected during road load conditions
Code 16 Knock sensor circuit—Open or short has been detected in the knock sensor circuit
Code 16 Battery input sensor—battery voltage sensor input below 4 volts with engine running
Code 17 Low engine temperature—engine coolant temperature remains below normal operating temperature during vehicle travel; possible thermostat problem
Code 21 Oxygen sensor signal—neither rich or lean condition is detected from the oxygen sensor input

Code 22 Coolant voltage low—coolant temperature sensor input below the minimum acceptable voltage/Coolant voltage high—coolant temperature sensor input above the maximum acceptable voltage

Code 23 Air Charge or Throttle Body temperature voltage HIGH/LOW—charge air temperature sensor input is above or below the acceptable voltage limits

Code 24 Throttle Position sensor voltage high or low. Code 25 -Automatic Idle Speed (AIS) motor driver circuit—short or open detected in 1 or more of the AIS control circuits

Code 26 Injectors No. 1, 2, or 3 peak current not reached, high resistance in circuit

Code 27 Injector control circuit—bank output driver stage does not respond properly to the control signal

Code 27 Injectors No. 1, 2, or 3 control circuit and peak current not reached

Code 31 Purge solenoid circuit—open or short detected in the purge solenoid circuit

Code 32 Exhaust Gas Recirculation (EGR) solenoid circuit—open or short detected in the EGR solenoid circuit EGR system failure—required change in fuel/air ratio not detected during diagnostic test

Code 32 Surge valve solenoid—open or short in turbocharger surge valve circuit—some 1993 vehicles

Code 33 Air conditioner clutch relay circuit—open or short detected in the air conditioner clutch relay circuit. If vehicle doesn't have air conditioning ignore this code

Code 34 Speed control servo solenoids or MUX speed control circuit HIGH/LOW—open or short detected in the vacuum or vent solenoid circuits or speed control switch input above or below allowable voltage

Code 35 Radiator fan control relay circuit—open or short detected in the radiator fan relay circuit

Code 35 Idle switch shorted—switch input shorted to ground -some 1993 vehicles

Code 36 Wastegate solenoid—open or short detected in the turbocharger wastegate control solenoid circuit

Code 37 Part Throttle Unlock (PTU) circuit for torque converter clutch—open or short detected in the torque converter part throttle unlock solenoid circuit

Code 37 Baro Reed Solenoid—solenoid does not turn off when it should

Code 37 Shift indicator circuit (manual transaxle)

Code 37 Transaxle temperature out of range—some 1993 models

Code 41 Charging system circuit—output driver stage for generator field does not respond properly to the voltage regulator control signal

Code 42 Fuel pump or no Auto shut-down (ASD) relay voltage sense at controller

Code 43 Ignition control circuit—peak primary circuit current not respond properly with maximum dwell time

Code 43 Ignition coil #1, 2, or 3 primary circuits—peak primary was not achieved within the maximum allowable dwell time

Code 44 Battery temperature voltage—problem exists in the PCM battery temperature circuit or there is an open or short in the engine coolant temperature circuit

Code 44 Fused J2 circuit in not present in the logic board; used on the single engine module controller system

Code 45 Turbo boost limit exceeded—MAP sensor detects overboost

Code 44 Overdrive solenoid circuit—open or short in overdrive solenoid circuit

Code 46 Battery voltage too high—battery voltage sense input above target charging voltage during engine operation

Code 47 Battery voltage too low—battery voltage sense input below target charging voltage

Code 51 Air/fuel at limit—oxygen sensor signal input indicates LEAN air/fuel ratio condition during engine operation

Code 52 Air/fuel at limit—oxygen sensor signal input indicates RICH air/fuel ratio condition during engine operation

Code 52 Logic module fault—1984 vehicles. Code 53—Internal controller failure—internal engine controller fault condition detected during self test

Code 54 Camshaft or (distributor sync.) reference circuit—No camshaft position sensor signal detected during engine rotation

Code 55 End of message

Code 61 Baro read solenoid—open or short detected in the baro read solenoid circuit

Code 62 EMR mileage not stored—unsuccessful attempt to update EMR mileage in the controller EEPROM

Code 63 EEPROM write denied—unsuccessful attempt to write to an EEPROM location by the controller

Code 64 Flex fuel sensor—Flex fuel sensor signal out of range—(new in 1993)- CNG Temperature voltage out of range—CN gas pressure out of range

Code 65 Manifold tuning valve—an open or short has been detected in the manifold tuning valve solenoid circuit (3.3L and 3.5L LH-Platform)

Code 66 No CCO messages or no BODY CCD messages or no EATX CCD messages—messages from the CCD bus or the BODY CCD or the EATX CCD were not received by the PCM

Code 76 Ballast bypass relay—open or short in fuel pump relay circuit

Code 77 Speed control relay—an open or short has been detected in the speed control relay

Code 88 Display used for start of test

Code Error Fault code error—Unrecognized fault 10 received by DRB

➥This list is for reference and does not mean that a component is defective. The code identifies the circuit and component that require further testing.

Dodge Feedback Carburetor System

Code 88 Display used for start of test—must appear or other codes aren't valid

Code 11 Carburetor oxygen solenoid

Code 12 Transmission unlock relay—3.7L and 5.2L

Code 13 Air switching solenoid—3.7L and 5.2L—or Vacuum operated secondary control solenoid—2.2L

Code 14 Battery feed to computer disconnected with 20–40 engine starts

Code 16 Ignore

Code 17 Electronic throttle control solenoid

Code 18 EGR or Purge control solenoid

Code 21 Distributor pick-up signal

Code 22 Oxygen feedback stays rich or lean too long -3.7L and 5.2L—or Oxygen feedback is LEAN too long—2.2L

Code 23 Oxygen feedback is RICH too long—2.2L

Code 24 Vacuum transducer signal problem

Code 25 Charge temperature switch signal—3.7L and 5.2L engine—or Radiator fan temperature switch signal—2.2L engine

Code 26 Charge temperature sensor signal—3.7L and 5.2L engine—or Engine temperature sensor signal—2.2L

Code 28 Speed sensor circuit (if equipped)

Code 31 Battery feed to computer

Code 32 Computer can't enter diagnostics

Code 33 Computer can't enter diagnostics

Code 55 End of message

Code 88 Display used for start of test

Code 00 Diagnostic readout box is powered up and waiting for codes

➥This list is for reference and does not mean that a component is defective. The code identifies the circuit and component that require further testing.

Jeep and Eagle Built Fuel Systems

1988–90 2.5L, 3.0L AND 4.0L ENGINE

Code 1000 Ignition line low

Code 1001 Ignition line high

Code 1002 Oxygen heater line

Code 1004 Battery voltage low

Code 1005 Sensor ground line out of limits

Code 1010 Diagnostic enable line low

Code 1011 Diagnostic enable line high
Code 1012 MAP line low
Code 1013 MAP line high
Code 1014 Fuel pump line low
Code 1015 Fuel pump line high
Code 1016 Charge air temperature sensor low
Code 1017 Charge air temperature sensor high
Code 1018 No serial data from the ECU
Code 1021 Engine failed to start due to mechanical, fuel, or ignition problem
Code 1022 Start line low
Code 1024 ECU does not see start signal
Code 1025 Wide open throttle circuit low
Code 1027 ECU sees wide open throttle
Code 1028 ECU does not see wide open throttle
Code 1031 ECU sees closed throttle
Code 1032 ECU does not see closed throttle
Code 1033 Idle speed increase line low
Code 1034 Idle speed increase line high
Code 1035 Idle speed decrease line low
Code 1036 Idle speed decrease line high
Code 1037 Throttle position sensor reads low
Code 1038 Park/Neutral line high
Code 1040 Latched B+ line low
Code 1041 Latched B+ line high
Code 1042 No Latched B+ 1/2 volt drop
Code 1047 Wrong ECU
Code 1048 Manual vehicle equipped with automatic ECU
Code 1949 Automatic vehicle equipped with manual ECU
Code 1050 Idle RPM less than 500
Code 1051 Idle RPM greater than 2000
Code 1052 MAP sensor out of limits
Code 1053 Change in MAP reading out of limits
Code 1054 Coolant temperature sensor line low
Code 1055 Coolant temperature sensor line high
Code 1056 Inactive coolant temperature sensor
Code 1057 Knock circuit shorted
Code 1058 Knock value out of limits
Code 1059 A/C request line low
Code 1060 A/C request line high
Code 1061 A/C select line low
Code 1062 A/C select line high
Code 1063 A/C clutch line low
Code 1064 A/C clutch line high
Code 1065 Oxygen reads rich
Code 1066 Oxygen reads lean
Code 1067 Latch relay line low
Code 1068 Latch relay line high
Code 1070 A/C cutout line low
Code 1071 A/C cutout line high
Code 1073 ECU does not see speed sensor signal
Code 1200 ECU defective
Code 1202 Injector shorted to ground
Code 1209 Injector open
Code 1218 No voltage at ECU from power latch relay
Code 1220 No voltage at ECU from EGR solenoid
Code 1221 No injector voltage
Code 1222 MAP not grounded
Code 1223 No ECU tests run

➡️**Prior to 1988 vehicles used an Off-Board Diagnostic system which required special diagnostic equipment to read codes. After 1991 Jeep and Eagle vehicles used the Chrysler Domestic Built Engine Control system. The code list for Chrysler Built Domestic Fuel injection System also covers 1991 and newer Jeep and Eagle vehicles.**

Ford Motor Company Truck

INTRODUCTION TO FORD SELF-DIAGNOSTICS

The engine control systems are used in conjunction with either a throttle body (CFI) injection or multi-point (EFI and SEFI) injection fuel delivery system or feedback carburetor systems depending on the year, model and powertrain. Although the individual system components vary slightly, the electronic control system operation is basically the same. The major difference is the number and type of output devices being controlled by the ECA.

Automotive manufacturers have developed on-board computers to control engines, transmissions and many other components. These on-board computers with dozens of sensors and actuators have become almost impossible to test without the help of electronic test equipment.

One of these electronic test devices has become the on-board computer itself. The Powertrain Control Modules (PCM), sometimes called the Electronic Control Assembly (ECA), used on toadies vehicles has a built in self testing system. This self test ability is called self-diagnosis. The self-diagnosis system will test many or all of the sensors and controlled devices for proper function. When a malfunction is detected this system will store a fault code in memory that's related to that specific circuit. You can access the computer to obtain fault codes recorded in memory by using an analog voltmeter or special diagnostic scan tool. This will help narrow down what area to begin testing.

Fault code meanings can vary from year to year even on the same model. It is extremely important after retrieving a fault code to verify its meaning with a proper manual. Servicing a fault code incorrectly will not only lead to the wrong conclusion but could also cause damage if tested or serviced incorrectly. There is a list of general code descriptions provide later in this manual.

What System Is On My Vehicle?

There are 3 electronic fuel control systems used by Ford Motor Company. These systems all operate using similar components and on-board computers. Self-Diagnostic on these systems will vary, but, the basic fuel control operation is the same. Ford uses the following systems:
- **EEC-IV and EEC-V** engine control system: used on most domestic built Ford vehicles since 1984.
- **Non-NAAO EEC** engine control system: used on import built Ford vehicles, referred to as Non-NAAO cars.
- **MCU** feedback carburetor system: used on most Ford vehicles before 1984 and some later model vehicles equipped with a V8 engine and feedback carburetor.

Most Ford vehicles made after 1983 use the 4th generation Electronic Engine Control system, commonly designated EEC-IV.

If you own a vehicle with a 2.0L, 2.2L, or 2.5L engine, then the fuel control system is referred to as NON-NAAO (Not North American Automotive Operations produced vehicles) system. The fuel system used on these vehicles is called Electronic Engine Control (EEC). This Non-NAAO EEC system components and operation are basically the same as the EEC-IV system. The self-diagnostic function on the EEC system differs from the EEC-VI system and is covered under NON-NAAO vehicle.

Most 1984–94 Ford domestic built vehicles employ the 4th generation Electronic Engine Control system, commonly called EEC-IV, to manage fuel, ignition and emissions on vehicle engines. In 1994 the EEC-V system was introduced on some models. The diagnostic system on EEC-V provides 3 digit codes in place of 2 digit codes, and it is capable of monitoring more inputs and outputs.

If your vehicle was made before 1984, or has a feedback carburetor equipped V8 engine, then it probably uses the Microprocessor Control Unit (MCU). The MCU system was used on most 1981-83 carburetor equipped vehicles, and 1984 and newer V8 engines with feedback carburetors. The MCU system uses a large six sided connector, identical to the one used with EEC-IV systems. The MCU system does NOT use the small single wire connector, like the EEC-IV system. The MCU system is covered in greater detail later in this manual.

EEC-IV & EEC-V DIAGNOSTIC SYSTEMS

Most 1984–94 Ford domestic built vehicles employ the 4th generation Electronic Engine Control system, commonly designated EEC-IV, to manage fuel, ignition and emissions on vehicle engines. In 1994 the EEC-V system was introduced on some models. The diagnostic system on EEC-V provides 3 digit codes in place of 2 digit codes and monitors more components.

Engine Control System

The Powertrain Control Modules (PCM), usually referred to as the Electronic Control Assembly (ECA) by Ford, is given responsibility for the operation of the emission control devices, cooling fans, ignition and advance and in some cases, automatic transmission functions. Because the EEC-IV oversees both the ignition timing and the fuel injector operation, a precise air/fuel ratio will be maintained under all operating conditions. The ECA is a microprocessor or small computer which receives electrical inputs from several sensors, switches and relays on and around the engine.

Based on combinations of these inputs, the ECA controls outputs to various devices concerned with engine operation and emissions. The engine control assembly relies on the signals to form a correct picture of current vehicle operation. If any of the input signals is incorrect, the ECA reacts to what ever picture is painted for it. For example, if the coolant temperature sensor is inaccurate and reads too low, the ECA may see a picture of the engine never warming up. Consequently, the engine settings will be maintained as if the engine were cold. Because so many inputs can affect one output, correct diagnostic procedures are essential on these systems.

One part of the ECA is devoted to monitoring both input and output functions within the system. This ability forms the core of the self-diagnostic system. If a problem is detected within a circuit, the controller will recognize the fault, assign it an identification code, and store the code in a memory section. Depending on the year and model, the fault code(s) may be represented by two or three digit numbers. The stored code(s) may be retrieved during diagnosis.

When the term Powertrain Control Module (PCM) is used in this manual it will refer to the engine control computer regardless that it may also be called an Electronic Control Assembly (ECA).

While the EEC-IV system is capable of recognizing many internal faults, certain faults will not be recognized. Because the computer system sees only electrical signals, it cannot sense or react to mechanical or vacuum faults affecting engine operation. Some of these faults may affect another component which will set a code. For example, the ECA monitors the output signal to the fuel injectors, but cannot detect a partially clogged injector. As long as the output driver responds correctly, the computer will read the system as functioning correctly. However, the improper flow of fuel may result in a lean mixture. This would, in turn, be detected by the oxygen sensor and noticed as a constantly lean signal by the ECA. Once the signal falls outside the pre-programmed limits, the engine control assembly would notice the fault and set an identification code.

Additionally, the EEC-IV system employs adaptive fuel logic. This process is used to compensate for normal wear and variability within the fuel system. Once the engine enters steady-state operation, the engine control assembly watches the oxygen sensor signal for a bias or tendency to run slightly rich or lean. If such a bias is detected, the adaptive logic corrects the fuel delivery to bring the air/fuel mixture towards a centered or 14.7:1 ratio. This compensating shift is stored in a non-volatile memory which is retained by battery power even with the ignition switched off. The correction factor is then available the next time the vehicle is operated.

➡ If the battery is disconnected for longer than 5 minutes, the adaptive fuel factor will be lost. After repair it will be necessary to drive the car at least 10 miles to allow the processor to relearn the correct factors. The driving period should include steady-throttle open road driving if possible. During the drive, the vehicle may exhibit driveability symptoms not noticed before. These symptoms should clear as the ECA computes the correction factor. The ECA will also store Code 19 indicating loss of power to the controller.

FAILURE MODE EFFECTS MANAGEMENT (FMEM)

The engine controller assembly contains back-up programs which allow the engine to operate if a sensor signal is lost. If a sensor input is seen to be out of range—either high or low—the FMEM program is used. The processor substitutes a fixed value for the missing sensor signal. The engine will continue to operate, although performance and driveability may be noticeably reduced. This function of the controller is sometimes referred to as the limp-in or fail-safe mode. If the missing sensor signal is restored, the FMEM system immediately returns the system to normal operation. The dashboard warning lamp will be lit when FMEM is in effect.

HARDWARE LIMITED OPERATION STRATEGY (HLOS)

This mode is only used if the fault is too extreme for the FMEM circuit to handle. In this mode, the processor has ceased all computation and control; the entire system is run on fixed values. The vehicle may be operated but performance and driveability will be greatly reduced. The fixed or default settings provide minimal calibration, allowing the vehicle to be carefully driven in for service. The dashboard warning lamp will be lit when HLOS is engaged. Codes cannot be read while the system is operating in this mode.

Dashboard Warning Lamp

The CHECK ENGINE or SERVICE ENGINE SOON dashboard warning lamp is referred to as the Malfunction Indicator Lamp (MIL). The lamp is connected to the engine control assembly and will alert the driver to certain malfunctions within the EEC-IV system. When the lamp is lit, the ECA has detected a fault and stored an identity code in memory. The engine control system will usually enter either FMEM or HLOS mode and driveability will be impaired.

The light will stay on as long as the fault causing it is present. Should the fault self-correct, the MIL will extinguish but the stored code will remain in memory.

Under normal operating conditions, the MIL should light briefly when the ignition key is turned ON. As soon as the ECA receives a signal that the engine is cranking, the lamp will be extinguished. The dash warning lamp should remain out during the entire operating cycle.

➡ On Continental, the CHECK ENGINE message is displayed on the message center. When a fault is detected, the message is accompanied by a 1 second tone every 5 seconds. The tone stops after 1 minute. When the Continental system enters HLOS, the additional message CHECK DCL is displayed. DCL refers to the Data Communications Link running between the engine controller and the message center.

EEC-IV & EEC-V SCAN TOOL FUNCTIONS

Although stored codes may be read by using a analog voltmeter, the use of hand-held scan tools such as Ford's Self-Test Automatic Readout (STAR) tester or the second generation SUPER STAR II tester or their equivalent is recommended. There are many manufacturers of these tools; the purchaser must be certain that the tool is proper for the intended use.

Both the STAR and SUPER STAR testers are designed to communicate directly with the EEC-IV system and interpret the electrical signals. The SUPER STAR tester may be used to read either 2 or 3 digit codes; the original STAR tester will not read the 3 digit codes used on many 1990 and newer vehicles.

The scan tool allows any stored faults to be read from the engine controller memory. Use of the scan tool provides additional data during troubleshooting but does not eliminate the use of the charts. The scan tool makes collecting information easier; the data must be correctly interpreted by an operator familiar with the system.

Electrical Tools

The most commonly required electrical diagnostic tool is the Digital Multimeter, allowing voltage, resistance and amperage to be read by one instrument. Many of the diagnostic charts require the use of a volt or ohm-meter during diagnosis.

The multimeter must be a high impedance unit, with 10 megohms of impedance in the voltmeter. This type of meter will not place an additional load on the circuit it is testing; this is extremely important in low voltage circuits. The multimeter must be of high quality in all respects. It should be handled carefully and protected from impact or damage. Replace the batteries frequently in the unit.

Additionally, an analog (needle type) voltmeter may be used to read stored fault codes if the STAR tester is not available. The codes are transmitted as visible needle sweeps on the face of the instrument.

Almost all diagnostic procedures will require the use of the Breakout Box, a device which connects into the EEC-IV harness and provides testing ports for the 60 wires in the harness. Direct testing of the harness connectors at the terminals or by back-probing is not recommended; damage to the wiring and terminals is almost certain to occur.

Other necessary tools include a quality tachometer with inductive (clip-on) pickup, a fuel pressure gauge with system adapters and a vacuum gauge with an auxiliary source of vacuum.

EEC-IV & EEC-V SELF-DIAGNOSTICS

Diagnosis of a driveability problem requires attention to detail and following the diagnostic procedures in the correct order. Resist the temptation to begin extensive testing before completing the preliminary diagnostic steps. The preliminary or visual inspection must be completed in detail before diagnosis begins. In many cases this will shorten diagnostic time and often cure the problem without electronic testing.

Visual Inspection

This is possibly the most critical step of diagnosis. A detailed examination of all connectors, wiring and vacuum hoses can often lead to a repair without further diagnosis. Performance of this step relies on the skill of the technician performing it; a careful inspector will check the undersides of hoses as well as the integrity of hard-to-reach hoses blocked by the air cleaner or other components. Wiring should be checked carefully for any sign of strain , burning, crimping or terminal pull-out from a connector.

Checking connectors at components or in harnesses is required; usually, pushing them together will reveal a loose fit. Pay particular attention to ground circuits, making sure they are not loose or corroded. Remember to inspect connectors and hose fittings at components not mounted on the engine, such as the evaporative canister or relays mounted on the fender aprons. Any component or wiring in the vicinity of a fluid leak or spillage should be given extra attention during inspection.

Additionally, inspect maintenance items such as belt condition and tension, battery charge and condition and the radiator cap carefully. Any of these very simple items may affect the system enough to set a fault.

Diagnostic Connector Location

▶ See Figure 11

The Diagnostic Link Connectors (DLC) are located a 6 basic locations:
• Near the bulkhead (right or left side of vehicle)

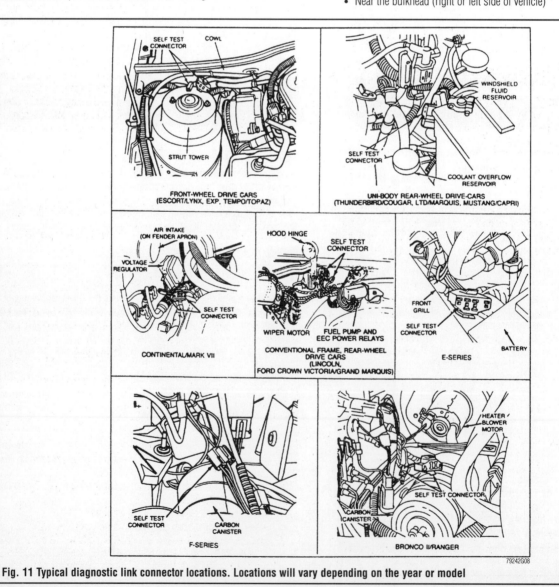

Fig. 11 Typical diagnostic link connector locations. Locations will vary depending on the year or model

- Near the wheel well (right or left side of vehicle)
- Near the front corner of the engine compartment (right or left side of vehicle)

EEC-IV & EEC-V READING CODES

The EEC-IV system may be interrogated for stored codes using the Quick Test procedures. These tests will reveal faults immediately present during the test as well as any intermittent codes set within the previous 80 warm up cycles. If a code was set before a problem self-corrected (such as a momentarily loose connector), the code will be erased if the problem does not reoccur within 80 warm-up cycles.

The Quick Test procedure is divided into 2 sections, Key On Engine Off (KOEO) and Key On Engine Running (KOER). These 2 procedures must be performed correctly if the system is to run the internal self-checks and provide accurate fault codes. Codes will be output and displayed as numbers on the hand scan tool, i.e. 23. Code 23 would be displayed as 2 needle sweeps and pause and 3 more needle sweeps. For codes being read on an analog voltmeter, the needle sweeps indicate the code digits in the same manner as the lamp flashes on other systems.

In all cases, the codes 11 or 111 are used to indicate PASS during testing. Note that the PASS code may appear, followed by other stored codes. These are codes from the continuous memory and may indicate intermittent faults, even though the system does not presently contain the fault. The PASS designation only indicates the system passes all internal tests at the moment.

Once the Quick Test has been performed and all fault codes recorded, refer to the code charts. The charts direct the use of specific pinpoint tests for the appropriate circuit and will allow complete circuit testing.

✳✳ CAUTION

To prevent injury and/or property damage, always block the drive wheels, firmly apply the parking brake, place the transmission in Park or Neutral and turn all electrical loads off before performing the Quick Test procedures.

Reading Codes With Analog Voltmeter

▶ See Figures 12 and 13

➡**There are inexpensive tools available at auto parts stores that make reading and clear Ford engine codes very easy. Reading the voltmeter needle sweeps is sometimes difficult. Always check the code more than once to make certain it was read correctly.**

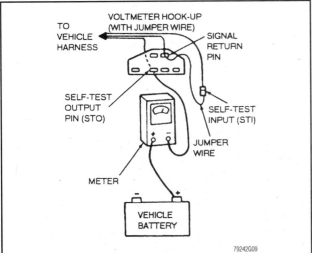

Fig. 12 Connect an analog voltmeter as shown to read diagnostic trouble codes

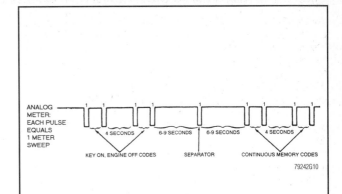

Fig. 13 Code transmission during KOEO test. Note the continuous memory codes are transmitted after a pause and a separator pulse

In the absence of a scan tool, an analog voltmeter may be used to retrieve stored fault codes. Set the meter range to read DC 0–15 volts. Connect the positive (+) lead of the meter to the battery positive terminal and connect the negative (-) lead of the meter to the self-test output pin of the diagnostic connector.

Follow the directions given for performing the KOEO and KOER tests. To activate the tests, use a jumper wire to connect the signal return pin on the diagnostic connector to the self-test input connector. The self-test input line is the separate wire and connector with or near the diagnostic connector.

The codes will be transmitted as groups of needle sweeps. This method may be used to read either 2 or 3 digit codes. The Continuous Memory codes are separated from the KOEO codes by 6 seconds, a single sweep and another 6 second delay.

KEY ON ENGINE OFF (KOEO) TEST

▶ See Figure 14

1. Connect the scan tool to the self-test connectors. Make certain the test button is unlatched or up.
2. Start the engine and run it until normal operating temperature is reached.
3. Turn the engine OFF for 10 seconds.
4. Activate the test button on the STAR tester.
5. Turn the ignition switch ON but do not start the engine. For vehicles with 4.9L engines, depress the clutch during the entire test. For vehicles with the 7.3L diesel engine, hold the accelerator to the floor during the test.
6. The KOEO codes will be transmitted. Six to nine seconds after the last KOEO code, a single separator pulse will be transmitted. Six to nine seconds after this pulse, the codes from the Continuous Memory will be transmitted.
7. Record all service codes displayed. Do not depress the throttle on gasoline engines during the test.

KEY ON ENGINE RUNNING (KOER) TEST

▶ See Figure 15

1. Make certain the self-test button is released or de-activated on the STAR tester.
2. Start the engine and run it at 2000 rpm for two minutes. This action warms up the oxygen sensor.
3. Turn the ignition switch OFF for 10 seconds.
4. Activate or latch the self-test button on the scan tool.
5. Start the engine. The engine identification code will be transmitted. This is a single digit number representing ½ the number of cylinders in a gasoline engine. On the STAR tester, this number may appear with a zero,

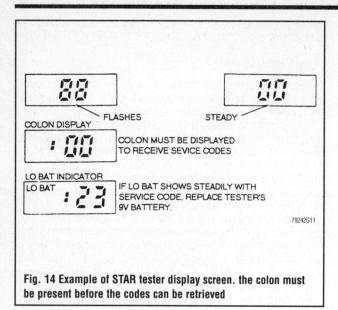

Fig. 14 Example of STAR tester display screen. the colon must be present before the codes can be retrieved

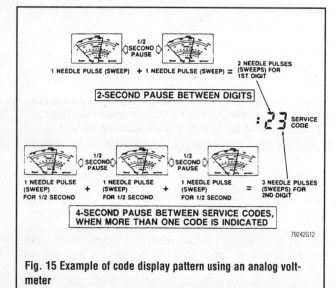

Fig. 15 Example of code display pattern using an analog voltmeter

i.e., 20 = 2. For 7.3L diesel engines, the 10 code is 5. The code is used to confirm that the correct processor is installed and that the self-test has begun.

6. If the vehicle is equipped with a Brake On/Off (BOO) switch, the brake pedal must be depressed and released after the 10 code is transmitted.

7. If the vehicle is equipped with a Power Steering Pressure Switch (PSPS), the steering wheel must be turned at least ½ turn and released within 2 seconds after the engine 10 code is transmitted.

8. If the vehicle is equipped with the E400 transmission, the Overdrive Cancel Switch (OCS) must be cycled after the engine 10 code is transmitted.

9. Certain Ford vehicles will display a Dynamic Response code 6–20 seconds after the engine 10 code. This will appear as one pulse on a meter or as a 10 on the STAR tester. When this code appears, briefly take the engine to wide open throttle. This allows the system to test the throttle position, MAF and MAP sensors.

10. All relevant codes will be displayed and should be recorded. Remember that the codes refer only to faults present during this test cycle. Codes stored in Continuous Memory are not displayed in this test mode.

11. Do not depress the throttle during testing unless a dynamic response code is displayed.

Advanced Test Modes

CONTINUOUS MONITOR OR WIGGLE TEST MODE

Once entered, this mode allows the technician to attempt to recreate intermittent faults by wiggling or tapping components, wiring or connectors. The test may be performed during either KOEO or KOER procedures. The test requires the use of either an analog voltmeter or a hand scan tool.

To enter the continuous monitor mode during KOEO testing, turn the ignition switch ON. Activate the test, wait 10 seconds, then deactivate and reactivate the test; the system will enter the continuous monitor mode. Tap, move or wiggle the harness, component or connector suspected of causing the problem; if a fault is detected, the code will store in the memory. When the fault occurs, the dash warning lamp will illuminate, the STAR tester will light a red indicator (and possibly beep) and the analog meter needle will sweep once.

To enter this mode in the KOER test:

1. Start the engine and run it at 2000 rpm for two minutes. This action warms up the oxygen sensor.

2. Turn the ignition switch OFF for 10 seconds.

3. Start the engine.

4. Activate the test, wait 10 seconds, then deactivate and reactivate the test; the system will enter the continuous monitor mode.

5. Tap, move or wiggle the harness, component or connector suspected of causing the problem; if a fault is detected, the code will store in the memory.

6. When the fault occurs, the dash warning lamp will illuminate, the STAR tester will light a red indicator (and possibly beep) and the analog meter needle will sweep once.

OUTPUT STATE CHECK

This testing mode allows the operator to energize and de-energize most of the outputs controlled by the EEC-IV system. Many of the outputs may be checked at the component by listening for a click or feeling the item move or engage by a hand placed on the case. To enter this check:

1. Enter the KOEO test mode.

2. When all codes have been transmitted, depress the accelerator all the way to the floor and release it.

3. The output actuators are now all ON. Depressing the throttle pedal to the floor again switches the all the actuator outputs OFF.

4. This test may be performed as often as necessary, switching between ON and OFF by depressing the throttle.

5. Exit the test by turning the ignition switch OFF, disconnecting the jumper at the diagnostic connector or releasing the test button on the scan tool.

CYLINDER BALANCE TEST

This test is only for SEFI engines. On SEFI engine the EEC-IV system allows a cylinder balance test to be performed on engines equipped with the Sequential Electronic Fuel Injection system. Cylinder balance testing identifies a weak or non-contributing cylinder.

Enter the cylinder balance test by depressing and releasing the throttle pedal within 2 minutes of the last code output in the KOER test. The idle speed will become fixed and engine mm is recorded for later reference. The engine control assembly will shut off the fuel to the highest numbered cylinder (4, 6 or 8), allow the engine to stabilize and then record the rpm. The injector is turned back on and the next one shut off and the process continues through cylinder No. 1.

The controller selects the highest rpm drop from all the cylinders tested, multiplies it by a percentage and arrives at an rpm drop value for all cylinders. For example, if the greatest drop for any cylinder was 150 rpm, the processor applies a multiple of 65% and arrives at 98 mm. The processor then checks the recorded rpm drops, checking that each was at least 98 rpm. If all cylinders meet the criteria, the test is complete and the ECA outputs Code 90 indicating PASS.

If one cylinder did not drop at least this amount, then the cylinder number is output instead of the 90 code. The cylinder number will be followed by a zero, so 30 indicates cylinder No. 3 did not meet the minimum rpm drop.

The test may be repeated a second time by depressing and releasing the throttle pedal within 2 minutes of the last code output. For the second test, the controller uses a lower percentage (and thus a lower rpm) to determine the minimum acceptable rpm drop. Again, either Code 90 or the number of the weak cylinder will be output.

Performing a third test causes the ECA to select an even lower percentage and rpm drop. If a cylinder is shown as weak in the third test, it should be considered non-contributing. The tests may be repeated as often as needed if the throttle is depressed within two minutes of the last code output. Subsequent tests will use the percentage from the third test instead of selecting even lower values.

Continuous Memory Codes

These codes are retained in memory for 80 warm-up cycles. To clear the codes for the purposes of testing or confirming repair, perform the KOEO test. When the fault codes begin to be displayed, de-activate the test by either disconnecting the jumper wire (meter, MIL or message center) or releasing the test button on the hand scanner. Stopping the test during code transmission will erase the Continuous Memory. Do not disconnect the negative battery cable to clear these codes; the Keep Alive memory will be cleared and a new code, 19, will be stored for loss of ECA power.

KEEP ALIVE MEMORY

The Keep Alive Memory (KAM) contains the adaptive factors used by the processor to compensate for component tolerances and wear. It should not be routinely cleared during diagnosis. If an emissions related part is replaced during repair, the KAM must be cleared. Failure to clear the KAM may cause severe driveability problems since the correction factor for the old component will be applied to the new component.

To clear the Keep Alive Memory, disconnect the negative battery cable for at least 5 minutes. After the memory is cleared and the battery reconnected, the vehicle must be driven at least 10 miles so that the processor may relearn the needed correction factors. The distance to be driven depends on the engine and vehicle, but all drives should include steady-throttle cruise on open roads. Certain driveability problems may be noted during the drive because the adaptive factors are not yet functioning.

To prevent the replacement of good components, remember that the EEC-IV system has no control over the following items:
- Fuel quantity and quality
- Damaged or faulty ignition components
- Internal engine condition—rings, valves, timing belt, etc.
- Starter and battery circuit
- Dual Hall sensor
- TFI or DIS module
- Distributor condition or function
- Camshaft sensor
- Crankshaft sensor
- Ignition or DIS coil
- Engine governor module

Any of these systems can cause erratic engine behavior easily mistaken for an EEC-IV problem.

NON-NAAO DIAGNOSTIC SYSTEM

The 2.0L, 2.2L and 2.5L engines are referred to by Ford Motor Company as NON-NAAO, indicating the vehicles and/or their engines originate outside North American Automotive Operations.

Although these vehicles share many similarities in their engine control systems, differences must also be considered. While the fault codes are almost standardized (i.e., Code 14 indicates the barometric pressure sensor), not all engines use the same components so a code may be unique to a particular engine or family. These procedures encompass both turbocharged and non-turbocharged engines.

Beside the engine diagnostic function, these procedures will also display codes related to the 4-speed Electronically-controlled Automatic Transaxle (4EAT) used in these vehicles. Note that the 4EAT codes are displayed by

these procedures even though retrieving the engine fault codes may require the North American procedures described at the beginning of this section.

Engine Control System

These vehicles employ the Electronic Engine Control system, commonly designated EEC, to manage fuel, ignition and emissions on vehicle engines. This system is not EEC-IV, but does share some similarities.

The engine control assembly (ECA) is given responsibility for the operation of the emission control devices, cooling fans, ignition and advance and in some cases, automatic transmission functions. Because the EEC oversees both the ignition timing and the fuel injector operation, a precise air/fuel ratio will be maintained under all operating conditions. The ECA is a microprocessor or small computer which receives electrical in-puts from several sensors, switches and relays on and around the engine.

Based on combinations of these inputs, the ECA controls outputs to various devices concerned with engine operation and emissions. The engine control assembly relies on the signals to form a correct picture of current vehicle operation. If any of the input signals is incorrect, the ECA reacts to what ever picture is painted for it. For example, if the coolant temperature sensor is inaccurate and reads too low, the ECA may see a picture of the engine never warming up. Consequently, the engine settings will be maintained as if the engine were cold. Because so many inputs can affect one output, correct diagnostic procedures are essential on these systems.

One part of the ECA is devoted to monitoring both input and output functions within the system. This ability forms the core of the self-diagnostic system. If a problem is detected within a circuit, the controller will recognize the fault, assign it an identification code, and store the code in a memory section. Most NON-NAAO vehicles use two-digit codes for both engine and 4EAT transaxle faults. The stored code(s) may be retrieved during diagnosis.

➡When the term Powertrain Control Module (PCM) is used in this manual it will refer to the engine control computer regardless that it may also be called an Electronic Control Assembly (ECA).

While the EEC system is capable of recognizing many internal faults, certain faults will not be recognized. Because the computer system sees only electrical signals, it cannot sense or react to mechanical or vacuum faults affecting engine operation. Some of these faults may affect another component which will set a code. For example, the ECA monitors the output signal to the fuel injectors, but cannot detect a partially clogged injector. As long as the output driver responds correctly, the computer will read the system as functioning correctly. However, the improper flow of fuel may result in a lean mixture. This would, in turn, be detected by the oxygen sensor and noticed as a constantly lean signal by the ECA. Once the signal falls outside the pre-programmed limits, the engine control assembly would notice the fault and set an identification code.

Dashboard Warning Lamp

The CHECK ENGINE dashboard warning lamp is referred to as the Malfunction Indicator Lamp (MIL). The lamp is connected to the engine control assembly and will alert the driver to certain malfunctions within the EEC system. When the lamp is lit, the ECA has detected a fault and stored an identity code in memory.

The light will stay on as long as the fault causing it is present. Should the fault self-correct, the MIL will extinguish but the stored code will remain in memory.

Under normal operating conditions, the MIL should light briefly when the ignition key is turned ON. As soon as the ECA receives a signal that the engine is running, the lamp will be extinguished. The dash warning lamp should remain out during the entire operating cycle.

Vehicles with a 4EAT transaxle also provide a manual shift light, indicating when the transmission is in manual shift mode.

NON-NAAO SCAN TOOL FUNCTIONS

Although stored codes may be read by using an analog voltmeter by counting the needle sweeps, the use of hand-held scan tools such as Ford's second generation SUPER STAR II tester or equivalent is recommended. There are many manufacturers of these tools; the purchaser must be certain that the tool is proper for the intended use.

➡The engine and 4EAT fault codes on NON-NAAO vehicles may only be read with the SUPER STAR II or its equivalent. The regular STAR tester or voltmeter may be capable not retrieve the stored codes.

The SUPER STAR II tester is designed to communicate directly with the EEC system and interpret the electrical signals. The scan tool allows any stored faults to be read from the engine controller memory. Use of the scan tool provides additional data during troubleshooting but does not eliminate the use of the charts. The scan tool makes collecting information easier; the data must be correctly interpreted by an operator familiar with the system.

An adapter cable will be required to connect the scan tool to the vehicle; the adapter(s) may differ depending on the vehicle being tested.

Electrical Tools

The most commonly required electrical diagnostic tool is the Digital Multimeter, allowing voltage, resistance and amperage to be read by one instrument. Many of the diagnostic charts require the use of a voltmeter or ohmmeter during diagnosis.

The multimeter must be a high impedance unit, with 10 megohms of impedance in the voltmeter. This type of meter will not place an additional load on the circuit it is testing; this is extremely important in low voltage circuits. The multimeter must be of high quality in all respects. It should be handled carefully and protected from impact or damage. Replace the batteries frequently in the unit.

Additionally, an analog (needle type) voltmeter may be used to read stored fault codes if the SUPER STAR II tester is not available. The codes are transmitted as visible needle sweeps on the face of the instrument.

Almost all diagnostic procedures will require the use of the Breakout Box, a device which connects into the EEC harness and provides testing ports for the 60 wires in the harness. Direct testing of the harness connectors at the terminals or by backprobing is not recommended; damage to the wiring and terminals is almost certain to occur.

Other necessary tools include a quality tachometer with inductive (clip-on) pickup, a fuel pressure gauge with system adapters and a vacuum gauge with an auxiliary source of vacuum.

NON-NAAO SELF-DIAGNOSTICS

Diagnosis of a driveability problem requires attention to detail and following the diagnostic procedures in the correct order. Resist the temptation to begin extensive testing before completing the preliminary diagnostic steps. The preliminary or visual inspection must be completed in detail before diagnosis begins. In many cases this will shorten diagnostic time and often cure the problem without electronic testing.

Keep in mind that all the things that previously went wrong with vehicles, before the age of electronics, can still go wrong and are still the cause of the majority of the driveability problems. The best diagnosis starts with a list of symptoms and possible causes, followed by careful checking of those causes in the most likely order. Eliminate all the possible mechanical causes before considering electrical faults.

Visual Inspection

This is possibly the most critical step of diagnosis. A detailed examination of all connectors, wiring and vacuum hoses can often lead to a repair without further diagnosis. Performance of this step relies on the skill of the technician performing it; a careful inspector will check the undersides of hoses as well as the integrity of hard-to-reach hoses blocked by the air cleaner or other components. Wiring should be checked carefully for any sign of strain , burning, crimping or terminal pull-out from a connector.

Checking connectors at components or in harnesses is required; usually, pushing them together will reveal a loose fit. Pay particular attention to ground circuits, making sure they are not loose or corroded. Remember to inspect connectors and hose fittings at components not mounted on the

engine, such as the evaporative canister or relays mounted on the fender aprons. Any component or wiring in the vicinity of a fluid leak or spillage should be given extra attention during inspection.

Additionally, inspect maintenance items such as belt condition and tension, battery charge and condition and the radiator cap carefully. Any of these very simple items may affect the system enough to set a fault.

NON-NAAO READING CODES

The EEC system may be interrogated for stored codes using the Quick Test procedures. If a code was set before a problem self-corrected (such as a momentarily loose connector), the code will remain in memory until cleared.

The Quick Test procedure is divided into 3 sections, Key On Engine Off (KOEO), Key On Engine Running (KOER) and the Switch Monitor test. These 3 procedures must be performed correctly if the system is to run the internal self-checks and provide accurate fault codes. Codes will be output and displayed as numbers on the hand scan tool, i.e. 23. If the codes are being read by an analog voltmeter, the codes will be displayed as groups of needle sweeps separated by pauses.

Code 23 would be shown as two sweeps, a pause and three more sweeps. A longer pause will occur between codes. Unlike the EEC-IV system, the EEC system does not broadcast a PASS designator or code. If no fault codes are stored, the display screen of the hand scanner will remain blank. Additionally, the EEC system does not operate switches or sensors during KOEO or KOER testing.

Once the Quick Test has been performed and all fault codes recorded, refer to the service code charts. The charts direct the use of specific pinpoint tests for the appropriate circuit and will allow complete circuit testing.

The EEC diagnostic connector is located at the left rear corner of the engine compartment on most vehicles. When connecting the test equipment and adapters, note that the Self-Test Input (STI) connector is separate from the main diagnostic connector on all NON-NAAO engines except for the 1.8L engine. The Self-Test Output (STO) connector is contained within the main diagnostic connector.

✳✳ CAUTION

To prevent injury and/or property damage, always block the drive wheels, firmly apply the parking brake, place the transmission in Park or Neutral and turn all electrical loads off before performing the Quick Test procedures.

Reading Codes With Analog Voltmeter

▶ See Figure 16

In the absence of a scan tool, an analog voltmeter may be used to retrieve stored fault codes. Set the meter range to read DC 0–20 volts. Connect the + lead of the meter to the STO pin in the diagnostic connector and connect the—lead of the meter to the negative battery terminal or a good engine ground.

Follow the directions given for performing the KOEO and KOER tests. To activate the tests, use a jumper wire to connect the STI connector to ground. The codes will be transmitted as groups of needle sweeps.

KEY ON ENGINE OFF (KOEO) TEST

1. Make certain the scan tool is OFF; connect it to the self-test connectors. Switch the scan tool to the MECS position. Except on 1.8L engines, make certain the adapter ground cable is connected to the negative battery terminal. On the 1.8L engine, make certain the switch on the adapter is set to EEC or ECA if engine codes are to be retrieved. The other switch position will retrieve codes from the 4EAT.

2. Make certain the scan tool test button is ON or latched down.

3. For all engine or 4EAT codes except 1.8L and 1.9L engines, turn the ignition switch ON but do not start the engine, then turn the scan tool ON. On 1.8L and 1.9L engines, turn the scan tool ON first, then turn the ignition switch ON.

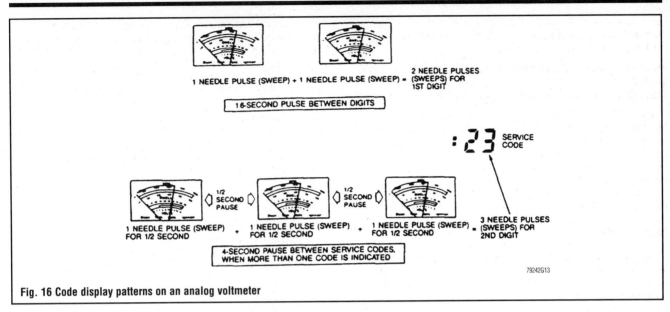

Fig. 16 Code display patterns on an analog voltmeter

4. Once energized, the tester should display 888 and beep for 2 seconds. Release the test button; 00 should appear, signifying the tool is ready to read codes.
5. Re-engage the test button.
6. The KOEO codes will be transmitted.
7. Record all service codes displayed.
8. After all codes are received, release the test button to review all the codes retained in tester memory.
9. Make sure all codes displayed are recorded. Clear the ECA memory and perform the KOEO test again. This will isolate hard faults from intermittent ones. Any hard faults will cause the code(s) to be repeated in the 2nd test. An intermittent which is not now present will not set a new code.
10. Record all codes from the 2nd test. After repairs are made on hard fault items, the intermittent ones must be recreated by tapping suspect sensors, wiggling wires or connectors or reproducing circumstances on a test drive.

➡ **For both KOEO and KOER tests, the message STO LO always displayed on the screen indicates that the system cannot initiate the Self-Test. The message STI LO displayed with an otherwise blank screen indicates Pass or No Codes Stored.**

KEY ON ENGINE RUNNING (KOER) TEST

1. Make certain the self-test button is released or de-activated on the SUPER STAR II tester and that the tester is properly connected.
2. Start the engine and run it at 2000 rpm for 2 minutes. This action warms up the oxygen sensor.
3. Turn the ignition switch OFF.
4. Turn the ignition switch ON for 10 seconds but do not start the engine.
5. Start the engine and run it at idle.
6. Activate or latch the self-test button on the scan tool.
7. All relevant codes will be displayed and should be recorded.

SWITCH MONITOR TESTS

▶ **See Figures 17 and 18**

This test mode allows the operator to check the input signal from individual switches to the ECA. All switches to be tested must be OFF at the time the test begins; if one switch is on, it will affect the testing of another. The test must begin with the engine cool. The tests may be performed with either the SUPER STAR II tester or an analog voltmeter. When using the scan tool, the small LED on the adapter cable will light to show that the ECA has received the switch signal. If the voltmeter is used, the voltage will change when the switch is engaged or disengaged.
1. The engine must be off and cooled. Place the transmission in Park or Neutral.
2. Turn all accessories OFF.

3. If using the SUPER STAR II, connect it properly. If using an analog voltmeter, use a jumper to ground the STI terminal. Connect the positive (+) voltmeter lead to the SML terminal of the diagnostic connector and connect the negative (-) lead to a good engine ground.
4. Turn the ignition switch **ON**. Engage the center button on the SUPER STAR II. Most switches can be exercised without starting the engine.
5. Operate each switch according to the test chart and note the response either on the LED or the volt scale. Remember that an improper response means the ECA did not see the switch operation; check circuitry and connectors before assuming the switch is faulty.
6. Turn the ignition switch **OFF** when testing is complete.

CLEARING CODES

Codes stored within the memory must be erased when repairs are completed. Additionally, erasing codes during diagnosis can separate hard faults from intermittent ones.
To erase stored codes, disconnect the negative battery cable, then depress the brake pedal for at least 10 seconds. Reconnect the battery cable and recheck the system for any remaining or newly-set codes.

EEC-IV SYSTEM DIAGNOSTIC TROUBLE CODES

The code definitions listed general 2-digit codes for Ford Vehicles using the Ford EEC-IV engine control system. In 1991 Ford started introducing vehicles that use 3-digit codes. The code definitions for both the 2 and 3-digit codes are found in this section. For a specific code definition or component test procedure consult your 'Chilton Total Car Care' manual for your vehicle. A diagnostic code does not mean the component is defective. For example a Code 29 is a vehicle speed sensor code. This does not mean the sensor is defective, but to check the sensor and related components. A defective speedometer cable or transmission problem will also set this code.

➡ **When the term Powertrain Control Module (PCM) is used in this manual it will refer to the engine control computer regardless that it may be a PCM or Electronic Control Module (ECM) or Electronic Control Assembly (ECA).**

2-Digit DTC'S

1984–94 Light Trucks:
Code 11 System Pass
Code 12 (R) Idle control fault—RPM Unable To Reach Upper Limit Self-Test
Code 13 (C) DC Motor Did Follow Dashpot
Code 13 (O) DC Motor Did Not Move

Switch	1.3L	1.6L	1.8L	2.2L	2.2L Turbo	SUPER STAR II Tester LED or Analog VOM Indications
Clutch engage Switch/Neutral Gear Switch (CES/NGS) (MTX only)	X	X	X	X	X	LED on or less than 1.5V in gear and clutch pedal released
Manual Lever Position Switch (MLP) (ATX Only)	X	X	X	X	X	LED on or less than 1.5V in P or N
Idle Switch (IDL)	X	X	X	X	X	LED on or less than 1.5V with accelerator pedal depressed
Brake On-Off Switch (BOO)	X	X	X MTX	X	X	LED on or less than 1.5V with brake pedal depressed (not fully)
Headlamps Switch (HLDT)	X	X	X	X	X	LED on or less than 1.5V with headlamp switch on
Blower Motor Switch (BLMT)	X	X	X	X	X	LED on or less than 1.5V with blower switch at 2nd or above position
A/C Switch (ACS)	X	X	X	X	X	LED on or less than 1.5V with A/C switch on and blower on
Defrost Switch (DEF)	X	X	X	X	X	LED on or less than 1.5V with defrost switch on
Coolant Temperature Switch (CTS)	X	X	X	X	X	LED on or less than 1.5V with cooling fan on
Wide Open Throttle Switch (WOT)	X	X	X	X		LED off or 0V with accelerator pedal fully depressed
Knock Control (KC)					X	LED on or less than 1.5V while tapping on engine

Fig. 18 Switch tests for 1991 and newer Ford Non-NAAO vehicles

Switch	1.3L	1.8L	2.2L	2.2L Turbo	SUPER STAR II Tester LED or Analog VOM Indications
Clutch engage Switch/Neutral Gear Switch (CES/NGS) (MTX only)	X	X	X	X	LED on or 12V in gear and clutch pedal released
Manual Lever Position Switch (MLP) (ATX Only)	X	X	X		LED on or 12V in P or N
Idle Switch (IDL)	X	X	X	X	LED on or 12V with accelerator pedal depressed
Brake On-Off Switch (BOO)	X	X MTX	X	X	LED on or 12V with brake pedal depressed
Headlamps Switch (HLDT)	X	X	X	X	LED on or 12V with headlamp switch on
Blower Motor Switch (BLMT)	X	X	X	X	LED on or 12V with blower switch at 2nd or above position
A/C Switch (ACS)	X	X	X		LED on or 12V with A/C switch on and blower on
Defrost Switch (DEF)	X	X	X	X	LED on or 12V with defrost switch on
Coolant Temperature Switch (CTS)	X	X	X	X	LED on or 12V with cooling fan on
Wide Open Throttle Switch (WOT)	X	X MTX	X		LED off or 0V with accelerator pedal fully depressed

Fig. 17 Switch tests for 1990 and early Ford Non-NAAO vehicles

Code 13 (R) Idle control fault—Cannot control RPM during Self-Test low RPM check

Code 14(C)—Engine RPM signal fault—Profile Ignition Pickup (PIP) circuit failure or RPM sensor.

Code 15 (C) EEC Processor, power to Keep Alive Memory (KAM) interrupted or test failed

Code 15 (O) Power Interrupted To Processor or EEC Processor ROM Test failure

Code 16 (O,R) RPM too low to perform Exhaust Gas Oxygen (EGO) sensor test or fuel control error.

Code 1 (O)7 CFI Fuel Control System fault—Rich/Lean condition indicated; 3.8L V-6/5.0LV-8 (1984).

Code 17 (R) RPM Below Self-Test Limit, Set Too Low. Code 18 (C)—Ignition diagnostic monitor (1DM) circuit failure, loss of RPM signal or SPOUT circuit grounded

Code 18 (O)—Ignition Diagnostic Monitor (1DM) circuit

Code 18 (R) SPOUT or SAW circuit open

Code 19 (C) Cylinder Identification (CID) Sensor Input failure

Code 19 (O) Failure in EEC Processor internal voltage. Code 19 (R)—Erratic RPM During EGR Test or RPM Too Low During ISC Off Test

Code 21 Engine Coolant Temperature (ECT) out of Self-Test range

Code 22 (O, R) Manifold Absolute Pressure (MAP)/Barometric Pressure (BP/BARO) Sensor circuit out of Self-Test range

Code 23 Throttle Position (TP) Sensor out of Self-Test range

Code 24 (O, R) Air Charge (ACT) or Intake Air (IAT) Temperature out of Self-Test range

Code 25 (R) Knock not sensed during dynamic response test

Code 26 (O, R) Transmission Fluid Temp (TFT) out of Self-Test range

Code 26 (O, R) Vane Air (VAF) or Mass Air (MAF) sensor out of self-test range

Code 28 (C) Loss Of Primary Tach, Right Side.

Code 29 (C) Insufficient input from Vehicle Speed Sensor (VSS) or Programmable Speedometer/Odometer Module (PSOM)

Code 31 EGR valve position sensor circuit below minimum voltage

Code 32 EGR Valve Position (EVP) sensor circuit voltage below closed limit

Code 33 (C) Throttle Position (TP) sensor noisy/harsh on line

Code 33 (R, C) EGR valve position sensor circuit, EGR valve opening not detected

Code 34 EGR valve circuit out of self-test range or valve not closing

Code 35 EGR valve circuit above maximum voltage -except 2.3L HSC with Feedback Carburetor System—or—Throttle Kicker on 2.3L HSC with Feedback Carburetor System.

Code 38 (C) Idle Track Switch Circuit Open.

Code 39 (C) AXOD Torque Converter or Bypass Clutch Not Applying Properly

Code 41 (R,C) Oxygen Sensor circuit indicates system always lean

Code 42 (R,C) Oxygen Sensor circuit indicates system always rich, right side if 2 sensors used

Code 43 (C) Oxygen Sensor Out Of Test Range—on 1992 and earlier vehicles—or—Throttle Position Sensor failure—on 1993 and newer vehicles

Code 43 (R) Exhaust Gas Oxygen (EGO) sensor cool down has occurred during testing—2.3L HSC and 2.8L FBC truck

Code 44 (R) Air injection control system failure (right side cylinders, if a split system)

Code 45 (C) Coil 1 primary circuit failure

Code 45 (R) Air injection control system air flow misdirected

Code 46 (C) Coil Primary Circuit failure

Code 46 (R) Thermactor air not bypassed during Self-Test

Code 47 (C) 4x4 switch is closed—on Truck.

Code 47 (R) Airflow low at idle—on fuel injected engines—or—4 x 4 switch is closed—on Truck—or—Fuel control system/Exhaust Gas Oxygen (EGO) Sensor fault—on 2.3L HSC and 2.8L FBC truck

Code 48 (C) Coil Primary Circuit failure; Except 2.3L Truck—or—Loss Of Secondary Tach, Left Side—with 2.3L Truck engine

Code 48 Airflow high at base idle

Code 49 (C) EI electronic Transmission Shift Error—on Truck and 1992 and later cars—or—SPOUT Signal Defaulted To 10 Degrees BTDC or SPOUT Open—Up to 1991 passenger cars

Code 51 (O, C) Engine Coolant Temperature (ECT) circuit open or out of range during self-test

Code 52 (O) Power Steering Pressure Switch (PSPS) circuit open

Code 52 (R) Power Steering Pressure Switch (PSPS) circuit did not change states

Code 53 (O, C) Throttle Position (TP) circuit above maximum voltage

Code 54 (O, C) Air Charge (ACT) or Intake Air (IAT) Temperature circuit open

Code 55 (R) Key Power Input To Processor—open circuit

Code 56 (O, C) Mass Air (MAF) or Vane Air (VAF) Flow circuit above maximum voltage—Port fuel injected engines—or—Transmission oil temperature (TOT) circuit open—on vehicles with automatic transaxle

Code 57 (C) AXOD Circuit failure—on vehicles with automatic overdrive transaxle—or—Octane Adjust Circuit failure—on some 1992 and newer cars

Code 58 (R) Idle Tracking Switch circuit fault.

Code 59 (C) Automatic Transmission Shift Error—on 1991 and newer—or—AXOD 4/3 or Neutral Pressure Switch Failed Open—on 3.0L EFI and 3.8L AXOD—vehicles with automatic overdrive transaxle

Code 59 (O) AXOD 4/3 Pressure Switch Failed Closed -on 3.8L engine AXOD—vehicles with automatic transaxle—or—Idle Adjust Service Pin In Use—on 2.9L EFI engine—or—Low Speed Fuel Pump Circuit failure—on 3.0L SHO engine

Code 61 (O, C) Engine Coolant Temperature (ECT) circuit grounded

Code 62 (C) Converter clutch error

Code 62 (O) Electronic Transmission Shift Error.

Code 63 (O, C) Throttle Position (TP) circuit below minimum voltage

Code 64 (O, C) Air Charge (ACT) or Intake Air (IAT) Temperature circuit grounded

Code 65 (C) Fuel System Failed To Enter Closed Loop Mode or key power

Code 65 (O) Key Power Check—Possible Charging System overvoltage condition

Code 65 (R) Overdrive Cancel Switch (OCS) circuit did not switch

Code 66 (C) Mass Air (MAF) or Vane Air (VAF) Flow circuit below minimum voltage—engine with Port fuel injection—or—Transmission Oil Temperature (TOT) circuit grounded—vehicles with automatic transaxle

Code 67 (O, C) Manual Lever Position (MLP) sensor out of range and A/C ON

Code 67 (O, C) Neutral/Drive Switch (NDS) circuit open/A/C on during Self-Test

Code 67 (O, R) Neutral Drive Circuit Failed or A/C Input High -or—Clutch Switch Circuit failed—on vehicles with manual transaxle -or—Manual Lever Position Sensor out of range—on vehicles with automatic transaxle

Code 68 (C) Transmission Fluid Temp (TFT) transmission over temp (over heated)

Code 68 (O) Idle Tracking Switch circuit—on 2.8L FBC truck only—or—Air temperature sensor—except FBC truck.

Code 68 (R, C) Air Temperature Sensor Circuit failure -on 1.9L EFI engine—or—Idle Tracking Switch Circuit failure—on CFI engine—or—Transmission Temperature Circuit

Code 69 (O, C) Transmission Shift Error

Code 70 (C) Data Communications Link Circuit failure

Code 71(C) SOftware Re-Initialization Detected—on 1 .9L EFI and 2.3L Turbo—or—Idle Tracking Switch failure—on CFI engine -or—Message Center Control Circuit failure—on vehicles with Message Center Control Center—or—Power Interrupt Detected—except vehicles with 3.8L AXOD (automatic overdrive transaxle)

Code 72 (R) Insufficient Manifold Absolute Pressure (MAP) change during Dynamic Response Test

Code 73 (R) Insufficient Throttle Position (TP) change during Dynamic Response Test

Code 74 (R, C) Brake On/Off (BOO) circuit open/not actuated during Self-Test

Code 75 (R) Brake On/Off (BOO) circuit closed/EEC processor input open

Code 76 (R) Insufficient Airflow Output Change During Test

Code 77 (R) Brief Wide Open Throttle (WOT) not sensed during Self-Test/operator error (Dynamic Response/Cylinder Balance Tests)

Code 78 (C) Power Interrupt Detected

Code 79 (O) A/C on/Defrost on during Self-Test

Code 81(C) MAP Sensor Has Not Changing Normally

Code 81(O) Air Management Circuit failure

Code 82 (O) Supercharger Bypass Circuit failure, 3.8L SC engine—or—Air Management Circuit failure, Except 3.8L SC engine—or—EGR Solenoid Circuit failure, 2.3L OHC engine

Code 83 OIC—Low speed fuel pump relay circuit failure

Code 83 (O) High Speed Electro Drive Fan Circuit failure, Except 2.3L OHC and 3.0L SHO engine—or—Low Speed Fuel Pump Relay Circuit failure, 3.0L SHO engine

Code 84 (O) EGR Vacuum Regulator (EVR) circuit failure

Code 84 (R) EGR Solenoid Circuit failure

Code 85 (C) Adaptive Lean Limit Reached

Code 85 (O) Canister Purge (CANP) circuit failure

Code 86 (C) Adaptive Rich Limit Reached

Code 86 (O) Shift Solenoid (SS) circuit failure—or—Wide Open Throttle (WOT) A/C Cutoff Solenoid circuit—on Carbureted engine

Code 87 Fuel Pump circuit fault

Code 88 (C) Loss Of Dual Plug Input control

Code 88 (O) Electro Drive Fan Circuit failure—fuel injected engine—or—Throttle Kicker, feedback carburetor system

Code 89 (O) Transmission solenoid circuit failure.

Code 89 (O) Clutch Converter Override (CCO) circuit failure—or—Exhaust Heat Control (EHC) Solenoid circuit—3.8L CFI engine

Code 91(C) No Heated Exhaust Gas Oxygen (HEGO) sensor switching detected—left HEGO

Code 91(O) Shift Solenoid 1 (SS1) circuit failure.

Code 91(R) Heated Exhaust Gas Oxygen (H EGO) sensor circuit indicates system lean—left HEGO

Code 92 (O) Shift Solenoid Circuit failure

Code 92 (R) Oxygen Sensor Circuit failure

Code 93 (O) Throttle Position Sensor (TPS) input low at maximum DC motor extension—OR—Shift solenoid circuit failure

Code 93 (O) Coast Clutch Solenoid (CCS) circuit failure

Code 94 (O) Torque Converter Clutch (TCC) solenoid circuit failure

Code 94 (O) Converter Clutch Control (CCC) Solenoid circuit failure

Code 94 (R) Thermactor Air System inoperative, left side

Code 95 (O, C) Fuel Pump secondary circuit failure/Fuel Pump circuit open—EEC processor to motor ground

Code 96 (O, C) Fuel Pump secondary circuit failure/Fuel Pump circuit open—battery to EEC processor

Code 97 (O) Overdrive Cancel Indicator Light (OCIL) circuit failure

Code 98 (R) Electronic control assembly failure

Code 98 (O) Electronic Pressure Control (EPC) Driver open in EEC processor

Code 98 (R) Hard fault is present—FMEM mode

Code 99 (O,C) Electronic Pressure Control (EPC) circuit failure

Code 92 (O) Shift Solenoid 2 (SS2) circuit failure.

Code 92 (R) Heated Exhaust Gas Oxygen (HEGO) sensor circuit indicates system rich—left HEGO

Code 93 (O) Throttle Position Sensor Input Low At Max DC Motor Extension, CFI engine—or—Shift Solenoid Circuit failure—Except CFI engine

Code 94 (O) Converter Clutch Solenoid Circuit failure

Code 94 (R) Thermactor Air System Inoperative

Code 95 (O, C) Fuel Pump Circuit failure, ECA To ground

Code 96 (O, C) Fuel Pump Circuit failure

Code 97 (O) Transmission Indicator Circuit failure

Code 98 (O) Electronic Pressure Control Circuit failure

Code 98 (R) Electronic Control Assembly failure

Code 99 (O, C) Electronic Pressure Control Circuit or Transmission Shift failure

Code 99 (R) EEC System Has Not Learned To Control Idle: Ignore Codes 12 & 13

No Code—Unable to Run Self Test or Output Codes, or list does not apply to vehicle tested, refer to service manual.

➡ **This list is to be used as a reference for testing and does not mean a specific component Is defective.**

(O)—Key On, Engine Off
(R)—Engine running
(C)—Continuous Memory

3-Digit DTC'S

1991–95 VEHICLES:

Code 111 System pass

Code 112 Intake Air Temperature (IAT) Sensor circuit below minimum voltage

Code 113 Intake Air Temperature (IAT) Sensor circuit above maximum voltage

Code 114 Intake Air Temperature (IAT) higher or lower than expected

Code 116 Engine Coolant Temperature (ECT) higher or lower than expected

Code 117 Engine Coolant Temperature (ECT) Sensor circuit below minimum voltage

Code 118 Engine Coolant Temperature (ECT) Sensor circuit above maximum voltage

Code 121 Closed throttle voltage higher or lower than expected

Code 121 Indicates Throttle Position voltage inconsistent with Mass Air Flow (MAF) Sensor

Code 122 Throttle Position (TP) Sensor circuit below minimum voltage

Code 123 Throttle Position (TP) Sensor circuit above maximum voltage

Code 124 Throttle Position (TP) Sensor circuit voltage higher than expected

Code 125 Throttle Position (TP) Sensor circuit voltage lower than expected

Code 126 Manifold Absolute Pressure/Barometric Pressure (MAP/BARO) Sensor higher or lower than expected

Code 128 Manifold Absolute Pressure (MAP) Sensor vacuum hose damaged/disconnected

Code 129 Insufficient Manifold Absolute Pressure (MAP)/Mass Air Flow (MAF) change during Dynamic Response Test-KOER

Code 136 Lack of Heated Oxygen Sensor (HO2S-2) switches during KOER, indicates lean—Bank # 2

Code 137 Lack of Heated Oxygen Sensor (HO2S-2) switches during KOER, indicates rich—Bank # 2

Code 138 Cold Start Injector (CSI) flow insufficient—KOER

Code 139 No Heated Oxygen Sensor (HO2NS-2) switches detected—Bank # 2

Code 141 Fuel system indicates lean

Code 144 No Heated Oxygen Sensor (HO2S-1) switches detected—Bank # 1

Code 157 Mass Air Flow (MAF) Sensor circuit below minimum voltage

Code 158 Mass Air Flow (MAF) Sensor circuit above maximum voltage

Code 159 Mass Air Flow (MAF) higher or lower than expected

Code 167 Insufficient Throttle Position (TP) change during Dynamic Response Test—KOER

Code 171 Fuel system at adaptive limits, Heated Oxygen Sensor (HO2S-I) unable to switch—Bank # 1

Code 172 Lack of Heated Oxygen Sensor (HO2S-1) switches, indicates lean—Bank # 1

Code 173 Lack of Heated Oxygen Sensor (HO2S-1) switches, indicates rich—Bank # 1

Code 174 Heated Oxygen Sensor (HO2S) switching time is slow—Right side—1992 vehicles only

Code 175 Fuel system at adaptive limits, Heated Oxygen Sensor (HO2S-2) unable to switch—Bank # 2

Code 176 Lack of Heated Oxygen Sensor (HO2S-2) switches, indicates lean—Bank # 2

Code 177 Lack of Heated Oxygen Sensor (HO$_2$S-2) switches, indicates rich—Bank # 2

Code 178 Heated Oxygen Sensor (HO$_2$S) switching time is slow—Left side—1992 vehicles only

Code 179 Fuel system at lean adaptive limit at part throttle, system rich—Bank # 1

Code 181 Fuel system at rich adaptive limit at part throttle, system lean—Bank # 1

Code 182 Fuel system at lean adaptive limit at idle, system rich—Right side—1992 vehicles only

Code 183 Fuel system at rich adaptive limit at idle, system lean—Right side—1992 vehicles only

Code 184 Mass Air Flow (MAF) higher than expected

Code 185 Mass Air Flow (MAF) lower than expected

Code 186 Injector pulse width higher or Mass Air Flow (MAF) lower than expected (without BARO Sensor)

Code 187 Injector pulse width lower than expected (with BARO Sensor)

Code 187 Injector pulse width lower or Mass Air Flow (MAF) higher than expected (without BARO Sensor)

Code 188 Fuel system at lean adaptive limit at part throttle, system rich—Bank # 2

Code 189 Fuel system at rich adaptive limit at part throttle, system lean—Bank # 2

Code 191 Adaptive fuel lean limit is reached at idle -Left side—1992 vehicles only

Code 192 Adaptive fuel rich limit is reached at idle—Left side—1992 vehicles only

Code 193 Flexible Fuel (FF) Sensor circuit failure

Code 211 Profile Ignition Pickup (PIP) circuit failure

Code 212 Loss of Ignition Diagnostic monitor (1DM) input to Powertrain Control Module (PCM)/SPOUT circuit grounded

Code 213 SPOUT circuit open

Code 214 Cylinder Identification (CID) circuit failure

Code 215 Powertrain Control Module (PCM) detected Coil 1 Primary circuit failure (EI)

Code 216 Powertrain Control Module (PCM) detected Coil 2 Primary circuit failure (EI)

Code 217 Powertrain Control Module (PCM) detected Coil 3 Primary circuit failure (EI)

Code 218 Loss of Ignition Diagnostic Monitor (1DM) signal left side (dual plug EI)

Code 219 Spark Timing defaulted to 10 degrees -SPOUT circuit open (EI)

Code 221 Spark Timing error (EI)

Code 222 Loss of Ignition Diagnostic Monitor (1DM) signal -right side (dual plug EI)

Code 223 Loss of Dual Plug Inhibit (DPI) control (Dual Plug EI)

Code 224 Powertrain Control Module (PCM) detected Coil 1, 2, 3 or 4 Primary circuit failure (Dual Plug EI)

Code 225 Knock not sensed during Dynamic Response Test—KOER

Code 226 Ignition Diagnostic Monitor (1DM) signal not received (EI)

Code 232 Powertrain Control Module (PCM) detected Coil 1, 2, 3 or 4 Primary circuit failure (EI)

Code 238 Powertrain Control Module (PCM) detected Coil 4 Primary circuit failure (EI)

Code 241 Ignition Control Module (1CM) to Powertrain Control Module (PCM) Ignition Diagnostic Monitor (1DM) Pulse Width Transmission error (EI)

Code 244 Cylinder Identification (CID) circuit fault present when Cylinder Balance Test requested

Code 311 Secondary Air Injection (AIR) system inoperative during KOER Bank # 1 with dual HO$_2$S

Code 312 Secondary Air Injection (AIR) misdirected during KOER

Code 313 Secondary Air Injection (AIR) not bypassed during KOER

Code 314 Secondary Air Injection (AIR) system inoperative during KOER—Bank # 2 with dual HO$_2$S

Code 326 EGR (PFE/DPFE) circuit voltage lower than expected

Code 327 EGR (EVP/PFE/DPFE) circuit below minimum voltage

Code 328 EGR (EVP) closed valve voltage lower than expected

Code 332 Insufficient EGR flow detected/EGR Valve opening not detected (EVP/PFE/DPFE)

Code 334 EGR (EVP) closed valve voltage higher than expected

Code 335 EGR (PFE/DPFE) Sensor voltage higher or lower than expected during KOEO

Code 336 Exhaust pressure high/EGR (PFE/DPFE) circuit voltage higher than expected

Code 337 EGR (EVP/PFE/DPFE) circuit above maximum voltage

Code 338 Engine Coolant Temperature (ECT) lower than expected (thermostat test)

Code 339 Engine Coolant Temperature (ECT) higher than expected (thermostat test)

Code 341 Octane Adjust service pin open

Code 411 Cannot control RPM during KOER low rpm check

Code 412 Cannot control RPM during KOER high rpm check

Code 415 Idle Air Control (IAC) system at maximum adaptive lower limit

Code 416 Idle Air Control (IAC) system at upper adaptive learning limit

Code 452 Insufficient input from Vehicle Speed Sensor (VSS) to PCM

Code 453 Servo leaking down (KOER IVSC test)

Code 454 Servo leaking up (KOER IVSC test)

Code 455 Insufficient RPM increase (KOER IVSC test)

Code 456 Insufficient RPM decrease (KOER IVSC test)

Code 457 Speed Control Command Switch(s) circuit not functioning (KOEO IVSC test)

Code 458 Speed Control Command Switch(s) stuck/circuit grounded (KOEO IVSC test)

Code 459 Speed Control ground circuit open (KOEO IVSC test)

Code 511 Powertrain Control Module (PCM) Read Only Memory (ROM) test failure (KOEO)

Code 512 Powertrain Control Module (PCM) Keep Alive Memory (KAM) test failure

Code 513 Powertrain Control Module (PCM) internal voltage failure (KOEO)

Code 519 Power Steering Pressure (PSP) Switch circuit open—KOEO

Code 521 Power Steering Pressure (PSP) Switch circuit did not change states—KOER

Code 522 Vehicle not in park or neutral during KOEO/Park/Neutral Position (PNP) Switch circuit open

Code 524 Low speed Fuel Pump circuit open—battery to PCM

Code 525 Indicates vehicle in gear/A/C on

Code 526 Neutral Pressure Switch (NPS) circuit closed; A/C on -1992 vehicles only

Code 527 Park/Neutral Position (PNP) Switch open—A/C on, KOEO

Code 528 Clutch Pedal Position (CPP) switch circuit failure

Code 529 Data Communications Link (DCL) or PCM circuit failure

Code 532 Cluster Control Assembly (CCA) circuit failure

Code 533 Data Communications Link (DCL) or Electronic Instrument Cluster (EIC) circuit failure

Code 536 Brake On/Off (BOO) circuit failure/not actuated during KOER

Code 538 Insufficient RPM change during KOER Dynamic Response Test

Code 538 Invalid Cylinder Balance Test due to throttle movement during test—SFI only

Code 538 Invalid Cylinder Balance test due to Cylinder Identification (CID) circuit failure

Code 539 A/C on/Defrost on during Self-Test

Code 542 Fuel Pump secondary circuit failure

Code 543 Fuel Pump secondary circuit failure

Code 551 Idle Air Control (IAC) circuit failure—KOEO

Code 552 Secondary Air Injection Bypass (AIRB) circuit failure—KOEO

Code 553 Secondary Air Injection Diverter (AIRD) circuit failure—KOEO

Code 554 Fuel Pressure Regulator Control (FPRC) circuit failure

Code 556 Fuel Pump Relay primary circuit failure

Code 557 Low speed Fuel Pump primary circuit failure

Code 558 EGR Vacuum Regulator (EVR) circuit failure -KOEO

Code 559 Air Conditioning On (ACON) Relay circuit failure-KOEO
Code 563 High Fan Control (HFC) circuit failure—KOEO
Code 564 Fan Control (FC) circuit failure—KOEO
Code 565 Canister Purge (CANP) circuit failure—KOEO
Code 566 3–4 Shift Solenoid circuit failure, A4LD transmission—KOEO
Code 567 Speed Control Vent (SCVNT) circuit failure -KOEO IVSC test
Code 568 Speed Control Vacuum (SCVAC) circuit failure—KOEO IVSC test
Code 569 Auxiliary Canister Purge (CANP2) circuit failure-KOEO
Code 571 EGRA solenoid circuit failure KOEO
Code 572 EGRV solenoid circuit failure KOEO
Code 578 A/C Pressure Sensor circuit shorted (VCRM) mode
Code 579 Insufficient A/C pressure change (VCRM) mode
Code 581 Power to fan circuit over current (VCRM) mode
Code 582 Fan circuit open (VCRM) mode
Code 583 Power to Fuel Pump over current (VCRM) mode
Code 584 Power ground circuit open (Pin 1) (VCRM) mode
Code 585 Power to A/C Clutch over current (VCRM) mode
Code 586 A/C Clutch circuit open (VCRM) mode
Code 587 Variable Control Relay Module (VCRM) communication failure
Code 593 Heated Oxygen Sensor Heater (HO$_2$S HTR)
Code 617 1–2 Shift error
Code 618 2–3 Shift error
Code 619 3–4 Shift error
Code 621 Shift Solenoid 1 (SS1) circuit failure—KOEO
Code 622 Shift Solenoid 2 (SS2) circuit failure—KOEO
Code 623 Transmission Control Indicator Lamp (TCIL) circuit failure
Code 624 Electronic Pressure Control (EPC) circuit failure
Code 625 Electronic Pressure Control (EPC) driver open in PCM
Code 626 Coast Clutch Solenoid (CCS) circuit failure—KOEO
Code 627 Torque Converter Clutch (TCC) solenoid circuit failure
Code 628 Excessive Converter Clutch slippage
Code 629 Torque Converter Clutch (TCC) solenoid circuit failure
Code 631 Transmission Control Indicator Lamp (TCIL) circuit failure—KOEO
Code 632 Transmission Control Switch (TCS) circuit did not change states during KOER
Code 633 4 x 4L Switch closed during KOEO
Code 634 Manual Lever Position (MLP) voltage higher or lower than expected/ error in Transmission Select Switch (TSS) circuit(s)
Code 636 Transmission Oil Temperature (TOT) higher or lower than expected
Code 637 Transmission Oil Temperature (TOT) Sensor circuit above maximum voltage/circuit open
Code 638 Transmission Oil Temperature (TOT) Sensor circuit below minimum voltage/circuit shorted
Code 639 Insufficient input from Transmission Speed Sensor (TSS)
Code 641 Shift Solenoid 3 (SS3) circuit failure
Code 643 Torque Converter Clutch (TCC) circuit failure
Code 645 Incorrect gear ratio obtained for first gear
Code 646 Incorrect gear ratio obtained for second gear
Code 647 Incorrect gear ratio obtained for third gear
Code 648 Incorrect gear ratio obtained for fourth gear
Code 649 Electronic Pressure Control (EPC) higher or lower than expected
Code 651 Electronic Pressure Control (EPC) circuit failure
Code 652 Torque Converter Clutch (TCC) Solenoid circuit failure
Code 654 Manual Lever Position (MLP) Sensor not indicating park during KOEO
Code 655 Manual Lever Position (MLP) Sensor indicating not in neutral during Self-Test
Code 656 Torque Converter Clutch (TCC) continuous slip error
Code 657 Transmission Over Temperature condition occurred
Code 659 High vehicle speed in park indicated
Code 667 Transmission Range sensor circuit voltage below minimum voltage

Code 668 Transmission Range sensor circuit voltage above maximum voltage
Code 675 Transmission Range sensor circuit voltage out of range
Code 691 4x4 Low switch open or short circuit
Code 692 Transmission state does not match calculated ratio
Code 998 Hard fault present—FMEM Mode

➡️If specific cylinder banks or sides are referred to in any of the above codes, but the vehicle code is being obtained from has a 4 cylinder engine, or only one Oxygen Sensor, disregard the bank side reference, but the code definition and components it pertains to is always the same.

EEC-V SYSTEM DIAGNOSTIC TROUBLE CODES

1994 Light Trucks

DTC P0102 Mass Air Flow (MAF) Sensor circuit low input
DTC P0103 Mass Air Flow (MAF) Sensor circuit high input
DTC P0112 Intake Air Temperature (IAT) Sensor circuit low input
DTC P0113 Intake Air Temperature (IAT) Sensor high input
DTC P0117 Engine Coolant Temperature (ECT) low input
DTC P0118 Engine Coolant Temperature (ECT) Sensor circuit high input
DTC P0122 Throttle Position (TP) Sensor circuit low input
DTC P0123 Throttle Position (TP) Sensor high input
DTC P0125 Insufficient coolant temperature to enter closed loop fuel control
DTC P0132 Upstream Heated Oxygen Sensor (HO$_2$S 11) circuit high voltage (Bank #1)
DTC P0135 Heated Oxygen Sensor Heater (HTR 11) circuit malfunction
DTC P0138 Downstream Heated Oxygen Sensor (HO$_2$S 12) circuit high voltage (Bank #1)
DTC P0140 Heated Oxygen Sensor (HO$_2$S 12) circuit no activity detected (Bank #1)
DTC P0141 Heated Oxygen Sensor Heater (HTR 12) circuit malfunction
DTC P0152 Upstream Heated Oxygen Sensor (HO$_2$S 21) circuit high voltage (Bank #2)
DTC P0155 Heated Oxygen Sensor Heater (HTR 21) circuit malfunction
DTC P0158 Downstream Heated Oxygen Sensor (HO$_2$S 22) circuit high voltage (Bank #2)
DTC P0160 Heated Oxygen Sensor (HO$_2$S 12) circuit no activity detected (Bank #2)
DTC P0161 Heated Oxygen Sensor Heater (HTR 22) circuit malfunction
DTC P0171 System (adaptive fuel) too lean (Bank #1)
DTC P0172 System (adaptive fuel) too lean (Bank #1)
DTC P0174 System (adaptive fuel) too lean (Bank #1)
DTC P0175 System (adaptive fuel) too lean (Bank #1)
DTC P0300 Random misfire detected
DTC P0301 Cylinder #1 misfire detected
DTC P0302 Cylinder #2 misfire detected
DTC P0303 Cylinder #3 misfire detected
DTC P0304 Cylinder #4 misfire detected
DTC P0305 Cylinder #5 misfire detected
DTC P0306 Cylinder #6 misfire detected
DTC P0307 Cylinder #7 misfire detected
DTC P0308 Cylinder #8 misfire detected
DTC P0320 Ignition engine speed (Profile Ignition Pickup) input circuit malfunction
DTC P0340 Camshaft Position (CMP) sensor circuit malfunction (CID)
DTC P0402 Exhaust Gas Recirculation (EGR) excess flow detected (valve open at idle)
DTC P0420 Catalyst system efficiency below threshold (Bank #1)
DTC P0430 Catalyst system efficiency below threshold (Bank #2)
DTC P0443 Evaporative emission control system Canister Purge (CANP) Control Valve circuit malfunction
DTC P0500 Vehicle Speed Sensor (VSS) malfunction
DTC P0505 Idle Air Control (IAC) system malfunction

DTC P0605 Powertrain Control Module (PCM)—Read Only Memory (ROM) test error
DTC P0703 Brake On/Off (BOO) switch input malfunction
DTC P0707 Manual Lever Position (MLP) sensor circuit low input
DTC P0708 Manual Lever Position (MLP) sensor circuit high input
DTC P0720 Output Shaft Speed (OSS) sensor circuit malfunction
DTC P0741 Torque Converter Clutch (TCC) system incorrect mechanical performance
DTC P0743 Torque Converter Clutch (TCC) system electrical failure
DTC P0750 Shift Solenoid #1(SS1) circuit malfunction
DTC P0751 Shift Solenoid #1(SS1) performance
DTC P0755 Shift Solenoid #2 (SS2) circuit malfunction
DTC P0756 Shift Solenoid #2 (SS2) performance
DTC P1000 OBD-II Monitor Testing not complete
DTC P1100 Mass Air Flow (MAF) sensor intermittent
DTC P1101 Mass Air Flow (MAF) sensor out of Self-Test range
DTC P1112 Intake Air Temperature (IAT) sensor intermittent
DTC P1116 Engine Coolant Temperature (ECT) sensor out of Self-Test range
DTC P1117 Engine Coolant Temperature (ECT) sensor intermittent
DTC P1120 Throttle Position (TP) sensor out of range low
DTC P1121 Throttle Position (TP) sensor inconsistent with MAF sensor
DTC P1124 Throttle Position (TP) sensor out of Self-Test range
DTC P1125 Throttle Position (TP) sensor circuit intermittent
DTC P1130 Lack of HO$_2$S 11 switch, adaptive fuel at limit
DTC P1131 Lack of HO$_2$S 11 switch, sensor indicates lean (Bank #1)
DTC P1132 Lack of HO$_2$S 11 switch, sensor indicates rich (Bank #1)
DTC P1137 Lack of HO$_2$S 12 switch, sensor indicates lean (Bank #1)
DTC P1138 Lack of HO$_2$S 12 switch, sensor indicates rich (Bank #1)
DTC P1150 Lack of HO$_2$S 21 switch, adaptive fuel at limit
DTC P1151 Lack of HO$_2$S 21 switch, sensor indicates lean (Bank #2)
DTC P1152 Lack of HO$_2$S 21 switch, sensor indicates rich (Bank #2)
DTC P1157 Lack of HO$_2$S 22 switch, sensor indicates lean (Bank #2)
DTC P1158 Lack of HO$_2$S 22 switch, sensor indicates rich (Bank #2)
DTC P1351 Ignition Diagnostic Monitor (1DM) circuit input malfunction
DTC P1352 Ignition coil A primary circuit malfunction
DTC P1353 Ignition coil B primary circuit malfunction
DTC P1354 Ignition coil C primary circuit malfunction
DTC P1355 Ignition coil D primary circuit malfunction
DTC P1364 Ignition coil primary circuit malfunction
DTC P1390 Octane Adjust (OCT ADJ) out of Self-Test range
DTC P1400 Differential Pressure Feedback Electronic (DPFE) sensor circuit low voltage detected
DTC P1401 Differential Pressure Feedback Electronic (DPFE) sensor circuit high voltage detected
DTC P1403 Differential Pressure Feedback Electronic (DPFE) sensor hoses reversed
DTC P1405 Differential Pressure Feedback Electronic (DPFE) sensor upstream hose off or plugged
DTC P1406 Differential Pressure Feedback Electronic (DPFE) sensor downstream hose off or plugged
DTC P1407 Exhaust Gas Recirculation (EGR) no flow detected (valve stuck closed or inoperative)
DTC P1408 Exhaust Gas Recirculation (EGR) flow out of Self-Test range
DTC P1473 Fan Secondary High with fan(s) off
DTC P1474 Low Fan Control primary circuit malfunction
DTC P1479 High Fan Control primary circuit malfunction
DTC P1480 Fan Secondary low with low fan on
DTC P1481 Fan Secondary low with high fan on
DTC P1500 Vehicle Speed Sensor (VSS) circuit intermittent
DTC P1505 Idle Air Control (IAC) system at adaptive clip
DTC P1605 Powertrain Control Module (PCM)—Keep Alive Memory (KAM) test error
DTC P1703 Brake On/Off (BOO) switch out of Self-Test range
DTC P1705 Manual Lever Position (MLP) sensor out of Self-Test range
DTC P1711 Transmission Fluid Temperature (TFT) sensor out of Self-Test range

DTC P1742 Torque Converter Clutch (TCC) solenoid mechanically failed (turns MIL on)
DTC P1743 Torque Converter Clutch (TCC) solenoid mechanically failed (turns TCIL on)
DTC P1744 Torque Converter Clutch (TCC) system mechanically stuck in off position
DTC P1746 Electronic Pressure Control (EPC) solenoid circuit low input (open circuit)
DTC P1747 Electronic Pressure Control (EPC) solenoid circuit high input (short circuit)
DTC P1751 Shift Solenoid #1(SS1) performance
DTC P1756 Shift Solenoid #2 (SS2) performance
DTC P1780 Transmission Control Switch (TCS) circuit out of Self-Test range

1995 Light Trucks

DTC P0102 Mass Air Flow (MAF) Sensor circuit low input
DTC P0103 Mass Air Flow (MAF) Sensor circuit high input
DTC P0112 Intake Air Temperature (IAT) Sensor circuit low input
DTC P0113 Intake Air Temperature (IAT) Sensor high input
DTC P0117 Engine Coolant Temperature (ECT) low input
DTC P0118 Engine Coolant Temperature (ECT) Sensor circuit high input
DTC P0121 In range operating Throttle Position (TP) sensor circuit failure
DTC P0122 Throttle Position (TP) Sensor circuit low input
DTC P0123 Throttle Position (TP) Sensor high input
DTC P0125 Insufficient coolant temperature to enter closed loop fuel control
DTC P0126 Insufficient coolant temperature for stable operation
DTC P0131 Upstream Heated Oxygen Sensor (HO$_2$S 11) circuit out of range low voltage (bank #1)
DTC P0132 Upstream Heated Oxygen Sensor (HO$_2$S 11) circuit high voltage (Bank #1)
DTC P0133 Upstream Heated Oxygen Sensor (HO$_2$S 11) circuit slow response (Bank #1)
DTC P0135 Heated Oxygen Sensor Heater (HTR 11) circuit malfunction
DTC P0136 Downstream Heated Oxygen Sensor (HO$_2$S 12) circuit malfunction (Bank #1
DTC P0138 Downstream Heated Oxygen Sensor (HO$_2$S 12) circuit high voltage (Bank #1)
DTC P0140 Heated Oxygen Sensor (HO$_2$S 12) circuit no activity detected (Bank #1)
DTC P0141 Heated Oxygen Sensor Heater (HTR 12) circuit malfunction
DTC P0151 Upstream Heated Oxygen Sensor (HO$_2$S 21) circuit out of range low voltage (Bank #2)
DTC P0152 Upstream Heated Oxygen Sensor (HO$_2$S 21) circuit high voltage (Bank #2)
DTC P0153 Upstream Heated Oxygen Sensor (HO$_2$S 21) circuit slow response (Bank #2)
DTC P0155 Heated Oxygen Sensor Heater (HTR 21) circuit malfunction
DTC P0156 Downstream Heated Oxygen Sensor (HO$_2$S 22) circuit malfunction (Bank #2)
DTC P0158 Downstream Heated Oxygen Sensor (HO$_2$S 22) circuit high voltage (Bank #2)
DTC P0160 Heated Oxygen Sensor (HO$_2$S 12) circuit no activity detected (Bank #2)
DTC P0161 Heated Oxygen Sensor Heater (HTR 22) circuit malfunction
DTC P0171 System (adaptive fuel) too lean (Bank #1)
DTC P0172 System (adaptive fuel) too rich (Bank #1)
DTC P0174 System (adaptive fuel) too lean (Bank #2)
DTC P0175 System (adaptive fuel) too rich (Bank #2)
DTC P0222 Throttle Position Sensor B (TP-B) circuit low input
DTC P0223 Throttle Position Sensor B (TP-B) circuit high input
DTC P0230 Fuel pump primary circuit malfunction
DTC P0231 Fuel pump secondary circuit low
DTC P0232 Fuel pump secondary circuit high
DTC P0300 Random misfire detected
DTC P0301 Cylinder #1 misfire detected

DTC P0302 Cylinder #2 misfire detected
DTC P0303 Cylinder #3 misfire detected
DTC P0304 Cylinder #4 misfire detected
DTC P0305 Cylinder #5 misfire detected
DTC P0306 Cylinder #6 misfire detected
DTC P0307 Cylinder #7 misfire detected
DTC P0308 Cylinder #8 misfire detected
DTC P0320 Ignition engine speed (Profile Ignition Pickup) input circuit malfunction
DTC P0340 Camshaft Position (CMP) sensor circuit malfunction (CID)
DTC P0350 Ignition Coil primary circuit malfunction
DTC P0351 Ignition Coil A primary circuit malfunction
DTC P0352 Ignition Coil B primary circuit malfunction
DTC P0353 Ignition Coil C primary circuit malfunction
DTC P0354 Ignition Coil D primary circuit malfunction
DTC P0400 Exhaust Gas Recirculation (EGR) flow malfunction
DTC P0401 Exhaust Gas Recirculation (EGR) flow insufficient detected
DTC P0402 Exhaust Gas Recirculation (EGR) excess flow detected (valve open at idle)
DTC P0411 Secondary Air Injection system incorrect flow detected
DTC P0412 Secondary Air Injection system control valve malfunction
DTC P0420 Catalyst system efficiency below threshold (Bank #1)
DTC P0430 Catalyst system efficiency below threshold (Bank #2)
DTC P0443 Evaporative emission control system Canister Purge (CANP) Control Valve circuit malfunction
DTC P0500 Vehicle Speed Sensor (VSS) malfunction
DTC P0505 Idle Air Control (IAC) system malfunction
DTC P0603 Powertrain Control Module (PCM)—Keep Alive Memory (KAM) test error
DTC P0605 Powertrain Control Module (PCM)—Read Only Memory (ROM) test error
DTC P0704 Clutch Pedal Position (CPP) switch input circuit malfunction
DTC P0703 Brake On/Off (BOO) switch input malfunction
DTC P0707 Manual Lever Position (MLP) sensor circuit low input
DTC P0708 Manual Lever Position (MLP) sensor circuit high input
DTC P0712 Transmission Fluid Temperature (TFT) sensor circuit low input
DTC P0713 Transmission Fluid Temperature (TFT) sensor circuit high input
DTC P0715 Turbine Shaft Speed (TSS) sensor circuit malfunction
DTC P0720 Output Shaft Speed (OSS) sensor circuit malfunction
DTC P0731 Incorrect ratio for first gear
DTC P0732 Incorrect ratio for second gear
DTC P0733 Incorrect ratio for third gear
DTC P0734 Incorrect ratio for fourth gear
DTC P0736 Reverse incorrect gear
DTC P0741 Torque Converter Clutch (TCC) system incorrect mechanical performance
DTC P0746 Electronic Pressure Control (EPC) solenoid performance
DTC P0743 Torque Converter Clutch (TCC) system electrical failure
DTC P0750 Shift Solenoid #1(SS1) circuit malfunction
DTC P0751 Shift Solenoid #1(SS1) performance
DTC P0755 Shift Solenoid #2 (SS2) circuit malfunction
DTC P0756 Shift Solenoid #2 (SS2) performance
DTC P0760 Shift Solenoid #3 (SS3) circuit malfunction
DTC P0761 Shift Solenoid #3 (SS3) performance
DTC P0781 1 to 2 shift error
DTC P0782 2 to 3 shift error
DTC P0783 3 to 4 shift error
DTC P0784 4 to 5 shift error
DTC P1000 OBD-II Monitor Testing not complete
DTC U1039 OBD-II Monitor not complete
DTC UIOS1 Brake switch signal missing or incorrect
DTC P1100 Mass Air Flow (MAF) sensor intermittent
DTC P1101 Mass Air Flow (MAF) sensor out of Self-Test range
DTC P1112 Intake Air Temperature (IAT) sensor intermittent
DTC P1116 Engine Coolant Temperature (ECT) sensor out of Self-Test range

DTC P1117 Engine Coolant Temperature (ECT) sensor intermittent
DTC P1120 Throttle Position (TP) sensor out of range low
DTC P1121 Throttle Position (TP) sensor inconsistent with MAF sensor
DTC P1124 Throttle Position (TP) sensor out of Self-Test range
DTC P1125 Throttle Position (TP) sensor circuit intermittent
DTC P1130 Lack of HO$_2$S 11 switch, adaptive fuel at limit
DTC P1131 Lack of HO$_2$S 11 switch, sensor indicates lean (Bank #1)
DTC P1132 Lack of HO$_2$S 11 switch, sensor indicates rich (Bank #1)
DTC U1135 Ignition switch signal missing or incorrect
DTC P1137 Lack of HO$_2$S 12 switch, sensor indicates lean (Bank #1)
DTC P1138 Lack of HO$_2$S 12 switch, sensor indicates rich (Bank #1)
DTC P1150 Lack of HO$_2$S 21 switch, adaptive fuel at limit
DTC P1151 Lack of HO$_2$S 21 switch, sensor indicates lean (Bank #2)
DTC P1152 Lack of HO$_2$S 21 switch, sensor indicates rich (Bank #2)
DTC P1157 Lack of HO$_2$S 22 switch, sensor indicates lean (Bank #2)
DTC P1158 Lack of HO$_2$S 22 switch, sensor indicates rich (Bank #2)
DTC P1220 Series Throttle Control malfunction
DTC P1224 Throttle Position Sensor (TP-B) out of Self-test range
DTC P1233 Fuel Pump driver Module off-line
DTC P1234 Fuel Pump driver Module off-line
DTC P1235 Fuel Pump control out of range
DTC P1236 Fuel Pump control out of range
DTC P1237 Fuel Pump secondary circuit malfunction
DTC P1238 Fuel Pump secondary circuit malfunction
DTC P1260 THEFT detected—engine disabled
DTC P1270 Engine RPM or vehicle speed limiter reached
DTC P1351 Ignition Diagnostic Monitor (1DM) circuit input malfunction
DTC P1352 Ignition coil A primary circuit malfunction
DTC P1353 Ignition coil B primary circuit malfunction
DTC P1354 Ignition coil C primary circuit malfunction
DTC P1355 Ignition coil D primary circuit malfunction
DTC P1358 Ignition Diagnostic Monitor (1DM) signal out of Self-Test range
DTC P1359 Spark output circuit malfunction
DTC P1364 Ignition coil primary circuit malfunction
DTC P1390 Octane Adjust (OCT ADJ) out of Self-Test range
DTC P1400 Differential Pressure Feedback Electronic (DPFE) sensor circuit low voltage detected
DTC P1401 Differential Pressure Feedback Electronic (DPFE) sensor circuit high voltage detected
DTC P1403 Differential Pressure Feedback Electronic (DPFE) sensor hoses reversed
DTC P1405 Differential Pressure Feedback Electronic (DPFE) sensor upstream hose off or plugged
DTC P1406 Differential Pressure Feedback Electronic (DPFE) sensor downstream hose off or plugged
DTC P1407 Exhaust Gas Recirculation (EGR) no flow detected (valve stuck closed or inoperative)
DTC P1408 Exhaust Gas Recirculation (EGR) flow out of Self-Test range
DTC P1409 Electronic Vacuum Regulator (EVR) control circuit malfunction
DTC P1414 Secondary Air Injection system monitor circuit high voltage
DTC P1443 Evaporative emission control system—vacuum system purge control solenoid or purge control valve malfunction
DTC P1444 4- Purge Flow Sensor (PFS) circuit low input
DTC P1445 Purge Flow Sensor (PFS) circuit high input
DTC U1451 Lack of response from Passive Anti-Theft system (PATS) module—engine disabled
DTC P1460 Wide Open Throttle Air Conditioning Cut-off (WAC) circuit malfunction
DTC P1461 Air Conditioning Pressure (ACP) sensor circuit low input
DTC P1462 Air Conditioning Pressure (ACP) sensor circuit high input
DTC P1463 Air Conditioning Pressure (ACP) sensor insufficient pressure change
DTC P1469 Low air conditioning cycling period
DTC P1473 Fan Secondary High with fan(s) off
DTC P1474 Low Fan Control primary circuit malfunction

DTC P1479 High Fan Control primary circuit malfunction
DTC P1480 Fan Secondary low with low fan on
DTC P1481 Fan Secondary low with high fan on
DTC P1500 Vehicle Speed Sensor (VSS) circuit intermittent
DTC P1505 Idle Air Control (IAC) system at adaptive clip
DTC P1506 Idle Air control (IAC) over speed error
DTC P1518 Intake Manifold Runner Control (IMRC) malfunction (stuck open)
DTC P1519 Intake Manifold Runner Control (IMRC) malfunction (stuck closed)
DTC P1520 Intake Manifold Runner Control (IMRC) circuit malfunction
DTC P1507 Idle Air control (IAC) under speed error
DTC P1605 Powertrain Control Module (PCM)—Keep Alive Memory (KAM) test error
DTC P1650 Power steering Pressure (PSP) switch out of Self-Test range
DTC P1651 Power steering Pressure (PSP) switch input malfunction
DTC P1701 Reverse engagement error
DTC P1703 Brake On/Off (BOO) switch out of Self-Test range
DTC P1705 Manual Lever Position (MLP) sensor out of Self-Test range
DTC P1709 Park or Neutral Position (PNP) switch out of Self-test range
DTC P1729 4X4 Low switch error
DTC P1711 Transmission Fluid Temperature (TFT) sensor out of Self-Test range
DTC P1741 Torque Converter Clutch (TOC) control error
DTC P1742 Torque Converter Clutch (TCC) solenoid mechanically failed (turns MIL on)
DTC P1743 Torque Converter Clutch (TCC) solenoid mechanically failed (turns TOIL on)
DTC P1744 Torque Converter Clutch (TCC) system mechanically stuck in off position
DTC P1748 Electronic Pressure Control (EPC) solenoid circuit low input (open circuit)
DTC P1747 Electronic Pressure Control (EPC) solenoid circuit high input (short circuit)
DTC P1749 Electric Pressure Control (EPC) solenoid failed low
DTC P1751 Shift Solenoid #1(SS1) performance
DTC P1756 Shift Solenoid #2 (SS2) performance
DTC P1780 Transmission Control Switch (TCS) circuit out of Self-Test range

General Motors Truck

SELF-DIAGNOSTICS

Automotive manufacturers have developed on-board computers to control engines, transmissions and many other components. These on-board computers with dozens of sensors and actuators have become almost impossible to test without the help of electronic test equipment.

One of these electronic test devices has become the on-board computer itself. The Powertrain Control Modules (PCM), sometimes called the Electronic Control Module (ECM), used on toadies vehicles has a built in self testing system. This self test ability is called self-diagnosis. The self-diagnosis system will test many or all of the sensors and controlled devices for proper function. When a malfunction is detected this system will store a code in memory that's related to that specific circuit. The computer can later be accessed to obtain fault codes recorded in memory using the procedures for Reading Codes. This helps narrow down what area to begin testing.

Fault code meanings can vary from year to year even on the same model. It is extremely important after retrieving a fault code to verify its meaning with a proper manual. Servicing a code incorrectly will not only lead to the wrong conclusion but could also cause damage if tested or serviced incorrectly.

Since the control module is programmed to recognize the presence and value of electrical inputs, it will also note the lack of a signal or a radical change in values. It will, for example, react to the loss of signal from the vehicle speed sensor or note that engine coolant temperature has risen

beyond acceptable (programmed) limits. Once a fault is recognized, a numeric code is assigned and held in memory. The dashboard warning lamp—CHECK ENGINE or SERVICE ENGINE SOON—will illuminate to advise the operator that the system has detected a fault.

More than one code may be stored. Although not every engine uses every code and the same code may carry different meanings relative to each engine or engine family. For example, on the 3.3L (VIN N), Code 46 indicates a fault found in the power steering pressure switch circuit. The same code on the 5.7L (VIN F) engine indicates a fault in the VATS anti-theft system. The list of codes and descriptions can be found in the 'Code Descriptions' section of the manual.

In the event of an PCM failure, the system will default to a pre-programmed set of values. These are compromise values which allow the engine to operate, although possibly at reduced efficiency. This is also known as the default, limp-in or back-up mode. Driveability is almost always affected when the PCM enters this mode.

Service Precautions

- Protect the on-board solid-state components from rough handling or extremes of temperature.
- Always turn the ignition OFF when connecting or disconnecting battery cables, jumper cables, or a battery charger. Failure to do this can result in PCM or other electronic component damage.
- Remove the PCM before any arc welding is performed to the vehicle
- Electronic components are very susceptible to damage caused by electrostatic discharge (static electricity). To prevent electronic component damage, do not touch the control module connector pins or soldered components on the control module circuit board.

Visual Inspection

This is possibly the most critical step of diagnosis. A detailed examination of all connectors, wiring and vacuum hoses can often lead to a repair without further diagnosis. Also, take into consideration if the vehicle has been serviced recently? Sometimes things get reconnected in the wrong place, or not at all. A careful inspector will check the undersides of hoses as well as the integrity of hard-to-reach hoses blocked by the air cleaner or other components. Correct routing for vacuum hoses can be obtained from your specific vehicle service manual or Vehicle Emission Control Information (VECI) label in the engine compartment of the vehicle. Wiring should be checked carefully for any sign of strain, burning, crimping or terminals pulled-out from a connector.

Checking connectors at components or in harnesses is required; usually, pushing them together will reveal a loose fit. Also, check electrical connectors for corroded, bent, damaged, improperly seated pins, and bad wire crimps to terminals. Pay particular attention to ground circuits, making sure they are not loose or corroded. Remember to inspect connectors and hose fittings at components not mounted on the engine, such as the evaporative canister or relays mounted on the fender aprons. Any component or wiring in the vicinity of a fluid leak or spillage should be given extra attention during inspection.

➡**There are many problems with connectors on electronic engine control systems. Due to the low voltage signals that these systems use any dirt, corrosion or damage will affect their operation. Note that some connectors use a special grease on the contacts to prevent corrosion. Do not wipe this grease off, it is a special type for this purpose. You can obtain this grease from your vehicle dealer.**

Additionally, inspect maintenance items such as belt condition and tension, battery charge and condition and the radiator cap carefully. Any of these very simple items may affect the system enough to set a fault.

Dashboard Warning Lamp

♦ See Figure 19

The primary function of the dash warning lamp is to advise the operator that a fault has been detected, and, in most cases, a code stored. Under normal conditions, the dash warning lamp will illuminate when the ignition

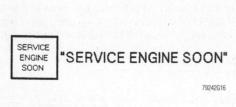

79242G16

Fig. 19 The Check Engine or Service Engine Soon (MIL) lamp is used for reading trouble codes

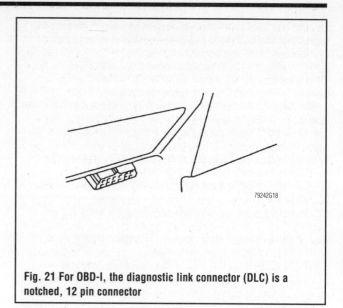

79242G18

Fig. 21 For OBD-I, the diagnostic link connector (DLC) is a notched, 12 pin connector

is turned ON. Once the engine is started and running, the PCM will perform a system check and extinguish the warning lamp if no fault is found.

Additionally, the dash warning lamp can be used to retrieve stored codes after the system is placed in the Diagnostic Mode. Codes are transmitted as a series of flashes with short or long pauses. When the system is placed in the Field Service Mode (available on fuel injected model), the dash lamp will indicate open loop or closed loop function.

Intermittent Problems

If a fault occurs intermittently, such as a loose connector pin breaking contact as the vehicle hits a bump, the PCM will note the fault as it occurs and energize the dash warning lamp. If the problem self-corrects, as with the terminal pin again making contact, the dash lamp will extinguish after 10 seconds but a code will remain stored in the PCM memory. When an unexpected code appears during an intermittent failure that self-corrected; the codes are still useful in diagnosis and should not be discounted.

Diagnostic Connector Location

▶ **See Figures 20 and 21**

The Assembly Line Communication Link (ALCL) or Assembly Line Diagnostic Link (ALDL) is a Diagnostic Link Connector (DLC) located in the

passenger compartment. It has terminals which are used in the assembly plant to check that the engine is operating properly before it leaves the plant.

This DLC is where you connect you jumper the terminals to place the engine control computer into self-diagnostic mode. The standard term DLC is sometimes referred to as the ALCL or the ALDL in different manuals. Either way it is referred to, they all still perform the same function.

READING CODES

▶ **See Figure 22**

Since the inception of electronic engine management systems on General Motors vehicles, there has been a variety of connectors provided to the technician for retrieving Diagnostic Trouble Codes (DTC)s. Additionally, there have been a number of different names given to these connectors over the years; Assembly Line Communication Link (ALCL), Assembly Line Diagnostic Link (ALDL), Data Link Connector (DLC). Actually when the system was initially introduced to the 49 states in 1979, early 1980, there was no connector used at all. On these early vehicles there was a green spade terminal taped to the ECM harness and connected to the diagnostic enable line at the computer. When this terminal was grounded with the key ON, the system would flash any stored diagnostic trouble codes. The introduction of

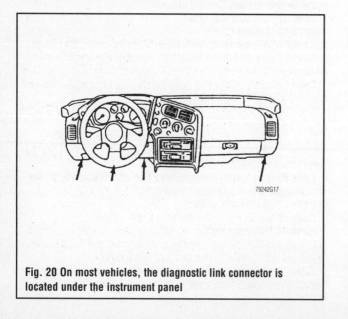

79242G17

Fig. 20 On most vehicles, the diagnostic link connector is located under the instrument panel

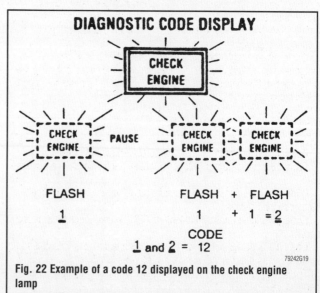

79242G19

Fig. 22 Example of a code 12 displayed on the check engine lamp

the ALDL was found to be a much more convenient way of retrieving fault codes. This connector was located underneath the instrument panel on most GM vehicles, however on some models it will not be found there. On early Corvettes the ALDL is located underneath the ashtray, it can be found in the glove compartment of some early FWD Oldsmobiles, and between the seats in the Pontiac Fiero. The connector was first introduced as a square connector with four terminals, then progressed to a flat five terminal connector, and finally to what is still used in 1993, a 12 terminal double row connector. To access stored Diagnostic Trouble Codes (DTC) from the square connector, turn the ignition ON and identify the diagnostic enable terminal (usually a white wire with a black tracer) and ground it. The flat five terminal connector is identified from left to right as A, B, C, D, and E. There is a space between terminal D and E which permits a spade to be inserted for the purposes of diagnostics when the ignition key is ON. On this connector terminal D is the diagnostic enable line, and E is a ground. The 12 terminal double row connector has been continually expanded through the years as vehicles acquired more on-board electronic systems such as Anti-lock Brakes. Despite this the terminals used for engine code retrieval have remained the same. The 12 terminal connector is identified from right-to-left on the top row A-F, and on the bottom row from left-to-right, G-L. To access engine codes turn the ignition ON and insert a jumper between terminals A and B. Terminal A is a ground, and terminal B is the diagnostic request line. Stored trouble codes can be read through the flashing of the Check Engine Light or on later vehicles the Service Engine Soon lamp. Trouble codes are identified by the timed flash of the indicator light. When diagnostics are first entered the light will flash once, pause; then two quick flashes.

This reads as DTC 12 which indicates that the diagnostic system is working. This code will flash indefinitely if there are no stored trouble codes. If codes are stored in memory, Code 12 will flash three times before the next code appears. Codes are displayed in the next highest numerical sequence. For example, Code 13 would be displayed next if it was stored in memory and would read as follow: flash, pause, flash, flash, flash, long pause, repeat twice. This sequence will continue until all codes have been displayed, and then start all over again with Code 12.

CLEARING CODES

To clear any Diagnostic Trouble Codes (DTC's) from the PCM memory, either to determine if the malfunction will occur again or because repair has been completed, power feed must be disconnected for at least 30 seconds. Depending on how the vehicle is equipped, the system power feed can be disconnected at the positive battery terminal pigtail, the inline fuseholder that originates at the positive connection at the battery, or the ECM/PCM fuse in the fuse block. The negative battery terminal may be disconnected but other on-board memory data such as preset radio tuning will also be lost. To prevent system damage, the ignition switch must be in the OFF position when disconnecting or reconnecting power.

When using a Diagnostic Computer such as Tech 1, or equivalent scan tool to read the diagnostic trouble codes, clearing the codes is done in the same manner. On some systems, DTC's may be cleared through the Tech 1, or equivalent scan tool.

DIAGNOSTIC TROUBLE CODES

Code 12 No engine RPM reference pulses—System Normal
Code 13 Oxygen Sensor (O2S) circuit open—left side on 2 sensor system
Code 14 Engine Coolant Temperature (ECT) sensor -possible circuit high or shorted sensor
Code 15 Engine Coolant Temperature (ECT) sensor -circuit low or open circuit
Code 16 Direct ignition system (DIS), fault line circuit or Distributor ignition system (low resolution pulse) or Missing 2x reference circuit or OPTI-Spark ignition timing system (low resolution pulse) or System voltage out of range

Code 17 Camshaft Position Sensor (CPS) or spark reference circuit error
Code 18 Crank/Cam error
Code 19 Crankshaft Position Sensor (CPS) circuit
Code 21 Throttle Position (TP) sensor circuit—signal voltage out of range, probably high
Code 22 Throttle Position (TP) sensor circuit—signal voltage low
Code 23 Intake Air Temperature (IAT or MAT) sensor circuit temperature out of range, low or Open or grounded M/C solenoid Feedback Carburetor system
Code 24 Vehicle Speed Sensor (VSS) circuit
Code 25 Intake Air Temperature (IAT or MAT) sensor circuit temperature out of range, high
Code 26 Quad-Driver Module #1 circuit or Transaxle gear switch circuit
Code 27 Quad-Driver Module circuit or Transaxle gear switch, probably 2nd gear switch circuit
Code 28 Quad-Driver Module (QDM) #2 circuit or Transaxle gear switch, probably 3rd gear switch circuit
Code 29 Transaxle gear switch, probably 4th gear switch circuit
Code 31 Camshaft sensor circuit fault or Park/Neutral Position (PNP) switch circuit or Wastegate circuit signal
Code 32 Exhaust Gas Recirculation (EGR) circuit fault or Barometric Pressure Sensor circuit low Feedback Carburetor system
Code 33 Manifold Absolute Pressure (MAP) sensor—signal voltage out of range, high or Mass Air Flow (MAF) sensor—signal voltage out of range, probably high
Code 34—Manifold Absolute Pressure (MAP) sensor—circuit out of range voltage, low or Mass Air Flow (MAF) sensor circuit (gm/sec low)
Code 35—Idle Air Control (IAC) or idle speed error or Idle Speed Control (ISO) circuit throttle switch shorted Feedback Carburetor system
Code 36 Ignition system circuit error or Transaxle shift problem—4T60E Transaxle
Code 38 Brake input circuit fault—Torque converter clutch signal
Code 39 Clutch input circuit fault—Torque converter clutch signal
Code 41 Cam sensor or cylinder select circuit fault ignition control (IC) reference pulse system fault or Electronic Spark Timing (EST) circuit open or shorted
Code 42 Electronic Spark Timing (EST) circuit grounded or Ignition Control (IC) circuit grounded or faulty bypass line
Code 43 Knock Sensor (KS) or Electronic Spark Control (ESC) circuit fault
Code 44 Oxygen Sensor (O2S), left side on 2 sensor system lean exhaust indicated
Code 45 Oxygen Sensor (O2S), left side on 2 sensor system rich exhaust indicated
Code 46 Personal Automotive Security System (PASSKey II) circuit or Power Steering Pressure Switch (PSPS) circuit
Code 47 PCM-BCM data circuit
Code 48 Misfire diagnosis
Code 51 Calibration error, faulty MEM-CAL, ECM or EEPROM failure
Code 52 Engine oil temperature sensor circuit, low temperature indicated or Fuel Calpac missing or Over voltage condition or EGR Circuit fault
Code 53 Battery voltage error or EGR problem or Personal Automotive Security System (PASS-Key) circuit
Code 54 EGR #2 problem or Fuel pump circuit (low voltage) or Shorted mixture control solenoid circuit Feedback Carburetor system
Code 55 A/D Converter error, PCM error or not grounded, EGR #3 problem, Fuel lean monitor, Grounded voltage reference, faulty oxygen sensor or fuel lean Feedback Carburetor system
Code 56 Quad-Driver Module (QDM) #2 circuit or Secondary air inlet valve actuator vacuum sensor circuit signal high 5.7L (VIN J)
Code 57 Boost control problem
Code 58 Vehicle Anti-theft System fuel enable circuit
Code 61 A/C system performance or Cruise vent solenoid circuit fault or Oxygen Sensor (O2S) degraded signal or Secondary port throttle valve system fault 5.7L (VIN J) or Transaxle gear switch signal
Code 62 Cruise vacuum solenoid circuit fault or Engine oil temperature sensor, high temperature indicated or Transaxle gear switch signal circuit fault

Code 63 Oxygen Sensor (O2S), right side circuit open or Cruise system problem (speed error) or Manifold Absolute Pressure (MAP) sensor circuit out of range

Code 64 Oxygen Sensor (O2S), right side—lean exhaust indicated

Code 65 Oxygen Sensor (O2S), right side—rich exhaust indicated or Cruise servo position circuit or Fuel injector circuit low current

Code 66 A/C pressure sensor circuit fault, probably low pressure or Engine power switch, voltage high or low or PCM fault 5.7L (VIN J)

Code 67 A/C pressure sensor circuit, sensor or A/C clutch circuit failure or Cruise switch circuit fault

Code 68 A/C compressor relay (shorted circuit) or Cruise system fault

Code 69 A/C clutch circuit or head pressure high

Code 70 A/C refrigerant pressure sensor circuit (high pressure)

Code 71 A/C evaporator temperature sensor circuit (low temperature)

Code 72 Gear selector switch circuit

Code 73 A/C evaporator temperature sensor circuit (high temperature)

Code 75 Digital EGR #1 solenoid error

Code 76 Digital EGR #2 solenoid error

Code 77 Digital EGR #3 solenoid error

Code 79 Vehicle Speed Sensor (VSS) circuit signal high

Code 80 Vehicle Speed Sensor (VSS) circuit signal low

Code 81 Brake input circuit fault—Torque converter clutch signal

Code 82 Ignition Control (IC) 3X signal error

Code 85 PROM error

Code 86 Analog/Digital ECM error

Code 87 EEPROM error

Code 99 Power management

➡ **This list is for reference and does not mean a specific component is defective.**

Honda Truck

GENERAL INFORMATION

Honda utilizes 2 types of fuel systems. The first is the feedback carburetor system of which there are 2 types; a 2 barrel down draft-fixed venturi type, and 2 side draft carburetors variable venturi type. The feedback carburetor was in use up to 1991 in Honda vehicles.

The second type fuel system is Programmed Fuel Injection (PGM-FI) system. As of 1992 all Hondas are fuel injected.

SELF-DIAGNOSTICS

Service Precautions

• Make sure all ECM harness connectors are fastened securely. A poor connection can cause an extremely high voltage surge and result in damage to integrated circuits.

• Keep all ECM parts and harnesses dry during service. Protect the ECM and all solid-state components from rough handling or extremes of temperature.

• Use extreme care when working around the ECM or other components. The airbag or SRS wiring may be in the vicinity. On these vehicles, the SRS wiring and connectors are yellow. Do not cut or test these circuits.

• Before attempting to remove any parts, turn the ignition switch OFF and disconnect the battery ground cable.

• Always use a 12 volt battery as a power source for the engine, never a booster or high-voltage charging unit.

• Do not disconnect the battery cables with the engine running.

• Do not disconnect any wiring connector with the engine running or the ignition ON unless specifically instructed.

• Do not apply battery power directly to injectors.

• Whenever possible, use a flashlight instead of a drop light.

• Relieve fuel system pressure before servicing any fuel system component.

• Always use eye or full-face protection when working around fuel lines, fittings or components.

READING CODES

▶ **See Figure 23**

1985–89 Vehicles

When a fault is noted, the ECU stores an identifying code and illuminates the CHECK ENGINE light. The code will remain in memory until cleared; the dashboard warning lamp may not illuminate during the next ignition cycle if the fault is no longer present. Not all faults noted by the ECU will trigger the dashboard warning lamp although the fault code will be set in memory. For this reason, troubleshooting should be based on the presence of stored codes, not the illumination of the warning lamp while the car is operating.

Stored codes are displayed by either a single flashing LED (Light Emitting Diode) light, or an illuminated light pattern of 4 LED lights on the ECU. When the CHECK ENGINE warning lamp has been on or reported on, check the ECU LED for presence of codes.

The location of the malfunction is determined by observing the LED display. Earlier Hondas used 2 types of LED displays: a single LED and a 4 LED display. After 1987 all models use the single LED display. Systems with a single LED indicate the malfunction with a series of flashes. The number of flashes indicates a code which identifies the location of the component or system malfunction. The code will flash, followed by a 2 second pause, repeat, followed by another 2 second pause, then move to the next code.

On systems with 4 LED's a display pattern identifies the malfunction. The LED's are numbered 1, 2, 4 and 8 as counted from right-to-left. The code is determined by observing which LED's are lit on the display. Each code is displayed once, followed by a 2 second pause, then the next code is displayed. The LED's are part of the Electronic Control Module (ECM).

Turn the ignition switch ON; the LED will display any stored codes.

When counting flashes to determine codes, a code not valid for the vehicle may be found. In this case, first recount the flashes to confirm an accurate count. If necessary, turn the ignition switch OFF, then recycle the system and begin the count again. If the Code is not valid for the vehicle, the ECU must be replaced.

➡ **On vehicles with electronically controlled automatic transaxles, the 5, D or D4 lamp may flash with the CHECK ENGINE lamp if certain codes are stored. If this does occur, proceed with the diagnosis based on the engine code shown. After repairs, recheck the lamp. If the additional warning lamp is still lit, proceed with diagnosis for that system.**

1990–95 Vehicles

When a fault is noted, the ECM stores an identifying code and illuminates the CHECK ENGINE light. The code will remain in memory until cleared. The

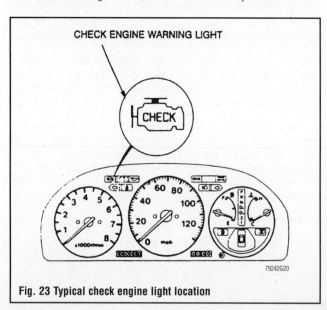

Fig. 23 Typical check engine light location

dashboard warning lamp may not illuminate during the next ignition cycle if the fault is no longer present. Not all faults noted by the ECM will trigger the dashboard warning lamp although the fault code will be set in memory. For this reason, troubleshooting should be based on the presence of stored codes, not the illumination of the warning lamp while the car is operating.

In 1990, the Accord and Prelude were equipped with a 2-pin service connector in addition to the LED. If the service connector is jumpered, with the ignition key in the ON position, the CHECK ENGINE lamp will display the stored codes in a series of flashes. The 2-pin service connector is located under the passenger side of dash on the Accord and behind the center console on the Prelude. As of 1992, the LED on the ECU was eliminated and all vehicles obtain codes by jumping the 2-pin connector when the ignition switch is ON. The CHECK ENGINE light will then flash codes present in the ECU memory.

Diagnostic Codes 1-9 are indicated by a series of short flashes; two-digit codes use a number of long flashes for the first digit followed by the appropriate number of short flashes. For example, Code 43 would be indicated by 4 long flashes followed by 3 short flashes. Codes are separated by a longer pause between transmissions. The position of the codes during output can be helpful in diagnostic work. Multiple codes transmitted in isolated order indicate unique occurrences; a display of showing 1-1-1 pause 9-9-9 indicates two problems or problems occurring at different times. An alternating display, such as 1-9-1-9-1, indicates simultaneous occurrences of the faults.

When counting flashes to determine codes, a code not valid for the vehicle may be found. In this case, first recount the flashes to confirm an accurate count. If necessary, turn the ignition switch OFF, then recycle the system and begin the count again. If the code is not valid for the vehicle, the ECM must be replaced.

➡ **On vehicles with electronically controlled automatic transaxles, the D4 lamp may flash with the CHECK ENGINE lamp if certain codes are stored. If this does occur, proceed with the diagnosis based on the engine code shown. After repairs, recheck the lamp. If the additional warning lamp is still lit, proceed with diagnosis for that system.**

CLEARING CODES

1985–87 Vehicles

The memory for the PGM-FI CHECK ENGINE lamp on the dashboard will be erased when the ignition switch is turned OFF; however, the memory for the LED display will not be canceled. Thus, the CHECK ENGINE lamp will not come on when the ignition switch is again turned ON unless the trouble is once more detected. Troubleshooting should be done according to the LED display even if the CHECK ENGINE lamp is off.

After making repairs, disconnect the battery negative cable from the battery negative terminal for at least 10 seconds and reset the ECU memory. After reconnecting the cable, check that the LED display is turned off.

Turn the ignition switch ON. The PGM-FI CHECK ENGINE lamp should come on for about 2 seconds. If the CHECK ENGINE lamp won't come on, check for:—Blown CHECK ENGINE lamp bulb—Blown fuse (causing faulty back up light, seat belt alarm, clock, memory function of the car radio) - Open circuit in Yellow wire—Open circuit in wiring and control unit.

After the PGM-FI CHECK ENGINE lamp and self-diagnosis indicators have been turned on, turn the ignition switch OFF. If the LED display fails to come on when the ignition switch is turned ON again, check for:—Blown fuses, especially No. 10 fuse—Open circuit in wire between ECU fuse.

Replace the ECU only after making sure that all couplers and connectors are connected securely.

1988–90 Vehicles

The memory for the PGM-CARB and PGM-FI CHECK ENGINE lamp on the dashboard will be erased when the ignition switch is turned OFF; however, the memory for the LED display will not be canceled. Thus, the CHECK ENGINE lamp will not come on when the ignition switch is again turned ON unless the trouble is once more detected. Troubleshooting

should be done according to the LED display even if the CHECK ENGINE lamp is off.

To clear the ECU trouble code memory, remove the ECU memory power fuse for at least 10 seconds.

➡ **Removing this fuse will also erase the clock, radio station presets, and the radio anti-theft codes. Make sure you have the anti-theft code and station presets before removing fuse so they may be reset when repairs are complete.**

1990–95 Vehicles

◗ See Figures 24 and 25

Stored codes are removed from memory by removing power to the ECU. Disconnecting the power may also clear the memories used for other solid-state equipment such as the clock and radio. For this reason, always make note of the radio presets before clearing the system. Additionally, some radios contain anti-theft programming; obtain the owner's code number before clearing the codes.

While disconnecting the battery will clear the memory, this is not the recommended procedure. The memory should be cleared after the ignition is switched OFF by removing the appropriate fuse for at least 10 seconds.

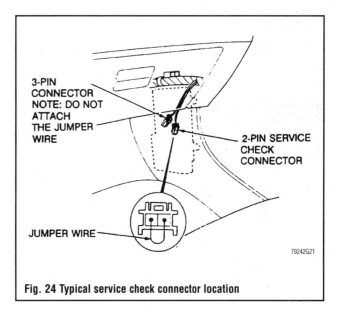

Fig. 24 Typical service check connector location

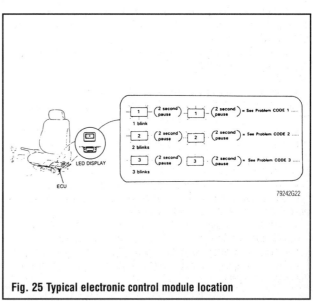

Fig. 25 Typical electronic control module location

➡Removing this fuse will also erase the clock, radio station presets, and the radio anti-theft codes. Make sure you have the anti-theft code and station presets before removing fuse so they may be reset when repairs are complete.

DIAGNOSTIC TROUBLE CODES

Code 0 Electronic Control Module (ECM)

Code 1 Heated oxygen sensor (or Oxygen content) or—Oxygen content A (A20A3, B20A5)

Code 2 Oxygen content B (A20A3, B20A5) or—Electronic Control Module (ECM) (BS, BT—1986 only) and (A20A3—1987 only)

Code 3 Manifold Absolute Pressure (MAP)

Code 4 Crankshaft position sensor or—Faulty ECU (BS, BT—1986 only) and (A20A3 -1987 only, B20A5, B21A1)

Code 5 Manifold Absolute Pressure (MAP)

Code 6 Engine coolant temperature (ECT)

Code 7 Throttle position sensor (TP sensor)

Code 8 Top dead center sensor (TDC sensor)

Code 9 No. 1 cylinder position sensor

Code 10- Intake air temperature sensor (IAT sensor)

Code 11- Electronic Control Module (ECM) (BS, BT -1986 only) and (A20A3—1987 only)

Code 12- Exhaust Gas Recirculation (EGR) System (except Del Sol and Civic & CRX 1 .6L DI 6A6)

Code 13 Barometric pressure sensor (BARO sensor)

Code 14—Idle air control (IAC valve) except 1987 -A20A3 engine. or—1986 BS, BT and 1987 A20A3 Engines, or high is possible faulty Electronic Control Module (ECM)

Code 15 Ignition output signal

Code 16 Fuel Injector

Code 17 Vehicle Speed sensor (VSS)

Code 19 NT lock-up control solenoid valve NB (D1SB1, D15B2, D15B6, D15B7, D15B8, D15Z1, D16A6, D16Z6)

Code 20 Electric load detector (ELD)

Code 21 V-TEC control solenoid (D15Z1, D16Z6, H22A1)

Code 22 V-TEC pressure switch (D15Z1, D16Z6, H22A1)

Code 23 Knock sensor (H22A1-DOHC—VTEC)

Code 30 NT FI Signal A (F22A1, F22A4, F22A6)

Code 31 NT FI Signal B (F22A1, F22A4, F22A6)

Code 41 Heated Oxygen Sensor Heater (F22A1, F22A4)

Code 43 Fuel supply system (except D1SB1, D15B2, D15B6, B20A5, B21A, D16A6)

Code 45 Fuel supply metering

Code 48 Heated oxygen sensor (D15Z1 engine only, except Calif. emission)

Code 61 Front Heated Oxygen Sensor

Code 63 Rear Heated Oxygen Sensor

Code 65 Rear Heated Oxygen Sensor Heater

Code 67 Catalytic Converter System

Code 70 Automatic Transaxle or A/F FI Data line

Code 71 Misfire detected; cylinder No. 1 or random misfire

Code 72 Misfire detected; cylinder No. 2 or random misfire

Code 73 Misfire detected; cylinder No. 3 or random misfire

Code 74 Misfire detected; cylinder No. 4 or random misfire

Code 75 Misfire detected; cylinder No. 5 or random misfire

Code 76 Misfire detected; cylinder No. 6 or random misfire

Code 80 Exhaust Gas Recirculation (EGR) system

Code 86 Coolant temperature

Code 92 Evaporative Emission Control System

Infiniti Truck

GENERAL INFORMATION

The Infiniti Electronic Concentrated Control System (ECCS) is an air flow controlled, sequential port fuel injection and engine control system. It is used on all models equipped with 2.0L, 3.0L and 4.5L engines. The ECCS electronic control unit consists of a microcomputer, an inspection lamp, a diagnostic mode selector and connectors for signal input and output, powers and grounds.

The safety relay prevents electrical damage to the electronic control unit, or ECU, and the injectors in case the battery terminals are accidentally connected in reverse. The safety relay is built into the fuel pump control circuit.

Ignition timing is controlled in response to engine operating conditions. The optimum ignition timing in each driving condition is pre-programmed in the computer. The signal from the control unit is transmitted to the power transistor and this signal controls when the transistor turns the ignition coil primary circuit on and off (hence, the ignition timing). The idle speed is also controlled according to engine operating conditions, temperature and gear position. On manual transmission models, if battery voltage is less than 12 volts for a few seconds, a higher idle speed will be maintained by the control unit to improve charging function.

There is a fail-safe system built into the ECCS control unit. This system makes engine starting possible if a portion of the ECU's central processing unit circuit fails. Also, if a major component such as the crank angle sensor or the air flow meter were to malfunction, the ECU substitutes or borrows data to compensate for the fault. For example, if the output voltage of the air flow meter is extremely low, the ECU will substitute a pre-programmed value for the air flow meter signal and allows the vehicle to be driven as long as the engine speed is kept below 2000 rpm. Or, if the cylinder head temperature sensor circuit is open, the control unit clamps the warm-up enrichment at a certain amount. This amount is almost the same as that when the cylinder head temperature is between 68–176°F (20–80°C).

If the fuel pump circuit malfunctions, the fuel pump relay comes on until the engine stops. This allows the fuel pump to receive power from the relay. The electronic control unit controls the following functions:

- Injector pulse width
- Ignition timing
- Intake valve timing control (045)
- Air regulator control (G20)
- Exhaust gas recirculation (EGR) solenoid valve operation
- Exhaust gas sensor heater operation
- Idle speed
- FICD solenoid valve operation (G20 and M30)
- Fuel pump relay operation
- Fuel pump voltage (M30 and 045)
- Fuel pressure regulator control (M30)
- AIV control (G20)
- Carbon canister control solenoid valve operation
- Air conditioner relay operation (During early wide-open throttle)
- Radiator fan operation (G20)
- Traction control system (TCS) operation (045, if equipped)
- Self-diagnosis
- Fail-safe mode operation

SELF-DIAGNOSTICS

Service Precautions

- Do not disconnect the injector harness connectors with the engine running.
- Do not apply battery power directly to the injectors.
- Do not disconnect the ECU harness connectors before the battery ground cable has been disconnected.
- Make sure all ECU connectors are fastened securely. A poor connection can cause an extremely high surge voltage in the coil and condenser and result in damage to integrated circuits.
- When testing the ECU with a DVOM make sure that the probes of the tester never touch each other as this will result in damage to a transistor in the ECU.
- Keep the ECCS harness at least 4 in. away from adjacent harnesses to prevent an ECCS system malfunction due to external electronic noise.
- Keep all parts and harnesses dry during service.
- Before attempting to remove any parts, turn OFF the ignition switch and disconnect the battery ground cable.
- Always use a 12 volt battery as a power source.

• Do not attempt to disconnect the battery cables with the engine running or the ignition key ON.
• Do not clean the air flow meter with any type of detergent.
• Do not attempt to disassemble the ECCS control unit under any circumstances.
• Avoid static electricity build-up by properly grounding yourself prior to handling any ECU or related parts.

READING CODES

▶ **See Figures 26 and 27**

➡**Diagnostic codes may be retrieved by observing code flashes through the LED lights located on the Electronic Control Module (ECM). A special Nissan Consult monitor tool can be used, but is not required- When using special diagnostic equipment, always observe the tool manufacturer's instructions.**

1990–95 Vehicles

2-Mode Diagnostic System

Infiniti vehicles use a 2-mode diagnostic system incorporated in the ECU which uses inputs from various sensors to determine the correct air/fuel ratio. If any of the sensors malfunction the ECU will store the code in memory.

An Infiniti/Nissan Consult monitor may be used to retrieve these codes by simply connecting the monitor to the diagnosis connector located on the driver's side near the hood release.

Turn the ignition switch ON and press START, ENGINE and then SELF-DIAG RESULTS, the results will then be output to the monitor.

The conventional CHECK ENGINE or red LED ECU light may be used for self-diagnostics. The conventional 2-mode diagnostic system is broken into 2 separate modes each capable of 2 tests, an ignition switch ON or engine running test as outlined below:

Mode I—Bulb Check

In this mode the RED indicator light on the ECU and the CHECK ENGINE light should be ON. To enter this mode simply turn the ignition switch ON and observe the light.

Mode 1—Malfunction Warning

In this mode the ECU is acknowledging if there is a malfunction by illuminating the RED indicator light on the ECU and the CHECK ENGINE light. If the light turns OFF, the system is normal. To enter this mode, simply start the engine and observe the light.

Mode 2—Self-Diagnostic Codes

In this mode the ECU will output all malfunctions via the CHECK ENGINE light or the red LED on the ECU. The code may be retrieved by counting the number of flashes. The longer flashes indicate the first digit and the shorter flashes indicate the second digit. To enter this mode proceed as follows:

1. Turn the ignition switch ON, but do not start the vehicle.
2. Turn the ECU diagnostic mode selector fully clockwise for 2 seconds, then turn it back fully counterclockwise.
3. Observe the red LED on the ECU or CHECK ENGINE light for stored codes.

Mode 2—Exhaust Gas Sensor Monitor

In this mode the red LED on the ECU or CHECK ENGINE light will display the condition of the fuel mixture and whether the system is in closed loop or open loop. When the light flashes ON, the exhaust gas sensor is indicating a lean mixture. When the light stays OFF, the sensor is indicating a rich mixture. If the light remains ON or OFF, it is indicating an open loop system. If the system is equipped with 2 exhaust gas sensors, the left side will operate first. If already in Mode 2, proceed to Step 3 for exhaust gas sensor monitor.

1. Turn the ignition switch ON.
2. Turn the diagnostic switch ON, by turning the switch fully clockwise for 2 seconds and then fully counterclockwise.
3. Start the engine and run until thoroughly warm. Raise the idle to 2,000 rpm and hold for approximately 2 minutes. Ensure the red LED or CHECK ENGINE light flash ON and OFF more than 5 times every 10 seconds with the engine speed at 2,000 rpm.

➡**If equipped with 2 exhaust gas sensors, switch to the right sensor by turning the ECU mode selector fully clockwise for 2 seconds and then fully counterclockwise with the engine running.**

CLEARING CODES

1990–95 Vehicles

All control unit diagnostic codes may be cleared by disconnecting the negative battery for a period of 15 seconds. The codes will be cleared when mode 1 is re-entered from mode 2. The Nissan Consult Monitor or equivalent can also be used to clear codes.

DIAGNOSTIC TROUBLE CODES

1990–95 Vehicles

Code 16 TCS Signal
Code 21 Ignition signal missing in primary coil
Code 31 ECM (engine ECCS control unit)
Code 32 EGR circuit

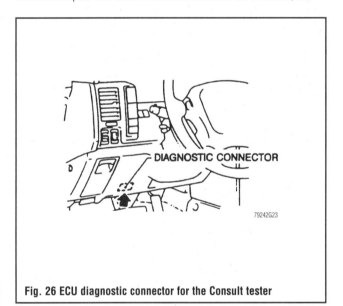

Fig. 26 ECU diagnostic connector for the Consult tester

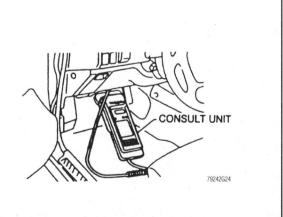

Fig. 27 Reading diagnostic codes using the consult tester

Code 33 Heated oxygen sensor circuit
Code 34 Knock Sensor (KS) circuit
Code 35 EGR temperature sensor circuit
Code 42 Fuel temperature sensor circuit
Code 43 Throttle sensor circuit
Code 45 Injector leak
Code 46 Secondary throttle sensor circuit
Code 51 Injector circuit
Code 53 Heated oxygen sensor circuit (right bank)
Code 54 NT controller circuit
Code 55 No malfunctioning in the above circuit
Code 11 Crankshaft position sensor
Code 12 Mass Air flow sensor
Code 13 Engine coolant temperature sensor circuit
Code 14 Vehicle speed sensor

Isuzu Truck

GENERAL INFORMATION

Isuzu vehicles may be fitted with either a Feedback Carburetor (FBC), a Throttle Body Fuel Injection (TBI) system or a Multi-port Fuel Injection System (MFI).

The Feedback Carburetor System (FBC) is primarily used on 1985 and earlier normally aspirated engines, although some engines may use this system up to 1993. The system Electronic Control Module (ECM) constantly monitors and controls engine operation by reading data from various sensors and outputting signals to the carburetor. This helps lower emissions while maintaining the fuel economy, driveability and performance of the vehicle.

The Throttle Body (TBI) fuel injection system was put into production in 1989. It is used on 2.8L and 3.1L engines. The system functions much the same as a multi-port fuel injection system but with one exception—fuel is injected into the intake manifold rather than into each individual cylinder. This system may also control the ignition system.

The 1-TEC Multi-port Fuel Injection (MFI) system was first used in 1985 and continues to be used today. The system constantly monitors and controls engine operation through the use of data sensors, an Electronic Control Module (ECM) and other components. Individual fuel injectors are mounted at each cylinder and provide a metered amount of fuel as required by current operating conditions. This system may also control the ignition system and, as equipped, the turbocharger system.

SELF-DIAGNOSTICS

All vehicles covered in this section have self-diagnostic capabilities. The ECM diagnostics are in the form of trouble codes stored in the system's memory. When a trouble code is detected by the control module, it will turn the malfunction indicator lamp ON until the code is cleared. An intermittent problem will set a code. The lamp will turn OFF if the problem goes away, but the trouble code will stay in memory until ECM power is interrupted.

Service Precautions

• Keep all ECM parts and harnesses dry during service. Protect the ECM and all solid-state components from rough handling or extremes of temperature.

• Use extreme care when working around the ECM or other solid-state components. Do not allow any open circuit to short or ground in the ECM circuit. Voltage spikes may cause damage to solid-state components.

• Before attempting to remove any parts, turn the ignition switch OFF or disconnect the negative battery cable.

• Remove the ECM before any arc welding is performed to the vehicle.

• Electronic components are very susceptible to damage caused by electrostatic discharge (static electricity). To prevent electronic component damage, do not touch the control module connector pins or soldered components on the control module circuit board.

READING CODES

➡**Diagnostic codes may be retrieve through the use of the CHECK ENGINE light or Malfunction Indicator Lamp (MIL). A special Scan tool can be used, but is not required. When using special diagnostic equipment, always observe the tool manufacturer's instructions.**

1982–86 Vehicles

The trouble code system is actuated by connecting a diagnostic lead to ground. The location of the diagnostic lead differs from model-to-model and, in some cases from year-to-year within the same model.

Trooper II for 1985; connect the diagnostic lead terminals together (1 male and 1 female). The terminals are located under dash, on the passenger's side, behind the radio. The terminal leads for 1986 models are located near the ALDL connector, under dash, on the driver's side behind the cigarette lighter.

Pick-up truck for 1982; connect the diagnostic lead terminals together (1 male and 1 female). The terminals are branched from the harness near the ECM, under the dash on the driver's side behind the hood release.

The trouble code is determined by counting the flashes of the 'Check Engine lamp. Trouble Code 12 will flash first, indicating that the self-diagnostic system is working. Code 12 consists of 1 flash, short pause, then 2 flashes. There will be a longer pause and Code 12 will repeat 2 more times. Each code flashes 3 times. The cycle will then repeat itself until the engine is started or the ignition switch is turned OFF. In most cases, the codes will be checked with the engine running since no codes other than 12 or 51 will be present on initial key ON.

1987–94 Vehicles

▶ **See Figures 28, 29, 30 and 31**

With Scan Tool
1. Turn the ignition key to the OFF position.
2. Connect the scan tool to the Assembly Line Diagnostic Link (ALDL).
3. Turn ON the ignition for scan tool to access engine computer.

1987–89 Vehicles

1. With the ignition turned ON, and the engine stopped, the CHECK ENGINE lamp should be ON. This is a bulb check to indicate the light is working properly.

2. For the Trooper and Pickup; connect the trouble code TEST lead (white cable) to the ground lead (black cable). It is located 8 in. from the ECM connector next to the clutch pedal or center console.

3. The CHECK ENGINE light will begin to flash a trouble Code 12. Code 12 consists of 1 flash, short pause and then 2 more flashes. There will be a longer pause and then a Code 12 will repeat 2 more times. The check indicates that the self-diagnostic system is working. This cycle will repeat itself

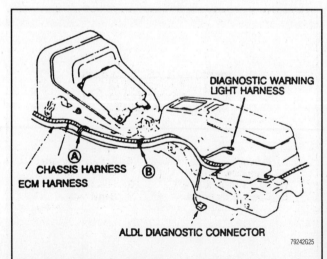

Fig. 28 Assembly Line Diagnostic link (ALDL) connector— 1988–91 Trooper with 2.6L engine

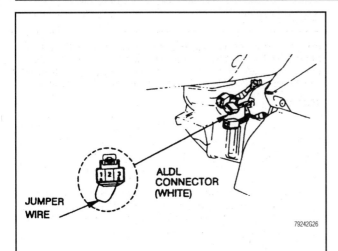

Fig. 29 Assembly Line Diagnostic link (ALDL) connector— 1992–94 Trooper with 2.6L engine

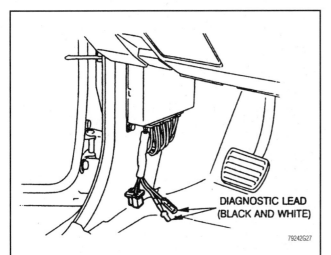

Fig. 30 Assembly Line Diagnostic link (ALDL) connector— 1990–94 Amigo, Pick-up and Rodeo (4 cylinder engines)

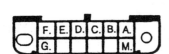

A. Ground
B. Diagnostic terminal
C. A.I.R system (if used)
D. Check engine light

E. Serial data
F. Torque Converter
   Clutch (TCC)
G. Fuel pump
M. Serial data

Fig. 31 Assembly Line Diagnostic link (ALDL) connector— 1990–94 Amigo, Pick-up and Rodeo (6 cylinder engines)

until the engine is started or the ignition switch is turned OFF. If more than a single fault code is stored in the memory, the lowest number code will flash 3 times followed by the next highest code number until all the codes have been flashed. The faults will then repeat in the same order. In most cases, codes will be checked with the engine running since no codes other than Codes 12 and 51 will be present on the initial key ON. Remove the jumper wire from the test terminal before starting the engine.

➡ **The fault indicated by trouble Code 15 takes 5 minutes of engine operation before it will display.**

1990–94 Vehicles

1. With the ignition turned ON and the engine stopped, the CHECK ENGINE lamp should be ON. This is a bulb check to indicate the light is working properly.
2. Enter the diagnostic modes as follows:
   a. For the Trooper; jumper the 1 and 3 terminals (outer terminals) of the white Assembly Line Diagnostic Link (ALDL). The connector for Impulse and Stylus is located behind the kick panel on the passenger side of the vehicle. On Trooper, the ALDL connector is located behind the left side of the center console.
   b. For the Amigo, Pickup, and Rodeo with 4 cylinder engine; connect the trouble code TEST lead (white cable) and a ground lead (black cable) together. It is located 8 in. from the ECM connector (next to the clutch pedal or brake pedal).
   c. For the Amigo, Pickup, and Rodeo with 6 cylinder engine; jumper wire the A and B terminals together of the Assembly Line Diagnostic Link (ALDL). The ALDL is located in the center console and is sometimes covered by a plastic cover labeled DIAGNOSTIC CONNECTOR. Read the trouble codes with the ignition switch ON and the engine OFF.
3. The CHECK ENGINE light will begin to flash a trouble Code 12. Code 12 consists of 1 flash, a short pause and then 2 more flashes. There will be a longer pause and a Code 12 will repeat 2 more times. Code 12 indicates that the self-diagnostic system is working. If any other faults are present, the faults will be displayed 3 times each in the same fashion. Fault codes are flashed from lowest to highest after the Code 12. Remember to remove the jumper wire from the ALDL connector before starting the engine. After all codes have been displayed, the cycle will repeat itself until the engine is started or the ignition switch is turned OFF.

➡ **The fault indicated by trouble Code 15 takes 5 minutes of engine operation before it will display (4 cylinder engine only).**

CLEARING CODES

1982–86 Vehicles

The trouble code memory is fed a continuous 12 volts even with the ignition switch in the OFF position. After a fault has been corrected, it will be necessary to remove the voltage for 10 seconds to clear any stored codes. Voltage can be removed by disconnecting the 14 pin ECM connector or by removing the fuse marked 'ECM' or fuse No. 4 on some models. Since all memory will be lost when removing the fuse, it will be necessary to reset the clock and other electrical equipment.

1987–94 Vehicles

The trouble code memory is fed a continuous 12 volts even with the ignition switch in the OFF position. After a fault has been corrected, it will be necessary to remove the voltage for 30 seconds to clear any stored codes. The quickest way to remove the voltage is to remove the ECM fuse from the fuse block or the MAIN 60A fuse for 10 seconds. The voltage can also be removed by disconnecting the negative battery cable. This will mean electronic instrumentation, such as a clock and radio, would have to be reset.

1987–89 Pickup and Trooper; turn the ignition switch OFF and disconnect the ECM 13-pin connector or remove the No. 4 fuse from the fuse block for 30 seconds.

The 60 amp slow blow fuse may be removed from the fuse block in the engine compartment. However, the electronic functions with memory have to be reset after removing the No. 4 fuse for 30 seconds.

1992–94 Amigo, Pickup, Rodeo and Trooper; To clear the trouble codes; turn the ignition switch OFF and remove the ECM fuse from the under-dash fuse block for 30 seconds. Removing the number 3 fuse from the under dash fuse panel will result in having to reset all the electronic functions with memory in the vehicle. This applies to trucks with 4-cylinder engines.

Removing the 60 amp slow blow fuse from the fuse block in the engine compartment will also erase codes.

DIAGNOSTIC TROUBLE CODES

1982–94 Vehicles

1982 1.8L FBC TRUCK ENGINE

Code 12 Idle switch is not turned ON
Code 13 Idle switch is not turned OFF
Code 14 Wide Open Throttle (WOT) switch is not turned ON
Code 15 Wide Open Throttle (WOT) switch is not turned ON
Code 21 Output transistor is not turned ON
Code 22 Output transistor is not turned OFF
Code 23 Abnormal oxygen sensor
Code 24 Abnormal Water Temperature Sensor (WTS) switch
Code 25 Abnormal Random Access Memory (RAM)
Code 12, 13, 14 and 15 Check Engine lamp not ON
Code 21, 22, 23, 24 and 25 Check Engine lamp ON

1985–89 1.SL FBC (VIN 7) ENGINE

1983 1.8L FBC ENGINE

1983–86 2.0L FBC (VIN A) ENGINE

1986–94 2.3L FBC (VIN L) ENGINE

Code 12 Normal
Code 13 Oxygen sensor circuit
Code 14 Coolant Temperature Sensor (CTS)—circuit shorted
Code 15 Coolant Temperature Sensor (CTS)—circuit open
Code 21 Idle switch—circuit open or Wide Open Throttle (WOT) switch—circuit shorted
Code 22 Fuel Cut Solenoid (FCS)—circuit open or grounded
Code 23 Mixture Control (M/C) solenoid—circuit open or grounded, or Vacuum Control Solenoid (VCS)—circuit open or grounded (1983 1.8L Truck, 1983–86 2.0L Truck, 1986–88 2.3L Truck)
Code 24 Vehicle Speed Sensor (VSS) circuit
Code 25 Air Switching Solenoid (ASS)—circuit open or grounded
Code 26 Vacuum Switching Valve (VSV) system for canister purge—circuit open or grounded
Code 27 Vacuum Switching Valve (VSV)-constant high voltage to ECM
Code 31 No ignition reference pulses to ECM
Code 32 EGR temperature sensor—system malfunction
Code 34 EGR temperature sensor—circuit failure electronic idle control
Code 42 Fuel Cut Relay and/or circuit shorted
Code 44 Oxygen Sensor circuit—lean indication
Code 45 Oxygen Sensor circuit—rich indication
Code 52 Faulty Electronic Control Module (ECM)—Random Access Memory (RAM) problem in ECM
Code 53 Shorted Air Switching Solenoid (ASS) or Air Injection System and/or faulty Electronic Control Module (ECM)
Code 54 Shorted Vacuum Control Solenoid (VCS) and/or faulty Electronic Control Module (ECM)
Code 55 Faulty Electronic Control Module (ECM)

1985–87 2.0L TURBO EFI (VIN F) ENGINE

1983–89 2.0L EFI (VIN A) ENGINE

1988–89 2.3L EFI (VIN L) ENGINE

1988–94 2.6L EFI (VIN E) ENGINE

Code 12 Normal
Code 13 Oxygen sensor circuit
Code 14 Engine Coolant Temperature (ECT) sensor -grounded

Code 15 Engine Coolant Temperature (ECT) sensor—incorrect signal (open circuit on 1988-94 2.6L)
Code 16 Engine Coolant Temperature (ECT) sensor -open circuit
Code 21 Throttle Valve Switch (TVS) system—idle contact and full contact made simultaneously
Code 22 Starter—no signal input
Code 23 Ignition power transistor—output terminal grounded
Code 25 Vacuum Switching Valve (VSV)—output terminal grounded or open
Code 26 Canister purge Vacuum Switching Valve (VSV)—open or grounded
Code 27 Canister purge Vacuum Switching Valve (VSV)—faulty transistor or bad ground circuit
Code 32 EGR temperature sensor—faulty sensor or harness
Code 33 Fuel injector system—output terminal grounded or open
Code 34 EGR vacuum switching valve—output terminal grounded or open
Code 35 Ignition power transistor—open circuit
Code 41 Crank Angle sensor (CAS)—no signal or faulty signal
Code 43 Throttle Valve Switch—idle contact closed continuously
Code 44 Fuel metering system—lean signal (Oxygen sensor-low voltage)
Code 45 Fuel metering system—rich signal (Oxygen sensor-high voltage)
Code 51 Faulty ECM
Code 52 Faulty ECM
Code 53 Vacuum Switching Valve (VSV)—grounded or faulty power transistor
Code 54 Ignition power transistor—grounded or faulty power transistor
Code 55 Faulty ECM
Code 61 Air Flow Sensor (AFS)—grounded, shorted, open or broken HOT wire
Code 62 Air Flow Sensor (AFS)—broken COLD wire
Code 63 Vehicle Speed Sensor (VSS)—no signal input
Code 64 Fuel injector system—grounded or faulty transistor
Code 65 Throttle Valve Switch (TVS)—full contact closed continuously
Code 66 Knock sensor—grounded or open circuit
Code 71 Throttle Position Sensor (TPS)—turbo control system -abnormal signal
Code 72 EGR Vacuum switching valve—output terminal grounded or open
Code 73 EGR Vacuum switching valve—faulty transistor or grounded system

1989–91 2.8L TBI (VIN R) ENGINE

1991–94 3.1L TBI (VIN Z) ENGINE

Code 12 Normal
Code 13 Oxygen sensor circuit
Code 14 Engine Coolant Temperature (ECT) sensor -high temperature indicated
Code 15 Engine Coolant Temperature (ECT) sensor -low temperature indicated
Code 21 Throttle Position Sensor (TPS)—voltage high
Code 22 Throttle Position Sensor (TPS)—voltage low
Code 23 Intake Air Temperature (IAT)—low temperature indicated
Code 24 Vehicle Speed Sensor (VSS)—no input signal Code 25—Intake Air Temperature (IAT)—high temperature indicated
Code 31 Turbocharger wastegate control
Code 32 EGR system fault
Code 33 Manifold Absolute Pressure (MAP) sensor -voltage high
Code 34 Manifold Absolute Pressure (MAP) sensor -voltage low
Code 42 Electronic Spark Timing (EST) circuit fault
Code 43 Electronic Spark Control (ESC)—knock failure circuit
Code 44 Oxygen sensor circuit—lean exhaust
Code 45 Oxygen sensor circuit—rich exhaust
Code 51 PROM error—faulty or incorrect PROM
Code 52 CALPAK error—faulty or incorrect CALPAK
Code 54 Fuel Pump Circuit—low voltage
Code 55 ECM error

1991–94 2.3L EFI (VIN 5/6) ENGINE
1992–94 3.2L EFI (VIN V/W) ENGINE

Code 13 Oxygen sensor circuit
Code 14 Engine Coolant Temperature (ECT) sensor -out of range
Code 21 Throttle Position Sensor (TPS)—out of range
Code 23 Intake Air Temperature (IAT)—out of range
Code 24 Vehicle Speed Sensor (VSS)—no input signal
Code 32 EGR system fault
Code 33 Manifold Absolute Pressure (MAP) sensor—out of range
Code 44 Oxygen sensor circuit—lean exhaust
Code 45 Oxygen sensor circuit—rich exhaust
Code 51 ECM failure

Mazda Truck

GENERAL INFORMATION

Mazda utilizes 2 types of fuel systems between the years 1984–94. The Feedback Carburetor (FBC) system and Electronic Gas Injection (EGI) system, or fuel injection system. The feedback carburetor system was used in the B2000, B2200 and B2600 pickup trucks between years 1984–92.

Electronic Gas Injection (EGI) was first available in the 1984 RX-7. 626 picked it up in 1986, 323 in 1987. In 1988 all models except B2200 and B2600 pickup trucks came equipped with fuel injection. Mazda uses various variations of EGI. Navajo uses the Ford EEC-IV system. However, the EEC-IV system will not be covered in this section.

SELF-DIAGNOSTICS

Service Precautions

• Before connecting or disconnecting the ECU harness connectors, make sure the ignition switch is OFF and the negative battery cable is disconnected to avoid the possibility of damage to the control unit.
• When performing ECU input/output signal diagnosis, remove the pin terminal retainer from the connectors to make it easier to insert tester probes into the connector.
• When connecting or disconnecting pin connectors from the ECU, take care not to bend or break any pin terminals. Check that there are no bends or breaks on ECU pin terminals before attempting any connections.
• Before replacing any ECU, perform the ECU input/output signal diagnosis to make sure the ECU is functioning properly or not.
• After checking through EGI troubleshooting, perform the EFI self-diagnosis and driving test.
• When measuring supply voltage of ECU controlled components with a circuit tester, separate 1 tester probe from another. If the 2 tester probes accidentally make contact with each other during measurement, a short circuit will result and may damage the ECU.

READING CODES

▶ **See Figure 32**

➡**Diagnostic codes may be retrieved through the use of the CHECK ENGINE light or Malfunction Indicator Lamp (MIL). Special System Checker No. 83, Digital Code Checker and a Self-diagnosis Checker are all special diagnostic equipment used to retrieve codes, however these tools are not required. When using special diagnostic equipment, always observe the tool manufacturer's instructions.**

1984–86 Vehicles With System Checker Tool 83

On 1986 B2000 Pick-up, the System Checker No. 83 (tool No. 49-G030-920), is used to detect and indicate any problems of each sensor, damaged wiring, poor contact or a short circuit between each of the sensor control units. Trouble is indicated by a red lamp and a buzzer. If there are more than 2 problems at a time, the indicator lamp turns ON in the numerical order of

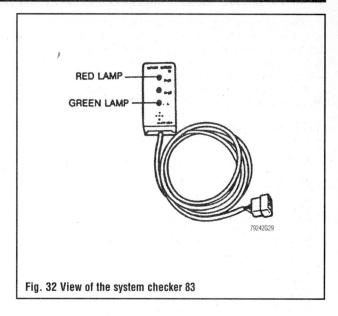

Fig. 32 View of the system checker 83

the code number. Even if the problem is corrected during indication, 1 cycle will be indicated, If after a malfunction has occurred and the ignition key is switched OFF, the malfunction indicator for the feedback system will not be displayed on the checker.

Read engine trouble codes using the following procedures:
1984–85 B2200
1. Operate the engine until normal operating temperatures are reached. Allow the engine to run at idle.
2. Connect System Checker tool No. 83 (49-G030-920) to the check connector, located near the ECU.
3. Check whether the trouble indication light turns ON.

If there is more than 2 problems at the same time, the indicator lamp lights on in the numerical order of the code number. Even if the problem is corrected during indication, 1 cycle will be Indicated. If after a malfunction has occurred the Ignition key is switched off, the malfunction indicator for the feedback system will not be displayed on the checker. The control unit has a built In fall-safe mechanism. If a malfunction occurs during driving, the control unit will on its own initiative, send out a command and driving performance will be affected. The commands are as follows:
   a. Water Thermo-Sensor—the control unit outputs a constant 176°F (80°C) command.
   b. Feed-Back Sensor—the control unit holds air/fuel solenoid to dwell meter reading 27° (duty 30%) for B2200.
   c. Vacuum Sensor—the control unit prevents operation of the EGR valve, and holds the air/fuel solenoid to a duty of 0%.
   d. EGR Position Sensor—the control unit prevents operation of the EGR valve.

➡**If the trouble code is code number 3 (feedback system), proceed as follows:**

4. Start the engine, letting it run until it reaches normal operating temperature. Connect a tachometer to the engine.
5. Connect a dwell meter (90 degrees, 4 cylinder) to the yellow wire in the service (check) connector of the air/fuel solenoid valve.
6. Run the engine at idle and note the reading on the dwell meter.
7. If the dwell meter reading is 0° degrees, the probable causes are as follows:
   a. The wiring harness from the IG to the check connector BrY terminal is open.
   b. The wiring harness from the check connector Y terminal to the control unit (F) terminal is grounded.
   c. The transistor in the control unit for the air/fuel solenoid is open.
8. If the dwell meter reading is 90°, the probable causes are as follows:
   a. The wiring harness from the IG to the check connector BrY terminal is open.

b. The wiring harness from the check connector BrY terminal to the control unit (F) terminal is grounded.

c. The transistor in the control unit for the air/fuel solenoid is short circuited.

9. If the dwell meter reading is 18°, check whether the green lamp (feedback signal) illuminates or does not illuminate.

10. If the oxygen sensor signal lamp does not illuminate, proceed as follows:

a. If the green lamp does not illuminate, the air is sucked from the intake system or the air is sucked from the exhaust manifold.

b. Carburetor jets are clogged.

c. The valve of the air/fuel solenoid is stuck to the lower position, giving a lean air/fuel mixture condition.

11. If the oxygen sensor signal lamp illuminates, proceed as follows:

a. If green lamp turns ON, the mixture is richer than stoichiometric air/fuel ratio.

b. If the green lamp turns ON and OFF, the O2 sensor signal is fed to the control unit.

c. If the green lamp turns OFF, the mixture is leaner than stoichiometric.

With Self-Diagnosis Checker

▶ See Figure 33

The self-diagnosis checker (49-HOI 8-9A1) and System Selector (49-BOI 9-9A0), are used to retrieve code numbers of malfunctions which have happened and were memorized or are continuing. The malfunction is indicated by a code number.

If there is more than 1 malfunction, the code numbers will display on the self-diagnosis checker in numerical order. The ECU has a built in fail-safe mechanism for the main input sensors. If a malfunction occurs, the emission control unit will substitute values. This will affect driving performance, but the vehicle may still be driven.

The ECU continuously checks for malfunctions of the input devices. But the ECU checks for malfunctions of the output devices within 3 seconds after the green (1 pin) test connector or TEN terminal of the diagnosis connector is grounded and the ignition switch is turned to the ON position.

Read engine trouble codes using the following procedures:

1992 MPV, B2200 and B2600i

The check connector is located at the rear of the left side wheel house on 626/MX-6, front of the left side wheel house on MPV, above the right side wheel house on B2200 and near the fuel filter on B2600i.

1. Connect the tester to the check connector and to ground.
2. Set the tester select switch to the A setting.
3. With a jumper wire, ground the 1 pin test connector.
4. Turn the ignition switch ON.

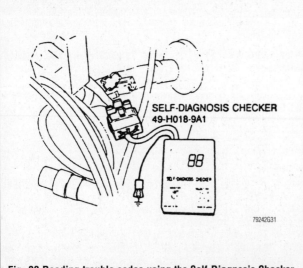

SELF-DIAGNOSIS CHECKER 49-H018-9A1

79242G31

Fig. 33 Reading trouble codes using the Self-Diagnosis Checker

5. Make sure that 88 flashes on the monitor and that the audible buzzer sounds for 3 seconds after turning the ignition switch ON.

6. If 88 does not flash, check the main relay, power supply circuit and the check connector wiring.

7. If 88 flashes and the buzzer sounds for more than 20 seconds, replace the engine control unit and perform steps number 1 through 6 again.

➡**Before replacing the ECU on the MPV or B2600i, check for a short circuit between ECU terminal IB for JE engine and 1F for G6 engine and the 6 pin check connector.**

8. Note and record any other code numbers that are present.

CLEARING CODES

1984–86 Vehicles

1. Turn the ignition switch OFF.
2. Disconnect the negative battery cable.
3. Depress the brake pedal for at least 5 seconds.
4. Reconnect the negative battery cable.

1987–91 Vehicles

1. Cancel the memory of the malfunction by disconnecting the negative battery cable and depressing the brake pedal for at least 20 seconds, then reconnect the negative battery cable.

2. Connect the Self-Diagnosis Checker 49-H018-9A1 to the check connector. Ground the test connector (green: 1 pin) using a jumper wire.

3. Turn the ignition switch ON, but do not start the engine for approximately 6 seconds.

4. Start the engine and allow it to reach normal operating temperature. Then run the engine at 2000 rpm for 2 minutes. Check that no code numbers are displayed.

1992–94 Vehicles

1992 B2200 (EGI) and B2600i
1. Disconnect the negative battery cable.
2. Press the brake pedal for at least 5 seconds.
3. Connect the negative battery cable.
4. Connect the self-diagnosis tester and ground the test connector.
5. Turn the ignition switch to the ON position for 6 seconds.
6. Start and warm-up the engine.
7. Run engine at 2,000 rpm for 2 minutes (3 minutes on truck).
8. Verify that no more codes are stored.

MPV (G6 engine)
9. Disconnect the negative battery cable for at least 20 seconds.
10. Connect the negative battery cable.
11. Connect the self-diagnosis tester and ground the test connector.
12. Turn the ignition switch to the ON position for 6 seconds.
13. Start and warm-up the engine.
14. Run engine at 2,000 rpm for 3 minutes.
15. Verify that no more codes are stored.

B2200 (FOC engine)
For the pickup with the feedback carburetor fuel system disconnect the negative battery cable for at least 5 seconds.

DIAGNOSTIC TROUBLE CODES

1984–94

1984–85 VEHICLES

2.0L ENGINE (CODE FE)
Code 01 Engine speed
Code 02 Water thermosensor
Code 03 Oxygen sensor
Code 04 Vacuum sensor
Code 05 EGR position sensor

1986–87 VEHICLES

1.6L, 2.0L AND Z2L ENGINES
Code 01 Ignition pulse
Code 02 Air flow meter
Code 03 Water thermosensor
Code 04 Intake air thermo or Temperature sensor
Code 05 Feedback system
Code 06 Atmospheric pressure sensor (1986 1 .6L)
Code 08 EGR position sensor
Code 09 Atmospheric pressure sensor
Code 22 No. 1 Cylinder sensor (2.2L turbocharged)

1988–94 VEHICLES

2.0L, 2.2L, 2.5L, 2.6L AND 3.0L ENGINES
Code 01 Ignition pulse
Code 02 Ne signal—distributor
Code 02 NE 2 signal—crankshaft (1994 2.0L, 1992–94 3.0L)
Code 03 Gi signal—distributor (1988–91 3.0L)
Code 03 G signal—distributor
Code 04G2 signal—distributor (1988–91 3.0L);NE 1 signal—distributor (1994 2.0L, 1992–93 3.0L)
Code 05 Knock sensor and control unit (Left side on 1992-94 3.0L)
Code 06 Speed signal
Code 07 Knock sensor; right side (1992-94 3.0L)
Code 08 Air flow meter
Code 09 Engine coolant temperature sensor (C IS)
Code 10 Intake air temperature sensor
Code 11 Intake air thermosensor—dynamic chamber (3.0L, 2.6L)
Code 13 Intake manifold pressure sensor (1 .3L)
Code 14 Atmospheric pressure sensor (in ECU on 2.6L and 1994 2.5L)
Code 15 Oxygen sensor
Code 15 Oxygen sensor; left side on 1994 2.5L, 1990-94 3.0L
Code 16 EGR position sensor
Code 17 Closed loop system
Code 17 Closed loop system; left side on 1993-94 2.5L 1990-94 3.0L
Code 23 Heated oxygen sensor; right side on 1992-94 1.8L V6, 1994 2.5L 1990-91 3.0L
Code 24 Closed loop system; right side on 1992-94 1 .8L V6, 1993 2.5L 1990-91 3.0L
Code 25 Solenoid valve—pressure regulator
Code 26 Solenoid valve—purge control
Code 26 Solenoid valve—purge control No. 2 (1988-89 3.0L)
Code 27 Solenoid valve—purge control No. 1 (1988-89 3.0L)
Code 27 Solenoid valve—No. 2 purge control (1989 1.6L)
Code 28 Solenoid valve—EGR vacuum
Code 29 Solenoid valve—EGR vent
Code 30 Relay (cold start injector 3.0L)
Code 34 ISC valve
Code 34 Idle air control valve (1993-94 2.0L and 2.5L, 1.6L, 1.8L, 2.6L, 3.1L)
Code 36 Oxygen sensor heater relay (1990 3.0L)
Code 36 Right side oxygen sensor heater (1 992-94 3.0L)
Code 37 Left side oxygen sensor heater (1 992-94 3.0L)
Code 37 Coolant fan relay
Code 40 Oxygen sensor heater relay (1991 3.0L)
Code 40 Solenoid (triple induction system) and oxygen sensor relay (1 988-89 3.0L)
Code 41 Solenoid valve—VRIS (1989–94 MPV 3.0L) Code 41—Solenoid valve—VRIS 1 (1992–94 1.8L V6, 1993 2.5L)
Code 41 Solenoid valve—VICS (3.0L)
Code 42 Solenoid valve—Waste gate (turbocharged)
Code 46 Solenoid valve—VRIS 2 (1992–94 1.8L V6, 1993 2.5L)
Code 65 C signal—PCMT (1 992-94 3.0L)
Code 67 Coolant fan relay No. 1 (1993 2.5L)
Code 67 Coolant fan relay No. 2 (1992–94 1.8L V6)
Code 68 Coolant fan relay No. 2, No.3 with ATX (1993 2.5L)

Code 69 Engine coolant temperature sensor—fan (1992–94 1.8L V6, 1993 2.0L and 2.5L)

Mitsubishi Truck

GENERAL INFORMATION

Mitsubishi uses 2 types of fuel systems. Feedback carburetor system and fuel injection. The type of fuel injection system is known as Electronic Controlled Injection (ECI).

Mitsubishi uses a conventional downdraft two-barrel compound type carburetor which incorporates an automatic choke, accelerator pump, and enrichment system. In addition, a deceleration device is provided.

The Electronic Fuel Injection (EFI) system, used on Mitsubishi vehicles, is classified as a Multi-Point Injection (MPI) system. The MPI system controls the fuel flow, idle speed, and ignition timing. The basic function of the MPI system is to control the air/fuel ratio in accordance with all engine operating conditions. An Electronic Control Unit (ECU) is the heart of the MPI system. Based on data from various sensors, the ECU computes the desired air/fuel ratio.

SELF-DIAGNOSTICS

Service Precautions

• Before connecting or disconnecting the ECU harness connectors, make sure the ignition switch is OFF and the negative battery cable is disconnected to avoid the possibility of damage to the control unit.
• When performing ECU input/output signal diagnosis, remove the pin terminal retainer from the connectors to make it easier to insert tester probes into the connector.
• When connecting or disconnecting pin connectors from the ECU, take care not to bend or break any pin terminals. Check that there are no bends or breaks on ECU pin terminals before attempting any connections.
• Before replacing any ECU, perform the ECU input/output signal diagnosis to make sure the ECU is functioning properly.
• When measuring supply voltage of ECU-controlled components with a circuit tester, separate 1 tester probe from another. If the 2 tester probes accidentally make contact with each other during measurement, a short circuit will result and damage the ECU.

READING CODES

▶ See Figure 34

➥All though the CHECK ENGINE light or Malfunction Indicator Lamp (MIL) will illuminate when there is trouble detected, diagnostic codes can only be retrieved with the use of either a analog voltmeter or a Multi-use Tester. When using diagnostic equipment, always observe the tool manufacturer's instructions.

1984–86 Vehicles

With ECI/MPI Tester
Refer to manufacturer's tester manual regarding diagnosis with this tester.

1985–94 Vehicles

With Analog Voltmeter
The voltmeter can be used to retrieve code numbers of malfunctions which have happened and were memorized or are continuing to happen. On the voltmeter, the malfunction is indicated by a sweep of the needle. The voltmeter should be connected to the data link connector located under the driver side dashboard. Connect the voltmeter between the Multi-Point Injection (MPI) terminal and the ground terminal. Turn the ignition switch ON if the normal condition exists, the voltmeter pointer will indicate a normal pattern. A normal pattern is indicated by constant needle sweeps. If a problem exists in the system the voltmeter pointer will indicate it in a series

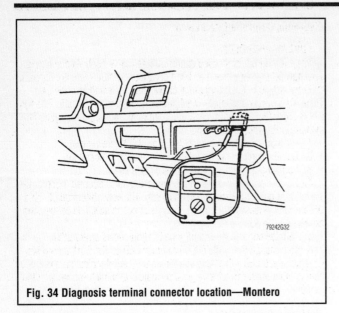

Fig. 34 Diagnosis terminal connector location—Montero

of pointer sweeps. For example, a Code 3 would be 3 consecutive short sweeps of the voltmeter needle.

If there is more than 1 malfunction, the low code numbers will first be indicated and after a 2 second pause (no code indication) the higher code will be indicated.

With Multi-Use Tester

To read the trouble codes using the Multi-Use Tester (MB991341 or equivalent) follow the steps below:

1. Turn the ignition switch OFF.
2. Insert the power supply terminal to the cigarette lighter socket.
3. Connect the tester connector to the diagnosis connector in the glove compartment, under the 'hood or under the driver side dashboard.
4. Turn the ignition switch ON and push the DIAG key.
5. Observe the trouble code and make the necessary repairs.

On most models the CHECK ENGINE malfunction indicator light will light up and remain illuminated to indicate that there is a problem in the system. After this light has been reported to be ON, the system should be checked for malfunction codes.

CLEARING CODES

Without Multi-Use Tester

1984–86 vehicles—engine codes can be cleared by disconnecting the negative battery terminal or by disconnecting ECU connector for 15 seconds or longer.

1987–94 vehicles—engine codes can be cleared by disconnecting the negative battery terminal for 10 seconds or longer.

With Multi-Use Tester

Engine codes may also be cleared by setting the ignition switch to the ON position and using the malfunction code ERASE signal.

DIAGNOSTIC TROUBLE CODES

1989–94 Vehicles

MONTERO, TRUCK AND VAN/WAGON

Code 11 Oxygen sensor
Code 12 Air flow sensor
Code 13 Intake Air Temperature Sensor
Code 14 Throttle Position Sensor (TPS)
Code 15 SC Motor Position Sensor (MPS)
Code 21 Engine Coolant Temperature Sensor
Code 22 Crank angle sensor
Code 23 No. 1 cylinder TDC (Camshaft position) Sensor

Code 24 Vehicle speed sensor
Code 25 Barometric pressure sensor
Code 31 Knock (KS) sensor
Code 32 Manifold pressure sensor
Code 36 Ignition timing adjustment signal
Code 39 Oxygen sensor (rear—turbocharged)
Code 41 Injector
Code 42 Fuel pump
Code 43 EGR-California
Code 44 Ignition Coil; power transistor unit (No. 1 and No. 4 cylinders) on 3.0L
Code 52 Ignition Coil; power transistor unit (No. 2 and No. 5 cylinders) on 3.0L
Code 53 Ignition Coil; power transistor unit (No. 3 and No. 6 cylinders)
Code 55 AC valve position sensor
Code 59 Heated oxygen sensor
Code 61 Transaxle control unit cable (automatic transmission)
Code 62 Warm-up control valve position sensor (non-turbo)

Nissan Truck

GENERAL INFORMATION

Nissan uses 2 types of fuel systems. Electronic Control Carburetor (ECC) system and Electronic Concentrated Control System (ECCS). The ECC system is a Feedback carburetor system. The ECCS is a fuel injected system which may be either throttle body injection or Multi-port injection. Both ECC and ECCS systems were available as of 1984.

SELF-DIAGNOSTICS

Service Precautions

• Do not disconnect the injector harness connectors with the engine running.
• Do not apply battery power directly to the injectors.
• Do not disconnect the ECU harness connectors before the battery ground cable has been disconnected.
• Make sure all ECU connectors are fastened securely. A poor connection can cause an extremely high surge voltage in the coil and condenser and result in damage to integrated circuits.
• When testing the ECU with a DVOM make sure that the probes of the tester never touch each other as this will result in damage to a transistor in the ECU.
• Keep the ECCS harness at least 4 in. away from adjacent harnesses to prevent an ECCS system malfunction due to external electronic noise.
• Keep all parts and harnesses dry during service.
• Before attempting to remove any parts, turn OFF the ignition switch and disconnect the battery ground cable.
• Always use a 12 volt battery as a power source.
• Do not attempt to disconnect the battery cables with the engine running or the ignition key ON.
• Do not clean the air flow meter with any type of detergent.
• Do not attempt to disassemble the ECCS control unit under any circumstances.
• Avoid static electricity build-up by properly grounding yourself prior to handling any ECU or related parts.

READING CODES

▶ See Figures 35, 36 and 37

➡ **Diagnostic codes may be retrieved by observing the code flashes through the LED lights located on the Electronic Control Module (ECM). A special Nissan Consult monitor tool can be used, but is not required. When using special diagnostic equipment, always observe the tool manufacturer's instructions.**

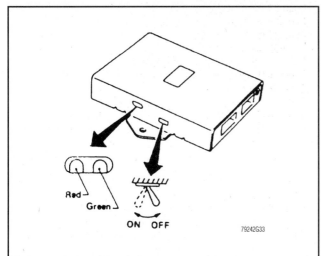

Fig. 35 Entering the self-diagnostics using the ON/OFF mode switch

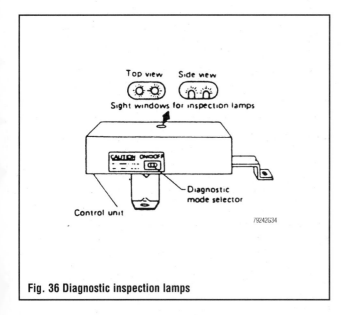

Fig. 36 Diagnostic inspection lamps

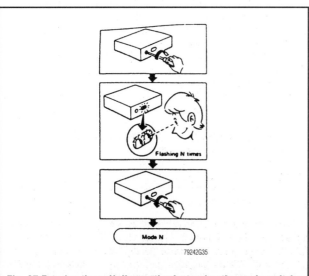

Fig. 37 Entering the self-diagnostics by turning the mode switch

Electronic Controlled Carburetor

1987–88 VEHICLES

The 1.6L (EI 6S) carbureted engine utilizes a duty-controlled solenoid valve for fuel enrichment and an Idle Speed Control (ISC) actuator for basic controls instead of the conventional choke valve plate and fast idle cam. There are several other inputs which further affect the air/fuel ratio. The system is controlled in 2 ways: open or closed loop. To inspect the system for malfunctions, proceed as follows:

1. Position the ECU so the red and green LED's are visible.
2. Run the engine until it is at normal operating temperature.
3. Verify the diagnosis switch on the ECU is OFF.
4. Run the engine 2000 rpm for 5 minutes. After 5 minutes, observe the green LED light while maintaining 2000 rpm. The light should be blinking ON and OFF at least 5 times in 10 seconds. If not as specified, inspect the exhaust gas sensor.
5. Turn the engine OFF and turn the ECU diagnosis switch ON.
6. Turn the ignition switch ON. The green LED on the ECU should stay ON and the red LED will either flash for a short period indicating a malfunctioning input sensor or for a longer time indicating a malfunctioning output sensor.

Electronic Fuel Injection

▶ **See Figures 38, 39, 40 and 41**

1984–94 VEHICLES

Two types of diagnostic systems are used in Nissan vehicles: the 2-mode diagnostic system and the 5-mode diagnostic system. The 2 mode system is used in some vehicles starting in 1990, ultimately, all vehicles used the 2-mode system after 1991 with the exception of 1991-94 Maxima (VG30E engine), Pathfinder and Truck. These vehicles continued to use the 5-mode system. The 5-mode system began in 1984.

The 5-mode diagnostic system is incorporated in the ECU which uses inputs from various sensors to determine the correct air/fuel ratio. If any of the sensors malfunction the ECU will store the code in memory. The 5-mode diagnostic system is capable of various tests as outlined below. When using these modes, the ECM may have to be removed from its mounting bracket to better access the mode selector switch.

➡**Vehicles are equipped with a CHECK ENGINE light on the instrument panel. If any systems are malfunctioning, the light will illuminate the same time as the red lamp while the engine is running and the system is in Mode 1.**

Mode 1—Heated Oxygen Sensor

During closed loop operation the green lamp turns ON when a lean condition is detected and turns OFF under a rich condition. During open loop the green lamp remains ON or OFF. This mode is used to check Heated Oxygen sensor functions for correct operation. To enter Mode 1, proceed as follows:

1. Turn the ignition switch ON.
2. Turn the diagnostic switch located on the side of the ECU ON by either flipping the switch to the ON position or turning the screw switch fully clockwise.
3. Turn the diagnostic switch OFF or fully counterclockwise as soon as the inspection lamps flash 1 time.
4. The self-diagnostic system is now in Mode 1.

Mode 2- Mixture Ratio Feedback Control Monitor

The green inspection lamp is operating in the same manner as in Mode 1. During closed loop operation the red inspection lamp turns ON and OFF simultaneously with the green lamp when the mixture ratio is controlled within the specified value. During open loop the red lamp remains ON or OFF. Mode 2 is used for checking that optimum control of the fuel mixture is obtained. To enter Mode 2, proceed as follows:

1. Turn the ignition switch ON.
2. Turn the diagnostic switch ON, by either flipping the switch to the ON position or use a screwdriver and turn the switch fully clockwise.
3. Turn the diagnostic switch OFF or fully counterclockwise as soon as the inspection lamps flash 2 times.

4. The self-diagnostic system is now in Mode 2.

Mode 3- Self-Diagnosis System

This mode of the self-diagnostics is for stored code retrieval. To enter Mode 3, proceed as follows:

1. Thoroughly warm the engine before proceeding. With the engine OFF, turn the ignition switch ON.

2. Turn the diagnostic switch located on the side of the ECU ON by either flipping the switch to the ON position or using a screwdriver, turn the switch fully clockwise.

3. Turn the diagnostic switch OFF or fully counterclockwise as soon as the inspection lamps flash 3 times.

4. The self-diagnostic system is now in Mode 3.

➡**When the battery is disconnected or self-diagnostic Mode 4 is selected after using Mode 3, all stored codes will be cleared. However if the ignition key is turned OFF and then the procedure is followed to enter Mode 4 directly, the stored codes will not be cleared.**

5. The codes will now be displayed by the red and green inspection lamps flashing. The red lamp will flash first and the green lamp will follow. The red lamp is the tens and the green lamp is the units, that is, the red lamp flashes 1 time and the green lamp flashes 2 times, this would indicate a Code 12.

Mode 4- On/Off Switches

This mode checks the operation of the Vehicle Speed Sensor (VSS), Closed Throttle Position (CTP) and starter switches. Entering this mode will also clear all stored codes in the ECU. To enter Mode 4, proceed as follows:

1. Turn the ignition switch ON.

2. Turn the diagnostic switch located on the side of the ECU ON by either flipping the switch to the ON position or turning the mode switch fully clockwise.

3. Turn the diagnostic switch OFF or fully counterclockwise as soon as the inspection lamps flash 4 times.

4. The self-diagnostic system is now in Mode 4.

5. Turn the ignition switch to the START position and verify the red inspection lamp illuminates. This verifies that the starter switch is working.

6. Depress the accelerator and verify the red inspection lamp goes OFF. This verifies that the CTP switch is working.

7. Raise and properly support the vehicle and verify the lamp goes ON when the vehicle speed is above 12 mph (20 km/h). This verifies that the VSS is working

8. Turn the ignition switch OFF.

Mode 5- Real Time Diagnostics

In this mode the ECU is capable of detecting and alerting the technician the instant a malfunction in the crank angle sensor, air flow meter, ignition signal or the fuel pump occurs while operating/driving the vehicle. Items which are noted to be malfunctioning are not stored in the ECU's memory. To enter Mode 5, proceed as follows:

1. Turn the ignition switch ON.

2. Turn the diagnostic switch located on the side of the ECU ON by either flipping the switch to the ON position or by turning the switch fully clockwise.

3. Turn the diagnostic switch OFF or fully counterclockwise as soon as the inspection lamps flash 5 times.

4. The self-diagnostic system is now in Mode 5.

5. Ensure the inspection lamps are not flashing. If they are, count the number of flashes within a 3.2 second period:

- 1 Flash = Crank angle sensor
- 2 Flashes = Air flow meter
- 3 Flashes = Fuel pump
- 4 Flashes = Ignition signal

2-MODE DIAGNOSTIC SYSTEM

The 1993-94 Quest uses a 2-mode diagnostic system incorporated in the ECU which uses inputs from various sensors to determine the correct air/fuel ratio. If any of the sensors malfunction the ECU will store the code in memory.

A Nissan Consult monitor, or equivalent may be used to retrieve these codes by simply connecting the monitor to the diagnostic connector located

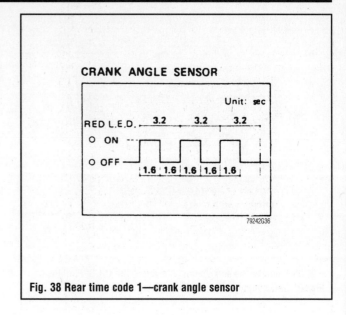

Fig. 38 Rear time code 1—crank angle sensor

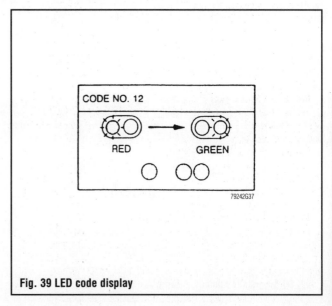

Fig. 39 LED code display

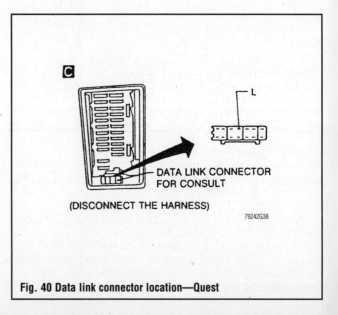

Fig. 40 Data link connector location—Quest

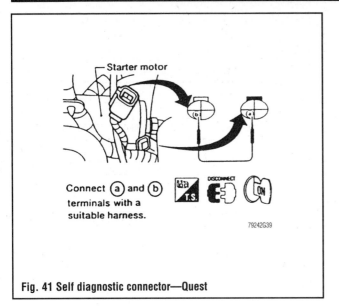

Connect (a) and (b) terminals with a suitable harness.

79242G39

Fig. 41 Self diagnostic connector—Quest

on the driver's side near the hood release. Turn the ignition switch to ON and press START, ENGINE and then SELF-DIAG RESULTS, the results will then be output to the monitor.

The conventional CHECK ENGINE or red LED ECU light may also be used for self-diagnostics. The conventional 2-Mode diagnostic system is broken into 2 separate modes each capable of 2 tests, an ignition switch ON or engine running test as outlined below:

Mode 1—Bulb Check
In this mode the RED indicator light on the ECU and the CHECK ENGINE light should be ON. To enter this mode simply turn the ignition switch ON and observe the light.

Mode I—Malfunction Warning
In this mode the ECU is acknowledging if there is a malfunction by illuminating the RED indicator light on the ECU and the CHECK ENGINE light. If the light turns OFF, the system is normal. To enter this mode, simply start the engine and observe the light.

Mode 2—Self-Diagnostic Codes—Quest
In this mode the ECU will output all malfunctions via the CHECK ENGINE light or the red LED on the ECU. The code may be retrieved by counting the number of flashes. The longer flashes indicate the first digit and the shorter flashes indicate the second digit. To enter this mode proceed as follows:
1. Turn the ignition switch ON, but do not start the vehicle.
2. Disconnect harness connectors and connect terminals A and B with a jumper wire.
3. Wait 2 seconds, remove the jumper wire and reconnect the harness connector.
4. Observe the CHECK ENGINE light for stored codes.

Mode 2—Exhaust Gas Sensor Monitor
In this mode the red LED on the ECU or CHECK ENGINE light will display the condition of the fuel mixture and whether the system is in closed loop or open loop. When the light flashes ON, the exhaust gas sensor is indicating a lean mixture. When the light stays OFF, the sensor is indicating a rich mixture. If the light remains ON or OFF, it is indicating an open loop system. If the system is equipped with 2 exhaust gas sensors, the left side will operate first. If already in Mode 2, proceed to Step C to enter the exhaust gas sensor monitor.
1. On all models except Quest, perform the following steps:
    a. Turn the ignition switch ON.
    b. Turn the diagnostic switch ON, by turning the switch fully clockwise for 2 seconds and then fully counterclockwise.
    c. Start the engine and run until thoroughly warm. Raise the idle to 2,000 rpm and hold for approximately 2 minutes. Ensure the red LED or CHECK ENGINE light flashes ON and OFF more than 5 times every 10 seconds with the engine speed at 2,000 rpm.

➡If equipped with 2 exhaust gas sensors, switch to the right sensor by turning the ECU mode selector fully clockwise for 2 seconds and then fully counterclockwise with the engine running.

2. On Quest models, perform the following steps:
    a. Turn the ignition switch ON.
    b. Disconnect harness connectors and connect terminals A and B with a jumper wire.
    c. Wait 2 seconds, remove the jumper wire and reconnect the harness connectors.
    d. Start the engine and run until thoroughly warm. Raise the idle to 2,000 rpm and hold for approximately 2 minutes. Ensure the red LED or CHECK ENGINE light flashes ON and OFF more than 5 times every 10 seconds with the engine speed at 2,000 rpm.

CLEARING CODES

Engine Codes

Except Mode 5, 3 and 2 Systems
All control unit diagnostic codes may be cleared by disconnecting the negative battery cable for a period of 15 seconds. Entering Mode 4 of the Electronic Fuel Injection system diagnostics will also clear stored ECM engine codes.

Mode 5, 3 and 2 Systems
On 5-mode systems, enter mode 4 immediately after using mode 3 and the codes will be cleared. On 2-mode systems, the codes will be cleared when mode 1 is re-entered from mode 2. The Nissan Consult Monitor or equivalent can also be used to clear codes on 2-mode systems.

DIAGNOSTIC TROUBLE CODES

1984–87 Vehicles

Code 11 Crankshaft position sensor circuit
Code 12 Mass Air flow sensor circuit
Code 13 Engine coolant temperature sensor circuit
Code 21 Ignition signal circuit
Code 22 Fuel pump circuit
Code 23 Idle switch circuit
Code 24 Transmission switch
Code 31 AC switch, fast idle control of load signal
Code 32 Starter signal
Code 33 EGR gas sensor
Code 34 Detonation (Knock) sensor
Code 41 Air or Fuel temperature sensor
Code 42 Throttle sensor (or BP sensor in Canada)
Code 43 Mixture feedback control slips out (or low battery in Canada)
Code 44 No Malfunctioning circuits

1988–94 Vehicles

Code 11 Crankshaft position sensor circuit
Code 12 Mass Air flow sensor circuit
Code 13 Engine coolant temperature sensor circuit
Code 14 Vehicle speed sensor circuit
Code 15 Mixture ratio feedback control slips out (1988)
Code 21 Ignition signal circuit
Code 22 Fuel pump circuit (to 1991)
Code 23 Idle switch circuit (to 1991)
Code 24 Fuel Switch circuit or OD. switch circuit (to 1990)
Code 25 AAC valve circuit (to 1991)
Code 31 Electronic Control Module (ECM) or A/C circuit
Code 32 Exhaust Gas Recirculation (EGR) function
Code 33 Oxygen sensor circuit (left side, if two)
Code 34 Knock sensor circuit
Code 35 Exhaust gas temperature sensor circuit
Code 41 Air temperature sensor circuit
Code 42 Fuel temperature sensor circuit
Code 43 Throttle position sensor circuit

Code 44 No malfunctioning circuits
Code 45 Injector leak
Code 51 Injector circuit
Code 53 Heated oxygen sensor circuit (right side)
Code 54 Signal circuit from NT control unit to ECM
Code 55 No malfunctioning in the above circuits

Suzuki Truck

GENERAL INFORMATION

▶ **See Figure 42**

Suzuki used both feedback carburetor and fuel injection systems.
Suzuki uses the Hitachi 2-barrel, downdraft type carburetor, which has both a primary and secondary system. A feedback system is provided to maintain the air/fuel ratio, to reduce emission levels and to improve fuel economy simultaneously.

The primary system operates under normal driving conditions and the secondary system operates under high speed-high load driving conditions. A choke valve is provided in the primary system.

The primary system is equipped with a choke system. The choke system is a fully automatic type using a thermo-wax. A mixture control solenoid valve is also incorporated which is operated by an electrical signal from the Electronic Control Module (ECM). The acceleration pump system and a fuel cutoff solenoid are also part of the primary system.

The secondary system is equipped with a secondary diaphragm through which vacuum is supplied from the primary side, via a Vacuum Switching Valve (VSV) and a Vacuum Transmitting Valve (VTV), to operate the secondary throttle valve. The VSV and VTV are used only on the Suzuki Samurai and have been eliminated on the Suzuki Sidekick 1300cc.

A Switch vent solenoid valve is provided on the top of the float chamber. Its purpose is to reduce the evaporative emissions. The 2-barrel, downdraft type carburetor is also equipped with a idle-up system.

This system operates at idle and compensates the idle speed when any of the following conditions exist:
• When any electrical load (lights, rear defogger, heater fan, etc.) is operating.
• When the vehicle is at a high altitude.
• When the engine temperature is below 44°F (7°C).
• When the engine speed is lower than 1500 rpm after the engine is started.

The Electronic Fuel Injection (EFI) system supplies the vehicle's combustion chambers with air/fuel mixture of optimized ratio under varying driving conditions. Fuel delivery through the injector is controlled electrically by the Electronic Control Module (ECM).

SELF-DIAGNOSTICS

Service Precautions

• Keep the ECM parts and harnesses dry during service. Protect the ECM and all solid-state components from rough handling or temperature extremes.
• Use extreme care when working around the ECM or other components.
• Disconnect the negative battery cable before attempting to disconnect or remove any parts.
a Disconnect the negative battery cable and ECM connector before performing arc welding on the vehicle.
• Disconnect and remove the ECM from the vehicle before subjecting the vehicle to the temperatures experienced in a heated paint booth.

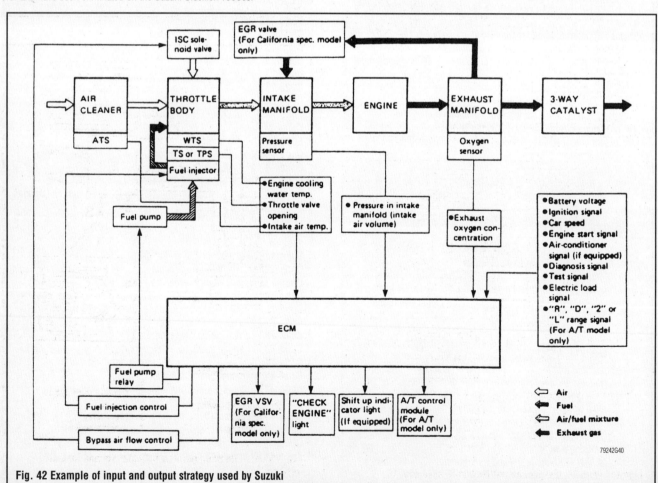

Fig. 42 Example of input and output strategy used by Suzuki

79242G40

READING CODES

1989–95 Vehicles

▶ See Figures 43, 44, 45 and 46

On Swift and Samurai, the ECM memory is activated by connecting the spare fuse to the diagnosis switch terminal and turning the ignition switch ON. The fuse panel is located under the instrument panel, near the driver's side kick panel. On Sidekick models the diagnostic terminals B and C must be grounded. The diagnostic terminal is located under the hood, on the right rear side.

The diagnostic codes are flashed by the CHECK ENGINE light or Malfunction Indicator Lamp (MIL) on the dash. The memory displays the codes in numerical order from lowest to highest. The order in which the codes are displayed does not necessarily indicate the order in which the malfunction occurred. The ECM displays each code 3 times, then moves on the next code in numerical order. The entire sequence is repeated as long as the diagnosis switch terminal is grounded and the ignition switch is in the ON position.

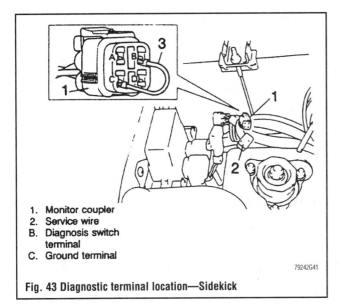

1. Monitor coupler
2. Service wire
B. Diagnosis switch terminal
C. Ground terminal

79242G41

Fig. 43 Diagnostic terminal location—Sidekick

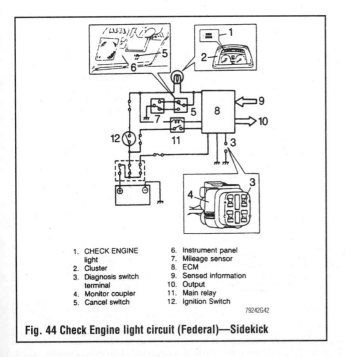

1. CHECK ENGINE light
2. Cluster
3. Diagnosis switch terminal
4. Monitor coupler
5. Cancel switch
6. Instrument panel
7. Mileage sensor
8. ECM
9. Sensed information
10. Output
11. Main relay
12. Ignition Switch

79242G42

Fig. 44 Check Engine light circuit (Federal)—Sidekick

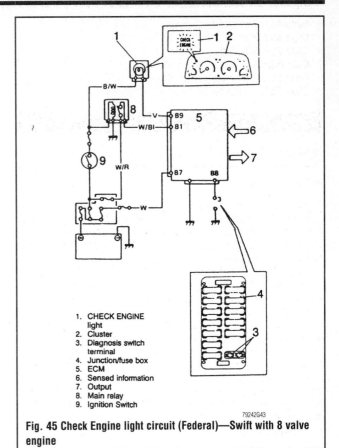

1. CHECK ENGINE light
2. Cluster
3. Diagnosis switch terminal
4. Junction/fuse box
5. ECM
6. Sensed information
7. Output
8. Main relay
9. Ignition Switch

79242G43

Fig. 45 Check Engine light circuit (Federal)—Swift with 8 valve engine

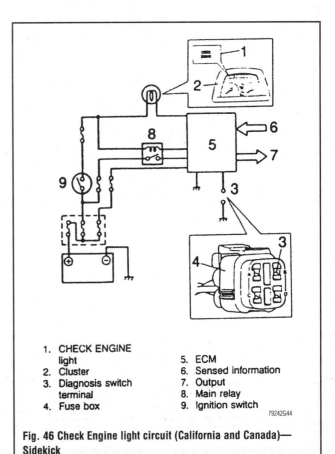

1. CHECK ENGINE light
2. Cluster
3. Diagnosis switch terminal
4. Fuse box
5. ECM
6. Sensed information
7. Output
8. Main relay
9. Ignition switch

79242G44

Fig. 46 Check Engine light circuit (California and Canada)—Sidekick

CLEARING CODES

1989–95 Vehicles

When repairs have been completed, erase the ECM back-up memory by disconnecting the negative battery cable or the ECM harness connector for 30 seconds or longer.

DIAGNOSTIC TROUBLE CODES

1986–95 Vehicles

Code 12 Normal
Code 13 Oxygen sensor circuit
Code 14 Engine Coolant Temperature (ECT) Sensor circuit—low temperature indicated, signal voltage high
Code 15 Engine Coolant Temperature (ECT) Sensor circuit—high temperature indicated, signal voltage low
Code 21 Throttle Position Sensor (TPS) circuit—signal voltage high
Code 22 Throttle Position Sensor (TPS) circuit—signal voltage low
Code 23 Air Temperature Sensor (ATS) circuit—low temperature indicated, signal voltage high
Code 24 Vehicle Speed Sensor (VSS) circuit
Code 25 Air Temperature Sensor (ATS) circuit—high temperature indicated, signal voltage low
Code 31 Pressure Sensor (PS) circuit—high pressure indicated, signal voltage high

Code 32 Pressure Sensor (PS) circuit—low pressure indicated, signal voltage low
Code 33 Mass Air Flow Sensor (MAS) circuit—signal voltage high
Code 34 Mass Air Flow Sensor (MAS) circuit—signal voltage low
Code 41 Ignition signal
Code 42 Crank Angle Sensor (CAS) circuit (except 1989–90 Sidekick) or Fifth switch circuit, Lock-up signal circuit (1989–90 Sidekick)
Code 44 Idle switch of Throttle Position Sensor (TPS) -open circuit
Code 45 Idle switch of Throttle Position Sensor (TPS) -shorted circuit
Code 51 Exhaust Gas Recirculation (EGR) system and/or Recirculated Exhaust Gas Temperature Sensor (REGTS) system—California vehicle
Code 52 Fuel Injector—California vehicle
Code 53 Ground circuit—California vehicle
Code 54 Fifth gear switch circuit
Code 71 Test switch circuit

Toyota Truck

GENERAL INFORMATION

♦ **See Figure 47**

Toyota vehicles may be fitted with either a Feedback Carburetor (FBC) or Multi-port Fuel Injection (MEI) system. The Toyota Feedback Carburetor (FBC) system was used on selected engines from 1983 1990. Two types of carburetors were used. The 3E engine used a variable venturi carburetor,

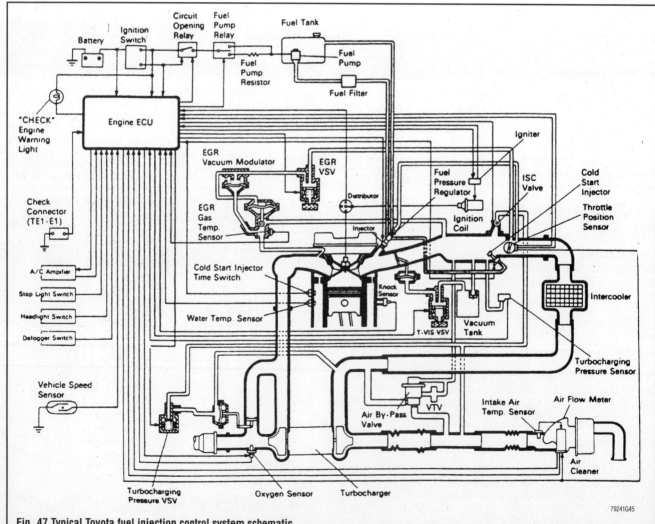

Fig. 47 Typical Toyota fuel injection control system schematic

79241G45

while all other engines used a more typical down draft style carburetor. The Multi-port Fuel Injection system was first used in 1980 and continues in use today.

SELF-DIAGNOSTICS

As the engine control computers became capable of more functions, self-diagnostic and memory circuits were added.

These systems allow the ECU to note a fault, assign an identity code and store the code in memory for later retrieval.

All fuel injected control engine units possess the ability to provide fault codes during diagnosis. The number, type and meaning of engine codes vary by year and model.

While most fault codes are held in an electronic memory and are retained even after the ignition is switched OFF, certain codes are only held or displayed as long as the ignition is ON. If the fault is present at the next restart, the code will reset.

When a controller or ECU notes a fault, the dash warning lamp for the appropriate system will be lit to advise the operator. If the dash lamp is normally lit during system operation, as in the case of cruise control, the lamp will flash when a fault is found. The illumination or flashing of the dash lamp indicates that the controller has detected a fault and placed itself into the back-up or default mode.

Beginning in 1995 some models were equipped with an on board diagnostic system known as OBD-II. To diagnose this system an OBD-II scan tool, complying with SAE J1978 or TOYOTA hand held tester is necessary to access codes and read data output from the ECM. This is a rather expensive tool and not cost effective for the general public. The following model and engine applications are equipped with the OBD-II system:

- 1995 Previa with a 2TZ-FZE engine
- 1995 Tacoma
- 1995 T100

Service Precautions

- Keep all ECU parts and harnesses dry during service. Protect the ECU and all solid-state components from rough handling or extremes of temperature.
- Before attempting to remove any parts, turn the ignition switch OFF and disconnect the battery ground cable.
- Make sure all harness connectors are fastened securely. A poor connection can cause an extremely high voltage surge, resulting in damage to integrated circuits.
- Always use a 12 volt battery as a power source.
- Do not attempt to disconnect the battery cables with the engine running.
- Do not attempt to disassemble the ECU unit under any circumstances.
- If installing a 2-way or CB radio, mobile phone or other radio equipment, keep the antenna as far as possible away from the electronic control unit. Keep the antenna feeder line at least 8 in. away from the EEI harness and do not run the lines parallel for a long distance. Be sure to ground the radio to the vehicle body.
- When performing ECU input/output signal diagnosis, remove the water-proofing rubber plug, if equipped, from the connectors to make it easier to insert tester probes into the connector. Always reinstall it after testing.
- When connecting or disconnecting pin connectors from the ECU, take care not to bend or break any pin terminals. Check that there are no bends or breaks on ECU pin terminals before attempting any connections.
- When measuring supply voltage of ECU-controlled components, keep the tester probes separated from each other and from accidental grounding. If the tester probes accidentally make contact with each other during measurement, a short circuit will damage the ECU.
- Use great care when working on or around air bag systems. Wait at least 20 seconds after turning the ignition switch to LOCK and disconnecting the negative battery cable before performing any other work. The air bag system is equipped with a back-up power system which will keep the system functional for 20 seconds without battery power.

- All air bag connectors are a standard yellow color; the related wiring is encased in standard yellow sheathing. Testing and diagnostic procedures must be followed exactly when performing diagnosis on this system. Improper procedures may cause accidental deployment or disable the system when needed.
- Never attempt to measure the resistance of the air bag squib; detonation may occur.

READING CODES

The following procedures are for all vehicles except those equipped with the OBD-II system. Accessing OBD-II system codes can only be accomplished with the use of a OBD-II scan tool, complying with SAE J1978 or TOYOTA hand held tester. This is a rather expensive tool and not cost effective for the general public. The following models are equipped with the OBD-II system:

- 1995 Previa with a 2TZ-FZE engine
- 1995 Tacoma
- 1995 T100

1983–86 Vehicles

♦ See Figures 48, 49, 50 and 51

The diagnostic codes can be read by the number of blinks of the 'Check Engine' warning light when the proper terminals of the check connector are short-circuited. If the vehicle is equipped with a super monitor display, the diagnostic code is indicated on the display screen. The initial conditions for entering the self-diagnostics are as follows:

1. The battery voltage of the vehicle should be above 11 volts. The throttle valve must be in a fully closed position (throttle position sensor IDL points closed).
2. If equipped with an automatic transmission, place it in P or N.
3. Turn the air conditioning switch OFF.
4. Start the engine and allow it reach normal operating temperature.

Except Super Monitor Display—Normal Mode

1. Turn the ignition switch to the ON position. Do not start the engine. Remove the protective rubber cap and, with a jumper wire connect the terminals of the check connector.
2. Read the diagnostic code as indicated by the number of flashes of the 'Check Engine' warning light.

➡**On some early models, install an analog voltmeter to the EFI service connector. Read diagnostic codes by voltmeter needle deflection between OV-2.5V-5V. The voltmeter needle will fluctuate between 5V and 2.5V every 0.6 seconds.**

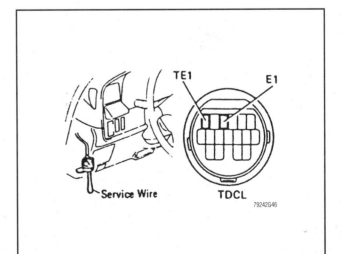

Fig. 48 Toyota Diagnostic Communication Link (TDCL)—normal mode

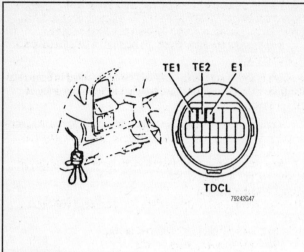

Fig. 49 Toyota Diagnostic Communication Link (TDCL)—test mode

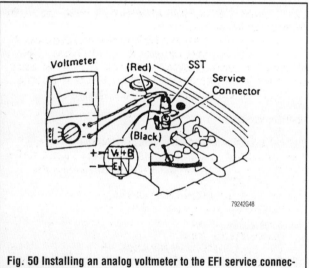

Fig. 50 Installing an analog voltmeter to the EFI service connector—early models

3. If the system is operating normally (no malfunction), the light will blink once every ¼ second. On single digit code number systems, the light will blink once every 3 or 4.5 seconds.

4. In the event of a malfunction, the light will blink once every ½ second (on some models it may be 1, 2 or 3 seconds). The 1st number of blinks will equal the 1st digit of a 2-digit diagnostic code. After a 1.5 second pause, the 2nd number of blinks will equal the 2nd number of a 2-digit diagnostic code. If there are 2 or more codes, there will be a 2.5 second pause between each. On single digit code number systems the light will blink a number of times equal to the malfunction code indication every 2 or 4.5 seconds.

5. After all the codes have been output, there will be a 4.5 second pause and they will be repeated as long as the terminals of the check connector are shorted.

➡**In event of multiple trouble codes, indication will begin from the smaller value and continue to the larger in order.**

6. After the diagnosis check, remove the jumper wire from the check connector and install the protective rubber cap.

Test Mode

1. Using a jumper wire, connect the TE2 and E1 terminals of the Toyota Diagnostic Communication Link (TDCL), then turn the ignition switch ON to begin the diagnostic test mode.

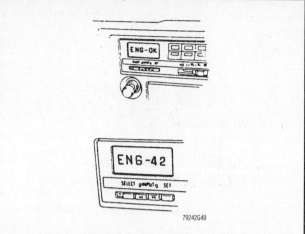

Fig. 51 Example of the Super Monitor display. When correctly engaged, the system will provide system identifiers such as ENG, ABS or ECT.

2. Start the engine and drive the vehicle at a speed of 10 mph or more. Simulate the conditions where the malfunction has been reported to happen.

3. Using a jumper wire, connect the TE2 and E1 terminals of the TDCL connector.

4. Read the diagnosis code as indicated by the number of 'Check Engine' light flashes.

5. After diagnosis check remove the jumper wires.

Super Monitor Display

The super monitor display system was offered as an option on some late model Toyota vehicles.

1. Turn the ignition switch ON but do not start the engine.

2. Simultaneously push and hold in the SELECT and INPUT M keys for at least 3 seconds. The letters DIAG will appear on the screen.

3. After a short pause, hold the SET key in for at least 3 seconds. If the system is normal (no malfunctions), ENG-OK will appear on the screen.

4. If there is a malfunction, the code number for it will appear on the screen. In event of 2 or more numbers, there will be a 3 second pause between each (example:EN-42).

1987–89 Vehicles

◆ **See Figures 52, 53 and 54**

Stored fault codes are transmitted through the blinking of the CHECK engine warning lamp. This occurs only when the system is placed into the diagnostic mode; it does not occur while the vehicle is being driven.

To read the fault codes:

1. The following initial conditions must be met:
   a. Battery voltage at or above 11 volts.
   b. Throttle fully closed.
   c. Transmission in N or P.
   d. All electrical systems and accessories OFF.

2. Turn the ignition ON but do not start the engine.

3. Use a jumper wire to connect terminals T and E1 at the diagnostic connector. On all 1989 vehicles except Corolla, MR2 and Tercel, connect terminals TE1 and Et. For 1988–89 Vans, jumper the 2 pins of the service connector. On 1989 Corolla, MR2 and Tercel, connect terminals T and E1.

4. The fault codes will be transmitted through the controlled flashing of the CHECK engine warning lamp.

5. If no malfunction was found or no code was stored, the lamp will flash 2 times per second with no other pauses or patterns. This confirms that the diagnostic system is working but has nothing to report. This light pattern may be referred to as the System Normal signal; it should be present when no other codes are stored.

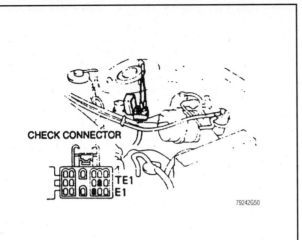

Fig. 52 To read the engine codes, the computer must be put into the diagnostic mode by connecting the proper terminals

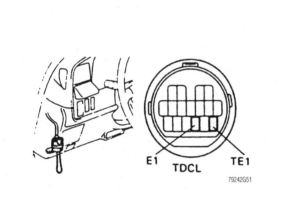

Fig. 53 Some vehicles are equipped with TDCL connector below the left dash

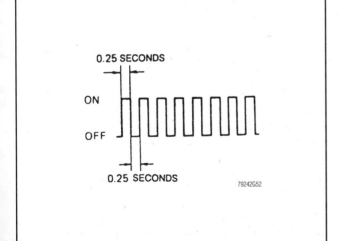

Fig. 54 The system normal signal is transmitted by a steady flashing of the lamp

6. The CHECK lamp will blink the number of the code(s). All codes are 2 digits; the pulsing of the light represents the digits, not the count. For example, Code 25 is displayed as 2 flashes a pause and 5 flashes.

7. If more than 2 codes are stored, the next will be transmitted after a 2½ second pause.

→If multiple codes are stored, they will be transmitted in numerical order from lowest to highest. This does not indicate the order of fault occurrence.

8. When all codes have been transmitted, the entire pattern will repeat after a 4½ second pause. The repeats continue as long as the diagnostic terminals are connected.

9. After recording the codes, disconnect the jumper at the diagnostic connector and turn the ignition OFF.

Super Monitor System

This procedure is used on Cressida and Supra equipped with Super Monitor.

10. The following initial conditions must be met:
   a. Battery voltage at or above 11 volts.
   b. Throttle fully closed.
   c. Transmission in N or P.
   d. All electrical systems and accessories OFF.

11. Turn the ignition ON but do not start the engine.

12. Simultaneously press and hold the SELECT and INPUT M keys for at least 2 seconds. The letters DIAG will appear on the screen, showing that the system is in the diagnostic mode.

13. After a short pause, hold in the SET key for at least 2 seconds.

14. If the system is normal, with no faults stored, the message ENG OK will appear on the screen. If faults are stored, the code number will appear on the screen with a system designator; for example, ENG-42. If 2 or more codes are stored, each will appear after a 3 second pause.

1990–95 Vehicles

Stored fault codes are transmitted through the blinking of the CHECK engine warning lamp. This occurs only when the system is placed into the diagnostic mode; it does not occur while the vehicle is being driven.

To read the fault codes:

1. The following initial conditions must be met:
   a. Battery voltage at or above 11 volts.
   b. Throttle fully closed.
   c. Transmission in N or P.
   d. All electrical systems and accessories OFF.

2. Turn the ignition ON but do not start the engine.

3. Use a jumper wire to connect terminals TE1 and E1 at the diagnostic connector in the engine compartment or at the TDCL connector below the left dashboard if so equipped.

4. The fault codes will be transmitted through the controlled flashing of the CHECK ENGINE warning lamp.

5. If no malfunction was found or no code was stored, the lamp will flash 2 times per second with no other pauses or patterns. This confirms that the diagnostic system is working but has nothing to report. This light pattern may be referred to as the System Normal signal; it should be present when no other codes are stored.

6. The CHECK lamp will blink the number of the code(s). All codes are 2-digit; the pulsing of the light represents the digits, not the count. For example, Code 25 is displayed as 2 flashes, a pause and 5 flashes.

7. If more than 1 code is stored, the next will be transmitted after a 2½ second pause.

→If multiple codes are stored, they will be transmitted in numerical order from lowest to highest. This does not indicate the order of fault occurrence.

8. When all codes have been transmitted, the entire pattern will repeat after a 4½ second pause. The repeats continue as long as the diagnostic terminals are connected.

9. After recording the codes, disconnect the jumper at the diagnostic connector and turn the ignition OFF.

CLEARING CODES

1986–95

Stored codes will remain in memory until cleared. The correct method of clearing codes is to turn the ignition switch OFF, then remove the proper fuse. On all vehicles except as noted below, remove the EEI fuse. Each fuse must be removed for at least 10 seconds. The time required may be longer in cold weather.

Disconnecting the negative battery cable will also clear the memory but is not recommended due to other on-board memories being cleared as well. Once the system power is restored, re-check for stored codes. Only the System Normal indication should be present. If any other code is stored, the clearing procedure must be repeated or additional repairs performed; the old code will remain stored along with any new ones.

After repairs, it is recommended to clear the memory before test driving the vehicle. Upon returning from the drive, interrogate the memory; if the original code is again present, the repair was unsuccessful.

DIAGNOSTIC TROUBLE CODES

1983–1984 Engine

Code 1 Normal operation
Code 2 Open or shorted air flow meter circuit—defective air flow meter or Electronic Control Unit (ECU)
Code 3 Open or shorted air flow meter circuit—defective air flow meter or Electronic Control Unit (ECU)
Code 4 Open Water Thermosnsor (THW) circuit—defective Water Thermosensor (THW) or Electronic Control Unit (ECU)
Code 5 Open or shorted oxygen sensor circuit—lean or rich indication—defective oxygen sensor or Electronic Control Unit (ECU)
Code 6 No ignition signal—defective ignition system circuit, Integrated Ignition Assembly (IIA) or Electronic Control Unit (ECU)
Code 7 Defective Throttle Position Sensor (TPS) circuit, Throttle Position Sensor (TPS) or Electronic Control Unit (ECU)

1985–1987 Engines

➡The 1985 2.0L (25-E and 3Y-EC) engines use 1984 Codes

Code 1 Normal operation
Code 2 Open or shorted air flow meter circuit—defective air flow meter or Electronic Control Unit (ECU)
Code 3 No signal from igniter 4 times in succession -defective igniter or main relay circuit, igniter or Electronic Control Unit (ECU)
Code 4 Open Water Thermosensor (THW) circuit—defective Water Thermosensor (THW) or Electronic Control Unit (ECU)
Code 5 Open or shorted oxygen sensor circuit—lean or rich indication—defective oxygen sensor or Electronic Control Unit (ECU)
Code 6 No engine revolution sensor (Ne) signal to Electronic Control Unit (ECU) or Ne value being over 1000 rpm in spite of no Ne signal to ECU—defective igniter circuit, igniter, distributor or Electronic Control Unit (ECU)
Code 7 Open or shorted Throttle Position Sensor (TPS) circuit, Throttle Position Sensor (TPS) or Electronic Control Unit (ECU)
Code 8 Open or shorted intake air thermosensor circuit -defective intake air thermosensor circuit or Electronic Control Unit (ECU)
Code 10 No starter switch signal to Electronic Control Unit (ECU) with vehicle speed at 0 and engine speed over 800 rpm—defective speed sensor circuit, main relay circuit, igniter switch to starter circuit, igniter switch or Electronic Control Unit (ECU)
Code 11 Short circuit in check connector terminal T with the air conditioning switch ON or throttle switch (IDL) contact point OFF—defective air conditioner switch, Throttle Position Sensor (TPS) circuit, Throttle Position Sensor (TPS) or Electronic Control Unit (ECU)
Code 12 Knock control sensor signal has not reached judgement level in succession—defective knock control sensor circuit, knock control sensor or Electronic Control Unit (ECU)
Code 13 Knock CPU faulty

1988–95 Engines except 1995 OBD-II

Constant blinking of indicator light: No faults detected
Code 11 Momentary interruption in power supply to ECU; up to 1991
Code 12 Engine revolution (NE or G) signal to ECU; missing within several seconds after engine is cranked
Code 13 Rpm NE signal to ECU; missing when engine speed is above 1000 rpm
Code 14 Igniter (IGE) signal to ECU; missing 4–11 times in succession
Code 16 ECT control signal—normal signal missing from ECT CPU (1990–94)
Code 16 A/T control system—normal signal missing from between the engine CPU and A/T CPU in the ECM (1995)
Code 21 Main oxygen sensor signal; voltage output does not exceed a set value on the lean and rich sides continuously for a certain period of time or open/short sensor heater circuit
Code 22 Water temperature sensor circuit (THW); open/short for 500 msec. or more
Code 23 Intake air temperature signal (THA)
Code 24 Intake air temperature sensor circuit (THA); open/short for 500 msec. or more
Code 25 Air/fuel ratio LEAN malfunction; Oxygen sensor output is less than 0.45 V for at least 90 seconds when oxygen sensor is warmed up (engine racing at 2000 rpm). California only: air/fuel ratio feedback compensation/adaptive control: feedback value continues at upper (LEAN) limit, or is not renewed, for a certain period of time.
Code 26 Air/fuel ratio RICH malfunction; California only: Air/fuel ratio feedback compensation/adaptive control: feedback value continues at lower (RICH) limit, or is not renewed, for a certain period of time.
Code 27 Sub-oxygen sensor signal; detection of sensor/signal deterioration or open/short sensor heater circuit (California only)
Code 28 No. 2 oxygen sensor signal/heater signal
Code 31 Air flow meter circuit; open or shorted when idle contacts are closed
Code 31 Vacuum (Manifold absolute pressure) sensor signal; open/short circuit
Code 32 Air flow meter circuit; circuit open or shorted when idling
Code 34 Turbocharging pressure signal; excessive pressure
Code 35 Altitude compensation (HAC) sensor signal; open/short
Code 35 Turbocharging pressure sensor signal; open/short
Code 36 Turbocharging pressure sensor signal; open or short detected for 0.5 sec or more in the turbocharging pressure sensor signal circuit; 1992–94
Code 41 Throttle position sensor circuit (VTA); open/short
Code 42 Vehicle speed sensor circuit
Code 43 No starter switch (STA) signal to ECU until engine speed reaches 800 rpm when cranking
Code 51 NC signal ON, DL contact OFF, or shift position in R, D, 2 or 1 range; with check terminals T and EI connected
Code 52 Knock sensor signal (KNK); open/short
Code 53 Knock control signal in ECU; ECU knock control faulty
Code 55 Knock sensor (rear side) signal in ECU; ECU knock control faulty
Code 71 EGR system malfunction; EGR gas temperature signal (THG) is below water temperature sensor signal or below intake air temperature sensor signal plus 86°F (30°C), after driving for 240 seconds in EGR operation range (California only)
Code 72 Fuel cut solenoid signal circuit (FCS) open; up to 1991
Code 78 Fuel pump control signal input circuit to pump (FPC) open
Code 81 TCM communication; open detected in ECT1 circuit for 2 or more seconds
Code 83 TCM communication; open detected in ESA1 circuit 0.5 sec after idle
Code 84 TCM communication; open in ESA2 circuit for 0.5 seconds after idle
Code 85 TCM communication; open in ESA3 circuit for more than 0.5 seconds after idle

OBD-II TROUBLE CODES

Introduction

The Federal Clean Air Act of 1990 mandated that all vehicles sold in the United States by the 1996 model year must adhere to the California Air Resources Board (CARB) requirements. These requirements took the form of a monitoring system that we now call OBD-II. The objective was to put into effect a method of monitoring the Electronic Engine Management and Emission Control Systems that would not only aid in their diagnosis, as was the case with OBD-I, but to also alert the driver of an OBD-II equipped vehicle of the early stages of an Emission Control component or system failure.

Diagnostic Test Modes

Common diagnostic test modes have been created in a way that makes them common to all manufacturers. What this means is that no matter what vehicle you're testing or which piece of scanning equipment you have, all the tests that you need to perform will be the same for all manufacturers using the same terms and trouble codes. There 6 Test Modes as follows:
- Mode 1—Parameter Identification (PID)—accessing of live data, digital and analog values for inputs and outputs etc. Mode 1 is very similar to OBD-I Data Scanning.
- Mode 2—Freeze Frame Data Access—This feature is a built-in freeze frame device right inside the control module. Data will be captured for all emissions related values at the time of a recognized fault, that will be available for the individual to retrieve at a suitable and convenient time.
- Mode 3—This enables all scan tools to retrieve stored DTCs. The DTC can be displayed alone or with descriptive text.
- Mode 4—This is ability of the scan tool to clear all control module emission-related diagnostic information. When the control module is reset like this, an Inspection/Maintenance Readiness code will be stored. (P1000) This only illustrates that the control module is awaiting further vehicle operating modes to complete further on-board monitoring and testing.
- Mode 5—This is the monitoring of the oxygen sensors to determine catalytic converter efficiency.
- Mode 6—Output State Mode (OTM)—allows the individual to energize and de-energize many of the controlled output devices. Through the use of the scanner, the devices can be manually controlled to determine real time functionality.

System Monitoring

To comply with EPA regulations, the OBD-II control module is equipped with software designed to allow it to extensively monitor vehicle emission control systems and components. Once the ignition is turned **ON** or the engine is started, and certain test conditions are met, the control module runs a series of monitors to test the emission control systems and components. Test conditions include different inputs such as time since startup, run-time, engine speed and temperature, transaxle gear position, and the engine open or closed loop status. Once the monitor is started, the control module attempts to run it to completion. If a particular monitor fails a test, a code is set and operating conditions at that time are recorded in memory. If the same component or system fails twice in succession, the Malfunction Indicator Lamp (MIL) is activated.

Monitors are divided into two types: Main Monitors and the Comprehensive Component Monitors.
- Catalyst Monitor
- EGR Monitor
- EVAP Monitor
- Fuel System Monitor
- Misfire Monitor
- Oxygen Sensor Monitor
- Oxygen Sensor Heater Monitor

Certain monitors, in particular the fuel system and misfire monitors, have limitations that are different from the others. The first time either of these monitors fail, the MIL is activated, and engine conditions at the time of the fault are recorded. In order for the control module to turn **OFF** an MIL related to these two monitors, it must determine that no faults are present with engine operating conditions similar to when it detected the fault. To qualify, the engine must be operated within a specified speed range, engine load range and temperature range. This is known as a drive cycle.

System monitoring has been improved over OBD-I by checking and double checking all input and output systems. The interesting thing about OBD-II is that this system has made it more difficult to illuminate the MIL by tightening up the parameters that causes the MIL to come on. Many of the conditions that cause the light to come on are now set out in what are referred to as the following:
- Warm-up Cycle—is operation of the vehicle to the point of warming the coolant by at least 40 degrees Fahrenheit over the last engine off and reaching at least 160 degrees Fahrenheit.
- Drive Cycles—take the warm-up cycle one step further by operating the vehicle to the point whereby it will go into closed loop and include the operating conditions that are necessary to initiate or even complete a specific OBD-II monitor or it will verify a symptom or its repair. A "monitor" is a new term that describes an operating strategy that can run internal tests of a specific system, component or function. This is very similar to on-board computer self tests.
- OBD-II Trip—is often referred to as a trip, and again takes the above mentioned steps further in progression. Beginning with an engine off period, after the engine is started, the vehicle must travel a specified distance to allow the following five OBD-II monitors to complete all of their tests:
  1. Misfires
  2. Fuel System
  3. Comprehensive components
  4. EGR
  5. HO2S

OBD-II Drive Cycle This is a very specific combination of driving conditions that have been set out by the Federal Clean Air Act. Completion of all the conditions of this cycle ensures that all monitors have completed their required tests. This cycle is the most comprehensive of all the cycles and is illustrated in repair and diagnostic manuals through the use of a chart. In order for all monitors to take place the following must happen:

1. Cold Start. In order to be classified as a cold start the engine coolant temperature must be below 50°C (122°F) and within 6°C (11°F) of the ambient air temperature at startup. Do not leave the key on prior to the cold start or the heated oxygen sensor diagnostic may not run.

2. Idle. The engine must be run for two and a half minutes with the air conditioner on and rear defroster on. The more electrical load you can apply the better. This will test the O2 heater, Passive Air, Purge "No Flow", Misfire and if closed loop is achieved, Fuel Trim.

3. Accelerate. Turn off the air conditioner and all the other loads and apply half throttle until 88km/hr (55mph) is reached. During this time the Misfire, Fuel Trim, and Purge Flow diagnostics will be performed.

4. Hold Steady Speed. Hold a steady speed of 88km/hr (55mph) for 3 minutes. During this time the O2 response, air Intrusive, EGR, Purge, Misfire, and Fuel Trim diagnostics will be performed.

5. Decelerate. Let off the accelerator pedal. Do not shift, touch the brake or clutch. It is important to let the vehicle coast along gradually slowing down to 32km/hr (20 mph). During this time the EGR, Purge and Fuel Trim diagnostics will be performed.

6. Accelerate. Accelerate at 3/4 throttle until 88-96 km/hr (55-60mph). This will perform the same diagnostics as in step 3.

7. Hold Steady Speed. Hold a steady speed of 88km/hr (55mph) for five minutes. During this time, in addition to the diagnostics performed in step 4, the catalyst monitor diagnostics will be performed. If the catalyst is marginal or the battery has been disconnected, it may take 5 complete driving cycles to determine the state of the catalyst.

8. Decelerate. This will perform the same diagnostics as in step 5. Again, don't press the clutch or brakes or shift gears.

Trouble Code Description

▶ **See Figure 55**

In the past, trouble code descriptions varied between manufacturers, years, makes and models. OBD-II requires that all vehicle manufacturers use a common Diagnostic Trouble Code (DTC) numbering system. Since the generic listing was not specific enough, most manufacturers came up with their own DTC listings which are called manufacturer specific codes. Both generic and manufacturer specific codes are 5 digits. The numbers can be decoded as follows:

The first digit is a letter which identifies the function of the device or circuit which has the fault. This digit can be either:

- P—Powertrain
- B—Body
- C—Chassis
- U—Network or data link code

The second digit is either a 0 or 1 and indicates whether the code is generic or manufacturer specific.

- 0—Generic
- 1—Manufacturer Specific

The third digit represents the specific vehicle circuit or system that has the fault. Listed below are the number identifiers for the powertrain system.

- 1—Fuel and Air Metering
- 2—Fuel and Air Metering (Injector Circuit Malfunctions Only)
- 3—Ignition System or Misfire
- 4—Auxiliary Emission Control
- 5—Vehicle Speed Control and Idle Control System
- 6—Computer and Auxiliary Outputs
- 7—Transmission
- 8—Transmission

The last two digits indicate the specific trouble code.

On OBD-II vehicles there are two different types of DTCs: Stored and Pending. For a DTC to become Stored, certain malfunction conditions must occur. The condition(s) required to Store codes are different for every DTC and vary by vehicle manufacturer.

In order for some DTCs to become Stored, a malfunction condition has to happen more than once. If the malfunction conditions are required to occur more than once, the potential malfunction is called a Pending DTC. The DTC remains pending until the malfunction condition occurs the required number of times to make the code stored. If the malfunction condition does not occur again after a set time the pending DTC will be cleared.

SAE Generic OBD-II Trouble Codes

On board diagnostic requirements have been defined by the OBD-II legislation in California and the Federal Clean Air Act. These requirements include the need for standardization of various parts of the system, including some of the Diagnostic Trouble Codes.

Prior to OBD-II, there was no uniformity in these numeric Diagnostic Trouble Codes (DTC) between manufacturers, and in some cases, even within the same manufacturer across different product lines. The Society of Automotive Engineers (SAE) codes from document J2012 provide some recommended uniformity for these codes.

In this section you will find the SAE recommended Industry Common Trouble codes for the powertrain control system. The fact that a code is recommended as a Industry Common Code does not imply that it is a Required Code (Legislated), an Emission Related Code, or that it indicates a fault that will cause the Malfunction Indicator Light to be illuminated.

In the following sections you will find the manufacturer specific codes. These are fault codes that will not generally be used by a majority of the manufacturers due to basic system differences, implementation differences, or diagnostic strategy differences. Each vehicle manufacturer or supplier who designs and specifies diagnostic algorithms, software, and diagnostic trouble codes have been strongly encouraged to remain consistent across their product line when assigning codes in the manufacturer controlled area.

P0100 Mass or Volume Air Flow Circuit Malfunction
P0101 Mass or Volume Air Flow Circuit Range/Performance Problem
P0102 Mass or Volume Air Flow Circuit Low Input
P0103 Mass or Volume Air Flow Circuit High Input
P0104 Mass or Volume Air Flow Circuit Intermittent
P0105 Manifold Absolute Pressure/Barometric Pressure Circuit Malfunction
P0106 Manifold Absolute Pressure/Barometric Pressure Circuit Range/Performance Problem
P0107 Manifold Absolute Pressure/Barometric Pressure Circuit Low Input
P0108 Manifold Absolute Pressure/Barometric Pressure Circuit High Input
P0109 Manifold Absolute Pressure/Barometric Pressure Circuit Intermittent
P0110 Intake Air Temperature Circuit Malfunction
P0111 Intake Air Temperature Circuit Range/Performance Problem
P0112 Intake Air Temperature Circuit Low Input
P0113 Intake Air Temperature Circuit High Input

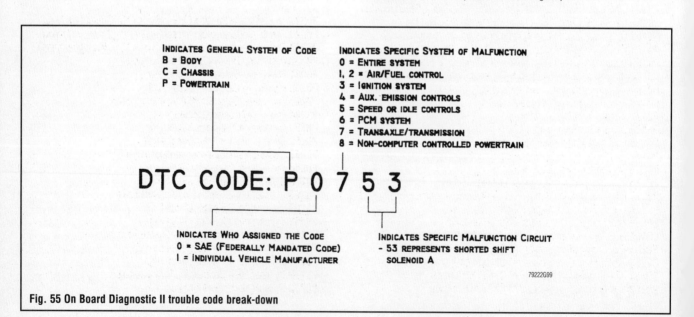

Fig. 55 On Board Diagnostic II trouble code break-down

P0114 Intake Air Temperature Circuit Intermittent
P0115 Engine Coolant Temperature Circuit Malfunction
P0116 Engine Coolant Temperature Circuit Range/Performance Problem
P0117 Engine Coolant Temperature Circuit Low Input
P0118 Engine Coolant Temperature Circuit High Input
P0119 Engine Coolant Temperature Circuit Intermittent
P0120 Throttle/Pedal Position Sensor/Switch "A" Circuit Malfunction
P0121 Throttle/Pedal Position Sensor/Switch "A" Circuit Range/Performance Problem
P0122 Throttle/Pedal Position Sensor/Switch "A" Circuit Low Input
P0123 Throttle/Pedal Position Sensor/Switch "A" Circuit High Input
P0124 Throttle/Pedal Position Sensor/Switch "A" Circuit Intermittent
P0125 Insufficient Coolant Temperature For Closed Loop Fuel Control
P0126 Insufficient Coolant Temperature For Stable Operation
P0130 O2 Circuit Malfunction (Bank no. 1 Sensor no. 1)
P0131 O2 Sensor Circuit Low Voltage (Bank no. 1 Sensor no. 1)
P0132 O2 Sensor Circuit High Voltage (Bank no. 1 Sensor no. 1)
P0133 O2 Sensor Circuit Slow Response (Bank no. 1 Sensor no. 1)
P0134 O2 Sensor Circuit No Activity Detected (Bank no. 1 Sensor no. 1)
P0135 O2 Sensor Heater Circuit Malfunction (Bank no. 1 Sensor no. 1)
P0136 O2 Sensor Circuit Malfunction (Bank no. 1 Sensor no. 2)
P0137 O2 Sensor Circuit Low Voltage (Bank no. 1 Sensor no. 2)
P0138 O2 Sensor Circuit High Voltage (Bank no. 1 Sensor no. 2)
P0139 O2 Sensor Circuit Slow Response (Bank no. 1 Sensor no. 2)
P0140 O2 Sensor Circuit No Activity Detected (Bank no. 1 Sensor no. 2)
P0141 O2 Sensor Heater Circuit Malfunction (Bank no. 1 Sensor no. 2)
P0142 O2 Sensor Circuit Malfunction (Bank no. 1 Sensor no. 3)
P0143 O2 Sensor Circuit Low Voltage (Bank no. 1 Sensor no. 3)
P0144 O2 Sensor Circuit High Voltage (Bank no. 1 Sensor no. 3)
P0145 O2 Sensor Circuit Slow Response (Bank no. 1 Sensor no. 3)
P0146 O2 Sensor Circuit No Activity Detected (Bank no. 1 Sensor no. 3)
P0147 O2 Sensor Heater Circuit Malfunction (Bank no. 1 Sensor no. 3)
P0150 O2 Sensor Circuit Malfunction (Bank no. 2 Sensor no. 1)
P0151 O2 Sensor Circuit Low Voltage (Bank no. 2 Sensor no. 1)
P0152 O2 Sensor Circuit High Voltage (Bank no. 2 Sensor no. 1)
P0153 O2 Sensor Circuit Slow Response (Bank no. 2 Sensor no. 1)
P0154 O2 Sensor Circuit No Activity Detected (Bank no. 2 Sensor no. 1)
P0155 O2 Sensor Heater Circuit Malfunction (Bank no. 2 Sensor no. 1)
P0156 O2 Sensor Circuit Malfunction (Bank no. 2 Sensor no. 2)
P0157 O2 Sensor Circuit Low Voltage (Bank no. 2 Sensor no. 2)
P0158 O2 Sensor Circuit High Voltage (Bank no. 2 Sensor no. 2)
P0159 O2 Sensor Circuit Slow Response (Bank no. 2 Sensor no. 2)
P0160 O2 Sensor Circuit No Activity Detected (Bank no. 2 Sensor no. 2)
P0161 O2 Sensor Heater Circuit Malfunction (Bank no. 2 Sensor no. 2)
P0162 O2 Sensor Circuit Malfunction (Bank no. 2 Sensor no. 3)
P0163 O2 Sensor Circuit Low Voltage (Bank no. 2 Sensor no. 3)
P0164 O2 Sensor Circuit High Voltage (Bank no. 2 Sensor no. 3)
P0165 O2 Sensor Circuit Slow Response (Bank no. 2 Sensor no. 3)
P0166 O2 Sensor Circuit No Activity Detected (Bank no. 2 Sensor no. 3)
P0167 O2 Sensor Heater Circuit Malfunction (Bank no. 2 Sensor no. 3)
P0170 Fuel Trim Malfunction (Bank no. 1)
P0171 System Too Lean (Bank no. 1)
P0172 System Too Rich (Bank no. 1)
P0173 Fuel Trim Malfunction (Bank no. 2)
P0174 System Too Lean (Bank no. 2)
P0175 System Too Rich (Bank no. 2)
P0176 Fuel Composition Sensor Circuit Malfunction
P0177 Fuel Composition Sensor Circuit Range/Performance
P0178 Fuel Composition Sensor Circuit Low Input
P0179 Fuel Composition Sensor Circuit High Input
P0180 Fuel Temperature Sensor "A" Circuit Malfunction
P0181 Fuel Temperature Sensor "A" Circuit Range/Performance
P0182 Fuel Temperature Sensor "A" Circuit Low Input
P0183 Fuel Temperature Sensor "A" Circuit High Input
P0184 Fuel Temperature Sensor "A" Circuit Intermittent

P0185 Fuel Temperature Sensor "B" Circuit Malfunction
P0186 Fuel Temperature Sensor "B" Circuit Range/Performance
P0187 Fuel Temperature Sensor "B" Circuit Low Input
P0188 Fuel Temperature Sensor "B" Circuit High Input
P0189 Fuel Temperature Sensor "B" Circuit Intermittent
P0190 Fuel Rail Pressure Sensor Circuit Malfunction
P0191 Fuel Rail Pressure Sensor Circuit Range/Performance
P0192 Fuel Rail Pressure Sensor Circuit Low Input
P0193 Fuel Rail Pressure Sensor Circuit High Input
P0194 Fuel Rail Pressure Sensor Circuit Intermittent
P0195 Engine Oil Temperature Sensor Malfunction
P0196 Engine Oil Temperature Sensor Range/Performance
P0197 Engine Oil Temperature Sensor Low
P0198 Engine Oil Temperature Sensor High
P0199 Engine Oil Temperature Sensor Intermittent
P0200 Injector Circuit Malfunction
P0201 Injector Circuit Malfunction—Cylinder no. 1
P0202 Injector Circuit Malfunction—Cylinder no. 2
P0203 Injector Circuit Malfunction—Cylinder no. 3
P0204 Injector Circuit Malfunction—Cylinder no. 4
P0205 Injector Circuit Malfunction—Cylinder no. 5
P0206 Injector Circuit Malfunction—Cylinder no. 6
P0207 Injector Circuit Malfunction—Cylinder no. 7
P0208 Injector Circuit Malfunction—Cylinder no. 8
P0209 Injector Circuit Malfunction—Cylinder no. 9
P0210 Injector Circuit Malfunction—Cylinder no. 10
P0211 Injector Circuit Malfunction—Cylinder no. 11
P0212 Injector Circuit Malfunction—Cylinder no. 12
P0213 Cold Start Injector no. 1 Malfunction
P0214 Cold Start Injector no. 2 Malfunction
P0215 Engine Shutoff Solenoid Malfunction
P0216 Injection Timing Control Circuit Malfunction
P0217 Engine Over Temperature Condition
P0218 Transmission Over Temperature Condition
P0219 Engine Over Speed Condition
P0220 Throttle/Pedal Position Sensor/Switch "B" Circuit Malfunction
P0221 Throttle/Pedal Position Sensor/Switch "B" Circuit Range/Performance Problem
P0222 Throttle/Pedal Position Sensor/Switch "B" Circuit Low Input
P0223 Throttle/Pedal Position Sensor/Switch "B" Circuit High Input
P0224 Throttle/Pedal Position Sensor/Switch "B" Circuit Intermittent
P0225 Throttle/Pedal Position Sensor/Switch "C" Circuit Malfunction
P0226 Throttle/Pedal Position Sensor/Switch "C" Circuit Range/Performance Problem
P0227 Throttle/Pedal Position Sensor/Switch "C" Circuit Low Input
P0228 Throttle/Pedal Position Sensor/Switch "C" Circuit High Input
P0229 Throttle/Pedal Position Sensor/Switch "C" Circuit Intermittent
P0230 Fuel Pump Primary Circuit Malfunction
P0231 Fuel Pump Secondary Circuit Low
P0232 Fuel Pump Secondary Circuit High
P0233 Fuel Pump Secondary Circuit Intermittent
P0234 Engine Over Boost Condition
P0261 Cylinder no. 1 Injector Circuit Low
P0262 Cylinder no. 1 Injector Circuit High
P0263 Cylinder no. 1 Contribution/Balance Fault
P0264 Cylinder no. 2 Injector Circuit Low
P0265 Cylinder no. 2 Injector Circuit High
P0266 Cylinder no. 2 Contribution/Balance Fault
P0267 Cylinder no. 3 Injector Circuit Low
P0268 Cylinder no. 3 Injector Circuit High
P0269 Cylinder no. 3 Contribution/Balance Fault
P0270 Cylinder no. 4 Injector Circuit Low
P0271 Cylinder no. 4 Injector Circuit High
P0272 Cylinder no. 4 Contribution/Balance Fault
P0273 Cylinder no. 5 Injector Circuit Low

P0274 Cylinder no. 5 Injector Circuit High
P0275 Cylinder no. 5 Contribution/Balance Fault
P0276 Cylinder no. 6 Injector Circuit Low
P0277 Cylinder no. 6 Injector Circuit High
P0278 Cylinder no. 6 Contribution/Balance Fault
P0279 Cylinder no. 7 Injector Circuit Low
P0280 Cylinder no. 7 Injector Circuit High
P0281 Cylinder no. 7 Contribution/Balance Fault
P0282 Cylinder no. 8 Injector Circuit Low
P0283 Cylinder no. 8 Injector Circuit High
P0284 Cylinder no. 8 Contribution/Balance Fault
P0285 Cylinder no. 9 Injector Circuit Low
P0286 Cylinder no. 9 Injector Circuit High
P0287 Cylinder no. 9 Contribution/Balance Fault
P0288 Cylinder no. 10 Injector Circuit Low
P0289 Cylinder no. 10 Injector Circuit High
P0290 Cylinder no. 10 Contribution/Balance Fault
P0291 Cylinder no. 11 Injector Circuit Low
P0292 Cylinder no. 11 Injector Circuit High
P0293 Cylinder no. 11 Contribution/Balance Fault
P0294 Cylinder no. 12 Injector Circuit Low
P0295 Cylinder no. 12 Injector Circuit High
P0296 Cylinder no. 12 Contribution/Balance Fault
P0300 Random/Multiple Cylinder Misfire Detected
P0301 Cylinder no. 1—Misfire Detected
P0302 Cylinder no. 2—Misfire Detected
P0303 Cylinder no. 3—Misfire Detected
P0304 Cylinder no. 4—Misfire Detected
P0305 Cylinder no. 5—Misfire Detected
P0306 Cylinder no. 6—Misfire Detected
P0307 Cylinder no. 7—Misfire Detected
P0308 Cylinder no. 8—Misfire Detected
P0309 Cylinder no. 9—Misfire Detected
P0310 Cylinder no. 10—Misfire Detected
P0311 Cylinder no. 11—Misfire Detected
P0312 Cylinder no. 12—Misfire Detected
P0320 Ignition/Distributor Engine Speed Input Circuit Malfunction
P0321 Ignition/Distributor Engine Speed Input Circuit Range/Performance
P0322 Ignition/Distributor Engine Speed Input Circuit No Signal
P0323 Ignition/Distributor Engine Speed Input Circuit Intermittent
P0325 Knock Sensor no. 1—Circuit Malfunction (Bank no. 1 or Single Sensor)
P0326 Knock Sensor no. 1—Circuit Range/Performance (Bank no. 1 or Single Sensor)
P0327 Knock Sensor no. 1—Circuit Low Input (Bank no. 1 or Single Sensor)
P0328 Knock Sensor no. 1—Circuit High Input (Bank no. 1 or Single Sensor)
P0329 Knock Sensor no. 1—Circuit Input Intermittent (Bank no. 1 or Single Sensor)
P0330 Knock Sensor no. 2—Circuit Malfunction (Bank no. 2)
P0331 Knock Sensor no. 2—Circuit Range/Performance (Bank no. 2)
P0332 Knock Sensor no. 2—Circuit Low Input (Bank no. 2)
P0333 Knock Sensor no. 2—Circuit High Input (Bank no. 2)
P0334 Knock Sensor no. 2—Circuit Input Intermittent (Bank no. 2)
P0335 Crankshaft Position Sensor "A" Circuit Malfunction
P0336 Crankshaft Position Sensor "A" Circuit Range/Performance
P0337 Crankshaft Position Sensor "A" Circuit Low Input
P0338 Crankshaft Position Sensor "A" Circuit High Input
P0339 Crankshaft Position Sensor "A" Circuit Intermittent
P0340 Camshaft Position Sensor Circuit Malfunction
P0341 Camshaft Position Sensor Circuit Range/Performance
P0342 Camshaft Position Sensor Circuit Low Input
P0343 Camshaft Position Sensor Circuit High Input
P0344 Camshaft Position Sensor Circuit Intermittent
P0350 Ignition Coil Primary/Secondary Circuit Malfunction
P0351 Ignition Coil "A" Primary/Secondary Circuit Malfunction

P0352 Ignition Coil "B" Primary/Secondary Circuit Malfunction
P0353 Ignition Coil "C" Primary/Secondary Circuit Malfunction
P0354 Ignition Coil "D" Primary/Secondary Circuit Malfunction
P0355 Ignition Coil "E" Primary/Secondary Circuit Malfunction
P0356 Ignition Coil "F" Primary/Secondary Circuit Malfunction
P0357 Ignition Coil "G" Primary/Secondary Circuit Malfunction
P0358 Ignition Coil "H" Primary/Secondary Circuit Malfunction
P0359 Ignition Coil "I" Primary/Secondary Circuit Malfunction
P0360 Ignition Coil "J" Primary/Secondary Circuit Malfunction
P0361 Ignition Coil "K" Primary/Secondary Circuit Malfunction
P0362 Ignition Coil "L" Primary/Secondary Circuit Malfunction
P0370 Timing Reference High Resolution Signal "A" Malfunction
P0371 Timing Reference High Resolution Signal "A" Too Many Pulses
P0372 Timing Reference High Resolution Signal "A" Too Few Pulses
P0373 Timing Reference High Resolution Signal "A" Intermittent/Erratic Pulses
P0374 Timing Reference High Resolution Signal "A" No Pulses
P0375 Timing Reference High Resolution Signal "B" Malfunction
P0376 Timing Reference High Resolution Signal "B" Too Many Pulses
P0377 Timing Reference High Resolution Signal "B" Too Few Pulses
P0378 Timing Reference High Resolution Signal "B" Intermittent/Erratic Pulses
P0379 Timing Reference High Resolution Signal "B" No Pulses
P0380 Glow Plug/Heater Circuit "A" Malfunction
P0381 Glow Plug/Heater Indicator Circuit Malfunction
P0382 Glow Plug/Heater Circuit "B" Malfunction
P0385 Crankshaft Position Sensor "B" Circuit Malfunction
P0386 Crankshaft Position Sensor "B" Circuit Range/Performance
P0387 Crankshaft Position Sensor "B" Circuit Low Input
P0388 Crankshaft Position Sensor "B" Circuit High Input
P0389 Crankshaft Position Sensor "B" Circuit Intermittent
P0400 Exhaust Gas Recirculation Flow Malfunction
P0401 Exhaust Gas Recirculation Flow Insufficient Detected
P0402 Exhaust Gas Recirculation Flow Excessive Detected
P0403 Exhaust Gas Recirculation Circuit Malfunction
P0404 Exhaust Gas Recirculation Circuit Range/Performance
P0405 Exhaust Gas Recirculation Sensor "A" Circuit Low
P0406 Exhaust Gas Recirculation Sensor "A" Circuit High
P0407 Exhaust Gas Recirculation Sensor "B" Circuit Low
P0408 Exhaust Gas Recirculation Sensor "B" Circuit High
P0410 Secondary Air Injection System Malfunction
P0411 Secondary Air Injection System Incorrect Flow Detected
P0412 Secondary Air Injection System Switching Valve "A" Circuit Malfunction
P0413 Secondary Air Injection System Switching Valve "A" Circuit Open
P0414 Secondary Air Injection System Switching Valve "A" Circuit Shorted
P0415 Secondary Air Injection System Switching Valve "B" Circuit Malfunction
P0416 Secondary Air Injection System Switching Valve "B" Circuit Open
P0417 Secondary Air Injection System Switching Valve "B" Circuit Shorted
P0418 Secondary Air Injection System Relay "A" Circuit Malfunction
P0419 Secondary Air Injection System Relay "B" Circuit Malfunction
P0420 Catalyst System Efficiency Below Threshold (Bank no. 1)
P0421 Warm Up Catalyst Efficiency Below Threshold (Bank no. 1)
P0422 Main Catalyst Efficiency Below Threshold (Bank no. 1)
P0423 Heated Catalyst Efficiency Below Threshold (Bank no. 1)
P0424 Heated Catalyst Temperature Below Threshold (Bank no. 1)
P0430 Catalyst System Efficiency Below Threshold (Bank no. 2)
P0431 Warm Up Catalyst Efficiency Below Threshold (Bank no. 2)
P0432 Main Catalyst Efficiency Below Threshold (Bank no. 2)
P0433 Heated Catalyst Efficiency Below Threshold (Bank no. 2)
P0434 Heated Catalyst Temperature Below Threshold (Bank no. 2)
P0440 Evaporative Emission Control System Malfunction
P0441 Evaporative Emission Control System Incorrect Purge Flow

P0442 Evaporative Emission Control System Leak Detected (Small Leak)

P0443 Evaporative Emission Control System Purge Control Valve Circuit Malfunction

P0444 Evaporative Emission Control System Purge Control Valve Circuit Open

P0445 Evaporative Emission Control System Purge Control Valve Circuit Shorted

P0446 Evaporative Emission Control System Vent Control Circuit Malfunction

P0447 Evaporative Emission Control System Vent Control Circuit Open

P0448 Evaporative Emission Control System Vent Control Circuit Shorted

P0449 Evaporative Emission Control System Vent Valve/Solenoid Circuit Malfunction

P0450 Evaporative Emission Control System Pressure Sensor Malfunction

P0451 Evaporative Emission Control System Pressure Sensor Range/Performance

P0452 Evaporative Emission Control System Pressure Sensor Low Input

P0453 Evaporative Emission Control System Pressure Sensor High Input

P0454 Evaporative Emission Control System Pressure Sensor Intermittent

P0455 Evaporative Emission Control System Leak Detected (Gross Leak)

P0460 Fuel Level Sensor Circuit Malfunction
P0461 Fuel Level Sensor Circuit Range/Performance
P0462 Fuel Level Sensor Circuit Low Input
P0463 Fuel Level Sensor Circuit High Input
P0464 Fuel Level Sensor Circuit Intermittent
P0465 Purge Flow Sensor Circuit Malfunction
P0466 Purge Flow Sensor Circuit Range/Performance
P0467 Purge Flow Sensor Circuit Low Input
P0468 Purge Flow Sensor Circuit High Input
P0469 Purge Flow Sensor Circuit Intermittent
P0470 Exhaust Pressure Sensor Malfunction
P0471 Exhaust Pressure Sensor Range/Performance
P0472 Exhaust Pressure Sensor Low
P0473 Exhaust Pressure Sensor High
P0474 Exhaust Pressure Sensor Intermittent
P0475 Exhaust Pressure Control Valve Malfunction
P0476 Exhaust Pressure Control Valve Range/Performance
P0477 Exhaust Pressure Control Valve Low
P0478 Exhaust Pressure Control Valve High
P0479 Exhaust Pressure Control Valve Intermittent
P0480 Cooling Fan no. 1 Control Circuit Malfunction
P0481 Cooling Fan no. 2 Control Circuit Malfunction
P0482 Cooling Fan no. 3 Control Circuit Malfunction
P0483 Cooling Fan Rationality Check Malfunction
P0484 Cooling Fan Circuit Over Current
P0485 Cooling Fan Power/Ground Circuit Malfunction
P0500 Vehicle Speed Sensor Malfunction
P0501 Vehicle Speed Sensor Range/Performance
P0502 Vehicle Speed Sensor Circuit Low Input
P0503 Vehicle Speed Sensor Intermittent/Erratic/High
P0505 Idle Control System Malfunction
P0506 Idle Control System RPM Lower Than Expected
P0507 Idle Control System RPM Higher Than Expected
P0510 Closed Throttle Position Switch Malfunction
P0520 Engine Oil Pressure Sensor/Switch Circuit Malfunction
P0521 Engine Oil Pressure Sensor/Switch Range/Performance
P0522 Engine Oil Pressure Sensor/Switch Low Voltage
P0523 Engine Oil Pressure Sensor/Switch High Voltage
P0530 A/C Refrigerant Pressure Sensor Circuit Malfunction
P0531 A/C Refrigerant Pressure Sensor Circuit Range/Performance
P0532 A/C Refrigerant Pressure Sensor Circuit Low Input

P0533 A/C Refrigerant Pressure Sensor Circuit High Input
P0534 A/C Refrigerant Charge Loss
P0550 Power Steering Pressure Sensor Circuit Malfunction
P0551 Power Steering Pressure Sensor Circuit Range/Performance
P0552 Power Steering Pressure Sensor Circuit Low Input
P0553 Power Steering Pressure Sensor Circuit High Input
P0554 Power Steering Pressure Sensor Circuit Intermittent
P0560 System Voltage Malfunction
P0561 System Voltage Unstable
P0562 System Voltage Low
P0563 System Voltage High
P0565 Cruise Control On Signal Malfunction
P0566 Cruise Control Off Signal Malfunction
P0567 Cruise Control Resume Signal Malfunction
P0568 Cruise Control Set Signal Malfunction
P0569 Cruise Control Coast Signal Malfunction
P0570 Cruise Control Accel Signal Malfunction
P0571 Cruise Control/Brake Switch "A" Circuit Malfunction
P0572 Cruise Control/Brake Switch "A" Circuit Low
P0573 Cruise Control/Brake Switch "A" Circuit High
P0574 **Through P0580** Reserved for Cruise Codes
P0600 Serial Communication Link Malfunction
P0601 Internal Control Module Memory Check Sum Error
P0602 Control Module Programming Error
P0603 Internal Control Module Keep Alive Memory (KAM) Error
P0604 Internal Control Module Random Access Memory (RAM) Error
P0605 Internal Control Module Read Only Memory (ROM) Error
P0606 PCM Processor Fault
P0608 Control Module VSS Output "A" Malfunction
P0609 Control Module VSS Output "B" Malfunction
P0620 Generator Control Circuit Malfunction
P0621 Generator Lamp "L" Control Circuit Malfunction
P0622 Generator Field "F" Control Circuit Malfunction
P0650 Malfunction Indicator Lamp (MIL) Control Circuit Malfunction
P0654 Engine RPM Output Circuit Malfunction
P0655 Engine Hot Lamp Output Control Circuit Malfunction
P0656 Fuel Level Output Circuit Malfunction
P0700 Transmission Control System Malfunction
P0701 Transmission Control System Range/Performance
P0702 Transmission Control System Electrical
P0703 Torque Converter/Brake Switch "B" Circuit Malfunction
P0704 Clutch Switch Input Circuit Malfunction
P0705 Transmission Range Sensor Circuit Malfunction (PRNDL Input)
P0706 Transmission Range Sensor Circuit Range/Performance
P0707 Transmission Range Sensor Circuit Low Input
P0708 Transmission Range Sensor Circuit High Input
P0709 Transmission Range Sensor Circuit Intermittent
P0710 Transmission Fluid Temperature Sensor Circuit Malfunction
P0711 Transmission Fluid Temperature Sensor Circuit Range/Performance
P0712 Transmission Fluid Temperature Sensor Circuit Low Input
P0713 Transmission Fluid Temperature Sensor Circuit High Input
P0714 Transmission Fluid Temperature Sensor Circuit Intermittent
P0715 Input/Turbine Speed Sensor Circuit Malfunction
P0716 Input/Turbine Speed Sensor Circuit Range/Performance
P0717 Input/Turbine Speed Sensor Circuit No Signal
P0718 Input/Turbine Speed Sensor Circuit Intermittent
P0719 Torque Converter/Brake Switch "B" Circuit Low
P0720 Output Speed Sensor Circuit Malfunction
P0721 Output Speed Sensor Circuit Range/Performance
P0722 Output Speed Sensor Circuit No Signal
P0723 Output Speed Sensor Circuit Intermittent
P0724 Torque Converter/Brake Switch "B" Circuit High
P0725 Engine Speed Input Circuit Malfunction
P0726 Engine Speed Input Circuit Range/Performance
P0727 Engine Speed Input Circuit No Signal
P0728 Engine Speed Input Circuit Intermittent
P0730 Incorrect Gear Ratio

P0731 Gear no. 1 Incorrect Ratio
P0732 Gear no. 2 Incorrect Ratio
P0733 Gear no. 3 Incorrect Ratio
P0734 Gear no. 4 Incorrect Ratio
P0735 Gear no. 5 Incorrect Ratio
P0736 Reverse Incorrect Ratio
P0740 Torque Converter Clutch Circuit Malfunction
P0741 Torque Converter Clutch Circuit Performance or Stuck Off
P0742 Torque Converter Clutch Circuit Stuck On
P0743 Torque Converter Clutch Circuit Electrical
P0744 Torque Converter Clutch Circuit Intermittent
P0745 Pressure Control Solenoid Malfunction
P0746 Pressure Control Solenoid Performance or Stuck Off
P0747 Pressure Control Solenoid Stuck On
P0748 Pressure Control Solenoid Electrical
P0749 Pressure Control Solenoid Intermittent
P0750 Shift Solenoid "A" Malfunction
P0751 Shift Solenoid "A" Performance or Stuck Off
P0752 Shift Solenoid "A" Stuck On
P0753 Shift Solenoid "A" Electrical
P0754 Shift Solenoid "A" Intermittent
P0755 Shift Solenoid "B" Malfunction
P0756 Shift Solenoid "B" Performance or Stuck Off
P0757 Shift Solenoid "B" Stuck On
P0758 Shift Solenoid "B" Electrical
P0759 Shift Solenoid "B" Intermittent
P0760 Shift Solenoid "C" Malfunction
P0761 Shift Solenoid "C" Performance Or Stuck Off
P0762 Shift Solenoid "C" Stuck On
P0763 Shift Solenoid "C" Electrical
P0764 Shift Solenoid "C" Intermittent
P0765 Shift Solenoid "D" Malfunction
P0766 Shift Solenoid "D" Performance Or Stuck Off
P0767 Shift Solenoid "D" Stuck On
P0768 Shift Solenoid "D" Electrical
P0769 Shift Solenoid "D" Intermittent
P0770 Shift Solenoid "E" Malfunction
P0771 Shift Solenoid "E" Performance Or Stuck Off
P0772 Shift Solenoid "E" Stuck On
P0773 Shift Solenoid "E" Electrical
P0774 Shift Solenoid "E" Intermittent
P0780 Shift Malfunction
P0781 1–2 Shift Malfunction
P0782 2–3 Shift Malfunction
P0783 3–4 Shift Malfunction
P0784 4–5 Shift Malfunction
P0785 Shift/Timing Solenoid Malfunction
P0786 Shift/Timing Solenoid Range/Performance
P0787 Shift/Timing Solenoid Low
P0788 Shift/Timing Solenoid High
P0789 Shift/Timing Solenoid Intermittent
P0790 Normal/Performance Switch Circuit Malfunction
P0801 Reverse Inhibit Control Circuit Malfunction
P0803 1–4 Upshift (Skip Shift) Solenoid Control Circuit Malfunction
P0804 1–4 Upshift (Skip Shift) Lamp Control Circuit Malfunction

Acura Truck

READING CODES

Reading the control module memory is one of the first steps in OBD-II system diagnostics.

This step should be initially performed to determine the general nature of the fault. Subsequent readings will determine if the fault has been cleared.

Reading codes can be performed by any of the methods below:
- Read the control module memory with the Generic Scan Tool (GST)
- Read the control module memory with the vehicle manufacturer's specific tester

To read the fault codes, connect the scan tool or tester according to the manufacturer's instructions. Follow the manufacturer's specified procedure for reading the codes.

CLEARING CODES

Control module reset procedures are a very important part of OBD-II system diagnostics. This step should be done at the end of any fault code repair and at the end of any driveability repair.

Clearing codes can be performed by any of the methods below:
- Clear the control module memory with the Generic Scan Tool (GST)
- Clear the control module memory with the vehicle manufacturer's specific tester
- Turn the ignition off and remove the negative battery cable for at least 1 minute.

Removing the negative battery cable may cause other systems in the vehicle to loose their memory. Prior to removing the cable, ensure you have the proper reset codes for radios and alarms.

➡**The MIL will may also be de-activated for some codes if the vehicle completes three consecutive trips without a fault detected with vehicle conditions similar to those present during the fault.**

ACURA SPECIFIC OBD-II TROUBLE CODES

P1106 Map Sensor Circuit Intermittent High Voltage
P1107 MAP Sensor Circuit Intermittent Low Voltage
P1111 IAT Sensor Circuit Intermittent High Voltage
P1112 IAT Sensor Circuit Intermittent Low Voltage
P1114 ECT Sensor Circuit Intermittent Low Voltage
P1115 ECT Sensor Circuit Intermittent High Voltage
P1121 TP Sensor Circuit Intermittent High Voltage
P1122 TP Sensor Circuit Intermittent Low Voltage
P1133 HO2S-11 Insufficient Switching (Bank 1 Sensor 1)
P1134 HO2S-11 Transition Time Ratio (Bank 1 Sensor 1)
P1153 HO2S-21 Insufficient Switching (Bank 2 Sensor I)
P1154 HO2S-21 Transition Time Ratio (Bank 2 Sensor 1)
P1171 Fuel System Lean During Acceleration
P1391 G-Acceleration Sensor Intermittent Low Voltage
P1390 G-Acceleration (Low G) Sensor Performance
P1392 Rough Road G-Sensor Circuit Low Voltage
P1393 Rough Road G-Sensor Circuit High Voltage
P1394 G-Acceleration Sensor Intermittent High Voltage
P1406 EGR Valve Pintle Position Sensor Circuit Fault
P1441 EVAP System Flow During Non-Purge
P1442 EVAP System Flow During Non-Purge
P1508 Idle Speed Control System-Low
P1509 Idle Speed Control System-High
P1618 Serial Peripheral Interface Communication Error
P1640 Output Driver Module 'A' Fault
P1790 PCM ROM (Transmission Side) Check Sum Error
P1792 PCM EEPROM (Transmission Side) Check Sum Error
P1835 Kick Down Switch Always On
P1850 Brake Band Apply Solenoid Electrical Fault
P1860 TCC PWM Solenoid Electrical Fault
P1870 Transmission Component Slipping

Chrysler Corporation Truck

READING CODES

Reading the control module memory is one of the first steps in OBD-II system diagnostics. This step should be initially performed to determine the general nature of the fault. Subsequent readings will determine if the fault has been cleared.

Reading codes can be performed by any of the methods below:
- Read the control module memory with the Generic Scan Tool (GST)
- Read the control module memory with the vehicle manufacturer's specific tester

To read the fault codes, connect the scan tool or tester according to the manufacturer's instructions. Follow the manufacturer's specified procedure for reading the codes.

CLEARING CODES

Control module reset procedures are a very important part of OBD-II System diagnostics. This step should be done at the end of any fault code repair and at the end of any driveability repair.

Clearing codes can be performed by any of the methods below:
- Clear the control module memory with the Generic Scan Tool (GST)
- Clear the control module memory with the vehicle manufacturer's specific tester
- Turn the ignition off and remove the negative battery cable for at least 1 minute.

Removing the negative battery cable may cause other systems in the vehicle to loose their memory. Prior to removing the cable, ensure you have the proper reset codes for radios and alarms.

➡**The MIL will may also be de-activated for some codes if the vehicle completes three consecutive trips without a fault detected with vehicle conditions similar to those present during the fault.**

CHRYSLER SPECIFIC OBD-II TROUBLE CODES

P1290 CNG Fuel System Pressure Too High—3.3L CNG vehicles only
P1291 No Temp Rise Seen From Intake Air Heaters
P1292 CNG Pressure Sensor Voltage Too High—3.3L CNG vehicles only
P1293 CNG Pressure Sensor Voltage Too Low—3.3L CNG vehicles only
P1294 Target Idle Not Reached
P1296 No 5-Volts To MAP Sensor
P1297 No Change In MAP From Start To Run
P1391 Intermittent Loss Of CMP Or CKP
P1398 Misfire Adaptive Numerator At Limit
P1486 EVAP Leak Monitor Pinched Hose Or Obstruction Found
P1491 Radiator Fan Control Relay Circuit
P1492 Battery Temp Sensor Voltage Too High
P1493 Battery Temp Sensor Voltage Too Low
P1494 Leak Detection Pump Pressure Switch Or Mechanical Fault
P1495 Leak Detection Pump Solenoid Circuit
P1498 Auxiliary 5-Volt Supply Output Too Low
P1697 PCM Failure SRI Mile Not Stored
P1698 PCM Failure EEPROM Write Denied
P1756 Governor Pressure Not Equal To Target @ 15–20 PSI
P1757 Governor Pressure Above 3 PSI In Gear With 0 MPH
P1762 Governor Pressure Sensor Offset Volts Too Low Or High
P1763 Governor Pressure Sensor Volts Too High
P1764 Governor Pressure Sensor Volts Too Low
P1765 Trans 12-Volt Supply Relay Control Circuit
P1899 P/N Switch Stuck In Park Or In Gear

Ford Motor Company Truck

➡**The Mercury Villager is covered under the Nissan section since it shares a platform with the Nissan Quest.**

READING CODES

Reading the control module memory is one of the first steps in OBD-II system diagnostics. This step should be initially performed to determine the general nature of the fault. Subsequent readings will determine if the fault has been cleared.

Reading codes can be performed by any of the methods below:
- Read the control module memory with the Generic Scan Tool (GST)
- Read the control module memory with the vehicle manufacturer's specific tester

To read the fault codes, connect the scan tool or tester according to the manufacturer's instructions. Follow the manufacturer's specified procedure for reading the codes.

CLEARING CODES

Control module reset procedures are a very important part of OBD-II System diagnostics. This step should be done at the end of any fault code repair and at the end of any driveability repair.

Clearing codes can be performed by any of the methods below:
- Clear the control module memory with the Generic Scan Tool (GST)
- Clear the control module memory with the vehicle manufacturer's specific tester
- Turn the ignition off and remove the negative battery cable for at least 1 minute.

Removing the negative battery cable may cause other systems in the vehicle to loose their memory. Prior to removing the cable, ensure you have the proper reset codes for radios and alarms.

➡**The MIL will may also be de-activated for some codes if the vehicle completes three consecutive trips without a fault detected with vehicle conditions similar to those present during the fault.**

OBD-II TROUBLE CODES

1995 Models

P1000 OBD-II Monitor Testing not complete
P1100 Mass Air Flow (MAF) sensor intermittent
P1101 Mass Air Flow (MAF) sensor out of Self-Test range
P1112 Intake Air Temperature (IAT) sensor intermittent
P1116 Engine Coolant Temperature (ECT) sensor out of Self-Test range
P1117 Engine Coolant Temperature (ECT) sensor intermittent
P1120 Throttle Position (TP) sensor out of range low
P1121 Throttle Position (TP) sensor inconsistent with MAF sensor
P1124 Throttle Position (TP) sensor out of Self-Test range
P1125 Throttle Position (TP) sensor circuit intermittent
P1130 Lack of HO2S 11 switch, adaptive fuel at limit
P1131 Lack of HO2S 11 switch, sensor indicates lean (Bank #1)
P1132 Lack of HO2S 11 switch, sensor indicates rich (Bank #1)
P1137 Lack of HO2S 12 switch, sensor indicates lean (Bank #1)
P1138 Lack of HO2S 12 switch, sensor indicates rich (Bank #1)
P1150 Lack of HO2S 21 switch, adaptive fuel at limit
P1151 Lack of HO2S 21 switch, sensor indicates lean (Bank #2)
P1152 Lack of HO2S 21 switch, sensor indicates rich (Bank #2)
P1157 Lack of HO2S 22 switch, sensor indicates lean (Bank #2)
P1158 Lack of HO2S 22 switch, sensor indicates rich (Bank #2)
P1220 Series Throttle Control malfunction
P1224 Throttle Position Sensor (TP-B) out of Self-test range
P1233 Fuel Pump driver Module off-line
P1234 Fuel Pump driver Module off-line
P1235 Fuel Pump control out of range
P1236 Fuel Pump control out of range
P1237 Fuel Pump secondary circuit malfunction
P1238 Fuel Pump secondary circuit malfunction
P1260 THEFT detected—engine disabled
P1270 Engine RPM or vehicle speed limiter reached
P1351 Ignition Diagnostic Monitor (IDM) circuit input malfunction
P1352 Ignition coil A primary circuit malfunction
P1353 Ignition coil B primary circuit malfunction
P1354 Ignition coil C primary circuit malfunction
P1355 Ignition coil D primary circuit malfunction
P1358 Ignition Diagnostic Monitor (IDM) signal out of Self-Test range
P1359 Spark output circuit malfunction

P1364 Ignition coil primary circuit malfunction
P1390 Octane Adjust (OCT ADJ) out of Self-Test range
P1400 Differential Pressure Feedback Electronic (DPFE) sensor circuit low voltage detected
P1401 Differential Pressure Feedback Electronic (DPFE) sensor circuit high voltage detected
P1403 Differential Pressure Feedback Electronic (DPFE) sensor hoses reversed
P1405 Differential Pressure Feedback Electronic (DPFE) sensor upstream hose off or plugged
P1406 Differential Pressure Feedback Electronic (DPFE) sensor downstream hose off or plugged
P1407 Exhaust Gas Recirculation (EGR) no flow detected (valve stuck closed or inoperative)
P1408 Exhaust Gas Recirculation (EGR) flow out of Self-Test range
P1409 Electronic Vacuum Regulator (EVR) control circuit malfunction
P1414 Secondary Air Injection system monitor circuit high voltage
P1443 Evaporative emission control system—vacuum system purge control solenoid or purge control valve malfunction
P1444 Purge Flow Sensor (PFS) circuit low input
P1445 Purge Flow Sensor (PFS) circuit high input
U1451 Lack of response from Passive Anti-Theft system (PATS) module—engine disabled
P1460 Wide Open Throttle Air Conditioning Cut-off (WAC) circuit malfunction
P1461 Air Conditioning Pressure (ACP) sensor circuit low input
P1462 Air Conditioning Pressure (ACP) sensor circuit high input
P1463 Air Conditioning Pressure (ACP) sensor insufficient pressure change
P1469 Low air conditioning cycling period
P1473 Fan Secondary High with fan(s) off
P1474 Low Fan Control primary circuit malfunction
P1479 High Fan Control primary circuit malfunction
P1480 Fan Secondary low with low fan on
P1481 Fan Secondary low with high fan on
P1500 Vehicle Speed Sensor (VSS) circuit intermittent
P1505 Idle Air Control (IAC) system at adaptive clip
P1506 Idle Air control (IAC) overspeed error
P1518 Intake Manifold Runner Control (IMRC) malfunction (stuck open)
P1519 Intake Manifold Runner Control (IMRC) malfunction (stuck closed)
P1520 Intake Manifold Runner Control (IMRC) circuit malfunction
P1507 Idle Air control (IAC) under speed error
P1605 Powertrain Control Module (POM)—Keep Alive Memory (KAM) test error
P1650 Power steering Pressure (PSP) switch out of Self-Test range
P1651 Power steering Pressure (PSP) switch input malfunction
P1701 Reverse engagement error
P1703 Brake On/Off (BOO) switch out of Self-Test range
P1705 Manual Lever Position (MLP) sensor out of Self-Test range
P1709 Park or Neutral Position (PNP) switch out of Self-test range
P1729 4X4 Low switch error
P1711 Transmission Fluid Temperature (TFT) sensor out of Self-Test range
P1741 Torque Converter Clutch (TCC) control error
P1742 Torque Converter Clutch (TCC) solenoid mechanically failed (turns MIL on)
P1743 Torque Converter Clutch (TCC) solenoid mechanically failed (turns TOIL on)
P1744 Torque Converter Clutch (TCC) system mechanically stuck in off position
P1748 Electronic Pressure Control (EPC) solenoid circuit low input (open circuit)
P1747 Electronic Pressure Control (EPC) solenoid circuit high input (short circuit)
P1749 Electric Pressure Control (EPC) solenoid failed low
P1751 Shift Solenoid #1(SS1) performance
P1756 Shift Solenoid #2 (SS2) performance
P1780 Transmission Control Switch (TCS) circuit out of Self-Test range

1996–99 Models

P1000 OBD-II Monitor Testing Not Complete More Driving Required
P1001 Key On Engine Running (KOER) Self-Test Not Able To Complete, KOER Aborted
P1100 Mass Air Flow (MAF) Sensor Intermittent
P1101 Mass Air Flow (MAF) Sensor Out Of Self-Test Range
P1111 System Pass 49 State Except Econoline
P1112 Intake Air Temperature (IAT) Sensor Intermittent
P1116 Engine Coolant Temperature (ECT) Sensor Out Of Self-Test Range
P1117 Engine Coolant Temperature (ECT) Sensor Intermittent
P1120 Throttle Position (TP) Sensor Out Of Range (Low)
P1121 Throttle Position (TP) Sensor Inconsistent With MAF Sensor
P1124 Throttle Position (TP) Sensor Out Of Self-Test Range
P1125 Throttle Position (TP) Sensor Circuit Intermittent
P1127 Exhaust Not Warm Enough, Downstream Heated Oxygen Sensors (HO2S) Not Tested
P1128 Upstream Heated Oxygen Sensors (HO2S) Swapped From Bank To Bank
P1129 Downstream Heated Oxygen Sensors (HO2S) Swapped From Bank To Bank
P1130 Lack Of Upstream Heated Oxygen Sensor (HO2S 11) Switch, Adaptive Fuel At Limit (Bank #1)
P1131 Lack Of Upstream Heated Oxygen Sensor (HO2S 11) Switch, Sensor Indicates Lean (Bank #1)
P1132 Lack Of Upstream Heated Oxygen Sensor (HO2S 11) Switch, Sensor Indicates Rich (Bank#1)
P1137 Lack Of Downstream Heated Oxygen Sensor (HO2S 12) Switch, Sensor Indicates Lean (Bank#1)
P1138 Lack Of Downstream Heated Oxygen Sensor (HO2S 12) Switch, Sensor Indicates Rich (Bank#1)
P1150 Lack Of Upstream Heated Oxygen Sensor (HO2S 21) Switch, Adaptive Fuel At Limit (Bank #2)
P1151 Lack Of Upstream Heated Oxygen Sensor (HO2S 21) Switch, Sensor Indicates Lean (Bank#2)
P1152 Lack Of Upstream Heated Oxygen Sensor (HO2S 21) Switch, Sensor Indicates Rich (Bank #2)
P1157 Lack Of Downstream Heated Oxygen Sensor (HO2S 22) Switch, Sensor Indicates Lean (Bank #2)
P1158 Lack Of Downstream Heated Oxygen Sensor (HO2S 22) Switch, Sensor Indicates Rich (Bank#2)
P1169 (HO2S 12) Signal Remained Unchanged For More Than 20 Seconds After Closed Loop
P1170 (HO2S 11) Signal Remained Unchanged For More Than 20 Seconds After Closed Loop
P1173 Feedback A/F Mixture Control (HO2S 21) Signal Remained Unchanged For More Than 20 Seconds After Closed Loop
P1184 Engine Oil Temp Sensor Circuit Performance
P1195 Barometric (BARO) Pressure Sensor Circuit Malfunction (Signal Is From EGR Boost Sensor)
P1196 Starter Switch Circuit Malfunction
P1209 Injection Control Pressure (ICP) Peak Fault
P1210 Injection Control Pressure (ICP) Above Expected Level
P1211 Injection Control Pressure (ICP) Not Controllable—Pressure Above/Below Desired
P1212 Injection Control Pressure (ICP) Voltage Not At Expected Level
P1218 Cylinder Identification (CID) Stuck High
P1219 Cylinder Identification (CID) Stuck Low
P1220 Series Throttle Control Malfunction (Traction Control System)
P1224 Throttle Position Sensor "B" (TP-B) Out Of Self-Test Range (Traction Control System)
P1230 Fuel Pump Low Speed Malfunction
P1231 Fuel Pump Secondary Circuit Low With High Speed Pump On
P1232 Low Speed Fuel Pump Primary Circuit Malfunction
P1233 Fuel Pump Driver Module Off-line (MIL DTC)
P1234 Fuel Pump Driver Module Disabled Or Off-line (No MIL)
P1235 Fuel Pump Control Out Of Range (MIL DTC)

P1236 Fuel Pump Control Out Of Range (No MIL)

P1237 Fuel Pump Secondary Circuit Malfunction (MIL DTC)

P1238 Fuel Pump Secondary Circuit Malfunction (No DMIL)

P1250 Fuel Pressure Regulator Control (FPRC) Solenoid Malfunction

P1260 THEFT Detected—Engine Disabled

P1261 High To Low Side Short—Cylinder #1 (Indicates Low side Circuit Is Shorted To B+ Or To The High Side Between The IDM And The Injector)

P1262 High To Low Side Short—Cylinder #2 (Indicates Low side Circuit Is Shorted To B+ Or To The High Side Between The IDM And The Injector)

P1263 High To Low Side Short—Cylinder #3 (Indicates Low side Circuit Is Shorted To B+ Or To The High Side Between The IDM And The Injector)

P1264 High To Low Side Short—Cylinder #4 (Indicates Low side Circuit Is Shorted To B+ Or To The High Side Between The IDM And The Injector)

P1265 High To Low Side Short—Cylinder #5 (Indicates Low side Circuit Is Shorted To B+ Or To The High Side Between The IDM And The Injector)

P1266 High To Low Side Short—Cylinder #6 (Indicates Low side Circuit Is Shorted To B+ Or To The High Side Between The IDM And The Injector)

P1267 High To Low Side Short—Cylinder #7 (Indicates Low side Circuit Is Shorted To B+ Or To The High Side Between The IDM And The Injector)

P1268 High To Low Side Short—Cylinder #8 (Indicates Low side Circuit Is Shorted To B+ Or To The High Side Between The IDM And The Injector)

P1270 Engine RPM Or Vehicle Speed Limiter Reached

P1271 High To Low Side Open—Cylinder #1 (Indicates A High To Low Side Open Between The Injector And The IDM)

P1272 High To Low Side Open—Cylinder #2 (Indicates A High To Low Side Open Between The Injector And The IDM)

P1273 High To Low Side Open—Cylinder #3 (Indicates A High To Low Side Open Between The Injector And The IDM)

P1274 High To Low Side Open—Cylinder #4 (Indicates A High To Low Side Open Between The Injector And The IDM)

P1275 High To Low Side Open—Cylinder #5 (Indicates A High To Low Side Open Between The Injector And The IDM)

P1276 High To Low Side Open—Cylinder #6 (Indicates A High To Low Side Open Between The Injector And The IDM)

P1277 High To Low Side Open—Cylinder #7 (Indicates A High To Low Side Open Between The Injector And The IDM)

P1278 High To Low Side Open—Cylinder #8 (Indicates A High To Low Side Open Between The Injector And The IDM)

P1280 Injection Control Pressure (ICP) Circuit Out Of Range Low

P1281 Injection Control Pressure (ICP) Circuit Out Of Range High

P1282 Injection Control Pressure (ICP) Excessive

P1283 Injection Pressure Regulator (IPR) Circuit Failure

P1284 Injection Control Pressure (ICP) Failure—Aborts KOER Or CCT Test

P1285 Cylinder Head Temperature (CHT) Over Temperature Sensed

P1288 Cylinder Head Temperature (CHT) Sensor Out Of Self-Test Range

P1289 Cylinder Head Temperature (CHT) Sensor Circuit Low Input

P1290 Cylinder Head Temperature (CHT) Sensor Circuit High Input

P1291 IDM To Injector High Side Circuit #1 (Right Bank) Short To GND Or B+

P1292 IDM To Injector High Side Circuit #2 (Right Bank) Short To GND Or B+

P1293 IDM To Injector High Side Circuit Open Bank #1 (Right Bank)

P1294 IDM To Injector High Side Circuit Open Bank #2 (Left Bank)

P1295 Multiple IDM/Injector Circuit Faults On Bank #1 (Right)

P1296 Multiple IDM/Injector Circuit Faults On Bank#2 (Left)

P1297 High Sides Shorted Together

P1298 IDM Failure

P1299 Engine Over Temperature Condition

P1309 Misfire Detection Monitor Is Not Enabled

P1316 Injector Circuit/IDM Codes Detected

P1320 Distributor Signal Interrupt

P1336 Crankshaft Position Sensor (Gear)

P1345 No Camshaft Position Sensor Signal

P1351 Ignition Diagnostic Monitor (IDM) Circuit Input Malfunction

P1351 Indicates Ignition System Malfunction

P1352 Indicates Ignition System Malfunction

P1353 Indicates Ignition System Malfunction

P1354 Indicates Ignition System Malfunction

P1355 Indicates Ignition System Malfunction

P1356 PIPs Occurred While IDM Pulse width Indicates Engine Not Turning

P1357 Ignition Diagnostic Monitor (IDM) Pulse width Not Defined

P1358 Ignition Diagnostic Monitor (IDM) Signal Out Of Self-Test Range

P1359 Spark Output Circuit Malfunction

P1364 Spark Output Circuit Malfunction

P1390 Octane Adjust (OCT ADJ) Out Of Self-Test Range

P1391 Glow Plug Circuit Low Input Bank #1 (Right)

P1392 Glow Plug Circuit High Input Bank #1 (Right)

P1393 Glow Plug Circuit Low Input Bank #2 (Left)

P1394 Glow Plug Circuit High Input Bank #2 (Left)

P1395 Glow Plug Monitor Fault Bank #1

P1396 Glow Plug Monitor Fault Bank #2

P1397 System Voltage Out Of Self Test Range

P1400 Differential Pressure Feedback EGR (DPFE) Sensor Circuit Low Voltage Detected

P1401 Differential Pressure Feedback EGR (DPFE) Sensor Circuit High Voltage Detected/EGR Temperature Sensor

P1402 EGR Valve Position Sensor Open Or Short

P1403 Differential Pressure Feedback EGR (DPFE) Sensor Hoses Reversed

P1405 Differential Pressure Feedback EGR (DPFE) Sensor Upstream Hose Off Or Plugged

P1406 Differential Pressure Feedback EGR (DPFE) Sensor Downstream Hose Off Or Plugged

P1407 Exhaust Gas Recirculation (EGR) No Flow Detected (Valve Stuck Closed Or Inoperative)

P1408 Exhaust Gas Recirculation (EGR) Flow Out Of Self-Test Range

P1409 Electronic Vacuum Regulator (EVR) Control Circuit Malfunction

P1410 Check That Fuel Pressure Regulator Control Solenoid And The EGR Check Solenoid Connectors Are Not Swapped

P1411 Secondary Air Injection System Incorrect Downstream Flow Detected

P1413 Secondary Air Injection System Monitor Circuit Low Voltage

P1414 Secondary Air Injection System Monitor Circuit High Voltage

P1442 Evaporative Emission Control System Small Leak Detected

P1443 Evaporative Emission Control System—Vacuum System, Purge Control Solenoid Or Purge Control Valve Malfunction

P1444 Purge Flow Sensor (PFS) Circuit Low Input

P1445 Purge Flow Sensor (PFS) Circuit High Input

P1449 Evaporative Emission Control System Unable To Hold Vacuum

P1450 Unable To Bleed Up Fuel Tank Vacuum

P1455 Evaporative Emission Control System Control Leak Detected (Gross Leak)

P1460 Wide Open Throttle Air Conditioning Cut-Off Circuit Malfunction

P1461 Air Conditioning Pressure (ACP) Sensor Circuit Low Input

P1462 Air Conditioning Pressure (ACP) Sensor Circuit High Input

P1463 Air Conditioning Pressure (ACP) Sensor Insufficient Pressure Change

P1464 Air Conditioning (A/C) Demand Out Of Self-Test Range/A/C On During KOER Or CCT Test

P1469 Low Air Conditioning Cycling Period

P1473 Fan Secondary High, With Fan(s) Off

P1474 Low Fan Control Primary Circuit Malfunction

P1479 High Fan Control Primary Circuit Malfunction

P1480 Fan Secondary Low, With Low Fan On

P1481 Fan Secondary Low, With High Fan On

P1483 Power To Fan Circuit Over current

P1484 Open Power/Ground To Variable Load Control Module (VLCM)

P1485 EGR Control Solenoid Open Or Short

P1486 EGR Vent Solenoid Open Or Short

P1487 EGR Boost Check Solenoid Open Or Short

P1500 Vehicle Speed Sensor (VSS) Circuit Intermittent

P1501 Vehicle Speed Sensor (VSS) Out Of Self-Test Range/Vehicle Moved During Test

P1502 Invalid Self Test—Auxiliary Powertrain Control Module (APCM) Functioning

P1504 Idle Air Control (IAC) Circuit Malfunction

P1505 Idle Air Control (IAC) System At Adaptive Clip

P1506 Idle Air Control (IAC) Overspeed Error

P1507 Idle Air Control (IAC) Underspeed Error

P1512 Intake Manifold Runner Control (IMRC) Malfunction (Bank#1 Stuck Closed)

P1513 Intake Manifold Runner Control (IMRC) Malfunction (Bank#2 Stuck Closed)

P1516 Intake Manifold Runner Control (IMRC) Input Error (Bank #1)

P1517 Intake Manifold Runner Control (IMRC) Input Error (Bank #2)

P1518 Intake Manifold Runner Control (IMRC) Malfunction (Stuck Open)

P1519 Intake Manifold Runner Control (IMRC) Malfunction (Stuck Closed)

P1520 Intake Manifold Runner Control (IMRC) Circuit Malfunction

P1521 Variable Resonance Induction System (VRIS) Solenoid #1 Open Or Short

P1522 Variable Resonance Induction System (VRIS) Solenoid#2 Open Or Short

P1523 High Speed Inlet Air (HSIA) Solenoid Open Or Short

P1530 Air Condition (A/C) Clutch Circuit Malfunction

P1531 Invalid Test—Accelerator Pedal Movement

P1536 Parking Brake Applied Failure

P1537 Intake Manifold Runner Control (IMRC) Malfunction (Bank#1 Stuck Open)

P1538 Intake Manifold Runner Control (IMRC) Malfunction (Bank#2 Stuck Open)

P1539 Power To Air Condition (A/C) Clutch Circuit Overcurrent

P1549 Problem In Intake Manifold Tuning (IMT) Valve System

P1550 Power Steering Pressure (PSP) Sensor Out Of Self-Test Range

P1601 Serial Communication Error

P1605 Powertrain Control Module (PCM)—Keep Alive Memory (KAM) Test Error

P1608 PCM Internal Circuit Malfunction

P1609 PCM Internal Circuit Malfunction (2.5L Only)

P1625 B+ Supply To Variable Load Control Module (VLCM) Fan Circuit Malfunction

P1626 B+ Supply To Variable Load Control Module (VLCM) Air Conditioning (A/C) Circuit

P1650 Power Steering Pressure (PSP) Switch Out Of Self-Test Range

P1651 Power Steering Pressure (PSP) Switch Input Malfunction

P1660 Output Circuit Check Signal High

P1661 Output Circuit Check Signal Low

P1662 Injection Driver Module Enable (IDM EN) Circuit Failure

P1663 Fuel Delivery Command Signal (FDCS) Circuit Failure

P1667 Cylinder Identification (CID) Circuit Failure

P1668 PCM—IDM Diagnostic Communication Error

P1670 EF Feedback Signal Not Detected

P1701 Reverse Engagement Error

P1701 Fuel Trim Malfunction (Villager)

P1703 Brake On/Off (BOO) Switch Out Of Self-Test Range

P1704 Digital Transmission Range (TR) Sensor Failed To Transition State

P1705 Transmission Range (TR) Sensor Out Of Self-Test Range

P1705 TP Sensor (AT) Villager

P1705 Clutch Pedal Position (CPP) Or Park Neutral Position (PNP) Problem

P1706 High Vehicle Speed In Park

P1709 Park Or Neutral Position (PNP) Or Clutch Pedal Position (CPP) Switch Out Of Self-Test Range

P1709 Throttle Position (TP) Sensor Malfunction (Aspire 1.3L, Escort/Tracer 1.8L, Probe 2.5L)

P1711 Transmission Fluid Temperature (TFT) Sensor Out Of Self-Test Range

P1714 Shift Solenoid "A" Inductive Signature Malfunction

P1715 Shift Solenoid "B" Inductive Signature Malfunction

P1716 Transmission Malfunction

P1717 Transmission Malfunction

P1719 Transmission Malfunction

P1720 Vehicle Speed Sensor (VSS) Circuit Malfunction

P1727 Coast Clutch Solenoid Inductive Signature Malfunction

P1728 Transmission Slip Error—Converter Clutch Failed

P1729 4x4 Low Switch Error

P1731 Improper 1–2 Shift

P1732 Improper 2–3 Shift

P1733 Improper 3–4 Shift

P1734 Improper 4–5 Shift

P1740 Torque Converter Clutch (TCC) Inductive Signature Malfunction

P1741 Torque Converter Clutch (TCC) Control Error

P1742 Torque Converter Clutch (TCC) Solenoid Failed On (Turns On MIL)

P1743 Torque Converter Clutch (TCC) Solenoid Failed On (Turns On TCIL)

P1744 Torque Converter Clutch (TCC) System Mechanically Stuck In Off Position

P1744 Torque Converter Clutch (TCC) Solenoid Malfunction (2.5L Only)

P1746 Electronic Pressure Control (EPC) Solenoid Open Circuit (Low Input)

P1747 Electronic Pressure Control (EPC) Solenoid Short Circuit (High Input)

P1748 Electronic Pressure Control (EPC) Malfunction

P1749 Electronic Pressure Control (EPC) Solenoid Failed Low

P1751 Shift Solenoid#1 (SS1) Performance

P1754 Coast Clutch Solenoid (CCS) Circuit Malfunction

P1756 Shift Solenoid#2 (SS2) Performance

P1760 Overrun Clutch SN

P1761 Shift Solenoid #(SS2) Performance

P1762 Transmission Malfunction

P1765 3–2 Timing Solenoid Malfunction (2.5L Only)

P1779 TCIL Circuit Malfunction

P1780 Transmission Control Switch (TCS) Circuit Out Of Self-Test Range

P1781 4x4 Low Switch, Out Of Self-Test Range

P1783 Transmission Over Temperature Condition

P1784 Transmission Malfunction

P1785 Transmission Malfunction

P1786 Transmission Malfunction

P1787 Transmission Malfunction

P1788 3–2 Timing/Coast Clutch Solenoid (3–2/CCS) Circuit Open

P1789 3–2 Timing/Coast Clutch Solenoid (3–2/CCS) Circuit Shorted

P1792 Idle (IDL) Switch (Closed Throttle Position Switch) Malfunction

P1794 Loss Of Battery Voltage Input

P1795 EGR Boost Sensor Malfunction

P1797 Clutch Pedal Position (CPP) Switch Or Neutral Switch Circuit Malfunction

P1900 Cooling Fan

General Motors Corporation Truck

READING CODES

Reading the control module memory is one of the first steps in OBD-II system diagnostics.

This step should be initially performed to determine the general nature of the fault. Subsequent readings will determine if the fault has been cleared.

Reading codes can be performed by any of the methods below:

• Read the control module memory with the Generic Scan Tool (GST)

• Read the control module memory with the vehicle manufacturer's specific tester

To read the fault codes, connect the scan tool or tester according to the manufacturer's instructions. Follow the manufacturer's specified procedure for reading the codes.

CLEARING CODES

Control module reset procedures are a very important part of OBD-II System diagnostics. This step should be done at the end of any fault code repair and at the end of any driveability repair.

Clearing codes can be performed by any of the methods below:
• Clear the control module memory with the Generic Scan Tool (GST)
• Clear the control module memory with the vehicle manufacturer's specific tester
• Turn the ignition off and remove the negative battery cable for at least 1 minute.

Removing the negative battery cable may cause other systems in the vehicle to loose their memory. Prior to removing the cable, ensure you have the proper reset codes for radios and alarms.

➡**The MIL will may also be de-activated for some codes if the vehicle completes three consecutive trips without a fault detected with vehicle conditions similar to those present during the fault.**

GENERAL MOTORS SPECIFIC OBD-II TROUBLE CODES

P1106 MAP Sensor Voltage Intermittently High (Except 2.2L)
P1107 MAP Sensor Voltage Intermittently Low (Except 2.2L)
P1111 IAT Sensor Circuit Intermittent High Voltage (Except 2.2L)
P1112 IAT Sensor Circuit Intermittent Low Voltage (Except 2.2L)
P1114 ECT Sensor Circuit Intermittent Low Voltage (Except 2.2L)
P1115 ECT Sensor Circuit Intermittent High Voltage (Except 2.2L)
P1121 TP Sensor Voltage Intermittently High (Except 2.2L)
P1122 TP Sensor Voltage Intermittently Low (Except 2.2L)
P1133 HO2S Insufficient Switching Bank #1, Sensor #1 (Except 3.4L & 4.3L)
P1133 HO2S Insufficient Switching Sensor (3.4L)
P1134 HO2S #1 Transition Time Ratio (3.4L)
P1134 HO2S Transition Time Ratio Bank #1, Sensor #1 (4.3L, 5.0L, 5.7L & 7.4L)
P1153 HO2S Insufficient Switching Sensor Bank #2, Sensor #1 (4.3L, 5.0L, 5.7L & 7.4L)
P1154 HO2S Transition Time Ratio Bank #2, Sensor #1 (4.3L, 5.0L, 5.7L & 7.4L)
P1345 Crankshaft/Camshaft (CKP/CMP) Correlation (4.3L, 5.0L, 5.7L & 7.4L)
P1350 Ignition Control (IC) Circuit Malfunction (3.4L)
P1351 Ignition Control (IC) Circuit High Voltage (4.3L, 5.0L, 5.7L & 7.4L)
P1361 Ignition Control (IC) Circuit Low Voltage (4.3L, 5.0L, 5.7L & 7.4L)
P1361 Ignition Control (IC) Circuit Not Toggling (3.4L)
P1380 Electronic Brake Control Module (EBCM) DTC Detected Rough Road Data Unusable
P1381 Misfire Detected, No EBCM/PCM/VCM Serial Data (Except "P" Series)
P1406 EGR Pintle Position Circuit Fault (Except "P" Series)
P1415 AIR System Bank #1 (Except "P" Series)
P1416 AIR System Bank #2 (Except "P" Series)
P1441 EVAP Control System Flow During Non-Purge
P1442 EVAP Vacuum Switch Circuit (3.4L)
P1450 Barometric Pressure Sensor Circuit Fault
P1451 Barometric Pressure Sensor Performance
P1460 Cooling Fan Control System Fault
P1508 IAC System Low RPM (4.3L, 5.0L, 5.7L & 7.4L)
P1509 IAC System High RPM (4.3L, 5.7L & 7.4L)
P1520 PNP Circuit (2.2L)
P1500 Starter Signal Circuit Fault
P1510 Back-up Power Supply Fault
P1530 Ignition Timing Adjustment Switch Circuit
P1600 PCM Battery Circuit Fault
P1635 5-Volt Reference "A" Circuit (3.4L)
P1639 5-Volt Reference "B" Circuit (3.4L)

P1641 MIL Control Circuit (3.4L)
P1651 Fan #1 Relay Control Circuit (3.4L)
P1652 Fan #2 Relay Control Circuit (3.4L)
P1654 A/C Relay Control (3.4L)
P1655 EVAP Purge Solenoid Control Circuit (3.4L)
P1672 Low Engine Oil Level Light Control Circuit (3.4L)

Honda Truck

➡**The Honda Passport is covered in the Isuzu section since it shares a platform with the Isuzu Rodeo.**

READING CODES

With Scan Tool

Reading the control module memory is one of the first steps in OBD-II system diagnostics. This step should be initially performed to determine the general nature of the fault. Subsequent readings will determine if the fault has been cleared.

Reading codes can be performed by any of the methods below:
• Read the control module memory with the Generic Scan Tool (GST)
• Read the control module memory with the vehicle manufacturer's specific tester

To read the fault codes, connect the scan tool or tester according to the manufacturer's instructions. Follow the manufacturer's specified procedure for reading the codes.

Without Scan Tool

Honda also provides a way of reading OBD-II trouble code equivalents using a service connector and viewing the MIL. This method is similar to the flash codes from non-OBD-II vehicles.

To read codes, plug the service connector into the service check connector and turn the ignition on. The MIL will flash any stored trouble codes.

CLEARING CODES

Control module reset procedures are a very important part of OBD-II System diagnostics.

This step should be done at the end of any fault code repair and at the end of any driveability repair.

Clearing codes can be performed by any of the methods below:
• Clear the control module memory with the Generic Scan Tool (GST)
• Clear the control module memory with the vehicle manufacturer's specific tester
• Turn the ignition off and remove the negative battery cable for at least 1 minute.

Removing the negative battery cable may cause other systems in the vehicle to loose their memory. Prior to removing the cable, ensure you have the proper reset codes for radios and alarms.

➡**The MIL will may also be de-activated for some codes if the vehicle completes three consecutive trips without a fault detected with vehicle conditions similar to those present during the fault.**

HONDA SPECIFIC OBD-II TROUBLE CODES

P1106 Barometric Pressure Circuit Range/Performance Problem
P1107 Barometric Pressure Circuit Low Input
P1108 Barometric Pressure Circuit High Input
P1121 Throttle Position Lower Than Expected
P1122 Throttle Position Higher Than Expected
P1128 Manifold Absolute Pressure Lower Than Expected
P1129 Manifold Absolute Pressure Higher Than Expected
P1259 VTEC System Malfunction
P1297 Electrical Load Detector Circuit Low Input
P1298 Electrical Load Detector Circuit High Input

P1297 Electrical Load Detector Circuit Low Input
P1298 Electrical Load Detector Circuit High Input
P1336 Crankshaft Speed Fluctuation Sensor Intermittent Interruption
P1337 Crankshaft Speed Fluctuation Sensor No Signal
P1359 Crankshaft Position Top Dead Center Sensor/Cylinder Position Connector Disconnection
P1361 Top Dead Center Sensor Intermittent Interruption
P1362 Top Dead Center Sensor No Signal
P1381 Cylinder Position Sensor Intermittent Interruption
P1382 Cylinder Position Sensor No Signal
P1456 Evaporative Emission Control System Leak Detected (Fuel Tank System)
P1457 Evaporative Emission Control System Leak Detected (EVAP Control Canister Leak)
P1491 EGR Valve Lift Insufficient Detected
P1498 EGR Valve Lift Sensor High Voltage
P1519 Idle Air Control Valve Circuit Failure
P1508 Idle Air Control Valve Circuit Failure
P1607 Powertrain Control Module Internal Circuit Failure A
P1705 Automatic Transaxle
P1706 Automatic Transaxle
P1753 Automatic Transaxle
P1768 Automatic Transaxle
P1790 Automatic Transaxle
P1791 Automatic Transaxle

HONDA OBD-II TROUBLE CODE EQUIVALENTS

If a scan tool is not available for code retrieval, the following codes may be retrieved without one.
1 02 Sensor Circuit High Voltage (Bank no. 1 Sensor no. 1)
1 02 Sensor Circuit Low Voltage (Bank no. 1 Sensor no. 1)
3 Manifold Absolute Pressure/Barometric Pressure Circuit Low Input
3 Manifold Absolute Pressure/Barometric Pressure Circuit High Input
4 Crankshaft Position Sensor "A" Circuit Malfunction **4** Crankshaft Position Sensor "A" Circuit Range/Performance **5** Manifold Absolute Pressure Higher Than Expected
5 Manifold Absolute Pressure Lower Than Expected
6 Engine Coolant Temperature Circuit High Input
6 Engine Coolant Temperature Circuit Low Input
7 Throttle Position Higher Than Expected
7 Throttle Position Lower Than Expected
7 Throttle/Pedal Position Sensor/Switch "A" Circuit High Input
7 Throttle/Pedal Position Sensor/Switch "A" Circuit Low Input
8 Crankshaft Position Top Dead Center Sensor/Cylinder Position Connector Disconnection
8 Top Dead Center Sensor Intermittent Interruption
8 Top Dead Center Sensor No Signal
9 Cylinder Position Sensor Intermittent Interruption
9 Cylinder Position Sensor No Signal
10 Intake Air Temperature Circuit High Input
10 Intake Air Temperature Circuit Low Input
12 EGR Valve Lift Insufficient Detected
12 EGR Valve Lift Sensor High Voltage
13 Barometric Pressure Circuit High Input
13 Barometric Pressure Circuit Low Input
13 Barometric Pressure Circuit Range/Performance Problem
14 Idle Air Control Valve Circuit Failure
14 Idle Air Control Valve Circuit Failure
14 Idle Control System Malfunction
20 Electrical Load Detector Circuit High Input
20 Electrical Load Detector Circuit High Input
20 Electrical Load Detector Circuit Low Input
20 Electrical Load Detector Circuit Low Input
22 VTEC System Malfunction
23 Knock Sensor no. 1—Circuit Malfunction (Bank no. 1 or Single Sensor)
80 Exhaust Gas Recirculation Flow Insufficient Detected

41 02 Sensor Heater Circuit Malfunction (Bank no. 1 Sensor no. 1)
45 System Too Lean (Bank no. 1)
45 System Too Rich (Bank no. 1)
54 Crankshaft Speed Fluctuation Sensor Intermittent Interruption
54 Crankshaft Speed Fluctuation Sensor No Signal
61 02 Sensor Circuit Slow Response (Bank no. 1 Sensor no. 1)
63 02 Sensor Circuit High Voltage (Bank no. 1 Sensor no. 2)
63 02 Sensor Circuit Low Voltage (Bank no. 1 Sensor no. 2)
63 02 Sensor Circuit Slow Response (Bank no. 1 Sensor no. 2)
65 02 Sensor Heater Circuit Malfunction (Bank no. 1 Sensor no. 2)
67 Catalyst System Efficiency Below Threshold (Bank no. 1)
70 Automatic Transaxle
70 Transmission Control System Malfunction
70 Input/Turbine Speed Sensor Circuit Malfunction
70 Output Speed Sensor Circuit Malfunction
70 Incorrect Gear Ratio
70 Torque Converter Clutch Circuit Malfunction
70 Shift Solenoid "A" Electrical
70 Shift Solenoid "B" Electrical
71 Cylinder no. 1—Misfire Detected
72 Cylinder no. 2—Misfire Detected
73 Cylinder no. 3—Misfire Detected
74 Cylinder no. 4—Misfire Detected
86 Engine Coolant Temperature Circuit Range/Performance Problem
90 Evaporative Emission Control System Leak Detected (EVAP Control Canister Leak)
90 Evaporative Emission Control System Leak Detected (Fuel Tank System)
91 Evaporative Emission Control System Pressure Sensor Low Input
91 Evaporative Emission Control System Pressure Sensor High Input

Isuzu Truck

➡**This section also provides coverage for the Honda Passport since it shares a platform with the Isuzu Rodeo.**

READING CODES

Reading the control module memory is one of the first steps in OBD-II system diagnostics. This step should be initially performed to determine the general nature of the fault. Subsequent readings will determine if the fault has been cleared.
Reading codes can be performed by any of the methods below:
• Read the control module memory with the Generic Scan Tool (GST)
• Read the control module memory with the vehicle manufacturer's specific tester
To read the fault codes, connect the scan tool or tester according to the manufacturer's instructions. Follow the manufacturer's specified procedure for reading the codes.

CLEARING CODES

Control module reset procedures are a very important part of OBD-II System diagnostics. This step should be done at the end of any fault code repair and at the end of any driveability repair.
Clearing codes can be performed by any of the methods below:
• Clear the control module memory with the Generic Scan Tool (GST)
• Clear the control module memory with the vehicle manufacturer's specific tester
• Turn the ignition off and remove the negative battery cable for at least 1 minute.
Removing the negative battery cable may cause other systems in the vehicle to loose their memory. Prior to removing the cable, ensure you have the proper reset codes for radios and alarms.

➡**The MIL will may also be de-activated for some codes if the vehicle completes three consecutive trips without a fault detected with vehicle conditions similar to those present during the fault.**

ISUZU SPECIFIC OBD-II TROUBLE CODES

P1106 Map Sensor Circuit Intermittent High Voltage
P1107 MAP Sensor Circuit Intermittent Low Voltage
P1111 IAT Sensor Circuit Intermittent High Voltage
P1112 IAT Sensor Circuit Intermittent Low Voltage
P1114 ECT Sensor Circuit Intermittent Low Voltage
P1115 ECT Sensor Circuit Intermittent High Voltage
P1121 TP Sensor Circuit Intermittent High Voltage
P1122 TP Sensor Circuit Intermittent Low Voltage
P1133 HO2S-11 Insufficient Switching (Bank 1 Sensor 1)
P1134 HO2S-11 Transition Time Ratio (Bank 1 Sensor 1)
P1153 HO2S-21 Insufficient Switching (Bank 2 Sensor I)
P1154 HO2S-21 Transition Time Ratio (Bank 2 Sensor 1)
P1171 Fuel System Lean During Acceleration
P1391 G-Acceleration Sensor Intermittent Low Voltage
P1390 G-Acceleration (Low G) Sensor Performance
P1392 Rough Road G-Sensor Circuit Low Voltage
P1393 Rough Road G-Sensor Circuit High Voltage
P1394 G-Acceleration Sensor Intermittent High Voltage
P1406 EGR Valve Pintle Position Sensor Circuit Fault
P1441 EVAP System Flow During Non-Purge
P1442 EVAP System Flow During Non-Purge
P1508 Idle Speed Control System-Low
P1509 Idle Speed Control System-High
P1618 Serial Peripheral Interface Communication Error
P1640 Output Driver Module 'A' Fault
P1790 PCM ROM (Transmission Side) Check Sum Error
P1792 PCM EEPROM (Transmission Side) Check Sum Error
P1835 Kick Down Switch Always On
P1850 Brake Band Apply Solenoid Electrical Fault
P1860 TCC PWM Solenoid Electrical Fault
P1870 Transmission Component Slipping

KIA Truck

READING CODES

Reading the control module memory is one of the first steps in OBD-II system diagnostics.

This step should be initially performed to determine the general nature of the fault. Subsequent readings will determine if the fault has been cleared.

Reading codes can be performed by any of the methods below:
- Read the control module memory with the Generic Scan Tool (GST)
- Read the control module memory with the vehicle manufacturer's specific tester

To read the fault codes, connect the scan tool or tester according to the manufacturer's instructions. Follow the manufacturer's specified procedure for reading the codes.

CLEARING CODES

Control module reset procedures are a very important part of OBD-II System diagnostics. This step should be done at the end of any fault code repair and at the end of any driveability repair.

Clearing codes can be performed by any of the methods below:
- Clear the control module memory with the Generic Scan Tool (GST)
- Clear the control module memory with the vehicle manufacturer's specific tester
- Turn the ignition off and remove the negative battery cable for at least 1 minute.

Removing the negative battery cable may cause other systems in the vehicle to loose their memory. Prior to removing the cable, ensure you have the proper reset codes for radios and alarms.

➡**The MIL will may also be de-activated for some codes if the vehicle completes three consecutive trips without a fault detected with vehicle conditions similar to those present during the fault.**

KIA SPECIFIC OBD-II TROUBLE CODES

P1102 HO2S-11 Heater Circuit High Voltage
P1105 HO2S-12 Heater Circuit High Voltage
P1115 HO2S-11 Heater Circuit Low Voltage
P1117 HO2S-12 Heater Circuit Low Voltage
P1123 Long Term Fuel Trim Adaptive Air System Low
P1124 Long Term Fuel Trim Adaptive Air System High
P1127 Long Term Fuel Trim Multiplicative Air System Low
P1128 Long Term Fuel Trim Multiplicative Air System High
P1140 Load Calculation Cross Check
P1170 HO2S-11 Circuit Voltage Stuck At Mid-Range
P1195 EGR Boost Or Pressure Sensor Circuit Fault
P1196 Ignition Switch Start Circuit Fault
P1213 Fuel Injector 1, 2, 3 Or 4 Circuit High Voltage
P1214 Fuel Injector 1, 2, 3 Or 4 Circuit High Voltage
P1215 Fuel Injector 1, 2, 3 Or 4 Circuit High Voltage
P1216 Fuel Injector 1, 2, 3 Or 4 Circuit High Voltage
P1225 Fuel Injector 1, 2, 5 Or 4 Circuit Low Voltage
P1226 Fuel Injector 1, 2, 5 Or 4 Circuit Low Voltage
P1227 Fuel Injector 1, 2, 5 Or 4 Circuit Low Voltage
P1228 Fuel Injector 1, 2, 5 Or 4 Circuit Low Voltage
P1250 Pressure Regulator Control Solenoid Circuit Fault
P1345 No SGC (CMP) Signal To PCM
P1386 Knock Sensor Control Zero Test
P1401 EGR Control Solenoid Circuit Signal Low
P1402 EGR Control Solenoid Circuit Signal High
P1402 EGR Valve Position Sensor Circuit Fault
P1410 EVAP Purge Control Solenoid Circuit High Voltage
P1412 EGR Differential Pressure Sensor Signal Low
P1413 EGR Differential Pressure Sensor Signal High
P1425 EVAP Purge Control Solenoid Circuit Low Voltage
P1449 Canister Drain Cut Valve Solenoid Circuit Fault
P1455 Fuel Tank Sending Unit Circuit Fault
P1458 Air Conditioning Compressor Clutch Signal Fault
P1485 EGR Vent Control Solenoid Circuit Fault
P1486 EGR Vacuum Control Solenoid Circuit Fault
P1487 EGR Boost Sensor Solenoid Circuit Fault
P1510 Idle Air Control Valve Closing Coil High Voltage
P1513 Idle Air Control Valve Closing Coil Low Voltage
P1515 A/T To M/T Codification
P1523 VICS Solenoid Valve Circuit Fault
P1552 Idle Air Control Valve Opening Coil Low Voltage
P1553 Idle Air Control Valve Opening Coil High Voltage
P1606 Chassis Accelerator Sensor Signal Circuit Fault
P1608 PCM Internal Fault
P1611 MIL Request Circuit Low Voltage
P1614 MIL Request Circuit High Voltage
P1616 Chassis Accelerator Sensor Signal Low Voltage
P1617 Chassis Accelerator Sensor Signal High Voltage
P1624 TCM to PCM MIL Request Circuit Fault
P1655 Unused Power Stage "B"
P1660 Unused Power Stage 'A'
P1660 Unused Power Stage 'B'
P1665 Power Stage Group 'A'
P1743 Torque Converter Clutch Solenoid Circuit Fault

P1794 Battery Or Circuit Fault
P1797 Clutch Pedal Switch (MT) Or PIN Switch Circuit Fault

Lexus Truck

READING CODES

Reading the control module memory is one of the first steps in OBD-II system diagnostics.

This step should be initially performed to determine the general nature of the fault. Subsequent readings will determine if the fault has been cleared.

Reading codes can be performed by any of the methods below:
- Read the control module memory with the Generic Scan Tool (GST)
- Read the control module memory with the vehicle manufacturer's specific tester

To read the fault codes, connect the scan tool or tester according to the manufacturer's instructions. Follow the manufacturer's specified procedure for reading the codes.

CLEARING CODES

Control module reset procedures are a very important part of OBD-II System diagnostics. This step should be done at the end of any fault code repair and at the end of any driveability repair.

Clearing codes can be performed by any of the methods below:
- Clear the control module memory with the Generic Scan Tool (GST)
- Clear the control module memory with the vehicle manufacturer's specific tester
- Turn the ignition off and remove the negative battery cable for at least 1 minute.

Removing the negative battery cable may cause other systems in the vehicle to loose their memory. Prior to removing the cable, ensure you have the proper reset codes for radios and alarms.

➡**The MIL will may also be de-activated for some codes if the vehicle completes three consecutive trips without a fault detected with vehicle conditions similar to those present during the fault.**

LEXUS SPECIFIC OBD-II TROUBLE CODES

P1100 Barometric Pressure Sensor Circuit Fault
P1200 Fuel Pump Relay Circuit Fault
P1300 Igniter Circuit Fault (Bank 1)
P1305 Igniter Circuit Fault (Bank 2)
P1335 Crankshaft Position Sensor Circuit Fault
P1400 Sub-Throttle Position Sensor Circuit Fault
P1401 Sub-Throttle Position Sensor Performance
P1500 Starter Signal Circuit Fault
P1510 Air Volume Too Low With Supercharger On
P1600 PCM Battery Back-up Circuit Fault
P1605 Knock Control CPU Fault
P1700 Vehicle Speed Sensor Circuit Fault
P1705 Direct Clutch Speed Sensor Circuit Fault
P1765 Linear Shift Solenoid Circuit Fault
P1780 Park Neutral Position Switch Fault

Mazda Truck

READING CODES

Reading the control module memory is one of the first steps in OBD-II system diagnostics.

This step should be initially performed to determine the general nature of the fault. Subsequent readings will determine if the fault has been cleared.

Reading codes can be performed by any of the methods below:
- Read the control module memory with the Generic Scan Tool (GST)
- Read the control module memory with the vehicle manufacturer's specific tester

To read the fault codes, connect the scan tool or tester according to the manufacturer's instructions. Follow the manufacturer's specified procedure for reading the codes.

CLEARING CODES

Control module reset procedures are a very important part of OBD-II System diagnostics. This step should be done at the end of any fault code repair and at the end of any driveability repair.

Clearing codes can be performed by any of the methods below:
- Clear the control module memory with the Generic Scan Tool (GST)
- Clear the control module memory with the vehicle manufacturer's specific tester
- Turn the ignition off and remove the negative battery cable for at least 1 minute.

Removing the negative battery cable may cause other systems in the vehicle to loose their memory. Prior to removing the cable, ensure you have the proper reset codes for radios and alarms.

➡**The MIL will may also be de-activated for some codes if the vehicle completes three consecutive trips without a fault detected with vehicle conditions similar to those present during the fault.**

MAZDA SPECIFIC OBD-II TROUBLE CODES

P1000 OBD-II Monitor Testing Not Complete More Driving Required
P1001 Key On Engine Running (KOER) Self-Test Not Able To Complete, KOER Aborted
P1100 Mass Air Flow (MAF) Sensor Intermittent
P1101 Mass Air Flow (MAF) Sensor Out Of Self-Test Range
P1110 Intake Air Temperature (IAT) Sensor Signal Circuit Fault
P1112 Intake Air Temperature (IAT) Sensor Intermittent
P1113 Intake Air Temperature (IAT) Sensor Intermittent
P1116 Engine Coolant Temperature (ECT) Sensor Out Of Self-Test Range
P1117 Engine Coolant Temperature (ECT) Sensor Intermittent
P1120 Throttle Position (TP) Sensor Out Of Range (Low)
P1121 Throttle Position (TP) Sensor Inconsistent With MAF Sensor
P1124 Throttle Position (TP) Sensor Out Of Self-Test Range
P1125 Throttle Position (TP) Sensor Circuit Intermittent
P1127 Exhaust Not Warm Enough, Downstream Heated Oxygen Sensors (HO2S) Not Tested
P1128 Upstream Heated Oxygen Sensors (HO2S) Swapped From Bank To Bank
P1129 Downstream Heated Oxygen Sensors (HO2S) Swapped From Bank To Bank
P1130 Lack Of Upstream Heated Oxygen Sensor (HO2S 11) Switch, Adaptive Fuel At Limit (Bank #1)
P1131 Lack Of Upstream Heated Oxygen Sensor (HO2S 11) Switch, Sensor Indicates Lean (Bank #1)
P1132 Lack Of Upstream Heated Oxygen Sensor (HO2S 11) Switch, Sensor Indicates Rich (Bank#1)
P1137 Lack Of Downstream Heated Oxygen Sensor (HO2S 12) Switch, Sensor Indicates Lean (Bank#1)
P1138 Lack Of Downstream Heated Oxygen Sensor (HO2S 12) Switch, Sensor Indicates Rich (Bank#1)
P1150 Lack Of Upstream Heated Oxygen Sensor (HO2S 21) Switch, Adaptive Fuel At Limit (Bank #2)
P1151 Lack Of Upstream Heated Oxygen Sensor (HO2S 21) Switch, Sensor Indicates Lean (Bank#2)
P1152 Lack Of Upstream Heated Oxygen Sensor (HO2S 21) Switch, Sensor Indicates Rich (Bank #2)
P1170 (HO2S 11) Signal Remained Unchanged For More Than 20 Seconds After Closed Loop
P1173 Feedback A/F Mixture Control (HO2S 21) Signal Remained Unchanged For More Than 20 Seconds After Closed Loop

P1195 Barometric (BARO) Pressure Sensor Circuit Malfunction (Signal Is From EGR Boost Sensor)

P1196 Starter Switch Circuit Malfunction

P1235 Fuel Pump Control Out Of Range (MIL DTC)

P1236 Fuel Pump Control Out Of Range (No MIL)

P1250 Fuel Pressure Regulator Control (FPRC) Solenoid Malfunction

P1252 Fuel Pressure Regulator Control (FPRC) Solenoid Malfunction

P1260 THEFT Detected—Engine Disabled

P1270 Engine RPM Or Vehicle Speed Limiter Reached

P1345 No Camshaft Position Sensor Signal

P1351 Ignition Diagnostic Monitor (IDM) Circuit Input Malfunction

P1351 Indicates Ignition System Malfunction

P1352 Indicates Ignition System Malfunction

P1353 Indicates Ignition System Malfunction

P1354 Indicates Ignition System Malfunction

P1358 Ignition Diagnostic Monitor (IDM) Signal Out Of Self-Test Range

P1359 Spark Output Circuit Malfunction

P1360 Ignition Coil "A" Secondary Circuit Fault

P1361 Ignition Coil "A" Secondary Circuit Fault

P1362 Ignition Coil "A" Secondary Circuit Fault

P1364 Spark Output Circuit Malfunction

P1365 Ignition Coil Secondary Circuit Fault

P1390 Octane Adjust (OCT ADJ) Out Of Self-Test Range

P1400 Differential Pressure Feedback EGR (DPFE) Sensor Circuit Low Voltage Detected

P1401 Differential Pressure Feedback EGR (DPFE) Sensor Circuit High Voltage Detected/EGR Temperature Sensor

P1402 EGR Valve Position Sensor Open Or Short

P1405 Differential Pressure Feedback EGR (DPFE) Sensor Upstream Hose Off Or Plugged

P1406 Differential Pressure Feedback EGR (DPFE) Sensor Downstream Hose Off Or Plugged

P1407 Exhaust Gas Recirculation (EGR) No Flow Detected (Valve Stuck Closed Or Inoperative)

P1408 Exhaust Gas Recirculation (EGR) Flow Out Of Self-Test Range

P1409 Electronic Vacuum Regulator (EVR) Control Circuit Malfunction

P1443 Evaporative Emission Control System—Vacuum System, Purge Control Solenoid Or Purge Control Valve Malfunction

P1444 Purge Flow Sensor (PFS) Circuit Low Input

P1445 Purge Flow Sensor (PFS) Circuit High Input

P1449 Evaporative Emission Control System Unable To Hold Vacuum

P1455 Evaporative Emission Control System Control Leak Detected (Gross Leak)

P1460 Wide Open Throttle Air Conditioning Cut-Off Circuit Malfunction

P1464 Air Conditioning (A/C) Demand Out Of Self-Test Range/A/C On During KOER Or CCT Test

P1474 Low Fan Control Primary Circuit Malfunction

P1485 EGR Control Solenoid Open Or Short

P1486 EGR Vent Solenoid Open Or Short

P1487 EGR Boost Check Solenoid Open Or Short

P1500 Vehicle Speed Sensor (VSS) Circuit Intermittent

P1501 Vehicle Speed Sensor (VSS) Out Of Self-Test Range/Vehicle Moved During Test

P1502 Invalid Self Test—Auxiliary Powertrain Control Module (APCM) Functioning

P1504 Idle Air Control (IAC) Circuit Malfunction

P1505 Idle Air Control (IAC) System At Adaptive Clip

P1506 Idle Air Control (IAC) Overspeed Error

P1507 Idle Air Control (IAC) Underspeed Error

P1508 Bypass Air Solenoid "1" Circuit Fault

P1509 Bypass Air Solenoid "2" Circuit Fault

P1521 Variable Resonance Induction System (VRIS) Solenoid #1 Open Or Short

P1522 Variable Resonance Induction System (VRIS) Solenoid #2 Open Or Short

P1523 High Speed Inlet Air (HSIA) Solenoid Open Or Short

P1524 Charge Air Cooler Bypass Solenoid Circuit Fault

P1525 ABV Vacuum Solenoid Circuit Fault

P1526 ABV Vent Solenoid Circuit Fault

P1529 Atmospheric balance Air Control Valve Fault

P1540 ABV System Fault

P1601 Serial Communication Error

P1602 Serial Communication Error

P1605 Powertrain Control Module (PCM)—Keep Alive Memory (KAM) Test Error

P1608 PCM Internal Circuit Malfunction

P1609 PCM Internal Circuit Malfunction

P1627 Serial Communication Error

P1628 Serial Communication Error

P1650 Power Steering Pressure (PSP) Switch Out Of Self-Test Range

P1651 Power Steering Pressure (PSP) Switch Input Malfunction

P1701 Reverse Engagement Error

P1703 Brake On/Off (BOO) Switch Out Of Self-Test Range

P1705 Transmission Range (TR) Sensor Out Of Self-Test Range

P1706 High Vehicle Speed In Park

P1709 Park Or Neutral Position (PNP) Or Clutch Pedal Position (CPP) Switch Out Of Self-Test Range

P1711 Transmission Fluid Temperature (TFT) Sensor Out Of Self-Test Range

P1720 Vehicle Speed Sensor (VSS) Circuit Malfunction

P1729 4x4 Low Switch Error

P1741 Torque Converter Clutch (TCC) Control Error

P1742 Torque Converter Clutch (TCC) Solenoid Failed On (Turns On MIL)

P1743 Torque Converter Clutch (TCC) Solenoid Failed On (Turns On TCIL)

P1746 Electronic Pressure Control (EPC) Solenoid Open Circuit (Low Input)

P1747 Electronic Pressure Control (EPC) Solenoid Short Circuit (High Input)

P1749 Electronic Pressure Control (EPC) Solenoid Failed Low

P1751 Shift Solenoid#1 (SS1) Performance

P1754 Coast Clutch Solenoid (CCS) Circuit Malfunction

P1756 Shift Solenoid#2 (SS2) Performance

P1761 Shift Solenoid #(SS2) Performance

P1780 Transmission Control Switch (TCS) Circuit Out Of Self-Test Range

P1781 4x4 Low Switch, Out Of Self-Test Range

P1783 Transmission Over Temperature Condition

P1794 PCM Battery Direct Power Circuit Fault

P1797 P/N Switch Open or Short Circuit Fault

Mitsubishi Truck

READING CODES

Reading the control module memory is one of the first steps in OBD-II system diagnostics. This step should be initially performed to determine the general nature of the fault. Subsequent readings will determine if the fault has been cleared.

Reading codes can be performed by any of the methods below:
- Read the control module memory with the Generic Scan Tool (GST)
- Read the control module memory with the vehicle manufacturer's specific tester

To read the fault codes, connect the scan tool or tester according to the manufacturer's instructions. Follow the manufacturer's specified procedure for reading the codes.

CLEARING CODES

Control module reset procedures are a very important part of OBD-II System diagnostics. This step should be done at the end of any fault code repair and at the end of any driveability repair.

Clearing codes can be performed by any of the methods below:
- Clear the control module memory with the Generic Scan Tool (GST)
- Clear the control module memory with the vehicle manufacturer's specific tester

• Turn the ignition off and remove the negative battery cable for at least 1 minute.

Removing the negative battery cable may cause other systems in the vehicle to loose their memory. Prior to removing the cable, ensure you have the proper reset codes for radios and alarms.

➡ The MIL will may also be de-activated for some codes if the vehicle completes three consecutive trips without a fault detected with vehicle conditions similar to those present during the fault.

MITSUBISHI SPECIFIC OBD-II TROUBLE CODES

P1100 Induction Control Motor Position Sensor Fault
P1101 Traction Control Vacuum Solenoid Circuit Fault
P1102 Traction Control Ventilation Solenoid Circuit Fault
P1103 Turbocharger Waste Gate Actuator Circuit Fault
P1104 Turbocharger Waste Gate Solenoid Circuit Fault
P1105 Fuel Pressure Solenoid Circuit Fault
P1294 Target Idle Speed Not Reached
P1295 No 5-Volt Supply To TP Sensor
P1296 No 5-Volt Supply To MAP Sensor
P1297 No Change In MAP From Start To Run
P1300 Ignition Timing Adjustment Circuit
P1390 Timing Belt Skipped One Tooth Or More
P1391 Intermittent Loss Of CMP Or CKP Sensor Signals
P1400 Manifold Differential Pressure Sensor Fault
P1443 EVAP Purge Control Solenoid "2" Circuit Fault
P1486 EVAP Leak Monitor Pinched Hose Detected
P1487 High Speed Radiator Fan Control Relay Circuit Fault
P1989 High Speed Condenser Fan Control Relay Fault
P1490 Low Speed Fan Control Relay Fault
P1492 Battery Temperature Sensor High Voltage
P1494 EVAP Ventilation Switch Or Mechanical Fault
P1495 EVAP Ventilation Solenoid Circuit Fault
P1496 5-Volt Supply Output Too Low
P1500 Generator FR Terminal Circuit Fault
P1600 PCM-TCM Serial Communication Link Circuit Fault
P1696 PCM Failure- EEPROM Write Denied
P1715 No CCD Messages From TCM
P1750 TCM Pulse Generator Circuit Fault
P1791 Pressure Control, Shift Control, TCC Solenoid Fault
P1899 PCM ECT Level Signal to TCM Circuit Fault

Nissan Truck

➡ This section also provides coverage for the Mercury Villager since it shares a platform with the Nissan Quest

READING CODES

With Scan Tool

Reading the control module memory is one of the first steps in OBD-II system diagnostics. This step should be initially performed to determine the general nature of the fault. Subsequent readings will determine if the fault has been cleared.

Reading codes can be performed by any of the methods below:
• Read the control module memory with the Generic Scan Tool (GST)
• Read the control module memory with the vehicle manufacturer's specific tester

To read the fault codes, connect the scan tool or tester according to the manufacturer's instructions. Follow the manufacturer's specified procedure for reading the codes.

Without Scan Tool

The ECM is capable of outputting data in four different modes, depending on the position of the mode switch and the ignition key. Modes are switched by turning the mode screw on the side of the ECM, near the red LED. Additional modes are accessed by turning the ignition key on or off.

The ECM is located forward of the center console, behind an access panel on the Altima, and in the passenger's side kick panel on the 240SX.

With the ECM set in Mode 1 and the ignition in the **ON** position, a malfunction indicator lamp bulb check may be performed. When the engine is started, the ECM will illuminate the indicator lamps as a warning of a fault in the system.

Mode 2 is set by turning the mode selector screw fully clockwise, waiting 2 seconds, then turning the screw fully counterclockwise. With the ignition in the **ON** position, self-diagnostic results will be output as a series of lamp flashes. When the engine is started, the oxygen sensor monitor function is enabled and the red LED on the ECM is used to determine proper oxygen sensor function.

1. Remove the access cover and locate the mode adjusting screw and LED on the ECM.

2. Turn the ignition switch **ON** , but do not start the engine. Both the LED and the malfunction indicator lamp on the instrument panel should be illuminated. This is a bulb check.

3. Start the engine.

➡ Switching modes is not possible while the engine is running.

4. If the LED or malfunction indicator lamp illuminates, there is a fault in the system.

5. Turn the mode selector screw fully clockwise. Wait 2 seconds, then turn the screw fully counterclockwise.

6. The diagnostic trouble codes will now be read from the ECM memory. They will appear as flashes of the malfunction indicator lamp, or the ECM's LED.

7. After all codes have been read, turn the mode selector screw fully clockwise to erase the codes.

➡ Turn the mode adjusting screw to the fully counterclockwise position whenever the vehicle is in use.

8. Turn the ignition **OFF**.

➡ When the ignition switch is turned OFF during diagnosis, power to the ECM will drop after approximately 5 seconds. The diagnosis will automatically return to Mode 1 at this time.

CLEARING CODES

With Scan Tool

Control module reset procedures are a very important part of OBD-II System diagnostics. This step should be done at the end of any fault code repair and at the end of any driveability repair.

Clearing codes can be performed by any of the methods below:
• Clear the control module memory with the Generic Scan Tool (GST)
• Clear the control module memory with the vehicle manufacturer's specific tester

➡ The MIL will may also be de-activated for some codes if the vehicle completes three consecutive trips without a fault detected with vehicle conditions similar to those present during the fault.

Without Scan Tool

The easiest way to clear trouble codes without a scan tool is to turn the mode selector screw fully clockwise after all codes have been read.

➡ Turn the mode adjusting screw to the fully counterclockwise position whenever the vehicle is in use.

Codes may also be erased by turning the ignition off and remove the negative battery cable for at least 1 minute. However, removing the negative battery cable may cause other systems in the vehicle to loose their memory. Prior to removing the cable, ensure you have the proper reset codes for radios and alarms.

NISSAN SPECIFIC OBD-II TROUBLE CODES

P1120 Secondary Throttle Position Sensor Circuit Fault
P1125 Tandem Throttle Position Sensor Circuit Fault
P1210 Traction Control System Signal Fault
P1220 Fuel Pump Control Module Fault
P1320 Ignition Control Signal Fault
P1336 Crankshaft Position Sensor Circuit Fault
P1400 EGR/EVAP Control Solenoid Circuit Fault
P1401 EGR Temperature Sensor Circuit Fault
P1443 EVAP Canister Control Vacuum Switch Circuit Fault
P1445 EVAP Purge Volume Control Valve Circuit Fault
P1605 TCM A~T Diagnosis Communication Line Fault
P1705 Throttle Position Sensor (Switch) Circuit Fault
P1760 Overrun Clutch Solenoid Valve Circuit Fault
P1900 Cooling Fan Control Circuit Fault

NISSAN OBD-II TROUBLE CODE EQUIVALENTS

If a scan tool is not available for code retrieval, the following codes may be retrieved without one.

0505 No Self Diagnostic Failure Indicated
0102 Mass or Volume Air Flow Circuit Malfunction
0401 Intake Air Temperature Circuit Malfunction
0103 Engine Coolant Temperature Circuit Malfunction
0403 Throttle/Pedal Position Sensor/Switch "A" Circuit Malfunction
0908 Insufficient Coolant Temperature For Closed Loop Fuel Control
0303 O2 Circuit Malfunction
0307 Closed Loop Control
0901 O2 Sensor Heater Circuit Malfunction (Bank no. 1 Sensor no. 1)
0707 O2 Sensor Circuit Malfunction (Bank no. 1 Sensor no. 2)
0902 O2 Sensor Heater Circuit Malfunction (Bank no. 1 Sensor no. 2)
0115 System Too Lean (Bank no. 1)
0114 System Too Rich (Bank no. 1)
0701 Random/Multiple Cylinder Misfire Detected
0608 Cylinder no. 1—Misfire Detected
0607 Cylinder no. 2—Misfire Detected
0606 Cylinder no. 3—Misfire Detected
0605 Cylinder no. 4—Misfire Detected
0304 Knock Sensor no. 1—Circuit Malfunction (Bank no. 1 or Single Sensor)
0802 Crankshaft Position Sensor "A" Circuit Malfunction
0101 Camshaft Position Sensor Circuit Malfunction
0302 Exhaust Gas Recirculation Flow Malfunction
0306 Exhaust Gas Recirculation Flow Excessive Detected
0702 Catalyst System Efficiency Below Threshold (Bank no. 1)
0104 Vehicle Speed Sensor Malfunction
0205 Idle Control System Malfunction
0301 Internal Control Module Read Only Memory (ROM) Error
1003 Transmission Range Sensor Circuit Malfunction (PRNDL Input)
1101 Inhibitor Switch Circuit
1208 Transmission Fluid Temperature Sensor Circuit Malfunction
1102 Output Speed Sensor Circuit Malfunction
1207 Engine Speed Input Circuit Malfunction
1103 Gear no. 1 Incorrect Ratio
1104 Gear no. 2 Incorrect Ratio
1105 Gear no. 3 Incorrect Ratio
1106 Gear no. 4 Incorrect Ratio
1204 Torque Converter Clutch Circuit Malfunction
1205 Pressure Control Solenoid Malfunction
1108 Shift Solenoid "A" Malfunction
1201 Shift Solenoid "B" Malfunction
0201 Ignition Control Signal Fault
0905 Crankshaft Position Sensor Circuit Fault
1005 EGR/EVAP Control Solenoid Circuit Fault
0305 EGR Temperature Sensor Circuit Fault
0804 TCM A~T Diagnosis Communication Line Fault

1206 Throttle Position Sensor (Switch) Circuit Fault
1203 Overrun Clutch Solenoid Valve Circuit Fault
1308 Cooling Fan Control Circuit Fault

Subaru Truck

READING CODES

Reading the control module memory is one of the first steps in OBD-II system diagnostics.

This step should be initially performed to determine the general nature of the fault. Subsequent readings will determine if the fault has been cleared.

Reading codes can be performed by any of the methods below:
• Read the control module memory with the Generic Scan Tool (GST)
• Read the control module memory with the vehicle manufacturer's specific tester

To read the fault codes, connect the scan tool or tester according to the manufacturer's instructions. Follow the manufacturer's specified procedure for reading the codes.

CLEARING CODES

Control module reset procedures are a very important part of OBD-II System diagnostics. This step should be done at the end of any fault code repair and at the end of any driveability repair.

Clearing codes can be performed by any of the methods below:
• Clear the control module memory with the Generic Scan Tool (GST)
• Clear the control module memory with the vehicle manufacturer's specific tester
• Turn the ignition off and remove the negative battery cable for at least 1 minute.

Removing the negative battery cable may cause other systems in the vehicle to loose their memory. Prior to removing the cable, ensure you have the proper reset codes for radios and alarms.

➡**The MIL will may also be de-activated for some codes if the vehicle completes three consecutive trips without a fault detected with vehicle conditions similar to those present during the fault.**

SUBARU SPECIFIC OBD-II TROUBLE CODES

P1100 Starter Switch Circuit Fault
P1101 Neutral Position Switch Circuit Fault (MT)

Suzuki Truck

READING CODES

Reading the control module memory is one of the first steps in OBD-II system diagnostics. This step should be initially performed to determine the general nature of the fault. Subsequent readings will determine if the fault has been cleared.

Reading codes can be performed by any of the methods below:
• Read the control module memory with the Generic Scan Tool (GST)
• Read the control module memory with the vehicle manufacturer's specific tester

To read the fault codes, connect the scan tool or tester according to the manufacturer's instructions. Follow the manufacturer's specified procedure for reading the codes.

CLEARING CODES

Control module reset procedures are a very important part of OBD-II System diagnostics. This step should be done at the end of any fault code repair and at the end of any driveability repair.

Clearing codes can be performed by any of the methods below:
- Clear the control module memory with the Generic Scan Tool (GST)
- Clear the control module memory with the vehicle manufacturer's specific tester
- Turn the ignition off and remove the negative battery cable for at least 1 minute.

Removing the negative battery cable may cause other systems in the vehicle to loose their memory. Prior to removing the cable, ensure you have the proper reset codes for radios and alarms.

➡**The MIL will may also be de-activated for some codes if the vehicle completes three consecutive trips without a fault detected with vehicle conditions similar to those present during the fault.**

SUZUKI SPECIFIC OBD-II TROUBLE CODES

P1250 EFI Heater Circuit Fault
P1408 Manifold Differential Pressure Sensor Circuit Fault

P1410 Fuel Tank Pressure Control Solenoid Circuit Fault
P1450 Barometric Pressure Sensor Circuit Fault
P1451 Barometric Pressure Sensor Performance
P1460 Cooling Fan Control System Fault
P1500 Starter Signal Circuit Fault
P1510 Back-up Power Supply Fault
P1530 Ignition Timing Adjustment Switch Circuit
P1600 PCM Battery Circuit Fault
P1700 TCM Throttle Position Sensor Circuit Fault
P1705 TCM ECT Circuit Fault
P1715 PNP Switch Circuit Fault
P1717 AT Drive Range Signal Circuit Fault

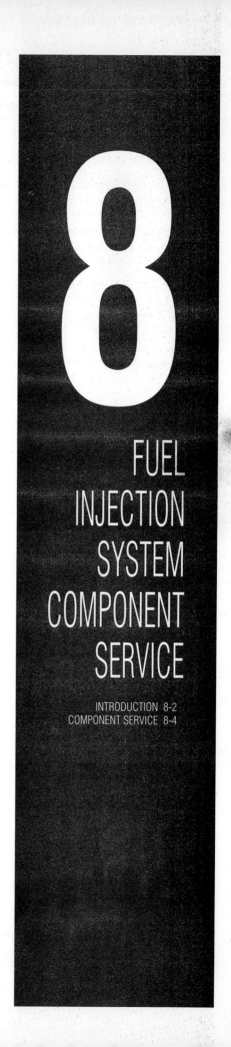

8

FUEL INJECTION SYSTEM COMPONENT SERVICE

INTRODUCTION

This section provides information for testing, replacement, and adjustment of the individual components. There are many different design fuel systems and components used on today's vehicles. It is not always possible to provide exact testing and replacement for every component. What this section will do is provide a generic test and replacement for most of the components related to your engine emission and electronic control system. For a description of how a component works, or it's function, please refer to Section 3. Once you have narrowed down the cause of the vehicle's problem, this section will enable you to perform the needed tests for each component. When a specific component test is discussed, this section will explain if the procedure is easy or difficult. The section will go on to explain how to perform the test or if specific tools may be required.

Some sensor or module tests may require specialty testers or tools. Check with the local automotive parts store, many times they offer to test these items (like ignition modules, etc.) for you, if you bring them in. Many auto part stores also rent testers and special test equipment. The auto parts counter person can be a valuable source of information. Before you make a purchase, describe the problem, they may have advice for testing that would be helpful.

Servicing Safely

▶ See Figures 1, 2, 3 and 4

It is virtually impossible to anticipate all of the hazards involved with automotive maintenance and service but care and common sense will prevent most accidents.

The rules of safety for mechanics range from "don't smoke around gasoline" to "use the proper tool for the job." The trick to avoiding injuries is to develop safe work habits and take every possible precaution.

DO'S

• Do keep a fire extinguisher and first aid kit handy.
• Do wear safety glasses or goggles when cutting, drilling, grinding or prying, even if you have 20–20 vision. If you wear glasses for the sake of vision, wear safety goggles over your regular glasses.
• Do shield your eyes whenever you work around the battery. Batteries contain sulfuric acid. In case of contact with the eyes or skin, flush the area

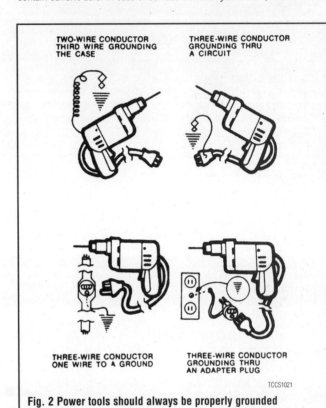

Fig. 2 Power tools should always be properly grounded

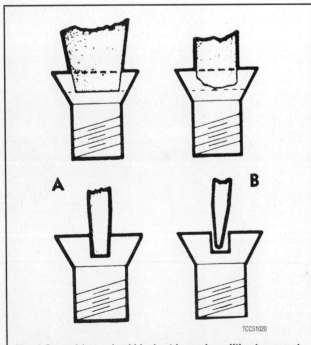

Fig. 1 Screwdrivers should be kept in good condition to prevent injury or damage that could result if the blade slips from the screw

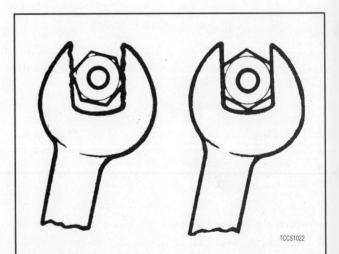

Fig. 3 Using the correct size wrench will help prevent the possibility of rounding-off a nut

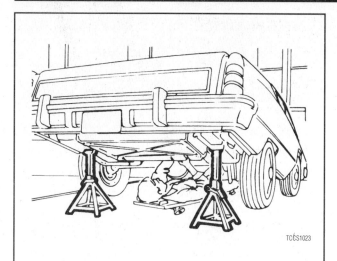

Fig. 4 NEVER work under a vehicle unless it is supported using safety stands (jackstands)

TCCS1023

with water or a mixture of water and baking soda, then seek immediate medical attention.

• Do use safety stands (jackstands) for any under vehicle service. Jacks are for raising vehicles; jackstands are for making sure the vehicle stays raised until you want it to come down. Whenever the vehicle is raised, block the wheels remaining on the ground and set the parking brake.

• Do use adequate ventilation when working with any chemicals or hazardous materials. Like carbon monoxide, the asbestos dust resulting from some brake lining wear can be hazardous in sufficient quantities.

• Do disconnect the negative battery cable when working on the electrical system. The secondary ignition system contains EXTREMELY HIGH VOLTAGE. In some cases it can even exceed 50,000 volts.

• Do follow manufacturer's directions whenever working with potentially hazardous materials. Most chemicals and fluids are poisonous if taken internally.

• Do properly maintain your tools. Loose hammerheads, mushroomed punches and chisels, frayed or poorly grounded electrical cords, excessively worn screwdrivers, spread wrenches (open end), cracked sockets, slipping ratchets, or faulty droplight sockets can cause accidents.

• Likewise, keep your tools clean; a greasy wrench can slip off a bolt head, ruining the bolt and often harming your knuckles in the process.

• Do use the proper size and type of tool for the job at hand. Do select a wrench or socket that fits the nut or bolt. The wrench or socket should sit straight, not cocked.

• Do, when possible, pull on a wrench handle rather than push on it, and adjust your stance to prevent a fall.

• Do be sure that adjustable wrenches are tightly closed on the nut or bolt and pulled so that the force is on the side of the fixed jaw.

• Do strike squarely with a hammer; avoid glancing blows.

• Do set the parking brake and block the drive wheels if the work requires a running engine.

DON'T'S

• Don't run the engine in a garage or anywhere else without proper ventilation—EVER! Carbon monoxide is poisonous; it takes a long time to leave the human body and you can build up a deadly supply of it in your system by simply breathing in a little every day. You may not realize you are slowly poisoning yourself. Always use power vents, windows, fans and/or open the garage door.

• Don't work around moving parts while wearing loose clothing. Short sleeves are much safer than long, loose sleeves. Hard-toed shoes with neoprene soles protect your toes and give a better grip on slippery surfaces. Jewelry such as watches, fancy belt buckles, beads or body adornment of any kind is not safe working around a vehicle. Long hair should be tied back under a hat or cap.

• Don't use pockets for toolboxes. A fall or bump can drive a screwdriver deep into your body. Even a rag hanging from your back pocket can wrap around a spinning shaft or fan.

• Don't smoke when working around gasoline, cleaning solvent or other flammable material.

• Don't smoke when working around the battery. When the battery is being charged, it gives off explosive hydrogen gas.

• Don't use gasoline to wash your hands; there are excellent soaps available. Gasoline contains dangerous additives that can enter the body through a cut or through your pores. Gasoline also removes all the natural oils from the skin so that bone dry hands will suck up oil and grease.

• Don't service the air conditioning system unless you are equipped with the necessary tools and training. When liquid or compressed gas refrigerant is released to atmospheric pressure it will absorb heat from whatever it contacts. This will chill or freeze anything it touches. Although refrigerant is normally non-toxic, R-12 becomes a deadly poisonous gas in the presence of an open flame. One good whiff of the vapors from burning refrigerant can be fatal.

• Don't use screwdrivers for anything other than driving screws! A screwdriver used as a prying tool can snap when you least expect it, causing injuries. At the very least, you'll ruin a good screwdriver.

• Don't use a bumper or emergency jack (that little ratchet, scissors, or pantograph jack supplied with the vehicle) for anything other than changing a flat! These jacks are only intended for emergency use out on the road; they are NOT designed as a maintenance tool. If you are serious about maintaining your vehicle yourself, invest in a hydraulic floor jack of at least a 1½ ton capacity, and at least two sturdy jackstands.

Relieving Fuel System Pressure

Relieving the fuel system pressure is also necessary on TBI, Bosch CIS, and other fuel injection systems that are not equipped with a Schrader valve type pressure test port. Without a Schrader valve, the system must be carefully relieved using the following method.

Furthermore, many TBI systems have a constant bleed passage which reduces the system's residual pressure to zero after the engine is shut off. However, it is still good practice to relieve the system pressure before opening it as a precaution to prevent an injury.

WITH SCHRADER VALVE

Since most fuel injection systems are highly pressurized, it is necessary to relieve the pressure prior to opening the system for repairs or testing. Multi-Port fuel injection systems are commonly equipped with a Schrader valve which, when used in conjunction with a fuel pressure gauge, allows the system pressure to be relieved.

WITHOUT SCHRADER VALVE

This procedure is generic and will work with most fuel injected vehicles. For specific procedures on your vehicle, consult a "Chilton Total Car Care (TCC) Manual".

1. Disable the fuel pump by one of the following methods:
• Remove the fuel pump fuse.
• Remove the fuel pump relay.
• Locate and disconnect the fuel pump wiring.

➡**When removing the fuel pump fuse or relay to disable the fuel pump, it is important to make certain that the fuel injectors are not part of this circuit. If the injectors do not operate the residual fuel system pressure will not be relieved.**

2. Start the engine and operate it until it stalls. Once the engine has stalled, crank the starter for an additional 10 seconds.

3. Place a rag over the connection in which you intend to disconnect and carefully separate the connections. Use the rag to absorb any remaining fuel.

SPECIAL CASES

▶ **See Figures 5, 6 and 7**

Removing the fuel pump fuse or relay from the fuse block is the most commonly used method. But this won't work for all vehicles because some fuses or relays protect the ignition and/or the fuel injector circuits as well. For example, on vehicles manufactured by Ford (all except Explorer), the fuel pump is disabled by disconnecting the inertia switch. In addition, on pre-1990 BMW models, the fuel pump can be disabled by disconnecting its ground.

When in doubt, always follow the manufacturer's recommended fuel pressure relief procedure. For specific procedures on your vehicle, consult a "Chilton Total Car Care (TCC) Manual" for your vehicle.

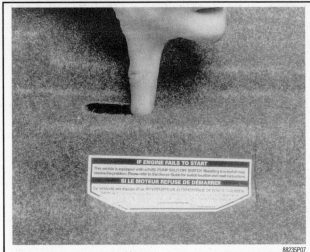

Fig. 6 Reset the switch by simply inserting a finger into the hole and push down on the switch

Fig. 5 The inertia or fuel pump shutoff switch on Ford vehicles has an access hole (arrow) usually located in the trunk or cargo area

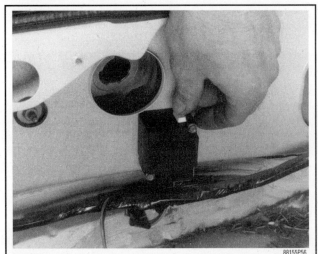

Fig. 7 The inertia switch can be used to shut down power to the fuel pump

COMPONENT SERVICE

Air Flow Sensor (CIS)

▶ **See Figures 8, 9 and 10**

This device measures the amount of air drawn in by the engine. It operates according to the suspended body principle, using a counterbalanced sensor plate that is connected to the fuel distributor control plunger by a lever system. A small leaf spring assures that the sensor plate assumes the correct zero position when the engine is stationary.

The air flow sensor consists of an air venturi tube in which an air flow sensor plate moves. The air flowing into the venturi from the air cleaner lifts the air flow sensor plate, allowing the air to flow through. The greater the amount of air, the higher the sensor plate will be raised.

The air flow sensor plate is fitted to a lever which is compensated by a counterweight. The lever acts on the control plunger in the fuel distributor which is pressed down by the control pressure, thus counteracting the lifting force of the air flow sensor plate.

The height to which the air flow sensor plate is raised is governed by the magnitude of the air flow.

The air/fuel mixture varies with the engine load. The inclination of the venturi walls therefore varies in stages in order to provide a correct air/fuel mixture at all loads. Thus, the mixture is enriched at full load and leaned at idle.

The lever acts on the control plunger in the fuel distributor by means of an adjustable link with a needle bearing at the contact point. The basic fuel setting, and thus the CO setting, is adjusted by means of the adjustment screw on the link. This adjustment is made with a special tool and access to the screw can be gained through a hole in the air flow sensor between the air venturi and the fuel distributor. The CO adjustment is sealed on later models.

A rubber bellows connects the air flow sensor to the throttle valve housing.

➡ **On KE systems, the sensor plate rest position is angled upward, not horizontal as is the K system.**

TESTING

The air flow sensor plate in the fuel distributor must operate smoothly in order to do a good job of measuring air. Remove the air boot and check the sensor plate movement. When released, the plate should fall freely with one

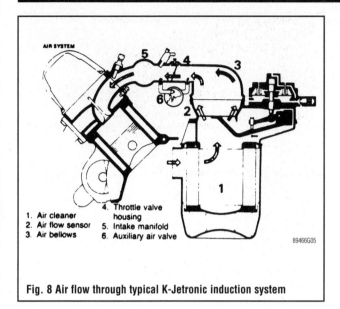

1. Air cleaner
2. Air flow sensor
3. Air bellows
4. Throttle valve housing
5. Intake manifold
6. Auxiliary air valve

89466G05

Fig. 8 Air flow through typical K-Jetronic induction system

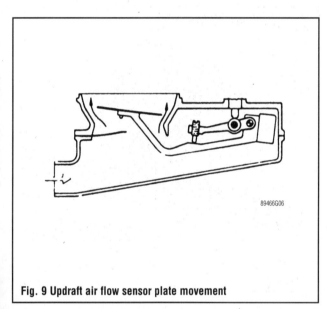

89466G06

Fig. 9 Updraft air flow sensor plate movement

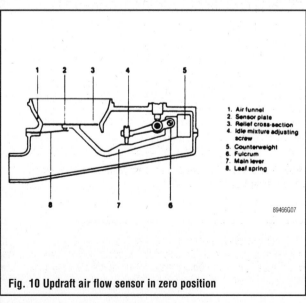
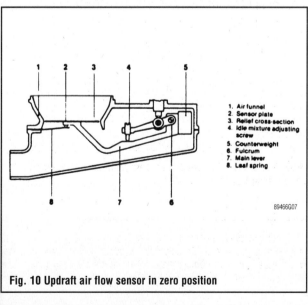

1. Air funnel
2. Sensor plate
3. Relief cross-section
4. Idle mixture adjusting screw
5. Counterweight
6. Fulcrum
7. Main lever
8. Leaf spring

89466G07

Fig. 10 Updraft air flow sensor in zero position

or two bounces. If the plate sticks, loosen the mounting screws and retighten them uniformly. Clean the funnel and sensor plate too, as these can get dirty from PCV fumes.

Check for leakage in the inlet system between the air flow sensor and the engine Air leaking into the system may result in poor engine performance, owing to the fact that it bypasses the air flow sensor, causing a lean mixture. Leakage can occur in the following places:

a. At the rubber bellows between the air flow sensor and the throttle valve housing.

b. At the gasket on the flange of the cold start valve.

c. At the gasket between the throttle valve housing and the inlet manifold.

d. At the gasket between the inlet manifold and the cylinder head.

e. At the hose connections on the throttle valve housing, auxiliary air valve or inlet manifold.

f. Via the crankcase ventilation hose from the oil filler cap, dip stick or valve cover gasket.

➡ Move the sensor plate gently with a small magnet.

The plate should not bind, and although the plate will offer some resistance when depressed (due to the control pressure), it should return to its rest position when released. Be careful not to scratch the plate or venturi.

To check the air flow sensor contact switch, depress or lift the sensor plate by hand. The fuel injectors should buzz, and the fuel pump should activate. If the pump operates, but the injectors do not buzz, check the fuel pressure. If the pump does not operate, check for a short in the air flow sensor connector.

SENSOR PLATE POSITION ADJUSTMENT

▶ See Figures 11 and 12

➡ The air flow sensor plate adjustment is critical. The distance between the sensor plate and the plate stop must be 0–0.2 in. The plate must also be centered In the venturi, and must not contact the venturi walls.

1. Remove the air cleaner assembly.

2. Using a 0.004 in. (0.10mm) feeler gauge, check the clearance around the sensor plate at four opposite points around the plate.

3. If necessary, loosen the bolt in the center of the sensor plate and center the plate. Torque the bolt to 3.6 ft. lbs. (4.9 Nm).

❊❊ WARNING

Do not scratch the venturi or the plate.

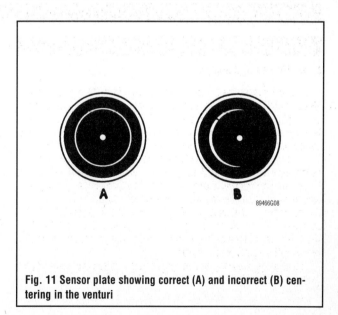

89466G08

Fig. 11 Sensor plate showing correct (A) and incorrect (B) centering in the venturi

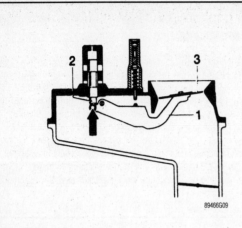

Fig. 12 Air flow sensor used on KE-Jetronic systems showing counterbalanced sensor arm (1), fuel distributor plunger (2) and angled air sensor plate (3)

SENSOR PLATE HEIGHT ADJUSTMENT

◆ **See Figures 13 and 14**

➡**The sensor plate height adjustment must be checked under fuel pressure.**

1. Install a pressure gauge in the line between the fuel distributor and the control pressure regulator as previously described.
2. Remove the rubber elbow from the air flow sensor assembly.
3. Remove the fuel pump replay from the fuse panel and install a bridge adapter on pre-1979 models. Check that the fuel pressure is within specifications.
4. The sensor plate should be flush or 0.02 in. (0.5mm) below the beginning of the venturi taper. If necessary to adjust, remove the mixture control from the intermediate housing and bend the spring accordingly.

➡**With the sensor plate too high, the engine will run on and with the sensor plate too low, poor cold and warm engine start-up will result. If the sensor plate movement is erratic, the control piston can be sticking.**

5. Recheck the pressure reading after any adjustments.

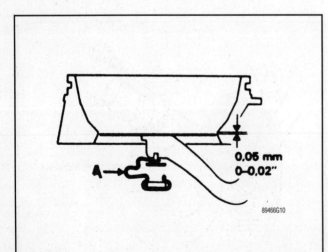

Fig. 13 Correct sensor plate height in venturi. Adjust by bending spring. (A)

0.05 mm
0–0.02"

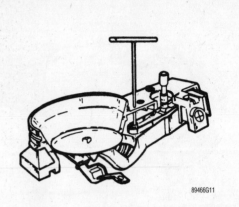

Fig. 14 Cutaway of the air flow sensor assembly showing the direction of air flow and proper placement of the mixture (CO) adjusting tool. Never accelerate the engine with the tool in place

6. Remove the pressure gauge, reconnect the fuel lines and install the fuel pump relay, if removed.
7. Reset the idle speed if necessary. See the individual car sections for details. Anytime an adjustment is made on the fuel system, or if a component is replaced, the idle CO should be reset with a CO meter.

REMOVAL AND INSTALLATION

1. Relieve the fuel system pressure.

➡**Wrap a cloth around the connection to catch any escaping fuel.**

2. Thoroughly clean all fuel lines on the fuel distributor and then remove them.
3. Remove the rubber air intake duct.
4. Remove the air flow sensor/fuel distributor as a unit.
5. Remove the three retaining screws and remove the fuel distributor.

➡**When installing the air flow sensor, always replace the O-ring and gaskets. Use Loctite® on all retaining bolts.**

6. Installation is in the reverse order of removal.

Auxiliary Air Regulator (CIS)

The auxiliary air regulator allows more air/fuel mixture when the engine is cold in order to improve driveability and provide idle stabilization. The increased air volume is measured by the air flow sensor and fuel is metered accordingly. The auxiliary air regulator contains a specially shaped plate attached to a bi-metal spring. The plate changes position according to engine temperature, allowing the moist air to pass when the engine is cold. As the temperature rises, the bi-metal spring slowly closes the air passage. The bi-metal spring is also heated electrically, allowing the opening time to be limited according to engine type. The auxiliary air regulator does not function when the engine is warm.

TESTING

◆ **See Figure 15**

➡**The engine must be cold to perform this test.**

1. Disconnect the electrical terminal-plug and the two air hoses at the auxiliary air regulator.
2. Voltage must be present at the terminal plug with the ignition switch **ON**. Check the continuity of the heater coil by connecting a test light or ohmmeter to the terminals on the regulator.

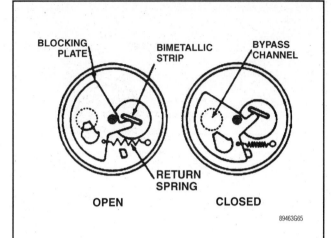

Fig. 15 Internal components of the auxiliary air regulator showing cold (open) and warm (closed) positions

3. Use a mirror to look through the bore of the regulator. If the air valve is not open, replace the auxiliary air regulator.

4. Connect the terminal plug and the two air hoses to the auxiliary air regulator.

5. Start the engine: the auxiliary air regulator bore should close within five minutes of engine operation by the cut-off valve.

➡**A quick check of the auxiliary air regulator can be made by unplugging the electrical connector with the engine cold. Start the engine and pinch the hose between the regulator and the intake manifold—the idle speed should drop. Reconnect the air regulator and allow the engine to warm up. With the engine at operating temperature, pinching the hose to the intake manifold should not affect the idle speed. If it does, replace the auxiliary air regulator.**

REMOVAL AND INSTALLATION

▶ See Figure 16

1. Locate the auxiliary air regulator on the rear of the intake manifold.
2. Disconnect the electrical connection and remove the air hoses.
3. Remove the mounting bolts and remove the regulator.
4. Installation is in the reverse order of removal.
5. Make sure all hose and electrical connections are tight.

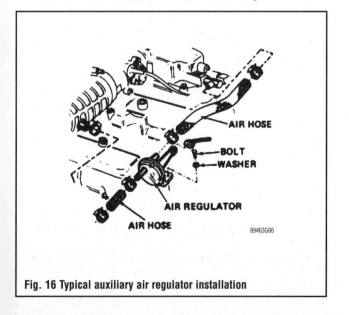

Fig. 16 Typical auxiliary air regulator installation

Camshaft Sensor

▶ See Figures 17 and 18

The Camshaft Position (CMP) sensor determines when Top Dead Center (TDC) compression of No. 1 cylinder occurs and then converts it into a pulse signal that is then sent to the control module. The control module uses the signal to determine correct injection sequence. The sensor may be located in the distributor housing, mounted on the cylinder head or in an assembly that replaces the distributor. In all cases, this sensor is driven by the camshaft.

Essentially, there are 2 types of camshaft sensors. One is a Hall Effect switch and the other is a magnetic reluctance sensor. The easiest way to distinguish the Hall Effect switch from magnetic sensors is the Hall Effect switch will have a three wire harness and the Reluctance sensors usually have 2 wires.

TESTING

Basic testing for each type camshaft sensor is covered under "Hall Effect Switch" or "Magnetic Reluctance Sensor" in this section. If you have spark at the coil or if the fuel injectors are injecting fuel, the problem is most likely not this sensor.

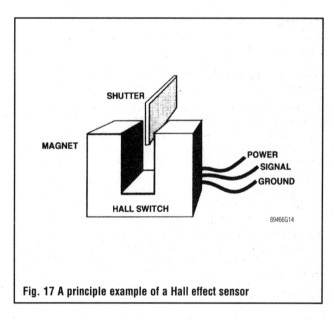

Fig. 17 A principle example of a Hall effect sensor

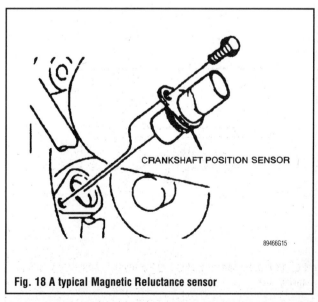

Fig. 18 A typical Magnetic Reluctance sensor

When suspecting a camshaft sensor problem, first perform a visual inspection, most problems can be found in wiring harnesses and connectors.

REMOVAL & INSTALLATION

▶ See Figures 19 and 20

On some engines the camshaft sensor may be a simple bolt on unit attached to the timing cover or cylinder head and is rather simple to replace. On other engines, it may be a part of the ignition distributor unit and not serviceable. For a specific procedure and further information about your vehicle, consult a "Chilton Total Car Care (TCC) Manual".

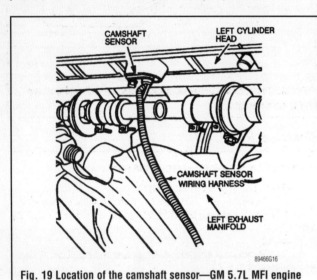

Fig. 19 Location of the camshaft sensor—GM 5.7L MFI engine shown

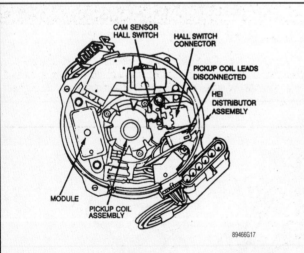

Fig. 20 Location of the camshaft sensor inside the distributor— GM 4.5L and 4.9L MFI engines shown

MAGNETIC RELUCTANCE SENSOR

This generic procedure covers the removal and installation of an engine mounted camshaft position sensor. This type of sensor usually does not require an adjustment. In the procedure for this engine application the sensor installation is a simple bolt in procedure.
1. Disconnect the negative battery cable.
2. Disconnect the electrical connector at the sensor.

3. Remove the camshaft sensor mounting bolt and remove the sensor from the engine cover.

To install:
4. Prior to installing the sensor, always inspect the O-ring seal and replace it as needed.
5. Position the camshaft sensor to the mounting position and carefully push it in place. Secure it in place with the mounting bolt.
6. Connect the electrical connector at the sensor.
7. Connect the negative battery cable.

HALL EFFECT SWITCH

This generic procedure covers the removal and installation of an engine mounted camshaft position sensor. This particular camshaft sensor is located in the distributor. Removal of the distributor will be necessary for this camshaft sensor.

This is a job that you can tackle with a little time and patience using the correct tools. Some sensors are obviously easy to replace, while others should be serviced as an assembly (by replacing the distributor).

➡**If you are going to tackle a distributor mounted sensor, it is highly recommended you refer to a "Chilton Total Car Care (TCC) Manual" for specific procedures.**

1. Disconnect the negative battery cable.
2. Prior to removing the distributor, mark it for installation position. You can use correction fluid, paint or scratch a line on the distributor. This will help provide the proper location during assembly.
3. Remove the ignition distributor assembly from the engine.
4. Secure the distributor in a holding device. Mark the distributor shaft and gear to ensure proper assembly.
5. Remove the gear roll pin and slide the gear from the shaft.
6. Align the flat on the timing core with the hall switch to allow removal.
7. Pull the shaft assembly from the distributor.
8. Remove the cam sensor retaining screws from the sensor. Disconnect the electrical connect from the sensor and remove the cam sensor from the distributor.

To install:
9. Connect the hall switch to the, electrical connector and place it in mounting position. Install the retaining screws.
10. Prior to installing the distributor shaft, inspect and ensure that all wires and connectors are intact.
11. Apply an appropriate distributor shaft lubricant to the shaft and install the distributor shaft. Align the flat on the timing core with the hall switch.
12. Install the gear and align the marks on the gear and shaft, made during disassembly. Secure the gear with the roll pin.
13. Install the distributor into the engine.
14. Connect the electrical connectors.
15. Connect the negative battery cable.
16. Start the engine and set the initial timing as required.

Cold Start Injector

TESTING

Only a few Multi-Point Fuel Injected (MFI) engines utilize a cold start injector to improve starting ability. The injector only injects fuel for a few minutes and only when the engine is cold. If there is no voltage present at the cold start injector when the engine is cold, the most likely problem is the cold start injector temperature time switch.
1. Check for power to the switch cold start switch with the key **ON**.
2. With the engine cold you should have power to the injector.
3. Start the engine, you should be able to hear or feel the injector clicking. The injector should shut off as the engine warms up or after a minute or two.

REMOVAL & INSTALLATION

▶ See Figure 21

1. Relieve the fuel system pressure.
2. With the ignition OFF, disconnect the electrical harness from the injector.
3. Disconnect the fuel line attached to the injector.

➡ **Some injectors are held in with clips.**

4. Using the proper sized wrench, carefully unscrew the injector or remove the attaching screws.
   To install:
5. Always use a new O-ring when you replace an injector.
6. Install the injector and tighten securely.
7. Connect the fuel line to the injector.
8. Connect the electrical harness.
9. Turn ignition **ON** with engine cold.
10. Check for proper operation and fuel leaks.

Cold Start Injector Time Switch

TESTING

▶ See Figure 22

Only a few Multi-Point Fuel Injected (MFI) engines utilize a cold start injector to improve starting ability. This switch controls the length of time the injector will stay on depending on engine temperature. The injector only injects fuel for a few minutes and only when the engine is cold. If there is no voltage present at the cold start injector when the engine is cold, the most likely problem is the cold start injector temperature time switch.

1. Check for power to the switch with the key **ON**.
2. With the engine cold you should have power on both sides of the switch, if not the switch is probably defective.
3. The switch should shut the power off as the engine warms up, or after a minute or two.
4. The resistance of some switches can also be tested. The switch may function but either too long or not long enough.
5. This test will vary on different engines. Check resistance between the terminals:
   • Terminals STA and STJ—approximately 20–40 ohms below 86°F (30°C) or approximately 40–60 ohms when above 104°F (40°C)
   • Terminal STA and ground—approximately 20–80 ohms.
6. If the resistance is not as specified, the switch may be faulty.

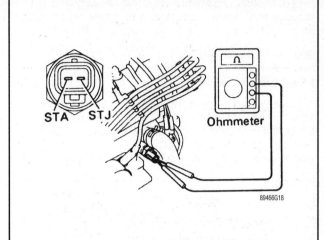

Fig. 22 The cold start injector time switch can be easily tested with an ohmmeter

REMOVAL & INSTALLATION

➡ **Perform this procedure only on a cold engine.**

1. Drain the cooling system as necessary.
2. With the ignition OFF, unplug the electrical connector to the switch.
3. Using the proper sized wrench, carefully unscrew the switch from the engine.
   To install:
4. Coat the threads of the switch with a sealant and install switch into engine. Tighten securely.
5. Plug the electrical connector into the switch.
6. Refill the coolant to the proper level.
7. Road test the vehicle for proper operation.

Cold Start Valve (CIS)

▶ See Figure 23

The cold start valve is mounted near the throttle valve housing and is connected to the pressure line. The valve, which is operated by a solenoid coil, is actuated by a thermo-time switch that is controlled by the engine temperature.

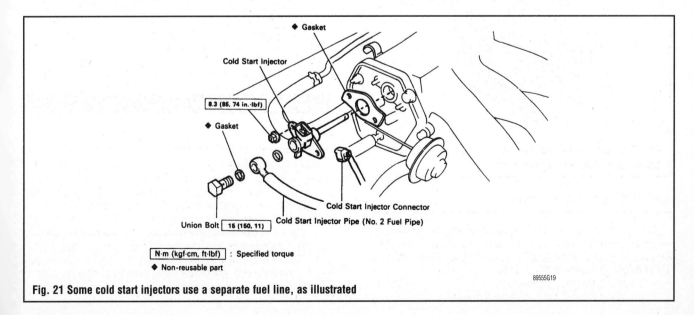

Fig. 21 Some cold start injectors use a separate fuel line, as illustrated

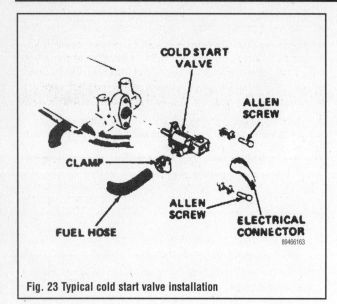

Fig. 23 Typical cold start valve installation

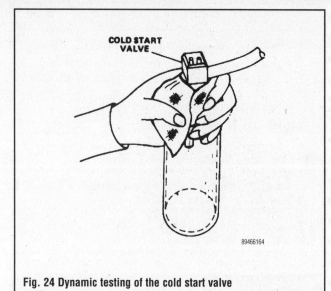

Fig. 24 Dynamic testing of the cold start valve

During cold starting, part of the fuel mixture is lost due to condensation on the cold cylinder walls. To compensate for this loss, extra fuel is injected by means of a solenoid-operated cold start valve. Fuel is delivered downstream of the throttle valve. A thermo-time switch determines the injection period of the cold start valve according to either engine temperature or an electrically heated bimetal strip that de-energizes the cold start valve after approximately 8 seconds to prevent flooding. The cold start valve does not function when the engine is warm.

REMOVAL & INSTALLATION

The cold start valve is mounted in the intake manifold, downstream from the air flow sensor. The valve is usually retained with two small Allen screws and can be removed for inspection without disconnecting the fuel line. When removing the valve, take care not to damage the valve body that is usually made of plastic. Make sure the valve is clean and the sealing O-ring is seated properly and in good condition when installing. Do not over-tighten the mounting screws.

✳ CAUTION

Always relieve fuel system pressure prior to servicing the system.

TESTING

▶ **See Figure 24**

Remove the cold start injector from the intake manifold and hold over a beaker. With a cold engine 95°F (35°C) or lower coolant temperature), the injector should spray during starter operation (max. 12 seconds). If not, check the voltage between the terminals of the injector when the starter is on. Voltage indicates a bad cold start injector. No voltage indicates a faulty thermo-time switch or wiring. Ground one terminal and connect the second to the positive side of the coil. When you run the pump, l0–30 seconds, you should get a good, cone-shaped spray. Dry the injector, disconnect jumpers, and energize the pump again. There shouldn't be any fuel. If it drips, replace it. Check the thermo-time switch when it's below 95°F (35°C). Disconnect the cold start valve and hook up a test light across its connector. Ground the No. 1 coil terminal and run the starter. The light should glow for several seconds and then go out. If not, replace the thermo-time switch.

➡**Remove the fuel pump relay and attach a bridging adapter to energize the fuel pump during testing.**

With the starter off, attach a test relay to operate fuel pump. Check for cold start valve leakage. Maximum allowable leakage is one drop per

minute. Any excessive leakage is reason enough to replace the cold start valve. Don't forget to wipe the valve nozzle with a clean towel after every test and before installing.

Coolant Temperature Sensor

TESTING

▶ **See Figures 25, 26 and 27**

The coolant temperature sensor's function is to advise the control module of changes in engine temperature by monitoring the changes in coolant temperature. The sensor must be handled carefully during removal. It can be damaged (thereby affecting engine performance) by impact.

The chart shown is a good guideline of what most coolant temperature sensor resistances will be. Specific resistance ranges may vary from engine to engine.

1. To test the sensor in the vehicle, with a cold engine, unplug the electrical connector from the sensor.

2. Using an ohmmeter, measure the resistance between both terminals. Refer to the chart for an example resistance reading.

Fig. 25 Measure the resistance between both terminals to test the coolant temperature sensor

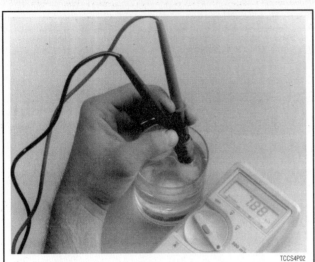

Fig. 26 Submerge the end of the sensor in hot or cold water and check sensor resistance

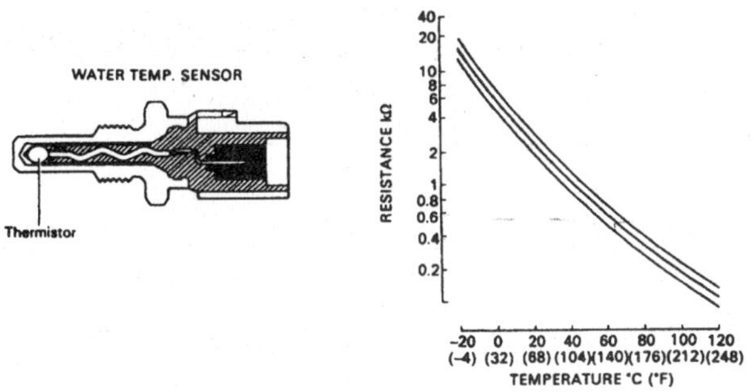

cylinder head or threaded into the radiator depending on your particular vehicle.

➡It is important not to confuse the coolant temperature sensor with the coolant temperature switch. For further information on your particular vehicle, always consult a "Chilton Total Car Care (TCC) Manual".

✳✳ CAUTION

Perform this procedure only on a cold engine. Attempting to remove any component that involves working with engine coolant can result in serious burns.

1. Drain the cooling system part way down.
2. With the ignition **OFF**, unplug the electrical connector to the sensor.
3. Using the proper sized wrench, carefully unscrew the sensor from the engine coolant passage.
   To install:
4. Coat the threads of the sensor with a sealant.
5. Install the sensor and tighten securely.
6. Plug the electrical connector into the sensor.
7. Refill the coolant to the proper level. Road test the vehicle for proper operation and check for leaks.

Fig. 27 Coolant temperature sensor resistance chart

Fig. 28 The coolant temperature sensor is always located in a coolant passage, shown here mounted on the side of the cylinder head

3. Reconnect the sensor, then run the engine until it reaches normal operating temperature.
4. Unplug the electrical connector from the sensor again.
5. Using an ohmmeter, measure the resistance between both terminals. Resistance values should change with temperature. Again, you can refer to the chart for examples of the resistance reading at different temperatures.
6. If the resistance does not change, the sensor is faulty.
7. A sensor may also be tested that has been removed from an engine. At room temperature, measure the resistance between both terminals with an ohmmeter.
8. Then place the sensor in a glass of ice water and measure the resistance between both terminals as it cools. The resistance should change smoothly as it cools. If resistance doesn't change, the sensor is faulty.

REMOVAL & INSTALLATION

▶ **See Figures 28, 29 and 30**

The following is a general procedure which should work for most applications. The sensor must be handled carefully during removal. It can be damaged (thereby affecting engine performance) by impact. The sensor may be located on the intake manifold, on the thermostat housing, on the

Fig. 29 This coolant temperature sensor is located at the back of an intake manifold

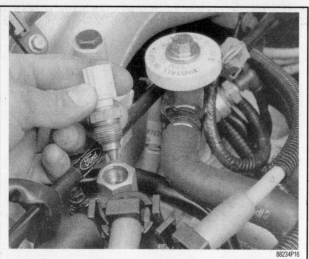

Fig. 30 Most coolant temperature sensors are located at the front of the intake manifold near the thermostat housing

Crankshaft Position Sensor

The crankshaft sensor generates a signal to the control module. The control module uses this signal to calculate crankshaft position and engine speed for ignition and injector operation.

Essentially, there are 2 types of crankshaft sensors. One is a Hall Effect switch and the other is a magnetic reluctance sensor. The easiest way to distinguished the switch designs is the Magnetic sensor is a 2 wire sensor and the Hall Effect switch will have a three wire harness.

There is also a crankshaft sensor called a Dual Crank sensor or Combination sensor. This design combines 2 sensors together and is normally mounted on a pedestal on the front of the engine, near the harmonic balancer. This type crankshaft sensor is usually a Hall Effect switch.

Crankshaft sensors are usually mounted near the crankshaft, either on the side or the front of the engine block. The sensors may also be a part of the distributor unit.

Relacement of typical crankshaft sensors if fairly straight forward. Replacement of distributor mounted types usually requires removing the distributor. However, if a distributor located sensor malfunctions, on some vehicles, the entire distributor unit must be replaced.

For more information on Hall switches and Magnetic sensors, see "Hall Effect Switch and Magnetic Reluctance sensor" in this section.

TESTING

Testing for each type crankshaft sensor is covered briefly under "Hall Effect Switch" or "Magnetic Reluctance Sensor" in this section. However, the procedure given is a general procedure and may not apply to the specific vehicle you are working with. If the fuel injectors are spraying fuel, then the crankshaft sensor is working.

When suspecting a crankshaft sensor problem, first perform a visual inspection, most problems can be found in wiring harnesses and connectors.

When diagnosing a suspected faulty crankshaft sensor, remember that a defective ECM or ignition module could also be related. Because of the relationship of these components, proper diagnosing should be accomplished by following the appropriate diagnostic procedures found in a "Chilton Total Car Care (TCC) Manual".

Magnetic Reluctance Sensor

◆ See Figures 31 and 32

The following procedure is general and should work for most applications. This particular crankshaft sensor is located on side of the engine, protruding into the block.

On some manufacturers, the crankshaft sensor requires an air gap adjustment. In this application, no adjustment is required. For more specific information on your vehicle, consult a "Chilton Total Car Care (TCC) Manual".

1. Disconnect the negative battery cable.
2. Disengage the sensor harness connector.
3. Remove the sensor-to-block retaining bolt.
4. Remove the sensor from the engine block.

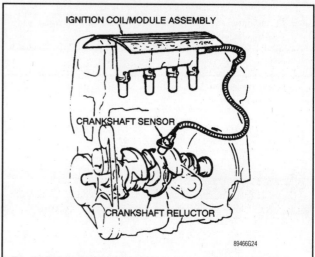

Fig. 31 Reluctance type crankshaft sensor mounted in the side of a 4-cylinder engine block

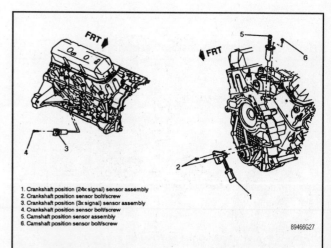

1. Crankshaft position (24x signal) sensor assembly
2. Crankshaft position sensor bolt/screw
3. Crankshaft position (3x signal) sensor assembly
4. Crankshaft position sensor bolt/screw
5. Camshaft position sensor assembly
6. Camshaft position sensor bolt/screw

Fig. 32 Reluctance type crankshaft and camshaft position sensors mounted at the front of the engine near the harmonic balancer

To install:

5. If equipped, inspect the sensor O-ring for wear, cracks or leakage and replace, if necessary.

6. Lightly coat the O-ring with clean engine oil, then install the sensor to the engine block.

7. Install the sensor-to-block retaining bolt.

8. Engage the sensor wiring harness.

9. Connect the negative battery cable.

Hall Effect Switch

▶ See Figure 33

The following procedure generic and covers the removal and installation of a Hall Effect switch type crankshaft sensor. This particular crankshaft sensor is located on a pedestal, on the front of the engine near the harmonic balancer.

1. Disconnect the negative battery cable.

2. Remove the serpentine belt from the crankshaft pulley.

3. Raise and support the vehicle safely.

4. Remove the right front tire and wheel assembly.

5. Remove the right inner fender access cover.

6. Using a correctly sized socket, remove the crankshaft harmonic balancer retaining bolt.

7. Remove the harmonic balancer. Remove crankshaft sensor/pedestal assembly from the engine.

8. Remove the sensor from the pedestal.

To install:

9. Loosely install the crankshaft sensor on the pedestal. Position the sensor/pedestal assembly on the special crankshaft sensor adjustment tool.

10. Position the special tool and pedestal assembly on the block. Install the retaining screws. Torque the mounting screws to specifications.

11. Torque the pedestal pinch bolt to the required torque according to specifications and remove the tool. The special tool will help place the sensor in the correct position.

12. Install the balancer onto the crankshaft and torque the bolt to specifications.

13. Install the inner fender shield. Install the tire and wheel assembly. Lower the vehicle and install the serpentine belt.

14. Connect the negative battery cable.

EGR Vacuum Switching Valve

TESTING

▶ See Figures 34, 35, 36, 37 and 38

Despite the impressive name, the Exhaust Gas Recirculation Vacuum Switching Valve (EGR-VSV) valve does nothing more than allow vacuum to flow through the system depending on engine coolant temperature. The bi-metallic element within the switch reacts to temperature changes, opening or closing the valve at a pre-determined level. To test the valve:

1. Drain the coolant from the radiator into a suitable container.

2. Label and disconnect the hoses from the VSV.

3. Remove the valve.

4. Using cool water, cool the threaded part of the valve to below 104°F (40°C).

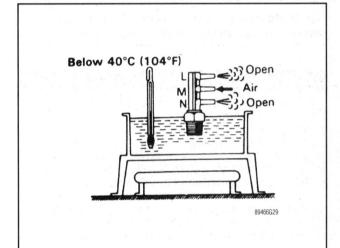

Fig. 34 Example of the VSV air flow when below its calibrated temperature—typical 3 hose valve shown

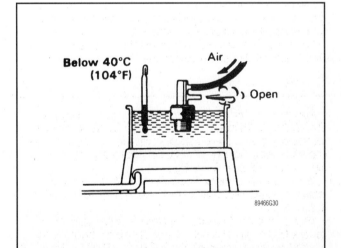

Fig. 35 Example of the VSV air flow when below its calibrated temperature—typical 2 hose valve shown

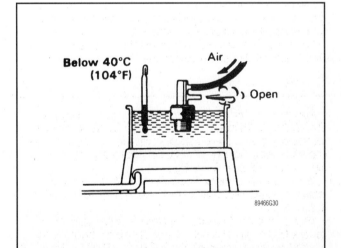

Fig. 33 Dual crankshaft sensor and special tool used to adjust the sensor

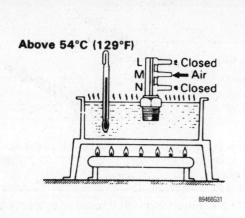

Fig. 36 Example of a the VSV air flow when above its calibrated temperature—typical 3 hose valve shown

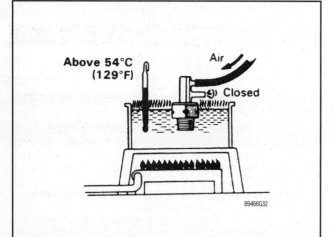

Fig. 37 Example of a VSV air flow when above its calibrated temperature—typical 2 hose valve shown

Fig. 38 Here is a good view of a VSV (left side) and a coolant temperature sensor (right on the thermostat housing)

a. M/T—check that air flows from port M to ports L and N.
b. A/T—check that air flows through the ports

➡ **The port letter identification is used for illustration only, there are many different designs of vacuum valves. Some vacuum valves will have 2 ports others may have 3 or more ports. The vehicle you are working with may have different port identification letters. Use this as an example, for the specifics on the vehicle you are working with consult a "Chilton Total Car Care (TCC) Manual".**

5. Using warm water, heat the threaded part of the valve to above 129°F (54°C) and blow into the ports again. The valve should not allow air to flow.
6. Apply liquid sealer to the threads of the VSV and reinstall it. Connect the vacuum lines.
7. Refill the radiator with coolant.

➡ **The underhood Vehicle Emission Control Information (VECI) Label may help determine which lines should have vacuum. The most common problem is incorrect routing of vacuum lines or broken vacuum lines.**

REMOVAL & INSTALLATION

▸ **See Figure 39**

The following procedure is general, consult a "Chilton Total Car Care (TCC) Manual" for further information on your particular vehicle.

✳✳ CAUTION

Perform this procedure only on a cold engine. Attempting to remove any component that involves working with engine coolant can result in serious burns.

1. Drain the cooling system as necessary.
2. With the ignition **OFF**, unplug the electrical connector to the sensor.
3. Using the proper sized wrench, carefully unscrew the sensor from the engine.
   To install:
4. Coat the threads of the sensor with a sealant. Install the sensor and tighten to specification.
5. Connect the vacuum hoses to the sensor.
6. Refill the coolant to the proper level.
7. Road test the vehicle for proper operation.
8. Check for leaks.

Fig. 39 Always label the vacuum lines prior to disconnecting them from the vacuum switching valve

EGR Valve Position Sensor

The EGR Valve Position (EVP) sensor, sometimes known as an EGR valve lift sensor, is mounted on EGR valve. It signals the computer of EGR opening so that it may subtract EGR flow from total air flow into the manifold. In this way, EGR flow is excluded from air flow information used to determine mixture requirements.

Most EGR position sensors are potentiometers or variable resistance sensors. Their operation is based on resistance changes caused by movement or position of the EGR valve. Electrical resistance within the valve changes as the EGR valve moves. On most systems, if the EGR valve is fully closed, the resistance reading is at maximum resistance. As the EGR valve begins to open the resistance reading decreases. When the EGR is a maximum open position, the reading is at its lowest specification.

TESTING

The type of EGR that the vehicle is equipped with will determine how it should be tested. The conventional way of testing the EGR valve does not apply to many of the systems today. On early model vehicles you can use a hand vacuum pump to apply vacuum to the EGR valve. If the valve didn't move it indicated either the valve was stuck or the diaphragm was defective.

Late model vehicles may use positive and negative back-pressure EGR valves and they respond to different types of tests. For example; engines equipped with a negative back-pressure EGR valve, applying vacuum to it with a vacuum pump should cause the EGR valve to open. If the valve fails to move, you know there is a problem with it. On the other hand, engines equipped with a positive backpressure EGR valve, this same test will not move the EGR valve. This is because it is not designed to function without backpressure. In order for a negative backpressure EGR valve to perform it requires a simulation of an exhaust restriction while using the vacuum pump to check movement. To simulate an exhaust restriction you would simply block the tail pipe and have a companion observe any movement of the EGR valve while vacuum was applied to it.

There are various tests required to successfully diagnose an EGR valve problem. To test the position sensor, you will need an ohmmeter and vacuum pump. Again, if the EGR valve is a negative backpressure type, simply disconnect the electrical connector at the position sensor. Check the resistance of the sensor when the EGR valve is closed. Remember, the resistance reading should be at its maximum specification when the valve is closed.

Gradually apply vacuum to the EGR valve and observe the resistance change. As the valve opens the resistance reading should began to decrease until fully open, then it should be at its minimum resistance. Most EGR position sensors have a resistance range of 500–800 ohms. Depending on the vehicle you are working with the specifications may be different. Because of the variety of different tests, when attempting to test the EGR position valve (EVP) or the EGR system consult a "Chilton Total Car Care (TCC) Manual" for your specific vehicle.

REMOVAL & INSTALLATION

The EGR position sensor is located on the EGR valve. Not all position sensors are removable. If found defective the EGR valve and sensor might be replace as an assembly. For those that are removable, it is a simple replacement.

Disconnect the electrical connector, remove the bolts attaching the sensor to the EGR valve and remove the sensor. No adjustment is required with the sensor. Simply bolt the new sensor on and plug in the connector.

EGR Check Valve

TESTING

♦ **See Figure 40**

Inspect the check valve (one-way valve) by gently blowing air into each end of the valve or hose. Air should flow from the orange or (light colored)

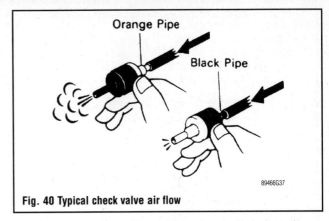

Fig. 40 Typical check valve air flow

pipe to the black pipe but SHOULD NOT flow from the black pipe to the orange or (light colored) pipe.

REMOVAL & INSTALLATION

The EGR check valve may be removed by simply disconnecting the vacuum hoses from either end of the valve. Use care if the hose should stick, excessive force could crack the plastic valve.

EGR Temperature Sensor

TESTING

➡**The EGR temperature sensor is usually used on certain models produced for sale in California.**

1. A sensor may be tested that has been removed from an engine. At room temperature, measure the resistance between both terminals with an ohmmeter.
2. Then place the sensor in a glass of ice water and measure the resistance between both terminals as it cools. The resistance should change smoothly with temperature. If resistance doesn't change, replace the sensor.
3. If the resistance value doesn't change as temperature changes, the sensor is faulty.

REMOVAL & INSTALLATION

♦ **See Figure 41**

1. With the ignition **OFF**, unplug the electrical connector to the sensor.

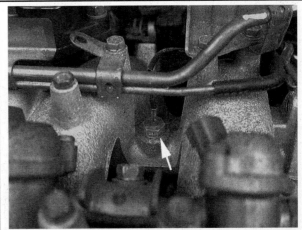

Fig. 41 EGR temperature sensors are located near the EGR valve. Resistance values of these sensors change with temperature

2. Using the proper sized wrench, carefully unscrew the sensor from the engine or EGR valve.

To install:

3. Install the sensor.
4. Plug the electrical connector into the sensor.
5. Road test the vehicle for proper operation.

EGR Vacuum Solenoid Valve

TESTING

▶ **See Figures 42, 43 and 44**

The EGR vacuum switching valve is very similar to the vacuum solenoid valve. They are both tested in the same fashion. Depending on the manufacturer, either of the devices may be used. Essentially the vacuum switching valve may not always be controlled by the control module as is the EGR solenoid. Its source of power may be energized through the activation of another component or system.

1. The vacuum switching circuit is checked by blowing air into the pipe under the following conditions:

   a. Connect the vacuum switching valve terminals to battery voltage.

   b. Blow into the tube and check that the VSV switch is open.

   c. Remove battery voltage from the terminals.

   d. Blow into the tube and check that the VSV switch is closed (no flow).

2. Check for a short circuit within the valve. Using an ohmmeter, check that there is no continuity between the positive terminal and the VSV body. If there is continuity, replace the VSV.

3. Check for an open circuit. Using an ohmmeter, measure the resistance between the 2 terminals of the valve. The resistance should be 38–44Ω 68°F (20°C). If the resistance is extremely out of range the VSV is probably bad.

➡ **The resistance will vary slightly with temperature. It will decrease in cooler temperatures and increase with heat, slight variations due to temperature range are not necessarily a sign of a failed valve.**

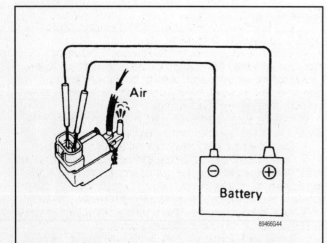

Fig. 42 On some models, air should pass through the VSV with battery voltage applied

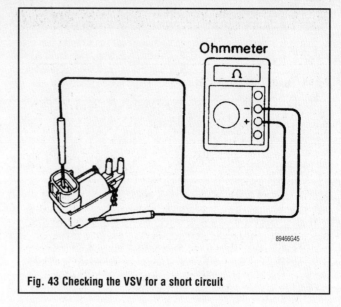

Fig. 43 Checking the VSV for a short circuit

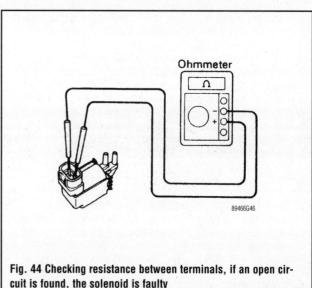

Fig. 44 Checking resistance between terminals, if an open circuit is found, the solenoid is faulty

REMOVAL & INSTALLATION

Removing an EGR Vacuum Switching Valve (VSV) is usually a simple matter of disconnecting the electrical connector and vacuum lines at the VSV and removing the retaining screw(s). On some models, it may be necessary to move a component for better access to the VSV. The VSV is usually mounted on a bracket located near the EGR valve.

1. Disconnect the electrical connector at the VSV.
2. Disconnect the vacuum hoses from the VSV.
3. Remove the EGR VSV retaining screw(s).

To install:

4. Install the EGR VSV and bracket and tighten the retaining screw(s) securely.
5. Connect the vacuum hoses to the VSV.
6. Connect the electrical connector at the VSV.

EGR (Exhaust Gas Recirculation) Valve

TESTING

▶ **See Figures 45, 46 and 47**

The type of EGR that the vehicle is equipped with will determine how it should be tested. The conventional way of testing the EGR valve does not apply to many of the systems today. On early model vehicles, you can use a hand vacuum pump to apply vacuum to the EGR valve. If the valve didn't move, it indicated either the valve was stuck or the diaphragm was defective.

Late model vehicles may use positive and negative back-pressure EGR valves and they respond to different type tests. For example; engines equipped with a negative backpressure EGR valve, applying vacuum to it with a vacuum pump should cause the EGR valve to open. If the valve fails to move, you know there is a problem with it. On the other hand, engines equipped with a positive backpressure EGR valve, this same test will not move the EGR valve. This is because it is not designed to function without backpressure. In order for a negative backpressure EGR valve to perform it requires a simulation of an exhaust restriction while using the vacuum pump to check movement. To simulate an exhaust restriction you would

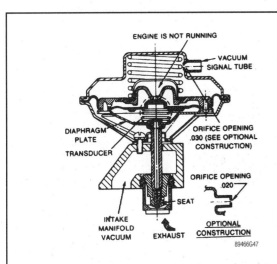

Fig. 45 This a cross sectional view of a negative backpressure EGR valve

Fig. 46 The EGR valve should be cleaned of carbon deposits

Fig. 47 You can test the condition of the EGR diaphragm by pushing it up with your fingers. If it is hard to move, the valve may be faulty

simply block the tail pipe and have a companion observe any movement of the EGR valve while vacuum was applied to it.

There are various tests required to successfully diagnose an EGR valve problem.

Functioning Test

WITHOUT SPECIAL TOOLS

1. Check to see if the EGR valve diaphragm moves freely. Use your finger to reach up under the valve and push on the diaphragm. If it doesn't move freely, the valve should be replaced. The use of a mirror will aid the inspection process.

✵✵ CAUTION

If the engine is hot, wear a glove to protect your hand.

2. Install a vacuum gauge into the vacuum line between the EGR valve and the vacuum source. Start the engine and allow it to reach operating temperature.

3. With the vehicle in either **P** or **N**, increase the engine speed until at least 5 in. Hg is showing on the gauge.

4. Remove the vacuum hose from the EGR valve. The diaphragm should move downward (valve closed). The engine speed should increase.

5. Install the vacuum hose and watch for the EGR valve to open (diaphragm moving upward). The engine speed should decrease to its former level, indicating exhaust recirculation.

6. If the diaphragm doesn't move, check engine vacuum; it should be at least 5 in. Hg with the throttle open and engine running.

7. Check to see that the engine is at normal operating temperature.

8. Check for vacuum at the EGR hose. If no vacuum is present, check the hose for leaks, breaks, kinks, improper connections, etc., and repair as necessary. Be aware that on some engines, computer controlled solenoids control the amount of vacuum to the EGR valve, depending on operating conditions.

9. If the diaphragm moves, but the engine speed doesn't change, check the EGR passages in the intake manifold for blockage.

10. Remove the EGR valve and check the valve and passages for damage or blockage.

11. It is a good idea to check the condition of the EGR diaphragm before buying a new valve.

12. Check the valve for sticking and heavy carbon deposits. If a problem is found, clean or replace the valve.

13. Reinstall the EGR valve with a new gasket.

WITH VACUUM PUMP

1. Install a vacuum pump into the vacuum line to the EGR valve. Start the engine and allow it to reach operating temperature.

2. Apply vacuum to the EGR valve.

3. On most vehicles you should be able to see the valve move and you should hear a change in the engine speed.

4. If you can not see the valve more or engine speed is not affected, the EGR valve is probably defective.

5. Remove the EGR valve and attach the vacuum pump to the valve.

6. Apply vacuum to the EGR valve and check that the it functions properly. It should not take more than 10 in. of vacuum to move the valve.

7. If the valve works okay removed from the vehicle, there probably is a blocked or leaking passage and the problem is not the valve itself.

REMOVAL & INSTALLATION

▶ **See Figures 48 and 49**

EGR equipment is generally simple to work on and easy to get to on the engine. On most vehicles, the air cleaner assembly will need to be removed. Always label each vacuum hose before removing it—they must be replaced in the correct position.

Most of the valves and solenoids are made of plastic. Be very careful during removal not to break or crack the ports; you have NO chance of gluing a broken fitting. Remember that the plastic has been in a hostile envi-

ronment (heat and vibration); the fittings become brittle and less resistant to abuse or accidental impact.

Most EGR valves are generally held in place by two bolts. The bolts can be difficult to remove due to corrosion. Once the EGR valve is off the engine, clean the bolts and the bolt holes of any rust or debris. Always replace the gasket any time the valve is removed.

Fuel Accumulator (CIS)

▶ **See Figure 50**

This device maintains the fuel system pressure at a constant level under all operating conditions. The pressure regulator, incorporated into the fuel distributor housing, keeps delivery pressure at approximately 5.0 bar (73 psi). Because the fuel pump delivers more fuel than the engine can use, a plunger shifts in the regulator to open a port which returns excess fuel to the tank. When the engine is switched off and the primary pressure drops, the pressure regulator closes the return port and prevents further pressure reduction in the system.

The fuel accumulator has a check valve which keeps residual fuel pressure from dropping below a pre-determined pressure when the engine or fuel pump are shut off.

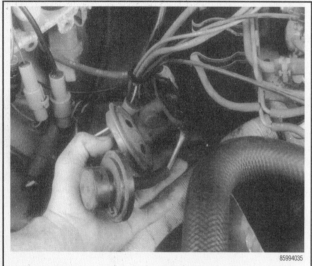

Fig. 48 EGR valves are usually secured with two bolts

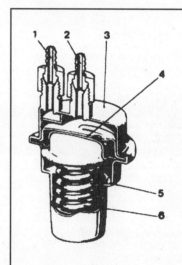

1. Inlet
2. Outlet
3. Accumulator housing
4. Diaphragm
5. Stop
6. Spring

Fig. 50 Cross section of a typical fuel accumulator

Fig. 49 Most EGR valves are attached to the intake manifold. Exhaust gasses are passed through a port (arrow) into the intake stream

TESTING

If the pump fails a volume test, raise the car and trace the fuel feed line back to the pump. Look for crimped fuel lines from a carelessly placed jack. Plug the accumulator return hose and repeat the volume test. If this yields good fuel volume, the accumulator diaphragm is ruptured. Soak a new fuel filter with clean gas and install it. Remember to wet the filter beforehand. When 80 psi of incoming fuel hits a dry filter, it can tear off some of the element and carry the paper debris into the rest of the system.

REMOVAL & INSTALLATION

✽✽ CAUTION

Relieve fuel system pressure before disconnecting any fuel lines.

The fuel accumulator is usually mounted near or on the fuel pump bracket somewhere near the fuel tank. It may be necessary to remove the fuel pump assembly to gain access to the fuel accumulator. Loosen the hose clamps and the retaining clamp and remove the accumulator. Reverse the procedure to install.

Fuel Distributor (CIS)

K-JETRONIC

The fuel distributor meters the correct amount of fuel to the individual cylinders according to the position of the air flow sensor plate. A control plunger opens or closes metering slits in the barrel, allowing more or less fuel to pass into the system. Control pressure assures that the plunger follows the movement of the sensor plate immediately. Control pressure is tapped from primary fuel pressure through a restriction bore. It acts through a damping restriction on the control plunger, eliminating any oscillations of the sensor plate due to a pulsating air flow. 1978 and later models incorporate a "push valve" in the fuel distributor to maintain pressure when the engine is switched off. The push valve is a one-way device mounted in the primary pressure regulator which is held open in normal operation by the pressure regulator plunger. Differential pressure valves in the fuel distributor hold the drop in pressure at the metering slits at a constant value.

KE-JETRONIC

The internal components and operation of the KE type fuel distributor are slightly different than the K model. With the engine running, a constant system pressure of approximately 79 psi (5.4 bar) is present at the fuel inlet. The plate valve is adjusted depending on current intensity and in this manner determines the flow rate, in combination with a fixed orifice (0.3mm in diameter) at the fuel distributor outlet. The pressure change in the lower chamber causes movement of the diaphragm and regulates the fuel volume flowing to the injectors.

During cold start and warm-up, current at the electro-hydraulic actuator (EHA) is approximately 8-120 milliamps. The plate valve is positioned in the direction of the intake port and the differential pressure drop in the lower chamber is approximately 6-22 psi (0.4- 1.5 bar). With increasing coolant temperature, the current at the actuator drops to approximately 8 milliamps and the differential pressure drops at the same rate, down to approximately 6 psi (0.4 bar). For acceleration enrichment, the current to the actuator is determined by the coolant temperature and the amount of sensor plate deflection. The plate valve is moved closer to the intake port and the differential pressure decreases by approximately 22 psi (1.5 bar).

➡**Acceleration enrichment is canceled at approximately 176° F (80°C).**

The airflow sensor position indicator operates with approximately 8 volts supplied constantly. During acceleration, a voltage signal is transmitted to the control unit, depending on the position of the airflow sensor plate. The control unit provides acceleration enrichment as an impulse that increases the instantaneous current value. During acceleration enrichment, Lambda (oxygen sensor) control is influenced by the control unit.

➡**With the accelerator pedal at idle, the micro switch on the side of the airflow sensor is closed and no enrichment is possible.**

The throttle valve switch receives a constant 8 volt signal from the control unit. With the throttle valve fully open (switch closed), approximately 8 mA of current flows to the electro hydraulic actuator, independent of engine speed. At full load enrichment, the plate valve moves in the direction of the intake port and the differential pressure in the lower chamber of the fuel distributor is approximately 6 psi (0.4 bar) below system pressure. Under deceleration, the circuit to the control unit is closed by the micro switch. The speed at which deceleration shutoff occurs depends on coolant temperature. The lower the temperature, the higher the speed at which restart of fuel injection begins. With the microswitch closed, the current at the actuator is approximately 45 mA and the plate valve moves away from the intake port. The pressure difference between the upper and lower chamber is canceled and system pressure is present in the lower chamber. Operational signals from the control unit will change the direction of the current flow at the actuator plate valve; the plate valve then opens. When the lower chamber pressure changes, pressure and spring force push the diaphragm against the ports to the injectors and cut off the fuel supply.

TESTING

Field testing of the fuel distributor as a single component is impractical. It is highly recommended that the entire fuel system be tested by a qualified mechanic who is experienced in CIS and CIS-E fuel injection systems.

REMOVAL & INSTALLATION

▸ **See Figure 51**

1. Release the pressure in the system by loosening the fuel line on the control pressure regulator (large connector). Use a clean rag to catch the fuel that escapes.
2. Mark the fuel lines in the top of the distributor in order to put them back in their correct positions.

➡**Using different colored paints is usually a good marking device. When marking each line, be sure to mark the spot where it connects to the distributor.**

3. Clean the fuel lines, then remove them from the distributor. Remove the little looped wire plug (the CO adjusting screw plug).
Remove the two retaining screws in the top of the distributor.

✱✱ WARNING

When removing the fuel distributor be sure the control plunger does not fall out from underneath. Keep all parts clean.

4. If the control plunger has been removed, moisten it with gasoline before installing. The small shoulder on the plunger is inserted first.

➡**Always use new gaskets and O-ring when removing and installing fuel distributor. Lock all retaining screws with Loctite® or its equivalent.**

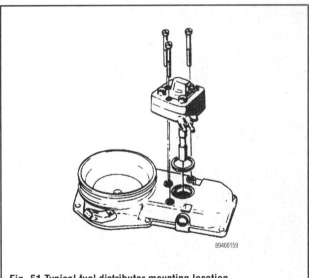

89466159

Fig. 51 Typical fuel distributor mounting location

Fuel Injectors (CIS)

▸ **See Figures 52 and 53**

The fuel injection valves are mounted in the intake manifold at the cylinder head, and continuously inject atomized fuel upstream of the intake valves.

A spring loaded valve is contained in each injector, calibrated to open at a fuel start pressure of 47–54 psi. The valves also contain a small fuel filter.

The fuel injector (one per cylinder) delivers the fuel allocated by the fuel distributor into the intake tubes directly in front of the intake valves of the

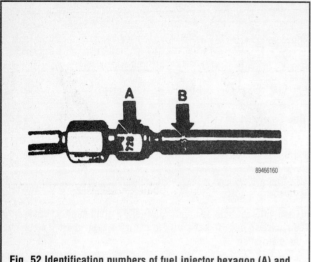

Fig. 52 Identification numbers of fuel injector hexagon (A) and shaft (B)

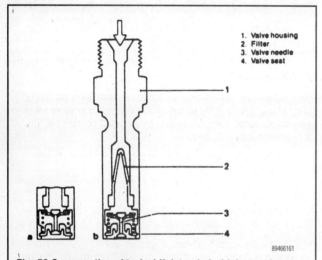

1. Valve housing
2. Filter
3. Valve needle
4. Valve seat

Fig. 53 Cross section of typical K-Jetronic fuel injector closed (A) and open (B) positions

cylinders. The injectors are secured in a special holder in order to insulate them from engine heat. The insulation is necessary to prevent vapor bubbles from forming in the fuel injection lines which would lead to poor starting when the engine is hot. The fuel injectors have no metering function: they open when the pressure exceeds 47–54 psi and are fitted with a valve needle that "chatters" at high frequency to atomize the fuel. When the engine is switched off, the injection valve closes tightly, forming a seal that prevents fuel from dripping into the intake tubes.

TESTING

▶ **See Figure 54**

➡ **Leave the fuel lines attached to the injectors for testing, but be careful not to crimp any metal fuel lines.**

Remove the rubber intake hose leading from the mixture control unit to the throttle unit. Expose the air flow sensor plate and bypass the safety circuit with a bridging adapter. Use a small magnet to lift the sensor plate during the test.

To check spray pattern, remove the injectors, one at a time, and hold them over a beaker. Switch the ignition key on and disconnect the electrical connector at the air-flow sensor to activate the fuel pump. Move the air flow

sensor plate. The injector should provide a dose of uniformly atomized fuel at about a 15-52 degree wide angle.

To check injection quantity, connect the removed injectors via hoses to equal sized beakers. Switch on the ignition. Disconnect the electrical connector at the airflow sensor to activate the fuel pump. Run the pump for approximately 30 seconds to pressurize the system, then connect the air flow sensor to stop the fuel pump. Lift or depress the airflow sensor plate halfway until one of the beakers fills up. Check the beakers. If injection quantity deviates more than 20~/o between injectors, isolate the problem by swapping the lowest and highest (in fuel quantity) injectors and repeating the test. If the same injector still injects less, clean or replace that injector and fuel supply line. If the other injector is now faulty, the fuel distributor is defective.

The check for injector leak-down (when closed) can now be conducted. Injector leakage (more than slight seepage) may be due to airflow sensor plate set to incorrect height, seizing of fuel distributor plunger, or internal leaks in the fuel distributor. Connect the airflow sensor connector to deactivate the fuel pump and switch off the ignition. Check for injector leakage at rest pressure. Depress the sensor plate to open the fuel distributor slots. Maximum permissible leakage is one drop per 15 seconds. If all injectors leak, the problem may be excessive rest pressure.

➡ **The injectors can be replaced individually.**

Fuel Injectors (MFI)

TESTING

▶ **See Figures 55 and 56**

On a multi-port fuel injection systems the injectors can be tested by installing a "Noid light" (a small tester bulb) into the injector electrical connector, which confirms voltage when the light flashes.

1. Start the engine and listen to each fuel injector individually for a "clicking" sound.
2. Turn the engine off and disconnect the electrical connector from the injector(s) that did not have a "clicking" sound.
3. Check the injector for continuity across the terminals. Compare the resistance value to a known good injector. The readings should be similar, if so proceed to the next step. If readings differ greatly, replace the injector.
4. Check between each injector terminal and ground. If continuity exists, replace the injector.
5. Disconnect the fuel injector connector and connect a Noid light to the wiring harness connector. Crank the engine, while watching the light. Perform this test on at least two injectors before proceeding. If the light does not flash, check the injector power supply and ground control circuitry. If the light flashes proceed to the next step.
6. If the light flashes, remove the fuel rail from the engine and following the procedure below check the injector operation:
   a. Using mechanic's wire, secure the injector to the fuel rail.
   b. Place a clear plastic container around each injector.

✳✳ CAUTION

Prior to performing this test, all fuel safety precautions must be followed. Make certain the container is approved to handle fuel and is securely positioned around the injector. Do NOT use a glass container. Glass containers can be easily damaged, resulting in a serious fire hazard.

   c. With the help of an assistant or using a remote starter button, crank the engine for 15 seconds while observing the injector operation. The injector should produce a cone shaped spray pattern and all containers should retain equal amounts of fuel.
   d. Once the cranking test is complete leave the fuel rail pressurized and observe the injectors for leakage.
7. Replace any injector which is leaking or fails to provide a cone shaped spray pattern when energized.

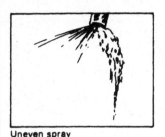 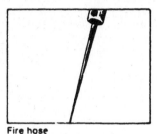  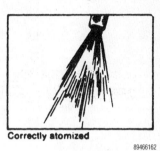

Uneven spray   Fire hose   Off center   Correctly atomized

89466162

Fig. 54 A correctly atomizing injector should have a fine spray pattern in a 45 degree fan

90915P14

Fig. 55 Using an ohmmeter to check fuel injector resistance

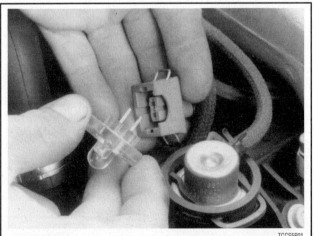

TCCS5P01

Fig. 56 Plugging a Noid light into the fuel injector harness on a MFI system. The Noid light illuminates when ever there is an injector pulse

For more comprehensive diagnosis on your specific fuel injection system, please refer to a "Chilton Total Car Care (TCC) Manual".

REMOVAL & INSTALLATION

▶ **See Figures 57 thru 62**

➡**Use care in removing injectors to prevent damage to the electrical connector pins and the nozzle. The fuel injector is serviced as a complete assembly only. Since it is an electrical component, DO NOT immerse it in a cleaner.**

1. Disconnect the negative battery cable.
2. Relieve the fuel system pressure.
3. You may need to remove the intake plenum and the fuel rail assembly.
4. Rotate the injector retaining clip to the release position.
5. Remove the fuel injector. Discard the O-rings and the retaining clip.

➡**Different injectors are calibrated for different flow rates. When ordering new injectors, be sure to order the identical part number that is inscribed on the old injector.**

To install:

✳✳ CAUTION

To reduce the risk of fire and personal injury, always install the injector O-rings in the proper position. If the upper and lower O-rings are different colors (black and brown in example), be sure to install the black O-ring in the upper position and the brown O-ring in the lower position. The O-rings are of the same size, but are made of different materials.

➡**The fuel injector lower O-ring uses a nylon collar, called the O-ring backup, to properly position the O-ring on the injector. Be sure to install the O-ring backup, or the sealing O-ring may move on the injector when installing the fuel rail. This can result in a vacuum leak and driveability problems will occur.**

6. Lubricate the new O-ring seals with clean engine oil and install them on the injector.
7. Assemble a new retainer clip onto the injector.
8. Install the fuel injector into the fuel rail socket with the electrical connections facing outwards.
9. Rotate the injector retaining clip to the lock position.
10. Install the fuel rail assembly.

Fig. 57 Fuel injectors are usually held into the intake manifold using O-rings

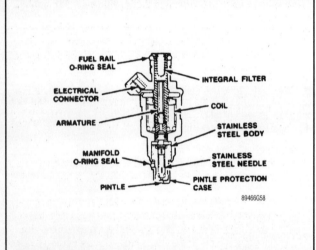

Fig. 58 Sectional view of a fuel injector showing internal components

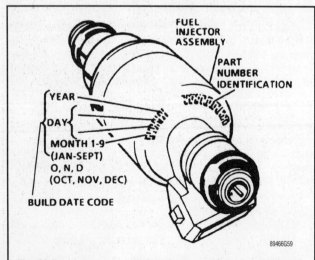

Fig. 59 Fuel injector part numbers are sometimes located at the top of the injector

11. Tighten the fuel filler cap and connect the negative battery cable.

12. With the engine **OFF**, turn the ignition switch to the **ON** position for 2 seconds, then turn it to the **OFF** position for 10 seconds. Again turn it to the **ON** position and check for fuel leaks.

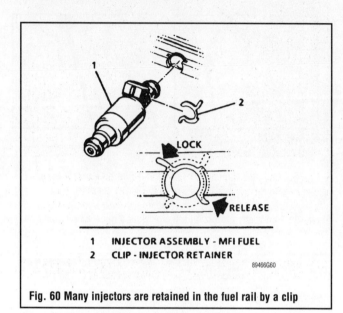

1   **INJECTOR ASSEMBLY - MFI FUEL**
2   **CLIP - INJECTOR RETAINER**

Fig. 60 Many injectors are retained in the fuel rail by a clip

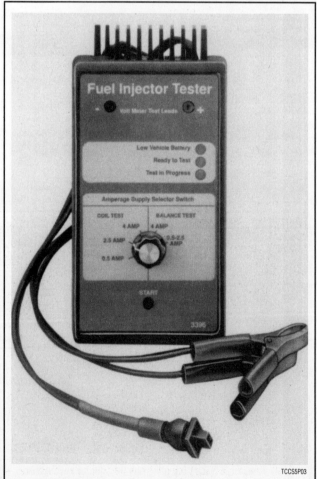

Fig. 61 Fuel injector testers are usually cost prohibitive for the do-it-yourselfer, but can sometimes be rented from local parts stores

Fig. 62 When testing fuel pressure, make sure your test gauge can handle the system pressure. Using a low pressure test gauge (note label on gauge) on a high pressure system is dangerous

Fuel Injectors (TBI)

TESTING

▶ **See Figure 63**

The Throttle Body Injection (TBI) system injector(s) can be tested by installing a "Noid light" (a small tester bulb) into the injector electrical connector, which confirms voltage when the light flashes. The injector can be checked by using a multi-tester. Disconnect the injector connector and check the resistance. This value is specific for each vehicle usually around 1–3 ohms. If you have more than one injector, they should read the same. If not, one of them is defective. When you purchase a new injector check it's resistance to confirm which of the old injectors is out of range.

You also need to check the injector's pattern. A flashlight and a timing light can help you view the fuel injector's operation and spray pattern. For more comprehensive diagnosis on your specific fuel injection system, please refer to a "Chilton Total Car Care (TCC) Manual".

REMOVAL & INSTALLATION

▶ **See Figures 64 thru 73**

The procedures given here are generic. Procedures differ according to manufacturer. For specific information your particular vehicle, consult a "Chilton Total Car Care (TCC) Manual".

➡ **Use care in removing injectors to prevent damage to the electrical connector pins on top of the injector, the fuel injector fuel filter and nozzle. The fuel injector is serviced as a complete assembly only and should never be immersed in any type of cleaner.**

1. Relieve the fuel system pressure.
2. Remove the air cleaner.
3. Disconnect the injector connector by squeezing the two tabs together and pulling straight up.
4. Remove the screws securing the fuel meter cover. Note the location of any short screws for correct placement during reassembly.

✸✸ CAUTION

DO NOT remove the four screws securing the pressure regulator to the fuel meter cover. The fuel pressure regulator includes a large spring under heavy tension that could cause personal injury if released.

5. With the old fuel meter gasket in place to prevent damage to the casting, use a screwdriver and fulcrum to pry the injector carefully until it is free from the fuel meter body.
6. Remove the injector.
7. Remove the large O-ring and steel back-up washer at the top of the injector cavity in the fuel meter body.
8. Remove the small O-ring located at the bottom of the injector cavity.

To Install:

9. Lubricate the new, small O-ring with automatic transmission fluid; then, push the new O-ring on the nozzle end of the injector up against the injector fuel filter.
10. Install the steel backup washer in the recess of the fuel meter body. Lubricate the new large O-ring with automatic transmission fluid, then install the O-ring directly above the backup washer, pressing the O-ring down into the cavity recess. The O-ring is properly installed when it is flush with the casting surface.

Fig. 63 The throttle body injectors can be seen after removing the air cleaner. Here an injector connector is being unplugged

Fig. 64 Unplug the injector connectors. You may have to squeeze a tab to release the connector

Fig. 65 Use clean rags to block the throttle openings. This will prevent dirt entering the intake manifold

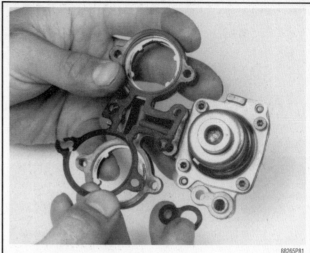

Fig. 68 Check the condition of the gaskets. This one is torn and would leak fuel if reused

Fig. 66 As required, remove the mounting screws from the top of the throttle body

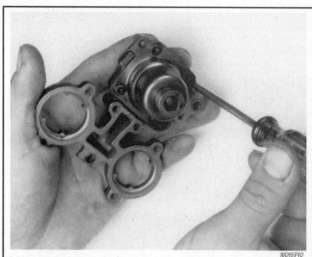

Fig. 69 The fuel pressure regulator can be removed from the meter cover

Fig. 67 Lift the metering body up and off the injectors. From this point the injectors can be removed easily

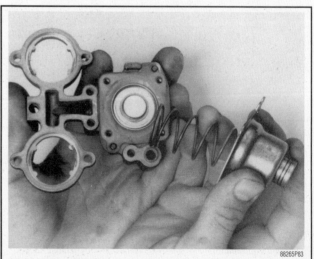

Fig. 70 The fuel pressure regulator diaphragm must be intact for proper operation

Fig. 71 Check the condition of the diaphragm and seating area prior to disassembly

Fig. 72 Exploded view of the fuel metering cover

Fig. 73 At this point the fuel injector are held in by O-rings. Always replace the O-rings when servicing the injectors

✳✳ WARNING

Do not attempt to reverse this procedure and install the backup washer and O-ring after the injector is located in the cavity. To do so will prevent proper seating of the O-ring in the cavity recess which could result in a fuel leak and possible fire.

11. Install the injector by using a pushing/twisting motion to center the nozzle O-ring in the bottom of the injector cavity and aligning the raised lug on the injector base with the notch cast into the fuel meter body. Push down on the injector making sure it is fully seated in the cavity. Injector installation is correct when the lug is seated in the notch and the electrical terminals are parallel to the throttle shaft.

12. Using new gaskets on the fuel meter cover and a new dust seal, install the cover to the fuel meter body. The two short screws are located adjacent to the injector.

13. Connect the injector electrical connector by pushing straight down until seated firmly in place.

14. Connect the negative battery cable.

15. With the engine **OFF** and the ignition **ON**, check for fuel leaks.

16. Install the air cleaner.

Fuel Pump

TESTING

Testing the fuel pump for operation and pressure output is not a complicated matter. You will want to observe the following precautions before getting started. These precautionary steps will prevent fire and or/explosion.

• Disconnect the negative battery cable, except when testing with the battery is required.

• Always relieve the fuel system pressure, using the proper procedures, before opening a fuel system.

• When possible, use a flashlight instead of a drop light.

(Many fires have been started because someone accidentally dropped a drop light, and the bulb broke igniting a few drips of fuel).

• Use eye protection. When working with high and low pressure fuel systems there is always a possibility of fuel either spraying, dripping or some debris dropping into the eyes.

• Always keep a dry chemical fire extinguisher in the service area.

• Keep all open flame and smoking material out of the area, this is especially important. Keep in mind that fuel vapors can be ignited if the area you are working in is not well ventilated.

• Use a shop cloth to catch fuel when opening the fuel system or relieving fuel system pressure.

If the engine does not start or occasionally stalls and the fuel pump is suspected, perform the following basic checks before condemning the fuel pump. Then proceed to further testing.

Voltage Checks

♦ **See Figures 74 and 75**

1. Check to make sure there is adequate fuel in the tank. Many incorrect diagnoses of a bad fuel pump have been made because this first and basic check is overlooked. If you are not certain add a gallon or two just to be sure.

➡**The procedure given here is a general procedure. For specific information for the vehicle you are working with, consult your "Chilton Total Car Care".**

2. If your vehicle has an internal fuel pump make this check. Unscrew the fuel fill cap and have an assistant turn the ignition switch **ON**. Listen to hear if the fuel pump turns on. On most vehicles, the electric fuel pump will energize for a few seconds every time the ignition switch is turned to the **ON** position. On others, it will be necessary to crank the engine a few revolutions. You will know the fuel pump is working by hearing an audible hum or whirling noise form the tank area.

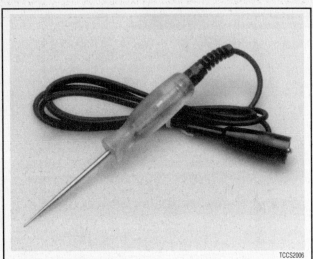

Fig. 74 A 12 volt test light, such as this one, can be used to check for voltage at the fuel pump

Fig. 75 Check the fuel pump connector terminals for corrosion or damage. Corrosion causes excessive resistance in the circuit and could hurt fuel pump performance

3. If your vehicle is equipped with an external electric fuel pump, make this check. In most cases, external fuel pumps are mounted under the vehicle, somewhere in proximity of the fuel tank on the frame of the vehicle. It will be necessary to raise and support the vehicle safely with good jackstands. Locate the fuel pump and have an assistant turn the ignition switch **ON**. Listen to hear if the fuel pump turns on. You should also be able to feel the fuel pump energize for a few seconds every time the ignition switch is turned to the ON position. If it does not it may be necessary to crank the engine a few revolutions.

4. If the fuel pump does not respond to the key on and crank test, you must now determine whether voltage is getting to the pump.

5. To check voltage supplied to the fuel pump, a systematic check will aid you in a quick and efficient diagnosis.

6. First, check the fuel pump fuse. In most cases, the fuse is located in the main fuse block either under the dash or in the engine compartment depending on the vehicle. Use a test light to check for voltage on both sides of the fuse. Turn the ignition switch to the ON position. Connect the test light to a suitable ground and probe each side of the fuse.

7. If there is voltage on both sides chances are the fuse is okay. However, don't take that for granted, remove the fuse anyway and inspect it for corrosion on the contact points. If there is corrosion, clean it and check it again to see if the pump responds.

8. If the fuse is blown, replace it and check the fuel pump operation. If there is voltage supply to the fuse and the fuse checks good, check the fuel pump relay and circuit.

9. Locate the fuel pump relay. The relay may be located in a variety of locations, it may be in the engine compartment mounted on a bracket on the strut tower, on the firewall or near the battery. On some vehicles, it will be located under the dash. It will be necessary for you to consult a "Chilton Total Car Care (TCC) Manual" for your specific vehicle. Sometimes the warranty book will give locations of the fuses and relays.

10. Once you have located the relay, remove it and check for voltage at the connector feed terminal. Turn the ignition switch **ON**. Using a test light, connect it to a suitable ground and probe the power feed terminal. If voltage exists, use a jumper wire to connect the power feed terminal and the fuel pump terminal circuit. It is best to have a diagram of which terminals are which. Each vehicle is different. It is important not to jump the wrong circuit and short or burn something out. However, some terminals are labeled to make this test simpler.

11. If you are sure of which terminals to jump, jump the terminals and have an assistant listen for fuel pump operation. If the fuel pump activates, chances are the relay is at fault. If fuel pump still does not activate, go directly to the fuel pump.

12. If you vehicle has a internal pump, locate the harness connection at the pump. Connect a 12 volt lead to the positive side of the pump and listen for the pump to activate. If the pump still does not activate, check the ground wire for a good clean connection. Clean the ground and connection and try to activate the pump again, if the pump still does not come on, chances are the pump is defective.

Pressure Checks

Proper fuel pressure is very important in the engine management system. Insufficient or excessive fuel pressure can cause many problems. Low fuel pressure can cause hard starting, stalling or engine surge problems, while excessive fuel pressure can cause flooding, poor gas mileage or poor performance, etc.

1. Connect a suitable fuel pressure gauge to the fuel tap line. This tap is located at different locations depending on the vehicle you are working with.

2. Turn ignition switch to the **ON** position, but do not start the engine, If the gauge registers fuel pressure, start the engine and observe the fuel pressure. You will need to check the specifications for the vehicle and system you are working with.

3. If pressure is within specifications, then the test is over. If fuel pressure is low, perform a fuel flow test.

4. If you find the fuel pressure is above specifications, check the fuel pressure regulator for proper operation, and check for a restriction in the return line to the gas tank.

5. If no fuel pressure was evident, when the switch was turned **ON**, check the operation of the fuel pump as mentioned earlier.

REMOVAL AND INSTALLATION

▶ **See Figures 76, 77, 78 and 79**

The internal fuel pump is a part of the fuel sender assembly located inside the fuel tank.

1. Release the fuel system pressure and disconnect the negative battery cable.

2. Drain the fuel tank, then raise and safely support the vehicle.

3. Remove the fuel tank from the vehicle.

4. Clean the areas surrounding the sender assembly to prevent contamination of the fuel system.

5. Remove the fuel sender from the tank as follows:

6. Use a special tool to remove the sender unit retaining cam. Remove the fuel sender and O-rings from the tank. Discard the O-rings.

7. If necessary, separate the fuel pump from the sending unit assembly.

To Install:

8. If removed, install the fuel pump to the sending unit. If the strainer was removed, it must be replaced with a new one.

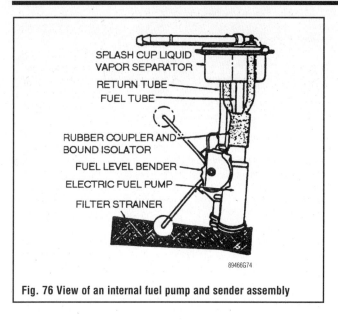

Fig. 76 View of an internal fuel pump and sender assembly

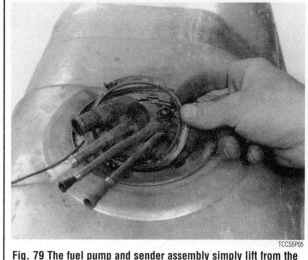

Fig. 79 The fuel pump and sender assembly simply lift from the fuel tank

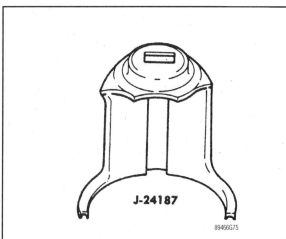

Fig. 77 On some vehicles, a special tool is used to remove and install the fuel pump locking cam

9. Inspect and clean the O-ring mating surfaces.
10. Install a new O-ring in the groove around the tank opening. If applicable, install a new O-ring on the fuel sender feed tube.
11. Install the fuel sender as follows:
   a. The fuel pump strainer must be in a horizontal position, and when installed, must not block the travel of the float arm. Gently fold the strainer over itself and slowly position the sending assembly in the tank so the strainer is not damaged or trapped by the sump walls.
12. Install the fuel tank assembly.
13. Lower the vehicle.
14. Fill the fuel tank, tighten the fuel filler cap and connect the negative battery cable.
15. Start the engine and check for leaks.

Fuses and Circuit Breakers

▶ See Figures 80, 81, 82 and 83

Protection devices are fuses, fusible links or circuit breakers. They are designed to open or break the circuit quickly whenever an overload, such as a short circuit, occurs. By opening the circuit quickly, the circuit protection device prevents damage to the wiring, battery and other circuit compo-

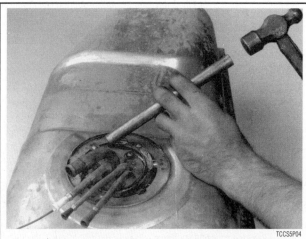

Fig. 78 On most vehicles, using a brass drift to loosen a fuel pump assembly is the method of choice. Take your time and work carefully

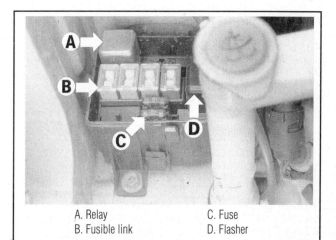

A. Relay   C. Fuse
B. Fusible link   D. Flasher

Fig. 80 Typical fuse and relay block located in the engine compartment. The block may be covered to protect the components but should be labeled

Fig. 81 This fusible link resembles a fuse . . .

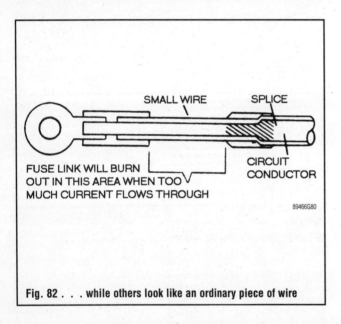

Fig. 82 . . . while others look like an ordinary piece of wire

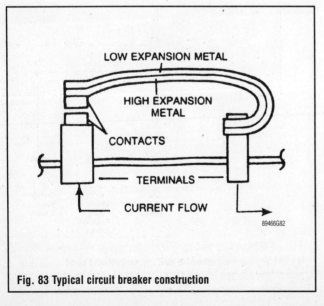

Fig. 83 Typical circuit breaker construction

nents. Fuses and fusible links are designed to carry a preset maximum amount of current and to melt when that maximum is exceeded, while circuit breakers merely break the connection and may be manually reset. The maximum amperage rating of each fuse is marked on the fuse body and all contain a see-through portion that shows the break in the fuse element when blown. Fusible link maximum amperage rating is indicated by the gauge or thickness of the wire. Never replace a blown fuse or fusible link with one of a higher amperage rating.

➡**Resistance wires, like fusible links, are also spliced into conductors in some areas. Do not make the mistake of replacing a fusible link with a resistance wire. Resistance wires are longer than fusible links and are stamped "RESISTOR-DO NOT CUT OR SPLICE."**

Circuit breakers consist of 2 strips of metal which have different coefficients of expansion. As an overload of current flows through the bi-metallic strip, the high-expansion metal will elongate due to heat and break the contact. With the circuit open, the bi-metal strip cools and shrinks, drawing the strip down until contact is re-established and current flows once again. In actual operation, the contact is broken very quickly if the overload is continuous and the circuit will be repeatedly broken and re-made until the source of the overload is corrected.

The self-resetting type of circuit breaker is the one most generally used in automotive electrical systems. On manually reset circuit breakers, a button will pop up on the circuit breaker case. This button must be pushed in to reset the circuit breaker and restore power to the circuit. Always repair the source of the overload before resetting a circuit breaker or replacing a fuse or fusible link. When searching for overloads, keep in mind that the circuit protection devices protect only against overloads between the protection device and ground.

TESTING

▶ **See Figures 84 and 85**

Testing fuses and circuit breakers is an easy task with a test light or voltmeter.

1. Connect a test light to a good ground.
2. Touch the test light to known good power source to make certain it lights.
3. Then touch the test light each side of the fuse or circuit breaker you want to test.
4. The test light should light up on both sides of the fuse or circuit breaker. If it only lights on one side, then the fuse or breaker is blown. If it doesn't light on either side there is a problem with power before the protection device.

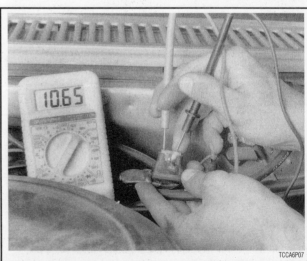

Fig. 84 Testing a fuse for voltage drop. If voltage drops too low, the fuse is broken

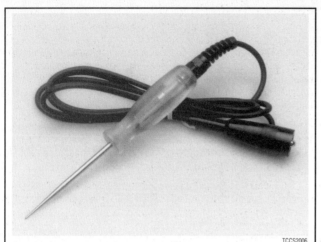

TCCS2006

Fig. 85 A test light, such as the one shown, can be used to check voltage drop across a fuse. If the light is dim or does not come on, the fuse may be faulty

For a problem where there is no power to the protection device you need to find the path that the circuit takes. Most circuits to fuses either come directly from a main fusible link connected to the battery. Remember many circuits are turned **OFF** when the ignition is turned **OFF**. For "IGN" hot circuits, make certain the ignition switch is **ON**. If there is still no power at the fuse box check the main breakers or fusible links near the battery. You may need to consult a "Chilton Total Car Care (TCC) Manual" for wiring diagrams.

REMOVAL & INSTALLATION

▶ **See Figure 86**

Replacing fuses and circuit breakers is usually easy. Simply pull the fuse or breaker from its contacts. Many newer vehicles have the fuse box in a location difficult to access. The fuses sometimes fit so flat against the fuse box you can't get your fingers on them. Most auto parts stores have fuse pullers that make this task a snap. A pair of needle nose pliers will also work, but if the fuse is the glass tube type you have to take care not to crush it.

8852DP01

Fig. 86 Special fuse pullers make changing fuses (especially the small ones) easy

Hall Effect Sensor

Hall effect sensors are used on some systems to determine speed and position of a rotating object. They can be distinguished from magnetic sensors by their three wire harness. The most common applications are as engine speed sensors mounted near the camshaft and crankshaft. On some engines, a Hall effect switch is located inside the distributor. These sensors can be tested using a digital multimeter. Common names of these sensors are camshaft sensor, crankshaft sensor and rpm sensors.

TESTING

▶ **See Figures 87 and 88**

1. Perform a visual inspection.
2. Disconnect the sensor connector and install jumper wires from the power and ground terminals of the sensor connector to the wiring harness. This permits the sensor to receive power and ground without signaling the ignition system during inspection.

➡ **Do not connect a jumper wire to the signal terminal on the Hall sensor. This will cause the engine to start. Use extreme caution while performing this test.**

3. Using a multimeter set to the volts setting, check the voltage between the power and ground wires. This voltage may be 4, 6, 8 or 12 volts depending on the system. Take note of this voltage reading. Refer to a "Chilton Total Car Care (TCC) Manual" for correct wire color, terminal location and recommended specifications.

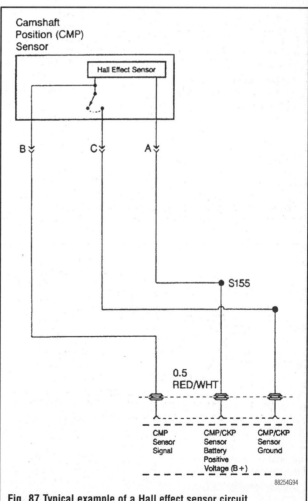

88254G94

Fig. 87 Typical example of a Hall effect sensor circuit

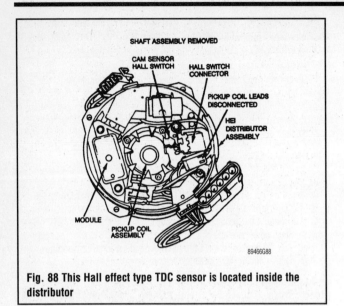

Fig. 88 This Hall effect type TDC sensor is located inside the distributor

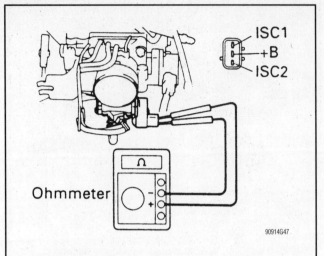

Fig. 89 Typical testing on an IAC valve involves checking resistance between the terminals

4. Connect the multimeter between the signal terminal and the ground wire. Rotate the engine by (tapping the ignition key) with the starter motor. When the engine is rotated, the signal should fluctuate between 0 volts and the system voltage noted in earlier step.

5. While rotating the engine, check for damaged shutter blades or any indication that the shutter blades are hitting the magnet.

REMOVAL & INSTALLATION

Depending on location, these sensors can be removed without too much difficulty. Removal usually involves disconnecting the electrical connector and unbolting the sensor. In some cases, the sensor must be aligned during installation. Refer to your vehicle service manual for proper adjustment procedure. Some manufacturers may have this sensor mounted behind the ignition module or inside the distributor. You may need to refer to a "Chilton Total Car Care (TCC) Manual", if this sensor is difficult to locate or is behind other components.

Idle Air Control (IAC) Valve

On fuel injected engines, engine idle speeds are controlled by the control module through the IAC valve. On most engines, the IAC valve is mounted on the throttle body, others may be mounted on the engine near the throttle body.

IAC valves mounted on the throttle body operate as follows. The control module sends voltage pulses to the AC motor windings causing the IAC motor shaft and pintle to move IN or OUT a given distance (number of steps) for each pulse (called counts). The movement of the pintle controls the airflow around the throttle plate, which in turn, controls engine idle speed. AC valve pintle position counts can be observed using a scan tool. Zero counts correspond to a fully closed passage, while 140 counts or more corresponds to full flow.

IAC valves that are mounted separately from the throttle body operate this way. Based on information the control module receives from the various sensors, it adjusts the opening of the IAC valve accordingly. When the engine is first started, it opens the IAC valve to its full amount. This causes the engine to run at a fast idle. As the engine temperature warms up the ECM signals the AC valve to close and open as increased air is needed. This maintains the idle speed at proper specification.

TESTING

▶ **See Figure 89**

When suspecting a IAC valve problem, first perform a visual inspection. Most problems can be found in wiring harnesses and connectors. An unstable idle or stalling condition could be caused by a vacuum leak or faulty PCV valve. In some cases, just dirty electrical connections at the IAC valve can cause a problem. Proper diagnosing can only be accomplished by systematic testing procedures. For specific information on the vehicle you are working with consult your "Chilton Total Car Care" or factory service manual. The following procedure is a general procedure and may not apply to the vehicle you are working with.

For the following test you will need a digital volt/ohmmeter.

1. Start with a cold engine.
2. Start the engine. Using a voltmeter check the volt reading by probing the feed circuit to the IAC valve.
3. Allow the engine to warm up while observing the voltmeter reading.
4. The initial reading should be high close to battery voltage. As the engine warms up the volt reading should gradually decrease to almost 0 volts.

Depending on the vehicle you are working with this voltage specification will vary. You will need to consult a "Chilton Total Car Care (TCC) Manual" for exact specifications. Another test that you can make is checking the resistance between the terminals of the IAC valve for an open circuit or checking the positive feed terminal to ground to see if the valve is shorted. These resistance values may vary, but should never be an open circuit.

REMOVAL & INSTALLATION

▶ **See Figures 90, 91 and 92**

The procedures given here are for various GM engines. Most valves simply unbolt or screw out.

➡ **On some models it may be necessary to remove the air inlet assembly.**

1. Disconnect the negative battery cable. Disconnect the AC valve electrical connector.
2. Remove the IAC valve by performing the following:
    a. On thread-mounted units, use a 1 ¼ in. (32mm) wrench.
    b. On flange-mounted units, remove the mounting screw assemblies.
3. Remove the IAC valve gasket or O-ring and discard.

To install:

4. Clean the mounting surfaces by performing the following:
    a. If servicing a thread-mounted valve, remove the old gasket material from the surface of the throttle body to ensure proper sealing of the new gasket.
    b. If servicing a flange-mounted valve, clean the AC valve surfaces on the throttle body to assure proper seal of the new O-ring and contact of the IAC valve flange.
5. If installing a new AC valve, measure the distance between the tip of the AC valve pintle and the mounting flange. If the distance is greater than

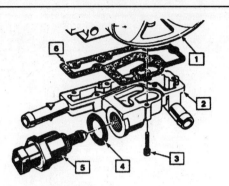

1. Throttle body assembly
2. IAC coolant cover
3. IAC cover assembly to throttle body screw
4. IAC valve gasket
5. Idle air control valve
6. IAC coolant cover to throttle body gasket

89466G94

Fig. 90 Exploded view of a screw-in type IAC valve

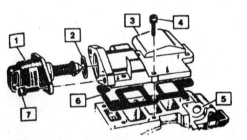

1. Idle air control (IAC) valve assembly
2. Idle air control valve O-ring
3. Idle air/vacuum signal housing assembly
4. Idle air/vacuum signal assembly screw
5. Throttle body assembly
6. Idle air/vacuum signal assembly gasket
7. Idle air control valve screw

89466G95

Fig. 91 Exploded view of a flange-mounted IAC valve. This type is retained by mounting screws

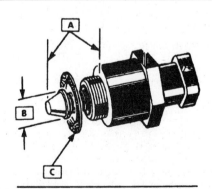

A. Distance of pintle extension
B. Diameter and shape of pintle
C. IAC valve gasket

89466G96

Fig. 92 It is important to measure the distance of pintle extension when installing a new IAC valve

1.102 in. (28mm), use finger pressure to slowly retract the pintle. The force required to retract the pintle of a new valve will not cause damage to the valve. If reinstalling the original IAC valve, do not attempt to adjust the pintle in this manner.

6. Install the AC valve into the throttle body by performing the following:

    a. With thread-mounted valves, install with a new gasket.

    b. With flange-mounted valves, lubricate a new O-ring with transmission fluid and install on the IAC valve. Install the IAC valve to the throttle body. Install the mounting screws using a suitable thread locking compound and tighten.

7. Connect the AC valve electrical connector.

8. Connect the negative battery cable.

9. No physical adjustment of the IAC valve assembly is required after installation. Reset the IAC valve pintle position by performing the following:

    a. Depress the accelerator pedal slightly.

    b. Start the engine and run for 5 seconds.

    c. Turn the ignition switch to the **OFF** position for 10 seconds.

    d. Restart the engine and check for proper idle operation.

Idle Speed Control Solenoid

The Idle Speed Control Solenoid (ISC) may be called different names depending on the manufacturer. It is referred as a Idle Speed Stepper Motor or an Automatic Idle Speed (AIS) Motor etc. In any event, they all perform the same purpose. Earlier solenoids were called Anti-dieseling solenoids or Idle Stop Solenoids. These earlier devices usually functioned whenever current was supplied to them as soon as the ignition switch was turn ON or when the air conditioning compressor was engaged. The Electronic Idle Speed Control Solenoid is controlled by the engine computer.

The Idle Speed Control Solenoid function is somewhat self-explanatory. It controls engine idle. The electronic idle solenoid is controlled by the control module. The control module has a specific idle specification programmed in memory. It determines the idle speed by calculating various information bits from engine sensors. It is also aware when the throttle stop is contacting the idle solenoid and when it is not.

By having this information, the control module is able to adjust the idle solenoid plunger to position the throttle for precise idle rpm conditions. If, for example, the air conditioning is switched **ON**, the extra load from the compressor slows the idle down, the control module therefore adjusts the idle solenoid to compensate for the added engine load and maintain proper idle speed.

TESTING

▶ **See Figure 93**

Since this device is controlled by the control module, complete testing, inspection and checks of the engine control system may be necessary. However, you can make a couple of basic checks to see if the idle speed control solenoid is working.

1. Remove the air cleaner to gain access to the solenoid.

2. Inspect the electrical connector at the idle speed control solenoid. Make sure the connection is clean and making good contact.

3. You will need a tachometer and idle specifications. Connect the tachometer and start the engine.

4. Allow the engine to warm up and allow the fast idle to drop. Observe the rpm reading at idle.

5. Turn the air conditioning ON, the tachometer may respond to the load change but the rpm should remain stable. If the vehicle is not equipped with air conditioning or it is not working, proceed to the next step.

6. Turn the steering from side-to-side or turn the headlights **ON**, the idle should remain stable.

7. If the vehicle is equipped with automatic transmission, apply the parking brake, apply the service brake pedal as you place the vehicle in drive position. Make sure no one is standing in front of the vehicle during this test. The tachometer may slightly change but the rpm should remain stable.

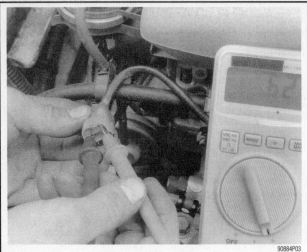

Fig. 93 Testing the idle speed control solenoid using a multimeter

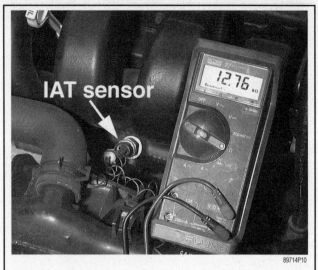

Fig. 94 Testing IAT sensor using an ohmmeter

8. If the engine idle rpm drops considerably or the engine stalls, further testing of the engine control system is required.

If the Idle Speed Control Solenoid is suspected, shut the engine **OFF**. Further testing of the solenoid will require a wiring chart to identify the proper terminals to test. When battery voltage is applied to the correct terminals the idle solenoid plunger will move out, when the alternated terminals are connected the plunger will move in.

➡**Do not apply battery voltage to any terminal unless you are sure it is the correct terminal to receive current. Otherwise you could burn out or short the component out. For specific checks and specifications on this device, consult a "Chilton Total Car Care (TCC) Manual".**

REMOVAL & INSTALLATION

Removal and installation of this device is pretty simple. Here is a general procedure that can be used for most vehicles.
1. Disconnect the negative battery cable.
2. Remove the air cleaner.
3. Disconnect the electrical connector at the ISC.
4. Remove the ISC bracket retaining screws and remove the ISC.

To install:
5. Install the ISC in position and secure it with the mounting screws.
6. Connect the electrical connector.
7. Connect the negative battery cable.
8. Start the engine and test ISC operation.
9. Install the air cleaner.

Intake Air Temperature (IAT) Sensor

TESTING

▶ **See Figures 94 and 95**

The IAT sensor advises the ECM of changes in intake air temperature (and therefore air density). As intake air temperature varies, the ECM, by monitoring the voltage change, adjusts the amount of fuel injection according to the air temperature.
1. Unplug the electrical connector from the IAT sensor.
2. Using an ohmmeter, measure the resistance between both terminals. The resistance should be approximately 3,000 ohms at room temperature (70°F). Refer to the chart for sample resistance readings.
3. The intake air temperature sensor and coolant temperature sensor resistance values are usually the same. Because of this, an easy test is, on a cold engine (sitting overnight), to compare the resistance values of the

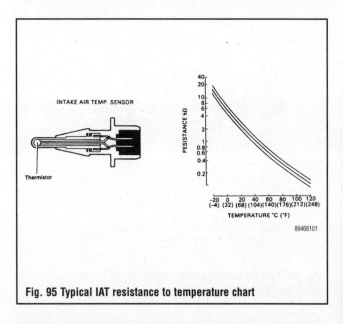

Fig. 95 Typical IAT resistance to temperature chart

two sensors. If the engine is cold, and both sensors are the same temperature, the resistances values should be about the same.
4. You can start the engine, and as it warms up check that the values change smoothly.
5. You can also heat the sensor using a hair dryer to see if the values change smoothly.
6. If the resistance value doesn't change, the sensor is probably defective. Some manufacturers built the intake air temperature sensor into the air flow sensor. In this case they are usually replaced as a unit. Since this type of sensor is expensive, you should perform air flow sensor testing to make certain it is defective.

REMOVAL & INSTALLATION

▶ **See Figures 96 and 97**

Most Intake Air Temperature (IAT) sensors screw or clip into the air intake stream. They are usually at the throttle body or air flow sensor.
1. Remove the air cleaner cover.
2. With the ignition **OFF**, unplug the electrical connector.
3. Remove the IAT sensor from inside the air cleaner housing or intake plenum.

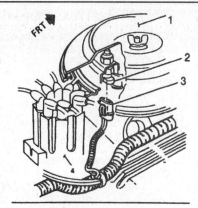

1. Air cleaner
2. Intake Air TGemperature (IAT) sensor
3. Harness connector to ECM
4. Distributor

89466104

Fig. 96 Typical Intake Air Temperature (IAT) sensor on Throttle Body Injected (TBI) engines

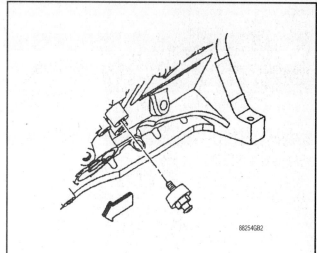

88254GB2

Fig. 98 Most knock sensors are mounted on the side of the engine block

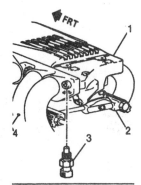

1. Intake manifold
2. Fuel rail
3. Intake Air TGemperature (IAT) sensor
4. Left intake runners

89466105

Fig. 97 Typical Intake Air Temperature (IAT) sensor on Multi-point Fuel Injected (MFI) engines

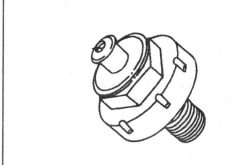

KNOCK SENSOR (KS)

89466107

Fig. 99 The typical knock sensor uses a single wire connection and is screwed into a boss on the engine

To install:
4. Install the sensor, making sure it is properly positioned and secure.
5. Connect the wiring harness, and install the air cleaner cover.

Knock Sensor

TESTING

▶ See Figures 98 and 99

The knock sensor is mounted to the engine block or manifold. When spark knock or pinging is present, the sensor produces a voltage signal that is sent to the ECM. The ECM will then retard the ignition timing based on these signals.

When suspecting a knock sensor problem, first perform a visual inspection. Most problems can be found in wiring harnesses and connectors.

Perform a basic knock sensor test as follows. To make this test you will need a timing light.
1. Connect a timing light to the engine.
2. Start the engine and allowing warm up sufficiently.

3. Position the timing light toward the timing marks on the harmonic balancer.
4. Locate the knock sensor, some engines may be equipped with 2 knock sensors.
5. Using a suitable metallic tool, tap on the intake manifold or side of the engine block which ever is closest to the knock sensor. Do not strike hard or hit the sensor directly, light tapping should cause the knock sensor to react.
6. If the knock sensor is working the ignition timing will begin to retard as you tap.

If the timing does not change, you will need to check voltage at the knock sensor harness connector. Also, make sure the connector is clean and making good connection. For specific testing for the vehicle you are working with, consult your "Chilton Total Car Care" or factory service manual.

REMOVAL & INSTALLATION

1. Disconnect the negative battery cable.
2. Drain the engine coolant.
3. Raise and properly support the vehicle.

4. Disconnect the knock sensor wiring harness.
5. Remove the knock sensor from the engine block.

✳✳ CAUTION

If the knock sensor is mounted in the engine block cooling passage, engine coolant will drain when the sensor is removed.

6. Installation is the reverse of removal.

Line Pressure Regulator (CIS)

◗ See Figure 100

The line pressure regulator ensures that the pressure in the circuit remains constant when the fuel pump is in operation and also controls the recirculation of fuel to the tank. When the fuel pump is switched off, the regulator will cause a rapid pressure drop to approximately 2.5 bar (kp/cm2, 35 psi), i.e. the rest pressure, which is maintained by means of the O-ring seal and the quantity of fuel contained in the fuel accumulator. The purpose of the rest pressure is to prevent the fuel from vaporizing in the circuit when the engine is warm, which would otherwise make restarting difficult.

The line pressure regulator forms an integral unit with a shut-off valve to which the return fuel line from the control pressure regulator is connected. When the fuel pump is operating, the shut-off valve is actuated mechanically by the control pressure regulator, whereupon the return fuel from the control pressure regulator bypasses the shut-off valve to the return line.

When the fuel pump stops running and the line pressure regulator valve is pressed into its seating, the shut-off valve is also pressed into its seating, preventing the fuel system from emptying through the control pressure return.

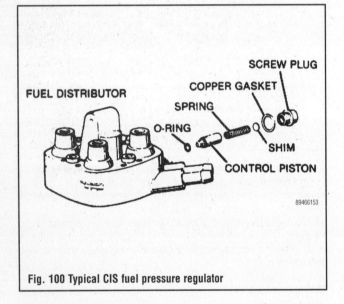

FUEL DISTRIBUTOR
SCREW PLUG
COPPER GASKET
SPRING
O-RING
SHIM
CONTROL PISTON

89466153

Fig. 100 Typical CIS fuel pressure regulator

REMOVAL & INSTALLATION

The pressure regulator is removed by loosening the screw plug on the fuel distributor and removing the copper gasket, shim, spring, control piston and O-ring. On 1979 and later systems, a push valve is attached to the large screw plug. Make sure all parts are kept clean and in order for assembly. Replace the O-ring and copper gasket, especially if any fuel leakage is noted.

✳✳ CAUTION

Relieve fuel system pressure before removing the screw plug.

➡**The piston in front of the shim is matched to the housing and is not replaceable.**

FUEL PRESSURE ADJUSTMENT

➡**On some early models, the fuel pressure can be adjusted on the regulator with the adjusting screw. Adjust to 28 psi. If a slight turn of the screw shows no change of pressure, replace the regulator.**

If the fuel distributor is fitted with a push valve, loosen the large screw plug with attached push valve assembly. Change the adjusting shim as required to raise or lower fuel system pressure. Each 0.1mm increase in shim thickness increases fuel pressure by 2.2 psi.

If the fuel distributor doesn't have a push valve, remove the screw plug and change the shim as required. Again, each 0.1mm increase is shim thickness will increase system pressure by 2.2 psi.

Magnetic Reluctance Sensor

Magnetic reluctance sensors are used to determine either position or speed. These sensors are commonly found on or near the camshaft and/or crankshaft. Some sensors may be located inside the distributor. They consist of a magnet assembly and a toothed ring commonly referred to as a reluctor. They can be tested by using a digital multimeter.

TESTING

1. Perform a visual inspection.
2. Disconnect the sensor connector.

➡**Never disconnect any connector with the ignition switch ON.**

3. Using a digital multimeter set to the ohms setting, check resistance across the sensor terminals. The resistance should be approximately 500–1200 ohms at 70°F. Resistance will vary with temperature.

➡**This test should be performed with the ignition ON and engine OFF.**

4. Using a thin piece of steel, check the tip of the sensor to see if it is magnetized.
5. Using a digital multimeter set to the millivolts AC scale, connect the test probes to the sensor.
6. Rotate reluctor ring to activate the sensor signal. On camshaft or crankshaft sensors, use the starter to crank the engine. Refer to a "Chilton Total Car Care (TCC) Manual" for correct wire color, terminal location and recommended specifications.
7. Voltage should be seen as the reluctor ring is rotated. If the reluctor is rotated quickly, a signal of at least 200 millivolts AC should be seen.

REMOVAL & INSTALLATION

◗ See Figures 101, 102 and 103

Depending on location, these sensors can be removed without too much difficulty. Removal usually involves disconnecting the electrical connector and unbolting the sensor. In some cases, the sensor must be adjusted during installation. Some manufacturers may mount these sensors behind other components, an example is that General Motors mounts the crankshaft position sensor on the 2.5L engine behind the DIS ignition module. If you can not locate this sensor, you may need to refer to a "Chilton Total Car Care (TCC) Manual". Some sensors may require a specific spacing adjustment. If necessary, this procedure is also provided in the "Chilton Total Car Care (TCC) Manual".

Manifold Absolute Pressure (MAP) Sensor

TESTING

◗ See Figures 104, 105 and 106

There are two types of Manifold Absolute Pressure (MAP) sensors. The analog signal type, which is tested with a voltmeter, is used on most General Motors, Chrysler and import vehicles. The frequency signal type, which is tested with a Hertz meter or digital tachometer is used on most Ford

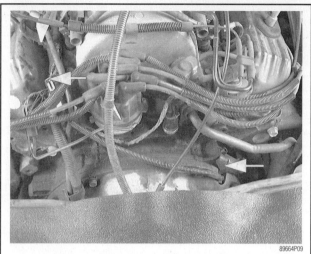

Fig. 101 Some magnetic reluctance crankshaft position sensors are mounted by the flywheel . . .

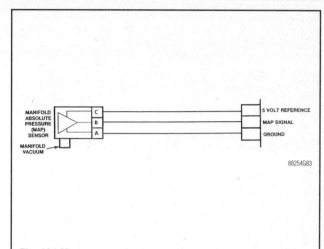

Fig. 104 Map sensors circuits usually contain three wires. A 5 volt reference signal, a ground and a signal wire back to the control module

Fig. 102 . . . while others are mounted at the front of the engine, like this one near the water pump

Fig. 105 Testing this MAP sensor with a voltmeter reveals a perfect 5.04 volt reference signal

CRANKSHAFT POSITION SENSOR

NOTCHES

FLYWHEEL

Fig. 103 Magnetic reluctance sensors require a tone ring with notches, like this flywheel, to function properly

vehicles. If you're not certain which type you have, check the reference voltage which is usually around 5 volts. Then check the signal voltage. If the signal voltage never changes from 2.5 volts, it is most likely a frequency type.

Analog Signal Type

▶ See Figure 107

➡The analog signal type MAP sensor is used most on General Motors, Chrysler and import vehicles.

These sensors are usually located in the engine compartment near the air cleaner, mounted on the inner fender or firewall. They can be checked using a digital voltmeter and a hand vacuum pump.

1. Disconnect the MAP sensor's electrical connector.
2. Connect one jumper wire from the connector to the MAP sensor's terminal A.
3. Connect the other wire from the connector to terminal C.
4. Connect the positive lead of a digital voltmeter to terminal B and the negative voltmeter lead to ground.
5. Turn the ignition key ON. If the reading falls in the voltage range of 4.6 to 5.0, the sensor is functioning properly, at this point.

Altitude—Meters	Altitude—Feet	Pressure—kPa	Voltage Range
Below 305	Below 1000	100—98	3.8—5.5V
305—610	1000—2000	98—95	3.6—5.3V
610—914	2000—3000	95—92	3.5—5.1V
914—1219	3000—4000	92—89	3.3—5.0V
1219—1524	4000—5000	89—86	3.2—4.8V
1524—1829	5000—6000	86—83	3.0—4.6V
1829—2133	6000—7000	83—80	2.9—4.5V
2133—2438	7000—8000	80—77	2.8—4.3V
2438—2743	8000—9000	77—74	2.6—4.2V
2743—3948	9000—10,000	74—71	2.5—4.0V

88144GC7

Fig. 106 Voltage at the signal terminal should change smoothly as altitude is changed. You can test this by applying vacuum to the sensor with a hand vacuum pump

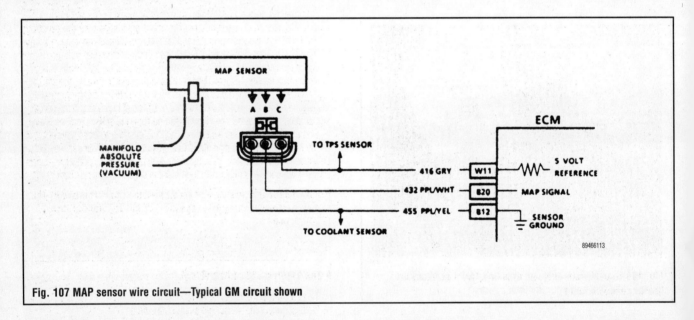

Fig. 107 MAP sensor wire circuit—Typical GM circuit shown

6. Start the engine and let it idle. An idling engine will produce a large amount of intake manifold vacuum, which should pull the MAP sensor's voltage down to a low reading of approximately 1–2 volts (reading will vary with altitude). This test indicates that the MAP sensor is responding to vacuum.

Frequency Signal Type

▶ See Figure 108

➡The frequency signal type MAP sensor is used on most Ford vehicles.

1. Set your digital tachometer on the 4 cylinder scale.
2. Start the engine and let it idle.
3. Connect the tachometer between the sensor's middle terminal and ground.
4. Take a reading and use the conversion chart to convert the tachometer reading to a frequency reading.

MAP sensor frequency can be measured with a digital tachometer. Never use an analog tachometer. A tachometer is a frequency counter. It measures pulses received per second (Hz) and converts them to revolutions per minute. We are going to use the RPM reading to measure the frequency. The following chart converts revolutions per minute into pulses per second.

	Tachometer 4-cyl. scale	Equivalent Frequency
0-In. vac	454-464	152-155 HZ
5-In. vac	411-420	138-140 HZ
10-In. vac	370-380	124-127 HZ
15-In. vac	331-339	111-114 HZ
20-In. vac	294-301	93- 98 HZ.

89466114

Fig. 108 Tachometer reading-to-frequency reading conversion chart

REMOVAL & INSTALLATION

Replacing the MAP sensor simply requires unplugging the vacuum and electrical connections, then unbolting the sensor. Inspect the vacuum hose over its entire length for any signs of crackin9 or splitting. The slightest leak can cause false messages to be send to the ECM.

Mass Air Flow (MAF) Sensor

TESTING

▶ **See Figures 109, 110 and 111**

The Mass Air Flow (MAF) sensor, found on some fuel injected engines, measures the amount of air passing through it. The control module uses this information to determine the operating conditions of the engine to control fuel delivery. A large quantity of air indicates acceleration, while a small quantity indicates deceleration or idle.

Most MAF sensors require special testing equipment or scan tools to help diagnose a problem. The MAF sensors used on most vehicles are some of the more complicated and expensive components.

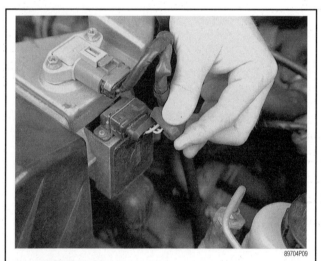

Fig. 109 To backprobe the sensor connector, first remove the rubber connector boot

Fig. 110 For this test vehicle, the voltage should be approximately 0.2 volts with the ignition ON. This sensor is within specifications

Fig. 111 With the engine running at operating temperature, the voltage should now be 0.85–1.35 volts. This sensor is on the high end of the specification

One method of checking a MAF sensor is to measure the voltage required to keep the sensor wire hot. As intake air rushes over the sensor, it cools the sensor wire. The control module then increases the voltage to the wire and calculates the volume of air based on this increased voltage.

Since the MAF must be connected during this test, backprobing is the only way to measure voltages. Measure voltage between ground the sensor signal wire. Voltage should be low the with engine **OFF**. Slightly higher with the engine idling and near 5 volts with the engine at high rpm. If the sensor signal does not increase linearly with engine rpm, the sensor may be faulty.

Some MAF sensors were sensitive to vibration. To test these sensors, can gently tap on the MAF, if the engine idle changes the MAF sensor may be defective. Another method is to jiggle the sensor connector and wires. Once again, if the engine hesitates or stumbles, the sensor may be defective.

➡**For specific information and recommended specifications on the vehicle you are working with, consult a "Chilton Total Car Care (TCC) Manual".**

REMOVAL & INSTALLATION

▶ **See Figures 112, 113 and 114**

1. Disconnect the negative battery cable.
2. Disconnect the sensor electrical connection.

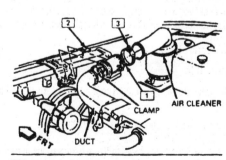

1	MAF SENSOR ASM (PONTIAC)
2	BRACKET MAF SENSOR
3	CLAMP 1.4-2.0 N·m (1-1.4 LBS. FT.)

Fig. 112 Mass airflow sensors are usually mounted in the air duct between the inlet and the throttle body

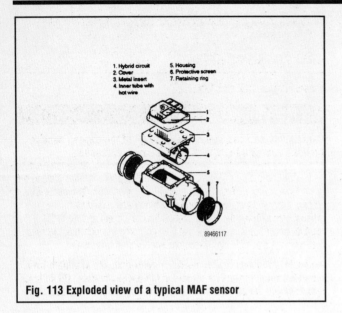

Fig. 113 Exploded view of a typical MAF sensor

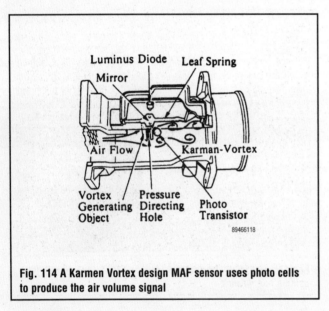

Fig. 114 A Karmen Vortex design MAF sensor uses photo cells to produce the air volume signal

3. Loosen the clamps and remove the air intake hoses from the MAF sensor

4. Remove the sensor from the vehicle. On some models, it will be necessary to remove the sensor-to-bracket attaching bolts.

5. Installation is the reverse of removal.

Oxygen Sensor

TESTING

♦ See Figures 115, 116, 117 and 118

The oxygen (O_2) sensor is located in the exhaust stream, ahead of the catalytic converter, usually on the exhaust manifold. Some vehicles use more than one sensor. Its function is to detect the concentration of oxygen in the exhaust gas. Using highly refined metals (zirconia and platinum), the sensor uses changes in the oxygen content to generate an electrical signal which is transmitted to the ECM. The computer in turn reacts to the signal by adjusting the fuel metering at the injectors or at the carburetor. More or less fuel is delivered into the cylinders and the correct oxygen level is maintained. The O_2 sensor can be checked using a multimeter set to the millivolt setting.

1. Perform a visual inspection. Black sooty deposits on the O_2 sensor tip may indicate a rich air/fuel mixture. White gritty deposits could be an internal antifreeze leak. Brown deposits indicate oil consumption.

➡**All of these contaminants will destroy a sensor, if problem is not repaired the new sensor will be destroyed too.**

2. Disconnect the O_2 sensor connector and install jumper wires from the sensor connector to the wiring harness. This permits the engine to operate normally while you check the engine.

❊❊ WARNING

Never disconnect any connector with the ignition switch ON.

3. Start the engine and allow it to reach operating temperature. This should take about ten minutes. Turn the engine **OFF**.

4. Connect the positive lead of a multimeter to the O_2 sensor signal wire and the negative lead to the engine ground. Re-start the engine.

➡**For specific information on wire color and terminal identification, it will be necessary to consult a "Chilton Total Car Care (TCC) Manual".**

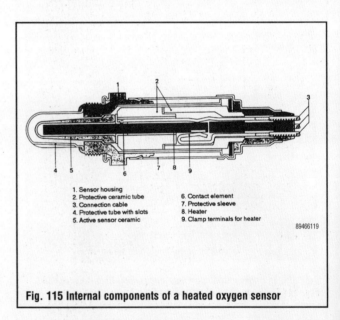

Fig. 115 Internal components of a heated oxygen sensor

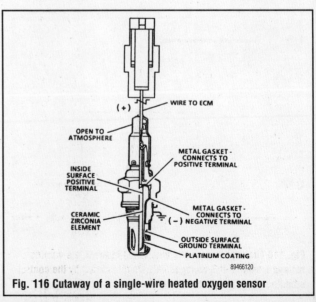

Fig. 116 Cutaway of a single-wire heated oxygen sensor

5. The voltage reading should be fluctuating as the O_2 sensor detects varying levels of oxygen in the exhaust stream.

6. If the O_2 sensor voltage does not fluctuate, the sensor may be defective or mixture could be extremely out of range.

7. If the O_2 sensor reads above 550 millivolts constantly, the fuel mixture is probably too rich. If the (O_2) sensor voltage reads below 350 millivolts constantly, the fuel mixture may be too lean or you may have an exhaust leak near the sensor.

8. Under normal conditions, the O_2 sensor should fluctuate high and low. Prior to condemning the O_2 sensor, try forcing the system rich by restricting the air intake or lean by removing a vacuum line. If this causes the oxygen sensor to momentarily respond, look for problems in other areas of the system.

REMOVAL & INSTALLATION

▶ **See Figures 119 and 120**

✵✵ WARNING

Care should be used during the removal of the oxygen sensor. Both the sensor and its wire can be easily damaged.

1. The best condition in which to remove the sensor is when the engine is moderately warm. This is generally achieved after two to five minutes (depending on outside temperature) of running after a cold start. The exhaust manifold has developed enough heat to expand and make the removal easier but is not so hot that it has become untouchable. Wearing heat resistant gloves is highly recommended during this repair.

➡**Special wrenches, either socket or open-end, are available from reputable retail outlets for removing the oxygen sensor. These tools make the job much easier and often prevent unnecessary damage.**

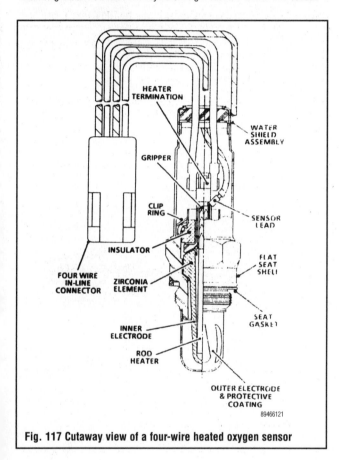

Fig. 117 Cutaway view of a four-wire heated oxygen sensor

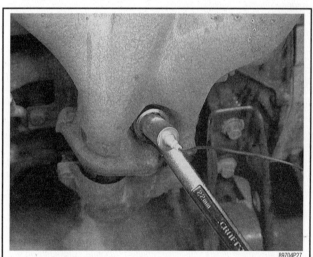

Fig. 119 Removing the oxygen sensor from the exhaust manifold using a line wrench

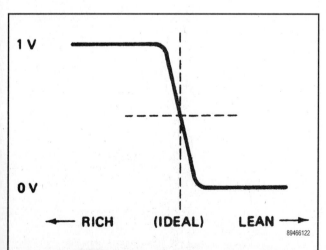

Fig. 118 The oxygen sensor's function is to provide a varying voltage from 0.1–0.9 voltage. This signal is used by the control module to keep the fuel mixture ideal

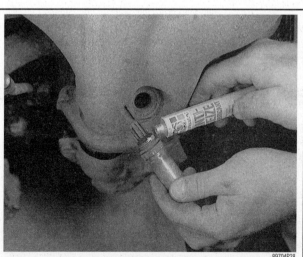

Fig. 120 Before installing an oxygen sensor, always coat the threads with anti-seize compound.

2. With the ignition **OFF**, unplug the connector for the sensor.

3. Unscrew the sensor or remove the two sensor attaching bolts.

4. Remove the oxygen sensor from the manifold.

To install:

5. During and after the removal, use great care to protect the tip of the sensor if it is to be reused. Do not allow it to encounter fluids or dirt. Do not attempt to clean it or wash it.

6. Apply a coat of anti-seize compound to the bolt threads but DO NOT allow any to get on the tip of the sensor.

7. Install the sensor in the manifold.

8. Reconnect the electrical connector and ensure a clean, tight connection.

Positive Crankcase Ventilation

▶ See Figure 121

A closed Positive Crankcase Ventilation (PCV) system is used on most vehicles. This system cycles incompletely burned fuel which works its way past the piston rings back into the intake manifold for reburning with the fuel/air mixture. The oil filler cap is sealed and the air is drawn from the top of the crankcase into the intake manifold through a valve with a variable orifice.

This valve (commonly known as the PCV valve) regulates the flow of air into the manifold according to the amount of manifold vacuum. When the throttle plates are open fairly wide, the valve is fully open. However, at idle speed, when the manifold vacuum is at maximum, the PCV valve reduces the flow.

A plugged valve or hose may cause a rough idle, stalling or low idle speed, oil leaks in the engine and/or sludging and oil deposits within the engine and air cleaner. A leaking valve or hose could cause an erratic idle or stalling.

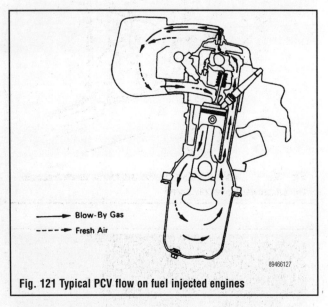

Fig. 121 Typical PCV flow on fuel injected engines

TESTING

▶ See Figures 122, 123 and 124

The PCV valve is easily checked with the engine running at normal idle speed (warmed up). Remove the PCV valve from the valve cover or intake manifold, but leave it connected to its hose. Place your thumb over the end of the valve to check for vacuum. If there is no vacuum, check for plugged hoses or ports. If these are open, the valve is faulty. With the engine off, remove the PCV valve completely. Shake it end to end, listening for the rattle of the needle inside the valve. If no rattle is heard, the needle is jammed (probably with oil sludge) and the valve should be replaced.

An engine which is operated without crankcase ventilation can be damaged very quickly. It is important to check and change the PCV valve at regular maintenance intervals.

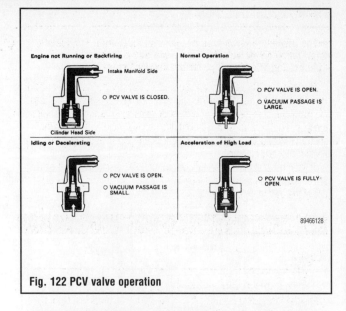

Fig. 122 PCV valve operation

Fig. 123 PCV valves are usually mounted using a grommet in the valve cover or in intake manifold

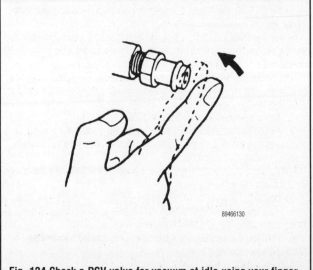

Fig. 124 Check a PCV valve for vacuum at idle using your finger

REMOVAL & INSTALLATION

➥The procedure given here is a general procedure. For specific information on the vehicle you are working with, consult your "Chilton Total Car Care" or factory service manual.

Remove the PCV valve from the cylinder head cover or intake manifold. Remove the hose from the valve. Take note of which end of the valve was in the manifold. This one-way valve must be reinstalled correctly or it will not function. While the valve is removed, the hoses should be checked for splits, kinks and blockages. Check the vacuum port (that the hoses connects to) for any clogging.

Remember that the correct function of the PCV system is based on a sealed engine. An air leak at the oil filler cap and/or around the oil pan can defeat the design of the system.

Control Module

TESTING

There are no methods currently available to test the control module in the field. Most testing involving the PCM usually involves testing of the components associated with the control module, and if all appears okay, substituting a known good unit is the common practice. Since the control module is a very expensive component to replace, accurate diagnosis of the engine management system is advised. Before condemning the control module, always perform extensive testing to be sure it is defective.

It is rare that control module is defective, and if found defective, usually a shorted or faulty actuator caused it to go bad. Consult a "Chilton Total Car Care (TCC) Manual" for additional information on this subject.

REMOVAL & INSTALLATION

♦ See Figures 125, 126, 127 and 128

The control module may be located in different locations depending on the manufacturer. The most common locations are: on the right or left side kick panels under the dash, under the driver's or passenger seat, or in the trunk area.

Before removing the control module, always adhere to the precautions given. The control module can be damaged very easily if not handled or removed properly. Observe the following precautions before attempting to remove any control module.

• Disconnect the negative battery cable, except when testing with battery voltage is required.

• Do not puncture the control module harness wires.

• To prevent internal control module damage, the ignition switch must be in the **OFF** position when disconnecting or reconnecting power to the computer.

• To prevent electrostatic discharge damage to the control module or other electronic components, do not touch the connector pins or soldered components on the circuit board.

The procedure given here is a general procedure. For specific information on the vehicle you are working with, consult a "Chilton Total Car Care (TCC) Manual".

1. Disconnect the negative battery cable.
2. Locate the control module and remove the protective covering.
3. Remove the mounting bolts and carefully pull the control module from its mounting location.
4. Carefully disconnect the harness connectors and remove the control module from the vehicle.

To install:

5. Carefully connect the harness connectors to the control module being very careful not to distort the prongs.
6. Position the control module its mounting location and secure it in place with the mounting bolts.
7. Install the protective cover.
8. Connect the negative battery cable.

Fig. 125 This Chrysler control module is located under the dash . . .

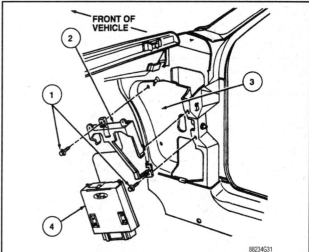

Fig. 126 . . . while this Ford control module is located behind the passenger's side kick panel

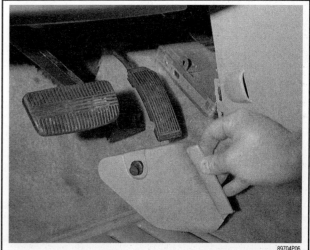

Fig. 127 This Nissan control module is hidden behind an access panel under the console

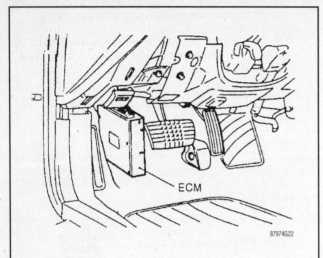

Fig. 128 This Subaru control module is located near the brake pedal under the driver's side of the dash

Thermo-Time Switch (CIS)

▶ See Figure 129

The thermo time switch, located on the cylinder head, actuates the cold start valve. It has a bi-metal spring that senses coolant temperature and an electric coil which limits the cold start valve spray to 12 seconds. A thermo-time switch also measures water temperature and opens the cold start valve, located on the intake header, a varying amount of each time the engine is started, depending on the conditions. With a hot engine, coolant temperature over 95°F (35°C), the injector should not operate. If it does, the thermo-time switch is defective. In addition, on a cold engine, the cold start valve should not inject fuel for more than 12 seconds (during starter cranking). If it does, the thermo-time switch is defective.

TESTING

➡To perform the following test properly, the engine must be cold with a coolant temperature below 95°F (35°C).

With the use of a test lamp, the switch can be tested at various temperatures for continuity. The operating time is eight seconds at -4°F (-20°C) and declines to 0 seconds at +59°F (+15°C).

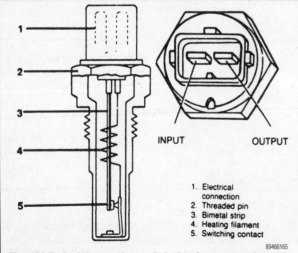

1. Electrical connection
2. Threaded pin
3. Bimetal strip
4. Heating filament
5. Switching contact

Fig. 129 Typical thermo-time switch showing construction and terminal location

When the engine temperature is below approximately 113°F (+45°C), current is allowed to flow for a certain period (depending on the temperature) while the starter motor is running.

Check that the switch closes when the engine is started by means of connecting a test lamp in series across the contacts of the cold start valve plug.

It is not possible to make a more accurate check of the cut-in time or temperature. If the condition of the switch is at all in doubt, it should be replaced.

1. With the engine cold, remove the harness plug from the cold start valve and connect a test light across the harness plug connections.
2. Connect a jumper wire from coil terminal No. 1 to ground.
3. Operate the starter. If the test light does not light for about 8 seconds, replace the switch. Removal of the switch requires that the engine is cold and the cooling system drained.

REMOVAL AND INSTALLATION

1. Disconnect the negative battery cable.
2. Drain the cooling system.
3. Locate the thermo-time switch on the left side of the engine block and disconnect the electrical connection.
4. Unscrew the switch and remove it.
5. Installation is in the reverse order of the removal. Refill the cooling system.

✳✳ WARNING

The engine must be cold when removing the switch.

Throttle Position Sensor

TESTING

▶ See Figures 130, 131 and 132

Throttle Position (TP) sensors are usually located on the side of the throttle body. TP sensors can be checked using a multimeter set to the Volts setting. TP sensor failure is common because it has parts that move each time the accelerator is depressed or released. This is one of the more common parts that require replacement or adjustment, due to the amount of movement this sensor endures every time a vehicle is driven. However, it is one of the easiest components to test and replace.

➡The procedure given here is a general procedure. For specific information on the vehicle you are working with, consult your "Chilton Total Car Care" or factory service manual.

1. Perform a visual inspection.

✳✳ WARNING

Never disconnect any connector with the ignition switch ON.

2. Disconnect the TP connector and install jumper wires from the sensor connector to the wiring harness. This permits the sensor to operate properly during testing.
3. Most TP sensors use 3 wires—a 5 volt reference wire, a signal wire to the computer and a ground wire. Some may have additional wires, used for integral switches in the sensor.

Refer to a "Chilton Total Car Care (TCC) Manual" for correct wire color, terminal location and recommended specification, if necessary.

4. Connect a multimeter set to the Volts setting between the signal wire (usually the center terminal) and the ground wire (one of the outside terminals) on the TP sensor.

➡This test should be performed with the ignition ON and the engine OFF.

5. Check the voltage reading with the throttle in the idle position. Usual voltage readings are approximately 0.45 volts.

Refer to your "Chilton Total Car Care" or factory service repair manual for specific voltages.

Fig. 130 Testing the throttle position sensor with the throttle closed shows a low voltage reading which is well within specification for this Nissan

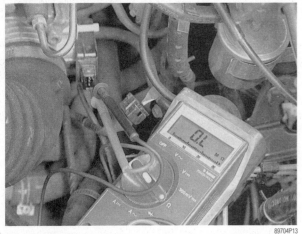

Fig. 131 Some throttle position sensors contain wide open throttle switches. With the throttle wide open, continuity should not exist, as indicated by the O.L ohms reading

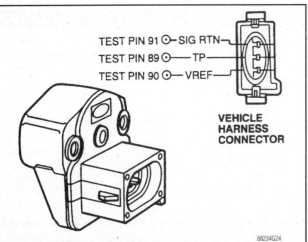

Fig. 132 Typical throttle position sensors use a three wire harness. Power and ground are supplied, while a signal wire returns the signals to the control module

6. Open the throttle slowly. The voltage increase smoothly as the throttle is moved to the Wide Open Throttle (WOT) position. Usual voltage at the WOT position is approximately 4.5 volts.

7. Release the throttle slowly. The voltage should decrease smoothly as the throttle is moved to the idle position. Erratic readings or a momentary infinite reading indicate a defective sensor.

REMOVAL & INSTALLATION

▶ **See Figure 133**

TP sensors are usually removed by disconnecting the electrical connector and unscrewing the mounting screws. If the screw holes are slotted, the sensor is adjustable. Please refer to your "Chilton Total Car Care" or factory service manual for the adjustment procedures. The specification is usually around 0.45 volts at closed throttle.

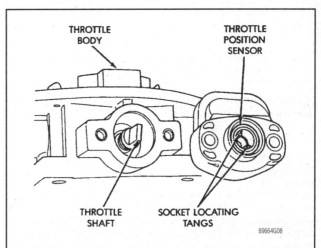

Fig. 133 Most throttle position sensors are bolted to the throttle body and are easily removed. Take care to align the tang with the slot in the sensor during installation

Throttle Valve (CIS)

The throttle valve housing is connected to the intake manifold and, in addition to the throttle valve, it contains the idling air passage and the idling adjustment screw, connections for the hoses to the auxiliary air valve, and the cold start valve and the vacuum outlet for ignition timing.

➡ **Some later models with electronic engine controls do not use vacuum advance units on the distributor.**

ADJUSTMENT

The stop screw is set by the factory and should not be moved. If for some reason it is moved, adjust as follows:

1. Turn the screw counterclockwise until a gap is visible between the stop and the screw.
2. Turn the screw until it just touches the stop.
3. Turn the screw clockwise an additional ½ turn.
4. Adjust the idle speed and CO and-check the linkage for proper operation and free movement.

IDLE ADJUSTMENTS

▶ **See Figure 134**

The idle speed screw (called a bypass screw by some manufacturers) on the throttle body housing of a K-Jetronic system bleeds air into the manifold when you increase idle speed—or cuts it off to slow the engine down. When idle speed changes the idle mixture always changes to some degree,

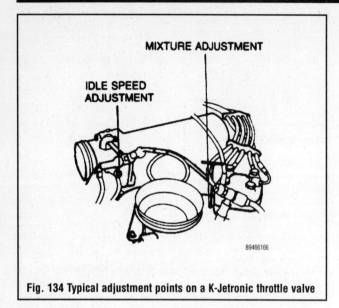

Fig. 134 Typical adjustment points on a K-Jetronic throttle valve

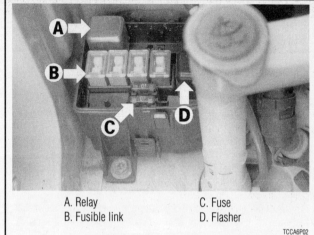

A. Relay   C. Fuse
B. Fusible link   D. Flasher

Fig. 136 In the past, relays were mounted in the engine compartment. Now, most relays are located in relay/fuse boxes mounted in the engine compartment (shown) or under the dash

and vice-versa. Therefore, you must juggle the speed and mixture adjustments back and forth to get the specified idle speed within the right range of CO. Unlike a carburetor, changing the idle CO changes the mixture throughout the entire rpm range. Never rev the engine with the Allen wrench sitting in the mixture screw or it may damage the air sensor plate.

Engine oil temperature is the most critical factor in getting an accurate CO adjustment on any K-Jetronic system. Don't touch the mixture screw until the oil temperature is between 140–176°F (60–80°C). CO adjustment is sealed on late K and all KE systems.

Relays

TESTING

▶ **See Figures 135 and 136**

These electrical protection devices are sometimes located in the convenience center, which is a swing down unit located under the instrument panel or under the hood along a fenderwell. The relays are generally serviced by plug-in replacements.

Relay testing may vary depending on the vehicle you are working with and the type of relay being used. On average, there are 2 common types of

relays used today. There is the Mechanical relay and the Solid state relay. Mechanical relays used on most cars come under 3 categories. There is the 3 terminal relay, 4 terminal relay and the multiple circuit relay.

Testing procedures will differ depending on what type of relay you are working with. Before trying to test a relay by supplying it with battery voltage to see if it will click, make sure you know if the type of relay you are testing will not be damaged by this. Solid state relays are not always 12 volts and can be damaged easily.

Usually mechanical relays can be tested in this fashion, but specific terminals must be energized to make these tests. If for an example; if you are working with a 4 terminal mechanical relay, 1 of the terminals is designated for power feed (voltage from the battery or ignition switch). The load terminal provides power to the component. One terminal comes from the control switch and one terminal is the ground. A basic test for this type of relay would be as follows:

First test to see if the relay is receiving voltage by using a 12 volt test light or voltmeter, and the grounded terminal has a good ground. Turn the component on and off to see if the relay clicks. If yes, check that voltage is applied to the component load terminal. If voltage is applied, the relay is okay. If no voltage was applied the relay is most likely defective. If the relay didn't click, and you have power and ground at the relay, check for a signal from the switch terminal of the relay. If you don't have a switch signal the problem is before the relay and may involve detailed electrical testing. You can also test some relays by removing the relay. Using a fused jumper wire, connect one end to the positive side of the battery and provide ground to the relay's ground terminal. Most relay terminals are marked. The relay should click. Connect another wire to the negative side of the battery and quickly ground the other component terminal. If it does not click reverse the wires and it should click. If there is still no response from the relay, chances are it is defective.

The other types of relays may require resistance or continuity checks between terminals when voltage is applied or when voltage is not applied. Resistance specifications are very important because although the relay may be working, it may have to much or not enough resistance. This could cause a specific problem with another unit that is dependent on the relay. This could result in the relay or the controlled unit failing prematurely.

Solid state relays should be tested only with special equipment as any other type of testing may damage this relay or a related circuit. Due to the wide variety of relay tests, consult a "Chilton Total Car Care (TCC) Manual" for the specific relay testing for the vehicle you are working with.

REMOVAL & INSTALLATION

Removal of a relay is pretty simple. Some relays are mounted on a bracket with 1 or 2 screws, just remove the screws and disconnect the connector. Others simply plug in. Care should be taken when disconnecting the connector as not to damage the relay terminals.

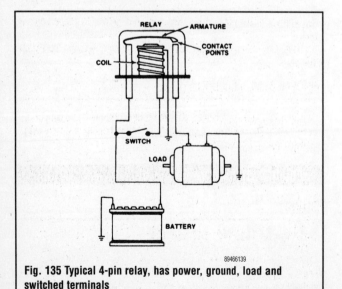

Fig. 135 Typical 4-pin relay, has power, ground, load and switched terminals

Vacuum Switch

TESTING

1 Wire Design

▶ **See Figures 137 and 138**

1. Using an ohmmeter, check for continuity between the switch terminal and body with the engine OFF and cold.
2. Start the engine and warm it to normal operating temperature.
3. Check that there is no continuity between the switch terminal and body, if continuity didn't change continue test.
4. Disconnect switch and apply a vacuum of 5 in. hg (12mm H2O) or greater to the port on the switch.
5. Check that there is a continuity change at switch, if not the switch is defective.

2 Wire Design

▶ **See Figures 139 and 140**

1. Using an ohmmeter, check for no continuity between the switch terminals.

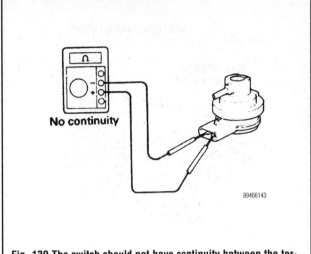

Fig. 139 The switch should not have continuity between the terminals without vacuum applied—2 wire design vacuum switch

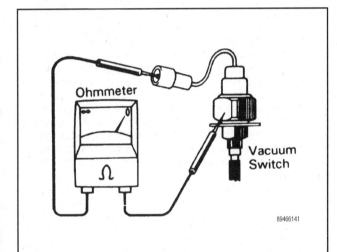

Fig. 137 With the engine off and cold, vacuum switch should have continuity—1 wire design vacuum switch

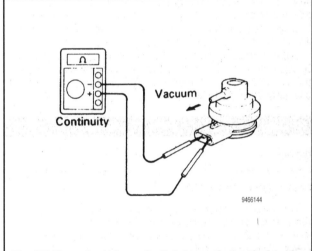

Fig. 140 There should be continuity between the terminals with vacuum applied—2 wire design vacuum switch8

2. Apply a vacuum of 5 in. hg (12mm H2O) or greater to the port on the switch.
3. Using an ohmmeter, check that there is continuity between the switch terminals.

REMOVAL & INSTALLATION

Vacuum switches are relatively easy to replace. Usually it is a simple procedure of disconnecting the vacuum hose and unbolting or unscrewing the switch from a bracket.

Vacuum Switching Valve

TESTING

▶ **See Figures 141, 142, 143 and 144**

The Vacuum Switching Valve (VSV) is used to provide vacuum to another component, either by command from the control module or it may energized through the activation of another component or system.

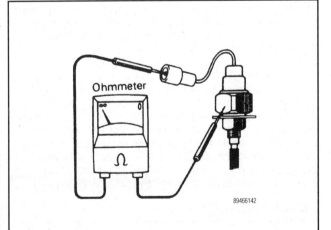

Fig. 138 Vacuum switch should not have continuity with the engine warm and running—1 wire design vacuum switch

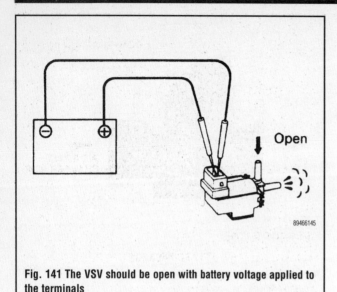

Fig. 141 The VSV should be open with battery voltage applied to the terminals

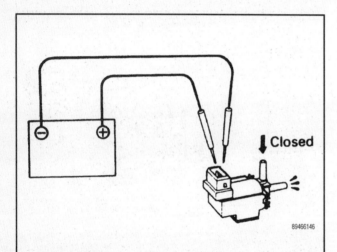

Fig. 142 Without battery voltage applied to the terminals, the VSV should be closed

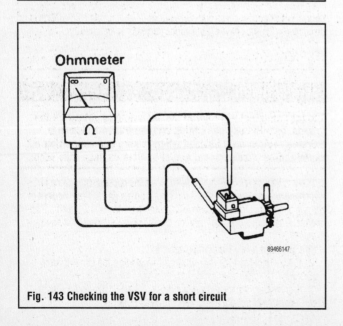

Fig. 143 Checking the VSV for a short circuit

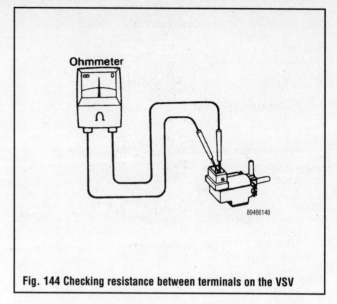

Fig. 144 Checking resistance between terminals on the VSV

1. The vacuum switching circuit is checked by blowing air into the pipe under the following conditions:
   a. Connect the vacuum switching valve terminals to battery voltage.
   b. Blow into the tube and check that the VSV switch is open.
   c. Remove battery voltage from the terminals.
   d. Blow into the tube and check that the VSV switch is closed (no flow).
2. Check for a short circuit within the valve. Using an ohmmeter, check that there is no continuity between the positive terminal and the VSV body. If there is continuity, replace the VSV.
3. Check for an open circuit. Using an ohmmeter, measure the resistance (ohms) between the two terminals of the valve. Resistance should be present. If no resistance is present the solenoid is open and should be replaced. Individual solenoids will have varying resistance readings. Consult a "Chilton Total Car Care (TCC) Manual" for the specifications for your vehicle.

➡**The resistance will vary slightly with temperature. It will decrease in cooler temperatures and increase with heat, slight variations due to temperature range are not necessarily a sign of a failed valve.**

REMOVAL & INSTALLATION

Removing a Vacuum Switching Valve (VSV) is usually a simple matter of disconnecting the electrical connector and vacuum lines at the VSV and removing the retaining screw(s). On some models it may be necessary to move a component for better access to the VSV. Vacuum switching valves are usually mounted on a bracket located on the fenderwell or near the component they control.

1. Disconnect the electrical connector at the VSV.
2. Disconnect and tag the vacuum hoses.
3. Remove the VSV retaining screw(s).
To install:
4. Install the EGR VSV and bracket and tighten the retaining screw(s) securely.
5. Connect the vacuum hoses to the VSV.
6. Connect the electrical connector at the VSV.

Vane Air Flow Meter

TESTING

◆ **See Figure 145**

The Vane Air Flow (VAF) meter senses the incoming volume of air before it enters the throttle body. Essentially, it is a spring loaded air flap with a

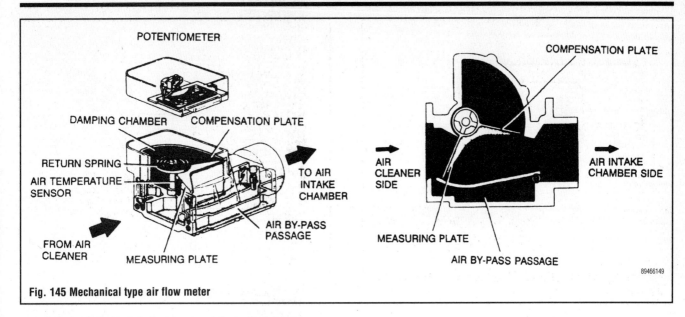

Fig. 145 Mechanical type air flow meter

potentiometer attached to it. As the incoming air forces the flap to open wider, the potentiometer changes resistance values, informing the PCM how far the air flap is open. With this information the PCM decides what the air/fuel ratio requirement should be.

Testing the VAF should first began with a visual inspection for dirt or contamination build-up on the air flap. This is critical to a VAF meter, and perhaps one of the most likely causes of malfunction. Inspect the air flap for movement, it should open and close freely without binding. If it binds, the hinges may be dirty causing it to stick. Spray some carburetor cleaner on the hinges and move it open and closed until it operates freely.

Disconnect the electrical connector from the VAF meter and check the resistance between the sensor terminals. As the flap is gradually moved open to closed, the resistance reading should change without fluctuation, If it the ohmmeter reading is not smooth and steady replace the VAF meter. Some VAF meters may be a frequency design. In this case, the ohmmeter reading will not change at all. Check with a "Chilton Total Care Car" or service manual if you suspect a frequency design meter.

The Vane Air Flow Meter (VAF) is used by early multiport fuel injected Import and some Domestic vehicles. The Mass Air Flow (MAF) sensor is also common on today's fuel injected engines.

REMOVAL & INSTALLATION

The VAF is located between the throttle body and air cleaner. It's usually easy to replace.
1. Disconnect the negative battery cable.
2. Disconnect the electrical connector from the VAF sensor.
3. Remove the air hose between the VAF and throttle body.
4. Remove the bolts attaching VAF to the air cleaner.
To install:
5. Position the VAF to the air cleaner and secure it with the retaining bolts.
6. Connect the air hose between the throttle body and VAF and secure it with the retaining strap.
7. Connect the electrical connect to the VAF sensor.
8. Connect the negative battery cable,

Vehicle Speed Sensor (VSS)

▶ **See Figure 146**

There are two types of Vehicle Speed Sensors (VSS). One type is a magnetic pickup that sends and small AC voltage signal, which is proportional to vehicle speed, to the control module to determine the transmission shift schedule. It also assists supplying information to the control module required by the Torque Converter Clutch (TCC) system. The other type is a reed switch

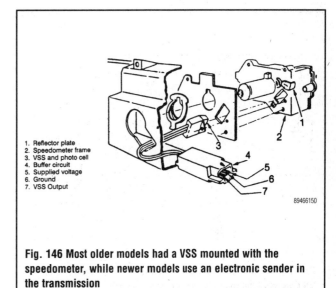

1. Reflector plate
2. Speedometer frame
3. VSS and photo cell
4. Buffer circuit
5. Supplied voltage
6. Ground
7. VSS Output

Fig. 146 Most older models had a VSS mounted with the speedometer, while newer models use an electronic sender in the transmission

design, which simply opens and closes a circuit as it is rotated. A defective or disconnect VSS will cause a tremendous decrease in fuel mileage.

TESTING

✷✷ CAUTION

The following test will require the vehicle to be raised off the ground, with the engine running and the transmission in D. Extreme caution must be used when raising and supporting the vehicle, otherwise personal and/or vehicle damage may occur.

A basic test for the switch type is to rotate the speedometer cable or wheel and with a ohmmeter see if the circuit opens and closes. Be sure to consult a "Chilton Total Car Care (TCC) Manual" for vehicle specific information. A basic test you can make on the AC generator design is as follows:
1. Raise and safely support the vehicle.
2. Disconnect the VSS wire connector located on the transmission housing.
3. Connect an ohmmeter between the terminals of the speed sensor. Most sensors will usually be between 190–250 ohms.

4. Place the vehicle in drive and allow the wheels to rotate. The ohmmeter should fluctuate. If it does not or the ohmmeter reading is not within specification, replace the sensor.

5. Apply the brake, place the vehicle in park and shut the engine off.
6. Connect the harness connector to the VSS.
7. Lower the vehicle.

REMOVAL & INSTALLATION

Removal and installation procedures may vary depending on the vehicle you are working with. Most are a simple "unbolt and pull out" removal. In any event, be sure to consult a "Chilton Total Car Care (TCC) Manual" for further information.

Warm-Up Regulator (CIS)

◗ See Figures 147, 148 and 149

When the engine is cold, the warm-up regulator reduces control pressure, causing the metering slits in the fuel distributor to open further. This enrichment process prevents combustion miss during the warm-up phase of engine operation and is continually reduced as temperature rises. The

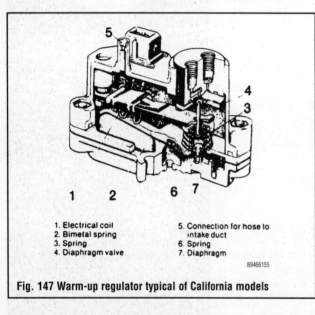

1. Electrical coil
2. Bimetal spring
3. Spring
4. Diaphragm valve
5. Connection for hose to intake duct
6. Spring
7. Diaphragm

89466155

Fig. 147 Warm-up regulator typical of California models

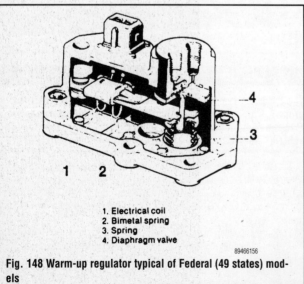

1. Electrical coil
2. Bimetal spring
3. Spring
4. Diaphragm valve

89466156

Fig. 148 Warm-up regulator typical of Federal (49 states) models

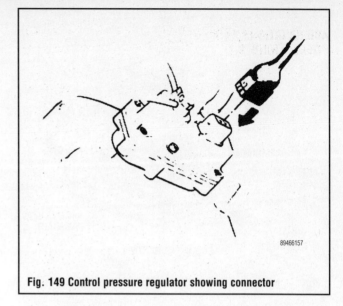

89466157

Fig. 149 Control pressure regulator showing connector

warm-up regulator is a spring controlled flat seat diaphragm-type valve with an electrically heated bi-metal spring. When cold, the bi-metal spring overcomes the valve spring pressure, moving the diaphragm and allowing more fuel to be diverted Out of the control pressure circuit thereby lowering the control pressure. When the bi-metal spring is heated electrically or by engine temperature the valve spring pushes the diaphragm up, allowing less fuel to be diverted thereby raising the control pressure. When the bi-metal spring lifts fully off the `valve spring the warm-up enrichment is completed and control pressure is maintained at normal level by the valve spring. The warm-up regulator should be checked when testing fuel pressure.

TESTING

1. Disconnect the terminal from the warm-up regulator and connect a voltmeter across the contacts in the connector. Ensure that the ignition is switched on and that the safety circuit connection at the air flow sensor has been bypassed. The lowest permissible voltage is 11.5 V.

2. Check that there are no breaks in the heater coil of the regulator by connecting a test lamp in series with the coil. If the coil is found to be damaged, the warm-up regulator should be replaced.

3. Connect an ohmmeter across the terminals in the regulator socket. Resistance must be 16–22 ohms. If the resistance is not within the specifications, the regulator will require replacement.

➡**The system is under considerable constant pressure. The only practical test that should be attempted is one using an ohmmeter. Be sure the engine is at normal operating temperature. There should be no loose fuel fittings or other fire hazards when the electrical connections are disengaged.**

REMOVAL & INSTALLATION

1. Disconnect the negative battery cable.
2. Unplug the electrical connector.
3. Depressurize the fuel system as previously described.

➡**Wrap a cloth around the connection to catch any escaping fuel.**

4. Remove both of the fuel lines.
5. Remove the vacuum hose.
6. Unscrew the four mounting bolts and remove the control pressure regulator.
7. Installation is in the reverse order of removal.

9

GLOSSARY

ABBREVIATIONS AND DEFINITIONS 9-2

ABBREVIATIONS AND DEFINITIONS

4EAT: Electronic automatic 4 speed transaxle.
4X4L: 4x4 Low input switch.
AC DV: Air Cleaner Duct and Valve motor.
A/C P: Air Conditioning Pressure cut-out switch.
A/C: Air Conditioning.
A/F: Air/Fuel Ratio.
A/T: Automatic Transmission.
A4LD: Ford automatic 4 speed lock-up converter drive.
AAC: Auxiliary Air Control Valve.
AAV: Anti-Afterburning Valve.
ABS: Anti-Lock Brake system.

89463P23

Absolute pressure sensor

ABSOLUTE PRESSURE: Pressure measured from the point of total vacuum. For instance, absolute atmospheric pressure at sea level is 14.7 psi (100 kPa, or 29.92 in. hg) at a temperature of 80° F (26.7° C).
ACC: Air Conditioning Clutch compressor signal input to the computer relating status of the air conditioning clutch.
ACCS: Air Conditioning Cycling Switch.
ACD: Air Conditioner Demand switch.
ACP: Air Conditioning Pressure sensor.
ACT: Air Charge Temperature sensor or its signal circuit.
ACTUATOR: One name for any computer-controlled output device, such as a fuel injector, an EGR solenoid valve, and EVAP solenoid purge valve, etc. The term also refers to a specific component, the pressure actuator, used on Bosch KE-Jetronic and KE-Motronic continuous injection systems. See Pressure actuator.
ACV: Air Control Valve or Thermactor Air Control Valve.
ADAPTIVE CONTROL: The ability of a control unit to adapt its closed-loop operation to changing operating conditions—such as engine wear, fuel quality or altitude—to maintain proper air-fuel mixture control, ignition timing or idle rpm. Also referred to as self-learning.
ADAPTIVE MEMORY: A feature of computer memory that allows the microprocessor to adjust its memory for computing open-loop operation, based on changes in engine operation.
AFC: Air Flow Controlled fuel injection.
AFS: Air Flow Sensor.
AHFSS: Air conditioning and Heater Function Selection Switch input to the computer.
AI: Air Injection.
AIC: Automatic Idling Control valve.
A.I.R.: Air Injection Reaction system. Injects air into the exhaust system to burn any remaining unburned fuel.

AISC: Air Induction System Control. Injects air into the exhaust system to burn any remaining unburned fuel.
AIR BPV: Thermactor Air Bypass Valve.
AIR FUEL RATIO: The amount of air compared to the amount of fuel in the air-fuel mixture, almost always expressed in terms of mass.
AIRFLOW METER: In Bosch systems, any device that measures the amount of air being used by the engine. The control unit uses this information to determine the load on the engine. The two most common examples of airflow meters are the airflow sensor used in the Bosch L-Jetronic and the air mass sensor used in the Bosch LH-Jetronic systems.
AIR GAP: The distance or space between the reluctor tooth and pick up coil.
AIR INJECTION: A way of reducing exhaust emissions by injecting air into each of the exhaust ports of an engine. The air mixes with the hot exhaust gasses and oxidizes the HC and CO to form H_2O and CO_2.
AIR MASS SENSOR: An airflow meter that uses the changing resistance of a heated wire in the intake air stream to measure the mass of the air being drawn into the engine. Also referred to as a hot-wire sensor.
AIR SENSOR: An air cone with a floating plate which measures air flow and determines plunger position on K-Jetronic type systems.
AIR VANE: The pivoting flap inside an L-Jetronic or Motronic airflow sensor that swings open in relation to the amount of air flowing through the airflow sensor.
AIS: Air Injection System or Automatic Idle Speed circuit and/or motor.
AIV: Air Injection Valve.
ALTERNATING CURRENT (AC.): An electric current that is constantly changing polarity from positive to negative and back again.
AMBIENT TEMPERATURE: Temperature of the air surrounding the vehicle being serviced.
AMMETER: An electrical meter used to measure current flow (amperes) in an electrical circuit. An ammeter should be connected in series and current flowing in the circuit to be checked.
AMPERE (AMP): The unit current flow is measured in. Amperage equals the voltage divided by the resistance.
AMPLITUDE: The maximum rise (or fall) of a voltage signal from 0 volts.
ANALOG: A voltage signal or processing action that is continuously variable relative to the operation being measured or controlled.
ANALOG VOLT-OHMMETER (VOM): A multi-function meter which measures voltage and resistance. Measurements are made with a D'arsenval meter movement (needle) instead of a digital display.
ANTI-BFV: Anti-Backfire Valve.
ANTI-KNOCK VALUE: The characteristic of gasoline that helps prevent detonation or knocking.
AOD: Automatic Over Drive transmission.
APC: Automatic Performance Control.
APS: Atmospheric Pressure Sensor. Sends information to the computer about pressure in the atmosphere to make correct fuel mixture calculations.
ASCD: Automatic Speed Control Device, often referred to as cruise control.
ASD: Automatic Shut-Down relay driver circuit, fuel pump relay.
ATDC: After Top Dead Center.
ATM: Actuator Test Mode.
ATMOSPHERIC PRESSURE: Normal pressure in the surrounding atmosphere, generated by the weight of the air pressing down from above. At sea level, atmospheric pressure is about 14.7 psi, above zero absolute pressure (100 kPa or 29.92 in hg.) at a temperature of 80°F (26.7°C).
ATS: Air Temperature Sensor.
AUTOMOTIVE EMISSIONS: Gaseous and particulate compounds (hydrocarbons, nitrogen oxides and carbon monoxide) that are emitted from a vehicle's crankcase, exhaust, and fuel tank.
AUXILIARY AIR REGULATOR: A rotary gate valve which stabilizes idle speed during engine warm-up.
AVOM: Analog Volt/Ohm Meter.
AWG: American Wire Gauge system.

AXOD-E: Electronic Automatic Overdrive transaxle.

AXOD: Automatic Overdrive transaxle.

BAC: Bypass Air Control system.

BACKFIRE: The accidental combustion of gasses in an engine's intake or exhaust manifold.

BACKPRESSURE: The resistance, caused by turbulence and friction, that is created as a gas or liquid is forced through a passage.

BAR: Unit of pressure measurement (1 bar is approximately 14.5 psi).

BARO: Barometric Pressure Sensor. Sends information to the computer about barometric pressure in the atmosphere.

BASE IDLE: Idle rpm determined by throttle switch with idle speed control fully retracted.

BATTERY-HOT: Refers to a circuit that is fed directly from battery voltage circuit. (eg. the starter relay terminal).

BATTERY VOLTAGE: Voltage measured between the two terminals of a battery, usually referring to 12–13 volts.

BCS: Boost Control Solenoid. Receives a voltage signal from the computer to adjust the amount of boost from the turbocharger.

BID: Breakerless Inductive Discharge ignition system.

BOB: Breakout Box. Device which connects in series with the control module and engine wiring harness. It permits measurements of the processor inputs and outputs.

BOO: Brake On-Off input to the computer.

BOOST: Turbo charger boost solenoid or its control circuit.

BOTTOM DEAD CENTER (BDC): The exact bottom of a piston stroke.

BP: Barometric Pressure sensor used to compensate for altitude variations.

BPA: Bypass Air Valve.

BPCSV: Bypass Control Solenoid Valve.

BREAKOUT BOX: A device sometimes call pin-out box, which connects in series with the computer and the harness and permits measurements of the processor inputs and outputs.

BTS: Battery Temperature Sensor sends information to the computer about the temperature of the battery.

BTDC: Before Top Dead Center.

BVT: Back-pressure Variable Transducer.

BYPASS: A passage inside a throttle body casting that allows air to go around a closed throttle valve.

CALIBRATE: To adjust the scale of any instrument given quantitative measurements.

CAMSHAFT OVERLAP: The period of camshaft rotation in degrees during which both the intake and the exhaust valve are open.

CANISTER: A container, in a evaporative emission system, that contains charcoal to trap fuel vapors from the fuel system.

CANP: Canister Purge solenoid.

CAPACITANCE: The ability of a condenser (capacitor) to receive and hold an electrical charge.

CAPACITOR: A device which stores an electrical charge.

CAPACITY: The quantity of electricity that can be delivered under specified conditions, as from a battery at a given rate of discharge in amp hours.

CARBON DIOXIDE (CO_2): One of the many by products of combustion.

CARBON MONOXIDE (CO): A colorless, odorless gas that is a by product of incomplete combustion of carbon. This gas is poisonous. NEVER run any vehicle in a confined space; breathing this gas can quickly prove to be fatal.

CAS: Crank Angle Sensor. Sends information to the computer about the angle of location of the crankshaft.

CATALYST: Special metals (i.e. platinum or palladium) within the catalytic converter that contact the hot exhaust gases and promote more complete combustion of the unburned hydrocarbons and reduction of carbon monoxide.

CATALYTIC CONVERTER: Muffler like assembly placed in the exhaust system that contains a catalyst to change hydrocarbons and carbon monoxide into water vapor and carbon dioxide.

CBD: Closed Bowl Distributor.

CC: Catalytic Converter.

CCC: Converter Clutch Control solenoid or its circuit.

CCD: Computer Controlled Dwell, used on Ford vehicles.

CCO: Converter Clutch Override output from the computer processor to the transmission.

CCS: Coast Clutch Solenoid or its circuit.

CEC: Computerized Emission Control.

CENTIGRADE: Unit of measuring temperature where water boils at 100° and freezes at 0° at sea level altitude (boiling points will decrease as altitude increases).

CER: Cold Enrichment Rod.

CES: Clutch Engage Switch.

CFC: Coasting Fuel Cut.

CFI: Central Fuel Injection. Another name for throttle body fuel injection.

CHARGE: Any condition where electricity is available. To restore the active materials In a battery cell by electrically reversing the chemical action.

CHECK ENGINE LIGHT: A dash panel light used either to aid in the identification and diagnosis of system problems or to indicate that maintenance is required.

CHECK VALVE: A one way valve which allows a vacuum or gas to flow in one direction only, preventing backflow.

CID: Cylinder Identification sensor or its circuit.

CIRCUIT: The path that electricity travels in route to component and back to power source.

CIS: Continuous Injection System, Bosch K-Jetronic type system.

CKP: Crankshaft Position Sensor.

CLEARANCE VOLUME: The volume of a combustion chamber when the piston is at top dead center.

CLC: Converter Lock-up Clutch.

CLOSED CIRCUIT: A circuit which is uninterrupted from the current source and back to the current source.

CLOSED LOOP: The mode of operation that a system with an oxygen sensor goes into once the engine is sufficiently warmed up. When the system is in closed loop operation, an oxygen sensor monitors the oxygen content of the exhaust gas and sends a varying voltage signal to the control unit, which alters the air/fuel mixture ratio accordingly.

CMH: Cold Mixture Heater.

CO: Carbon monoxide.

COC: Conventional Oxidation Catalyst.

COLD START INJECTOR: A solenoid type injector installed in the intake plenum that injects extra fuel during cold engine starts. Also referred to as a cold start valve.

COLD START VALVE: See cold start injector.

COMBUSTION CHAMBER: Space left between the cylinder head and the top of the piston at TDC where combustion of the air fuel mixture takes place.

COMPRESSION RATIO: The ratio of maximum engine cylinder volume (when the piston is at the bottom of its stroke) to minimum engine cylinder volume (with the piston at TDC). Thus, the theoretical amount that the air fuel mixture is compressed in the cylinder.

COMPUTER TIMING: The total spark advance in degrees before top dead center. Calculated by the Ford EECIV processor, based on sensor input.

COMPUTER: Any device capable of accepting information, comparing, adding, subtracting, multiplying, dividing and integrating this information and then supplying the results of these processes in proper form.

CONDENSER: A device for holding or storing an electric charge.

CONDUCTOR: Any material through which an electrical current can be transmitted easily.

CONTINUITY: Continuous or complete circuit. The type of circuit that can be checked with an ohmmeter.

CONTINUOUS INJECTION SYSTEM (CIS): A Bosch developed fuel injection system that injects fuel continuously. Unlike an electronic injection system, which uses a computer to control the pulse width of electronic solenoid injectors, CIS uses hydraulic controls to alter the amount of fuel injected. There are four basic types of CIS: K-Jetronic, K-Jetronic with Lambda (oxygen sensor), KE-Jetronic and KE Motronic.

CONTINUOUS SELF-TEST: A continuous test of the Ford EEC-IV system conducted whenever the vehicle is in operation.

CONTROL MODULE: A transistorized device that processes electrical inputs and produces output signals to control various engine functions. One of several names for a solid state micro computer.

CONTROL PLUNGER: In Bosch CIS, the component inside the fuel distributor that rises and falls with the airflow sensor plate lever, which controls fuel flow to the injectors.

CONTROL PRESSURE REGULATOR: In Bosch CIS, the control pressure regulator is a thermal hydraulic device that alters the control pressure by returning the excess fuel from the control pressure circuit to the fuel tank. The control pressure regulator controls the counter force pressure on top of the control plunger. Also referred to as the warm up regulator.

CONTROL UNIT: An electronic computer that processes electrical inputs and produces electrical outputs to control a series of actuators which alter engine operating conditions. Also referred to as an Electronic Control Assembly (ECA), Electronic Control Module (ECM), Electronic Control Unit (ECU), logic module, or simply, the computer.

CONVENTIONAL THEORY: The flow of current in an electrical circuit in which the direction is from positive to negative.

CORE: The center conductor part or wire of the iron magnetic material or a solenoid magnet.

COUNTERFORCE: The force of the fuel pressure applied to the top of the control plunger to balance the force of the airflow pushing against the sensor plate.

CPS: Crankshaft Position Sensor. Provides the ECU with engine speed and crankshaft angle (position).

CPU: Central Processing Unit.

CTS: Coolant Temperature Sensor.

CURB IDLE: Computer controlled idle rpm.

CURRENT: Amount or intensity of flow of electricity. Measured in amperes.

CURRENT FLOW: The current flow theory which says electricity flows from positive to negative. Also called positive current flow theory.

CVR: Control Vacuum Regulator.

CWM: Cold Weather Modulator.

CYCLE: A complete alternation in an alternating current.

CYL SENSOR: Crankshaft Angle Sensor.

CYLINDER IDENTIFICATION SIGNAL (CID): A signal generated by the crankshaft timing sensor, that is used to synchronize the ignition coils, due to the fact that some models use a 2 ignition coil pack DIS system.

DAMPENER: A device, sometimes called an accumulator, installed in-line between the fuel pump and the fuel filter on many fuel injection systems, which dampens the pulsations of the fuel pump. The accumulator also maintains residual pressure in the fuel delivery system, even after the engine has been turned off, to prevent vapor lock.

DCL: Data Communications Link is a terminal used to access the computer codes.

DFS: Decel Fuel Shut-off.

DI: Direct Ignition system, each spark plug has its own ignition coil.

DIAGNOSTIC MODE: This operation mode is used by the Engine Control Computer (ECU) and provides historical data to the technician that indicates any malfunctions or discrepancies that have been stored in memory.

DIAPHRAGM: A component which moves a control lever accordingly when supplied with a vacuum signal.

DIELECTRIC SILICONE COMPOUND: Non-conducting silicone grease applied to spark plug wire boots, rotors and connectors to prevent arcing and moisture from entering a connector.

DIESELING: A condition in a gasoline engine in which extreme heat in the combustion chamber continues to ignite fuel after the ignition has been turned off.

DIFFERENTIAL PRESSURE: In Bosch KE-Jetronic systems, the difference between actuator fuel pressure in the lower chambers of the differential pressure valves and the system pressure entering the pressure actuator.

DIGIFANT: Volkswagen collaborated with Bosch to develop this electronic injection system. Digifant is similar to a Motronic system, except that its timing control map is less complicated than the Motronic map. Also, a knock sensor is not used.

DIGIFANT II: A refined version of Volkswagen's Digifant. This system has some control improvements and uses a knock sensor for improved timing control.

DIGITAL: A two level voltage signal or processing function that is either **ON/OFF** or **HIGH/LOW**.

DIGITAL CONTROL: Circuits which handle information by switching the current **ON** and **OFF**.

DIGITAL FUEL INJECTION (DFI): A General Motors system, similar to earlier electronic fuel injection systems, but with digital microprocessors. Analog inputs from various engine sensors are converted to digital signals before processing. The system is self monitoring and self diagnosing. It also has the capabilities of compensating for failed components and remembering intermittent failures.

DIODE: An electrical device that will allow current to flow in one direction only.

DISPLACEMENT: A measurement of the volume of air displaced by a piston as it moves from the bottom to the top of its stroke. Engine displacement is the piston displacement multiplied by the number of pistons in an engine.

DIRECT CURRENT (DC): An electrical current which flows in only one direction.

DIS: Distributorless Ignition System.

DLC: Data Link Connector.

DOL: Data Output Link. Fuel calculation data from the EEC-IV processor to the trip computer.

DRB II: Diagnostic Readout Box tester, for Chrysler system testing. Determines sensor voltage, degrees F, vacuum, rpm and mileage reading with vehicle's engine both on and off.

DRIVEABILITY: The operating characteristics of a vehicle.

DSV: Deceleration Solenoid Valve.

DTC: Diagnostic Trouble Code.

DUAL CATALYTIC CONVERTER: Combines two converters in one shell. Controls NOx, HC and CO. Also called TWC.

DUAL-POINT INJECTION SYSTEM: A computer regulated system, that provides precise air/fuel ratio under all driving conditions. Same as throttle body with 2 injectors.

DUTY CYCLE: Many solenoid-operated metering devices cycle on and off. The duty cycle is a measurement of the amount of time a device is energized or turned on expressed as a percentage of the complete on-off cycle of that device. In other words, the duty cycle is the ratio of the pulse width to the complete cycle width.

DV TW: Delay Valve, 2 Way.

DV: Delay Valve.

DVOM: Digital Volt/Ohm Meter.

DWELL: The amount of time that primary voltage is applied to the ignition coil to energize it. Dwell is also a measurement of the duration of time a component is on, relative to the time it's off. Dwell measurements are expressed in degrees (degrees of crankshaft rotation, for example).

DWELL METER: Measures the amount of time, recorded in degrees, that current passes through a closed switch.

E/L: Electrical Load control unit.

E4OD: Ford Electronic 4 speed Overdrive transmission.

EACV: Electronic Air Control Valve.

ECA: Electronic Control Assembly. Ford's engine controlling computer.

ECCENTRIC: Off center. A shaft lobe which has a center different from that of the shaft.

ECCS: Electronic Concentrated Control System.

ECI: Electronic Control Injection.

ECIT: Electronic Control Ignition Timing.

ECM: Electronic Control Module.

ECS: Emission Control System.

ECT: Engine Coolant Temperature sensor or its circuit, could also be Electronic Control Transmission.

ECU: Electronic Control Unit or Engine Control Unit. Processes input information to trigger the ignition control module.

EDF: Electro-Drive Fan relay or its circuit.

EEC-IV: Electronic Engine Control design 4. A computer controlled system of engine control used on Ford and some Mazda vehicles.

EEC-V: Electronic Engine Control design 5. A computer controlled system of engine control used on Ford and some Mazda vehicles.

EEC: Evaporative Emission Control.

EEGR: Electronic Exhaust Gas Recirculation valve (Sonic).

EET: Electronic Exhaust Gas Recirculation Transducer.

EFC: Electronic Fuel Control.

EFE: Early Fuel Evaporation.

EFI: Electronic Fuel Injection. A computer controlled fuel injection system. On Ford, EFI uses injectors in each intake port and CFI uses an injector in the throttle body.

EGI: Electronic Gasoline Injection.

EGO: Exhaust Gas Oxygen sensor.

EGOG: Exhaust Gas Oxygen Ground.

EGR S/O: Exhaust Gas Recirculation Shut-Off.

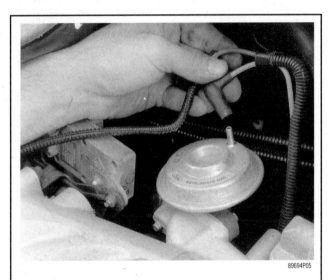

Typical ported vacuum EGR valve

EGR: Exhaust Gas Recirculation. System is designed to allow the flow of inert exhaust gases into the combustion chamber to cool combustion and thus reduce nitrous oxides in the exhaust.

EGRC: Exhaust Gas Recirculation Control vacuum solenoid valve or its control circuit.

EGRV: Exhaust Gas Recirculation Vent solenoid valve or its circuit.

EHC: Exhaust Heat Control vacuum solenoid or its circuit.

EICV: Electronic Idle Control Valve.

EIS: Electronic Ignition System which uses a reluctor and a pick up coil along with a module to replace the ignition points and condenser.

ELCD: Evaporative Loss Control Device.

ELECTRON THEORY OF CURRENT FLOW: The current flow theory which says electricity flows from negative to positive.

ELECTRONIC CONTROL UNIT (ECU): On board computer module, used to control ignition, fuel or other engine function.

ELECTROMAGNETIC: Refers to a device which incorporates both electronic and magnetic principles together in its operation.

EMISSIONS: Unburned parts of the air fuel mixture released in the exhaust. Refers mostly to carbon monoxide (CO), hydrocarbons (HC), and nitrous oxide (NOx).

EMR: Emissions Maintenance Reminder.

EMW: Emission Maintenance Warning.

ENGINE MAPPING: Vehicle operation simulation procedure used to tailor the on-board computer program to a specific engine! power-

train combination. This program is stored in a PROM or calibration assembly.

ENVIRONMENTAL PROTECTION AGENCY: Federal agency having responsibility for administering congressional programs relating to the protection of the environment.

EPA: Environmental Protection Agency.

EPROM: Erasable Programmable Read Only Memory.

EPS: Engine Position Sensor. Sends information to the computer about the crankshaft's angle of location.

ER: Engine Running. Mode used on some Ford system tests.

ERS: Engine RPM Sensor.

ESA: Electronic Spark Advance.

ESC: Electronic Spark Control.

ESS: Engine Speed Sensor.

EST: Electronic Spark Timing.

ETS: Exhaust Temperature Sensor.

EVAP: Evaporative Emission system.

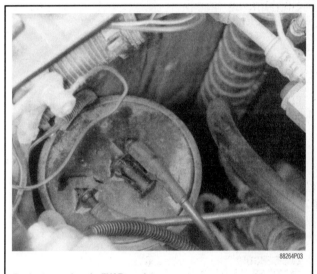

Typical round style EVAP canister

EVAPORATIVE EMISSION CONTROL (EEC): A way of controlling HC emissions by collecting fuel vapors from the fuel tank and directing them through an engine's intake system.

EVP: EGR Valve Position sensor or its circuit.

EVR: EGR Vacuum Regulator or its circuit.

EXHAUST GAS OXYGEN SENSOR: Sensor that changes its voltage output as exhaust gas oxygen content changes as compared to the oxygen content of the atmosphere. The constantly changing electrical signal is used to control fuel mixture.

EXHAUST GAS RECIRCULATION: A procedure where a small amount of exhaust gas is readmitted to the combustion chamber to reduce peak combustion temperatures, thus reducing NOx.

FAHRENHEIT: Unit of measuring temperature where water boils at 212° and freezes at 32° at sea level altitude (boiling points decrease as altitude increases).

FAULT CODES: A series of numbers representing the results of On Board Diagnostic or Vehicle Diagnostics. The computer communicates this service information via the diagnostic connector as a series of timed pulses read either on a scan tool or as flashes of the "Power Loss or Check Engine" light.

FCS: Fuel Control Solenoid.

FCV: Float Chamber Ventilation system.

FEED CIRCUIT: The power supply or hot wire.

FICB: Fast Idle Cam Breaker.

FIPL: Fuel Injection Pump Lever sensor or its circuit.

FIRING ORDER: The order in which combustion occurs in the cylinders of an engine.

FMEM: Failure Mode Effects Management. Sometimes referred to limp-in mode.

FOM: Fix Operating Mode, limp-in mode.

FOS: Front Oxygen Sensor. Sends information to the computer about the amount of oxygen in the front exhaust manifold.

FPM: Fuel Pump Monitor. A circuit in the Ford EEC system used to monitor fuel pump operation.

FREQUENCY: The number of cycles (complete alterations) of an alternating current per second.

FREQUENCY VALVE: On Bosch CIS, a device that regulates pressure in the lower chamber of the differential pressure valve, in response to a signal from the Lambda (oxygen) sensor. Also referred to as a Lambda valve or a timing valve.

FTO: Filter Tach Output. An output from the Ford DIS TFI IV module which provides a filtered ignition signal to the processor in order to control dwell.

FTS: Fuel Temperature Sensor.

FUEL ACCUMULATOR: Diaphragm unit which helps maintain residual fuel pressure for hot starting on CIS type fuel system.

FUEL DISTRIBUTOR: The component which feeds fuel to the individual engine cylinders corresponding to the air flow rate metered by the air flow sensor on CIS systems.

FUEL METERING: Control of the amount of fuel that is mixed with engine intake air to form a combustible mixture.

1. Fuel injector
2. Fuel rail
3. Fuel pressure regulator
4. Fuel feed hose

Typical MFI fuel rail and components

FUEL RAIL: The hollow pipe, tube or manifold that delivers fuel at system pressure to the injectors. The fuel rail also serves as the mounting point for the upper ends of the injectors, and for the damper (if equipped) and the pressure regulator.

FULL LOAD: The load condition of the engine when the throttle is wide open. Full load can occur at any rpm.

FULL LOAD ENRICHMENT: The extra fuel injected during acceleration to enrich the mixture when the throttle is wide open. On some systems, the computer goes open loop during full load enrichment.

FUSIBLE LINK: A device that protects a circuit from damage if a short to ground occurs or if the polarity of the battery or charger is reversed.

GND, GRD or GRND: Ground. Common line leading to the negative side of the battery.

GULP VALVE: A valve used in an air injection system to prevent backfire. During deceleration it redirects air from the air pump to the intake manifold where the air leans out the rich air fuel mixture.

GVW: Gross Vehicle Weight.

HAC: High Altitude Compensation sensor.

HACV: High Altitude Compensation Valve.

HAI: Hot Air Intake.

HALL EFFECT PICK-UP ASSEMBLY: Used to input a signal to the electronic control unit. The system operates on the Hall Effect principle whereby a magnetic field is blocked from the pick-up by a rotating shutter assembly.

HALL EFFECT: A process where current is passed through a small slice of semi-conductor material at the same time as a magnetic field to produce a small voltage in the semi-conductor.

HBV: Heater Blower Voltage input to the ECC-IV processor reflecting heater blower voltage demand.

HC: Hydrocarbons. Any compound composed of hydrogen and carbon, such as petroleum products, that is considered a pollutant.

HCV: Exhaust Heat Control Valve.

HEDF: High-speed Electro-Drive Fan relay or its circuit.

HEGO: Heat Exhaust Gas Oxygen sensor or its circuit.

HERTZ (Hz): The term meaning the cycles per second.

HIC: Hot Idle Compensator.

HICAS: High Capacity Active Controlled Suspension.

HIGH SPEED SURGE: A sudden increase in engine speed caused by high manifold vacuum pulling in an excess air fuel mixture.

HIGH SWIRL COMBUSTION (HSC) CHAMBER: A combustion chamber in which the intake valve is shrouded or masked to direct the incoming air/fuel charge and create turbulence they will circulate the mixture more evenly and rapidly.

Hg (MERCURY): A calibration material used as a standard for vacuum measurement.

HLOS: Hardware Limited Operation Strategy. Certain types of computer malfunctions will place the EEC-IV system into HLOS mode. Output commands are replaced with fixed values. Sometimes referred to as limp-in mode.

HT: High Tension.

HYDROCARBON: Any compound composed of carbon and hydrogen, such as petroleum products. Excess amounts are considered undesirable contaminants.

I/O: Input/Output, for computer data transmission.

IAC: Idle Air Control solenoid.

IAS: Inlet Air Solenoid valve or its circuit.

IAT: Intake Air Temperature sensor.

IBP: Integral Back Pressure.

IC: Integrated Circuit.

ICM: Ignition Control Module. Used by Chrysler to supply voltage for spark plug firing.

ICV: Induction Control Valve. Receives a voltage signal from the computer to adjust the air induction into the engine.

IDLE AIR STABILIZATION VALVE: Electronically controlled valve used to maintain idle speed at a predetermined level.

IDLE LIMITER: A device to control minimum and maximum idle fuel richness. The idle limiter is intended to prevent unauthorized persons from making mixture adjustments.

IDLE SPEED STABILIZER: An electronically controlled air bypass around the throttle. Also referred to as an idle speed actuator or a constant idle system.

IDLE TRACKING SWITCH: An input device that sends a signal to the computer to indicate a closed throttle condition.

IDM: Ignition Diagnostics Monitor. A continuous monitor of the ignition input to the EEC-IV processor used to detect intermittent ignition faults.

IG: Ignition.

IGNITER: Term used by Japanese automotive and ignition manufacturers for the electronic control unit or module.

IGNITION COIL: Step-up transformer consisting of a primary and a secondary winding with an iron core. As the current flow in the primary winding stops, the magnetic field collapses across the secondary winding inducing the high secondary voltage. The coil may be oil filled or of an epoxy type design.

ILC: Idle Load Compensation solenoid receives a voltage signal from the computer to adjust the engine idle when the engine is under load.

IMA Sensor: Idle Mixture Adjuster Sensor.

IMPEDANCE: The total opposition a circuit offers to the flow of current. It includes resistance and reactance and is measured in ohms (i.e. 20 megohms.)

IMPELLER: A rotor or rotor blade (vane) used to force a gas or liquid in a certain direction under pressure.

IMS: Inferred Mileage Sensor: A circuit using a E-cell which deflates its state with the application of a current. As the vehicle ages, the EEC-IV processor compensates for aging by changing calibration parameters.

INDUCTION: A means of transferring electrical energy in the form of a magnetic field. Principle used in the ignition coil to increase voltage.

INDUCTIVE DISCHARGE IGNITION: A method of igniting the air fuel mixture in an engine cylinder. It is based on the induction of a high voltage in the secondary winding of a coil.

INFINITE READING: A reading on an ohmmeter that indicates an open circuit or infinite reading.

INFINITY: An ohmmeter reading which indicates an open circuit in which no current will flow.

INJECTION VALVE: Same as an injector.

INJECTOR: A solenoid or pressure-operated fuel delivery valve used for fuel injection systems.

INTERCOOLER: An air to air or air to liquid heat exchanger used to lower the temperature of the air/fuel mixture by removing heat from the intake air charge.

INTEGRATED CIRCUIT (IC): Electronic micro-circuit consisting of a semi-conductor components or elements made using thick-film or thin-film technology. Elements are located on a small chip made of a semi-conducting material, greatly reducing the size of the electronic control unit and allowing it to be incorporated within the distributor.

INTERMITTENT: Occurs now and then (not continuously). In electrical circuits, it refers to an occasional open, short, or ground.

IRCM: Integrated Relay Control Module, used on some Ford systems.

ISA: Idle Speed Actuator. Extends or retracts to control engine idle speed and to set throttle stop angle during deceleration.

ISAV: Idle Speed Air Valve.

ISC: Idle Speed Control, this could be a computer controlled motor, air bypass valve, or any device used to control idle rpm.

ITS: Idle Tracking Switch. An input device that sends a signal to the control module to indicate throttle position.

JSV: Jet Mixture Solenoid Valve.

JUMPER WIRE: Is used to bypass sections of a circuit. The simplest type is a length of electrical wire with an alligator clip at each end.

KAM: Keep Alive Memory. Battery power memory locations in the computer used to store failure codes and some diagnostic item meters.

KAPWR: Keep Alive Power, used to power the KAM circuit of the processor.

KDLH: Kick-Down Low Hold.

KNOCK: A sudden increase in cylinder pressure caused by preignition of some of the air/fuel mixture as the flame front moves out from the spark plug ignition point. Pressure waves in the combustion chamber crash into the piston or cylinder walls. The result is a sound known as knock or pinging. Knock can be caused by using fuel with an octane rating that's too low, overheating, by excessively advanced ignition timing, or by a compression ratio that's been raised by hot carbon deposits on the piston or cylinder head.

KNOCK SENSOR: An input device that responds to spark knock, caused by over advanced ignition timing.

KOEO: Key On/Engine Off.

KOER: Key On/Engine Running.

KS: Knock Sensor. An input device that responds to spark knock caused by excessively advanced ignition timing.

LAMBDA (I): Expresses the air/fuel ratio in terms of the Stoichiometric ratio compared to the oxygen content of the exhaust. At the Stoichiometric ratio, when all of the fuel is burned with all of the air in the combustion chamber, the oxygen content of the exhaust is said to be at lambda = 1. If there's an excess of fuel in the exhaust (a shortage of air rich mixture), then lambda is less than 1.

LEAN MIXTURE: An air/fuel mixture that has excessive oxygen left after all the fuel in the combustion chamber has burned, 1 part fuel to 15 or more parts air.

LEAN SURGE: A change in rpm caused by an extremely lean fuel mixture.

LED: Light Emitting Diode.

LIMP-IN MODE: Is the attempt by the SMEC/SBEC to compensate for the failure of certain components by substituting information from 6ther sources. Used in the Chrysler self diagnostic system.

LOAD: Any electrical device that provides resistance to current flow.

LOBES: The rounded protrusions on a camshaft that force, and govern, the opening of the intake and exhaust valves.

LOGIC PROBE: A simple hand held device used to confirm the operational characteristics of a logic (On/Off) circuit.

LOS: Limited Operation Strategy.

LUS: Lock-Up Solenoid.

M/C: Mixture Control.

M/T: Manual Transmission.

MAF: Mass Airflow sensor. A device used to measure the amount of intake air entering the engine on some fuel injection systems.

MAGNETIC FIELD: The area in which magnetic lines of force exist.

MAGNETIC PICK UP COIL: Coil used in the electronic distributor ignition system to determine exactly when to switch off the coil secondary.

MAP: Manifold Absolute Pressure sensor or its circuit.

MAS: Mixture Adjust Screw.

MAT: Manifold Air Temperature.

MCS: Mixture Control Solenoid. Receives a voltage signal from the computer to adjust the air to fuel mixture (air/fuel ratio).

MCT: Manifold Charge Temperature sensor.

MCV: Mixture Control Valve.

MFI: Multiport Fuel Injection.

MICRON: A unit of length equal to one millionth of a meter, one one-thousandth of a millimeter.

MICROPROCESSOR: A miniature computer on a silicone chip.

MIL: Malfunction Indicator Light. Check engine light.

MILLIAMPERE (mA): One one-thousandth of one ampere. The current flow to the pressure actuator in KE systems is measured in milliamps.

MLP: Manual (shift) Lever Position sensor or its circuit.

MODE: An operating state i.e. closed loop vs. open loop.

MODULE: Electronic control unit, amplifier or igniter of solid state or integrated design which controls the current flow in the ignition primary circuit based on input from the pick-up coil. When the module opens the primary circuit, the high secondary voltage is induced in the coil.

MONITOR BOX: An optional Ford EEC-IV test device which connects in series with the EEC-IV processor and its harness, and permits measurements in various units of the processor inputs and output.

MPC: Manifold Pressure Controlled.

MPFI: Multi-Point Fuel Injection.

MPS: Motor Position Sensor.

MRL: Maintenance Reminder Light.

MS: Millisecond.

MSD: Multiple Spark Discharge.

NDS: Neutral/Drive Switch.

NGS: Neutral Gear Switch or its circuit.

NITROUS OXIDES (NOx): A compound formed during the engine's combustion process above 2500° F (1382° C), when the oxygen combines with nitrogen to form nitrous oxides. This contributes to photochemical smog.

NPS: Neutral Pressure Switch or its circuit.

NTS: Negative Temperature Coefficient Resistor.

OBD: On Board Diagnostics.

OCC: Output Cycling Check.

OCT ADJ: Octane Adjust device which modifies ignition spark.

OCT: Octane Switch.

OCTANE RATING: The measurement of the anti-knock value of gasoline.

OHM: The standard unit for measuring the resistance to current flow.

OHMMETER: The electrical meter used to measure the resistance in ohms. Self-powered and must be connected to a voltage free circuit or damage to the ohmmeter will result.

OPEN CIRCUIT: A circuit which does not provide a complete path for the flow of current.

ORIFICE: The calibrated fuel delivery hole at the nozzle end of the fuel injector.

OSC: Output State Check.

OSCILLATING: Moving back and forth with a steady rhythm.

OSCILLOSCOPE: An electric testing device that shows a pattern wave form of an electrical occurrence. Used to test ignition, fuel injection, alternator and other electrical devices.

OVCV: Outer Vent Control Valve.

OVERLAY CARD: A plastic card used for the Ford Breakout or Monitor box to identify connections for each engine tested.

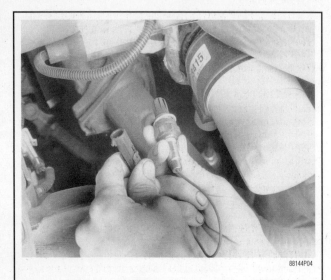

88144P04

Typical 1-wire oxygen sensor

OXYGEN (O₂) SENSOR: Used with the feedback system to sense the presence of oxygen in the exhaust gas and signal the computer which can reference the voltage signal to an air/fuel ratio.

PAIR: Pulsed Air Injection system.

PARALLEL CIRCUIT: A circuit with more than one path for the current to follow.

PART LOAD ENRICHMENT: Extra fuel injected during throttle opening to enrich the mixture during transition. Usually occurs during closed loop operation.

PA SENSOR: Atmospheric Pressure Sensor.

PCV: Positive Crankcase Ventilation. A system that controls the flow of crankshaft vapors into the engine intake manifold where they are burned in combustion rather then being discharged into the atmosphere.

PFE: Pressure Feedback EGR sensor or its circuit.

PGM-FI: Programmed Fuel Injection system.

PGM-IG: Programmed Ignition system.

PHENOMENA: Basis of symptoms; a significant occurrence.

PICK-UP COIL: Inputs signal to the electronic control unit to open the primary circuit. Consists of a fine wire coil mounted around a permanent magnet. As the reluctor's ferrous tooth passes through the magnetic field an alternating current is produced, signaling the electronic control unit. Can operate on the principle of metal detecting, magnetic induction or Hall Effect. Is also referred to as a stator or sensor.

PIP: Profile Ignition Pickup.

PLENUM: A chamber that stabilizes the air/fuel mixture and allows it to rise to a pressure slightly above atmospheric pressure.

PORT INJECTION: A fuel injection system in which the fuel is sprayed by individual injectors into each intake port, upstream of the intake valve.

PORTED VACUUM: The low pressure area (vacuum) just above the throttle body plate.

PORTED VACUUM SWITCH: A temperature actuated switch that changes vacuum connections when the coolant temperature changes.

POSITIVE POLARITY: Also called reverse polarity. An incorrect polarity of the ignition coil connections. Coil voltage is delivered to the spark plugs so that the center electrode of the spark plugs is positively charged and the grounded electrode is negatively charged.

POTENTIOMETER: A variable resistor used to change a voltage signal.

PRC: Pressure Regulator Control solenoid.

PRE-PUMP: In-tank fuel pump.

PRESSURE REGULATOR: A spring loaded diaphragm type pressure relief valve which controls the pressure of fuel delivered to the fuel injector(s) by returning excess fuel to the tank.

PRIMARY CIRCUIT: Is the low voltage side of the ignition system which consists of the ignition switch, ballast resistor or resistance wire, bypass, coil, electronic control unit and pick-up coil as well as the connecting wires and harnesses.

PROFILE IGNITION PICKUP: A hall effect vane switch that furnishes crankshaft position data to the EEC-IV processor.

PROM: Programmable Read Only Memory.

PSP: Power Steering Pressure Switch. The signal is used by a computer to compensate for power steering loads.

PTC HEATER: Positive Temperature Coefficient Heater.

PULSED INJECTION: A system that delivers fuel in intermittent pulses by the opening and closing of solenoid controlled injectors. Also referred to as electronic fuel injection (EFI).

PULSE GENERATOR: Also called a pulse signal generator. Term used by Japanese and German automotive and ignition manufacturers to describe the pick-up and reluctor assembly. Generates an electrical pulse which triggers the electronic control unit or igniter.

PULSE WIDTH: The amount of time the control unit energizes the fuel injectors to spray fuel into the intake manifold, usually measured in milliseconds.

PURGE VALVE: A vacuum operated valve used to draw fuel vapors from a vapor canister.

PVS: Ported Vacuum Switch. A temperature-activated switch that changes vacuum connections when the coolant temperature changes.

QUICK TEST: A functional diagnostic test for Ford EECIV system, consisting of test hookup, key on engine off, engine running and continuous self test modes.

RAD: Radiator Temperature Switch.

RAM: Random Access Memory.

RATIO: The proportion of one value divided by another.

RECORDER: A device used to record the electronic signals sent to and from the engine computer. Sometimes referred to as a flight recorder, because it works similar to aircraft recording device; to store what the last functions of the engine computer that where performed over a 1 minute or some other time period.

REFERENCE VOLTAGE: A constant voltage signal (below battery voltage) applied to a sensor by the computer. The sensor alters the voltage according to engine operating conditions and returns it as a variable input signal to the computer which adjusts the system operation accordingly.

RELAY: A switching device operated by a low current circuit, which controls the opening and closing of another higher current circuit.

RELIEF VALVE: A pressure limiting valve located in the exhaust chamber of the thermactor air pump. Its function is to relieve part of exhaust airflow if pressure exceeds a calibrated value.

RELUCTOR: Also called an armature or trigger wheel. Ferrous metal piece attached to the distributor shaft. Made up of teeth of which the number are the same as the number of engine cylinders. As the reluctor teeth pass through the pickup magnetic field, an alternating current is generated in the pick-up coil.

RESIDUAL PRESSURE: Pressure remaining in the fuel system after the engine has been shut off.

RESISTOR: Any electrical circuit element that provides resistance in a circuit.

RESISTANCE: The opposition to the flow of current through a circuit or electrical device, and is measured in ohms. Resistance is equal to the voltage divided by the amperage.

RICH MIXTURE: An air/fuel mixture that has more fuel than can burn completely, 1 part fuel to 14 or less parts air.

RMS: Root Mean Square (effective): The square root average of the squares of the instantaneous amplitudes taken over the duration of the pulse. Example; the wave pattern on a 110vac house receptacle would be 300vac peak-to-peak, 300vac divided by 2 times 0.70 equals 105vac RMS.

ROM: Read Only Memory.

RPM: Revolution Per-Minute.

RXD: Receive data line.

SAE: Society of Automotive Engineers.

SAS: Speed Adjusting Screw.

SATURATION: The state of a coil when current flow has reached the design maximum and the magnetic field has reached its maximum strength.

SBEC/SMEC: Single Board Engine Controller/Single Module Engine Controller used on Chrysler vehicles. Both regulate ignition timing, air-fuel ratio, emission control devices, cooling fan, charging system idle speed and speed control.

SBS: Supercharger Bypass Solenoid or its circuit.

SCC: Spark Control Computer.

SCS: Speed Control Solenoid receives a voltage signal from the computer to control the engine idle speed.

SCSV: Slow Cut Solenoid Valve.

SDS: Service Data and Specifications.

SDV: Spark Delay Valve.

SECONDARY: The high voltage side of the ignition system, usually above 20,000 volts. The secondary includes the ignition coil, coil wire, distributor cap and rotor, spark plug wires and spark plugs.

SEFI: Sequential Electronic Fuel Injection. Injectors located in intake ports that inject fuel triggered by ignition timing.

SELF-TEST: One of the 3 subsets of the Ford EEC-IV Quick Test modes.

SENSOR PLATE: A round plate bolted to the air flow sensor lever which floats in the stream of intake air on the CIS type systems.

SENSOR: Also called the pick-up coil or stator. See pick-up coil for definition.

SENSOR TEST MODE: This mode of diagnosis used to read the output signal of a specific sensor when the engine is not running. Specific codes are used to select a specific sensor on the scan tool. The output of this mode is actual output of the selected sensor (temperature, voltage, speed, etc.).

SHORT CIRCUIT: An undesirable connection between a circuit and any other point.

SHUTTER: Also called the vane. Used in a Hall Effect distributor to block the magnetic field from the Hall Effect pickup. The shutter is attached to the rotor and is grounded to the distributor shaft.

SIG RTN: Signal Return circuit for all sensors except HEGO.

SIL: Shift Indicator Light. Indicates to driver optimum time to shift gears.

SIS: Solenoid Idle Stop.

SM: Stepper Motor. Receives a voltage signal from the computer to control engine idle speed.

SMJ: Super Multiple Junction, the main harness connector through the bulkhead for the engine controller circuits.

SOLENOID: A wire coil with a movable core which changes position by means of electromagnetism when current flows through the coil.

SOS: Sub Oxygen Sensor.

SPARK ADVANCE: Causing spark to occur earlier.

SPARK DURATION: The length of time measured in milliseconds the spark is established across the spark plug gap.

SPARK RETARD: Causing less spark advance to be added, resulting in a spark which is introduced later.

SPARK VOLTAGE: The inductive portion of a spark that maintains the spark in the air gap between a spark plug's electrodes. Usually about one quarter of the firing voltage level.

SPFI: Single Point Fuel Injection.

SPI: Single-Point Injection system, same as throttle body injection.

SPOUT: SPark OUTput signal from the EEC-IV processor to the TFI-IV module, used to control amount of timing retard.

SQUARE WAVE: An essentially square or rectangular shaped wave. A wave that alternately assumes 1 to 2 fixed values with a negligible transition time between the 2 values.

SRI: Service Reminder Indicator. The SRI light is used to inform the driver that the vehicle is due for service. Prior to 1993, it was commonly called the Maintenance Reminder Light.

SSI: Solid State Ignition system.

SST: Special Service Tool, or special test equipment to be used for testing or repairs.

STAR: Self Test Automatic Readout (Ford), used to access codes from the EEC-IV processor.

STARTER SAFETY SWITCH: A neutral start switch. It keeps the starting system from operating when a car's transmission is in gear.

STATOR: Another name for a pick-coil. See pick-up coil for definition.

STEPPER MOTOR: Are digital devices actuators, (motors that work with DC current), that move in a fixed amount of increments from the off position.

STI: Self Test Input (Ford) circuit in the EEC-IV systems. Used to place the computer into testing mode.

STO: Self Test Output (Ford) circuit in the EEC-IV systems. Used by the computer to send testing and fault codes to tester.

STOICHIOMETRIC: in general, the precise mixture for the most efficient process of conversion. In automotive use, a ratio of 14.7 parts air to 1 part fuel. This ratio yields the highest combustion efficiency and therefore, the lowest emissions.

STROKE: One complete top to bottom or bottom to top movement of an engine piston.

SUB OXYGEN SENSOR: The second oxygen sensor, (after the catalytic converter), which monitors catalytic converter efficiency.

SWITCHING TRANSISTOR: Used in some electronic ignition systems, it acts as a switch for high current in response to a low voltage signal applied to the base terminal.

TV: Throttle Valve.

TA SENSOR: Intake Air Temperature Sensor.

TAB: Thermactor Air Bypass solenoid.

TACH INPUT: An engine rpm signal sent to the computer from the ignition coil primary circuit.

TAD: Thermactor Air Diverter solenoid.

TAS: Throttle Adjust Screw.

TBI: Throttle Body Injection (Fuel).

TCA: Thermostat Controlled Air Cleaner.

TCM: Throttle Control Module.

TCP: Temperature Compensated Accelerator Pump.

TCS: Traction Control System.

TDC: Top Dead Center.

TERMINAL: A connecting point in a electrical circuit, where the circuit can be disconnected or tested.

TES: Thermal Electric Switch.

TEMPERATURE SENSOR: A special type of solid state resistor, known as a thermistor. Used to sense coolant and, on some systems, air temperature also.

TFI: Thick Film Ignition module. Controls the coil and ignition operation on most Ford vehicles.

THERMACTOR AIR CONTROL VALVE: Combines the function of a normally closed air bypass valve and an air diverter valve in one integral valve.

THERMACTOR AIR SYSTEM: The efficiency of the catalytic converter is dependent upon temperature and the chemical makeup of the exhaust gases. These requirements are met by the thermactor air injection system.

THERMISTOR: A device that changes its resistance with temperature.

THERMOSTATIC: Referring to a device that automatically responds to temperature changes in order to activate a switch.

THERMO-TIME SWITCH: A switch which interrupts the electrical circuit of the cold start injector based on temperature and time.

THREE-WAY CATALYST (TWC): Combines two converters in one shell. Controls NOx, HC and CO. Also called dual catalytic converter.

THROTTLE BODY: The carburetor-like aluminum casting that houses the throttle valve, the idle air bypass (if equipped), the throttle position sensor (TPS), the idle air control (IAC) motor, the throttle linkage and on TBI systems, one or two injectors.

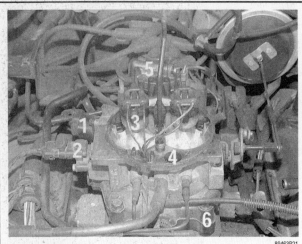

89463P21

1. IAC Valve
2. TP sensor
3. Fuel Injector
4. Throttle body
5. Fuel pressure regulator
6. Fuel heater

Typical dual injector TBI unit

TIMING: Relationship between the spark plug firing and the piston position.

TK or TKS: Throttle Kicker Solenoid. An actuator that moves the throttle linkage to increase idle rpm.

TKS: Throttle Kicker Solenoid. When energized, it supplies manifold vacuum to the throttle kicker actuator, as directed by the computer, to compensate for engine loads. Also called the idle-up system.

TOT: Transmission Oil Temperature sensor.

TP or TPS: Throttle Position Sensor or its circuit. Used to signal computer the position of the throttle plates.

TPI: Tuned Port Injection.

TRANSDUCER: A transducer converts or transduces a form of energy to another. All of the sensors or actuators are transducers.

TRANSFER PUMP: Fuel pump located in the fuel tank, usually used with a 2 pump system.

TRANSISTOR: A semiconductor device that can control an electrical current by varying a smaller base current. This device acts like a mechanical relay with a variable resistor at the points.

TRIGGER WHEEL: See Reluctor for definition.

TTS: Transmission Temperature Switch.

TVS: Temperature Vacuum Switch.

TVSV: Thermostatic Vacuum Switching Valve.

TVV: Thermal Vent Valve.

TW SENSOR: Coolant Temperature Sensor.

TWC: Three-way catalyst, sometimes referred to as a dual catalytic converter. Combines two catalytic converters in one shell to control emissions of NOx, HC and CO.

TWSV: Three Way Solenoid Valve.

TXD: Transmitted data line.

UIM: Universal control unit.

VACUUM ADVANCE: Advances the ignition timing with relation to engine load or computer signals.

VACUUM: A term side to describe a pressure that is less than atmospheric pressure.

VAF: Vane Air-Flow sensor or its circuit.

VAPOR LOCK: A condition which occurs when the fuel becomes so hot that it vaporizes, slowing or stopping fuel flow in the fuel lines.

VARIABLE DWELL: The ignition dwell period varies in distributor degrees at different engine speeds, but remains relatively constant in duration or actual time.

VAT: Vane Air-flow Temperature sensor.

VB VOLTAGE: Battery Voltage.

VBAT: Vehicle Battery voltage.

VCM: Vehicle Condition Monitor.

VCV: Vacuum Control Valve.

VECI LABEL: Vehicle Emission Control Information label, located under the hood.

VENTURI: A restriction in an airflow, such as in TBI, that speeds the airflow and creates a vacuum.

VF VOLTAGE: Battery Voltage.

VIS: Variable Induction System.

VISCOSITY: The tendency of a liquid, such as oil, to resist flowing.

VLC: Vacuum Sensor and Vacuum Line Charging solenoid valve.

VM: Vane Meter.

VOLT: The unit of electrical pressure or electromotive force.

VOLTAGE DROP: The difference in voltage between one point in a circuit and another, usually across a resistance. Voltage drop is measured in parallel with current flowing in the circuit.

VOLTMETER: An electrical meter used to measure voltage in a circuit. Voltmeters must be connected in parallel across the load or circuit.

VOM: Volt/Ohm Meter. Used to measure voltage and resistance.

VOTM: Vacuum Operated Throttle Modulator. Also referred to as throttle kicker or idle-up system.

VPWR: Vehicle Power supply voltage. 10–14 volts DC.

VREF: The reference voltage or power supplied by the computer control unit to some sensors regulated at a specific voltage.

VRS: Variable Reluctance Sensor.

VSC: Vehicle Speed Control sensor or its circuit.

VSS: Vehicle Speed Sensor.

VSV: Vacuum Switching Valve.

VTV: Vacuum Transmitting Valve.

VVC: Variable Voltage Choke.

WARM UP REGULATOR: On Bosch CIS, the original name for the control pressure regulator.

WAC: Wide open throttle Air Conditioning cut-off.

WOT: Wide Open Throttle or Wide Open Throttle switch.

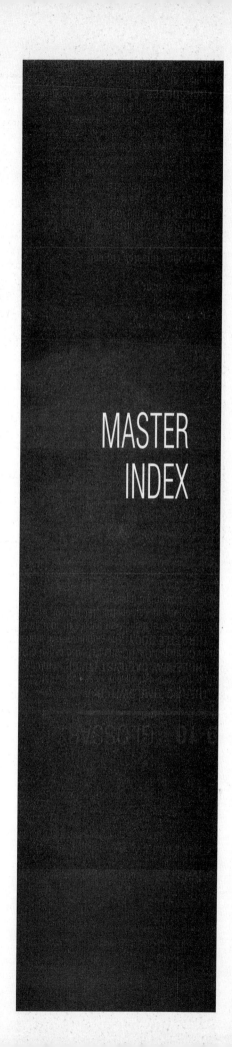

MASTER

INDEX